Contemporary
Literary Criticism
Yearbook 1997

Guide to Gale Literary Criticism Series

For criticism on	Consult these Gale series
Authors now living or who died after December 31, 1959	*CONTEMPORARY LITERARY CRITICISM (CLC)*
Authors who died between 1900 and 1959	*TWENTIETH-CENTURY LITERARY CRITICISM (TCLC)*
Authors who died between 1800 and 1899	*NINETEENTH-CENTURY LITERATURE CRITICISM (NCLC)*
Authors who died between 1400 and 1799	*LITERATURE CRITICISM FROM 1400 TO 1800 (LC)* *SHAKESPEAREAN CRITICISM (SC)*
Authors who died before 1400	*CLASSICAL AND MEDIEVAL LITERATURE CRITICISM (CMLC)*
Black writers of the past two hundred years	*BLACK LITERATURE CRITICISM (BLC)*
Authors of books for children and young adults	*CHILDREN'S LITERATURE REVIEW (CLR)*
Dramatists	*DRAMA CRITICISM (DC)*
Hispanic writers of the late nineteenth and twentieth centuries	*HISPANIC LITERATURE CRITICISM (HLC)*
Native North American writers and orators of the eighteenth, nineteenth, and twentieth centuries	*NATIVE NORTH AMERICAN LITERATURE (NNAL)*
Poets	*POETRY CRITICISM (PC)*
Short story writers	*SHORT STORY CRITICISM (SSC)*
Major authors from the Renaissance to the present	*WORLD LITERATURE CRITICISM, 1500 TO THE PRESENT (WLC)*
Major authors and works from the Bible to the present	*WORLD LITERATURE CRITICISM SUPPLEMENT (WLCS)*

ISSN 0091-3421

Volume 109

Contemporary Literary Criticism

Yearbook 1997

The Year in Fiction, Poetry, Drama, and
World Literature and the Year's
New Authors, Prizewinners, Obituaries,
and Outstanding Literary Events

**Jeffrey W. Hunter
Deborah A. Stanley
Timothy J. White**
EDITORS

**Pamela S. Dear
Catherine V. Donaldson
Daniel Jones
John D. Jorgenson
Jerry Moore
Polly A. Vedder
Thomas Wiloch
Kathleen Wilson**
ASSOCIATE EDITORS

GALE

DETROIT · LONDON

STAFF

Library of Congress Catalog Card Number 76-46132
ISBN 0-7876-2032-7
ISSN 0091-3421

Printed in the United States of America
10 9 8 7 6 5 4 3 2 1

Contents

Preface vii

Acknowledgments xi

THE YEAR IN REVIEW

The Year in Fiction 3
by Bruce Allen

The Year in Poetry 12
by Allen Hoey

The Year in Drama 24
by Julius Novick

The Year in World Literature 31
by William Riggan

Notes on Contributors 35

NEW AUTHORS

Daniel Akst 1956- 39
American novelist; *St. Burl's Obituary*

Lan Cao 1961- 43
Vietnamese-American nonfiction writer,
novelist, and professor of law; *Monkey
Bridge*

Charles Frazier 1950- 47
American novelist; *Cold Mountain*

Ha Jin 1956- 52
Chinese-American poet and short story
writer; *Ocean of Words: Army Stories*

Sebastian Junger 1962- 56
American nonfiction writer; *The Perfect
Storm*

Nora Okja Keller 19??- 63
Korean-born American novelist; *Comfort
Woman*

Arundhati Roy 1960- 68
Indian novelist; *The God of Small Things*

PRIZEWINNERS

Prizewinners Announced in 1995 81

Gina Berriault 1926- 89
American novelist and short story writer;
National Book Critics Circle Award for
*Women in Their Beds: New and Selected
Stories*

Dario Fo 1926- 99
Italian dramatist and essayist; Nobel
Laureate in Literature

Frank McCourt 1930- 147
Irish-born American memoirist; Pulitzer
Prize in Biography, National Book Critics
Circle Award for *Angela's Ashes*

Steven Millhauser 1943- 156
American novelist and short story writer;
Pulitzer Prize for fiction for *Martin
Dressler: The Tale of an American
Dreamer*

IN MEMORIAM

William S. Burroughs 1914-1997 179
American novelist, essayist, critic, poet,
and scriptwriter

James Dickey 1923-1997 234
American poet, novelist, critic, essayist,

scriptwriter, and author of children's books

Michael Dorris 1945-1997 295
American novelist, short story writer, nonfiction writer, and author of children's books

Allen Ginsberg 1926-1997 315
American poet, essayist, playwright, and nonfiction writer

James A. Michener 1907-1997 374
American novelist, short story writer, memoirist, nonfiction writer, essayist, and art historian

Mike Royko 1932-1997 392
American newspaper columnist and biographer

Obituaries 413

TOPICS IN LITERATURE: 1997

Memoirs of Trauma 419

Literary Criticism Series Cumulative Author Index 469

Literary Criticism Series Cumulative Topic Index 537

CLC Cumulative Nationality Index 547

CLC-109 Title Index 563

Preface

A Comprehensive Information Source
on Contemporary Literature

Scope of the *Yearbook*

*C*ontemporary Literary Criticism Yearbook is a part of the ongoing *Contemporary Literary Criticism (CLC)* series. *CLC* provides a comprehensive survey of modern literature by presenting excerpted criticism on the works of novelists, poets, playwrights, short story writers, scriptwriters, and other creative writers now living or who died after December 31, 1959. A strong emphasis is placed on including criticism of works by established authors who frequently appear on syllabuses of high school and college literature courses.

To complement this broad coverage, the *Yearbook* focuses more specifically on a given year's literary activities and features a larger number of currently noteworthy authors than is possible in standard *CLC* volumes. *CLC Yearbook* provides students, teachers, librarians, researchers, and general readers with information and commentary on the outstanding literary works and events of a given year.

Format of the Book

CLC, Volume 109: *Yearbook 1997,* which includes excerpted criticism on seventeen authors and comprehensive coverage of a key issue in contemporary literature, is divided into five sections—"The Year in Review," "New Authors," "Prizewinners," "In Memoriam," and "Topic in Literature: 1997."

- **The Year in Review**—This section consists of specially commissioned essays by prominent writers who survey the year's works in their respective fields. Bruce Allen discusses "The Year in Fiction," Allen Hoey "The Year in Poetry," Julius Novick "The Year in Drama," and William Riggan "The Year in World Literature." For introductions to the essayists, please see the Notes on Contributors.

- **New Authors**—This section introduces seven writers who received significant critical recognition for their first major work of fiction in 1997 or whose work was translated into English or published in the United States for the first time. Authors were selected for inclusion if their work was reviewed in several prominent literary periodicals.

- **Prizewinners**—This section begins with a list of literary prizes and honors announced in 1997, citing the award, award criteria, the recipient, and the title of the prizewinning work. Following the listing of prizewinners is a presentation of four entries on individual award winners, representing a mixture of genres and nationalities as well as established prizes and those more recently introduced.

- **In Memoriam**—This section consists of reminiscences, tributes, retrospective articles, and obituary notices on six authors who died in 1997. In addition, an Obituary section provides information on other recently deceased literary figures.

- **Topic in Literature**—This section focuses on a literary issue of considerable public interest, the growth in popularity of memoirs of trauma.

Features

With the exception of the four essays in "The Year in Review" section, which were written specifically for this publication, the *Yearbook* consists of excerpted criticism drawn from literary reviews, general magazines, newspapers, books, and scholarly journals. *Yearbook* entries variously contain the following items:

- An **Author Heading** in the "New Authors" and "Prizewinners" sections cites the name under which the author publishes and the title of the work discussed in the entry; the "In Memoriam" section includes the author's name and birth and death dates. The author's full name, pseudonyms (if any) under which the author has published, nationality, and principal genres are listed on the first line of the author entry.

- The **Subject Heading** defines the theme of each entry in "The Year in Review" and "Topic in Literature" sections.

- A brief **Biographical and Critical Introduction** to the author and his or her work precedes excerpted criticism in the "New Authors," "Prizewinners," and "In Memoriam" sections; the subjects, authors, and works in the "Topic in Literature" section are introduced in a similar manner.

- A listing of **Principal Works** is included for all entries in the "Prizewinners" and "In Memoriam" sections.

- A **Portrait** of the author is included in the "New Authors," "Prizewinners," and "In Memoriam" sections.

- The **Excerpted Criticism,** included in all entries except those in the "Year in Review" section, represents essays selected by editors to reflect the spectrum of opinion about a specific work or about an author's writing in general. The excerpts are typically arranged chronologically, adding a useful perspective to the entry. In the "Year in Review," "New Authors," "Prizewinners," and "In Memoriam" sections, all titles by the author being discussed are printed in boldface type, enabling the reader to more easily identify the author's work.

- A complete **Bibliographical Citation,** designed to help the user find the original essay or book, precedes each excerpt.

- **Cross-references** have been included in the "New Authors," "Prizewinners," and "In Memoriam" sections to direct readers to other useful sources published by Gale. Previous volumes of *CLC* in which the author has been featured are also listed.

Other Features

The *Yearbook* also includes the following features:

- An **Acknowledgments** section lists the copyright holders who have granted permission to reprint material in this volume of *CLC*. It does not, however, list every book or periodical reprinted or consulted during the preparation of this volume.

- A **Cumulative Author Index** lists all the authors who have appeared in the Literary Criticism Series published by Gale, with cross-references to Gale's Biographical and Autobiographical Series. A full listing of series referenced in the index appears at the beginning of the index. Readers will welcome this cumulated author index as a useful tool for locating an author within the various series. The index, which lists birth and death dates when available, is particularly valuable for locating references to those authors whose careers span two periods. For example, Ernest Hemingway is found in *CLC,* yet a writer often associated with him, F. Scott Fitzgerald, is found in *Twentieth-Century Literary Criticism.*

- Beginning with *CLC,* Vol. 65, each *Yearbook* contains a **Cumulative Topic Index,** which lists all literary topics treated in *CLC* as well as the topic volumes of *Twentieth-Century Literary Criticism, Nineteenth-Century Literature Criticism,* and *Literature Criticism from 1400 to 1800.*

- A **Cumulative Nationality Index** alphabetically lists all authors featured in *CLC* by nationality, followed by numbers corresponding to the volumes in which the authors appear.

- A **Title Index** alphabetically lists all titles reviewed in the current volume of *CLC*. Listings are followed by the author's name and the corresponding page numbers where the titles are discussed. English translations of foreign titles and variations of titles are cross-referenced to the title under which a work was originally published. Titles of novels, novellas, dramas, films, record albums, and poetry, short story, and essay collections are printed in italics, while all individual poems, short stories, essays, and songs are printed in roman type within quotation marks. When published separately, the titles of long poems (e.g., T. S. Eliot's *The Waste Land*) are printed in italics.

Citing *Contemporary Literary Criticism*

When writing papers, students who quote directly from any volume in the Literary Criticism Series may use the following general forms to footnote reprinted criticism. The first example is for material drawn from periodicals, the second for material reprinted from books:

[1]Alfred Cismaru, "Making the Best of It," *The New Republic, 207,* No. 24, (December 7, 1992), 30, 32; excerpted and reprinted in *Contemporary Literary Criticism,* Vol. 85, ed. Christopher Giroux (Detroit: Gale Research, 1995), pp. 73-4.

[2]Yvor Winters, *The Post-Symbolist Methods* (Allan Swallow, 1967); excerpted and reprinted in *Contemporary Literary Criticism,* Vol. 85, ed. Christopher Giroux (Detroit: Gale Research, 1995), pp. 223-26.

Suggestions Are Welcome

The editors hope that readers will find *CLC Yearbook* a useful reference tool and welcome comments about the work. Send comments and suggestions to: Editors, *Contemporary Literary Criticism,* Gale Research, 27500 Drake Rd., Farmington Hills, MI 48331-3535.

Acknowledgments

The editors wish to thank the copyright holders of the excerpted criticism included in this volume and the permissions managers of many book and magazine publishing companies for assisting us in securing reproduction rights. We are also grateful to the staffs of the Detroit Public Library, the Library of Congress, the University of Detroit Mercy Library, Wayne State University Purdy/Kresge Library Complex, and the University of Michigan Libraries for making their resources available to us. Following is a list of the copyright holders who have granted us permission to reproduce material in this volume of CLC. Every effort has been made to trace copyright, but if omissions have been made, please let us know.

COPYRIGHTED EXCERPTS IN *CLC*, VOLUME 109, WERE REPRODUCED FROM THE FOLLOWING PERIODICALS:

The American Poetry Review, v. 4, July-August, 1997 for "Allen Ginsberg: An Interview" by Gary Pacernick. Copyright © 1997 by Gary Pacernick. First published by The American Poetry Review. Reprinted by permission of the Ellen Levine Literary Agency, Inc/v. 4, July-August, 1997 for "Howl Revisited: The Poet as Jew" by Alicia Ostriker. Copyright © 1997 by World Poetry, Inc. Reproduced by permission of the author.—*The Armchair Detective,* v. 27, 1994. Copyright © 1994 by The Armchair Detective. Reproduced by permission.—*Associated Press*, April 14, 1997; October 17 1997. Copyright © 1997 Associated Press. All rights reserved. Both reproduced by permission.—*The Atlantic Monthly*, June, 1996 for a review of 'St. Burl's Obituary' by Phoebe-Lou Adams. Reproduced by permission of the author.—*Belles Lettres: A Review of Books By Women*, Spring, 1995. Reproduced by permission.—*The Bloomsbury Review*, May/June, 1995 for a review of 'Working Men' and 'Paper Trail' by Stephen Lyons. Copyright © by Owaissa Communications Company, Inc. 1995. Reproduced by permission of the author—*Book World—The Washington Post*, October 14, 1984; October 16, 1994; May 26, 1996; September 29, 1996; February 2, 1997; July 6, 1997. Copyright © 1984, 1994, 1996, 1997 Washington Post Book World Service/Washington Post Writers Group. All reproduced by permission.—*Booklist*, March 15, 1996; March 15, 1997; June 1 & 15, 1997; July, 1997. © 1996, 1997 by the American Library Association. All reproduced by permission.—*Chicago Tribune*, September 19, 1993 for "A Walk on the Dark Side" by Greg Johnson; June 11, 1995 for "Bits From a Beat: Sorting Through Allen Ginsberg's Mid-50's Odds and Ends" by Alexander Theroux; December 24, 1996 for "Beating the Odds" by Jocelyn Lieu; March 2, 1997 for "Michael Dorris Explores the Power of Family" by Sandra Scofield; April 6, 1997 "Fear of Father," by Conan Putnam; April 20. 1997 for "Novelist Kathryn Harrison's Memoir of Her Affair With Her Father" by Joanne Kaufman; April 27, 1997 for "Dark Angels" by Carolyn Alessio. © copyrighted 1993, 1995, 1996, 1997 Chicago Tribune Company. All rights reserved. All reproduced by permission of the respective authors./ August 5, 1990;October 22, 1996; April 29, 1997; August 4, 1997. © copyrighted 1990, 1996, 1997, Chicago Tribune Company. All rights reserved. All used by permission.—*The Christian Century*, v. 14, May 21-28, 1997. Copyright (c)1997 Christian Century Foundation. Reproduced by permission from *The Christian Century.*—*Concerning Poetry*, v. 2, Spring, 1969. Copyright © 1969, Western Washington University. Reproduced by permission.—*Contemporary Literature*, v. XXXI, Summer, 1990. Copyright © 1990 by the Board of Regents of the University of Wisconsin System. Reprinted by permission of The University of Wisconsin Press.—*Contemporary Literature*, v. XXXVI, Spring, 1995. Copyright © 1995 by the Board of Regents of the University of Wisconsin System. Reprinted by permission of The University of Wisconsin Press.—*The Drama Review*, v. 30, Spring, 1986. Copyright © 1986, *The Drama Review*. Reproduced by permission of The MIT Press, Cambridge, MA.—*Entertainment Weekly*, August 1, 1997. Copyright © 1997 Entertainment Weekly, Inc. Reproduced by permission.—*The Explicator*, v. 54, Winter, 1996. Copyright © 1996 Helen Dwight Reid Educational Foundation. Reproduced with permission of the Helen Dwight Reid Educational Foundation, published by Heldref Publications, 1319 18th Street, NW, Washington, DC 20036-1802.—*Italica*, v. 65, Summer, 1988. Copyright © 1988 by The American Association of Teachers of Italian. Reproduced by permission.—*Kirkus Reviews*, March 15, 1997; June 1, 1997; July 1, 1997. Copyright © 1997 The Kirkus Service, Inc. All rights reserved. All reproduced by permission of the publisher, *Kirkus Reviews* and Kirkus Associates, LP.—*Library Journal*, February 1, 1996 for A review of 'St. Burl's Obituary' by Dean James; March 1, 1996 for A review of 'Women in Their Beds: New and Selected Stories' by Janet Ruth Heller; May 15, 1997 for A review of 'Cold Mountain' by David A. Beronä.

COPYRIGHTED EXCERPTS IN *CLC*, VOLUME 109, WERE REPRODUCED FROM THE FOLLOWING BOOKS:

PHOTOGRAPHS AND ILLUSTRATIONS APPEARING IN *CLC*, VOLUME 109, WERE RECEIVED FROM THE FOLLOWING SOURCES:

The Year in Review

The Year in Fiction
by Bruce Allen

The year 1997 was highlighted by new books from several of the English-speaking world's indisputably major writers. And no reappearance was more surprising than that of the late Anthony Burgess (1917-93), whose last completed fiction, **Byrne** ("a novel in verse"), was published posthumously to high praise in Great Britain and rather more tempered admiration in the U.S.

Byrne relates, primarily in *ottava rima* (the verse form most famously employed in Byron's *Don Juan*), the rambunctious artistic and amatory career of Michael Byrne, the scion of Irish potato farmers and shopkeepers, a gifted composer and a great success throughout Europe—most notoriously in Nazi Germany, where he successfully collaborates with a musical Joseph Goebbels. Then, in a surprising about-face, the focus shifts to Byrne's middle-aged children ("the fruits of my insemination"), struggling with unresolved feelings about their scapegrace parent as they journey to London for the reading of his will. This gloriously entertaining portrait of the artist spares neither its probably autobiographical protagonist (who knows he's at best a flawed genius) nor the twentieth century, which Burgess seems not to have liked much. But few readers will resist its resourceful and often quite brilliant versifying (for example, this, of a Russian physician: "His origin was Minsk or Pinsk or Moscow. Pe / Rusing Tim's chart he called for a bronchoscopy"). To the end, Anthony Burgess remained a vital, restless, mischievous creative force. Byron would have approved.

Three worthy novels by major Welsh writers made their first U.S. appearances. **Monica,** by critic and journalist Saunders Lewis, details the romantic unhappiness of a housewife betrayed by her romantic imagination with a frankness (doubtless inspired by *Madame Bovary*) that made it a *succès de scandale* upon its publication in 1930. Poet Caradog Prichard's **One Moonlit Night** (1961) skillfully fictionalizes the inhibiting parental and cultural environment that stifles its dreamy protagonist's desires to escape his moribund village. And **Ram with Red Horns** by Rhys Davies, a fine, flinty novel unpublished during his lifetime (1903-78), traces in striking realistic and symbolic detail the psychological deterioration of a long-married woman who murders her unfaithful husband, then tries to make peace with her (vividly characterized) neighbors as well as her own guilt and fear. Arguably unfinished (its ending is rushed), this is nevertheless a gripping fiction and a perfect introduction to Davies's justly celebrated novels and stories of rural Wales.

The Springs of Affection collects the short stories of the late Maeve Brennan, a longtime American citizen and *New Yorker* staff writer whose fiction endures as unmistakably (and irrepressibly) Irish. These twenty-one tales, which all appeared in Brennan's two published collections, include precisely detailed sketches of her girlhood in Dublin (**"The Devil in Us"** is especially acute about Catholicism and its discontents) and ampler studies of adult marital unhappiness and detente—most memorably the long title story's complex, elegiac portrayal of a troubled couple who are even in death the objects of lingering family resentments.

Penelope Fitzgerald, who began publishing fiction at the age of sixty, has in the twenty years since produced half a dozen sophisticated and surprisingly widely ranging novels; none is more accomplished than her newest, **The Blue Flower.** This is a character study of Friedrich von Hardenberg, a late eighteenth-century German idealist and visionary (en route to becoming the Romantic poet Novalis) as restless seeking intellect, perversely unconventional son and brother, and worshipful suitor to a beautiful young girl who dies in adolescence. Fitzgerald here evokes with masterly concision both the intellectual ferment of "Fritz's" time and the awkward development of his own Romantic temperament in a perfectly calculated little novel that speaks densely packed volumes about its remote and immensely appealing subject.

Fitzgerald's **The Bookshop,** a 1978 novel previously published only in Great Britain, is a slighter though scarcely less resonant story of a well-meaning widow (Florence Green) whose title venture, which she establishes in an abandoned house in Eastern England's rural marshland country, falls afoul of local myopia and philistinism, and—in the person of a Machiavellian retired general's wife, the formidable Mrs. Gamart—deeply vested conflicting interests. It's a social comedy that deftly analyzes the fate of culture in its time (1959), and, surely, ours—another virtuosic demonstration of its invaluable author's alert wit and becoming humanity.

A rather more acerbic tone sounds throughout **Part of the Furniture,** another hilariously brusque *bildungsroman* from octogenarian Mary Wesley (who first published at seventy; Penelope Fitzgerald must wonder what took her so long). She is an elliptical writer, who scorns conventional exposition, description, and pacing, and is something of an acquired taste. But readers attuned to her crisp rhetoric will find much to enjoy in this tart comedy, whose events occur (as in many of her novels) during the Second World War and long thereafter, and which examines the maturing of its young heroine (drolly named Juno) through a cataclysmic loss of innocence, peaceful country life with its own surreal dimensions, and a perfectly credible romance with a much older man. It is as urbane a pastoral as can be found; a refreshingly saturnine comic blend of the idyllic with the everyday.

Fay Weldon files more of her fetchingly murderous field reports on the battle of the genders in **Wicked Women,** a vigorous collection (her fourth) of tonally varied and often very entertaining short stories. The usual suspects include adulterous or indifferent husbands and wives slow to assert their rights, and the reader occasionally feels he's re-entering overfamiliar territories. But all the stories are sharply written, and two belong among her best work: a harrowing portrait of a teenaged girl stunted by her parents' incompatibility (**"Heat-Haze"**) and the delicious **"Not Even a Blood Relation,"** about the tug of wills, so to speak, between a feisty widow and her three greedy adult daughters.

Muriel Spark's *Open to the Public* offers such "New and Collected Stories" as her classic long tales **"Bang Bang You're Dead"** and **"The Go-Away Bird"** and a miscellany of briefer stories that play sophisticated (and often arch) variations on what seems her abiding theme: the inherence of the grotesque and fantastic within the mundane, as observed by a knowing, preternaturally keen, and oddly detached eye.

Spark's new novel, **Reality and Dreams,** adroitly wraps enigma within riddle in the story of a prominent film director and writer (Tom), crippled by an accident on the set, whose recovery—and Olympian plans for future films, in which he effectively plays God—contrasts amusingly with the job-related and other catastrophes that befall all those within his extended family and orbit. Spark gives nothing away, allowing the delighted reader to wonder whether it is Tom's bland appropriation of others' lives that sets the tone for their decline (thrown into wry relief by his continuing good fortune)—or if all is, indeed, accident. The novel's very elusiveness underscores, as it magnifies, its very considerable quirkiness and charm.

Sardonic wit is the chief virtue of Margaret Drabble's novel **The Witch of Exmoor,** an overwritten portrayal of a prototypically contemporary middle-class English clan whose only really interesting member is the eponymous matriarch, a "mad" recluse whose disgust with her acquisitive family is much more tolerable than Drabble's omniscient authorial scorn. Edna O'Brien's **Down by the River** is an uncharacteristically leaden variant of her usually razor-sharp studies of rural Irish poverty and despair—a story of the consequences of paternal sexual abuse too discursive and accusatory to be effective fiction.

Altered States is another of Anita Brookner's dry anatomies of timid souls whose waking lives never fulfill their day-

dreams—unusual in that its protagonist, Alan Sherwood, stimulates the same microscopic attention to emotional detail most often lavished on her women characters. Though not essentially different otherwise from her earlier novels, it's a haunting character study, beautifully done.

Carol Shields's **Larry's Party** boldly follows her award-winning novel *The Stone Diaries* with a warmly funny in-depth portrayal of a middle-aged landscape designer (and, most notably, "maze maker") awkwardly coming to terms with the puzzles of his own career and romantic insecurities and confusions. The novel feels rather too rigidly structured and patterned, though Larry Weller is one of Shields's most attractively humanly fallible creations.

Penelope Lively's clever studies of embattled domesticity are collected in **The Five Thousand and One Nights,** a scattershot volume redeemed by a powerful portrait of a woman's unease when out of her comfortably familiar environment (**"The Slovenian Giantess"**), and the, uh, lively title story, which reinvents Scheherazade as an overworked supermom.

A. S. Byatt's collection **The Djinn in the Nightingale's Eye** offers both the colorful pleasures of the traditional fairytales it expertly recreates (**"The Story of the Eldest Princess"** is especially spellbinding) and some very clever speculations on the question of whether stories do (or should) "imprison" characters, hence denying their freedom to act. The relevant convolutions appear most teasingly, and pleasingly in the title story's confrontation between a traveling folklorist and the genie who more than satisfies her scholarly and womanly needs.

Other writers of established reputation who published new work in 1997 include former (surprise) Booker Prize winner, Scotland's James Kelman, whose **Busted Scotch** gathers "selected stories" from twenty years' worth of this defiantly abrasive writer's tightly focused character studies. Derelicts and drifters aren't the only victims of circumstance observed in these bleak, lyrically foulmouthed dramas (many are monologues) which concentrate on the resentful emotions of people who sense, even when they cannot articulate, their connections with others (**"Greyhound for Breakfast"** and the superb **"Pictures"** are especially rewarding). Kelman probably won't be invited to high tea with the Queen Mum, but that's her loss. He's a very skillful and distinctive writer.

William Boyd's cosmopolitanism (and unevenness) are typically displayed in **The Destiny of Nathalie X and Other Stories,** a geographically and tonally varied collection which ranges over three continents and a thematic gamut embracing Ludwig Wittgenstein, a fashion designer's World War

II, and, most amusingly, an African film director's blithe conquest of Hollywood.

Australian David Malouf's *Conversations at Curlow Creek* effectively superimposes a history of Irish resistance to British oppression over another of his intense studies of the permutations of masculine friendship. Though it's really only an extended anecdote, J. P. Donleavy's *The Lady Who Liked Clean Restrooms,* which portrays a Scarsdale matron dumped by her husband and educating herself to life outside her privileged world, draws a cartoon that blossoms into an immensely likable character. And Barry Unsworth's *After Hannibal* is a vigorous social comedy about latter-day "invasions" of Italy's Umbrian region by a multinational gaggle of tourists skillfully manipulated by an urbane, amoral attorney. It reads much like Muriel Spark in one of her sunnier moods.

More serious matters are examined in Nicholas Mosley's *Children of Darkness and Light,* a crabbed and surprisingly absorbing story of a veteran journalist investigating an alleged "miracle" in a northern England backwater, and thence his own moral nature; Hans Koning's *Pursuit of a Woman on the Hinge of History,* a suave and cryptic account of a millennarian leftist group's plot to redistribute the world's wealth and reorganize its power structures; and especially *The Untouchable,* Irish novelist John Banville's expert fictionalization of the life of British art historian—and Russian spy—Anthony Blunt (as protagonist Victor Maskell). It's an ingenious restoration, one might say, which vividly traces the biographical and emotional connections among politics, art, sex, and a fragmented psyche's quest for authenticity.

A refreshing touch of exoticism enlivens *Salt,* a pleasant, borderline-sentimental tale of Caribbean folk culture at odds with "civilizing" British interests, set in its author Earl Lovelace's native Trinidad. Better still are two novels from Guyanese-born British writer Roy Heath, set in his homeland and focused on an endearing hustler, Kwaku Cholmondeley, a comically harried husband, father, and self-justifying opportunist. *Kwaku,* first published in 1982, offers a vivid picaresque introduction to its eponymous "shoemaker . . . , inveterate liar, would-be photographer, near-bigamist and father of eight children." Its successor, *The Ministry of Hope,* memorably recounts Kwaku's adventures as a self-created "faith healer," failed bureaucrat, and spy. No one writing today can match Roy Heath's perfect lightness of touch and infectious love for his characters. He's an international treasure awaiting the acclaim he deserves.

West Indian Caryl Phillips's *Nature of Blood* comprises three murky interwoven novellas (including a retelling of "Othello") that demonstrate all too shrilly the effects of ethnic and racial injustice. Hanif Kureishi's stories in *Love in a Blue Time* modify his trademark comedies of Pakistanis

making it (or not) in London, in a comparatively dour series of portraits of middle-aged compromise and malaise.

Jeanette Winterson's *Gut Symmetries* received a mixed press, but struck this reader as willfully dense postmodernist caterwauling about the impossibility of writing stories (the earlier Winterson simply went ahead and wrote them). Canadian Guy Vanderhaeghe's ambitious novel *The Englishman's Boy* is a strongly imagined story that yokes together with only middling success a satirical portrait of Hollywood in the 1920s and the eerie piecemeal saga of a massacre of Indians fifty years earlier. It's a novel that keeps threatening to become wonderful, but sadly, remains curiously uninvolving.

Patrick McGrath's *Asylum* is much better: a subtle and really rather frightening analysis (by the doctor who only imperfectly comprehends her) of a woman mental patient's distracted surrender to evil in the person of the murderous sculptor for whom she has abandoned all others and all else. A grim, fascinating, beautifully controlled fiction.

Will Self, that cheeky Pretender to the maverick throne pretty much conceded to Martin Amis, reaffirms his iconoclastic credentials with *Great Apes,* an impish reversal of "the natural order" in which the title creatures are evolution's masterpiece and humanity of a far lower mental and moral order. A virtual anthology of clever gags and, at its best, something more: an oddly moving story of a troubled simian's efforts to subdue his baser (human) impulses.

Geoff Nicholson's *Bleeding London,* a tightly plotted romp about three variously obsessed misfits seeking love, revenge, and avocational fulfillment in the city of Dickens and Margaret Thatcher, while dependably entertaining, is both a little more dryly schematic and a little less rudely inventive than one expects from the comic surrealist who gave us *Still Life with Volkswagen* and *Footsucker.*

A Change of Climate, a 1994 novel by Hilary Mantel (whose more recent *An Experiment in Love* was successfully published in the U.S.), describes with skillfully understated wit and empathy the comic-horrible loss of illusions experienced by an idealistic English couple who journey as hopeful missionaries to the hell of South Africa. And Shena Mackay's *An Advent Calendar,* which appeared in Great Britain in 1971, expertly records the emotional and sexual misadventures involving an ill-matched married pair, a vulnerable teenager, and their even more ill-chosen various lovers, in a savage comedy that climaxes with a thoroughly satisfying quiet resolution. Many people are beginning to believe, with good reason, that Mackay is one of the best writers around.

Interesting second books from newer writers included Neil

Bartlett's meticulously rendered, almost neo-Victorian story of homosexual love in 1920s London (*The House on Brooke Street*); Kate Atkinson's delectable mixture of pastoral romance and family chronicle (*Human Croquet*); and Vikram Chandra's accomplished *Love and Longing in Bombay,* five linked tales of ghostly visitation, sexual conflict, and murder. Beautifully written, and filled with superbly realized characters and dramatic scenes, this was one of the year's very best books.

Notable first novels included *The Jade Peony,* Chinese Canadian Wayson Choy's intelligently textured tale of emigrant siblings growing up a half-century ago in Vancouver's Chinatown; Scot Alan Warner's sardonic portrayal of a resourcefully amoral young woman (*Morvern Callar*); Robert McLiam Wilson's anatomy of working-class ennui and despair vis-à-vis IRA violence in contemporary Belfast (*Eureka Street*); and—the most substantial of these four—Niall Williams's *Four Letters of Love,* a complex story of thwarted passion set in Dublin and near Galway, in which the fates of withdrawn Nicholas Coughlan and troubled Isabel Gore are slowly, quite believably knitted together. This is a carefully structured, deeply reflective novel (much of its important "action" contained in letters that never reach their intended readers), well worth the time and effort required to enter its deliberately dreamlike, somewhat insubstantial world.

Andrew Miller's *Ingenious Pain* spins a bizarre period tale (reminiscent of Patrick Suskind's *Perfume*) of an eighteenth-century physician's development from a paragon of objectivity (who, remarkably, cannot feel either pain or pleasure) into a suffering, and therefore more sentient specimen of humanity. It's a richly imagined and often very funny portrayal of the limitations of Reason in a culture that pretends to prize it above all other virtues.

Mick Jackson's *Underground Man* offers a stunning portrait of nineteenth-century England as well as an ingenious imagining of the life of William John Cavendish Bentinck-Scott, Duke of Portland and a fabulously wealthy eccentric who builds for himself an escape from the world in a series of vast tunnels dug beneath his Nottinghamshire manor. Lengthy excerpts "From His Grace's Journal" are balanced against accounts of (and speculations about) the nobleman's "madness" by various tradesmen, miscellaneous social acquaintances, and townspeople in a beautifully crafted Chinese-box puzzle of a novel that makes of its unlikely protagonist a sympathetic and very nearly heroic character.

There were three other superb first novels from abroad. *Fugitive Pieces,* by Canadian poet Anne Michaels, employs amazingly precise language and gorgeous imagery to tell the story of Jakob Beer, a Polish orphan who survives the Holocaust and, under the tutelage of the polymath Greek ge-

ologist who rescues him from the Nazis, becomes an accomplished poet. In a brilliant shift of focus, it is also a story of the aesthetic and moral awakening of a young scholar who, years afterward, discovers the late Jakob's journals. It's a subtle and very involving story about how memory both does and does not help endangered people to survive.

A similar theme informs Irish poet and critic Seamus Deane's *Reading in the Dark,* a wonderfully written story of a Northern Ireland (Derry) family, destroyed, though still clinging stubbornly together, by a relentless succession of deaths and by betrayals that have set brother against brother and will affect forever its young narrator's fumbling efforts to understand his relatives' violence and despair. A virtually perfect construction, and one of the year's most moving books.

One of the most warmly praised was Indian film writer Arundhati Roy's novel *The God of Small Things,* an intricate and absorbing tale, crammed with colorful local detail and extravagant figurative language, about a young twin brother and sister brought up among a rich, eccentric Kerala family, a forbidden liaison that defies boundaries of caste and class, and the connected aftermaths of two mysterious deaths that haunt the twins Estha and Rahel long years afterward. Roy's fragmented, almost surreptitious approach to her novel's hidden center is itself a thing of beauty; the story becomes both teasingly diffuse and nerve-wrackingly suspenseful. One understands why it won last year's Booker Prize and established Roy as one of the English-speaking world's most promising younger novelists.

The most highly praised American novel of 1997 was Charles Frazier's *Cold Mountain,* a story set during the final days of the Civil War and unmistakably modeled on Homer's *Odyssey.* It describes the harrowing return homeward of Inman, a wounded Confederate soldier whose destination is Cold Mountain in North Carolina, and also a reunion with Ada, the city-bred girl he left behind and aims to marry. Frazier juxtaposes Inman's often interrupted journey with Ada's slow maturing as she learns to run the moribund farm left her by her late father. The novel's texture is movingly deepened by echoes of the wisdom of Ralph Waldo Emerson (whom Ada's preacher father had revered) and eighteenth-century naturalist William Bartram, whose *Travels* is the book that sustains Inman through the perils and disillusionments he must endure before his odyssey is concluded. *Cold Mountain* is a masterly performance—a haunting image of America in its greatest time of travail.

A comparatively neglected debut novel that has much in common with Frazier's triumph, Howard Bahr's *The Black Flower,* explores with impressive delicacy and power the ordeal of a veteran Confederate soldier whose confusion of allegiances climaxes at the battle of Nashville. And Tom Dyja's *Play for a Kingdom* fashions moving drama as well as a convincing panoramic view of the Civil War's conclusion from its ingenious premise: the accidental meeting of Confederate and Union troops on a makeshift baseball field and the series of "matches" that absorb these players as they await a crucial meeting on the battlefield. It belongs with Frazier's and Bahr's novels among the year's most unexpectedly welcome surprises.

Another was **In the Memory of the Forest,** a fine first novel by the late newspaper correspondent Charles T. Powers, about Poland in the wake of Communism's demise and a murder in a rural village. The solution of the murder discloses the painfully lingering presences of divisive old fears and superstitions.

Joseph Skibell's *A Blessing on the Moon* effectively uses magical realism in a haunting tale of a Polish Jew killed during the Second World War by German soldiers, whose body rises from a mass grave and travels through the ongoing carnage toward "the World to Come." A most unusual memorial to the many million dead, it's a thoroughly convincing fantasy.

Nora Okja Keller's **Comfort Woman** skillfully employs two narrators, a Korean-American girl growing up in Hawaii and her traumatized mother, to tell the harsh yet dreamy and lyrical tale of a naive village girl made into a "comfort woman" (prostitute) in wartime Japan's "recreation camps," the vengeance she later exacts, and the complex legacy thus passed on to her daughter. A deeply felt and beautifully constructed first novel.

Memoirs of a Geisha by Arthur Golden is packed with fascinating information about the life of Chiyo, a Japanese girl sold into slavery who later becomes a pampered, prosperous geisha—but its heroine is so gentle and passive (albeit credibly so) that the novel is virtually devoid of tension. Its most dramatic pages are those that describe Chiyo's victimization by her rival Hatsumomo, a *femme fatale* who might have dropped in out of one of Sax Rohmer's overheated melodramas. She shakes the novel, if only intermittently, into furious life.

Patricia Chao's debut, **Monkey King,** vividly explores the complicated self-healing undertaken by Sally Wang, a Chinese-American woman whose fulfilling new life in New York City is troubled by memories of childhood sexual abuse at the hands of her late father. This is a remarkably fair-minded novel, grimly unsparing in its portrayal of family horrors and both perceptive and forgiving toward disoriented immigrants who seek "control" over their lives in the only ways they know.

A more benign look at the immigrant experience is offered in **The Chin Kiss King,** Ana Veciana-Suarez's infectiously warmhearted tale of a Cuban-American family threatened and unified by the birth of a seriously handicapped baby. The characters of the baby's courageous mother Maribel, her firebrand mother Adela, and distracted grandmother Cuca form the solid center of a life-affirming novel that's far less sentimental and romantic than are its endearingly crazy women. A real charmer.

Aryeh Lev Stollman's **The Far Euphrates** movingly relates the coming-of-age of Aryeh Alexander, a rabbi's son growing up in Windsor, Ontario, in the 1960s. Aryeh's gradual understanding of the extremity of his father's (and others') sufferings during the Holocaust and acceptance of his homosexuality help him to see how one may "retreat" from "reality" in order to better comprehend it. Aryeh's own accommodation to the mysteries of God's creation brings this freshly imagined and admirably intelligent novel to an inconclusive ending that nevertheless feels like an honestly earned victory.

No such satisfaction awaits Elizabeth Taube, the beleaguered protagonist (she'd laugh if you called her a heroine) of Amy Bloom's **Love Invents Us,** an episodic novel (presumably developed from stories in her first book, *Come to Me*) which tracks Elizabeth's unhappy sexual adventures, beginning with the elderly furrier who gently abuses her and ending, many men later, with her realization that "I've been alone my whole life." Though Elizabeth's confusion and pain are very feelingly rendered, one finishes this rather bitter novel not quite sure what it was all about or why we should care about its morose main character.

The episodic nature of Julie Hecht's **Do the Windows Open?** is the great strength of a sequence of crisp stories that subtly reveal the inner emotional world of their common narrator: a fortyish woman photographer who accepts the staleness of her marriage and the fact of her childlessness, while observing with a hilariously rendered sardonic ennui the exasperating plenitude of others' lives in her several (New York and Nantucket) environments. A very funny book with a very convincing serious undertone.

The same is true of the exhilarating stories (many won literary prizes) in Sharon Solwitz's debut collection **Blood and Milk,** which celebrates in wry, combative colloquial voices the getting and spending and enduring of domestic and marital minutiae and crises. **"Mercy"** and **"Polio"** are especially compelling, but there isn't a dud—or an experience to which any reader can remain indifferent—in this accomplished book.

In **Horace Afoot,** Frederick Reuss contrives to interest readers in a character (who has adopted the name of the Roman poet mentioned in the title) stubbornly at odds with his hometown (Oblivion, somewhere in the midwest) and indeed the present century. Horace's somewhat pedantic broadsides against American materialism and shallowness are, fortunately, modified by a simple but serviceable plot that takes him outside his own psyche and into hesitant, and finally committed involvement with others. It's as if the hero of *A Confederacy of Dunces* had actually met people he *liked.*

The year's most entertaining first novel—and one that made my shortlist of the five best novels, period—was *The Wishbones,* Tom Perrotta's follow-up to his delightful story collection *Bad Haircut,* likewise set in suburban New Jersey and focused on amiable young layabouts unwilling to grow up. Footloose Dave Raymond's musical escapism playing with a local "wedding band," resigned surrender to his longtime girlfriend, and precipitous fall into love with another woman just as marriage rears its ugly head are the stuff comic dreams are made of—and the beguiling matter of a jaunty novel that's as knowledgeable about prolonged adolescence as it is about "classic" rock 'n' roll. Irresistible.

In a different vein, Ann Harleman's *Bitter Lake* turns what might have been conventional domestic melodrama into an engrossing portrait of relations among a middle-aged woman (Judith Hutchins) whose husband has left her, her embittered teenaged daughter (Lil), and the fugitive husband and father (Gort), whose flight from the exigencies and constrictions of family becomes the paradoxical source of this excellent novel's unusual and affecting resolution.

In *Willy Slater's Lane,* first-novelist Mitch Wieland draws a vivid contrast between sixtyish Erban Kern and his choleric older brother Harlan, with whom he has lived all his life—and convincingly portrays Erban's gradual separation from Harlan and emergence into the fuller life he'd believed would always be denied him. It's a book whose grip on the reader grows stronger as its plainspoken, moving story proceeds. And Tom Kelly's *Payback* evokes memories of 1930s movies with its tightly plotted, suspenseful account of two brothers, Paddy and Billy Adare, who go their separate ways (toward crime and respectability, respectfully) in a vigorously realized New York world of construction workers, Mafiosi, and dedicated lawmen. It's a familiar story nicely reimagined in contemporary terms.

Suzanne Berne's novel *A Crime in the Neighborhood* expertly plaits together the 1972 murder of a small boy in a Washington suburb, narrator Marsha Eberhard's confusion as her family recovers from her father's abandonment of them, and the country's dawning realization of what the Watergate burglary meant—in a fascinating novel that memorably analyzes "crimes" that plague us and how we survive and learn from them.

The "criminals" are, in a way, the heroes of Bruce Duffy's

long-awaited second novel (following his spectacular 1987 debut *The World as I Found It*), *Last Comes the Egg.* They include teenaged Frank Dougherty, his sociopathic buddy Alvy, and a black kid named Sheppy on an odyssey southward from their Maryland hometown in 1960, the year Frank's mother died—surviving an adventure remembered twenty-six years later and offered up as a kind of tribute to the passionate, perhaps slightly crazy Julie Dougherty. This journey, which echoes Huck Finn's progress, is a (rather overargued) object lesson in racial understanding, and a funny, entertaining, and endearing expression of its bright young narrator's uneasy assumption of maturity.

Pete Hamill's *Snow in August* knowingly traces the moral growth of eleven-year-old Michael Devlin in a postwar (1947) Brooklyn whose ethnic insularity is ruffled by both Jackie Robinson's unforeseen celebrity and acts of sickening antisemitic violence from which its young hero learns he cannot hold himself apart. Allen Hoffman's *Big League Dreams,* a winning successor to his earlier *Small Worlds,* continues an absorbing chronicle of the lives of Polish Jews transplanted to America. Here, the year is 1920 and the yearnings of Hoffman's characters to preserve their cultural heritage are severely (and comically) tested by moral crises related to the government's treatment of Native Americans and the temptations of major league baseball. Admirably constructed and teeming with life, this is a very ingratiating and possibly very important work in progress.

The Mercy Seat by Rilla Askew is a superbly dramatic (and offbeat) family chronicle set in the Oklahoma Territory in the 1880s and narrated by Mattie Lodi, a spirited girl forced into premature womanhood by the death of her mother during their family's westward traveling. A long-simmering conflict between her peace-loving father (a superlative gunsmith, ironically) and his dishonest brother makes for a marvelous recasting of the Cain and Abel story, and a painstaking, painful depiction of Mattie's beleaguered ingenuity and survival skills.

The three novellas in Rick Bass's collection *The Sky, the Stars, the Wilderness* aren't especially dramatic, but explore with seductive precision the varied worlds of a Texas ranch stubbornly maintained by the woman who loves it (the title story), Mississippi oil country (**"Where the Sea Used to Be"**), and the Yukon Territory decades ago (in the wonderful **"The Myths of Bears"**) as home to a taciturn "Trapper" so attuned to his environment's rhythms that his human presence is effectively subsumed into, and becomes part of its untamed animal life. Beautiful writing, of a visionary intensity shared probably only by Bass's contemporary Cormac McCarthy.

Small-town America is skillfully evoked and satirized in National Public Radio maven Garrison Keillor's delightful

Wobegon Boy, an amiably loose portrayal of Minnesotan John Tollefson's escape from the provinces to a nondescript New York State campus, a maddening job at (what else?) a public radio station, and an agreeably frustrating affair with a Modern Woman who won't take any guff from him. It really is a shame Sinclair Lewis never lived to meet Garrison Keillor.

Similar pleasures await the reader of John Dufresne's bittersweet second novel, *Love Warps the Mind a Little,* a beguiling portrait of a mediocre youngish writer who's both shattered and, eventually, matured by the agonizing death of the courageous, infuriating woman he can't help loving.

The crises are more manageable—as well as hilariously interconnected—in *Straight Man,* Richard Russo's ingratiating anatomy of exurban (Pennsylvania) campus life, held together (sort of) by principal character Hank Devereaux Jr.: a middle-aged one-book author and tenured professor buffeted among academic confrontations and scandals (including—I'm not making this up—the murder of a goose), half-serious sexual fantasies, and unresolved feelings toward his variously deranged relatives. It's a terrific comic novel, powered by narrator Hank's wry, irreverent, appealingly world-weary voice.

Laurence Naumoff's *A Plan for Women* works frustratingly less well, mainly because its deliciously unconventional portrayal of a loving couple who bring a little too much uncomfortable baggage to their tenuous union is interrupted by far too many authorial asides about the sexes' inevitable (and, when you come right down to it, irrelevant) incompatibility. Naumoff knows the territory all right, but he places a few too many roadblocks and potholes along the reader's path to it.

A powerful sense of the mysterious natures of ordinary lives permeates the stories in Charles Baxter's strong fourth collection, *Believers.* His characters are midwesterners stunned (in **"Time Exposure"** and **"Kiss Away"**) by the closeness of violent or bizarre forces to their innocent routines or, conversely, soothed and empowered (especially in **"The Cures of Love"**) by affirmative images beckoning from earlier times and other places. And the title novella, in which an American priest's experience of prewar Europe first distorts, then deepens his understanding of how good and evil are mingled together in the world, is a milestone in Baxter's work thus far.

Similar depth distinguishes the seven long stories in Deborah Eisenberg's *All around Atlantis.* These are lavishly described accounts of rites of passage whose most memorable participants are children or adolescents adapting themselves to the compromises adulthood seems to require (**"Mermaids," "The Girl Who Left Her Sock on the Floor"**) and

deracinated tourists who discover in alien surroundings their own vulnerability and unresolved strangeness (**"Tlaloc's Paradise," "Someone to Talk To"**). Demanding and thoughtful fiction, very much worth the close attention it asks of the reader.

The sophisticated characters who populate Allan Gurganus's vivid second novel, *Plays Well with Others,* embody both the colorful flair of gay artistic culture in the 1980s and the defiant spirit of victims of the plague (AIDS) that relentlessly strikes down New York City's brightest and most beautiful. The novel's effectiveness is vitiated by Firbankian campiness, but no praise is too high for the astonishing wit and vigor of its elegiac colloquial prose. The same cannot be said for *The Farewell Symphony,* Edmund White's heartfelt but overlong conclusion to the autobiographical trilogy he began with *A Boy's Own Story.* As much memorial to those who died of AIDS as it is character study of its fascinating and eloquent protagonist, it's a good novel which, had it been less explanatory and argumentative, might well be a far better one.

Francisco Goldman's *The Ordinary Seaman* ingeniously creates arresting drama from its literally static premise: a ship manned by Central American refugees moored in Brooklyn harbor. Its characters' tentative, frustrated efforts to assimilate into a world that won't permit them to come ashore comprise a provocative allegory of the immigrant experience of America.

Starling Lawrence's *Montenegro* creates a rich character in Auberon Harwell, an Englishman whose business trip to the Balkans (early in the century) is subverted by his attachment to an endangered, courageous people—and a consequent change of heart that makes him, in spite of himself, a man of principle. A rather different, and enormously appealing, adventure absorbs the eponymous twelve-year-old heroine of Brian Hall's *Saskiad.* Bookish and imaginative Saskia ventures beyond the upstate New York commune where she lives with her mother, inspired by an exotic new schoolmate and also the reappearance of her vagrant father, a self-styled "eco-warrior" whose fantasies nicely counterpoint Saskia's dreams of inhabiting the far-off lands and emulating the epic heroes she compulsively reads about. It's an utterly original portrayal of adolescence, and one of the year's most likable novels.

Sheer creative ingenuity distinguishes new novels from two very underrated American writers. The versatile Carol Dawson spins in *Meeting the Minotaur* a disarmingly bizarre yarn about young Texan Taylor Troys's adventures as a cat burglar and industrial spy as he seeks to make peace with his absentee father by undertaking a dangerous journey—into the subterranean bowels of a Japanese conglomerate's maze-like office building. The novel is both a comic reworking of classical myth and a laid-back, enjoyably sprawling coming-of-age tale. Harvey Jacobs's *American Goliath* retells the story of the Cardiff Giant, a marvelous hoax perpetrated on the spectacle-hungry populace in post-Civil War America. P. T. Barnum, Cornelius Vanderbilt, and other historical figures join such splendid invented ones as wiseacre journalist Barnaby Rack and criminally inclined cigarmaker George Hull in an exuberant carnival of Americana flavored with authoritative period detail and slang. It's hard to believe this hasn't been recognized as one of the year's best novels.

If veteran Harvey Jacobs remains underappreciated, there was ample critical attention paid to Kurt Vonnegut's "novel" *Timequake*, a fitfully amusing piece of whimsy purporting to describe life during a rerun of the 1990s occasioned by "a sudden glitch in the space-time continuum," but instead offering an autobiographical patchwork coyly explaining why this was all Vonnegut could make out of that promising premise. *Timequake* has its shaggy charms, but it's an annoyingly self-indulgent farrago in which the old familiar jokes are better than the new ones.

Other so-so books from big-name writers included John Hawkes's oddball tale of a suggestible girl's dreamlike romantic and sexual maturing (*An Irish Eye*); Joyce Carol Oates's disturbingly intense but hasn't-she-written-this-book-already? portrayal of a believably troubled girl bedeviled by cartoonishly violent men (*Man Crazy*); Denis Johnson's also over-familiar "California Gothic" (*Already Dead*) *noir*-derived tale of drug- and sex-addicts in surreal conflict, and—1997's damnedest surprise—*The Gospel According to the Son*, Norman Mailer's flat retelling of the life and martyrdom of Jesus as told by h/Himself. Except for its protagonist's Mailer-like fascination with the eternal struggle between God and the Devil, it's an altogether conventional, seemingly pointless book, which one reads with mounting confusion, wondering why in hell it was written and published.

Another career iconoclast, Robert Coover, fared better with his very amusing and highly sexed postmodernist retelling of a familiar fairytale in *Briar Rose*, a lovely old story to which he adds some hair-raising metafictional speculations about the limitations and very nature of storytelling.

Paul Theroux (whose cosmopolitan and darkly humorous *Collected Stories* also appeared in 1997) produced in *Kowloon Tong* one of his better (if only too characteristic) novels in some time: a portrayal of the English in Hong Kong on the eve of its reunification with China that offers both acute observations on the theme of cultural dislocation and simplistic ethnic characterisations that seem to this reader borderline racist.

Ward Just's *Echo House,* which analyzes the political and sexual involvements of three generations of a prominent Washington family, exudes a weary, sardonic knowledgeability about exactly what power brokers and office seekers do, and how our institutions are run, that makes it this ex-political correspondent's best novel yet. And Diane Johnson's *Le Divorce,* a witty tale of a hopeful young American woman's imperfect conquest of Paris, specifically evokes Henry James's *Portrait of a Lady* and *The Ambassadors* and, astonishingly, compares rather favorably with those masterpieces.

Cynthia Ozick was in top form with *The Puttermesser Papers,* a compound volume including previously published stories about as well as further adventures (extending into the afterlife) of her irresistible ater ego: frazzled bureaucrat, lover of literature, onetime Mayor of New York, and indomitable romantic. Hortense Calisher returned, with an unfortunately sluggish and attenuated tale of a misfit's rehabilitation among Manhattan's homeless (*In the Slammer with Carol Smith*), and, triumphantly, with her collected *Novellas,* a dazzling display of verbally rich and intricately interwoven narratives that restores to print such gems as **"Tale for the Mirror"** and **"The Railway Police."**

Ann Beattie's *My Life, Starring Dara Falcon* contrasts at excessive length its subdued narrator with the (eponymous) mercurial sophisticate she admires and abhors, in an otherwise well-plotted story about a woman learning to separate herself from others' claims on her. John Updike's ruminative *Toward the End of Time* is a disappointment: a vision of future America following a disastrous nuclear war with China that forsakes its interesting premise for a tedious reiteration of the opinions and fantasies of its sexually obsessed sexagenarian protagonist.

Frederick Busch's *Girls,* on the other hand, is one of this prolific author's best books: the story of a campus security guard whose shouldering of others' burdens makes painfully real to him how dangerous a place the world is, while making him a more sensitive and stronger man. But Peter Matthiessen's sprawling *Lost Man's River,* part of a long work in progress about familial mysteries, corruption, and murder in Florida's Everglades, is seriously weakened by discursive and hyperbolic authorial intrusions.

Bear and His Daughter collects stories written over a thirty-year period by the increasingly accomplished Robert Stone. These tense, disturbing studies of introverted characters compelled to test their courage and decency while unmanned by their various addictions are among the most powerful fiction of our time (**"Helping"** and **"Absence of Mercy"** are particularly noteworthy). The three novellas of Philip Caputo's *Exiles* are similar: tales of interior conflict that burst into violent confrontation, set in the contrasting locales of suburban Connecticut, an Australian off-island, and the jungles of Vietnam. Caputo's best book yet.

Old master Saul Bellow's novella *The Actual* is a *jeu*—another canny portrayal of high-energy Jewish moguls and intellectuals whom society and circumstance ineluctably, amusingly draw together. Louis Auchincloss's *The Atonement* contains twelve smoothly polished stories of social and moral *contretemps* among the wealthy and privileged that make the romance of old money seem enchantingly new. And *The Collected Stories* of Bernard Malamud ought to be an occasion for national rejoicing: fifty-five joyously colloquial, surreally comic stories of Jewry *in extremis,* including previously uncollected early work along with such familiar wonders as **"Idiots First," "The Jewbird,"** and **"The Magic Barrel."** A treasure house of fiction.

Finally, three novels that should be remembered when lists of the decade's best are compiled. *American Pastoral* is Philip Roth's uncharacteristically plaintive story (told, and in part imagined, by his recurring character novelist Nathan Zuckerman) of a life well lived—and, by extension, a prosperous and complacent society—rent irrationally asunder. The downward path to rueful wisdom trod by Zuckerman's old schoolmate Seymour "Swede" Levov, a paragon of athletic prowess and high lifetime achievement, whose beloved daughter becomes a terrorist and murderer, is traced with remorseless clarity and subtle empathy in a powerful accusatory narrative that rests on the unanswerable question "What the hell is wrong with doing things right?" The novelist capable of both *Portnoy's Complaint* and this masterpiece is unquestionably one of our best.

So, of course, is Thomas Pynchon, who emerged from another of his lengthy literary hibernations with the long-promised *Mason & Dixon.* A very imitation of the eighteenth-century novel, this wonderful historical romance tells the story of the British astronomer-surveyors whose demarcation of the line between America's northern and southern states is only one of their astonishing intellectual adventures in various climes and among a bevy of "enlightened" souls whom Pynchon presents (often with the help of enjoyably deranged anachronisms) as seekers, in their different ways, after knowledge, and *as* freedom. As always, Pynchon's polymathic fluency is brilliantly displayed, especially in a vivid account of his protagonists' sojourn in South Africa to observe the transit of Venus—an astral phenomenon scarcely more remarkable than the spectacle of this one-of-a-kind book itself: the work of a great writer at the height of his powers.

Mason & Dixon's only rival as the novel of the year was Don De Lillo's *Underworld,* a dazzlingly rich portrait of cold war America that begins with Bobby Thomson's pennant-winning home run in 1951, then exfoliated to embrace the creation of the atomic bomb and the subsequent shock waves that transformed our culture over the following forty years. Protagonist Nick Shay, a specialist in "waste management" and another of De Lillo's watchful solitaries, is the fulcrum for a complex envisioning of recent history that patiently, conclusively demonstrates how people are all simultaneously divided from one another and united by the forces ever at work around and beneath them, preparing a mass destiny in which all will unknowingly share.

Both apocalyptic and oddly reassuring (it stresses human interconnectedness in a way that's new in De Lillo's fiction), *Underworld* is a generously detailed panoramic synthesis of America approaching the century's, and perhaps our species's, end. It defies summary, but few readers who make their way through its densely dramatic opening pages will be able to resist the dark-hued millennial spell it casts. It's a novel that belongs on the same shelf with *Mason & Dixon,* and I can't imagine higher praise than that.

The Year in Poetry
by Allen Hoey

At the conclusion of "The Poet as Translator," the most intelligent and savvy essay on the topic, Kenneth Rexroth notes one reason why poets try translation:

> Translation saves you from your contemporaries. You can never really model yourself on Tu Fu or Leopardi or Paulus the Silentiary, but if you try you can learn a great deal about yourself. It is all too easy to model yourself on T. S. Eliot or William Carlos Williams or W. H. Auden or Allen Ginsberg—fatally easy—thousands do it every day. But you will never learn anything about yourself.

Updating the list of contemporaries (Robert Bly, John Ashbery, and, probably still, Allen Ginsberg), this passage retains its common-sense appeal. Given that, if anything, the demand for "practically unrelieved intensity in poetry" has increased in the 36 years since Rexroth wrote this piece, we have even greater need not only for the forum in which to practice our art when our capacity for intensity fails but the need for the "nice class of people" we meet in this way.

Few living poets have translated as widely and prolifically as Rexroth (W. S. Merwin comes to mind), but many poets test their skills against the challenge, as a cursory glance at the Table of Contents of *Dante's Inferno: Translations by 20 Contemporary Poets* (Ecco, 1993) reveals. More recently, Stephen Berg's **The Steel Cricket: Versions 1958-1997** (Copper Canyon) seems to rival Rexroth in terms of diversity and range. Like Rexroth, Berg is not conversant (or even literate) in most of the languages represented; he indicates in his "Preface," most of these pieces are "based on the English translations of scholars." However, much as Rexroth suggests, Berg's compulsion to work with these texts was born of a desire for self-discovery: the texts "touched me," he writes, "they offered fresh experience, unexpected imagery, strange logic. Often I heard a music that took over and led me to remake the texts." Hence, Berg calls these "versions" rather than translations, much as Lowell referred to his efforts as "imitations." The product of his forty years at this effort (with a few omissions, most notably his probing versions of Zen Master Ikkyu, *Crow with No Mouth,* recently reissued by Copper Canyon) is a mixed bag in more ways than one.

Berg's versions range from Buddha to Octavio Paz; from Aztec to Tlinget to Eskimo; from French, German, Spanish, and Italian to Hungarian and Japanese. The volume's scope rivals Pound's *From Confucius to Cummings,* except that

Berg does not confine his attention to the anthologized elite. The forms and styles are equally eclectic. Versions from modern European or Latin American texts tend to be written in fairly conventional lineation and syntax, while the shapes he uses to present the more "primitive" texts or texts from non-Western languages reflect the difficulties inherent in such transposition. At their most extreme, Berg's versions almost force us to occupy a middle ground between the original and its English equivalent, a position he describes as part of his process in making some of these poems:

> During the process of struggling for the English version of a poem you want to re-create and make exciting reading, there is no language exactly, only broken webs, shadow accuracies, error enraged and impatient—you become anonymous and then leap out into a new attempt.

This sounds very much like the kind of "sympathy" Rexroth felt necessary to successful translation: "the identification of another person with oneself, the transference of his utterance to one's own utterance."

Individual readers will need to judge how successfully Berg "advocates" (to use Rexroth's term) for these originals. My own familiarity with many of the Japanese texts makes me a little impatient with his efforts; I would rather he had brought the ideas a little closer to English, but then I'm struck by the recognition that Berg probably has brought these as close to his own experience as he can. His own impulse in these pieces is expressed in a line from Paz's "Altar of the Sun": "I come to life in someone else." Further, the raw power of the originals often shines through because of his minimal intrusion, as in this Aztec song:

> only we come to make songs on earth
> to know each other in the place of drums
> you are a friend!
> nothing is so far away
> and nothing breaks

At times, however, one is uncertain where the original stops and Berg begins. His version of Leopardi's "To the Moon" exceeds the original five times over in length and incorporates elements of biography nowhere present in Leopardi's lyric. On the other hand, he has rendered Leopardi's famous **"L'Infinito"** as a powerful contemporary statement:

> That hill out there—I've always loved it!—

and this hedge, cutting in front of me,
blocking the horizon, the last step to infinity
Sitting here, stunned by a dream of space
beyond all hills and hedges, I hear
silence erasing man's possibilities.
A calm starts inside me and stays for a while.
Wind roughing the trees, weighed against silence,
is eternity.
This is the season of the mind—
the dizzying gulf of sky, the abyss of self—
one distant, visible; one close as my own skin—
each impossible to know or to touch,
this is the time when consciousness and thought
and I
are nameless, nothing, not here. I love it—
the one true freedom: letting my mind sink
like a ship in midocean whose keel
is smashed by some invisible
fist and goes down with the sweet ease of a rock.

The idiom floats somewhere between Leopardi's Romanticism and our own post-modern, self-conscious variation on Romanticism. For readers interested in the shape and range of poetry and poetic expression, this volume is a must.

Very much more scholarly, **Leopardi: Selected Poems** (Princeton UP), translated by Irish poet Eamon Grennan, provides a representative sampling of this poet whose contribution to the contemplative lyric is too little appreciated. Grennan, in addition to his considerable talent as a poet, also brings his undergraduate study of Italian to bear on these versions, and he produces a volume of highly readable poetry to introduce readers to or expand their understanding of Leopardi's work. Both the introduction by John C. Barnes and Grennan's own introduction provide valuable insight into the milieu in and from which Leopardi wrote and the process of bringing these poems into English. Here is Grennan's translation of **"L'Infinito"**:

I've always loved this lonesome hill
And this hedge that hides
The entire horizon, almost, from sight.
But sitting here in a daydream, I picture
The boundless spaces away out there, silences
Deeper than human silence, an unfathomable hush
In which my heart is hardly a beat
From fear. And hearing the wind
Rush rustling through these bushes,
I pit its speech against infinite silence—
And a notion of eternity floats to mind,
And the dead seasons, and the season
Beating here and now, and the sound of it. So,
In this immensity my thoughts all drown;
And it's easeful to be wrecked in seas like these.

Line for line, this is certainly a closer equivalent than Berg's rendition. The best sense of the original may be gleaned from comparing the two and extrapolating one's own sympathetic "take" on Leopardi's mood. (For further comparison, see Rexroth's translation in his *Collected Shorter Poems.*)

A measure of cultural difference can be gleaned by comparing Leopardi's work with that of his Japanese contemporary, Kobayashi Issa. In **The Spring of My Life and Selected Haiku** (Shambhala) Sam Hamill offers a wholly satisfying selection of Issa's work, including the only easily available version of his best-known haibun, *Oraga haru,* a diary-like collection of observations and anthology of other poets' haiku. The most familiar example of the form is Matsuo Basho's *Narrow Road to the Interior.* Issa's gathering is much different, much more apparently a vade mecum than Basho's carefully wrought spiritual allegory. In fact, Issa tends to be much more genuinely popular than Basho, in general; his concerns are the concerns of the common man, his eye more concentrated on the mundane minutia without deliberate regard for its artistic potential. The inherent problem in Issa's way is the frequent lapses into sentimentality and mere trivia. At heart, however, he is committed to the Buddhist way, and that devotion shines through his work. In the twelfth section, after considering his "bad karma," he continues:

In the midst of my confession, moonlight falls over the gate like a cool breath. A group of dancing children suddenly begins to sing. My daughter drops her bowl and crawls out on the porch and joins her voice to the others, lifting her hands to the moon. Watching, I forget my advancing age and worldly ways. I daydream about a time when she'll be old enough for long waves of hair, when we encourage her to dance. Surely she could outshine the music of two dozen heavenly maidens. Day in, day out, her legs never rest. By nightfall, she's exhausted and sleeps deeply until the sun is high. While she sleeps, her mother cooks and cleans. Only then can her mother find a moment's rest before she awakens again with a cry. Her mother carries her out to the yard to pee, then nurses her. Our daughter sucks with a smile, poking the breast happily. Her mother then forgets the weariness and pain of having carried her in the womb, she forgets the dirty diapers she washes every day, lost in the supreme joy of having such a child, more precious than jewels.

Nursing, mother counts
the fleabites on her daughter's
small white body.

A measure of Issa's artistry and design of the volume is that within a few months the child will be dead. We glimpse this reprieve from contemplation of karma, then we see with heart-breaking clarity the price of cherishing.

In his versions, Hamill seeks to capture the wide-eyed simplicity of Issa's deep and complicated vision. Overall, his accomplishment is more evident in his rendering of Basho's haibun, a task that shows off his skill as a translator in more apparent ways; the very understatement of Issa's poems might cause Western readers to dismiss Hamill's felicity. His versions are fuller and more realized than those of other translators who have sought to duplicate in stripped-down English the literal effect of the Japanese verse. That is not, however, the way that native readers of Issa would experience the poems. If Hamill's commitment to retaining the syllabic armature of the Japanese form occasionally leads him astray, his devotion to the work more than compensates in providing this marvelous example of a master artist.

Very different in tone are David R. Slavitt's translations of John Owen's Latin epigrams, which comprise the first half of *Epic and Epigram: Two Elizabethan Entertainments* (LSU). If, as Rexroth has elsewhere suggested, **"L'Infinito"** serves as a kind of stepping stone between Romanticism and the kind of poetic reverie typical of contemporary poetry, the epigram, with its laconic, balanced incisiveness, is a far remove from what we expect from a poem. Slavitt admits as much in his introduction and provides a further insight into the "elitist" esthetic involved particularly in Owen's epigrams: an Elizabethan headmaster, he deliberately wrote in Latin at a time when some of the masterworks of modern English were being produced. The form Slavitt chooses for his translations speaks volumes about the distance we have come from Owen's sensibility; in place of the carefully balanced Latin elegiac distichs, Slavitt often opts for longer stanzas, frequently irregular in shape though always metrically sound. As in the following example, **"Contemptus Mundi,"** the losses in Slavitt's strategy sometimes outweigh the gains:

> Felicem vitam vis vivere? spernito vitam:
> Vivit enim misere, cui sua vita placet.

> Ya want to be happy
> as Mr. Clam?
>   Then you've got to learn how
>   not to give a damn.

> The fellow who frets
> and worries all night
>   is the one who is hanging
>   on too tight,

> counting his blessings,
>   his children, his wife,

> his nice house
>   and his lovely life . . .

> He knows he is going to kick the bucket.

>   He's got to learn how
>   to shrug and say, "Fuck it."

To appreciate that Slavitt's "translation" may be a more trenchant comment on our lives is not to diminish the distance between his piece and the original. At other times, happily, Slavitt has reproduced both the bite and the balance, as in **"To Germanicus, January 1, 1600"**:

> Vel munus donato mihi, vel reddito versus:
>   Quos hac donavi condicione tibi.

> Send me the damned gift, you incompetent hack.
> Otherwise, send me my New Year's poem back.

Unfortunately, the "Entertainment," variations on Spenser featuring a cast of characters that includes the contemporary royal family, partakes more of the first translation than the second.

Finally, Stephen Mitchell has published what is to my ear the single best selection of Pablo Neruda's poetry in English. The most significant complaint I have with ***Full Woman, Fleshly Apple, Hot Moon*** (HarperCollins) concerns the selection itself rather than the translation. Not surprisingly for someone who has rendered some of the best translations of Rilke and arguably the best version of *The Duino Elegies,* Mitchell has an astute ear for both idiom and music. The American English of his versions is not marred by lapses in diction or awkward constructions; he finds an appropriate balance between the Latinate and Anglo-Saxon. As importantly, one never senses that any of his rearrangement of lines to make the poems successful in English alter the emphasis or focus of the originals. Most of the selections are long, skinny odes, which makes excerpting difficult. This brief poem from late in the book, however, should give some sense of Mitchell's accomplishment; titled **"Nace,"** he translates it as "It Is Born":

> Here, I came to the boundaries
> where nothing needs to be said,
> everything is learned with weather and ocean,
> and the moon returned
> with its lines silvered
> and each time the shadow was broken
> by the crash of a wave
> and each day on the balcony of the sea
> wings open, fire is born
> and everything continues blue as the morning.

Readers acquainted with Mitchell's long-time interest in Eastern religions will sense the appeal of this for the translator.

In his Forword, Mitchell notes that he "made no effort to be representative"; instead, he "just took what [he] loved most." What he loved most, it turns out, are poems from a scant eight years of Neruda's fifty-year career, poems beginning with his first collection of *Odas Elementales* (1954) through until *Plenos poderes* (1962). And even these eight years are not fully represented, since during this period he published at least four collections which Mitchell has entirely ignored: *Navegaciones y regresos* (1959), *Las piedras de Chili* (1960), *Cantos ceremoniales* (1961), and the almost completely neglected *Canción de gesta,* Neruda's book that details the subjection and revolutionary action in Latin America that culminated in Castro's overthrow of Batista's regime. Since Mitchell's interest seems far removed from the political, his eschewing of this volume is hardly surprising, and the circumscribed criteria for inclusion do not detract from his achievement; primarily I would like to register my small general complaint against the short shrift given *Canciòn de gesta* and my more specific complaint about not having a more widely representative selection of Neruda's poetry in Mitchell's translation.

After completing the beginning of this review, I began reading Jane Hirshfield's collection of essays, ***Nine Gates: Entering the Mind of Poetry*** (HarperCollins), which includes the piece "The World Is Large and Full of Noises: Thoughts on Translation." That Hirshfield, herself an accomplished translator, shares the gist of Rexroth's attitude toward the art and craft is signaled by her epigraph, taken from the Preface to the King James Bible: "Translation it is that openeth the window to let in the light; that breaketh the shell, that we may eat the kernel." For Hirshfield, translation "play[s] an essential role in the innumerable conversations between familiar and strange, native and import, past and future, by which history and culture are made." Echoing the impulse that draws Berg to translation, she writes, "A great poem creates in its readers the desire to know it more thoroughly, to live with it in intimacy, to join its speaking to their own as fully as possible." For the translator, the process is one of mutual seduction: something in the poem seduces the reader to want to engage it fully; then, the reader attempts to seduce the poem into his or her native tongue.

Given the erotic (in the fullest sense) nature of the act, the poet/translator bears considerable responsibility, not the least of which is "to convey each poem's particular strength." This challenge increases proportionate to the poem's distance across culture or time:

> An older poem's increasing strangeness of language
> is part of its beauty, in the same way that the cracks

and darkening of an old painting become part of its luminosity in the viewer's mind: they enter not only the physical painting, but our vision of it as well. This is why seeing an old painting suddenly "restored" can be unnerving—we recognize a tampering with its relationship to time, miss the scented smoke of the centuries' passage.

The second half of the essay details the ways in which her own process in bringing the works of Ono no Komachi and Izumi Shikibu (*The Ink Dark Moon,* with Mariko Aratani) reveal the challenges and rewards of this labor. The passionate, caring, and careful sensibility demonstrated is similarly at work in the other eight essays gathered in the volume.

Concurrently, Hirshfield published her fifth collection of poems, ***The Lives of the Heart*** (HarperCollins). The poems in this volume show maturation of craft from her previous book, *The October Palace,* but the specificity and delicacy of focus, particularly on the natural world, are consistent. If these poems display a little less erudition than those in *The October Palace,* the gain is an intensified presence and increased acuity of metaphor. A practicing Zen Buddhist, Hirshfield shares that discipline's perception that the sacred and the profane, the worldly and the spiritual are not separable realms. Among the finest examples of this insistence on "not one, not two" gathered here is "If the Rise of the Fish":

> If for a moment
> the leaves fell upward,
> if it seemed a small flock
> of brown-orange birds
> circled over the trees,
> if they circled then scattered each in
> its own direction for the lost seed
> they had spotted in tall, gold-checkered grass.
> If the bloom of flies on the window
> in morning sun, if their singing insistence
> on grief and desire. If the fish.
> If the rise of the fish.
> If the blue morning held in the glass of the
> window,
> if my fingers, my palms. If my thighs.
> If your hands, if my thighs.
> If the seeds, among all the lost gold of the grass.
> If your hands on my thighs, if your tongue.
> If the leaves. If the singing fell upward. If grief.
> For a moment if singing and grief.
> If the blue of the body fell upward, out of our
> hands.
> If the morning held it like leaves.

From these few, relatively simple elements, Hirshfield creates a complex music of variation, complete in its insistent lack of completion.

For all their gorgeousness, Hirshfield's poems too often leave out the shared quotidian, the hallmark of Issa's haiku. As with a still life painter who includes fruit and flowers—not necessarily rare beauties; day lilies and asters will do—the sense of the disarray of human use is often lost. She articulates an awareness of this in **"Letter to Hugo from Later,"** a form appropriate to her recognition:

> I envy the way you managed to pack so many parts
> of the world
> in such a little space, the way you'd go from
> pouring a glass
> of beer to something American and huge. I don't
> write much
> about America, or even people. For you, people
> were what there was:
> you talked with and about them and stayed up late
> to love those high-lobbed lives. I'd often enough
> rather
> talk to horses.

Interestingly, in using the shape of Hugo's letter poems, she imitates as well the too-often dull prosody, the lapse into prose energized, when at all, by sentiment rather than emotion. The danger for Hirshfield if, as this poem suggests, she hopes to find a way to incorporate more of that world within her poems, is to get the force of contingency without the slackening of acuity.

In *The Monarchs: A Poem Sequence* (LSU), Alison Hawthorne Deming displays a similar clarity of focus when regarding the natural world. Rather than viewing nature through a spiritual lens, however, Deming more often studies the workings of nature, process, and intelligence through a lens ground from a compound of literary naturalism and science. This is perhaps not surprising for a poet whose first collection bore the title *Science and Other Poems.* Science for Deming is not the test-tube remove of the laboratory chemist but the expanse of the ethnobiologist, and, if the canny intelligence of the monarch butterflies lends a through-line to the sequence, she spends more time noting the peculiarities of human intelligence and emotions. Running at a glancing parallel to the recurrent motif of the monarchs are moments from the life of a rather typical end-of-the-century woman, including the broken or failed relations, the efforts at justifying love, and the essays at making intelligence, emotion, and other manifestations of art and nature cohere. Throughout, Deming displays a range of styles, from slender lyrics to longer lined poems to prose poems. Section 44 provides an example of her compression:

> Night. A woman betrayed.

> Insects gather
> on the cabin window
> so that all she can see
> is a plague of gray moths.
> She's sick of the body's
> dumb song, the frenzy
> of insects for light.
> Why does a moth do that
> if it's nocturnal?
> If it woke up in the daytime,
> it could simply
> have what it wants.

The juxtaposition of "the body's / dumb song, the frenzy / of insects for light" provides the basis for a metaphor that extends far beyond the surface of the poem; if we read it fully, we extrapolate a world of wondering. Just how far can this analogy be stretched? What exactly is it about our "body's / dumb song" that so resembles "the frenzy / of insects"? What might our equivalent be to simply waking in daylight to "have what [we] want . . ."? The balancing of "dumb song" and "the frenzy" in a single line demonstrates a mastery of the effects that an accomplished versifier can achieve in free verse.

Interspersed through the sixty poems of the sequence are seven "Essays on Intelligence" which draw together the threads of the varied discourse. These are usually the most "scientific" of the pieces. Deming's ability to modulate technical vocabulary into poetic lines is impressive; we can become so accustomed to the narrow semantic and syntactic lexicon of contemporary poetry that we forget the wealth of possibilities our language offers. Here is the opening of section 24, **"Essay on Intelligence: Two"**:

> Language has been the central
> event in human evolution.
> Simple emotional utterances
> evoked in sex, anger, and fear
> activate the primitive area
> near the *corpus callosum,*
> that ribbon tying together
> the hemispheres. No one knows
> how our ancestors got beyond
> the scream, grunt, and moan
> to string meaningless phonemes
> together until the sounds
> meant something in tandem
> they didn't mean alone.

In this volume Deming has succeeded at incorporating into poetry, with no loss of emotive power or linguistic music, a sensibility firmly rooted in the protocols of science. And nowhere does Deming seem tempted to applaud her achievement.

Rather more modest in scope, the poems in *Sky and Island Light* (LSU) nonetheless persuade that Brendan Galvin consistently keeps both eyes trained on the natural world while he allows his imagination to play. Anyone who has lived the country life, spent time in field and forest and on the water, will trust the accuracy of Galvin's perceptions and, hence, follow his fancy where it leads. **"Wild Blackberries,"** one of the shorter lyrics, displays his skill:

> There are places where things
> tie a knot between seasons—
> back of fern beds, for instance,
> against a steepness
> of trees, places you watch
> your step, risking ticks,
> snakes, maybe tentacles of
> something escaped
> or paroled from the mind
> as too difficult to manage.
> Here, for instance (I will not
> tell you where), you taste
> and look both ways, each bleb
> a sweet completion and tart
> finality, a trap for
> solstice light, a lamp
> down hollow, faint in early dark.

Small moments here that please include the nod toward the countryman's reticence to disclose his trove and the self-deprecating acknowledgment that even for the experienced outdoorsman the imagination projects the greatest dangers. If Galvin does not show leaps of improvement in craft or a wide range of either technical skill or subject, his work continues to please.

As usual, the year produced a bumper crop of selected poems. Since I've groused about this previously, I'll hold my grumbling to a minimum. Clearly, many presses, especially the university presses so necessary to poetry's survival, employ the selected edition for a plethora of purposes, which include preserving work that has otherwise gone out of print, consolidating the work of one of their stable under a single imprint, and promoting one of theirs as a candidate for the majors. Even considered from this last standard, however, some selectees seem less warranted than others. If one reads James Seay's **Open Field, Understory** (LSU) in this light, one might conclude that this was not the best pitch to make on Seay's behalf. The book's first disservice is its reverse chronological ordering; Seay's most recent work is strong and individual, an interesting voice and intelligence playing with strategies of narrative disclosure. The earliest work, drawn from his two Wesleyan University collections, is indistinguishable from the period style. On the other hand, the selection of new poems, the work excerpted from *The Light as They Found It* (1990), and the long sequence *Said There*

Was Somebody Talking to Him Through the Air Conditioner (1985), drew me in. The language is more supple and the forms more responsive to his more complex undertakings. Seay's serpentine handling of narrative threads is suggested by the opening lines of the sequence:

> There is always one fiction or another trying to
> trade for real
>   skin and bone,
> just to turn around and drive that taken character
> back over
> the border into phenomena with the story every-
> where around him
>   alive.
> The charge is to claim whatever needs to be freed
> from fact: road,
>   ruin, stretch of river
> known by heart, ring or pendant, torn flag, fist in
> the face,
>   ticket stub,
> family plot, love and grief so riddled one with the
> other there
>   isn't even a choice.
> The character he's become says he doesn't want to
> die, but he's got
>   only one foot in the fiction,
> everlasting, the other in the grave of this life. And
> he needs us
>   conscripted alongside him.

Had LSU issued a volume that consisted of only new poems and *Said There Was Somebody* (issued only in limited edition), Seay would have delivered a collection to claim attention on the basis of growth.

While Margaret Gibson's case is less cautionary than Seay's, one still wonders why the volume was entirely necessary given the strength of the newest poems collected in **Earth Elegy: New and Selected Poems.** Perhaps LSU, which holds the rights to all of Gibson's work, hoped to capitalize on the attention *The Vigil* garnered as 1993 National Book Award finalist. As near as I can determine, three of her five previous volumes remain in print, including the two book-length sequences, *The Vigil* and *Memories of the Future: the Daybooks of Tina Modotti.* This is particularly good since the former, especially, is not well represented in this collection; in general, long poems or sequences are not easily digested into selected volumes. In Gibson's case, *The Vigil* represents, more than any other of her collections, the scope and variety of which she is capable. The four speakers in the sequence are each presented in different forms and distinctive voices to delineate character. It shows maturation in this regard from the earlier sequence which presented only one character, Tina Modotti, and that representation at times, even in the samples included in this volume, seems generic, wooden, although the verse itself is generally supple and well-crafted.

In fact, what strikes the reader most about Gibson's work is less the dramatic improvement or evolution of form and style but, like Brendan Galvin's, the consistent consolidation of craft and sensibility across her career. Her concerns remain constant; her sense of language and line, although refining from volume to volume, similarly demonstrates consistency throughout her career. This is not to condemn or criticize either Gibson's art or craft; her accomplishment is evidenced in the complex, lengthy syntax and verbal and aural play in these opening lines of **"At the Ravine"**:

> Within the interpreted world of stone
> walls and a bougainvillea trained to bloom
> into the body and beak of a bird,
> exotic plumage kept to hand
> and rooted, you have pointed out
> the prickets of epiphytic bromeliad
> kindled by early sun in the spreading tree
> across the ravine—candlelabra,
> you say, smiling to recall
> how your mother, new to the language,
> said *candle bras*—and so
> the conversation rambles into a thicket
> of resemblances, nothing singular
> but ourselves, and we hide our light.

Many poets consolidate rather than display radical shifting of style and concern. As an observation, however, it leads me to wonder what about Gibson's career, sure and steady as it may have been, warrants the valediction of a selected poems. In many ways her most notable achievements—the two book-length sequences—have been truncated such that we cannot measure that accomplishment. Instead, we are left with evidence of one more journeyman poet among many, which is not slighting praise but not convincing rationale for a selected poems, either.

The rationale for Brenda Marie Osbey's *All Saints: New and Selected Poems* (LSU), her fourth collection, seems stronger. Her previous collections have passed with little notice and are available, if at all, from small presses. Still, the label is a bit misleading; the volume seems of a piece, with no apparatus—no indication anywhere, in fact, which poems are old and which new. These twenty poems, many lengthy narratives, are organized such that they resemble the selection a poet makes to assemble a collection rather than a retrospection. The poems are spoken by a variety of personae, male and female, spanning from youth to age. All of them, however, are steeped in the redolence of New Orleans: the mythology of jazz, the folklore and faith of New World African religions, and the living history of slave culture. The mix is compelling. Characters speak, articulating the lives

behind their lives, the foundation of the dead who remain vital ingredients of the present. The overlapping realms are evoked in the incantatory opening of **"Peculiar Fascination with the Dead"**:

> light candles to honor the dead.
> set flowers on the altars of the dead
> which must be raised in your home.
> wear the memory of the dead plainly
> so anyone looking will see
> how the decent do not forget.
> speak of the dead
> as though you thought they might hear
> from the adjoining room.
> keep mourning portraits
> always about your home.
> marry memory to the dead.

Osbey uses the sinewy, largely unpunctuated line well; I particularly admire the specificity of the turn into the line, "as though they might hear / from the adjoining room." The dead are not merely a presence; they are that absolutely present. This collection should achieve wider recognition for Osbey's considerable talent.

Finally, although only a selection of poems written since his 1992 *Collected Poems* gathered into a single volume, James Laughlin's **The Secret Room** (New Directions) serves as a fitting testament to his career. Few have devoted their lives to the service of poetry as Laughlin did over his 83 years. New Directions brought into and kept in print a greater number of masterworks of the twentieth century than any other single publisher. The works of Pound, Williams, H. D., Rexroth, Duncan, and Levertov, to cite only the cream, have been shepherded through numerous editions; the re-edited volumes of Williams' complete poems, including the tireless restoration of *Paterson,* alone would be worth tribute. Beyond that, although never of the first rank, Laughlin has served considerable yeoman duty in his own verse. The poems gathered in this volume represent a variety of forms: the "typewriter metric" whose shape is lost in set type, syllabics, a three-stress line modeled after Rexroth, and the variably metered "pentastich" are only a few of the shapes Laughlin employs to explore his musings and reminiscences. The voice is that of the poetic elder, unabashedly personal in reference but also modest in its claims. For this, Laughlin is best served by his shorter, more epigrammatic lyrics:

SOME PEOPLE THINK

> that poetry should be a-
> dorned or complicated   I'm
>
> not so sure   I think I'll
> take the simple statement

in plain speech compress-
ed to brevity   I think that

will do all I want to do.

Such wit and modesty will be missed.

Casual readers who mistake Charles Wright for C. K. Williams and vice versa suffer an understandable confusion; their
names are quite similar, they're roughly of an age, they've
been publishing for about the same span of time, their works
often turn up in the same magazines, and both are published
by Farrar, Straus and Giroux. Beyond that, similarities are
few. True, both write rather extended, often non-linear meditative lyrics. Williams, however, retains at base a commitment to narrative disclosure, oblique and looping as it may
be, as well as a concern for the human contingencies. In
Black Zodiac, his tenth separate collection of poems,
Charles Wright demonstrates a knack for the abstract realm
of rumination that leaves one wondering whether the poet
has a life beyond his wooded backyard; does he converse
with anyone outside his recollection or imagination? Do the
terms "form," "structure," and "measure" refer to anything
more concrete than artistic templates? In **"The Appalachian
Book of the Dead"** (a promising title), the poet invokes
Pound's caution, then dismisses it:

> *Go in fear of abstractions . . .*
> > > Well, possibly. Meanwhile,
> They *are* the strata our bodies rise through, the
> > sere veins
> Our skins rub off on.
> For instance, whatever enlightenment there might
> > be
> Housels compassion and affection, those two
> > tributaries
> That river above our lives,
> Whose waters we sense the sense of
> > > > late at night, and later still.

This passage may exemplify what Pound meant by
logopoeia, "the dance of intellect among words," but it demonstrates the danger as well as the appeal, for, as Pound
notes, "It is . . . perhaps [the] most tricky and undependable
mode." This dance runs the risk of violating one of Pound's
fundamental touchstones: "One 'moves' the reader only by
clarity. In depicting the motions of the 'human heart' the durability of the writing depends on exactitude." However exactly Wright may delimit the condition of his own heart, once
we get beyond his word-drunk momentum, what remains to
clarify the state of our souls?

In *The Vigil,* his seventh collection, C. K. Williams at times
seems as apt to lose us, but his poems reward the return
reader with glimpses beyond the lap and swell of language

across the page. Entering his sixth decade, he entertains an
elegiac note more often than before, though his concerns are
less to mourn the lost than to explore the complexities of
time and memory. In fact, the four poems titled "Time," each
marked with a specific year, are among the most engaging
in the collection. **"Time: 1976"** provides the model. Walking "down the hallway towards the living room," the poet
has a momentary flash forward in time that provokes "as violent and rending a regret as anything [he's] ever felt." From
this, the poem leaps forward:

> Ten years from now, or twenty; I'm walking down
> the same hallway,
> > I hear the same music,
> the same sounds—Catherine's story, Jed's chirps
> of response—but
> > I know with anxiety
> that most of this is only in my mind: the reality is
> that Catherine
> > and Jed are no longer there,
> that I'm merely constructing this—what actually
> accompanies me
> > down that corridor is memory:
> here, in this tentative but terribly convincing
> future I think to
> > myself that it must be the music—
> the Bach surely is real. I can *hear* it—that drives
> me so
> > poignantly, expectantly back
> to remember again that morning of innocent peace
> a lifetime ago
> > when I came towards them;
> the sunny room, the music, the voices, each more
> distinct now:
> > *Voilà le château, voilà Babar . . .*

That this occurs, occurs to all of us, only in our minds is
no great relief; Williams evokes the helplessness we experience in the drift of our imaginations toward loss anticipated and, as well, the redemptive grounding we can
find in the actual.

The actual does not provide the same measure of redemption for Marie Howe in her second collection, *What the Living Do* (Norton). As an incest survivor and sister of a young
man dead of AIDS, she needs to find consolation, as slender as it may be, in the ephemeral threads of relationship—
to the commonplace and those who share it with her. The
dilemma, as for most of us, is how to extricate ourselves
from cocoons of self-absorption, especially intellectual in-
sulation, to get to that comfort. Howe presents a portrait of
that fix in **"Memorial,"** a poem about the aftermath of her
brother's death. She inhabits her own grief-stricken egoism
ruthlessly, laying it bare for us to see:

When James comes in from plowing for hours,
stomping
his big boots by the open door, he's beautiful,

but I don't tell him that. I say: aren't you going to
your music lesson?
Thinking: why don't you make more money?

When I tell him about post-modern brokenness in
Caroline [*sic*] Forche's poems,
that can't be repaired, he stirs the old fire with a
stick,

and reaches in with his hands and moves one log
so it sits
on top of the other. Then I think: James is stupid,

he doesn't know that the personal narrative is
obsolete. And I think
about how Billy used to call me Angel Face—

how after he died we found out that he called a lot
of us that.
I don't know the meaning of my own life anymore,
is what I tell James,

and he says, Yes you do. You've forgotten, but
you'll remember again.
And when I stare at him steadily, he rises

from where he's crouching by the fire and leans
over my chair,
and opens and closes his eyes so his lashes brush
my throat and lips and cheek

I'm hungry, he says. What do you want to eat?

Although the dramatic unfolding is less masterful than
Frost's handling of star-crossed grief in "Home Burial,"
Howe nonetheless frames the tension in drama, trusting the
reader to understand the subtext that emerges from the scraps
of conversation, how, despite the apparent denigration of
James by the speaker, the poem presents James as the one
able to derive and offer such solace as heat and food—the
basic creature comforts—allow. Although not all the poems
are this successful, this collection provides many such rewards.

The substance of Christopher Bursk's fifth full-length collection, *The One True Religion* (QRL), is precisely the sort
of personal narrative lyric that Howe claims is obsolete. The
dramatic interplay evident in the best of Howe's poems is
not the staple of Bursk's book; rather, he relies on a good
ear and skilled sense of how to balance the free verse line
to frame some of the finest evocations of the imaginary

realms of childhood I've encountered in a long time. In his
"Afterword," Bursk reveals the autobiographical basis for
the volume: the child's imagined empire, complete with histories, maps, treaties, and genealogies, that served as a refuge for two brothers whose mother suffered from madness
and whose father was ill-equipped (as almost all are) to "deal
with his wife's brilliant refusal to accept the world's injustices." On this foundation, the older brother created and
elaborated the world of Brem; the younger, the poet, had the
duty "to witness, remember, and believe." Part of the ritual
was the periodic devastation of all they had created and its
resurrection through the agency of the younger brother's
mourning. One of the most moving poems in the collection
describes the final destruction of Brem, an inevitable rite of
passage the older brother requires sooner than the younger.
They gather "everything to do with *pretend*" and burn it in
the backyard. "It was time [he] learned the difference / between reality and make believe," the older brother said; the
younger believed it merely another move in the game:

As he held the match to all our heaped-up
riches, our secret documents, our years of labor,
I refused to worry.
The point of our games had always been ruin,
to bring the empire to the edge of extinction.
No one returned from the dead
more often than my brother.
Bored with one world, he'd invent another.
The bonfire was just another stroke of genius.

The fourth section moves away from **"The Life of the
Imagination,"** as Bursk aptly titles one poem, into the world
he experiences teaching in a local prison. The connection
between the childhood realms of imaginative play as refuge
and the sorts of refuge the inmates sought is not as clearly
delineated as the relationships explored in the earlier sections. At times the clarity of perception and expression that
crystallize the suffering of child and family blur ever so
slightly, leading away from compassion, difficult enough to
feel for oneself, into the sentimental. Still, this collection
confirms Bursk as a poet worth reading and watching.

Brenda Hillman is another poet I have been watching for
some time. *Loose Sugar* (Wesleyan UP), her fifth full-length
collection, is the third of her volumes I've reviewed since I
began this enterprise in 1991. Her two previous collections,
Death Tractates (1992) and *Bright Existence* (1993), derive
their foundations from Hillman's study of Gnosticism; in this
book, she moves a step further into esoterica, building the
poems around the metaphysics and psychology of alchemy.
Readers familiar with the works of C. G. Jung, Marie-Louise
von Franz, and James Hillman will understand that the true
prima materia of alchemists was the self, at least from a
twentieth-century perspective, so the exploration of this
realm as trope or correspondent art is not as extreme as it

may seem. Still, however much the language of alchemy was grounded in the elemental (materials were not to be heated to a specific temperature measured in degrees but, for example, to the heat of fresh horse dung), the cumulative effect is—designedly—hermetic. Mystery religions and mysticism (the terms derive from words that recognize the closed and secretive nature of these enterprises) have always been for the elite; their knowledge is revealed and imparted only to those who need to know, those who have been initiated into the ranks. Twentieth-century psychoanalytic mysteries differ little from the Orphic or Eleusinian mysteries; the codices may be more widely published, but Tarot decks demonstrate how hermetic knowledge may be preserved by broadcast yet retain their privilege by withholding the key to the arcanum. Codices, as the name suggests, are written in code.

All of the preceding is especially germane to the attempt to penetrate this newest collection of Hillman's. Scattered throughout are relatively "normal" poems in terms of look and texture; occasionally, however, the volume is "interrupted" by brief passages, fragments apparently interjected by a "visitor" who had first appeared during the writer's "mediations on depression and alchemy . . . a figure with the eyes of an owl or a walnut half who could come inside a circle and withdraw." Not quite a muse, the figure, I infer, represents a manifestation of what some psychoanalysts call "anima," a feminine principle one of whose tasks is to initiate us into a deeper, imaginal understanding. As Hillman notes, the visitor "came when I asked her / but left at her own pleasure. . . ." This notion is reinforced by the volume's final poem, **"world/axis"**:

> The visitor comes,
> not an invention but
> an axis of something already invented—
>
> (even memory is sometimes an invention
> as are dreams)

At the end, Hillman explicitly invites us to read her book— and I refer to the book as a composition entire rather than to the individual poems—in the ways we might approach dream analysis, alert to archetypes, to mysteries, to antinomy.

The problem with such a strategy is that many readers will be left to scratch their heads in confusion while others may scurry off into arcana, contemporary or archaic. Hillman recognizes some of the difficulty of the path she's chosen in the poem **"The Mysteries"**:

> Writing about the mysteries
> you can't quite say what they were.
> Sacrifices? fasting? walking below
> or sprinkling drops of water near

the marriage bed where the celebrants lay
briefly with the sacred one before
the raising up of objects?

These represent signs only, symptoms of what have driven humans over the centuries to "suffer / over the mysteries" although they "learn / nothing new." The "emblem" is not what's sought; the ineffable is, and it is not disclosed through "research / among the transcripts of the institution," because all one finds is "the breath of another person . . ." The poem concludes:

> Belief in the subterranean rooms
> has haunted you. Not finding them
> isn't it the same as if you had?
> We know you through your writings
> and your complaints. Of course
> she found you, though you believed
> she loved you less than she should have—
> your short smile, your long tears,
> your fingers exiting the page,
> the chords of your mysteries
> absolute and wild and brief—

The interrupted end is typical of Hillman's work, as if to indicate that whatever can be said remains inconclusive.

At the center of the book is "blue codices," "a cycle of poems on depression and alchemy," apparently the fruit of her meditations. The epigraph, an alchemical theorem, clearly signals the obscurity of the endeavor: "Explain the unknown by the more unknown." The very look of the poems on the page underscores their method; at the bottom of the page, three columns of "footnotes" appear, imaging the process: "Below the furnace, ash." The seventh of thirteen poems, hence the heart of the cycle, provides an example of the group. Occuring midway, it marks the turning point of the process, explicitly identified in the notes as correlate to the stages of alchemical transmutation:

below below

> In the corner of the heart
> reserved for action, a pig is eating
> the poppies of hell;
>
> it doesn't look up when I come in;
> it doesn't need
> a confirming ideal. If there are flowers
>
> there must be dirt below hell
> where power has no meaning
> but growth comes out of it.
>
> Now a door blows open

and this sound starts coming in
till enough of the candles are lit—

```
stage 7—the thought                              red-breasted nuthatch—
of sorrow not as an event   the alchemist grew hopeful   hello you wonderful!
                      as the vapor rose            (then, the federal
                                                   deficit. . . )
```

If we hope to penetrate this (not unpack or untangle), we need to work within the parameters James Hillman suggests in *Re-Visioning Psychology:*

> The alchemical psychologists worked with intense discipline, with ethical devotion to their work, careful formulae, and high purposes. Yet the entire alchemical operation was marked by freedom and diversity, with full place for the bizarre and heretical. Each alchemist worked with his images in his own way and none would think that repeatability and conformity of an operation was the main mark of its success. We learn from the alchemical psychologists to let the images work upon the experimenter; we learn to become the object of the work—even an object, or objectified image, of the imagination.

Later, he argues that the true work involved "the transmutation, within the alchemist himself, of the natural viewpoint into the imaginal viewpoint."

This leaves Brenda Hillman's reader with a clear choice: skim the volume, appreciating her craft with line and language, or plunge in, join the process, risking the transformation. This volume, like the closed alembic of the alchemists, is a "solemn and rare" space of the sort Albertus Magnus recommended for the work. It marks a further step in Hillman's development, one that will gather some readers further in but effectively closing the door to others.

Kenneth Rexroth's lifelong project was making sacred the profane, as the title of his new selection of love poems makes clear; in *Sacramental Acts* (Copper Canyon), editors Sam Hamill and Elaine Laura Kleiner gather from almost the entire range of Rexroth's work to bring together a superb volume of both the poet's original compositions and his translations. The only phase of Rexroth's long career given short shrift is his last, the final two volumes posthumously combined as *Flower Wreath Hill*. In a collection of Rexroth's love poems, the decision not to include any of his marvelous "Love Poems of Marichiko," the sequence by the fictitious contemporary Japanese woman poet in which Rexroth most fully realizes a totally human sense of the erotic, seems puzzling, not to mention the exclusion of many other fine poems that manifest a culminating synthesis of the erotic and the sublime. Ultimately, however, such cavils should not dis-

tract from the service the editors and publisher have done for both Rexroth and the poetry reading public.

Rexroth is one of our most under-appreciated major American poets. I suspect that his neglect owes as much to the little apparent work left to critics (or work of a nature and scope most academicians are prepared to undertake) as to his "antiestablishmentarianism," as the editors note in their Introduction. He was a self-styled renegade, both poetically and politically, and determinedly went his own way, sparing few feelings in his commitment to advocate the truth, at least so far as he saw it. And, as the editors note, this is truly sad, for one will look long and far before finding another poet as dedicated to humane causes and revolutionary ideals, both in politics and in poetry, for, ultimately, Rexroth saw such distinctions as distractions. His early and most trenchant masters were the great T'ang poets, especially Tu Fu and, although not as widely appreciated, Yuan Chen. This provided him with a poetics both synthetic and syncretic, a way of perceiving the world, and expressing that perception, that saw the personal, the political, the philosophical, and the poetic as—not so much intertwined—interfused. My only other small disappointment with this gathering is that many of the "political" poems which flow as clearly from Rexroth's encompassing erotic sensibility as the overt love poems have also been left out, for love is more than the romantic ideal. I recommend to interested readers especially his wonderful "Climbing Milestone Mountain, August 22, 1937," addressed to Bartolomeo Vanzetti on the tenth anniversary of his execution.

A hallmark of Rexroth's love poems is that, even in poems to women, he is as apt to write about filial or parental love as sexual or romantic. *Sacramental Acts* contains one of several poems Rexroth wrote to his mother and a generous sampling of poems written to and about his daughter Mary, including sections from **"Mary and the Seasons"** and the entire sequence **"The Lights in the Sky Are Stars,"** in which this poem appears:

"A Maze of Sparks of Gold"

Spring—the rain goes by, the stars
Shine pale beside the Easter
Moon. Scudding clouds, tossing leaves,
Whirl overhead. Blossoms fall
In the dark from the fragrant
Madrone trees. You lie beside
Me, luminous and still in sleep.
Overhead bees sleep in their
Tree. Beyond them the bees in
The Beehive in the Crab drift
Slowly past, a maze of points
Of fire. I've had ten times your
Years. Time holds us both fixed fast

Under the bright wasting stars.

In addition to the clear expression of devotion, we see Rexroth's characteristic sense of correspondence, almost in the Scholastic sense: that which is below echoes that which is above. As Goethe wrote, "*Alles Vergängliches ist nur ein Gleichnis*": everything fleeting is but a metaphor.

For Rexroth, eros was as much elegiac as immediate. He continued to write passionate poems to Andrée, his first wife who died at an early age, throughout his career. In their evocation of their love, his tenderness extends beyond memory to a literal recalling of the past with all its emotional and sensual amplitude. Most often, these poems, as most of his erotic poems, are set in nature, where the distinctions between human emotion and the natural processes are blurred, of no consequence except to intensify the sensations:

ANDRÉE REXROTH

died October, 1940

Now once more grey mottled buckeye branches
Explode their emerald stars,
And alders smoulder in a rosy smoke

Of innumerable buds.
I know that spring again is splendid
As ever, the hidden thrush
As sweetly tongued, the sun as vital—
But these are the forest trails we walked together,
These paths, ten years together.
We thought the years would last forever,
They are all gone now, the days
We thought would not come for us are here.
Bright trout poised in the current—
The raccoon's track at the water's edge—
A bittern booming in the distance—
Your ashes scattered on this mountain—
Moving seaward on this stream.

As the Introduction points out, remembered love was often easier for Rexroth to celebrate; a difficult man drawn to strong-willed women, his marriages often ended disastrously. But the over-arching passion and compassion, even if only this available across distance and through his art, bleeds through the words. Once more, Copper Canyon has done wonderful service in preserving and presenting the work of an American master in an elegant, readable, and affordable edition. May it continue do so for many years, and may many new readers come to appreciate the work of Kenneth Rexroth.

The Year in Drama

by Julius Novick

The year in drama was a year of big musicals and (mostly) small plays. Mega-musicals grew ever more mega-, playing, if they were successful, to large and well-heeled audiences on Broadway (where they comprise one of New York City's main tourist attractions) and on the road. Meanwhile, new non-musical plays continued to emerge from non-profit theaters in New York (mainly off-Broadway) and around the country, playing to vastly smaller audiences, taking in vastly less money, receiving vastly less attention—although small-scale work of admirable quality was, as always, in evidence.

The most prominent Broadway musicals of the previous year were transfers from downtown, bringing with them different sounds from those heard in conventional musicals: *Rent* had an eclectic rock score, and *Bring in da Noise, Bring in da Funk,* driven by virtuoso tapping, was a festival of percussion. Both of them ran through 1997 on Broadway, and spawned touring companies as well. But 1997 was a year when corporate power asserted itself in the American musical theater as never before, as two entertainment-world giants established flagship Broadway theaters facing each other across brightly-rehabilitated 42nd Street. (Both theaters, along with state-of-the-art technical facilities and lavishly decorated public areas, feature large retail stores on the premises peddling souvenir merchandise.) There was much hoopla as the Disney organization opened the elaborately refurbished New Amsterdam Theater with **The Lion King,** and Livent, Inc. (bankrolled by former movie-theater magnate Garth Drabinsky) inaugurated its Ford Center for the Performing Arts with **Ragtime**—mega-musicals distinctly not from downtown.

But this new age of double-digit-million-dollar musicals produced by giant entertainment corporations—and by other managements trying to keep up with them—is not an age of mere commercialism. Far from it. Critics used to inveigh against the frivolity of "musical comedy," but old-fashioned "musical comedy" appears to be dead. Nobody is producing anything like *Guys and Dolls* or *A Funny Thing Happened on the Way to the Forum* any more—except when those shows are revived, to the delight of many people who love their wit and exuberance. The Broadway musicals of 1997 are earnest, ambitious, serious—even downright somber. The first-act finale of **Ragtime** is a funeral. The first act of **Titanic** ends with the sighting of the fatal iceberg. The first act of **The Capeman** ends with the hero being led off to jail. The rejection of frivolity is emphatic, and ultimately praiseworthy. But whether any of the 1997 shows entirely fulfills its ambitions is another matter.

The theatrical event of the year was unquestionably **The Lion King,** the musical-theater version of the hugely successful Disney animated film. It marked the most extraordinary union of mass culture and high culture since Marilyn Monroe married Arthur Miller. *Beauty and the Beast,* the previous Disney stage musical recycled from a Disney movie, was a ponderously literal reproduction of the film, directed by a long-time Disney apparatchik. To direct **The Lion King,** however, Disney hired Julie Taymor, a director, designer, and puppeteer deeply influenced by Asian theater, who had worked extensively off-Broadway and in opera, but had never staged a commercial Broadway show. It was an astonishing move. Even more astonishing, when she set to work according to her own long-held aesthetic principles and practices, Disney did not fire her. And more astonishing yet, the result is a huge, huge hit. The commercial lion, it seems, can lie down with the avant-garde lamb, without the result being blood on the ground in the morning.

The Lion King has a book credited to Roger Allers and Irene Mecchi, both of whom worked on the film, and it uses the five songs that Elton John and Tim Rice wrote for the film. But Ms. Taymor, credited as director, costume designer, mask and puppet designer (with Michael Curry) and lyricist for one of several new songs, was clearly the shaping force behind the show. "At every turn," she has written, "I was looking for that which would make this **Lion King** a live theater event and not a duplication of the film onstage." The characters in **The Lion King** are animals (plus a bird or two)—very human animals, but animals, without a single literal human being among them. How should they appear onstage? Ms. Taymor was determined "not to hide the actor behind a whole mask or inside a bodysuit. I wanted the human being to be an essential part of the stylization, creating a double event where the audience can watch the actor and the animal simultaneously." And so her giraffes, stepping imposingly but precariously across the stage, are obviously men in yellow costumes with stilts strapped to their hands and feet. Sculpted antelopes are supported on the heads and arms of leaping dancers. Other animals are puppets, manipulated by actors or dancers standing in plain sight behind them. The lions wear magnificent masks positioned *above* their heads. "When the human spirit visibly animates an object," Ms. Taymor writes, "we experience a special, almost life-giving connection. We become engaged by both the method of storytelling as well as by the story itself [sic]." Syntax aside, yes! The opening of the show, when elephant and rhino parade down the aisles of the theater, and magically simple birds, suspended on strings from poles, fly out over the audience, and all the animals throng the stage to behold their new-born future king, is one of the great theatrical moments.

Unfortunately, the story itself does not altogether measure up to the method of storytelling. Mufasa the lion king is killed by his evil brother Scar, and Mufasa's son Simba goes through various adventures before he defeats Scar and takes the throne. Beginning with King Mufasa showing baby Simba to his loyal subjects, and ending with King Simba, all grown up, showing his baby son to his loyal subjects, *The Lion King* seems to be the first monarchist musical. Sample dialogue:

> Simba: I really missed you.

> Nula [his destined lioness]: I missed you too.

Sample joke:

> "Mufasa's as mad as a hippo with a hernia."

Moreover, except for the African chants contributed by Lebo M (far more prominent than in the film), the music is undistinguished.

There are high-minded messages about the "Circle of Life," and about the necessity of hanging in there and hitching up your self-esteem so you can fulfil your destiny. But the real artistic ambition of *The Lion King* is in its evocation of the power of visual imagination. Even Aristotle had to admit that spectacle was an integral part of drama (though he wasn't happy about it). *The Lion King* restores wonder—sheer, open-mouthed wonder—to our theater.

The most overtly and grandly ambitious of the new musicals, however, is *Ragtime,* loyally adapted from E. L. Doctorow's ambitious novel, which opened in Toronto in December, 1996, opened in Los Angeles in June, 1997, and came to Broadway in December, 1997 for an official opening in January, 1998. *Ragtime* unmistakably aims to be a great American musical—if not The Great American Musical. Garth Drabinsky, its producer, has said, "What especially excites us is putting America onstage—both its past and its present." Frank Galati, its director, has said, "*Ragtime* can be, and I think should be, an important part of the national discourse." The official *Ragtime* sweatshirt (on sale at the theater) is emblazoned with an American flag.

Ragtime begins with a Little Boy who tells us, "In 1902 Father built a house at the crest of the Broadview Avenue hill in New Rochelle, New York, and it seemed for some years thereafter that all the family's days would be warm and fair." But of course we know better. And sure enough, in an opening number (choreographed by Graciela Daniele) that vividly sets out the characters and themes of the show, the stage on which the WASP gentry genteely parade is quickly invaded by a livelier group of black men and women from Harlem, and then by a huddled mass of immigrants from Europe, as the lyrics (by Lynn Ahrens) for the title song tell us of "distant music" coming closer:

> It was the music
> Of something beginning,
> An era exploding,
> A century spinning . . .
> The people called it ragtime . . .

Ragtime clearly means to dramatize the great social changes that marked the beginning of the twentieth century in America—changes that continue to shape our lives at the century's end.

Like Mr. Doctorow's novel, Terrence McNally's book for the musical intertwines the story of three emblematic families. The lives of Father, Mother, Mother's Younger Brother, and The Little Boy, WASP gentry of New Rochelle, are changed by their involvement with Coalhouse Walker Jr., a black ragtime pianist, his fiancee Sarah, and their little son. But the Coalhouse story tends toward not-quite-convincing melodrama. When Coalhouse's gleaming new Ford is trashed by some cliché bigots, Coalhouse demands justice, and declares that he will not marry Sarah until he gets it. When Sarah is rather arbitrarily killed, Coalhouse becomes a revolutionary terrorist. Sarah and Coalhouse voice their agonized feelings in a series of impassioned songs, most of which remain stubbornly unmoving. Moreover, the third story, about a Jewish immigrant and his little daughter, is never fully integrated with the other two, with only a few points of somewhat forced connection. As in the novel, a number of real historical characters make their appearance, but onstage it is not always clear why they are there. At the end, the survivors of all three groups, white and black, Christian and Jew, come together into—literally—one big happy family: a pious hope belied by the action of the show (injustice, violence, betrayal, death) and by twentieth-century American reality.

Still, there is much to be said for *Ragtime:* it is intelligent, graceful, variegated; handsomely and inventively designed and staged; admirably acted, sung, and danced; with glints and gleams in which history does come alive. The growing distance between old-fashioned, patriarchal Father and restless, independent Mother is finely marked in their songs; some of the anthems are rousing; the comic numbers have wit. Stephen Flaherty's music adroitly embraces both old-timey popular and folk idioms and up-to-date, sometimes Sondheimesque modes, in one of the more listenable Broadway scores of recent years. If greatness eludes *Ragtime,* it is still an impressive achievement.

By some, or no, coincidence, *Ragtime* was not the only Broadway musical of 1997 that looked back to the early part of this century; there was also *Titanic* (unrelated to the blockbuster film, except that they both stemmed from the same historical source), with a book by Peter Stone, and music and lyrics by Maury Yeston. In previews, *Titanic* the musical was the butt of many jokes; there was trouble with its technical apparatus, and there were rumors that it would never open. But open it did, and it won the 1996-97 Tony Award as Best Musical (*The Lion King* and *Ragtime* opened too late to be eligible) and became a hit. It begins with a series of songs in praise of the great ship—its size, its speed, its invulnerability—that brilliantly expresses the technological hubris of the early twentieth century, since of course everyone in the audience and no one among the characters knows of the disaster (and many subsequent twentieth-century disasters) to come. The historical irony in these few minutes is keener than anything in *Ragtime.* Unfortunately, the stories that Mr. Stone has made up about various individuals on board are uninspired, and after its arresting opening the show sags until the irony, terror, and pathos of the great shipwreck exert their effect in the second act. But like both *The Lion King* and *Ragtime,* it offers its own kind of admirable, elaborate, expensive spectacle; the technical apparatus that misbehaved so embarrassingly during previews turned out to be worth the trouble it caused.

Another less-than-cheerful Broadway musical of 1997 was *The Life* (music by Cy Coleman, lyrics by Ira Gasman, book by David Newman, Ira Gasman and Cy Coleman), about the prostitutes and pimps who inhabited 42nd Street in the pre-Disney days. It has some shrewd and lively moments, and a lot of hokey melodrama. Clichés abound. While she's out hooking, he takes the money that they've saved to buy a little house and raise kids, and spends it on cocaine. "He's no good," she sings, "But I'm no good without him. . . Don't matter what he's done before, / I keep coming back for more." *The Life* would be enjoyed, however, by anyone who likes to see women beaten up.

And still another: *The Capeman,* with music by Paul Simon, and book and lyrics by Paul Simon and the Nobel-Prizewinning poet Derek Walcott: two eminent gentlemen with little in common except that neither had ever worked in musical theater before. (Like *Ragtime,* it began New York previews in December, 1997 for an opening in January, 1998.) Salvador Agron, known as the Capeman, was a real person: a teen-ager who made headlines in New York in 1959 by killing two other teen-agers. The show, a pet project on which Mr. Simon had worked for years, takes Agron from childhood to middle age and death (he is played at various stages of his life by three actors), but fails to get inside his head, falling back instead on the kind of sentimental excuses satirized forty years ago in West Side Story by the kid who said, "I'm depraved on account I'm deprived." *The*

Capeman was understandably savaged in the press, and not only because its authors had loftily proclaimed their contempt for the Broadway musical-theater tradition. It has some seductive fifties-style songs, very Paul Simon, especially one called "Satin Summer Nights"; but satin summer nights are not what Salvador Agron was about.

In a year of very big musicals came one extraordinary small musical. In 1995 a country-rock musician named Steve Schalchlin, suffering from AIDS, began writing songs about how he felt—songs in which self-pity and sententiousness are held in check by tough, ironically playful wit:

> There's a woman named Louise
> Tells me my immunities . . .
> She sells T-cells by the seashore.

Mr. Schalchlin's partner, Jim Brochu, turned the songs into a five-character musical called *The Last Session,* which moved from the off-off-Broadway Currican Theater to a commercial off-Broadway house. Its hero is a singer-songwriter named Gideon, a gay man with AIDS—clearly a kind of alter ego for Mr. Schalchlin—who summons a few colleagues for a recording session. Gideon intends to make a valedictory album of songs for his lover, and then to commit suicide.

Into the studio comes a substitute backup singer, a brash, naive country boy named Buddy, religiously homophobic, who is aghast to discover that Gideon, his boyhood hero, is one of *them*. This plot-premise, under the circumstances, has a certain predictability about it. The callow Christian kid who thinks homosexuality is an abomination is unlikely to convert the suicidal AIDS victim to his point of view—not in a show written by an AIDS sufferer and his domestic partner. In fact the show has gentle fun with Buddy's appalled innocence, and Gideon does get the best of the argument:

> Buddy: I'm trying to love the sinner and hate the sin.
>
> Gideon: So am I. I'm trying to love the bigot and hate the bigotry.

But Buddy is neither a monster nor a fool, and the process by which he comes gradually, reluctantly, to accept and (metaphorically) embrace Gideon's humanity, is convincing and touching.

Similarly, it is not exactly a surprise when Gideon decides to live after all, but it would take a hard heart to complain. Invigorating, hopeful without being soppy, *The Last Session* achieves its intentions more completely than any of the big musicals discussed above.

As far as non-musical drama is concerned, it was a quiet year. The best of the new plays were mainly modest affairs, finely turned individually—but collectively, something was lacking: wildness, boldness, fierceness. There were no major new plays. Presumably it was similar considerations that induced the Pulitzer Prize Drama Jury to vote not to give an award for 1997. A stunning revival of *A View from the Bridge,* seldom considered one of Arthur Miller's best, at New York's (non-profit, of course) Roundabout Theatre, made clear by contrast what the new plays, fine as some of them were, lacked in sheer emotional power.

As always these days, most of the year's interesting non-musical plays were produced off-Broadway. The most unexpected of the year's artistic and popular triumphs was ***Gross Indecency: The Three Trials of Oscar Wilde,*** written—or perhaps "compiled" would be a better word—and directed by Moises Kaufman. Staged off-off-Broadway by the Tectonic Theatre Project, a hitherto-obscure enterprise founded and led by the hitherto-obscure Mr. Kaufman, it moved to a commercial off-Broadway house for a long run, and other companies were formed to play it in San Francisco and Los Angeles.

Mr. Kaufman puts the documentary aspect of his play literally front and center. Facing the audience, downstage of the raised platform that represents the courtroom, is a long table at which several actors sit, punctuating the proceedings (themselves taken from trial records) by quoting various commentators. Sometimes they positively brandish the books and newspapers they read from. Questions of art, love, and morality are cogently raised. But because Wilde was such a mass of contradictions, and because what happened to him, brought on by the fatal collision of homophobic bigotry with his own irresistible urge for self-display (and self-destruction), was so terrible—and because Mr. Kaufman has selected his material so deftly—*Gross Indecency* is no less gripping and moving for being, for the most part, literally true. (It is not, however, altogether cricket to quote Frank Harris without adding that he was the biggest liar in London.)

Because Wilde is so richly complicated, the play necessarily leaves a lot unprobed, but the intercutting of the trials with his writings is finely done, particularly the juxtaposition of brutal hectoring by the prosecutor in the third trial with Wilde's pathetic avowal of eternal love for Lord Alfred Douglas, and his even more pathetic vaunting of what he had been in the world—what he had thrown away. Michael Emerson, the previously-unknown actor who plays Wilde, looks nothing like him, but he knows how to take stage, as Wilde must have known, and he gives us, poignantly, Wilde's haughty frivolity collapsing into terror and grief. Wilde said that he put his talent into his work and his genius into his life. *Gross Indecency* sug-

gests that perhaps this great comic writer's greatest achievement was his own tragedy.

From the Vineyard Theatre, off-Broadway, came a small, quiet, amazing play—funny, touching, riveting—entitled with ironic understatement, ***How I Learned to Drive,*** by Paula Vogel. With perfect sure-handedness, it neither sensationalizes nor mitigates its subject, which is child molesting. It offers no pious horror, no callous attempts to shock, and no excuses. It won the New York Drama Critics Circle Award and the Drama Desk Award as Best Play of 1996-97, and the Pulitzer Prize for 1998.

The play follows its protagonist, a country girl from Maryland nicknamed Li'l Bit, from childhood to the edge of adulthood, shifting easily back and forth through time and space, with a cast of five, on a bare thrust stage furnished only with four kitchen chairs and a table. It is the story of a long, slow, patient attempt at seduction. Li'l Bit's Uncle Peck likes to go fishing, and he plays her the way an expert fisherman plays a fish, through driving lessons and other meetings, over many years, exerting shrewd and subtle, gentle but unrelenting sexual pressure. "Nothin's gonna happen between us, until you want it to. . . . Do you want something to happen?" Uncle Peck is not a stereotypical molester: Li'l Bit is unmistakably the love of his life, and he loves her no less as she matures. She is unnerved, but attracted, and, especially given David Morse's quiet, subtle performance as Uncle Peck, it is easy to see why.

Ms. Vogel is wonderfully perceptive about the delicate ways in which one human being can manipulate another, and without for a moment justifying Uncle Peck, she enables us to sympathize with him as a man who misuses his fine sensitivity in the service of a warped, life-long obsession. In a way, the play is his tragedy. The realistic, finely observed scenes between Li'l Bit and Uncle Peck are distanced, kept in check, by the ironic Brechtian announcements and comments that surround them, and by the simplicity of the staging. ***How I Learned to Drive*** transferred from the Vineyard to a commercial off-Broadway house for a long and well-deserved run.

A traditional American comic plot—George S. Kaufman used and re-used it for decades—is the one about a young man with artistic ambitions who is tempted off the straight and narrow by a flashy dame who represents money, glamor, fame, or all three. But he comes to his senses just in time, and ends up with the sweet gal who really loves him. A typical example is *June Moon* (1929) by Ring Lardner and George S. Kaufman, charmingly revived off-Broadway by a new group that calls itself Drama Dept. A thoroughly up-to-date variation on this theme, ***As Bees in Honey Drown*** by Douglas Carter Beane—presented, neatly enough, by

Drama Dept., of which Mr. Beane is artistic director—is by all odds the funniest play of 1997.

Mr. Beane's protagonist is a young first-novelist named Eric Wollenstein, who has already changed his name to the more euphonious Evan Wyler, and reluctantly agreed to pose shirtless for a gossipy magazine feature, when Alexa Vere de Vere enters his life. Alexa is a dazzling creature, a self-creation inspired by flamboyant literary (and movie) hero-ines: Sally Bowles, Holly Golightly, Auntie Mame. She is a manic motor-mouth, a bundle of fantastic affectations, shoot-ing off enthusiasms and dropping names like a fireworks dis-play.

> The reason I called you [she says to Evan] is that I have been struggling—looking for the genius young writer to write this mouthwatering movie idea I have up my peplum sleeve. David Bowie, no less, wants to play my father. He's a dear friend. David Bowie, not my father. . . . You see I want this film to be the story of my life which is too entrancing, almost even for me . . .

Evan is duly dazzled, delighted to be caught up in the whirl-wind of wealth, fame, and glamor that Alexa offers him, will-ing to lose himself in more ways than one. This of course is an old story, far older even than George S. Kaufman—Alexa is really Mephistopheles in a Louise Brooks bob—but Mr. Beane has one original, very nineties twist. In accordance with the formula, Evan falls for Alexa's sophisticated charms, and breaks the spell just in time. But her traditional rival, the sweet gal who truly believes in the hero, has un-dergone a metamorphosis, and become a man. As part of the process of losing himself, Evan lays aside his homosexual-ity to make love to Alexa, but at the end of the play, we hear that he has written a second novel, entitled *As Bees in Honey Drown* (Alexa's catch-phrase), and on the jacket it says, "Eric Wollenstein's debut novel, *Pig and Pepper,* was pub-lished under the pseudonym Evan Wyler. . . . He resides in New York City with painter Mike Stabinsky." A new-old happy ending.

But more important, Mr. Beane's hilarious exaggerations and condensations express a shrewd, unhackneyed understand-ing of the preposterous apparatus of late-twentieth-century celebrity—and the deep thirst that impels so many people, even talented people who know better, toward that celebrity. Alexa is no fool; she knows what she stands for: "fame with-out achievement." Mr. Beane is a genuine satirist, and there are never many of them around.

David Ives is another kind of comic writer. None of his full-length plays have won—or deserved—much admiration, but along with Christopher Durang, he is our leading writer of brief comic sketches. An evening of these, entitled *All in the*

Timing, was a hit a few years ago, and its 1997 successor, *Mere Mortals (and Others),* has transferred from the tiny Primary Stages for a commercial off-Broadway run. Mr. Ives's most characteristic sketches are quirky, off-beat, rather delicate, independent of conventional comic formulas. A playlet called **"Time Flies,"** for instance, presents us with two mayflies, Horace and May, who are aghast to discover, by watching Sir David Attenborough on television, that may-flies live for only one day. But the funniest piece in this cur-rent collection is **"Speed-the-Play,"** a no-holds-barred David Mamet parody.

Two sober, realistic plays, commissioned and first produced by the South Coast Repertory in Costa Mesa, California, were presented off-Broadway in New York by the Manhat-tan Theater Club. Both are graceful, intelligent, finely writ-ten, small-scale works by distinguished writers who are not yet (and may never be) well-known to the general public. The first to reach New York was *Collected Stories* by Donald Margulies, author of *Sight Unseen* and *The Loman Family Picnic:* a two-character play about two writers (both women), and the elder writer's difficulty in dealing with the younger one's success. How does it feel when your admir-ing, adoring follower becomes your rival? How does it feel, if you are a writer, when your life turns up in the fiction of someone else—someone so close to you, who owes you so much? Delicately, shrewdly, precisely, Mr. Margulies ex-plores the ambiguities of the teacher-student, mentor-prote-gee relationship. The older writer, sharp-tongued, demanding, defensive, lonely (and admirably played by Maria Tucci), is a particularly vivid and sympathetic pres-ence.

Later in 1997 came *Three Days of Rain* by Richard Greenberg, author of *Eastern Standard* and *Night and Her Stars.* His new play has a neat gimmick that is more than just a gimmick: in the second act, its three actors play par-ents of the characters they play in the first act. In the first act we meet Walker, his sister Nan, and their friend Pip. Walker is unhappy to the point of madness; rational Nan copes with him as best she can; cheerful Pip admits, "I strove to sustain some level of unhappiness, but I just couldn't." The father of Walker and Nan, and Pip's father, were archi-tects, and partners; who will inherit the house that is their masterpiece? The younger generation is deeply involved with—and deeply marked by—what happened among their elders; in the second act we find out that the truth is very different from what its heirs conceive it to be. All six char-acters are involved in a dense web of family and romantic relationships, their lives entangled in artfully complicated, ironic ways; Mr. Greenberg's dialogue is abundantly witty and unfailingly graceful, but what powers it is the emotional intensity of his characters.

Lanford Wilson is another quiet, serious, graceful writer. The

Circle Repertory Theater, his long-time artistic home, being now defunct, his new play, *Sympathetic Magic,* was given an impeccable off-Broadway production at the Second Stage Theater. The new work is not one of his best. The relationships among the characters are confusing, as are the author's attempts to combine the home life of his protagonist, an astrophysicist, with murky observations on the nature of the cosmos. But Mr. Wilson's dialogue has not lost its peculiar charm; his characters are not particularly witty or eloquent, but it is a pleasure to listen to them. It is amazing that a play so unclear can be so absorbing.

A few non-musical plays worth noting did come to Broadway, rather than off-Broadway, in 1997—most of them (unlike the musicals) from non-commercial sources. If *Gross Indecency* was the year's surprise success, *An American Daughter* by Wendy Wasserstein was, as far as the public and many of the critics were concerned, the year's surprise failure. Over the past few years, Ms. Wasserstein, the author of *The Heidi Chronicles* and *The Sisters Rosensweig,* has probably been the most commercially successful of all American playwrights. Like all her major plays, *An American Daughter* is a comedy about the tribulations of highly intelligent, highly educated, highly privileged American women. It has in ample measure the special Wasserstein combination of wit and warmth. It ends, like the others, with her heroine determined to soldier on into the future. But it is still a new departure for her: it is her most political play, the one most concerned with res publica, and it is, strikingly, her angriest. Perhaps the anger is one reason why this play, admirably staged (in a rented Broadway house) by the non-profit Lincoln Center Theatre Company, proved so much less popular than her others.

Lyssa Dent Hughes, her heroine—with Ms. Wasserstein it is always a heroine—is, like Heidi Holland of *The Heidi Chronicles,* "a serious good person": not only smart but principled, dedicated, humane. She has been nominated by the president to be the surgeon general of the United States—a position she desires passionately, not out of personal ambition, but because of what it would enable her to accomplish. But her nomination runs into trouble when she describes her mother as "the kind of ordinary Indiana housewife who took pride in her icebox cakes and cheese pimento canapes." On top of this, a supposed friend reveals that she once threw away a jury-duty notice. After which, the latest poll reveals that the women of America, for whom Lyssa has fought all her professional life, have decided that she is "condescending and elitist." Replying to this charge on national television, she lashes back with scathing sarcasm:

Oh we all understand it now! She must have hated her mother! That's why she's such a good doctor! She must be a bad cold person. That's why she achieved so much!

After this outburst, she is forced to ask the president to withdraw her nomination. Lyssa is defeated because, according to Ms. Wasserstein, even after so many decades of feminism, strong, effective professional women are still regarded with deep suspicion—especially by women.

Lyssa is obviously meant to remind us of Hillary Rodham Clinton, a strong, effective, professional woman who was induced to try to placate the suspicious American public by releasing her recipe for cookies, and also to remind us of the strong, effective professional women whose nominations for attorney general were stymied by revelations that they paid their servants off the books. But thanks in good part to Kate Nelligan's performance, she becomes a sympathetic human being, not just an instrument for scoring points.

An American Daughter is somewhat overloaded with contemporary political and social phenomena. Lyssa's best friend, Dr. Judith B. Kaufman, is an infertile Jewish African-American oncologist struggling with her inability to "make life or stop death": a few too many Issues of the Day stuffed, over-cutely, into one character. Judith's appearance sopping wet, after an unsuccessful attempt to commit suicide by jumping into the Potomac, is a bit much. But—again with substantial help from the actress, in this case Lynne Thigpen—she too turns into a person. Too neatly for complete plausibility, liberal Lyssa's father is a staunchly conservative senator. It would have been easy, given Ms. Wasserstein's liberal sentiments, for her to caricature him as a bigoted neanderthal. But instead she makes him a shrewd, charming, urbane old gent who genuinely loves his daughter. This is a rich, funny, keenly intelligent play, its anger finely expressed and never shrill, about the human cost of idealism in our society, especially when the idealist is a woman.

It was not, all told, a happy year for well-known American playwrights, especially on Broadway. *Proposals,* Neil Simon's new comedy, came and went without causing much excitement, even though it was his first play with an African-American central character. Has Mr. Simon's talent ebbed, or has he merely outlived his historical moment?

David Mamet is a generation younger than Mr. Simon, and unquestionably more in tune with the current zeitgeist, which may not be such a nice thing to say about Mr. Mamet, or perhaps about the zeitgeist. His new play *The Old Neighborhood,* which came to Broadway from the American Repertory Theater in Cambridge, Massachusetts, is about a middle-aged man named Bobby Gould, who has evidently come to a crisis in his life. He has left his wife and returned to his home town—clearly Mr. Mamet's Chicago—to rethink, reevaluate, remember, reconnect.

The play consists of three episodes, each with its own title.

In the first, "The Disappearance of the Jews," Bobby sits around reminiscing with Joey, a boyhood friend, about growing up Jewish. Joey feels trapped in a barren, meaningless life, and spins fantasies about the ancestral shtetl. "You think they fooled around?" Bobby wants to know. There is plenty of comedy in the conjunction of Jewish references—rare in Mamet's plays until now—with the staccato rhythms, the pauses, the sentence fragments, the percussive obscenities, of characteristic macho Mamet-speak. In "Jolly," the second episode, Bobby visits his sister, an angry, bitter woman who complains, and complains, and complains about their mother and stepfather. (Patti LuPone manages to make this drab litany compelling.) In "Deeny," the final episode, Bobby listens to a former girlfriend talk about gardens and other things, after which the two of them say goodbye.

Mr. Mamet has acknowledged that Bobby is his alter ego. In the program for the play, he reprints a fierce attack on the Reform Judaism of his youth: "It was a religion in a plain brown wrapper, a religion the selling point of which was that it would not embarrass us." The question of Jewish-American identity, of whether assimilation has gone too far, is much in the news these days, but *The Old Neighborhood* engages it only glancingly.

In general, this is a play of not much substance. Information is doled out sparingly. Bobby is agreeable, supportive, but frustratingly passive. Nothing happens to him, or to anyone else. The character—and the playwright—are so reserved, so unforthcoming, that if there is a real play in this material, it never reaches the stage.

The Last Night of Ballyhoo by Alfred Uhry, author of *Driving Miss Daisy,* is a more accessible—and more revealing—play about being Jewish in America. Commissioned for the Olympic festivities in Atlanta, it came to Broadway from Atlanta's Alliance Theater, and won the 1996-97 Tony Award for Best Play. It presents us with a genteel, prosperous Atlanta family, circa 1939, whose members are far more uncomfortable about being Jewish than anybody in *The Old Neighborhood.* According to Sunny, the family's bright, re-bellious daughter, the annual "Ballyhoo" ball at their exclusive upscale-Jewish club consists mainly of "A bunch a' dressed-up Jews dancin' around wishin' they could kiss their elbows and turn into Episcopalians." Sunny clearly has their number. After a slow start, the plot kicks in when Sunny's Uncle Adolph, the family breadwinner, brings home a new employee, a personable young man from Brooklyn with no pretensions to Episcopalian-style gentility—clearly "the other kind" of Jew. As the young man leaves, Adolph's sister says, "Adolph, that kike you hired has no manners." It is a chilling moment.

Of course Sunny and the young man from Brooklyn fall in love, quarrel, and are reunited in time for a happy ending. *The Last Night of Ballyhoo* is a conventional, predictable, old-fashioned light comedy, not always convincing in its dramaturgy, but amiable and charming—we want those two nice kids to get together—and also very sharply observed.

Thus much for American drama. As always, there were foreign plays, mostly from England, but this year's crop was a poor one. *Stanley,* by Pam Gems, about the peculiar life of the twentieth-century English painter Stanley Spencer, was notable mainly for Antony Sher's performance in the title role. (It was the last production of the Circle in the Square, a non-commercial management that made history off-Broadway, moved to Broadway, and ultimately went broke.) *My Night with Reg* by Kevin Elyot (The New Group) and *Mojo* by Jez Butterworth (Atlantic Theatre Company) were given off-Broadway productions with American casts. Each won an Olivier Award as Best Comedy of its year in London, which suggests that British comedy has fallen on hard times. *Goose-Pimples* (also The New Company) by Mike Leigh, the film-maker, was a labored, repetitive farce, its attempt at social criticism undermined by its implausibility. Meanwhile, new plays in London by Tom Stoppard and David Hare, and the emergence of a widely-hailed new Irish-English playwright named Martin McDonagh, offered hope for the future.

But there is always that.

The Year in World Literature
by William Riggan

In 1997, India and the West Indies led the way in a superb literary year which saw virtually every major Western literature and several Eastern ones as well produce at least one runaway critical *and* popular success.

Perhaps the single biggest literary sensation of 1997 was the young South Indian writer Arundhati Roy's debut novel, *The God of Small Things,* a sensuously magical and intricately dreamlike tale of sexual and caste conflict in exotic, communist-infiltrated Kerala of the late 1960s. In recounting the far-flung travails of a sprawling Syrian Christian family from the southern village of Ayemenem, including painful childhood experiences, broken marriages, turbulent relocations across three continents, and a profane love between an untouchable and a respectable lady, Roy produces a narrative that is splashed with humor and irony and marked by a linguistic verve and felicity strongly reminiscent of Salman Rushdie's best work. The awarding of the U.K.'s prestigious Booker Prize to *Small Things* both confirmed and augmented the overwhelmingly positive worldwide reaction to this remarkable first novel.

When Memory Dies, another brilliant and moving debut novel, this time from the pen of the Sri Lankan writer A. Sivanandan, moves majestically through three generations of a Ceylonese/Sri Lankan family from the subservient 1920s, to independence in 1948, to the neoliberal communalism of the 1980s. A political novel as told by unpolitical men, the work "mulls over colonial pain with deep investment in its dramas of labor strife," wrote one admiring critic. "But what grips here is the calm and the charm, the momentous ordinariness of a life on edge."

In the stories of *Love and Longing in Bombay,* Vikram Chandra followed up the explosive novelistic success of 1996's mythic/exotic *Red Earth and Pouring Rain* with a series of chronicles about glitzy urban sophisticates, high finance, high society, and generally high times in a bewildering array of exclusive clubs and arty private parties. Like Roy and Sivanandan, Chandra belongs to a new generation of Indian writers in English who, in Rushdie's considerable wake, are enriching anglophone literature by reinventing the subcontinent in the cadences of English prose: "Through their writing, they have colonized the literary world of their colonizers," in the words of another fine younger Indian writer, Shashi Tharoor.

From elsewhere in Asia, two important mid-1980s novels from mainland China made their first appearance in the West in 1997. *The Castle,* by southeastern regionalist writer Jia Pingwa, weaves a complex tale about the doomed efforts of a talented and energetic young entrepreneur to reopen an abandoned antinomy mine and turn it into a provincial town's biggest economic success in more than a century. The novel suggests that however impressive China's cultural inheritance may be in its embodiment of the old fortress (the eponymous "castle") that dominates the town, at another level it can destroy individual initiative and deny the achievements of both talented contemporaries like the energetic young protagonist and famous visionaries of the past like the Legalist overlord and intellectual from 338 BCE who was executed in this very locale on trumped-up charges after a distinguished career as a court advisor.

Virgin Widows by Gu Hua follows its vibrant and vital heroine, Yao Guihua, through an oppressive failed marriage and her subsequent attempts to achieve both economic independence and cultural-social liberation from traditional restraints against the remarriage of widows and against assertive women in general. Interspersed with Yao Guihua's story is a parallel narrative set in the very same town one hundred years earlier in which the widowed young protagonist chooses a life of enforced chastity rather than a return to poverty, thus bringing honor to her husband's family and memory but ensuring herself only a lonely, loveless, barren future. A comparison of the two stories guides the reader forcefully toward an enlightened acceptance of the modern-day Yao's desire to remarry.

Japan witnessed a recurrence of "Bananamania" in 1997 with the publication of Banana Yoshimoto's newest novel, *Amrita,* yet another earnest and quirkily ingenious foray into the adolescent soul-searchings of a Generation-X twenty-something, this time a woman trying to come to terms with the sudden death of her actress sister. The dialogue rarely rises above comic-book level ("Wow! Wow! Wow!"), but an effortless lyricism infuses the work with an often surprising weightiness and charm.

In *The Wind-Up Bird Chronicle* Haruki Murakami, Japan's hippest and currently most successful male writer, is quite obviously making a concerted effort to publish a big, ambitious, heavy book that will refute the widespread critical opinion of him in Japan as a lightweight literary wiseguy who takes nothing seriously except the detritus and vacuities of Western pop culture. In following the unemployed and alienated man-child narrator through a convoluted, hallucinatory series of bizarre searches in the alternately dreamlike and nightmarish suburbs of modern-day Tokyo, the novel almost self-consciously takes up a wide range of weighty topics such as the transitory nature of romantic love, the baseness of contemporary politics, and the legacy of Japanese aggression in World War II. The result is a huge (600-plus pages) and hugely flawed compendium that nevertheless makes up for its structural shortcomings and wildly uneven design through the sheer brilliance of its invention and the author's almost Joycean exuberance for the widest possible range of literary forms and styles.

From the anglophone Caribbean in 1997 came *The Nature of Blood* by Caryl Phillips of St. Kitts, a brilliant evocation of the Holocaust experience told in flashback through the voice and discontinuous memories of a young female Jewish death-camp survivor. Undercutting and occasionally glossing this main narrative line are such improbable interpolations as a retelling of *Othello* in the Moor's own voice and an account of the persecution of Jewish moneylenders in fifteenth-century Italy. Phillips makes little effort to impose coherence on all these intermingled narrative threads or to tie up all the loose ends they leave; yet in this, his sixth novel, he brilliantly captures the voices of his various protagonists, "evoking their common humanity as they struggle with and against social definitions of the nature of their blood," as one early reviewer aptly stated.

Nobel laureate Derek Walcott of St. Lucia brought out *The Bounty,* his first collection of new verse since the 1990 epic poem *Omeros,* revealing anew his unmatched talent among English-language poets of the late twentieth century for creating dazzling verbal textures and the richest imagery imaginable. From the francophone Caribbean came wonderfully original novels by two younger Martinican writers: *Chimères d'En-Ville* (*Urban Chimeras*) by Raphaël Confiant recasts his own 1985 Creole novel of socioeconomic exploitation, survival, and assimilation in early colonial times in and around Fort-de-France; and *L'esclave vieil homme et le molosse* (*The Old Slave and the Mastiff*) by recent Goncourt Prize winner Patrick Chamoiseau (of *Texaco* fame) recounts an archetypal tale of slavery, attempted escape, and pursuit and recapture by the oppressive forces of darkness and dominion.

Two of Israel's premier writers brought out superb new works in 1997. A. B. Yehoshua's novel *Masa el tom ha-elef: Roman bi-shlasha halakim* (*Voyage to the End of the Millennium: A Novel in Three Parts*) looks backward rather than forward, to the end of the *first* millennium--specifically, the year 998--as it tracks the relationship between a prosperous Jewish merchant of Tangier and his beloved nephew and commercial partner, a young European Jew who sells the merchant's exotic wares in Paris and the Rhineland. Through these two the novelist meditates on the nature and future of Jewish identity in the contrast between the vital,

sophisticated, urbanized "Oriental" Judaism and the austere, persecuted, inward-turned "European" variety.

Amos Oz's *Panther in the Basement,* set in 1947 Jerusalem, chronicles the adolescence of a precociously word-obsessed twelve-year-old called "Proffy" (short for "Professor"), particularly his "fraternizing" with the British occupiers and the question of whether such close contact constitutes treason or betrayal of his people and their heritage. As one perceptive critic has commented: "The now grown-up narrator knows that war is sometimes necessary, that there is a time for choosing sides. Rather, this writer is provoked by the way a precious solidarity can excite a lethal mistrust, and by the way the memory of absolute powerlessness can corrupt absolutely. He seems to be implying that when public obsessions rule private life, the human quality of that life is reduced to ashes."

Even if Yashar Kemal, Turkey's grand old man of letters and perennial Nobel candidate, had not been arrested and tried in 1996 for his outspoken defense of his country's Kurdish minority, the allegory of the ethnic rifts afflicting modern Turkey would be unmistakable in his 1980 novel, *Salman the Solitary,* at last made available in English in late 1997. Delivered in an old-fashioned epic voice and in Kemal's typically digressive campfire-storyteller style, the novel follows the fateful courses of two brothers, one adopted and one natural, as they weave their way toward an inevitably violent final clash. A certain shimmering yet austere lyricism mutes the tension between the brothers somewhat and sets the characters and events at some remove from the reader, unlike the wholly absorbing tragedy of Kemal's classic 1955 novel, *Memed, My Hawk.*

The New Life, the third and latest novel by Kemal's younger countryman Orhan Pamuk, became a runaway best-seller despite the surrealistic phantasmagoria of its story line and the extended Borgesian ambiguity of its narrative, charting the metamorphoses in the life of a young engineering student following his perusal of a certain mysterious book.

Among a good crop of 1997 releases by African authors, two stand out, as much for their strong sociopolitical relevance as for their artistic merit. *Le Lys et le Flamboyant* (*The Lily and the Flamboyant*) by the francophone Congolese writer (and associate director of UNESCO) Henri Lopes purports to be an account of the life and career of the beautiful and talented African-born mulatta singer Kolélé, as told by her former lover, the African-Chinese-European writer Victor Houang. Houang's manuscript is rejected by French publishers, however, since one "Henri Lopes" had published his own version of this story nearly twenty years earlier. Still, we get to read that manuscript, and even to compare it with its "Lopes" predecessor, which it significantly updates and expands into a treatise focused primarily on the new, latter-day hybridization of African identity and the corruption, pretensions, and hypocrisy of most modern African rulers. In the short stories of *Awaiting Court Martial* the prizewinning Nigerian author Festus Iyayi paints a numbingly and unrelentingly horrific portrait of human irrationality, immorality, and cruelty. His is a world where the prominent may kill with total impunity, where kindly little old grandmothers decoy unsuspecting good Samaritans into traps for armed robbers, and where supposedly loving relatives circle a patriarch's deathbed in anticipation of their inheritance once he finally expires. It is a sad, existential world of blurred beauty, of blighted dreams and ambitions, of futile struggles and empty accomplishments, a world where the grail of secret hopes lies always just beyond reach.

From the Romance-language literatures of Europe and the Americas came several outstanding new works of fiction in 1997. The Russian-born French writer Andreï Makine dazzled readers and critics alike with *Le testament français* (*Dreams of My Russian Summers*), a haunting autobiographical novel of personal and collective hardship in early-twentieth-century Russia and in Western exile, and also the first work ever to win *both* the Prix Goncourt and the Prix Médicis. As told by the Russian narrator's French-born grandmother, the tale moves from the deliciously decadent realm of 1920s Paris, to the intense hardships endured as a nurse in Russia as the catastrophic events of the thirties, forties, and fifties explode all around her, to her eventual separation from her husband and arbitrary banishment to Siberia. In her, Makine has created a living symbol of a suffering, divided Europe in the twentieth century.

J. M. G. Le Clézio's new novel, *Poisson d'or* (*Golden Fish*), recounts in the first person the kidnapping, sale, and peripatetic experiences of a young North African woman who endures the harsh realities of exclusion and marginalizing prejudice on three continents (Africa, Europe, North America) before her eventual return "home" to where her life and lineage began. Many of the themes present in the author's previous works over the last thirty years are evident here once again: the fate of the oppressed, the tension between First and Third World societies, the physical *and* spiritual journey of self-discovery. Particularly noteworthy are the numerous affinities with Le Clézio's acclaimed 1980 novel *Désert,* which also focuses on the life of a young North African woman who, like Laïla in *Poisson d'or,* leaves Africa only to return in the end, abandoning an unsatisfying Western world in order to rediscover her true origins and identity.

In *Noticia de un secuestro* (*News of a Kidnapping*) the Colombian Nobel laureate Gabriel García Márquez combines the precision of first-rate journalism with the imaginative flair of the finest fiction writing to produce a classic and compelling narrative of several fateful political kidnappings

orchestrated by the late Medellín drug king Pablo Escobar. The limit experience of living with one's potential executioners is rendered in prose that is as precise and clinical as a medical report, and the unimaginably fantastic is made thereby to seem quite ordinary. It is all, in other words, classic García Márquez: at once comic, tragic, and all too human.

Portugal's José Saramago, in *The History of the Siege of Lisbon* (orig. *História do Cerco de Lisboa,* 1989), weaves a cryptic, ingenious tale about two humble yet whimsically subversive proofreaders who rewrite one of the seminal events of early Portuguese history through the smallest and most subtle of alterations in the standard texts on which they are assigned to work. Their collaborative intrigue both derives from and fuels the growing attraction between the two, and their courtship, rendered in lengthy and virtually unpunctuated paragraphs of dazzling verbal virtuosity and unstable attribution, superbly reproduces "the tantalizing delirium of desire," as one admiring critic so aptly phrased it.

Portugal--the port city of Oporto, specifically--also provides the setting for the most recent novel by Italy's supremely talented Antonio Tabucchi, *La testa perduta di Damasceno Monteiro* (*The Lost Testament of D.M.*). The cultured journalist-narrator Firmino, dispatched by his circulation-conscious editor to investigate a gruesome murder (based on an actual 1996 case), uncovers a teeming underworld of poverty, corruption, and crime that permeates all layers of Oporto society, from the most hapless indigents to the most powerful leaders of government and industry. For its insistence that even in such evolved societies as those of contemporary Portugal and Italy a kind of lowercase fascism not only continues to flourish but is too often supported by the supposedly antiauthoritarian forces that control the levers of power, the novel is likely to be one of Tabucchi's most controversial works yet.

Austria's Peter Handke returned to the storytelling ways of his earliest novels and novellas with *In einer dunklen Nacht ging ich aus meinem stillen Haus* (*On a Dark Night I Left My Quiet House*), a wonderfully light and inventive account of a fantastic journey into alien territories beyond the "border," undertaken by a lonely but resourceful pharmacist in company with a former ski champion and a once-famous poet for much of the way. Nothing in this delightful book can be anticipated or guessed, and almost every page contains new surprises in both plot and poetic style. There is much worldly concern, and many troublesome facts and bitter truths of our lives are touched upon, such as the painfully relevant passages about the new relationships between men and women. Nevertheless, as one sympathetic reader noted, "We find everywhere a redemption of our common lot."

The late Nobel Prize-winning poet Joseph Brodsky was honored with the posthumous release of his last unpublished poems, together with a good many earlier selections, in *Peizazh s navodneniem* (*Landscape with Floods*), a collection that is nothing short of outstanding in the richness of its lyric expression and the depth and originality of its content. The landscapes here as often as not are those of the spirit and the soul as of topography and the physical world, and they are as threatened by the "flooding" of emotions and death as by rainstorms and meteorological deluges.

The Life of Insects by the younger Russian writer Victor Pelevin is set entirely within the fetid subworld of mosquitoes, flies, cockroaches, ants, and dung beetles, a seedy and lawless sphere saturated by cynicism, raw self-interest, authoritarian bullying, and the unchecked brutality of rapacious capitalists and petty hoodlums. Never strictly fable-like, parabolic, or even satiric in any sustained manner, the work fashions a universe wholly unto itself, though one which possesses definite similarities to post-Soviet Russia as that country transforms itself pell-mell from a hidebound and repressive society into one in which virtually anything goes, even sucking the lifeblood out of one's fellow creatures for one's own benefit and advancement.

Hungarian author Péter Nádas's monumental 1986 novel

Emlékiratok könyve finally made its debut in English in 1997 as *A Book of Memories,* introducing a wealth of new readers to the stylistic brilliance and Joycean linguistic brio of this multilevel *bildungsroman* that moves seamlessly from the revolutionary days of 1956 to the mid-nineteenth century and back in charting the growing-up experiences of its three very different protagonists: the son of a communist prosecutor who commits suicide after the 1956 uprising; a flamboyantly gay nineteenth-century esthete; and a childhood friend of the first protagonist, who retells the latter's story from an altogether different perspective.

And lastly, in *Spiritus,* Albania's Ismail Kadare again attempts to come to terms with the unspeakably evil and oppressive nature of the Enver Hoxha dictatorship in an imaginative and solidly constructed work focusing on the motives and machinations of several secret-service operatives enthralled with the power of their electronic eavesdropping equipment and the secrets they are able to unearth through its use. Several characters from earlier Kadare works reappear here, and readers will readily recognize such familiar Kadarean elements as Albania viewed through foreign eyes, bumbling secret agents doting parentally over their technological gear, and a sizable admixture of Balkan and Albanian legendry.

Notes on Contributors

Bruce Allen is a contributing editor to *Kirkus Reviews,* and also writes for the *Boston Globe,* the *New York Times Book Review,* and numerous other publications.

Allen Hoey is the author of *A Fire in the Cold House of Being,* chosen by Galway Kinnell as the 1985 Camden Poetry Prize winner. A professor in the Department of Language and Literature at Bucks County Community College outside of Philadelphia, Hoey has contributed poems and essays to such journals as *American Poetry Review, Diacritics, The Hudson Review, Poetry,* and *Shenandoah. What Persists,* his most recent collection of poems, was published in 1992.

Julius Novick is Professor of Literature and Drama Studies at Purchase College of the State University of New York. The author of *Beyond Broadway: The Quest for Permanent Theatres,* Novick has written theatre criticism for *The Village Voice, The Nation, The New York Times,* and many other publications, and is a winner of the George Jean Nathan Award for Dramatic Criticism.

William Riggan is *Editor of World Literature Today* and an expert on Third World, Slavic, Anglo-American, and smaller European literatures. The author of *Picaros, Madmen, Naïfs, and Clowns: The Unreliable First-Person Narrator,* Riggan has written extensively on the history of both the Nobel and Neustadt International Prizes in Literature. He also regularly reviews new foreign poetry and fiction for several journals and newspapers.

New Authors

Daniel Akst

St. Burl's Obituary

Akst is an American novelist.

INTRODUCTION

Akst's first novel, *St. Burl's Obituary* (1996), focuses on Burl Bennett, a reporter who writes obituaries for *The New York Tribune*. An obese man who enjoys lavish meals and takes immense pleasure in eating, Burl's life is changed when he enters a restaurant and witnesses a murderer attempting to escape a mob hit. After several threats from the Mafia, Burl flees west, where he works on an epic poem about the life and death of Mormon leader Joseph Smith. In Utah, Burl finds acceptance with Engel, a man who manages a laundromat and whose culture worships people of great weight; Burl leaves Utah, however, when he discovers Engel's interest in him is sexual. After losing a large amount of weight, Burl returns to Utah and wins the heart of a waitress, only to learn that, like Engel's, her interest in him is purely sexual. A member of a cult whose main purpose is procreation, she uses Burl to father a child and then throws him out. Burl finally returns to New York and faces the truth behind his weight problem. Akst was nominated for the PEN/Faulkner Award for fiction for *St. Burl's Obituary*, which drew comparisions to Dante and *The Divine Comedy*. Charles Monaghan stated, "With its delicately handled echoes of Dante, and its unblinking look at contemporary America, *St. Burl's Obituary* is ingenious and thought provoking. . . . Bizarre and ambitious the plot may be, but Akst tells his tale in no-nonsense, journalistic prose that keeps the story moving at a swift clip." Most critics commented on Akst's unusual and extended descriptions of food. A *Publishers Weekly* reviewer asserted that "Akst handles the labyrinthian plot twists deftly, employing a style that is at once literate and funny as he explores contemporary links among food, sex, identity and death."

CRITICISM

Dean James (review date 1 February 1996)

SOURCE: A review of *St. Burl's Obituary*, in *Library Journal*, February 1, 1996, p. 96.

[*In the following review, James asserts that "Akst offers an amusing story" in his* St. Burl's Obituary.]

[In *St. Burl's Obituary*] Burl Bennett is an overweight obituary writer for a New York paper who stumbles into

the aftermath of a mob killing in the restaurant he co-owns with an uncle. Eventually, intimidated by threats against his life, Burl leaves New York and heads out West on a bizarre odyssey. He winds up in Salt Lake City, where his weight continues to increase, until he literally gets stuck in the door of his hotel room. Burl has various adventures as his girth expands and contracts along with his economic status, and he explores every nuance of his own identity and what it means to be fat in contemporary America. The story comes full circle when Burl, having assumed someone else's identity, returns to New York, where he finally faces the issue of who he really is. Akst offers an amusing story; he writes lovingly about food, but Burl is by turns an engaging and repulsive hero. It's hard to predict what kind of audience this quirky novel will attract. Recommended for large fiction collections.

Publishers Weekly (review date 1 April 1996)

SOURCE: A review of *St. Burl's Obituary*, in *Publishers Weekly*, April 1, 1996, p. 58.

[*In the following review, the critic states that "Akst handles the labyrinthian plot twists deftly, employing a style that is at once literate and funny as he explores contemporary links among food, sex, identity and death."*]

Transcending both the usual boundaries of the genre and the standard flaws of first novels, Akst's comic debut [*St. Burl's Obituary*] begins as a thriller about a journalist who witnesses a mob killing, then slowly evolves into an exploration of identity as experienced by a delightful protagonist who will invite comparisons to John Kennedy Toole's Ignatius Reilly. Burl Bennett is the 300-pound journalistic force of nature who's been banished to the obituary desk at the *New York Tribune* because of his cantankerous response to being edited. En route to a typically gourmet meal, Burl stumbles into a gangland-style slaying. After a brief period of enduring mob threats—and suffering through a failed stab at romance with fellow *Trib* reporter Norma Ruifelen—Burl vanishes, heading west to Las Vegas and then to Utah, where he hopes to research his epic poem about the life of Mormon leader Joe Smith. Instead, he becomes the object of affection for a gay Salt Lake City laundromat owner with a fat fetish. Alarmed at his rapidly expanding girth, Burl undergoes stomach reduction surgery, then engages in a spirited affair with a female cultist. When that romance fails, he takes on a new identity and returns to New York, where he attends his own funeral and begins anew his affair with Norma, who remains unaware that her lover is, in fact, Burl. *Los Angeles Times* reporter Akst handles the labyrinthian plot twists deftly, employing a style that is at once literate and funny as he explores contemporary links among food, sex, identity and death. But the true star here is Burl, whose appetites, charm, intellect and Houdini-like ability to get himself in and out of tight situations will win readers' minds and hearts.

Charles Monaghan (review date 26 May 1996)

SOURCE: "The Weight of the Matter," in *Washington Post Book World,* May 26, 1996, p. 5.

[*In the following review, Monaghan praises Akst's* St. Burl's Obituary *as "ingenious and thought-provoking."*]

St. Burl's Obituary starts out like a thriller. The hero, Burl Bennett, savoring his approaching meal, enters a New York Italian restaurant where he brushes by a small, intense man who looks as if "he must have just killed somebody." And indeed he has. In the dining room are three bodies, victims of a Mafia rubout. The staff is in the kitchen, cowering face down on the floor.

But despite this opening, the novel is only tangentially a thriller. Rather, it is a map of the contemporary world, a black comedy that carries Burl, fearfully fleeing the Mafia, into the belly of the American beast. A newspaperman specializing in thoughtful obituaries, Burl is also a writer who has been working on an epic poem, in Dantesque *terza rima,* about the killing of Mormon leader Joseph Smith in Illinois. (There are echoes throughout the novel of Dante and *The Divine Comedy*). Burl's descent into Hell retraces Smith's journey from Palmyra, N.Y., where Mormonism was founded, to Nauvoo, Ill. Then Burl pushes on, as the Mormons did, to Utah, the American utopia.

But neither is this picaresque journey the main business of Akst's book. At its core is Burl's personal Purgatory, a feverish wrestling match with his immense appetite, a mystery in its own right because his parents are so thin and abstemious. The novel lavishes continuous loving detail on Burl's prodigious meals at restaurants and at home. Fat drips, sugar abounds, the scale groans. Burl is the American consumer par excellence.

In Utah, Burl discovers his own utopias. The first is friendship with Engel, the son of Mormon immigrants from the island of Tonga. In Tonga, the royal family is admired for

its fatness. Engel, derided by a relative as "Mr. Tongan Culture, the Franz Fanon of the islands," is deeply unhappy because he himself weighs only 150 pounds (his German grandfather, he believes, "polluted the gene pool, man"). Engel gives the ever more adipose Burl the nickname "Rex" and worships him for his greasy bulk. Miraculously, Burl has discovered a place where the ordinary world's distaste for fatness is turned on its head.

But the friendship ends badly, as Engel's interest in Burl turns out to be mainly sexual. (Not the least hint of homophobia here, by the way.) Burl continues his gargantuan eating. The apotheosis of all his meals is dinner at a restaurant called The Grail. It takes eight pages to savor. Guided by his waitress, Wanda, he consumes, among other courses, scallops atop a tomato concasse with fresh basil; a whole foie gras in an Armagnac and quince sauce; Maine lobster "shelled and reassembled with beurre scented with ginger and lime"; filet of Utah beef; risotto Milanese with grated truffles; and lamb cooked in a thick crust of kosher salt, flour and thyme. We won't discuss the veggies, desserts and wines, but Akst labors hard and makes them all sound delicious.

Back in his motel called the Chrysalis, Burl continues to gobble food, growing wider and wider. Finally, he is so fat he gets stuck in the door of his room, and the fire department is summoned to cut him out. A butterfly of sorts emerges from this Chrysalis, as Burl is transported to a hospital where, as warning signs point to his imminent demise, his stomach is stapled. His days as a fatty are over—science has conquered gluttony.

There is one more, nutty utopia to come. The slimmed down Burl is taken into a feminist commune led by Janet David Witness, an obvious parody of the religious mini-movement led by Elizabeth Clare Prophet. The Witness movement is yet another cult of personality in the great American tradition. Burl, a virgin when the book opens, gets his fill of sex from his charming commune companion, Wanda, who had been his waitress at the great feast. It soon becomes evident, however, that Wanda's main interest like that of the Witness movement, is procreation. ("The alternative," Wanda explains, "is Shakerdom. People would remember us for our furniture.") Once his work as stud leads to an apparently fruitful outcome, Burl is shown the door.

His encounters with the Scylla of homosexuality and the Charybdis of radical feminism behind him, his appetite curbed by science, his very appearance altered, our hero returns to New York from his Western odyssey under the alias Abe Alter. As the book draws to a culmination, he finds courage, settles his business with the mob, discovers the genetic reason for his raging appetite, regains his identity as

Burl Bennett, makes peace with his parents, and settles down to the Paradise of a normal married life.

With its delicately handled echoes of Dante, and its unblinking look at contemporary America, *St. Burl's Obituary* is ingenious and thought-provoking. But the book is in no way difficult reading. Bizarre and ambitious the plot may be, but Akst tells his tale in no-nonsense, journalistic prose that keeps the story moving at a swift clip. It goes down as easily as cotton candy, one of the few foods that Burl Bennett does not down in this epic of consumption.

Phoebe-Lou Adams (review date June 1996)

SOURCE: A review of *St. Burl's Obituary,* in *The Atlantic Monthly,* June, 1996, p. 126.

[*In the following review, Adams complains that Akst's* St. Burl's Obituary *is "ultimately disappointing."*]

Mr. Akst's novel starts with a provocative problem: how does a spectacularly obese man disappear? Burleigh Bennett, an obituary writer for a New York newspaper, lumbers out for a late dinner at the restaurant he has inherited and walks into a gangland execution. Unfortunately, he gets a good face-to-face look at the hit man. It becomes advisable to vanish. His adventures on the run are grotesque, elaborately gastronomic, and ultimately disappointing—at least for the reader. After all the ingeniously contrived to-do, one expects something more than a picnic in a graveyard.

Stewart M. Lindh (review date 11 August 1996)

SOURCE: "Shedding the Weight of the Past," in *Los Angeles Times Book Review,* August 11, 1996, p. 8.

[*In the following review, Lindh lauds Akst's* St. Burl's Obituary *as "a remarkable novel."*]

In *St. Burl's Obituary,* Daniel Akst has crafted a remarkable novel that gives life to Cyril Connolly's adage that "imprisoned in every fat man, a thin one is wildly signaling to be let out."

The protagonist, Burl Bennett, is marooned inside a morbid obesity. A prolonged celibate, his only joy occurs with fork in hand. Burl, 35, writes obituaries for a New York newspaper, and he ascribes all sensations to taste. On the way to repast, he imagines the fare:

He would have the fried squid in hot sauce, a Cae-

sar salad, clams in that gray salty broth so good you used bread to sop up the liquor, and finally the veal *saltimbocca,* slender elegances of flesh blanched in wine and butter, draped in mozzarella and crowned with swirls of salty red and white prosciutto. . . .

Burl's lone friendship is with a female colleague. Yet rather than move forward romantically, his relationship with Norma remains stalled at arm's length, separated by his girth. "Can't a fat man love?" he wonders, leaving her apartment sideways in order to wedge through the door.

Burl is sinking inside a sea of sauces and self-pity, and a life preserver is needed. Fate throws him one when by chance he enters a restaurant just as the killer of three diners is fleeing. The encounter triggers events that undermine the gluttonous inertia of Burl's world.

Realizing he can identify the killer, Burl worries he may be silenced in turn. Panicked, he embarks on a fugue across America, a Rabelaisian journey punctuated not by tourist sites but by roadside restaurants. At the end, he is a completely transformed person, both spiritually and physically. Rather than simply portray Burl's world realistically, Akst's stunning allegory of self-transformation goes one step further: We decipher the hidden meanings, the concealed patterns, of our own lives by watching Burl dramatically change his.

In Salt Lake City, he finds work at a Laundromat, where the slender Tongan manager adores fat men. Eluding his clutches, Burl is soon befriended by a waitress who is part of a local cult. He knows he doesn't stand a chance of winning her as long as he resembles a human balloon. So, responding to a newspaper advertisement seeking obese volunteers for an experimental weight-loss program. Burl decides it's time for a big change.

He undergoes banded gastroplasty and begins to shed pounds. Within a few months, Burl loses an average man's body weight. Yet, "even though the transformation he saw was gradual," writes Akst, a Los Angeles Times columnist, "it came upon him with the force of a death."

The void that Burl once silenced with food now needs spiritual nourishment. Ultimately, he returns home and, mistakenly thought to be dead, he reads his own obituary in the paper for which he once worked. Bearded, wearing glasses, a sliver of the man he once was, Burl turns up at his own memorial service. In a final scene, he confronts the great secret of his life—the reason why he became fat. Only then does he shed the literal and figurative weight of the past.

Pascal once wrote: "No two men differ as much as one man does from his former self." He might have added that such transformation owes less to will than it does to acceptance. That's one of the lessons of **St. Burl's Obituary,** the tale of a man slipping away from the fortress of his body to find freedom and love in the world beyond.

For readers, it's a journey worth taking.

Lan Cao
Monkey Bridge

Cao is a Vietnamese-American nonfiction writer, novelist, and professor of law.

INTRODUCTION

Monkey Bridge (1997), Cao's first novel, tells the story of a Vietnamese mother and daughter who leave their homeland shortly after the Vietnam War to immigrate to the United States, where they confront a clash of cultures and generations, as well as secrets from their own family's past. Thirteen-year-old Mai arrives in the United States in 1975, followed shortly afterward by her mother, Thanh, and the two settle in an area heavily populated by other Vietnamese outside Washington, D.C., known as "Little Saigon." Mai quickly adjusts to American life, learning English and adopting American social conventions, but she is at once embarrassed and amused by her mother's difficulty assimilating, and feels herself acutely torn between the two worlds. Not long after their arrival, Mai discovers that mystery surrounds her missing father and grandfather, and that her mother is somehow haunted by the past. While Mai is the primary narrator of *Monkey Bridge,* Cao uses the device of a diary within the text to tell the story of Mai's mother, who records not only her confusion and apprehension about her new country, but also painful details about the family's past. Cao herself immigrated to the United States from Vietnam in 1975 and now teaches international law at Brooklyn Law School. In 1996 she published *Everything You Need to Know about Asian-American History* with Himilee Novas. With *Monkey Bridge,* Cao is one of the only Vietnamese-Americans to explore the war—called the "American War" by the Vietnamese—and the ensuing immigrant experience in fiction. Critics have almost unanimously praised Cao's evocation of the Vietnamese landscape and culture as well as her depiction of the simultaneous feelings of alienation and hope experienced by immigrants to the United States. Many reviewers have been less enthusiastic about Cao's narrative structure and plot development, finding her use of two narrators—Mai and her mother in the diary—awkward. Nevertheless, *Monkey Bridge* is considered an important contribution to both Vietnam War literature and immigrant literature, giving voice to a little-explored part of one of America's most painful historical events.

CRITICISM

***Kirkus Reviews* (review date 15 May 1997)**

SOURCE: A review of *Monkey Bridge,* in *Kirkus Reviews,* May 15, 1997, p. 736.

[*The following review provides a mixed opinion of* Monkey Bridge, *noting that Cao's evocation of pre-war Vietnam is beautifully written, but finding her plot "lifeless."*]

A wonderfully written but unengaging first novel about a young Vietnamese refugee who, in 1975, is airlifted from Saigon and only later learns of her family's dark past.

Mai, whose family befriended Michael MacMahon, an American Colonel in Saigon, comes to the States as a 13-year-old. After staying with the MacMahons for six months, she moves to Washington, D.C., joined there by her widowed mother. The two make their home in "Little Saigon," the years pass, Mai is soon fluent in English, and though mindful of her past—she nostalgically recalls traditional myths and customs—she adjusts to the new country. Her mother doesn't, though, and a bad fall, followed by a disabling stroke, seems to push her even further into the past. Mai hears her talk fretfully in her sleep of her father, Baba Quan, who was to accompany her to the US but never arrived at the agreed-upon rendezvous. Mai tries to contact him, but her mother is curiously discouraging. As Mai prepares to go to college, her mother seems happier, but the secret letters Mai finds her writing are less cheerful. While the letters at first retell old legends and beliefs and describe life in her native village, the last entries, her legacy to Mai, tell a darker and more complex story. Mai learns that her grandmother had been the landlord's concubine and he, not Baba Quan, was her grandfather; Baba Quan was actually a brutal, bitter man, and a Vietcong leader; moreover, her mother had been neglected by her intellectual husband and suffered many miscarriages. Convinced that she and the family have bad karma, Mai's mother acts—successfully—to free her daughter so that she may have a "different heritage, an unburdened past."

Heartfelt evocations of a different time and place aren't enough here to give vigor to a beautifully rendered but disappointingly lifeless story of the Vietnamese American experience.

Michiko Kakutani (review date 19 August 1997)

SOURCE: "The American Dream with a Vietnamese Twist,"

in *The New York Times,* August 19, 1997, p. C13.

[In the following review, Kakutani writes that Cao's development of her characters and evocation of time and place "more than make up for" weaknesses in her plot.]

"My dilemma," says Mai, the narrator of Lan Cao's affecting first novel, "was that, seeing both sides to everything, I belonged to neither." Mai lives at once in the past and the present, haunted by the memories of her Vietnamese youth and determined at the same time to create a new life for herself in America. On one hand, she shares the immigrant fears of her mother; on the other, she shares the shiny teen-age dreams of her friends—college, a career, hanging out at the mall.

In **Monkey Bridge,** Ms. Cao, who left Vietnam in 1975 and now teaches international law at the Brooklyn Law School, tells the story of a family fractured by the Vietnam War (or, as the Vietnamese call it, the American war) It is a story about immigrants grappling with the mind-boggling possibilities and confusions of American life, reinventing themselves as they go along. But is also a story about the collision of public events and private lives, and the devastating consequences of cultural and emotional dislocation on the members of a single family.

Moving back and forth between Mai's first-person reminiscences and journals written by her mother, Thanh, Ms Cao does a sensitive job of delineating the complicated relationship between a mother and a daughter, a relationship that has been turned upside down by their move to the United States. Back home in Saigon, Mai not only found comfort in "the solid geometry" of her mother's life, but also deferred to her politely like a model Confucian daughter. Here in the Virginia suburbs, Mai is the one who quickly masters the language; she is also the one who tells her mother what is "acceptable or unacceptable behavior"

In Saigon, Thanh would buy dozens of hummingbirds and canaries and release them in the garden to generate positive karma for the family. Here in America, such charming gestures, along with her belief in curses and countercurses, are rejected by her teen-age daughter as "bad fortune-cookie advice." Mai's impatience will turn to concern, however, when a stroke sends Thanh to the hospital, and Mai is forced to become her caretaker, overseeing her convalescence and guarding her fragile emotional health.

Their relationship is hardly the only thing to undergo a sea change. As Mai observes, many Vietnamese immigrants arrived in the United States without identification papers, and the lack of proper documentation has conferred on them the ability to invent themselves anew. Sometimes the changes are cosmetic ones, made for simple vanity's sake: a woman who doesn't like having been born in the Year of the Rat gives herself a new birthday in the Year of the Tiger when she applies for a Social Security card. Sometimes the changes are more fundamental: a bar girl who once worked in a nightclub frequented by American soldiers gives herself a new past as a virtuous Confucian teacher from a small village in a distant province.

"Here, in the vehemently anti-Vietcong refugee community," Ms. Cao writes, "draft dodgers and ordinary foot soldiers could become decorated veterans of battlefields as famous as Kontum and Pleiku and Xuan Loc. It was the Vietnamese version of the American Dream; a new spin, the Vietnam spin, to the old immigrant faith in the future."

Intent on shielding her daughter from the brute reality of her family's history, Thanh, too, has put a spin on her past. The story she tells Mai, the story she has presented to the world, is a fairy tale with a tragic ending: poor peasant girl is adopted by a rich landlord, sent to convent school and married off to a handsome intellectual. She leaves behind the green rice fields of the delta for a custard yellow house on a Saigon boulevard and gives birth to a beautiful baby girl.

It is only as the war escalates that Thanh's world begins to fall apart: after her husband suddenly dies in his sleep, Thanh decides to move the family to the United States. With the help of one of her husband's friends who is an American military officer, she sends Mai to the United States; she and her aged father, Baba Quan, will follow in a few months. The day they are to leave, however, something terrible happens: Baba Quan does not arrive at the appointed meeting place, and Thanh is forced to leave without him.

As Mai begins to look into her mother's past, she slowly discovers that this official version of their family's history conceals an even sadder, darker story—a story involving marital betrayal, political intrigue and coldblooded revenge. Although Ms. Cao's orchestration of these melodramatic revelations is far from fluent—incongruous developments and clumsy foreshadowings making us suspect that something is afoot long before we're supposed to—she more than makes up for this weakness with her authoritative and subtly nuanced delineation of character and place.

Mai, Thanh and their family and friends are rendered with fierce, unsentimental detail, and the disparate worlds they have called home—from the tiny villages of the Mekong Delta to the bustling streets of Saigon to the air-conditioned malls of Virginia—are made equally palpable to the reader. With **Monkey Bridge,** Ms. Cao has not only made an impressive debut, but also joined writers like Salman Rushdie and Bharati Mukherjee in mapping the state of exile and its elusive geography of loss and hope.

Judith Coburn (review date 14 September 1997)

SOURCE: "Starting Over," in *Los Angeles Times Book Review,* September 14, 1997, p. 10.

[*In the following review, Coburn praises Cao's insightful and at times lyrical writing, despite the flaws she finds in the plot.*]

A monkey bridge—three bamboo stalks lashed with vines—figures in two of this novel's turning points. Apparitions: A man first sees his wife-to-be in white silk fluttering above him on such a bridge; a trapped American Marine glimpses through the mist the figure of a Vietnamese friend floating above a minefield and signaling the way out of the lethal maze.

In *Monkey Bridge,* the first novel by Vietnamese American writer Lan Cao, Vietnamese refugees, the relatives they left behind and the Americans they meet reach for each other across just such a simple and magical connection.

It's the late 1970s, and teenager Mai Nguyen has been settled in northern Virginia with her mother since fleeing Vietnam in 1975 during the fall of Saigon. They live in what the refugees call "Little Saigon" where they can talk, eat and shop Vietnamese under the watchful eyes of their own fortunetellers. Just like the old country.

But it wasn't a clean getaway; it never is. Family, friends and the native land still haunt them. Somehow, in the rush to escape from Vietnam, Mai's grandfather Baba Quan didn't make the rendezvous point, and there's been no word of his whereabouts. The American post-war fever of revenge prevents any telephone calls, mail or visits between the Americans and Vietnamese. A curtain of stars and stripes has fallen, and Baba Quan is all but dead to his daughter and granddaughter. And like other ghostly visitations recalled in the story, he hovers over Mai's and her mother's dream-life as if on a monkey bridge.

In America, the generation gap that inevitably opens up in immigrant families divides Mai and her mother. While her mother and her friends build Little Saigon into a sanctuary, Mai wants to be American, chattering in English, mastering the supermarket check-out line and hanging out in fast-food restaurants with new, non-Vietnamese friends. Cao movingly evokes the cultural gap between teenager Mai's bedazzlement at Safeway's air-conditioned efficiency and its produce embalmed in plastic and her mother's longing for the hustle, bustle and bargaining of Saigon's open-air markets. Mai, like most immigrant children, becomes the go-between, translating Vietnamese and American languages, customs and laws. The child becomes the parent and the parent the child, as everything new must be interpreted and explained.

As do all teenagers, Mai tries to put over what she can on the grown-ups, telling her mother that American custom requires students to go to college far from their families, "the equivalent of a martial artist leaving her village to study Kung Fu at the Shaolin Temple or even Siddharta Gautama going away to seek enlightenment under the bo tree." She's too guilty to tell her mother that Little Saigon is a prison to her, not an oasis. In one of the book's most moving chapters, Mai brings her American friend Bobbie to watch a Vietnamese fortuneteller minister to a reverent crowd of her mother's friends. To the older refugees, the fortuneteller's prognostications are gold. But to Mai, who already has crossed over into the new world, it's just a fun scene.

In Cao's hands, there is sometimes a hilarious cast to these cross-cultural matings. When her mother is hospitalized with a stroke, Mai discovers that the older woman's favorite TV show is *The Bionic Woman.* It seems the character's Bionic ears remind Mai's mother of her own long ears, or the Buddha's, which droop halfway down the side of his face. Such ears are to the Vietnamese a sign of longevity and luck. But as for the program's actual plot, the teenager must translate:

> The Bionic Woman had just finished rescuing a young girl, from drowning in a lake where she'd gone swimming against her mother's wishes. Once out of harm's way, Jaime made the girl promise she'd be more careful next time and listen to her mother.

> Translation: the Bionic Woman rescued the girl from drowning in the lake, but commended her for her magnificent deed, since the girl had heroically jumped into the water to rescue a prized police dog.

> "Where's the dog?" my mother would ask. "I don't see him."

> "He's not there anymore, they took him to the vet."

Traditionalists, both Vietnamese and American, may bristle at such cultural mish-mashing. But Cao, one of the first Vietnamese American novelists to publish in English, shows, as do other immigrant writers before her, how the new Americans believe far more fervently in the American dream than do longtime citizens. Mai's mother and her friends may cling to their old language and their fortuneteller, but they're just as avid about the "possibility for rebirth, reinvention and other euphemisms for half-truths and outright lies" that starting over in America promises.

The novel's weaknesses oddly recapitulate the cost of the immigrants' protean approach to life in America. The novelist overreaches wildly, especially at the end of the novel, where she attempts to condense Vietnamese history and the war with the Americans into a few hyperactive pages. After early chapters of lyrical and subtle writing, the novel rockets to a close with so many plot developments that it's more like a bodice-ripper than like literary fiction. The voice of the narrator, supposedly Mai's, is too knowing and literary to be a teenager's. And her mother's journal is too close to the narrator's densely metaphoric style to ring anything but false. There are patches of psychobabble and metaphors repeated so many times that the storyteller's spell is broken. Has becoming an American converted Cao to a culture in which big dams wash out fragile monkey bridges?

But then, even in the unconvincing mother's journal, there are insights: "Why do children resemble their parents? . . . In my daughter's reasoning, it is a fact, intangible but scientific, that the child can inherit the fact of the parent, but not the parent's karmic history. . . . Yet karma, my child, is nothing more than an ethical, spiritual chromosome, an amalgam of parent and child, which is as much a part of our history as DNA strands. There is no escaping it, the fact of mother and child, as synchronous and inseparable as left and right, up and down, back and front, sun and moon."

Such writing makes the reader look forward to Cao's next novel.

Charles Frazier
Cold Mountain

Frazier is an American novelist.

INTRODUCTION

Frazier chose a difficult and expansive setting for his debut novel, the 1997 National Book Award-winning *Cold Mountain* (1997), set in the South and based on a family story about Frazier's great-great-grandfather who deserted during the Civil War. Frazier wrote *Cold Mountain* by researching the time period and the landscape of the North Carolina mountains, then allowing his knowledge of the natural world and his imagination to fill in the rest. In response, many critics have described Frazier as a natural-born storyteller. *Cold Mountain* follows Inman, a Confederate soldier wounded in battle who deserts before his injury heals enough to force him back to war, and Ada, the woman he loves and to whom he sets out to return. As the daughter of a minister, Ada lived in genteel Charleston society until her father brought her to the remote mountains of North Carolina to live on a farm into which he put some indifferent effort, but not enough to make it a successful venture. When her father dies, Ada, ignorant of farm management, soon finds herself starving but unwilling to return to city life and dependence upon her father's friends. Help arrives in the form of a local girl named Ruby, who knows everything Ada needs for the farm's and her own survival. As Ada learns of manual labor and daily subsistence, Inman encounters a number of people, both friend and foe, on his way to her. Among them are bounty hunters hoping to return him to the war, a widow and her child whom he saves from Yankee soldiers, and a goat-herding woman who heals his wounds.

Reviewers have made note of the parallels between *Cold Mountain* and Homer's *Odyssey,* with Inman as Odysseus journeying home to Ada, his Penelope. Critics have also mentioned Frazier's skill with antiquated language in *Cold Mountain,* many of them asserting that it contributes to the understanding of the story, slowing the pace and forcing the reader to savor each scene. Additionally, many reviewers have praised Frazier's ability to capture the natural world. Claire Messud stated, "He writes evocatively about the region's flora and fauna and about man's relationship to it."

CRITICISM

David A. Berona (review date 15 May 1997)

SOURCE: A review of *Cold Mountain,* in *Library Journal,* May 15, 1997, p. 100.

[*In the following review, Berona lauds* Cold Mountain *as a work that "will enrich readers not only with its story but with its strong characters."*]

This monumental novel is set at the end of the Civil War and follows the journey of a wounded Confederate soldier named Inman as he returns home. Interwoven is the story of Ada, the woman he loves. Ada, who was raised in genteel society, cannot cope with the rigors of war until a woman called Ruby arrives to help her. Inman comes across memorable characters like the goatwoman, who lives off the secret herbs in the woods and Sara, a woman stranded with an infant who is assaulted by Yankee soldiers whom Inman later kills. After a long, threatening journey, Inman finally arrives home to Ada, "ravaged, worn ragged and wary and thin." His momentary homecoming, however, comes to a tragic end. A remarkable effort that opens up a historical past that will enrich readers not only with its story but with its strong characters. Highly recommended for all collections.

Mary Carroll (review date 1/15 June 1997)

SOURCE: A review of *Cold Mountain,* in *Booklist,* June 1/ 15, 1997, p. 1656.

[*In the following review, Carroll calls* Cold Mountain *"a satisfying read."*]

The Civil War's last months are the setting for this first novel by Frazier, erstwhile college teacher and author of travel books and stories. Inman, a wounded Confederate soldier, leaves the hospital before his gashed neck heals enough to get him sent back to war. Still weak, he heads for the mountains, where a minister's daughter named Ada is his objective. Inman's return could hardly be timelier for the Charleston-raised Ada: her father has died, and she finds she knows little about operating a farm. Frazier blends the story of Inman's journey with that of Ada's efforts, with the help of a drifter named Ruby, to wring a subsistence living from the neglected land; in the background are the yelping dogs of war (most dramatically, gangs chasing Confederate deserters like Inman), as well as hints of changes the end of war will bring. *Cold Mountain,* based on a Frazier family story, is a satisfying read, though for some readers elements of the story (e.g., Ada's dependence) are anachronistic.

Malcolm Jones Jr. (review date 23 June 1997)

SOURCE: "A Yarn Finely Spun," in *Newsweek,* June 23, 1997, p. 73.

[*In the follwoing review, Jones offers a highly positive review of* Cold Mountain.]

Novelists are never in short supply. Natural-born storytellers come along only rarely. Charles Frazier joins the ranks of that elite cadre on the first page of his astonishing debut, *Cold Mountain.* A Civil War soldier, Inman, is recuperating from a gunshot wound in an army hospital in Raleigh, N.C., where he passes the time reading naturalist William Bartram's *Travels* and staring out the window. "The window was tall as a door, and he had imagined many times that it would open onto some other place and let him walk through and be there." That sentence is like a hand in the small of your back. At the end of that chapter, when Inman skips out of the hospital and heads for home in the mountains near Asheville, you're as ready to roam as he is.

Frazier based his novel on family stories told about W. P. Inman, the author's great-great-grandfather, who deserted in the midst of the Civil War and walked home. Around that armature he wraps a narrative that is equal parts adventure yarn, war novel and love story. Those elements have been the ingredients of many a potboiler, but no hack ever dreamed up a protagonist like Inman. The horrors of war have hollowed him out, leaving him to ponder how "a man's spirit could be torn apart and cease and yet his body keep on living." Two things keep him going: the thought of Ada Monroe, an unapproachable beauty for whom he'd fallen before the war, and the memory of Cold Mountain. For Inman, this peak looming over his home symbolizes all that's right with the world, "a place where all his scattered forces might gather."

> **Novelists are never in short supply. Natural-born storytellers come along only rarely. Charles Frazier joins the ranks of that elite cadre on the first page of his astonishing debut, *Cold Mountain.***
> **—*Malcolm Jones Jr.***

Nature, though, is never simple in Frazier's cosmos. Inman nearly starves and almost freezes to death contending with nature on his way home. And while he constantly dodges vigilante posses, men as evil as any you'd ever want to meet, it's the natural world in the end that constitutes his greatest foe. And his greatest friend. *Cold Mountain*'s best lesson is that the natural world is not something to be conquered but something before which we must humble ourselves. "The creek's turnings," Frazier writes, "marked how all that moves must shape itself to the maze of actual landscape, no matter what its preferences might be."

Frazier's descriptions of farmwork and animals are the work of a man with first-hand knowledge, and it is no surprise to discover that the 46-year-old author raises horses for a living. But where he learned to conjure war's horror with a poet's economy ("the mere existence of the Henry repeating rifle or the eprouvette mortar made all talk of spirit immediately antique") is anyone's guess.

The pleasure of Frazier's language—forceful and perfectly cadenced to capture the flavor of a long-gone era—is merely a side dish. Inman's trek and Ada's struggle to manage a small mountain farm are told in alternating chapters. As these narratives converge, their yearning for each other grows more intense, and so does our suspense. The genuinely romantic saga of Ada and Inman is a page turner that attains the status of literature. In a closing note of acknowledgment, Frazier apologizes for taking liberties with "W. P. Inman's life and with the geography surrounding Cold Mountain (6030 feet)." One must assume that he is merely being polite. This writer owes apologies to no one.

Claire Messud (review date 6 July 1997)

SOURCE: "Tried in the Fire," in *The Washington Post Book World,* July 6, 1997, p. 6.

[*In the following review, Messud praises the lyricism and language of Frazier's* Cold Mountain, *but complains that the ending "relies unabashedly on the conventions of romance."*]

Contemporary fiction continues to tackle the Civil War because its ramifications are ubiquitous still: That brutal conflict marks the watershed of American modernity, as the First World War marks Europe's. Significantly, Charles Frazier's rich first novel addresses that watershed not only in its themes but in its very structure.

Cold Mountain comprises the interwoven narratives of a Confederate soldier named Inman and his intended, a young woman named Ada Monroe. Wounded at Petersburg and transferred to a Tennessee hospital in the summer of 1864, Inman deserts and heads for his home in the mountains of North Carolina. His journey is fraught with adventures and pitfalls, with curious characters who unburden their stories to him, and with villains whose aim is to recapture and make him fight again.

Meanwhile, Ada, the well-born daughter of a Charleston minister whose mission took him to Cold Mountain, struggles to reconstruct her life after her father's death, opting to remain at her remote farm in the lee of the mountain rather than return to the city dependent upon her father's friends. Joined by a tough local girl named Ruby, Ada comes to value nature and its gifts, the fruits of hard labor and the intensity of the seasons. As the lovers' reunion approaches, both are aware of their internal (and external) transformations, irrevocable changes that reflect those of the country in which they live.

Their stories, in spite of the overlapping menace of the war, are very different. Inman's is emphatically picaresque, a progression of grotesque and fantastic encounters reminiscent of Fielding or Richardson. He saves a woman from a murderous preacher; he falls into the clutches of a bloated fellow named Junior and his harem of sluttish women, who turn him over to the Home Guard; he stumbles upon a goat-keeping hermit woman who heals his wounds; he takes refuge in the home of a frail widow and saves her and her infant from marauding Federals. Inman moves through these adventures like a cipher, alternately a hero and a victim of action.

Ada's chapters, focused on the farm and her reflections upon it, and upon her growing friendship with Ruby, form a more contemporary tale, the exploration of a woman's psychological development in communion with the stable but seasonal natural world in which she is immersed. Ada and Inman's union is, in a sense, the literary confrontation of history and the present. Readers impatient with the relentless linearity of Inman's progress will find respite in Ada's concentric growth, and vice versa.

Throughout, Frazier has adopted an antiquated style to authenticate the 19th-century Southern world. His locutions sound unnatural to the contemporary ear—"There was scant humidity in the air for a change and all the colors and edges of things seemed crisp beyond the natural"—and his vocabulary thrills in its oddity. He has captured his characters' lost quotidian speech, and the novel's pages are peppered with words such as "hinnies," "spavins," and "taliped."

This rhetorical analepsis alone makes **Cold Mountain** an exciting work of fiction, but Frazier's prose, consistent and precise, goes further. He writes evocatively about the region's flora and fauna and about man's relationship to it. When Ada observes a heron, he notes that "the beak of it was black on top and yellow underneath, and the light shone off it with muted sheen as from satin or chipped flint." When Inman encounters a catfish, Frazier records: "It was stout as a tub. It was ugly in the face with its tiny eyes and pale barbels run out from its mouth and wagging in the current. Its lower jaw was set back to make sucking up bottom trash easier, and its back was greeny black and gritty-looking." The use of plants for medicinal purposes, the calculation of time and seasons by the movement of the stars, the foraging for and preparation of food—all are reconstructed and conveyed in meticulous detail. **Cold Mountain** delights, above all, as an exceedingly free natural history, in which Frazier's characters learn and live by their surroundings.

What disappoints, in this fine debut, is its cinematic conclusion, a carefully contrived display of the bittersweet. It is an ending that relies unabashedly on the conventions of romance; and while Frazier has drawn on other literary conventions—the picaresque and the psychological novel—one might have hoped that their daring conflation would produce a less predictable result. This said, the fate of Frazier's human protagonists is not, perhaps, so important. He notes that "Inman had seen so much death it had come to seem a random thing entirely," and the narrative reinforces this sentiment. Ultimately, it is not the people who endure but the locale: Cold Mountain is the novel's true core and, fittingly, its title.

James Polk (review date 13 July 1997)

SOURCE: "American Odyssey," in *The New York Times Book Review,* July 13, 1997, p. 14.

[In the following review, Polk considers numerous second-ary elements of Cold Mountain, *but notes that "however strongly the side issues resonate, they are never allowed to interfere with the main thrust of the plot. The author's focus is always on Ada and Inman."]*

For a first novelist, in fact for any novelist, Charles Frazier has taken on a daunting task—and has done extraordinarily well by it. In prose filled with grace notes and trenchant asides, he has reset much of the *Odyssey* in 19th-century America, near the end of the Civil War.

Although too much can be made of the Homeric parallels, they are obvious, and they echo through the narrative. The author's Ithaca lies deep within the Carolina mountains and is the elusive goal of his Odysseus: a wounded Confederate veteran named Inman who "had seen so much death it had come to seem a random thing entirely." Because it had, he resolves to reclaim himself and his humanity by fleeing the hospital where he is recovering, returning to his home and to Ada, his Penelope, whom he intends to make his wife.

At the same time, Ada, a city girl "educated beyond the point considered wise for females," must deal with being suddenly alone in the backwoods. Her father, Monroe, has died, leaving her with an indifferently maintained property and little idea how to manage it. A preacher come to the mountains for his health, Monroe was far more interested in his God and his Emerson—Ralph the horse and Waldo the cow are part of his legacy—than in operating a farm that actually worked. Ada remains on Cold Mountain partly to wait for Inman but also because, however vaguely, that's where she has glimpsed her destiny. She never really fit into the elegant pettiness of Charleston society and has always wanted something else, something she suspects might lie in the Blue Ridge Mountains.

So both of Frazier's characters are between their pasts and their futures, escaping the former and traveling toward the latter. Although Inman's journey (which, he tells himself, "will be the axle of my life") covers more physical distance and has more immediate drama, Ada's is richer and deeper; in the end, perhaps it is she who travels farther.

Setting out armed with a pistol and a tattered copy of the 18th-century naturalist William Bartram's *Travels,* Inman takes leave of a "country of swill and sullage, sump of the continent," and heads off into the new sunrise of his life. Along the way, he encounters wonders and deadly threats that, while of less mythological weight than the trials of Odysseus, carry mystical overtones that are particularly American.

He meets other travelers who threaten him, strangers who take him in and guide him, vigilantes who shoot at him. But most of all, he confronts the land. Accompanied by random selections from Bartram, Inman's close observations of the countryside and its creatures make *Cold Mountain* read at times like a novelistic version of Annie Dillard's *Pilgrim at Tinker Creek.* These passages also make the journey home seem like a Whitmanesque foray into America: into its huge-ness, its freshness, its scope and its soul.

Meanwhile, as Inman struggles toward her, Ada engages in an internalized journey of no less grandeur. By the novel's end, she has successfully "made her way to a place where an entirely other order prevailed from what she had always known." Helped by Ruby, a tiny country woman who joins her as a companion and teacher, this well-bred child of the city becomes a woman of strength and consequence. In her quest, "Ruby was her principal text," but the final achievement is all her own.

A wealth of finely realized supporting characters gives Frazier's novel a subtext of richness and subtlety. The account of the reclamation of Ruby's layabout father, the drunkard Stobrod, through music and the fiddle, for instance, is memorable and inspired. Yet however strongly the side issues resonate, they are never allowed to interfere with the main thrust of the plot. The author's focus is always on Ada and Inman. It is their movement toward each other that always remains central, and that finally makes *Cold Mountain* such a memorable book.

Christina Patterson (review date 20 July 1997)

SOURCE: "Hope Is Where the Hearth Is," in *The Observer,* July 20, 1997, p. 17.

[In the following excerpt, Patterson asserts that Cold Mountain *"presents the terrible, discordant reality of life in a war."]*

God, sex, pigs, mountains and cheese feature heavily in [*Cold Mountain*], offering enough sexual titillation and metaphysical speculation for the most guilt-ridden survivor of a Catholic childhood. The God of Charles Frazier's *Cold Mountain,* set in the American Civil War, is the squeaky-clean Protestant model of the pioneers. However, as the story unfolds, with its bewildering array of lives wrecked by the random ravages of war, perceptions of God, like everything else in the American Dream, become more complicated. Wounded on the Confederate side in the battle of Petersburg, Inman decides to desert and return to his sweetheart, Ada, at Cold Mountain. She has been alone on the family farm since the death of her wealthy father, suffering genteel hun-ger and nibbling only the odd tomato. Luckily, help arrives in the form of feisty Ruby, who knows everything there is to know about survival. Soon the two women are sowing, hoeing and ploughing with the gusto of characters from *The Little House on the Prairie* and then sinking down exhausted at sunset to eat hearty meals with 'gobs of biscuit dough the size of cat heads'.

While Ada is experiencing the novelty of labour, independence and a life in touch with the rhythms of nature, Inman is nursing his neck wound, scratching around for food and enduring one life-threatening encounter after another on his tortuous journey home. Not surprisingly, his American optimism and belief in progress has been replaced by the idea that 'at the rate we're going we'll be eating each other raw'. Only his hope of being reunited with Ada allows him to dream that 'his despair might be honed off to a point so fine and thin that it would be nearly the same as vanishing'.

As this quotation makes clear, the narrative voice is ponderous and archaic, full of words and phrases like 'somewhat', 'smote' and 'neither mark nor impress'. This initially feels like rather hard work, making it a difficult book to gallop through. Instead, the reader is forced to take it all at a slightly slower pace, to savour each episode of this magnificent adventure story and to allow the magic of the prose to work in its own way. It does. Full of graphic, unflinching details, striking concrete images and lyrically precise descriptions of the natural world, this wonderful novel presents the terrible, discordant reality of life in a war. Profoundly moving, it raises all the big questions, but offers no answers other than the recognition that 'what you have lost will not be returned to you. It will always be lost. . . . All you can choose to do is go on or not'. ***Cold Mountain*** has, apparently, just been picked up as the next Anthony Minghella big-screen weepie. It certainly has all the right ingredients.

Ha Jin
Ocean of Words

Born in 1956, Jin is a Chinese-American poet and short story writer.

INTRODUCTION

Jin was raised in China during the Cultural Revolution and immigrated to the United States in 1985. He chose to write in English, despite the challenges this presented to him, since "it would be impossible for him to write honestly in China," Jocelyn Lieu has reported. The author of two collections of poetry (*Between Silences,* 1990, and *Facing Shadows,* 1996), Jin gained critical attention, and the 1997 Hemingway/PEN Award for First Fiction, with his short story collection, *Ocean of Words* (1996). Set on the forbidding Chinese-Russian border in the early 1970s, the stories in *Ocean of Words* focus on longing, loss, betrayal, and rivalry. Jin has observed about his own writing: "As for the subject matter, I guess we are compelled to write about what has hurt us most." In "Dragon Head," widely considered the best piece in *Ocean of Words,* an elderly iconoclastic veteran recounts a battle of wits between an army officer and a local militia commander involving betrayal, political machinations, and the truth about Mao Tse-tung's regime. Jin's fictional world also incorporates humor and irony into its Maoist milieu. "Miss Jee" centers on a less-than-sturdy soldier targeted by his joking comrades, while "Too Late" comically portrays a political instructor who interferes in a love affair between a young soldier and an orphaned girl. Jin has recently released a second collection of stories, *Under the Red Flag* (1998), which won the 1997 Flannery O'Connor Award; a third book, *In the Pond,* is due out in 1998. Overall, reception of Jin's work has been positive. Andy Solomon determined that Jin's stories are "powerful in their unity of theme and rich in their diversity of styles." Lieu expressed admiration for Jin's "laconic, luminous prose" in *Ocean of Words,* which she designates "a nearly flawless treasure." A *Publishers Weekly* reviewer concluded that "Jin's characters make hard choices that will move not just readers interested in China or the army life, but any reader vulnerable to good writing and simple human drama."

CRITICISM

Publishers Weekly (review date 26 February 1996)

SOURCE: A review of *Ocean of Words,* in *Publishers Weekly,* February 26, 1996, p. 98.

[*In the following review of* Ocean of Words, *the writer notes Jin's "talent for humor" and "good writing."*]

Set on the Chinese-Russian border in the early 1970s, these short stories by this poet (***Between Silences***) and veteran of the People's Army, quickly draws the reader into Chinese army life with all its rivalries, propaganda and poignancy. **"Dragon Head"** follows a fascinating battle of wits between an army commander and a local militia commander ("If this were the Old China, no doubt Dragon Head would become a small warlord") through the twists and turns of betrayal and political intrigue. In **"Miss Jee,"** about a soldier who is the helpless butt of his comrades' jokes, Jin also shows a genuine talent for humor. But the author is at his best when telling the stories of soldiers forced to choose between ideology and love. Whether it is love of a woman or love of knowledge, Jin's characters make hard choices that will move not just readers interested in China or the army life, but any reader vulnerable to good writing and simple human drama.

Andy Solomon (review date 2 June 1996)

SOURCE: A review of *Ocean of Words,* in *The New York Times Book Review,* June 2, 1996, p. 21.

[*In the review below, Solomon summarizes the themes and tone of* Ocean of Words.]

A veteran of the People's Army, the Chinese poet Ha Jin (who now teaches at Emory University) has produced a compelling collection of stories [*Ocean of Words*], powerful in their unity of theme and rich in their diversity of styles. Set along the Chinese-Russian border in the early 1970's, they range from a droll sketch of an affectionately derided, delicate young soldier to a painfully iconoclastic parable in which an old veteran reveals the ugly truth of Mad's Long March. Warily eyeing Soviet troops from their watchtowers, the characters in these stories believe that "they were barbarians and Revisionists, while we were Chinese and true Revolutionaries." But what they are all revealed to be is achingly human. Whether nurturing lifelong grudges against enemy soldiers, aiding vagabond neighbors who once betrayed them or witnessing the slaughter of an ox, these men isolated in a forbidding landscape are brought together to form a group portrait that suggests how an entire people struggles to keep its basic humanity within the stiff, unnatural confines of Maoist ideology.

Jocelyn Lieu (review date 24 December 1996)

SOURCE: "Beating the Odds," in *Chicago Tribune Books,* December 24, 1996, p. 6.

[*In the following review, Lieu compares and contrasts Jin's* Ocean of Words *with Chinese writer Wang Ping's* Foreign Devil.]

These are two extraordinary, original works of fiction, similar in subject and spirit, by two Chinese American writers. Wang Ping, who was born in 1957, and Ha Jin, born in 1956, both grew up in China during the turbulent Cultural Revolution. Both emigrated to America in 1985 and began writing—and publishing—thereafter. (Ha has written two books of poems, **Between Silences** and **Facing Shadows.** Wang's critically acclaimed short-story collection, *American Visa,* was published in 1994. A collection of her poems—she has won a National Endowment for the Arts fellowship for her poetry—is due out from Coffee House next spring.)

Both also have chosen to write in English, which in Ha's case is based on more than just geography. About his decision to emigrate and leave behind his native tongue, Ha has said, alluding to restrictions of freedom of speech in his homeland, that he realized it would be impossible for him to write honestly in China. Writing in English "meant a lot of labor

and some despair—but also, freedom."

Wang, in *Foreign Devil,* her first novel, and Ha, in his story collection **Ocean of Words,** explore the upheavals that transformed lives in the China they knew—the seemingly arbitrary reversals that turned friends, family and allies into "class enemies" overnight. Their stories are about the power of the regime, of any regime, to subvert tenderness—yet Ha and Wang also insist on the possibility of love and of human connection despite almost overwhelming harshness.

Their approaches differ dramatically, however. **Ocean of Words** consists of 12 carefully crafted stories that arise from Ha's six years of service in the Chinese army. The voices of young recruits, Communist Party secretaries and officers are beautifully knit together in a way that, like Isaac Babel's *Red Cavalry* stories, makes the most of irony. (Unlike Babel, Ha is consistently open-hearted, even when navigating his way through narratives of bitter betrayal and lost hope.) Together, the stories in **Ocean of Words** present a powerful, humane portrait of a group of military men.

Although *Foreign Devil* focuses on a single narrator, a young woman named Ni Bing, it may be even more ambitious in scope than **Ocean of Words.** A passionate, sprawling, coming-of-age novel that jumps back and forth through time, *Foreign Devil* charts Bing's progress from her severe, Cinderella-like childhood (territory familiar to readers of *American Visa*) to the day she boards a plane to emigrate to America. Along the way, we see her as daughter, granddaughter, a "model educated youth" laboring in the countryside, a Communist Party member, a college student, a schoolteacher and, in the months before she emigrates, a homeless woman who falls through the system's cracks almost to her death.

Her given name, Bing, means "ice," which is appropriate because of the emotional distance she often feels regarding those close to her. (During the novel's opening scene, when she gives up her stubborn virginity to a married man, she wonders if she isn't a *shinu,* "a stone girl, whose hymen can never be broken.")

But her chilly name is ironic as well, because of her ability to empathize. As a schoolgirl, she earns the nickname "Foreign Devil" by inappropriately crying during the screening of a film that shows Chinese women boxing the faces of captured Japanese soldiers. Her teacher tells her classmates that by weeping for the Japanese "foreign devils," Bing not only aligns herself with them but becomes one. Bing is at a loss to explain her feelings. "I knew that I should hate those invaders and killers. But I couldn't stop shedding tears for them."

When as a young schoolteacher she is ordered to participate

in the interrogation of the school's disgraced former party secretary, Bing feels the dangerous urge to comfort and side with her instead. Asking herself why she feels sympathy for a woman who had tormented others during the Cultural Revolution, she thinks: "Perhaps it was . . . physical closeness that made me sentimental. Whenever I moved my legs, our knees would touch."

Wang's unflinching, unsparing voice saves Bing's story from sentimentality. So, too, does the fact that Bing's personal crises—family and friends who appear to love and support her one moment, reject and brutally punish her the next—echo the larger historical moment. The times when the personal and the public converge are unforgettable, as in a stunning scene early in the novel, when 10-year-old Bing watches her mother humiliated by the Red Guard as an enemy of the people, paraded publicly as a "Beauty Snake."

Along with *American Visa, Foreign Devil* establishes Wang as an exciting, important voice among a generation of American writers working to enlarge and change our ideas of who we are.

Although Ha also writes eloquently about societal harshness and the subversive power of tenderness, he takes a different approach. Whereas Wang uses the urgent voice of a woman telling her life's story, Ha employs a mosaic of men's and boys' voices, often allowing the "misunderstandings" that arise from limited points of view to speak for him.

For example, **"A Report,"** the opening work in this collection of linked stories set near the Russian border in the 1970s, is written in the form of an official report from the party secretary of a reconnaissance company. He must explain to his superiors how a mournful marching song sung by the young soldiers—"Good-bye, mother, good-bye, mother"—caused the whole company to break down in tears. While Chen Jun, the author of the report, blames the composers of the "contagious song" for infecting the troops, we see, over his shoulder, as it were, that the contagion is nothing more—or less—than longing and love.

Against the odds, many of Ha's characters become infected by longing. Sometimes love wins, as in **"Too Late,"** a wryly funny love story told from the point of view of a political instructor who tries unsuccessfully to derail an affair between a young soldier, Kong Kai, and an orphaned girl named An Mali.

More often, though, longing exacts a terrible price. In **"My Best Soldier,"** a sex-obsessed recruit helps bring about his own violent death. The protagonist of **"Love in the Air,"** a slow-witted telegraph operator, becomes obsessed with the "gold fingers" and telephonic voice of a female operator in another unit. Though they never meet, he falls so deeply in love with the unseen woman that he withdraws from his army career and, he believes, ruins his future.

The best piece in the collection is a longer story titled **"Dragon Head."** Narrated by an ineffectual commander named Old Gao, it is the story of a powerful militiaman named Dragon Head, who enters into an uneasy alliance with the army. Eventually, his passion for battle and his treatment at the hands of an opportunistic commissar lead to his downfall, and he is executed as a scapegoat when Russia and China turn from enemies to allies.

Like Isaac Babel, Ha lets silence speak for him, allowing the sometimes hilarious, sometimes terrible truth to sink in without commentary.

—Jocelyn Lieu

Also like Isaac Babel, Ha lets silence speak for him, allowing the sometimes hilarious, sometimes terrible truth to sink in without commentary. A parting ironic jab comes with the title story, **"Ocean of Words,"** which is also the title of a Chinese dictionary. In the story's final line, the protagonist, Zhou, who is leaving the army, makes up his mind to become "a socialist man of letters, fighting with the Revolutionary Pen for the rest of his life." If we are to see Zhou as a stand-in for the author, the fight took an unexpected turn. The result is a wonderful Chinese American writer whose laconic, luminous prose makes *Ocean of Words* a nearly flawless treasure.

Peter Bricklebank (review date 11 January 1998)

SOURCE: A review of *Under the Red Flag,* in *The New York Times Book Review,* January 11, 1998.

[*In the following review, Bricklebank faults the "political exigencies" of the themes and Jin's narrative technique in* Under the Red Flag.]

Dismount Fort is a country town ruled under the red flag of China's Cultural Revolution, a place where feudal custom has been further warped by the political dogma of a new social order. Ha Jin's dozen stories about Dismount Fort [in **Under the Red Flag**], which won the 1997 Flannery O'Connor Award, inform us that noble goals do not prevent many of these country people from scrambling for wealth, revenge and prestige, or from seeking the opportunity to address lingering resentments. In one story, an arrogant and miserly Communist finds that as small a thing as an accidentally smashed Mao button can lead to his downfall. In another, a widow who in the course of a rape kills the nephew of a party boss poses a terrible problem—until her actions can be recast into patriotic propaganda. Unfortunately, these sorts of political exigencies seem awfully familiar, especially when used in the service of well-worn themes. And Ha Jin's narrative style isn't much of a help. As plain and stiffly serviceable as a Mao uniform, it lacks expressive elegance and leaves the reader wishing for greater psychological richness, for colors other than red.

Additional coverage of Jin's life and career is contained in the following source published by Gale: *Contemporary Authors,* **Vol. 152.**

Sebastian Junger
The Perfect Storm

American nonfiction writer.

INTRODUCTION

Before he became a writer, Sebastian Junger made a living as a climber for a tree-removal company. After suffering a serious injury, he turned his attention to writing. Junger reports having always had a fascination with men facing extreme situations, and his first book, *The Perfect Storm* (1997), expresses this interest. The book follows the true story of a swordfishing boat, the *Andrea Gail,* and her crew as they face one of the worst storms in the last hundred years, a gale that one meteorologist termed a "perfect storm." In October of 1991, two storm fronts joined with the remnants of Hurricane Grace to create 70- to 100-foot waves and 100-mile-per-hour winds. On October 28, the *Andrea Gail* was returning to her port in Gloucester, Massachusetts, after a successful trip and was carrying 40,000 pounds of swordfish and tuna in her hold; she was halfway home near the coast of Nova Scotia when the storm began. The captain sent one final radio message and was never heard from again. Though no first-hand accounts of the *Andrea Gail's* final hours exist, Junger attempts to relate the ship's last voyage by piecing together stories of survivors caught in the same storm, adding meteorological information about the force of the storm and the effect it was likely to have had on the *Andrea Gail.* Junger also traces the lives of the crew before they left on the trip and recounts the history of the fishing industry in Gloucester. Many reviewers noted the ambitious research and technical information that went into *The Perfect Storm.* Anthony Bailey asserted that "not all of Junger's information is vital to his task," but most critics found the technical information helpful to the story and praised Junger for his masterful handling of it. Richard Ellis stated, "In less competent hands, this abundance of information might impede the progress of the narrative. But, for the most part, the book—like the storm it describes—rolls along toward its inevitable conclusion: the sinking of the *Andrea Gail* and the death of its crew." Reviewers also lauded Junger for his ability to create a vivid, though imagined, picture of the event. Bailey said, "just as he has kept us hooked so far, despite our knowing from the start that the *Andrea Gail* and her crew are doomed, so he manages with considerable reporting skill to conjure up their last hours." Sandy Bauers described *The Perfect Storm* as "a cross between a meteorological whatdunnit and a high-seas drama."

CRITICISM

Richard Ellis (review date 25 May 1997)

SOURCE: "Sturm und Drang," in *Los Angeles Times Book Review,* May 25, 1997, pp. 8-9.

[*In the following review, Ellis lauds Junger's* The Perfect Storm *as "a wild ride that brilliantly captures the awesome power of the raging sea and the often futile attempts of humans to withstand it."*]

In October 1991, Sebastian Junger was standing on the shore of Gloucester, Mass., as winds howled, waves crested at 100 feet, ships were overturned, rescues were effected, men died. In *The Perfect Storm,* he writes: "A mature hurricane is by far the most powerful event on Earth; the combined nuclear arsenals of the United States and the former Soviet Union don't contain enough energy to keep a hurricane going for one day. A typical hurricane encompasses a million cubic miles of atmosphere and could provide all the electric power needed by the United States for three or four years. During the Labor Day hurricane of 1935, winds surpassed 200 miles an hour and people caught outside were sandblasted to death."

Junger investigated the lives and deaths of six fishermen who went down with their fishing boat, the 72-foot *Andrea Gail,* off the coast of Nova Scotia; he tracked the course of the storm, investigated other vessels caught in the storm, researched the training of rescue jumpers and interviewed meteorologists. The "perfect storm" of the title was bestowed on the Halloween Gale of 1991 by a meteorologist named Bob Case, who saw "perfection in strange things, and the meshing of three completely independent weather systems to form a hundred-year event is one of them. My God, thought Case, this is the perfect storm."

I once sailed to Antarctica across the Drake Passage, that infamous 600-mile strait between the southern tip of South America and the Antarctic peninsula, generally considered to be the roughest, windiest body of open water for sailing in the world. It may very well be, but we were aboard a cruise ship and, although we were all seasick as we shared stories about the dangers of open water sailing, we were in danger only of losing our lunches, not our lives. The Drake Passage is that region where so many sailing ships ran into trouble trying to round Cape Horn, and our stories imparted to our voyage a historical sense of danger, almost all of it imaginary. There is nothing imaginary about Junger's book; it is all terrifyingly, awesomely real.

The Perfect Storm is actually several stories, interlarded with the history of New England fisheries; explanations of wind, wave and weather phenomena; a detailed discussion of the phenomenon of drowning; and the training work of rescue jumpers, all of which helps us to understand and follow the narrative without having to stumble over arcane definitions.

In less competent hands, this abundance of information might impede the progress of the narrative. But, for the most part, the book—like the storm it describes—rolls along toward its inevitable conclusion: the sinking of the *Andrea Gail* and the death of its crew. If we didn't know the story of technological advances in fishing and the diminishing fish stocks that resulted, we wouldn't understand why these men had risked their lives so far offshore. And if we didn't understand the complex, sometimes lethal interactions between waves and wind, we would be denied the very heart of the story.

Billy Tyne, Bobby Shatford, David Sullivan, "Bugsy" Moran, Dale Murphy and Alfred Pierre died when the *Andrea Gail* went down. These men were not noble heroes but ordinary working fishermen, accustomed to living and drinking hard, who chose this dangerous line of work for the money. (On a successful voyage, a hand might earn $5,000 for a month's work; more if the fishing was particularly productive.) But while the story is about their brief lives and violent deaths, it is also about the sea—the irrepressible, all powerful, unforgiving sea.

The scale of the subject matter overpowers us: not only the vastness of the ocean as compared with the puny works of man but also waves and winds that roar outside the range of our comprehension. Waves as high as a 10-story building! Winds that can destroy any instrument designed to measure them! What is surprising is not that the *Andrea Gail* went down, but that any man—or for that matter anything made by man—could possibly survive such a violent merging of the elements.

Junger also follows what happened to the Satori, a 32-foot sailboat, sailed by a crew of two, Karen Stimson and Sue Bylander, with Ray Leonard, the boat's owner, also aboard. During the storm, the Satori was knocked down, righted and then, in response to its mayday signal, found by a Coast Guard air-sea rescue unit. Conditions were too dangerous for a helicopter rescue, so two life rafts were dropped, but they exploded upon hitting the water. The rescue cutter Tamaroa was also dispatched; when it finally arrived on the scene, two inflatable boats were launched. In the maelstrom, one of the inflatables was punctured by the bow of the lurching Satori. Suddenly six people needed rescuing. With waves cresting at 50 feet, the seas were too rough for these little boats. Finally, Dave Moore, a Coast Guard rescue swimmer,

was dropped into the water from the hovering helicopter and assisted the terrified crew of the Satori into a rescue basket dangling from the chopper.

Moore is one of an elite crew of rescue jumpers, men who jump from helicopters to rescue people in these impossible conditions. They take a six-month trauma medicine course, a water survival course and a "dunker" training course in which they are strapped into a helicopter simulator and have to escape from it underwater, upside-down and blindfolded. During one exercise, the instructor throws his whistle into the pool and the jumpers-in-training fight for it in the water. Once a swimmer obtains the whistle, he comes out of the pool. When there are only two men left fighting for the whistle, the loser of the last battle flunks out of the course.

We can only imagine what it must have been like as the gale-force winds tossed the *Andrea Gail* around, blowing out its windows and plunging the rails under, until the vessel filled with water and sank to the bottom: "On a steel boat the windows implode, the hatches fail, and the boat starts to flood. The crew is prevented from escaping by the sheer force of the water pouring into the cabin—it's like walking into the blast of a fire hose."

Junger cannot know the specific details of the last moments of the lives of the *Andrea Gail's* crew, but he has assembled a version of it from knowledge of the ship's construction and from accounts of other seamen who survived the storm. A Canadian woman who signed aboard a Japanese fishing vessel as an observer recorded her experiences as that ship almost went down in the storm. In 1892, a Scottish doctor named James Lowson was aboard a steamship bound for Ceylon when it encountered a typhoon that sank the ship. Lowson, who washed ashore on an island, described his near-drowning in the Edinburgh Medical Journal. From this and other medical references, Junger explains in frightening clinical detail how people drown.

The Perfect Storm is a wild ride that brilliantly captures the awesome power of the raging sea and the often futile attempts of humans to withstand it.

Christopher Lehmann-Haupt (review date 5 June 1997)

SOURCE: "The Shipwreck Story No One Survived to Tell," in *The New York Times*, June 5, 1997, p. C20.

[*In the following review, Lehmann-Haupt praises Junger for "nicely pac[ing] his narrative" in* The Perfect Storm.]

The title of Sebastian Junger's powerful book, ***The Perfect***

Storm: A True Story of Men Against the Sea, is not meant to be celebratory. Rather, Mr. Junger, a freelance journalist, intends the phrase "perfect storm" to be read "in the meteorological sense: a storm that could not possibly have been worse."

As he reports at the height of his gripping story, when Bob Case, a meteorologist in the Boston office of the National Weather Service, observed the satellite imagery of three storm systems colliding off New England in late October 1991, he experienced a dreadful thrill.

"Meteorologists see perfection in strange things," Mr. Junger writes, "and the meshing of three completely independent weather systems to form a hundred-year event is one of them. My God, thought Case, this is the perfect storm."

To be out at sea in the path of such an event would be a catastrophic experience. And so it evidently proved for the six men aboard the *Andrea Gail,* a 72-foot swordfish boat that disappeared off the coast of Nova Scotia on Oct. 28, leaving behind only fuel drums, a propane tank and sundry radio equipment that were found weeks later. To dramatize the incredible fury of a severe storm at sea, Mr. Junger reconstructs the fatal voyage of the *Andrea Gail.*

How does he manage to do this with no survivors to interview and with no details available about the ship's final hours of existence? A good deal is known up to a certain point: the layout of the *Andrea Gail;* the routine of a previous outing; how the crew members spent their time before leaving Gloucester, Mass., their home port; the pressure they were under to fill their hold with swordfish; the high risk of injury or death in the business; the bad feelings about the coming trip that drove two crew members to walk away before it began.

Mr. Junger nicely paces his narrative by interrupting it with histories of Gloucester, of the New England fishing industry and its gradual decline, and of the development of longline fishing—dragging a 40-mile-long monofilament with up to 1,000 baited hooks.

He creates a distinct atmosphere when he writes: "At dinner the crew talk about what men everywhere talk about—women, lack of women, kids, sports, horse racing, money, lack of money, work. They talk a lot about work; they talk about it the way men in prison talk about time. Work is what's keeping them from going home, and they all want to go home." You can sense the coming storm when he writes: "The sunset is a bloody rust-red on a sharp autumn horizon, and the night comes in fast with a northwest wind and a sky riveted with stars. There's no sound but the smack of water on steel and the heavy gargle of the diesel engine."

For information beyond what is known of the *Andrea Gail*'s destruction, Mr. Junger turns to "people who had been through similar situations and survived." From such interviews he learns what an 80-mile-an-hour wind sounds like and what it feels like to be tossed by waves 100 feet high.

Perhaps most compelling of all, he explains in concrete detail why hurricanes blow, how waves rise, what happens to boats in a storm and the way human beings drown. Thus he is able to reconstruct what he calls "the zero-moment point." When drowning, he writes in this frightening chapter, "the body could be likened to a crew that resorts to increasingly desperate measures to keep their vessel afloat." He concludes, "Eventually the last wire has shorted out, the last bit of decking has settled under the water." The crew members of the *Andrea Gail* "are dead."

After this calamity, the narrative of *The Perfect Storm* abruptly shifts its focus to describe a couple of heart-stopping rescue attempts, one of them successful, the other a costly fiasco by pararescue teams from the New York State Air National Guard. What is particularly impressive here is the dedication of professional storm watchers to save any human life at sea, no matter what foolishness or bad luck led to the trouble.

Despite the upbeat ending of *The Perfect Storm,* what lingers is a sense of the cruel indifference of nature. One chapter's epigraph quotes *Moby Dick:* "All collapsed, and the great shroud of the sea rolled on as it had five thousand years ago."

Even more chilling is the lack of closure that the families of the victims experienced. Mr. Junger writes:

> If the men on the *Andrea Gail* had simply died, and their bodies were lying in state somewhere, their loved ones could make their goodbyes and get on with their lives. But they didn't die, they disappeared off the face of the earth and, strictly speaking, it's just a matter of faith that these men will never return. Such faith takes work, it takes effort. The people of Gloucester must willfully extract these men from their lives and banish them to another world.

To have to strive for a belief in death and oblivion: a perfect conclusion to *The Perfect Storm.*

Anthony Bailey (review date 22 June 1997)

SOURCE: "The Tempest," in *New York Times Book Review,*

June 22, 1997, p. 8.

[In the following review, Bailey asserts that Junger "manages with considerable reporting skill to conjure up [the crew's] last hours," but complains that "Not all of Junger's information is vital to his task."]

For several hundred years men have been going out from Gloucester, Mass., to fish in near and distant waters, and not all have come home: some 10,000 Gloucestermen have died at sea since 1650. Even today, commercial fishing is one of the most dangerous occupations in this country that men—and now women—can take up. In *The Perfect Storm,* which chronicles the havoc caused by a monster gale off the coast of New England in 1991, Sebastian Junger tells us that, per capita, more people are killed working on fishing boats than in any other job in the United States. It's safer to parachute into forest fires or be a cop in New York City. Time was when the prime danger for New England fishermen was getting run down on the foggy Grand Banks by an ocean liner or finding oneself adrift in a dory in a January snowstorm, unable to reach one's schooner. Nowadays the perils of fishing lie in highly mechanized gear—hooks running out on fast-moving lines, for instance—or in powerfully engined boats. Meant to bring home the increasingly elusive, perishable catch at speed, such craft can yet find themselves—perhaps overloaded, overstretched—in horrendous sea conditions. No wonder that fishermen suffer from frequent premonitions of disaster; as Junger says, "The trick is knowing when to listen to them."

> In *The Perfect Storm* . . . Junger tells us that, per capita, more poeple are killed working on fishing boats than in any other job in the United States. It's safer to parachute into forest fires or be a cop in New York City.
> —*Anthony Bailey*

The first half of Junger's book follows a 72-foot steel swordfishing boat named the *Andrea Gail* on a voyage 1,200 miles into the Atlantic in 1991. It is late in the season, and the *Andrea Gail*'s captain, Billy Tyne, has problems rounding up a full crew of six. Some men have misgivings about the trip; one, Adam Randall, turns up to replace Doug Kosco, who has walked off the boat "because he got a bad feeling," but Randall himself looks the *Andrea Gail* over, has "a funny feeling" and instead of signing on goes off to a Gloucester bar. At the last minute Tyne gets David Sullivan to take his place. Gloucester bars, in fact, have a grip on the Gail's crew that Tyne has trouble breaking. Junger homes in on the crew in the Crow's Nest Inn, one of three bars that form "the Bermuda Triangle of downtown Gloucester." Swordfishermen

are high rollers; they can make $5,000 or so for a 30- or 40-day hard-working trip, but quite a lot goes for continuous hard drinking during the five or six days in port, leaving not much change once child-support and ex-wife-maintenance payments have been deducted. We meet Bobby Shatford, separated, with two children, and about to make his second trip on the Gail, in bed upstairs at the Crow's Nest with his girlfriend, Chris. It is the morning of sailing, they are hung over and somehow during the night she has given him a black eye. Bobby doesn't want to go and Chris says, Well, don't go then. But he goes—for the money; he has to.

Junger, a contributing editor at Men's Journal, gets the *Andrea Gail* out to sea and in the course of the six-day passage divulges much about fish, weather systems and the fishing grounds. He adds to the weight of premonition by telling us how the Gail was rebuilt in 1986 by "eyeball engineering," lengthened and—most seriously—with heavy equipment added and windage increased above decks. But we know from the start that there's going to be no happy ending to this voyage, and it is almost as a member of a coroner's jury that the reader feels bound to take in the relevant facts while the Gail rolls out to the Grand Banks at eight knots and the men prepare the fishing gear, eat, sleep, watch videos and read Dick Francis novels. The Grand Banks are dangerous "because they happen to sit on one of the worst storm tracks in the world." The Gail goes out in fair weather. Then, from Sept. 27 to Oct. 18, working 20-hour days, the Gail fishes, and doesn't do well; the trip is shaping up to be a bust. But in the next week the men's luck changes, and when Tyne sets course for home on Oct. 25 the Gail has 40,000 pounds of swordfish and tuna in her hold, worth about $160,000. She should reach port (and high prices) while most of her rivals are well out to sea. If the fishing had been better earlier, she would have been back in Gloucester by now.

As it is, on Oct. 28 the *Andrea Gail* is about halfway home, south of Nova Scotia, when she runs into a meteorological nightmare. A violent nor'easter out of Canada merges with the remnants of Hurricane Grace and is squeezed by high pressure from the north back toward the New England coast. In weather-expert terms, it is a once-in-a-hundred-years event, a "perfect storm." What this means at sea is over 100-mile-per-hour winds and waves 70 to 100 feet high for about 17 hours. The *Andrea Gail* enters the first stages of this storm "the way one might step into a room." The screaming wind is instant and unnerving. Just after 6 P.M. on the 28th, Billy Tyne talks on the radio to a fellow skipper who is anxious to know about the approaching weather, and Tyne tells him that it's blowing 50 to 80, and the seas are already 30 feet. A bit later in a message to the other boats, he says, "She's comin' on, boys, and she's comin' on strong." That is the last that is heard from the *Andrea Gail.*

You might think that Junger has an irresolvable problem at this point, halfway into his book: no Mayday message, no log recovered; only some fuel cans later found floating. But just as he has kept us hooked so far, despite our knowing from the start that the *Andrea Gail* and her crew are doomed, so he manages with considerable reporting skill to conjure up their last hours. He has evidence from other boats that survive. He has the tale of those on board the yacht Satori, who come to grief in the Great South Channel off Cape Cod. He has access to the log of the Contship Holland, a 10,000-ton vessel that loses rudder control (and 36 cargo containers overboard). He has the experience of a Canadian fishery observer, Judith Reeves, on board a battered, flooded and drifting Japanese long-liner, the Eishin Maru. He follows the efforts of the Coast Guard to rescue a man and two women on the Satori and the travails of the Air National Guard hoping to pick up a Japanese yachtsman in trouble farther south. The Satori mission is a heart-in-the-mouth success; the other is not. Conditions make a pickup impossible. Although the yachtsman is later taken off by a cargo ship, the Air National Guard helicopter is unable to refuel in the air, in zero visibility, on the way back to base on Long Island, and has to ditch. After a heroic search operation, four of its men are picked up; one is not seen again. Even if you have never been to sea, Junger's account will put the frighteners on you. If you have been offshore in bad weather—as I have, in 75-m.p.h. winds and 35-foot seas—and vowed to sail in sounds, ponds and creeks thereafter, it will make you renew your vows.

Not all of Junger's information is vital to his task. His analysis of increases in wave energy is strong in math but may distract from the violent wind-backed weight of water he is trying to convey. Similarly, when he is attempting to get across what it may have been like for someone actually drowning, a little less scientific jargon might have helped—for example, "voluntary apnea" and "laryngospasm." It may be, as one skipper says, that you're too busy at such moments to think about drowning.

For all that, the reader is with the ditched helicopter crewmen in the avalanching seas, and willing them to hang on to the lines and nets thrown over the side of the nearly capsizing Coast Guard cutter Tamaroa, which pulls them out. We are with the partners and relatives of the *Andrea Gail's* crew as they wait for news in Gloucester. Bobby Shatford's girlfriend, Chris, has a nightmare on the night of Oct. 29 that involves filthy weather and a boat and Bobby's body. Soon, although there's no news, a wake begins at the Crow's Nest. Chris says, "Everybody was drunk cause that's what we do." Meanwhile, the storm, to be recorded as the Halloween Gale, the most powerful nor'easter of the century, strikes the New England coast, destroying houses, ripping up streets, killing sightseers and surfers; the damage is $1.5 billion.

Sebastian Junger declares that his own confrontation with the storm was limited to standing on the backshore of Gloucester, watching 30-foot swells approach Cape Ann. But he clearly went on to experience it through the words of the storm's survivors and those connected with the *Andrea Gail.* Interviewing them must have been a difficult, even intrusive job, but the result is thrilling—a boat ride into and (for us) out of a watery hell.

John Sutherland (review date 18 July 1997)

SOURCE: "The Same Cruel Life," in *Times Literary Supplement,* No. 4920, July 18, 1997, p. 8.

[*In the following review, Sutherland calls Junger's* The Perfect Storm *"a fine and moving book, which deserves to succeed."*]

Sebastian Junger's publishers describe him as "a writer and adventurer". That is not, one suspects, exactly what he enters under "occupation" on his IRS tax forms, but it creates the necessary authorial *bona fides* for "A True Story of Men against the Sea". *A Perfect Storm* is, we are informed, the culmination of the author's lifelong interest in men in extreme circumstances, "out beyond where society can help them". Junger himself apparently used to earn a manly living as a climber for tree-removal companies, "scaling 100-foot trees and taking them down section by section with ropes and a chainsaw". Injury turned him to a more benign assault on the world's forests. *A Perfect Storm,* his first book, received "terrific" reviews in America and went straight into the bestseller lists; it may well do the same in Britain.

The title is paradoxical. "Perfect" is used in its meteorological sense of "as bad as can be". In October 1991, the collision of two gigantic weather systems generated Hurricane Grace off the American north-eastern coast, a Force Twelve, "hundred year" weather event. The awesome storm wrecked a seventy-two-foot swordfishing boat, the *Andrea Gail,* as she was powering back with 40,000 pounds of catch [worth $160,000] in her hold to her home port of Gloucester, MA. All that was ever found of the craft and her six-man crew were some fuel drums off the Georges Bank fishing-grounds. Junger's narrative reconstructs the last voyage of this ill-starred vessel.

The Perfect Storm approaches its central episode from different angles. Historical retrospects recall the long and amazingly dangerous history of the eastern-seaboard fishing industry. Junger's epigraph—"It's no fish ye're buying, it's men's lives"—is from Walter Scott. Another country, another time, the same cruel life for the fisherman. Lightly, but effectively, Junger sketches the current degraded state of the industry: the depleted stocks, the gross marine pollution (prudent American diners avoid the mercury-saturated swordfish), and the increasingly aggressive competition from foreign fleets which has driven down American catches and wages. Nowadays, when we eat fish, we buy men's lives at bargain price. There is nothing glamorous in the trade of a modern fisherman, nothing to inspire a latter-day Melville, Dana, Conrad, or Jack London: "Most deck-hands", Junger records, "have precious little affection for the business; for them, fishing is a brutal, dead-end job that they try to get clear of as fast as possible. . . .By and large, young men from Gloucester find themselves at sea because they're broke and need money fast."

The money is certainly fast and, when it comes, goes the same way. Had she made port, the *Andrea Gail's* crew would have been millionaires for a week. As Junger portrays it, the hard-won share-out would have been spent in drunken riot and in getting laid. And then, after their brief furlough as "high rollers", back to sea. Given the boom-bust income cycle and the short working career (if you don't drown, aren't injured, or don't lose your nerve, the work will break you by forty), stable family relationships are rare. Human interest in *The Perfect Storm* focuses on one of the ship's hands, Bobby Shatford, whose common-law wife, Chris, was evidently one of Junger's principal sources. The narrative opens, novelistically, with Bobby's waking with a hangover, a black eye (Chris's work) and a very bad feeling about the impending voyage. Wise sailors should heed such premonitions. Bobby doesn't.

In the subsequent narrative, Junger offers vivid technical descriptions of storm systems, the complex business of baiting hooks and hauling back the line (swordfish do not "school", and have to be caught individually), the hydrodynamics of seventy-foot waves and what they do to seventy-two-foot craft, the harsh economics of modern blue-water fishing. In *The Nigger of the Narcissus,* Conrad noted that the common sailor's favourite reading-matter at sea was, incredibly, the fiction of Bulwer-Lytton. Junger records that the current favourite is Dick Francis: "Francis writes about horse racing, which seems to appeal to swordfishermen because it's another way to win or lose huge amounts of money."

What Junger does not do is reconstruct, except by tentative hypothesis, the last hours of the *Andrea Gail.* Like the hurricane itself, *The Perfect Storm* has a hollow eye at its centre—the unnarratable tragedy. Like everything in this terse, extraordinarily readable "true story", it witnesses to an authorial honesty and disinclination to glamorize. This is a fine and moving book, which deserves to succeed.

Tom De Haven (review date 1 August 1997)

SOURCE: "'Gail'-Force Wins," in *Entertainment Weekly,* August 1, 1997, pp. 66-7.

[*In the following review, De Haven asserts that Junger's* A Perfect Storm *is "[f]erociously dramatic and vividly written."*]

Who'd have figured that bad weather—*really* bad weather—would enthrall beach readers this summer? In late October 1991, the *Andrea Gail,* a swordfishing boat out of Gloucester, Mass., was returning home when a freak convergence of three storm systems engulfed it several hundred miles off the coast of Nova Scotia. With shrieking winds and waves like piggybacked dinosaurs, the "Halloween Gale" was a once-in-a-century event, a fisherman's worst nightmare, or, as Sebastian Junger calls it, **The Perfect Storm.** While Junger's surprise best-seller (no serial killers! no sex! no Hollywood!) encompasses everything from meteorology to shipbuilding to the rough-and-tumble sociology of New England port towns, his focus never strays far from the promise of his subtitle: *A True Story of Men Against the Sea.* In the clash between the sea and the men of the *Andrea Gail,* it was no contest—the sea won.

Unlike mariners in the fiction of Melville or Hemingway, few of the *Andrea Gail's* fishermen seem to have had any mystical attachments to the ocean. (Depending on seniority, a crewman on a sword boat can make between $5,000 and $10,000 a month—or if the fishing is bad, he can earn practically nothing.) It was the lure of fast money that persuaded Billy Tyne, Michael Moran, Dale Murphy, Alfred Pierre, David Sullivan, and especially young Bobby Shatford (who was being threatened with jail for nonpayment of child support) to ignore any misgivings they had about fishing the Grand Banks so late in the season.

As Junger re-creates the crew's last, anxious day in port—their time divided almost equally between barhopping and preparing for the trip—it might strike you that not much about a fisherman's life has changed in 100, even 200 years. For all of a modern boat's high-tech trappings (including a VCR and plenty of movies), its crew is still prone to hard drinking, black moods, and superstition. And when bad weather blows—as it did four weeks into the *Andrea Gail's* ill-fated voyage—six able-bodied seamen inside a 72-foot-long welded-steel vessel are scarcely less vulnerable than their ancestors were on wooden ships.

"More people are killed on fishing boats, per capita, than any other job in the United States," Junger tells us. But lest we romanticize the "clean" death of fishermen at sea, he also tells us, in horrific detail, precisely what it's like to drown: "When the first involuntary breath occurs most people are still conscious, which is unfortunate, because the only thing more unpleasant than running out of air is breathing in water." The excruciating description, more nightmare inducing than anything Stephen King ever cooked up, continues for several more pages.

Once the Halloween Gale—which included Hurricane Grace among its component weather systems—slammed into the North Atlantic, the men of the *Andrea Gail* were doomed. Except for a floating cluster of fuel barrels, a propane tank, and a radio beacon picked up days later, the fishing boat vanished completely, and its small crew joined the estimated 10,000 Gloucestermen who have died at sea over the past three centuries. Reports of ghostly visitations to loved ones at home add a shuddering, almost mythic coda to the shipwreck, though they can't mitigate the tragedy.

But Junger's riveting account of this savage nor'easter has its share of triumphs as well; and because it includes a number of "meanwhiles"—intercut stories of other ships and aircraft caught in the same fury, with miraculous in-the-nick-of-time rescues—the narrative exhilarates as often as it terrifies. Well, nearly as often.

Ferociously dramatic and vividly written, *The Perfect Storm* is not just the best book of the summer. It's an indelible experience.

Nora Okja Keller
Comfort Woman

Born in Korea, Keller is an American novelist.

INTRODUCTION

Keller was born in Korea to an American father and Korean mother. She grew up in Hawaii where her mother, hoping to help her daughter fit in with mainstream America, chose not to teach Keller the Korean language. Consequently, Keller felt alienated from her Korean heritage. While attending a symposium on human rights at the University of Hawaii in 1993, Keller heard the story of a Korean woman who had been a "comfort woman" during World War II; she felt the story should be told and began writing *Comfort Woman* (1997), her first novel. Comfort women were sex slaves imprisoned in "recreation centers" and forced to serve Japanese soldiers. In the novel, described by a *Publishers Weekly* reviewer as "an intense study of a mother-daughter relationship," the protagonist, Beccah, grows into adulthood feeling both protective of and embarrassed by her eccentric mother, Akiko, a spirit medium prone to long trances and terrifying battles with Saja the Death Messenger, from whom she perpetually attempts to protect her daughter. The author alternates Beccah's story with Akiko's, and the reader comes to realize the extent of the horror Akiko experienced as an adolescent sold into prostitution and forced to become a comfort woman, an element of her past that Beccah learns only after her death. Although Akiko escaped and married one of her rescuers, a missionary who became Beccah's father but died when Beccah was five, her spirit died in the camp and the experience haunted her for the rest of her life. Beccah must come to terms with her mother's past in order to define her own identity and choose her future. *Comfort Woman* received much positive critical response, with reviewers pointing out the sensitive portrayal of a woman's search for identity and the exploration of the mother-daughter relationship. Many critics described Keller as a gifted writer and storyteller. Merle Rubin stated, "Strongly imagined, well-paced and written with eloquently restrained lyricism that conveys the subtleties of feelings as well as the harshness of facts, *Comfort Woman* is a poignant and impressive debut."

CRITICISM

Publishers Weekly (review date 6 January 1997)

SOURCE: A review of *Comfort Woman,* in *Publishers*

Weekly, January 6, 1997, p. 61.

[*In the following review of* Comfort Woman, *the critic states,* "Though piercing and moving in its evocation of feminine closeness, . . . the narrative becomes somewhat claustrophobic."]

This impressive first novel [*Comfort Woman*] by a Hawaii-based writer of mixed Korean and American ancestry depicts one of the atrocities of war and its lingering effects on a later generation. An intense study of a mother-daughter relationship, it dwells simultaneously in the world of spirits and the social milieu of the adolescent schoolgirl who later becomes a career woman with lovers. Beccah is a youngish, contemporary Hawaiian whose Korean mother, Akiko, was sold into prostitution as a young woman and sent to a "recreation camp" to service the occupying Japanese army. Akiko developed a resilience that allowed her to distance herself from the daily plundering of her body; she also developed an intense communication with the spirit world that helped her survive the horror of her experience—and helped her, too, to catch the attention of a visiting American missionary, who married her and fathered Beccah. After his death, mother and daughter live together in Honolulu, Beccah striving for a normal life, Akiko, often possessed, screaming and wailing, by her ghosts and visions. With the help of a flamboyant, ultra-worldly friend who calls herself Auntie Reno, Akiko becomes a seer and fortune-teller. Akiko's flashbacks to her haunted past and Beccah's account of their lives together are told alternately, and it is one of Keller's several triumphs that she is able to render the two worlds so powerfully and distinctly. Though piercing and moving in its evocation of feminine closeness, however, the narrative becomes somewhat claustrophobic, so that the occasional interventions of the cheerfully vulgar Auntie Reno are hugely welcome. A striking debut by a strongly gifted writer, nonetheless.

Joanne Wilkinson (review date 15 March 1997)

SOURCE: A review of *Comfort Woman*, in *Booklist*, March 15, 1997, p. 1226.

[*In the following review, Wilkinson lauds the lyricism and humor of Keller's* Comfort Woman.]

In her haunting debut novel [*Comfort Woman*], Korean American Keller tells of the complex, loving bond between a mother and daughter. Akiko had been sold into prostitution during World War II when still a child. Her harsh memories of her experiences as a "comfort woman" to the Japanese army alternate with her daughter Beccah's more straightforward account of her attempts to fit in with the popular kids at the local high school. Completely ignorant of her mother's history, Beccah is ashamed of her mother's spiritual "trances," in which she seems to commune with the spirit world, leaving Beccah to fend for herself. When an enterprising Filipino woman successfully markets Akiko as a gifted fortune-teller, their finances improve dramatically, but Beccah is still confused by her mother's strange behavior. In the powerful, moving conclusion, Beccah finally discovers the truth about her family history. With a deft and subtle use of humor and an assured, lyrical prose style, Keller threads her graceful narrative with themes of identity and the search of self.

Merle Rubin (review date 23 March 1997)

SOURCE: "The Haunting," in *The Los Angeles Times Book Review*, March 23, 1997, p. 9.

[*In the following review, Rubin calls Keller's* Comfort Woman *"a poignant and impressive debut."*]

The ugly story of the women and girls forced to serve as "comfort women" in the "recreation camps" designed to accommodate the sexual needs of Japanese soldiers during World War II took a long time to come to light. Women who had been victimized in this way were devalued not only in the eyes of their communities but often in their own eyes. This bitterly ironic paradigm is not limited to traditional sexist cultures. Almost everywhere, it seems, far too many victims struggle with feelings of shame and despair, while too few victimizers are troubled by guilt.

This powerful first novel [*Comfort Woman*] by a young writer born in Korea and raised in Hawaii tells the intertwined stories of a Korean-born woman sold into the sexual slavery of the Japanese camps and of the woman's American-born daughter, who discovers the secret of her mother's harrowing past after her death.

Rebeccah Bradley, known as Beccah, grows up in Hawaii, where she enjoys a relatively normal life—or, at any rate, a life blessedly free from the shocking dislocations and acute suffering experienced by her mother, Akiko. But in some respects, Beccah's childhood is abnormal. Her mother is given to strange fits, falling into trances, dancing on tabletops and communing with invisible spirits. Beccah's father, an American Protestant missionary, died when she was 5. Five years later, while dutifully commemorating the anniversary of his demise by preparing a sacrificial offering of his favorite food (shrimp), Akiko tells her daughter that she killed him.

Beccah, however, has learned to take many of her mother's pronouncements with a grain of salt. She knows that in the eyes of her classmates at school, Akiko is the "crazy lady," and there are times when she feels powerfully alienated by her mother's outlandishness. Yet in other ways, Beccah's perceptions and emotions have been deeply colored by Akiko's confused yet potent mixture of folklore, superstitions and passionately held beliefs.

Akiko warns the little girl about Saja the Death Messenger. When the child awakens in the middle of the night screaming that Saja is after her, the mother grabs a butchered chicken, tears off her daughter's nightgown, wraps it around the chicken and throws the bloody bundle out of doors to "fool" the hungry demon.

As Beccah grows older, her mother's strange beliefs seem deluded, yet oddly plausible. There seem to be any number of bizarre unseen powers capable of threatening happiness and well-being. "Red Disaster, the way my mother explained it, was like the bacteria we learned about in health class: invisible and everywhere in the air around us; *honyaek* was contagious and sometimes deadly. Burning the red items from our apartment was my mother's version of washing my hands."

Akiko's weird behavior is not without redeeming financial value. The proprietress of a local eatery, having given the poor widow a job, recognizes her employee's oracular potential. She sets her up as a spiritual advisor and clients flock from miles around.

As a mother, Akiko can be fiercely protective but at other times neglectful and withdrawn. Beccah's account of growing up in this eccentric household is interwoven with chapters in which Akiko relates the appalling story of her wartime experiences as a comfort woman. As we find out what she has endured, her apparent "craziness" begins to look mild in comparison.

The youngest daughter of a poor Korean family, Akiko was born with the name Soon Hyo. Barely into her adolescence, she was orphaned and sold to raise money for her oldest sister's dowry: It was known that the Japanese were looking for pretty girls. On arriving at the recreation camp, she was still so young that they assigned her to work as a maid to the other women, cleaning their rooms and emptying their chamber pots. Before long, however, she is made to take over for one of the previous comfort women, who spoke out one night and was killed for it. The memory has been branded into her brain:

> To this day, I do not think Induk—the woman who was the Akiko before me—cracked. Most of the other women thought she did because she would not shut up. One night she talked loud and nonstop. In Korean and Japanese, she denounced the soldiers, yelling at them to stop their invasion of her country and her body. Even as they mounted her, she shouted: I am Korea, I am a woman, I am alive. I am seventeen, I had a family just like you do, I am a daughter, I am a sister. . . . Just before daybreak, they took her out of her stall and into the woods, where we couldn't hear her anymore. They brought her back skewered . . . like a pig ready for roasting. A lesson, they told the rest of us, warning us into silence. That night, it was as if a thousand frogs encircled the camp. They opened their throats for us, swallowed our tears, and cried for us. All night, it seemed, they called, Induk, Induk, Induk, so we would never forget.

Even after her eventual escape from the camp, Akiko feels unable to assume her former name or identity. She is rescued from her war-torn country by an American missionary. Their marriage is based on a kind of love and furtive lust on his side, resignation and silent hatred on hers and a mutual lack of understanding. Yet despite the damage inflicted on her by a crude abortion in the camp, Akiko manages to conceive and bear Beccah. She loves her daughter with a passionate intensity that transcends the enormous gap between their universes. She hates her husband so much she feels responsible for his death.

Writing from Beccah's perspective, Keller effectively conveys the daughter's ambivalence, the mixture of embarrassment and protectiveness she feels toward her mother. Gradually, the slight touch of irony in her tone gives way to a deeper understanding and a wholehearted attempt to identify with her mother's sufferings and struggles. In the chapters given over to Akiko's recounting of her painful history, Keller's achievement is still more remarkable. By the time Beccah—and the reader—have learned Akiko's story, it is clear why this daughter cannot turn her back on her mother, for all that she lost, endured and hoped to pass on to her child.

Strongly imagined, well-paced and written with an eloquently restrained lyricism that conveys the subtleties of feelings as well as the harshness of facts, *Comfort Woman* is a poignant and impressive debut.

Laura Shapiro (review date 28 April 1997)

SOURCE: "They Gotta Be Making This Up," in *Newsweek*, April 28, 1997, p. 78.

[*In the following review, Shapiro asserts that in* Comfort Woman, *Keller has "an emotional touch so sure and a sense of language so precise she seems to have sprung into print full-grown as a novelist."*]

Her name is Akiko, or so her daughter Beccah has always believed. Not until her mother's death does Beccah learn that Akiko's real name was torn from her at the age of 12, when she was sold from a Korean village to be a "comfort woman"—a sex slave for Japanese troops in World War II. These two stories, Akiko's and Beccah's, make up the somber skeins that Nora Okja Keller beautifully weaves together in *Comfort Woman,* her first novel.

Akiko's harrowing memories of the "recreation center" are seared into her brain and soul, from the first night she is raped—"It was a free-for-all, and I thought I would never stop bleeding"—until she escapes after the camp doctor gives her an abortion.

"He did not bother tying me down. . . . Maybe he knew I had died and that ropes and guards couldn't keep me anyway." Rescued by missionaries, she marries one of them and moves to America but never really returns to life. The gods and spirits who swarmed into her consciousness at the camp and helped her survive don't let go: they keep command of her ever after. Beccah grows up both protective and resentful of the mother who guards her from Saja the Death Messenger by wrapping the child's nightie around a raw chicken and flinging the bundle out the door.

Like Amy Tan—in another now legendary debut, *The Joy Luck Club*—Keller skillfully mingles the Asian past and the American present, the earthly world and the spiritual one, a mother's trauma and a daughter's quest. But she is very much her own writer, with an emotional touch so sure and a sense of language so precise she seems to have sprung into print full-grown as a novelist. The gods in charge of terrific new fiction must be very pleased.

Christopher John Farley (review date 5 May 1997)

SOURCE: "No Man's Land," in *Time,* May 5, 1997, pp. 101-2.

[*In the following excerpt, Farley asserts that "although Keller's prose, at a few points, has more ambition than lyricism, overall* [Comfort Woman] *is a sturdy, eloquent book."*]

Nora Okja Keller used to think real writers looked like Ernest Hemingway. Gruff, bearded, white, male. She was none of those. She was an immigrant, born in Seoul to a Korean mother and a white American father, and raised in Hawaii. But Keller's image of herself started to change in 1993, when she went to a symposium on human rights at the University of Hawaii at Manoa; there she heard an elderly Korean woman tell her true story of being a "comfort woman" during World War II, when she was one of the many foreigners forced by the Japanese into prostitution camps that serviced their soldiers. The story haunted Keller. Who would pass it on? Who would write it down? The old woman came to her in nightmares. "Finally, I got up in the middle of the night and started to write down my dreams," says Keller. Those notes became a book. And she became a writer.

> **I went through a period of feeling really embarrassed and alienated from things that were Korean. So I write now, in part, to go back to that Korean perspective and try to reclaim what I denied for so long.**
> **—*Nora Okja Keller***

Keller's book, ***Comfort Woman,*** is one of a trio of powerful debut novels by Asian-American women to arrive in bookstores lately. The others: *Monkey King* by Patricia Chao (of Chinese and Japanese descent) and *The Necessary Hunger* by Nina Revoyr (whose mother and father are Japanese and Polish-American, respectively). Although these books

share some themes—all of them deal with parents and children in conflict over such issues as cultural and sexual identity—each author has a sharp, specific vision.

Keller's story is the most harrowing. The book, narrated in the alternating voices of a Korean comfort woman named Akiko and her Korean-American daughter Beccah, delivers a wrenching view of war and its lasting intergenerational impact. Akiko, driven half-mad by the war, is haunted by the ghost of a woman from the camp and becomes a sought-after mystic after moving to America. But to call this a ghost story is to miss the point: ***Comfort Woman*** is really about pain, the kind that haunts and is handed down, like old, sad clothes. Writes Akiko: "I knew what it felt like to stretch open for many men . . . about pain sharp enough to cut your body from your mind." Although Keller's prose, at a few points, has more ambition than lyricism, overall this is a sturdy, eloquent book.

Keller says her own mother was not a comfort woman, but served as an inspiration. "My mom didn't really speak Korean to me," says Keller. "She was so conscious of her own difference that she didn't want me to learn Korean and make me something different, 'the other' . . . I know I went through a period of feeling really embarrassed and alienated from things that were Korean. So I write now, in part, to go back to that Korean perspective and try to reclaim what I denied for so long."

Lise Funderburg (review date 31 August 1997)

SOURCE: A review of *Comfort Woman,* in *The New York Times Book Review,* August 31, 1997, p. 14.

[*In the following review, Funderburg calls Keller's* Comfort Woman *"accomplished."*]

A mother and daughter wrestle with the mother's plagued past in Nora Okja Keller's accomplished first novel [***Comfort Woman***]. The daughter, Beccah, comes of age in Hawaii, where she is taunted by other children because she is poor, because she is of Korean and American heritage, and because her mother, Akiko, seems to be mentally imbalanced. (When she isn't falling into trances, Akiko is performing strange rituals meant to protect Beccah from Saja, the Death Messenger, or *honyaek,* the cloud of Red Disaster.) The reader learns long before Beccah does that Akiko was sold away from her Korean family during World War II—as a sister's dowry—and forced into a "recreation center" run by the Japanese Army. There she was renamed and remade into a "comfort woman," a prostitute for Japanese soldiers. Akiko escaped after a clumsy abortion and was taken in by American missionaries, one of whom, Beccah's father, married her and brought her to the United States. But by the time we meet them he has died, leaving Akiko and Beccah to live in their own tormented private world. Moving between the mother's voice and the daughter's, Keller beautifully evokes both their anguish and their love. "I wanted to help my mother, shield her from the children's sharp-toothed barbs," Beccah tells us when Akiko descends on the local elementary school, intent on purifying it by tossing handfuls of grain from a sack. "And yet I didn't want to. Because for the first time as I watched and listened to the children taunting my mother, using their tongues to mangle what she said into what they heard, I saw and heard what they did. And I was ashamed."

Arundhati Roy

The God of Small Things

Born in 1960, Roy is an Indian novelist.

INTRODUCTION

In *The God of Small Things* (1997) Roy creates a microcosm that encompasses wife battering, infidelity, molestation, emotional insecurity, pride, and death within one family in the southern Indian state of Kerala. Through this microcosm, Roy explores the often chaotic social and political history of India. Written in a style verging on magical realism, the novel features nonlinear chronology and fragmented flashbacks so that the reader must unravel the story from its conclusion to its source. Roy herself grew up in Kerala, where she witnessed the disarray of Indian politics and the quiet violence of the Indian upper classes against the Untouchables—the lowest stratum in the strict Indian caste system. She studied to be an architect before writing screenplays for several successful Indian films and now resides in New Delhi. Her story of the Kochamma family addresses the sweeping problems and complexities of twentieth-century India as the country struggled for independence from British colonialism. Lingering Anglophilia among Indians and its resultant shame and self-loathing inform the better part of the novel, in which Indians are caught between upholding narrow English standards of beauty and conduct, and confronting their own history of class prejudice and misogyny. Consequently, it is the children of the story—the fraternal twins Estha and Rahel—who are left irreparably scarred by their tumultuous family and society. Critical response to *The God of Small Things* has been largely positive. Critics have praised Roy's lush and sensuous prose and her handling of such a wide range of personal and social issues, and have noted similarities in her writing to that of Salman Rushdie, William Faulkner, and James Joyce. Other critics have argued that such comparisons are premature and that, while the novel shows tremendous promise, it is too self-consciously literary to be considered a masterpiece. Nonetheless, Roy is lauded for undertaking to examine the turbulence of India on such a large scale. She won Britain's prestigious Booker Prize for *The God of Small Things* in 1997.

CRITICISM

***Publishers Weekly* (review date 3 March 1997)**

SOURCE: Review of *The God of Small Things,* in *Publishers Weekly,* March 3, 1997, p. 62.

[*In the following review, the critic praises Roy's subtle handling of complex issues and her masterful storytelling.*]

With sensuous prose, a dreamlike style infused with breathtakingly beautiful images and keen insight into human nature, Roy's debut novel [***The God of Small Things***] charts fresh territory in the genre of magical, prismatic literature. Set in Kerala, India, during the late 1960s when Communism rattled the age-old caste system, the story begins with the funeral of young Sophie Mol, the cousin of the novel's protagonists, Rahel and her fraternal twin brother, Estha. In a circuitous and suspenseful narrative, Roy reveals the family tensions that led to the twins' behavior on the fateful night that Sophie drowned. Beneath the drama of a family tragedy lies a background of local politics, social taboos and the tide of history—all of which come together in a slip of fate, after which a family is irreparably shattered. Roy captures the children's candid observations but clouded understanding of adults' complex emotional lives. Rahel notices that "at times like these, only the Small Things are ever said. The Big Things lurk unsaid inside." Plangent with a sad wisdom, the children's view is never oversimplified, and the adult characters reveal their frailties—and in one case, a repulsively evil power—in subtle and complex ways. While Roy's powers of description are formidable, she sometimes succumbs to overwriting, forcing every minute detail to symbolize something bigger, and the pace of the story slows. But these lapses are few, and her powers coalesce magnificently in the book's second half. Roy's clarity of vision is remarkable, her voice original, her story beautifully constructed and masterfully told.

Kirkus Reviews (review date 15 March 1997)

SOURCE: Review of *The God of Small Things*, in *Kirkus Reviews*, March 15, 1997, p. 412.

[*In the following review, the critic commends Roy's "spectacular" first novel.*]

A brilliantly constructed first novel that untangles an intricate web of sexual and caste conflict in a vivid style reminiscent of Salman Rushdie's early work.

The major characters are Estha and Rahel, the fraternal twin son and daughter of a wealthy family living in the province of Kerala. The family's prosperity is derived from a pickle factory and rubber estate, and their prideful Anglophilia essentially estranges them from their country's drift toward Communism and their "inferiors'" hunger for independence and equality. The events of a crucial December day in 1969—including an accidental death that may have been no accident and the violent consequences that afflict an illicit couple who have broken "the Love Law"—are the moral and narrative center around which the episodes of the novel repeatedly circle. Shifting backward and forward in time with effortless grace, Roy fashions a compelling nexus of personalities that influence the twins' "eerie stealth" and furtive interdependence. These include their beautiful and mysteriously remote mother Ammu; her battling "Mammachi" (who runs the pickle factory) and "Pappachi" (an insufficiently renowned entomologist); their Oxford-educated Marxist Uncle Chacko and their wily "grandaunt" Baby Kochamma; and the volatile laborite "Untouchable" Velutha, whose relationship with the twins' family will prove his undoing. Roy conveys their explosive commingling in a vigorous prose dominated by odd syntactical and verbal combinations and coinages (a bad dream experience during midday nap-time is an "aftermare") reminiscent of Gerard Manly Hopkins's "sprung rhythm," incantatory repetitions, striking metaphors (Velutha is seen "standing in the shade of the rubber trees with coins of sunshine dancing on his

body") and sensuous descriptive passages ("The sky was orange, and the coconut trees were sea anemones waving their tentacles, hoping to trap and eat an unsuspecting cloud").

In part a perfectly paced mystery story, in part an Indian *Wuthering Heights:* a gorgeous and seductive fever dream of a novel, and a truly spectacular debut.

Alice Truax (review date 25 May 1997)

SOURCE: "A Silver Thimble in Her Fist," in *New York Times Book Review,* May 25, 1997, p. 5.

[*In the following review, Truax notes that* The God of Small Things *is at times painful and difficult to read, but maintains that the reader is richly rewarded for finishing the novel.*]

There is no single tragedy at the heart of Arundhati Roy's devastating first novel. Although ***The God of Small Things*** opens with memories of a family grieving around a drowned child's coffin, there are plenty of other intimate horrors still to come, and they compete for the reader's sympathy with the furious energy of cats in a sack. Yet the quality of Ms. Roy's narration is so extraordinary—at once so morally strenuous and so imaginatively supple—that the reader remains enthralled all the way through to its agonizing finish.

This ambitious meditation on the decline and fall of an Indian family is part political fable, part psychological drama, part fairy tale, and it begins at its chronological end, in a landscape of extravagant ruin. When 31-year-old Rahel Kochamma returns to Ayemenem House, her former home in the south Indian state of Kerala, its elegant windows are coated with filth and its brass door-knobs dulled with grease; dead insects lie in the bottom of its empty vases. The only animated presence in the house seems to be great-aunt Baby Kochamma's new television set—in front of which she and her servant sit day after day, munching peanuts.

Rahel has come back to Ayemenem not to see her great-aunt however, but because she has heard that her twin brother, Estha, has unexpectedly returned. Estha and Rahel were once inseparable, but now they have been apart for almost 25 years—ever since the winter of 1969, when their English cousin, Sophie Mol, drowned in the river with their grandmother's silver thimble in her fist.

"Perhaps it's true that things can change in a day," Ms. Roy's narrator muses. "That a few dozen hours can affect the outcome of whole lifetimes. And that when they do, those few dozen hours, like the salvaged remains of a burned house—the charred clock, the singed photograph, the scorched furniture—must be resurrected from the ruins and examined. Preserved. Accounted for." And this is precisely Ms. Roy's undertaking as, throughout her book, she shuttles between the twins' past and present, continually angling in, crabwise, toward the night of Sophie Mol's death.

Unlike most first novels, **The God of Small Things** is an anti-*Bildungsroman,* for Estha and Rahel have never properly grown up. Whatever the nature of their crimes, it is almost immediately apparent that they have never recovered from their punishments, and present-day Ayemenem—with its toxic river fish and its breezes stinking of sewage—seems to reflect their poisoned and blighted lives. The Ayemenem of the twins' aborted childhood, however, is a rich confusion of competing influences. Bearded Syrian priests swing their censers while *kathakali* dancers perform at the temple nearby; the Communists are splintering, the Untouchables are becoming politicized and *The Sound of Music* is wildly popular. Life has an edgy, unpredictable feel.

The twins are only 7 years old in 1969; and—affectionate, contentious, indefatigable—they still live almost entirely in a world of their own making. They are at Ayemenem House because their proud and beautiful mother, Ammu, made the unforgivable mistake of marrying badly: when her husband began hitting the children as well as her she returned, unwelcome, to her parents' home.

Ammu's status within the family is tenuous because of her marital disgrace, but a certain aura of eccentricity and defeat clings like a smell to all the residents of Ayemenem House, rendering them alternately comic, sympathetic and grotesque. There is the twins' elegant grandmother, Mammachi, with her skull permanently scarred from her dead husband's beatings and her bottle of Dior perfume carefully locked up in the safe. Then there is scheming Baby Kochamma, who once tried to become a nun but—her faith inspired less by God than by a certain Father Mulligan—lasted only a year in the convent. And there is the house servant, Kochu Maris, who thinks that Rahel is ridiculing her when she announces that Neil Armstrong has walked on the moon.

Finally, there is the twins' charming uncle, Chacko, the Oxford-educated Marxist who has returned from his failed marriage in England and taken over Mammachi's chutney business—which, with cheerful ineptitude, he is running into the ground. Comrade Chacko means to organize a trade union for his workers, but he never quite gets around to it; instead he philosophizes, flirts with his female employees and assembles tiny balsa airplanes that immediately plummet to the ground. Chacko commends his ex-wife, Margaret, for leaving him, but he pines for her and their little daughter, Sophie Mol, just the same.

It gradually becomes clear to the reader that only Velutha, an Untouchable who serves as the family carpenter, is competent enough to transform life rather than simply endure it—but, of course, as he's an Untouchable, endurance is supposed to be all he's good for. Velutha fixes everything around Ayemenem House, from the factory's canning machine to the cherub fountain in Baby Kochamma's garden. He is both essential and taken for granted in the twins' existence, like breathing. He is "the God of Small Things."

Estha and Rahel are accustomed to life under the umbrella of their elders' discontent; it is only after Chacko invites Margaret and Sophie Mol to come to India for Christmas that the twins gain a fresh appreciation for their second-class status. Baby Kochamma makes Estha and Rahel memorize a hymn and fines them whenever they speak in Malayalam instead of English. Kochu Maria bakes a great cake; Mammachi plays the violin and allows Sophie Moi to make off with her thimble. When Chacko angrily refers to the children as millstones around his neck, Rahel understands that her light-skinned cousin, on the other hand, has been "loved from the beginning."

In the following weeks, the smoldering longings and resentments at Ayemenem House will be ignited by larger historical pressures—the heady promises of Communism, the pieties of Christianity, the rigidities of India's caste system—and combust with catastrophic results. And if the events surrounding the night of Sophie Mol's death form an intricate tale of crime and punishment, Ms. Roy's elaborate and circuitous reconstruction of those events is both a treasure hunt (for the story itself) and a court of appeals (perhaps all the witnesses were not heard; perhaps all the evidence was not considered).

Are the twins responsible for Sophie Mol's death? Why is Baby Kochamma so terrified of the Communists? What happened to Velutha at the police station? Why does jolly Chacko batter down the door to Ammu's room, threatening to break every bone in her body?

What sustains us through this dread-filled dance between the calamitous past and the bleak present is the exuberant, almost acrobatic nature of the writing itself. Ms. Roy refuses to allow the reader to view the proceedings from any single vantage point: time and again, she lures us toward some glib judgment only to twist away at the last minute, thereby exposing our moral laziness and shaming us with it. But Ms. Roy's shape-shifting narrative is also tremendously nourishing, crammed not only with remonstrances but also with inside jokes, metaphors, rogue capital letters, nonsense rhymes and unexpected elaborations. Even as the Kochamma family seems to be withering before our eyes, the story of the family is flourishing, becoming ever more nuanced and intricate.

Very early on in *The God of Small Things,* the grown-up Estha is caring for an ancient dog when he glimpses the shadow of a bird in flight moving across the dying animal's skin: "To Estha—steeped in the smell of old roses, blooded on memories of a broken man—the fact that something so fragile, so unbearably tender had survived, had been *allowed* to exist, was a miracle." The end of this novel also describes a brief interlude of intense happiness, and it evokes in the reader a similar feeling of gratitude and wonderment: It's as if we had suddenly stumbled upon something small and sparkling in all this wreckage. By now we know what horrors await these characters, but we have also learned, like Estha, to take what we can get. And so we hold on to this vision of happiness, this precious scrap of plunder, even as the novel's waters close over our heads.

Laura Shapiro (review date 26 May 1997)

SOURCE: "Disaster in a Lush Land," in *Newsweek,* May 26, 1997, p. 76.

[*Shapiro is an American journalist. In the following review, she offers praise for* The God of Small Things, *in particular Roy's playful use of language and development of eccentric characters.*]

After you turn the last page and start thinking back on *The God of Small Things,* Arundhati Roy's glowing first novel, you find you're still deep inside it. You can feel against your skin the lush vines and grasses, smell the pickled mangoes and sweet banana jam, hear the children singing as their uncle's car carries them home to disaster. Disaster was waiting from the start, for the novel begins with a little girl's funeral. Sophie Mol, almost 9, has drowned; and her twin cousins and their mother are mysteriously, horribly implicated. The details don't fall into place until the end of the book. But making our way there, we move through a landscape of sensory imagery so richly evocative that, like the 7-year-old twins, we seem to have lived the tragedy long before we can understand it.

Roy, 37, grew up in Kerala, the state in southwest India where her novel is set. She's been through architecture school and written the screenplays for two highly regarded Indian films; and now she proves herself to be an extraordinary novelist. Inevitably she will be compared with Salman Rushdie, whose novels (*Midnight's Children, The Satanic Verses*) were the first to carve out a definitive place in English fiction for books about India by Indians. Indeed, hardly a season seems to go by now without a talented young writer emerging from the Subcontinent with a new book and a bid for Rushdie's mantle. It's true that like Rushdie, Roy plays often and delightfully with language, loves songs and jingles

and doggerel, and scatters capital letters where they're bound to startle. Some of her characters, too, are very much in his vein, off-beat and emotionally gnarled. The twins, for instance: forcibly separated after the tragedy, they grow up with jagged edges that never heal. Eventually the boy, Estha, stops speaking and the girl, Rahel, stops feeling.

But Roy is no disciple of anyone: a distinctive voice and vision rule this book. Her sentences, though drenched in unforgettable metaphor, are perfectly chiseled. "Once the quietness arrived, it stayed and spread in Estha," she writes. "It sent its stealthy, suckered tentacles inching along the insides of his skull, hoovering the knolls and dells of his memory, dislodging old sentences, whisking them off the tip of his tongue . . . He grew accustomed to the uneasy octopus that lived inside him and squirted its inky tranquilizer on his past."

Sophie Mol's death is only one of the disasters spawned by history, love and human cruelty here, yet *The God of Small Things* is never grim. It's way too full of life for that. Much of the narrative is filtered through Rahel's perspective, and the girl's imagination gives a wonderfully magic buoyancy to the page. At an airport where she's behaved so badly her only allies are the cement kangaroos that serve as trash receptacles, Rahel glances at them as the family leaves. "Cement kisses whirred through the air like small helicopters," writes Roy, and the pleasure she takes in such imagery is contagious. This outstanding novel is a banquet for all the senses we bring to reading.

Richard Eder (review date 1 June 1997)

SOURCE: "As the World Turns," in *Los Angeles Times Book Review,* June 1, 1997, p. 2.

[*Eder is an American journalist and critic. In the following review, he commends Roy's evocative treatment of social upheaval and personal tragedy, but dislikes her narrative nonlinearity and experimentation with language.*]

A decaying South Indian royalty, its wealth and hegemony in drastic decline, its princess caught in a scandalous affair with an Untouchable carpenter. Punishment, exile, death and the downfall and scattering of the regal line.

Royalty in this case consists of the proprietors of Paradise Pickles, the industrial mainstay of the small Kerala town of Ayemenem. Their tragedy, though, is played out as ornamented princely melodrama: a lush modern fictional equivalent of classical Kathakali theater.

Arundhati Roy, a young Indian writer, has devised a novel

of poignancy and considerable sweep, along with some serious weaknesses. Among the appealing elements are a wit that is sardonic and whimsical by turns, a portrait of social change in rural India in mid-century and both sympathy and harsh judgment for a doomed small-town upper class. Above all, Roy evokes the premonitory pain of the two children through whose eyes the story is told—spectators of their family catastrophe and its victims.

The God of Small Things is the story of three generations of the Kochamma family. The grandfather, a distinguished entomologist—and a sadistic tyrant within his family—is eclipsed upon his retirement by the enterprise of his hitherto docile wife, Mammaji. She builds a few recipes into a thriving pickle and jam business and makes a family fortune.

Her two children, by contrast, are stumblers. The loquacious Chacko goes off to Oxford on a Rhodes scholarship, marries an Englishwoman, has a child and promptly falls into apathy. After putting up with him for a while, his wife divorces him and marries another man. Chacko returns home and intervenes in the family business with ruinously expansive ideas. Ammu, his beautiful and rebellious sister, has also returned home from a disastrous marriage, bringing two babies, Rahel and her twin brother, Estha.

When the twins are 7, everything falls to pieces. It is the confluence of currents of personal, familial and social decay. Estha, in a scene of brilliant horror, is sexually abused by the candy vendor at a movie house. Ammu, who has lived in a kind of caged heat within the constrictions of the family, has a passionate affair with the factory carpenter, a brilliant, handsome man and a friend of her children. At the same time, Chacko's ex-wife, now a widow, arrives for a visit along with their beloved little daughter, Sophie.

In a complex, violent climax, Sophie drowns while playing with the twins. Ammu's affair is discovered. Chacko, distraught with grief and fury, orders her out of the house and separates the twins by sending Estha to live with his father in Calcutta. The carpenter dies from a brutal police beating instigated by a vicious Kochamma aunt. Ammu, living in a furnished room and struggling to make a living, sickens and dies, and the bright and imaginative Estha falls into irrecoverable silence.

The starting point for the story is Rahel's return, years later, from her own blighted life in America. The house is a ruin; the only ones left are the aunt, who spends the day watching television serials with her maid, and the silent Estha.

Much of *The God of Small Things* is told as the children saw, and failed to see, what went on. There are some beautifully written scenes. The family goes by car to the movies in Cochin, from where they will pick up Chacko's wife and

his daughter the next day at the airport. It is a precursor moment—of Estha's sexual abuse, the beginning of Ammu's affair, Sophie's drowning two weeks later and all that follows.

The car is stopped at a railroad crossing and overtaken by a left-wing political march. With a brief rendering of that heat-stricken wait, Roy weaves together the visible and implicit strands of her story: India at that time and place and two restless children growing into life.

"With a desultory nod of his bored and sleepy head, the Level Crossing Divinity conjured beggars with bandages, men with trays selling pieces of fresh coconut, parippu vadas on banana leaves, and cold drinks. Coca-Cola, Fanta, Rosemilk." And Rahel and Estha watching, "cloudy children at car windows with yearning marshmallow noses."

There is a lively portrait of Chacko, the beloved son spoiled by his mother, Mammaji. She is disablingly jealous of Margaret, his English wife. When Margaret comes on a visit, early in the marriage, Mammaji sneaks money into the pockets of her dresses so that she can think of her as a prostitute, not as someone her son loves. Chacko is well-meaning and weak, a spinner of theories. His fearful violence with Ammu at the end comes from the manipulation of his grief by mother and aunt.

There is the heartbreaking moment when Estha is put on the train by Ammu. They hold hands through the window; as the train begins to move, Estha voices his familiar complaint when in need of his mother. "I feel vomity," he says, as the train bears him off into the night.

Unfortunately, Roy has dressed much of her book in an ambitious gorgeousness that she often lacks the dexterity to manage. She inflates story into epic, the modest magic of perception into an occasional clumsy piece of magic realism, and the erotic current between pickle princess and carpenter into an avalanche, resembling a Hollywood musical crescendo. For example, when they meet the first night at the river:

> Biology designed the dance. Terror timed it. Dictated the rhythm with which their bodies answered each other. . . . Behind them the river pulsed through the darkness, shimmering like wild silk. Yellow bamboo wept. Night's elbows rested on the water and watched them.

Roy scrambles chronology, saws her revelations into jigsaw hints and scatters the hints throughout. What in more skillful hands may sustain tension and mystery buckles into narrative cacophony. She bends and teases language. Sometimes the result is a prism that breaks light into new colors; more often it is a self-reflecting mirror. She will fuse two words into one: "hardsounds," "wetgreen," "thunderdarkness"—sucking up the oxygen-pocket that allows an adjective to ignite a noun. Sometimes the noun is sucked up as well: "cementy."

Inventing as much as evoking her Indian-English patois, Roy invents cute and with cloyed self-indulgence. "Stoppited," Margaret tells Sophie at one point and, we read, the child "stoppited." This reader stoppited too, if only for a moment. The book has far too many such moments.

Michiko Kakutani (review date 3 June 1997)

SOURCE: "Melodrama as Structure for Subtlety," in *The New York Times,* June 3, 1997, p. C15.

[*In the following review, Kakutani praises Roy's keen observation of human nature.*]

The God of Small Things, Arundhati Roy's dazzling first novel, begins as a sort of mystery story. What caused the boy named Estha to stop talking? What sent his twin sister, Rahel, into exile in the United States? Why did their beautiful mother, Ammu, end up dying alone in a grimy hotel room? What killed their English cousin, Sophie Mol? And why has a "whiff of scandal" involving sex and death come to surround their bourgeois family?

While such questions may sound crudely melodramatic, they provide the narrative architecture of a novel that turns out to be as subtle as it is powerful, a novel that is Faulknerian in its ambitious tackling of family and race and class, Dickensian in its sharp-eyed observation of society and character.

A screenwriter who grew up in Kerala, India, Ms. Roy creates a richly layered story of familial betrayal and thwarted romantic passion by cutting back and forth between time present and time past. Set in southern India against a backdrop of traditional religious and caste taboos, her story depicts the tragic confluence of events—both personal and political, private and public—that bring about the murder of an innocent man and the dissolution of a family.

Although Ms. Roy's musical, densely patterned prose combines with the mythic power of her tale to create the impression of magical realism (her work has already been compared in India to that of Gabriel García Márquez), the most fantastical events in *God of Small Things* are not the products of a fevered imagination; they are simply the byproducts of everyday passions. As one of her characters observes: "Anything's possible in human nature. Love. Madness. Hope. Infinite joy."

Writing largely from the point of view of the twins, Estha and Rahel, Ms. Roy does a marvelous job of conjuring the anamolous world of childhood, its sense of privilege and frustration, its fragility, innocence and unsentimental wisdom. She shows us the twins' uncanny spiritual connection with each other and their longing for their mercurial mother's approval. Even at age 7, Estha is the reserved one, dignified in his Elvis pompadour and pointy beige shoes. Rahel is the curious one, wayward, ardent and solitary in her pride.

Through the twins' eyes, we are introduced to their relatives and neighbors in the small Indian community of Ayemenem. There's their mother, Ammu, a lonely, secretly rebellious woman who feels that her failed marriage to a drunkard has ruined her chances of happiness and flight. There's their uncle, Chacko, a former Rhodes scholar who has returned home from Oxford to run his mother's pickle factory. And there's their great-aunt, Baby Kochamma, a mean, petty behemoth of a woman whose unrequited love for a priest has permanently warped her life. We meet Comrade Pillai, a local politician willing to sacrifice people to principles ("the old omelette-and-eggs thing"). And we meet Velutha, the handsome son of a family of untouchables, a skilled carpenter whom the twins and their mother adore.

Ms. Roy gives us a richly pictorial sense of these characters' daily routines and habits, and she delineates their emotional lives with insight and panache, revealing the fatal confluence of jealousy, cruelty and naiveté that shapes their destinies forever. Dozens of small details pin her characters to the page and insinuate them into our minds: the family matriarch, Mammachi, blind behind her rhinestone studded glasses, playing the violin: Chacko, carefully building model planes of balsa and watching them crash into the town's lush green fields of rice and Rahel, her unruly pulled back into a ponytail, making mental foes of people she loves in an effort to quiet her fears.

The world these characters inhabit is made equally palpable to the reader. On the surface, it is a modern world of populist politics and entrepreneurial zeal, a world in which American cars are status symbols and workers' rights are a fashionable cause. At the same time, it is a world in which divorced women are looked upon with scorn and romances between members of the bourgeoisie and the so-called untouchable castes are considered an unthinkable sin. In Ayemenem there are rigid, unspoken rules, and as the twins learn, history "collects its dues from those who break its laws."

If Ms. Roy is sometimes overzealous in foreshadowing her characters' fate, resorting on occasion to darkly portentous clues, she proves remarkably adept at infusing her story with the inexorable momentum of tragedy. She writes near the beginning of the novel that in India, personal despair "could never be desperate enough," that "it was never important enough" because "worse things had happened" and "kept happening." Yet as rendered in this remarkable novel, the "relative smallness" of her characters' misfortunes remains both heartbreaking and indelible.

John Updike (review date 23 June 1997)

SOURCE: "Mother Tongues," in *The New Yorker*, June 23 & 30, 1997, pp. 156-59.

[*Updike is an American novelist, critic, essayist, and short story writer. In the following review, he lauds Roy's achievements in* The God of Small Things *despite what he considers her "overwrought" passages and self-conscious "artiness."*]

The spread of English throughout the world, via commerce and colonialism and now popular culture, has spawned any number of fluent outriggers capable of contributing to English literature. Some, like most Australians and Americans, write English with no thought of an alternative; others, like certain inhabitants of the Caribbean, Ireland, Anglophone Africa, and India, write it against a background of native tongues or patois that are abandoned or suppressed in the creative effort—an effort that to a degree enlists them in a foreign if not enemy camp, that of the colonizer. *The God of Small Things* by Arundhati Roy, a work of highly conscious art, is conscious not least of its linguistic ambivalence. It takes place in India's southern state of Kerala, where the local language is Malayalam; phrases and whole sentences of Malayalam, sometimes translated and sometimes not, seep into the book's English, whose mannerisms—compound and coined words, fragmentary sentences, paragraphs a word or a phrase long, whimsical capitalization—underline the eccentricity of the language in relation to the tale's emotional center. Estha and Rahel, male and female dizygotic twins who serve as the central characters, remember how their great-aunt Navomi Ipe, incongruously called Baby Kochamma, inflicted English upon them, making them write "I will always speak in English" a hundred times and practice their pronunciation by singing, "Rej-Oice in the Lo-Ord Or-Orlways / And again I say rej-oice." The twins' sensibilities, uncannily conjoined, are expressed in a confidently unorthodox prose that owes something to Salman Rushdie's jazzy riffs:

> Their lives have a size and a shape now. Estha has his and Rahel hers.
>
> Edges, Borders, Boundaries, Brinks and Limits have appeared like a team of trolls on their separate horizons. Short creatures with long shadows, patroling

the Blurry End. Gentle half-moons have gathered under their eyes and they are as old as Ammu [their mother] was when she died. Thirty-one.

> Not old.
>
> Not young.
>
> But a viable die-able age.

The main events of the novel, to which everything harks back, occur in December of 1969, when the twins' English cousin, Sophie Mol, arrives for a two-week Christmas vacation. She is the daughter and only child of their uncle Chacko, who met his English wife at Oxford, and who, divorced, has returned to live with his mother, his aunt, and his sister, Ammu—herself divorced—in the big family house in Ayemenem. They are Syrian Christians; Baby Kochamma's father was the Reverend E. John Ipe, a priest personally blessed by the Patriarch of Antioch. His son, the twins' grandfather Pappachi, was an Imperial Entomologist under the British and after Independence assumed the title of Joint Director of Entomology. But a rare moth he discovered was not named after him, and this moth, with "its unusually dense dorsal tufts," consequently "tormented him and his children and his children's children." He beat his wife, Mammachi, with a brass flower vase every night until Chacko, burly from rowing for Oxford, put a halt to the practice; then Pappachi took his favorite mahogany rocking chair into the middle of the driveway and smashed it with a plumber's monkey wrench. His black rages were partly the fruit of spousal jealousy: Mammachi in her youth was a violinist of potential concert calibre, until he forbade further lessons; in her middle age, though virtually blind, she created from some of her recipes a successful business, named (by Chacko) Paradise Pickles and Preserves. The pickle plant with its employees, the great old house, the river beyond, a deserted house and rubber plantation on the other side of the river (once owned by the Black Sahib, a fabled Englishman who had "gone native" and committed suicide), the Ipe heritage of backward looking Anglophilia, a sky-blue Plymouth that Pappachi spitefully bought for himself after his rebuke from Chacko—these are the data that Arundhati Roy revolves before us as she spins her circuitous tale. The twins were seven when nine-year-old Sophie Mol visited; now they are thirty-one, and Rahel has returned from America upon learning that Estha has been sent back to Ayemenem by his father and stepmother, who have wearied of his withdrawn and virtually demented behavior.

Roy takes her time exploring the past by means of the present. Her novel provides one more example of William Faulkner's powerful influence upon Third World writers; his method of torturing a story—mangling it, coming at it roundabout after portentous detours and delays—presumably strikes a chord in stratified, unevenly developed societies that feel a shame and defeat in their history. The narrator works as hard to avoid as to reach her destination of forbidden sex and atrocious violence. As we read *The God of Small Things,* we know that Sophie Mol died during her Christmas vacation in India, but we don't know why. We know that Rahel and Estha were exposed to something dreadful, but we don't know what. Roy peels away the layers of her mysteries with such delicate cunning, such a dazzlingly adroit shuffle of accumulating revelations within the blighted House of Ipe, that to discuss the plot would violate it.

> **Roy takes her time exploring the past by means of the present. Her novel provides one more example of William Faulkner's powerful influence upon Third World writers; his method of torturing a story—mangling it, coming at it roundabout after portentous detours and delays—presumably strikes a chord in stratified, unevenly developed societies that feel a shame and defeat in their history.**
> **—*John Updike***

Treading Roy's maze, we learn a great deal about India—a "vast, violent, circling, driving, ridiculous, insane, unfeasible, public turmoil of a nation." We learn foremost that in 1969 it was not a safe place. Though Kerala, unlike "a small country with similar landscape" to the east, is not being bombed by the forces of capitalism, it holds a large number of Communists, whose machinations threaten the solvency of Paradise Pickles and Preserves, and whose angry marches shatter the peace of an upper-class Syrian Christian family on its way, in its big blue Plymouth, to Cochin to see the movie *The Sound of Music.* The young nation seethes with the violence of its long history, its resentments, its prejudices, going back to a time "before Vasco da Gama arrived, before the Zamorin's conquest of Calicut." Husbands beat wives, women have no *locus standi,* and Ammu, divorced from her alcoholic Hindu husband, spends hours "on the riverbank with her little plastic transistor shaped like a tangerine": "A liquid ache spread under her skin, and she walked out of the world like a witch, to a better, happier place." The liquid ache of longing is widespread, and dangerous. The Black Sahib committed suicide because "his young lover's parents had taken the boy away from him." Chacko still loves his pale English wife; fat old Baby Kochamma was once fanatically in love with a Catholic priest; and little Estha, banished to the empty lobby of Abhilash Talkies during *The Sound of Music,* is coerced into masturbating the man behind the refreshment counter. This horrific scene, with its inordinately vivid molester ("He looked like an unfriendly jeweled bear. . . . His yellow teeth were magnets. They saw, they

smiled, they sang, they smelled, they moved. They mesmerized"), is one of the novel's flashing lunges outside the suffocating circle of Anglophile Syrian Christians into the Indian masses, in their poverty and dynamic, Dickensian color.

Occidental readers who imagined that untouchability was banished by Mahatma Gandhi will find the caste onus cruelly operative in 1969, and not just in the memories of the aged:

> Mammachi told Estha and Rahel that she could remember a time, in her girlhood, when Paravans were expected to crawl backwards with a broom, sweeping away their footprints so that Brahmins or Syrian Christians would not defile themselves by accidentally stepping into a Paravan's footprint. In Mammachi's time, Paravans, like other Untouchables, were not allowed to walk on public roads, not allowed to cover their upper bodies, not allowed to carry umbrellas. They had to put their hands over their mouths when they spoke, to divert their polluted breath away from those whom they addressed.

Velutha, a clever Paravan child who lives in Ayemenem, brings to Ammu, a child three years older, little toys he has made—"tiny windmills, rattles, minute jewel boxes out of dried palm reeds"—and presents them "holding them out on his palm (as he had been taught to) so she wouldn't have to touch him to take them." This sad detail, of the child taught to give without being touched, has a comic counterpart later in the novel, when Velutha's father, the subservient Vellya Paapen, is knocked down by an angry push: "He was taken completely by surprise. Part of the taboo of being an Untouchable was expecting not to be touched." In a century scarred by racial genocides, in a country no stranger to formal and informal racial segregation, Hinduism's creation of a vast loathed underclass still has the power to shock, as if it held a magnifying glass to our own inner discriminations and dismissals.

Rahel, studying in Delhi to be an architect, meets and marries an American, who brings her to Boston. But, though adoring, he can't break through her pre-occupation with the past; after her divorce, she works for several years as the night cashier in a bulletproof booth at a gas station outside Washington, where "drunks occasionally vomited into the till, and pimps propositioned her with more lucrative job offers." One of her recurrent visitors, a "punctual drunk with sober eyes," shouts, "Hey, you! Black bitch! Suck my dick!" This is not so far from Baby Kochamma's thinking of the twins as "Half-Hindu Hybrids whom no self-respecting Syrian Christian would ever marry." Neither India nor the world is an easy melting pot.

Roy manages to catch, in the skein of the Ipes' haunted history, a sense of India's deep past, the mingling of dark inhabitants and light invaders going back to the Aryan authors of the Vedas, the roots of Hinduism. She brings us, in her ecstatically written last pages, into the heart of human love and the mythic past: Krishna, as it were, couples with Radha on the riverbank, and, when the lover makes the beloved dance, it is the dance of Kali, of death and coming destruction. There is even a magic-realist touch: he folds his fear into a rose, and she wears it in her hair. Such dark bliss is akin to that sought by a group of male kathakali dancers who, unsatisfied and humiliated by the truncated performances they put on for the guests at a tourist hotel that by 1993 has arisen on the Black Sahib's old plantation, give the full performance, in an all but empty temple, until dawn.

Since **The God of Small Things** delivers so much terror and beauty, and so omniscient a view of modern India, it is perhaps ungrateful to complain of the novel's artiness. But the prose, shuttling back and forth among its key images and phrases, rarely lets us forget that we are in the company of an artificer: Roy caresses her novel until it seems not merely well wrought but overwrought. Much of our mental energy is spent in recalling where insistently repeated phrases like "Locusts Stand I" and "Esthapappychachen Kuttappen Peter Mon" and "Sourmetal Smells" first occurred, and what they signify. A Joycean passage like

> A carbreeze blew. Greentrees and telephone poles flew past the windows. Still birds slid by on moving wires, like unclaimed baggage at the airport.

> A pale daymoon hung hugely in the sky and went where they went. As big as the belly of a beer-drinking man

arguably transports us into the mind of a seven-year-old, but arch modifiers like "dinner-plate-eyed" and "slipperoily" and palindromic formations such as "Dark of Heartness tiptoed into the Heart of Darkness" put us squarely on a writer's desk. Well, a novel of real ambition must invent its own language, and this one does. Arundhati Roy, the elegant dust jacket tells us, has worked as a production designer and has written two screenplays; this experience shows in the skill with which she sets and lights her scenes, as well as in such touches of special jargon as "mosaic blur," "gofers on a film set," and "a test tube of sparkling, backlit urine." Her scenes get replayed in both the reader's memory and the characters'. This is a first novel, and it's a Tiger Woodsian début—the author hits the long, socio-cosmic ball but is also exquisite in her short game. Like a devotionally built temple, **The God of Small Things** builds a massive interlocking structure of fine, intensely felt details. A rosary is held up to the light: "Each greedy bead grabbed its share of sun."

Amanda Craig (review date 27 June 1997)

SOURCE: "But What about this Year's Barbados Novel?" in *New Statesman,* June 27, 1997, p. 49.

[*Craig is a South African-born English journalist. In the following review, she contends that, while* The God of Small Things *suffers from Roy's somewhat overwrought style, the book demonstrates the author's talent and promise.*]

This year's India novel is ... but stop. Where did that sneering phrase creep in? We do not speak of this year's Ireland novel, or Africa novel, or any other former British colony on which our culture was imposed.

The Indian novelist is confronted with a paradox. Our feelings about India are so complex that a novel is rarely judged on its own merits rather than on a mixture of guilt, anger, defiance and sneaking envy. Those such as Rushdie, who stress the exotic, profit by it; Rohinton Mistry, on the other hand, is accused of writing flat prose—presumably because critics, when confronted with a thick book about poor people, simply cannot cope with too much reality.

Arundhati Roy, whose first novel (**The God of Small Things**) has excited much interest, is getting both ends of it, as an Indian and as a woman. With her advance of £500,000, her photogenic face and big coverage in this month's *Vogue* and *New Yorker,* the British critical response has been predictably hostile. So, is she any good?

Her novel, like most such debuts, is a mixture of outstanding promise and wonky style. Roy badly needs a good editor to sieve the gold from the chaff, because her response to her culture is both overwhelmed and overwhelming. The melding of cultures produces a periodic sub-Joycean meltdown of language; the English reader who has rejoiced in the absurdities and felicities of Indian English will find this almost as irritating as the author's fondness for capitalised clichés, such as "Things Can Change in a Day". Yet she has wit, intelligence and a sensuous love of words.

The plot, which is difficult to disentangle because the novel uses fractured time, concerns a pair of twins, Estha and Rahel, and their family. They spend their childhood in Cochin, Kerala, and live with their beautiful mother, Ammu, and their blind grandmother, Mammachi. The latter has started the Paradise Pickle Factory and, under the influence of the twins' uncle Chacko, promoted a Harijan (Untouchable) within it, much to the horror of the other workers.

At first the novel seems to be about the twins, their innocent precocity and comic delight in the English language. Yet we know that something terrible will happen. Quite soon the twins (who, we are told, share one soul) will be separated and Estha rendered mute. The adult Rahel has a husband who cannot understand the expression in her eyes: "He put it between indifference and despair. He didn't know that in some places, like the country that Rahel came from, various kinds of despair competed for primacy. And that personal despair could never be desperate enough."

Only the God of Small Things can help you survive, by becoming resilient and truly indifferent.

The twins' mother and their Harijan friend, Velutha, fall in love. Their first, cataclysmic love-making is not described until the end of the novel, after we have been told of the suffering it causes—how Velutha has been beaten to death and falsely accused of kidnap and murder, how the twins' cousin has drowned, how the communists of Cochin have utterly failed in their promise, and innocent lives been ruined.

Despite Roy's defects of style, this is a sumptuous portrait of a family, a community and a tragic love affair. Fractured time has been employed by writers as diverse as Pinter, Spark and Barbara Vine. When successfully handled, it is both affecting and aesthetically satisfying to a high degree. *The God of Small Things* is not just this year's India novel. Nor is it, as its publishers unwisely proclaim, a masterpiece. It is, however, written by someone who shows every promise of being capable of producing such a thing in the future.

Amitava Kumar (review date 29 September 1997)

SOURCE: "Rushdie's Children," in *The Nation,* September 29, 1997, pp. 36-38.

[*In the following review, attempts to place* The God of Small Things *within the tradition of modern Indian literature written in English.*]

"India: The Fiction Issue" sang the cover of *The New Yorker* at the newsstand run by a Gujarati man inside Penn Station. On the bright cover, topped with turmeric sunset hues, sat a stone Lord Ganesha browsing through a couple of books, the task made easier because He has more than two hands. And emerging from a thicket, dressed for a safari, were a white couple, mouths agape.

This has been the season of the discovery of India—presumably because it is the fiftieth-anniversary year of Indian independence and not because India, under World Bank-I.M.F. dictates, has introduced wide-scale "structural adjustments," exponentially increasing the commercial traffic between India and the United States. (Jesse Helms, whose conservatism is old enough to deserve an anniversary of its own,

congratulated an Indian-American audience recently for its enthusiasm for U.S. capitalism: "Everything that you good friends who are citizens of this country of ours have worked for—opening the Indian economy and improving relations—is coming to pass.") Welcome to the literature of the New Economic Policy.

I grew up in India under the stultifying shadow of the nationalist myth that we were all the children of Mahatma Gandhi. Now, if *The New Yorker* is to be believed, we are all the children of Salman Rushdie. A bit extreme, perhaps, but indulge me, dear reader. For we live in an extreme world. And one of the features of this world is that publications from Western metropoles have the power to be the god of all things—especially things from the famished, resourceful regions of the Third World.

In one such powerful venue, *The New York Times,* the publication of Rushdie's *Midnight's Children* was characterized as "a Continent finding its voice." The Delhi-based critic Aijaz Ahmad remarked caustically, "As if one has no voice if one does not speak in English."

In the editorial introduction to *The New Yorker,* Bill Buford repeated the same fiction, talking of what he calls "Indian fiction" as the literary output in only one language, English, and that too by recent, mostly expatriate, authors. In his own survey of Indian writing in the same issue, Rushdie rather briskly and a bit disingenuously brushes away post-independence writing in other languages of India as not being as "strong" or "important" as the literary output in English during the same period. "Admittedly," he says, "I did my reading only in English, and there has long been a genuine problem of translation in India." But this confession isn't intended as a genuine qualification, it would seem, and it only inoculates his judgment against further inquiry. No mention is made of the explosion of Dalit (literally, the oppressed, referring to the untouchable castes) writing in Marathi, for example, which represents a radical rewriting not only of the canon but of the very notion of the literary.

Like the *Times,* Buford reduces the history of writing in India—in at least eighteen other languages but also in a variety of other contexts, not the least of which was the nationalist movement—to one single publication in the West, as cozily close to the present as the year 1981, the year "that Salman Rushdie published *Midnight's Children,* a book that . . . made everything possible."

Even if that were true, such a contention would beg the question: Why is it so? Or, what does it say about the historical invisibility of others and their languages? But Buford's statement isn't true. Even if we take novels written only in, say, Hindi or Urdu, around the singular event of the partition of India in 1947—the event that constitutes the bloody underside of what we're celebrating this year—very little that has been written in English in India approaches the eloquent expressions in those novels of the woes, the divided hopes, or the numb, demented silences of 10 million uprooted lives.

And yet there is an undeniable force to several new novels written in English by Indian novelists. How are we to read them outside the ignorant and self-congratulatory rhetoric of Western publishing? How can we frame this writing with issues that join, rather than separate, them from other milieus both in India and the world?

Arundhati Roy's moving first novel, *The God of Small Things,* has created a publishing sensation not only in the West but also in India—where, of course, some gods fare far better than others. But, this is not a novel about those gods that dwell in temples or mosques. The violence at the heart of the novel has nothing to do with, for instance, the demolition in 1992 of a mosque by right-wing Hindu zealots in the Indian town of Ayodhya. The communal frenzy in Hindu-Muslim riots had led the historian Gyan Pandey to comment that violence in Indian historiography is often "written up" only as "aberration" and "absence." So that an interrogation of an experience like the trauma of Ayodhya makes it essential, as the critic Rustom Bharucha has put it, to produce another kind of historiography, one that "do[es] not neutralise the necessity of writing, but acknowledge[s], nonetheless, the gaps and holes in it."

I invoke the Ayodhya violence here because Roy engages the recall of—rather, the recoil from—violence and the difficulty of ever articulating its trauma. Her novel is set in a small town in Kerala where the police inspector taps the breasts of a divorced, upper-class woman, in front of her small children, when she comes to inquire after her jailed lover, a Communist worker from an untouchable caste. The policeman uses his baton to touch Ammu's breasts: "Gently. Tap tap. As though he was choosing mangoes from a basket. Pointing out the ones that he wanted packed and delivered."

We are offered this in the first pages of the book. The rest of the novel is not only a keen, unremitting revelation of the jagged edges of the holes in memory, it's also a nearly visible attempt by Ammu's two little kids, a pair of dizygotic twins, to grasp the meaning of those events and the words that surround their mother. Words like "illegitimate children" and "veshya" (whore). That long journey leads to the slow madness of language and to silence, to deaths from lonely griefs, and the sweet, small, bitter consolations of incestuous caring.

Writing about the traditional Indian dance form Kathakali,

Roy says "the Great Stories are the ones you have heard and want to hear again. . . . You know how they end, yet you listen as though you don't." In *The God of Small Things,* you know "who lives, who dies, who finds love, who doesn't. And yet you want to know again."

It is possible that the novel can't tell more because it discovers its own post-colonial heart of darkness in caste violence and the humiliation of domestic abuse. ("The hidden fish of shame in a sea of glory.") But, perhaps connected with that is also the possibility that Roy refuses to hope for anything beyond the horror she contemplates. Those who had fought are now dead; those who are alive only happen to be survivors. The untouchable barely speaks in the narrative, and it's likely that when the story is over, all you can remember of him is his glittering smile. The subaltern with perfect teeth.

Sarah Lyall (article date 15 October 1997)

SOURCE: "Indian's First Novel Wins Booker Prize in Britain," in *The New York Times,* October 15, 1997, p. A4.

[*In the following article, Lyall reports on Roy's winning of the Booker Prize for* The God of Small Things.]

An Indian writer, Arundhati Roy, was awarded England's prestigious Booker Prize this evening for her first novel, *The God of Small Things,* a soaring story about a set of twins struggling to make sense of the world, themselves and their strange and difficult family in southern India.

The international best seller, published by Random House, created a star when Ms. Roy's combined advances reportedly came to more than $1.6 million. Ms. Roy, who is 37, lives in New Delhi.

Gillian Beer, a professor of English literature at Cambridge and the chairman of the Booker judges, said the book was written with "extraordinary linguistic inventiveness."

The Booker Prize, worth more than $32,000, is awarded annually to a novel published in the past year by a writer from Britain or one of the Commonwealth countries. It is considered Britain's most distinguished literary prize. But the award is usually riven by controversy, with people criticising the judges for not naming one book or another to the six-book short list and the judges themselves, who plowed through 106 novels this year, often failing to reach a happy consensus.

Prizewinners

1997 Literary Prizes and Honors

Academy of American Poets Fellowship
Established in 1946 to reward one American poet per year "for distinguished poetic achievement"; $20,000 stipend.

John Haines

American Academy of Arts and Letters Awards in Literature
Bestowed annually by the Academy to honor and encourage writers in their creative work; includes $7500 prize for each honoree.

Charles Baxter, Maureen Howard, Jayne Anne Phillips, and Jane Smiley
In fiction
Allen Grossman
In poetry
Luc Sante
In nonfiction

American Academy of Arts and Letters New Members in Literature
Elected annually to fill vacancies in the academy's membership.

Philip Levine, *poet*
Albert Murray, *novelist*
Studs Terkel, *nonfiction writer*

American Book Awards
Established in 1978 by the Before Columbus Foundation, in recognition of the excellence and multicultural diversity of American writing, to reward outstanding literary achievement by contemporary American authors without restriction to race, sex, ethnic background, or genre.

Alurista
For *Et Tu . . . Raza*
Dorothy Barresi
For *The Post-Rapture Diner*
William M. Banks
For *Black Intellectuals: Race and Responsibility in American Life*
Derrick Bell
For *Gospel Choirs: Psalms of Survival in an Alien Land Called Home*
Thulani Davis
For *Maker of Saints*
Tom De Haven
For *Derby Dugan's Depression Funnies*
Martin Espada
For *Imagine the Angels of Bread*
Montserrat Fontes
For *Dreams of the Centaur*
Guillermo Gomez-Pena
For *The New World Border: Prophecies, Poems & Loqueras for the End of the Century*
Noel Ignatiev and John Garvey
For *Race Traitor*
Brenda Knight
For *Women of the Beat Generation*

American Book Awards, continued

Shirley Geok-Lin Lim
For *Among the White Moon Faces: An Asian-American Memoir of Homelands*
Sunaina Maira and Rajini Srikanth
For *Contours of the Heart: South Asians Map North America*
Louis Owens
For *Nightland*

ALA Gay, Lesbian & Bisexual Book Awards

Established in 1971 by the GLBTF, a unit of the American Library Association's Social Responsibilities Round Table, to recognize the best works of fiction and nonfiction dealing with gay, lesbian, and bisexual themes.

Fenton Johnson
In nonfiction, for *Geography of the Heart: A Memoir*
Emma Donoghue
In literature, for *Hood*

Alice Fay Di Castagnola Award

Awarded by the Poetry Society of America for a work in progress by a poet at a crucial stage in his or her work; includes $1000 prize.

Chase Twichell
"The Snow Watcher"

Antoinette Perry ("Tony") Awards

Established in 1947 and bestowed by the American Theatre Wing in recognition of outstanding Broadway plays.

Peter Stone
For best musical, *Titanic*
Alfred Uhry
For best play, *The Night of Ballyhoo*

Barbara Goldsmith Awards

Awarded by the PEN American Center to "writers either in prison or facing imprisonment for exercising their right to freedom of expression"; includes $3000 prize for each honoree.

Godwin Agbroko, *Nigerian*
Ayse Nur Zarakolu, *Turkish*

BCALA Literary Awards

Administered by the Black Caucus of the American Library Association to recognize excellence in adult fiction and nonfiction by African American authors published in the previous year; includes $500 prize for each honoree.

Florence Ladd
In fiction, for novel *Sarah's Psalm*
Nell Irvin Painter
In nonfiction, for *Sojourner Truth: A Life, A Symbol*

Booker Prize for Fiction

Britain's major literary prize for fiction, established in 1969; £20,000 awarded annually.

Arundhati Roy
For *The God of Small Things*

Bram Stoker Award

Annual award of the Horror Writers of America.

Thomas H. Cook
For *The Chatham School Affair*

Chekhov Prize for Short Fiction

Annual award of $500 given by The Crescent Review *for a short story of 7000 words or less.*

Paddy Reid
"Faces"

Edgar Allan Poe Awards

Bestowed by the Mystery Writers of America in recognition of achievement in mystery, crime, and suspense writing.

Thomas H. Cook
For best novel, *The Chatham School Affair*
Harlan Coben
For best original paperback, *Fade Away*
John Morgan Wilson
For best first novel, *Simple Justice*
Michael Malone
For best short story, "Red Clay"

E. M. Forster Award in Literature

Established in 1972 by Christopher Isherwood and bestowed by the American Academy of Arts and Letters to enable a young English, Scottish, Irish, or Welsh writer to travel to the U.S.; $15,000 awarded annually.

Glyn Maxwell, *poet and playwright*

Ernest Hemingway Foundation Award for First Fiction

Established in 1976 in memory of Ernest Hemingway and bestowed by the PEN American Center to recognize the first publication of a young or developing writer; $7500 awarded annually.

Ha Jin
For short story collection *Ocean of Words*

Frost Medal

Bestowed by the Poetry Society of America to recognize lifetime achievement in poetry; includes $2500 prize.

Josephine Jacobsen

Governor General's Literary Awards

Established in 1936 by the Canadian Authors Association and bestowed by the Canada Council for the Arts; $10,000 awarded to each honoree.

Jane Urquhart
In fiction, for *The Underpainter*
Aude
In fiction, for *Cet imperceptible mouvement*
Dionne Brand
In poetry, for *Land to Light On*
Pierre Nepveu
In poetry, for *Romans-fleuves*
Ian Ross
In drama, for *fareWel*
Yvan Bienvenue
In drama, for *Dits et Inédits*
Rachel Manley
In nonfiction, for *Drumblair—Memories of a Jamaican Childhood*
Roland Viau
In nonfiction, for *Enfants du néant et mangeurs d'âmes*

Guggenheim Fellowships
*Awarded by the
Guggenheim Memorial Foundation
in recognition of
"unusually distinguished
achievement in the past
and exceptional promise
for future accomplishments."*

**Rafael Campo, James Lasdun, Khaled
Mattawa, Naomi Shihab, Jacqueline Osherow,
Carl Phillips, Peter Sacks, Arthur Sze**
In poetry
**Andrea Barrett, Rick Bass, Lydia Davis, Judith
Freeman, Elizabeth Graver, Margot Livesay,
Susan Straight**
In fiction

Harold D. Vursell Memorial Award
*Bestowed by the American Academy of Arts and Letters to
recognize writers for "the quality of their prose style";
$5000 awarded annually.*

Elizabeth McCracken
For *The Giant's House*

Hugo Awards
*Established in 1953 and
administered by
the World Science
Fiction Society;
also known as
the Science Fiction
Achievement Awards.*

Kim Stanley Robinson
For novel *Blue Mars*
George R. R. Martin
For novella "Blood of the Dragon"
Bruce Sterling
For novelette "Bicycle Repairman"
Connie Willis
For short story "The Soul Selects Her Own Society . . ."

James Dickey Prize for Poetry
*Annual award of $500 and publication
of the honoree's poems in* Five Points.

Michael McFee
"To Work" and "Treadmill"

James Laughlin Award
*Established in 1954 and administered by the Academy of
American Poets; $5000 award to recognize and
support a poet's second book.*

Tony Hoagland
Donkey Gospel

James Tiptree Jr. Awards
*Recognizing works of science
fiction or fantasy which best explore
and expand gender roles.*

Candas Jane Dorsey
For novel *Black Wine*
Kelly Link
For short story "Travels with the Snow Queen"

Kate Tufts Discovery Award
*Bestowed by Claremont Graduate University for a first or
very early book of poetry, published in the previous year,
by an emerging poet; $5000 awarded annually.*

Lucia Perillo
The Body Mutinies

Kingsley Tufts Poetry Award
*Bestowed by Claremont Graduate University;
$50,000 awarded annually to a mid-career poet.*

Campbell McGrath
Spring Comes to Chicago

Kiriyama Pacific Rim Book Prize

Founded in 1996 and co-sponsored by the Kiriyama Pacific Rim Foundation and the Center for the Pacific Rim at the University of San Francisco; $30,000 awarded annually for the book that best contributes to greater understanding among Pacific Rim nations and peoples.

Patrick Smith

Japan: A Reinterpretation

Lambda Literary Awards

Awarded annually to recognize excellence in gay and lesbian writing and publishing in the U.S. during the previous year; sponsored by the Lambda Book Report.

Achy Obejas

In lesbian fiction, for *Memory Mambo*

Shyam Selvadurai

In gay men's fiction, for *Funny Boy*

Bernadette J. Brooten

In lesbian studies, for *Love between Women*

Patrick Merla

In gay men's studies, for *Boys Like Us*

Robin Becker

In lesbian poetry, for *All-American Girl*

Rafael Campo

In gay men's poetry, for *What the Body Told*

Doris Grumbach

In lesbian biography/autobiography, for *Life in a Day*

Fenton Johnson

In gay men's biography/autobiography, for *Geography of the Heart: A Memoir*

Lawrence O'Shaughnessy Award for Poetry

Annual award of $5000 to an Irish poet.

Eavan Boland

Lenore Marshall Poetry Prize

Established in 1975 and administered by the Academy of American Poets and The Nation *magazine; $10,000 award which recognizes the most outstanding book of poetry published in the United States in the previous year.*

Robert Pinsky

The Figured Wheel

Miles Franklin Award

Endowed by Australian author Stella Maria Sarah Miles Franklin and awarded annually to an Australian author for a novel or play published during the previous year which is of the highest literary merit and presents aspects of Australian life.

David Foster

The Glade within the Grove

National Book Awards

Administered by the National Book Foundation; $10,000 awarded in each of three categories.

Charles Frazier

In fiction, for *Cold Mountain*

Joseph Ellis

In nonfiction, for *American Sphinx*

William Meredith

In poetry, for *Effort at Speech*

National Book Critics Circle Award

Established in 1974
and awarded annually
to recognize
outstanding books
in five categories.

Gina Berriault

In fiction, for *Women in Their Beds*

Jonathan Raban

In general nonfiction, for *Bad Land*

Frank McCourt

In biography/autobiography, for *Angela's Ashes*

Robert Hass

In poetry, for *Sun under Wood*

William Gass

In criticism, for *Finding a Form*

National Book Foundation Medal

For distinguished contribution to American letters.

Studs Terkel

Nebula Awards

Established in 1965 and
administered by the
Science Fiction Writers
of America to honor
significant works of
science fiction
published in the U.S.

Vonda McIntyre

For novel *The Moon and the Sun*

Jerry Oltion

For novella "Abandon in Place"

Nancy Kress

For novelette "Flowers of Aulit Prison"

Jane Yolen

For short story "Sister Emily's Lightship"

Poul Anderson

Grand Master

Nobel Prize for Literature

Awarded annually to recognize an author's distinguished
achievement; established in 1901 and
administered by the Swedish Academy.

Dario Fo, *Italian playwright*

Orange Prize

Established in 1996; celebrates fiction written by women
and published in the United Kingdom.

Anne Michaels

Fugitive Pieces

PEN/Faulkner Award for Fiction

Bestowed by the PEN American Center; includes $15,000
award to winner and $5000 to each of four runners-up.

Gina Berriault

For short story collection *Women in Their Beds*

Premio Aztlán Literary Prize

Established in 1993 and administered by the University of
New Mexico; $1000 annual prize recognizing a Chicano
or Chicana fiction writer who has published
no more than two books.

Wendell Mayo

For short story collection *Centaur of the North*

Pulitzer Prize

Awarded annually by Columbia University on the recommendation of the Pulitzer Prize board; includes a $3000 award in each category.

[Note: No award was given in the drama category in 1997.]

Frank McCourt

In biography/autobiography, for *Angela's Ashes*

Steven Millhauser

In fiction, for *Martin Dressler: The Tale of an American Dreamer*

Jack N. Rakove

In history, for *Original Meanings: Politics and Ideas in the Making of the Constitution*

Richard Kluger

In nonfiction, for *Ashes to Ashes: America's Hundred-Year Cigarette War, the Public Health, and the Unabashed Triumph of Philip Morris*

Lisel Mueller

In poetry, for *Alive Together*

Richard and Hilda Rosenthal Foundation Award in Literature

Bestowed by the American Academy of Arts and Letters for a work of fiction considered a literary achievement but not a commercial success; $5000 awarded annually.

Mary Kay Zuravleff

For novel *The Frequency of Souls*

Rome Fellowship in Literature

Bestowed by the American Academy of Arts and Letters to allow a year of study at the Academy in Rome.

Fae Myenne Ng, *fiction writer*

Ruth Lilly Poetry Prize

Established by Lilly in 1986 and bestowed by Poetry *magazine to honor a U.S. poet "whose accomplishments warrant extraordinary recognition"; $75,000 awarded annually.*

William Matthews

Sue Kaufman Prize for First Fiction

Established in 1979 in memory of Kaufman and bestowed by the American Academy of Arts and Letters; $2500 awarded annually.

Brad Watson

For short-story collection *Last Days of the Dog-Men*

Tanning Prize

Established in 1994 with an endowment from painter Dorothea Tanning; $100,000 prize given by the Academy of American Poets "to recognize outstanding and proven mastery in the art of poetry."

Anthony Hecht

United States Poet Laureate

Established by the Library of Congress in the 1930s to recognize an outstanding American poet.

Robert Pinsky

Walt Whitman Award

Established in 1975 and administered by the Academy of American Poets to encourage the work of emerging poets and to enable the publication of a poet's first book.

Barbara Ras

Bite Every Sorrow

Whitbread Prize

Awarded each year in five categories to honor works by authors who have lived three or more years in Great Britain or Ireland; includes £30,500 divided among honorees.

Ted Hughes

In poetry and Book of the Year, for *Tales from Ovid*

Jim Crace

For best novel, *Quarantine*

Pauline Melville

For best first novel, *The Ventriloquist's Tale*

Graham Robb

In biography, for *Victor Hugo: A Biography*

Andrew Norriss

For best children's novel, *Aquila*

William Carlos Williams Award

Bestowed by the Poetry Society of America for the best book published in the previous year by a small, nonprofit, or university press; $500 awarded annually.

David Ignatow

I Have a Name

Witter Bynner Poetry Prize

Established in 1980 and bestowed by the American Academy of Arts and Letters; $2500 awarded annually to support the work of a young poet.

Mark Doty

Gina Berriault

Women in Their Beds: New and Selected Stories

Award: National Book Critics Circle Award

Berriault is an American novelist and short story writer.

For further information on her life and career, see *CLC,* Volume 54.

INTRODUCTION

Writing about *Women in Their Beds: New and Selected Stories* (1996), Berriault's prizewinning collection, Tobin Harshaw asserted: "In these 35 stories, one struggles to find a sentence that is anything less than jewel-box perfect. And the author uses her gift for language to do more than show us the world through her characters' eyes; we are also forced to think about it from their point of view—no small feat for someone who favors third-person narration." A reviewer in *Publishers Weekly* stated: "Each story is constructed so gracefully that it's easy to overlook how carefully crafted Berriault's writing is. Her lilting, musical prose adds a sophisticated sheen to the truths she mines." Yet Berriault, who has been writing for more than three decades, is not widely known. She has, says Lynell George, "achieved the dubious distinction of a writer's writer, praised to the heavens in literary circles, but who moves outside of that orbit incognito." George, like many other critics, considers this an unfortunate situation for such a talented writer. "Her writing," he remarked, is "imbued with a haunting resonance, is like a secret accidentally spilled. A poltergeist, she moves lives off foundations, so doors don't shut as cleanly or securely as before." Utilizing some common, recurring themes, many of Berriault's short stories deal with the ambiguous feelings of failed relationships and the pain of loss. Many of the women in her stories are preyed upon by men. Yet Berriault does not resort to stock characters or stereotypical stories. Gary Amdahl said, "One of the most notable features of her work is the absence of categorization, of description by quick (lazy) reference. There are no brand names, trademarks, franchises, buzz words or jargon here, no free rides on fads, no trading on popular issues or current affairs." Amdahl concluded, "Berriault does not imitate, cater, affect or posture. She deepens reality, complements it and affords us the bliss of knowing, for a moment, what we cannot know."

PRINCIPAL WORKS

The Descent (novel) 1960

Conference of Victims (novel) 1962
The Mistress, and Other Stories (short stories) 1965
The Son (novel) 1966
The Infinite Passion of Expectations: Twenty-five Stories (short stories) 1982
The Light of Earth (novel) 1984
The Stone Boy (screenplay) 1984
Women in Their Beds: New and Selected Stories (short stories) 1996

CRITICISM

Gina Berriault with Bonnie Lyons and Bill Oliver (interview date Summer 1994)

SOURCE: "'Don't I Know You?': An Interview with Gina Berriault," in *The Literary Review,* Vol. 37, Summer, 1994, pp. 714-23.

[*In the following interview, Berriault discusses her writing and motivation.*]

Gina Berriault has been writing stories, novels, and screenplays for more than three decades. Best known and most honored as a short story writer, she has published two volumes of stories, *The Mistress and Other Stories* (1965) and *The Infinite Passion of Expectations: Twenty-Five Stories* (1982). Called "exquisitely crafted," and "without exception, nearly flawless," her stories are remarkable for their subtle craft and the variety of characters, settings, and subject.

Her first novel, *The Descent* (1960), is about a Midwestern college professor appointed the first Secretary for Humanity, a Cabinet position designed to help prevent nuclear war. A plea for disarmament, *The Descent* depicts politicians militarizing the economy, harassing dissidents and promoting theories of winnable nuclear wars. *Conference of Victims* (1962), her second novel, explores the effects of the suicide of Hal Costigan on his family and mistress. *The Son* (1966), Berriault's third novel, is the account of the devastating effects of a woman's dependence on men for meaning in her life. This need to attract men eventually leads to a disastrous seduction of her teenage son. Her fourth novel, *The Lights of Earth* (1984), focuses on Ilona Lewis, a writer whose sense of self is undermined by the end of her relationship with a lover who has recently become a celebrity. Initially feeling unmoored, Ilona is finally drawn back into the world by the death of her brother, whom she has neglected.

In response to critics who have referred to Berriault's stories as "miniatures" or "watercolors," Berriault has said, "whenever I was referred to as a miniaturist or a watercolorist, I wondered if those labels were a way of diminishing a woman's writing. I believe that, now, because of the feminist movement, no reviewer would use those comparisons without hesitation." She added, "I hope my stories reveal some depths and some strengths, but if those virtues are not to be found in my work, then at least the intentions and the effort ought to call up a comparison with 12' x 12' acrylic."

Berriault also rejects any category more limited than "writer," saying, "I found my sustenance in the outward, the wealth of humankind everywhere, and do not wish to be thought of as a Jewish writer or a feminist writer or as a California writer or as a left-wing writer or categorized by any interpretation. I found it liberating to roam wherever my heart and my mind guided me, each story I've ever written."

Although she has received many fellowships and awards, is currently under contract with Pantheon for another story collection, and *The Infinite Passion of Expectation* has been called "the best book of short stories by a living American writer," we believe that Berriault's work has yet to receive the attention it deserves.

We talked with Gina Berriault in the Sausalito apartment of her daughter, Julie Elena. Although she was initially reticent about talking about herself and her work, her comments have the same honesty, depth, and humanity as her fiction.

[*Lyons and Oliver:*] *How do you think your childhood reading affected you as a writer?*

[Berriault:] That little girl who was me was a restless spirit, confined in a classroom and yearning to be out and roaming, either in the landscape or in her own imagination, and that restlessness was channeled into reading. I read more books than any other student in grammar school, roaming everywhere the persons in the stories roamed; I was those persons. Among the earliest books was *Water Babies* (that one belonged to the family across the alley and I remember climbing in through their kitchen window when they were away on vacation, reading it over and over, sitting on the floor in a corner) and George McDonald's great-hearted books, especially *At the Back of the Northwind* about a poor family and their love for one another. That deepened me. I began to know who I was, and that kids in poor families were worthy of books about them. And A. A. Milne, who wakened in me a delight in dialogue, an intuitive ear for what goes on between us and our beloved small animals—conversations of pretend naivete and subtle wit, that can make a child feel she knows more than adults think she knows. And later, in the novels of I. Zangwill, who wrote about Jewish families in Europe, I found a secret kinship, and I found that Jewish persons were worthy of being in novels. No one, all through my school years (except for a teacher who must have felt a kinship with Hitler) suspected that I was Jewish, and I must have been one-of-a-kind in that small California town. An insatiable reader, I began early to write my own stories, because, when you find yourself enthralled by their marvelous manipulation of language, when you find your wits sharpened, your heart stirred, your conscience revealed, then those writers become your guardian angels. They bring you to see your own existence as valuable—why else would they write their stories for you?—and they seem to be giving you their blessing to write your own. They seem to be blessing all children, even those who can't read a word.

Do you remember how you actually began writing?

My father was a free-lance writer for trade magazines and he had one of those old, stand-up-high typewriters. So I began to write my stories on it.

So you began writing when you were very young?

Yes, I began to write on that typewriter when I was in grammar school. I also wanted to be an artist and an actress. A drama teacher in high school offered to pay my tuition to an excellent drama school, but just at that time my father died and it was necessary for me to support my mother, brother, and sister. I never had any formal training as a writer, either.

Do you remember anything specific about how you taught yourself to write?

I simply wrote and wrote, and I was an avid reader. One thing I'd do was put a great writer's book beside the typewriter and then I'd type out a beautiful and moving paragraph or page and see those sentences rising up before my eyes from my own typewriter, and I would think "Someday maybe I can write like that."

You mean you'd type the words of someone else's story?

Yes, to see the words coming up out of my typewriter. It was like a dream of possibilities for my own self. And maybe I began to know that there was no other way for that sentence and that paragraph to be and arouse the same feeling. The someone whose words were rising from that typewriter became like a mentor for me. And when I went on with my own work, I'd strive to attain the same qualities I loved in that other person's work. Reading and writing are collaborations. When you read someone you truly love, their writing reaches your innermost self. You're soulmates.

How old were you when you did that experiment with your father's typewriter?

In my teens. I did it a few times. You shouldn't do it more than a few times because you must get on with your own.

Could you talk a bit more about how you began writing and publishing?

My experiment with my father's typewriter was going on at the same time I was writing my own stories. Rejection cards and letters with hastily scribbled encouragement helped to convince me that I existed. I remember a letter from an elegant, slick magazine, asking me to make a change or two and offer the story again. I did that, and when it was returned I cried for hours. By that time my parents had lost their house and the orange tree and the roses, and I wanted to earn enough with my writing to buy a farm for them. (I'd always wanted to live on a farm.) My father died before I could be of any help to him with my stories.

Elsewhere you mentioned that your mother began to go blind when you were fourteen. Could you talk about how that affected you as a person and as a writer?

As I wrote in my essay for *Confidence Women,* my blind mother sat by her little radio, listening to those serial ro-

mances and waving her hand before her eyes, hoping to see it take shape out of the dark. That could be a metaphor for my attempt to write, hoping to bring forth some light from out of the dark. I haven't yet.

How much formal education did you have?

After high school I took over my father's job. Then after work I'd roam through the Los Angeles public library and pick out whatever names or titles intrigued me. Having no mentor to guide me through that library, I just found writers by myself.

Do you regret not having a mentor?

My father was mentor for my spirit, I can say, and there were others from whom I learned about the world. I regret not having a formal, organized education. I wish I'd studied world history, philosophy, comparative literature, and I wish I'd learned several languages. Really, there is no excuse for my lack of those attainments, of that intellectual exploring, except as it is with every unschooled person—the circumstances of each one's life.

You don't say you regret not having gone through a creative writing program. Suppose a young writer wrote to you and said, "I admire your work and I want to write, Should I get a degree in creative writing?" What would you say?

I'd tell that person to learn more about everything, to rove, to be curious, and to read great writers from everywhere. If there's a true compulsion to write, a deep need, that person will write against all odds. And if that person enters a creative writing program, it would be for the purpose of learning how to shape what's already known and felt. Sometimes, when I taught workshops, I was glad I hadn't subjected myself to the unkind criticism of strangers. There's so much competitiveness, concealed and overt, among those who want to be writers and those who are writers. In Unamuno's *Tragic Sense of Life* he speaks about poets' desperate longing to be remembered, to be immortal. I think that concept of immortality is long past, long gone from our consciousness. Such immense change going on in the world, so much that will be irretrievable. So now the vying with one another is only for present gain. When I asked the students if they'd read this-or-that great writer, most had read only contemporary writers, and if the ads and the reviews praised those writers, the students accepted that evaluation. Ivan Bunin, for example, has been almost forgotten, and what a writer he was!

Speaking of contemporary writers, whose work do you admire?

Nabokov, Primo Levi, Jean Rhys—aren't they contemporary

still? And to go a little further back, but still within my view contemporary, Chekhov, Turgenev, Gogol, Bunin. They are my first and last deep loves. I liked Raymond Carver's first collection best. Those stories were like underground poetry. He must have felt that the reader possessed an intuitiveness like his own, and picked up on the meaning, just as with poetry.

Isn't that a way of taking your reader as equal?

And when you take the reader as your equal, your work isn't affected or false. You establish that collaboration, that shared intuitiveness.

In your career there's a big gap between **The Son** *and* **The Infinite Passion of Expectation.** *Why?*

That's a question that should never be asked. It opens a wound. What can a writer say about gaps and silence? The question can't be answered because the answer involves the circumstances of a lifetime and the condition of the psyche at one time and another. How can a writer possibly answer it without the shame of pleading for understanding of one's confusions and limitations and fears? You call it a gap, but that's the time between publications. There is no measurable gap. I never ceased writing, but I destroy much of what I write or I can't work out what I want to say and I put the piece aside. The longing to write and the writing never cease. When I taught to make a living, evenings and years were given over to guiding students through their own imagination, to the neglect of my own. And there's the disbelief, so often at my elbow as I write, that I can write at all.

Do you see yourself primarily as a short story writer rather than a novelist?

Oh, yes. When my first stories were published, there was a lot of enticement from editors to write novels. But I wish I'd written twenty stories to one novel, instead. Short stories and some short novels are close to poetry, with the fewest words they capture the essence of a situation, of a human being. It's like trying to pin down the eternal moment.

Many critics have praised your work for the extraordinary variety of characters and settings, including characters of various races and classes. Do you think your life experience was important in developing that wide scope?

I never thought I had a wide scope. The way to escape from the person who you figure you may be is to become many others in your imagination. And that way you can't be categorized as a regional writer or a Jewish writer or a feminist writer, and even though you may be confined by the circumstances of your life, you're roaming out in the world, your imagination as your guide. I haven't roamed far

enough.

You've said, "Between the lines of every story, readers write their own lines, shaping up the story as a collaborative effort." As the writer, are you concerned about controlling or directing the reader's lines, with the question of a "correct" interpretation?

Of course the writer wishes to compel and persuade and entice and guide the reader to a comprehension of the story, but there's no such thing as a "correct" interpretation of a piece of fiction. That's demanding a scientific precision of the writer. Each reader's interpretation originates in his or her life's experiences, in feelings and emotions of intensely personal history. You get more from what you read as you grow older, and your choices change, and, wiser, you bring more to that collaborative effort.

How about screenplays?

They're so mechanical to write, and you must leave out the depths you try to reach when you're writing your stories. A screenplay is a simplification and an exaggeration at the same time. By contrast, if you slip in a false note in a story, the whole thing falls. But a film can be packed with other persons' demands upon it, become a falsification of the writer's original idea, and then be hailed as one of the year's best—the usual. What makes a film work are the magnified, publicized, idolized actors moving around up there on the screen. And because the influence and the gain from movies are made to seem more real than from your obscure small stories, so many young writers think it's the highest achievement in life to write a movie script.

Were any of the interviews you wrote for Esquire in the Sixties memorable to you? To whom did you talk? In addition to your story **"God and the Article Writer"** *did they have any lasting influence or effect?*

Whom did I interview? I interviewed the topless dancers, the first nightclub topless dancers, not first in the world, of course, but in San Francisco. I remember that an editor at *Esquire* asked me to write an article; they had published some stories of mine, and he said that fiction writers write better articles. So I offered the idea of the topless dancers, who had only recently stepped out onto the stages in North Beach. His "Okay" sounded tentative to me, and so I was very surprised when he phoned a few weeks later wanting to know where the article was. I had only a week in which to research and write, and I got it to them in time. Synchronicity is at work when you're writing an article. Pertinent things—overheard conversations, random meetings—are attracted by your task as by a magnet, and the article shapes up in a surprising way. That's not always the case, but it happens. Then an editor at *Esquire* asked me to interview someone or two who were fallen from the heights and so I found a very elderly couple, man and wife, who had been Broadway entertainers in their youth, and, in their shabby apartment, I looked through their piles of old newspaper clippings and photos; I was moved. I interviewed the student at Stanford who was a leader of demonstrations opposed to the Vietnam War, and I interviewed the men who were the firing squad executioners in Utah, the last firing squad that wasn't, after all, the last. They all wanted anonymity—shame, I suppose—and the photographer took their picture together in silhouette, dark, against a yellow sunset, out in a field. Since I am an outsider, an observer at heart, not an interrogator, I'm not facile at asking people about themselves. And protective as I am of my own secret self, my own personal life, I am reluctant to inquire of others, even though I find that some others don't mind at all telling about themselves. Pride intervenes, too; you feel subservient, at times, to the person you're interviewing, and it was this attitude, this uneasiness, this feeling of being an intruder, that brought about the story **"God and the Article Writer,"** wherein the lowly article writer transcends himself by becoming one with God. It's a bit of a satire and it amused me as I wrote it.

In the more than thirty years you've been writing and teaching, what do you think has been the most significant change in fiction?

One thing that dismays is the cruel pornography of recent novels and how they're considered an honest probe of these desecrating times. What's inspiring is the work of more Black writers and Hispanic writers, and the availability of the small presses and quarterlies. But most of the short stories in most of the large circulation magazines seem about the same as they always were—about the middle class, their mishaps and misapprehensions. An elitism in a vacuum. There's no sorrow and no pity. We're far from writers like Steinbeck and Dos Passos and Nelson Algren. I remember reading *In Dubious Battle* all through the night, I remember just where I was and what period of my life—like a vivid fragment. There's been an intimidation of writers in this country. We write to be acceptable. Some things I wanted to write about, I haven't because I was afraid I wouldn't be published, and writing has been and is my livelihood. I supported myself and my child with my writing. I like to believe that I never misled and that I wrote truthfully, but I've always felt the presence of anonymous and not-so-anonymous authority.

Do you think there is a connection between the superficiality you find in so much writing today and the fact that many writers are academically trained and remain in academia as teachers?

It may be that superficiality results from covert or implicit censorship of our work. The academe isn't to blame, I think. Some very fine writers, prose and poetry, are teaching in universities to keep a roof over their heads and to find pleasure in teaching. Superficial writers seem to make a good living and don't need to teach.

Right now, a first person, present tense style is very popular. How do you feel about it?

I don't look over my past work, or I don't like to. I want to look over my future work. If there is a recurring theme, it's an attempt at compassionate understanding. Judgment is the prevalent theme in our society, but it's from fiction we learn compassion and comprehension.
—Gina Berriault

I imagine that the first person, present tense is the easiest way to write. But to me it seems to contain the most emptiness. It brings a sense of immediacy, and with immediacy you think you've got hold of the truth and the real, and so there's a touch of satisfaction about it, a conceit. Just recently I was looking at Sebastiao Salgado's book of photos, *An Uncertain Grace,* and there was a short introduction by Eduardo Galeano, who wrote "Salgado shows us that concealed within the pain of living and the tragedy of dying there is a potent magic, a luminous mystery that redeems the human adventure in the world." When I read that I thought that's what great writers have always done. Salgado lived in Africa with those suffering people and he lived in Central America. He was right there, where the truth and the real and that luminous mystery are found. It can all be found in this country.

Do you see yourself as a woman writer or as a writer who happens to be a woman? And has your gender affected your career at all, caused you any difficulties?

I've known and still know a fear of men's judgments and ridicule and rejection. At the same time I've been acutely aware of the oppression and abuse and humiliation that men endure and struggle against, the same that women endure and now know they don't have to endure. In other words, I'm a humanist, I guess.

How do you think of your work in relationship to the Women's Movement?

Most of my stories, early ones and later ones, are about women. My wonder and my concern over women are present always in the natural course of my writing.

When you look at your own work, do you think there are

recurring themes?

I don't look over my past work, or I don't like to. I want to look over my future work. If there is a recurring theme, it's an attempt at compassionate understanding. Judgment is the prevalent theme in our society, but it's from fiction we learn compassion and comprehension. In Gogol's great story, "The Overcoat," there's a description of the poor copying clerk's threadbare overcoat, how the cold wind got in across his back. I don't know why those lines move me so much, except when you visualize how the cloth has worn out without his knowing until suddenly one day he's surprised by that cold invasion—isn't that a description of an entire life? That copying clerk is always ridiculed and insulted by the younger clerks. I guess that in my work, in my way, I attempt to rouse compassion for those who are called demented or alien or absurd or ridiculous, for those who are beyond the pale.

I think you do that wonderfully well in your work, especially with the brother in **The Lights of Earth.**

That *was* my brother, and though I told only part of the story, it was the most grueling work I've ever attempted.

Because it is about a woman writer, set in California, and many of the details seem to parallel your life, Lights of Earth seems to be autobiographical. How autobiographical is that novel?

Lights of Earth was an attempt to redeem and forgive myself, and maybe that's what autobiographical novels are all about. But it's impossible that characters and situations and scenes and plots be absolutely true to life. If you attempt that truth then you may be false to your creative spirit which knows how to handle truths in its own way.

Toward the end of **Lights of Earth** *when Ilona receives that healing letter from her daughter, Antonia, the narrator says "For a moment now the earth was hers to know, even as it was known to everyone to whom the earth with all its wonders appeared to belong. A child out in the world can do that for you, can bring you to belong in the world yourself." That second sentence seems to leave Ilona and speak to the reader about life in general in your own personal voice. Is that so?*

Yes, I suppose, and that's probably why, when you first came in and before the interview began, I spoke about my daughter. My child and my writing and others' writings and everyone I've loved, all have brought me to belong in the world.

It seems to me that although your writing is never propaganda, it is indirectly quite political and that you see social or political engagement as essential to serious litera-

ture. Do you agree?

Engagement is the only word you need, because it explains why some of us must write. And political engagement is essential to serious literature as design or perspective or materials are essential to any work of art, but only as an integral part of that engagement, that dedication.

What do you make of the idea, popular in some circles today, that writers should only write about people like themselves, people of their own ethnicity, class, gender, and sexual preference?

How limiting that is—to write only of your own ethnicity, class, gender, sexual preference. Your imagination is left to hang around the sidelines. Say that you're crammed in at a restaurant table with your ethnic friends or friends of the same preferences as yourself, all speaking the same language, and you notice someone, a stranger, out on the street, who's glancing through the window, and your eyes meet his, and you want to get up and go out and say to that stranger, "Don't I know you?"

Publishers Weekly (review date 5 February 1996)

SOURCE: A review of *Women in their Beds: New and Selected Stories,* in *Publishers Weekly,* February 5, 1996, p. 77.

[*The following review provides an evaluation of the collection* Women in their Beds *and short plot summaries of some of the stories.*]

Whether focusing on yuppies or drifters, social workers or Indian restaurateurs, heroin addicts or teenage baby-sitters, Berriault (*The Lights of Earth*) writes with great psychological acuity and a compassion that comes always from observation, never from sentimentality. These 35 short stories have been published in magazines ranging from the *Paris Review* to *Harper's Bazaar,* 10 of them are here issued in book form for the first time. In **"Who Is It Can Tell Me Who I Am?"** the dapper Alberto Perera, "a librarian who did not look like one," fears that the young drifter who has befriended him, wishing to discuss the Spanish poetry he carries in his pockets, is out to kill him; but the drifter is only trying to understand how—both literally and philosophically—to live. A 79-year-old psychologist woos a young, pragmatic waitress in **"The Infinite Passion of Expectation."** When she meets his ex-wife and witnesses the selfishness spawned by a life spent in deferment, she flees. In the clever **"The Search for J. Kruper,"** an extremely famous and narcissistic novelist, noted for writing grand, poorly disguised autobiographical confessions, learns of the possible whereabouts of one of the few remaining living novelists as famous as he, a recluse who betrays nothing of himself in his writings. Each story is constructed so gracefully that it's easy to overlook how carefully crafted Berriault's writing is. Her lilting, musical prose adds a sophisticated sheen to the truths she mines.

Janet Ruth Heller (review date 1 March 1996)

SOURCE: A review of *Women in their Beds: New and Selected Stories,* in *Library Journal,* March 1, 1996, pp. 107-08.

[*In the following review, Heller provides a brief discussion of the collection* Women in Their Beds.]

Despite the title, these stories are not about sex. Using primarily third-person narration, Berriault places her introspective characters in interesting situations to explore a range of themes: dealing with loss, gaining self-knowledge, overcoming mental illness, coping with poverty, and living alone. For instance, **"The Stone Boy,"** which became the basis for a screenplay, concerns the emotional estrangement caused by a boy's accidental killing of his brother. Although most of these 35 stories have been previously published in magazines like *Esquire, Paris Review,* and *Ploughshares,* they are not all successful; some are merely vignettes, lacking conflict and full character development. Recommended for larger fiction collections.

Donna Seaman (review date 15 March 1996)

SOURCE: "The Glory of Stories," in *Booklist,* March 15, 1996, p. 1239.

[*Below, Seaman favorably reviews* Women in Their Beds.]

Berriault's title story contains all the key elements of her metaphysical, compassionate fiction. Angela is deeply affected by the women she works with in a city hospital. Their fates make her think not only about her own sorrows, but about all the complex consequences of what happens to women in beds, from dreaming to sex, childbirth, and death. This elevation from the particular to the universal is a hallmark of Berriault's finely wrought stories. Another motif is a life-altering confrontation with a stranger, such as when a librarian talks about poetry with a homeless man in **"Who is it Can Tell Me Who I Am?"** and a magazine writer attempts to interview a recalcitrant physicist in **"God and the Article Writer."** Outsiders intrigue Berriault; her insights intrigue us.

Tobin Harshaw (review date 5 May 1996)

SOURCE: "Short Takes," in *New York Times Book Review,* May 5, 1996, p. 22.

[*Below, Harshaw gives a mixed review of* Women in Their Beds. *He praises the prose, but finds the characters too static.*]

As an alternative to those trivial compendiums of literary opening passages sold near bookstore cash registers, how about a collection of last lines from Gina Berriault's very short stories, **Women in Their Beds: New and Selected Stories.** Consider this stand-alone triumph: "He lay facedown under the tree and bit off some grass near the roots, chewing to distract his smile, but it would not give in, and so he lay there the entire day, smiling into the earth." Or: "She heard his breath take over for him and, in that secretive way the sleeper knows nothing about, carry on his life." Ms. Berriault is nothing if not consistent. In these 35 stories, one struggles to find a sentence that is anything less than jewel-box perfect. And the author uses her gift for language to do more than show us the world through her characters' eyes; we are also forced to think about it from their point of view—no small feat for someone who favors third-person narration. These are complex characters, and although many stories run only a few pages Ms. Berriault never falls back on clichés: an aging male librarian, for example, is no shrinking violet; instead, he sports "a Borsalino fedora" and "English boots John Major would covet." Most of Ms. Berriault's characters are caught at moments of divergence: in **"Soul and Money,"** a lapsed Communist confronts God and Mammon in Las Vegas; in **"Lives of the Saints,"** the son of a famous religious artist undertakes his own sort of pilgrimage, visiting his father's works, and discovers that life is more lasting than art. Yet in the smooth flow of Ms. Berriault's writing, few of these people manage to register the emotional pitch needed to transcend their crises. It is not a matter of stoicism; instead, most seem dizzyingly unaware of the option to act on their own behalf. Thus the stories, so exquisite to wend through, leave one a little cold. Like their characters, they seem trapped by the perfection of Ms. Berriault's prose.

Lynell George (review date 26 May 1996)

SOURCE: "Secrets Accidentally Spilled," in *Los Angeles Times Book Review,* May 26, 1996, p. 7.

[*In the following favorable review of* Women in Their Beds, *George praises the vivid precision of Berriault's work.*]

In stories that are part trance, part cinema, Gina Berriault writes about the beds we make and are forced to lie in. She explores he choices we squeeze ourselves into, like shoes much too tight; the choices forced upon us by ill timing or unfortunate station.

The homeless "sidewalk sleeper" of **"Who Is It Can Tell Me Who I Am"** shuffling into a San Francisco library with scraps of poetry stuffed into his pockets, demands an explanation. At least someone who can shed light on the enigma of himself. He locks his gaze on a librarian, Alberto Perera, who is peppered with affectation, but full of book-learned philosophy.

Perera, standing at the dawn of retirement—without much self-confrontation—is tidying up his already tidy life. "If you can't, halloo the sun, if you can't go chirpity chirp to the moon . . . what're you doing around here anyway?" demands the homeless man, younger but standing at the twilight of his life.

There is the lonely existence of an anonymous 63-year-old woman, of **"The Diary of K. W.,"** who makes her bed beneath the shared ceiling and floor of the young man with whom she's grown mortally obsessed. Instead of filling a psychiatrist's ear, she crowds the pages of a journal. Her life, like crumbling plaster, rains down on her with each of his heavy footsteps.

These lives in tumult are ostensibly western tales, not romantic elegy but raw testimony from regions that border the Pacific. They are the terrain of extremes—physical as well as emotional—mysterious gray jagged coast robed in fog or the thirsty; sun-bleached deserts that defy anything to grow or prosper.

Berriault explores the roots set down amid the fault lines. She writes of families jolted by unexpected tremors of love and absence, of displaced people marooned on the peripheries.

Much of the body of ***Women in Their Beds*** was resurrected from now out-of-print North Point Press editions amid a sprinkling of newer work. Berriault, whose most famous work, **"The Stone Boy"** is also included in this volume, has achieved the dubious distinction of a writer's writer, praised to the heavens in literary circles, but who moves outside of that orbit incognito.

Her writing, imbued with a haunting resonance, is like a secret accidentally spilled. A poltergeist, she moves lives off foundations, so doors don't shut as cleanly or securely as before. They commence from the middle—after the deed's done, the truth spoken, the promise broken.

This is Berriault's power: poetically interpreting the vivid arc of raw emotion, articulating what hangs in that cramped balance—after revelation and before resolution. Although there are moments when the stories feel so finely tuned that the dialogue too closely matches the cadence of the narrative, she is the master of the poetic utterance of suggestion and what lies in the small space of secrets.

In **"The Houses of the City,"** a little boy, some afternoons after school, shadows his cleaning woman mother. Acutely aware of but too young to fully digest the meaning of the mother's coat and hat draped over a bedroom chair or the bared thigh of the man of the house, the boy accepts the hot chocolate and the conversation. But clues fuel the child's suspicions. He feels his borders threatened, his fear gains life as jealousy. "By such devout observance of her presence," plots the son, "he was proving to her that he was a more loving son than the young man could ever be, no matter how hard the other tried."

Children, in Berriault's vignettes, often trip unexpectedly into the dimly lit living rooms of adult worlds—on the jagged edges of arguments and accusations. The extramarital affairs of parents become the burdensome affairs of the children. It is a theme that occupies Berriault. In the **"Woman In the Rose Colored Dress"** the child overhears the sketchy details of a past planned rendezvous between her father and his lover. In **"The Sublime Child,"** the daughter of a dead mistress and the adulterer fill the space of loss for one another—until bounds are over-stepped. And a long-abandoned paramour at a party confronts the son of an old lover, fishing for her effect, her ultimate impact at the expense of the son and his pain in **"The Mistress."**

But here weakness isn't a mark of evil, it is a sign of humanity, a wound earned in the struggle toward self. It's the parents who break down under the eyes of their children or who fail them (as in **"The Bystander"** or **"The Overcoat"**), daughters who attempt to remove themselves from the folds of their families, the perceived curses of their blood (**"Felis Catus," "Anna Lisa's Nose"**).

Ghosts, impostors, pariahs, Berriault's characters move like somnambulists through their lives. These are the beds, prompts her protagonist from the title story, "Where you wished you weren't and the beds where you wished you were. . . ." Memory recalls the rote particulars, but Gina Berriault's great gift is summoning the pitch and roll of restlessness within which we lie in them.

Gary Amdahl (review date 24 June 1996)

SOURCE: "Making Literature," in *The Nation,* June 24, 1996, pp. 31-32.

[In the following review, Amdahl strongly praises Berriault's

work and asserts that she is a powerful force against the mediocrity of modern fiction.]

In the absence of a certain peculiar force, the American short story declines swiftly toward the uniform. This may be true of all human endeavor, but in the case of our short fiction, the degenerate form has been made to seem the acme of the art. The teaching of it is liturgical, the writing pious and intolerant of deviation, the reading devotional, the publishing straight-faced. It has been one of the most relentlessly banal decades in the history of U.S. literature, but, I'm happy to say, it's over: A collection of new and selected stories by Gina Berriault (serious readers in the late fifties and early sixties will know this name—she wrote three novels and a volume of stories by 1966, another novel and collection after that—but most will not) is good enough not only to be read enthusiastically, reviewed widely and cheered wildly but to inspire as well, and to be as broadly influential as, perhaps, Ray Carver was (the one guy who could do what he did; and I don't mean to imply that Carverism—Raymond as Jesus with Tobias Wolff the Pope presiding over a bureaucracy of celibate workshop directors—is the only thing wrong with short fiction). If she does get the wide notice she deserves, it will have been a long time coming: Having written so beautifully and so consistently for nearly forty years, she ought to be as familiar to us as Toni Morrison and John Updike.

How she does what she does is less easy to say than that she does it magnificently. It is, for instance, difficult to quote her. She does not indulge in fits of fine language connected by ligamentary plot development. Each sentence is as good, as subtly evocative, as poised and full of import and pleasure as the next. Nevertheless, from **"The Island of Ven,"** in which a terribly ill woman visits the Tycho Brahe museum on an island in the Baltic: "a picture of the Astronomer composed itself for her eyes and for her hand someday: up in his observatory, the young Brahe, his face lifted to that brilliancy, to that inescapable portent, its reflection floating in his eyes, and in the gems on his plump fingers, and in the waters of a fountain, and on every leaf turned toward the heavens." And this, from **"Stolen Pleasures,"** a poor young girl's contemplation of her wealthier friend's piano: "The piano, a huge, flat, forbidding face, until her best friend, Ellsworth, across the alley, sat down before it, lifted the long upper lip, baring the long rows of black and yellow teeth clamped together in an unsightly grin, and with nervous fingers picked out cajoling sounds that meant *Please piano, piano, open up a happy future for me, for me, piano, please, for me, for me.*"

Berriault's imagination and her prose (both are cause and effect at once) are as carefully ambitious and elaborate as Henry James's, her meanings and rhythms as closely allied as Cynthia Ozick's. She reminds me too of Barry Hannah,

not so much in the prose itself—Berriault makes a virtue of calm, while Hannah makes one of fever—but in the sense they both give of being somehow unable not to write: A sentence appears before them, and the world spills out of it. Finally it's Chekhov she most calls to mind: Her characters, for the most part, are entrancingly anonymous.

So much current fiction depends on a very narrow understanding of character. Blurb after blurb, review after review, we are assured we will encounter characters we really care about. We will identify with these people because they are just like us. We will bond with them, and share. Berriault, on the other hand, creates characters whom we emphatically do not recognize—or whom we recognize, rather, only in ways that have nothing to do with superficial similarities. (I have had *that* experience! I have known *those* mixed feelings!) Describe them how you will—a struggling actress doing social work in a hospital in the title story; a fussy, overly cautious dandy librarian in **"Who Is It Can Tell Me Who I Am?"**; a classical guitarist at midlife in **"Nights in the Gardens of Spain"**; a fired school food-service worker in **"The Diary of K.W."** (one of my favorites)—these are people we do not know, just as we do not know any but an infinitesimal fraction of the people we see each day. They are not "likable," nor are they "unlikable."

Ozick once wrote of Chekhov that when "his characters strike us as unwholesome, or exasperating, or enervated, or only perverse (especially then), we feel Chekhov's patience, his clarity, his meticulous humanity," and this applies perfectly to Berriault as well. She deals with the inner lives of the perforce invisible, and sees no need to force familiarity upon us. One of the most notable features of her work is the absence of categorization, of description by quick (lazy) reference. There are no brand names, trademarks, franchises, buzz words or jargon here, no free rides on fads, no trading on popular issues or current affairs. No one is "alcoholic" or "abused," much less "recovering." Even age, race and gender are more elusive than you expect them to be. This is not slacker fiction or cyberfiction or domestic fiction, not K Mart realism or minimalism, not magic realism, not postmodernism, not avant-pop. It's not multicultural in the corporate sense, it's unicultural, if you will: not monocultural, not balkanized and not exclusive.

Which is not to say the work is not direct, detailed, specific: "Anonymous" does not mean "general" (or "downtrodden" or "neglected" or "residing on the margins of society"—inner lives do not recognize class distinctions), as this quote should make clear:

> The Judge's voice was cleaving its way through the soiled air, asking legalese questions and informing each of his destination, which asylum, what refuge. Like a scene in any number of plays, where an as-

sassin or a priest comes to tell the prisoner what his future looks like, this was a scene in a debtors' prison for those who couldn't pay back all that civilizing invested in them. She'd been in even closer proximity to this Judge. A wedding reception at the Stanford Court Hotel atop Nob Hill, where she'd carried trays loaded with prawns and oysters up to that buttoned-up belly.

Over in a few minutes, this orderly dispersal of the deranged. The Judge left and she followed at a discreet distance, noting his brisk sort of shuffle, a slight uncertainty of step that came from sitting in judgment for so many years. If she were ever to play a high-court judge on the stage in the park, she'd stuff a bed pillow vertically down her front and take those small steps, the uncertainty in the head repressed all the way down to the feet.

Fiction has never been so poorly read, poorly understood and poorly represented as it is right now: made up, not true, diverting, entertaining, escapist, therapeutic—this is mock fiction, imitations of a thing easily imitated (by the carefree).

Consider the following, from **"The Light at Birth,"** in which a woman, renting a room on the ocean, apprehends the last moments of a very old woman one floor beneath her:

She was wakened in the night by the strangers at the old mother's garden party. Visions of light and of luminous strangers in that light, that was what the dying saw. She knew who they were, those strangers. They were the first of all the many strangers in your life, the ones there when you come out of the dark womb into the amazing light of earth, and never to be seen again in just that way until your last hours. She got up and walked about, barefoot, careful to make no sound that would intrude on that gathering of strangers in the little room, below.

While it may seem a lot to ask of some short stories, **Women in Their Beds** could conceivably vindicate the art, and thereby participate in the saving of the Republic. Whether or not certain kinds of novels and stories train readers in the sympathetic imagining of others' lives—from which spring the civic virtues of tolerance and concern for the welfare of all—can be debated. What is incontrovertible is that Berriault writes real fiction.

The epigraph of her previous collection, **The Infinite Passion of Expectation,** is from Neruda: "and that's how we are, forever falling / into the deep well of other beings." Berriault does not imitate, cater, affect or posture. She deepens reality, complements it and affords us the bliss of knowing, for a moment, what we cannot know.

Additional coverage of Berriault's life and career is contained in the following sources published by Gale: *Contemporary Authors,* Vols. 116 and 129; and *Dictionary of Literary Biography,* Vol. 130.

Dario Fo

Nobel Prize for Literature

Born in 1926, Fo is an Italian dramatist and essayist.

For further information on his life and career, see *CLC,* Volume 32.

PRIZEWINNER

In bestowing the 1997 Nobel Prize for Literature on Italian dramatist, actor, and director Dario Fo, the Awards Committee said, "He if anyone merits the epithet of jester in the true meaning of that word. With a blend of laughter and gravity he opens our eyes to abuses and injustices in society and also the wider historical perspective in which they can be placed." The Committee's award is one of the most controversial decisions in the history of the Nobel Prize. While his broad farce, wild slapstick, and earthy irreverence have made him one of the world's most widely produced contemporary playwrights, Fo's political ideology as a proponent of proletarian revolution has earned him the enmity of the rich and powerful objects of his social and political satires. His style has also deeply divided critical response to his work along political lines. The Swedish Academy addressed this aspect of his work as well: "Fo is an extremely serious satirist with a multifaceted oeuvre. His independence and clear-sightedness have led him to take great risks, whose consequences he has been made to feel while at the same time experiencing enormous response from widely differing quarters." Such divergent groups as the Italian government and police, the Italian Communist Party, the Vatican, and the U.S. State Department have denounced and sanctioned Fo.

Fo's artistic style consists of elements as antipodal as the responses to his work. He draws on the venerable Italian traditions of the medieval *giullari,* itinerant street entertainers, and the more polished ensemble *commedia dell'arte* of the Renaissance to stage polemical works rooted in Marxist ideology. His own background mirrors his antiquarian sources. Fo began his career as an actor shortly after the end of World War II, performing one-man comedy shows in nightclubs and theaters. In the 1950s, in collaboration with his wife, actress Franca Rame, Fo established a touring company, and the couple appeared on Italian television in a popular comedy revue. By the 1960s, the couple was censored for the explicit political content of their routines, and Fo vowed to "stop playing the jester of the bourgeoisie." Amidst the social and political turmoil in Europe in 1968, Fo and Rame formed a new troupe under the sponsorship of the Italian Communist Party. Fo's criticism of the party bureaucracy, however, soon led to a split, and the Fos formed *Il colletivo*

teatrale la comune in 1970.

La comune's explicit goal was to raise the consciousness of the working classes and encourage the overthrow of the bourgeois state to bring about a socialist government. Fo's best-known works come from the early years of this troupe. His signature piece *Mistero buffo* (*Comic Mystery*), first produced in 1969, consists of a series of skits that satirize Italy's institutions of power, including the government and the Pope, as well as farcical inversions of traditional folk tales and biblical morality lessons. Fo's broad international acclaim came with *Morte accidentale di un anarchico* (*Accidental Death of an Anarchist*) in 1970. This was Fo's first play to be produced in both England and the United States, and while the London production was a great success, the Broadway version failed. *Non si paga, non si paga* (1974; *We Won't Pay! We Won't Pay!*), a farce lampooning consumer economics, made its New York debut in 1980. *Clacson, trombette e pernacchi* (1981; produced as *Trumpets and Raspberries* in England and *About Face* in the United States) reworks the Aldo Moro kidnapping into a satire on capitalist/worker relations. During the

1980s, Fo increasingly collaborated with Franca Rame, and their productions have featured Rame's feminist perspective while focusing on male/female relationships. Fo explained the more personal focus of these works when he said, "In the face of the failure of revolutionary ideals, the basic problem is how people relate to one another." Because all of Fo's works rely so heavily on improvisation and audience interaction, each production bears only a general similarity to its published text.

In its zany humor and slapstick exaggeration, Fo's work has been compared with that of Charlie Chaplin, the Marx brothers, and Monty Python. His biting satire and scatological humor have led many to liken him to Lenny Bruce. Some critics have praised Fo's abilities as both writer and performer. "Imagine a cross between Bertolt Brecht and Lenny Bruce, and you may begin to have an idea of the scope of Fo's anarchic wit," said Mel Gussow in *The New York Times* in 1983. Robert Brustein compared Fo's receipt of the Nobel Prize with "giving the prize to Charlie Chaplin. . . . Lenny Bruce also comes to mind, as does Richard Pryor." Italy's best-known theater director, Giorgio Strehler, said, "With Dario Fo, we feel honored as Europeans and as men of the theater." On the other hand, based on the themes of his productions and his explicit political views, the United States refused to allow him into the country, considering him a supporter of terrorism; though he and Rame were allowed to enter for brief visits in 1984 and 1986, the laws under which Fo had been excluded were changed only in 1990. Conservative voices have expressed consternation and even outrage at Fo's selection. Italian literary critic and senator Carlo Bo said, "No one expected this. . . . What does this mean? Everything changes, even literature changes." Marcello Veneziano, editorial writer for the Roman newspaper *Il Messagero*, thought the announcement of Fo as Nobel laureate was a misprint. The Roman Catholic Church, a frequent target of Fo's satire, has been denouncing Fo's works at least since the appearance of *Mistero buffo* in 1969. In 1977, the Vatican called the televised version of the play the "most blasphemous show in the history of television." A spokesperson for the Vatican newspaper *L'Osservatore Roman* said the organization was shocked by Fo's selection for the Nobel Prize: "Giving the prize to someone who is also the author of questionable works is beyond all imagination," the paper read. Stephen Schwartz, as spokesman for another target of Fo's satires, capitalist business, called Fo "an unrepentant hater of capitalism, religion, and common decency." Fo's own response to receiving the award bears no trace of his onstage jester persona: "I'm flabbergasted," he is reported to have said. "I'd be a hypocrite if I told you that I counted on it. I didn't. I didn't expect it at all."

PRINCIPAL WORKS

Gli arcangeli non giocano a flipper [*Archangels Don't Play Pinball*] (drama) 1959

Isabella, tre caravelle, e un cacciaballe [*Isabella, Three Ships, and a Con Man*] (drama) 1963

Mistero buffo [*Comic Mystery*] (drama) 1969

Morte accidentale di un anarchico [*Accidental Death of an Anarchist*] (drama) 1970

Tutti uniti! Tutti insieme! Ma scusa quello non e il padrone? [*United We Stand! All Together Now! Oops, Isn't That the Boss?*] (drama) 1972

Non si paga, non si paga [*We Won't Pay! We Won't Pay!*] (drama) 1974

Il Fanfani rapito (drama) 1975

La giullarata (drama) 1975

Storia della tigre [*The Tale of a Tiger*] (drama) 1977

Tutta casa, letto e chiesa [with Franca Rame; translation published as *Orgasmo Adulto Escapes from the Zoo*] (drama) 1978

Clacson, trombette e pernacchi [*Trumpets and Raspberries*; later *About Face*] (drama) 1981

Female Parts: One Woman Plays (with Franca Rame) (drama) 1981

The Open Couple—Wide Open Even (with Franca Rame) (drama) 1984

Quasi per caso una donna: Elisabetta [*A Woman Almost by Chance: Elizabeth*] (drama) 1984

Harlequin (drama) 1985

Manuale minimo dell'attore [*Basic Handbook for the Actor*] (essays) 1987

The Pope and the Witch (drama) 1989

Il diavolo con le zinne [*The Devil with Boobs*] (drama) 1997

CRITICISM

Ron Jenkins (essay date Spring 1986)

SOURCE: "The Roar of the Clown," in *The Drama Review*, Vol. 30, No. 1, Spring, 1986, pp. 171-80.

[*In the following essay, Jenkins analyzes Fo's "fusion of subversive politics and poetic slapstick."*]

The intellectual complexity and bacchanalian passions of Dario Fo's epic comedy are usually reduced in translation to the flatness of a political cartoon. Even successful productions like Rennie Davis' version of *We Won't Pay! We Won't Pay!* leave the audience with the impression of Fo as a clever satirist whose work can be comfortably categorized as political theater. This limited view ignores the subtler dimensions of Fo's talents. In their original versions Fo's plays are dense with poetic wordplay, visual references to medieval paintings, and sophisticated rhythmic structures that are lost by translators and directors who focus single-mindedly on Fo as a political clown.

Of course, there is a fundamentally political dimension to all of Fo's work, which includes mocking references to police brutality, government fraud, and social injustice. His recurring theatrical allusions to current events reflect Fo's commitment to a theater that is politically relevant, but during the three months that I traveled with him and his company, he rarely spoke explicitly about politics. Rehearsals, seminars, and casual mealtime conversations revolved around topics like the theatricality of regional dialects and the actor/audience relationship. Artistic concerns like these are linked to political issues, but Fo manages to make the connections without waving flags as blatantly as do some of his adaptors abroad. An actress in the New York production of *We Won't Pay* referred to it as a "spoon waving" version of the play, because she was directed to play the role of a housewife by standing on the edge of the stage and waving a spoon at the audience as she lectured them on the evils of capitalism.

Fo's outrage against political and social injustice emerges more obliquely, as in the moment at the dinner table when the company's electrical technician asked him if he believed that people spoke regional dialects because they were too ignorant to speak "proper Italian." Fo responded with a spirited defense of the inherent beauty of the dialects and an attack on the Italian school system's policy of branding the variations as inferior. In his plays Fo uses a poetic blend of regional dialects, and it is clear that the choice reflects his commitment to the celebration of working class popular culture. What Fo's audiences hear onstage, however, is not a didactic manifesto about the "language of the people," but a magnificent cascade of coarse poetry that is an indirect tribute to the lyricism of the dialects spoken in Italy's village markets.

Fo's fusion of subversive politics and poetic slapstick is exemplified in his portrayal of Harlequin. Having been sent by his master to fetch a love potion, Harlequin uses it himself in a visit to a prostitute. When he returns home, Harlequin's disobedience is betrayed by the fantastic and uncontrollable growth of his penis. Using his mimetic talents, Fo creates the illusion that his organ has become almost as big as Harlequin himself. To avoid detection he wraps it in a blanket and pretends it is a baby. All the women in the neighborhood coo and stroke it, resulting in a great comic situation. The focus of the comedy is ostensibly erotic, but at the heart of the piece is the servant's revolt against his patron, the refusal of the impoverished Harlequin to submit to the master's repressive rules. The humor is generated by the tension between Harlequin's fear of his tyrannical master and his pleasure over his enhanced potency. Fo's performance is an allegory of rebellion camouflaged behind a

mask of crude buffoonery. The politics are clear, but they never overwhelm the piece's exquisite slapstick poetics.

Fo blends politics and art with an effortless eloquence that makes him a Brechtian clown. Frequently describing the style of his theater as "epic," Fo borrows Brecht's terminology, but his points of reference go back to the medieval town jesters (*giullari*) and the commedia dell'arte players who were the originators of Italy's epic comedy tradition. Looking to these models for inspiration, Fo has developed a modern style of epic performance that speaks to his audience with the immediacy of a newspaper editorial, shifts perspectives with the fluidity of cinematic montage, and pulsates with the rhythmic drive of a jazz improvisation.

A good example of Fo's epic clowning can be found in his play about the relationship between Shakespeare and Queen Elizabeth, *Elisabetta: Quasi per Caso una Donna.* Shakespeare never appears on stage, but Fo, playing a maidservant, acts out the entire plot of *Hamlet* for the head of Elizabeth's secret police as he explains that it is a veiled satire of the Queen's regime. Playing all the parts himself, Fo uses gestures and gibberish to re-enact the high points of Shakespeare's tragedy in less than two minutes, as if the action were unfolding on high-speed film. The police captain is totally bewildered, and Fo has structured the episode so that the audience identifies the official's dullness with the thickheadedness of modern Italian police investigators. Angered by the abusive mockery of her policies, Elizabeth tries to prevent Fo from recounting his secondhand Hamlet, but the clown is unstoppable. When she grabs his left hand, he continues miming the story behind his back with his right hand, and when she manages to tie up both his arms, he continues gesturing with his feet. The comedy of the scene is rooted in the muscular rhythms of Fo's performance. The Queen's clumsy attempts at physical censorship are no match for the irrepressible satiric impulses of the clown.

This style of densely-layered comedy appears frequently in the plays that Fo writes for his theater ensemble, but the simplest way to isolate the essential techniques of Fo's epic clowning is to look at examples drawn from his solo comic performances. In one-man plays like *Mistero Buffo, Fabulazzo Osceno,* and *Storia della Tigre* Fo demonstrates most clearly his genius for creating theater that unites art and politics in a seamless comic blend. Among the key elements that give Fo's performances their distinctive power are his musically orchestrated rhythms, his montage-like use of multiple perspectives, and the intimately immediate quality of his relationship with his public.

When Fo directs rehearsals of his plays or critiques the work of his students, he always stresses the importance of rhythm. Fo is a musician as well as a playwright, and his theater flows with a dynamic musicality that is generated by the basic emotional impulses of the situations he enacts. For example, his portrayal of a starving man in **The Grammelot of the Zanni** is structured around the rhythms of hunger as experienced by a 14th-century peasant.

The hungry Zanni is so famished that he begins to eat his own body, popping his eyeballs into his mouth and slurping up his disemboweled intestines as if they were pasta in a bowl. The action could easily become mired in infantile grotesquerie, but Fo makes it comic by cannibalizing himself with the rhythmic joy of a big band leader in full swing. The body parts are devoured with tempos of building excitement that culminate in percussive burps or climactic sighs of contentment. Although the piece is extremely funny, there is nothing frivolous about the mood Fo's rhythms evoke. There is never any doubt that the man is in pain, that he suffers not only a hunger for food but also a hunger for dignity and justice.

After consuming himself, the peasant challenges the complacency of God and the audience by threatening to eat them next, but he gets side-tracked by the dream of cooking a feast in an overstocked kitchen. His delirious fantasies are accompanied by the syncopated sounds of gurgling stews and sizzling oils. Fo creates all the effects himself with musical vocalizations that resemble a jazz singer scatting his way through a song. The piece concludes when the famished man wakes up from his dream and satisfies his cravings by eating a fly. He sucks the juice off the wings and savors each morsel of the insect with a primal howl of delight. Fo's performance is comparable to Chaplin's classic routine of eating a boiled shoe in *The Gold Rush*.

Fo's rhythmic pantomime is antithetical to the style of a performer like Marcel Marceau. There is nothing refined, delicate or quiet about a performance by Dario Fo. It is full of crude sounds and coarse gestures expressing human desires and needs. Marceau's technique of pure mime calls attention to itself as something apart from everyday gesture. Fo submerges his technique in a flurry of sounds and movements. He seems to have just come off the subway and invented it all on the spot. Fo is full of passions, obscenities, odors, growls, and desires that could not exist in the rarified world of classical mime. These irrepressible urges give Fo's performances their inner pulse. The comic cadences of the hungry Zanni's actions are inseparable from his struggle to survive.

The earthy rhythms of Fo's style are complemented by his ability to present a story from several perspectives successively rather than from a single point of view. In the enactment of the Zanni's hunger, for instance, Fo first offers the grotesque fantasy of the man eating himself, then shifts to the pleasurable dream of a giant kitchen, and concludes with the stark portrait of a starving man eating a fly. All of this

is presented in the context of a political/historical explanation for the man's hunger presented by Fo in his introductory prolog.

The shifts of perspective are intentional. Like Brecht, he wants his audience to see a situation from a variety of viewpoints so they can reflect on its multiple aspects, instead of simply losing themselves in empathy for a single point of view. In describing the way his epic style of characterization differs from traditional acting, Fo uses the analogy of a sculptor carving a statue. As a performer he circles a situation the way a sculptor circles an unfinished statue, examining the way the lights and shadows are formed when viewed from different directions.

Fo's technique of shifting perspectives is equivalent to cinematic montage. One of the most vivid examples of Fo's multiple-perspective storytelling is his satire of the attempted assassination of the Pope. Alone on the stage without props, Fo recreates the scene of the Pope's arrival in Spain. Fo becomes the people shouting their greetings in the welcoming crowd. Fo becomes the Pope's airplane, advertising its sacred passenger with a giant papal cap on top of its wings. Fo becomes one of the peasants explaining to another that the magnificently attired plane is not the Pope, but that the Pope is inside the plane. Images and characters appear and dissolve with a rapidity that gives the audience the impression of watching a televised news report of the event, with the camera angles changing every few seconds.

The Pope emerges from the door of the plane. Fo both portrays and describes him, presenting the scene in first and third person simultaneously. After showing the Pope in all the splendor of his jewels and colored robes, Fo slips out of the story completely to recount a newspaper article he had read recently that criticized the Pope's taste for opulence as the opposite of Christ's renunciation of material pleasures. Fo then quotes the Bible story in which Jesus was tempted by the devil with the power to fly all over the world. "Jesus said no to the devil," quips Fo, "but the Pope says 'yes'." Continuing to mock the Pope's incessant world travels, Fo jokes that "God is everywhere, but the Pope's already been there."

Moving back to the newsreel images of the Pope, Fo portrays the gunman, the Bulgarian agents with walkie-talkies directing the gunman, the police asking the gunman what he is doing with the bullets, and the gunman replying that they are a new kind of rosary bead. He says a prayer as he loads each one into the chamber, and the guards leave him alone. Fo then resumes the role of narrator to wonder aloud why no one was able to stop the gunman, given that so many photographs were taken of him in varying phases of preparation for the assassination. Fo becomes a series of still photographs leading up to the gunshots, and he then acts out the fall of the wounded Pope, the television commentators announcing that the Pope has been shot in the sphincter, and the outraged Vatican spokesman who refuses to acknowledge that the Pope has a sphincter, insisting instead that the Pope's bowels should be referred to as a divine conduit.

Fo's looney tune version of the shooting leads to another quick change of perspective, this one more drastic, taking the audience to the twelfth century and the Papacy of Pope Boniface VIII. Fo's story is a 12th-century illustration of the 20th-century newspaper column describing the Pope as the opposite of Christ. Boniface is presented as he prepares himself for a public appearance, adorning himself in fine clothes, expensive rings, and elegant robes. When the Pope's procession meets the humbler procession of Jesus, Fo portrays Boniface's hypocrisy by showing him unrobing and covering himself with mud in feigned humility before Christ.

Up until the meeting with Jesus, Boniface has been satirized for his vanity and arrogance. When altar boys wrinkle his clothes he threatens to hang them by their tongues, a punishment, Fo explains, actually used by Boniface to deal with religious dissidents. Fo uses this graphic image as a recurring bit of black comedy. Each time the altar boys displease him, Boniface mimes hanging them by their tongues. Fo mimes hammering the tongue into the wall, then his hands become the tongue swinging in the wind. Next he transforms himself into a boy as he would appear if his body were hanging suspended from the tongue.

By shifting from the subject to the object of the threat and from the close-up of the tongue to a long shot of the hanging victim, Fo tells the story as if he were a camera shooting the scenes. The sequence is repeated several times throughout the piece from different angles and for shorter durations, as if miniature flashbacks of the original threat were inserted into a corner of the stage. With such montage techniques Fo insures that the audience never gets lost in the characterization of the Pope and is continually reminded of the contextual frame of religious tyranny within which the action takes place.

Fo talks to the public directly through prologs, intentional narrative interruptions, and improvised responses to spontaneous situations that arise onstage. Fo's intimate rapport with large crowds gives his performances an immediacy that elicits the public's active involvement in an ongoing dialog of ideas. Fo challenges the audience with a phrase or gestures, and they respond with laughter or applause. Using his public as a collaborator, Fo structures his monologs with the rhythms of their responses in mind. During his performances the integration of the audience seems unplanned, but when Fo advises other actors of his material in rehearsals, he explicitly directs them to anticipate the public's response at specific moments. Rehearsing monologs with student actors,

Fo will play the role of the audience responding to each line, so that the student learns to transform the monologs into a dialog with the public.

The immediacy of the audience is central to Fo's retelling of the miracle when Jesus turns water into wine. Fo initially presents two competing storytellers. One is an angel who tells the official version of the story in a detached style that does not take into account the public's desires. The other storyteller is a drunk who claims to have been present at the miracle and offers an earthy account of the celebration that speaks more directly to the audience's spirit of revelry. The drunk plucks the angel's feathers, chases him away, and proceeds to tell his Dionysian version of the miracle, emphasizing the pleasures of drinking wine with an inebriated ecstasy that serves as a direct call to the senses of his audience. He invites them to feel, smell, and taste the wine with him as he relives the pleasures of Jesus' miracle. In one sequence he drinks wine as if bathing in it, mimes the passage of the red liquid as it seeps through his veins, and expresses the depth of his pleasure with a gigantic burp that sends the aroma of the wine across the countryside. In a cinematic transition the expansive burp opens up the landscape of the action, and Fo presents the trail of the wine's aroma leading to a man on horseback who smells it and shouts out with gratitude, "Jesus sei di / vino" ("Jesus you are divine / of wine"). Fo's vocal and visual shifts have been building up to this climactic shout, which inevitably results in applause from the audience appreciating the pun. The sequence is structured in a way that would render its rhythms incomplete without the culminating punctuation of the audience's gleeful response.

Arguing that drinking wine could never be a sin if Jesus offered it to his mother, the drunk is implicitly urging the public to challenge the angel's pious attitudes and celebrate the liberating effects of wine. To strengthen his argument, the drunk reasons that Adam and Eve would never have been tempted by the snake to eat the apple if there had been wine in the garden for them to drink. The performance is a masterpiece of comic rhetoric designed to persuade the audience to abandon the angel's puritan point of view and accept a more joyous vision of religion. As the story progresses, the drunk's argument becomes funnier and more reasonable at the same time. The public is swayed by his comic logic about Adam in the garden of Eden: if Adam had been like the drunk, the human race would still be living in Paradise. Fo's success in persuading the audience can be measured in their roars of laughter and applause at moments like the horseman's yell.

Fo weaves the technical elements of his epic clowning into a dense theatrical tapestry in which politics and poetry are inseparable. His comic rhythms grow out of the dialectic between freedom and oppression that is at the core of the stories he tells. Each slapstick crescendo is orchestrated around a liberating triumph over injustice. Generated by the conflict between the powerful and the powerless, the frantic tempo of Fo's farces is an implicit tribute to his characters' abilities to outwit their oppressors and survive.

Fo's montage-like use of shifting perspectives is linked to his political beliefs. Presenting a situation from multiple points of view enables him to emphasize the relationship between individual behavior and its cultural context. The theatrical jump-cuts in Fo's performances suggest a complex interaction between history, economics, religion, morality, and mundane current events. Fo's comedy exists at the overlap between the private and the public domains.

The relationship between Fo and his audiences reveals another aspect of this overlap. The public is included in the performance because Fo believes in their intelligence. He speaks to them with a direct and candid simplicity that transforms spectators into Fo's co-conspirators against injustice.

All of Fo's techniques coalesce in the powerful conclusion to his story of Jesus and the wine. Having just presented Adam's rejection of the Serpent in favor of a glass of wine, the drunk offers a toast to God, the audience, and the earth beneath his feet. Tilting the glass to the public, Fo is graciously thanking them for their involvement. Pouring a few drops on the ground he is paying homage to the earthy impulses that stand in opposition to the repressive censorship of the angel he battled at the beginning of the piece. And raising the glass toward heaven he shifts the focus from the mundane to the spiritual world. This simple, skyward motion is the last gesture of the story, and it is charged with startling eloquence. Having defied the authority of heaven, the buffoon strikes a pose that momentarily transforms him into an angel in spite of himself. The closing sequence epitomizes the spirit of Fo's epic clown in the breadth of its vision, the depth of its feeling, and the generosity with which it embraces the world beyond the stage.

Pina Piccolo (essay date Summer 1988)

SOURCE: "Dario Fo's *giullarate:* Dialogic Parables in the Service of the Oppressed," in *Italica,* Vol. 65, No. 2, Summer, 1988, pp. 131-43.

[*In the following essay, Piccolo focuses on the binary theatrical technique,* giullarata, *which alternates between a narrative voice and quotes from various characters, and examines the connection between dialogue structure and the type of knowledge it yields.*]

The production of knowledge useful to the oppressed has

been one of Dario Fo's foremost concerns throughout his career. While the grotesque has been his all-encompassing paradigm and demystification his main aim, in his post-1968 production Fo uses two distinct dramatic structures to convey different types of knowledge. Elements of the farce and of the *giullarata* are present and mixed in all of his works, but Fo predominantly uses the former structure when he wishes to provide counter-information about specific political events. The latter structure is more useful in conveying a general type of knowledge stemming from universal divisions, as, for example, the dichotomy oppressor/oppressed, dominant/subordinate, hero/villain, and so on.

Thus, for example, the farce structure is used to demystify the events surrounding Pinelli's death (***Morte accidentale di un anarchico***), the historical repercussions of pursuing a class-collaborationist policy (***Tutti uniti! Tutti insieme! Ma scusa quello non è il padrone?***), or to expose the power base of and the divisions in the Christian Democratic party (***Il Fanfani rapito***). The mechanical qualities of the farce, its paroxystic rhythm, and its alogical sequences aptly reproduce the modus operandi specific to contemporary bourgeois politics. However, when problems related to an ideological stand and a world view arise, the dialogic structure of the *giullarata* provides the binary framework needed to focus attention on the clash of interests between oppressor and oppressed.

Closer investigation of the link between type of knowledge and dramatic form is useful to a better understanding of Fo's choices as well as to the exploration of issues that have been neglected in the study of popular theater. In attempting to formulate a typology of Fo's *giullarate,* this article will examine the connection between dialogue structure and the type of knowledge it yields. Bakhtin's findings on the grotesque in general and on the Menippean satire in particular will serve as backdrops against which to project Fo's indebtedness to tradition as well as to explore his innovative contributions.

Mistero buffo

Staged for the first time in 1969, **Mistero buffo** is one of Fo's most performed and better known theatrical pieces. It represented the culmination of years of experimentation as well as the re-elaboration of theatrical techniques that were part of Fo's own cultural background. It is in the preparatory stages of **Mistero buffo** that the figure of the *giullare* made his first appearance as the Fo-Rame theater company consciously began to research and explore the significance of popular culture. The company was not isolated in these efforts. In fact the 60s were years in which Gramsci's theory of cultural hegemony and his formulations on the creation of an autonomous proletarian culture prior to and as a prerequisite for a political revolution were being debated and applied by thousands of progressive intellectuals.

In previous years both Fo and Rame had collaborated with musicologists and ethnographers in the travelling show series *Ci ragiono e canto,* a very successful nation-wide attempt to salvage songs belonging to the popular tradition. In Fo's case, exposure to the oral tradition of the *fabulatori* was an integral part of his personal background both as a child and as a young man. Sediments of the *fabulatori*'s tales were in fact at the base of his early reversals of point of view as expressed in the radio show *Poer nano* (1952), which earned him broad artistic recognition for the first time. In the show Fo used the structure of a narrator's running commentary, punctuated by the voicing of the characters' exchanges in an "in quote" fashion. The dialogues aimed at reversing traditional verdicts given on historical or mythological figures such as Cain and Abel, Isaac and Jacob, Garibaldi, and so on. This structure was to serve as a rudimentary base for Fo's later *giullarate.*

In **Mistero buffo** this spontaneous alternation between narrator and quoted dialogue found a theoretical justification. According to Fo, the task of contemporary progressive artists was, in fact, to ally themselves with the cause of the oppressed by lending their artistic skills to express the experiences and point of view of the underdog. Using Gramscian analytic categories, Fo insisted that historically the *giullari* were a type of intellectual with organic ties to the oppressed classes; consequently, the artistic structures they create were "of the people" rather than "for the people." Similarly, Fo wished to become a modern day *giullare del popolo,* relying on forms developed by popular tradition and that were being destroyed by the advent of mass culture created by the bourgeoisie. In **Mistero buffo,** Fo appeared in the role of a modern day *giullare,* alone on the stage, in a bare setting, lending his voice both to the commentator and to characters "quoting" from the Bible. The latter were recreated through a mixture of dialogues taken from medieval texts steeped in the grotesque of the carnivalesque tradition while making references to contemporary events. The bareness of the stage helped keep the focus on the actor, who, through a shifting of the body and a change in facial expression, signaled that different characters were being quoted. Fo's device required an active type of listening on the part of the audience and helped concentrate attention on the relation between the dialoguing voices by pursuing relentlessly the differences in social position, objectives, and class interests as they became manifest in the development of a particular situation.

According to Bakhtin, the dialogue has been used since antiquity as an especially effective tool in focusing philosophical questions; suffice it to think of the Socratic dialogues. In those works, the literary form of dialogue had been posited not so much as an aesthetic device but rather as part of the epistemological process itself. In fact, one of the premises set in those narratives was that knowledge was not an "object" already possessed by any of the dialoguing voices, but rather it was to be discovered in the process of clashing views. In the Menippean satire, a later development of the Socratic dialogues, usually a wise man would be placed in a threshold situation, i.e., in an extraordinary set of circumstances such as the moments preceding one's own death, in which one is freed from a mechanical and objectified participation in life. From this "cleansed" perspective, then, the character would engage in a dialogue with the dead or with other unusual interlocutors, debating deep philosophical questions. The loftiness of the undertaking was usually counterbalanced by what Bakhtin calls elements of slum naturalism, as, for example, the use of everyday language or references to contemporary events. These lessons from the popular traditions reached Fo through his exposure to the *fabulatori* who employed similar techniques.

In the pieces composing **Mistero buffo** Fo used as his foundation theatrical pieces, poems, and narratives from medieval popular tradition collected in various parts of Europe and in various regions of Italy. Such heterogeneity was counterbalanced by Fo's uniform use of an invented fourteenth-century dialect that utilized the syntax and words found in the Po Valley. Following the style of Menippean satire, the halo of loftiness potentially deriving from the antiquity of the texts was mitigated by continuous reference to contemporary events and issues.

Significantly, in the introduction, Fo gave a justification for his enterprise: the necessity for the Marxist movement to form an alliance with the progressive grassroots Catholic movement so that "the rich will inherit neither the kingdom of heaven, nor this world." This call for a programmatic alliance brought to the fore ideological questions connected to the tradition of resistance shared by both the workers' movement and the grassroots Catholic movement in regards to power and institutions. Thus, a concrete dialogue between these two very important trends in Italian society was aptly initiated in the form of a theatrical dialogue.

When observed from the point of interlocution and content, the dialogues composing **Mistero buffo** can be divided into three broad categories: (1) the two-voiced dialogues of clashing interests; (2) the two-voiced dialogues leading to the banding together of the oppressed; (3) polyphonic dialogues creating a choral sense of the experiences of the oppressed. Thus, in the first category the dialogic, binary structure emphasizes division, dissent, and irreconcilability. In the latter two, instead, it underlines unification and a blending of the diverse. These two operations can fundamentally be linked to the functioning of the grotesque, the underlying paradigm of Fo's entire work.

In keeping with the Menippean tradition, the dialogues of *Mistero buffo* confront rather broad issues, all of which converge on and center around the question of power. In contrast to the farce which mobilizes its proteiform inclination for coup de théâtre, quick tempo, disguise, and the alogical, all of which lead to dispersion, the dialogue has the power to concentrate, to keep the focus on a particular relation. In this case, the binary oppression/resistance is the dominant one. In fact, Roberto Nepoti has observed that in spite of their seemingly historical focus, in the *giullarate* counter-history is not the primary aim, but rather the challenge to point of view, imposed by those in power and in many cases unquestioningly accepted by those in a subordinate position.

Unlike the Socratic dialogues which posited a lack of a prior truth, in *Mistero buffo* the oppressed are the holders of truth while the powerful represent its negation and usurpation by force. This conflict-laden division is particularly true in the dialogues of the first type, while the possibility of ignorance or error is more likely to be found in the absence of the oppressor, in the dialogues of "banding together."

Thus, the conduct of the oppressed, rather than performing a counter-information function, acts as a parable to the modern day inheritors of the oppressor/oppressed division. Fo's understanding of the importance of exampla perhaps explains the preference he accords to the reversal of historical, biblical, or mythological episodes. Because of the weight of tradition exampla from the past have usually been incorporated at a very deep, almost unconscious, level and serve as stronger models of behavior than episodes of contemporary life.

Mistero buffo: *The Conflict*

The episode in *Mistero buffo* that perhaps is based most explicitly on the clash of point of view is the altercation between the Angel and the drunkard as each tries to recount the miracle performed by Christ at the wedding at Cana. The winged, elegant creature starts off with a lofty, condescending prologue aimed at gathering the people to hear the story: "Deime rason . . . bona zente . . . 'scoltime con atenzion imparchè ve voj contare. . . ." Interrupted by the loud remarks of the drunk who is praising the effects of the abundant libations in which he himself indulged at the wedding, the Angel loses his initial magnanimous tone and escalates his threats against the drunk, first with a "in silensio," then "cito," and finally with a "vaj si no te vol che at trage fora a pesciadi. . . ." Seizing the opportunities offered by the physical attributes of the celestial creature, the drunk starts defeathering him and then launches into a first person, earthy description of the wedding. In contrast to the Angel who had declared that his story was true because it was taken from the Holy Book, the drunk relies on his own experience. Thus, from the start the truth is established not through authority but through experience. Furthermore, the discourse of power is shown to be double-faced, pretending loftiness and magnanimity but in reality resorting to force.

Even though the latter part of the altercation episode is an *a solo* by the drunk, the implied contrasting voice is the New Testament version of the facts. The wealth of observations deriving from the grotesque's "lower bodily stratum" in the monologue of the drunk can be seen as a parody of the lofty monologues concerning deep philosophical questions or tragic choices typical of the monologues of the elevated tradition. Oppression is experienced by Fo's characters as a class phenomenon rather than as an individual condition. Thus, the monologues are not structured as "internal debates"; they are never soliloquies but, rather, narrations directed to others.

Another important altercation in *Mistero buffo* involves the Madonna and the Archangel Gabriel at the foot of the cross. God's emissary approaches Mary to give his condolences, and fearing that he won't be recognized, reintroduces himself with a lofty speech: "Gabriel, l'angiol de deo, sent mi quelo vergen, ol nunzi d'ol to solengo e delicat amor." Unmoved by the lyrical tone, the Madonna responds with an invective, relying again on the opportunities afforded by Catholic iconography: "Torna a slargat i ali Gabriel, torna indre al to bel ciel zojoso che no ti g'ha riente a far chi loga in sta sgarosa tera, in stu turmento mundo." With the obtuseness typical of power, the Archangel continues his consolatory rhymes: "Dona indulurada . . . che fin 'ndol venter t'ha scarpada ol patiment, oh mi ol cognosi ciaro sto turment che t'hait catat mirand ol segnor zovin deo inciudat. . . ." Undaunted, the Madonna rebuffs the Angel's claim to equal suffering: "At n'è sgagniat ti i labri par no criar di duluri 'ndol parturil? At l'ahit nutregat ti? Dait de teta ol latt, ti, Gabriel?"

As in the previous episode, the oppressed relies on the data of his/her own experience while the powerful rely on vicarious, surrogate knowledge. The diversity in the experience of the oppressed also gives the playwright varied materials to compose his examples of resistance: thus the drunk relies on scatological metaphors of abundance, the *mater dolorosa* on the pain and sacrifice of a woman's biological experience. This diversity contributes to mitigate the didactic weightiness of each parable.

In the farce, on the other hand, exchanges of contrast exhibit greater mobility. For example, in *Morte accidentale di un anarchico,* both in the monologues and in the exchanges, Il Matto relies on a multiplicity of discourses to subvert point of view: one need only think of his appropriation of the specialized languages of the grammarian, of the psychologist, of police bureaucracy, of the army, of the church. While in the *giullarate* there is a certain uniformity within each episode so that one can expect a response deriving from the direct experience of each character, the farce is freed from such logical limitations, as is expected from a genre that is dispersive in character. Even in the monologues present in the piece, one can detect a broader range of experiences. For example, in the monologue leading to the description of judges, Il Matto gives the audience an entire catalogue of the effects of old age on workers ranging from miners to bank clerks. In contrasting the credibility of retired workers vs. old tycoons in the eyes of the law, Il Matto relies not on direct experience but on lists of popular images of the lifestyles of each category as the purpose of the play is counter-informational rather than exemplary.

Mistero buffo: The Alliances

The episode of the blind man and of the lame man belongs to the category of "alliance" dialogues. Two beggars, one blind and the other lame, are stranded in a square; each laments his misfortune to a passerby. As the lame man invokes the wheels of God, the blind man nears him and devises a system by which they can assist one another: the blind man will carry the lame man who in turn will guide them both. The language of the lower bodily stratum dominates as the maneuverability of the human machine proves problematic; however, the mood of alliance between the two eventually prevails. The alliance increases as they realize they are approaching Jesus, a warlock with a great reputation for healing the unfortunate. The lame man, particularly mindful of his long-range interests, suggests that they move on quickly: "Pensaghe un poc, se davero ghe cata a tuti e doj la desgrazia de ves liberadi di nostri desgrazi. D'un boto ag strovariam in la cundision d'es obligat a tor via un mestier per impoder campare." Both of the marginalized characters concur in their assessment of the reaction of the world of labor to an eventual healing:

> At gnirat miracolat, bon, e at tocherà crepar de fame
> . . . che toeti i te criaran: vagj'a lavorar!
>
> . . . Vagj a lavorar vagabondo . . . i te diserà . . .
> brasce robade a la galera . . . e a perderesmio ol gran
> previlez che g'avemo in pari ai siori, ai paroni, de
> tor gabela: lori col slongar i truchi de la lege,
> nojaltri con la pità. Li doi a gabar cojoni!

In the dialogue one clearly hears a common heritage on the part of the beggars as they confront the question of work. A communion of interests sets them apart both from the workers and the masters, and from the vantage point of their marginality they can mimic the voices of the other classes. Commonality also reigns in the polyphonic dialogues, for example, in the resurrection of Lazarus. It opens with the protests of a late spectator who is confronted at the gate of the cemetery by the avaricious custodian who wants to

charge him both an entrance and a seating fee. As the place begins to fill, a woman warns: "uei scomingion mica a spinger," while other smothered voices speculate about the Messiah's arrival. As Christ appears on the scene one hears his description from the point of view of the dialoguing spectators:

> —Ol riva!! a l'è chi . . .
>
> —L'è quelo là? . . .
>
> —Si, quelo cont la barbeta bionda . . . oh me l'è
> zovin . . . ol par un bagai . . . E quela l'è la sua
> mama de lu . . . voj!! Bela dona eh?

As attention moves to the miracle about to be performed, one complaining voice alludes to the forward movement of the crowd: "No sti a sping . . . am versit buta anc mi la tomba?" Meanwhile, other voices are heard complaining on account of the stench of the decomposing body, and others bet on Jesus' ability to perform a miracle. However, not everybody is fully satisfied by Jesus' miraculous performance: a chronic complainer prefers John the Baptist's showman qualities: "o quel si che ne faseva de quei . . . che miracol fioi! Roba de no crederghe! pecad che g'han taiad ol colo. . . ." It is the human demand for the marvelous of the transcendent invoked to counter human limitations that brings together the world of spectacle and of magic. It allows Fo to be ironical as he gives a choral representation of the world of the oppressed in which idiosyncrasies, ignorance, and quirks are admitted in the absence of the voice of power that needs to be contrasted.

The sense of dispersion typical of the farce can also be found in the choral dialogues, in contrast with the fixed focus of the contrast dialogue. In the choral dialogues, one can observe a great degree of mobility, and the tendency for dispersion is encouraged by the great number of voices heard. For example, lines are not necessarily a reply to a previous one; in fact, they often lead to changes in direction that seem homologous to the coups de théâtre of the farce.

The enthusiasm for challenging the oppressor's point of view that characterizes especially the "conflict dialogues" can be put in relation to the tendencies of the historical period in which they were performed. A fertile terrain for parables of resistance with positive outcomes for the oppressed was provided by the experiences of the Chinese Cultural Revolution and by the 1968 widespread rebellion of the youth in Europe and in the U.S. The focus on common elements present in the experience of the oppressed, whether they be the resistance of Catholics held down by the institution of a Church favorable to the rich (illustrated by the Boniface VIII episode in *Mistero buffo*), or the insubordination of workers, was aimed at forming an alliance in the name of defiance of power. At a time when on a world-wide scale powerful institutions and nations were being challenged (the resistance of the Vietnamese people, the Cultural Revolution, Black struggles in the U.S., etc.), Fo dramatized through his parables the strength of the people when it is defiant, united, and cognizant of its interest. Already by the mid-seventies, however, a new set of ideological problems would beset the revolutionary movement and its theatrical space.

Parables of the 70s and of the 80s

The shift in the ideological climate of the revolutionary movement was already very evident by 1977. This change could also be noticed in the tone of the dialogic parables that Fo performed in that period. *Storia della tigre* was first performed at a nation-wide meeting of different anti-institutional organizations and individuals which met in Bologna in September 1977 in a convention against repression.

The protagonist and narrator of *Storia della tigre* is a Chinese soldier, wounded and left behind by his comrades during the Long March. The soldier finds refuge in a cave and falls asleep, only to be awakened by the loud return of its legitimate occupants, a tiger and her half-drowned cub. A rather inarticulate exchange ensues between man and beast, an exchange based on fear and misunderstanding. Gradually the model switches to one of "skeptical" cooperation as the tiger and the soldier discover they can be of mutual help. In fact, the tiger heals the soldier by licking the wound with her medicinal saliva and in turn the soldier introduces the wild beasts to the refined taste of cooked meat. When the soldier is well enough, he leaves the cave and attempts to find his guerilla detachment. Angered by the sudden departure of the soldier, the tigers follow him into town and they help him drive away the Kuomintang forces that had descended into the village. The tigers are then borrowed by all neighboring villages whenever the Kuomintang tries to invade. The dialogue then switches to one of conflict when local party authorities insist that the tigers be sent away; their vigilance is no longer needed because the party, now in power, will rule in the interest of the people:

> Bravi, bravi! Questa invenzion de la tigre l'è straordinaria. Il popolo ha un inventiva e un'immaginazione, una fantasia che nessun g'ha! Bravi! Bravi! Adesso le tigri però, non si possono più tenere con voi, bisogna mandarle nella foresta come erano prima.

Disregarding the people's protests, the bureaucrat insists:

> Non possiamo, le tigri, sono gente anarcoide, mancano di dialettica, non ci possiamo dare un ruolo alla tigre nel partito, e se non può star nel partito, non può star neanche nella base. Dialettica

non g'ha. Ubbidite al partito. Mettete le tigri nella foresta. (*Storia della tigre* 56)

Feigning obedience to the authorities, the cunning people hide the tigers in a chicken coop and camouflage them as roosters. This causes the formalistic-minded bureaucrat who is inspecting the chicken coop to record them as specimens of "Gallo tigrato." The story continues with other episodes that illustrate the necessity to be self-reliant and to never delegate one's interests and power to the authorities. Fo's shift from an optimistic call to defy authority to one to be self-reliant and resist the attacks of the powerful seems to stem from changes occurring in the world situation, such as the setbacks suffered in China by the revolutionary forces after Mao's death, and in the Italian situation, of increased repression following the Legge Reale, as well as the ideological confusion within the movement.

A further menace to the weakened movement was the defection of many youths who reacted to the setbacks by escapism and utopian solutions. Fo addressed this problem by relying directly on and re-elaborating a dialogue of the Menippean tradition. The dialogues written by Lucian of Samosata consisted of exchanges between Icarus and Lucian himself. Fo's revised version starts on the model of a family altercation as Icarus reproaches his father for having built the labyrinth in which they are imprisoned. After numerous unsuccessful attempts to find the way out, they are able to emerge into the open air, and attracting the birds passing by, they gather raw materials to make the wings needed to escape. Icarus seeks (literally) a flight to utopia. Upon seeing an island at a distance, he says: "Che bela è! Gh'è pescadori . . . varde, dei contadini . . . Varda, anco qui a gh'è i solda! Varda che i masa! E le preson piene! Patre, scapemo! Dai, patre, andemo, scapo!"

Dedalus tries to counter his son's impulse to flee from conflict by advising him to land on the problem-ridden island:

> Perchè a l'è inutile andare cercando un'altra isola nova . . . bela . . . dove tuto l'è aprontà, tranquilo. Dove te rive e i te dise: "Bona sera, vegne, te speciava!" No! No! troverai gimai l'isola tranquila già fata! Ne toca farla . . . farla co' le mani dentro la palta . . . dentro el sangu . . . nei sogni trovar isole. Vegne, 'des.

The allegorical stance of both pieces, the first recommending self-reliance, the second persistence, unmistakenly refers to contemporary problems then facing the movement. The shift was also one in which conflict among the oppressed as to how to proceed replaced the unified version of *Mistero buffo* in which the main division was between oppressor and oppressed.

In later *giullarate* and monologues like ***Fabulazzo osceno*** and ***Una madre*** the situation of confusion and retreat among the revolutionary forces was mirrored by both the heterogeneity of Fo's material and changes in the structure of the monologues, giving more space to the reflections of the commentator. For example, in ***Fabulazzo osceno*** Fo's programmatic intention is to harness the liberating effect of the obscene as a revolt against the methods and categories deemed respectable by the authorities. The materials gathered for this purpose are extremely heterogeneous, ranging from a Provençal fabliau and a Menippean tale by Lucian of Samosata, both based on issues of sexual politics, to a chronicle of the "revolt of Bologna," based on a medieval historian's counter history, to the imagined monologue of Ulrike Meinhoff in her final hours before her "suicide" by the West German State. The elaboration of themes that are not "political" in the institutional sense of the word suggest the influence of issues brought to light by the feminist movement and by various post-structuralist currents originating in France. The fragmentation and lack of organic center mirror in a sense the loss of the fairly unified version that had characterized the early stages of the '68 révolts. In fact, as the optimistic unitary focus on example of defiant and victorious resistance shifted to more problematic grounds, the situation in Fo's fables shifts to ones in which the hero's or the heroine's relation to knowledge as well as his/her relation to power is tested. Thus the Menippean wise man is increasingly transformed in Fo's stock naïve/cunning characters whose relation to knowledge grows in the course of a journey (as, for example, "il Lungo" of ***Gli arcangeli non giocano a flipper***).

In the monologue ***Una madre,*** co-authored with Franca Rame, (1983) Fo seems to combine the counter-informational qualities of the farce with the prescriptive bent of the *giullarata*. A more complex approach towards knowledge is seen in *Una madre,* whose protagonist is a mother who has just learned from a newscast that her son has been arrested and charged with membership in the Red Brigades. As she travels through the world of emergency legislation, she faces isolation from her former comrades, who buckling under the pressure of the backlash, proclaim they understood the naiveté and futility of the '68 movement, that they foresaw its inevitable culmination in terrorism. Unlike the heroines of ***Mistero buffo,*** the mother does not rely solely on her own experiences. In fact, throughout the story, to illustrate the desperate situation of Italian youth, she draws a continuing parallel between her situation and that of the mother of a young drug addict, another victim of the political and economic crisis. Once again the form of the dialogue is used to express a shared sense of suffering. As she faces the judge in the final lines, she also raises a critique of the institutional role of motherhood:

"Signora, dovè il detenuto bambino? Lei è responsible . . . lo aveva in custodia!"

Affondo la mano sotto il livello della nebbia: "Eccolo! L'ho preso! Signor giudice!"

Ma questo non è mio figlio! È il ragazzo drogato . . . Sanguina! Ha il corpo cosparso di ustioni! Che è successo?!

"Mi hanno torturato! Mi hanno bruciato anche i testicoli! Voglio sporgere denuncia contro cinque poliziotti!"

"Taci! È mio figlio! L'ho preso signor giudice! Ho catturato mio figlio! Ho fatto il mio dovere di cittadina democratica che ha fiducia nelle istituzioni! Oh! Mi spiace . . . L'ho stretto troppo! L'ho strangolato! È MORTO!"

In ***Una madre*** the mood has decidedly changed from optimism to a more problematic reflection: while praising and prescribing resistance, other issues are raised which are not easily answerable and are part of the struggle to resolve the ideological crisis of the revolutionary left.

The repercussions of the loss of a unified center are observable also in Fo's later farces, which, unlike the ones with a unified theme characteristic of the late sixties and early seventies, are more dispersive, strike out in several directions at once, and often raise the issue of "personal" politics (***Clacson trombette e pernacchi*** [1981] or ***Coppia aperta*** [1983]).

To date, Fo's farces have mainly been indicators of the latest political intrigues and scandals, whereas the monologues have served as a barometer of the ideological climate and situation in the revolutionary movement. His latest production, including both the *giullarate* and the farces, at first sight appear less refined and more fragmentary in respect to his earlier work. These changes have been interpreted by some as signs of tiredness, confusion, and the author's inability to keep up with the times. Although elements of this critique are valid, one can see in some of Fo's later production an attempt to achieve artistic and ideological growth, the acknowledgment of the need to develop more complex approaches to the question of power and knowledge. Keeping in mind the flexible "in progress" nature of Fo's style of work one can hope that his latest experimentations are signs of new, improved, and more mature plays.

Ed Emery (essay date November 1988)

SOURCE: "Dario Fo's *Trumpets and Raspberries* and the Tradition of Commedia," in *The Commedia Dell'Arte: From the Renaissance to Dario Fo,* November, 1988, pp. 330-34.

[*In the essay below, Emery analyzes Fo's* Trumpets and Raspberries *in relation to the use of masks, the nature of characters, the use of stock gags, and the representation of power as in the commedia tradition and carnival celebrations.*]

My subject is the Dario Fo play, **Clacson, trombette e pernacchi,** in its English translation, **Trumpets and Raspberries.**

The play presents, in farcical vein, a variation on the theme of the kidnaping and killing of Aldo Moro. This time the victim of the kidnaping is the owner of FIAT, Gianni Agnelli.

In some senses we should trace the roots of the play to the classical tradition. Fo's earlier attempt to deal with the Moro kidnap had taken him to the model of Sophocles' *Philoctetes*; and the roots of **Trumpets ...** owe much to Plautus, in particular the *Menaechmi,* the classic tale of mistaken identity involving two twin brothers.

However, here we are concerned more with the relation to the *Commedia* tradition, and carnival.

That this relation is to Carnival is obvious from numbers of textual references in the play. For example, the paramedics at the Hospital are carnival characters, dressed in surgeons' masks that are also clown masks. Then, in Act Two Scene Two we have the appearance (excised from the English version) of a café waiter in a Pulcinella mask, offering the assembled company ersatz champagne in celebration of Carnival, "even if it is Lent". The title of the piece, too, together with the music and dance that is in the play ("All the furniture begins whirling round like a carousel; lights flash on and off; the music gets louder; there is shouting and laughter as at an amusement park") are strongly suggestive of carnival.

As regards the relation to *Commedia,* here we are on interesting ground, because Fo takes aspects that are familiar from *Commedia* and performs his own very characteristic inversion of them. I shall look briefly at some of them; the use of mask; the nature of his characters; the use of stock gags; and the representation of power.

The Mask

As anyone who has been to the Venice Carnival recently can testify, there has been a great revival in the art of the Mask in Italy. The mask, as an object, has been transformed, in an artisanal sense. Most particularly by the pioneering work of Donato Sartori.

However, the Mask is not simply a physical *thing*. It has an extremely complex set of representations and social relations embodied in it, and nowhere more so than in the theatre. The fact that a given society chooses to use *mask* in its dramatic representations is a very pregnant socio-political fact.

The play **Clacson ...** is remarkable for its reworking of the set of representations traditionally embodied in the mask. What happens is that Gianni Agnelli is badly disfigured in a car crash. Through a mistaken identity mechanism, the hospital which does the plastic surgery on him takes him for one of his own car workers, and remodels his face in the image of the car worker. Then follows the comedy of errors.

What happens here? We see the same actor appearing as both Agnelli and as Antonio the car worker. When the Agnelli figure appears, we are asked to believe that the face we see is a mask, transformed by plastic surgery. Complete with scars, stitches and visible joins. Of course, there is no mask; the actors face is the same in both appearances. The trick here is that the actual physical mask has been done away with; the mask is a fictional entity, which the audience is asked to recreate in its imagination. This is a novel extension of the commedia form.

There are further instances in the play, of a reworking of the Mask. First, when Agnelli appears with his face completely swathed in bandages, which are then removed. A powerful moment of horror. Later too, when the carworker's wife attempts to feed him stewed meat through a meat-mixer facial contraption that resembles an instrument of torture. Here we have an interplay between horror and farce.

The use of the Mask was, by the way, a live political issue in Italy in the late 1970's. In the mass-movement of the revolutionary left, face masks and kerchiefs were widely used as disguises in street confrontations and moments of political violence. A law was passed specifically banning the covering of the face in public places. And, incidentally, the style of the street-fighting face mask then passed into European fashion as the kerchief knotted round the neck, as popularised by Benetton.

The Characters

Another element that links **Trumpets ...** with the world of *Commedia* is the presentation of its characters and the interplay that takes place between them.

The characters come close to being stock characters of the *Commedia.* Rosa, for instance, could be Colombina: good-looking, flirtatious, quick-tempered, with a sharp wit and an equally sharp turn of phrase, joined with a ready ability to lie when and where necessary. Antonio, too, is a stock figure—the servant-figure—he's a womaniser, he's astute but slightly obtuse, he hates his master but has inadvertently saved his life, and he reveals a marked instinct for self-preservation.

As in the traditional *Commedia,* these characters ask to be played not naturalistically, not realistically, but as *maschere,* as more or less traditional archetypes. What we have here is *not* the inner complexities of human intercourse, or probings of the human psyche. The action of the play is determined by a series of mechanisms (some of them coming from a stock repertoire of theatrical mechanisms), which trip from one to another, and which finally end up in a resolution (the classical "recognition scene"), the "touch of the magic wand", so to speak, which gives the action its unity and restores everything to its rightful place.

As in traditional *Commedia,* the structure of the play is an elaborate interweaving of intrigues and misunderstandings. In traditional *Commedia,* the cement that holds this structure together, the mainspring that motivates it is love. Affairs of the heart. In *Trumpets . . . ,* though, the mainspring that motivates the action and drives it forward is the dialectic of repression . . . police action, government action. The constant linking thread is the action by, or the imminent arrival of, the police. This is a novel adaptation of the commedia form.

The Use of Gags

In *Trumpets . . .* there are explicit references to, and borrowings from, the traditional gags and *lazzi* that were the stock in trade of popular theatre and of *Commedia.* For example, on page 48 of the Italian edition, the jacket-swap routine. Or, on page 49, the injection-in-the-bum-of-the-wrong-person routine, which Fo lifts wholesale from an earlier play of his, *Gli Imbianchini.* There is also the point where Antonio comes on, spouting water from his mouth. The stage direction reads: "Col trucco della spugnetta"—"by using the sponge trick . . ."—a direct reference to the comic actor's stock in trade.

There is also the gag which Fo has made all his own—the Window which acts as a character in its own right—dashing in to centre stage at a moment's notice, as if it had a mind of its own. "Entra in proscenio la solita finestra . . ." (Enter the usual window). This gag occurs five times in *Trumpets . . .* Another of the *mechanisms* which trip the action from one moment to the next.

I, by the way, am still of the opinion that someone should write a learned thesis on The Use of the Window in the Works of Dario Fo. The use of the window is a fundamenal part of Fo's method of organising his theatrical space.

The Representation of Power

The classical societal context of the *Commedia* play is in the relations between classes—the upper and the lower—the gentlemen and ladies, and their respective serving people. This context is carried over into *Trumpets . . .* where the discourse is more explicitly one of class power. We have the owner of the car factory, who has contempt for his workers, and we have the car worker, who hates his boss. By a classic *coup de théâtre*—the mistaken identity mechanism and the plastic surgery—they are forced to change roles. Here we have one of the favorite themes of carnival—the servant playing the part of the master and vice-versa. But more to the point, Fo steps out of the relatively safe conventions of the *Commedia* form—in which the structure of societal power is taken more or less for granted—and addresses himself directly to the nature of power. He takes the occasion of the final scene to question what is societal power, and what are the forces that embody it—police, state, capital . . . etc. In all of what I have said, what is interesting is the way that Fo has taken the traditions of *Commedia,* and has reworked them, making his own very characteristic inversions of them. This makes *Trumpets . . .* a remarkable piece of writing. In addition it is a very *tight* and well-structured piece of writing. It deserves to be taken a lot more seriously than it has been.

European theatre seems to have caught commedia-mania. Every other actor seems to have done courses in *Commedia* technique, and *Commedia* shows are popping up all over the place. My own feeling is that this mania has a lot in it that is conservative, ossificatory and unhealthy. Unless *Commedia* is approached in Fo's sense of *reworking Commedia within a framework of radicalism,* then I suspect that the present wave of commedia-mania is going to leave us with yet another theatrical millstone around our necks.

Joseph Farrell (essay date November 1988)

SOURCE: "Dario Fo: *Zanni* and *Giullare,*" in *The Commedia Dell'Arte: From the Renaissance to Dario Fo,* November, 1988, pp. 315-29.

[*In the following essay, Farrell presents Fo as a political revolutionary but a theatrical conservative in that he employs traditional characters and styles dating from the Medieval performers,* giullare, *to promote his radical politics.*]

The affection for, and identification with, figures from Italian theatrical tradition, be it *Arlecchino* or the *giullare,* are perfect illustrations of one of the most striking and paradoxical features of the work of Dario Fo—his relentless search for models from the past with whom he can identify. If on the one hand Fo is customarily seen, and indeed goes out of his way to present himself, as the subversive, the iconoclastic revolutionary, the admirer of Marx and Mao, the writer who dramatizes the dilemmas, the struggles, the controversies of today, or as the clown who lampoons and lambasts the politicians and the Popes who hold sway in contemporary society, at the same time his theatrical style is based not on any avant-garde, but on the approaches and techniques practiced by performers of centuries past. It is not too much to present Dario Fo as a political progressive but as a theatrical conservative, and his plays and performances as a unique combination of the two.

In itself, his path has few parallels in the world of political theatre. In their different ways, Mayakowski and his use of clowns and circus techniques, Brecht and Piscator with their notions of epic theatre, were attempting to forge new forms and create new techniques appropriate to changed times. Other companies established in the aftermath of the convulsions of 1968—at exactly the moment when Dario Fo made his own break with bourgeois theatre' to play on an "alternative circuit"—were often frankly uninterested, at least in their early stages, in theatrical language as such. One of the most renowned, and one whose choices can be regarded in many ways as emblematic, was the Het Werktheater of Holland who announced, at the time, that for them the message, the content was everything and the theatrical means were unimportant, it is true that in a debate following a production of *Tutti unitil tutti insiemel ma scusa quello non e'il padrone?* at Adria in 1971, Dario Fo came close to this position.

> Il problema del metodo e dello stile di esporre è, a
> nostro avviso, del tutto secondario. A noi interessa
> il disccrso che dobbiamo fare.

Nevertheless, on the same occasion, Fo went on to discuss his own use of farce, to admit that "ci interessa ancora eseguire il discorso attraverso il teatro" and to quote Mao Tse Tung to the effect that any performer incapable of the proper use of artistic means should content himself with direct public speeches, otherwise he would do a disservice to both art and politics. For the whole of his own varied career, Fo has always been attentive to theatrical techniques.

The choice of popular theatre was crucial, and separated him from others of his contemporaries who chose to express themselves in experimental theatrical techniques and, thereby, restrict their audience to an alert and, hopefully, socially aware intelligentsia. Jean Paul Sartre and, even more significantly, Pier Paolo Pasolini chose a demanding and at times arcane theatrical, or cinematic, language which *de facto* debarred all except the minority who had the neces-

sary, acquired familiarity with that language. Pasolini hated Fo's popular approach, and dismissed him as "una peste" for Italian theatre, whereas Fo, in more measured terms insisted that Pasolini, in his own plays, was incapable of freeing himself from the requirements of literature and had no understanding of the real nature and demands of theatre.

The dispute with Pasolini was over theatrical language and not over political ideology. Fo insisted that the only valid choice for anyone who wished to use theatre as a vehicle for political debate was popular theatre, something which Pasolini denied. Further, Fo chose to use dialect at a time when Pasolini, among others, decided that dialect had lost its drive.

Not all critics and commentators have accepted Fo's distinctions (deriving, ultimately, from Gramsci) between upper-class, dominant and oppressive culture on the one hand, and lower-class, subaltern, liberating culture on the other, but the stance was fundamental for his career post 1968. At the very moment of making his celebrated (and, in retrospect, exaggerated) break with bourgeois theatre, he chose to explain himself in a language which identified himself with a specific figure from the traditions of Italy. He repeated the words, in slightly different forms on various occasions:

> Noi per anni abbiamo fatto i giullari della borghesia,
> andavamo a dare scarpate in faccia ai borghesi . . .
> Eravamo l'Alka Seltzer, credevamo di essere dei
> fustigatori dei costumi, di incidere: nossignore li
> aiutavamo a divertirsi e a sentirsi democratici . . .
> abbiamo pensato di fare i giullari per la classe a cui
> noi sentiamo di appartenere, cioè il proletario.

The figure of the *giullare* provides Fo with a focus and a model for all his vast and varied theatrical activity-as a writer, performer, song-writer, actor, designer, fool. No doubt the 1968 break has been over-done, inasmuch as a great deal of his output from his first steps in theatre, with the reviews such as *Dito nell' occhio,* had already been of this type, but over the years Fo's researches into theatre had been deep and wide-ranging.

The *giullare* is a quintessentially medieval figure, who flourished approximately from the Tenth to the Fifteenth centuries, in other words in the period before the blossoming of *Commedia dell'arte.* Some commentators have tried to read some significance into that fact. Tony Mitchell writes:

> A common misconception is that the theatrical tra-
> ditions of farce and comedy in Fo's theatre stem
> from the *commedia dell'arte,* but the giullari are es-
> sentially pre-commedia, the popular, unofficial
> mouthpieces of the peasant population. while the
> performers of the commedia are regarded by Fo as

the professional 'court jesters' officially recognised by the ruling class.

From the point of view of theatre history, Mr Mitchell is right to underline this distinction but there are few other critics who agree that such rigidity is helpful when applied to Fo's own brand of theatre, Paulo Puppa, discussing **Mistero buffo,** puts the two elements together as phases of a common undercurrent:

> Questo enorme collage sproloquiante ... rappresenta, certo, una rilettura colta, teatralmente parlando, della tradizione bassa, fantastica-popolare della vulgata, attraverso modi espressivi multipli, grazie a una mescolanza tra la memoria guittesca degli zanni, delle maschere cioè della Commedia dell'arte, con i loro precedenti goliardico-giullareschi.

Maurizio Ponzi makes the same coupling of the same two disparate elements in his own critique of some of the individual sketches which make up **Mistero buffo.** Noting that Fo moves between two registers, leaving straight performance to engage in direct dialogue with the spectator, he writes:

> Tali passaggi, tale uso del doppio registro, non sono una novità assoluta nella storia del teatro, nel senso che i giullari e i comici dell'arte, cui Fo fa riferimento, li usavano come cardine della loro tecnica recitativa.

Dario Fo's search was for a working model, for something which would live and work onstage now, and there is no greater justification for dispute over the validity of his historical recreation of the *giullare,* or of the *zanni* than of his portrait of Christopher Columbus in his play **Isabella, tre caravelle e un cacciaballe.** Fo makes various internal distinctions and judgements inside the category of *giullare* or commedia performer, and it is these which are of greater moment than any distinction between the categories themselves. For both the *zanni* and the *giullare,* the basis of the judgement is identical. In perfect coherence with his overall political and theatrical stance, his preference is for those who adopted the popular approach and performed in the piazza, as against those who adopted a more aesthetic or aristocratic style and accepted invitations to court.

The matter is better documented with regard to commedia troupes, and it may even be that *Commedia dell'arte* is too all-embracing a term if it has to encompass both companies like the *Gelosi,* the official troupe-in-residence at the court of the Duke of Ferrara, and writer-performers like Ruzante. Ruzante is one of the more prominent landmarks along the line Fo wishes to mark out. In his *Due dialoghi,* for instance, Ruzante presents an unromantic, unheroic view of war, and writes from the point of view of the footsoldiers and not of the captains and the kings. It is this attitude which draws Fo's appreciation, whether it appears in a medieval *giullare* or in a performer from the age of commedia, like Ruzante.

Among the *maschere* of commedia, it is, of course, Arlecchino with whom he can most easily be compared. In his recent **Manuale minimo dell' Attore,** he offers a re-appraisal of the figure of Arlecchino, urging that he be viewed not, (in his ordinary light, as the comically, ever-greedy and crafty rascal on the make, but as a representative of a class accustomed to hunger. The greed portrayed with such comic effect by actors from Tristano Martinelli in the sixteenth century onwards derived from the genuine experience of famine. (It had, in Marxist terms, a material base.) Arlecchino was an authentic underling, with an outlook and culture to match. Fo explained to Mario Verdone both the attraction of Arlecchino for him, and his own identification with him:

> Io ho sempre fatto Arlecchino, che lo volessi o no. Pur non facendo saltelli o doppi passi, i miei personaggi sono stati sempre in questa chiave. Di Arlecchino mi affascina la sua caratteristica di distruttore di tutte le convenzioni.

Earlier however he had used very similar language, to Chiara Valentini, to describe the historical function of the giullare:

> Fin dal Mille, il giullare andava in giro per i paesi, per le piazze a recitare le sue clowneries, che erano delle vere e proprie tirate grottesche contro i potenti. Perfino uno storico reazionario come Ludovico Antonio Muratori riconosce che il giullare era una figura che nasceva dal popolo, che dal popolo prendeva la rabbia per ritrasmettergliela, mediata dal grottesco.

There begins to emerge a wholly coherent view of a tradition of popular theatre of today and of the past. Fo picks and chooses, among writers and performers, excluding Pasolini of the twentieth century and, on different criteria, the Geloso company from the sixteenth but admitting, to name a few at random, certain unnamed *giullari* the character of Arlecchino, Ruzzante, and some figures from Neapolitan theatre. The standards he employs are a mixture of the political and the theatrical, but admission to his personal Pantheon is not easy to obtain.

At different points in his life, he has spoken more of Arlecchino or of the *giullare,* and has done more or less original works of his own featuring the one or the other. The period immediately following 1968, ushering in the most *explicitly* political period of his theatrical activity, was undoubtedly a period most dedicated to the *giullare.* He used the *giullare* to explain his political and theatrical moves that year, identified the giullare as giving the essential performance key for the whole of **Mistero buffo,** one of whose central sketches has the title *Nascita del giullare.* He referred to the work of the *giullare* endlessly in the debates with the audience which were a feature of the performances of the *Nuova Scena* and *La Comune* years and gave the title **La giullarata** to the work he wrote, together with the Sicilian singer-songwriter Cicciu Busacca in 1975.

It is noteworthy that he underlines that in the heyday of *Commedia dell'arte,* the very name giullare had become a term of abuse. In the *Convegno Sulla Cultura* held in the occupied Palazzina Liberty in Milan he quoted an incident involving the famous Andreini company of commedia players. Francesco Andreini had tried to train his company in new acting techniques, and to familiarise them with a new kind of relationship with the audience. He experienced exactly the difficulties which Goldoni, at the other end of the tradition would encounter. The actors simply could not adapt to a type of theatre for which they had not been trained, so that when Andreini fell ill, they reverted to their old ways. A letter from Andreini roundly abusing them for their failings is still extant, and Andreini resorted to the worst of the insults within his vocabulary. He called them "*giullari*", and this because they had returned to the tradition of "lazzi, degli incidenti, degli a parte diretti". Finally he told them:

> Dovete dimenticarvi che il pubblico e' in platea:
> siete in teatro e non in una piazza.

During the days of his alternative circuit. Fo was more likely to be in a piazza than in a regular theatre, and asides and improvised tricks were an integral part of his stock-in-trade. It is curious that the term *giullare* degenerated so rapidly, and came to represent, for 'straight' actors, an inferior kind of performer and an illegitimate style of theatre. Something of that reputation has remained, and no less an organ than the *Encyclopedia Italiana* carries this definition:

> giullare è sinonimo di mimo e di istrione con un
> senso più volgare e ristretto.

The same article adds that *giullari*

> vivone in margine alla vita morale e rappresentano
> il divertiment e la dissipazione

That attitude towards the *giullare* is precisely the one which has been, in Fo's view, expressed by the ruling culture at every stage in history. Precisely because he has been the proponent of a different culture, or the spokesman for an alternative set of values, the *giullare* has been invariably reviled and abused by the official representatives of the régime. Fo has pointed to the edicts of the Medieval Church and the laws of the kingdoms and republics of the same epoch as proof of the status of the *giullare* as illegitimate or as the quintessential outsider. Others have mentioned Fo's own brushes with censureship and the Law as establishing a continuity between his experiences and those of his precursors.

Historically, in the Middle Ages, the *giullare* represented lay drama, as opposed to the Mysteries or Miracle plays which represented religious drama. The word derives from the Latin *iocus,* and has the same roots as the French *Jongleur* but since the English word "juggler", which has the same origin, now has a more restricted sense, it is difficult to find a precise English equivalent. "Minstrel" is probably the closest, although a case could be made for "fool", but "jester", with its aristocratic connotations has the wrong associations. The *giullare* was an all-round entertainer, whose talents were not expected to be restricted to any one style. The English word "performer" is a more convenient term than the Italian *attore,* for the giullare would be stand-up comic, tumbler, juggler, mime, singer, dancer, clown, satirist, actor and would have to draw up his own material. Since the sketches or texts were intended for immediate use and not for enduring literary glory, they were rarely written out, and very few have come down to us. Even those which are extant give little flavour of the original, since their impact derived from a unique dialectic between actor and author. What the celebrated Harlequin, Evaristo Gherardi, said of commedia texts—non hanno alcun risalto sulla carta—is equally true of the *guillarate.*

The *giullare* had much in common with the Elizabethan strolling player, except that he is to be seen not in the palace of a Prince Hamlet but in the street outside, and had, of course, counterparts in most countries. All of Dario Fo's descriptions and definitions are, typically, partial and incomplete, and reflect the topic foremost in his mind at the time, or the aspect of the question put to him: Fo is not a man for the systematic, exhaustive treatment of a subject, nor should it be asked of him. He is a theatre worker, not a critic or historian. Thus, his most recent definition of the *giullare* reads:

> È un mimo che, oltre ad usare il gesto, si avvale
> della parola e del canto, e che, nella maggior parte
> dei casi, non si serve della scrittura per i propri testi,
> ma li rimanda oralmente, andando a memoria e
> spesso anche improvvisando.

To this "aesthetic" definition, must be added the elements, previously quoted, from Muratori, dealing with the sense of anger which the giullare takes from the people and gives back in a transformed state. Fo is fond of the phrase "*riso con rabbia*" to describe his own activity, and these elements are present in his version of the activities of the *giullare.* The entertainment is never escapism or distraction, while the anger is never mere shapeless posturing or denunciation.

It is precisely this mission which is given to the protagonist of the sketch *Nascita del giullare,* the heart and core of *Mistero buffo.* Few of his other works are so imbued with a sense of compassion and of fellow suffering. And here the atmosphere of the grotesque is toned down. Perhaps this is the work which should stand as prelude to all his political theatre.

The *giullare* tells his own tale, and rises to the status of representative of the oppressed everywhere. Once he had been a peasant, supporting himself and his family by his labours, but his efforts were undone by the overbearing tyranny of the local lord who slaughtered his wife and children and evicted him from his land. In despair, he contemplated suicide, when a stranger, who turned out to be Jesus Christ, comforted and encouraged him and, by a kiss on the mouth, endowed him with new and explosive talents—the ability to entertain, spread enjoyment but also enlightenment—with the ability, in other words, to be a *giullare,* to speak for and to the underlings, the oppressed, the exploited. His tongue, transfixed by the contact with the Almighty, would become a weapon to lacerate and ridicule injustice and oppression.

> Gesù Cristo sono io, che vengo a te a darti la parola. E questa lingua bucherà e andrà a dar contro ai padroni. . . . Che non è che col ridere che il padrone si fa sbracare. Che se si ride contro i padroni, il padrone da montagna che è diviene collina, e poi più niente.

The humour of the *giullare* was essentially corrosive satire, the most fundamental characteristic of Fo's own comedy. Although he has often discussed popular theatre, satire, catharsis, comedy, and although a whole genre of didactic farce has been developed—often calamitously—by writers who follow his example, Dario Fo has never written any systematic manifesto of theatre, comparable with, for instance, Brecht's *Novum Organum,* and his basic beliefs have to be put together from a series of lectures, workshops, interviews and occasional, often highly polemical, articles. The *giullare* crystalises much that is distinctive in his own view of the function and potential of theatre. Thinking about the historical role of that medieval figure forced this most twentieth century of playwright-performers to develop, and justify, an approach of his own.

The *giullare* gave him an onstage style. Initially it was his plan to have the scenes and sketches of *Mistero buffo* performed by a company of actors in the usual way, but in rehearsal this proved impossible and he reverted to the one-man style of the *giullarata.* The *Storia di una tigre,* even if the material comes from China, was developed with the same model in mind, with Fo himself playing all the parts, including that of the tiger. The giullare can be detected, very obviously, in *La giullarata,* but also behind the condemned actor on *Isabella, tre carabelle e un cacciaballe* as well as in the "medieval" spirit of *La colpa è sempre del diavolo.*

The *giullare* operated within specific parameters of popular theatre. Plainly popular culture is a vague, imprecise term, covering a vast gamut of meaning and embracing a wide range of attitudes, and popular theatre too can be of the most widely differing stamp. Common to all forms of popular theatre, including, for example, music hall, *avanspettacolo* and pantomime, is the acknowledgment of the presence of the audience, and a willingness to address them directly. In other words, the fiction that the stage was a magical space, hidden behind a mythical "fourth wall" was restricted to "teatro borghese". In Fo's scornful words:

> Dice Stanislavski che quando un attore recita leve fare in modo che il pubblico che sta ascoltando si trovi per caso li.

The rejection of the famous 'fourth wall' makes possible, indeed almost obligatory, a different style of acting and a different kind of relationship with the audience. Specifically, the *giullare* was able to make free use of the "aside", to comment on the action of the play as it is unfolded, and to come in and out part as he acts. Lanfranco Binni sees parallels with the tenets of Brechtian-style epic theatre:

> Cosi il "teatro epico" dei giullari medievali, in cui il giullare si poneva come espressione corale e dialettica dell' intera comunità, dei sentimenti, della rabbia, della speranza . . . ma sempre *comunque* vivo di una passione disperatamente umana.

The *giullare* can present a character without altogether representing it. He can, and will, strive to function as a mediating force, putting forward action, situation and character, but not insisting on the fictional, temporary identification between the actor and the character. This approach both allows the *giullare* a collective (choral) role, which is wider than that of a conventional character in a conventional theatre, and goes a long way to avoiding catharsis, "*uno dei pericoli maggiori* ". Once again, the confrontation with the giullare brings out a theoretical position, this time vis-à-vis acting method. Fo's beliefs on acting are plainly far removed from Stanislavsky's or from the Method school, but are not at all identical with Brecht's. If he rejects a Stanislavskian actor-character identification, he has, as an actor, doubts about the possibility of achieving Brechtian alienation or "third person" acting. The example of the *giullare* offers a third way. It offers the possibility of occasional identification together with the chance of standing outside the character, the means of linking performance of a fiction with commentary of the performance and its meaning.

The most obvious commentary to works which involve an entire company of actors is the prologue, which Fo considers indispensable—and which are often comic masterpieces in themselves. Acting with other actors does not give the same opportunity for improvisation or for off-the-cuff comments—although Fo will not always resist the temptation—so the prologue is the ideal place for setting a play in history, discussing its contents and, if necessary, pointing up contemporary parallels. The prologue, when Fo-*giullare* is onstage alone, is the preferred moment for improvisation and caricaturing of contemporary attitudes. In delivering his prologues to **Quasi per caso una donna Elisabetta,** he draws attention to similarities between the court of Queen Elizabeth I and the contemporary Italian State, making reference to the development of the secret police and comparing the situation of Essex with that of Aldo Moro in captivity. Conversely, he once criticised Giogio Strehler harshly for "mystification" in presenting Ruzante without any form of prologue. In this form, the work of the arch-anarchist was reduced to banality and the cutting edge was lost.

Fo's debt to the *giullare* and the traditions which that figure incarnated has been profound. He provided Fo with a framework for much of his thinking on the theatre, as well as with a stimulus for much of his original work. On the other hand, the *giullare* of other times owe a debt to Fo, for he has rescued them from obscurity and shadows, and given them back a central role in Italian theatre.

Mimi D'Aponte (essay date December 1989)

SOURCE: "From Italian Roots to American Relevance: The Remarkable Theatre of Dario Fo," in *Modern Drama,* Vol. XXXII, No. 4, December, 1989, pp. 532-44.

[*In the following essay, Fo is viewed as a successor to earlier twentieth-century "Italian geniuses of the comic spirit" Totò and Eduardo De Filippo.*]

> Clowns are grotesque blashpemers against all our pieties. That's why we need them. They're our alter egos.
>
> —Dario Fo, Cambridge, May 1987

Americans writing about theatre have been pronouncing Dario Fo's work extraordinary, whether for performance or political reasons, or for both. "For the past decade," claimed Joel Schechter in 1985, "Dario Fo has been Europe's most popular political satirist." "So many theatres have included Fo in their recent seasons," wrote Ron Jenkins in 1986, "that

he has become the most-produced contemporary Italian playwright in the U.S." American producers interested in social satire seem to have become less leery of this zany Italian genius who publicly thanked his "fellow actor," Ronald Reagan, for the marvelous promotion afforded his work when the State Department denied him an American visa for several years.

Dario Fo is the brilliant successor of a comic tradition of mime and improvisation which extends not only back to Greek *phlyakes* and Roman *fabulae,* but also includes both medieval *giullari* (to whom he so often refers) and Italian *commedia dell' arte.* He is, in addition, the heir of two twentieth-century Italian geniuses of the comic spirit—Totò and Eduardo. The first connection is evident from the transcription of Fo's remarks filmed to honor Totò (1898-1967) in 1978 and published in English translation last year. He pronounces Totò an "epic actor" (nomenclature he often applies to his own technique)—"he uses all the elements which allow a break with naturalism." Fo also states that Totò is true to the *commedia dell'arte* tradition since, by using body and face in opposition to one another, he creates a true mask (Fo's use of masks and puppets in the 50s and 60s was extensive). Finally, Fo celebrates gleefully Totò's destruction of the fourth wall by citing an example of Totoian conversation with a tardy audience member:

> If someone arrived late when the show had started. Totò interrupted everything and said: "So you've come at last? . . . We were really worried . . . Do sit down . . ."

This dialog is identical to one which Fo engaged in with a late-comer to the James Joyce Theater in New York City during a May 1986 performance of his signature piece, **Mistero buffo.**

> You will find a[n] . . . authentic . . . version of its [commedia dell'arte's] artificial clowning in the Neapolitan comedian Totò. And for another side of the tradition—not famous at all unfortunately—you must go to Eduardo.

The other twentieth-century figure with whom Fo must be compared is Eduardo De Filippo (1900-84). Referred to familiarly by Italians as "Eduardo," and by Eric Bentley as the "Son of Pulcinella," this prolific Neapolitan actor/playwright exemplified a strongly realistic tradition of acting. In 1950 Bentley identified Eduardo as perhaps the finest actor in Italy today "more likely . . . to be the heir of *commedia dell'arte* than any other important performer now living." There was a precision to Eduardo's performances which was uncanny, which left the viewer with the sense of having witnessed the quintessential interpretation of the character in question. This "polish" seems to be what Fo, in speaking to acting students in London. termed "*souplesse.*"

> What makes . . . great swimmer[s] is the fact that they have coordination. You're hardly aware of how their bodies move . . . you hardly see them breathe. . . . *That* is *souplesse.* It's the same *souplesse,* litheness, that great actors have. They don't show that they are exerting themselves. They make you forget that they are acting.

Fo possesses "*souplesse*" to an astonishing degree and he practises a performance style probably closer to the "Ruzzante" form of *commedia* which he admires than "any other important performer now living." Fo sees himself as the inheritor of the "realistic" acting style of the Italian popular theatre which, he explains, encompasses an epic dimension as well:

> The epic style derives from realism. But it is characterised by the self-aware detachment of the actor; the actor is critical of what he acts. He does not confine himself to conveying information, to telling something, and then letting the audience sort it all out. He seeks to provide the audience with the necessary data for a reading of the piece.

As I hope to demonstrate later in this paper. Fo's performance style also exemplifies Bentley's admiring words about Eduardo: "a series of statements, vocal and corporeal . . . beautiful in their clean economy . . . in [their] relation to each other and to the whole."

Like Eduardo before him, Fo is a highly successful Italian playwright who has created excitement in international theatre circles. Eduardo wrote domestic tragi-comedies produced in translation around the world which, as Bentley put it, were both traditional and original and in which he "put his finger on the black moral spot." Fo's theatre has been defined at various times as agit-prop, throw-away, political, improvisational, a theatre of blasphemy, and popular. His first translator in the United States, Suzanne Cowan, wrote in 1979:

> To give a full account of Dario Fo's theatrical career would really be tantamount to writing a history of postwar Italy, because his work can only be understood as a continuous, uniquely creative response to the major social and political developments of the past thirty years.

Like Eduardo before him, Fo has been greeted with instant popularity in many countries while being given, initially at least, a somewhat cooler reception in the U.S. The failure, for example, of Eduardo's *Saturday, Sunday and Monday* in 1974 Broadway production despite its huge British success in 1973 seems to have been a virtual blueprint for Fo's British-American experience with **Accidental Death of an Anarchist.** This "grotesque" farce about a "tragic farce" achieved tremendous success in London during 1979-81, only to open and close rapidly on Broadway in Fall of 1984.

What seems clear, however, is that Fo's work has created an ongoing interest in American university and repertory theatres which Eduardo's did not. This is due in part to an increased American awareness of international theatre trends fostered by the academy's more frequent conference and exchange programs, and also perhaps by more frequent mass-media culture coverage. Continued American interest in Fo's work springs also from our desire to stay abreast of such trends: Tony Mitchell, in the first English-language book devoted to Fo, states flatly that by 1978, "Fo was already the most widely performed playwright in world theatre." But it is the fact that Fo and Rame have finally been able to practise their crafts of acting and directing in this country that has led to acclaim in the American theatre about this extraordinary team.

Dario Fo's performance of **Mistero buffo (Comic Mystery Play)** and Franca Rame's performance of *Tutta casa, letto, e chiesa* (*It's All Bed, Board and Church*) at the James Joyce Theatre after a tour which played in Boston, New Haven, and Washington, D.C. were remarkably different from usual Off-Broadway fare. Two immediate adjustments of perspective were built into this Obie-award-winning experience. The verbal comedy of these one-person shows, performed on alternate evenings, worked through instant translation (Ron Jenkins as translator for Fo took on the persona of straight-man) and projected overhead sub-titles. Also, the house remained half-lit throughout performance in order to permit interaction with the audience, something accomplished with ease and intimacy despite the "language barrier." Rame's work was a series of monologs treating the "sexual slavery of women" and played "in a style that recalls the sexy, comic intelligence of Mae West." "Dario Fo mesmerizes in **Mistero buffo**" began *The Boston Globe* review, for each audience was treated to an astounding range of both physical comedy and historical context, which Fo wove anew each evening as he proceeded deftly through the fresh improvisation of a show encompassing a dozen texts.

> For several of the scenes, Fo employs "grammelot"— a nonsense language he invents phonetically as if it were Northern Italian dialect, English, French, Italian. He becomes transformed, before our eyes and without costume or prop, from a chatty fellow letting us in on historical gossip, into an Italian peasant, a French advisor to the king, an English lawyer of high place, a pope. Each sketch is politi-

cally biting, physically hilarious and theatrically successful in its maintenance of character.

In reviewing **Mistero buffo** for *The New York Times,* Mel Gussow introduced Fo as "an outrageous gadfly" and mentioned Richard Pryor, Father Guido Sarducci and Monty Python by way of comparison. Mr. Gussow concluded with mention of other names:

> With his mobile face and body, he is a cartoon in motion, loping across the stage with the antelopean grace of Jacques Tati, doing a Jackie Gleason away-we-go to demonstrate the Italian perfection of the art of women-watching.

Both sets of references are on target. Fo's performance was unforgettable because it conjured up a complex battery of historical and cultural perspectives, while simultaneously satirizing their contingent political realities. Clad in black work-day jersey and slacks and sharing a bare stage with only his translator, Fo created in the mind's eye of his audience chaotic crowds, lavish costumes, and dramatic conflicts resolved by the machinations of a laughing clown-narrator in favor of those without power.

Fo's formidable powers of persuasion through laughter illuminate his on-stage persona. These same powers are seen from another perspective in his work as teacher and director. Most immediately obvious is the appeal of the comradeship and community which Fo creates about him, beginning with that strong emotional, intellectual, and artistic partnership which he and Franca Rame, his wife, have shared for thirty-four years. This partnership extends not only to their own acting company, currently La Comune of Milan, but also to the manner in which Fo and Rame interact with any company. While Western theatre is by definition an art form organized in hierarchical fashion, Fo's concept of how to work in the theatre appears consistently egalitarian. This philosophy ultimately translates into a specific reality: everything which appears on stage and/or takes place on stage is in some fashion touched by Fo. Whatever the form of this nurturing, its manner is one of co-authorship, of "we" rather than of "I" and "you."

Along with this comradeship comes a powerful charisma which Dario Fo possesses and uses automatically, effortlessly in his quest for the ideal performance of his troupe. He is a director whose every syllable and step on stage are noted by everyone, near and far. Members of the American Repertory Theatre, a young, vital professional company with excellent credentials, spoke glowingly of their learning under Fo's tutelage during rehearsals for **Archangels Don't Play Pinball** in Spring 1987. "Dario exerts an amazing influence—he has a way of working with actors. No one at ART has ever attained this popularity." "I want to get a grant

to follow Dario Fo around. This is the guy I've been waiting to learn from all my life." A visiting university director added, "I'm on leave this year. I'd be in Milan if Dario were in Milan. I'm in Cambridge because he's here." Such remarks take on additional weight when one realizes that they represent English-speaking theatre folk describing their Italian-speaking theatre mentor. Dario's ability to communicate goes beyond the limitation of language.

Then there is the power of example. Fo the performer is able to illustrate what Fo the director has to say. Fo and Rame conducted five theatre workshops in London in late spring 1983 the transcripts of which were subsequently published and translated. The student/teacher exchanges during these sessions underscore the credibility in the theatre of a director who practices in his own performances what he preaches to his students. For example:

> [*QUESTION*] *When you did the three situations exercise earlier, the only way that we spectators could laugh at the comedy of it was because we already understood the situation, because you had explained it to us. But how, then, if you are the actor, creating the situation, how do you express it without using even more obvious methods of expression?*

> [DARIO FO] Theatre has always had *prologues,* even when they are not declared as such. There is an old tradition of theatre in Italy, which had prologues which were really masterpieces. In fact, the rest of the plays has often been lost, and the prologues have remained in their own right. There is, for example, the famous prologue: . . . "Ah, if I could only become invisible." The situation is already presented in it . . . in that one sentence it already gives you the situation. The actor comes on and explains the things he could do if he was invisible. (*He acts out the prologue*)

The enjoyment of watching the persuasive power of Fo's directing and teaching is enhanced by the knowledge that what he offers his actors and students alike is empowerment—empowerment as actors and empowerment as authors. The answer to two questions posed to him demonstrate something of the private Dario Fo's modest character and a sense of the public Fo's ability to teach effortlessly, with "*souplesse.*"

> [*QUESTION*] *What influence do you want your work to have on American theatre?*

> [DARIO FO] I don't know.

> *What is the connection between political theatre and improvisation?*

The choice of an improvisational form of theatre is already a political one—because improvisational theatre is never finished, never a closed case, always open-ended.

Improvisational theatre is open on a space level. If we are performing in a large theatre, a stadium which seats 5000 in one night and in a factory which accommodates 300 the next, we must improvise, by necessity, and without a dozen rehearsals. Out of necessity we signal to one another and stretch out what we do to fill the stadium or contract it to fit into the factory.

Improvisational theatre is open on an emotional level. Audiences are not the same every evening. Different things have happened to them on a political level. Someone may have been shot, someone may have died: an audience is an emotionally different entity every night. The actor in an improvisational theatre is open to audience mood and builds upon it, using it as a springboard for what he is going to do.

Improvisational theatre is open on an intellectual level. New events happen every day. These events can't be ignored, but must be included, and the old ones, if they are no longer useful, put aside. The commedia dell'arte troupes were often the chroniclers of their times, bringing to their often ill-informed audiences up-dates of what was going on in the country of the audience that evening and of what was going on in outlying countries. Improvisational theatre must be a theatre of ideas, not merely of technique.

Fo's last statement holds the heart of the matter. It is clear that his concept of theatre is both improvisational and political, and it is also clear that he demands a body of knowledge, a challenge to the intellect, from a theatrical event. So do many theatre artists. What is unique about Fo is that, rather than coveting that creative act known as "playwriting" as is traditional, he asks of his actors that they become his co-writers. "After I leave [the actors] must read newspapers every day and listen to and watch news broadcasts every day, and include pertinent material into the *Archangel* performances." When an actor had suggested that perhaps one person be put in charge of updating the text, this was Fo's reply: "No, no, no one has to be in charge—you all do it! Every actor must practice self-discipline, trying out material and judging its effectiveness carefully, eliminating it if audience reaction is not favorable." It is in this manner that Fo empowers his actors to grow, to stretch, to develop, for he invites them not simply to interpret someone else's ideas, but also to initiate their own.

Which brings us to Dario Fo, playwright, produced in translation in the United States. How, given Fo's convictions concerning improvisation about current political events, does this work? A quick production/publication profile offers several revealing statistics. To date there have been American, English-language productions mounted of six full-length works by Fo (*We Won't Pay! We Won't Pay!, Accidental Death of an Anarchist, Almost By Chance A Woman: Elizabeth, Archangels Don't Play Pinball, About Face* and *A Day Like Any Other*) and two full-length works by Fo and Rame (*Orgasmo Adulto Escapes from the Zoo* and *Open Couple*). Since 1979 there have been at least one, but as many as three American productions of these works annually. Fo's plays have been mounted by regional theatres, touring groups, university theatres, Off-Broadway and Broadway producers. In addition to numerous texts imported from Great Britain, there are currently available American publications of five of the works produced here. Plans are in progress for an American translation of Fo's four-hundred-page theoretical work on theatre, *Manuale minimo dell'autore.* Finally, both American journalists and scholars have begun writing about Fo to the extent that their major contribution to an already impressive European bibliography of secondary sources about his work appears imminent.

Each published introduction or preface to a Fo work contains some reference to the need to update or adapt material, while at the same time preserving the playwright's intention. Such directives suggest the problems inherent in revision. "A Note on the Text," which introduces Samuel French's edition of *Accidental Death of an Anarchist,* for example, reads in part:

> For the Arena Stage production and the subsequent Broadway production . . . Nelson [the adaptor] revised the dialogue for the American stage, and added some references to current politics. . . . Subsequently, Fo asked for further changes. . . . Future productions may require further alteration of political references, unless our President is elected for a life term, and outlives the century.

Ron Jenkins' "Translator's Preface," which introduces Theater's edition of *Elizabeth,* offers both directive and sound explanation:

> For the American version of the play Mr. Fo and I have substituted references to American politics for the original references to Italian politics. This text is presented only as a record of what was prepared for the Yale Repertory Theater production. It should not be performed without prior approval from the translator and playwright. . . . Their [Fo's and Rame's] work cannot be translated without reference to their performance technique, and transla-

tions of their work should not be performed without taking their performance style into account. It is delicately balanced between detachment and passion, tragedy and comedy, intimacy and showmanship.

A perusal of American reaction to Fo's work indicates frequent critical reference, both positive and negative, to the current American politics alluded to during the course of a Fo play. Three writers had three different reactions to this question when they reviewed the Broadway production of *Accidental Death* in 1984:

> The play may have deserved to be successful in Italy, where its dealing with an actual case of police defenestration was doubtless audacious and salutary. But it has far less resonance here, and the manner in which Nelson has dragged in American references is obvious and safe.

> Although it's ostensibly an Italian subject, the play has been given emphatic contemporary American application by adaptor Richard Nelson, whose version includes some hilarious speeches for the masquerading hero about current U.S. politics.

> There are references to the Great Communicator's belief that trees pollute the air and to his habit of sleeping in cabinet meetings. . . . Not all of these jokes take wing, but it is somewhat refreshing on Broadway to hear political subjects mentioned at all.

Despite the ongoing need for relevant revision, *We Won't Pay, Accidental Death,* and *About Face* are, thanks to multiple American productions, "here to stay." These three plays appear to have graduated from the stage of "experimental" or "alternative" theatre and, will, I believe, be accepted as an integral part of contemporary international repertory desirable in American theatre schedules. Fo has in essence, during the period 1979-1988, established a base, a modest body of dramatic literature which is recognized by the collective American theatre mind.

This base of three dramatic works realistically represents Fo's social and political concerns while at the same time appropriately casting him as a writer of comedy and satire. In *We Won't Pay,* the richness of which as a drama has been competently described in this journal, the grave social question of economic ineptitude on a national scale is lampooned by the madcap manner in which Mr. everyman worker and Mrs. everywoman wife deal with insufficient salaries and inflationary prices. The hilarity of the piece is caught in the unforgettable image of women leaving the supermarket with goods they have refused to pay for and which they eventually transport as unborn "babies" beneath their coats.

In *Accidental Death of an Anarchist* the frightening specter of institutional "justice" applied to an innocent victim is raised to the high art of grisly grotesque as an actual case becomes the focus of farce. Real-life anarchist Giuseppe Pinelli was arrested in late 1969, erroneously accused of having planted a bomb which killed sixteen people in a Milan bank, and "fell" to his death from a window of the Milan police station. The Fool of Fo's play portrays a mad graduate of many an asylum who arrives to interrogate police hierarchy about this scandal, who stays to re-enact Pinelli's "fall," and who seems to re-appear once again before the horrified police personnel.

In *About Face* the limitations of both management and underdog perspectives on life and love are broadly satirized by a series of fabulous switches of fate. Caricatured Fiat magnate, Gianni Agnelli, becomes, thanks to an auto accident, amnesia, and the wrong plastic surgery, a factory worker in his own plant. He is eventually "exchanged" out of this humdrum existence by both the return of his memory and the co-operation of government officials to whom he writes threatening letters.

In the first two plays the principal key, both to socio-political bite and to hilarity, is the mistaken identity of the protagonist. In *Accidental Death* police officials on stage labor under the delusion that a bureau inspector is creating havoc in their midst, while we in the audience know that a mad, self-styled investigator come from a paradise where real justice reigns is loose on the boards. In *About Face* some characters work to improve the health of someone they take for an injured factory worker, while others discover and then protect the Agnelli identity behind the surgically applied incognito. In *We Won't Pay* a series of chaotic misunderstandings pave a double-edged path to social criticism and to side-splitting laughter. In an amazing scene from Act II, the police lieutenant casing the protagonist's flat searches the "pregnant" women he finds there; he is rewarded by imagined blindness when they tell him about a pregnant saint's husband who lost his sight and when, coincidentally, the long-unpaid-for electric lights suddenly dim.

When each play's ruse has been stretched to the most insane absurdity imaginable, Fo snaps us back to epic disengagement, usually through a long-winded speech delivered by a leading character which jars us into remembering a current political problem. In *About Face,* for example, Antonio/Agnelli offers a final diatribe about the power of the state equaling the power of money and caps it with, "So Aldo Moro gets 15 bullets in his gut to protect me." And from the seemingly safe shores of such "reality," we laugh madly at the horrific foibles of human society.

As suggested at the start of this essay, Fo's performance style is reminiscent of Totò and of Eduardo, While the contours of his double life as actor and internationally acclaimed playwright also recall Eduardo's career. Fo's playwriting evokes the works of two other countrymen, one of the Roman era and the other of ours. His consistent reliance upon the dramaturgical misreading of the who and the what harkens back to those comedies of Plautus from whose brilliant feats of mistaken identity and misunderstanding Shakespeare was to borrow liberally. It is also relevant to point out the common fixation about identity which Fo shares with Luigi Pirandello, whose characters' tortured peregrinations lead us finally to learn only that neither we nor they are certain of who they are. When questioned by a Harvard student as to whether Pirandello had influenced him, Fo replied: "Pirandello and I deal with the same themes [illusion and reality] but I'm an optimist.

In considering Fo's impact on theatre in the United States, it seems that two developments are taking place, the direction of which, attributable to a variety of forces, is surely Foian. The first is a new awareness, for us, that the actor need not necessarily put his own ideas aside or neglect to have ideas of his own. During his and Franca's London workshop of May 1983, Fo asserted:

> In my opinion it is more important for actors to learn to invent roles for themselves . . . to learn to be authors . . . *all* actors should do this. In my opinion, the most important criterion for any school of drama is that it should teach its actors to be authors. They must learn how to develop situations.

A *New York Times* issue chosen at random in January 1988 describes the Actors Studio search for a new direction which will include "a mandate to revive the Actors Studio's Playwright-Director's Unit and integrate its work with that of the actors." After more than fifty years of proclaiming the primacy of the actor's individual self-expression, the American citadel of "the method" has come to recognize, for instructional purposes at least, the natural relationship between acting and playwriting. The same issue of the *Times* includes Mel Gussow's enthusiastic review of the American Place Theatre's *Roy Blount's Happy Hour and a Half:* "For 90 minutes we are, figuratively, at a bar with the author and raconteur as he expounds wittily on his shaggy life and his and our hard times."

American actors who author and American authors who act have been aided and abetted by a rich backdrop of vaudeville history and its subsequent chapters in television and radio shows. More recent sources of inspiration have been our own inventive brand of improvisational group theatre (beginning with Chicago's original Second City company in the early sixties and for two decades receiving multiple resurrections around the country) and our new brand of solo, mimetic clowning (the work of the West Coast's "New Vaudevillians" in the eighties). It is fascinating, in this latter connection, to note a clear example of Fo's direct influence. The actor Geoff Hoyle, who played the lead in the 1984 San Francisco Eureka Theatre production of *Accidental Death,* was subsequently invited to play the lead in the 1987 ART production of *Archangels Don't Play Pinball* directed by Fo. During my interviewing in Cambridge, two actors made mention of Fo's considerable influence on Hoyle. Later the same summer, *New York Times* reviewer Jennifer Dunning offered accolades to Hoyle for his part in the "New Vaudevillian" *Serious Fun!* Festival at Lincoln Center.

The second development in contemporary American theatre which reflects a Foian flavor is our renewed awareness of a need for theatre which speaks frequently to social and political concerns. The Eureka Theatre Company mentioned above has produced four of Fo's plays to date and has recently been awarded a substantial federal grant specifically earmarked to develop new American plays dedicated to social concerns. The recent outpouring of powerful political theatre from South Africa, the growing awareness of the impact of the AIDS epidemic around the world, the fear of nuclear holocaust shared by all nations have brought to the American theatre a new sense of urgency about the subject matter of our plays. Examining our own psyches is no longer enough.

On the broad canvas of world theatre, Dario Fo's mark is visible. He has chosen to place his enormous talents at the service of everyman and everywoman, making it plain that those who have no power are his concern. He supports the have-nots by using the theatre as a forum for paring the powerful down to size. His arms are those available to the economically and politically powerless: physical agility and intellectual wit. In Fo's version of stage reality, presidents and popes are adroitly relieved of prestige and power as ordinary people become aware of their own potential. Fo synthesizes past, present, and future concerns of society as he weds an appreciative sense of tradition with satirical but hilarious situations in which bureaucratic bunglings of immense proportions victimize the common people.

To a student in London who asked him if theatre could change the world. Fo responded: "I believe that neither theatre, nor any form of art, can, in itself, change anything . . . Not even great art." But Dario Fo is a performance artist and a playwright whose comically costumed message, *beware institutional power,* has been heard around the world. Both his comedy and his message are nourishing our theatre today.

Leah D. Frank (review date 24 November 1991)

SOURCE: "Dario Fo's Outraged Housewives," in *New York Times,* Long Island Weekly Section, November 24, 1991, p. 23.

[*In the following review of the Arena Players Repertory Theater production of* We Won't Pay! We Won't Pay!, *Frank lauds the play's humor but finds the story itself lacking verisimilitude.*]

Dario Fo is Western Europe's most widely produced playwright. This phenomenally successful Italian satirist, actor, painter, musician, cinematographer, director, set and costume designer and political activist has been in the forefront of world theater for the last 40 years.

His creative social commentary has been condemned by groups as divergent as the Vatican, the Italian Communist Party and our own State Department, which continues to deny Mr Fo a visa on the grounds that his presence is powerful enough to constitute a "clear and present danger" to the stability of the United States.

Free speech and a free flow of ideas are still paramount, so fortunately the fruits of Mr. Fo's labor regularly slip across our borders. If State Department bureaucrats attended the theater, they might be comforted to discover that in practice, at least in many American productions, Mr. Fo's plays may be the cutting edge of political bubble bursters, but they are often too long to sustain the passionate waving of the red flag of revolution.

In *We Won't Pay! We Won't Pay!* Mr. Fo's play at the Arena Players Repertory Theater in East Farmingdale through Dec. 15, the working class expresses its dissatisfaction with consumer-price increases that are not keeping up with workers' wages.

This farce about outraged housewives had its English language debut in London in 1978, and what is both interesting and tragic at the same time is that the issues it raises seem to come right out of contemporary American newspapers.

We Won't Pay! We Won't Pay! may be set in Milan, but the economic problems facing two women and their overworked husbands are no longer defined by national boundaries.

Yet, as in so many political plays, the problems are defined, high cost of living and exploitation of the working classes, but solutions are given in amorphous terms. To suggest that Utopia will arrive when power is given to the people makes no more sense dramatically than it does economically or politically. In any case, a total suspension of disbelief is required.

It does not, however, take a Marxist bent or even that of a moderate Democrat to appreciate the broadsided political humor in a Fo play. Serious situations, in this case economic recession, are pushed to the limits of absurdity.

In this play, several women in a grocery store decide to stage an impromptu revolt against rising prices. They decide not to pay for their groceries, and in the ensuing confusion they walk off with any edible item they can grab.

Frederic De Feis, who has directed the Arena production, has trimmed the script to good effect and has chosen a gentle approach to the sometimes heavy-handed political farce.

The overall result is good fun, rather than left-wing theoretical bludgeoning, and although the approach dulls the satiric edge, it allows the genuine charm in the script to come through.

Sunny Taylor handles the role of one of the rebellious housewives with cunning and wit. Her Antonia is a fast-talking quick-thinking woman who does not allow idealism to interfere with her pragmatic approach to life.

Stephanie Bianca gives Margherita, the friend who follows Antonia into a cauldron of economic uprising, a fixed expression not unlike that of a deer caught in the headlights of a speeding automobile.

Joseph Senzone is the blustery, law-and-order-comes-first husband of Antonia, a man who finally sees the need for a people's uprising, Patrick Burchill as Luigi, Margherita's husband, is a mirror image of his stunned wife. Joseph M. Mantello gives a rounded, zesty performance in the dual role of a sympathetic police sergeant and his hard-hearted lieutenant.

We Won't Pay! We Won't Pay! is a delightful example of political theater and a gentle reminder that the more things change, the more they seem to remain mired in the same clichés.

J. L. Wing (essay date October 1993)

SOURCE: "The Iconicity of Absence: Dario Fo and the Radical Invisible," in *Theatre Journal,* Vol. 45, No. 3, October, 1993, pp. 303-15.

[*In the following essay, Wing argues that, especially in his one-man skits, Fo causes the visible to become invisible, requiring the audience's participation to fill the gaps.*]

In demonstration of the mysterious power of *absence* as a

staging technique, Italian playwright/performer Dario Fo recounts an intriguing tale of a performance at a mental institution for "untreatable cases" in Turin, Italy. Fo was in the midst of a skit involving an archangel and a drunk, in which he, himself, played both characters, a task which compelled him continuously to speak to the empty spot where he had just "placed" his antagonist. At one point, as he was impersonating the drunk who was trying to get a word in edgewise, a patient began berating the (absent) archangel for stifling the drunk's story, screaming," Let him talk, you bastard! Otherwise I'll come up there and give you a kick in the halo!" Somewhat astonished at this response from a spectator he was told hadn't spoken in years, Fo told a group of acting students, "The amazing thing was that she was raging at the character whom I had sketched out in the air; she was pointing at the spot where I had left him." Later other inmates who had been tied to their beds expressed a desire to get up on stage and speak out against oppressive conditions in the hospital. This astonishing response raises questions not only about the nature of "insanity," but also about an art form based fundamentally on presence. How did Fo shape his staging so that absence signified profoundly, so much so that, in this case at least, it induced the mute and powerless to speak? And what are the theoretical implications of this iconic nothingness?

If theatre is an iconically dense representational medium, as many theorists indicate, interpretation of that iconicity has become increasingly open to debate. As a signifier, the icon is a tease: there is simply too much there. Since, as Keir Elam tells us, "the governing principle in iconic signs is similitude," our tendency as spectators is to naturalize the icon—to assume that it *means* what it *is*. This essentialist temptation is especially apparent when considering the phenomenon of the actor. In a valuable discussion of the slippery relation between the icon and its referent in various theatrical genres, for example, Marvin Carlson contends that "the one element which almost invariably involves iconic identity—is the actor, a human being who represents a human being." Having made this assertion, Carlson hastens to cite the exception of puppetry, much as Elam, wrestling with the same problem ten years earlier, came up with immediate contradictions involving Elizabethan boy actors and Greeks playing gods.

The troubling link between iconicity as "the visual component of meaning" and the physical presence of the actor has proved to be an especially rich source of analysis for feminist theorists, who problematize the social and psychological constructions of the subject in relation to the female body displayed on the stage (or screen). As Laura Mulvey pointed out in her influential essay on film theory in 1975, visibility and pleasure are inextricably linked in the Western configuration of the unconscious. Whether considered from a Freudian or Lacanian perspective, this link is devastating to the female subject, so much so that Mulvey proposes deleting pleasure from the representational configuration altogether.

> It is said that analysing pleasure, or beauty, destroys it. That is the intention of this essay. The satisfaction and reinforcement of the ego that represent the high point of film history hitherto must be attacked; not in favor of a reconstructed new pleasure, which cannot exist in the abstract, or of intellectualized unpleasure, but to make way for a total negation of the ease and plenitude of the narrative fiction film.

Since the pleasure/vision collusion derives from psychological theories which are fundamentally ideological in nature, as Kaja Silverman demonstrates (because they are configured within a culture which already valorizes the male), the most promising approach for a feminist critique of theatrical representation would seem to involve a radical deconstruction of its ideological apparatus. But is this possible without condemning us all to what Mulvey calls "intellectual unpleasure"?

Such a deconstruction is, of course, precisely the project to which Bertolt Brecht addressed himself, when he proposed foregrounding the mechanics of theatrical production in order to break with what he called "culinary theatre," which he equated to an illusionistic meal, easily digested and forgotten. According to Brecht, holistic representation of character or narrative is objectively, *realistically* misguided:

> The continuity of ego is a myth. A man is an atom that perpetually breaks up and forms anew. The bourgeois theatre's performance always aim at smoothing over contradictions.... Conditions are reported as if they could not be otherwise.... If there is any development it is always steady, never by jerks.... None of this is like reality, so a realistic theatre must give it up.

Brecht's solution to bourgeois realism—what might be called his "atomic theory" of representation—features a radical perceptual realignment, which, through various "distancing" techniques, co-opts the spectator as collaborator, rather than passive witness to the performance event. In Walter Benjamin's terms, the spectator in Brecht's configuration in fact co-produces the event, a concept which has ethical implications:

> *An author who teaches nothing, teaches no one.* What matters, therefore, is the exemplary character of production, which is first able to induce other producers to produce, and second to put an improved apparatus at their disposal. And this apparatus is better the more consumers it is able to turn

into producers—that is readers or spectators into collaborators. We already possess such an example. . . . It is Brecht's epic theatre.

According to Roland Barthes, this process implies a disruption of the standard semiotic equation, in which the signifier flows inexorably toward the signified on an ideologically closed circuit:

> Consciousness of the unconsciousness, consciousness that the audience should have of the unconsciousness which prevails on stage: this is the theatre of Brecht. . . . The function of the system here is not to hand on a positive message (it is not a theatre of signifieds), but to make it understood that the world is an object that must be deciphered (it is a theatre of signifiers).

The perceptual "gap" which results from Brecht's denaturalized signification strategy has been appropriated by both film and theatre scholars recently in order to conceptualize an alternative to the ideological entanglements of subjectivity and the gaze. For example, Elin Diamond has shown how the Brechtian "alienation" strategy can be applied to a feminist theatre critique:

> *Verfremdungseffekt* . . . challenges the mimetic property of acting that semioticians call iconicity, the fact that the performer's body conventionally resembles the object (or character) to which it refers . . . by alienating (not simply rejecting) iconicity, by foregrounding the expectation of resemblance, the ideology of gender is exposed and thrown back to the spectator.

In a series of incisive articles, Diamond has applied her observations to show how Caryl Churchill's theatre, in particular, uses a Brechtian approach to challenge ideological presumptions, especially those involving gender construction. Among other considerations, Diamond analyzes how Churchill's dramaturgy makes visible what is normally *in*visible (showing us Val's perceptions as a Ghost in *Fen,* for example) as a means of rupturing a perceptual complacency which equates icon with identity. In this paper, I want to consider how Dario Fo uses the Brechtian formulation to do just the opposite—to make the normally visible *in*visible—in pursuit of a similar goal: to force the spectator into an active and critical collaboration with the representational process in order to challenge "the ideological nature of the seeable."

Fo's manipulation of absence is most apparent in the one-actor skits he regularly performs under the aegis of ***Mistero buffo*** (the title refers to the medieval mystery plays which are his source material). For Fo, the crucial common factor of all these skits is their historical lineage in the medieval craft of the wandering players, or *giullari,* which he attempts to reconstruct in his performances. This reconstruction centers initially not on visual gaps but on historical gaps in surviving texts, which Fo claims have been sentimentalized and mystified for centuries by academics who were complicitous with power structures which squelched dissent. To recover the original vitality and intent of the medieval pieces, it is necessary to reconstitute the performative elements that linger between the words, the gestural traces that functioned as, "*the* determining part of the representation, precisely to get across to the public those allusions which it was too dangerous to write down in full." Fo contends that to take everything literally is to misrepresent it:

> The text belongs to a precise social class, the one which controls the power. Opposed to it there is another theatric lexicon composed of text, pause rhythm; a lexicon in which many times the word is dependent on a situation."

Fo's insistence on the "theatric lexicon" links up handily with the argument against "privileging the text," flourishing for some time now among Italian semioticians, such as Marco de Marinis and Franco Ruffini who both insist on the importance of evaluating the entire theatrical process rather than focusing on either a text or a definitive production. De Marinis's objection to the idea that a virtual performance is somehow already prefigured within each dramatic text—a necessary condition for the reduction of theatre to a set of codifiable sign systems which can then be definitively analyzed—parallels Fo's notion that the key to a performance lies in the absence between the words. If absence is the uncodifiable, creative core of the performance, then its very unpredictability is potentially threatening to a structure (academic or political) that thrives on codes.

However, Fo's appropriation of absence transcends an opposition to text alone. In the process of attempting to recover the original gestural satire latent in the medieval pieces, to reconstruct absence, he has uncovered a representational strategy which, like Brecht's, fundamentally destabilizes the semiotic foundation of illusionistic representation. Ironically, given Fo's forthright Marxist epistemology, the primary source for his gestural reconstruction is the rich iconography of religious paintings of the period. Fo claims that many of these paintings, which he likens to medieval cartoon strips, represent a synchronomous and multi-faceted narrative, embodying what Fo sees as an optimum epic style which transcends the merely linguistic. "When (medieval) painters tell a story they are outside language," Fo suggests. "They don't show the perspective of only one person. They show diverse points of view . . . the same scene from behind, from the front, from a distance."

Obviously this simultaneous, multiple perspective has ideological implications for theatrical representation. On the one hand, the sense of multiplicity, of cacophony, of popular culture represented by a performer in the public marketplace recalls Bakhtin's theory of the carnivalesque; both Fo and Bakhtin identify an anarchical exuberance in the type of public performance which "precisely because of its unofficial existence was marked by an exceptional radicalism, freedom and ruthlessness." This theatrical exuberance is anything but benign; indeed, according to Bakhtin, it poses an explicit threat to any power structure which depends on its representation as "eternal, immovable, and absolute."

For Fo, however, the practical challenge which presents itself is precisely one of performance: how does one reconstruct this rich iconography, this popular, pluralistic perspective? A tempting solution would be to attempt a kind of literal mimesis, to reconstitute the original image, using one actor per figure. In the case of the *Mistero buffo* sketches, however, Fo came to the conclusion that the pieces were clearly intended to be performed by one actor alone. According to Fo:

> The giullari almost always worked on their own; we can see this from the fact that, in the text, things that happen tend to be indicated by the actor splitting himself between (the) parts, and by allusion, so that the full comic and poetic weight of the piece is heightened by the free play of (the spectator's) imagination.

The requisite representational strategy, then, would need to insure that the spectator's imagination is engaged in maximum movement, in order to create the necessarily simultaneous and multiple iconicity. This prescription calls for a kind of "motion picture," and indeed Fo deliberately incorporates cinematic techniques into his performance. A closer look at a few of the *Buffo* pieces will serve to illustrate Fo's approach.

Fo claims that **"The Resurrection of Lazarus,"** was a *piece de resistance* among medieval *giullari,* requiring an astounding virtuosity, in which one actor would represent some fifteen different characters in succession. "The principal theme of the piece," according to Fo, is "a satirization of everything that passes for the moment of mystery:

> The satire is aimed at the miracle mongers, the magicians, the conjurer's art of the miraculous, which is an underlying feature of many religions, including Catholicism ... here though, the story of the miracle is told from the standpoint of the people. The scene is set as though it were about to be performed by a great conjurer, a great magician, some-

body who is able to do extraordinary and vastly entertaining things.

Clearly the "vastly entertaining conjurer" in question is analogous to Fo, himself, and indeed Fo's strategy depends on a kind of theatrical sleight of hand which needs to be "set up" as meticulously as a magic trick. To emphasize the deliberate derivation from religious icons, and to entice audience collaboration in a "pictorial" reconstruction, Fo always precedes the Mystery sketches with slides. In the case of **"Lazarus,"** he often shows one of his own drawings, which he claims to have copied from the original sketches for a fresco in a Pisa cemetery. Fo's drawing represents part of a crowd scene, which features one of the figures picking the pocket of another. Although this particular action clearly serves Fo's intention of irreverent demystification, his general configuration of the "Lazarus" is remarkably similar to many versions extant throughout southern Europe and the Near East. According to Emerson Swift, in *The Roman Sources of Christian Art,* the resurrection of Lazarus is one of the most frequently painted scenes in medieval Christian iconography, many versions of which feature the multiple perspective of a crowd of people. The action is invariably more or less centripetally focused—that is, the figures are grouped in semi-circular arrangements around a central axis, that of the "miracle." But perhaps more significant than the striking similarities between all these scenes and Fo's enactment of them, is Fo's one glaring omission: although the paintings invariably feature the figures of Jesus and Lazarus as protagonists of the figural narrative, Fo notably does *not* embody either of these characters; rather, he quite deliberately chooses to restrict his impersonation to the crowd witnessing the event: Jesus and Lazarus may be at the center of the iconic text, the visual narration, but in Fo's demystified version, they are significantly demoted to mere projected absences.

Fo "positions" the fifteen odd characters he chooses to indicate in a semi-circular configuration around an invisible gravesite which he "places" center front. He effects these characters with a kind of staccato, strobe-light effect, introducing them through a precise, swift gestural technique he calls the *invito,* a kind of shorthand acting notation:

> [the *invito* is a] synthesis created by the shortening of the rhythm of images. For the audience, therefore, the transition whereby the character comes onto the stage does not exist; it has been cut out, shortened out ... [in this way] the description [of the character is] made by the movement of the actor's body even before he [says] the words describing what [is] happening.

By using this *invito* technique, Fo manages to engage spectatorial collaboration in the creation of a three-dimensional, virtually cinematic "crowd scene" perspective. The mood of the piece, decidedly more carnivalesque than sublime, reflects Fo's contention that the skit is a "satire of everything that contributes the mystical experience" A gatekeeper haggles with the crowd over attendance fees, hawkers sell chairs and refreshments ("Getcha redhots! Hot n' delicious! Bring you right back from the dead!"), latecomers fight with earlybirds for the best seats and old codgers gossip about Jesus's family ("they don't let him go out alone, because he's a little crazy"). When Lazarus's corpse is finally uncovered, reeking and crawling with worms, one entrepreneur takes advantage of the spirited debate over whether Jesus can pull the miracle off by calling for bets. The sketch peaks at the moment of the resurrection, with shouts of celebration, interspersed with the cries of the woman who discovers that her purse has been snatched in the commotion: the final words, ringing out in a kind of staccato opposition are: "Bravo! . . . Ladro (thief) . . . Bravo! . . . Ladro . . . Bravo . . . Ladro!"

In Fo's incredibly complex configuration, then, the very core of the piece, the miracle, is represented by absence—absent protagonists (Jesus and Lazarus), witnessed by a crowd of spectators, which at any given moment exists almost entirely in the imagination of the theatrical spectator, who is thus mirrored, but in a manner which would seem to have escaped at least some of the ideological constraints of a literal mimesis. Meanwhile, the miracle itself, which could be said to represent a liberation from death (significantly linking ancient fertility rituals to the Christian ritual to the theatrical ritual) is undercut by the theft; and it is *precisely* this subversion of the miraculous by the profane which serves as the basis for Fo's own dialogic theatricality. Whether Fo's strategy is ultimately constraining or liberating is a question which is often lost in the dazzling virtuosity of Fo's performance, as he both evokes and exorcises the crowd of characters with such speed and precision that the mind of the spectator is set on a collision course within itself to reconstruct a known event from proffered puzzle pieces that are contradictory, irreverent and finally profanely seductive. French critic Bernard Dort describes the process of piecing together Fo's Lazarus as an adventure in semantics:

> At each moment a double (or triple or quadruple) play of meaning is invested in an image or emotion. . . . By his gestures which remain unfinished— as though suspended between the past and the present—and his words which recall the gestures but which never completely resolve them . . . , Fo addresses nothing but the imagination of the spectator: he literally puts the spectator into movement. He obliges him to adapt himself ceaselessly, to multiply his points of view and perspectives. He forces him into debate.

Fo's dynamic montage is a result of a confluence of carefully constructed framing strategies which are largely borrowed from film techniques, although Fo claims a theatrical lineage for them:

> . . . long before the invention of cinema with all its up-to-date equipment every actor worth his salt managed to compel every spectator with any sensitivity or culture to employ the identical camera, the identical fields and counter-fields of vision, identical universal focus, identical wide-angle lens. . . .

"Compel" would seem to be the operative word here, and indeed Fo's appropriation of filming strategy leads to an interesting dilemma: if, as Laura Mulvey tells us, "cinematic codes create a gaze, a world, and an object, thereby producing an illusion cut to the measure of desire," then does Fo's utilization of cinematic techniques render him complicitous in the illusion/desire entanglement? Certainly he controls the site of the gaze, but what does it mean when the object "to-be-looked-at," the theatrical icon, is absence, nothingness? To what extent is the *manner* in which he compels focus fundamentally different from that of the filmic "eye"? It is certainly the case that Fo's intervention in the interpretation of his *mise-en-scène,* although intensively manipulative, is nevertheless absolutely dependent on an on-going co-conspiracy with the audience which is absent in the cinematic relationship.

Orchestration of the spectatorial "lens" to which Fo refers requires an acting technique which could be described in semiotic terms as somewhat more indexical than iconic. That is to say that within this configuration, it is the actor's job not to create character or essence, but rather to set up an interpretive code and to act as the mediator of that code for the audience. Again, Fo shapes this role of mediator in cinematic terms, exercising a canny adaptation of the link between ideology and perception

> [which] arises from a particular psychological attitude which on different occasions compels the spectators, almost as though they were using a series of lenses, to frame the images produced by the actors in different ways. The decisive factor is the way the audience is persuaded by the actor to focus on one detail of the action or on the totality of the action, by the use of the lenses unknowingly stored in the individual brain.

This notion of an individual perceptual "lens" links up with De Lauretis's contention that perception is relative to context, a context that must be destabilized in order to break ideology's stranglehold on iconicity; and it is precisely *context,* or conceptual framing, which is the key to Fo's theatrical technique. Fo ensures the perceptual collaboration of his working-class audience by employing a traditional actor's trick he calls the *intervento* to insinuate himself as the crucial intermediary between historical oppression and theatrical liberation. In order to establish this intermediary function, Fo uses the context of medieval fables featuring a *giullare* who is "born without a soul," and can therefore speak out against oppression by refusing to "give into the blackmail of a good conscience." Fo's analogy features himself as the *giullare* while the medieval peasant for whom the *giullare* speaks is clearly Fo's own working-class audience. Within this equation, Fo then manipulates the *intervento,* or disruptive commentary, as a kind of ideological tracking device, to foreground the trans-historical parallels.

An example of this "metatheatrical" manipulation occurs in "*La Nascita del Villano*" ("The Birth of the Peasant"), a text which Fo incorporates virtually intact from a piece done by the *giullare,* Matazone da Caligano, in the sixteenth century. It features the "miraculous" birth of a peasant from a donkey's fart, followed by the appearance of an angel who stipulates a "dress code" for the peasant, requiring a garment with a convenient slit so he can relieve him without losing time from his work:

> As soon as he's born, in the buff
> Give him an old piece of cloth
> To bag him up with a few stitches
> And make him a good pair of britches
> Pants with a slit—no zipping
> So he doesn't waste any time pissing.

At this point in the presentation, Fo abandons the character of the angel and addresses the audience directly: "You know, this guy seems to have a lot in common with the bosses today!" After telling about a factory in Verona, where the management declared 11:25 a.m. to be the only time for a bathroom break and where the workers went on strike, according to Fo, "[t]o be allowed to pee when they felt the urge," Fo leads the audience back to a historical perspective by proceeding to impersonate both the landlord and the angel. When the landlord justifies his exploitation by telling the peasant that this is his fate on earth but his immortal soul will transcend terrestrial suffering, the angel unwittingly subverts the religious blackmail by blurting out, "How can this stupid serf have a soul when he was blown out by a donkey's fart?"

What the authoritative angel sees as a critical absence, however, Fo identifies as a source of power, forging a bond between the peasant and the *giullare* as blood brothers inn a material struggle; for the immortal soul that they both lack is really nothing more than a kind of spiritual blackmail used to ensure passive behavior on the parts of those who "buy into it." But even more important to the dialectical process than the declarative climax is a catalytic *intervento,* through

which Fo has deftly compelled a perceptual link between the medieval peasant and the contemporary factory worker, a configuration which, as one critic notes, is differentiated from a fundamentally static vision ("*Plus ca change . . .*") by the "continuous mobility of the text" which sets itself up as constant interruption, opposition and debate. The complexity of this representational structure undergoes individual permutations in each of Fo's **Mistero buffo** skits.

In Le nozze di Cana ("The Wedding at Cana"), for example, the skit which somehow impelled the mute to speak at the Turin mental hospital, Fo creates a direct dialectical opposition between two ideological "matrices," in this case representing divergent interpretations of a biblical story. As in all the medieval pieces, the underlying theme here is the overturning of officially sanctioned, "authorized" versions of gospel stories and church history, to be replaced with a populist notion of religious tradition in which the character Jesus is seen as a working-class hero, described by one observer as "a human, exploited peasant Christ who refutes the injustices of the hypocritical religion of the rich." Again Fo constricts interpretation by constructing a didactic framework for the piece, insuring a perceptual link between Christ and fertility rituals by showing a slide of a *sacre rappresentazione,* depicting a Palm Sunday procession, in which Dionysus, Bacchus and Christ all take part. Using the Brechtian device of eliminating the suspense by telling the fable before enacting it, Fo then explains the significance of the earlier deities to his proposed skit:

> Jesus Christ became Bacchus [who] at a certain point is seen standing on a table, shouting to all the celebrants, "Drink, gentlemen, be merry." Be happy, that's what counts: don't wait for paradise hereafter, paradise is here on earth. [This is] exactly the opposite of the doctrine they teach you from childhood on, when they explain that one must endure, that we are in a vale of tears . . . not everyone can be rich, there are those who do well and those who do poorly, but everyone will be compensated when we are in heaven . . . be calm, be good, and don't rock the boat. . . . Now instead this Jesus Christ of the giullarta says, "Rock the boat and be happy!"

In this irreverent configuration, then, Fo represents Christ not only as "just another god," but as an ill-behaved one at that, a rabble rouser, the veritable life of comedy's requisite party. As in the other *giullaresque* sketches, however, the Christ of "The Wedding at Cana" is not directly impersonated by Fo, but is rather a projected absence, an invisible referent of the two oppositional characters alternately "placed" onstage by Fo. Using a technique which Fo calls, *sdoppiamento,* or splitting, Fo sets up a dramatic confrontation between two unlikely antagonists: the first is the archangel, who speaks in the polished Venetian dialect of an aristocrat and affects, as Fo says, "pretty gestures;" he is, of course the alazon, or pretender, in the archetypal configuration. Opposing him is a subarticulate, drunken oaf, who speaks in a coarse, peasant dialect peppered with obscenities, and who is barely able to hold himself upright due to his inebriated condition. For the archangel, authority and text are inseparable. As the two struggle for the audience's attention, the archangel repeatedly intones the same litany, as though repetition itself increased credibility:

> (To the drunkard) Be quiet! I must begin because I'm the prologist. (To the audience) Good people, everything that I tell you is true, because it all comes from books and from the Gospels. What comes from them is not fantasy. . . .

The drunkard, on the other hand, appeals only to his own experience for veracity:

> Me too, what I want to tell you isn't fantasy. I enjoyed a drunkenness so sweet, so beautiful, that I never want to get drunk in this world again, so I won't forget this fantastic drunkenness that is on me now!

However "well-spoken" the angel, however, his supposedly divinely sanctioned text is no match for the corporeal subversion of the drunkard. In an apparently benign attempt to cooperate with the edicts of censorship, the drunkard, explores the possibilities of non-verbal communication:

> Drunkard: . . . I'll think, think, think, and use my eyes . . . and they'll understand.
>
> Archangel: No.
>
> D: But I don't make noise with my brain.
>
> A: You're making noise!
>
> D: I'm making noise with my brain? Dammit! I must really be drunk! Holy shit!
>
> A: Don't breathe!
>
> D: What? I can't breathe? Not even with my nose? I'll burst!
>
> A: Burst!
>
> D: Ah . . . but if I burst, I'll make noise, huh?

Here physical excess and textual purity are in direct conflict and the constant play between the presence and absence of each creates a troubling tableau indeed if Fo's configuration

is in any sense "an illusion cut to the measure of desire." According to comic convention, however, the implications are somewhat more direct: forbidden to express himself through his own body, the drunkard proceeds to subvert the physical authority of the angel plucking his feathers, and eventually kicking him offstage. Thus far, the structure of the piece follows the pattern that Ron Jenkins has identified as "a dialectic between freedom and oppression [in which] each slapstick crescendo is orchestrated around a liberating triumph over injustice." Again Fo plays both parts, using the *invito* to defy conventional standards of iconicity: at any given moment, he is a presence addressing an absence, which he has established as a presence in the spectator's imagination. That the "absent" figure is every bit as "real" to the audience as the (temporarily) incarnated one is evidenced by Fo's experience at the mental hospital, which would certainly seem to indicate that his configuration of the absent Other is an empowering strategy for his audience. The voiceless in this case not only identified with the oppressed clown, they were actually enticed by the empty space to join in his revolutionary behavior. On this evidence alone, one might conclude that although Fo's ideological framing devices constrict interpretation somewhat, his use of absence produces a kind of iconic undetermination, which would seem to invite participation. This is true, not only in the "Cana" dialogue, but also in Fo's staging of the story of the medieval Pope, Boniface.

If the sanctimonious posture of the authoritative archangel is subverted by the finally triumphant voice of the opposing clown in "The Wedding at Cana," the representational dialectic of "Bonifacio VIII" is somewhat more complex. Iconographically, Fo structures the piece as a processional, although it is important to keep in mind that this configuration is indeed "in mind"—the only figure actually on stage at any given time is Fo himself. Unlike the "heteroglossia" of "Lazarus," or the dialectical opposition of "The Wedding of Cana," "Boniface" is a true monologue—only the protagonist of the piece, the medieval Pope of the title, has a voice. Nevertheless, the silent, subversive forces of a procession of choirboys in the background are no less potently evoked in the minds of the spectators than the irrepressibly voluble drunkard of Cana.

As in the other skits, Fo straddles theatrical "frames," functioning alternatively as the craftsman and the character. As the storyteller with a microphone, he introduces his subject by recounting historical horror tales of Boniface's repressions of both penitential religious orders and the early communards of Lombardy and Piedmont, gleefully punctuating the narration by miming Boniface's grotesque torture techniques, which included nailing dissenters by their tongues to the doors of offended nobility. Then, in a sly shift of historical perspective, Fo assures the audience that the present Pope has nothing whatsoever in common with

Boniface, after which he proceeds to tell "Pope stories" which imply just the opposite. Having thus set up a vivid and grotesque analogy between the present Pope and his medieval counterpart, Fo launches into his impersonation of Boniface, who is in the process of getting dressed for an important procession: as he is weighted down by increasingly more opulent garments, Boniface irritably interrupts his liturgical chant to berate his incompetent choirboys, finally threatening one with a tongue hanging. The dialectic in this representation involves an opposition which is set up within the figure of Boniface, himself. Fo foregrounds the Pope and then situates the choirboys behind him, so that Boniface effectively upstages himself each time he turns to admonish them, a configuration which causes him to subvert himself as the voice of authority. In addition, the opulent signs of wealth and power, progressively accumulated upon his body, cause him to be grotesquely weighted down, and finally, literally "tripped up," as one of the choirboys steps on his mantle.

This vision of an arrogant, cruel and grotesquely ornamented Pope is suddenly interrupted when Boniface sees Jesus coming up another street, leading a procession of penitents. When one of his underlings points out that it would be wise to be seen as a humble servant of Christ (in whose name, after all, he supposedly derives his own spiritual authority) Boniface throws off his jewels, smears mud on his face and obsequiously presents himself to Jesus, who doesn't recognize him ("What do you mean, what's the Pope?") After several ludicrous attempts at self-abnegation, the Pope becomes increasingly more impatient ("Pay attention to me, you twit!") Finally he goes too far and is seen to be "flung a long way by a terrible kick in the butt."

Like the clown/drunkard of Cana, "Christ" has presumably been pushed too far. In this case, however, the only visible representation of his revenge, is enacted by the character, Boniface, on himself, as he stumbles grotesquely across the stage, consumed by humiliation and rage. In Fo's brilliant staging configuration, the power that pushes this raging alazon out—the triumphant comic empowerment—emanates from nothing other than absence, an iconicity of nothing. One could argue that Fo has infused this nothing, this absence, with a "Christ" character, but it is clear that whatever is there, it is nowhere if not in the mind of the spectator. If it is a "signifying space," it would seem to signify a force created by the collaborative imagination of performer and audience together, a force which is seen to eject an agent of oppression. Because it is not embodied, this force evades overdetermination. If Fo's use of "iconized absence" is an effective strategy for "denaturaliz[ing] identity," in Kaja Silverman's terms, "by emphasizing at every conceivable juncture its imaginary bases," then it would certainly seem to be a promising scheme for breaking down an oppressively encoded entanglement of iconicity and ideology in theatrical representation. By emphasizing the mechanics of perception, Fo has transferred the "burden of iconicity from the representation to the viewer's judgement," and it would seem that he has considerably empowered the viewer's judgement in the process.

As I have indicated throughout this essay, Fo's theatrical framing devices create a deliberate interpretative constraint, a kind of "forced perspective," which is scarcely free of ideological entanglements. Nevertheless, Fo has succeeded, at the very least, in setting up an extraordinarily dynamic theatrical dialogue. Indeed Fo has said that the purpose of his theatre is to create a debate, that he doesn't want his theatre to "rain down vertically on people's heads." By presenting a kind of fragmented iconicity—fragments of characters, fragments of actions and interactions—Fo has shaped a dramatic montage in which the shifting perspectives force a sense of community. There is no time to identify privately with one character or point of view; the spectator is too busy in every given moment, working on the collective creation of the event, an event which is tossed back and forth through the time and space of the theatrical protoplasm like Brecht's atomic particles of humankind.

Christopher Cairns (essay date 1993)

SOURCE: "Dario Fo and the *commedia dell'arte*," in *Studies in the Commedia Dell'Arte,* edited by David J. George and Christopher J. Gossip, University of Wales Press, 1993, pp. 247-265.

[*In the following essay, Cairns focuses on Fo's 1985* Harlequin *production and examines his contemporary adaptation of commedia techniques.*]

The extraordinary vogue for the *commedia dell'arte* as a performance language in the contemporary theatre has given rise to two distinct conventions. First, the 'archaeological' reconstruction of the working methods, costumes, masks and relationships between the well-known stereotype characters, refined and polished to a high degree of professional performance by such companies as TAG Teatro of Venice and the Carrara family, who tour Europe with their re-elaborations of classic scenarios such as *La Pazzia di Isabella.* Secondly, we have the adaptation or 'selection' of styles from past traditions of *commedia* for modern uses: a bringing face to face with contemporary social and political causes of a deep-rooted European theatrical tradition, particularly since the 1960s. It is to this second *modern* convention that Dario Fo's **Harlequin** belongs, a convention that has seen many and diverse experiments, such as the adaptation of *commedia* to a travelling show, in which the poet and teacher Giuliano Scabia has appeared in Italy as a kind of Harlequin-devil;

or the depiction of Harlequin as a very modern Algerian immigrant into France in Ariane Mnouchkine's *L'Age d'or,* first presented at the Théâtre du Soleil in Paris in 1975. And there have been other adaptations, such as those of the more radically innovative San Francisco Mime Troupe, El Campesino, and Schumann's Bread and Puppet Theatre in the United States. The *commedia dell'arte* is a style and performance language in these adaptations, taking contemporary social and political issues by the throat, as it were (American involvement in Vietnam is an example), but selectively adapting the traditional attributes of mime and improvisation to the contemporary world, or inventing new character-stereotypes of decisively modern relevance, such as the San Francisco Mime Troupe's creation of the Lawyer, Politician, College Student and Feminist.

Dario Fo's relationship with the *commedia dell'arte* came to a head in 1985 but grew from a long-standing similarity between the *commedia's* dependence on audience reaction and Fo's own background as a performer. His emphasis on mime (originally from Lecoque) and ability to improvise in direct address to the audience are all characteristics which derived from his background in variety, but which he and his company developed from the sixties onwards. When their new ideological stance prompted an even closer relationship with the audience in discussions after or during the show of the issues it raised, this was also, in a sense, a further sophistication of *commedia* techniques. In London in 1988, Fo admitted that he had come late to the formal study of the *commedia dell'arte,* but had found with some surprise that he had been involved in similar theatrical practice (with different roots, in variety, the circus, the silent film) already for many years.

Against this background of instinctive sympathy for the *commedia dell'arte* (and research is showing how many commedia characteristics had appeared in his previous productions), Dario Fo came to his **Harlequin** production in 1985 as a result of the promptings of academics. He admits that:

> When Ferruccio Marotti and Franco Quadri asked me to undertake a 'Laboratory [workshop] on **Harlequin**', and a show to be performed at the Venice Biennale, I accepted at once: I have always been interested in the *commedia dell'arte,* it's my territory.

He goes on to define the ideological parameters of his standpoint, showing his particular Harlequin to be an evolution from the *giullare* of **Mistero buffo,** since

> The *commedia dell'arte* companies were, after all, giullari organised into groups. During the Renaissance, in harmony with the spirit of the times (this

was the era in which the arts, trades and business began to be organised) even the theatre began to organise itself. At a certain moment, those who had been dilletanti travelling players went to a notary and constituted theatre companies with contracts.

In the same interview, Fo admitted that he had gone back to the roots of the *commedia dell'arte* in the creation of the Harlequin show. He had started with the basic *canovaccio* or synthesis, and improvised on the basis of this, seeking the starting point for the evolution of each situation or gag in ancient models, often building on a terse citation of an object or prop (for instance the *lazzo* of the ladder, which he was to build into a long episode in the final show). Ferruccio Marotti has said that the original scenarios were provided for Dario Fo by Delia Gambelli (whose researches on the classical figure of Harlequin are well known) and himself. But he also stresses the consonance of Fo's (radical left-wing) ideological stance from the seventies, and what he considers to be the ancient roots of *commedia.* Marotti spoke to Sergio Parini in these terms in 1985, stressing that Harlequin was never a stereotype susceptible of facile classification like Zanni (a servant from Bergamo) or Pantaloon (a merchant from Venice), and was not limited to a recognizable type, language or regional place of origin. Secondly, Harlequin was a universal gadfly, a creature *di disturbo,* and far from the polished stereotype immortalized by Goldoni in the eighteenth century.

> The reinterpretation of Harlequin as a figure *di disturbo* was based on some documents discovered by Delia Gambelli and myself. Witness the first document which exists on the character. This is an anti-Harlequin libel written at the end of the sixteenth century by a French comedian who, eaten up by jealousy at the success of Martinelli [Harlequin] makes Harlequin descend into Hell in search of the proprietor of a well-known brothel. Martinelli replied to this affront by reaffirming his own artistic superiority: 'It is true he said to his colleague [and enemy]—I did go down into Hell, but even there, I made everyone laugh, even the devils.

Marotti went on to show that this aggressive, almost anarchic line was followed above all by the two earliest famous Harlequins, and two of the most celebrated, Tristano Martinelli and Dominique Biancolelli, who broadened the function and applicability of the stereotype from Zanni (who must always be the servant, always inferior, physically and visually 'lower' than the Magnifico) to play potentially many parts, impersonating not only the servant, but also an inquisitor, even a woman. And since it is these two Harlequin actors who were principally the subject of Delia Gambelli's researches, it is not hard to see where Fo's authentication lies for his own distinctively subversive Harlequin. This image also fits his own 'subversive' personality as a theatre performer—from the politically downtrodden *giullare* of *Mistero buffo,* or indeed from the early Chaplinesque *Poer nano* to (perhaps its other extreme) a Pope who can similarly turn the tables on the conservative establishment in the cause of social justice (of 1990). And just as this is firmly in tune with the downtrodden cult of the 'little man' of the twentieth century, the anti-hero of many guises and forms, it is also reminiscent of the many other *engagé* and newly radical adaptations of *commedia,* such as those of the San Francisco Mime Troupe that we have noted. Thus it can be seen how relatively little distance separates the committed left-wing Dario Fo (who will send up and satirize almost any received orthodoxy, including that of the Italian Communist Party) and a slightly anarchic universal type reminiscent of the earliest Harlequins in their stage personalities whose most obvious modern incarnation is Chaplin.

The 'Laboratory on Harlequin' took place at Sta Cristina (near Gubbio) in Italy, where, over a six-week period, academics would read examples of early scenarios (such as those by Flaminio Scala, or the notebooks of Biancolelli), and Fo would make sketches of many of the *lazzi.* He was then left entirely free to improvise on the basis of this evidence, noting down his impressions in this graphic form. The whole process was monitored by technicians, TV cameramen and others, so that the resulting tapes could be played back in the evenings and the improvisations assessed. This body of filmed material is a precious resource which will one day allow the process of evolution to be observed very closely, just as the notes taken by two Rome university students (along with hundreds of photographs) will shortly be published in book form. Marotti's summing-up shows exactly where this initiative was driving in the early summer of 1985, and reflects the result: a show that (even if it seems to lack some structural unity to an audience expecting a 'play') is nonetheless consistent with its ambition:

> The objective was to overturn the official concept according to which the *commedia dell'arte* is tied to the idea of 'comedy', that is a performance in three or four acts. Our researches in the University of Rome in recent years show that the majority of the pieces for the great Harlequins of the sixteenth and seventeenth centuries (Martinelli and later Biancolelli) were a collection of farces, comic situations of 10-20 minutes' duration, the 'Comedy' was only the container of these various farces, of the *lazzi.* This is the Harlequin I am referring to in this show.

Before considering the show itself, we should mention that there were two further products from the fruitful collaboration of Dario Fo with the groves of academe: the first is Fo's *Manuale minimo dell'attore* (**The Tricks of the Trade**),

published in 1987, but clearly written during the period (more or less) of the gestation and performance of the Harlequin show. There is substantial evidence in its pages—indeed the whole first book is devoted to *commedia*—of the theories elaborated during the summer of 1985; the Italian edition carries a drawing of Harlequin by Fo on its front cover, and the English edition (imminent as this goes to press) has a number of photographs from the show itself. Secondly, Fo was asked to direct and design productions of Molière's *Le Médecin malgré lui* and a rarely performed Molière farce, *Le Médecin volant,* at the Comédie-Française in Paris in the summer of 1990. The latter is barely a scenario-synthesis, and Fo was able to fill this out with elaborations on *lazzi* drawn from antique Italian *commedia* scenarios. Importantly, just as the process of evolution of **Harlequin** was visualized through sketches (published in *Alcatraz News*), so too was the preparation process for the Molière production, the results of which are to be published in Paris. The benefits of this process of 'physical visualization', for the observation of the creative process of theatre, from the hand of an actor who is also an artist, can hardly be overstressed.

But there is one other way of considering the period Harlequin 'selected' by Dario Fo for his own *commedia* performance: a consideration of the tradition's modern derivatives. If the lessons of the *commedia dell'arte* have come down to us (archaeology apart) directly and most explicitly through farce, pantomime, the circus, music hall and the various performance uses of the clown image and survival of mime (not excluding Punch & Judy), why should not Fo, argues Ugo Volli, reinvent the tradition in terms of these modern derivatives? Even if, as he also suggests, the results show some fallback on gags and theatrical devices already used before, and seen in other contexts, this is precisely what Fo freely admits in his accounts of his late arrival at historical *commedia.* His discovery, as we have seen, was that *commedia*-derived skills were already in his repertoire, having been acquired through his experience of mime and variety. In fact he remains faithful to his own performance roots which themselves facilitated his adoption of the mask of Harlequin—a mask uncluttered with the narrowness of stereotype characteristics, or regional (and linguistic) stamp, and a Harlequin who is, in the end, Fo himself, as he must be.

> Naturally [speaking of early Commedia actors] they were people who had at least 2,000 gags and jokes under their belt. I would never have been able to carry out this task [Harlequin] at twenty years of age. I can only do it now thanks to all the research I have done on this theatre.

And Fo spoke in 1988 of being able to improvise on a theme

with few or no notes precisely because of a lifetime's activity as a performer in the theatre.

Turning now to the **Harlequin** show, first performed at the Venice Biennale on 10 October 1985, and on tour in Italy until March 1986, there is much evidence of development from the early draft of the script (which Dario Fo's son, Jacopo, confessed 'my father has not finished writing' when the first number of *Alcatraz News* went to press in November), to the version which was being performed in February and March 1986. Of course, this is entirely characteristic of Fo: the adaptation of material, addition of scenes and detail, in response to audience reaction is as much part of the working methods of Dario Fo and Franca Rame as it must have been for the earliest *commedia* troupes. 'The audience is the sole arbiter' is a sentiment often expressed down the long history of the tradition. In fact the edition of the script now considered definitive by the author (my copy marked: *aggiornata, aprile* 86) represents the *end* of the performance schedule, not the beginning, and is a transcript made from a recording of the performance given at the Teatro Ciak, Milan on 2 March 1986. Comparing these two versions makes it clear that the 'laboratory' yielded much that never reached final performance, just as many of the sketches already referred to have no tangible relationship with the show performed, for the same reason. Finally (as if to prove the truth of an infinitely variable and volatile text) we have the inclusion in an early script of two observers of the 'laboratory' of a sketch ('The Flying Car') *as if* performed but which had gone from the performance by February 1986, as well as the example of *Arlecchino fallotropo*, which was included in the Milan performance on 15 February, but excluded on 25 February, possibly to leave time for an increased volume of situations related to references to current affairs. Thus we have a shifting volume of material, true to the spirit of the *commedia dell'arte* ('feeding off' its audience in every respect), always related to the performers' perceptions of audience reception. For the purposes of the present discussion, therefore, four versions of the script have been used: the early draft published in *Alcatraz News* in November 1985, a sound tape of the show performed on 15 February 1986, a videotape of that performed on 25 February and the performance script (transcript) of 2 March 1986. In what must be an economical description, there is clearly no space here for a discussion of all the many minor variants, destined elsewhere, in any case.

The prologue in front of the curtain is a feature of all modern performances by Dario Fo (often a hilarious performance in itself), testing the vibrations of the audience, settling people into their seats as has become traditional, and itself echoes *commedia dell'arte* practice in the character's self-introduction to the audience alone on stage. In the case of **Harlequin** it takes the form of a 'lecture' on the *commedia dell'arte* with a collection of masks displayed on a screen

and costumes for Harlequin in different periods—from Martinelli in the sixteenth century to Goldoni's in the eighteenth—as well as costumes for Colombina and Franceschina. Fo explains that his own leafy costume indicates an 'early' Harlequin, the subversive one, *di disturbo,* and not later versions made famous by Goldoni. The prologue, then, is the prologue to the show, not an integral part of the *commedia dell'arte* storyline, which comes afterwards. It defines Fo's own interpretation of the arch-subversive, the defender of obscenity and scurrility (he claims that Harlequin used to defecate on stage, then pelt the audience with the fruits of his labours, shouting: 'Good luck! It brings good luck!'). He explains how the *canovaccio* (scenario) was used, how the indications of *lazzi* are built on in performance, using the 'Phallicthropic Harlequin' sketch as an example, in which a monster Phallus grows and grows as a result of drinking an overdose of his master's love (virility) potion. The sketch employs a full range of Fo's talents with mime (attempts to conceal the 'monster' from curious female onlookers include camouflage as a cat and as a baby), and he afterwards performed the sketch in London in 1988. Fo then proceeds to illustrate moments from the history of the *commedia dell'arte,* sometimes substituting the names of contemporaries (such as Italian cabinet ministers) for historical personages for topical effect, in a process which seems entirely gratuitous and linked to the 'lecture' situation by the slenderest of threads. The following priceless morsel (which had the audience in stitches) is based on the 'cartoon' image of the subject in the minds of the audience, and is linked to its situation only by a gag about the electric chair, which is gratuitously anachronistic anyway:

> It's amazing isn't it? We must have a highly developed sense of humour, mustn't we? To accept . . . as a Minister of Defence: just think of it! Incredible! All fact and buttery! A soft and fluttering defence, an elastic defence! Imagine giving . . . a kick! Buaah! Your foot would sink right in and come out all sticky and covered with pudding and creme caramel, glue, honey; after a week you'd still be covered in sticky. . . !

The prologue proper now begins as a prelude to the *commedia dell'arte* performance, with music, tumbling, acrobatics and song, in a colourful interlude which has Fo playing (or making noises with) an antique all-enveloping trombone. The whole of the prologue scene is based not (as traditionally) on an explanation in summary of the period story to be recounted by the play (although the earliest script did have a sketch-version of this that was later abandoned), but on the situation-comedy of the stage itself: the curtain has got stuck. Marcolfa (played by Franca Rame) is discovered mopping the stage floor, and protests that the audience seem like voyeurs; a ladder must be sought to mend the curtain, and the source, acquisition and description of this, as well as its eventual raising, are an opportunity for a string of surreal jokes attending this oldest of stage props (the ladder, pole or plank, from Charlie Chaplin to Benny Hill), which are yet entirely consistent with the surreal and magical world inhabited by this early Harlequin. First it is so long that the actor holding either end will disappear into the wings (only to reappear on the wrong side); then it is erected, and becomes a lookout mast on a fishing vessel; erected with the help of guy ropes, it metaphorically and physically draws in the audience, as two ropes are held by members of the audience: 'No! don't give it to him; he's an intellectual; they always let go when things get interesting!' Finally, Fo pretends almost to let it fall onto the front stalls, claiming four dead the previous evening, a gag (potential danger for the audience) used by him both before and since, importantly when an extended piece of ladder-play threatens to precipitate the actress into the audience in his direction of the Molière farces at the Comédie-Française. As we have seen before, in **Harlequin,** this situation is the hook for a string of organ transplant jokes, topical for 1985, again involving certain venerable senior politicians.

In all this, the very structure of the stage and its props are the situation: the 'prologue' itself never gets off the ground. In the show performed in the winter of 1986, an extended monologue was inserted for Franca Rame, in which she relates the story of the Magnifico's wife Isabella, sexually frustrated, who must learn from the prostitute her husband is known to frequent how to win back her husband. The lesson given to the wife by the prostitute, Eleanora, provides the actress with a unique opportunity to deliver to all women in the audience a lesson (replete with mime, obscene detail and voice-effects, such as sighs and sobs) in the techniques of seduction—and this is openly addressed to the audience when she advises them to take notes, quells an objection from the second row, and changes her mind about the number of times they made love that night when she realizes it is unrealistic. The monologue is a translation into period costume, with the licence conferred by the *commedia dell'arte,* of the love-chase from a female standpoint, reminiscent, in some respects, of Franca Rame's monologues and one-act plays, but here almost an ironic treatment of feminist polemic. Significantly, apart from the one moment when she rebukes the protester in the audience, the scene is played wholly in character and in *grammelot:* Marcolfa as the washerwoman is perhaps closer to the working-class origins of *A Woman Alone* than the more sophisticated protagonists of *The Open Couple* and *An Ordinary Day.*

So the story of Isabella's reconquest of her husband, the Magnifico, is all that remains of the original prologue storyline from the first draft script. Originally, the 'plot' told of young Flavio (disguised as a woman to avoid conscription into the Flanders wars), who goes into service in Pantaloon's house and falls in love with Isabella, dropping

all 'her' pots and pans with the emotion of meeting her. All this disappeared in performance (although a Pantaloon with stinking breath does survive in a sketch), and the period 'story' surfaces only very occasionally during the ladder episode, such as when a *zanni* is reminded by Fo-Harlequin that he cannot protest he is overworked because trade unions had not been invented in 1585.

By now it is clear that the **Harlequin** show was a series of situation gags (originating from antique models) but based loosely on the characteristics of Harlequin, and only linked with the Renaissance *commedia* theme by the situation of performance itself (the stage, costume, Fo's mask, stage props). It comments on the *commedia dell'arte,* in a sense, rather than reliving or reinventing it. Harlequin himself is its only connecting thread in the end. His 'paradoxes'—the extension of the real into an imaginary surreal or grotesque, such as when he 'rubs out' the audience offending Marcolfa by watching her work with a mime of cleaning a blackboard—are typical of the characteristics described by scholars like Molinari, or of the Harlequin described by Fo himself, who will mime being a chair to embrace his love when she sits down. Another example, from later in the show, is where Fo-Harlequin puts half a cold chicken to his ear, claiming to be able to hear the sea. The action of the mime associates the actual object the audience sees with another, similar one it knows well.

The characteristics for which Harlequin was famous also include hunger, and the original script included an episode in which Harlequin discovers a heap of rubbish, thanking God for such a precious find. Sifting through the remains of countless meals, he identifies the different social classes whose meals he now shares, doubtless with liberal doses of mimed attributes, and comes upon an unused candle, which he eats as a great delicacy. The scene was cut from the final performance but echoes the famous *zanni* hunger scene (in which Harlequin or a *zanni* mimes eating parts of himself, so great is his hunger) that Fo performed at the National Theatre in London in January, 1991. Hunger, too, was the initial theme of the *Cantata dei Pastori* ('Song of the shepherds'), present in the first draft, but abandoned in performance. Two *zanni* spy a blackbird, then a cat, then a dog, waiting for each animal to eat up the former in order to catch them all at once. Predictably, the animals escape and the *zanni* have to be content with the crumbs the blackbird was pecking. This is followed by the arrival of the Virgin Mary *en route* for Jerusalem and needing porters. Understanding *Pellestrina* (on the coast not far from Venice) for *Palestina,* the *zanni* attempt to take her there by a boat which is almost wrecked in a storm and only saved by invocations to the Virgin (who of course is present). Thus the mistaken-identity gag is sustained to the end, supported by songs sung in chorus. Apparently from an original by Perrucci, and analysed with variants by the authors of *Io Fo Arlecchino,* who style it an 'operetta', the whole episode was no longer in the show in performance.

The same fate befell 'The Flying Cat', a sketch which appears in the early draft as the triumph of Harlequin's astuteness and cunning over received wisdom. Harlequin quizzes Eularia, who appears to be a walking dictionary: he bets with her that she cannot answer all his questions; she raises the stakes by prevaricating with answers *around* the question, while he mimes various chronometers to indicate the passage of time. This guessing game, with Eularia now asking the questions, goes on through a rising crescendo of mimed attributes of the fabulous animal—called, in the end, the flying cat—until the monster appears from the wings of the finale blowing bubbles as part of the world of fantasy and imagination that Harlequin inhabits, and the triumph of childlike fantasy over conventional wisdom is complete. Harlequin is vanquished on this occasion by Eularia's superior tactics. The sketch was clearly a powerful vehicle for the mime talents of Dario Fo, and appears, as we have seen, as if in performance in the summary of lo Fo *Arlecchino,* though not in the final performance.

The sketch entitled 'The Gravediggers' did survive into final performance and endured, with variants, down to the end of the performance schedule. It takes place in a graveyard where Harlequin and Razzullo are digging the grave for a man who drowned himself in a bowl of water. But the fable Harlequin now recounts is of a suicide in a vat of wine (the opportunity for mime and voice-effects), and the episode is a comic *tour de force* of Harlequin's traditional assaults on conventions, a surreal circus of obscenities (Harlequin explains the derivation of 'scatology' in a mock-serious discourse, and urinates on a skull), pantomime effects (two skulls speak and a skeleton emerges), physical business (skulls are slapped and thrown about like footballs), and a mock-serious funeral conducted by a homosexual priest which ends in a fight, further deaths, and dinner with the 'despairing' widow. The whole is commented on by Fo-Harlequin in a systematic dismantling of conventional taboos: death, the Church, the family, with surreal touches like the following:

> WIDOW Aahh! I've been widowed a second time. [the widow's lover has just been killed in a fight]
> HARLEQUIN God, for a hundred performances now, the dead man's brother has ended up dead—with his head resting on the priest's buttocks!

This episode—alone in Fo's *Harlequin*—is self-contained and moves from the situation of the suicide by drowning to the fable of the wine suicide, to knockabout with clown-skulls (who ironically play the part of respect for the dead),

and ends in a mini-farce of the funeral, complete with *De Profundis* and music, in which Fo-Harlequin mercilessly lampoons the solemnity and gravity of such occasions. Just as the many uses of the ladder prop in the prologue (secured with guy ropes) echo many of Fo's favourite stage effects using theatrical devices before and since *Harlequin,* so too the animation of the skulls, in a sort of ludicrous parody of the scene from *Hamlet,* re-uses the puppet and marionette effects from other times and contexts. Here, more than elsewhere, Harlequin is, in Fo's words: 'destroyer of conventions. His interventions are often completely gratuitous, and his morality always derives from paradox. . . .'

The second half of Fo's *Harlequin* contained the episode of the Key and the Lock, a classic sexual metaphor, and the sketch with the animals, which builds on Harlequin's traditional fear. The Key episode begins with a device typical of the bizarre logic of paradox in the world Harlequin introduces: a joke with a table and the attempt to lift it with a lever. Once again, the *situation* causes the table to be brought onstage; the result is mockery of the pretensions of science to accomplish miracles. The table will bear the Lock (a giant stage-prop some three feet square,) tended, oiled and decorated by Franceschina (played by Franca Rame), while Harlequin's Key is on a similar scale, carried like a rifle over the shoulder. Endless elaborations of the predictable scenario follow: Harlequin supplies oil for cleaning the Lock, it is tempted by a *zanni* with a golden key, until, refusing penetration by Harlequin's key, the Lock is finally persuaded by the traditional blackmail when Harlequin produces a picnic lunch, and Franceschina realizes she is hungry. In the early version of the script, conception followed penetration, and five little keys clatter onto the stage, but in performance Harlequin returns to his key to find a substitute rubber floppy inflatable key in its place—it has died—and the sketch ends as a tragedy of love.

In the concluding episode, Harlequin's traditional fear of animals provides the excuse for a variety of pantomime beasts and a play on the fiction/reality dualism of men and animals. Harlequin illustrates this by fear of a dog, conversation with a donkey (in the fantasy world of magic that pantomime confers), finding that it had formerly belonged to a drunken priest who had suffered a heart-attack after making love to a girl! Anticlericalism apart, the climax comes after a practical joke played on Harlequin by two *zanni* who impersonate a pantomime lion to frighten him. Determined on a show of courage to win the love of Franceschina, Harlequin undertakes feats of bravado with the lion, believing it contains his two friends, while in reality, a *real* lion has escaped from a ship in port. A number of jokes derive from this situation of 'mistaken identity', including such circus favourites as the head (or hand) in the lion's mouth, 'feeding' sausages to the animal's 'rear actor' and a lesson in roaring.

Looking back on Fo's **Harlequin,** one is struck again by Marotti's claim that the essence of the *commedia dell'arte* was the *lazzi,* never the story, which was only their shell, Practitioners of 'strict tempo' *commedia* like Carlo Boso teach young actors never to lose sight of the storyline—or you will lose your audience. The format chosen by Dario Fo, utilizing, as we have seen, all the resources of his performance experience and background, does move the Harlequin show perceptibly nearer the relative structural anarchy of music-hall. And yet the audience in the circus tent will react with wide-eyed delight at clowns and a high-wire act without worrying about hypothetical organic connections. Alone among the sketches—tied in a loose bundle by Harlequin's traditional attributes, in a word, his biography—is Franca Rame's monologue, which is both period-orientated (as built on 'Renaissance' concepts of corsetry), and in tune with the storyline (the relationship between Isabella and Eleanora). For the rest, costume, spirit, the paradox and the imagination, the authentic sources of *lazzi,* are all part of the *commedia dell'arte,* but mingle irresistibly with other undeniable strengths of Fo's comic stage personality, which no amount of justification and research in the world will turn into a Harlequin of history. The very twentieth-century targets, from the anachronisms of satire of cabinet ministers to Fo's propensity for 'gags off the wall', are, in the end, the result of Fo's stage personality, as robustly satisfying as it ever was, which tends to spill out in performance and breaks free from the 'academic' framework of the *commedia dell'arte,* in an instinctive rapport (itself authentic) with audiences in the here and now, which will not be boxed and pigeon-holed. And in the end, this is itself what the *commedia dell'arte* means today: the *freedom* to adapt to 'modern' purposes a pan-European theatrical tradition which encompasses experiments as diverse as the *Age d'or* of Ariane Mnouchkine, the complexities and multi-discipline approach of Eugenio Barba, and the determinedly 'modern' innovations of the San Francisco Mime Troupe. With the innate subversive charge of the radical, Fo *is* today's Harlequin (at least since the death of Chaplin), and the encounter (confrontation?) in 1985-6 with academic pretensions was a liberating of his stage personality, not a caging of it.

Typically, in his **Manuale minimo** . . . , he begins precisely with a satirical treatment of the scholarly controversy surrounding the *commedia dell'arte,* in a sense, distancing himself from it as from all the pedantries of academically disputed orthodoxies:

> Yet, where I succeeded in reaching the sublimely impossible was the point in which Meldolesi of Dams at the University of Bologna, although he was giving a course on avant-garde theatre at the time at Holstbro in Denmark, was made to leap here to Rome by my magic, and obliged to take part in a

debate which, in reality, will take place at Stresa next year. In this case I simply speed up time by 10,000 light-units and make the event happen when it suits me . . . here in Rome, for example . . . I get loads of people together and without even seeking their approval, I throw them into the audience.

> Taviani, up you get! . . . Come on, no 'buts', I know you're actually in Palermo at this minute . . . and you can't see how I managed to get you here . . . I can't explain, it's a trade secret. Come on, repeat word for word your lecture from Pistoia. . . . What do you mean, which one? The one on Harlequin, of course, where you said you thought he was a character extraneous to the *commedia dell'arte,* so much so that you said he wasn't even Italian but French in origin. . . . There, good . . . now you stay put while I get Eugenio Barba to reply to you, who at the moment is in New York. . . . Don't worry about the time difference. . . . Here he is, Eugenio, reply to him. . . . You don't want to? Well, I'll make you say what you wrote in your essay three years ago . . . in the chapter: *Harlequin—an oriental mask.*

> Stop, everyone, there's Marotti asking to speak . . . he's speaking from Bali where he's on holiday at present. . . .

In the end, Fo makes them all go to lunch—in their respective places and time-zones, and exclaims: 'Ah, at last! A bit of peace and quiet and *normality!*'

Joel Schechter (essay date 1994)

SOURCE: "Dario Fo: *Trumpets and Raspberries,*" in *Satiric Impersonations: From Aristophanes to the Guerrilla Girls,* Southern Illinois University Press, 1994, pp. 92-106.

[*In a close examination of Fo's* Trumpets and Raspberries *and* Almost by Chance a Woman: Elizabeth, *Schechter argues for Fo's timeliness as a humorist and his identification as perhaps the last great theatrical satirist.*]

Few comedians in our century besides Chaplin have been better known than Dario Fo. The Italian satirist's plays are staged around the world. He has directed comic opera at La Scala in Milan. His own one-man shows have been applauded everywhere from China to New York.

Unfortunately, Fo may also be one of the theater's last great satirists. Comic broadsides against abusive power and wealth are rarely heard on stage anymore. Producers avoid controversial subjects, especially those that offend wealthy patrons. Even when playwrights are able to stage satire, if they produce it themselves as Fo has, it remains difficult to compete with actuality. We live in an age when presidents, generals, financiers, and journalists offer the public statements outrageous enough to rival the inventions of the most imaginative playwrights.

Fortunately, one of Dario Fo's gifts as actor and author is the ability to impersonate public leaders on stage. He does not have to invent outrageous statements; instead, during the performance of a farce, he repeats public leaders' statements. "I call my work farce," he once said. "What they call comedy today has lost the rebellious strain of ancient times. In farce, you have the possibility of going beyond character. You can comment on the situation while you are in it." Fo is "in" his situations as satirist and political activist. Onstage he is able to renew the ancient, Aristophanic art of topical satire with references informed by post-Marxist political theory as well as a praxis that has led him to perform plays inside occupied factories, outside courthouses, and on more conventional stages.

Fo has publicly acknowledged debts to the comedy of wandering medieval jesters (*giullari* in Italy), commedia dell'arte slapstick, nineteenth-century Italian storytellers, and Brecht's epic theater. But the plays also frequently employ high court judges, prime ministers, and millionaires as their "coauthors." Rather than debate these influential leaders in media that favor them, Fo brings them—or rather their doubles—into his stage world, where they live in his inventive impersonations, quotations and parodies of official language. Through impersonations the satirist can say what his adversaries only imply and repeat what they already said to the press in a manner that underscores its preposterousness. The stage becomes his alternative press, his low (as opposed to high) court tribunal, where the audience is invited to judge history and current events anew.

More than once Fo has been compared to the Marx Brothers, as well as Karl, and he has acknowledged their diverse traditions. "We have always taken situations of struggle as our point of reference," he once said in response to a question about his study of Marx. But while he has read Karl Marx and quotes the man in a play, Fo says of his theater collective: "We . . . are not 'serious' Marxists. In fact, we are a mass of 'villains' and, like all villains of this world, we enjoy smiling and mockery, being grotesque, vulgar and at times, scurrilous." Its members sound more like Groucho Marxists; their "situation of struggle" sets Fo the clown in a world of economic law and order that he cannot take seriously and that he prefers to portray with mockery.

Fo insures that villains are seen from his perspective by performing the lead role (of high court judge, millionaire, general) himself, comically embodying the attributes of wealth, power, and authority to which he objects. Anyone who has seen Dario Fo perform in Italy, in front of thousands of cheering spectators, understands the force of his satire; large crowds join his side and laugh at those in power. He creates a pleasurable, partisan event that his opponents cannot control, although they have tried through legal actions and harassment.

On stage Fo is a clown who needs no greasepaint or red nose to signal his love of low comedy; his gleeful eyes, toothy smile, deft hand and leg movements, topped by a balding pate make him look like a cherub past sixty, joyously racing through a repertory of pranks that have increased in number with the passage of time. He is a Falstaff minus potbelly and beard, quick in movements as well as wit, able to break into a crazy jig without warning and answer hecklers so fast it seems rehearsed. He is a one-man chorus, too, with a voice rich in its range of tempos, tones and personae. The actor can hold a conversation with himself, which permits him to play two or more roles in more than one play.

Taking on multiple roles in a single play also allows Fo to embody his commitment to communal forms of living. As he says:

> We find ourselves completely opposed to the idea of identifying the actor with the character: the actor is ME, I try to identify with him or her, and inside myself all the fripperies, the innards, all my defects, all my qualities in an attempt to dress up the character as myself. That's what Stanislavsky's all about, and it's the worst type of reactionary, conservative, bourgeois position in history.

> If instead I try to create the vision of a community, a chorus, a communion obviously I'm not going to be too concerned about talking about myself—I'm talking about collective problems. If I seek out collective problems, what I'm saying and the language I use will be different: it'll be forced to be epic. This is why all the popular theater is always epic, because it's based on a clear ideological fact—the idea of community, of a communion of interests, social interests, interests of living together, producing together, and sharing proceeds.

In plays Fo initiates a more even distribution of power and wealth by turning policemen into anarchists and industrialists into wage laborers, at least temporarily. He becomes a high court judge, defends the innocent, and persuades the police to sing anarchist songs in *Accidental Death of an Anarchist*. He portrays a kidnapped millionaire who secures the freedom of suspected terrorists in *Trumpets and Rasp-*

berries. Perhaps it would be more accurate to say that the millionaire secures his own freedom in the latter play, since Fo portrays both an alleged hostage and an alleged terrorist, neither of whom are what is alleged.

When Fo first performed **Trumpets and Raspberries** in 1981 (retitled **About Face** for its American premiere in 1983), he portrayed one of Italy's wealthiest men, Gianni Agnelli, and one of Agnelli's employees, Antonio Berardi. Agnelli, owner of the Fiat auto company and a national celebrity, is shown by Fo to be the victim of a Red Brigades kidnaping. In fact, Agnelli never was kidnapped; the plot is a fantasy based on another actual kidnaping.

After Agnelli's rescue, described in the prologue of the play, his face requires plastic surgery. By mistake surgeons give him a worker's face—Berardi's—since the employee left his photo behind. Fo's Agnelli suddenly finds himself facing the indignities of wage labor and police surveillance, to which the leftist workers in his factories have been subjected for years.

The real-life Agnelli is a white-haired, large-nosed gentleman whose appearance resembles Fo's and a few Italians familiar with the original model for Fo's impersonation might have briefly wondered on opening night if Agnelli, not Fo, was performing for them. A few minutes of Fo's anticapitalist jests, and their doubts would have disappeared.

Fo Kidnaps the Prime Minister

Agnelli's kidnaping was not the first act of terrorism Fo imagined. In 1975 he wrote *Fanfani Abducted,* a satiric fantasy about the kidnapping of the man who was then Italy's prime minister. Fo portrayed the diminutive leader as a dwarf, by holding shoes in front of his knees while another actor behind him performed the character's arm movements. A living cartoon, Fanfani walked walls, flew, became hysterically pregnant, and gave birth to a puppet. The prime minister who had opposed abortion in Italy was subjected to the same labor he wanted to force upon women, and his body, like theirs, became a toy for men to play with. Prior to that abduction, Fanfani had never been kidnapped, much as Agnelli had never been kidnapped when the later play was written about him. Unfortunately, reality intervened between plays with a violent crime. Christian Democratic party leader Aldo Moro was kidnapped by the Red Brigades in 1978. Fo's fantasy about Fanfani was no longer so funny after Moro was executed by terrorists.

In response to the kidnapping, Fo initially turned to politics, not theater. He joined with the president of Catholic Action, some priests, and Radical party leader Marco Pannella to publish an appeal for Moro's release. The coalition, which called itself the Party of Negotiation, thought that the sanc-tity of human life should override everyday politics and that the government should negotiate with the terrorists for Moro's release. The government refused. Only one radical leftist newspaper, *Lotta Continua,* agreed to publish the appeal to which Fo was signatory; in part it may have been the refusal of other media to allow for expression of his view that led Fo to write a play about the event and to address a larger public directly with his comic commentary. Before and after Moro's murder, thousands of Italian leftists were arrested and questioned in a campaign to end terrorism. The threat of terrorism was exaggerated by prosecuting officials, and the imagined danger gave Italy's right wing an excuse to disregard civil rights and suppress leftist dissent.

Prominent political activists were arrested not on the basis of crimes committed but because of statements they had spoken and published. Franca Rame, the actress and wife of Dario Fo, noted in a 1982 interview: "Now we have more than 4,500 political prisoners. In the last six years, more than 15,000 have been arrested and then released because they [the charges] were completely irrelevant and [the accused were] innocent." She and Fo collected funds to insure fair trials and prevent police torture of suspected terrorists, and for this the couple was accused by the United States State Department of supporting terrorism. The State Department denied them entry into the United States in 1980 and 1983 when they were invited to perform their one person shows in New York. Finally, they were admitted in 1984 but continued to face questions about their attitude toward terrorism. In fact, they never supported terrorism, quite the contrary. Fo explains:

> Terror never destabilizes the established rule; rather it strengthens it, it destabilizes the opposition (even when the opposition is most moderate) which is thus forced, in order to avoid being suspiciously drawn in as a cover to terrorism, to accept, support and allow those laws and those uncontrollable, violent acts which will be used against citizens and workers. . . . Power has no real interest in fighting terrorism.

Terrorism is accepted by power in **Trumpets and Raspberries,** when Fo's version of Gianni Agnelli pretends to be kidnapped in order to test the limits of his own power. He asks the state to release political prisoners in exchange for his freedom and to negotiate with terrorists on his behalf, although it refused to do so for Aldo Moro's release. Agnelli, called the Double throughout the play, is jubilant when his demands are met. He announces to all present: "Listen, the whole Cabinet has met and issued a communique. Here it is, under the headline: 'Kidnap Chaos. Cabinet Caves In. Yes. In the Moro Case, the State Answered: No Exchange. This Time It Must Answer: Yes.'" The release of prisoners in exchange for his alleged release (alleged because he is free) persuades the Double that he is the state. He repeats the words of France's Sun King. "I am the state," suggesting that today wealth can purchase the power formerly inherited by kings. Aldo Moro "was sacrificed in order to save the respectability of the . . . financial state"—Agnelli's state—according to the Double. He also claims Karl Marx as an ally here, quoting lines from *Das Kapital* to assert that "the only true power . . . is financial-economic power."

The lines attributed to Marx in this speech may have been invented by Fo. Several Marxist scholars have failed to find the source for this speech, which should be fully quoted here: "The only true power in this world is financial-economic power, the power of cartels, multinational industries, banks, markets and manufactured goods—that is, Capital!" Fo's Agnelli then asks astounded listeners onstage, "What's wrong with you? That's Karl Marx. What, only industrialists read Marx nowadays?" He resumes the text allegedly authored by Marx to assert that "the filigreed paper on which banknotes are printed bears the sacred laws of the state, of the economic state. Governments and institutions are nothing other than props for the economic state." Agnelli says these lines ought to be memorized and sung by children. They have been memorized by actors around the world, who recite them in a political farce. If, as Marx once wrote paraphrasing Hegel, history repeats itself as farce, it could be added that Fo has actors repeat Marx as farce.

With provocative humor, For attributes a thorough knowledge of Marx to a leading capitalist and cites Marx as proof that Agnelli is all-powerful. Marxism, like terrorism, exists to serve and confirm the power of the wealthy in Fo's satire; by extension, the ruling class would also applaud poverty, illness, and ignorance as sources of its strength. The play offers a vision of a world much like our own, except that its contradictions become grotesquely comic in Fo's depiction of them. Wealth and power depend on their opposites for their continued existence. And occasionally they turn into their opposites, thanks to Fo's portrayal of multiple roles. (In light of the 1991 transformation of Russian Marxists into capitalists—discussed in an earlier chapter—it might be said that Fo's Agnelli read Marx quite correctly, prophetically, in fact, although his reading seemed quite funny in the early eighties.)

"Auto-Terrorism"

Fo's Agnelli turns into a terrorist, self-kidnapped, once he decides to see if he is more respected than Aldo Moro. He commits "auto-terrorism," since he, Gianni Agnelli, is the only terrorist who holds Agnelli hostage. As grotesque as this development seems, Fo's humor has a basis in actuality. Agnelli's company, Fiat, was accused by one of its workers of being a terrorist organization in 1979. Giampaolo Pansa was fired for union activities, including a call for safer working conditions at Fiat. Afterwards he wrote: "I am evidence that Fiat is a terrorist organization. By eliminating people like me, Fiat wants to eliminate those who can speak on behalf of the others, those who do not bow their heads." When he was wrongly accused of terrorism by Fiat, Pansa began to sense that Agnelli's company was much closer than he was to terrorism, as it drove law-abiding men like himself out of the factory, out of unions, until they had nowhere to turn but the unemployment line or the Red Brigades. In that sense, Agnelli's plant was recruiting terrorists and its owner had sided with the Red Brigades.

Fo, too, was turned into a terrorist through an unsought transformation when the United States State Department accused him of supporting terrorism in 1980. He and his wife had asked for Italian laws to be observed, with the same legal rights accorded everyone, including suspected terrorists. In turn, Fo and Rame were accused of acting unlawfully. Fo forces Agnelli to undergo the same transformation from lawful citizen into terrorist in his play. His satire could be regarded as an act of counter-counterterrorism, as it suggests that counter-terrorist actions by industry and state actually create terrorism.

Calling Mrs. Moro

In one of the play's hospital scenes, a doctor analyzing the patient he believes to be Antonio Berardi says that after months of "chewing over his hatred toward the person who, in his opinion, is responsible for his tragedy . . . in other words, Agnelli . . . [he] ended up identifying with him." In fact Fo's Agnelli has ended up identifying with himself, remembering who he is after months of amnesia. But the doctor, and Fo himself as satirist, deny this identity to Agnelli. Much as Fo in his acting theory opposes the idea of identifying actor with character, he also denies his characters a single, fixed identity. They are too dependent on one another—boss on worker, policeman on anarchist—to be completely separated or contradictory. The doctor decides Agnelli is a Fiat worker, and in another scene, the wealthy man is regarded as a terrorist by the police.

During a comic interrogation, conducted in the hospital while Agnelli is still suffering from amnesia, the Fiat magnate cannot recall what work is. One implication is that the wealthy man has never had to work in his life. Another, less obvious possibility, is that he is a worker active in the Autonomia movement, which encourages its members to refuse work and reduce their weekly hours of labor through strikes, new contracts, and even industrial sabotage. Fo's Agnelli sounds much like an Autonomia activist when he states that "work . . . labour. . . . These words have no meaning for me." His refusal to acknowledge that work and labor are meaningful sum up *Semiotext*(e) creditor Christian Marazzi's description of the Autonomia movement's goal: "the refusal of work." "Only when the worker's labor is reduced to the minimum is it possible to go beyond, in the literal sense, the capitalist mode of production. Only when 'non-worker's labor' becomes a generalized reality and enjoying life a productive fact in itself, does freedom from exploitation become not only possible but materially achievable."

Italy's Autonomia activists are by no means the same as the Red Brigades terrorists, though the police in Fo's play and in Italy have mistakenly equated the two. The Italian police mistook identities in a manner far less comic than the scene of interrogation in **Trumpets and Raspberries.** Fo's farce follows a similar illogical course, however. Discussing Autonomia with Christian Marazzi, *Semiotext*(e) co-editor Sylvere Lotringer argues that Italy had become a "non-Aristotelian state," defying Aristotelian logic in its violation of "the principle of identity (A is always A, never B)." The usual concept and logic of identity are overthrown when the state (not Fo) equates Autonomia with the Red Brigades and refusal of work with terrorism.

At the trial of Autonomia theorist Toni Negri in 1979, the judge repeatedly asked the defendant to explain the difference between Autonomia and Red Brigades philosophies. The judge kept mistaking one for the other, despite Negri's explanations. Some lines in the courtroom dialogue could have been written by Dario Fo. When the judge told Negri, "You should be able to remember who these people were who gave you these documents and asked for your support," Negri replied, "I repeat I cannot answer. Terrorists never introduce themselves as such." The public prosecutor, desperately wanting to have a terrorist introduce himself in court, then suggested Negri was the mysterious Red Brigades member who had telephoned Mrs. Moro. "When you speak in this excited tone," he told the defendant, "you remind me of the voice in that phone call to Mrs. Moro." The taped, anonymous call had not yet been analyzed in a lab when the prosecutor offered his observation to the court, but the prosecutor wanted, needed, identities mistaken here to prove the state's case.

Fo's play conveys in comic form the non sequiturs of Italian politics, in which almost anyone on the left with an excited voice could be accused of phoning Mrs. Moro. When Fo's Agnelli extends the process of unsubstantiated accusations to those involved in a right-wing plot and begins to identify them ("Generals, ministers . . . then everything was exposed, and then covered up again"), he is told to shut up. Terrorism of the right and state terrorism are not acknowledged by those in power in the play's parody of actual government dispositions.

In "The Sandstorm Method," Fo notes that Power or the Power Party is interested in perpetuating "the spectacle and the emotional participation of the spectator citizen in a continuous merry-go-round of bombastic facts, much like a television 'mystery' where everyone is the suspect, everyone is the murderer. . . . In this 'blizzard' where everyone is screaming 'He has the plague,' Power has freed itself. . . ." The spectacle is replicated with fervor in Fo's play, revealing what Lotringer has called a society of "celebrated falsifications." Lotringer illustrates the term with an anecdote about the arrest of actor Ugo Tognazzi. Tognazzi was not arrested as chief of the Red Brigades, but when a satiric journal, *Il Male,* published photographic evidence of the arrest, "the public took this simulation for the literal truth." The distinction between satire and actuality was abolished not by the satiric journal or an actor playing a role, but by a public willing to accept fantasy as reality. In his play, Fo also invites the public to collaborate in a fabrication of reality, to see Agnelli rather than Tognazzi as a leading terrorist.

Is Italy's Wealthiest Man a Communist?

One would expect most Italians to find it implausible that Agnelli is a terrorist. After all, they see photographs of him diving off his yacht, dining in chic restaurants, driving sports cars—hardly the imagery of terrorism. Yet some Italians took Fo seriously enough to attack his play. One of its most vocal opponents was a communist member of Parliament who called for the work to be censored. At first it may sound surprising—that a communist would defend Agnelli. But Agnelli—the real Agnelli—had more or less approved of the Italian Communist party's program around the time Moro was kidnapped. In the seventies, the PCI (Italian Communist party) initiated its "historic compromise" with the Christian Democratic party in order to secure more power. While Agnelli approved of the compromise, Fo did not, particularly when it meant that the PCI supported centrist leaders in their refusal to negotiate for Aldo Moro's release. Fo said in an interview:

> The Communist Party wanted in any way they could to be involved in the direction of the Italian government. To compromise with the Christian Democratic government in order to share power, and to exploit the horror story of Moro, they did something oriented toward the so-called "National Unity." The workers always felt the state was an oppressive machine against them, and now they suddenly find that the Communist Party is holding it [the state] sacred. When we turned over all this ideology and spat it back out so it could be seen as babbling hypocrisy, it made the Communist Party lose their heads.

Fo also noted that his play revealed "the hypocrisy of the state which cynically allowed the life of Moro to be sacrificed. Aldo Moro would have been rescued if he had been more like Agnelli, argues Fo, but the cynicism here is that of leading politicians, not the playwright. They took a hard line against terrorists because they had nothing to lose but Moro's life, and they had a reputation as supporters of "national unity" and "historic compromise" to gain.

In letters written while he was held hostage, Moro called on Italy's leaders to negotiate for his release and criticized their lack of compromise: "An institutional 'compromise' that does not include the political and social forces outside those in power is a puny accomplishment." He had begun to see the inadequacy of the "historic compromise," when he saw it might exclude him as well as Autonomia and other extraparliamentary organizations. The response to Moro's letters at the time he wrote them was as grotesque as anything Fo could suggest. "Who has written this letter?" a leading daily, *Corrier Della Sera,* asked, before answering its own question: "Aldo Moro, president of the Christian Democrats, statesman, maximum mediator and inspiration of Italian politics, cautious strategist . . . in normal conditions, would never have suggested . . . the yielding to terrorists." Fo's whole play might have been based on another phrase in the same daily paper's doubt about the letter: "Has it been written by a man who has the same name, the same face, still Aldo Moro, but reduced to impotence by cruel imprisonment, isolated and perhaps dulled by drugs?" Fo's Agnelli is dulled by amnesia and has a new face after he is allegedly kidnapped, but the letters he writes are as sharp and provocative as those written by Moro. In fact, they copy Moro's, as he admits.

Although he copies some lines from the letters of Aldo Moro, Agnelli alters the text enough so that history will turn into farce when it is repeated. His kidnaping is far more comic and happy than Moro's, in part because his letters are more imaginative. He writes not only for himself but also on behalf of a terrorist organization—his own. His letters convince Italy's leading politicians and ministers that they will lose more than his life from his kidnaping. They might lose their own lives or, worse yet, their reputations as honest men, after he accepts their offers to sacrifice their lives in place of his. The politicians thought their offers would never be accepted by the Red Brigades, but Agnelli accepts them on behalf of his own (self-) terrorist organization.

The Double in the play sees another reason for those in power to seek his freedom: he is more important than Moro, since the state exists to serve his financial empire. "It does not matter which face I have. I am Power," he concludes, as he ascends toward heaven by climbing up the scenery.

The Quack Doctor's Prognosis

Early in act 1, Fo's injection-loving doctor—a modern version of Italian Commedia's quack Il Dottore—offers an analysis of his patient that sounds persuasive. He describes the human "fiction mechanism" as the "most exposed and ephemeral part of the brain," and claims it is the first part of the brain to be destroyed by a violent trauma. Patients are incapable of telling lies or pretending after losing their fiction mechanism. Such a loss would be disastrous for an actor. For a politician, asserts Fo's doctor, the loss is impossible: "For them, traumas have no effect." They continue to lie. This explains why politicians can be actors, and perhaps this is the reason politicians inspire so many of the wonderful fools Fo portrays onstage.

Fo's Hamlet

Fo returned to the Moro kidnapping in another, later satire, ***Almost by Chance a Woman: Elizabeth.*** The 1983 play, based on historical documents and *Hamlet,* concerns the last years of Elizabeth I. The queen fears that Shakespeare wrote *Hamlet* as a satire on her own indecisive character around the same time the Earl of Essex led a rebellion against her majesty. In drawing on history, Fo explodes any myths that may remain about Elizabeth being a virgin queen or a mere woman dependent on the advice of men for her political survival. In the play, she relies primarily on women for support, as she acquiesces to the fact that she must execute her lover, Robert of Essex, to stay in power.

Fo himself played the role of the queen's beautician, a sorceress, in woman's dress. Much as Elizabeth has to reject the "weak," stereotypical behavior expected of women and steel herself against rebels, Fo becomes a woman in order to serve the queen's needs and comically question gender roles. When Elizabeth suspects that someone in her chamber may not be a woman, the beautician replies, "Don't be so hard on yourself." Fo is hard on both of them as he reverses gender roles and the servant-master (or mistress) relationship.

In this play, as elsewhere, Fo manages to infuse history with a sense of continuity and present-tense activity, a sense that while offering the story of Queen Elizabeth's last years, his play is simultaneously examining our own culture and its origins. The empire collapsing around Elizabeth is not exactly the same as Italy or America in the past decade. But the tendency of state rulers to overextend themselves, foster rebellion by suppressing dissent, and lose contact with democratic principles while allegedly defending those principles was not uniquely Elizabeth's.

She and similar, later rulers neglect to hear the voices of the underclass—voices like that of the vulgar beautician Fo portrays or of Martha, Elizabeth's other servant in the play. Martha has watched *Hamlet* with the groundlings at the Globe, and her love of popular entertainment enables her to allay Queen Elizabeth's fears that Hamlet is a caricature of the queen herself.

> ELIZABETH: This entire play is an attack against my character and my politics. Every night at the Globe this theatrical tub-thumper [Shakespeare] spits in my eye.
> MARTHA: Listen, Elizabeth, by chance I happened to see a performance of *Hamlet* a few days ago, and I assure you that I saw no attack on you.

Elizabeth's sentiment here is not necessarily Shakespeare's, perhaps not his at all, but it is Dario Fo's. With an elaborate comic theory based on history, he suggests Shakespeare was a subversive author who should have been beheaded with the Earl of Essex for attempting to overthrow the state. Elizabeth's fears that Hamlet the Dane is a caricature of her reflect Fo's own perception of theater as an art that disturbs unjust rulers and places them and scenes of their defeat onstage.

Theater historians have argued that Shakespeare's company revived *Richard II* with its deposition scene at the Earl of Essex's prompting in 1601 so that it might encourage the deposition of Elizabeth. But prior to Fo's play, it has rarely been proposed that Hamlet was created as a satiric impersonation of the Virgin Queen.

Shakespeare's panorama of an unruly Danish state, where assassination and revenge erupt, is received as a portrait of her own reign by Fo's Elizabeth. The imagined threat *Hamlet* poses to her is reduced considerably in one comic scene in which Fo as beautician tells the entire story of *Hamlet* very quickly (in three minutes) so the court police chief can judge whether Shakespeare is a subversive author. Elizabeth keeps asking her servant to keep quiet and stop his pantomime: in doing so, she censors Shakespeare and Fo at the same time. Rarely has the state placed Fo in such august company.

Terrorism arrives when a religious fanatic attempts to kill the Queen, and fails, and when the Earl of Essex then takes several of the Queen's messengers (lords) hostage as if he were a member of the Red Brigades. Suddenly, Queen Elizabeth begins to sound like a Christian Democrat prime minister, as she announces that her government "cannot give in to their demands" and that "this is a moment that calls for strength." Her lines originally echoed those of the Italian government during the Moro crisis, but in the 1987 American premiere of the play at Yale, Fo and translator Ron Jenkins ingeniously revised the references so they addressed another crisis—the Iran/Contra scandal. At the time the play opened, the Reagan administration was being called to account for its secret exchange of weapons for hostages in Iran after it had publicly announced it would not negotiate with

terrorist states. Fo anticipated the revelations before he knew them; his play showed Elizabeth deciding that although she secretly loved Essex, she had to show strength by publicly refusing to negotiate with him over hostages and finally by executing him.

At the Yale Repertory Theatre, audiences laughed as anachronistic references to the ongoing Iran/Contra scandal surfaced in Queen Elizabeth's dialogue. "The poor fellows can't be held accountable for themselves anymore," said the Queen of her advisers, adding that one of them "spends hours ripping paper into tiny shreds: maybe they've all gone mad." (The night after Oliver North confessed to Congress that he had shredded many secret documents, this line was especially popular.) The timeliness of the satire, featuring new lines by Fo and translator Jenkins, indicated how the playwright himself succeeds as an actor-author: his plays provide the framework for a continually changing commentary on political events. The topical American references fit into Yale's production because Fo intuited in advance of the opening that Western governments, from Shakespeare's time to our own, have engaged in a shared scenario of dramatic state pronouncements against terrorism and insurrection spoken by leaders who employ secret police and covert military operations themselves.

Queen Elizabeth's fear that Shakespeare's play will subvert her leadership reflects a consciousness that her role in history—her future—will be shaped by theatrical flourishes of rhetoric (hers or Shakespeare's) and swift, violent action (hers or Shakespeare's). Asked if her statement about the balance of justice hanging from a butcher's hook was written by Shakespeare, Fo's queen replies: "It's mine. . . . [But] in a few days you'll find the line in one of his plays. He gets all his best ideas from me." So, perhaps, did Dario Fo.

Celestine Bohlen (essay date 10 October 1997)

SOURCE: "Italy's Barbed Political Jester, Dario Fo, Wins Nobel Prize," in *The New York Times,* October 10, 1997, pp. A1, A10.

[*In the following essay, Bohlen emphasizes the controversy created by the Nobel Committee's selection of Fo as the 1997 laureate in literature.*]

Dario Fo, an iconoclastic Italian playwright-performer known for mixing wacky social farce with sharp political satire, was awarded the Nobel Prize in Literature today, to the guarded amazement of Italy's literary establishment and the outright dismay of the Vatican.

In its announcement of the $1 million prize, the Swedish

Academy likened the 71-year-old Mr. Fo to the "jesters of the Middle Ages" who relied on wit, irreverence and even slapstick humor to poke fun at authority while "upholding the dignity of the downtrodden."

Critics have praised Mr. Fo's rare abilities as both writer and performer. "Imagine a cross between Bertolt Brecht and Lenny Bruce, and you may begin to have an idea of the scope of Fo's anarchic wit." Mel Gussow wrote in *The New York Times* in 1983.

His one-man tour de force, *Mistero buffo* (*Comic Mystery*), written in 1969, finally had its United States premiere at the Joyce Theater in Manhattan in 1986. It has its stylistic roots in the strolling players and minstrels of the Middle Ages. But it was also a timely satirical blast at religion and politics, delivered in Grammelot, a kind of double-speak masquerading as a language, wholly invented by Mr. Fo himself.

The Roman Catholic Church has been a frequent target of Mr. Fo's satire, and the Vatican newspaper *L'Osservatore Roman* said it was flabbergasted by his selection. "Giving the prize to someone who is also the author of questionable works is beyond all imagination," the paper said.

Mr. Fo, a longtime member of the Communist Party, and his wife, the writer and actress Franca Rame, were refused entry into the United States in the 1980's under longstanding laws denying visas to people who took part in anti-government activities or belonged to the Communist Party.

But the State Department twice granted them waivers, the first in 1984, for the premiere of his play *Accidental Death of an Anarchist* on Broadway, where it failed. (The 1970 play had already been a hit in Italy and Britain.) The couple were again allowed to visit the United States in 1986. In 1990, the United States Congress rewrote the laws, eliminating many of the prohibitions on entry, including those that applied to Mr. Fo.

In 1962, Mr. Fo, then a young actor, provoked his first major controversy with a sketch about Italian workers that was censored by Italian television. His politics became increasingly radical, and he did not appear again on television in his country until 1977, when *Mistero buffo* was first broadcast there. The Vatican called it the "most blasphemous show in the history of television."

Twelve years later, Mr Fo unveiled another impertinent play, *The Pope and the Witch,* featuring a news conference at which the Pope confuses a children's gathering in St. Peter's Square with an abortion rights rally. The play again became a lightning rod for anger when it was staged in San Francisco in 1992.

In Italy, where his popularity peaked in the 1970's, Mr. Fo remains a well-known personality whose strong political views win him both friends and enemies. Not long ago, at a rally in Milan called to defend Italian unity against the threats of northern secessionists, he criticized the adulation given Italy's flag of red, white and green, which he said had been used to cover up "thefts, private interests and the blood of innocents."

News of the Nobel Prize reached Mr. Fo as he was driving from Rome, where he had finished filming a television special, to Milan, where he lives with Ms. Rame.

News agencies reported that he said, "I am flabbergasted," after a car pulled up alongside his with a sign in the window saying, "Dario, you have won the Nobel Prize."

Mr. Fo later told reporters over the telephone that he found out 15 days ago that he was a Nobel finalist along with the Portuguese writer Jose Saramago.

"Certainly it gives me a certain sensation to be in the company of people like Pirandello and Beckett," Mr. Fo said. "I'd be a hypocrite if I told you that I counted on it. I didn't. I didn't expect it at all."

The astonishment extended to Italian writers, critics and theatergoers, who in some cases expressed pleasure, in others outrage, at the news that one of the country's playwrights had been so honored.

"No one expected this," said Carlo Bo, an Italian literary critic and senator. "What does this mean? Everything changes, even literature changes."

Marcello Veneziano, a right-wing intellectual and editorial writer for the Roman newspaper *Il Messaggero,* insisted that the prize for Mr. Fo was a misprint. "I think he is a great actor, but everyone has to be recognized for their own worth," he said.

But Giorgio Strehler, Italy's best-known theater director, said the prize to Mr. Fo "can only give further prestige to Italian literature and our theater." Mr. Strehler, the longtime director of the Piccolo Teatro in Milan, said, "With Dario Fo, we feel honored as Europeans and as men of the theater."

The prize to Mr. Fo, while among the most unexpected and controversial in the 97-year history of the award, is not the only one to draw criticism in recent years.

The selection of the Japanese writer Kenzaburo Oe in 1994 drew complaints that other Japanese writers were more deserving and that the academy was, perhaps, caving into complaints that few Asian writers had been selected. In 1989, some complained that the Spanish writer Camilo José Cela did not deserve the prize because he had written little of significance since the mid-1950's.

But the biggest recent dispute over the award came in 1983, with the selection of the British writer William Golding; critics charged that he wrote little of lasting significance beyond one book, *The Lord of the Flies.*

Complaints continue that the award has rarely gone to women or writers from Africa and Asia, but the academy seemed to be trying to address those complaints in recent years with awards to writers like Mr. Oe and Nadine Gordimer, a South African.

There was concern in the Swedish press that support for Mr. Fo had come from a relatively small number of voting members of the Swedish Academy, though Sture Allen, the academy secretary, denied that there had been any problem.

The academy has 18 members, appointed for life, and Mr. Fo was awarded his prize by a vote of 13 members. At least 12 votes are needed to select a winner.

In 1989 two members began a boycott of academy proceedings after Mr. Allen refused to issue a statement condemning the Government of Iran for calling for the death of the British author Salman Rushdie. That boycott continues. A third member announced last year that he, too, would boycott this year's vote after a dispute with Mr. Allen, whom he accused of being dictatorial.

Two members of the academy have died in the last year; only one was replaced, but too late to take part in the vote.

Maria Schottenius, the culture editor of the Stockholm evening paper *Expressen,* said of the academy, "if they want the prize to be considered as the highest literary award, they take a great risk."

She continued: "I know that already quite a few of the world's most prestigious literary writers are questioning the prize, wondering what they are doing now. But I think that the academy felt that they could not afford another unknown poet. They need some love from the people."

Mr. Fo was born on March 24, 1926, in the tiny town of Leggiuno Sangiano on the banks of Lake Maggiore where his father was a railway stationmaster and part-time actor.

"Culturally, I have always been part of the proletariat," Dario Fo told *The Guardian,* the British newspaper, last year. "I lived side by side with the sons of glassblowers, fishermen and smugglers. The stories they told were shaper satires about the hypocrisy of authority and the middle classes, the two-facedness of teachers and lawyers and politicians. I was born politicized."

Ms. Rame, his wife since 1953, has been his frequent collaborator and co-author of the feminist play *It's all Bed, Board and Church* in which she played the sole role.

His best-known play, ***Accidental Death of an Anarchist,*** which has been translated into dozens of languages, was based on a real event in 1969: a young anarchist, under interrogation by the police as a suspect in a bombing in Milan, fell four stories to his death in what was officially called an accident, although many on the Italian left called it murder. The play takes the plot from there, creating a fictional Hamlet-like character known as the fool who exposes the lies and hypocrisy of officialdom.

Mr. Fo's other plays include ***Can't Pay, Won't Pay*** (1974), a broadside against capitalism in which housewives strike against. Another, ***About Face,*** performed by the Yale Repertory Theater in 1982, fantasizes about the possible kidnapping of Giovanni Agnelli, one of Italy's pre-eminent industrialists, and turns into a satire that wraps in mistaken identities, the C.I.A., macrobiotics and the Soviet leader Yuri Andropov.

Mr. Fo's most recent work, ***The Devil with Boobs,*** which had its premiere in the Sicilian city of Messina in August, is a comedy set in the Renaissance featuring a zealous judge and a woman possessed by the devil.

In announcing the selection of Mr. Fo, the Swedish Academy called him a playwright whose influence had been considerable.

"He if anyone merits the epithet of jester in the true meaning of that word," the academy said, "With a blend of laughter and gravity, he opens our eyes to abuses and injustices in society and also the wider historical perspective in which they can be placed. Fo is an extremely serious satirist with a multifaceted œuvre."

Stephen Schwartz (essay date 13 October 1997)

SOURCE: "Foo on Fo, an Ignoble Prize Winner," in *Wall Street Journal,* October 13, 1997.

[*Below, Schwartz identifies Fo as undeserving of the Nobel Prize because he has "dedicated his life to the promotion of everything discredited, despicable, and socially destructive in modern culture."*]

In an incident reported in *The Washington Post,* and too

good to have been invented, the famous writers at a Library of Congress luncheon last Thursday confessed they knew little or nothing about this year's Nobel laureate in literature, Italian theater performer Dario Fo. But one person recognized his name: Jane Alexander, outgoing head of the National Endowment for the Arts. "A very good choice," trilled America's art commissar. "He's one of our greatest living playwrights."

Excuse me, our? As a former actress, Ms. Alexander must know something about theater, which probably explains why she had heard of him. But how is Mr. Fo, who has dedicated his life to the promotion of everything discredited, despicable, and socially destructive in modern culture, "our" playwright?

Mr. Fo remains an anti-American extremist almost 10 years after the fall of the Berlin Wall—an unrepentant hater of capitalism, religion, and common decency. In a century marked above all by the twin human tragedies of fascism and communism, Mr. Fo insists the real enemy is the supermarket. In a world groping for a return to morality and religiosity, Mr. Fo indulges in primitive anticlericalism of a kind that was already passé a generation ago.

Leftist drama critic Robert Brustein, naturally, chimed in with encomia similar to that offered by Ms. Alexander, comparing Mr. Fo's award with "giving the prize to Charlie Chaplin. . . . Lenny Bruce also comes to mind, as does Richard Pryor." So the Nobel Prize, which has been awarded to authors of such significance as Octavio Paz, Isaac Bashevis Singer, and Saul Bellow, is now to be considered a kind of super-classy Oscar for stand-up comics?

In fact, Mr. Fo's works are not literature, if what is meant by literature is the refinement of language, perception, and reflection. His plays are unwatchable for anybody but those wanting to hear and see a recitation of the biases, myths, and cliches of the left. His monologues are so tedious and predictable that they have more in common with radio advertising jingles than with the works of Samuel Beckett and Luigi Pirandello, prior Nobel recipients in theater to whom Mr. Fo tries to compare himself.

No normal theater fan would go to see *We Won't Pay! We Won't Pay!*—which glorifies the looting of a supermarket—to say nothing of Mr. Fo's more pretentious anti-religions works, such as *The Pope and the Witch,* in which the pope is portrayed as turning pro-abortion and pro-drug legalization after the administration of a "truth serum." *The Pope and the Witch* is so offensive that it stirred outrage even in ultraliberal San Francisco when it was performed there in 1992. It was correctly viewed by critics as nothing more than a riot of Catholic-baiting prejudice that, if applied to, say, Judaism, would never have been performed.

Mercenary politics has already rendered the Nobel Peace Prize, which is awarded by Norway, contemptible. This year's recipient, leftist anti-mine campaigner Jody Williams, had been preceded by Yasser Arafat as a co-recipient in 1991 and by yet another apologist for terror, Guatemalan Rigoberta Menchu, in 1992.

A singular mentality on the part of the Swedes next door now threatens to render the literary Nobel meaningless once and for all. For although it has been granted to writers as great as Messrs. Paz and Bellow, it was also given, for purely ideological reasons, to the Russian novelist Mikhail Sholokhov and to the Chilean "poet" and part-time Soviet secret-police terrorist Pablo Neruda. The problem is not, as many complain, that the Swedish Academy often recognizes obscure authors. In fact some less famous honorees—e.g., the Czech poet Jaroslav Seifert and the Balkan-British prose writer Elias Canetti—have been writers of genius. The problem is that political considerations often trump literary ones.

In a category by herself stands the 1993 laureate, Toni Morrison, one of the few awarded the Nobel literature prize in the middle rather than at the end of a career, simply because she is an African-American woman. Stanley Crouch commented at the time. "I hope this prize inspires her to write better books."

It is not hard to guess what motivates the Swedes in such behavior. They are, when it comes down to it, brooding nostalgics, irritable that the rest of the world has abandoned the verities that help comfort them in their long winters: guilt about wealth, resentment of success, and rejection of the values of a market economy.

Similar sentiments move Mr. Fo. In *Accidental Death of an Anarchist,* Mr. Fo insightfully described his own type, as well as his patrons in Stockholm: "They're just poor, sick, manic depressives, hypochondriacs, gloomy people, who disguise themselves as revolutionaries." Now this radical has donned the best disguise of all: Noble Prize winner.

Mel Gussow (essay date 15 October 1997)

SOURCE: "The Not-So-Accidental Recognition of an Anarchist," in *The New York Times,* October 15, 1997, p. E2.

[*In the essay below, Gussow sees Fo's award as an expansion of the boundaries of literature, legitimation of the world of performance, and recognition of the contribution of comedy, especially political satire.*]

When Dario Fo was awarded the Nobel Prize in Literature last week, it was the first time the honor had been given to an actor and clown. Mr. Fo is, of course, also a playwright, but it is as a performer of his own comedies that he has achieved his greatest international celebrity. His primary distinction is in combining all his diverse theatrical roles—he is also a director and designer—into a single act of comic self-creation.

For more than 40 years, he has been a court jester, a professional gadfly with a stinging sense of satire, attacking corruption, greed and hypocrisy, especially in high places. As a mime and mimic, he is a throwback to the giullari, medieval strolling players, but with a very contemporary political purpose.

Next to such esteemed Nobel laureates as Samuel Beckett and Luigi Pirandello, Mr. Fo seems like an alien, even an accidental choice. His response was characteristic: He said that to be in their company gave him "a certain sensation." One can imagine that the sensation was a combination of disbelief and pride, seasoned by a hearty Fovian laugh, an awareness of the irony of it all.

By recognizing Mr. Fo, the Swedish Academy expands the boundaries of literature and underscores the immediacy of theater. It legitimizes the world of performance and recognizes the contribution of comedy, and, in particular, of political satire All outspoken monologuists, clowns and cartoonists should be aware of the importance of the award. Jonathan Swift takes his position in the pantheon with Shakespeare.

Mr. Fo has written more than 40 plays, some in collaboration with his wife, Franca Rame. Three of them (*Accidental Death of an Anarchist, We Won't Pay! We Won't Pay!* and *About Face*) and his one-man show *Mistero buffo* (*Comical Mystery*) are the cornerstones of his career, but none of the work is a sacred text, least of all to the author. Those who stage his plays are encouraged to take liberties, as Mr Fo does when he performs them *Accidental Death* would have been duck soup to the Marx Brothers.

His work is not easy to translate or to perform, which is why his plays have had such mixed success in the United States On Broadway, *Accidental Death* lost the sheer zaniness that another version had in London. On the other hand, the Off Broadway production of *We Won't Pay,* a scathing broadside about consumerism, seemed as relevant as it must have been in Italy; and the Yale Repertory Theater version of *About Face* was a delirious animated cartoon. Mr. Fo partly solves the language problem by performing *Mistero buffo* in a language called grammelot, doubletalk that could have been ciphered by Sid Caesar.

One of the oddities of his career is that he is a fringe experimental artist with enormous popular appeal, at least in Italy and other European countries. He has appeared in football stadiums, circus tents and public squares as well as in intimate theaters. He is always dedicated to destroying the mythical fourth wall of theater. Bringing his art to the people, he is the performance artist as populist.

It was not surprising that the award was greeted with astonishment by the Roman Catholic Church. Years ago, the Vatican called *Mistero buffo* the "most blasphemous show in the history of television." He has also been attacked by the Italian Communist Party. With Mr. Fo, few take a neutral position. Throughout his life, he has thumbed his nose at tradition and offended sensibilities as his God-given right.

Those who disparage him overlook his effervescent wit and his moral purpose. At heart, he is a social reformer. In common with the character of the Fool in *Accidental Death,* he throws all secret files out the window and proclaims that "justice has arrived."

In 1984, when he was finally allowed to come to the United States after twice being denied a visa on political grounds, he said to me, "I came without a sense of euphoria, with the nonchalance of a slave who has become free" He denied that he was anti-American, saying that he had always criticized "all people who are in charge of any country."

It is no great leap of the imagination to suggest that if earlier Nobel electors had been as free-spirited and open-minded as current members of the academy, radical writers like the futurist poet and playwright Vladimir Mayakovsky might have won the literature prize. The award widens the door for this and related honors to go to other innovative theater artists.

Although Mr. Fo had apparently been nominated (by Simone de Beauvoir and Alberto Moravia) as early as 1975, his name would probably not have appeared on many short lists of the most deserving candidates, alongside V.S. Naipaul, William Trevor and Mr. Fo's friend and countryman Umberto Eco, among others. In the world of theater, playwrights like Athol Fugard, Fernando Arrabal and Harold Pinter would certainly merit the most serious consideration. But taken on its own terms, the naming of Mr. Fo is an act of boldness. In elevating a grand clown, the Swedish Academy reveals that it has an irreverent sense of humor.

A tantalizing question remains as to what Mr. Fo will say in his acceptance speech. How can he, or anyone, follow the eloquence of William Faulkner? When he plays Stockholm, will he perform a new version of *Mistero buffo,* and, if so, will members of the august academy, his captive audience, collapse in helpless laughter?

Perhaps he will begin with one of his favorite quotations

from Mayakovsky: "The end of satire is the first alarm bell signaling the end of real democracy." Then, dashing in and out of guises, using his expressive face and body and speaking in grammelot so that everyone can understand him, he might improvise. That would surely be a Nobel first, like the winner himself.

FURTHER READING

Criticism

Saccocia, Susan. "Italy's Rubber-faced Mime Dario Fo Un-hinges Audiences with Comedy." *Christian Science Monitor* (28 September 1994): 13.

Gives a brief biographical overview and provides an account of some of Fo's projects and explanation of his style and technique.

Scuderi, Antonio. "Dario Fo and Performance Theory." *Italian Culture* XII (1994): 239-46.

Emphasizes the central importance of popular tradition in Dario Fo's uncodified performance theory, extrapolating its elements of formulas, frame, and humor from Fo's introductions to his plays and from transcripts of Fo's lectures, workshops, and interviews.

Frank McCourt

Angela's Ashes

Awards: Pulitzer Prize for Biography, National Book Critics Circle Award

Born in Brooklyn, New York and raised in Ireland, McCourt is an American memoirist.

INTRODUCTION

McCourt's childhood, recounted in his critically acclaimed autobiography, *Angela's Ashes* (1996), was so bleak and impoverished that the months he spent in a hospital recovering from typhoid fever seemed like a vacation. His parents, Malachy and Angela, were Irish immigrants who met and married in the slums of New York during the Depression; after several years and the births of several children, McCourt's father chose to move the family back to Ireland. It was an ill-fated decision: The fortunes of the family did not improve, largely due to Malachy's heavy drinking and inability to hold a job, and they found themselves living in an unheated room with no running water and the neighborhood latrine right next door. Despite the desperation that marks his story, McCourt writes of positive, even humorous, events along with the horrible. Malcolm Jones Jr. observed: "The genius of the book is that the tears and laughter are rarely separated by so much as a comma." Jones further praised McCourt for enabling readers to "care not just about little Frank but about his brothers, his mother and even his good-for-nothing father." Many critics have suggested that McCourt's storytelling ability is a legacy from his father, who often burst into the house in the middle of the night, having drunk his last penny at a local pub, and woke his sons to regale them with stories of Irish folk heroes and patriotic songs. Michiko Kakutani remarked: "With *Angela's Ashes,* [McCourt] has used the storytelling gifts he inherited from his father to write a book that redeems the pain of his early years with wit and compassion and grace." Kakutani noted that McCourt's affinity for descriptive prose "does for the town of Limerick what the young [James] Joyce did for Dublin: he conjures the place for us with such intimacy that we feel we've walked its streets and crawled its pubs." Although *Angela's Ashes* is filled with examples of typical Irish stereotypes—the drunken father, the mother burdened with too many children—critics felt McCourt successfully avoided reinforcing them. Nina King commented: "*Angela's Ashes* . . . confirms the stereotypes at the same time that it transcends them through the sharpness and precision of McCourt's observation and the wit and beauty of his prose."

PRINCIPAL WORKS

Angela's Ashes (memoir) 1996

CRITICISM

Malcolm Jones Jr. (review date 2 September 1996)

SOURCE: "Hard Luck, Good Tales," in *Newsweek,* September 2, 1996, pp. 68-9.

[*In the review below, Jones praises McCourt's memoir but notes that the author's fast-paced narrative belies a desire to rid himself of his memories.*]

In its barest outline, Frank McCourt's memoir, *Angela's Ashes,* looks like an encyclopedia of Irish cliché. His account of an impoverished Irish Catholic childhood gives us the drunken father bawling patriotic songs at all hours of the night, the poor sainted mother weeping by the fire and the wee lads without a crust between 'em. The odd thing is, while you're reading you hardly notice that some of this material has come your way before. Taking up the staples of Irish family sagas, McCourt uses virtuosic black humor and a natural-born storyteller's instincts to induce in his readers a blissful literary amnesia. By the time you're done, you've come to wonder if he didn't invent Ireland all by himself.

From the first page, it's easy to see why literary insiders have been buzzing about McCourt since early summer, after advance copies of his book started circulating and *The New Yorker* ran a long excerpt. Musical, intelligent, confiding, his confident voice belies the fact that this is the first book from a former New York City schoolteacher. "When I look back on my childhood I wonder how I survived at all," he writes. "It was, of course, a miserable childhood: the happy childhood is hardly worth your while. Worse than the ordinary miserable childhood is the miserable Irish childhood, and worse yet is the miserable Irish Catholic childhood."

Born in Brooklyn to Irish immigrants who soon returned to Ireland, McCourt grew up in Limerick, a soggy city where the pervasive wet "created a cacophony of hacking coughs, bronchial rattles, asthmatic wheezes, consumptive croaks." His baby sister had died in America; his little twin brothers died soon after the family arrived in Ireland. His mother suffered through pneumonia, and McCourt survived typhoid. When the dad did find the infrequent job, he drank his paycheck on the way home, leaving the family to depend on charity and the grudging help of relatives. The McCourts' rented house sat beside the only outhouse for a whole lane of houses. When it rained, their downstairs, dubbed "Ireland," flooded. Upstairs, marginally warmer, they called "Italy."

With a keen memory for character and the music of Irish speech, McCourt can climb inside a boy's head and piece the world together with a child's illogic. He writes about his bout with typhoid: "It's dark and Dr. Campbell is sitting by my bed. He's holding my wrist and looking at his watch. . . . He sits now and hums and looks out the window. His eyes close and he snores a little. He tilts over on the chair and farts and smiles to himself and I know now I'm going to get better because a doctor would never fart in the presence of a dying boy."

Conversation in *Angela's Ashes* is rendered without quotation marks, and McCourt is almost as sparing with commas, as though he were anxious that nothing, not even punctuation, should slow the telling of these tales. Given the oceans of suffering he unleashes, that speed is a blessing. But it leaves no room for reflection, and in the end McCourt's haste—to escape childhood and Limerick, to return to

America—gets the best of him. He has taught us to care not just about little Frank but about his brothers, his mother and even his good-for-nothing father, but he can't take the time to tell us what happened to those people. One suspects that for McCourt, memoir is not about getting the facts straight but a way of putting esthetic distance between himself and the pain of his past. The biographical note on the book's jacket tells us that the author and his brother Malachy have performed a musical review, "A Couple of Blaguards," about their childhood—another hint that McCourt is an old hand at defusing bad memories by turning them into entertainment. And given his childhood circumstances, one can hardly blame him. Indeed, the craving for more that we feel at the end of this book is less McCourt's fault than it is to his credit. It is only the best storyteller who can so beguile his readers that he leaves them wanting more when he's done. With *Angela's Ashes,* McCourt proves himself one of the very best.

Denis Donoghue (review date 15 September 1996)

SOURCE: "Some Day I'll Be In Out of the Rain," in *The New York Times Book Review,* September 15, 1996, p. 13.

[*In the following review, Donoghue summarizes* Angela's Ashes *and reflects on the Irish childhood experiences he shares in common with McCourt.*]

All happy childhoods are the same; every unhappy childhood is unhappy in its own way. In *Angela's Ashes* Frank McCourt maintains that "worse than the ordinary miserable childhood is the miserable Irish childhood, and worse yet is the miserable Irish Catholic childhood." My own childhood was Irish and Catholic, a combination I didn't find especially disagreeable; but then I had certain advantages. I lived in Warrenpoint, then as now a far more salubrious place than Mr. McCourt's Limerick. I had the advantage of steady parents. My father was a sober man, hard working, domestically reliable, cautious about money, an ungregarious character, a minder of his own business. My mother was a frail creature, often ill, but the only fault she had was on evidence in the kitchen: she was a terrible cook; in every other respect, she was fine.

Mr. McCourt's mother was woebegone for good reason and as if on principle. His father, Malachy McCourt, was an idler, a drunkard, a layabout, a singer of patriotic ballads, a praiser of gone times, a sentimentalist, a slob, a sot addicted to the company of sots. So the miseries of Frank McCourt's childhood are attributable to his father. A more generous welfare system would have helped, but de Valera's Ireland was in the throes of the "economic war" with England, and life was hard. Nonetheless, neither Ireland nor Catholicism was to blame; Malachy McCourt was the sole miscreant. He would have done the same damage to wife and children if he had given up the Faith and stayed in Brooklyn. Fair is fair.

To start at the beginning: Malachy McCourt was born and reared on a farm in Toome, County Antrim. We are asked to believe that he joined the old I.R.A. and committed such gory deeds that a price was put on his head. It may be true, but I doubt it. Maybe he took up arms in the Rising of Easter Week 1916 or in the Troubles of the years leading to the Anglo-Irish Treaty of 1922. Maybe he chose the Republican side in the civil war of 1922-23 and thought it wise to clear off to America in 1923 or later. Frank McCourt gives no evidence, no detail. His father's name does not appear in the list of those who fought in 1916 and were later given pensions for their services. I suspect that the whole story of escaping from Ireland is a fabrication on his father's part, a tale of derring-do recited and repeated with an air of drama to impress the children.

All we know is that at some point—the first chapter is tellingly short on dates—Malachy McCourt immigrated to America. Later he met Angela Sheehan, a recent emigrant from the slums of Limerick. They married on March 28, 1930, and had their first child, Frank, on Aug. 19 of the same year. A year later they had another boy, Malachy. Then twins, Oliver and Eugene, and a girl, Margaret. Their prospects in Brooklyn being poor, the family decided to go back to Ireland, first to Toome, then to Limerick. Relatives provided them with tickets. *Angela's Ashes* is a memoir of the years in Limerick from 1934, by my count, to 1948 or thereabouts. Angela and Malachy had two more children, Michael and Alphonsus, but they lost Margaret and the twins. Eugene died (like my own brother John) of pneumonia, Oliver probably of the same disease. The book ends in 1948 with Frank fulfilling his father's dream of the boy's going back to America:

> "And some day I'll go back to America and get an inside job where I'll be sitting at a desk with two fountain pens in my pocket, one red and one blue, making decisions. I'll be in out of the rain and I'll have a suit and shoes and a warm place to live and what more could a man want? He says you can do anything in America, it's the land of opportunity. You can be a fisherman in Maine or a farmer in California. America is not like Limerick, a gray place with a river that kills."

Frank McCourt lives in New York still, a teacher, husband, father, grandfather, occasional actor; in short, a personage.

The one clear fact about the years in Limerick is that they were dreadful. Malachy McCourt rarely had a job. When he had one, he lost it. He got the dole—19 shillings and sixpence a week—but he drank it. No wonder Frank

McCourt reports these domestic events in the continuous present tense:

> "I'm 7, 8, 9 going on 10 and still Dad has no work. He drinks his tea in the morning, signs for the dole at the Labor Exchange, reads the papers at the Carnegie Library, goes for his long walks far into the country. If he gets a job at the Limerick Cement Company or Rank's Flour Mills he loses it in the third week. He loses it because he goes to the pubs on the third Friday of the job, drinks all his wages and misses the half day of work on Saturday morning."

When the United States joined the Allies in 1941 to defeat Hitler, the Germans and the Japanese, Malachy McCourt decided that the war was not England's usual mischief but a worthy cause. He went to Coventry, ostensibly to work in a munitions factory and send back large sums of money for the support of his family. Instead he bummed around, drank whatever wages he earned and forgot to mail the money. In the end he went to Belfast and died there in the Royal Victoria Hospital. Meanwhile his wife and children lived on loans, debts, the charity of the St. Vincent de Paul Society and petty thefts when the going was particularly rough.

The most touching chapters of the book deal with Frank McCourt's schooling and his illnesses. He attended Leamy's National School, a decent enough institution and just as good as the Christian Brothers' School in Newry that I attended during the same years. I recognize many of the types of pedagogy; Mr. Benson, for instance:

> "If he had his way we'd be learning our religion in Latin, the language of the saints who communed intimately with God and His Holy Mother, the language of the early Christians, who huddled in the catacombs and went forth to die on rack and sword, who expired in the foaming jaws of the ravenous lion. Irish is fine for patriots, English for traitors and informers, but it's the Latin that gains us entrance to heaven itself."

Patrick Crinion, the best teacher I had in Newry, taught me Irish and Latin with similar fervor, though his terms of exaltation were national and civic rather than religious. I recognize, too, Frank McCourt's Mr. O'Neill, who thought that the true basis of education was the geometry of Euclid:

> "Without Euclid, boys, mathematics would be a poor doddering thing. Without Euclid we wouldn't be able to go from here to there. Without Euclid the bicycle would have no wheel. Without Euclid St. Joseph could not have been a carpenter for carpentry is geometry and geometry is carpentry."

Frank McCourt was not sickly by nature or heredity, but he contracted typhoid from contaminated food or water, I assume, and appalling sanitary arrangements in his various lodgings. He also suffered a bad dose of conjunctivitis. For the typhoid, he spent 14 weeks in the Fever Hospital at the City Home. The hospital was well managed by nuns, but it was not medically advanced. With the introduction of the Irish Hospital Sweepstakes and better funding, hospitals gradually improved. But they had to wait for the invention of penicillin and the development of other antibiotic drugs: in the meantime, proper food and rest were nearly the only treatment for typhoid fever. In the hospital, young Frank was next-door to a girl, Patricia Madigan, who was dying of diphtheria. She had two books by her bedside, one an anthology of English poetry that I also had in Newry, *The Poet's Company,* from which Mr. McCourt committed to memory—as I did—a poem called "The Highwayman." Her other book was a short history of England that happened to contain the first lines of Shakespeare that Mr. McCourt read, the Queen's rebuke to Cardinal Wolsey in Act II, Scene 4 of *King Henry VIII*:

> I do believe,
> Induced by potent circumstances,
> That thou art mine enemy.

Not a bad introduction to a certain style of English. Frank McCourt's prose has other sources. For the most part, his style is that of an Irish-American raconteur, honorably voluble and engaging. He is aware of his charm but doesn't disgracefully linger upon it. Induced by potent circumstances, he has told his story, and memorable it is.

Michiko Kakutani (review date 17 September 1996)

SOURCE: "Generous Memories of a Poor, Painful Childhood," in *The New York Times,* September 17, 1996.

[*In the review below, Kakutani asserts that McCourt's father bequeathed to him "two things: a childhood of awful, bone-chilling poverty and illness, and a magical gift for storytelling."*]

"I know when Dad does the bad thing," Frank McCourt writes of his father in this remarkable new memoir [*Angela's Ashes*]. "I know when he drinks the dole money and Mam is desperate and has to beg at the St. Vincent de Paul Society and ask for credit at Kathleen O'Connell's shop but I don't want to back away from him and run to Mam. How can I do that when I'm up with him early every morning with the whole world asleep? He lights the fire and makes the tea and sings to himself or reads the paper to me in a whisper that won't wake up the rest of the family."

Frankie's father tells him stories about great Irish heroes like Cuchulain and makes up stories about their neighbors down the street. He tells Frankie about "the old days in Ireland when the English wouldn't let the Catholics have schools," and he tells him about the world beyond the shores of Ireland where men like Hitler, Mussolini and "the great Roosevelt" make history. He bequeaths to Frankie two things: a childhood of awful, bone-chilling poverty and illness, and a magical gift for storytelling.

Frank McCourt, who taught writing for many years in the New York public school system, waited more than four decades to tell the story of his childhood, and it's been well worth the wait. With *Angela's Ashes,* he has used the storytelling gifts he inherited from his father to write a book that redeems the pain of his early years with wit and compassion and grace. He has written a book that stands with *The Liars Club* by Mary Karr and André Aciman's *Out of Egypt* as a classic modern memoir.

There is not a trace of bitterness or resentment in *Angela's Ashes,* though there is plenty a less generous writer might well be judgmental about. Indeed Mr. McCourt's childhood is, as he has said, "an epic of woe." Besides a father who drank away the family's meager food money and a mother who was reduced to begging, there were three siblings who died in infancy from illness. The McCourts were too poor to afford sheets or blankets for their flea-infested bed, too poor to buy new shoes for the children, too poor to get milk for the new baby. A boiled egg was considered a luxury, a bit of discarded apple peel a coveted treat.

Mr. McCourt's parents started out as immigrants in New York, but America hadn't turned out to be the promised land they'd hoped. Not only was the family trying to cope with the Depression, but Malachy McCourt also had a way of taking his sporadic paychecks to the local bar and not returning home. It wasn't long before the family was headed back across the Atlantic to Ireland, where there were relatives who could help out with the four children.

Things, however, were considerably worse in Limerick than they were in Brooklyn. No work for Frankie's Dad, no decent place to live. After a series of moves, the family ends up in a ramshackle apartment that reeks from the public lavatory next door. The downstairs (known as Ireland) is unlivable: flooded in the winter and overrun with rats and flies in the summer; the upstairs (known as Italy) is where the family spends most of its time, burning wood from one of the walls whenever it gets cold. The three months Frankie spends in the hospital with typhoid fever feel like a vacation: a bed with real sheets, a bath with hot water and even books to read.

"The rain dampened the city from the Feast of the Circumcision to New Year's Eve," Mr. McCourt writes. "It created a cacophony of hacking coughs, bronchial rattles, asthmatic wheezes, consumptive croaks. It turned noses into fountains, lungs into bacterial sponges."

"From October to April the walls of Limerick glistened with the damp," he goes on. "Clothes never dried: tweed and woolen coats housed living things, sometimes sprouted mysterious vegetations. In pubs, steam rose from damp bodies and garments to be inhaled with cigarette and pipe smoke laced with the stale fumes of spilled stout and whisky."

During the war, Frankie's father leaves home to take a job at a munitions factory in England, but the paychecks he's supposed to send home never arrive. Frankie starts stealing bread and milk so the family will have something to eat. He dreams of growing up and getting a job so his mother will have money for eggs and toast and jam. He dreams of buying his younger brothers shoes that aren't patched with tire treads and clothes that aren't riddled with holes. He dreams of escaping to America to make a new life.

Writing in prose that's pictorial and tactile, lyrical but streetwise, Mr. McCourt does for the town of Limerick what the young Joyce did for Dublin: he conjures the place for us with such intimacy that we feel we've walked its streets and crawled its pubs. He introduces us to the schoolmasters who terrorized (and occasionally, inspired) their pupils, the shopkeepers who extended credit to the poor and the priests who listened to the confessions of young boys preoccupied with sex and sin and shame.

Mr. McCourt's own relatives form a Dickensian gallery of characters. There's his hideous Aunt Aggie, who calls him "scabby eyes" and predicts he'll "run off and marry an English tart" and cover his house "with pictures of the royal family." There's Cousin Laman, who lost his commission with the Royal Navy when his unrequited crush on Jean Harlow drove him to drink and ruin. And there's Frankie's long-suffering mother, Angela, who tries to hold together a family of five on 19 shillings a week.

In the end, of course, Mr. McCourt's memoir is not just the story of his family's struggles, but the story of his own sentimental education: his discovery of poetry and girls, and his efforts to come to terms with God and death and faith. By 11, he's the chief breadwinner for the family. By 15, he's lost his first girlfriend to tuberculosis. By 19, he's saved enough money to make his escape to the States.

The reader of this stunning memoir can only hope that Mr. McCourt will set down the story of his subsequent adventures in America in another book. *Angela's Ashes* is so good it deserves a sequel.

Nina King (review date 29 September 1996)

SOURCE: "With Love and Squalor," in *Washington Post Book World,* September 29, 1996, pp. 1, 10.

[*In the review below, King describes* Angela's Ashes *as "an instant classic of the genre—all the more remarkable for being the 66-year-old McCourt's first book."*]

> "When I look back on my childhood I wonder how I survived at all. It was, of course, a miserable childhood: the happy childhood is hardly worth your while. Worse than the ordinary miserable childhood is the miserable Irish childhood, and worse yet is the miserable Irish Catholic childhood."

It takes a tough reviewer to resist quoting this paragraph from the opening page of *Angela's Ashes,* and it takes a splendid writer to fulfill the promise of those lines. I am not that reviewer, but Frank McCourt is definitely that writer. This memoir is an instant classic of the genre—all the more remarkable for being the 66-year-old McCourt's first book.

The story McCourt tells was a familiar one to earlier generations of Irish and Irish Americans. McCourt was just 4, the oldest of Angela and Malachy McCourt's four living children, when the family left the land of his birth to seek a better life across the sea. They were, however, reversing the usual path—returning to Ireland, where both parents had been born, from the States, where they had met and married and where Malachy's drinking, the death of a baby daughter, and other misfortunes had reduced them to an existence so squalid that even Limerick in the 1930s seemed more promising. Besides, they were embarrassing their respectable relatives, who conspired to ship them back to the Old Country.

There things got worse. The chief cause of their woes was "the curse of the Irish," "the craving," Malachy McCourt's alcoholism. On the rare occasions when he had a job, Malachy was likely to have spent his weekly paycheck long before reaching the stinking lane where the family lived. When he didn't have a job, there was the national "dole" or the charity of institutions or individuals or, at the nadir of their need, begging (Angela) and stealing (Frank). Few writers have written as powerfully of hunger as experienced by the young. In one vivid scene, a ravenous Frank dines on the grease from the discarded newspaper wrapping of an order of fish and chips. "I lick the front page, which is all advertisements for films and dances in the city. I lick the headlines. I lick the great attacks of Patton and Montgomery in France and Germany; I lick the war in the Pacific. I lick the obituaries and the sad memorial poems, the sports pages, the market prices of eggs, butter and bacon. I suck the paper till there isn't a smidgen of grease."

Conversely, never has a boiled egg seemed so appealing as when the elder McCourt divides his into five slices for his wife and children. Such scenes of paternal solicitude are rare, however. Though Frank listened enchanted to his father's tales of the mythical Irish hero Cuchulain, much more common were the Thursdays

> when Dad gets his dole money at the Labour Exchange and a man might say, Will we go for a pint, Malachy? and Dad will say, One, only one, and the man will say, Oh, God, yes, one, and before the night is over all the money is gone and Dad comes home singing and getting us out of bed to line up and promise to die for Ireland when the call comes. He even gets Michael up and he's only three but there he is singing and promising to die for Ireland at the first opportunity. . . . I'm nine and [his brother] Malachy is eight and we know all the songs. We sing all the verses of Kevin Barry and Roddy McCorley, "The West's Asleep," "O'Donnell Abu," "The Boys of Wexford".

Meanwhile, Angela, the mother, makes ineffectual threats and finds her only solace in smoking cigarettes and gazing into the ashes of the fire. (Whence, I suppose, the not very satisfactory title.)

Angela's Ashes confirms the worst old stereotypes about the Irish, portraying them as drunken, sentimental, bigoted, bloody-minded dreamers, repressed sexually and oppressed politically, nursing ancient grievances while their children (their far-too-many children) go hungry. It confirms the stereotypes at the same time that it transcends them through the sharpness and precision of McCourt's observation and the wit and beauty of his prose.

For if the physical conditions of Frank McCourt's Limerick childhood were appalling—fleas, rats, a single malodorous toilet for 11 families, TB, typhoid fever, diphtheria and the deadly damp from the River Shannon—and the emotional conditions were impoverished by his family's inability to express love, he emerged with at least one great inheritance: the Irish gift for, and love of, language and music. His father's favorite political dirges echo throughout the book.

> On Mountjoy one Monday morning
> High upon the gallows tree,
> Kevin Barry gave his young life
> For the cause of liberty . . .

Or:

> When all around a vigil keep,
> The West's asleep, the West's asleep—
> Alas, and well may Erin weep

> When Connacht lies in slumber deep . . .

Hospitalized with typhoid fever, Frank learns his first lines of Shakespeare, and "it's like having jewels in my mouth when I say the words." During that same hospital stay, an illiterate janitor memorizes Alfred Noyes's "The Highwayman" to please him.

McCourt was still a teenager when he fled Limerick for New York. There he taught writing at Stuyvesant high school and, according to the dustjacket, "performed with his brother Malachy in a musical review about their Irish youth." This memoir is good enough to be the capstone of a distinguished writing career; let's hope that it is only the beginning of Frank McCourt's.

Malcolm Jones Jr. (essay date 25 August 1997)

SOURCE: "From 'Ashes' to Stardom," in *Newsweek,* August 25, 1997, pp. 66-70.

[*In the following essay, Jones discusses the popular and literary success of* Angela's Ashes, *describing the book as "the publishing event of the decade."*]

Frank McCourt is not without sin. But no one could confess with more charm. In the course of defending the accuracy of his memoir, *Angela's Ashes,* McCourt admits that he erred at least once, a mistake he discovered last October when he traveled back to Limerick, the Irish city where his Pulitzer Prize-winning account of growing up poor is set. He was autographing books in a bookstore when a man approached and introduced himself as Willie Harrell, one of the boys that little Frankie McCourt grew up with. "Weak and leaning on a stick and looking like he was 100 years old," Harrell congratulated McCourt on a fine job of writing. Then he leaned across the table and said, "In your book you give me a sister, and Frankie, I had no sister." McCourt shakes his head. "This was true. Somehow or other, I invented a sister for him who had none. But we chatted awhile, and finally Willie says, 'Frankie, I'd love a copy of your book. But I'm on the pension these days, and I was wondering, could you see letting me have a copy?'" And McCourt, still embarrassed, says of course he can. "That's fine, then," Willie says, "you let me have this book, Frankie, and we'll be forgetting about the sister."

Since then, this 67-year-old former schoolteacher has done very little apologizing for the book that has become the publishing event of the decade. Scribner has printed more than 1.3 million copies. It's been on *The New York Times* bestseller list for nearly a year; on July 13 it jumped back to No. 1 for the fifth time, and is there still. It won both the

National Book Critics Circle Award and the Pulitzer Prize. American booksellers named it their favorite book of 1997.

Reduced to its essentials, *Angela's Ashes* looks like an encyclopedia of Irish cliché—the alcoholic pa, the long-suffering ma, the wee lads without a crust between 'em. A natural storyteller and wit, McCourt sidesteps sentimentality with a litany of hardship that would make a cynic flinch. "My father and mother should have stayed in New York where they met and married and where I was born," his book begins. By the time the family moved back to Ireland in 1934, 4-year-old Frank had gained three brothers and lost a sister. Two more brothers would be born, and two would die. The father drank his paycheck and eventually wandered off for good during World War II. The mother, the Angela of the title, begged for charity and lived off the mingy help of relatives, at one point sleeping with a cousin so that her children might have a place to live. People who haven't read the book always ask, "Isn't it awfully depressing?" Yes, but it's also awfully funny. The genius of the book is that the tears and laughter are rarely separated by so much as a comma.

The success this book is having isn't supposed to happen in modern publishing, a world where "literary" and "best seller" are never used in the same sentence. U.S. tradebook sales have been off as much as 12 percent this year. This summer HarperCollins, one of the nation's largest publishers, lopped more than 100 titles off its trade list and then announced that it would take a $270 million charge against earnings this fiscal year. Meanwhile, independent booksellers—the very people publishers count on to handsell literary work like McCourt's—continued to lose market share, while chain stores and book clubs kept getting fat. "If you have only a few copies of a book in a huge store, none of the help knows what it is," says one publicity director. "You need Barnes & Noble to take 50,000 copies so the book will be in evidence." That's gloomy news for a book like *Angela's Ashes,* which had a first printing of 27,000—a healthy first printing for an unknown author. But as Patricia Eisemann, publicity director at Scribner, puts it, "The rules only apply when the rules apply, and in Frank's case, none of the rules apply."

For example, he got very little television exposure at first—the *Today* show didn't book him until he won the Pulitzer Prize, and he's never been on *Oprah*—but that didn't matter. Old-fashioned bookselling—excitement inside the publishing house, enthusiastic booksellers and lots of good reviews—sent McCourt onto the best-seller list. Once that happened, the chains started to pay attention. That's when sales hit warp speed.

"One of the great things about the chain stores is that you have very good bookstores in communities that really never had bookstores," observes Morgan Entrekin, publisher of Grove/Atlantic. "So you have the ability every once in a while—with David Guterson, with Carol Shields, with Annie Proulx—to sell huge numbers of a serious book. Seven to 10 years ago, you could never have conceived of selling 2.5 million copies of *Snow Falling on Cedars* in trade paperback; 300,000 would have been a giant number."

Self-effacing to a fault, McCourt claims not to understand why his book is so popular. "I thought it might appeal to women who had been through childbirth and some adversity," he says dryly. But the fact is, McCourt himself is the not-so-secret ingredient in the book's success. He's a publicist's dream: a first-rate writer with stage presence. He knows just how much personal lore to confide in an interview—he's had a couple of bad marriages, he's a lapsed Roman Catholic, he can take a drink without any problem—but he's never embarrassingly indiscreet. Throw in a slight Irish brogue, offset it with a sardonic sense of his own heritage—"A well-placed bomb at the New York St. Patrick's Day parade would wipe out the cream of Irish mediocrity"—and you can see why Scribner's Eisemann says, "Frank and *Angela's Ashes* are a majestic combination: a book that talks and an author who talks."

His schedule—bookstore signings, readings, interviews—is a half-inch thick, and he's booked through April 1998. McCourt's only grumble is that he has no time to write, but he grumbles with a grin. With seven-figure deals for paperback rights, movie rights and the rights to his next book (an *Angela* sequel), he's bought plusher digs in Manhattan and daydreams of buying a place in Ireland. With a horse on it. Meanwhile, he's seeing the world at his publishers' expense.

This summer he addressed the graduating class of Stuyvesant High School, where he taught for 18 years until he retired in 1987. He put in a good-natured appearance as himself on the daytime soap opera *One Life to Live*—his brother, the actor Malachy McCourt, plays a freelance anarchist on the show. *Esquire* has just paid him $1,000 to begin a story that will be completed a sentence at a time by other writers. And he had his first taste of raw celebrity in a New York restaurant when a woman swooped down and demanded his autograph. "I don't know who you are," she said, "but I know you're somebody."

In July he was back in Ireland, where his book is a No. 1 best seller, signing books and giving readings. Throughout the week, from Dublin to Belfast to Sligo to Galway, store after store, he was unflappable, agreeably chatting, signing, answering questions from reporters, fans and the merely curious. But the fifth stop was Limerick, his hometown, and the very fount of memory. And it made him uneasy. Driving in that morning, he'd said, "It's Limerick you worry about. Limerick is where the experts are."

Sure enough, at O'Mahony's bookstore, there was Billy Campbell, little Frankie's boyhood friend all grown up and wearing an L.A. Dodgers cap and looking bored when asked if McCourt got it right in his book. "Accurate enough," he murmurs at first. Then, as if he's afraid he's sounded stingy, he says, "Frankie has the gift. He brought it all back. There's a lot in there we hadn't remembered." Before he can go on, a man comes up, throws a yellowed photograph on the table and says, "Do you know what that is?" McCourt says of course, it's the picture of his class at Leamy's National School, the picture in the front of his book. "Which one am I?" the man demands to know. McCourt can't say. This provokes a tirade. "You've insulted the fair name of Ireland, you've besmirched the fair name of Limerick, and you've insulted your poor dead mother. Here's what I think of your book." Thereupon he tore his copy in two.

McCourt's voice takes on a hard edge when he starts to address the crowd a few minutes later. "I can do no more than tell the truth," he begins. "People who think I have insulted Ireland or Limerick or my family HAVE NOT READ THE BOOK!" An ovation drowns out whatever he says next. Then he begins to read, and the rancor evaporates from his voice.

"When I look back on my childhood I wonder how I survived at all. It was, of course, a miserable childhood: the happy childhood is hardly worth your while. Worse than the ordinary miserable childhood is the miserable Irish childhood, and worse yet is the miserable Irish Catholic childhood." As always, this line gets a big laugh, but the mood of this reading is different from all the others. The bleak passages that McCourt picks to read far outnumber the funny stories, beginning with the ingredients of his childhood—"the poverty; the shiftless loquacious alcoholic father; the pious defeated mother moaning by the fire; pompous priests; bullying schoolmasters." He stops and tells of going through his mother's things after she died. "She kept a sort of diary, and the very first thing she wrote in there was 'I must have been the most unfortunate creature God ever made'." Hearing this—and maybe it's hearing this in Limerick—you realize that for McCourt, *Angela's Ashes,* for all its art, is first and last the marrow of his life and the life of his family.

McCourt has a child's eyes, merry and quizzical, and when he's showing a stranger around Limerick, it's the city of half a century ago that he sees. "There were no stoplights in Limerick when I was a boy," he recalls. "People drove cattle and sheep down the street." On Barrack Hill, where much of *Angela's Ashes* takes place, the slums were razed long ago, but the humiliating memories of poverty and a censorious middle class are not so easily erased. "The frown. Everything then was a frown. All these people had was tremendous dignity, but I don't know how my generation survived. Today I saw [one of the boys from the book]. He told me that a day doesn't go by that he doesn't think of suicide."

People are always asking, how does he remember so much? And how much is an Irish storyteller's embroidery? The earliest memory in his book takes place when he's 3—64 years ago. "We had nothing, no television, no radio, nothing to get in the way," McCourt replies. "We read by the street light at the top of the lane, and we acted out the stories. Malachy and I would do P.G. Wodehouse, still do. But otherwise there was no secondhand material. You saw the various habits and conditions of your neighbors. The uncluttered life is the key to a good memory."

"When I came to America, all I had was this story," McCourt says. "It took me two years and all my life to write it." He took a stab at a fictional version in the '60s but stuck it in a drawer. He had arrived in America at 19 in 1949 and worked at a variety of jobs, from hotel porter to dockworker. After the Korean War, he used the GI Bill to put himself through New York University, and then he began to teach. He started out at vocational schools and then, for 18 years, taught English at prestigious Stuyvesant High, where he is still a legend among the alumni. "When we were in 12th grade," recalls Maura Whalen, who studied with him in the '70s, "we started calling him Frank. He said this was undignified and we weren't to do it. We could call him Fra, he said, and when we graduated we could call him the full Frank."

Whalen remembers McCourt's funny stories about his past, "but not learning about the depths of the hardship and the sadness." Nor does Jack Deacy, deputy press secretary to the mayor of New York, who first hung out with McCourt in the '60s at the Lion's Head bar in Greenwich Village. By then, all four McCourt boys and their mother had been living in New York, and it was Malachy, according to Deacy, whom people thought of when they thought of a McCourt. Malachy was the man who started New York's first singles bar, the raconteur famous for his monologues on Jack Paar's show and, everyone assumed, the most important member of the duo when he and Frank put together their cabaret revue, "A Couple of Blaguards," a series of autobiographical comic sketches they performed in New York, Chicago and San Francisco in the '80s. Malachy, who is writing his own memoir, "A Monk Swimming," smiles wistfully when he says, "Frank was always the brother of Malachy McCourt. Now I'm the brother of Frank McCourt."

Immigrating to New York, McCourt says, was like discovering oxygen, and he sees his life there as a series of turning points, Joycean epiphanies. "Whatever I discovered about myself, I discovered in New York, reading, talking to kids, getting a sense of accomplishment from being a teacher." There was his third marriage, in 1994, to Ellen Frey, who, he says, "taught me to be a grown-up." And then there was Chiara, his 5-year-old granddaughter. "I was babysitting her one day when she was 2, and I began to notice how she talked. You gave her a ball, and said, 'Ball,' and she said it after you and you could see her file this piece of information away. Kids take what they need. And they talk in the present tense. So I began to think about how I could use this." A few days later, he found himself writing, "I'm in a playground on Classon Avenue in Brooklyn with my brother, Malachy. He's two, I'm three. We're on the seesaw"—early lines in the book. The child's voice, the innocent eye through which we see the world of *Angela's Ashes,* was born then and there. "It was like a gift," McCourt says. "This was one of those books that had to be written. If I'm happy now, it's because I wrote that book and it's successful and I'm embraced all over the place. If I hadn't written it, I'd probably be sitting around thinking about going back to teaching. I'd feel unfulfilled, as they say. And I'd die howling."

Angela's Ashes was written, in large part, to lay ghosts to rest, and in that sense it was a failure. Every time he goes back to Limerick, McCourt realizes that he has no armor against the past. "I'm haunted by the place. I know every street, every door, because I delivered telegrams all over. That was the most emotional, most hopeful time of my life. I would be struck with such ecstasy that I would cry out in the street." The past, he has come to realize, is not something to banish but something to be lived with. "It's very satisfying to come home now," he says, staring out the window of the car that's taking him away, to Cork and the next round of book signings. "The city has changed and I've changed. I don't go home with that chip on my shoulder. I used to get off the plane at Shannon and I'd get very angry about my past. I'd see a priest and I'd want to haul him off his bicycle." But was there no sense of release when he finished the book? He doesn't answer immediately. Limerick is sliding away in the rearview mirror. "There was no sense of release. As long as you have memory there's no catharsis." Objects in the mirror are closer than they seem.

Additional coverage of McCourt's life and career is contained in the following source published by Gale: *Contemporary Authors,* Vol. 157.

Steven Millhauser

Martin Dressler: The Tale of an American Dreamer

Award: Pulitzer Prize for Fiction

Millhauser is an American novelist and short story writer.

For furtherl information on his life and career, see *CLC,* Volumes 21 and 54.

INTRODUCTION

Steven Millhauser writes of the world of the imagination. The subject of his stories is frequently the artist and the dreamer, the illusionist who creates worlds to satisfy the needs of others for fantasy. Millhauser's artistic motivation is summarized in the opening line of his short story, "Eisenheim the Illusionist" from the collection *The Barnum Museum* (1990): "Stories, like conjuring tricks, are invented because history is inadequate to our dreams." Millhauser's lauded first novel, a mock biography, *Edwin Mullhouse: The Life and Death of an American Writer, 1943-54, by Jeffrey Cartwright* (1972), is the story of Mullhouse, an eleven-year-old novelist, as told by his twelve-year-old biographer, Cartwright. The novel, which examines the wonder of childhood and imagination and suggests that all biography is inherently fiction, won the Prix Medicis Etranger. A *Washington Post* reviewer said of the novel: "It is at once a satire of literary biography, an evocation of childhood and an exploration of the creative mind; it is clever without being showy, its intelligence is daunting, and it has a surprisingly powerful effect upon the reader's emotions." Millhauser continued his examination of childhood with *Portrait of a Romantic* (1977), a fictional account of the narrator's life from ages twelve to fifteen. He followed that book with another novel, but the publisher balked at the 1,000-page manuscript and Millhauser refused to cut it. Eventually he did shorten the story and *From the Realm of Morpheus* (1986) was finally published in the same year as his short story collection, *In the Penny Arcade.* The collection, like the ones that followed—*The Barnum Museum* (1990) and *Little Kingdoms* (1993)—explored illusion, fantasy and modern mythology. A reviewer for *The Washington Post* said, "In those books Millhauser was experimenting with ways of treating American mythology, of intermingling the realistic and the fantastic into a unique fabric that might help us see ourselves in a clearer and more revealing light." Individually the stories were largely praised, but several critics felt they were too much alike. Douglas Balz observed that "many of the stories bear an uncomfortable resemblance to each other. Read one too many stories about a character's escape from the solid world of appearances—by falling

down a rabbit hole ("Alice, Falling") or slipping past a theater curtain ("Behind the Blue Curtain")—and their impact is diminished." However, Balz praised Millhauser's examination of the imagination and his ability "to take us inside the labyrinth of prose," making comparisons to Jorge Luis Borges and Italo Calvino. Some critics view Millhauser's short stories as too static. Michiko Kakutani said, "While the reader delights in Mr. Millhauser's meticulously detailed descriptions, one waits and waits for something to occur." Millhauser brought the themes of illusion, fantasy, and what he called "the myth of the self-made man in America" into his next novel, *Martin Dressler: The Tale of an American Dreamer* (1996). Set in what Jennifer Schuessler described as "a precisely evoked, but oddly ethereal, New York City," *Martin Dressler* is the story of a sort of Horatio Alger of the imagination. Dressler rises from cigar store clerk to hotel magnate by being closely attuned to the needs of his customers' imagination. At the apex of his career, Dressler creates the ultimate fantasy land—The Grand Cosmo—a combination hotel and theme park. Diana Postlethwaite described the facility as "an amalgam of hotel, museum, department store, amusement park and theater—twenty-three levels underground, thirty above—containing (and I offer only the most partial of lists): rustic cottages, caves, a New England Village, a Moorish Bazaar, a Seance Parlor, a Temple of Poesy, an Asylum for the Insane, a Theatrum Mundi, stage sets of the solar system and 'black gardens of imagination' in a subterranean labyrinth. Millhauser's powers of description in this section of the book astound and delight." However, Millhauser does not portray the life of the imagination as perfect. Dressler's personal life and marriage are unsatisfactory. He overlooks a plain but interesting woman to marry her beautiful but vacuous sister who appeals to his fantasy. In what some critics consider the most telling development of the book, the hotel fails to attract customers, and Dressler allows actors to live there free of charge while they pretend to be customers. Janet Burroway concluded: "*Martin Dressler* coolly explores this American Dream in all its manifestations as aim, vision, intention, nightmare, hallucination, delusion, death. The great city—and by extension America, with its ever more exotic immigrants, its ever more hyperbolic advertising, its voracious ambition, its headlong rush into the 20th century—becomes 'a fever patient in a hospital, thrashing in its sleep, erupting in modern dreams.'" The book was awarded the 1997 Pulitzer Prize for fiction and Millhauser was somewhat taken aback by the honor. Dinitia Smith related that Millhauser, who was told of the prize while lecturing to a class at Skidmore College, remarked, "I told my students that a grotesque error had been committed, and that I had to straighten it out."

PRINCIPAL WORKS

Edwin Mullhouse: The Life and Death of an American Writer, 1943-54, by Jeffrey Cartwright, (novel) 1972
Portrait of a Romantic (novel) 1977
From the Realm of Morpheus (novel) 1986
In the Penny Arcade (short stories) 1986
The Barnum Museum (short stories) 1990
Little Kingdoms (novellas) 1993
Martin Dressler: The Tale of an American Dreamer (novel) 1996
The Knife Thrower and Other Stories (short stories) 1998

CRITICISM

Michiko Kakutani (review 12 June 1990)

SOURCE: "Where Everyday Life Intersects with the Magical," in *The New York Times,* June 12, 1990, p. C17.

[*Below, Kakutani reviews several of Millhauser's short story collections, praising the writing style but finding several of the stories lacking in character or plot development.*]

To read Steven Millhauser's fiction is to enter a fairy-tale kingdom of "the mysterious, the magical, the unexpected." Like his earlier books (*In the Penny Arcade, From the Realm of Morpheus*), *The Barnum Museum* is crammed full of amazing events, perplexing characters, strange exercises in sleight of hand. A magician conjures up the head of a girl named Greta, who takes on a life of her own ("**Eisenheim the Illusionist**"). A merchant sailor visits a distant country that is besieged by a giant bird ("**The Eighth Voyage of Sinbad**"). A lonely, unhappy man buys a postcard that slowly comes to life ("**The Sepia Postcard**").

Nearly all the stories in this collection are concerned with two worlds (the familiar, sunlit world of everyday life and the dark, intriguing world of the imagination) and the boundaries that lie between them. In "**Alice, Falling**"—a kind of annotation of the first chapter of Lewis Carroll's *Alice in Wonderland*—the heroine notices that a change comes about as she falls down the rabbit hole: "the mysterious shaft or vertical tunnel through which she is falling begins to seem familiar to her, with its cupboards, its shelves, its lamplit bumps and hollows, while the upper world grows shadowy and strange; and as she falls she has to remind herself that somewhere far above, suddenly the air is blinding blue, white-and-yellow daisies grow in a green field, on a sloping bank her sister sits reading in sun-checked shade."

"**Behind the Blue Curtain**" and the title story of this collection similarly delineate the world of wonders that lies just on the other side of our workaday world. In the first, Mr. Millhauser uses the metaphor of a movie theater, taking us behind the screen to reveal a backstage realm in which characters step out of their film roles to hold conversations with one another. In the next, he compares the realm of the imagination to a fantastical museum—a museum of infinite rooms, wings and exhibits, which like Jorge Luis Borges's famous library contains all the secrets of the universe.

Though this museum is enjoyed by children and boasts many joyful diversions (a flying carpet, a winged horse, leprechauns, jugglers and peanut vendors), there is a darker, more sinister aspect to it as well. There are said to be subterranean levels in the museum presided over by bands of swarthy dwarfs, and black caverns containing "disturbing creatures dangerous to behold." Visitors can easily become lost in the museum, and those who completely succumb to its seductive charms often lose touch with their real lives, abandoning everything they know and love to wander its many towers and halls.

"If the Barnum Museum is a little suspect, if something of the sly and gimcrack clings to it always, that is simply part of its nature, a fact among other facts. We may doubt the museum, but we do not doubt our need to return. For we are restless, already we are impatient to move through the beckoning doorways, which lead to rooms with other doorways that give dark glimpses of distant rooms, distant doorways, unimaginable discoveries."

The problem with this story, like many in this collection, is that it's almost completely static. While the reader delights in Mr. Millhauser's meticulously detailed descriptions, one waits and waits for something to occur. No character of any significance is introduced, no moral—save the obvious one that the imagination can be both enervating and spiritually sustaining—is ever drawn. Instead, we are simply given a laundry list (albeit a prettily written laundry list) of marvels, most of them already highly familiar to us from mythology, fairy tales and the works of other writers.

"The Eighth Voyage of Sinbad" even more pointedly recycles earlier tales, namely the adventures of Sinbad the Sailor as recounted in the *Arabian Nights,* though it does so in the guise of providing a commentary on the nature of storytelling. **"Alice, Falling"** does little more than embroider Lewis Carroll's well-known story with some of Alice's own musings. And **"The Invention of Robert Herendeen"** simply gives the Frankenstein story a predictable twist, turning the man-made monster into a pretty girl. Such exercises convince the reader that Mr. Millhauser can write. Unlike the stories in his last collection (**In the Penny Arcade**), however, they do not persuade the reader that he has much to say.

Fortunately, several other tales in this volume evince a little more originality. **"Eisenheim the Illusionist"** recounts the story of a turn of the century magician capable of inventing people out of thin air, and it becomes a resonant fairy tale about the unreckoned consequences of art.

"A Game of Clue" similarly explores the connections between the real world and the world of fiction by using the anxieties and concerns of a family playing the board game Clue as counterpoint to the anxieties and concerns of the characters in the game (Mrs. Peacock, Miss Scarlet, Mr. Green, Colonel Mustard etc.). In this tale, Mr. Millhauser demonstrates his proven talent for inventing fanciful, fairytale-like characters, but at the same time he also displays—for the first and only time in this volume—an ability to conjure up some believable flesh-and-blood human beings. It's a skill he might well want to explore further.

Jay Cantor (review date 24 June 1990)

SOURCE: "Free Fall to Wonderland," in *The New York Times Book Review,* June 24, 1990, p. 16.

[*Cantor is an author and a MacArthur Prize Fellow. Below, he reviews Millhauser's collection* The Barnum Museum.]

"Imagination dead, imagine," Samuel Beckett moaned, dismayed to discover that even to write the demise of the imagination would be the imagination's work. Would this endless, pointless chase after imaginary rabbits never cease?

Whoa, you moody Irish brooder! Steven Millhauser, inhabitant of a sunnier, more American frame of mind, also takes the imagination as his subject [in ***The Barnum Museum***], attempting, in this tightly focused collection of stories, to stage it, allegorize it, track its motives, delineate its solace, seek its limits. Unlike Beckett, though, Mr. Millhauser celebrates the times when, dissatisfied with life or our previous imaginings, we turn to . . . our imaginings.

In Mr. Millhauser's first story he imagines a game as the stage the imagination constructs for itself. The children of a suburban family play Clue to forget their family tangles, their father's illness. As they play, Mr. Millhauser creates lives for the game's characters—Professor Plum, Colonel Mustard, Miss Scarlet—as confused as the players', as given to imaginings, as much in need of games. For the imagination has no limits, it reaches all the way down—though I wished that I might have sensed a thicker web of connection between the family and the Clue troupe, to complicate the game for the reader.

Mr. Millhauser also imagines the imagination as a junk shop with a warren of rooms, one chamber linked to another without any reason except the bewildering reason of the heart. The shop's seeming confusion reminds us of the possibility of surprise the imagination offers—the once discarded thing that has undergone a sea change, and emerged rich with an as yet unacknowledged desire. The unhappy lover in **"The Sepia Postcard"** plucks from the shop's bins an image of a man and a woman in a romantic setting, but when he gazes at the card alone in his rented room, the picture shows not romance but his own terrifying anger: the swain's "slightly raised right hand grasped a small sharp rock."

And Mr. Millhauser allegorizes the imagination as a **"Barnum Museum,"** named for the patron saint of charming bunco, and filled with seemingly magical displays, flying carpets, half-glimpsed mermaids that disappear into a haze and invisible beings that "brush lightly against our arms." The museum's air of trickery—it's just your imagination!—only calms the patron as she wanders through its maze of halls, allowing her more easily to fall into the museum's dreams.

Or Mr. Millhauser imagines the imagination as secret apartments within the movie theater, where the film characters continue their lives offscreen, as if projected on air. When a boy on the verge of his sexuality reaches out to touch his beloved star, he feels his hand "sinking through melting barriers." Perhaps Freud's right, and love begins again in imaginings, because we cannot possess the forbidden love of childhood and so we project her, or him, onto another. But that other cannot truly be our lost beloved, and our hand moves through our projection grasping only air.

Dissatisfied with life, or our previous imaginings, we fantasize, providing ourselves with an uncertain supplement to life, like the man in **"The Invention of Robert Herendeen,"** a sad sort who invents in exacting detail a romantic friend for himself. His amour is disrupted by an uncalled-for, equally imaginary intruder, Orville, a post-modern demon, who pulls up his trouser legs to show he has no shins underneath. For the imagination delights in calling attention to its powers, even if that means undermining its own creations. Such illusion-destroying mockery recalls Herendeen to life—where he still must "imagine what would happen to me next."

The best of Mr. Millhauser's stagings of the imagination are hardly stories at all, but extended reflections on the imagination, as he walks about the Barnum Museum, or examines and re-examines the voyages of Sinbad, or wonders what the moment of free fall was like as Alice descended the rabbit hole to Wonderland. Dodgson, you see, momentarily stumbled in his invention, making Alice, his character, feel her fall might last forever. Mr. Millhauser provides the invention that fills in until Dodgson invents a place for Alice to land.

No doubt the bunny Alice chases is the very same rabbit that Pascal imagines a king chasing in his "Pensees"—a goal not worth a king's effort, except that the game keeps the king's mind from his life's unintended goal, his death. "Alice tries to recall her feeling of restlessness on the bank. . . . She felt that at any moment she was going to split open, like a seed pod. That was when . . . she heard the noise in the grass." Our restlessness—our yearning for a lost object, our murderous violence that should only be expressed in stories, our unappeasable fear of death—these cause our endless imaginings, even an author's restless multiplication of representations of the imagination. It creates the noise in the grass that Alice chases after.

The author's faith in the imagination sometimes has an air of the sheltered existence. Sinbad's voyages resolve themselves to a boy reading on the beach in Connecticut, beside his "mother's straw beach bag and her white rubber bathing cap. He would like to prolong this moment, when the two worlds are held in harmony, he would like this moment to last forever." In such protected places imagination has its efflorescence, develops its amplitude, but I occasionally wished that Mr. Millhauser's stories had had more of the

bluster and intrusion of history, those unhappy collective imaginings. And Mr. Millhauser's work has the difficulties of farming the self-regarding terrain that has become a staple of modern art, producing, for example, Beckett's and Nabokov's and Italo Calvino's masterpieces. But Mr. Millhauser's elegantly told, charming stories about the nature and muscle of storytelling often provided me with delight.

Douglas Balz (review date 5 August 1990)

SOURCE: "A Collection of Cunning Escape Routes for Fleeing the Mundane," in *The Chicago Tribune,* August 5, 1990, p. 7.

[*In the following review, Balz favorably assesses* The Barnum Museum.]

Among the pleasures of literature, and there are many, is one that is absent from much of the self-conscious fiction of recent years. It is what made readers of most of us when we were too young to know better, but that doesn't make it just a childish delight. It may, in fact, be the root of the storytelling impulse; the desire to escape a humdrum world of ordinary appearances for one where anything and everything is possible.

Steven Millhauser's new book, **The Barnum Museum,** pays homage to this type of writing in the most direct way possible, by recreating those delicious sensations in his readers. But Millhauser is hardly an archaeologist of fiction. His short stories are old-fashioned and avant garde at the same time; they tip their hat to the past, but are on speaking terms with contemporary fiction, too.

"The Eighth Voyage of Sinbad" is a good example of Millhauser's blend of old and new literary strategies. **"Sinbad"** is actually three stories in one: a third-person narration of Sinbad's voyage, the same story told through Sinbad's eyes and a scholar's critical gloss on *The Arabian Nights,* in which the Sinbad story appears.

Millhauser accomplishes this by devoting separate paragraphs to each voice, and advancing the story in three-paragraph clusters. The effect is unsettling, for just as one voice begins to weave its spell, another intrudes. Where, the reader wonders, does authority reside? What is the truth about this piece of fiction?

This kind of self-awareness can be a crippling liability, but Millhauser has a knack for satisfying both the mind and the imagination. Like Jorge Luis Borges (and Italo Calvino), he takes us inside the labyrinth of prose, but never at the expense of those shivery pleasures that fiction can provide.

In **"A Game of Clue"** the reader spends an evening playing that well-known game with the Ross family: 15-year-old David, who is celebrating his birthday; his older sister Marian; and David's older brother, Jacob, who has arrived hours late for the party with his girlfriend, Susan.

At first, it seems to be a conventional story. The narrator sets the scene, describes the mechanics of the game and the clues each person is holding, and then explores the private thoughts of each player. Will Jacob be forgiven for arriving hours late and spoiling David's birthday party? Will Susan be accepted into the circle of the family? But then Millhauser goes one step further. His narrator takes us onto the game board itself and inside the minds of the playing pieces, too. Will Colonel Mustard succeed in his attempted seduction of Miss Scarlet?

Where does the "fiction" begin and end in a story like this? Who is more real, the players or the playing pieces? Intriguing questions, certainly, but Millhauser is too clever to allow them to intrude on his story. They come to mind only after the story is finished and the narrator's spell is broken. **"Clue,"** then, is an irresistible blend of adult enthusiasms and childish pleasures, including the chance to solve the game's murder.

Not every one of Millhauser's stories succeeds as well as these two. **"Klassik Komix #1,"** which turns *The Love Song of J. Alfred Prufrock* into a sequence of panels from a comic book, is merely clever. **"Rain,"** in which the elements conspire to make the world dissolve, is slight. And many of the stories bear an uncomfortable resemblance to each other. Read one too many stories about a character's escape from the solid world of appearances—by falling down a rabbit hole (**"Alice, Falling"**) or slipping past a theater curtain (**"Behind the Blue Curtain"**)—and their impact is diminished. Readers are advised to savor these stories slowly; there is too much rhetorical sleight-of-hand and too many exotic worlds for a single sitting.

Then again, exotic worlds may not be enough for some readers. Where are the commentaries on contemporary society, the truths about the larger world? Is Millhauser's work nothing but escapist fantasy? In his title story, the author provides an answer.

"The Barnum Museum" is a vast palace of numberless delights, a kind of gaudy, extravagant cousin of the Museum of Science and Industry: part science, part sideshow. The story is more a catalog than a narrative, a tour of the place in the company of a guide who not only describes its attractions but also explains its appeal: "In the branching halls of the Barnum Museum we are never forgetful of the ordinary world, for it is precisely our awareness of that world which permits us to enjoy the wonders of the halls. Indeed I would argue that we are most sharply aware of our town when we leave it to enter the Barnum museum; without our museum, we would pass through life as in a daze or dream."

Is it necessary to say that the Barnum Museum is the house of fiction (the house of art, for that matter) and Millhauser is our tour guide? Probably not. Though it is worth adding that a splendid guide he is, a writer who vivifies the act of reading. For those who must attach importance to a collection of stories, that ought to do the trick.

Aram Saroyan (review date 30 September 1990)

SOURCE: "The Surreal as Substance," in *The Los Angeles Times,* September 30, 1990, p. 11.

[*Below, Saroyan gives a mixed review of the stories in* The Barnum Museum.]

In more than a few of the 10 stories that comprise **The Barnum Museum** it's as if a prodigious, bizarre and photographic imagination is struggling mightily to pin itself to the mat of the post-modern story as practiced, for example, by the late Donald Barthelme. Steven Millhauser does his best to distance his art, to make it cool in the manner of accomplished predecessors, but the effect is sometimes like seeing a gorgeous butterfly—say a tiger-swallow-tail—mounted under glass, and then catching a slight twitch in one of its wings.

He can be witty. **"Klassik Komix #1"** is a comic-book version—the prose divided into sections labeled "Cover" and "Panels" numbered 1 through 44—of *The Love Song of J. Alfred Prufrock,* in which the anti-hero is seen regarding a beautiful woman at a party without being able to muster the courage to engage her socially, and is rendered climactically on the cover as "a creature part crustacean and part man" lying on his stomach on the ocean floor. So much for hesitation.

"A Game of Clue," a novella that opens the collection, alternately evokes a family of grown and almost grown siblings as they play the board game one evening just after being newly reunited at the family house in Connecticut, and the characters, architecture, furnishings and situations unfolding in the English mansion that is the setting of the game. Millhauser charts a seduction between the game-board figures of Colonel Mustard and Miss Scarlet that has unexpected emotional nuances. Finding herself reduced to an object under the gaze of this stalwart, heartless womanizer:

She feels, in that pause of inspection, that she has achieved the condition of utter banality. It is a condition more extreme than death, for to die is to continue to exist in the body; but she has ceased to exist in the body, she is impalpable, the cells of her flesh have dissolved in the solvent of a trite imagination. Despite her revulsion for the vulgar Colonel, Miss Scarlet is grateful to him for permitting her to savor this annihilation.

The board game has taken a turn into a parlor out of a macabre Henry James. And overlooking this action—to which they remain oblivious—are David Ross, 15; his older brother, Jacob—with his girlfriend Susan—and his older sister, Marian. Millhauser renders their interpersonal complexities with a touch as gentle as it is evocative, and in this dimension the narrative has a fluent realism reminiscent of William Maxwell.

The other, briefer stories seem less involved with relationships per se than with the artist, in various guises and incarnations, and with the power and position of art in the larger community within which it exists. **"The Barnum Museum,"** the title story, seems an elaborately tedious conceit on this order, the museum being a sort of local circus of freaks and wonders, about which the locals feel, yes, ambivalent.

In another story, a man buys a postcard that seems to change on successive viewings. In **"Alice, Falling,"** the famous Alice has a nap after a picnic with her sister beside a lake and dreams of falling down the rabbit hole without ever reaching wonderland. In **"The Eighth Voyage of Sinbad,"** the old wanderer at home in his garden in Baghdad dreams another journey while recalling earlier ones with his memory playing an elusive role of its own.

In these works, the odd, remote, supernatural or surreal seems to be perceived as the primary substance of art, a notion that has its most popular literary incarnation in the genre of science fiction, which Millhauser flirts with and never quite embraces. This is a notion that might be argued, but in the end it may come down to a difference in taste. Just how great a writer *is* Edgar Allan Poe?

The final two stories, **"The Invention of Robert Herendeen"** and **"Eisenheim the Illusionist,"** make it clear that Millhauser perceives the artist as a magician, one who works wonders that society and the artist himself may have trouble keeping in proper perspective. In the first story, an unpublished writer imagines into actual being a young woman, her family, and even a male rival for her attention. As things start to go out of control, the narrator concludes: "If only I could remain calm remain calm remain calm then I might be able to imagine what would happen to me next."

In the final story, Eisenheim, the most celebrated magician of *fin de siècle* Vienna as the Hapsburg empire nears its end, is able by concentration to create living presences on stage who prove to be impalpable when members of the audience try to touch them. When the chief of police and 12 policemen come to the theater to arrest him, it is because he is guilty of "shaking the foundations of the universe, of undermining reality, and in consequence of doing something far worse: subverting the Empire." When the police get on stage to take the magician into custody, Eisenheim himself proves to be impalpable, disappears, and is never seen again.

One realizes we are living in a *fin de siècle* period of our own when the American empire is no longer what it once was, and there is particular resonance to this tale in our day of Jesse Helm's pronouncements on the proper functioning of the National Endowment for the Arts and the recent arrests for the selling of the 2 Live Crew album. Then too, **"Eisenheim the Illusionist"** is the narrative in which Millhauser seems finally at home with his vision, masterfully evoking the charged interactions at the crossroads of history and art, a grim face-off between the officialdom of the timebound and an alchemist of the eternal. Technically conventional, employing none of the post-modernist literary devices the writer uses elsewhere, it is at once the most readable, complex and uniquely daring story of the book.

Jens Rieckmann (essay date 1994)

SOURCE: "Mocking a Mock Biography: Steven Millhauser's *Edwin Mullhouse* and Thomas Mann's *Doctor Faustus*," in *Neverending Stories: Toward a Critical Narratology,* edited by Ann Fehn, Ingeborg Hoesterey, and Maria Tatar, Princeton University Press, 1994, pp. 62-9.

[*Below, Rieckmann uses* Edwin Mullhouse *and Thomas Mann's* Doctor Faustus *to examine the literary role of the mock biography.*]

When Steven Millhauser's first novel, ***Edwin Mullhouse: The Life and Death of an American Writer (1943-1954), by Jeffrey Cartwright*** was published in 1972, several reviewers remarked on its Nabokovian qualities and pointed to *Pale Fire* as the most likely model for Millhauser's mock-biography. The very title of Millhauser's novel, however, seems to point to another possible model: Thomas Mann's *Doctor Faustus: The Life of the German Composer Adrian Leverkühn, as Told by a Friend.* In fact, a comparison of these two fictional witness biographies leads this reader to conclude that Millhauser's novel, in some of its themes and motives as well as in the person of its fictional biographer and in its parody of the conventions of biographical writing, bears more of a mockingly distorted resemblance to Mann's text than to that of Nabokov.

Millhauser's novel, which won the Prix Medicis Etranger, is ostensibly the biography of the prodigious writer Edwin Mullhouse, who meets a premature death at the age of eleven. Millhauser's novel focuses as much on Edwin's life as on the efforts of his biographer, Jeffrey Cartwright, Mullhouse's eleven-and-a-half-year-old friend, to shape Edwin's life into a meaningful whole. As Edwin's next-door neighbor, Cartwright is a privileged observer of his friend's life, and his desire to write his biography becomes an all-consuming passion. Compared to his "zealous sense of purpose, his industrious concentration on his subject's infinite variety and plenitude of sameness," Pearl Bell wrote in a review of the novel, "James Boswell seems inattentive, Richard Ellman's *Joyce* slipshod, Leon Edel's *James* cursory."

The subjects of Mann's and Millhauser's mock-biographies, the modernist composer Adrian Leverkühn and the eleven-year-old writer Edwin Mullhouse, represent in the eyes of their fictional biographers the artist as genius. They give occasion for reflection on the nature of genius and the proximity of disease and creativity. Both novels are what Hoberman terms "mediated biographies"; Mann and Millhauser put particular emphasis on their fictional biographers' perception of their subjects. "It is as if these narrators were standing in front of a slide projector: they are themselves immediately present to the viewer, and thus experienced dramatically, unmediatedly, but the slides themselves [Leverkühn and Mullhouse in our case] are now visible only in relation to [the narrators]." Hoberman's comparison very aptly captures the peculiar stance of narrators in mock biographies. On the one hand, they are aware of their subservient role; on the other hand, their marked presence provides the opportunity for self-dramatization.

Edwin Mullhouse's brief life, culminating in the writing of his "immortal novel" *Cartoons,* is told by his friend Jeffrey Cartwright. For him as for Zeitblom, the narrator in *Doctor Faustus,* the writing of the biography becomes a "mission" that gives "meaning" to his life. This sense of mission awakens early in both biographers. When Leverkühn chooses the University of Halle as his alma mater, Zeitblom follows him there "to keep a constant eye" on his friend, motivated by personal solicitude but even more by "something like a premonition of the fact that it would one day be my task to set down an account of the impressions that moulded his [Leverkühn's] early life." Similarly, yet carrying the parody of the biographer's sense of mission further, Millhauser has Cartwright observe his subject "from the beginning"—from the day Mullhouse is eight days and Cartwright six months old, "with the fond solicitude of an older brother and the scrupulous fascination of a budding biographer."

The biographer's mission thus becomes all-consuming and virtually takes over his life. "It should be said once more," Zeitblom confesses, implicitly boasting of the sacrifice of self involved in the biographer's task, "that I led my own life, without precisely neglecting it, only as if it were an aside, with half my attention, with my left hand; that my real concern and anxiety were centered upon the existence of my childhood friend." Again, in *Edwin Mullhouse* the biographer's vicarious existence is carried to its extreme. When Mullhouse withdraws from the world to write his "immortal novel," Cartwright's own life is reduced to a void. His many "attempts to escape into sham hobbies" are futile, and the biographer's obsessive watchfulness, which is the content of his life, is hilariously spoofed when Cartwright attempts to witness his novelist friend's progress: "Often at night, unable to sleep, I would creep into my kitchen and watch Edwin's light until it went out: at 1:26, at 2:03, at 2:55. I even made a game of it, thrilling each time he broke a record. Once I watched from 3:27 (his previous record) to 5:06 . . . before I had to crawl back to bed, exhausted, though his light still burned; but that morning Edwin looked surprisingly well-rested, and I realized that he had fallen asleep with his light on."

Both narrators, then, emphasize their subservient roles. Zeitblom, the self-styled "simple man," feels privileged to be the witness of the "life of an artist . . . this unique specimen of humanity," just as Cartwright seems to be imbued with the sense that his subject is "the special one," and not he, although he is "an unusually bright child." Ostensibly they know that for the biographer it is only fitting to assume "a place in the background of these memoirs," as Zeitblom puts it, or to "huddle modestly in the background," which is Cartwright's declared policy. An inkling of the biographer's desire to be emancipated from a subservient role is provided by Cartwright's observations on the relationship between biographer and subject:

> Edwin looked up to me as a prince looks up to a
> trusty servant; there was never any question of a
> clash of privileges. In bitter loneliness the prince
> asks his man to decide a subtle question of policy,
> and so the unseen man has a hand in the affairs of
> state. Then perhaps the prince forgets the existence
> of his man for a week or weeks or months at a time,
> until suddenly he needs him again. But the man
> never forgets his prince, and in the servant's cham-
> ber, which the prince never enters, who can tell
> what strange midnight thoughts flit through a skull?

The extended metaphor reveals the tendency on the part of most narrators in mock-biographies to assert themselves, despite their protestations to the contrary. Although Zeitblom assures the reader in the opening sentence of his account of Leverkühn's life "that it is by no means out of any wish to bring my own personality into the foreground that I preface with a few words about myself and my own affairs this report on the life of the departed Adrian Leverkühn," he does bring himself into the foreground to a degree that no narrator in a factual biography ever would. In this respect Cartwright is modeled directly on Zeitblom. Recalling his first meeting with the eight-day-old Mullhouse, he observes: "It is with no desire of thrusting myself forward, but only of presenting the pertinent details of a noteworthy occasion, that I thus intrude my personal history into these pages." Yet intrude he does, and, as we shall see, not only "into these pages." The prominent role biographers assume in mock-biographies ultimately leads the reader to question the narrator's reliability and disinterestedness to such an extent that the focus tends to shift away from the account of the subject's life to its narrator.

In psychological terms, the biographer's need to assert himself can be seen as part of a compensation syndrome. Zeitblom and Cartwright both claim the same motivation for writing their respective biographies: the desire to preserve for posterity the details of their friends' lives. Ultimately, however, both Zeitblom's and Cartwright's motives for rendering an account of their friends' lives stem from unrequited love. Zeitblom can barely hide his hurt feelings occasioned by the "friendly" and "objective" mention of himself in the note with which Leverkühn assigns his sketches and journals to him; neither can he deceive the reader about the intensity of the jealousy aroused in him by Leverkün's homosexual relationship with Rudi Schwerdtfeger. Similarly, Cartwright cannot disguise his jealous disapproval of Mullhouse's two loves, Rose Dorn and Arnold Hasselstrom, and his feeling of rejection when Mullhouse includes him only as an afterthought among those who had influenced his life. It is this rejection that motivates Cartwright's most extreme statement of the biographer's need for self-assertion, made on behalf of all witness biographers who are tied to their subjects by a "burdensome friendship." In his response to Mullhouse's critical comments on the fictionality of biography he notes: "But I take this opportunity to ask . . . : isn't it true that the biographer performs a function nearly as great as, or precisely as great as, or actually greater by far than the function performed by the artist himself? For the artist creates the work of art, but the biographer, so to speak, creates the artist. Which is to say: without me, would you exist at all, Edwin?"

The rhetorical question of course reveals the very fictionality of biography it is intended to refute, and at the same time it draws attention to the chief characteristic of all mock biographies: through placing a greater emphasis on the supposed biographer than factual or "straight" fictional biographies do, they stress the act of mediation and reveal to the reader, as Petrie has pointed out, the problems inherent in all biographical narration. Mann's comments on his choice of Zeitblom

as narrator reveal his consciousness that this choice foregrounded the act of mediation and determined the hybrid character of his work. In *The Story of a Novel: The Genesis of Doctor Faustus* he writes: "My diary of the period does not record exactly when I made the decision to interpose the medium of the 'friend' between myself and my subject; in other words, not to tell the life of Adrian Leverkühn directly but to have it told, and therefore not to write a novel but a biography with all its trappings." And rereading the fourteenth chapter of *Doctor Faustus,* he was struck by the degree to which he had realized his goal. In his diary, he noted: "Read in the evening the discussions among the students in the novel. The unnovelistic, strangely real biographical [sonderbar real Biographische] that nevertheless is fiction." He did not anticipate, however, that some readers might be duped by the "sonderbar real Biographische," among them Arnold Schönberg, who feared that future generations of musicologists would read Mann's novel as a factual biography and assume that Leverkühn and not Schönberg was the actual creator of the twelve-tone system. What Schönberg failed to see was the "mimicking of the biographer [Biographen-Mimik]," the parody of the conventions of biographical writing. This among other features of *Doctor Faustus* establishes its fictionality and in its turn casts doubts on the nonfictional quality of factual biographies.

It is exactly this point that is made in Mullhouse's critical comments on the art of writing lives. In a conversation with his biographer, Mullhouse claims that

> the very notion of biography was hopelessly fictional, since unlike real life, which presents us with question marks, censored passages, blank spaces, rows of asterisks, omitted paragraphs, and numberless sequences of three dots trailing into whiteness, biography provides an illusion of completeness, a vast pattern of details organized by an omniscient biographer whose occasional assertions of ignorance or uncertainty deceive us no more than the polite protestations of a hostess who, during the sixth course of an elaborate feast, assures us that really, it was no trouble at all.

Cartwright, anxious to protect the dignity of his trade, dismisses these comments as the "typical mixture of subtlety and inanity" characteristic of the thought processes of creative people, but Mullhouse has of course put his finger on a problem that has received much attention in the critical discourse of the recent past.

The validity of Mullhouse's questioning of the biographer's trade is ironically confirmed by Cartwright's critical reflections on the methodological problems he encounters in the reconstruction of his subject's life, and once again these reflections mirror in a mockingly distorted fashion those of his predecessor Zeitblom. As we have seen, the weakest chinks in the biographer's armor are, according to Mullhouse, his imposition of a meaningful pattern on his subject's life, his desire to shape the life into an aesthetic whole, and his concealed claim to omniscience. As biographers, Zeitblom and, to a larger extent, Cartwright are guilty on all three counts. Zeitblom assures the reader that the account of his friend's life is necessarily limited to those parts of it he could witness. He ostentatiously renounces the novelist's omniscience and skillfully tries to disarm any doubts the reader may harbor concerning the extent of his *Zeugenschaft* by raising the issue himself: "May not my readers ask whence comes the detail in my narrative, so precisely known to me, even though I could not have been always present, not always at the side of the departed hero of this biography?" Zeitblom tries to meet such possible objections by an array of statements interspersed throughout the text, such as frequent references to his excellent memory, the notes he took on conversations, and Leverkühn's "priceless sketches," letters, and diary pages that are in his possession. Yet when it serves his purpose, he oversteps the bounds of the witness biographer, though he himself had established them in a kind of contract with the reader. Although Zeitblom exclaims at one point that he is not writing a novel "in whose composition the author reveals the hearts of his characters indirectly, through scenic presentation" (my translation), this fictional technique abounds in *Doctor Faustus.* Significantly, it is not only employed for the presentation of scenes Zeitblom witnessed, but also for those he admittedly did not. In the latter instances the disavowed omniscience of the novelist is embraced by the witness biographer apparently because of a *horror vacui* shared by most biographers, and justified on the basis of the witness biographer's "frightful intimacy," which "makes him an eye-and ear-witness even to [the story's] hidden phases."

There is, however, yet another kind of omniscience that novelists and biographers share, and it is this kind of omniscience Cartwright alludes to when he enumerates the preoccupations of Mullhouse's early childhood: "Comic books, cameras, photographs, Viewmaster reels—such were his simple games, but what omens for the omniscient biographer!" The biographer's relationship to the life he narrates is a retrospective one, and this puts him perilously close to the novelist's omniscience, as Cartwright puts it in one of his many futile attempts to draw a clear distinction between the biographer's art and that of the novelist. It is this retrospective omniscience that accounts for a dual perspective in both historical (biographical) and fictional narration. The narrator, as Paul Hernadi points out, sustains a delicate balance between a retrospective point of view and the point of view of one immersed in the events as they occur. The two perspectives correspond to what Hernadi calls logos and mythos: the narration of events in terms of causality versus their narration in terms of intention or teleology. No matter how much Zeitblom and Cartwright protest that they are writing biographies and not novels, they are caught up in the quandary created by this dual perspective. For the witness biographer, the quandary is exacerbated by the treacherous tricks memory is wont to play on the biographer's recollections. This added predicament is reflected in Cartwright's self-admonishing statement: "The true course of events must always be carefully distinguished from memory's false fusion, lest biography degenerate into fiction."

The tensions created by this dual perspective are reflected in the oppositional directions in which Zeitblom and Cartwright feel themselves pulled as biographers. On the one hand, they labor under the obligation to narrate their subjects' lives chronologically, hence Zeitblom's misgivings at "jumping the gun" in the opening pages of the novel through his premature revelation of Leverkühn's pact with the devil. In a lengthy disquisition on the advantages of biographical writing as compared to fictional writing, Cartwright observes:

> God pity the poor novelist. Standing on his omniscient cliff, with painful ingenuity he must contrive to drop bits of important information into the swift current of his allpowerful plot. . . . The modest biographer, fortunately, is under no such obligation. Calmly and methodically, in one fell swoop, in a way impossible for the harried novelist who is always trying to do a hundred things at once, he can simply say what he has to say, ticking off each item with his right hand on the successively raised fingers of his left.

On the other hand, to adhere to the chronological straitjacket conflicts with the biographer's desire to impose a pattern on what Cartwright equates with "the stupid wretched pretense that one thing follows from another thing, as if on Saturday a man should hang himself because on Friday he was melancholy." What Hernadi calls mythos is super-imposed on logos, and this superimposition ultimately causes the degeneration of historical "truth" into fiction. Again, it is Cartwright, the more self-conscious of the two biographers, who, in the course of writing his life of Edwin Mullhouse, is forced to confirm the verdict of biography's enemies, "its helpless conformity to the laws of fiction." This truth is brought home to him when he realizes that the "curse of chronology" threatens the biographer's ultimate goal: to write the life of his subject in such a way that "each date, each incident, each casual remark contributes to an elaborate plot that slowly and cunningly builds to a foreknown climax: the hero's celebrated deed."

Closely connected to the interplay between logos and myth

is the biographer's desire to subsume the "question marks, censored passages, blank spaces, rows of asterisks, omitted paragraphs, and numberless sequences of three dots trailing into whiteness" of real life into an aesthetic whole. Cartwright's endeavor in this respect represents the ultimate, mockingly distorted reflection of Zeitblom's labor of love and at the same time the slighted biographer's revenge on his subject. Whereas Zeitblom as biographer is motivated by, among other things, his hope that Leverkühn may find grace, if not in the eyes of God, then in the eyes of posterity once an account of his friend's life has been rendered, Cartwright, increasingly troubled that the "design" of his biography is "marred somewhat by Edwin's indefinitely continued existence," conceives and carries out the ingenious plan of killing off his subject, thus providing an aesthetically pleasing end to this "throbbing book." At the same time he fulfills his labor of love, for had not Mullhouse told him shortly before his death that Cartwright had "saved his soul . . . by making him think of his life as biography, that is, a design with a beginning, middle, and end"? As mock-biographies both *Doctor Faustus* and to a larger extent ***Edwin Mullhouse*** should be read, as I have tried to show, at least on one level as Cartwright would have us read Mullhouse's "immortal novel" *Cartoons:* "By the method of scrupulous distortion, Edwin draws attention to things that have been rendered invisible to us by overmuch familiarity."

Publishers Weekly (review date 25 March 1996)

SOURCE: A review of *Martin Dressler: The Tale of an American Dreamer,* in *Publishers Weekly,* March 25, 1996, pp. 62-3.

[*Below, the critic provides a brief plot summary and favorable review of* Martin Dressler.]

Literature's romance with the building-as-metaphor earns new energy through Millhauser's latest novel [***Martin Dressler: The Tale of an American Dreamer***] (after ***Little Kingdoms,*** 1993), which quietly chronicles the life of an entrepreneur whose career peaks when he builds a fabulous hotel in turn-of-the-century Manhattan. Beginning with his first jobs—in his father's cigar shop and as a bellhop—young Martin's rise is fueled by a happy blend of pragmatism and imagination. Both inform the design of the cafes and hotels he builds as an adult, though the latter seems to gain sway in the construction of his magnum opus, the Grand Cosmo. Within the rusticated walls of that grand hotel, one floor's elevators open onto "a densely wooded countryside" dotted with cottages; another floor simulates a rugged mountainside, featuring "caves" furnished with beds, plumbing and "refrigerated air." For recreation, guests can wander in the artificial moonlight of the Pleasure Park or visit the Temple of

Poesy, where young women in Green tunics will recite poetry, 24 hours a day. Such amenities speak of Dressler's view of the hotel as "a world within the world, rivaling the world." In deliberate contrast stands Millhauser's cooler evocation of his protagonist's private life. The magnate's genial sister-in-law works for him, while the troubles of his neurasthenic wife—"his sister's sister, his tense, languous, floating, ungraspable bride"—reflect his increasingly manic, untethered imaginings. Millhauser's characteristic fascination with the material artifacts of the vanished past—and the startling deftness with which he can describe the street, the carnival, the hotel that never existed—marks him as a cultural historian as well as an idiosyncratic fabulist. Taking its place alongside other fine tales of architectural symbology, from Poe to Borges to Ayn Rand, this enticing novel becomes at once the tale of a life, a marriage and a creative imagination in crisis.

Washington Post (review date 28 April 1996)

SOURCE: "When Fairy Tales Come True," in *The Washington Post,* April 28, 1996, p. 3.

[*In the following review, the critic provides a plot summary and positive review of* Martin Dressler.]

Steven Millhauser is a wonderfully gifted and original writer who had the rather considerable misfortune to write an absolutely brilliant first novel. ***Edwin Mullhouse: The Life and Death of an American Writer, 1943-54*** was published in 1972—it has just been reissued in paperback by Vintage—and was reviewed with near-universal enthusiasm. It is at once a satire of literary biography, an evocation of childhood and an exploration of the creative mind; it is clever without being showy, its intelligence is daunting, and it has a surprisingly powerful effect upon the reader's emotions.

The problem with writing so thoroughly accomplished a first novel is that it arouses undue expectations about those to follow. In a literary culture such as ours, one that bestows fame hastily and withdraws it cruelly, this can have devastating effects. At its worst, as recounted by John Leggett in *Ross and Tom,* it can lead to despair and suicide, as happened to both Ross Lockridge and Thomas Heggen, the authors, respectively, of *Raintree County* and *Mister Roberts.* More typically, it leads writers down various paths in search either of ways to repeat that first success or of ways to depart from it.

In the case of Steven Millhauser, the splendid first book was followed by several others, most recently two collections of stories, ***The Barnum Museum*** and ***Little Kingdoms.*** Although they did not, alas, make much of a dent, we can see now that in them Millhauser was steering himself toward *Martin Dressler,* a book quite different from *Edwin Mullhouse* but similarly accomplished. In those books Millhauser was experimenting with ways of treating American mythology, of intermingling the realistic and the fantastic into a unique fabric that might help us see ourselves in a clearer and more revealing light.

Martin Dressler is the culmination of that undertaking. It tells the story of the ultimate American archetype, the dreamer, forever imagining "something else, something great, something greater, something as great as the whole world." The novel's opening paragraph establishes its themes and tones with a sureness that few writers could hope to achieve:

"There once lived a man named Martin Dressler, a shopkeeper's son, who rose from modest beginnings to a height of dreamlike good fortune. This was toward the end of the 19th century, when on any street corner in America you might see some ordinary-looking citizen who was destined to invent a new kind of bottlecap or tin can, start a chain of five-cent stores, sell a faster and better elevator, or open a fabulous new department store with big display, windows made possible by an improved process for manufacturing sheets of glass. Although Martin Dressler was a shopkeeper's son, he too dreamed his dream, and at last he was lucky enough to do what few people even dare to imagine: he satisfied his heart's desire. But this is a perilous privilege, which the gods watch jealously, waiting for the flaw, the little flaw, that brings everything to ruin, in the end."

There you have it, almost literally in a nutshell. On the first page, Millhauser announces that this is to be an American fairy tale, one steeped in the mythology of American success and offering, at its end, a cautionary moral. That Millhauser then proceeds to deliver as advertised is no mean accomplishment, especially when one considers that in addition he tells an engaging story and brings turn-of-the-century Manhattan to life with precision and affection. In this latter respect *Martin Dressler* may remind some readers of *Ragtime,* but it is a far less self-conscious book than E. L. Doctorow's best-seller, and its purposes are far more serious.

Young Martin Dressler gets his first taste of business working at his father's cigar store, where he displays "a gift that surprised people: he could swiftly sense the temperament of a customer and make sensible, precise suggestions." He soon moves into the hotel business, where customers sense "some quality of sympathy or curiosity that made him concentrate his deepest attention on them, made him sense their secret moods." His rise is swift, from running a hotel-lobby cigar stand to managerial positions of steadily greater authority to opening his first lunchroom and billiard parlor to becom-

ing a hotel magnate on his own; all this happens while he feels himself "being led by friendly powers toward a destination they had marked out for him."

His story is a mixture of Horatio Alger and Theodore Dreiser—Dressler/Dreiser doubtless is no accident—told in language out of the Brothers Grimm. Early in his career he is lured into the bed of a hotel guest, Mrs. Hamilton, who introduces him to the mysteries of love and tells him: "Everything seems like a dream. That's what they say, you know: life is a dream. As in that child's song—how does it go? Merrily merrily. Life is but a dream." As his career unfolds Martin's dreaming turns upon him; falling in with an attractive woman and her two marriageable daughters, he chooses the one so lost in dreams that she is disconnected from reality; then he embarks on successive hotel projects that aim not merely to provide lodging but to transport their customers into "a world within the world, rivaling the world; and whoever entered its walls had no further need of that other world."

When the story of Martin Dressler reaches this point it takes no great leap of the imagination to realize that it is, in mythical form, the story of Walt Disney, of all those American dreamers for whom fantasy—unreality—becomes the ultimate reality. Martin hires an advertiser who could as well be a promoter for Disney World: "it was Harwinton's belief that every city dweller harbored a double desire: the desire to be in the thick of things, and the equal and opposite desire to escape from the horrible thick of things to some peaceful rural place with shady paths, murmuring streams, and the hum of bumblebees over vaguely imagined flowers."

Millhauser has taken on big themes in *Martin Dressler*. These include not merely the American longing for illusion and excape, but also the pitfalls of great ambition and the rise and fall of the modern city.
—*Washington Post*

As should be self-evident, Millhauser has taken on big themes in *Martin Dressler.* These include not merely the American longing for illusion and escape, but also the pitfalls of great ambition and the rise and fall of the modern city. In embracing these themes it is therefore, a transparently American novel, and a most convincing one, well worth the long wait since *Edwin Mullhouse.*

Diana Postlethwaite (review date 6 May 1996)

SOURCE: "Cities of the Mind," in *The Nation,* May 6, 1996, pp. 68-72.

[In the following review, Postlethwaite compares the development of the theme of the world of the imagination in Edwin Mullhouse *and* Martin Dressler.*]*

On the surface, Steven Millhauser's first novel, *Edwin Mullhouse: The Life and Death of an American Writer 1943-1954,* and his most recent, *Martin Dressler: The Tale of an American Dreamer,* appear radically different in subject and scope. *Edwin Mullhouse*—the outrageously exhaustive literary biography (written by an 11-year-old!) of a writer whose "Early," "Middle" and "Late" periods span kindergarten through fifth grade—counts the angels on the head of a pin. *Martin Dressler,* in contrast, constructs a grand cosmology (a vast, turn-of-the-century New York City hotel named—what else?—The Grand Cosmo) to rival Dante's road map of heaven and hell. But both Edwin Mullhouse's biography and Martin Dressler's hotel are really cities of the mind, archeologies of the imagination.

Steven Millhauser's previous novels include *Little Kingdoms* and *The Barnum Museum.* The re-publication of his 1972 novel, *Edwin Mullhouse,* in conjunction with the appearance of *Martin Dressler,* provides an opportunity to discover patterns that have shaped the writer's ongoing aspirations and inspirations from beginning to end.

Edwin Mullhouse is a hoot of a book. Not since Vladimir Nabokov set Dr. Charles Kinbote loose to wreak havoc on poet John Shade's heroic couplets in *Pale Fire* has there been a more deliciously loony literary critic than Jeffrey Cartwright, the "real" author of *Edwin Mullhouse.*

You have to suspend your disbelief a bit, of course, to enjoy this *Bugsy Malone* of literary biographies. The truly annoying Jeffrey Cartwright, detecting signs of genius in his friend Edwin since birth, decides at age 5 that he will play a pint-sized Boswell. (Edwin's first, infant memory of Jeffrey is, appropriately, "a vague sensation of someone bending too close to me"). Jeffrey, a young fellow with apparently total recall, faithfully catalogues the titles of Edwin's 200 favorite cartoons, provides an exhaustive summary of "juvenilia"—thirty-one stories from a family newspaper, "an event of major significance in the spiritual history of my artistic friend"—and records Edwin's every word. Edwin Mullhouse's literary career climaxes with his one and only book, *Cartoons* (published posthumously in 1958). Ironically, the writer's death makes possible the biographer's *Life.*

Is it any coincidence that *Edwin Mullhouse,* with its lambent prose, flights of speculative free association and novelistic probings, was originally published in the same year as the final tome of Leon Edel's five-volume, bazillion-page

life of Henry James? But then, why pick on Edel? Scores of literary biographers could be models for Millhauser's dead-on satire of the form.

Shrunk to the scale of Edwin Mullhouse's brief life span, childhood events loom large as defining moments: At 6 months, we learn, "Edwin was always sleeping"; "colds always took him by surprise"; "third grade surprised me: I had not anticipated desks." When a cohort hits the skids, "she drifted into the middle reading group and at last into the lowest reading group, from which she never emerged."

A big joke, of course (one Jeffrey shares with Kinbote) is that this unreliable narrator/biographer has no idea how deluded he is. Jeffrey's unctuous self-effacement is hollow to the core: "It has been my policy in this work to huddle modestly in the background." Who's the biographer really writing about? Why, himself, of course: "I, for one, can testify that even a modest biographer can be driven to strange devices for the sake of his throbbing book."

The even bigger joke, though—one it may take the reader longer to figure out—is the fact that Jeffrey Cartwright is correct: Edwin Mullhouse is a genius. And so is Jeffrey Cartwright (Steven Millhauser, too).

"Biography is so simple. . . . All you do is put in everything," says Edwin. And that's just what Jeffrey does, with mad abandon. There are wonderful pages on the poetry of Edwin's pre-verbal burbles (James Joyce meets Mister Rogers), and the miracle that happens in first grade: "Words were springing up all around him. . . . They grew on pencils, on lamps, on clocks, on paper bags, on cardboard boxes, on carpet sweepers, on the brass prongs of all plugs, on the bottom of plates, on the backs of spoons. They grew on his sneakers, in his underpants, on the inside of his shirt behind his neck."

"For what is genius," Millhauser writes, "but the capacity to be obsessed? Every normal child has that capacity . . . but sooner or later it is beaten out of us, the glory faded." What if, contrary to the Wordsworthian dictum that we must inexorably trade the heaven which "lies about us in our infancy" for the "light of common day," we could fully recall the wondrous way we saw the world as a child?

That's the imaginative premise of *Edwin Mullhouse*—and the grim joke behind Edwin's early death, which saves him from "the obscenity of maturity." It's also a clue to the main character's name, that seductive echo between "Edwin Mullhouse" and "Steven Millhauser." Not to wax biographical (*pace,* Jeffrey Cartwright!), but surely Mullhouse is Millhauser's childhood self—just as Cartwright is a darkly comic parody of the adult writer, shaping childhood memories to the procrustean bed of literary form.

Like *Edwin Mullhouse,* Millhauser's new novel, *Martin Dressler,* is a story of genius and obsession, in which an amazing world is built to the dictates of an unfettered imagination. It's a tale as American as a Horatio Alger. A German immigrant lad in New York City at the turn of the century rises from rolling cigars in his father's store to out-trumping The Donald as the builder of the most astounding hotels the world has ever seen.

At age 13, Martin takes the Prospect Park & Coney Island Railroad to West Brighton, where he has a transforming vision of the modern age: "Iron piers stretched out over the ocean, iron towers pierced the sky, somewhere under the water a great telegraph cable longer than the longest train stretched . . . and Martin had the odd sensation . . . that the world, immense and extravagant, was rushing away in every direction." The rest of the novel (which takes place between 1881 and 1905) chronicles Dressler's attempts to harness and contain that pulsing energy in a series of ever-grander business and building enterprises.

As a youth, Dressler wanders the "vast stretch of land" between the Hudson River and Central Park, a patchwork of row houses, vacant lots, chateaux, squatters' shacks and farms. As the city grows, so does Dressler's imagination: "It was as if the West End had been raked over by a gigantic harrow and planted with seeds of steel and stone; now as the century turned, the avenues had begun to erupt in strange, immense growths: modern flowers with veins of steel, bursting out of bedrock."

Historic New York has been the focus of popular novels from the nostalgic (Jack Finney's *Time and Again*) to the nasty (Caleb Carr's *The Alienist*). Martin Dressler's Manhattan joins the fantastic ranks of meta-cities as a worthy companion to Mark Helprin's *Winter's Tale* and E. L. Doctorow's *The Waterworks*. If you're a fan of the time-travel genre, you'll relish the vivid detail with which Millhauser re-creates a bygone era: a flash of high-seated cyclists, distant sounds of an organ grinder, the smell of horse manure in the air. In contrast to the Joycean excess of *Edwin Mullhouse, Martin Dressler*'s prose is spare, but still sensuous, as rich as a Tiffany lampshade "hand-painted with Nile-green sailboats, its gleam of slender glasses holding amber and emerald and ruby liquids."

Martin Dressler's astounding success comes from his uncanny ability to intuit the temper of an era still in its infancy. His restaurants flourish on prescient principles: relentless print advertising, linked stores with similar decor, name recognition, "five-minute" breakfasts (guaranteed), free prizes for the kids. Not content to invent the McDonald's of the horse and buggy set, however, he restlessly seeks out ever-more difficult and daring endeavors. Dressler rises inexorably from desk clerk at the Vanderlyn Hotel to developer of a chain of "Metropolitan Lunchrooms" to innovator of the grandest of grand hotels.

In the hotel business, Martin Dressler finds his true métier. An epiphany sets the tone for the fantastical ventures that follow: "At once he saw: deep under the earth, in darkness impenetrable, an immense dynamo was humming . . . it was as if the structure were his own body, his head piercing the clouds, his feet buried deep in the earth, and in his blood the plunge and rise of elevators . . . a wild, sweet exhilaration." The self-contained universe of the hotel will literally body forth its creator's imagination.

I can't help but think of Martin Dressler's contemporary, Henry Adams, speculating in his *Education* that "the new American—the child of incalculable coal-power, chemical power, electric power, and radiating energy, as well as of new forces yet undetermined—must be a sort of God."

Just as Jeffrey Cartwright "creates" Edwin Mullhouse, so Martin Dressler realizes American dreams in concrete and steel. The apex of his creation, the Grand Cosmo itself, is an amalgam of hotel, museum, department store, amusement park and theater—twenty-three levels underground, thirty above—containing (and I offer only the most partial of lists): rustic cottages, caves, a New England Village, a Moorish Bazaar, a Seance Parlor, a Temple of Poesy, an Asylum for the Insane, a Theatrum Mundi, stage sets of the solar system and "black gardens of imagination" in a subterranean labyrinth. Millhauser's powers of description in this section of the book astound and delight.

The Grand Cosmo cleverly embodies the most profound contradictions of the modern American sensibility: our yearning for the nostalgic and the new, the exotic and the utterly familiar; a place at the very heart of the city—and a place where we can get away from it all. (I write this review a stone's throw from the Mall of America, that Grand Cosmo of the Upper Midwest!)

Yet Martin Dressler, man of his age with the Midas touch, builds the Grand Cosmo to his heart's desire—and it fails miserably. Why? Is Dressler being punished by a jealous God for satanic overreaching? Is there a fatal flaw in this creator that leads to the downfall of his creation? One clue may be found in his disastrous marriage. Dreams make terrible lovers, as he discovers after wedding the languorous beauty Caroline Vernon, a woman whose lotus-eating sensibility ("a sweet, melting melancholy, a dissolving shadowy sweetness of vague regret and dim longing") would seem at utter odds with Martin's go-getting ambition. His ill-fated attraction to Caroline suggests the darker proclivities of an obsessive imagination: Vigorous cities of the mind can also become entropic, escapist prisons.

Another clue to the fate of the Grand Cosmo can be found near the novel's end. Martin strolls the streets of his old neighborhood to discover that his first residence, the Bellingham Hotel, has vanished without a trace: "That was the way of things in New York. . . . Even as his new building rose story by story it was already vanishing, the trajectory of the wrecker's ball had been set in motion as the blade of the first bulldozer bit into the earth." Millhauser here takes a page from Prospero's book: "The cloud-capped towers, the gorgeous palaces . . . the great globe itself" must inevitably dissolve as we awake from artifice to reality.

But I doubt Steven Millhauser is about to abjure his rough magic just yet. *Edwin Mullhouse* ends with Jeffrey bumping into yet another "interesting little fellow . . . I expect to be seeing more of . . . in the near future." At the conclusion of *Martin Dressler,* its hero ambles away from his failed hotel into the light of common day: "For the time being he would just walk along, keeping a little out of the way of things, admiring the view. . . . He was in no hurry." The year is 1905; Martin Dressler, the suggestive age of 33. I eagerly await another biography, another hotel, another novel.

Steven Millhauser with Jennifer Schuessler (interview date 6 May 1996)

SOURCE: "Steven Millhauser: The Business of Dreaming," in *Publishers Weekly,* May 6, 1996, pp. 56-7.

[In the following interview, Millhauser provides some insight on his perspectives regarding the creative process.]

Saratoga Springs, in upstate New York, is perhaps best known as the home of the oldest racetrack in America, where Texans in the obligatory ten-gallon hats and the more genteel traditional horsey set gather each August for the Travers Stakes. But Steven Millhauser's imagination is captured more by structures like the old Batchelor mansion, an elaborately painted and turreted Victorian folly a few blocks off the main drag. "The man who built that was not thinking just of a practical dwelling," Millhauser tells *PW* on a brilliant early spring day. "He was a dreamer."

In seven novels and short-story collections, Millhauser has made a considerable reputation writing about the inner lives of novelists, painters, puppeteers and other assorted inventors. His latest novel, *Martin Dressler: The Tale of an American Dreamer,* out last month from Crown, depicts a turn-of-the-century entrepreneur caught up in "a long dream of stone," building an increasingly fantastical series of hotels in a precisely evoked, but oddly ethereal, New York City. His ambitions culminate in the Grand Cosmo, a monstrously rococo pleasure dome that combines elements of the hotel,

the department store, the carnival and the museum in its endlessly mutating interiors. This shadow city, "in comparison with which the actual city was not simply inferior, but superfluous," is the dreamer's greatest success, and the businessman's undoing.

But when attention turns to himself and his own creative impulses, Millhauser insists writers are the most boring people imaginable. "I'm assuming everything I say is of no interest whatsoever, and that's what allows me to say it," he warns. "If I thought it was of interest, I'd immediately be silent."

Tall and thin, with graying hair and a gently exacting professorial manner, Millhauser, 52, is disarmingly voluble even when threatening to revert to the public silence he has kept for most of his career. With few exceptions, he has scrupulously avoided interviews—"that means I'm now unscrupulous," he deadpans—and the biographical sheet on file in his publicist's office is revealingly blank. "You know, I was convinced you were going to describe my shirt. So I chose the least noticeable, the blandest one possible," he says of his (heretofore unnoticed) blue and purple plaid flannel.

Millhauser's playful mockery of his own public non-persona belies the persistent melancholy of his artist tales. His first novel, *Edwin Mullhouse: The Life and Death of an American Writer 1943-1954 by Jeffrey Cartwright,* published in 1972 (and reissued this month by Vintage), was a dark elegy for the creative genius of childhood, a portrait of the artist as a 12-year-old boy written by an overly literal, secretly envious best friend. The stories gathered in collections with names capturing Millhauser's fascination with the fantastic and the outmoded—*The Barnum Museum, In the Penny Arcade, Little Kingdoms*—often returned to the theme of the solitary inventor or artist, stranded both ahead of and behind his own time, gradually fading out of the real world and into the imaginary.

Now, after 25 years of making dreamers his business, Millhauser has made the dreamer a businessman. "I wanted to write about something as different from my earlier stories about artists as possible," he tells *PW* in a coffee shop across from the Adelphi, the only hotel remaining from Saratoga's heyday as a summer playground for the likes of J. P. Morgan, Diamond Jim Brady and Lillian Russell. (Millhauser has lived in this historic town with his wife and two young children since the late 1980s). "And the thing most different from an artist is a businessman, someone who looks at the world practically. Now I have a feeling that as I did this I was secretly turning him into an artist, trying to find the place where his imagination touched mine, because I wanted it to be a sympathetic view. I've always liked the myth of the self-made man in America."

The novel grew out of research Millhauser did for a story

called **"Paradise Park,"** a long fantasy on turn-of-the-century Coney Island published in *Grand Street* in 1993. Millhauser had found a historical moment in which time itself seemed out of joint. "The grand hotels, the great department stores," Millhauser says, "always combined the most modern mechanisms—elevators, vacuum-cleaning systems—with deliberate imitations of old-fashioned European features. It's a wonderful contradiction—looking back over your shoulder at something that is passing and also at everything that is aggressively modern in America."

Since the market forces that spectacularly reward and punish such dreamers in stone as Martin Dressler are generally oblivious to novelists of a serious bent, Millhauser has, since the late 1980s, taken four months out of each writing year to teach at Skidmore College. For him, teaching writing is an odd, paradoxical business, but he throws himself into it. "Writing can't be taught," he insists, "and if you know that you'll suffer much less confusion. But what can be taught is a certain kind of attentive, skillful reading. If you want to write, you absorb literature. And then you can't *stop* writing."

Millhauser recalls wanting to write stories ever since he could read them. "When I was seven years old," he in-tones, pausing with a mock portentousness worthy of Edwin Mullhouse's preadolescent biographer. "But seriously, I guess I always thought from childhood that I wanted to write. But then many children think that."

After finishing college at Columbia, Millhauser took part-time jobs, shuttled back and forth between New York City and his parent's house in Stratford, Conn., and completed numerous stories and a novel. An agent circulated the novel, and while Knopf rejected it, an editor did express interest in seeing his next book. In the meantime, Millhauser enrolled in the English Ph.D. program at Brown, working, over two summers, on the book that became *Edwin Mullhouse.* It was accepted "instantly," he says, by Knopf's Robert Gottlieb in 1971 and published to rave reviews in 1972.

Edwin Mullhouse is a not-so-gentle satire on the savage art of literary biography, which—quite literally, in the novel—murders genius in its very attempt to anatomize it. Jeffrey Cartwright, playing Boswell to the 12-year-old author of a hallucinatory masterpiece called *Cartoons,* documents everything from Edwin's earliest burblings to his schoolyard crushes on his most disturbed classmates. It's a dizzying, uncannily vivid elaboration of what Holden Caulfield memorably dismissed as "all that David Copperfield kind of crap," transplanted to suburban Connecticut of the 1940s. But in the end, our brief glimpse of *Cartoons* suggests that Jeffrey's biography—and the real world itself—is merely a "scrupulous distortion, a specious clarity and hardness imposed on mists and shadows."

While the novel is a wicked indictment of biography's excesses, Millhauser says, its mists and shadows are drawn straight from his own past. The book, he says, "has a deliberately implausible premise, which was what released me into being able to write about my childhood at all. I did Zola-like research, interviewing my third-grade teacher to find out exactly what happened. But within that, I invented wildly. The book imitates a certain kind of realistic novel, and pushes more and more toward the extravagant."

Millhauser followed up his debut with ***Portrait of a Romantic*** in 1977 and ***In the Penny Arcade*** in 1984, both from Knopf. When Knopf rejected an early version of ***From the Realm of Morpheus,*** his agent, Amanda Urban, took the book to Morrow, which published it in 1986. But Millhauser, desiring a smaller house that could give him more attention, subsequently went to Ann Patty's S&S imprint, Poseidon Press, which brought out ***The Barnum Museum*** in 1990. After Poseidon folded in 1993, just as ***Little Kingdoms*** was being published, Millhauser followed Patty to Crown. "So I've had a checkered past," he laughs.

Asked about connections between his first and latest novels, Millhauser admits there are "patterns I helplessly follow. I'm attracted to extreme things, and I see extreme things in a deeply practical culture doomed to failure. There's a place where things go too far, become too much of themselves. I seek out that place always. But on a technical level, with Martin Dressler's last hotel, I wanted to stretch the real into the fantastic without actually snapping it."

On the whole, Millhauser is reluctant to discuss openly the tasks he sets for himself as an artist, hewing to a highly articulate, grown-up version of "the maddening evasiveness" that bedeviled Edwin Mullhouse's fictional biographer. It's as if he doesn't want to let readers into the innermost chamber, to reveal just how the man behind the curtain is controlling the men behind their own curtains in his stories. "There's something so intimate about my imagination that I don't want to tamper with it."

Asked about the nature of fiction in a rare 1982 interview with *Contemporary Authors,* Millhauser made a typically firm, and typically evasive, declaration: "Unless a writer is a trained aesthetician, his opinion concerning the nature of fiction is of no more interest than his opinion concerning the nature of the economy." In other words, as one skeptical academic supposedly said of efforts to bring Nabokov to Harvard in the 1950s: "Why would you hire an elephant to teach zoology?"

While reluctant to identify himself with "the person representing Stephen Millhauser in that interview," the author backs up his old disclaimer. "Most writers are not terribly interesting when it comes to describing the nature of what they do. What you learn from a writer, as a rule, is what his passions are. If I wanted to learn how to think about art theoretically, I would not go to a writer. I would go to a philosopher. And then I would find the philosopher dry and dull and I would finally go back to the works of the writer."

But even as Millhauser asserts that artists as people are not interesting, that they have little of value to say about their own work, he finds their creative drive endlessly fruitful as a subject for his own art. "Artists are not terribly interesting if you observe them from the outside. But they're interesting insofar as they represent a refusal to behave the way conventional people behave. What artists do, if they're the real thing, is shut themselves off secretly in a room and ask not to be disturbed while they pursue waking dreams. This is a very curious way of behaving over a lifetime. It's very close to lunacy, in fact."

Does Millhauser really believe himself to be a lunatic? "Yes and no," he says. "It's as if my fear with each new book is that 'Oh, now I've really stepped over the edge. Now they'll know the truth about me, that I'm a screaming madman who spends all day having pictures in my mind and writing them down.' The only comfort a review has ever given me is that feeling that 'Ah, I'm allowed to do this. I can do this again.'"

But in characteristic style, Millhauser can't resist going on, pulling the rug out from under himself, wriggling out of one statement about his art with another, equally adamant declaration.

"As I say this, something else rises in me, which is the opposite of that—to assert the absolute validity of what I do. I have no doubts about it; I never have. Dreaming is the healthiest possible thing to do. It sounds arrogant, but when I make up these tales, I'm not removing myself from reality. I'm pointing myself absolutely toward the center."

He pauses. "Of course, I'm also aware that this may be a terrible delusion. I'm involved in a very peculiar human activity. But I'll never stop."

Janet Burroway (review date 12 May 1996)

SOURCE: "Heartbreak Hotel," in *The New York Times Book Review,* May 12, 1996, p. 8.

[*In the following review, Burroway favorably assesses* Martin Dressler.]

"Stories, like conjuring tricks, are invented because history is inadequate to our dreams." So says the narrator of Steven

Millhauser's story **"Eisenheim the Illusionist,"** and that claim, might stand as an epigraph to his new conjuring trick of a novel, *Martin Dressler: The Tale of an American Dreamer.*

This wonderful, wonder-*full* book is a fable and phantasmagoria of the sources of our century "There once lived a man named Martin Dressler, a shopkeeper's son, who rose from modest beginnings to a height of dreamlike good fortune . . . But this is a perilous privilege, which the gods watch jealously." "Perilous privilege" is the core of Mr. Millhauser's analysis of that subgenre of fairy tale, the American Dream.

The setting is late-19th-century New York, a place where, like third sons in the tales of the brothers *Grimm.* Horatio Alger heroes hang out "on any, street corner" Martin's story is quickly told. He begins as a helper in his father's Broadway cigar store, does a clever kindness for an acquaintance and as a result becomes a bellboy at a nearby hotel. He is diligent, good-looking, inventively attentive and reserved, he rises to day clerk, then becomes the manager's private secretary. He takes over the lobby cigar stand as a sideline, opens a lunchroom, then another, becomes tempted by the idea of chain, or "linked," stores and eventually acquires the hotel he originally worked for. He is always interested in the larger scheme, both in the sense of manipulating many elements into a harmonious whole and of working toward something bigger and better. He builds a hotel of his own that goes underground and up in the air. Taken by the new notions of subway and skyscraper, he goes farther underground and farther up, and then farther, and then too far.

Running concurrently with this expansion of Martin's ambitions is the progress of his love life, which begins with his seduction by a voluptuous hotel guest. He proceeds through the usual sexual awakening, the usual whorehouse experience, then meets a trio of gentlewomen, a mother and two daughters, all of whom attract him in some way He charms the mother, Margaret, marries the languid Caroline and takes the plain but vibrant Emmeline into his business ventures. However, his wedding night is consummated not in his marriage bed but up in the hotel attic, with a thick-legged immigrant maid whose friendship he needs and whom he later abandons. Exhilarated by his sister-in-law and her "brave plunge into the world of work," aroused only by his monosyllabic wife, who is always at the edge of "thick, sticky sleep," he watches the sisters strangely merge and interchange. It appears that desire, too, elaborates itself in ever more rarefied and labyrinthine ways.

Martin Dressler is full of favorite Millhauser images: caves, castles, forests, clairvoyants, nickelodeon parlors, fortunetellers, photography studios, waxworks, conjurers, dragons and vampires. Set against these slightly tawdry fancies, however, is another hallmark of this writer—the flat, convincing grit of workaday experience, the machine behind the magic. Like his hero, Mr. Millhauser moves in two directions, toward the fantastical and the mundane, and for this the faux-naif tone of the fairy tale serves very well.

Martin himself is not a parody but a paradigm of the bootstrap capitalist. He might with perfect sensitivity have served—and got rich on—Edith Wharton's characters. He is the apogee of all that Willy Loman would admire. His early genius is for the nuances of servitude, a consciousness that the customer is not only always right but always vulnerable. Therefore, Martin tries to "imagine, the confusion of strangers, satisfy their desires, make things simple and orderly." As his skills develop and his dreams inflate, this shop-clerk sense becomes fabulous as he seeks to cater—with under-city waterfalls and Hindu temples—to "the hotel guest's need for solitude and mystery."

Martin is not so much interested in wealth as he is in making an alternate world, an ambition that is at once attractive and overweening. His passion is for the way things work and for making them work—for pattern, arrangement, combination, for solving the structural puzzle and the marketing enigma. He is quick to understand in this new age of telephones and dynamos, when, nonetheless, goats still roam behind the ramshackle fences of the West 70's, that people want "to move in both directions at once—to introduce every mechanical improvement without fail, and at the same time to emphasize the past," to preserve "an older world of stone arches and hand-carved wood." Through his architect partner, he becomes obsessed with the notion of "inner eclecticism"—the structural fusion of disparate elements, the stone and steel equivalent of a mall-order catalogue.

Of course, "inner eclecticism" bears a striking resemblance to post-modernism, but **Martin Dressler** is not a story that parallels our world. Rather, the novel X-rays it in utero, showing how the ideas and infatuations of our lives were already fully formed at the turn of the century. Here the advertising man is already God, the developer already insatiable. At the moment of each leap up the entrepreneurial ladder, Martin is visited by a surge of dissatisfaction. Others pull out, take their money and run. "Was there then something wrong with him, that he couldn't just rest content? Must he always be dreaming up improvements? And it seemed to Martin that if only he could imagine something else, something great, something greater, something as great as the whole world, then he might rest awhile." The ultimate enterprise is the Grand Cosmo, "not a hotel at all" but an experiment in enclosed community, something like a vertical city and something like a global village—and finally a dystopian disaster of clash, uncertainty and confusion.

One of the novel's marvelous motifs is a cigar-store Indian,

nicknamed Tecumseh, that it is the boy Martin's pleasure to wheel out in front of his father's shop every morning. As Martin becomes more successful, so do his props, and this icon of Americana transmutes into a Pilgrim emblem for the restaurant chain, turns to stone on the facade of the Hotel Dressler as a group of massive statues of Pilgrims and Indians, then proliferates in a museum-like display with a wigwam, a wax squaw and a chief smoking a pipe. Later it turns robotic in a carefully counterfeited Grand Cosmo Cigar Store, which also houses "authentic German cigar makers," and finally fuses with Martin's dream as an image of doom.

Mr. Millhauser's story often suggests an affiliation with philosophy rather than folklore, and in particular brings to mind the French critic Guy Debord's perception that in our world the artificial and the real have exchanged places. (In a culture of electricity and annual holidays, for example, to pace one's work to the rhythm of the seasons or daylight would amount to affectation)

Very early in the novel, when Martin is still employed by his father, the day clerk of the Vanderlyn Hotel takes him up in an elevator and through a series of corridors They turn a corner and come upon a surreal collection of people, including a woman who wrings her hands, weeps and falls to the floor. A silk-hatted man goes to her aid, but the others merely sit and stand around, seemingly indifferent; one concentrates on peeling an orange. Like Martin, we learn with shock that these are actors in rehearsal. Late in the novel, when the Grand Cosmo begins to fall, he offers free accommodation to actors to make it look as if the rooms were taken—which, naturally, they then are, producing "the rather complicated little effect of false life that, in the acting, became less false, that spilled into the real, since the actors knew each other and were pleased to talk, to walk about, to go on with their lives in a pleasant new setting."

Throughout the capitalist enterprise, a dangerous, magical and mundane exchange takes place between the found and the fabulated worlds, and both these worlds are finite: "The trajectory of the wrecker's ball had been set in motion as the blade of the first bulldozer bit into the earth." **Martin Dressler** coolly explores this American Dream in all its manifestations as aim, vision, intention, nightmare, hallucination, delusion, death. The great city—and by extension America, with its ever more exotic immigrants, its ever more hyperbolic advertising, its voracious ambition, its headlong rush into the 20th century—becomes "a fever patient in a hospital, thrashing in its sleep, erupting in modern dreams."

R. Z. Sheppard (review date 10 June 1996)

SOURCE: "Trump, the Early Days," in *Time,* June 10, 1996,

pp. 82-3.

[*In the following review, Sheppard discusses* Martin Dressler, *suggesting that the architectural structures in the story are metaphors for American culture.*]

Why do novelists like to stereotype American entrepreneurs as single-minded and heartless? Perhaps because so many are. Herman Melville set the tone in 1857 with *The Confidence-Man.* Mark Twain later brought the national style of go-getting to popular perfection in *Huckleberry Finn.* An adult rereading of that masterpiece reveals a hierarchy of hustlers, from runaway slave Jim and his fortune-telling hair ball to the outlandish charlatans calling themselves the King and the Duke.

At the other literary extreme, Horatio Alger's heroes triumphed through trustworthiness, diligence and stupefying practicality. As usual, the truth about the business world lies somewhere between comic cynicism and Rotarian sentimentality, in a psychological wilderness area now artfully surveyed by Steven Millhauser's *Martin Dressler: The Tale of an American Dreamer.*

Set in New York City at the turn of the century, this tale of a young man, a real-estate dreamer, embodies both the realities and the fantasies of a growing nation infatuated with its own possibilities. Dressler is only nine years old when he builds a display that makes the 5 cent cigars in his father's tobacco shop look more expensive. As a teenage bellhop, he boosts sales at a hotel concession. In 1894 at the age of 22, he opens the Metropolitan Lunchroom and Billiard Parlor, a winning concept that is expanded northward into the newly developing acreage bordering Central Park.

Among the pleasures of Millhauser's fourth novel, which continues in the author's previous vein of treating American history with dreamlike obsession, are descriptions of Manhattan as it began to transform its landscape into a 20th century skyline: an eruption of "modern flowers with veins of steel, bursting out of bedrock." It does not take a Viennese mind doctor to find eroticism in such charged imagery. Building cities is a procreative business, and Dressler is an evocative example of a breed driven to reproduce itself in concrete. A decision to marry a withdrawn woman of no discernible personality is a strong indication of his diverted passions.

In such respects *Martin Dressler* is an urban fable about civilization and its discontents, the repression of instincts in the service of progress. Yet this commercial hero also represents a period of social history when ambition and new wealth outstripped utility and taste. Dressler's Grand Cosmo, an architectural and cultural Tower of Babel, is part residence and part theme park. Within its 30 stories and two sub-terranean levels are a beach, a lake, a model New England village, a Moorish bazaar and a simulated asylum for the insane. Criticized as an example of "the worst excesses of late Victorian eclecticism," Dressler's folly fails spectacularly, a case of too much too late. In the end Dressler completes the illusion and his ruination by hiring actors to play customers.

Turning real estate into a reflection of a mind that in turn mirrors a society is a tricky literary feat. Millhauser pulls it off by lowering the barriers between realism and myth. The effect is also to remove artificial distinctions between the entrepreneur and the artist. Both, this well-told tale of obsession suggests, are gripped by demonic energies and grand schemes. And both take big risks, not the least of which is to be consumed by their own creations.

Dinitia Smith (essay date 9 April 1997)

SOURCE: "Shy Author Likes to Live and Work in Obscurity," in *The New York Times,* April 9, 1997, pp. C13, C18.

[*In the following essay, Smith provides some biographical information about the author and a summary of his works.*]

The writer Steven Millhauser was teaching his fiction workshop class at Skidmore College in Saratoga Springs, N.Y., on Monday afternoon when the chairman of his department entered the classroom and handed him a note asking him to call a reporter from a local newspaper "re: Pulitzer." "I told my students that a grotesque error had been committed," Mr. Millhauser said yesterday, "and that I had to straighten it out."

Of course, it was no error. Mr. Millhauser had received the Pulitzer Prize for fiction for his novel *Martin Dressler: The Tale of an American Dreamer,* published last year. But his suspicions were understandable. Until today, few but readers of serious fiction had heard of Mr. Millhauser, a shy, 53-year-old author of seven books, including four novels.

Known primarily for his 1972 novel, *Edwin Mullhouse: The Life and Death of an American Writer, 1943-1954, by Jeffrey Cartwright,* the fictional-biography of a cartoon-obsessed 11-year-old written by his best friend, Mr. Millhauser has deliberately kept himself out of the mainstream, preferring to type out his novels in solitude, first in his parents' attic, and since the late 1980's in his home in Saratoga Springs. His books have received relatively low advances, and his new novel was published by Crown rather than by Knopf, which has been a bulwark of prize-winning literary fiction and published some of his earlier work.

Mr. Millhauser's *Martin Dressler* is the story of a self-made man in 19th-century New York City, a kind of phantasmic hero out of Dreiser, Martin begins by helping out in his father's cigar store and becomes an entrepreneur whose career is a metaphor for the construction of the modern city. He is a builder, retailer and hotel owner who tries to satisfy his guests' needs "for solitude and mystery," with under-city waterfalls and Hindu temples. Martin's goal is "to imagine the confusion of strangers, satisfy their desires, make things simple and orderly." He wants "to move in both directions at once—to introduce every mechanical improvement without fail, and at the same time to emphasize the past."

In many ways, *Martin Dressler* is a typical Millhauser book, reflecting the author's obsession with popular culture, with labyrinths and dreams, and portraying a world in which the real and the fabricated have become intermingled.

When the novel was published last year, Janet Burroway, writing in the New York Times Book Review called it a "wonderful, wonder-full book." The novel, she wrote, shows "how the ideas and infatuations of our lives were already formed at the turn of the century." The book was a finalist for this year's National Book Award for fiction.

"I've always been interested in the American myth of the self-made man." Mr. Millhauser said in a telephone interview, "the idea you can work your way up the ladder. It's as central to our culture as the Faust myth is to Germany. I wanted to confront the fable head on."

Mr. Millhauser was born in 1943 in New York City, where his father was a professor of English at City College. He spent some of his childhood in Brooklyn before his father became, a professor at the University of Bridgeport in Connecticut. He attended high school in Fairfield and went on to Columbia University. A three-year period as a graduate student at Brown University followed. Mr. Millhauser planned to get a Ph.D. in medieval and Renaissance literature; indeed, Spenser's "Fairie Queene" has been one of the influences on his work. "I was someone who wanted to be a novelist, but I was having trouble writing." Mr. Millhauser said. "I was wandering around, wondering what to do. I have a scholarly strain in me. I was officially at school, but secretly writing at night."

The book he was secretly writing was *Edwin Mullhouse.* It is a strange work, a biography of a baseball-obsessed child who dies at 11 written by his envious best friend. It is both a sardonic portrait of an artist and a parody of literary biography. William Hjortberg, writing in the New York Times Book Review, called it "a mature, skillful, intelligent and often very funny novel."

Mr. Millhauser spent the following years "dimly earning a living," he said, and continuing to write in his parents' attic. In 1977 came *Portrait of a Romantic,* a fictitious account of the narrator's life from ages 12 to 15, published by Knopf. *In the Penny Arcade,* a collection of stories and a novella appeared in 1986. He wrote a third novel. *From the Realm of Morpheus,* in which a man watching a softball game follows the ball down a hole into the realm of dreams, but the manuscript was over 1,000 pages long, and Mr. Millhauser refused to cut it. Robert Gottlieb, then an editor at Knopf, turned it down.

Eventually, however, Mr. Millhauser agreed to cut the manuscript, and it was published by Morrow in 1988. Next came *The Barnum Museum,* a collection of stories, in 1990. The title story was about a museum with fantastic rooms that "represents the imagination," he said. The book reflected Mr. Millhauser's love of popular culture and was published by Poseidon Press, an imprint of Simon & Schuster, where his editor was Ann Patty.

In 1993 *Little Kingdoms,* another collection, was published. When the Poseidon imprint folded that year, Mr. Millhauser decided to follow Ms. Patty, his editor, to Crown, an imprint of Random House. "Steven has been published by a lot of houses," said Carolyn Reidy, the current president and publisher of Simon & Schuster's trade division. "It shows you editorial passion counts, no matter what house you're in."

Martin Dressler, which was chosen for the Pulitzer over *Unlocking the Air and Other Stories,* by Ursula K. LeGuin, and *The Mannikin,* by Joanna Holt, took two years to write. Though Mr. Millhauser knew he wanted to write about New York at the turn of the century, his knowledge of the era was limited.

"My immediate problem was ignorance," he said. "I had chosen to write a period piece. I researched the necessary time and place—what does the front of a cigar store in 1890 look like, for instance? A writer has to steep himself in research. But he must also be free to play with it and twist it. The turn of the century in New York was an era of astonishing physical changes—Manhattan was slowly marching uptown. I read novels of the times, Howells, Wharton."

Today, Mr. Millhauser teaches at Skidmore one full semester each year, and spends the rest of the time writing. His wife, Cathy, creates crossword puzzles. They have two children. "I don't anticipate the Pulitzer will change my life at all," he said. "I dare it to change my life!"

FURTHER READING

Criticism

Birkerts, Sven. A review of *Martin Dressler: The Tale of an American Dreamer,* by Steven Millhauser. *The Yale Review* 85, No. 1 (January 1997): 144-49.

> A review of *Martin Dressler* in which Birkerts calls the book a "Horatio Alger novel with a twist, a bildungs-roman of American capitalism."

Kunkel, Benjamin. A review of *The Knife Thrower and Other Stories,* by Steven Millhauser. *The Nation* 266, No. 19 (25 May 1988): 33-5.

> A positive review of *The Knife Thrower and Other Stories* in which Kunkel praises Millhauser's prose as "lucid, exact and formal," and compares the author to Nathaniel Hawthorne.

Additional coverage of Millhauser's life and work is contained in the following sources published by Gale: *Contemporary Authors,* Vols. 110 and 111; *Contemporary Authors New Revision Series*, Vol. 63; and *Dictionary of Literary Biography*, Vol. 2.

In Memoriam

William S. Burroughs

1914-1997

American novelist, essayist, critic, poet, and scriptwriter.

For further information on Burroughs's life and career, see *CLC*, Volumes 1, 2, 5, 15, 22, 42, and 75.

INTRODUCTION

A homosexual drug addict turned experimental novelist, Burroughs embodied for many observers the artist as outsider and rebel. As a Beat generation writer and avant-garde theorist, Burroughs greatly influenced the hippie and punk movements of the 1960s and 1970s, while making an important contribution to gay literature. Born in 1914 in St. Louis, Missouri, Burroughs was the grandson of the inventor of the adding machine and founder of the Burroughs Corporation. After graduating in 1936 from Harvard University, Burroughs worked odd jobs until the mid-1940s, when he became addicted to morphine and other drugs. In 1946 he met and married Joan Vollmer, who introduced him to fledgling Beat writers Jack Kerouac and Allen Ginsberg. They rekindled Burroughs's college dream of becoming a writer, and later facilitated the publication of *Junkie* (1953), Burroughs's memoir of his drug addiction. Under constant threat of arrest for drug offenses, Burroughs moved around the United States and eventually to Mexico, where in 1951, after a day of drinking and drugs, he accidentally shot and killed Vollmer in a game of William Tell. Shortly after his wife's death, Burroughs dealt indirectly with the incident in *Queer,* a novel that was not published until 1985. Burroughs next went to South America in search of the legendary hallucinogen *yage;* his correspondence with Ginsberg during this trip became the basis for *The Yage Letters* (1963). In 1953, Burroughs joined a community of expatriate American writers and artists in Tangiers, Morocco. Over the next four years he indulged his drug habits to the point of aimless inactivity, but still was able to compile a mass of notes based on his drug-induced experiences and fantasies; these notes were later collected and published in France as *The Naked Lunch* (1959). Composed of loosely related sections containing graphic descriptions of drug use, murder, and sadomasochistic homosexual acts, *The Naked Lunch* aroused critical debate in the United States in advance of its 1962 American edition, which appeared only after three years of court trials for obscenity. In 1957 Burroughs traveled to London to undergo treatment for drug addiction using the non-addictive drug apomorphine; after several relapses he was cured in 1959. Using leftover material from his Tangiers notebooks, Burroughs applied the "cut-up" technique that he had used in *Naked Lunch*—derived from the collage method

used in visual arts—and produced three books: *The Soft Machine* (1961), which outlines the use of control systems throughout human history; *The Ticket That Exploded* (1962), which borrows concepts from science fiction to illustrate linguistic control systems; and *Nova Express* (1964), which introduces the idea that writing is a powerful tool to resist control. Throughout the 1960s Burroughs experimented with cut-ups in fiction, film, and tape recordings, while gradually becoming aware of the cult figure status accorded him by "underground" culture. Burroughs abandoned the cut-up method in favor of a more conventional narrative style with *The Wild Boys* (1971), but his concerns about personal freedom, the control systems of society, and efforts to free oneself from social restrictions remained and continued in *Exterminator!* (1973), *Port of Saints* (1973), and *Ah Pook Is Here* (1979). During the 1980s Burroughs began a second career as a visual artist, which included such pursuits as painting, calligraphy, and writing screenplays and a libretto, as well as appearing in the films *Drugstore Cowboy* and *Twister* and a television ad for Nike shoes. Burroughs's most significant literary work of this period comprises the so-called "Red Night trilogy," and includes *Cities of the Red*

Night (1981), *The Place of Dead Roads* (1983), and *The Western Lands* (1987), the latter of which many critics thought would be his last book. But Burroughs continued to write into the 1990s, producing *Ghost of a Chance* (1991) and *My Education* (1995). He died after a heart attack on August 2, 1997, in Lawrence, Kansas, where he had lived since 1981. Despite Burroughs's undeniable influence in the arts and popular culture, his works as a whole have not received widespread academic acceptance. *The Naked Lunch,* however, has received critical praise from most quarters and is considered a classic of American literature by some scholars. James McManus has said, "He's turning out to have been enormously influential, especially on artists who go into the inferno and report back. He was into sex and drugs and rock n' roll before anybody else. And his influence on gay literatuure is immeasurable."

PRINCIPAL WORKS

Junkie: Confessions of an Unredeemed Drug Addict [under the pseudonym William Lee] (novel) 1953; also published as *Junky* [unexpurgated edition], 1977

*The Naked Lunch (novel) 1959; also published as *Naked Lunch,* 1962

Minutes to Go [with Brion Gysin, Sinclair Beiles, and Gregory Corso] (poems) 1960

The Soft Machine (novel) 1961; revised edition, 1966

The Ticket That Exploded (novel) 1962; revised edition, 1967

The Yage Letters (letters) 1963

Nova Express (novel) 1964

Time (poems) 1965

The Job: Interviews with Williams S. Burroughs (interviews) 1970

The Last Words of Dutch Schulz: A Fiction in the Form of a Film Script (screenplay) 1970

Third Mind (novel) 1970

The Wild Boys: A Book of the Dead (novel) 1971; revised edition, 1979

Exterminator! (novel) 1973

Port of Saints (novel) 1973

Ah Pook Is Here and Other Texts (prose) 1979

Blade Runner: A Movie (novel) 1979

Cities of the Red Night (novel) 1981

The Burroughs File (prose and diaries) 1984

The Place of Dead Roads (novel) 1983

The Adding Machine: Collected Essays (essays) 1985

†*Queer* (novel) 1985

The Western Lands (novel) 1987

Interzone (novel) 1989

Ghost of a Chance (essays) 1991

The Letters of William S. Burroughs, 1945-1959 (letters) 1993

My Education: A Book of Dreams (sketches and prose) 1995

*This work was adapted for film by David Cronenberg in 1991.

†This work was originally written in 1953.

OBITUARIES

Richard Severo (obituary date 3 August 1997)

SOURCE: "William S. Burroughs Dies at 83; Member of the Beat Generation Wrote *Naked Lunch,*" in *The New York Times,* August 3, 1997, p. B5.

[*In the following obituary, Severo reviews Burroughs's life and literary achievements.*]

William S. Burroughs, a renegade writer of the Beat Generation who stunned readers and inspired adoring cultists with his 1959 book *Naked Lunch,* died yesterday afternoon at Lawrence Memorial Hospital in Lawrence, Kan. He was 83.

The cause of his death, at Lawrence Memorial Hospital, was a heart attack that he suffered on Friday, his publicist, Ira Silverberg, said.

Over the years, Mr. Burroughs had lived in such places as New York, London, Paris, Mexico City and Tangier. But since 1981 he maintained a house in Lawrence, where he lived simply with three cats and indulged his interests in painting and photography and in collecting and discharging firearms.

Mr. Burroughs had undergone triple bypass surgery in 1991. He quit smoking after the operation. And though he continued to suffer from a leaky heart valve, from all reports, he regained robust health quickly for a man of his years.

His recovery was all the more noteworthy since he had spent so many of his younger days engulfed in narcotics addiction, an imperative so demanding that in 1954, while living in London, he sold his typewriter to buy heroin, although he kept working in longhand. He spent years experimenting with drugs as well as with sex, which he engaged in with men, women and children.

Naked Lunch, first published in Paris, and later by Grove Press in New York, was hailed as a masterly definition of what was hip, although the critics were not sure how to define the definition. Herbert Gold, writing in *The New York Times,* said that the book was "less a novel than a series of essays, puns, epigrams—all hovering about the explicit subject matter of making out on drugs while not making out in either work or love." Mr. Gold called the book "booty brought back from a nightmare."

Newsweek said that **Naked Lunch** possessed a "strange genius" and was a masterpiece "but a totally insane and anarchic one, and it can only be diminished by attempts to give it a social purpose or value whatever."

For his part, Mr. Burroughs said he agreed with the writer Mary McCarthy, who thought that **Naked Lunch,** and his other books, had a deep moral purpose.

"I do definitely mean what I say to be taken literally, yes, to make people aware of the true criminality of our times, to wise up to the marks," Mr. Burroughs told an interviewer in 1970.

Nobody found it especially easy to impose literality on Mr. Burroughs's sentences, either written or spoken. He described **Naked Lunch** as "a frozen moment when everyone sees what is on the end of every fork."

His work was not for traditionalists who loved a well-developed narrative. Dame Edith Sitwell was among those who demurred from the critics' praise, denouncing **Naked Lunch** as psychopathological filth. And even those who admired Mr. Burroughs's iconoclasm and his ruthless honesty had to admit that they could see flaws in the man. He was, in the final analysis, an alien among aliens, the ultimate odd duck.

"Just because he sleeps with boys, takes drugs and smokes dope doesn't mean that he tolerates or supports the majority of junkies, homosexuals or potheads," wrote Barry Miles in his 1993 biography, *William Burroughs,* which was subtitled *El Hombre Invisible* and published by Hyperion. "Bill simply doesn't like most people."

William Seward Burroughs was born on Feb. 5, 1914, in St. Louis, the son of Mortimer P. Burroughs, the owner of a plate-glass company, and Laura Lee Burroughs, who came from a prominent Southern family. His grandfather, for whom he was named, invented the perforated, oil-filled cylinder that made the Burroughs adding machine add and invariably get the right answer. The machine became a standard fixture in small and large businesses everywhere.

Mr. Burroughs's parents sold their stock in the Burroughs Company shortly before the stock market crash of 1929, and the $200,000 they received saw them nicely through the Depression. It did not leave the author with much of a legacy; his mother died in 1970, and what was left of her share of the estate was $10,000.

When Mr. Burroughs was a teen-ager, he read *You Can't Win,*

an autobiography of Jack Black, a drifter who took drugs and pilfered his way through a sordid, predatory life. The book made a considerable impression on him and became grist for his own books years later. It was around this time that he, too, started experimenting with drugs.

Mr. Burroughs was educated, not happily, in private schools in St. Louis and in Los Alamos, N.M.

He was sent to Harvard University, which he did not like any better than he had his preparatory schools, although the time spent reading pleased him. His favorite writers gave no hint of what was ultimately to come out of his typewriter. They included Shakespeare, Coleridge and DeQuincy. Other writers he came to admire included James Joyce, Joseph Conrad, Jean Genet, Franz Kafka, Graham Greene and Raymond Chandler. He received a baccalaureate degree from Harvard in 1936.

He took a vacation to Europe after graduation and in Dubrovnik met Ilse Klapper, a German Jew who had fled the Nazis. She was stranded, unable to renew her Yugoslav passport and unable to go to the United States. To accommodate her, he married her. They never lived together, and dissolved the marriage almost immediately upon returning to the United States, but they remained friends.

After his return to the United States, he worked at many jobs, including bartender, private detective, factory worker and insect exterminator. Except for exterminating, which he rather enjoyed, these jobs bored him.

He later recalled his experiences in *Exterminator!* published by Viking in 1973.

In the years before World War II, he returned to Harvard and did some graduate work in cultural anthropology and ethnology. After the war began, he was drafted into the Army but got out after only three months. According to the Miles biography, his mother used her influence to win his discharge for physical reasons.

By 1944, Mr. Burroughs had an apartment on Bedford Street in Greenwich Village and developed an addiction to heroin. Among those he befriended in New York in the 1940's were Allen Ginsberg and Jack Kerouac. It was from these three and their friends and acquaintances that the term Beat Generation would later be applied. And it was Mr. Ginsberg who, several years later, inadvertently came up with the title **Naked Lunch.** He got it from misreading a bit of manuscript in Mr. Burroughs's scrawl, which actually referred to "naked lust."

Mr. Burroughs's first book, published by Ace in 1953 under the pseudonym William Lee, was called *Junkie* and told of his years as an addict.

The writing of *Junkie* came after what was arguably the saddest part of Mr. Burroughs's life. He had married Joan Vollmer in 1945 and in 1951 they were living in Mexico City. He was then using drugs heavily and had returned to Mexico City from a trip to Ecuador, where he had tried to learn more about a hallucinogen called yage. His wife was addicted to Benzedrine and, according to Barry Miles, did not mind Mr. Burroughs's homosexual interests. Indeed, she had borne him a son.

Their life in Mexico City was not especially happy. One September afternoon in 1951, they began to drink with friends. Eventually, Mr. Burroughs, who was quite drunk, took a handgun out of his travel bag and told his wife, "It's time for our William Tell act." There never had been a William Tell act but his wife laughed and put a water glass on her head. Mr. Burroughs fired the gun. The bullet entered her brain through her forehead, killing her instantly. Mexican authorities concluded that it was an accident; Mr. Burroughs was convicted only of a minor charge and served little time in jail.

Years later, he would say that he would never have become a writer had it not been for her death. His wife's death, he said, "brought me into contact with the invader, the Ugly Spirit and maneuvered me into a lifelong struggle, in which I have had no choice but to write my way out."

The incident did not stop his drug use, and in his introduction to *Naked Lunch,* he describes his addiction: "I have smoked junk, eaten it, sniffed it, injected it in vein-skin-muscle, inserted it in rectal suppositories. The needle is not important." Mr.. Burroughs wrote that during the time he was an addict, he did "absolutely nothing." He said, "I could look at the end of my shoe for eight hours." When he was 45 years old, he ended 15 years of addiction by taking apomorphine, a chemical compound developed in Britain.

His son, William, died in 1981. He is survived by his companion and manager, James Grauerholz, who remained at Lawrence Hospital and declined to take phone calls.

No other Burroughs book attracted the attention of *Naked Lunch,* but his works always interested the critics. In 1960, he started inserting shards of sentences and paragraphs from newspapers and other authors into his own prose because, he said, he wanted to break the patterns that one normally finds in a book and emulate the peripheral impressions experienced in life itself.

"I don't plan a book out. I don't know how it's going to end,"

he told one interviewer. He readily admitted there was considerable overlap of material in his books.

In 1989, he collaborated on a comic opera, **The Black Rider,** which was performed at the Brooklyn Academy of Music Opera House by the Thalia Theater of Hamburg and was based on *Der Freischutz,* a folk opera by Carl Maria von Weber. Mr. Burroughs wrote the libretto; Tom Waits wrote the songs, and it was staged by Robert Wilson. It was also produced in Europe. There were many other projects but some, like **Ruski** (1984), **The Cat Inside** (1986) and **Ghost of a Chance** (1991) were limited editions.

In his later years, he spent a great deal of time as a painter and calligrapher. He said he did a lot of painting "with my eyes closed," but there was interest in his art and sales of his works helped bail him out of the tough financial situation in which he found himself in the mid-1980's.

Only a week before his death, Mr. Burroughs had been helping to prepare selected writings to be published next year by Grove Press, Mr. Silverberg, the publicist, said. A reprinting of a novel, **The Third Mind,** is also scheduled by Grove Press for next year and last year Viking Press reissued **My Education: A Book of Dreams.**

A self-avowed animal-rights activist and environmentalist, he had been supporting a Duke University foundation dedicated to the survival of lemurs.

In a rare interview last November, Mr. Burroughs told *The New York Times* that he made entries in a journal each day but had given up formal writing, adding quietly, "I guess I have run out of things to say." He also said that he had temporarily given up painting. "I don't want to keep repeating myself," he said.

Several of his friends, fellow drug-users and contemporaries have died in the last two years, including Timothy Leary, Herbert Huncke and Allen Ginsberg.

To the end of his life, Mr. Burroughs remained pessimistic about the future for humankind. In **Ghost of a Chance,** he lamented the destruction of the rain forests and their creatures and wrote: "All going, to make way for more and more devalued human stock, with less and less of the wild spark, the priceless ingredient—energy into matter. A vast mudslide of soulless sludge."

The London Times (obituary date 4 August 1997)

SOURCE: An obituary for William Burroughs, in *The London Times* (online publication), August 4, 1997.

[In the following obituary, the writer provides an overview of Burroughs's life and career.]

William Burroughs saw himself as a campaigner against destruction of the self by all the agents that he believed were conspiring to depersonalize it. His metaphor for this was junk addiction. By junk, the one-time drug-addict meant anything that put a person's life beyond his or her control. He saw the world in the despairing terms of addiction and fragmentation of the psyche, and his vision made him one of the most controversial writers of the second half of the century. Described as "the big daddy of the Beats", he influenced much of the "underground" of the 1950s which became the mainstream of the 1960s, from Norman Mailer and Anthony Burgess to Allen Ginsberg and R. D. Laing.

William Seward Burroughs was born in St Louis, Missouri, into the family of a famous industrialist. At Harvard during the New Deal years he studied poetry, ethnology and yoga, and gained a reputation for his wide-ranging knowledge. He travelled in Europe, studying medicine at Vienna University, and returned to Harvard to study postgraduate anthropology. He then rejected the bourgeois academic and scholarly life and entered the *demi monde* that was to shape his life.

Rejected for the US Army, he went through a variety of jobs, including those of private detective, pest controller, bartender, factory and office worker, advertising and "the edge of crime". It was a good training for a writer of his social range and peculiar gifts of mimicry. He developed his first drug habit at this time, and its frightening effects became central to his life and work. His experiences of drugs, crime and the police were fully documented in his first book, *Junkie: Confessions of an Unredeemed Drug Addict* (1953), published under the pseudonym William Lee.

Addiction and withdrawal or cure were the central metaphors of his career. His concern with the analysis of power was based largely on his drug-dependence and concomitant dependence on pushers, and on his antagonism to narcotics agents.

After some time in New Orleans and Texas, he made anthropological journeys to South America in search of alien cultures and new varieties of drugs. In the later 1950s he lived in Tangier, and after a crisis there in 1956 he underwent the apomorphine cure under Dr John Yerbury in London. *The Naked Lunch* (1959), his most famous book, was written largely in Tangier afterwards. "I awoke from the Sickness at the age of forty-five," he wrote, "calm and sane, and in reasonably good health except for a weakened liver and the look of borrowed flesh common to all who survive the Sickness."

The Naked Lunch—an aleatory, anarchic fantasy about ad-

diction and homosexuality—was acclaimed by Norman Mailer and Robert Lowell, but its monotonous and nauseating violence, scatology and sadism ensured that it was banned in America until 1962. It did not appear in Britain until 1964, by which time the failure of the *Lady Chatterley* case had freed publishing from most taboos. Like other "underground" writers, such as Henry Miller and Samuel Beckett, Burroughs was published by Olympia Press in Paris, Grove Press in America and John Calder in Britain. But Burroughs was no Beckett. While Beckett became famous for his fastidiousness about words, Burroughs used them casually, flippantly, and without compassion.

His ideas were shocking but shallow. "The whole system is completely wrong and heading for unimaginable disasters," he said. He claimed that there was a "necessity of deconditioning people from their whole past", and argued that "words are thought control". For a writer, who must begin with the inherited resources of language, this wholesale rejection was not promising.

His major theme was power as the manipulation of pleasure and pain in the human body. Around him he saw a systematic degradation in which people willingly submitted to becoming hosts of the parasites of rule. His targets were gangsters, judges, doctors, psychiatrists, policemen and servicemen. Fake sacrifices and cures, phoney panaceas and causes were his satirical targets, and yet he believed that people volunteered for exploitation. His work may have been a warning against the nature of power, but he saw human beings as irrevocably addicted to victimization by their overlords.

The Naked Lunch was followed by *The Soft Machine* (1961, final version 1968), *The Ticket That Exploded* (1962) and *Nova Express* (1964). Julian Symons's review of *The Soft Machine* summed up Burroughs's world: "The lovers bugger each other desperately, have nightmares in which they are violated by centipedes, and endure painful fantasies about the terminal erections of a hanged man. Out of the dirt, the excrement, the couplings, the repetitious confusion with which they are described, Burroughs makes a kind of dismal and disgusting urban poetry."

The confusion and repetition stemmed from Burroughs's "cut-up" method, which involved slicing up his typescripts and reassembling them—techniques demonstrated in two books of examples, *The Exterminator!* (1960, written with Brion Gysin) and *Minutes To Go* (1960, written with Brion Gysin, Sinclair Beiles and Gregory Corso). This form of dislocation was supposedly influenced by film and recording methods, but after *Finnegans Wake* and Gertrude Stein it was perhaps not so revolutionary and exciting as was made out.

Burroughs's subsequent career was spent between Tangier,

Paris, New York and London, the main scenes of what Mary McCarthy called his carnival world. His experiences of South America emerged in *The Yage Letters* (1963), written to Allen Ginsberg, who contributed a letter of his own, and Burroughs also wrote of his drug experiences in a number of articles, the most significant of which was **"Deposition: Testimony Concerning a Sickness"** (1960).

Newspaper column formats and ticker-tape structures appear in his *Time* (1965) and again in *Apo-33 Bulletin A Metabolic Regulator* (1967), which sought a way to re-establish individuality in the face of ideologies, miseducation and advertising.

Burroughs wrote a large number of shorter fictional pieces and articles on drug addiction and cure, but never, despite the popular myth, encouraged the indiscriminate use of drugs. He was, however, deeply interested in transformations of consciousness through both drugs and meditation. For a while he associated with Scientologists, in order to discover whether their methods were useful for the development of the self. His criticism of all such educational programs, plus some account of his own schemes for retraining the mind and body, are contained in the conversations of *The Job* (1970). *The Wild Boys* (1972) imagines a youth organization which has gained sole political power, a Spenglerian coming of the New Barbarians, self-generative and asexual.

His film script *The Last Words of Dutch Schultz* (1970) is based on the delirious dying testimony of the celebrated gangster, and reflects Burroughs's lifelong interest in cinema (he took part in two films based on his own work) and in the criminally pathological mind.

In his later work, science fiction techniques extended his vision of perpetual terrestrial strife into galactic conflicts, but in the 1970s his reputation and readership began to decline. His style and compositional method had been highly influential, but were more and more evidently one of modernism's culs-de-sac. The Burroughs family fortune had been based on the invention of the adding machine, but although he continued to write and publish into his eighties, it is unclear what it all added up to.

William Burroughs married Joan Vollmer in 1945, but in Mexico in 1951 he accidentally shot her, reportedly while playing William Tell. His son died in 1981.

Achy Obejas (obituary date 4 August 1997)

SOURCE: "Beats' Burroughs Survives in Pop, Gay Culture," in *Chicago Tribune* (online publication), August 4, 1997.

[*In the following obituary, Obejas appreciates Burroughs's influence on modern music and art.*]

"But I'm dying," says William Burroughs in his flat, unflinching voice on the song, "Interlude 3 (The Vultures are Gone and Will Never Come Back)," a collaboration with the Disposable Heroes of Hiphoprisy. Then, with just a hint of a smirk in his voice, Burroughs adds, "No, you're not."

Burroughs, one of the founding figures of the Beat Generation, actually died Saturday in Lawrence, Kan., after a heart attack. He was 83. But anyone who thinks that's the end of him doesn't understand the effect Burroughs continues to have on literature and popular culture.

"He's turning out to be have been enormously influential, especially on artists who go into the inferno and report back," said James McManus, author of the novel *Going to the Sun,* last year's Carl Sandburg award winner. "He was into sex and drugs and rock n' roll before anybody else. And his influence on gay literature is immeasurable."

Burroughs' *Naked Lunch* is considered a landmark book, even though its publication in 1959 prompted Dame Edith Sitwell to label it "filth." Other writers, including Mary McCarthy and Norman Mailer, hailed Burroughs as a genius.

"It's a satire on the evils of government and the uniquely American conflict between independence and control," said Barry Silesky, a magazine editor and author of a biography of Lawrence Ferlinghetti, another Beat Generation writer.

Naked Lunch was nonetheless the subject of a long-running obscenity trial, which concluded in 1962, generating enough publicity for a re-issuing of the book by Grove Press, literary home of both Burroughs and Beat pal Allen Ginsberg. Ginsberg died four months ago.

Burroughs' third book is a hallucinogenic feeding frenzy, with unlikely characters such as the Shoe Store Kid and the Lobotomy Kid. In one passage, a man is consumed by his own anus; in others, mad scientists perform a series of parodic operations. Burroughs' over-the-top style, influenced by his longtime heroin addiction, often bypassed literary staples such as plot, narrative and characterization in favor of an urgent, visceral approach.

"The study of hieroglyphic languages shows us that a word is an image," said Burroughs in 1969. "The written word is an image."

In that vein, Burroughs pioneered a writing style called "Cut-Ups," in which he cut up pieces of his own writing, mixed it with text from other sources, then glued it back together.

For all the surreal and shocking subject matter of his work, Burroughs' tall, trim figure served as contrast. Often wearing white suits and a fedora, Burroughs rarely smiled, preferring instead an affectless demeanor that suggested gentility.

In 1981, he was invited to read from *Naked Lunch* and another work, *The Soft Machine,* on *Saturday Night Live.* As Burroughs read, "The Star Spangled Banner" played.

In recent years, Burroughs had been collaborating with musicians, including Sonic Youth, John Cale, Donald Fagen, Marianne Faithful, Brian Jones, Tom Waits, Kurt Cobain, Michael Franti, Ravi Shankar, and Laurie Anderson. He had a significant influence on others such as Lou Reed, Throbbing Gristle, Bob Mould, Jesus Lizard and producer Steve Albini.

His last CD, *Spare Ass Annie,* was released in 1993, a pulsating, danceable collection of stories told in Burroughs' staticky voice.

"It's one of the great American voices of the century, in terms of its tonal qualities—literally, how it sounded, regardless of what he said," explained McManus, a writing professor at the School of the Art Institute and whose own works, particularly *Chin Music,* were inspired in part by Burroughs.

One rocker who certainly thought of Burroughs' voice as unique is Chicagoan Al Jourgensen of Ministry, who used the Beat poet on a CD single called "Just One Fix." "Smash the control images, smash the control machines," intones Burroughs on the 1992 release.

Burroughs' rock n' roll legacy, however, goes beyond his vocalizing. He is credited as the first person to use the term "heavy metal" in relationship to music. The Mugwumps, a 1963 band formed by the Lovin' Spoonful's John Sebastian, took its name from a Burroughs novel. Steely Dan was named after a metallic dildo in *Naked Lunch.* And '70s progressive band Soft Machine won Burroughs' permission to name itself after his novel.

Since the beginning of his writing career, Burroughs also demonstrated a separate interest in visual arts. He did the first dust jacket for *Naked Lunch*; the cover of "Just One Fix" is a Burroughs painting titled "Last Chance Junction and Curse on Drug Hysteria." Last year, the Los Angeles County Museum of Art organized his one-person show of works on paper, collage, photography, installation and paintings.

In *Man from Nowhere,* a biography of Burroughs by Joe Ambrose, Terry Wilson and Frank Rynne, the authors describe how Burroughs discovered one of his painting techniques: "In 1982, (he was) trying out some guns at a friend's place, using a double-barreled 10 gauge shotgun with an 18 inch barrel. . . . He had been shooting at pieces of plywood, and he found that different layers of wood had been exposed on different parts of the plywood . . . He tied cans of spray paint in front of the pieces of wood and blasted away with the gun. The inevitable explosions of garish and tactile color pleased Burroughs . . . Burroughs had changed writing with the Cut-Ups. Now he was applying the same random spirit to the world of art."

His first customer was Timothy Leary, who paid $10,000 for a painting. Cobain and other members of Nirvana were later customers. In his October 1988 show in Chicago, his works sold at prices between $1,500 and $10,000.

Burroughs was born February 5, 1914 in St. Louis, grandson and heir of the inventor of the Burroughs adding machine. He was educated in private schools and served as a glider pilot trainee for three months during World War II. Burroughs claims he began writing after shooting his second wife, Joan Vollmer, to death while playing a William Tell game. Their son William died in 1981 of cirrhosis of the liver. Burroughs is survived by longtime companion James Grauerholz.

Tunku Varadajan (obituary date 4 August 1997)

SOURCE: "America's Original Hippy Dies at 83," in *The Times* (online publication), August 4, 1997.

[*In the following obituary, Varadajan offers highlights of Burroughs's career.*]

The writer William Burroughs, widely acknowledged as the world's first hippy, has died, aged 83.

Burroughs, whose life was a melange of self-abuse and self-satisfaction, founded the "beat" movement with the novelist Jack Kerouac and the poet Allen Ginsberg.

A junkie, homosexual and brilliant writer, Burroughs was also famous for shooting his partner in the head in a drug-addled attempt to recreate the apple episode from *William Tell.* She balanced a glass on her head at a party in Mexico City, but Burroughs' aim let him down. Her death was to be the most famous case of wife-killing until O. J. Simpson.

Burroughs' most famous work, *Naked Lunch,* is a rollercoaster ride through the psyche of a drug addict and a deviant world of junkies, perverts and hucksters. The book was the subject of numerous censorship trials. Although written in 1959, it did not go on sale in America until 1962.

Although many found it unreadable at first, *Naked Lunch* eventually came to be recognized as a "stream of consciousness" classic. Critics have described Burroughs' his style as "non-linear", which is an elegant way of saying anarchic.

Burroughs also wrote *Junkie* (1953), *The Soft Machine* (1961), *The Ticket that Exploded* (1962) and *Nova Express* (1964).

Burroughs' happiest times were spent in Tangier in the 1950s, where he had easy access to drugs and boys. He befriended a Dutch sea-captain who ran a male brothel, moved into his home, and scoured the alleyways. "I get averages of ten very attractive propositions a day," he said.

Martin Weil (obituary date 4 August 1997)

SOURCE: "Beat Author William S. Burroughs Dies at 83," in *The Washington Post,* August 4, 1997, p. B4.

[*In the following essay, Weil summarizes the highlights of Burroughs's life and career.*]

William S. Burroughs, 83, whose efforts to transmute into literature the events and visions of a tormented life earned him fame as an artistic innovator and a founder of the Beat Generation, died Aug. 2 in Kansas.

Mr. Burroughs, who had resided since the early 1980s in Lawrence, Kan., after a knockabout life on four continents, died at Lawrence Memorial Hospital. He had been admitted Aug. 1 after a heart attack.

Much of Mr. Burroughs's enduring literary fame rests on *Naked Lunch,* the controversial 1959 novel that was hailed for groundbreaking creativity and denounced as vile filth.

In that book and in later writing, Mr. Burroughs employed a highly personalized stream-of-consciousness style to which literary critics have traced much of the work that characterized the authors of the Beat Generation.

Along with Jack Kerouac and Allen Ginsberg, whom he was credited with introducing to each other, Mr. Burroughs was regarded as one of the three literary mainstays of the Beat movement. That movement exercised a profound effect on the culture of young people in the 1960s and ultimately on the wider culture, as well.

Filled with nightmarish, surreal, corrupt images of living matter, *Naked Lunch* seemed off-putting and even revolting to many students of literature. Others, however, believed that Mr. Burroughs used his surreal imagery, its polymor-

phous insects and intestines, to serve as a vast metaphor for his central vision.

It aimed, British critic Tony Tanner once said, to stand for the variety of ways mankind is devoured in the modern world, and, according to New York literary scholar Morris Dickstein, it served as a model "for younger writers trying to break through the standard realistic method."

Mr. Burroughs's work was in many ways closely connected with a life that included firsthand familiarity with society's underside, years of heroin addiction and a tragic incident in Mexico in which, after hours of taking drugs and drinking, he accidentally shot and killed his wife.

Just the same, Mr. Burroughs's own life was one of paradox and of unexpected departures and deviations from the images and expectations created by his art and vision. St. Louis-born, he was the grandson and namesake of the man who invented the adding machine, or at least, said Mr. Burroughs, "the gimmick that made it work."

The literary, personal and psychological odyssey of his life, a voyage through New York's literary communities, to Mexico, to the jungles of the Amazon basin, to the exoticism of Tangiers, finally took him to Lawrence.

A friend, Richard Gwin, a photographer for the *Lawrence Journal-World* newspaper, said Mr. Burroughs had a bungalow with a large yard "and sort of faded into the community." One of Mr. Burroughs's cats was buried in the yard under a tombstone with the cat's name on it, Gwin said.

In the 1980s, Gwin said, Mr. Burroughs and Ginsberg, wearing ear protectors, would shoot at targets with a pistol when Ginsberg came to visit.

Mr. Burroughs had a circle of friends but lived in seclusion "in a lot of ways," Gwin said. "Maybe that's what he wanted."

Indeed, in his speech, appearance and demeanor, Mr. Burroughs appeared to belie his reputation for iconoclasm and the unconventional. While his fellow Beats were histrionic in declaiming their work from the lecture platform, Mr. Burroughs presented "very much a style of his own," said Dickstein, a professor of literature at City University of New York, who wrote a book on the literature of the 1960s.

He was dry, poker-faced, antiseptic and "always very well dressed," Dickstein said. And in his quiet way, Dickstein said, Mr. Burroughs was "very funny."

Not even Mr. Burroughs's descent from a member of the nation's pantheon of industry and achievement counted for much in his life. Only vestiges of the family fortune survived the Wall Street crash of 1929. His mother, described as a member of the southern aristocracy, may, according to students of his work, have cultivated in him a degree of misogyny that marked his life.

He attended private schools, found his way as a young man to the fringes of the drug world and, in 1936, graduated from Harvard University with a degree in English. Afterward, he traveled to Europe, where he met and married a woman of Jewish extraction to help her emigrate and escape the Nazis. The marriage was dissolved after they reached this country.

Mr. Burroughs served briefly in the Army during World War II, was discharged for medical reasons and, by 1944, had become addicted to heroin; concern about legal problems prompted his move to Mexico with his second wife, Joan Vollmer, whom he later shot.

They had a son who died in 1981.

Eventually, a British doctor was credited with breaking Mr. Burroughs of his heroin addiction, ending what he said were years of "staring at the toe of my foot" and opening the way for him to write. *Naked Lunch* appeared in Europe in 1959 and, after overcoming efforts to censor it, was published in the United States three years later.

His work often incorporated random observations sometimes inserted into the manuscript with scissors and paste, creating a stream-of-consciousness style. It all had an overarching purpose, he once said:

"To make people aware of the true criminality of our times. To wise up the marks."

OVERVIEW

Thomas Parkinson (essay date Spring 1980)

SOURCE: "Critical Approaches to William Burroughs, or How to Admit an Admiration for a Good Dirty Book," in *Poets, Poems, Movements,* UMI Research Press, 1987, pp. 313-20.

[*In the following essay, which originally appeared in 1980 in* Occidem, *Parkinson approaches* Naked Lunch *as continuing the "peculiar American tradition of hilarity" in literature.*]

I want to begin by giving a retrospective view of my own relations to Burroughs. First, I saw both the *Yage Letters* and

Naked Lunch before publication. In 1955 Allen Ginsberg lived in a little cottage four houses south of us on Milvia Street in Berkeley. He came to see me first in my office before we realized that we were neighbors, and he enrolled for graduate study at Berkeley. Kenneth Rexroth had advised him to see me, and together we worked out the best possible program that our graduate school would allow: required courses in bibliography and Anglo-Saxon and a special studies course in the prosody of Whitman. At first we talked incessantly about Whitman, and practically every day he came to the house and read Whitman aloud, and we discussed and argued. At that time Ginsberg was much taken with Richard Chase's book on Whitman and kept arguing for Whitman's sense of humor. At first I was amused and suggested that he could also write on intentional jokes in the *Faerie Queene.* Later we came to agreement, but I insisted he use the term *hilarity* rather than humor—a concept that I shall return to later.

Ginsberg did not trust academic figures, but he gradually came to the conclusion that I was not really a bad sort and showed me some of his poems. I thought that those weak imitations of Andrew Marvell were pretty dreadful and told him so directly, advising him to follow Whitman. That came as a relief to him, and since that moment we have been good friends. He showed me parts of a long poem that he was working on, and he began talking about Kerouac and Burroughs. He showed me a typescript of *On The Road* and segments of what would become *Naked Lunch.* The long poem was *Howl,* which he would read aloud later in the year at several places in the Bay Area. The little cottage in Berkeley has since been torn down, but though it was extremely tiny, about fifteen by fifteen feet, Ginsberg lived there, Kerouac visited for periods, Phil Whalen was a constant resident, and, when Ginsberg lived for a week or more at a time in San Francisco, the only resident. Gary Snyder was a frequent visitor, and they often overflowed into the old farm house—now torn down—where I lived with my wife and our first daughter. Mine is the melancholy fame of being the professor that the narrator of *The Dharma Bums* claimed to have scared the shit out of, with his customary elegance. The truth is that I threw Kerouac out of the house one evening because he was drunk, obscene, and was frightening my five-year-old daughter. In those days I stood six feet seven inches tall, weighed about two hundred and twenty pounds, was only 35 years old, quicker than most bears and as strong as some, and it would have been a pleasure to throw Kerouac physically out of the house, but he went mumbling away. Another piece of mythology about that period is that Ginsberg quit graduate school, though I encouraged him to stay, because Kerouac told him to quit. This is simply not true. Ginsberg on the way back from San Francisco one night asked me whether he should leave graduate school because, in his words, he could not twist his mind to work in the grammatical categories of Anglo-Saxon and the systematic procedures of bibliographical study. I told him that if he tried to orient himself toward something alien to his being, he would be making a mistake. But he insisted that he could not let down some of the professors who had been kind to him, and I answered that perhaps he should think of his well being rather than theirs. Finally I lost my temper and told him that he was a grown man, should certainly know his own mind, and should get out of graduate school as soon as possible because he was only making himself miserable. Kerouac may have said something to him, but the day after our conversation Ginsberg withdrew from graduate school.

In 1957-58 Ginsberg spent several weeks at our house in London, where Donald Carne-Ross recorded the whole of *Howl* for BBC and I included part of it in a broadcast on American poetry. In spring of 1958 I met Burroughs in the hotel on 9 rue Gît-le-Coeur and found him charming, gentle, and kind. He had just returned to Paris from London where he had undergone the apomorphine treatment and was free of drugs, very calm and gently didactic in conversation with Ginsberg, who was deep in the writing of *Kaddish* and in one of the manic phases which affected him occasionally during that period. That was my only meeting with Burroughs, though I have followed his career with attentive respect.

In 1959 while writing my second book on Yeats, I was also compiling the *Casebook on the Beat.* When I was being considered for a promotion my then chairman asked for a description of recent publications and current research, and after I handed him a bibliography, I remarked that I was compiling an anthology on the Beat writers. He replied that it would be wiser not to mention it because there might be somebody on the Budget Committee who lacked a sense of humor. I have always treasured that moment. That was the first critical approach to the Beat writers—ignore them, don't take them seriously, they are a bunch of clowns. But the fact is that they could not be ignored, that they went on to become the common reading of millions of young people, and my chief pride in the *Casebook* is that not one of the writers included in it has failed to be continuously productive, that Gary Snyder won the Pulitzer Prize and Ginsberg the National Book Award and that, alas, those writers have become part of academic study.

I say alas, because there is something mildly depressing in considering the distance from 1959 to 1977, from the chairman who thought the Beat writers were funny to the full majesty of the Modern Language Association turned toward the study of William S. Burroughs. *Naked Lunch* is now, in Chaucer's terms, to be considered by the members of "A solempne and a great fraternitee," rather than in unpublishable form by a few young people reading a typescript.

The danger in making the contemporary respectable is that we might at the same time make it dull. Serious study tends toward solemnity, and I have the uneasy feeling in reading Eric Mottram's *William Burroughs* that a handful of very uneven books and a rather goofy theory of composition are being treated as if they were the major works and theories of a Conrad, Hardy or James. I am mildly relieved when I note that Mottram has absolutely no clue about how to handle routine matters like bibliographies and notes and is no scholar, but when the question of Burroughs' world view is given so Germanic a presentation, I become irreverent, as I do at times with Professor Tytell's excellent long essay on Burroughs in his *Naked Angels.*

> **The primary critical problem is what is the ground of the appeal of this work? . . . Do we read *Naked Lunch* because it is one phase in the development of a vision of defiance against cosmic authoritarianism? . . . I suspect . . . that we read *Naked Lunch* because it is outrageously funny.**
> **—*Thomas Parkinson***

The primary critical problem is what is the ground of the appeal of this work? Does *Ulysses,* for instance, get its overwhelming charm from the series of literary and philosophical and historical correspondences that can be found through patient labor and a little bending of the truth? Does Yeats' later poetry appeal to us because of the endless delight of comparing perfectly clear poems with irrelevant and obscure prose selected from *A Vision*? Do *The Tropic of Cancer* and *The Tropic of Capricorn* command attention because of their Emersonean vision of individual value? Do we read *Naked Lunch* because it is one phase in the development of a vision of defiance against cosmic authoritarianism? Do we read the notes to *The Waste Land* rather than the poem because we don't want to face the funny frightening poem that Eliot actually wrote? I suspect that we read Yeats because he is bold, sexy, and wise, and that we read *Naked Lunch* because it is outrageously funny.

This brings us back to Ginsberg's perception of the funny side of Whitman. What he had in mind can be epitomized in a single line: "I dote on myself. There is that lot of me and all so luscious." This is on the surface as hilarious as Mark Twain's essay on the literary offenses of James Fenimore Cooper or Faulkner's "Spotted Horses" episode from *The Hamlet.* The English are capable of humor, the French of wit, but only Americans are capable of hilarity: boisterous merriment. I am speaking of literature not life; the English are capable of boisterous merriment, but except for the Anglo-Irish, notably Joyce, it is beyond them in literature. "No, Sir; wine gives not light, gay, ideal humour; but tumultuous, noisy, clamorous merriment" (O.E.D.). Outrageous fun.

Humor for Dr. Johnson was ideal; he loved Shakespeare's comedies and had little use for the tragedies. Burroughs is frequently compared to Swift, especially the Swift of *A Modest Proposal,* but there is a more appropriate sense in which he should be compared to Twain and Faulkner, and perhaps most of all to Henry Miller, all part of that special tradition of hilarity that distinguishes American literature and would seem hopelessly out of place in English or French, not to mention our earnest German and Russian friends. When Russian writers are hilarious, the tone is entirely different, and there are many times when to think of their work as hilarious is to insult them. Woody Allen's *Love and Death* is a marvelous parody of an American trying to keep a straight face when he treats characteristic situations and plots in Russian fiction. Even so solemn a fellow as Woody Allen cannot quite bring it off.

What is the special hilarious quality of American humor? It has not been defined, though my suspicion is that many members of this audience have an immediate reaction to the effect that, yes, the same tradition that produced Hemingway's "Today is Friday" could as properly produce the famous hanging cum buggery/fornication scenes of *Naked Lunch.* It is hard to believe, however, that Hemingway would excuse his travesty of the crucifixion as an argument against capital punishment. Burroughs says of the disgusting and fascination hanging cum buggery/fornication passages that they were written ". . . as a tract against Capital Punishment in the manner of Jonathan Swift's Modest Proposal. These sections are intended to reveal capital punishment as the obscene barbaric and disgusting anachronism that it is. . . ." Now this is hogwash. Swift's *Modest Proposal* is written in a somberly rational tone, and it is a kind of hoax writing—like [Daniel] Defoe's *The Shortest Way with Dissenters* (suppress them totally, even if the cost is mass slaughter)—that was taken literally by part of its audience, even though it was written by the Dean of Dublin's St. Patrick's Cathedral, just as Defoe's ironic tract was written by a notorious dissenter. Now nobody in his right mind would take Burroughs' "tract" as in any way a literal or probable recommendation. It boggles my mind to imagine any reader of the text, without Burroughs' intervention, stumbling unaided on the notion that those obscene, barbaric and disgusting passages are anything more than an exhibit of the kind of depravity that the human mind can sink to, and of which to the guilt and sorrow of humanity, we are all capable. But the text itself gives no clue to Burroughs' intended effect. If Burroughs really intended to write an attack on Capital Punishment, what he managed was a much more fundamental indictment of humanity. That he did so through savage hilarity superficially comparable to that of Apollinaire's *The Debauched Hospodar* and his *Memoirs of a Young*

Rakehell (which have absolutely no redeeming social importance, except that they were written by a great poet) places him firmly in the tradition of Miller and the late Twain. Burroughs is not a social critic but a nihilist intent on wiping out all conventional and civilized human values.

The appeal of **Naked Lunch** resides in the fact that it expresses the plight of a decadent capitalist culture in which the audience does not believe. The conventional and civilized values that it flouts are accepted superficially by the audience, and they delight in seeing them reduced to sexual and violent horror. The same principle makes the figure of Doctor Benway so numbingly funny:

> Dr. Benway is operating in an auditorium filled with students: "Now, boys, you don't see this operation performed very often and there's a reason for that. . . . You see it has absolutely no medical value. No one knows what the purpose of it originally was or if it had a purpose at all. Personally I think it was a pure artistic creation from the beginning.

> "Just as a bull fighter with his skill and knowledge extricates himself from danger he has himself invoked, so in this operation the surgeon deliberately endangers his patient, and then, with incredible speed and celerity, rescues him from death at the last possible split second. . . . Did any of you ever see Dr. Tetrazzini perform? I say perform advisedly because his operations were performances. He would start by throwing a scalpel across the room into the patient and then make his entry like a ballet dancer. His speed was incredible: 'I don't give them time to die,' he would say. Tumors put him in a frenzy of rage. 'Fucking undisciplined cells!' he would snarl, advancing on the tumor like a knife-fighter."

> A young man leaps down into the operating theatre and, whipping out a scalpel, advances on the patient.

> Dr. Benway: "An espontaneo! Stop him before he guts the patient!"

> (Espontaneo is a bull-fighting term for a member of the audience who leaps down into the ring, pulls out a concealed cape and attempts a few passes with the bull before he is dragged out of the ring.)

> The orderlies scuffle with the espontaneo, who is finally ejected from the hall. The anesthetist takes advantage of the confusion to pry a large gold filling from the patient's mouth. . . .

Now, does anybody in the audience think that this is an argument for socialized medicine? It is an hilarious presentation of all our unconscious fears of doctors, their absolute authority over life and death, their indifference to their patients, their pride in their skill, even their vainglory, and finally the opportunistic greed of the anesthetist. Since modern medicine has saved my life on three separate occasions because of its recent technological developments, I respect it immensely, and number among my friends several devoted radiotherapists and surgeons. But this episode makes me laugh heartily and with a sense of relief. Burroughs writes many such brilliant scenes in *Naked Lunch,* including the unprintable (!) section on the day that Roosevelt appointed nine baboons to the Supreme Court. Is this a satire on the judicial system? Or is it a terribly funny presentation of the fears that Roosevelt haters had of him and his intentions? Anybody who understands or remembers the New Deal will also understand why otherwise rational men in their seventies will drool with rage at the mention of NRA, WPA, and FDR. And much of *Naked Lunch* is full of such topical fun. I find it hard to think of it, however, as satirical. Burroughs and his readers are just having a good time. But since this means that we share low motives and are capable of being moved by gleefully unrestricted obscenity, we try to convince ourselves that we are reading a noble tract against Capital Punishment or the AMA or the judicial system. I think that one deficiency in criticism of *Naked Lunch* is that critics are wary of being caught appreciating the book for laughs. Hence the "solempne" tone. And until some serious critic of Burroughs writes a frank and uninhibited appreciation of the book, really serious criticism of Burroughs cannot begin.

When it does, I think that certain results will follow, and one of them will be a depreciation of the succeeding books. I am a tireless reader of science fiction, and Burroughs apparently has also read E. E. (Doc) Smith's *Lensman* series. Those books with their Intergalactic Patrol, their Arisians contemplating the Cosmic All, the monstrous Eichs who cut their victims to pieces molecule by molecule and then assimilate them by a gruesome method that a Burroughs character would characterize as "disgustin"—they are the exact and adequate parallel to the "serious" novels that follow *Naked Lunch* and strike me as pretentious bores.

As for critical approaches to Burroughs, my own feeling is that the central need for determining the ground of the work's appeal has not been satisfied. First, I should suggest that evaluations of the individual books have not seriously been entertained. The negative critics merely call names; the friendly critics take refuge in allegories that, to my mind, inhabit the banks of the Nile. The special humor of Burroughs has not been defined, and his place in the history of the peculiar American tradition of hilarity not approached. In contemplating the subject for the purposes of this brief chapter, I have concluded that wit divides man from

man; humor brings them together in a community of biological good sense; hilarity destroys the individual person as the author transcends and violates reality by a sense of outrageously uninhibited fun. Burroughs is no Swift or Defoe. Works like the *Bickerstaff Papers, A Modest Proposal,* or *The Shortest Way with Dissenters* are rational wit with a certain extravagance. Burroughs belongs with the authors of *The Mysterious Stranger, Pudd'nhead Wilson, Fenimore Cooper's Literary Offenses, The Tropic of Cancer* and *The Tropic of Capricorn,* and Faulkner's classic *The Hamlet.*

Beyond that, there simply has to be some more rational examination of science fiction that would clarify what Burroughs is up to in his cosmic works. There is a special genre of science fiction that can only be called fascist—some of the works of Robert Heinlein (especially *Farnham's Freehold*), most of the grand panoramic works, but especially Doc Smith's *Lensman* series. Burroughs uses many of Smith's devices for anarchist purposes, and this seems to have evaded sensible notice.

Finally, there is the entire question of Burroughs' theories of composition. They are goofy, and the cut-up method and all the nonsense about electronic fooling around neglect the fact that Burroughs' sensibility is what makes the work interesting, not all the gimmicks. The trouble is that there is no young Kenneth Burke around to make a responsible analysis of the folly of the entire theory. My own experience with Ginsberg, Kerouac, and Burroughs is that they rationalize their practice when they theorize, and with the exception of Ginsberg—who has real knowledge of the poetic tradition—they lack the training and good sense to shape any kind of rational and usable theory. There is something dreary in watching that chameleon Norman Mailer try to use Burroughs' style in *Why We Are in Viet Nam.* All that Mailer proves in that book is that Burroughs' manner is peculiarly suited to his sensibility, not to Mailer's.

In my view the best description of Burroughs' idea of the novel is Wyatt Blassingame's conclusion that Mark Twain "was not so interested in the novel as a compact whole as in the individual scenes on which he could release his full flamboyant genius."

Hence there is a great deal to re-think about Burroughs, evaluatively, with some sense of literary continuities and parallels, socially with some sense of the post-fascist nature of the later works. A good Marxist critique of Burroughs might also clarify matters. But above all, I should like to see the serious students of Burroughs confess that they like *Naked Lunch* because it is outrageously funny, hilarious in the manner of Faulkner, Miller, and Twain. Seriousness about hilarity becomes unconsciously hilarious. Years ago I consented to do an individual study project on Miller with a rather solempne student. Finally, at one of our weekly conferences,

I asked him with a feeling of despair, why he liked Miller. He looked shifty and said, "Well, remember the passage at the Paris Opera where the soprano has an immense menstrual flow that inundates the orchestra and boxes and leaves the audience floundering for their lives? Well, I used to have visions like that all the time, and until I read Miller, I thought I was abnormal." All right, I could understand that, but he was deeply offended when I said that I liked Miller because he was hilariously funny. I hope that nobody in the audience is offended when I affirm that in approaching *Naked Lunch,* we should keep our real motives in mind.

Gregory Stephenson (essay date 1990)

SOURCE: "The Gnostic Vision of William S. Burroughs," in *The Daybreak Boys: Essays on the Literature of the Beat Generation,* Southern Illinois University Press, 1990, pp. 59-73.

[*In the following essay, Stephenson discusses Burroughs's middle and late works in the context of Gnostic thought, focusing principally on the themes of* The Soft Machine.]

In the following I want to consider what I call the Gnostic vision of William S. Burroughs and to trace its development in his work with particular attention to his key novel *The Soft Machine.* I do not mean to suggest that William Burroughs is an adherent of Gnosticism or even that he would endorse or concur with its tenets and practices. I do, however, find that there are significant parallels and points of contact between Burroughs' writing and Gnostic thought, and that these provide a framework in which aspects of his work may be clarified.

Fundamental to religion, philosophy, and other modes of human enquiry is the problem of the relationship of the self to the physical body, of spirit to matter. The spectrum of opinion with regard to this problem varies from the absolute materialist position at one extreme, through the immanentist position in the center, to the position of the absolute transcendentalist at the other extreme. The ideas of the Gnostic and of William Burroughs are situated at this latter extreme. Both view the material world as illusory, the body as the primary impediment to true being and identity, and escape from the body and the world of the senses as humankind's paramount concern. The terms in which they characterize their beliefs and the proposals they advance to further their goals have much in common. To this extent they share a vision of the universe and of the human situation.

Gnosticism was a religious movement that flourished in the Middle East and in the Roman world approximately during A.D. 80-200. Gnosticism incorporated elements of Hellenis-

tic philosophy, Oriental religion, Judaism, and Christianity together with magical practices and mystical traditions from diverse cultures including Babylon, Persia, and India. Orthodox Christians considered it heretical and blasphemous, and they persecuted and finally suppressed the movement.

There were a number of different sects and systems of Gnosticism: the Simonian, Saturnian, Ophite, Naasene, Valentinian, Basilidian, Marcionite, Peratikite, Encratite, Docetist, Haimatitite, Cainite, Entychite, Carpocratian, and others. These systems had varied emphases and approaches, different terminologies and mythologies to the extent that, as one scholar has stated, "There is no one uniform set of ideas that may be singled out as gnostic; rather it is a matter of a type of thought that manifests itself in different ways in different groups."

Essentially though, the attitude that characterizes all the Gnostic systems is that the world, the body, and matter are unreal and evil. They are illusions that are the products of malevolent powers called Archons, chief among whom is Sammael (the god of the blind or the blind god), also called Ialdabaoth or the Demiurge. These creator-gods are not the Deity or the Supreme Being, though they make claim to being so. The Deity is completely transcendent—absolutely distinct, apart, and remote from the created universe. However, a portion of the divine substance, called the pneuma, is enclosed in the human body—within the human passions and the human appetites where it is "unconscious of itself, benumbed, asleep, or intoxicated by the poison of the world." The aim of Gnosticism is to liberate the pneuma from its material, delusional prison and to reunite it with the Deity. The Archons seek to obstruct this liberation and to maintain their dominion.

The tyrannical rule of the Archons is called *heimarmene,* which manifests itself through natural law, through human governments, institutions, laws, and conventions. It even extends to the afterlife where the escape of the soul and its return to God is prevented. In the Gnostic cosmology the universe is a closed domain, ruled by forces hostile to man, where ordinary life is spiritual death.

The situation would be entirely without hope were it not for "a messenger from the world of light who penetrates the barriers of the spheres, outwits the Archons, awakens the spirit . . . and imparts to it the saving knowledge. . . ." This saving knowledge is gnosis, which means knowledge or insight. Gnosis is distinct from rational, philosophical, or scientific knowledge. It is an ecstatic, transcendent knowledge of the nature of the self and of reality, an enlightenment that redeems the pneuma from the body and from the realm of matter and allows it to escape the control of the Archons.

Gnosis may be achieved in many ways. A knowledge of the

nature of the Archons, their spheres and their powers, and a ritual renunciation of their dominion is basic to the quest for gnosis. Gnosis may be the result of a long process of self-knowledge or of the correct understanding of spiritual texts, or the receipt of knowledge may be swift and revelatory. The knowledge may be attained through ascetic discipline or by means of a systematic licentiousness. Whatever means break the illusion of the body-self and the material world, whatever acts repudiate the authority of the Archons and affirm the pneuma, are paths to gnosis.

The Gnostics were strictly antihierarchical in their approach to their religion and to the social and political situation of their time. They viewed all rulers and powers on the earth as servants of the Demiurge. The distinctions between clergy and laity and the relationships of superiors and subordinates were seen as reflections of the principles of the Archons from which the Gnostic was redeemed. Elaine Pagels notes that "instead of ranking their members into superior and inferior orders within a hierarchy, they followed the principle of strict equality. All initiates, men and women alike, participated equally in the drawing; anyone might be selected to serve as priest, bishop or prophet. Furthermore they cast lots at each meeting, even the distinctions established by lot could never become permanent ranks." In this way, resistance to the blind god and his minions was total, and each human was an agent of either the Deity or the Demiurge.

In a similar manner, the universe of William Burroughs' writing is also dualistic, a universe of warring powers and their agents on earth. At the highest level of abstraction, Burroughs exhibits in his novels a struggle between freedom and control, whose representatives in the universe are often portrayed as the Nova Police and the Nova Mob. The Nova Mob, also called the Board, enforces limit, authority, and single vision, while the regulatory, redemptive Nova Police have as their goal the restoration of multitudinousness, the liberation of consciousness from matter.

The head of the Nova Mob, which has occupied earth for thousands of years, is Mr. Bradly Mr. Martin, also called Mr. & Mrs. D or the Ugly Spirit. Of him Burroughs writes:

> Mr. Bradly-Mr. Martin, in my mythology, is a God that failed, a God of conflict in two parts, so created to keep a tired old show on the road, The God of Arbitrary Power and Restraint, Of Prison and Pressure, who needs subordinates, who needs what he calls his "human dogs" while treating them with the contempt a con man feels for his victims—But remember the con man needs the mark—The mark does not need the con man—Mr. Bradly-Mr. Martin needs his "dogs" his "errandboys" his "human animals." He needs them because he is literally blind. They do not need him. In my mythological

system he is overthrown in a revolution of his "dogs."

Burroughs' blind god, like the Gnostic Demiurge, enforces his dominion over man through the human body and brain. By means of manipulation and control he keeps human consciousness confined to the body and reduced to the body consciousness of the ego self. His Archons include: "Sammy the Butcher," "Green Tony," "the Brown Artist," "Jacky Blue Note," "Limestone John," "Izzy the Push," "Iron Claws," "Hamburger Mary," "Paddy the Sting," "the Subliminal Kid," and "the Blue Dinosaur." The agents of Mr. Bradly Mr. Martin on earth are all the authorities and all the establishments and all the systems—the military, the police, business and advertising, religion, and such individuals as customs inspectors, con artists, politicians, pushers, all those who coerce and con, anyone in a position to impose and enforce a reality on another.

The key technique of the Nova Mobs control is image, especially as it is communicated through language. Through the manipulation of word and image an illusory reality is created and maintained. This is what Burroughs refers to as "the Reality Film." It is scripted and directed by the Nova Mob and we are the unconscious, involuntary actors. The script, "the Board Books," calls for the deliberate creation and aggravation of insoluable conflicts, which serve both to keep the actors unaware of their position and to move the planet slowly, inexorably toward the Nova State that is the climax of the entertainment for the Nova Mob. "The angle on planet earth was birth and death—pain and pleasure—the tough cop and the con cop. . . ." By these means the earth is kept as a sealed colony, exploited viciously and controlled totally by Bradly Martin and the Board."

As in Gnosticism, it is "a messenger from the world of light who penetrates the barriers of the spheres" to bring the message of liberation. The Nova Police break through the blockade around the earth, infiltrate Nova Mob operations, and with the help of local partisans, eventually overthrow the rule of Mr. Bradly Mr. Martin.

The message of the Nova Police is, "This is war to extermination—Fight cell by cell through bodies and mind screens of the earth . . . Storm the Reality Studio and retake the universe." Their plan calls for "total exposure—Wise up all the marks everywhere Show them the rigged wheel." And their strategy is to "cut the word lines—smash the control images."

This program of the Nova Police is equivalent to gnosis, for it provides a way of breaking through the illusion of the material world and escaping from the body and the limits of ego consciousness. The specific method to implement the strategy is the cut-up.

The cut-up is quite simply the cutting up and rearranging of written material. There are variations such as the fold-in method or the use of tape recordings, but the intention and the effect is the same: to decondition perception, to destructure and restructure reality.

Burroughs' premises for his theory of the cut-up are these: language is a system that carries implicit patterns of perception and thought that are largely unconscious in the user of the language; these patterns are the assumptions of the system; and all patterns, all systems are reductive. We experience ourselves and the world through language, but language limits our experience to its implicit patterns. Our life within the limits of our language is our reality. If we wish to discover what other realities may exist outside of the patterns of our language reality, then we must break out of our language.

For Burroughs the cut-up method is a tool of escape from language reality into a multiverse. The cut-up can release us from the discreetness, the exclusiveness of an either/or universe into a multivalent infinity where all sets intersect. By cutting the word lines we can restructure our reality, our consciousness.

Colin Wilson has distinguished between two planes of consciousness that he names the horizontal and the vertical. "The plane of everyday experience is horizontal, static," he writes, "and my ordinary thinking moves on this plane. On the other hand, experiences of intensity tend to penetrate vertically into consciousness, and make us aware of consciousness *as freedom* instead of as passive perception." This is precisely Burroughs' direction with the cut-up—from the horizontal to the vertical plane. His concern is the liberation of consciousness and its extension beyond language.

For Burroughs the cut-up is not primarily an act of destruction but an act of creation. The cut-up creates by permitting multiple connections and by unifying. Specifically, the cut-up unifies time, identity, and perception. In the multiverse of the cut-up all time is simultaneous. The past, present, and future are exploded as arbitrary and artificial distinctions. Events occur in what scientists call Absolute Elsewhere. The ego identity is likewise discovered to be an arbitrary and nonexistent limit. Self and other and *it* melt and merge in the cut-up. The modes of sense perception overlap and fuse into synaesthesia. Thus, the cut-up provides access to a new clarity, a new lucidity.

In this regard, there is an affinity between Burroughs ideas and Aldous Huxley's view (based on the ideas of C. D. Broad and Henri Bergson) of the human central nervous system as a "reducing valve" that processes information according to its pertinence to physical survival, restricting "Mind At Large" to ego identity.

Clearly though, there is a more direct line from Burroughs back to Rimbaud. Burroughs has acknowledged the relationship of his cut-ups to Rimbaud. "Images shift sense under the scissors smell images to sound sight to sound sound to kinesthetic. This is where Rimbaud was going with his color of vowels. And his 'systematic derangement of the senses. . . .'"

Burroughs refers, in the above quote, to Rimbaud's poem "Voyelles," in which the poet explores the correspondences between color and sound. The same correspondence is referred to again in the "Alchemie Du Verbe" section of *Une Saison En Enfer*. Like Burroughs, Rimbaud felt that true being and true identity were elsewhere and other than ego identity. ("Je est un autre." "La vraie vie est absente.") And he believed that in order to attain experience of the unknown, visionary self, the ego identity and its perceptions must be destructured. ("Il s'agit d'arriver à l'inconnu par le déreglement de tous les sens." "Le poète se fait voyant par un long, immense et raisonné déreglement de tous les sens.")

The cut-up for Burroughs is a way of knowledge, a method of resistance, and a tool of escape readily available to everyone.

The extent to which Burroughs became convinced that cut-ups represented a radical and effective solution to the human predicament is evidenced in his letter of 21 June 1960 to Allen Ginsberg. Ginsberg had written to Burroughs on 10 June 1960 from Pucallpa, Peru, describing a terrifying experience with the drug ayahuasca and its disorienting aftermath. Fearing madness, Ginsberg appealed to Burroughs for aid and advice. Burroughs replied, instructing his friend to cut-up the enclosed copy of the letter, cut-up his own poems, cut-up "any poems any prose." His message is unequivocal and is striking in its resemblance to the Gnostic vision.

> WHAT SCARED YOU INTO TIME? INTO BODY? INTO SHIT? I WILL TELL YOU. THE WORD. THE-THEE WORD. IN THEE BEGINNING WAS THE WORD. SCARED YOU ALL INTO SHIT FOREVER! COME OUT FOREVER, COME OUT OF THE TIME WORD THE FOREVER. COME OUT OF THE BODY WORD THEE FOREVER. COME OUT OF THE SHIT WORD THE FOREVER. ALL OUT OF TIME AND INTO SPACE.

Apart from its insistence on language as the principal device of control, Burroughs' statement is very close in tone and sentiment to a phrase in a Gnostic text: "Why did ye carry me away from my abode into captivity and cast me into the stinking body?"

Beyond the cut-up, beyond language and image, is silence, which Burroughs describes as "the most desirable state" because it leads to "non-body experience." In Burroughs' view man must move from speech to silence, from image to awareness, from body identity to disembodied self, from time to space. This is the direction of human evolution as he assesses it, and these ideas are the central themes of Burroughs' middle and late work, beginning with his novel *The Soft Machine.*

The Soft Machine is a pivotal work in Burroughs' oeuvre and as distinct from *Naked Lunch* as was that book from *Junkie.* In *The Soft Machine* all that has preceded in Burroughs' work is summarized and extended, and all that is to come is forespoken. In *The Soft Machine* Burroughs introduces his new technique, the cut-up; employs a new central image, parasitism; and outlines his cosmic myth, the Nova Police versus the Nova Mob. And in contrast to his earlier works in which he restricted himself to description and detached observation, in *The Soft Machine* the author himself becomes a prescriptive and an active agent, a partisan saboteur working against the occupying forces of the enemy.

The Soft Machine was printed in three different versions, the first of which was published in Paris by the Olympia Press in 1961. The second rearranged, recombined, altered text, with deletions and additions, was published in New York in 1966 by Grove Press. Apparently, as correspondence in the Grove Press collection indicates, the author was not satisfied with this edition even at the time that it was typeset for publication and wished to make further revisions. However, the editor insisted on a cutoff date for revisions, and the book was published without incorporating Burroughs' final revisions. The third version of *The Soft Machine,* the final and definitive text, was published by Calder & Boyars in London in 1968 and is still unavailable in the United States. This version contains about thirty pages of new text plus an appendix and additional material following the text.

The new technique, new imagery, and new vision of *The Soft Machine* may already be discerned in Burroughs' contributions to *Minutes to Go.* In these short pieces, the author's first cut-ups, he discovers his central metaphor, that of parasite and host; some of his most important characters, including Mr. Bradly Mr. Martin; and the dominant themes of *The Soft Machine* and his subsequent novels.

Burroughs' collaborators in *Minutes to Go,* Brion Gysin, Gregory Corso, and Sinclair Beiles, use literary, religious, or political material for their cut-ups, while Burroughs uses medical articles, especially those concerning virus. "These individuals are marked foe," pronounces one text referring to the medical profession. Other texts disclose diseases and

viruses as "deals," while another ominously reveals the "agent at work" behind cancer. Burroughs' final contribution to the volume presents a comprehensive delineation of the theories that inform *The Soft Machine:* "The word was a virus . . . virus made man . . . man is virus. . . ." The addictions to language, body, ego identity, sex, religion, and drugs are exposed as one addiction: image addiction, a virus parasitism. The Native Guide, who becomes a recurrent figure in Burroughs' mythology, is introduced as is Hassan i Sabbah and his maxim, "Nothing is true—everything is permitted." And finally, Burroughs presents his countermeasure to the agents, the deals, the addictions, and the parasites that infest human consciousness: "Rub Out The Word."

The Soft Machine is a full-length treatment of the ideas, images, and characters introduced in the pieces in *Minutes to Go.* Burroughs has described the book as "an obstacle course. Basic training for space." The episodic structure, together with the use of cut-ups, effects a spatial and temporal dislocation, a breakdown of sequential, linear perception, inducing a sort of dream state in the reader. The recurrence of words, phrases, places, images, situations, and characters without forward narrative movement contributes further to a sense of an utter otherness that is almost familiar, almost recalled. In this manner the book fulfills its intended "training" function.

The first version of *The Soft Machine* was divided into four large sections or Color Units: Unit I, Red; Unit II, Green; Unit III, Blue; Unit IV, White. This structure was abandoned in the second and third versions of the book but it remains embedded in the text. The reference is to Rimbaud's color vowels (alluded to in the text) and the intention is, again, that of an "obstacle course." Color imagery dominates in *The Soft Machine* and is used most frequently to produce the effect of synaesthesia. Burroughs hopes to train the reader to perceive and to conceive in larger terms than the discreetness permitted by the five senses. The program, which is Burroughs' systematic derangement of the senses, is aimed at deconditioning and reconditioning consciousness to permit nonbody experience.

The Soft Machine portrays a world of violence, viciousness, mendacity, and manipulation. The earth is a planet approaching nova state as a result of the deliberate design of the Nova Mob. The first section. "Dead on Arrival," depicts the hopelessness of the human condition in images of junk, parasitism, and death. Desperate junkies wait in downtown cafeterias for "the Man," and in the suburbs "antennae of TV suck the sky" in images of addiction. Man is at the mercy of biology ("running out of veins") and of the authorities (pushers, croakers, the heat) and is receiving a short count of junk and of time. Parasitism is the principle of survival; the hosts attach themselves to other hosts; the junkie becomes pusher or turns stool pigeon. The strategy of parasitism is "INVADE. DAMAGE. OCCUPY.," and the pusher, promising "freedom," moves into his host with the junk. Death by overdose, by drowning, by hanging, by murder, by accident, by one's own hand, or at the hand of another, physical death and psychic death: we are all, by the nature of the setup, "Dead on Arrival."

Human history is a "penny arcade peepshow long process in different forms" for Mr. Bradly Mr. Martin and the Board, and they are preparing to bring it to the Grand Finale of nova when the Nova Police arrive. Arrests are made, and one Board member "Willy the Rat" turns stool pigeon. Partisans undertake sabotage, and agents infiltrate and destroy Board operations past and present (the Mayan control system and Trak News Agency). As the total control of the Nova Mob begins to crumble, the situation report of the conflict is, "Word falling—photo falling—breakthrough in grey room." The tyranny of image is being subverted. The Reality Studio, the "grey room," is under siege.

A final apocalyptic overthrow of Mr. Bradly Mr. Martin is presented in the section titled "Gongs of Violence."

> Police files of the world spurt out in a blast of bone meal. . . . Wind through dusty offices and archives—Board Books scattered to rubbish heaps of the earth—Symbol books of the all-powerful board that had controlled thought feeling and movement of a planet from birth to death with iron claws of pain and pleasure—The whole structure of reality went up in silent explosions—Paper moon and muslin trees and in a black silver sky great rents as the cover of the world rained down—Biologic film went up.

Having shown us the end, Burroughs then shows us the beginning in the final section of *The Soft Machine,* "Cross the Wounded Galaxies." We are presented with the moment in prehistory when herbivore apes were first invaded by the parasitic consciousness of the Nova Mob. Migrating during a period of glacial advance, a band of apes is suddenly afflicted with "the talk sickness," which causes both interior and exterior transformations.

Whereas previously the apes had no sense of individual identity, no "me" but only "we," the "talk sickness" precipitates a radical change in consciousness, creating ego identity. (It may be, as Eric Mottram has suggested, that this passage owes something to William Golding's *The Inheritors* [1955], but it is not a cut-up of Golding's book.) This alteration of consciousness is accompanied by a physical metamorphosis: "hair and ape flesh off in screaming strips, stood naked human bodies. . . ."

The parasite invasion of consciousness also manifests itself

in the awareness of "the white worm-thing inside" that feeds off the fear and the pain of others and that changes the dietary practices of the ape-men to carnivorousness and cannibalism. The ape-men become hunter-killers, practicing ritual hunting magic. This first tribal religion quickly evolves into social hierarchy and monotheism when one of the creatures tells another, "I am Allah. I made you." Thus, in Burroughs' view, human religion and class structures are the extensions of psychic parasitism.

The Soft Machine ends with a coda in which the events of the myth are condensed and fragmented. Bradly Martin's arrival on earth, his long reign, his pursuit by the Nova Police, and his final overthrow are presented in twenty-two lines of cut-up prose-poetry.

The incidents and essential situations of *The Soft Machine* are repeated, developed, and further clarified in the author's next two novels. *The Ticket That Exploded* (1962, rev. ed. 1967) and *Nova Express* (1964). Subsequent novels such as *The Wild Boys* (1971), *Exterminator!* (1973), and *Port of Saints* (1970, rev. ed. 1980) also treat aspects of Burroughs' Gnostic vision but do so using different characters and situations. The problem of image and body is resolved most conclusively in *The Wild Boys,* in which all existing institutions, systems, and cultural and biological patterns are overthrown, and there is a return to a preverbal tribalism as an evolutionary medium to a nonmaterial state of being.

As the central work of Burroughs' oeuvre, *The Soft Machine* is itself centered around Mr. Bradly Mr. Martin. His phantom and elusive presence, his dual nature (as his name suggests), is the informing principle of the story.

Mr. Bradly Mr. Martin may be related to the figure of "Bradly the Buyer" in *Naked Lunch,* but he first appears under his own name in *Minutes to Go* in a piece titled **"Reactive Agent Tape Cut by Lee the Agent in Interzone."** The context of his appearance is a précis of his history and his ultimate fate in Burroughs' mythology. "He had to use junk somewhere. Mr. Bradly Mr. Martin—slotless fade out in sick streets of cry—."

Bradly Martin, the god of image and of reality, is himself addicted to image. He is junk in all its manifestations. Without his human hosts he is literally nowhere. He cannot exist without a medium. So he has to use junk somewhere. (We learn later that earth is not the first host planet for Bradly Martin. He has left a trail of novas behind him in space, across "the wounded galaxies." The fade-out image foretells his ultimate disappearance following his overthrow on earth.

Bradly Martin is also in *Minutes to Go* associated with Yves Martin, a member of an actual expedition composed of four scientists and a guide that met with disaster in the Egyptian desert. The bodies of four of the members were recovered; one person remained missing. Positive identification of the bodies proved impossible due to their decomposition and due to the sharing and exchange of clothing, documents, and diaries by members of the expedition. This curious event intrigued Burroughs and contributed to his conception of Bradly Martin as a ruthless survivor of an interplanetary spaceflight, who, after a forced landing on the planet earth, assimilated and subsumed the other crew members. Burroughs refers to the Yves Martin expedition in *The Soft Machine* and again in *Nova Express.* Bradly Martin describes his arrival on earth in **"The Beginning Is Also the End."**

In developing Bradly Martin ("God of Conflict . . . God of Arbitrary Power and Restraint, of Prison and Pressure"), Burroughs also drew on other sources. He has stated, "My conception of Mr. Bradly-Mr. Martin is similar to the conception developed by William Golding in *Pincher Martin.*"

The similarity between the two figures, Christopher Hadley "Pincher" Martin and Mr. Bradly Mr. Martin, extends beyond the obvious resemblance of their names. Their situations are essentially the same, for they are both godlike creators of a reality, the product of their remorseless will to survive. Both are eaters—viciously self-assertive, parasitic, aggressive, greedy, without scruples, and ready to survive at all costs. Pincher Martin is an actor by profession; Bradly Martin repeatedly refers to himself in the narratives as "just an old showman." Both are marooned: Pincher Martin on his island and Bradly Martin on earth. And both are erased finally, unable to completely control and thus maintain the reality that they have created.

As an avid reader of science fiction, Burroughs may also have been influenced in the construction of his cosmic myth by J. B. Priestley's short story "The Grey Ones" (1953) or by Jack Finney's *The Body Snatchers* (1955), in both of which the takeover of human consciousness by alien intelligence is depicted; by Kurt Vonnegut's *The Sirens of Titan* (1959) in which all of human history is the product of alien control; and by Brian W. Aldiss' novelette *Hothouse,* which first appeared in the early sixties, in which the human brain and intelligence are presented as being derived from and susceptible to parasitic invasion. It is also interesting to note that Colin Wilson adopted Burroughs' metaphor for his philosophic science fiction novel *The Mind Parasites* (1967), and that Lawrence Durrell's latest series of novels, of which the first two constituents are *Monsieur* (1974) and *Litia* (1978), is centered on Gnosticism.

In the second century Tertullian wrote contemptuously of the Gnostics: "They meet together to storm the center of the one only truth. . . ." In 1960 William Burroughs wrote on a New

Year's card to his friend Brion Gysin, "Blitzkrieg the citadel of enlightenment!" This sense of urgency, of impatience with anything less than direct and immediate action, characterizes, at the deepest level, the vision of the Gnostics and of William Burroughs. In addition, as we have seen, they share an essentially pessimistic view of the material world, a radical dualism, a sense of alienated existence, a principle of the negation of physical experience, an antihierarchical approach to human organization, an urge to transcendence by means of saving knowledge, a willingness to pursue extreme measures to achieve such saving knowledge, and the predisposition to express their vision through a mythology rather than an ordered theology.

The recurrence in a twentieth-century American writer of the essential ideas and attitudes of a long vanished religion is not as surprising nor as unlikely as it may at first seem. Scholars have long recognized that art and religion share a good deal of common ground, and the problem with which the Gnostics and Burroughs have dealt may be seen as "the basic problem of the universe, the relationship between good and evil, between man and this seemingly evil cosmos." Furthermore, the type of thought or vision that may be called Gnostic is not an isolated phenomenon; but rather, it is a universal and recurrent tendency. "Manichaeism among the Persians, hermeticism among the Greeks, the Ismaelites in Islam, the Jewish Kabbala, medieval alchemy, the theosophy of the Romantics, modern occultism and contemporary surrealism" have all been seen as descendants of the Gnostics. Although there is no direct continuity from one movement to the next, Gnostic thought has been seen as "a religious ideology which always tends to reappear . . . in times of social and political crisis."

Although we must recognize that the political and social climate in which Burroughs writes is one of crisis, we need not accept the implication that Gnostic thought is therefore a hysterical and desperate psychological reaction to unstable historical conditions. The periodical recurrence of Gnostic thought may well be due to its relevance to the human situation or due to its not having truly been addressed and considered but only repressed and anathematized by the dominant orthodoxy.

In his essays "Passage to More Than India" and "Why Tribe," the poet Gary Snyder posits the existence of what he calls the "Great Subculture"—a tradition of thought extending back to the late Paleolithic era and resurfacing at various times in various guises. "In China it manifested as Taoism, not only Lao-tzu but the later Yellow Turban revolt and medieval Taoist societies, and the Zen Buddhists up till early Sung. Within Islam the Sufis; in India the various threads converged to produce Tantrism. In the West it has been represented largely by a string of heresies starting with the Gnostics. . . ."

I believe that Burroughs' work can most properly be understood and appreciated in the context of this tradition—in the esoteric, heretical modes of thought that constitute a suppressed and subversive unconscious beneath the accepted and orthodox social, philosophical, and religious structures of civilization.

Within this tradition of Snyder's "Great Subculture" Burroughs' work serves two key functions, both essentially shamanistic in nature.

First, it exorcises "the negative and demonic potentials of the unconscious" by presenting them in symbolic form. Thus, the violence, obsessive sexuality, and nightmare horror that are so often characteristic of Burroughs' work represent an attempt to purge the psyche of these influences by means of their symbolic enactment. The Hungarian psychoanalyst Géza Róheim has observed: "The shaman makes public the systems of symbolic fantasy that are present in the psyche of every adult member of society. They are . . . the lightning conductors of common anxiety. They fight the demons. . . ." Or, as the *Gnostic Gospel* of Thomas states: "If you bring forth what is within you, what you bring forth will save you. If you do not bring forth what is within you, what you do not bring forth will destroy you."

The second function of Burroughs' writing, is to provide a new cosmology. The author's space-age mythology, together with his experimental prose technique, introduces a new view of time, space, and identity, a new map of the cosmos and of our psychic geography. "In my writing," Burroughs has stated, "I am acting as a map maker, an explorer of psychic areas . . . as a cosmonaut of inner space. . . ."

Both functions of Burroughs' writing, expressed in a manner similar to that of the ritual practices and mythological systems of the Gnostics, serve to effect self-knowledge, internal transformation, and transcendence. In this sense his work occupies a position in that zone of contemporary culture that is still being defined—where anthropology, philosophy, religion, psychology, and literature overlap and merge into a single discipline: human liberation.

Daniel Punday (essay date Spring 1995)

SOURCE: "Narrative after Deconstruction: Structure and the Negative Poetics of William S. Burroughs's *Cities of the Red Night*," in *Style*, Vol. 29, No. 1, Spring, 1995, pp. 36-57.

[*In the following essay, Punday analyzes the meaning of the narrative structure of* Cities of the Red Night *based on lin-guist A. J. Greimas' theoretical construction of the semiotic square.*]

William Burroughs's recent writing poses problems for critics. Traditionally Burroughs is known for a negative poetics that assaults the word and all continuity for the sake of breaking down social controls. His recent writing attempts to balance this negative poetics with a narrative continuity previously foreign to his writing. Burroughs remarked in a recent interview, for example, "I don't think there's any substitute for [narrative structure]. I mean—people want some sort of story in there. Otherwise they don't read it. What are they going to read? That's the point." This shift towards increased narrative cohesion is one that we can observe in most postmodern authors. Thomas Pynchon shifts from the radical discontinuity of *Gravity's Rainbow* (1973) to the more cohesive style of *Vineland* (1990); Ishmael Reed moves from absurd parody in *Mumbo Jumbo* (1972) and *Yellow Back Radio Broke-Down* (1969) to somewhat more realistic social satire in *The Terrible Twos* (1986); Kathy Acker quiets some of the radical discontinuity of works like *The Childlike Life of the Black Tarantula* (1973) in her recent *In Memoriam to Identity* (1990). Burroughs and these other writers can be seen as working through the deconstructive impulse that dominated writing of the 1970s and searching for some way of reintroducing narrative structure without rejecting that deconstruction wholesale. Because Burroughs's writing was, perhaps, more radically deconstructive than any of these other writers, his movement towards a narrative continuity is more pronounced and promises to be particularly revealing. Our challenge is to explain how Burroughs can adopt a narrative structure without renouncing his confrontational, negative poetics.

Burroughs's recent writing is primarily "scenic": that is, it moves away from the linguistic basis of his experimental "cut ups" of the 1960s to concern itself with the dynamics of individual episodes. *The Place of Dead Roads* (1983), for example, begins and ends with the same scene recast with a different ending and significance. These scenes differ from the often individual comic and stylized pieces of *Naked Lunch* (1959) in that Burroughs's recent scenes recast the same characters and situations in a variety of combinations, drawing attention to how characters and their goals are structured by their situation and its narrative presentation. Situation also appears as a plot issue in this recent fiction. Characters search for a way of transcending the traditional conceptualization of the human situation. Burroughs speaks, for example, throughout *The Place of Dead Roads* and *The Western Lands* (1987) of the need for humans to "evolve" out of their bodies in order to move beyond the earth into space. Thus, in reading this recent fiction, we need to bring together an understanding of the dynamics of scenes and a consideration of how this scenic structuring reflects the more abstract construction of the human universe. We must account for both the concrete scenes and the abstract values that stand behind them.

Burroughs demands a narrative model that emphasizes the play between surface and depth but rejects the notion that narrative can remain under the control of some deep "core."

—Daniel Punday

This scenic and abstract narrative seems to push us back towards an older structuralist model, in which a narrative balances abstract deep structural values with their manifestation into concrete situations and narrative. At the same time, however, one of Burroughs's principle themes is the danger of universalizing systems that reduce the world to an abstract machine, exactly the complaint raised against narrative structuralism. In other words, Burroughs demands a narrative model that emphasizes the play between surface and depth but rejects the notion that narrative can remain under the control of some deep "core." Burroughs can be seen as returning to a notion of narrative structure that he has rejected in the past just as current theorists reject structuralists' accounts of narrative in the hopes of reworking this model as the basis of a new narrative form. Thus, in describing Burroughs's narrative we will need both to employ and to critique the structural narrative model that these scenic and abstract repetitions play out. The closest theoretical analogue to Burroughs's scenic, conceptual narrative is the structural semantics of A. J. Greimas. Greimas has theorized the abstract bases of the fictional universe and has concerned himself, like Burroughs, with the structural roles within narrative scenes. Greimas is best known for his attempt to synthesize abstract binary semiology and Vladimir Propp's theory of characters and their formal functions within narrative. Thus, more than any narrative theorist, Greimas balances "deep" abstract values and "surface" narrative characters and situations. Greimas thus offers a theoretically explicit analogue against which we can define the nature of Burroughs's approach to narrative. We need to ask not only what Greimas can reveal about Burroughs's fiction, but also what aspects of Greimas's theory Burroughs accepts or rejects. In doing so, we will sketch a narrative that employs a structural model without accepting it fully; how structure and critique are balanced is the key to Burroughs's movement beyond the negative poetics for which he is principally known. To simplify this inquiry, I would like to focus on one novel in particular, *Cities of the Red Night* (1981). This novel is the first of Burroughs's recent trilogy (which includes *Place of Dead Roads* and *Western Lands*) and is grounded as much in Burroughs's 1960s experimentalism as in the narrative co-

hesion of the later books of the trilogy. As such, it offers a natural starting point for considering Burroughs's more recent constructive works.

1. DEEP STRUCTURES

For Greimas, the most basic level of any narrative consists of "[d]eep structures [which] define the fundamental mode of existence of an individual or a society, and subsequently the conditions of existence of semiotic objects." This abstract mapping—a term Burroughs often uses to describe his own writing—is particularly appropriate for Burroughs since he himself is interested in the invisible conceptual grounding of reality. Burroughs's description of language and power as a "virus," for example, implies a hidden, logically replicating structure that gives rise to everyday relations. Greimas's analytical model for this deep structure is the "semiotic square," which Ronald Schleifer defines as "a logical mapping out of structural possibilities: for any content which can be understood as itself analyzable into binary oppositions (S vs. non S), the square, repeated and superposed, will exhaust the logical structural relations between its minimal elements." Greimas's square takes an abstract term and discloses the three terms logically opposed to it (which, consequently, define it). In doing so, it presents a four-part schema of what Greimas calls a "semantic category." To take a simple example, black can only be understood in contrast not only to white, but to the very possibilities of "coloredness" and "noncoloredness." The latter two elements can be thought of as metaterms, elements that comment on the possibility of the simple black-white opposition. Greimas represents the semiotic square in its most basic terms as follows:

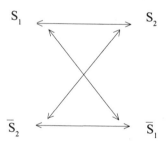

Figure 1: Semiotic Square

Here S_1 is the positive simple term (i.e., s), S_2 the negative simple term (i.e., non-s, the opposite of s), $\overline{S}_1$ the positive complex term (both s and non-s), and $\overline{S}_2$ the negative complex term (neither s nor non-s). It should be obvious that $\overline{S}_1$ is not simply equivalent to S_2; the former represents a distinct step outside the basic opposition of s and non-s. One of Greimas's more concrete examples, "The Social Model of Sexual Relations," should clarify the interrelation of these terms:

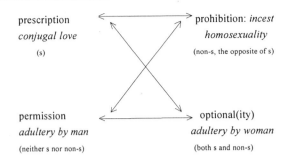

Figure 2: Semiotic Square of Social Relations

I note in italics how Greimas applies to "traditional French society" his general mapping out of possible social attitudes towards sexual relations. Thus the simple opposition between prescribed and prohibited love (in Greimas's application, matrimonial and deviant sexual behavior such as homosexuality or incest) is complemented in the square by the complex form of this binary relationship. The positive complex term is that which is both prescribed and prohibited, "adultery by woman." Greimas suggests that traditional French society generally emphasizes sexuality as an element of female social identity yet prohibits extramarital expression of that sexuality in adultery; thus this term combines the accepted and rejected elements of social relations and exposes the mixed signals sent by this society to its female members. This positive complex term is counterbalanced by that which is neither prohibited nor prescribed, "adultery in man." Greimas implies that this society neither ties sexuality so closely to the social identity of males nor bans so forcefully extramarital sexual relations; this society thus largely frees its males from the opposition of accepted and deviant social relations.

In this opening section I will establish what I take as the novel's fundamental stratum of values and analyze them by means of a semiotic square. We will find these values by looking at the dynamics of individual scenes. Burroughs's recent writing increasingly relies on discrete scenes or groups of related scenes. Indeed, at one point in *Cities,* characters put on a play called "Cities of the Red Night," suggesting that this model of discrete noncontinuous bits of narrative with individual dramatic foci represents the novel's structure as a whole. *Cities* is a composite of independent episodes and groups of related scenes; both share typical themes and methods of progression. The three most developed of the larger subplots are Clem Snide's investigation of Jerry Green's murder (set in the present); the more elaborate tale of the "Cities of the Red Night," a chaotic civilization that became "addicted" to death (set in the futuristic ancient past); and the story of Noah Blake, a Boston gun maker who falls into the hands of pirates and eventually helps to found a utopian civilization in South America (set in the nineteenth century). We can group these subplots and other independent scenes into types of episodes according to their concern with one of two basic goals: either an attempt to transcend the physical or a quest for something lost. Indeed, these goals support each other and run throughout Burroughs's career. Burroughs's fiction is characterized by the attempt to return to the past—in *The Western Lands* to ancient Egypt, in *The Soft Machine* to Mayan civilization, in *Place of Dead Roads* to the American west—for the sake of physical transcendence of which we no longer seem capable. This search for transcendence seems to reach a pitch of explicitness and centrality in Burroughs's most recent novel, *The Western Lands,* in which characters search for a way to evolve into "space" just as fish evolved in order to leave the seas and move onto land. In *Cities,* the first type of episode is best represented by the story of Noah, and the second by the story of Clem Snide's search for Jerry Green. Both of these types of subplots have their own set of "deep structural" values. I will eventually return to consider how these two groups of values interact and suggest that the two groups of values are intertwined.

Let us begin, then, by looking at episodes concerned with transcending the physical. Burroughs's episodes fall into patterns of progression that have little to do with the desires or choices of the individual characters: one of Burroughs's principle themes is how individuals are controlled by powers so pervasive as to be part of the world itself. The first episode in the novel, "The Health Officer" (unrelated to any of the novel's major subplots), is a particularly clear example of the stages through which these scenes progress. This is the novel's first instance of homosexual sex and instances the metaphysical issues that Burroughs attaches to these couplings. Such scenes, although rarely discussed in detail by critics, comprise a large portion of Burroughs's fiction and are the single most consistent and repeated event in his writing. Any method of reading Burroughs must account for these repeated scenes, but in Burroughs's turn to narrative, the details of how these scenes progress become particularly significant. Like many of the independent episodes, this episode mirrors in miniature the progression that the larger subplots will carry out across many individual scenes. This episode ends as follows:

> Farnsworth lay down on his shirt and pants and fell into a wordless vacuum, feeling the sun on his back and the faint ache of the healing scratch. He saw Ali sitting naked above him, Ali's hands massaging his back, moving down to the buttocks. Something was surfacing in his body, drifting up from remote depths of memory, and he saw as if projected on a screen a strange incident from his adolescence. He was in the British Museum at the age of fourteen, standing in front of a glass case. He was alone in the room. In the case was the figure, about two feet long, of a reclining man. The man was naked, the right knee flexed, holding the body a few

inches off the ground, the penis exposed. The hands were extended in front of the man palms down, and the face was reptile or animal, something between an alligator and a jaguar.

The boy was looking at the thighs and buttocks and genitals, breathing through his teeth. He was getting stiff and lubricating, his pants sticking out at the fly. He was squeezing into the figure, a dream tension gathering in his crotch, squeezing and stretching, a strange smell unlike anything he had ever smelled before but familiar as smell itself, a naked man lying by a wide clear river—the twisted figure. Silver spots boiled in front of his eyes and he ejaculated.

Ali's hands parted his buttocks, he spit on his rectum—his body opening and the figure entering him in a silent rush, flexing his right knee, stretching his jaw forward into a snout, his head flattening, his brain squeezing out the smell from inside . . . a hoarse hissing sound was forced from his lips and light popped in his eyes as his body boiled and twisted out scalding spurts.

This blending of sex and dreams is common in Burroughs's fiction and often related to characters' attempt to transcend and transform the body. New in *Cities* is the explicitness and significance of the stages through which the characters pass. In this section Farnsworth progresses through four distinct stages, which are consistent through all episodes concerned with the physical. At the beginning of this section, Farnsworth rests in a normal state, vaguely remembering a past episode. Then he dreams, mixing self-abstraction with the increased physicality of "a dream tension gathering in his crotch, squeezing and stretching." Farnsworth then ejaculates, "his body opening," and finally merges with the vision. The same type of four-part movement occurs throughout *Cities.* Clem Snide's assistant becomes possessed by Jerry Green's spirit and moves to the "stretching" of his body ("he's half in and half out and it hurts") through the expulsion of the spirit through a homosexual coupling that "opens" the body and provides some magical vision ("For a split second Jerry's face hung there, eyes blazing green light"). Similarly, Noah is able to see into the future of weaponry through a similar process of bodily merging: he couples with Hans, and the "explosion" of their bodies allows him a vision of the use of gunpowder. This pattern also appears above the level of individual scenes in overall plot patterns. Burroughs's history of the Cities of the Red Night itself repeats the movement from the physical balance ("no one was born unless someone died") to the "explosion" of these bodies through the use of slaves as "receptacles" for the spirits of dying inhabitants of the cities to the visionary confrontation of the moment of conception.

Greimas's structural model offers us a way of understanding how these four parts of the scene are related. Indeed, the mechanical, automatic progression of this scene implies that Burroughs sees these four stages as somehow logically inevitable. Central to the scene is the issue of physicality: the "solidity" of our body and the validity of the inside-outside dichotomy. The first and third stages seem to represent a basic opposition. The first stage instances the clear presence of physicality, "feeling the sun on his back and the faint ache of the healing scratch," where Farnsworth's body is present to him. Here, as in everyday life, we sense the connection between what happens to our body and what we feel, and we assume that the body is exterior but accessible to our mental life. The third stage, conversely, seems to represent a lack of that physicality as his body "opens," directly negating the strong sense of physical presence and continuity between inside and outside that we saw in the first stage. The semantic category of "physicality" could be analyzed, therefore, as a primary opposition:

physicality
continuity between interior and exterior
(e.g., everyday experience of the body)

nonphysicality
break between interior and exterior
(e.g., amputation, numbness, death)

Figure 3: Basic Opposition of Category "Physicality"

If these two stages represent the "positive simple" and the "negative simple" terms of Burroughs's approach to the physical, the other two stages of this scene represent the "positive complex" and "negative complex" terms. The positive complex term is the second stage, dream and recollection. This stage blends the physical and the nonphysical: "Something was surfacing in his body, drifting up from remote depths of memory, and he saw as if projected on a screen a strange incident from his adolescence." Here Farnsworth moves away from the physical by leaving the present, but the dream is still described in terms of his body as something "surfacing." This stage can be described as "antiphysicality": it negates the physical in its own terms and in the process retains the physical as part of its definition. Conversely, the negative complex term, the fourth stage of the passage, is transcendence, the direct confrontation and negation of physicality. In contrast to the previous stage, this one negates the physical but also rejects rejection: that is, it refuses an adversarial stance and in the process escapes both simple terms. Physicality is transcended not as simple "nonphysicality" (that is, a loss or void), but by confronting and expelling physicality: "his brain squeezing out the smell from inside." For this reason, we might call this stage "aphysicality" since it seems to stand outside the physical-nonphysical opposition. We can represent this four-part

structure graphically as shown in figure 4, below. I have itali-
cized the four primary terms of the square and will use them
throughout this article to refer to these structural relations
specifically. Already it should be clear that these various
forms run throughout the novel. Burroughs's fiction in general is dominated by people and things in various forms of
physicality: ghosts, missing persons, visions, memories,
vaguely human powers from beyond.

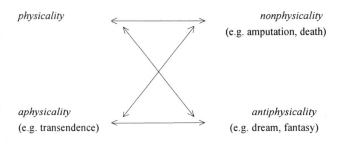

Figure 4: Semiotic Square for Category "Physicality"

Burroughs's second group of episodes and the semiotic
square it implies are more straightforward, in part because
Greimas himself has provided us with a discussion of this
type of semantic category. Episodes of this type follow the
common quest pattern of loss and reclaiming. Following the
hero's relation (conjunction) with his or her object or goal,
Greimas has sketched the structure of the quest as shown in
figure 5, below. The search for Jerry Green begins with
simple terms: the family used to "have" him and now they
have lost him. Greimas uses the terms "conjunction" and
"disjunction" for these simple states of relation to a desired
object. The quest for Jerry veers off into more complex terms
early in the novel. Shortly after Snide is hired to find him,
Green is discovered murdered and decapitated. Snide's quest
consequently becomes a search for Green's head, which
promises to explain the mystery behind his disappearance
and the ritualistic manner of his murder. Green as a desirable object thus becomes more complicated; in addition to
the simple states of "conjunction" and "disjunction," we discover positive complex and negative complex forms of relation to him as a desirable object. The positive complex
state is defined by the complication that Green undergoes
when he is murdered: he is both now "possessed" by the family (his body is returned) but "lost" in that his desirability
as an object is transformed and integrated within a ritual that
the family does not understand and has no part in. The negative complex term arises in that Snide's investigation attempts, at least in part, to uncover the ultimately
metaphysical implications of Green's disappearance. Snide's
quest for knowledge of the ritual attempts to transcend
Green's "loss" and "return" and ends up evoking the powers at work in Jerry's death. The same complicated and
problematized quest recurs in Snide's later attempt to "re-
write" the lost book, "The Cities of The Red Night." Indeed,
throughout the trilogy Burroughs returns to older mytholo-

gies and genres—particularly the western of *Place of Dead
Roads* and the Egyptian mythology of *Western Lands*—in
order to reclaim and transform possibilities and ideas lost
in the past.

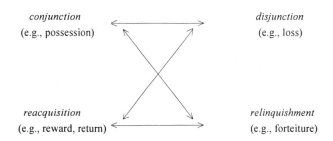

Figure 5: Semiotic Square for the Quest

These two models trace out the basic values of the novel. It
is already clear that they must be interrelated. The quest for
physical transcendence is, of course, a quest and thus relies
on conjunction and disjunction. Similarly, the quest for
Jerry Green is a quest for a head, an emblem of physicality and
its rational transcendence. How these two squares come together is an issue of the novel's movement towards a "story"
level, to which we now turn.

2. STORY LEVEL

In narratology, the "story" level of a narrative traditionally
refers to what happens in a narrative, its plot. This story level
is distinguished both from the ways those factual events are
told by the narrator and the more abstract deep-structural
values that the story instances. Greimas attends to this
"story" level in terms of his fairly well-known theory of
"actants." Based on Propp's folklore functions, actants are
abstract actors necessary in the structural logic of the text.
Individual characters within a story need not have a one-to-
one relation to that story's actantial structure. Thus, two characters may split the "opponent" role, or one character may
play the story's "opponent" role and then later, perhaps after a change of heart, play the "helper" role. By formulat-
ing character in this abstract way, Greimas hopes to connect
these characters to the deeper, logical relations that we examined in the previous section. According to Greimas,
actants act out the confrontation and exchange of values defined in the work's implicit deep level.

Most noticeable in Burroughs's novel is the fact that an explicit actantial manifestation of these deep-structural values
is lacking and, indeed, unnecessary. As I have already argued, Burroughs's characters seem to fall into patterns of
development that have little to do with their own individual
goals and choices. Indeed, as we have already seen, these
patterns of development seem to contain within themselves
their own narrative development before ever being inserted
into the "story" level. Because Burroughs accepts Greimas's

theory of semiotic values but disregards Greimas's theory of how these values are manifested actantially, his use of Greimas resembles that of Jameson. Jameson has argued that any semiotic square can act as a model of plot development towards a goal state. According to Jameson, every semiotic square has the seeds of a quest implicit in it; this quest can be read without reference to the actantial structures Greimas proposes. Jameson argues that the semiotic square generally privileges the negative complex term towards which the artistic composition strives. This model applies particularly well to Burroughs's use of the physicality square. Burroughs's preface to *Cities,* "Fore!", which in one sense summarizes the novel, exemplifies the movement in individual episodes towards this fourth term of the physicality square. This preface tells the story of Captain Mission, who attempts to establish an innovative social state in South America in the nineteenth century. Mission's problem is a more general, social form of the "personal" physicality I sketched in the first section: he simply does not have enough troops to withstand the attack of the South-American natives and European invaders. To escape such a population disadvantage, this preface suggests moving out of the simple terms of the physical-nonphysical split:

> Fortified positions supported by and supporting guerrilla hit-and-run bands; supplied with soldiers, weapons, medicines and information by the local populations . . . such a combination would be unbeatable. . . . Consider the difficulties which such an invading army would face: continual harassment from the guerrillas, a totally hostile population always ready with poison, misdirection, snakes and spiders in the general's bed, armadillos carrying the deadly earth-eating disease rooting under the barracks and adopted as mascots by the regiment as dysentery and malaria take their toll.

Traditionally, militaries rely on their size and fortifications, their presence. Good military strategy is the effective use of finite troup resources, the best system of "presences" and "absences" within a battlefield. Captain Mission's guerrilla troups depart from their model of physical presence and location and make it difficult to locate the army itself as a distinct entity. Mission here defines an army that is neither "present" in the traditional sense, and hence not susceptible to traditional military counterattack, nor simply "absent" since these forces can have a direct effect. What Burroughs suggests for this historical situation applies to individual characters as well: they must move to aphysicality, to transcendence if they are to achieve success. This valuation is built into Burroughs's general interest in "evolving" out of the body to move into space and to the physicality square's fourth term, aphysicality.

The similarities between Burroughs's and Jameson's uses of Greimas force us to recognize that, while both squares are important to Burroughs, physicality represents the more distinctive organizing issue of the novel's composition. While "reacquisition" may be built into nearly any narrative, Burroughs's concern for transcending the physical is more distinctive and related to the interests that have run throughout his career. Conversely, how Burroughs deviates from Jameson's theory makes clear why Burroughs needs the second quest square. Unlike Jameson, Burroughs is far more interested in why natural progression does not occur. The emphasis on failure and entrapment is clear throughout all of Burroughs's novels. Burroughs emphasizes not how the physical and nonphysical are reconciled and escaped, but why characters fail to reach transcendence. Such misguided striving is clear in how the Transmigrants (inhabitants of The Cities of the Red Night) attempt to escape from the body by dying and "transmigrating" into new, young bodies. The narrator summarizes this and the problems involved with it: "This was the basic error of the Transmigrants: you do not get beyond death and conception by reexperience any more than you get beyond heroin by ingesting larger and larger doses. The Transmigrants were quite literally addicted to death and they needed more and more death to kill the pain of conception. They were buying parasitic life with a promissory death note to be paid at a prearranged time." Burroughs clearly shows here an antiphysicality that cannot move to aphysicality, cannot transcend the physical. Unlike Captain Mission's guerrilla army, which escapes from the conventional ways of understanding the physical existence of military forces, the Transmigrants' attempt to escape from the body simply repeats the conventional forms of death. The Transmigrants' attempt to escape physicality, to move to aphysicality, is tied to the physical in the terms of its rejection and thus remains antiphysicality. The investigations of Yen Lee (another one-time character related to the Health-Officer scenario) best exemplify the limitations of antiphysicality. Yen Lee's astral projection enables him to conduct "an out-of-body exploration of the village," but he is unable to complete such an exploration because of the physicality implicit in this antiphysicality: "He did not push himself, knowing that a biologic protective reaction was shielding him from knowledge he was unable to assimilate and handle."

Because antiphysicality provides a false transcendence, characters have difficulty distinguishing genuine and illusory attempts at aphysicality; this confusion represents the central danger in the novel. In this sense the rituals that permeate the novel, such as the "series of theatrical performances" designed to impregnate the women in Port Roger (in the Noah subplot), prove misguided attempts to transcend the physical and to achieve aphysicality. Regardless of the degree to which "the faces of the boys are remote and impersonal . . . their bodies quiver and shake as if possessed by wild spirits." As such we see one reason why sex and drugs pervade the novel: they are often examples of antiphysicality, attempts to negate the physical that are inescapably tied to that very physicality. These means contrast sharply with those that genuinely lead to aphysicality, the transcendence of physicality. Dink Rivers, the character who spurs Noah on to aphysicality, is noted for his body control. By mixing dreams and conscious physicality, this control stresses the use and eventual transcendence of the physical: "In order to achieve orgasm [without physical stimulus], it is simply necessary to relive a previous orgasm. So while awake, I would endeavor to project myself into sexual dreams, which I was not having several times a week. It was some months before I acquired sufficient concentration to get results."

Burroughs's narrative differs from that explained by either Jameson's or Greimas's theory. Although Jameson's theory deviates from Greimas's formulation of how deep-structural values are inserted into the text (bypassing any systematic theory of actants and the modalities of action), like Greimas, Jameson sees the tension of the work arising out of how the logical relations of the square are manifested in a plot and whole narrative. Narrative tension for Burroughs, conversely, arises out of the contradiction of textual logic. Burroughs shows us characters caught within a text whose logic seems to turn back on itself and deny the progression it demands. Presenting such self-contradiction can be seen as the principal challenge of the novel's composition. Burroughs employs two squares in order to separate the text's values with their implicit natural progression from the characters' actual position in relation to those values. Burroughs's episodes consequently arise out of the combination of the two squares. More specifically, Burroughs creates two types of episodes: one that follows the ideal, expected model of progression and another that offers a real but self-contradictory movement. I will call the combination of these two squares "plot structures" and argue that these two types of plot structures represent, respectively, the two types of episodes mentioned at the beginning of this essay.

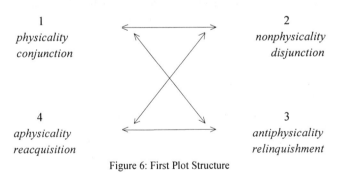

Figure 6: First Plot Structure

To start from seeing oneself as a unified self whose exterior is controlled by one's interior is the more "obvious" and basic view on physicality in the novel. This notion entails pairing simple physicality with simple conjunction and seeing nonphysicality as a matter of disjunction (to see, for example, amputation or death as a simple and unproblematic

loss). This view is the way that we assume physicality should be. To pair these squares in this way results in the following plot structure.

The subplots that obey this first plot structure develop along the values of the primary (physicality-nonphysicality) square, moving from the simple terms to the negative complex term (aphysicality). We have already seen this in the Farnsworth example above. I have numbered the positions on the square as the stages of progression through this plot structure although the second stage rarely is distinct and usually combines with the first to form a simple starting point.

The pirates (in the Noah subplot) for example, begin in a state of conjunction and physicality and move towards a final reacquisition of that conjunction on a higher, decentered level (and thus aphysicality). Noah, in this sense, begins in the simple conventionality of Boston with its strict social codes that enforce a very definite view of the physical individual and his or her responsibility, adopts the defiant freedom of the pirate ship where the notion of "body" and "individual" is turned upside down (particularly in transvestitism), and finally helps to establish the utopia of Port Roger, which represents a society that has transcended issues of individual bodies.

Obviously, Burroughs's view of physicality is often considerably more complex; when trying to express such complexity, he resorts to a second plot structure. In contrast to this ideal vision, Burroughs presents another physicality that is far from simple and under control of a unified self. Specifically, this second view of physicality begins with an understanding of physicality based on loss. This loss does not take the form we might expect (amputation, death) but rather, while retaining the form of physical control, implies that the body is somehow forfeit to powers beyond itself. Thus, the simple terms of the basic square (physicality and nonphysicality) are paired not with the simple terms of the quest (conjunction and disjunction) but with the complex terms of the quest. Characters are, in a sense, always already in the middle of the quest. This leads to the second plot structure:

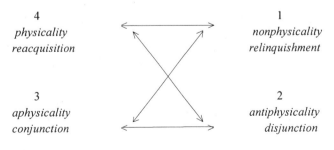

Figure 7: Second Plot Structure

We can see this attempt at reunion at work in Clem Snide's

detection system. Snide's attempt to "reacquire" Green represents, *en abyme,* the characters' more general attempt to "reacquire" simple physicality. Let us look specifically at Snide's method, which will reveal the implications of this second plot structure:

> I will explain exactly how these recordings are made. I want an hour of Spetsai: an hour of places where my M.P. [missing person] has been and the sounds he has heard. But not in sequence. I don't start at the beginning of the tape and record to the end. I spin the tape back and forth, cutting in at random so that *The Magus* may be cut off in the middle of a word by a flushing toilet, or *The Magus* may cut into sea sounds. It's a sort of *I Ching* or table-tapping procedure. How random is it actually? Don Juan says that nothing is random to a man of knowledge: everything he sees or hears is there just at that time waiting to be seen and heard.

Snide moves from the nonphysicality of the missing character to the antiphysicality of cutting up the recorded material (a rejection of its physicality in its own terms) towards the aphysicality of the insight provided by the merging of all these materials (the transcending of the physical materials). Although this second plot structure repeats the same terms and direction of progression as the first, Snide's position and overall goals are different. Noah's story begins in a state of conjunction and moves through relinquishment finally to reacquisition in the position of aphysicality. Snide attempts, instead, to use aphysicality as a way to return Jerry to his family (and thus achieve normal physicality). For this reason, I have numbered the second plot structure as I have. Characters in this plot structure do not strive towards a new relation to their goal as in the first plot structure (aphysicality), but instead attempt to return to an ideal situation of simple physicality postulated before the action of the plot. We thus contrast the more adventurous first plot structure with its bold rejection of the norm to the more hesitant second plot structure; the characters generally want, in this second structure, simply to return to the security of an unproblematic norm. As Snide investigates Jerry's abduction, however, he discovers Jerry's hidden past, suggesting that such an unproblematic normal situation is illusory. Relinquishment invalidates the previous stage by revealing the flaws in that norm, and characters are never able to reach the fourth stage. Characters are thus caught, in this second plot structure, tragically relinquishing without ever being able to reacquire.

For this reason the second plot structure places more emphasis on the quest since physicality is more the means to the end of finding what is lost. The first plot structure, conversely, places more emphasis on physicality because the quest structure is not problematic here and can be assumed.

This contrast helps to account for why these two types of episodes seemed to have distinct thematic foci at first. Both plot structures, however, work with the same elements, and the meaning of the novel results from their interaction.

3. STRUCTURALIST READING AND DECONSTRUCTIVE STYLE

We have already discovered that we must read Burroughs's basic "story" and its abstract structures in a different way from how we read traditional narrative. I would like to suggest that this analysis also models the overall trajectory of the reader's interaction with the novel. Indeed, Burroughs himself has described his narrative as something we can feel with our body: "I think it is possible to create multilevel events and characters that a reader could comprehend with his entire organic being." Consequently I would like to argue that in reading **Cities** we are implicitly trying to use and transcend the physical limits of his text. Understanding this parallel will allow us, finally, to explain what role the structural analysis we have just completed plays within the whole meaning of Burroughs's antistructural text.

In order to understand fully how Burroughs means us to read, we must turn to consider how Burroughs understands language. The response from the Santa-Claus figure to Toby's Christmas wish (another brief and unrelated character set more or less in the present) is one of the clearest examples of the pervasiveness of language and how language limits characters' attempts to reach their goals: "Yes, Toby, people do ask for silly things. They want to live forever, forgetting or not knowing that forever is a time word and time is that which ends." Language in this sense forms a network of terms without which the characters cannot express themselves yet which necessarily limits their ability to get outside their physical location and state. The notion of a limiting but inescapable linguistic and conceptual system runs throughout the novel. Peterson's response to Dr. Pierson's lecture (an early episode that sets up Burroughs's general attitude towards the problems that characters face in the novel) suggests the larger context of linguistic limitation:

> "Why should this virus be an exception?"

> "Because it is the *human virus.* After many thousands of years of more or less benign coexistence, it is now once again on the verge of malignant mutation. . . . The whole human position is no longer tenable."

Humanity itself is a problematic concept with which we are nonetheless stuck at least for the present. Language is for Burroughs a virus that replicates itself and homogenizes the organism it inhabits. Indeed, we can go so far as to characterize language as a kind of "antiphysicality," both physicality and nonphysicality. Language is omnipresent and inescapable (physical) yet inadequate and finally illusory (nonphysical). The presence of this linguistic system distinguishes the first and second plot structures. We saw above that antiphysicality often provides a false transcendence; this linguistic antiphysicality is the reason that characters of the second plot structure are unable to progress fully through the square. Characters of the first plot structure can free themselves from this linguistic control. We see this state in Dink Rivers's explanation of body control, which stands as the clearest statement of the conditions of aphysicality in this first plot structure: "Having brought sexual energy under control I now had the key to body control. Errors, fumbles, and ineptitudes are caused by uncontrolled sexual energy which then lays one open to any sort of psychic or physical attack. I went on to bring speech under control, to be used when I want it, not yammering in my ear at all times or twisting tunes and jingles in my brain. I used the same method of projecting myself into a time when my mind seemed empty of words." Snide's second plot-structure investigations, conversely, lead him to the book "The Cities of the Red Night," suggesting that language and textuality are the heart of the second plot structure. Burroughs clearly sees this first plot structure as desirable but unattainable; consequently, the second plot structure models the situation of his reader.

This inescapable linguistic system helps to explain Burroughs's direct presentation of abstract deep-structural relations in lieu of an actantial textual level. Greimas devotes so much of his theory to actants, in part because the transition from deep to actantial level reflects the whole metalinguistic functioning of semiotic analysis. Ricoeur's analysis of Greimas on this tricky subject is worth quoting at some length:

> The initial model must from the outset present an articulated character, if indeed it is going to be able to be narrativized. The stroke of genius—and this is not too strong—is to have sought this already articulated nature in a logical structure that is as simple as possible, that is, the "elementary structure of signification." This structure has to do with the conditions of grasping of meaning, any meaning. If something—anything at all—*signifies,* it is not because one might have some intuition as to what it signifies, but because one can lay out [through a semiotic square] . . . an absolutely elementary system of relations. . . . The mutual defining of its four poles presents an absolutely static network of relations. But one can represent the model dynamically. One just has to move from the morphological point of view to the syntactic one, that is, treat the constituent *relations* of the taxonomic model as being *operations.*

Indeed, syntax is no more than a regulating of these operations.

Greimas's theory can be seen as an attempt to define the essence of narrative in such a way as to justify its translation into a semiotic metalanguage. Ricoeur bases the essential narrative function of a text on the continuity between analytical metalanguage and textual, actantial representation. Because the actantial story model is simply another version of sentence syntax, narrative structuring can be reduced to the metalinguistic semiotic analysis of deep-structural values. Greimas has been criticized for assuming without justification this homology of sentence syntax, narrative structure, and the deep structures of the text. Burroughs's use of Greimas's square can be seen as an indirect response to this problem, an attempt to analyze essential workings of language without relying on such presumed homologies. In representing the squares directly, Burroughs admits the artificiality of these structures and separates true linguistic functioning from these structural overlays. Consequently, the plot structures discussed above outline this linguistic functioning but do not fully define it or reduce it to a metalanguage.

In order to stress the autonomy of linguistic play from the structures that can be isolated in the text, Burroughs attempts to cast language as something with its own motivation: language almost becomes an independent character in the novel. To understand how he does this, let us return to the analysis we have already carried out and consider how it departs from Greimas's own theory. In Greimas's theory, the combination of semiotic squares I employed in the second section occurs only in describing modalities of character predisposition and ability to act and not in describing the deep structures of texts. For Greimas, modal homologation is possible in a way that combining textual deep structures is not because, while we can imagine a situation in which we are expected but unable to do something (modal categories of prescription and competence), textual deep structures must provide a simple scheme of opposed values that the actants will embody. For Greimas, without deep-structural values in direct and simple opposition, actants lack the basis for interaction, and narrative is impossible. These two squares can be combined for Burroughs, conversely, because his text has no actantial narrative and therefore does not need a simple deep-structural opposition. The structure we have discussed in the previous two sections is thus merely a potential for character action, rather than a genuine narrative of conflict between deep-structural oppositions worked out in the confrontation of actants. The novel's locus of conflict—its narrative—is not in the conflicts between characters, but in how the characters are elaborated within the scenes according to the text's contradictory semiotic predispositions. The text, the process of articulation, is the real actor in **Cities.** This is consistent with Burroughs's definition of language as a virus. To call language a virus is to attribute to it a crude motivation (of self-preservation and propagation) that we do not normally recognize. A virus both obeys a logic for self-preservation and repeats that logic as it spreads into a new organism. So too, the text both functions within a predisposing modal structure and represents that logic within the text as the scope of characters' actions. Burroughs seems to want us to recognize the parallel between the text's functioning and what it describes for characters as a clue for glimpsing the methods of textual self-motivation and self-begetting.

We get a model of how we should read this linguistic self-motivation in those characters who successfully confront these linguistic problems in *Cities* and learn to "exist" in Burroughs's textual environment. For episodes of the first plot structure, aphysicality occurs by two characters blending physically. Noah's "initiation" by Dink Rivers into body control is described as follows: "He is getting stiff and so am I, the feeling of weakness now like death in the throat as we both are fully erect. Silver spots boil in front of my eyes and I have a feeling of squeezing into his nuts and cock as I lie on the pallet and Dink fucks me." The aphysical vision that results from this scene brings an understanding beyond the temporal limits of the characters; thus, as a result of this transcendence Noah glimpses the future of weaponry and works to bring these new weapons into existence. For the second plot structure, the circumstances are subtly different and reflect the way the antiphysical quality of language (omnipresent but hollow) problematizes transcendence. Characters do not use this blending to see into another narrative situation; instead, that blending itself is with characters in other such situations. Audrey's problems of temporal disorientation, for example, seem to dissipate when, late in the novel, he is given a "separator": "Might come in handy if you ever need to be in two places at once." Similarly Toby gains the power to travel in time by moving into conjunction with people who already exist and who are active during Toby's "residence." This method implies less an escape from body to body than a merging of characters who are equally bound. Because characters' thoughts and actions are always already defined by language in the second plot-structure, their movement between scenes is not a way of glimpsing something beyond the scene, as it is in the first plot structure, but merely a way of circulating within a network of scenes and characters. Such a closed network of scenes and the repetition it leads to parallels the finite, all-encompassing linguistic system in which characters find themselves. In this sense, the characters of the second plot structure are always dependent on other characters, are always both present and absent, and hence antiphysical.

Burroughs believes, I think, that the direct experience of this disjointed text, understood properly, will provide an ineffable but real insight into linguistic self-construction that paral-

lels but also extends the insight of characters in the second plot structure. Like Audrey and Toby, we learn to straddle narrative situations. As we move from seeing characters as splintered and disjoint, we begin to gain insight into how language and context create character and self. Unlike the specific and summarizable meaning provided by the play of plot structures, this insight derives from experience and cannot be summarized and translated into a semiotic metalanguage. Throughout the novel Burroughs shifts the same character to another manifestation within another narrative context in order to provide us with a glimpse of the structuring process itself. Thus Audrey is a teenager in Greece, a fighter in the Cities of the Red Night, and the detective Clem Snide, none of which have ontological priority but all of which rely on similar situations. These characters (and they often realize it themselves) cannot stand on their own, but are always the products of forces and parallels only barely glimpsed. In following these disjunctions, we should gradually progress from seeing them as negations, to attempting to find that which is not simply "physically" present in any of the individual subplots and thus limited by preexisting social, linguistic, and narrative structures; instead we find the gaps between these episodes and subplots and thus glimpse something beyond this structuring. This movement from seeing characters as both parallel to and distinct from each other to seeing the process of that structuring in the abstract is similar to the movement from the antiphysicality to aphysicality of character. At this moment the active structuring of characters by a self-motivated language becomes equivalent to the characters represented. In this aphysicality of character, Burroughs seems to promise insight into the nature of language. Farnsworth, as quoted above, senses "a strange smell unlike anything he had ever smelled before but familiar as smell itself"; and as the *mise-en-abyme* text of "Cities of the Red Night" says, "At one time a language existed that was immediately comprehensible to anyone with the concept of language."

We find, then, that Burroughs's structural narrative does not "contain" its meaning as a traditional narrative might. Structural analysis cannot reduce the novel to a simple core statement, as Michael Riffaterre's *Semiotics of Poetry* might, nor reveal an ideological tension frozen in the text's structure, as Jameson's use of Greimas would. Rather, Burroughs's strictly controlled structural play is a pattern that points beyond itself. The real meaning of Burroughs's text does not rest in the plot structures themselves, but in how those structures provide a pattern for a reading of linguistic play that is beyond Burroughs's or our own control. Burroughs's text, then, does not merely set up oppositions to tear them down, as a deconstructive critic might read his play with abstractions and shifting repetitions. Instead, these oppositions stand as a form in which a much more intuitive reader response occurs, giving a meaning to the text shaped by, but not equivalent to, a narratological structure.

4. CONCLUSION

Greimas has provided us with a crucial formulation of how narrative balances surface and depth for a whole textual meaning. This surface-depth opposition has allowed us to recognize a structure within Burroughs's narrative that is not available to the more descriptive and currently popular narratologies concerned with speakers, narratees, and types of discourse. The movement back towards this more structural narrative theory is part of postmodernism's recent search for some form amid the deconstructive play that has concerned it in the past. Burroughs does not simply accept Greimas or the metalinguistic structure that he offers. Instead, as we have seen, the structure in Burroughs's novel is "self consuming": it makes visible something within the text that cannot be reduced to the structure and even stands as a critique of that structure. Thus, Burroughs's recent turn to narrative is not a rejection of his earlier experimentalism and antagonism to language. Rather, it is a recognition that he can confront the issues of language not only on the level of words in his "cut-up" technique, but also on the level of the narrative structures that this language gives rise to. The increased cohesion of Burroughs's recent narrative implies no more trust of language than it ever did. It does, however, locate the aporia of language and the text's representation in a different and more carefully constructed position within the text. Burroughs no longer assaults language directly, but now constructs a carefully structured narrative that turns back and points beyond itself to the language within which both reader and text operate. Postmodern writers, Burroughs suggests, will attend to narrative structures and how they open up a language play that they cannot fully circumscribe.

Brent Wood (essay date March 1996)

SOURCE: "William S. Burroughs and the Language of Cyberpunk," in *Science-Fiction Studies,* Vol. 23, No. 1, March, 1996, pp. 11-26.

[*In the following essay, Wood explains the connection between Burroughs's works and cyberpunk writing.*]

The work of William S. Burroughs has often been credited as a primary influence on cyberpunk writing. The connection between the two, however, is more often cited than explained. Burroughs' "science-fiction" work (***Nova Express, The Soft Machine,*** and ***The Ticket That Exploded,*** 1964-1967) was more experimental poetry than conventional science fiction, and had already come in and out of style by the time science fiction became theory-worthy. Times have changed. Today, theorists not only feel sf to be worthy of theory, but theory to be worthy of sf. To this end, Istvan

Csicsery-Ronay, Jr. has invited Jean Baudrillard and Donna Haraway into the sf fold; Scott Bukatman has extended a similar invitation to Gilles Deleuze and Félix Guattari. In this essay I would like to argue for the inclusion of William S. Burroughs as a diner at the sf theory dinner-party, especially to hear his theories of poetic action in a world where science fiction has become reality.

In spite of the riotous dark comedy and starkly innovative character of his writing, Burroughs' reputation has been chiefly as the writer whose book ***Naked Lunch*** (1959) challenged the conservative mores of post-war America. In recent years, many cuttings from Burroughs' texts have emerged in commercial culture as soundbites and cryptic political slogans. This phenomenon supports Burroughs' claims about the way language functions, and reflects the things he has tried to do with it. Laurie Anderson's *Home of the Brave* (1984) repopularized Burroughs' slogan "language is a virus," which had first reached into popular consciousness over a decade before through *Harper's* magazine and *Rolling Stone.* The vogue which Burroughs' texts and ideas currently enjoy around the fringes of mainstream culture belies their continuous influence on the counter-culture since the 1950's. Their relevance to an understanding of post-modernity is confirmed by their intimate relationship with the generally fashionable texts of Guattari, Deleuze, Baudrillard, and Derrida. Burroughs is of course also one of William Gibson's principal sources, and the Burroughs fold-in method is a part of the history of cyberspace. The link that Burroughs makes between theory and sf lies in his understanding of the force of language, the danger it poses to free and evolving life, and just what a writer is supposed to do about it anyway.

In an issue of *Science-Fiction Studies* devoted to postmodernism and science fiction (1991), Istvan Csicsery-Ronay Jr. raised the issue of the "operationality" of language in sf and in the "sf theory" of Baudrillard and Haraway. This concern with the effect of the written word is related to his argument that the texts of Baudrillard and Haraway constitute, in effect, a deconstruction of the terms "science" and "fiction." Csicsery-Ronay argues that for these writers "the boundary between sf and social reality is an optical illusion." He classes both Baudrillard and Haraway as sf theorists whose texts operate in a hyperreality in which the categories of subject, body, machine, and text have become thoroughly confused by the evolution of technology and its discursive ripples.

The question to be asked of these "theoretical" texts, then, is not "are they true" or "are they accurate" but rather, "what do they do?" Scott Durham's essay "The Technology of Death and Its Limits" (1993), an attempt to reconcile Baudrillard with J. G. Ballard, asks just this question of Baudrillard. Ballard's novel *Crash* (1966), which one might consider a bridge between Burroughs and contemporary cyberpunk fiction, deals in part with the "precession of simulacra" as expressed through "planned" automobile accidents. Durham uses *Crash* to illustrate a sort of comic failing that is characteristic of the actual functioning of cybernetic systems. Ballard, he argues, explores the leftover "reality" that Baudrillard dismisses as a desert. This interest in exploring society's marginalia, those events, spaces and characters that have slipped through the cracks in the planner's model—in Baudrillard's terminology, the "outside" of the simulation model—is essential to a "punk" ethos, and typical of the cyberpunk literature which Burroughs' texts indirectly foreshadow. While Burroughs uses the same black humour as does Ballard; explores the same marginal territory and like Ballard offers an antidote to totalitarian cybernetic systems, the absolute dismembering of conventional narrative in Burroughs' science-fictional works indicates a self-consciously *operational* inspiration, as opposed to a metaphoric one. The anti-narrative in his sf-derived works is what sets Burroughs apart from the science-fiction writers whose work he appropriated and those he has influenced, and is the reason Ballard has called Burroughs "the most important writer to emerge since the Second World War."

Durham concludes that the force of Baudrillard's hyperreality hyperbole, especially as expressed in "The Precession of Simulacra" (trans. 1983) and "The Ecstasy of Communication" (trans. 1988), is to effect a sort of supplication to the control system that is made comic by the revenge of the real—in the case of *Crash,* the accidental of the planned "accidents." In other words, despite the apparent infallibility of the simulation model, the desired life on the far side of the screen will not be manifested as planned. In the end, Durham concludes, "there is no real other than the relation to the spectacle he [Vaughn] has shared all along with his fellow victims." Denied by *Crash,* Baudrillard's texts become for Durham just so many "soft machines," confounding and contradicting their own revelations and necessarily failing in their attempts at totality.

Accepting that we do live in a world rapidly being enclosed by massive interconnected cybernetic machines, and that our words have no recourse to truth or accuracy as guarantors of their behavior, a question of pragmatics arises. How are we cyborg-writers to understand the effects of our words such that we are not unwittingly or unconsciously participating in the kinds of cybernetic machines we would prefer to avoid? In other words, since resistance implies an opposition of sorts, how can one mobilize one's forces when it is so difficult to tell who is "them" and who is "us"? Csicsery-Ronay describes this problem by imagining conventional language as a Trojan Horse which is carried into a utopian future and proceeds to disgorge the very same social relations which characterize the (dystopian) present. This is the situation which led Frederic Jameson, as Csicsery-

Ronay notes, to call language the "informing aporia of sf." Haraway's response, Csicsery-Ronay argues, is to protect her imagined future from corruption by refusing to make it explicit or give it a name. Baudrillard's response, on the other hand, is to create a "logical delirium" in the reader through his hyperbolic prose. Both these strategies typify a reaction to cybernetic domination which Burroughs refers to, in Cageian terms, as Silence. The silence demanded by Burroughs is not a passive, a quietist, or a conservative silence, but rather a *generative* silence, a silence on the part of those faculties that manage representational meaning and enforce a controlling order on experience.

1. *Burroughs and Derrida: The Anarchist Use of Language.*

Burroughs is a key figure in the history of theoretical and textual resistance. A generation ago, we would not have been thinking about Gibson and Baudrillard, but if we were of a particular mind we might have been drawing connections between the experimental "science fiction" of Burroughs and the critique of logocentrism forwarded by Jacques Derrida. Although Burroughs and Derrida seem to make strange bedfellows, there is much that might have attracted them to one another. Each sought to challenge the reading and thinking habits of his audience and to shake the foundations of "totalitarian" systems of thought; since the 1960s, each has also become an iconic figure whose reputation threatens to outgrow his actual work. The two line up on the same side of most issues, the most noteworthy exception being their differing conceptions of the role of writing with respect to those totalitarian systems. Because writing confuses the defining categories of absence and presence, Derrida considers the very idea of writing to be a threat to metaphysically-based modes of Western thought (including structuralism) and the social order associated with them. Burroughs, on the other hand, understands writing as essentially a force *alien* to the human. He refers to it as "a virus that made the spoken word possible," and fingers it as the culprit responsible for the growth of totalitarian control systems of all shapes and sizes.

At first glance, Burroughs' categorical separation of language and human being invites the same sort of deconstructive treatment Derrida gives other Western writers and thinkers. If language is not part of the human, just how does Burroughs define the human? Not as body; Burroughs is as famous as Gibson's console cowboys for his disdain of the human body. But if the body is nothing but an obsolete artifact, and language a virus infecting that artifact, just what is it that Burroughs feels so strongly about rescuing? I propose that Burroughs is attempting to direct us to the energy of continuous evolution, or mutation, which, temporarily embodied in the human, is in Burroughs' view under siege by the insidious self-replication of language.

One might conceivably relate Burroughs' ideal of continuous evolution to Deleuze-Guattari's "continuous variation" and even to *différance,* Derrida's playful neologism conflating the concepts of difference (in space) and deference (in time). The function of *différance* is to act as a sort of anti-origin that, far from keeping any given thought-system stable, keeps everything moving and off-kilter. By temporarily "inhabiting" structuralist philosophical modes, Derrida does with traditional philosophy what Burroughs does with conventional science fiction. Burroughs twists the words of those fiction writers who imagine that humans can live in outer space like fish in a tank; Derrida critiques those philosophers who seek to revolutionize philosophy while repeating the same old (logocentric) thought-patterns. The governing structures of thought, both writers argue, must be shaken from within the communication networks through which they perpetuate themselves.

Derrida's "trick," if I may be allowed such a crude reduction, is to work through the texts of the masters with one eye peeled for a seam to slip into. Once in, his meticulous scholarship is set to work stretching and reshaping the fabric not along normal patterns of use, but along lines of tension never tested by its creator, using the seam as a fulcrum. When challenged on his having made the seam into a center, Derrida quickly moves his work elsewhere. His philosophical practice is not unlike the musical practice of an early twentieth-century composer, endlessly modulating at the very moments that tonal centers threaten to establish themselves. Through this mobile deconstruction, Derrida seeks to turn hierarchy into anarchy. Burroughs' approach to his source material is somewhat less intellectual, but the result, for the reader, is not dissimilar. Rather than looking for seams, Burroughs simply cuts and sews the garments randomly, keeping an eye out for the hidden patterns which begin to reveal themselves when the rationalist filters of everyday perception are removed.

Perhaps the following well-known expression best relates Burroughs to Derrida: "'Nothing Is True—Everything Is Permitted—' Last Words Hassan I Sabbah" (*Nova Express*). Burroughs here locates the notion of "truth" as a device that acts to suppress possibility. For Derrida, this is the "transcendental signified"; for Haraway, it is "the one code that translates all meaning perfectly." Just as Haraway finds her freedom in living as a cyborg in a cybernetic system that can't quite be closed, so did Derrida once find that, when nothing is true, the world becomes text. Conversely, everything is permitted when the "absence of the transcendental signified extends the domain and the play of signification infinitely." When everything is permitted, the result is anarchy. And anarchy is precisely what a cyberpunk aims at.

What Burroughs terms the viral function of language is its ongoing ordering of reality toward the limit of total control,

the opposite of anarchy. He employs the figure of the *virus,* a force hovering between evolving being and mere replicator, to problematize conventional definitions of living and non-living. In Burroughs' cosmos, one must always remember that the words one transmits can never be neutral moves in the universal language-game; even if misfiring, *some* sort of force is necessarily being transmitted. This is the very problem addressed by Csicsery-Ronay when he cites Jameson's skepticism over sf's linguistic aporia. It is exceptionally difficult for any resistant message to avoid complicity with the dominant communication systems in whose language it is composed. If "a butterfly flapping its wings in Tokyo can cause a tornado in Toledo," who knows what havoc a few well-chosen words could wreak in the infosphere? As responsible cyborg-writers, we'd best have a good idea how the "techsts" we use are going to function out there before we turn them loose. The trick, argues Burroughs, is to transmit a kind of force that doesn't immediately contribute to the virus-effect but can actually help work against it. The fold-in is the principle textual method of *guerrilla* resistance against the virus (or, as Burroughs puts it in his science-fictional work, against the Nova Conspiracy); one takes a strongly linear form like the typewritten word, cuts it, and reassembles it such that its ordinative powers are deactivated. As apomorphine was Burroughs' antidote to morphine addiction, so silence is the antidote to word-addiction and the fold-in to order-addiction. This resistance, in Burroughs' work, is the only option under the circumstances of total occupation by Control.

2. *Burroughs as Body without Organs.*

Scott Bukatman is another writer who has taken the role of language in contemporary sf as an issue to be addressed. In his article "Postcards from the Posthuman Solar System" (1991) and later in his book *Terminal Identity* (1993), Bukatman describes cyberpunks as "taking their cues from Burroughs and Pynchon as well as from Bataille and Breton and Dali and Man Ray." In Bukatman's opinion, one of the principal tactics of cyberpunk writers is to, like Derrida and Burroughs, temporarily inhabit the "rational structures of technological discourse" in order to transform them into a "highly poeticized, dreamlike liberation." Like Csicsery-Ronay, Bukatman would like to extend the boundaries of sf to include his own favorite theorist(s), Deleuze and Guattari. "Deleuze and Guattari are cyberpunks, too," he writes, "constructing fictions of terminal identity in the nearly familiar language of techno-surrealism."

Bukatman is interested in Deleuze and Guattari primarily for their idea of the "Body without Organs" (BwO), which he uses as a way to understand the non-unitary cyborg body. He argues that Ballard's Vaughan "seeks to crash through to attain that state of being without organs," and that a comic-book character who is an android reproduction of Andy

Warhol has in fact already attained it. To illustrate the tricky (anti-)concept of the BwO, Bukatman resorts to the same passage from Burroughs' *Naked Lunch* as do Deleuze and Guattari:

> In his place of total darkness mouth and eyes are one organ that leaps forward to snap with transparent teeth . . . but no organ is constant as regards either function or position . . . sex organs sprout anywhere . . . rectums open, defecate and close . . . the entire organism changes color and consistency in split-second adjustments.

The Body without Organs, in this illustration, is a sort of *ad hoc* body, one whose configuration can change according to present need. Bukatman uses it as a way to explain what happens when the human is sublimated entirely into technology or text. In *Terminal Identity* Bukatman correctly concludes that the "BwO stands against the telos of theology and the order of instrumental reason" and that "it is also anti-armor," but then is misled by Deleuze and Guattari's use of the passage from *Naked Lunch.* Bukatman defines the BwO as "a heterogenous system defined by the malleability of the organs and not just their absence" and cites Cronenberg's *Videodrome,* Ballard's *Crash,* and performance artist Stelarc as exemplifying this "malleability of organs." In Deleuze and Guattari's use of terminology like "machine," "appendix," "spare part," he argues, they are following the steps of Burroughs and Ballard in making use of technological language to create their own brand of sf theory. Bukatman then cavalierly claims that "the BwO is the state in which we aspire to dissolve the body and regain the world." This allows him to segue into a chat about surface vs. depth, and to make the claim that "the surface of the body becomes the arena for dissolving the governing instrumental reason of the organism."

To my mind Bukatman is off course in his concern with the malleability of bodies. The Body without Organs is more than a figure useful for illustrating the intermingling of the human body and technology. Its principle import is as one of the many deconstructive "sets of practices" Deleuze and Guattari advocate as a way to dismantle the (ideologically-determined) "self" in its relationship to organization and judgement. The BwO, they write, is a "practice," not a "concept"; a "limit," not a "goal"; the "full egg before the extension of the organism and the organization of the organs." They relate it specifically to what they call "desire," which is "a process without telos, intensity without intention." The BwO is deconstructive in that one can never achieve it; it is "always swinging between the surfaces that stratify it and the plane that sets it free." Their translator, Brian Massumi, paraphrases bodies without organs as "bundles of virtual affects" (93) in his discussion of the making-monstrous of a man who tries to become a dog. My own preference is to

understand the BwO as a sort of ideal anarchist or Taoist existence in which energy flows freely within and through the individual, moving one between order and chaos; one works at it but can never completely achieve it.

Deleuze and Guattari theorize various BwOs at various stages of "fullness." The full BwO, as opposed to the empty, "drugged body" or "masochist body," is illustrated by the already quoted passage drawn from the opening routine of *Naked Lunch.* On the way to the full BwO, one encounters several types of "emptied" bodies, bodies without organs whose circulation of intensities nevertheless remains blocked. Deleuze and Guattari turn once again to Burroughs for an example of an empty body: "the drugged body, the experimental schizo," indicated by the iteration of a scheme by Dr Benway's colleague Dr Schaefer, also drawn from *Naked Lunch.*

> "the human body is scandalously inefficient. Instead of a mouth and an anus to get out of order why not have one all-purpose hole to eat and eliminate? We could seal up the nose and mouth, fill in the stomach, make an air hole direct into the lungs where it should have been in the first place."

Before further explicating the "empty" BwO, it is instructive to return to the first quotation from *Naked Lunch* which Deleuze and Guattari and Bukatman use to illustrate the "full" BwO and put it in context. In this passage, a character referred to as "the Vigilante" has been sentenced to the Federal Nut House, an institution designed to contain ghosts. Alone in his cell, with nothing to organize or subdivide his need, the Vigilante has, in Deleuze and Guattari's reading, become the very image of a BwO, an undifferentiated body able to mobilize portions of itself *ad hoc.* The Vigilante is thus a figure of Deleuzian desire suspended in a moment of temporary isolation, eventually to return to the drugged body from which he emerged.

One clue to the relevance of the second quotation is the later citing by Deleuze and Guattari of *Speed,* a book written by Burroughs' (amphetamine-addicted) son, William Jr., as an expression of a "paranoid point, a point of blockage" that prevents circulation at the level of the BwO. The junky (also exemplified by the pre-*Naked Lunch* Burroughs, Sr.) is thus defined as one who has moved toward the limit of the BwO but "botches" the job by achieving a body in which the intensities that pass are equal to zero. By "wildly destratifying," the emptied bodies have made the mistake of emptying themselves of their own organs rather than seeking a point where they could momentarily dismantle the true enemy—organization itself. Burroughs himself worried about his extensive cut-up experiments ending up in just this way. It is not enough, obviously, to simply be done with the organs themselves, for when they are gone there is nothing from which to gain leverage. Deleuze and Guattari state that there is a fascist use of drugs and this is clearly the use Burroughs sees in the function of junk.

Burroughs is an appropriate choice for Deleuze and Guattari not because these particular passages happen to be suitable illustrations of the BwO, but because Burroughs' own life experiences and theoretical orientation make him a model case for many of their ideas. As already noted, Burroughs himself shows an intense lack of interest in the human body, which he identifies as a sort of weakness, a foothold for the forces of control. Most of his writing, however, is intensely visceral in its imagery, relying heavily on descriptions of sexual interplay, deformed bodies, and especially olfactory experience. The sorts of "monsters" envisioned in the foregoing passages from *Naked Lunch* are quite typical of the imagery of that book, and would not be out of place in certain parts of his later, more "realistic," writing also. These mixed-up bodies, however, are not what the BwO is all about; they are merely symptoms of Burroughs' own quest for the BwO. Burroughs originally made contact with junk in his attempts to throw off his stratified and stifling upper-class St. Louis upbringing, only to find that junk itself became a blockage point, preventing the circulation of desire because it in fact replaces desire itself. Drifting from one misadventure to another in his early adult years, Burroughs eventually found himself playing at the life of a small-time criminal and junkie in New York City, and the heroin habit he developed there lasted fifteen years. Unlike the crowd that started him on heroin, Burroughs continued to receive a monthly allowance from his parents of $200. This was more than just a symbol of his upbringing; it was a long, flexible tentacle of upper-class judgement keeping Burroughs in a state of arrested development. It was only when the allowance was cut off that he finally sought the infamous apomorphine cure and detoxified himself by writing the chaos of material that eventually became *Naked Lunch.* In becoming a writer, and in writing material to aid his own (Deleuzian) "becoming" and that of his readers, Burroughs can be counted among the few who have made it past the "drugged" BwO to approach the "full." Burroughs' experimental texts are evidence of his conviction in the power of continuous mutation through freedom from what Deleuze and Guattari might call "the molar order."

3. *Chaos—Anarchy—Enlightenment.*

The Body without Organs is not only a figure through which to grasp the import of Burroughs' work, but also one which can be used to understand Deleuze and Guattari's own work, especially *A Thousand Plateaus* (trans. 1987), a text in which the BwO is prominently featured. In this case, however, it may be easier to make use of another of Deleuze and Guattari's figures, the "rhizome," which is related to the

BwO but is more readily applicable to texts; in fact, Deleuze and Guattari do just this in their introduction to *A Thousand Plateaus.* Like Burroughs' work, *A Thousand Plateaus* is an attempt to function on the margin of both the medium (book) and the genre (philosophy, science fiction) by letting the conventions that define those discourses act as leverage points for resistance. Where Burroughs uses imitation and recombination to defuse the forces of push-button mind-and-body control, Deleuze and Guattari look past the sender-receiver relationship altogether and constitute their own work as a middle.

> A plateau is always in the middle, not at the beginning or the end. A rhizome is made of plateaus. Gregory Bateson uses the word "plateau" to designate something very special: a continuous, self-vibrating region of intensities whose development avoids any orientation toward a culmination point or external end.

Eschewing mechanical randomizing technique (such as the fold-in), Deleuze and Guattari find their own method of making their text a multiple: "Each morning we would wake up, and each of us would ask himself what plateau he was going to tackle, writing five lines here, ten there." Their motive was not to make their book grow from the roots up, but from the middle out. *A Thousand Plateaus* is thus "in assemblage" with its own outside, acting on "semiotic flows, material flows and social flows simultaneously." Its translator, Brian Massumi, states that the book should be approached with the "plateau" in mind. The best way to read it, he argues, is to

> pry open the vacant spaces that would enable you to build your life and those of the people around you into a plateau of intensity that would leave afterimages of its dynamism that could be reinjected into still other lives, creating a fabric of heightened states between which any number, the greatest number, of connecting routes would exist.

"Some might call that promiscuous," Massumi writes. "Deleuze and Guattari call it revolution." In their creation of an "open system" that levers itself against the borders of the domain of philosophy, Deleuze and Guattari have developed their own parry to what Burroughs identifies as control. As Burroughs writes chaos to engender silence, Deleuze and Guattari write a rhizome to engender anarchy.

This notion of generative chaos is crucial to the "punk" aspect of cyberpunk writing. The understanding of chaos as a positive force in organisms and systems has gained acceptance with the popularizing of Ilya Prigogine's work, which in sf circles has been facilitated in part by Gibson, Sterling, and others, including Porush and Fischlin. It is equally important to understand the importance of chaos to experimental, subversive, or resistant communication strategies. Massumi refers extensively to Prigogine's theories in his *User's Guide to A Thousand Plateaus* (1993), particularly with respect to Deleuze-Guattari's underlying theory of language acquisition and development of the "self." In *A Thousand Plateaus,* Guattari and Deleuze, like Baudrillard and even Burroughs, rely on a sort of "logical delirium" as a way to bring their work in touch with the generative powers of chaos. In their own way, they, like Burroughs, are writing silence—a silence that is not equal to zero, but rather is unrepresentable in a conventional cybernetic model of communication. The reason is that conventional cybernetic theory, drawn as it is from thermodynamic theory, equates order with life and disorder with death, in stark contrast with the theories of Burroughs, who sees a fixation with order as strangling the forces of life as they seek to mutate. As Massumi writes, Deleuze and Guattari understand chaos as a sea of virtuality which beings need to come in contact with in order to evolve. To this end, they intend their work to function as a "rhizome," a multiplying multiplicity opening up the reader to the infinite possibility of becoming.

Though happy to borrow from Burroughs' texts to illustrate their ideas, Deleuze and Guattari, in *A Thousand Plateaus,* are skeptical that his work actually succeeds in doing what he intends it to. Before explicitly defining what they mean by their term "rhizome-book," they identify two other models: the "root-book," which is organized like a dichotomous tree in which one becomes two, two become four, and so on; and the "radicle-system," in which the principle root has been aborted and a multiplicity of secondary roots have been grafted onto it. Burroughs' work is held up as an illustration of the radicle model:

> Take William Burroughs' cut-up method: the folding of one text onto another, which constitutes multiple and even adventitious roots (like a cutting), implies a supplementary dimension to that of the texts under consideration. In this supplementary dimension of folding, unity continues its spiritual labor.

Burroughs' cut-ups are thus consigned to the museum of modernist obsolescence along with Joyce and Nietzsche. In their respective works, "the world has become chaos, but the book remains the image of the world: radicle chaosmos rather than root-cosmos." Deleuze and Guattari argue that the multiple is not made by adding more dimensions, but by subtracting a dimension from the number given in order to open the work to the forces of chance. Burroughs is thus figured as a mere "adding machine" (an ironic comment on his family heritage and his creation of the "Third Mind" with friend and collaborator Brion Gysin).

The model put forth to supplant both the tree and the radicle-system is the rhizome. "Certain approximate characteristics" of the rhizome are cited:

> 1 and 2. Principles of connection and heterogeneity: any point of a rhizome can be connected to anything other, and must be.
>
> 3. Principle of multiplicity: it is only when the multiple is effectively treated as a substantive, "multiplicity," that it ceases to have any relation to the One as subject or object, natural or spiritual reality, image and world.
>
> 4. Principle of asignifying rupture: against the oversignifying breaks separating structures or cutting across a single structure. A rhizome may be broken, shattered at a given spot, but it will start up again on one of its old lines, or on new lines.
>
> 5 and 6. Principle of cartography and decalomania: a rhizome is not amenable to any structural or generative model . . . a map and not a tracing. . . . The map has to do with performance, whereas the tracing always involves alleged "competence."

Despite Deleuze and Guattari's reservations, the relationship between chaos and life finds, to my mind, an enlightening expression in Burroughs' experimental sf texts. Living in the space between order and chaos, working within the tensions resulting from their interaction, Burroughs offers not merely the rhetoric of resistance, but sets his texts in motion as "soft machines" operating to deconstruct systematized communication. Although Burroughs has often been presented to the public as a writer of "new kinds of novels," it is seldom emphasized that the "novel" form functions only as a margin that can be turned back on itself, used as a lever to create a tension between the expected order and the actual text that "spill[s] off the page in all directions."

> **The importance of the texts . . . is not to be found in their immediate consumption, but in whatever the lasting effects they have on their reader's lives.**
> —*Brent Wood*

Using Deleuze and Guattari's terminology, one might think of Burroughs' texts, at their best, as also comprised of plateaus. Any given "chapter" of *Naked Lunch, Nova Express, The Soft Machine,* and *The Ticket That Exploded* may contain a number of plateaus which occur as intensities build between a text comprised of fold-ins of outlandish comedy routines, poetry, quotations and reports, the reader's gut reactions, and the rational mind searching fruitlessly for order. Initial exposure to the shocking or disgusting images Burroughs commonly employs might result mainly in a series of jolts to the nervous system, while prolonged exposure to severely cut-up text may leave one simply cross-eyed. The importance of the texts, however, according to the theories explored here, is not to be found in their immediate consumption, but in whatever the lasting effects they have on their readers' lives. As noted earlier, much of the "word horde" which came out of Burroughs' typewriter in the late 1950's was in fact designed to liberate Burroughs himself from his own upper class midwestern upbringing. In playing with (stereo)typical sf images, the sf works represent an attempt to re-write *Naked Lunch* in order to deal specifically with the kinds of technological and communicational crises which Burroughs, like Gibson a generation later, sensed were occurring all around him.

I have written about Burroughs' work largely in the past tense, but both he and his texts are very much alive, stimulating thinkers, writers and anarchists of all stripes. Though his books returned to a more narrative form in the 1970s and 1980s, he continued his experimentation with chaos in the 1960s through graphic collage and in the 1980s through shotgun-painting. His skill at using the spoken word has led to a proliferation of sound recordings and a corresponding invitation to the cyberpunk dance party just down the hall. And, like any counter-cultural icon, his image has finally been appropriated by consumer culture as a Nike television advertisement. If Warhol-as-reproducible-android represented the achievement of the BwO, then certainly Burroughs' living texts will soon qualify him as at least approaching that limit. Perhaps the best tribute to Burroughs' work along these lines is given by Gibson in *Neuromancer,* where he casts Burroughs' voice, personality and wisdom as McCoy Pauley, the Dixie Flatline. A ROM construct, the Flatline guides Gibson's protagonist in his cyberspatial mission. The resulting union of Wintermute and Neuromancer, though accomplished under duress, provides at least the birth of a new form of life even as it totalizes the Matrix. If we anarchist cyborgs similarly keep our ears tuned to Burroughs' voice, and consider its advice, we may be able to hope that our own science-fiction realities will result in a revolution of happy accidents instead of the world of corporate control which was the subject of Gibson's speculation.

Jonathan Paul Eburne (essay date Spring 1997)

SOURCE: "Trafficking in the Void: Burroughs, Kerouac, and the Consumption of Otherness," in *Modern Fiction Studies,* Vol. 43, No. 1, Spring, 1997, pp. 53-92.

[*In the following essay, Eburne examines the influence of* the Cold War-era ideological construct of "otherness" in Naked Lunch *and in Jack Kerouac's* The Subterraneans, *comparing its effect on the subjectivity of each novel.*]

Divulging his latest platform as crime-and-commie-busting director of the FBI, J. Edgar Hoover claimed at the 1960 Republican National Convention that "beatniks" were, alongside communists and liberal "eggheads," one of the three greatest menaces to U.S. National Security. Using "beat-*nik*" rather than "beat" to describe the group of writers, poets, and bohemians known as the Beat Generation, Hoover's semantic slide—or push—seemed to implicate beat "niks" as petty communists who threatened to enervate America's welfare. Both a terrible menace and a crude joke, the Beat Generation elicited similar disdain across a vast cultural front—from Hoover, mainstream culture, and "eggheads" alike.

Notorious for its resistance to conventional sexual and moral practices, the Beats' literary solicitation of breaches and breakdowns within the social fabric garnered obscenity charges for much of their written work. What these charges signified, according to the Supreme Court, was that their work itself was "patently offensive because it affront[ed] contemporary community standards" and that "the material [was] *utterly* without redeeming social value." At issue was the imputation that the Beats radically and deliberately affronted firmly installed notions of decency and thus threatened to undermine the basic integrity of a nation that was already nervous about its internal security.

The broad aim of the following paper will be to examine this subversive element in William Burroughs's *Naked Lunch* (1959) and Jack Kerouac's *The Subterraneans* (1958, written in 1952), both of which faced obscenity charges or censorship in some form. These two works confront, and seek to disrupt, what their authors considered to be a cultural environment in which individual identity had become inexorably bound up within stifling artistic, societal, and existential norms. Keeping in mind Judith Butler's contention that "identity" itself operates not as a predeterminate ontological category but as a regulatory, and often oppressive, practice of cultural formation, I will argue that the two novels seek to "trouble" such regulatory practices within the context of the postwar U.S. By casting the "self"—as the privileged signifier of narrative and cultural identity—into serious contention, they each attempt to drain identity of its fixity as a locus of coercive standards. In doing so, they also attempt to contest the very discursive practices of Cold War-era identity configuration themselves.

What troubles such efforts most immediately, however, is that the very idiom of dissent from these norms was prefabricated by a "liberal" intelligentsia with its own set of governing standards and expectations. Indeed, novels such as *Naked Lunch* and *The Subterraneans* were considered "obscene" by many of the "eggheads"—liberal intellectuals, literary critics, and scholars—in whose eyes their dissent was not formulated cogently enough to qualify their writing as truly "radical." Both grotesque and stylistically discombobulated, this writing seemed so immersed in remonstrating the personal that it fell victim to a damning romance of the apolitical. Writers like Burroughs and Kerouac were little more than incoherent, and therefore obscene in the sense that they merely channeled the confusion of the society that distressed them. Their confusion deviated distinctly from the more lucidly formulated "pragmatism" of critics like Lionel Trilling, who argued that by introducing "alterity" and "conflict" as incorporable challenges to the mind of the individual, a true radical could be jostled free from the forces of conformity and repression which characterized Cold War normalcy. The Beats, however, scoured city streets in order to find alterity and conflict in the form of a racial, cultural, and ethnic minority, an anthropomorphized strategy of dissent by means of which incorporation and control became a calamitous impossibility.

However, any such means of evacuating a bankrupt subject position by identifying with the "otherness" of the American cultural margins ends up, as Burroughs and Kerouac realize with increasing distress, implicating themselves in the same process of normativity and containment that they attempt to leave behind. Since the identification with "otherness" operates as a power-play relying upon specifically conceived notions of what this "otherness" consists of, it proves to be an elaborate fantasy by which Burroughs and Kerouac themselves end up performing the coercive work of identity configuration. My specific aim in this paper, then, will be to examine how this latter instance of containment comes about and becomes yet another subject position to be evacuated. In other words, I aim to show how "making trouble" for identity becomes a fundamental and deeply complex problem in the two novels, a problem which necessitates not merely a rethinking of "identity" as a discursive concept but, in fact, a radical complication of notions of the process of identity *refiguration* that would rely upon the commodification of otherness as its fundamental mechanism of change.

1.

    "I can feel the heat closing in. . . ."
           —William Burroughs, *Naked Lunch*

This first line of *Naked Lunch* leaps out, in medias res, from a hardboiled melodrama which bears an acute sense of imminent constriction. For Burroughs's narrator/protagonist, this encroachment is not merely the legalistic menace of stalking detectives but, more broadly, the tightening grip of an entire network of heirarchized systems of containment and control. In the opening lines of *The Subterraneans,*

Kerouac's narrator/protagonist exposes a similarly constricting (albeit less evidently "political") web of limitations: his loss of youth, his obfuscatory need for "literary preambles," and a perplexing trap of self, this being the story of "an unself-confident man, at the same time of an egomaniac." What is most striking about the near-paranoiac sense of confinement and constraint at the opening moments of these novels is precisely their immediacy: the narrational "I" appears as already caught up within such strictures. The novels thus bear the traces of a complex drama of escape—not merely from "the heat" but from a notion of selfhood caught in a network of temporal, spatial, and narrative constraints: aging and the passage of time, the "literary preambles" of style, and the subject positions determined by U.S. culture and national policy in the post-World War II years.

Much of this evacuative work is attempted stylistically. The majority of critical work written about *Naked Lunch* addresses, in some fashion, Burroughs's full frontal assault on textual "control systems." As a brutal subversion of accepted notions of narrative unity, character cohesiveness, and linguistic propriety, Burroughs's writing slashes vertiginously through space and time. Thomas Hill Schaub, among others, reads this radical disruptiveness as a search "for some means of achieving 'nakedness' or immediacy without succumbing to the atrophy or imposition of form. . . ." Burroughs's solution is to distill a "language of consciousness" by zooming in on a first-person narrator's subjective relation to experience. Schaub maintains that the authority of Burroughs's work relies in part upon this subjective language's claim to immediacy, its reduction of rhetorical mediation. He cites a passage from *Naked Lunch*'s "Atrophied Preface" which appears in the novel's final pages: ". . . I am a recording instrument . . . I do not presume to impose 'story' 'plot' 'continuity.' . . . Insofar as I succeed in *Direct* recording of certain areas of psychic process I may have limited function. . . . I am not an entertainer. . . ." While Schaub focuses on Burroughs's claim to impose as little structure and mediation as possible, any claim to "immediacy" here seems to be cut short—not just by the ambiguity of the passage, but by the very positioning of this claim: as an atrophied preface, its presence is suspect. Is this passage itself an attempt to impose structure and continuity by means of explanation? How structured, or how atrophied, is its own value? This suspicion is fed by the narrator's later claim that he has written many prefaces which atrophy and amputate spontaneously. As we'll see, the very idea of "stripping down" narrative to a naked prose-consciousness is itself a treacherous process; Schaub's argument that this has to do with immediacy assumes the presence of a subjective logos, some "naked" core of consciousness that can be served up to readers as the "naked lunch" itself.

Such a stripping down, though, is done only at the expense of the speaking subject: as noted above, any claim to immediacy threatens the narrator with the eradication of his authorial function. It is not merely the preface(s) that are at risk of atrophy and amputation, but the narrator—or even the writer—himself. Indeed, in *Naked Lunch,* the narrational "I"s clash and commingle to such a degree that the didactic voice of "William Burroughs" the author (or author-function), "William Lee" the protagonist/narrator, and the "Master Addict" of the appendix are conflated yet maintain specific relationships to the body of the text. These disjunctions open up a discursive space inside which the constructedness of the so-called narrative "self" can be scrutinized, thrown into disarray, subverted.

This "discursive space" to which I am referring is not a clean, open, locatable area made possible by a simple division of the narration into different voices, each relaying separate and differentiated subjective consciousnesses. Rather, the novel is a total disarray; it is more a recombination, a juxtapositioning of narrative selves than a stripping down to individual consciousness. Indeed, "William Lee" is not only Burroughs's protagonist but his own alter-ego—the name with which he closes many of his letters as well as, in fact, the pseudonym under which he published his first book, *Junky,* in 1953. Nor is William Lee, within the novel itself, an unflappable narrational presence: the text fades in and out of first-person and third-person narration, just as Lee himself drifts in and out of the book's mosaic fragments. Lee's function as a storyteller is also complicated, threatened by the suspicion that he is expendable. Many passages throughout the novel narrate him rather than vice versa; others are narrated in spite of his absence. Thus, rather than adopting a first-person narrative style as a direct mainline into the "language of consciousness" of the individual subject, Burroughs wreaks havoc upon the possibility of such a subject ever being an embraceable totality.

Kerouac effects a similar breach in the narrative subject's claim to immediacy and presence. As a fictionalized yet thinly veiled autobiographical novel, *The Subterraneans* unlocks a fictive space in which the primary identifications of the narrative "self" as author (or author-function), narrator, and protagonist are at once advertised and suspended, deferred and yet more or less immediately available. Commenting on the stylistic background of the novel, Kerouac writes that "the form is strictly confessional in accordance with the confessional form of Fyodor Dostoyevsky's *Notes from Underground.*" But any claim to directness or emotional immediacy that his modeling of Leo Percepied after Dostoyevsky's nameless anti-hero bears is, as in the case of Burroughs's atrophy-prone storytellers, undermined by Kerouac's choice of literary model. Dostoyevsky's speaker is no simple "confessor"; ruthlessly self-effacing, frequently infuriating, never to be fully trusted, his presence in Kerouac's text speaks of more than merely assertion and disclosure.

Percepied's frequent self-depreciating slashes and rebuttals—as well as the shadowy intertextual presence of Dostoyevsky's madman himself—call a significant amount of attention to how much his narration is tied up, reflexive, mediated; this mediation becomes as conspicuous, and as necessary, to Kerouac's prose as the emotional unguardedness of its attempt at spontaneity. And yet, the novel's "spontaneous prose method" has often been read as an attempt to *eliminate* temporal and emotional distance between the writing of the novel and the experiences it narrates: *The Subterraneans* was written in three grueling, Benzedrine-compelled days almost immediately after the events described in the novel took place. The novel ends, too, narrating its own (fictionalized) conception: Percepied goes home to write "this book." However, the deeply engaged, intricately entangled narrative that results only serves, conversely, to dramatize the distance between speaking and spoken subjects, a distance which Kerouac realized to be a function of "the limitations of time flying by as our mind flies by with it." Indeed, Kerouac's writing faces the broader problem of control involved in eliminating distance—embedding his narration within the mechanics of representation, the sticky limitations of expression, and the fracturing of the possibility of an omnipotent literary *auteur* able to convey successfully "the language of consciousness." Instead of using fast work and fast language as a "way in" to the immediate experience it promises, Kerouac's prose cleaves apart the very fabric of the narrative "self" assumed by such a language's metaphysics of presence to be a coherent possibility.

I have deliberately simplified Schaub's notion of the "language of consciousness's" claim to immediacy here for the sake of highlighting an effect of Burroughs's and Kerouac's writing whereby "the way OUT is the way IN" (*Naked Lunch*). Their attempt to escape temporal and rhetorical limitations by zeroing in on an "immediate" language ironically, and traumatically, necessitates an evacuation of the "self" as a fixed narrational category. As we've seen, though, this effect is itself as much the result of limitation and entanglement as it is of efficient self-evacuation.

Schaub, however, argues otherwise: the conscious move of many post-World War II writers to "subjectivize" the novel was itself a "voice of resistance to general pressures, both popular and critical, for political conformity and controlled, crafted form. The discourse of resistance and reform was no longer dominated by the language of social and economic forces, giving way, instead, to explanatory models based in psychology—to a renewed focus upon the mind." According to Schaub, the first-person affords a means for dramatizing a subjective view of experience, a focus on "the ongoing dialectic of consciousness." Such points-of-view not only relieved the stifling artistic bane of conformity, but also had a more legitimate access to "reality" and "authenticity" within their highly individualized contexts. "The subject" thus became a highly motivated—and, it seems, highly fashionable—literary trope for a postwar novel in search of the voice of subversion "within the postwar discourse of 'mass society,' 'conformity,' and 'totalitarianism,' which governed thinking about society for writer and critic alike in the forties and fifties. . . ."

However, in *Naked Lunch* and *The Subterraneans,* this move fails to claim coherence or even authority; rather, the use of a first-person narrator in these two novels serves more to alienate the self from the self than to distance the "rebel" self from postwar society. As Schaub points out, both novels often dramatize the vicissitudes of the subjective voice. However, if the novels in some way approach the naked immediacy of consciousness, they expose a realm so turbulent as to rip apart the subjective voice altogether.

Nonetheless, both novels remain deeply committed to confronting the social and political modalities of the selfhood they subvert: namely, the images of U.S. postwar "normalcy" which privileged a virulently anticommunist white, middle-class, heterosexual male. Burroughs and Kerouac resisted, and attempted to evacuate, this position of artistic and experiential subjectivity which, in their eyes, had become a real drag. This evacuation implicated not merely the existential drudgery that conformity entailed but, in fact, the whole notion of "fitting in" altogether. In the discursive climate of the early postwar years, "fitting in" already carried an onerous amount of ideological baggage. As we will see below, conformity implied complicity with a U.S. social and political orthodoxy intent on stamping out difference and "deviance" by means of the Cold War politics of personal containment.

2.

> Little Surrealist sketch. A woman in white uniform with a chrome-plated machine appears in J. E. Hoover's office: "I have come to give Mr. Hoover a sample high colonic wash courtesy of the Fox Massage Studios Inc." She plants a time bomb up his ass. High up.
>
> —William Burroughs, Letter to
> Allen Ginsberg, 24 Dec. 1952

Naked Lunch and *The Subterraneans* nosed their way into the literary market at a period—the Cold War 1950s—in which a remarkably hegemonic cultural and political body had fashioned a narrative of opposing internal and external forces, positioning "us" versus "them." The national fixation upon internal security, operating not only within U.S. Government policy but, to an unprecedented degree, within the private sector, implemented an alarmingly pervasive political consensus which would define the affairs of the state

in "human" terms. Under this consensus, a mass of "anxieties" drawn from foreign and domestic policy alike—the fear of communism, the Bomb, homosexuality, sexual chaos and moral decrepitude, aliens (foreigners and extraterrestrials)—became condensed with a nightmarish lucidity upon a unifying rhetorical figure: a festering and highly contagious disease which threatened the national "body" with pollution. Andrew Ross aligns the widespread use of such rhetoric

> to the chorus of similar hysterical discourses that contributed to the Cold War culture of germophobia, and the many fantasmatic health concerns directly linked to the Cold War—Is Fluoridation a Communist Plot? Is your washroom breeding Bolsheviks? Cold War culture is rich with the demonology of the "alien," especially in the genre of science fiction film, where a pan-social fear of the Other—communism, feminism and other egalitarianisms foreign to the American social body—is reproduced through images drawn from the popular fringe of biological or genetic engineering gone wrong.

Implicit in Ross's explication of the language of germophobia is the work being done in the Cold War imagination to transform "egalitarianisms" into something "alien"; indeed, what is most interesting in such a transformation is that the most damning aspect of the "Other"—of "It," "The Thing," and other manifestations of alien presence—was not its sameness but its seemingly ineluctable *difference.* As Ross suggests, behind the figuration of this difference was the danger of usurpation, the systematic transformation of "us" into "them" which would, in fact, result in a perverse sort of egalitarianism whereby American self-identity would dissolve. More specifically, it was the fear of infection, of the infiltration of a foreign pollutant into the American social body, which figured as this demonization's fundamental rhetorical anxiety. Such invasive rhetoric was most visible in J. Edgar Hoover's massively publicized agenda as FBI director, which co-opted his antebellum campaign to stamp out "degenerates" for the sake of maintaining U.S. internal security against the "trojan horse of Communism" in the postwar years. Though more moderate, George Kennan's 1947 article, "The Sources of Soviet Conduct," makes a similar move, allegorizing the threatening spread of communism as a contaminating "fluid stream." In face of this spreading ooze of Soviet expansionism, Kennan calls for a form of "containment" which would counterbalance its external threat by means of a reinforcement of the "*integral integrity*" of the country. It is by strong counterexample, by an American *self* enclosure—that is, by "good health"—that the Communist danger could be kept at bay.

The "integral integrity" or American social body at stake in this drama of corrupting influence formed the contrary figure upon which was condensed an equally astounding number of concentric structures of self-enclosure, from the most personal to the most public. Conflating the languages of physical, psychic, and public health with the language of national security, an American "self" was formulated as a dominant subject position designed to withstand the threat of outside pollution. This "self" was compound, a set of varying spatial boundaries and bulwarks, each protecting another's integrity. The versions of subjectivity at stake were liable to change and slide into multiple configurations; depending on the situation, depending on the concurring cultural and political contexts called upon for legitimacy, the "self" at stake could be private, public, national, or all at once.

The master metaphor of this struggle to preserve the "integrity" of the American subject position from the contamination by the Other was the drive to preserve the body from the corrupting influences of "unnatural" bodily acts: the advances of "loose" women, sexual perverts and deviates, and, most emphatically, homosexuals. To engage in such "unnatural" sexual practice was symptomatic of a transgression into pathological *deviance*. As Elaine Tyler May writes, unfettered female promiscuity figured as the "explosive issue" which plagued male sexual health with venereal diseases—May's term "explosive issue" calling to mind both a Kennanesque metaphor of communist infection as an "issue" or seminal fluid, as well as the notion of the "bombshell," the pin-up siren registering atomic destruction in female form. An even more explosive issue in the immediate postwar years was the juridical linkage of sexual deviance to political deviance, a move which, Robert Corber attests, "not only politicized the sexual practices of an indeterminate group of gay men and women by linking them directly to the growing crisis over national security, but also coerced heterosexuals into policing their own behavior." This implication of homosexuals as a communist threat to American integrity came scandalously at the heels of a full-blown investigation, launched by Senator Joseph McCarthy and the Senate Appropriations Committee, which sought to confirm allegations that "sexual deviates" were employed by the federal government. This infiltration, or, in the Senate's terms, this "pollution" of the federal government (Hoover, too, would revise his own "trojan horse" metaphor to the suggestively phallic "trojan snake") provoked a metaphor of anal penetration which, in turn, could be co-opted for the purposes of further hystericizing the Communist "pollution" of the United States as a national body.

Furthermore both the natal—and thus "natural"—origin of the individual body as well as its most intimate social milieu, the family, was posted as a version of the self similarly at risk on a national level. The family as a state apparatus—an image reiterated not just by the state itself but also by the popular media at least since World War II—existed not just as an endangered social unit but as a protective struc-

ture that was itself essential to national security. Such structural units were considered to be endangered as much from within as from without. Bad parenting, which threatened a family with the lurking danger of an "Oedipal complex"—or what Philip Wylie called "momism"—risked producing psychologically damaged "mother-lovers" destined to become criminals, drug addicts, or (worst of all) sissies. The latter were especially demonized since, as likely homosexuals, they thus became susceptible to suspicions of communistic subversion as well. Indeed, in his 1944 article entitled "Mothers . . . Our Only Hope," J. Edgar Hoover posits "crime" and "perversion" as the consequences of "parental incompetence and neglect." It thus became the father's role—and the State's—to contain the mother's influence over her children, a further bulwark of internal security. This regulatory family structure was crucial to the rearing of "healthy" and "decent" children.

What is interesting here is that, in adopting developmental psychology as a means of describing domestic relations, there arose a widespread clinical prognostication of "deviance"—crime, drugs, perversion, homosexuality—as a psychological sickness. A "maladjusted" child could become Hoover's "degenerate" "afflicted with diseases which only recently have been discussed in public." Psychoanalysts such as Edmund Bergler, too, lumped homosexuals in "among swindlers, pseudologues, forgers, lawbreakers of all sorts, drug purveyors, gamblers, pimps, spies, brothel owners, etc.," as deviants with fundamental psychological problems. Once again, we find what Andrew Ross called the "pan-social fear of the Other" condensed onto the figure of disease, this time with the aid and clinical authority of doctors, psychoanalysts, and other "experts."

In terms of this vision of the individual American subject as a body perpetually at risk of pollution, the enemies who posed this threat lurked not only outside of the various physical and psychic bulwarks (and fallout shelters) of the U.S. identity-structures, but often from *within* these boundaries. Yet what this rhetoric of disease (whether mental or physical) and vampiric infiltration provided within the ideology of containment was a way of locating "internal" difference as the result of outside influence. The demonology of the "alien" or "the Thing" as a generalized Other served as a strategy for abjecting integral difference within a U.S. national identity, projecting such difference upon all kinds of shadowy figures of negative influence. Such figures, whether the nuclear warhead or the covert homosexual, were recast in the dominant public eye not merely as "Others" but, it seems, as perversely *phallic* Others with the ability and will to penetrate into the national fabric and disrupt its integrity. More precisely, such figures became the symbolic repositories of what Julia Kristeva describes as the abject: the fundamental *lack* (in this case, of health, of normality, of "American-ness") which is "what disturbs identity, system, order. What does not respect borders, positions, rules." In the shifting images of personal, familial, and national security, the discourse about such "dejects" of U.S. national culture provided a brilliant strategy for maintaining the rhetoric of containment. The importance of such demonized figures was due not to their fundamental positioning "outside" U.S. culture, but because of the ability of their essential "otherness" to be compounded into an "abject" which could be located as the source of internal differences within the U.S. self.

3.

> "I always told you Trilling was a shit."
> —William Burroughs, Letter to
> Allen Ginsberg, 1956.

Foreshadowing Burroughs's and Kerouac's reactions to this national narrative were the counter-narratives of the "liberal" literary critics of the Cold War period who, though virulently anticommunist as well as homophobic, wished to distance themselves from the conservative preoccupation with rooting out subversives. However, for such intellectuals the conception of a society—and especially of an individual subject position—organized in response to traumatic difference nevertheless remained a key concept in their critical imagination. Rather than adhering so rigorously to the importance of the subject's "integral integrity," though, the Cold War liberals redefined the subject to present a more "realistic" picture of U.S. culture. No longer at constant risk of penetration by an "abject," the subject became, in a sense, always already polluted by the homeopathic strains of difference; "reality" was the perpetual struggle of the self with this trauma, and thus the "abject" became a fundamental, internal property of this reality.

Though indeed anticommunist, the Cold War intellectuals were emphatically critical of the "conservative" official and popular-media ideas of national security on the home front. The rigorously normative strategies of containment and defense represented, in their eyes, less security than "a shadow-world of political sectarianism and sheer obsession" as well as "an hysteria through which . . . foreign policy has been frozen into an inflexible rigidity." In other words, the conservative compulsion to attack communism on the home front had become a form of mass-manipulation, an ideological "false consciousness" which lured the U.S. population into a state of conformity which could drain individuals of the will to resistance necessary to free democracy. The national fixation with its own health was symptomatic of a broader fascination with the homogenizing appeal of "mass culture." Indeed, the watershed *Partisan Review* symposium "Our Country and Our Culture" (1952) mobilized the majority of Cold War Intellectuals under Dwight Macdonald's argument that mass culture was the very "spreading ooze"

of conformity and commodification which threatened to engulf the possibility of individualism altogether. And yet, while Macdonald's "spreading ooze" certainly reiterates the germophobic language of anticommunist hysteria, rhetorically it represented a fear of mind control rather than of a physical penetration and a fear of sameness rather than the fear of "deviance" voiced by pundits such as Hoover and McCarthy.

What was at stake in the liberals' struggle against the "spreading ooze" of conformity was still the individual self which the fixation upon National Security wished to protect. Yet it was a "self" figured differently: on one hand, the language of hegemonic representations of individual subjectivity tended to conflate "self," "Nation," and "family" as allegories of each other, condensing geopolitical and psychoanalytical language under the master-signifier of the male body; the Cold War intellectuals, on the other hand, saw the self as an emphatically psychological entity. Indeed, the Cold War liberals mobilized psychic criteria to dramatize the susceptibility of an unconscious, mass-culture-desublimated populace to the deadly "false consciousness" of ideology. Controlled and manipulated by forces of social repression, an individual consciousness would lose its fundamental autonomy and capacity to think, since it no longer had access to "reality."

The project foreseen by Cold War critics, such as Lionel Trilling, was to devise a critical methodology which could reinstall an essential complexity within the American intellectual milieu, emphasizing the power of "high" (complex) cultural artifacts to offset the dangerous repressions lurking beneath mass culture's simplicity. As he writes in the 1949 preface to *The Liberal Imagination,* "[t]he job of criticism would seem to be . . . to recall liberalism to its first essential imagination of variousness and possibility, which implies the awareness of complexity and difficulty." For Trilling, the Cold War intellectual closest and most influential to the Beats in their early years, "reality," as the first essential imagination of complexity, gains a transcendental potential for resistance. In rendering the struggle against conformity an essentially subjective project, Trilling locates reality in the individual mind's ability to internalize the conflict, or the dialectic, of culture. As he writes in "Reality in America," the form of culture's existence is

> struggle, or at least debate—it is nothing if not a dialectic. And in any culture there are likely to be certain artists who contain a large part of the dialectic within themselves, their meaning and power lying in their contradictions; they contain within themselves, it may be said, the very essence of the culture, and the sign of this is that they do not submit to serve the ends of any one ideological group or tendency.

That Trilling lends to "reality" the power to transcend the ideological constraints of a given historical moment suggests a sublime quality: as simultaneously "really real" and beyond normal (mass) experience. Trilling's dialectical struggle possesses the power to remain precarious, to be an "essential core" which forever resists hardening into ideology.

As a kernel of reality which escapes resolution and thus possesses a destructive power over ideological tendencies, Trilling's "reality" appears, as Slavoj Zizek writes, as the Lacanian "rock upon which every attempt at symbolization stumbles, the hard core which remains the same in all possible worlds." Fortunately for Trilling, such a notion of "reality" can never actually be identifiable as an actual material thing; rather "[a]ll its effectivity lies in the distortions it produces in the symbolic universe of the subject: the traumatic event is ultimately just a fantasy-construct filling out a certain void in a symbolic structure and, as such, the retroactive effect of that structure." The ability of this version of reality to cause trouble—that is, its sublime power to disrupt totalization—is precisely the concept Trilling is looking for. Indeed, the ability of dialectical reality's "sublime" nature to create distortions in the "symbolic universe" allows Trilling a mechanism for disrupting an American cultural "universe" at risk of stasis. As Zizek suggests, the "void" in the symbolic structure created by the Real fulfills the Cold War liberal fantasy of maintaining an essential complexity within U.S. culture.

Ironically, though, what Daniel O'Hara calls Trilling's "romance of reading" requires a forceful limitation of reality's disruptive potential. Ultimately, Trilling must reformulate the sublime effect of culture's dialectic as something assimilable; since he assumes reality to be something containable within literature, its effect must thus be capturable, expressible through writing. Connecting the "trauma" (or "trouble") of remaining faithful to dialectic with Freud's concept of neurosis as the "conflict" facing "genius," Trilling argues that neurosis—while indeed essential—is *not,* in fact, the source of genius at all. Rather, it becomes the material upon which a genius "exercises his powers." What allows the genius to transcend ordinary madness is his ability, through struggle, to gain command over the trauma. In other words, the essential, disruptive nature of traumatic neurosis—its sublime effect—invokes, but must be mastered by, the "power" of genius. This mastery—Trilling even calls it "dominion," citing Charles Lamb—is a process of colonization which becomes a much different kind of "struggle" essential to his thinking.

I have opened the previous two sections with William Burroughs's opinions of both Trilling and Hoover to show, through his anal-izations of these two figures, how their respective models of identity are interconnected. If, in Burroughs's terms, Hoover's ass—an available synecdoche

for the FBI as both the "head" and the "seat" of government—is clinically sodomized by the very fear it systematically locks out and pathologizes (the bomb, subversion, anal penetration), then Trilling's colonization of abjection gets, shall we say, *colon-ized.* As "a shit," Trilling becomes the internalized abject which Hoover's time-bomb artificially supplants: Trilling's narratively contained dialectic represents an already digested, internalized "hard kernel," an abject substance that is the evidence and essence of psychic/cultural production. In other words, the liberal response to anticommunist, homophobic, nuclear-age hysteria does not reverse that systematic rejection of invading substances (difference, the abject, disease, trauma), but, rather, positions "difference" as an essential but consumed, digested, and containable abject. But by calling Lionel Trilling "shit," Burroughs allows me to voice the suspicion (both Burroughs's and my own) that any attempt to contain the "sublime" potency of the abject is destined to fail: it's got to come out sometime.

4.

Of course, it is much easier to look at Burroughs's attack on Trilling as "a shit" simply as a rejection of his criticism. But if my hyperbolic treatment of this attack suggests anything else at all, it is that the Beats did *not* reject Trilling's insistence upon the sublime effect of "reality" as the shock to the system U.S. culture desperately needed in order to transcend conformity, but found him rather hopelessly constipated. Moving "reality" from the University to the city, and from the mind to the body, as the sites of culture's essential conflict, the Beats developed a much more radical idea of what this reality—and the plural possibility it promised—meant.

Thrown into the context of postwar New York City, what this "reality" came to represent was not simply a *deviance* from standard cultural formations but a "discovery" of an American racial, ethnic, and cultural underclass who lived in a manner very much at odds with mainstream culture. That is, the Beats encountered a city loaded with all kinds of demographic "others"—down-and-outs, drug addicts, homosexuals, criminals, political subversives, and other such undesirables against whom the National Security State was protecting itself, as well as the jazz legends, hipsters, and African Americans whom the U.S. refused to recognize and had relegated to the ghetto. Such social "dejects" became the Beats' "secret heroes" whose access to social objection was construed as a privilege which allowed them, it seemed, to contain the dialectic of culture within their minds as something immediate, powerful, and *real.*

For Burroughs and Kerouac, the refusal, or inability, of such figures to be assimilated into mainstream culture volunteered them as models of resistance able to disrupt the stylistic and existential rules of white, middle-class America. For the most part, the Beats' desire for the privileged experience such "secret heroes" supposedly possessed played itself out vicariously as a drive to plug into the lifestyles, imitate the speech and music, and inhabit the marginalized cultural realm of such figures.

This desire to identify sinks deeper, though: the desire for otherness figures in their texts not as identification *with* "secret heroes," but as identification as "other"—a move which even relies on hegemonic stereotypes of who "dejects" were for the very sake of rejecting societal typecasting. Burroughs thematizes his own homosexuality and drug use; Kerouac writes in *On the Road* of "wishing I were a Negro." The question of identification becomes, in their work, that of how to gain access to this paradoxically privileged experience of cultural subversion, how to modulate one's own subject position by means of it. One argument shows this romance of abjection playing itself out sexually, as if "the dialectic" experience were physically accessible. As Catharine Stimpson suggests, this took place as a sexual trafficking of "ethnic" women—or in Burroughs's case, of young boys from Tangiers, Mexico, and Peru. As she writes, "If a chick were black, Chicana, Native American, or Mexican, her grooving and swinging were all the more mythic because she was displaying a 'primitive' force that all those in flight from bourgeois society so wishfully craved." Stimpson's take is particularly useful here in showing sexual co-optation as a mechanism for meeting a deeper desire to rebel against mainstream conventions. Such sexual appropriation points to a conflation of the "abjecting" effect of racial and ethnic otherness with the human object of desire herself, which charts this appropriation as a fantasy-identification by means of which the object—the "chick" or young boy—becomes the repository of what the subject lacks. This implication within Stimpson's criticism suggests an already deep difficulty, yet it does not fully realize the extraordinary degree of appropriation and romantization involved in this scenario.

Norman Mailer, however, does fully realize—and fully perpetuates—the deep implications of the consumption of otherness. In his 1959 essay "The White Negro," Mailer's endorsement of the kind of racial cross-dressing suggested by the title posits "race"—figured as blackness—as a metaphor for the abject. In effect, Mailer's essay responds directly to Lionel Trilling's invocation of the sublime effect of "reality" as the way to subvert conformity; the difference is that Mailer—one of the youngest and most "hip" of the Cold War intellectuals—uses the Beats as his medium and blackness as his master trope. Indeed, in "The White Negro," Catharine Stimpson's explication of the Beats gender politics modulates to a full-blown narrative of miscegenation:

> In such places as Greenwich Village, a ménage-à-trois was completed—the bohemian and the juve-

nile delinquent came face-to-face with the Negro, and the hipster was a fact in American life. If marijuana was the wedding ring, the child was the language of Hip for its argot gave expression to abstract states of feeling which all could share, at least all who were hip. And in this wedding of the white and the black it was the Negro who brought the cultural dowry.

That "the Negro" occupies the feminine position in this marriage typifies Mailer's double configuration of the black male at once as active—the locus of cultural and sexual potency—and as passive, the courted object of desire. Both phallus and lack, the "Negro" appears homosexually available as capital; and yet, what is charging this configuration is not so much homoerotic desire but rather "what the Negro had to offer": the "cultural dowry" offered in this "wedding." This dowry—literally the object of exchange in this eroticized instance of homosexual/cross-racial desire appears as some essence intrinsic to race for which blackness is the synecdoche and whose power is the sublime. Moreover, the "sublime" registers as an inflated, accelerated version of Trilling's sublime effect: it has the power not merely to critique society but to evoke total removal of all social restraint. This makes Mailer's White Negro literally a psychopath whose sublime power—repositioned as "hip" and avant-garde—fulfills the role of the specter plaguing the National Security State: psychopath, sexual deviant, juvenile delinquent, drug user.

Indeed, for Mailer, the "White Negro" represents not merely a radical cross-identification but a whole reconfiguration of a "new white man" as a sort of bomb-era Nietzschean Dionysus, whereby, in Toni Morrison's words, onto the master trope of blackness is transferred "the power of illicit sexuality, chaos, madness, impropriety, anarchy, strangeness, and helpless, hapless desire." The consumption of such romanticized attributes of racial otherness, which Mailer advertises as "Hip" or "Beat," promises not only self-marginalization from the constraints of "square" mainstream culture but, as Eric Lott notes in his tremendous essay "White Like Me," caters also to a "dream of freedom and play" beyond the rational constraints of Cold War society.

As we can see, such an example of binarized "cross-identification," though bound to Trilling's concept of reality, is not "real" at all but relies instead upon deeply mythologized constructions of "otherness" formed directly from the mainstream rhetoric of subjectivity. At the same time, these constructions are made to retain the privileged status of "reality" as well as its apparently sublime power to subvert the "false consciousness" of normalcy. Such disquieting strategies of "self-othering" run into very serious trouble in the mediated narratives of **Naked Lunch** and *The Subterraneans.* In these two texts "the void" of Otherness ceases to function merely as a commodity that exists (in the words of bell books) "solely to suggest new aesthetic and political directions white folks might move in" and becomes a category as inadequate—and indeed as suspect—as that of the white, middle-class, heterosexual male "self" which Burroughs and Kerouac attempt to deconstruct.

5.

> " . . . break the shell of body."
> —William Burroughs, *Naked Lunch*

At the obscenity trial for *Naked Lunch,* Norman Mailer testified (in defense of the novel) that its value springs from its ability to envision a bomb-era "descent into Hell." Calling Burroughs "essentially a religious writer," Mailer attempted to get the book out of trouble by underwriting its "obscenity" as allegory, as something assimilable into the national literary imagination. But in terms of its relationship to nationalized as well as "liberal" enforcements of subjectivity, Burroughs's book was not so easily digested. As Lydenberg argues, *Naked Lunch* adamantly resists such allegorization, stripping down writing to a "naked lunch, a revelation of what is really going on and not an allegorical evasion." Such an argument is especially useful when we understand "naked" to refer to a radical divestment of the moral and rhetorical "dressing" of the National Security State—as well as from Mailer's own dressing up of the novel. However, Lydenberg's further argument, that such nakedness creates "a materiality of absence, a literal mysticism which opens up the possibility of a 'non-body experience,'" disregards the extent to which *Naked Lunch* not only relies on the body to perform its subversive work, but in fact relies on the very "allegories" of self and subversion—the very tropological system—it wishes to destroy.

Continuing the character of William Lee from his two earlier and more personal novels, *Junky* (1953) and *Queer* (1985, written in 1953), Burroughs retains these two titular identifications as the two societal "Sicknesses," as he (not uncritically) calls them, which not only act as primary contexts of identification for Lee himself but also enshroud the very writing process of *Naked Lunch.* As we have seen, the pathologization of drug use and homosexuality took place in the Cold War imagination as patently *psychological* ailments; ailments which, moreover, represented criminal breaches in the public health. Indeed, Allen Ginsberg himself was institutionalized for psychoanalytical treatment of his homosexuality in 1949. Burroughs met the notion of such a "cure" with ample sarcasm and hostility: "By the way what ever became of Als normality program? . . . I thought the nut croakers had fucked him up permanent and reconstructed him in their own dreary image." His words on psychological treatments for junk addiction, though less charming, are just as harsh: "Morphine addiction is a metabolic illness

brought about by the use of morphine. In my opinion psychological treatment is not only useless it is contraindicated." As this suggests, Burroughs vehemently resisted treating such "illnesses" as psychological, insisting instead that they be viewed as primarily physical, metabolic phenomena.

To do otherwise is to impose psychological tyranny; thus, in *Naked Lunch,* there are figures such as Dr. Benway, who, though he strikes away concentration camps and mass arrests in the name of democracy, is "a manipulator and coordinator of symbol systems, an expert on all phases of interrogation, brainwashing and control." Benway's philosophy: "He [the subject] must be made to feel that he deserves *any* treatment he receives because there is something (never specified) horribly wrong with him." As such, the "technological psychiatry" of *Naked Lunch* erupts in a form of violence that, ultimately, ends up being physical anyway.

Just as his anger at "Als normality program" soon shifts in his letters to a rhetorical arrogation of homosexuality-as-disease for his own satirical purposes, in *Naked Lunch,* Burroughs transforms what was considered an emphatically mental disease into a physical "sickness." He retains the National Security trope of homosexuality figured as a physical penetration that would threaten the integrity of the subject with annihilation, breaking up the "shell of body." This effect whereby "the way OUT is the way IN" requires, as Lee Edelman writes, that homosexuality be figured as sodomy, thus producing this disruptive effect by "Confounding the distinction between coming in and going out, between consumption and expulsion, between the public and the private, and thereby transgressing the definitional boundaries that underwrite social identities. . . ." Rather than a "nonbody" experience, sodomy figures as a physical disruption that takes over the body and destabilizes it. Thus suspending the biological and social logic of "integral" identity, Burroughs's sodomy files in the face of hegemony, "washing away the human lines" of body, compulsory heterosexuality, family values, and other nationalized metaphors of identity. *Naked Lunch*'s polymorphous perversity becomes, in fact, the platform of a political party—the Liquefactionists—which embodies decadence in all its senses: "Liquefaction involves protein cleavage and reduction to liquid which is absorbed into someone else's protoplasmic being." Satirizing both Kennan's language and Hoover's, Burroughs's reduction of the human body to liquid and protoplasm offers a hedonistic subversion of the possibility of an "integral" social being.

Similarly, Burroughs retains the pathology of heroin intoxication as a sickness with a similarly profound potential for physical and ontological disruption. Lee describes one such "attack," which results in a condition whereby: ". . . no organ is constant as regards wither function or position . . . sex organs sprout anywhere . . . rectums open, defecate and close

. . . the entire organism changes color and consistency in split-second adjustments. . . ." An extreme example because it describes the first high after a long withdrawal, this passage nevertheless dramatizes junk's radical subversion of the metaphor of bodily integrity, compounding severe disruption with a kind of drastic, eroticized *jouissance* as the effects of the same act. Ironically, the "afflicted" member's attack transforms the symptomology of heroin *withdrawal*—which Burroughs describes in his early work as a transfigurative metabolic craving—into the pathology of intoxication. Feeding and hunger, cellular production and consumption, are conflated in *Naked Lunch* in favor of a different "prescription": a version of intoxication that rewrites the bodily script as a polymorphous entity.

The "act" which induces such alterations occurs, moreover, as a consumption—that is, as the result of an injection of "the junk virus" which produces an alternate version of experience in which "identity" is not evacuated but rather repossessed. The process of "in/toxication"—the internalization of an abject substance; a pollution conflating desire, pleasure, and violence—occurs not only in the intravenous injection of the needle into the skin but by multiple penetrating instruments (needles, droppers, jagged glass, morphine and heroin in any form, including anal suppositories) into multiple orifices. The performance of a self-othering process as both penetration and consumption reveals its subversive nature—it involves, as does sodomy, breaking into and disrupting the "integral integrity" of the body.

At the same time, though, this penetration into the body is not the sole cause of intoxication's altering effects, but rather the material exchange which catalyses this disruption. As Avital Ronell writes, "drugs" are only a material *logos* used only to catalyze, and signify, a chemical reaction that occurs inside the body. The injection only serves to activate a pathology that is already rooted in the human cellular structure: "Drugs are excentric. They are animated by an outside already inside. Endorphins relate internal secretion to the external chemical." As a pathologized form of bodily communication (between "inside" and "outside"), junk—which Burroughs tropes both as a virus and as a form of textuality—is, like sodomy, at once a penetration and an internal awakening. This intoxication presents a form of exchange, an intercourse, which changes the body both from within and from without.

But it is not this easy. Such a "way out" of the Cold War self confronts serious limitations in Burroughs's text. As a kind of consumption, sex results not only in the "absorption of liquid" but in the irreversible commodification of the (homo- or hetero-) sexual partner. Indeed, "going all the way" in *Naked Lunch* means literally killing, using up the sexual "object" in an ultimate ejaculatory moment. Rather than reverting to the homophobic Cold War ideology, imagining death as the end result of desire reveals the complicity of such a commodification of human life with systems of power and control. Desire, always ready to run out of control, threatens to become an automatic mechanism of domination.

The stakes of "junk" consumption, too, run the risk of conflating total excess with the perpetuation of control. As an addictive quantity, heroin is at once eminently consumable and all-consuming—Burroughs portrays it as a commodity of a heirarchized and violently repressive exchange structure. If it does somehow succeed in "evacuating" the self, its seduction of "being other" yields a state of addiction whereby, as Ronell writes, Being itself (*Dasein*) "has become blind, and puts all possibility into the service of the addiction." Under the specter of addiction, junk's sublime promise of alterity, and thus transcendence, threatens always to end up as automatism, as subservience to an ethic of domination. What is at stake in the commodification of otherness, the trafficking of "ways out," is a terrifying conflation of power with powerlessness: addiction produces not merely "sick people who cannot act other than they do," but, more precisely, people who are utterly controlled. *Naked Lunch* dramatizes how the sublime and the desublimating constantly threaten to merge into one another.

In order to realize fully the complexity and danger of this slippage, Burroughs extends the conflict outwards, configuring the transitivity of sublimity and addiction as a place he calls "the City of Interzone." As he writes in letters to Kerouac and Ginsberg in 1955: "The meaning of Interzone, its space-time location is at a point where 3-dimensional fact merges into dreams, and dreams erupt into the real world. In Interzone dreams can kill . . . and solid objects and persons can be as unreal as dreams." An ontologically transitive state as well as a city, Interzone creates a site at which Burroughs's "self-othering" problematic becomes racialized. He explains: as a space of racial and national transitivity "Interzone is very much modeled on Tangier in the old international days: it was an Inter-Zone, it was no country." Resisting total identification either as vision of a real city or as an allegory of a mental state, Interzone is neither an inner space nor an outer space. Rather, it is a between space, a crossroads at which textuality, alterity, and identity collide:

> The blood and substance of many races, Negro, Polynesian, Mountain Mongol, Desert Nomad, Polyglot Near East, Indian—races as yet unconceived and unborn, combinations not yet realized pass through your body. Migrations, incredible journeys through deserts and jungles and mountains (stasis and death in closed mountain valleys where plants grow out of genitals, vast crusta-

ceans hatch inside and break the shell of body)
across the pacific in an outrigger canoe to Easter
Island. The Composite City where all human potentials are spread out in a vast silent market. . . .

. . . Cooking smells of all countries hang over the
City, a haze of opium, hashish, the resinous red
smoke of Yage, smell of the jungle and salt water
and the rotting river and dried excrement and sweat
and genitals. . . .

The City is visited by epidemics of violence, and
the untended dead are eaten by vultures in the
streets. Albinos blink in the sun. Boys sit in trees,
languidly masturbate. People eaten by unknown diseases watch the passerby with evil, knowing eyes.

Much like the junk-virus and Burroughs's repathologization
of homoerotic desire, this "Composite City" promises a market of human potential where identities—figured as the
"blood and substance" of "race"—can be trafficked like opi-
ates. The sublime quality of Trilling's "plural possibility" is
offered in a vast carnal buffet of alterity, wherein "abject"
identities are consumed, sacrificed, and used up. At the same
time, while it would be inaccurate to conflate Interzone with
junk and sodomy as direct allegories of each other, they each
furiously insist that the consumption of otherness is not a
simple capitalist exchange; rather it is a fantasy whose transitivity engenders confusion, violent conflict, and illness.

Burroughs suspends moral judgment of the commodification
of otherness as a "starting point for white self-criticism" by
representing racial cross-identification as an addiction: he
terms it in the language of need, a consuming need that *requires* identification—"wouldn't you?" he asks in the introduction. "Yes, you would," is the imposed, unspoken,
response, his one absolute. For Burroughs, the state of being addicted to cross-identification is also a sickness, a virus, indicating its violence not only to the subjective carrier,
but to those he comes in contact with, a violence at every
intersection.

The injection/intersection point does not generate space of
freedom and play immune to the violence of repressive cultural formations or of rebellions against them. The potentially deadly dream-state is, at best, a space of *potential,*
fantasized play, the space of distant masturbation, of spectacle rather than true intercourse. This interzone, neither fully
formed nor immaterial, is a crossroads whereby the attractions, the addictions, of either side of the binary are
traffickable as commodities—indeed, the *perfect* commodities, since they require no advertising in order to be ferreted
out by desperate consumers—but only at the price of deferral, violence, and the endless craving of metabolic addiction.

6.

> "I would have preferred the happy man to the un-
> happy poems he's left us."
>
> —Jack Kerouac, *The Subterraneans*

In Kerouac's more intimate and sentimental novel, *The
Subterraneans,* Interzone's potentially deadly dream-state of
endless deferral becomes instead an emotional crossroads
which compounds loss, paranoia, obsession, and the lingering emotions of a relationship gone hopelessly awry. This
traumatic juncture haunts the entire novel, since *The
Subterraneans* consistently wrestles with failure and
breakup; indeed, as a narrative of the broken love affair between Leo Percepied and Mardou Fox, a part-Cherokee,
part-African American woman ten years his junior, the novel
is less about a romance than about its failure. And as a bro-
ken-up book itself, it becomes increasingly aware of the
breakdown of "romance" as a cultural and literary apparatus, the failure of the romance of abjection.

The Subterraneans, then, seems less directly concerned with
consuming "otherness" for the sake of self-evacuation than
with managing the interpersonal and narrative consequences
of such a Romance of dissent. As if realizing the inadequa-
cies of a Maileresque project—a project which includes several of Kerouac's earlier novels—*The Subterraneans*
struggles to configure the relationship between Percepied and
Fox in a way that doesn't merely involve "sucking her dry"
of her othering power. Likewise, the "self" Kerouac wishes
to evacuate here isn't merely the Maileresque "white man
disillusioned" of *On the Road,* fleeing from the constraints
of Cold War expectations. Rather, the trap of "self" in *The
Subterraneans* expands beyond these constraints to include
the sexually appropriative "White Negro" rebellion against
them as well. Such reflexivity confounds the efficiency of
the latter's romance of the racial sublime and, simultaneously, lodges their relationship at a perpetual scene of
anxiety.

Ineffably confused as to what to do with his feelings of desire and sexuality towards Mardou other than being "crudely
malely sexual," Percepied interrogates his own motives for
attraction: is his love for Mardou merely a romance of the
other's abject power? This consternation and ambiguity toward the sources of his own desire plays itself out repeatedly in scenes of paradox and conflict wherein Percepied
seems unable to come to grips with the possibility of racial
and gender difference, whether to embrace it or to eradicate
it. First making, then abnegating, horrified confessions of
"male self-contained doubts" about Mardou and "doubts
about her race," Percepied asks himself if the reason for his
attraction to her is, conversely, *because* of her race, because
of her exotic otherness.

This anxiety in the face of the inevitable specter of difference continues to manifest itself throughout the novel; even in one of the most secure moments of their relationship, it arises as a paranoid attempt to deny their racial difference altogether. Kerouac tells of "my fear of communicating WHITE images to her in our telepathies for fear she'll be (in her fun) reminded of our racial difference, at that time making me feel guilty." This guilt over racial difference, it seems, represents less Percepied's reluctance to dissolve a fantasy identification with blackness than it does his compulsion to perform for Mardou's love. Unlike Burroughs, who deploys "race" to connote difference, Kerouac struggles with an inability to conceptualize race as anything *but* difference, in a situation—the intimacies of telepathy and love—where the two people are presumably bound by similarity.

However, by casting Mardou as at risk of being "reminded" of difference, when it is Percepied himself who seems unable to forget it, the passage suggests that something further is in play. What seems to be Percepied's own fear of judgment retroactively casts Mardou as his judge, thus re-igniting the problem of agency and appropriation that the novel otherwise tries to leave behind: the question is not only about who is judging whom, but about who is narrating whom. This crisis in textual power arises as an immediate concern over how to "tell" Mardou: "But now let me tell Mardou herself (difficult to make a real confession and show what happened when you're such an egomaniac all you can do is take off on big paragraphs about minor details about yourself and the big soul details about others go sitting and waiting)." Implicit in this struggle to sort out who should or should not be narrated lurks a deceptively forceful clash of complex subjectivities. Though he berates his own self-absorption, the very process of writing out an evacuation of this selfishness still amounts, narratively, to self-absorption. Moreover, lingering within this admonishment of his own selfishness is an indicative, albeit tender-hearted, trace of the romance of abjection as the "way out." As he comes to grips with the differences between representation and forms of narrative domination, Kerouac seems to trip over his own internalized romances in an effort to avoid them—as with *Naked Lunch,* the attempt to evacuate a bankrupt subject-position becomes a further bind.

This kind of conflict occurs with greater severity once Percepied's initial attempts to deny difference fail, and he resorts to imposing textual control over the language which structures his relationship with Mardou. The explosion of contradictory exchanges resulting from this struggle with control and failure occurs not only within Kerouac's narrative discourse, but also at the intersections of this voice and Mardou's "own" words. The clash is twofold: it involves both Percepied's persistent drive to fashion his relationship into a mythological binary, as well as the secondary clash of subjectivities in which Mardou rejects this essentializing and deeply normative structuration. The normative value of such myths reverberates throughout the whole series of imposed configurations in which Percepied and Mardou are cast, respectively, as "jazz poet" and "child of bop," phallus and womb, tower and well, and Adam and Eve—constructions whose motives swing back and forth between tenderness and panic, between desire and fear. Again, Percepied is critically aware of the artificial nature of such "big abstract constructions" and attributes his tendency as a writer to "erect" these constructions as "the stupid neurotic nervousness of the phallic type, forever conscious of his phallus, his tower, of women as wells." Yet these images, compounded by the gender-, race- and ethnicity-related power differential implicit in their polarity, recur throughout the novel as the conceptual apparatus for dealing with the difference that Kerouac cannot seem to avoid.

The result is a changing series of constructions all reiterating the same theme. Relegated to "womb" and "well," Mardou is allegorized as an orifice whose primitive and generative nature is corroborated by her mythologization as Eve, and made doubly disturbing by its racial and ethnic overtones of darkness and indigenousness. At the same time, this synecdochal orifice is invested with the abject power of the sublime: Mardou becomes the object upon whom Percepied projects not only the vitality and darkness of "bop" but a deep fear of being consumed and used up. At once beautiful and fearful, Mardou-as-womb suggests the power both to rebirth and to destroy. Like Burroughs's orifice, where identity becomes amorphous and volatile, Kerouac's neurotic figuration of Mardou as womb and as well hovers between the primordinacy of birth and the destructiveness of a *vagina dentata*. This representation figures most paranoically in a passage where, borrowing roles from Tennessee Williams's "Desire and the Black Masseur," Mardou becomes "the big buck nigger Turkish bath attendant, and I the little fag who's broken to bits in the love affair and carried to the bay in a burlap bag, there to be distributed piece by piece and broken bone by bone to the fish." Percepied's fear of being used up by Mardou—of being chewed up and devoured by the *vagina dentata*—represents the flip side of the romance of blackness which seems most actively at work in Kerouac's acceptance of its promise of rebirth and self-evacuation in the first place. Furthermore, the terminologies at work in this example from Williams are charged with particular Cold War resonances: as we saw earlier, the "fag" dominated by a "phallic" maternal, or pre-oedipal, presence (Mardou-as-womb) was a favored iteration both of psychoanalysis in general, and of Hoover-era "experts" in particular; furthermore, "nigger" carries in this context an indelible brand of racism which simultaneously bows its head to the power-play at work in Williams's story. That Kerouac *would* position Percepied and Mardou in this manner not only suggests a deep anxiety over his own sexuality and desire, but intensifies the volatile ambiguity with which their relationship is represented.

Whether neurotic, well-intended, or self-pitying, such binary constructions are each painfully invalidated, either by the self-conscious paranoia and hyperbolic hatefulness of Percepied's language or by Mardou's "own" resistance to them. In another—though presumably tender—instance, Percepied tells Mardou: "'because as part Negro somehow you are the first, the essential woman, and therefore the most, most originally most fully affectionate and maternal'—there now is the chagrin too, some lost American addition and mood with it—'Eden's in Africa,' I'd added one time—." In response to which Mardou later adds, in a parenthetical aside: "'Look man,' she'd said only a week before when I'd suddenly started talking about Adam and Eve and referred to her as Eve, the woman who by her beauty is able to make the man do anything, 'don't call me Eve.'" Mardou's blunt censure of this romanticized notion is, to some extent, echoed by the narration's own self-destructive reflexivity. Indeed, Percepied seems aware that his association is a loaded one; for in calling Mardou "Eve" he knows he is engendering it with "some lost American addition and mood," by means of which Mardou is transmuted from lover to allegory. Mardou's aspersion is, furthermore, surrounded by the narrator's own reasons for the objectionability of the myth. He revises the "story" of Adam and Eve to fit this awareness: in the second passage what is of concern is not Eve's "original" nature but, again, her "sublime" power to manipulate and use up Adam. The breakdown of this myth is compound: effected most explicitly by Mardou, its artifices are also disclosed by Percepied's self-reflexive narration.

The disintegration of such essentialist myths in which women are symbolized as wells—or, as Mardou later argues, as prizes—do not only occur within this double context of dialogic confrontation, but also in the inability of the relationship to remain a private binary. Again dramatizing the possibility that their relationship may not just be about love but about Percepied's desire for self-evacuation, the novel's binarisms tend to evolve into threesomes. Indeed, throughout the text their relationship is framed as a shifting love-triangle, whereby Percepied's relationship with Mardou exists only in oppositional exchange with a third party.

Such imaginary triadic constructions—and Kerouac, each time, struggles in his indirect discourse with the suspicion that they are constructions—engender a homosocial rivalry between Percepied and a shifting series of male characters, even by the rumor and possibility of Percepied's own homosexuality. Most significantly, though, it is a young poet, Yuri Gligoric, who becomes Percepied's final obsession and thus the third-party rival whom he continually fantasizes to

be sleeping with Mardou. The novel ends with a contemplation of this triadic obsession:

> . . . I curled her on my lap, and she talked about the war between men—"They have a war, to them a woman is a prize. . . ."

> "Yeah," I say, sad, "but I should have paid more attention to the old junkey nevertheless, who said there's a lover on every corner—they're all the same, boy, don't get hung-up on one."

> "It isn't true, it isn't true, that's just what Yuri wants is for you to go down to Dante's now and the two of you'll laugh and talk me over and agree that women are good lays and there are a lot of them.— I think you're like me—you want one love—like, men have the essence in the woman, there's an essence" ("Yes," I thought, "there's an essence and that is your womb") "and the man has it in his hand, but rushes off to build big constructions." (I'd just read her the first few pages of *Finnegan's Wake* and explained them and where Finnegan is always putting up "buildung supra buildung supra buildung" on the banks of the Liffey—dung!)

> . . . And I go home having lost her love.

> And write this book.

Mardou's rejection of being trafficked as bounty in the war between men finally shuts down the long series of romances which have appropriated her as symbolic property. Appealing to essentialism as a version of reality preferable to Percepied's "big constructions," Mardou attempts to focus Percepied's attention back on their relationship and to dislodge it from the coercive identifications his narrative attempts to impose.

Though it concludes with Mardou's resistance to commodification as a "prize," this very resistance raises yet a further question: does "this book" itself become another construction, another monument of "the war between [white] men," another figuration of Mardou as sublime object? Mardou's suspicion seems to introduce the question of how much her influence—her own voice and the way she resists symbolization throughout the text—is itself a textual consumption of her "sublime" ability to disrupt it. Does Kerouac use her merely in order to break up the unity of his prose and "make trouble" for his sense of identity as a nonconformist writer of "bop prosody"? Even if, as I suggested earlier, Mardou figures as an "ideal ego" and not as a mere object of consumption, she still serves narratively as the "object" to his "subject," and her "voice" could seem to serve as the *petit objet a* of identification which Kerouac ultimately covets, the "sublime object" which breaks up totality and escapes symbolization. In a refrain of his intimations of rebirth through Mardou's sublime womb, Kerouac appears to ponder this latter possibility when he cites Joyce's revision of the *Bildungsroman* of personal development as "buildung supra buildung." In this final image, juxtaposing textuality, construction, and dung, he questions the tractability of any such project of containment and control: is he just another Trilling, using Mardou to access a textual sublime; is he, too, in Burroughs's words, merely "a shit"?

Kerouac's project diverges significantly from Trilling's, though. *The Subterraneans* is charged with a traumatic awareness of its own failure, acting out and disinheriting a vast array of identity strategies, myths, and structures whose coerciveness and propensity for damage become glaringly apparent. And unlike Trilling's idea of the "conflicted" artist who contains the dialectical essence of culture in his mind, Kerouac/Percepied cannot master that conflict, either in his head or in his prose: Percepied's relationship with Mardou disintegrates alongside the mythologies used to frame it.

Though it dramatizes Kerouac's discovery of the emotional violence and breakup forever imminent in imposed configurations of identity, the "failed romance" of *The Subterraneans* engenders a self-destructive poetics that does *not,* however, court the righteous possibility of "self-deconstruction" by castrating its own phallic tower of typological constructions. Gerald Nicosia writes that Kerouac somehow turns loss into gain through art, that "this book" feeds upon the sadness within it and assimilates the tragic outcome as an element of the master-narrative the book itself represents. However, the narrative control over events Nicosia implies is only ever lost, never gained: Kerouac is neither completely able to escape his own entangled illusions nor to identify with Mardou's "language of bop." I am tempted, for sentimental reasons, to say that there lies in the structural dynamics of *The Subterraneans* an internalization of Mardou's subjective influence—that ultimately, the novel works as a *true* romance in a more spiritual sense by showing Kerouac to "really understand" Mardou's take on their relationship. Any such self-righteousness, though, is inevitably disqualified; the damage is done. *The Subterraneans,* like *Naked Lunch,* represents a crisis, a trafficking of the interzone between the traumatic inadequacy of identity impositions and the harsh narrative and emotional violence that comes in realizing this inadequacy.

The possibility that this latter notion of a "textual sublime"—which Kerouac broaches in order to transcend the constraints he seems unable to escape otherwise—would also play itself out as a commodification of otherness seems to have been lurking all along. Like Burroughs, who constructs a sublime, orifice-like textual space as an alternative to the limitations of Cold War existence, Kerouac attempts to co-opt Mardou's voice in order to sever—or at least to mediate—his ambivalent position "within" and "without" the dominant U.S. culture. Such an ambivalence, suggested in *On the Road* by Kerouac's use of the "Interstate" to allow him to leave and return home, cannot fully evolve into a space free of cultural determination without the disruption the sublime entails. As we've seen, though, in both Kerouac's and Burroughs's cases this very promise lands them in a further bind, a place no longer "on the road" or a utopian "outside," but at a crossroads.

And despite Trilling's claims to the contrary, such a crossroads does not proffer transcendence. Burroughs and Kerouac do indeed "make trouble" for dominant Cold War constructions of "self"—that is, their attempts to forge a notion of identity, or at least subjectivity, as a volatile site of contested meanings were indeed disruptive—but the effectiveness of "trouble" must also take into account whom one makes trouble *for.* The "sublime" performs useful work in Burroughs's and Kerouac's fiction insofar as its power to disrupt is used to keep meanings and identities in a state of flux and contestation—that is, when it works toward the acceptance and generation of difference. However, implicit in locating the sublime as an inherent property of another person's being is a power-play which brings this very work of contestation and flux to a crashing halt. As Timothy Engström writes, "the subversive thrill of undermining identities with the help of the sublime may be itself the repetition—by inversion—of a rather classical philosophical project: to establish identities." The risk of such an inversion, in the case of *Naked Lunch* and *The Subterraneans,* is of accidentally performing the containment work of the Cold War.

And yet, I have argued that Burroughs and Kerouac both become painfully aware of this inversion, aware that, as Lee Edelman writes, "producing different notions of subjectivity is not the same thing as occupying a different position as a subject." In order to read their fiction outside of the repressive forces of consumption and containment that lurk within it, we must read the use of the sublime in a way that foregrounds its tendency to be the stumbling point of representation, a tendency which best expresses frustration rather than mastery or control. The rhetorical deployment of sublimity we've witnessed in *Naked Lunch* and *The Subterraneans* is most useful in its capacity to mediate relationships which, as Engström argues, "reside for some time in an awkward orbit around the normalcy of any given narrative. . . ." As something always inassimilable into the narrative of mainstream culture, the sublime can be liberating if activated as a way of mediating the unknown and generating a familiarity with difference. Burroughs's and Kerouac's "interzones," however, gain their volatility and propensity for violence at the moment when they try to "score"—and become addicted to—the myth of someone else's intransigence, and thus refuse to accept its conceptual value as something that cannot be fully abstracted as a commodified racial, ethnic, or gendered attribute. Such a transaction results in an inability to vacate the confines of the subject position with which they are most critically at odds, an inability which leaves indelible traces of an inherited rhetorical agenda of coercion and containment. Ill at ease with either situation, and thus neither ever truly "in" nor ever truly "out," Kerouac and Burroughs find themselves instead—to use the Cold War idiom—painfully "out in the cold."

REVIEWS OF BURROUGHS'S RECENT WORKS

James Campbell (review date 15 October 1993)

SOURCE: "The Bare Facts," in *Times Literary Supplement,* October 15, 1993, p. 22.

[*In the following review of the first volume of* The Letters of William S. Burroughs, *Campbell gleans the "facts" of Burroughs's early writing career from his correspondence, observing its relation to specific works and other Beat writers.*]

There is no such thing as a Naked Lunch. In keeping with its conception as a fluid event rather than a frozen artefact ("the usual novel has happened", the author wrote. "This novel *is happening*"), William Burroughs's purgative, funny, wholly original book has continued to exhibit new forms over the years. As successive editions have followed the Paris one of 1959, passages which once appeared as footnotes have been integrated into the text or else excluded from it; new prefaces and appendices have been grafted on to the narrative, each becoming in the process an organic part. Even the title eludes definition, the American publishers offering plain old *Naked Lunch,* while the British, following the Paris original, garnish it with an article. Now, from this first volume of Burroughs's correspondence [*The Letters of William S. Burroughs*], a different shape emerges: *Naked Lunch* is actually a letter to Allen Ginsberg.

In the late 1940s, Ginsberg, Jack Kerouac and their friends would not have seemed unlike any other group of white, New York low-lifes, except that they read books and aspired to write them, and also that their assaults on the sacred cow of respectability led them to more than usually unrespectable behavior. Ginsberg staggered from mental hospital to law court (petty theft) as he fought with the unwelcome fact of his homosexuality. Neal Cassady, the original for Dean Moriarty in Kerouac's *On the Road,* was a larger-than-life,

irresponsible sponger, with an appetite for women (and occasionally for Ginsberg). Lucien Carr was in prison, having killed a man who made sexual advances towards him. (The case later inspired James Baldwin to write *Giovanni's Room.*) Gregory Corso had also spent time in prison, for lesser offenses. Kerouac, the legendary lonesome traveller, was actually cripplingly dependent on his mother, and later on drink.

Burroughs was different: older than the rest by about a decade, he was Harvard educated and heir to a fortune (his grandfather invented the Burroughs Adding Machine). He was not seduced by the accessories of hip: the dress, the jazz, the argot; in letters written from New Orleans and Mexico in the early part of this fascinating book, he comes across more as a gun-toting, lawless frontiersman than an imitator of Brando and black cool. "Dear Jack," he writes from Mexico City on January 1, 1950, "Every time I receive a communication from the U.S. I congratulate myself on being here. Nigra laws eh? That really is the pay off."

Despite the grey suit and the somber countenance ("his whole person", he wrote of himself, "seemed at first glance completely anonymous"), Burroughs was even more given to extremes of behavior than the others. Variations on the phrase "I mean business" pop up regularly throughout these letters. It might refer to anything, from cutting off a finger-joint to impress a lover, as he did in the early 1940s, to cutting up his pages to usurp the forces of "thought-control" lurking in conventional grammar, a campaign we find him embarking on as this book ends. In 1952, he wrote to Ginsberg that he was not really meant to be a writer. "I am essentially active and will always seek solution in activity."

This is strictly true, even though the man of action was to spend much of the remainder of the decade, in his own description, staring at the end of his shoe. If his activity was destined to be in the literary arena, then he wanted, so he told Ginsberg (to whom the vast majority of these letters are addressed), to practice a form of writing that had "the urgency of bullfighting". In so far as it makes sense at all to say so, in *Naked Lunch* he succeeded.

Stranded in Tangier during the second half of the 1950s, addicted to heroin, lovesick for Ginsberg with whom he had been briefly partnered in New York (the pair were not to meet for six years), gorging himself on paid-for sex with Spanish boys, Burroughs began to record his impressions of the city in a series of bulletins to the poet. Tangier was then an "international zone", colonized by eight foreign powers, and technically not part of Morocco. Eager and admiring but also critically objective, Ginsberg was felt to be the perfect "receptor" for what Burroughs called his "routines": short, phantasmagorical prose pieces, usually involving mutations of people and events seen or experienced in Tangier. Dr

Benway, A.J., The Lobotomy Kid, and other weird beings from *Naked Lunch,* all have real-life originals. Over time, a book began to emerge from the impressionistic mass, to which Burroughs gave various titles: "Interzone", "Ignorant Armies", etc. (By a curious coincidence, the latter was also an early title for Baldwin's novel based on the Lucien Carr case. Was "Dover Beach" the hip poem of the 1950s?)

Whenever Burroughs tried to turn his hand to other types of writing—for a magazine, for instance, in the hope of earning some money—he only had to begin typing to find he was writing another routine. In December 1954, he told Ginsberg that he had

> sat down seriously to write a best-seller Book of the Month Club job on Tanger [*sic*]. So here is what comes out in the first sentence:
>
> "The only native in Interzone who is neither queer nor available is Andrew Keif's chauffeur, which is not an affectation on Keif's part but a useful pretext to break off relations with anyone he doesn't want to see: 'You made a pass at Aracknid last night. I can't have you in the house again.' . . ."

Vile grotesquerie ensues, and the passage was later refined and used to form the opening of the "interzone" section of *Naked Lunch.* (In a PS, Burroughs adds: "Andrew Keif is Paul Bowles, of course.")

The early letters mainly concern the composition and publication of *Junkie,* his first novel. Burroughs began writing seriously in 1950, when in his late thirties, possibly in an effort to displace one type of occupation—the all-absorbing inaction of the drug-addict—by another. A more or less straightforward account of the drug-addict's life in New York, *Junkie* (later *Junky*) was published in 1953 under the pseudonym William Lee—the name Burroughs later used to represent himself in his own fiction. The novel was presented as a "confessions of . . ." sort of book by its nervous publishers, who packaged it in one volume with the memoirs of a narcotics agent. A first attempt, it falls on to the page in a style fully formed. The original intention was to follow it with *Queer,* a companion-piece on the theme of homosexual obsession. But after the completion of *Junkie,* Burroughs's ideas about writing changed. It is interesting to learn that as early as 1952 he was persuaded of his need for medium-as-message innovation. "A medium suitable for me does not yet exist, unless I invent it", he told Ginsberg in May of that year. Three years later, fully committed to his new style, he wrote: "It's almost like automatic writing produced by a hostile, independent entity who is saying in effect, 'I will write what I please' . . . only the most extreme material is available to me."

The hostile entity drew him towards horrors greater than what was to become *Naked Lunch.* In 1951, in a now notorious incident, Burroughs killed his wife Joan while aiming to shoot a champagne glass off her head in a game of "William Tell". "The idea of shooting a glass off her head had never *entered my mind,* consciously, until, out of the blue so far as I can recall—I was very drunk, of course—I said 'It's about time for our William Tell act. . . . Put a glass on your head, Joan.' Nothing led up to the idea." It was an accident all right, but four years later Burroughs remained haunted by murmuring voices from his subconscious. "I am quite a good shot and accustomed to handle guns. I aimed *carefully at a distance of 6 feet for the very top of the glass."*

That there might be a connection between this incident and the violent reconstruction of his consciousness which Burroughs afterwards began to pursue in literary strategies—obscene fantasy, cut-up or whatever—is touched on in the letters. It was made explicit, though, in the introduction to *Queer,* which was finally published in 1985:

> I am forced to the appalling conclusion that I would never have become a writer but for Joan's death, and to the realization of the extent to which this event has motivated and formulated my writing. I live with the constant threat of possession, and a constant need to escape from possession, from Control. So the death of Joan brought me into contact with the invader, the Ugly Spirit, and maneuvred me into a lifelong struggle, in which I have no choice but to write my way out.

In a letter to Ginsberg published here, he writes: "I am trying *to create something that will have a life of its own, that can put me in a real danger, a danger which I willingly take on myself."* Burroughs begins to sound increasingly like some demonic performance artist, for whom each act—wilful drug addiction, a jungle expedition to meet Indian tribes, a game of William Tell, and finally writing itself—involves a struggle with the Ugly Spirit, which will bring him face to face with death, but also offers the possibility of total release.

At the same time, we see him working methodically on his prose, sometimes writing more than one draft of a letter, and quite aware of the nature of the book emanating from his transmissions. The picture often drawn by chroniclers of the Beat Generation, of Burroughs friendless and penniless in Tangier, floating on a raft of junk amid the scattered pages of *Naked Lunch,* without a clue as to how to put them together, should gain revision from the publication of these letters. When he wrote to Ginsberg, "Read in any order. It makes no difference", it was not lack of interest but the affirmation of a surrealist aesthetic of chance: "The selection chapters form a sort of mosaic, with the cryptic significance of juxtaposition, like objects abandoned in a hotel drawer, a form of still life" (October 21, 1955). Two years later, he wrote: "I am beginning to see now where I have been going all along. It's beginning to look like a modern Inferno." The Inferno, he might have added, "c'est moi".

Here and there, some harsh light is cast on the romance of the Beats. For all his way-out behavior, Burroughs often exhibits a sympathetic conventionality. At the beginning of 1949, he wrote in a tone of annoyance to Ginsberg of a journey being planned by Cassady and Kerouac:

> Neal is, of course, the very soul of this voyage into pure, abstract, meaningless motion. He is The Mover, compulsive, dedicated, ready to sacrifice family, friends, even his very car itself to the necessity of moving from one place to another. Wife and child may starve, friends exist only to exploit for gas money. . . . Neal must move.

So much for *On the Road.* Two years later, he is no more tolerant:

> I can not understand Neal's passion for travel—especially under the disagreeable conditions you run into in the States. What does he do to eat?

As for Kerouac, "To be blunt, I have never had a more inconsiderate and selfish guest under my roof." By the end of the decade, Kerouac's crude opinions and dependency on his mother had marginalized him from Burroughs's field of vision: "If he is content to be treated like a child and let his mother open his mail and tell him who to see and correspond with, he is a lost cause."

Burroughs's expensive drug habit was financed by a private income, regulated by his parents, who, exasperated though they were, subsidized his repeated attempts to find a "cure". They were also, of course, subsidizing his addiction, and the composition of *Naked Lunch.* It's interesting to discover how often, and from what an early stage, Burroughs tried to kick the habit. The second letter in the volume (September 1, 1946) contains the sentence, "I have given up junk entirely and don't miss it at all." The refrain is then repeated throughout, sometimes backed up by one of the medical theories or systems for which he had great fondness. Like any quack, he was never discouraged by their exposure. He was convinced he had discovered cures for schizophrenia and cancer, involving narcotics and the withdrawal process, and circulated them to medical practitioners. In 1956, he was introduced to Dr. John Yerbury Dent of London, who succeeded in freeing him from his addiction by means of apomorphine treatment, though not at the first attempt.

When this volume comes to a close, Burroughs is in Paris, working out new ways of assaulting language, in this case actually involving sharp implements. With the aid of Brion Gysin, whom he had met in Tangier and who was starting to replace Ginsberg as his number one receptor, Burroughs developed the cut-up technique, which he used in his next three books, **The Soft Machine, The Ticket that Exploded,** and **Nova Express.** The cut-ups, which were to occupy him for the next decade, and for which he was to make grand psychic claims, mostly read like a waste of time now in a writer who could show language such care and consideration. But Burroughs is one of those artists whom the reader has to swallow whole, lean, fat and offal together in a mad new recipe, or probably not at all. What this collection displays, above all, is the integrity of his experimentation; it's plain, as he reels off the routines, that he has faint hope of seeing the results in print. When Ginsberg suggested putting the material into a shape which would give it linear continuity, Burroughs replied that he regarded "any attempt at chronological arrangement extremely ill-advised". This was in September 1957, after his manuscript had been rejected by the Olympia Press, which Burroughs had held as his only hope. (They took it at second submission.)

To read these letters is to be, in a Burroughsian phrase, in possession of the facts. It is like reading Burroughs in the original, of which the published texts seem like translations. Oliver Harris's editing is in general exemplary, though he reproduces the error—first propagated by Maurice Girodias, Burroughs's roguish publisher—that Graham Greene mounted his defence of *Lolita* in 1956 in the *TLS* (it was in the *Sunday Times*). I look forward to a second instalment, which will tell the story of the 1960s in Burroughs's own words—published complete with a pair of scissors.

Robert Cohen (review date 15 January 1995)

SOURCE: "Dispatches from the Interzone," in *The New York Times Book Review,* January 15, 1995, pp. 9, 11.

[*In the following review, Cohen detects an "autumnal, elegiac" tone in the imagery of* My Education.]

William S. Burroughs is now 80. Is this a shock? Certainly his skeletal, impassive, thin-lipped mask of a face—sort of a cerebralized Buster Keaton—has always looked old. At the same time Mr. Burroughs's iconic stature among the young, for whom he is arguably the most influential American prose writer of the last 40 years, remains undiminished. The heavy metal traces of his singular vocabulary can be seen glowing darkly at the edges of our cultural landscape: In Thomas Pynchon, Hunter S. Thompson, J. G. Ballard, Philip K. Dick and countless other writers; in avant-garde music, painting and film; and in all the successive new waves of Beats, hippies and punks (what Newt Gingrich—a Burroughsian construct if ever there was one—likes to call the counterculture) who have made withdrawals from his well-endowed image bank.

And yet at the end of the day, after the lights have gone off and the noisy admirers have departed, there is simply what there was in the beginning: a man alone at his desk, spinning dreams into words and words into dreams. "Survival is the name of the game." Mr. Burroughs writes in *My Education: A Book of Dreams.* "It's all a film run backward."

Readers of Mr. Burroughs's previous novel, *The Western Lands* (1987), may recall a certain last-testament quality in the final passage—the old writer signing off, perhaps for good, with a line appropriated from another literary St. Louisan: "Hurry up, please. It's time."

Yet each new book in the Burroughs *oeuvre* overlaps with the last. His ongoing project—a kind of multidimensional map of his own mythology—refuses to complete itself. How can it, you find yourself wondering, while he's still alive? And yet small changes can be registered. Dream fragments and direct autobiography, present in the novels since the beginning, have been infiltrating Mr. Burroughs's late work more and more; now they appear to have won the day. These pages reveal how thin the membrane is that separates the writer's fictional conceits from the life he has lived, asleep and awake (we can see the flow in both directions) and how this flow is itself perhaps Mr. Burroughs's real subject. The loose, seemingly casual form of a dream journal is ideal for such purposes; here he can eschew fictional routines altogether, offering instead a whirlwind valedictory tour—*hurry up, please*—of his own unconscious.

For those who have traveled this territory before, certain features are reliably prominent. Dreams, guns, sea disasters, fringe science, conspiratorial struggles for control—the familiar obsessions are still around. One of this book's more touching suggestions is that *everything* is still around: the things we've seen, the places we've lived, the lovers we've had, the friends we've lost, the books we've written. All exist in a kind of eternal Interzone, in which the line between the dead and the living is as indistinguishable as that between dream and waking, autobiography and fiction, past and present. "There is no line between the dream world and the actual world," Mr. Burroughs has said. "Of course if you get to the point where you find it difficult to cross the road then you should see a doctor."

This brand of satiric duality—Kafka on the one hand, W. C. Fields on the other—is a Burroughs trademark, a shrewd small-town sheriff's approach to abstraction, one that allows him to observe without judgment or interpretation. "The danger," he writes, "is to walk through life without seeing anything."

Indeed, one of the pleasures of this book, as the title suggests, is its depiction of an artist's endless self-education, the various processes—"cut-ups," most famously, in which fragments of text from wildly disparate sources are juxtaposed on a single page—by which Mr. Burroughs has trained his perceptions to yield fresh and often startling observations. As far back as 1959, with *Naked Lunch,* he claimed to be "a recording instrument . . . not an entertainer." In truth, he is both. His gaze is dry, laconic, corrosive, at once playfully inventive and coolly subversive: there has always been something of the carny in him, and more than a little Tod Browning—as in this droll digression, apropos of nothing: "And here, you young lions, is a recipe for making botulism, used with conspicuous success by Pancho Villa against the Federal troops in Mexico." Or: "It always makes me nervous to see a cat on a ledge. . . . Suppose a bird flew by?"

It must be said that this method of inclusive neutrality has its cost. There is nothing to be found here, for example in the way of story. "Plot," "character development," "continuity," "context," "exposition"—none of what we like to think of as the novel's featured players so much as put in a cameo appearance. Readers unfamiliar with Mr. Burroughs's work and life will find a maze of involuted references that go unexplained, and will quickly resort to skimming.

But even skimming has its rewards—particularly in a mulligan stew like this, studded with dreams, memories, apocalyptic reflections, digs at old friends and critics, and meditations on art and science. "The fragile lifeboat between this and that," Mr. Burroughs writes, rather tenderly, of his own craft. "Your words are the sails." Some entries are as brief and instructive as Zen koans: "The answer to any question will be revealed when you stop asking questions and wipe from your mind the concept of question." Some are vivid but glancing: "I have what I suspect to be a live cockroach stuck in my ear." And some remain, for this reader anyway, stubbornly opaque, the unconscious flexing its muscles in an empty gym.

"For years I wondered why dreams are so often so dull when related," Mr. Burroughs tells us early on, anticipating such a problem. "*No context* . . . like a stuffed animal on the floor of a bank."

Fair warning some of the dreams that follow are dull. A considerable number concern "the unsuccessful attempt to obtain breakfast or any other kind of food for that matter, except very occasionally some utterly unpalatable dish." This unsatiated quest becomes a kind of running joke—a portrait of the hunger artist, that rudely ignored customer at life's bad restaurant—until, like so much else in this slippery and provocative little book, it becomes by the end oddly moving. "An old man's hunger," Mr. Burroughs writes, with no trace of his usual irony, "is precious."

Though his book has more than its share of lively, often hilarious bits, the prevailing tone is autumnal, elegiac. This is truly a place of dead roads. Many of the settings—Kansas (where Mr. Burroughs now lives), Tangier, Paris, New York, St. Louis—have a vacant, Edward Hopperish feel, ghost towns full of "empty houses, leaves blowing and drifting like shreds of time." Even the occasional bout of dreamed sex is a halfhearted, somewhat vestigial affair ("We sort of make it," runs a typical entry); it fails to console. Nothing offered here is free of doubt or self-subversion.

At its heart, *My Education* is an intensely personal book, so much so that it leaves the usual forms of personality behind. It depicts a life seen almost from beyond itself, through a dense field of shifting, associational patterns, but behind it there is a naked weight of loss and regret. Since accidentally shooting his wife in 1951 in a notorious drunken game of William Tell, Mr. Burroughs has been struggling with what he calls "the Other Half Boy," his own "Ugly Spirit." The deeper the plunge into the unconscious, the larger its shadows. Thus the book as it unfolds takes on a painful gravity. Mr. Burroughs writes with uncharacteristic directness about the past, the "cold hate" he showed his father, his detachment in the face of his mother's death. The final image is of his mother in a packing crate, frozen.

From a man who once claimed that "anything in the past as far as I'm concerned is of no importance," such passages come as a shock. But then age can do funny things. At the end, we are left with the writer as a diminished Prospero, under overhead lights that "sputtered out like an old joke," pleading for a chance to complete his education and wondering if it's still possible to "get it all straight."

Benjamin Weissman (review date 18 June 1995)

SOURCE: "Dream Control," in *Los Angeles Times Book Review,* June 18, 1995, p. 15.

[*In the following review, Weissman assesses the dream-like aspects of* My Education.]

William Burroughs has the greatest speaking voice I've ever heard in my life. A gravelly deadpan, direct from the chest cavity. Think of a goat with a large vocabulary. Burroughs was and is the wild alternative to his spiritual, stream-of-con-

fessional beat brothers of the 1950s and '60s. With the publication of *Junky* and *Naked Lunch,* he locked himself and his readers into a blasted, playful zone, a sort of Jonathan Swift-meets-Marquis de Sade "humanoidspeak." The voice of Burroughs' prose is a profound and prophetic dementia that continually blows people away, and like all great writing it disturbed a lot of people (got banned, of course; this is America), including his immediate fans who had a gut need for disturbance. A surreal maelstrom of sex, violence and drugs all swirled together in a levelheaded cowboy vernacular—an American viewpoint as fresh and unpredictable as a can of gray (his favorite color) paint poured over your head. His sense of humor was another thing that threw people off. Writers usually aren't funny about those dire sorts of things, and Burroughs' writing seemed a little like prose from the devil. He was very weird in the most exciting ways, articulated the queerest levels of behavior and narration, and became his own American avant-garde (a position he held/ holds all by his little lonesome).

At 81 years old he's very much alive but it seems more natural to talk about him in the past tense; maybe because that's where his great books and contributions reside. All the greats who were affected by Burroughs have also, politely, left him behind. What else can you do with a hero but say thanks, kick him in the pants and leave? Think about writers such as Denis Johnson, William Gibson, Jeanette Winterson and Stephen Wright (the list is long and there are more obvious, regularly cited, examples), or underground comics, or rock bands from the Sex Pistols to Sonic Youth. Most of these fiery things came out of the flaming pit of Burroughs. History seems to be muttering that his influence on fiction and pop culture is much more significant than the gargantuan monoliths of the same period (John Barth, Joseph Heller, Norman Mailer), or the minimalists (Donald Barthelme, Raymond Carver, Grace Paley).

My Education is subtitled *A Book of Dreams,* which it is, in part. It's also a notebook of story sketches and odd little prose chunks. Every Burroughs novel reeks of dreams; the imagery, the illogic, the unexplainable, the violent. *My Education* has moments of being a fragmented memoir with highly distorted sequences. He writes about Joan, his wife, whom he shot and killed accidentally in 1951 during a game of William Tell, trying to shoot an apple off her head—but he writes of her only as she appears in dreams of no particular consequence. It may be a subject too painful and tricky to handle any other way, and it's information that a Burroughs reader craves, especially a version of the story straight from the shooter's mouth. Burroughs explains at the book's beginning that he dreams during sleep and also has waking dreams that are more real than real life or more like dreams than dreams, and that he also experiences a third type of dreaming. This sets the table for the many non-dream entries, general notations on things such as therapy, gun enthusiasts or on being a writer (the world's most natural type of freak).

In the end, the book's strongest feature is Burroughs' language. His blunt, grumpy vocabulary. It's hugely satisfying to read something approaching nonfiction from Burroughs simply because it's good to know what he thinks, curious to see what his language is like with his fictional guard down. He is very straightforward. Here is a recipe for making botulism, "used with conspicuous success by Pancho Villa" against federal troops in Mexico:

> Fill a water canteen to the top with freshly cooked and drained green beans. Close it and put aside for several days. A few slivers of rotting pork are then added, and the canteen sealed tightly. Ten incubators are buried underground. After seven days most will be swollen, indicating a thriving botulism culture.

> Can be smeared on any fruit, meats, or vegetables, dabbed on thornbushes and fragments of glass. Guerrilla children sniped sentries with pottery shards or with obsidian chips dipped in botulism. A little ingenuity. There are many ways and it takes such a little to do the Big Job. A woman opened a can of home-canned beans. Put one bean in her mouth, spit it out and washed her mouth out with mouthwash. She died three days later from botulism poisoning.

And there are wonderfully cryptic moments, like this one, that occur regularly:

> All abilities are paid for with disabilities. Perfect health may entail the heavy toll of bovine stupidity. Insight in one area involves blind spots in another. I could not have done what I have done as a writer had I been a gifted mathematician or physicist.

> Honesty wrung out of him by pain, he cried out with a loud voice.

What haunts Burroughs in dreamland is an amusing parallel cartoon version of what obsesses him during waking, working hours. (His favorite thing on earth might be cats.) It's not too surprising that the dreams of William Burroughs would be filled with paranoia, but a small disappointment flares up over how undetailed his dreams are. It's far from a rigorous documentation. In most cases the dreams are vaguely remembered, void of nuance and of the pleasure of kicking around oddities one expects from Burroughs' fiction. On the other hand, the general tone, which lacks specificity

and detail, has the appealing feel of folk tales, and reeks of whacked-out lessons and upside-down morality tales.

Four pages from the end of the book there is a black-and-white photograph of a sweet, curly-haired boy with big ears. Under the picture a caption reads "Michael Emerton [to whom the book is dedicated] August 1985, aged nineteen." Preceding that page is an entry about crashing a car followed by a classified ad taken in a Kansas newspaper expressing thanks to two motorists who helped the victims out of their car. Followed by an entry stating that Emerton shot himself seven weeks later. Burroughs writes: "An experience most deeply felt is the most difficult to convey in words. Remembering brings the emptiness, the acutely painful awareness of irreparable loss." And then a paragraph about losing his cat Ruski and how empty that made him feel.

Passages like these, about real people and events, bring up some revealing aspects of his personality. A familiar detachment keeps the reader at arm's distance. Burroughs is unwilling to go where things are emotionally dangerous. He's not going to go in. His dreams reveal aspects of his psyche, but in the telling he will not let anything get out of control. Family and loss are slippery. Even with sex he's extremely modest (his term for it is "making it"). There's rarely a genital in view, a smell of any kind. Those wild things are off-limits, avoided. He won't take us there. And that's a huge shame, because it's the humbling humiliation of dreams that makes being on earth exhilarating and horrible—just what a Burroughs reader has learned to love.

FURTHER READING

Criticism

Mannes-Abbott, Guy. "The Beats Go On." *New Statesman & Society* (27 October 1995): 47-8.
>   Reviews *My Education,* suggesting that Burroughs's "carefully forged work will prove the accompaniment to [T. S.] Eliot's evocation of our century's waste lands."

Vickers, Scott. "Summer Reading." *The Bloomsbury Review* (May-June 1994): 7.
>   Details the insights on Burroughs's life and writings provided by *The Letters of William S. Burroughs* and *William Burroughs: El Hombre Invisible.*

White, Edmund. "This Is Not a Mammal: A Visit with William Burroughs." In *The Burning Library,* edited by David Bergman, pp. 107-14. New York: Alfred A. Knopf, 1994.
>   Recounts a visit to Burroughs's residence shortly after reading *Cities of the Red Night,* commenting on its themes and relation to other works.

Additional coverage of Burroughs's life and career is contained in the following sources published by Gale: *Authors in the News*, Vol. 2; *Contemporary Authors*, Vols. 9-12R; *Contemporary Authors New Revision Series*, Vols. 20 and 52; *DISCovering Authors*; *DISCovering Authors: British*; *DISCovering Authors: Canadian*; *DISCovering Authors Modules: Most-studied Authors, Novelists, Popular Fiction and Genre Authors*; *Dictionary of Literary Biography*, Vols. 2, 8, 16, and 152; *Dictionary of Literary Biography Yearbook*, 1981; *Major Twentieth-Century Writers*; and *World Literature Criticism.*

James Dickey

1923-1997

(Full name James Lafayette Dickey) American poet, novelist, critic, essayist, scriptwriter, and author of children's books.

For further information on Dickey's life and career, see *CLC*, Volumes 1, 2, 4, 7, 10, 15, and 47.

INTRODUCTION

A prominent figure in contemporary American literature, Dickey is best known for his intense exploration of the primal, irrational, creative, and ordering forces in life. Often classified as a visionary Romantic in the tradition of Walt Whitman, Dylan Thomas, and Theodore Roethke, Dickey emphasized the primacy of imagination and examined the relationship between humanity and nature. He frequently described confrontations in war, sports, and nature as means for probing violence, mortality, creativity, and social values. In his poetry, Dickey rejected formalism, artifice, and confession, favoring instead a narrative mode that features energetic rhythms and charged emotions. Dickey once stated that in his poetry he attempted to achieve "a kind of plain-speaking line in which astonishing things can be said without rhetorical emphasis." In addition to his verse, Dickey authored the acclaimed novels *Deliverance* (1970) and *Alnilam* (1987) as well as the less well-received *To the White Sea* (1993), symbolic works that explore the extremes of human behavior.

Dickey, who died of complications of lung disease on January 19, 1997, commonly drew upon crucial events in his life for his subject matter. His early poetry, for example, is infused with guilt over his role as a fighter pilot in World War II and the Korean War, ruminations on his older brother's death, and reflections upon his Southern heritage. In his first three volumes of verse—*Into the Stone, and Other Poems* (1960), *Drowning with Others* (1962), and *Helmets* (1964)—Dickey explored such topics as war, family, love, death, spiritual rebirth, nature, and survival. These poems are generally arranged in traditional stanzaic units and are marked by an expansive and affirmatory tone. James Schevill observed such characteristics of Dickey's early verse as "a unique unmistakable tone, an awareness of the physical forces of the world that flow beyond time, beyond history." These volumes also contain several poems about the wilderness in which Dickey stressed the importance of maintaining the primal physical and imaginative powers that he believed are suppressed by civilization. *Buckdancer's Choice* (1965), which won the National Book Award, signaled a shift

in Dickey's verse to freer, more complex forms. Employing internal monologues, varied spacing between words and phrases in place of punctuation, and subtler rhythms, *Buckdancer's Choice* investigates human suffering in its myriad forms. Dickey expressed ambivalence toward violence, most notably in "The Firebombing," a long poem that juxtaposes the thoughts of a fighter pilot as he flies over Japan and his memories twenty years later. *Poems, 1957-1967* (1968) encapsulates what most critics consider Dickey's strongest phase as a poet.

In the novel *Deliverance,* which was adapted into an acclaimed film, Dickey reiterated several themes prevalent in his verse, primarily the rejuvenation of human life through interaction with nature. This work concerns four suburban men who seek diversion from their unfulfilling lives by canoeing down a remote and dangerous river. The characters encounter human violence and natural threats, forcing them to rely on primordial instincts in order to survive. Many initial reviews assessed *Deliverance* as a sensational adventure story that exalts violence and machismo. Subsequent evaluations, however, noted Dickey's skillful use of myth, biblical references, and Jungian archetypes, and several critics compared *Deliverance* to Mark Twain's *Adventures of Huckleberry Finn* and Joseph Conrad's *Heart of Darkness*. Despite growing belief in the book's value as legitimate literature, however, many schools refuse to include *Deliverance* in curricula. William G. Tapply, in a highly favorable analysis of the work, recounted being denied permission to teach to his high-school English students "a book in which the plot pivots on a scene where a man is sodomized at gunpoint, in which the heroes 'get away' with murder, in which verboten vocabulary words appear." Dickey's second novel, *Alnilam,* is an ambitious experimental work centering on a blind man's attempts to uncover the mysterious circumstances of his son's death. The man's son had been a charismatic leader of an elite corps of army pilots who held vaguely sinister revolutionary aspirations. While the book celebrates the pleasures of flying with vivid imagery, it denounces the misuse of power, becoming what Robert Towers described as "a vast, intricate work distinguished not by its forward momentum but by its symbolic suggestiveness and its bravura passages, some of which rise to visionary heights."

Dickey's *To the White Sea,* the story of a seemingly sociopathic soldier forced to parachute into Japan during World War II, received less favorable critical attention than his earlier novels. Greg Johnson reported that Dickey, "long acknowledged as one of our finest contemporary poets, with *Deliverance* . . . produced one of the most celebrated novels of its decade. Although his hefty second novel, *Alnilam,* garnered a mixed response, its ambitious scope and often dazzling use of language furthered his reputation as a novelist of considerable powers. Dickey's new work of fiction, *To the White Sea,* probably will not harm that reputation, though it is less ambitious and in some ways less accomplished than his previous novels." Thick with overtones of primitive survival and the natural world, *To the White Sea* follows Sergeant Muldrow on his trek from Tokyo to Japan's northern wilderness. Muldrow's desire to commune with nature as he travels is frequently interrupted by unwelcome human beings, most of whom he murders in cold blood and with sadistically creative techniques. This unsettling and central element of *To the White Sea* was frequently cited by critics as the basis for the book's lukewarm reception among readers, who found themselves unable to muster any sympathy toward the story's protagonist. "Any reader approaching *To the White Sea* in the hope of finding a traditional war story or an adventure novel will be sharply disappointed," Johnson concluded. "But the book will surely please admirers of Dickey's poetry and of his harsh, unsettling vision of natural savagery."

PRINCIPAL WORKS

Into the Stone, and Other Poems (poetry) 1960
Drowning with Others (poetry) 1962
Helmets (poetry) 1964
The Suspect in Poetry (criticism) 1964
Two Poems of the Air (poetry) 1964
Buckdancer's Choice (poetry) 1965
Babel to Byzantium: Poets and Poetry Now (criticism) 1968
Poems, 1957-1967 (poetry) 1968
*Deliverance (novel) 1970
The Eye-Beaters, Blood, Victory, Madness, Buckhead, and Mercy (poetry) 1970
Self-Interviews (monologues) 1970
Sorties: Journals and New Essays (essays) 1971
The Zodiac [based on Hendrik Marsman's poem of the same title] (poem) 1976
The Strength of Fields (poem) 1977
Tucky the Hunter (children's poetry) 1978
The Strength of Fields [poetry collection; title poem published separately in 1977] (poetry) 1979
Scion (poetry) 1980
Falling, May Day Sermon, and Other Poems (poetry) 1981
Puella (poetry) 1982
The Central Motion (poetry) 1983
Alnilam (novel) 1987
The Eagle's Mile [poetry collection; title poem published separately in 1981] (poetry) 1990
The Whole Motion: Collected Poems, 1945-1992 (poetry) 1992
To the White Sea (novel) 1993

*Dickey also wrote the screenplay for the 1972 movie.

INTERVIEW

James Dickey with Ernest Suarez (interview date August 1989)

SOURCE: "An Interview with James Dickey," in *Contemporary Literature,* Vol. 31, No. 2, Summer, 1990, pp. 117-32.

[*In the following interview, conducted in August, 1989, Dickey discusses his work, his life, and his political and literary ideas.*]

At the age of thirty-five, James Dickey, in the poem **"The Other,"** wrote of building his body so as to "keep me dying / Years longer." When I arrived at his house on Lake Katherine in Columbia, South Carolina, on August 8, 1989, Dickey asserted, with both eagerness and desperation in his voice, "There is so much I can write, if life will give me the time." An acute awareness of mortality and of its counterpart—the desire to create the illusion that death can be conquered—is never far from the heart of Dickey's work, which is pervaded by thoughts of a brother who died before Dickey was born, the deaths of his parents and friends, the carnage he witnessed in World War II and the Korean War, and his own bouts with serious illnesses.

The death of Dickey's close friend Robert Penn Warren in October 1989 leaves Dickey as the last living member of a long line of influential poets to emerge from Vanderbilt University in the first half of this century. During his often spectacular and always controversial career, now in its fifth decade, Dickey's achievements have been recognized widely. He has won numerous prestigious awards, including the National Book Award, *Poetry*'s Levinson Prize, a Guggenheim Fellowship, the Melville Cane Award, the Longview Foundation Prize, and the Vachel Lindsay Award. He has twice been named Consultant in Poetry to the Library of Congress and was elected to the American Academy of Arts and Letters and to the National Academy of Letters and Sciences. Dickey has written a dozen books of poetry, two novels, two books of criticism, and several acclaimed screenplays. He has held the chair of Carolina Professor of English at the University of South Carolina since 1969 and has won several teaching awards. Despite these successes, Dickey remains convinced his best work is yet to come. In Dickey's work, death is combated—and courted—through action, and, at age sixty-seven, Dickey is still living and working at a vigorous pace, with an impressive new book of poems, *The Eagle's Mile,* ready for publication, another, *Real God, Roll,* well under way, and two novels, *To the White Sea* and *Crux* (a sequel to *Alnilam*) in progress.

Dickey is nothing if not passionate, engaged, and acutely aware of the possibilities life affords, as well as intensely disturbed—even insulted—at the loss of those possibilities when life ends.
—Ernest Suarez

This interview was conducted during my stay with Dickey in August 1989. Following an evening with the writer and his family in Columbia, he and I drove to his second home at Litchfield Plantation on Pawley's Island, where we remained for six days. A tranquil, remote, timeless atmosphere seeped from the lush grounds, a strangely meditative setting in which to interview a man whose art brims with vigor and sensation. With a tape recorder and a bottle of Wild Turkey to keep us company, we sat in the living room and talked, pausing occasionally to look out at a heron fly by or perch in a tree shrouded in Spanish moss. Though our nightly conversations sometimes continued hours into the early morning, Dickey was always up and striking the typewriter keys

by seven or eight o'clock. On several occasions he bounded down the stairs to read me a scene or a line or a phrase that pleased him. Dickey is nothing if not passionate, engaged, and acutely aware of the possibilities life affords, as well as intensely disturbed—even insulted—at the loss of those possibilities when life ends.

[*Suarez:*] *You began to compose the poems that appeared in your first book,* **Into the Stone,** *about the time you met Ezra Pound. What would you say you picked out from Pound?*

[Dickey:] What I would call an extreme magical directness. That ability to take something which is factual and make a simple, highly imaginative statement out of it.

So you are specifying Pound's use of the image?

Yes, a very clear, concrete, simply stated and highly original, highly imaginative but simple quality. What I'm looking for in my own work more than anything else is a kind of deep simplicity. I was raised with the notion that as far as literary judgments are concerned, complexity is desirable. I. A. Richards or William Empson, for example, assert that more appetencies are satisfied with more economy by complexity. I don't think so. I like the thing that comes like a lightning flash, that is vivid and momentarily there and intense and unmistakable and doesn't require a great deal of ratiocination. When William Empson talks about a line of [William] Shakespeare's, like "Bare ruined choirs where late the sweet birds sang," he goes into this long peroration of all the things the mind calls up by means of this image of the birds—the fact that real choirs require sitting in rows with their own wooden benches like the branch a bird sits on and this and that and the other. The ingenuity just to conjure all that up is wonderful, but I get none of that at all—none of it, and I don't want it. The point is that criticism can proliferate endlessly on the slightest text, or sometimes, by theorizing endlessly, even on no text at all. Unlike most people I know, I like to read boring books, and I've never read a more boring book than Empson's *Structure of Complex Words.* It's extremely boring, and yet he is a brilliant man, and he says some good things that even I can assimilate every now and then. But to spend one's life doing that, or being in an area where that sort of activity is of a great deal of importance, is not to my liking at all. Thank God I'm at the age now where I don't have to give lip service to anything. If my opinions are those of an aging jerk, then so be it!

Can you think of any of your own poems where you use the Poundian conception of the image?

Yes, though you can't tell where Pound's or Eliot's influence is going to be. It takes place on such a subliminal level that you can never really say that this is directly influenced by one or the other. I think Pound's influence is deeper and more pervasive than anything I can directly lay a finger on. But I can pick out a number of lines of mine that have the kind of simplicity, the imaginative simplicity, that I learned more from Pound than from anyone else. One is from **"Drinking from a Helmet,"** where the soldier picks up the dead soldier's helmet, which is filled with water, and looks inside it. He says, "I drank with the timing of rust." I could look through my work and show you plenty of places where I think that happens.

Thank God I'm at the age now where I don't have to give lip service to anything. If my opinions are those of an aging jerk, then so be it!
—*James Dickey*

I think that this conception of the image is the very core of your work.

That's the guts of it for me. The image and the dramatic development—the dramatic aspect of what is actually going on in the poem. I think that too much poetry is being written about trivialities, with the attempt to pump up the triviality into something of consequence. But a triviality is a triviality. One gets a little tired of Blake seeing heaven in a wild flower and eternity in a grain of sand. That is all very well for [William] Blake and very well for some poets some of the time, but not for all poets all of the time. When Adrienne Rich gives an account of a cockroach in a kitchen cupboard, it's interesting momentarily, but one doesn't really in one's heart believe it's that important.

Much of your poetry involves transcending the mundane world. Do you see yourself as a visionary poet?

Well, one doesn't like to make such wild claims as that, but any original insight that any poet has is in a sense a vision. But in the sense that Blake is a visionary poet, I'm not at all. I don't really believe that I can see God sitting up in that tree yonder, you know. Or any of the things, any of the visions that Blake said he saw or claimed to see. I'm sure he did. I hope he did. I would like to see something like that. Somebody said to Blake, "Now when you look at the sun do you see a disc about the size of a florin?" Blake said, "No, I see a great multitude of the heavenly hosts singing hosannas unto the most high." Now, I don't see that when I see the sun. It would be great if I did, but a visionary poet in that sense, I'm not.

You place great emphasis on the poet as a "maker."

Yes, I do. That's something I firmly believe in.

In what sense do you see the poet as a "maker"? What consequences does "making" have for the world at large?

I don't know how the world is affected by it. I don't know because in some sense it's biblical. The Bible is always talking about the Lord working in mysterious ways. So does poetry, and you can't chart those. I. A. Richards talks about appetency and about this response or that response called forth by these words and so on. That is an attempt to make a scientific discipline of something that is profoundly unscientific. Poetry is not really subject to such investigation beyond a certain very rigid border. For example, if in a poem I mentioned the word "tree," what would you see? What would that call up in your mind? What is your tree?

An oak.

Wrong. Because the only tree, the archetypal, the Platonic tree, is definitely a pine tree. You bring your life to the image, to create the image that the word suggests, and nothing can legislate that.

Robert Lowell's poetry is interesting because he is a powerful, tearing writer. I mean he can write like a streak, and all that desperate neuroticism has infinite ramifications. He can do a lot with it, but ultimately it comes back to him and his situation in life—his condition, his personality. And it is no good to say that Lowell takes on all this agony and grief for all of us. He does not take it on for all of us. He takes it on for himself; it is his life. It is not the life of twentieth-century humankind. It's his personal life, and too much of that is wearing. You're asked to give too much credence to it.

How would you say your work differs from that?

I'd like to think that it differs from it in opening out rather than closing down on the pinpoint of one person. I like to give. As I once said in an essay on Ted Roethke—he does this kind of opening out—if you have heard wind, you have heard Roethke's wind, but because you know about Roethke's wind, the wind he has put down in words, the wind to you has another dimension—something creative and positive that accrues to you. You are deepened and expanded because of the words.

In "Approaching Prayer" you write that "reason" must be slain for vision to occur. Is that essential?

Well, I don't know if it is essential or not. But I think that there are certain circumstances in a person's experience where it is better to participate in the experience by means of simple gut reactions and not through reasoning. Not through intellectualization about the experience but to just be in it and feel what you honestly feel as a response. That is essentially what I mean.

Earlier you mentioned a conversation you had with Yvor Winters many years ago where he called you an Emersonian because of your emphasis on directly experiencing things. Winters was very wary of that Emersonian doctrine.

I don't remember the conversation perfectly, but it seems to me he said something about my being essentially an American decadent romantic poet following [Ralph Waldo] Emerson. Yes, he was wary of Emersonianism. I hate to use such a loaded word, but Winters was a fascistic type who believed in order and the establishment of very rigid standards, largely determined by him. This is the stuff of dictators, is it not? To him I would compare a critic who is more flexible and who is willing to be wrong, like Randall Jarrell or John Berryman—somebody who is willing to say, "I thought this last year, but I've changed my mind." I've changed my mind many times, and I think that is a privilege. If you lock yourself into your own doctrines, then you lose the flexibility of the moment to moment ability to respond.

Is that why you think Emerson was a greater man than [Henry David] Thoreau?

I think he is because he opens up more territory than Thoreau. Thoreau is too much of a doctrine giver. Emerson is a presenter of possibilities. I like that.

Which, as you have expressed, is essentially the poetic enterprise.

It would seem to me to be so. Opening up possibilities. Thoreau is too concerned with laying down the law about everything. Thoreau says some good things. That people lead lives of quiet desperation. Things about stepping to a different drummer. These are wonderful statements, great stuff. But honest reaction to experience, intuitive reaction—nothing is of greater consequence than that. Emerson had a curious relationship to religion, although he was at one point a Unitarian minister. His idea was that you could have a direct line to God. That you don't have to go through the church or follow any dogma. That God comes straight to you like a ray of light—and so do you to Him. I think that is fine. I don't believe it. I would like to believe it, and I'm glad somebody said it. I'm glad he said it.

What do you believe? Do you believe there is any moral force governing the universe?

No, I don't believe in that at all. I'm writing a long poem

now, *Real God, Roll,* where a father watches his son pumping iron and exercising on the beach, and he feels it's all part of the whole thing, of the real god. The waves coming in, his death, his father's death, the son's physique are all part of the whole thing. The real god is what causes everything to exist, like the laws of motion. The humanization of God in the Bible I find absurd. I love the Bible like I love Greek mythology, though Greek mythology is far more imaginative than the Bible is.

In your war poems, like "The Performance" or "Between Two Prisoners," you never seem to take sides or make moral judgments.

I suppose in those poems there is an implicit moral stance, I guess you could say. Obviously, I don't think it is right for the Japanese to behead Don Armstrong, who was my best friend. Obviously, I'm against it. Anybody would be. Or in "The Fire Bombing," which is based on a kind of paradox based on the sense of power one has as a pilot of an aircrew dropping bombs. This is a sense of power a person can otherwise never experience. Of course this sensation is humanly reprehensible, but so are many of the human emotions that one has. Judged by the general standard, such emotions are reprehensible, but they do happen, and that is the feeling. Then you come back from a war you won, and you're a civilian, and you begin to think about the implications of what you actually did do when you experienced this sense of power and remoteness and godlike vision. And you think of the exercise of authority via the machine that your own government has put at your disposal to do exactly what you did with it. Then you have a family yourself, and you think about those people twenty, thirty, forty years ago—I was dropping those bombs on them, on some of them. Suppose somebody did that to me? It was no different to them. All of that went into "The Fire Bombing."

Yet some people at the time, the mid-to-late sixties, did not read the poem as an antiwar poem.

Well, you do yourself a disservice if you blink the real implications of a situation like that. It is a poem about the guilt at the inability to feel guilty because you have not only proved yourself a patriot but something of a hero. You've been given medals for doing this. Your country has honored you—but there are those doubts that stay with you. You feel as a family man what all those unseen, forever unseen, people felt that you dropped those bombs on. You did it. The detachment one senses when dropping the bombs is the worst evil of all—yet it doesn't seem so at the time.

The poem ends with the narrator still unable to imagine "nothing not as American as / I am, and proud of it." What do you see as the meaning of those lines?

You are a patriot. You have fought in a war. You have fought for freedom and risked your life not once but many times for the cause of peace and freedom. It might be a Pax Americana, like the Pax Romana, the Roman peace—imposed peace by force of arms. In other words, you be peaceful or we will blow your heads off. In our times we will atomic bomb you. Even if that is the case, still peace is peace. If you have a home in the suburbs and a lawn to cut, you are able to have it because forty years ago you had to do something else when the world's historical situation called for it. And you're not ashamed of it no matter who says what. Suppose we hadn't stood against [Adolf] Hitler? We would be in a different world.

What other historical events do you see as most significant for American culture?

I'm not a historian; I'm just an ordinary citizen. But I suppose since the Second World War the whole concept of limited war, like Korea and Vietnam, has been the most important thing, because the balance of world power is involved. One hundred and fifty years ago a guy named Karl Marx wrote a treatise on economics based on the Hegelian dialectic. I don't mean to be so academic, but—and this is changing—the world has been largely divided in two because of economic and political doctrines. We're on the side of freedom, but for us freedom means capitalism. They are on the side—you can't say oppression but that's what is the result of it—of, theoretically at least, equal distribution. The state dictating everything, including salaries, living quarters, food rationing, and the rest of it. Marx says everything is determined by the economic situation—everything, even the quality of the mind. I don't think so. I think capitalism and democracy enable you to have more of that elusive quality called "freedom" in your life.

I took an awful lot of flak for ["Notes on the Decline of Outrage"]. I didn't get a job I wanted with an advertising agency in Atlanta because the people were so rabidly pro-Southern and antiblack. I came out for black citizens and said that if it took repudiating part of my so-called Southern heritage in order for blacks to have an equal chance, I would do it—and I advised other people to do it also.
—*James Dickey*

You wrote an overtly political essay, "Notes on the Decline of Outrage," which involved the civil rights movement.

Martin Luther King [Jr.] quoted from the end of that essay in his speeches—that for white southerners "it can be a greater thing than the South has ever done" to discover that blacks are our "unknown brothers." That was written back in the 1950s, which as far as the civil rights movement was concerned was practically prehistory. I took an awful lot of flak for that. I didn't get a job I wanted with an advertising agency in Atlanta because the people were so rabidly pro-Southern and antiblack. I came out for black citizens and said that if it took repudiating part of my so-called Southern heritage in order for blacks to have an equal chance, I would do it—and I advised other people to do it also.

Racism has ruined so many people's lives, white and black. Donald Davidson was one of my teachers at Vanderbilt. Davidson was a remarkable man. He was in many ways one of the most humane, sensitive, and caring persons I ever knew—and intelligent, too. He was a man who had great gifts but who ruined his life—especially the latter part of his life, which should have been the most productive—over the question of racism. You could not imagine that a sensitive and retiring and responsible man like Don Davidson could have these fanatical beliefs about blacks. He actually deeply believed that the Caucasian race was demonstrably superior to the Negro race, and that the laws and ethos and mores of society should reflect that. He thought the laws shouldn't militate against blacks—although that is inevitably the result of Don Davidson's ideas—but that these divisions should be recognized, to use a favorite phrase of his, "for what they are." Now, he wasn't anyone who wanted to go out and lynch people or anything like that. His beliefs were quite sincere. He was in many ways a brilliant guy and a wonderful teacher. He had a great ability to communicate one on one with a student. He had scholarly knowledge and was quite a good poet—much better than he has ever been given credit for being. He was overshadowed by [John Crowe] Ransom and [Allen] Tate, and especially by Warren. He was in many ways a very worthy person, but you could not get him on the subject of race, or allow him to get on the subject of race, without everything degenerating. It just went bad, and when it went bad you didn't want to be around him. He ended up allying himself with all these "white citizens" councils and the most dubious kinds of redneck racist groups. He spent his time and energy doing that; it was a terrible mistake.

What prompted you to write the essay?

I wanted to write it. It seemed necessary. Louis Rubin was putting together an anthology of essays, *South,* and asked me to do something—anything that I wanted to do—and I chose to write about the racial situation in the South.

Why didn't you do anything like that again?

Because I would then seem to be trading on it. I made all

the statements I wanted to make there, and if people wanted to know my opinion about the subject, they could go there.

You were later involved in and helped write speeches for both Eugene McCarthy's and Jimmy Carter's political campaigns. What prompted your involvement?

When I was in Washington, as Consultant in Poetry to the Library of Congress, Eugene McCarthy became my closest friend. I felt he was a political leader that this country hardly deserved because he had a tremendous commitment to the life of the mind—especially to poetry. He was a poet himself, and some of his things are not bad. I became devoted to him: his cause seemed right because he wanted to end the Vietnam War and was a positive politician. He didn't just condemn, but said we have to go forward—that we're going to upgrade the whole national sensibility so that people can live more and have more of themselves. I loved the man. I think he stood for the right things. I wish he had become president.

Jimmy Carter I loved because of the morality factor. I think he is a very kind man. Who else could have achieved the peace he helped manage to establish—even if some of it was just temporary—in the Middle East? We were really not that close, although I spoke at his inauguration.

Although you worked for McCarthy in the sixties, you never wrote any anti-Vietnam poetry. What are your thoughts on the protests that were going on in the sixties?

Well, man is a political animal. As far as it concerns the poets and writers involved in sixties protests, I would say two different aspects should probably be considered. First are the poets and writers who were acting as outraged citizens, who felt that Vietnam was a tragic mistake for this country and wished to speak out. All of that is really good, even noble. The other thing is the poets and writers who seized on this political and national crisis to aggrandize themselves because they could not earn recognition by means of their talent. You get up on the podium and start spouting forgettable poetry in the name of the cause. Poetry against death. How can anyone be pro death? It's against slaughter; it's against the killing of women and children by fire bombing and so on. How can't you be against that? You're stacking the hand like a card game, stacking your hand in your favor. Who would be in favor of the slaughter of women and children? And yet the poetry that resulted from it is dead before it hits the page. It's topical, and when the historic occasion that called it forth has passed, so has the poetry. It's easy, it's wonderful, it's inspiring to have all the right opinions—and to put down words on a page that capitalize on those opinions, that identify you as being a right guy because you're against death. You're against torture—but that is just another version of being in favor of mom's apple pie.

What do you think is the relationship between poetry and culture?

I would pin it down to our time because I'm functioning in our time. I don't know what it is in the various eras of history. Our age, the age of Marshall McLuhan, is an age dominated by the media. McLuhan believes that print will eventually be superseded by TV, and that words will no longer be printed but that there will only be spoken words, and that they will only be apprehensible by means of personal communication and by means of the electronic media, and that on that basis we'll all be together in the global village. I think the poet needs to stand forthrightly against that notion because words themselves have enormous potency. Language is the greatest gift that mankind has ever received or has given to itself. Language has made everything else possible. One generation can build on the discoveries of the previous one. This makes libraries possible, and all the information that you need to know to build rockets, conquer cancer and polio, and so on. Language makes it possible for all the professions and the arts to go forward. Language. The word. In the beginning was the Logos. The most mysterious statement of human history is "In the beginning was the word"—not the thing—the word, Logos. The supreme custodian of the word, the one who uses it with the most eloquence, the most meaning, the most consequentiality, is the poet. The poet is the one who has the most command of the word and of all strata and substrata of language, of all meanings and all connotations. There is something in the human soul that will respond to that kind of use of language because it is our most precious gift. There is something that will respond to it no matter how rudimentary the intellect of the responding person. Through such use words can reach a person in a way that is particularly intimate and individual. My main disappointment in this culture that I live in is the low level of sensibility. D. H. Lawrence says somewhere, "I will show you how not to be a dead man in life." Too many of us approximate the state of being dead in life, and the more mechanized a culture becomes, the more mechanical the people become. I believe there is value in feelings and in responsiveness and in the contribution of the imagination to those things. So many of our students are brainwashed. They don't give a shit—that's a favorite expression of our time. "I don't know about you, but I don't give a shit." And they don't. But I do give a shit. I don't want to "come off of it," I want to get on with it.

Do you feel that in other eras people did "give a shit"? In the sixties, for instance?

Yes, especially in the sixties. That shows us that there is an underlying stream of available emotion that simply needs a channel. In that era the energy was funneled into social protest. In my novel *Alnilam,* all Joel Cahill has to do is appear and all that loose, wandering emotion in the young people focuses on him, and he becomes their channel. That is what made John F. Kennedy, for example, or Hitler, for that matter. These leaders provide people's suppressed emotions with an image, a channel, to focus on. We all need that, and it is very inspiring in the case of great leaders and very terrifying in the case of sinister leaders. Leaders like Hitler, Frederick the Great, and Napoleon tap in on the same kind of emotion that enables someone like [Abraham] Lincoln or [George] Washington or [Thomas] Jefferson to be a leader. There is a charismatic quality in the leaders who are focused on that is indigenous to them.

Aside from such a leader's charismatic quality, do you feel that the moral underpinnings of the leader's message are arbitrary? Do you think that a negative leader like Hitler is just as likely to be focused on as a more positive figure?

I don't think these things are completely arbitrary. For instance, one thing these matters depend on is the historical situation at the time. But it does also depend on something that is basically fundamental in human nature that wants such things to happen. The reason that the people join the Alnilam conspiracy, that the plotters join up with Joel Cahill, is that they believe that he is initiating them into an elite which everyone wants to be in. It is like a college fraternity. A college fraternity is not based on what the word "fraternity" suggests; it is not based on brotherhood and inclusion but on exclusion.

Earlier you made the statement that you felt World War II was the last just war America was involved in. Why do you feel that way?

There was no enemy or villain in the Vietnam or Korean war—no enemy as profoundly evil as Hitler. The supposed villain was collectivism. The communist state. But that doesn't have the solidity of an actual figure like Hitler. The baleful fascination of that guy—I don't think it will ever diminish. There are people in this country right now who are worshipers of Hitler. People don't only worship him because of his political and military deeds, but because he represented some kind of mystical force that only occasionally shows itself. People, the human race, want some kind of inspired, charismatic leader. Whether it's Alexander the Great, Caesar, Frederick II, Napoleon, Hitler, John F. Kennedy, or Joel Cahill, it satisfies some deep hunger in people that somebody has got hold of a truth and a way of life that they themselves cannot command.

*Tell me more about that idea in the context of **Alnilam**.*

Joel Cahill is that kind of a figure. Joel is the young college-boy mystic raised to the nth power. He is a genius in an airplane. Even the instructors are afraid to fly with him because he's so much better than they are. They don't want

to be humiliated by this guy who seems to have been born not *in* an airplane but *as* an airplane. The whole mysticism of the air, of flight, gives credence and weight to his political feelings. He's someone everyone remembers. He is a [Arthur] Rimbaud or [Percy Bysshe] Shelley of the air. A Jesus Christ or Messiah figure that one would follow to the grave because one's whole existence is justified by contact with this extraordinary person.

How does this relate to the things you say about poetry and the creative act in the novel?

I think the power of the word is great. Poetry makes plenty happen. In **Alnilam** the figure of Joel Cahill has a powerful effect on people. Not only on people who love him and follow him, but also on the people who hate him but can't ignore him. Part of his power is based on language. When he has the Alnilam plotters recite the lines from Shelley about the young charioteers drinking the wind of their own speed, the effect is hypnotic. This effect on the followers of Joel Cahill is made possible by means of language. "Drinking the wind of their own speed / And seeing nothing but the keen stars, / They all pass onward." It's the power of the words. Poetry is the ultimate; it has a powerful effect on people. It can have a satirical effect. Look at [Alexander] Pope. Pope says, "I stood aghast to see / They were not afraid of God, but afraid of me." Now this is power. [W. H.] Auden be damned. This is power. Part of Joel's power comes from the word, from language itself.

You equate Joel Cahill with Shelley at some points in the novel.

Yes, I do. Shelley is the ultimate beatnik. What a mind! What a mind! I wish I liked his poetry better. I keep reading Shelley, but there are only a few lines of Shelley's that I really care for. He is wonderful on the effects of the ephemeral qualities of air and light. The great type of Shelley image is that of a sunrise over the mountains.

But it's Shelley's personality that most interests you.

I love Shelley because he represents an extreme, like Joel Cahill represents an extreme. He's the ultimate youthful idealist with a great mind, completely unorthodox.

Yet he also has a potentially destructive side. I'm thinking of Joel Cahill.

Yes, there is also that side of him, as well. He is an overreacher.

How does this relate to our culture?

There is something about the excessive that appeals to

people. Excess. As Oscar Wilde, a favorite of mine, says, nothing succeeds like excess. You look at movements—like the John Birch Society. Who is John Birch? Nobody knows that much about John Birch—and nobody gives a shit. He was a martyr—a martyr like John Kennedy. He has that charisma that comes down through successive generations. He becomes a legend. The greatest of legends in Western culture is who? Jesus. Now, I was talking to Jesus the other day. He's a very good fellow—sympathetic, interesting, and something of a philosopher. But Jesus Christ had only the simplest of doctrines! The Bible is a desperate attempt by the human race, which is a product of the animal world. A dead dog crushed on the highway has the same organs as you. It's got a heart, liver, kidneys, bowels, all that. It's no different from you. All the difference is that you have evolved into something that can think of and conceive of the idea of God. A dog can't do that. If I had a dog who had the notion of God, I would fall to my knees and worship. Well, the dog does not have the concept of God. We have the concept of God. Genesis says God formed people in his own image. But it's actually the reverse of what Genesis says: we have formed God in our own image. As Russell says, if horses had gods, the gods would look like horses.

Joel Cahill speaks in parables. He talks about precision mysticism. What the hell does that mean? You don't know what it means, and in the novel it's not explained. Yet I intended to implant that in the reader's mind. Precision mysticism. When you relate that to an airplane engine and to Joel's relationship to flight, it takes on another meaning, but you're never able to understand exactly what. The Alnilam plotters think it's something that may be beyond anything that they have ever been able to perceive. That's the fascination of Joel Cahill. He's able to formulate these weird, strange, provocative, evocative notions. And he can get up there in an airplane and prove them—or what he does in an aircraft seems, to the Alnilam fliers, to bear out everything he talks about.

Does Joel have a specific political position?

No—only one statement. He says to his followers, We're going to make it like it should have been at the beginning. But you don't know what that is. He talks about existence as seen from an aircraft, the great blue field and the purple haze and so on. My point here is, that if you have somebody as charismatic as Joel Cahill, his followers follow him toward his ultimate goal not *despite* the fact it's vague, but *because* it's vague. It's like Tertullian's proof of God. He says, I don't believe in God's existence despite the fact that it's absurd; I believe it because it is absurd. The more vague and problematical the end of the Alnilam plot, the more fanatical the followers become.

Let's switch gears. In your work you place great emphasis

on the "creative lie," creating an illusion that becomes, in your words, "better than the truth." Can you relate this notion to the creation of your public personality?*

I think I can. When we were out on the west coast, a university, I believe it was Oregon State, offered me one hundred dollars to read some of my poetry. My wife, Maxine, told me, "Jim, we need the money, so you have to do it." At the time I didn't even know if I had enough poetry to give an hour-long program. Although I had been a teacher, the idea of getting up to read my own stuff in front of all those people seemed unthinkable. But Maxine insisted. She said, "Jim, you get out there and you do this. Those people at Oregon State want to hear what you have to say." Well, this was a monstrosity to me. I couldn't imagine getting up there. I told her I would be paralyzed with stage fright and self-consciousness. She told me, "If you are a teacher and can get up in front of your class every day, you can get up in front of an audience. Just get up there and be yourself." Which sounded fine to me until I began thinking, "Yeah, but what self, which one?" I had to invent a self. The twentieth century has produced two great invented selves, people who wished to become other than they really were and who wrote and acted out of the assumed personality. The first is T. E. Lawrence, who was a timid fellow who became a superman in warfare because he willed the personality that he wished to be. Instead of being a little, weak guy he became a military genius and a wonderful writer. But the self he was writing out of was not his real personality. The other person I think of is [Ernest] Hemingway. The real Hemingway was not the public Hemingway. The assumed personality. I have a great deal of that.

In what ways?

Because I'm essentially a coward, so therefore I flew with the night fighters in the Pacific, or in football I hit the guy especially hard because essentially I was afraid of him. I think you must turn these things to your favor.

How does this work for you poetically?

Essentially I was a timid, Ernest Dahlson type—a "days of wine and roses," decadent, late-romantic poet—so therefore I go for force and vigor. And it works. My assumed personality is working for me just as much as Lawrence's worked for him or Hemingway's worked for him.

Characterize that assumed personality for me.

That is easy to do. Very easy. All I have to do is turn it back to you and ask what you have heard about me. That's the assumed personality: big, strong, hard drinking, hard fighting. Nothing could be less characteristic of the true James Dickey, who is a timid, cowardly person.

I don't think many people would agree with you there.

Well, maybe not, but you can't fool yourself, so you spend your life fooling yourself. The self that you fool yourself into is the one that functions. Isn't that so?

OBITUARY

Albin Krebs (obituary date 21 January 1997)

SOURCE: "James Dickey, Two-Fisted Poet and the Author of *Deliverance,* is Dead at 73," in *The New York Times,* January 21, 1997, p. C27.

[*In the following obituary, Krebs presents a detailed review of Dickey's life and career.*]

James Dickey, one of the nation's most distinguished modern poets and a critic, lecturer and teacher perhaps best known for his rugged novel ***Deliverance,*** died on Sunday in Columbia, S.C. He was 73.

He died of complications of lung disease, The Associated Press reported.

Mr. Dickey, a big, sprawling, life-loving, hard-drinking man once described as "a bare-chested bard," was a prolific poet whose work was admired for its "intense clarity," its "joyous imagination" and its "courageous tenderness."

His poems often sang the praises of fighter pilots, football players and backwoods Southerners, but, as one critic put it, they were also "deceptively simple metaphysical poems that search the lakes and trees and workday fragments of his experience for a clue to the meaning of existence."

In addition to books of essays and what he called self-interviews, Mr. Dickey turned out some 20 volumes of poetry, many of them vividly muscular and passionate, almost always composed in a solidly purposeful English. He avoided the affected, and he celebrated the ordinary along with the sublime. His collection ***Buckdancer's Choice*** received the National Book Award for poetry in 1968.

There were few subjects Mr. Dickey would not tackle. In 1966, for example, he covered the launching of the Apollo 7 spacecraft for *Life* magazine and, while other journalists concentrated on the blastoff's scientific implications, he stressed the human drama:

> as they plunge with all of us—up from the
> flame-trench, up from the Launch
>   Umbilic Tower,

up from the elk and the butterfly,
  up from
the meadows and rivers and
  mountains and the beds
of wives into the universal cavern,
  into the
mathematical abyss, to find us—
  and return,
to tell us what we will be.

In 1970, after working seven years at it, Mr. Dickey finally published his first novel, ***Deliverance,*** a gripping, thrilling and highly praised account of a harrowing, disastrous canoe trip four friends take down a rolling north Georgia river.

The book was a best seller, and the 1972 film based on it, for which Mr. Dickey supplied the screenplay, was one of the most popular of its decade. The film starred Jon Voight and Burt Reynolds, and Mr. Dickey, already known for his several other talents, appeared in the featured role of the portly sheriff.

In 1977 Mr. Dickey was asked by his fellow Georgian, Jimmy Carter, to compose a poem for Mr. Carter's Presidential Inauguration. The poet read the work **"The Strength of Fields"** at the Inaugural gala, speaking in sonorous tones of "the profound, unstoppable craving of nations" that was part of the challenge facing Mr. Carter.

The poet was the winner of many awards, including *Sewanee Review* and Guggenheim fellowships for study and travel in Europe and the Longview, Vachel Lindsay and Melville Cane Awards for poetry.

James Dickey was born in an Atlanta suburb on Feb. 2, 1923, the son of Eugene and Maibelle Swift Dickey. His father was a lawyer fond of reading to his son, with rich rhetorical flourishes, the speeches of Robert Ingersoll, the 19th-century agnostic orator who relished personal confrontations with the fundamentalist preachers of his day.

Although the younger Dickey was more interested in sports at the time, his father's admiring readings of the Ingersoll speeches must have influenced him, for he was to be known in later years as an eloquent college lecturer and gifted reader of his own poetry.

Starting with his freshman year at Clemson College, where he was a varsity wingback on the football team, Mr. Dickey showed a fondness for risk and action, taking up canoeing, archery, weight lifting and other sports, all of which would interest him for the rest of his life. He also became an excellent guitarist and played a passable banjo.

He quit college after a year, in 1942, enlisted in the Army

Air Corps and volunteered for the 418th Night Fighter Squadron, for which he flew more than 100 missions in the Pacific theater of operations.

He later wrote often about his war experiences, for example in **"The Firebombing,"** the opening poem in his 1966 collection, *Buckdancer's Choice.* The poem read in part:

> Snap, a bulb is tricked on in the cockpit
> And some technical-minded stranger with my
>   hands
> Is sitting in a glass treasure-hole of blue light,
> Having potential fire under the undeodorized arms
> Of his wings, on thin bomb-shackles,
> The "tear-drop-shaped" 300-gallon drop-tanks
> Filled with napalm and gasoline.

Mr. Dickey found combat "viscerally exhilarating," he said, "like being on a big football team you knew was going to win." Yet his experiences in World War II, and when he was recalled to duty in the Korean War, taught him, he said, that life must be savored. "I look on existence from the standpoint of a survivor," he said.

It was while trying to bridge the gaps of wartime boredom that Mr. Dickey turned toward "tinkering" with literature, he said. "At first I spent most of my time writing erotic love letters to girls back in Atlanta and Montgomery," he said later. "I guess I started being a writer the day I found myself thinking, 'Gosh, that's pretty good,' instead of, 'That ought to knock her dead.'"

And so, at wartime base libraries, Mr. Dickey began a mission of self-teaching. "I sensed immediately that writers like [William] Faulkner or [Thomas] Wolfe had a different orientation with language than, say, [W. Somerset] Maugham. I kept looking for writers who had this thing. [Herman] Melville, James Agee. I felt writers like this were sort of failed poets but were trying to use prose for higher things. I thought that was the direction to go. I began reading anthologies of poetry."

It finally struck him, Mr. Dickey said, that "I had as much claim to saying or writing about my existence as anyone else had. I was just as much alive in my own way and if I did make my life speak, the possibilities of poetry were just as great as they were with [John] Donne or [John] Keats or Shelley."

After World War II, Mr. Dickey majored in English at Vanderbilt University in Nashville and, as a track star, won the Tennessee state championship in the 120-yard high hurdles. He graduated magna cum laude in 1949 and earned his master's degree the following year.

Then there was an English teaching job at Rice Institute, and the call back to duty in the Korean War, during which he had sold his first poem, **"Shark in the Window,"** to *The Sewanee Review* for $28.50. In 1954 the magazine awarded him a $3,500 fellowship, which gave him a year of writing in Europe.

Back home, Mr. Dickey, who had married Maxine Syerson in 1948 and become the father of two sons, Christopher and Kevin, found it difficult supporting a family as a teacher at the University of Florida.

He went to work for the McCann-Erickson advertising agency in Manhattan, leaving behind his poetry to praise in prose the glories of Coca-Cola. He was to remain in advertising, writing copy about fertilizer, potato chips and air travel for nearly six years, confining his poetry writing to evenings and weekends.

Into the Stone and Other Poems, Mr. Dickey's first collection, was published by Charles Scribner's Sons in 1960. (Some poems had already appeared in magazines like *The New Yorker* and *Harper's.*)

"It is when he yokes the natural and the mechanical, the antipodes of our folklore, he really sings," wrote the critic Geoffrey A. Wolff. "In this he resembles Hart Crane: wedding the machine to the natural, taking all things for what they are and explaining their shapes and motives."

As he grew more successful in advertising, working for agencies in New York and Atlanta, Mr. Dickey said, he realized he was "living half a life," stealing time for poetry. He was also feeling guilty, looking on advertising as a corrupter of the values of both its creators and the public. "I knew how to manipulate those poor sheep," he said, "but the fact I felt that way about them was an indication of my own corruption."

In 1961, Mr. Dickey chucked it all, went on welfare briefly, then received a $5,000 Guggenheim grant and sold his home in Atlanta. After spending a year in Italy, he was for the next few years poet in residence at Reed College in Portland, Ore.; San Fernando Valley State College in Los Angeles, and the University of Wisconsin. He also published volumes of poetry in 1962 (*Drowning With Others*) and in 1964 (*Helmets, Two Poems in the Air*).

He also published a selection of his critical essays, *The Suspect in Poetry,* in which Mr. Dickey ventured some ornery judgments. He classified John Milton, for example, among "the great stuffed goats of English literature," showed scant enthusiasm for Ezra Pound and T. S. Eliot, and dismissed altogether such contemporaries as Allen Ginsberg.

In 1966 Mr. Dickey succeeded Stephen Spender as consultant in poetry to the Library of Congress and held the post—at the time, the rough American equivalent of Britain's poet laureate—for two years. He enlivened the library with his unbridled opinions, as illustrated at a news conference in which he described Dylan Thomas's poetry reading style as "too actorish," called Theodore Roethke "immensely superior to any other poet we have in this country," denounced the Beat poets as "awful, ludicrously inept, hopelessly bad" and pronounced Vietnam War protest poems mere "tracts—messages with a capital 'M,' propaganda."

Mr. Dickey finally settled, in 1968, at the University of South Carolina in Columbia, where he was poet in residence and a professor of English. A popular teacher who dressed habitually in blue jeans, he became locally renowned for his epic capacity for consuming liquor and attracting the attention of women. He liked to advise his creative-writing students to tune into their recalcitrant unconsciousness or, as he put it, the "celestial wireless."

His favorite pastime was archery, a sport in which he excelled and which figured prominently in the plot of *Deliverance.*

Mr. Dickey said writing that novel was one of the most challenging experiences of his life. He admitted that his poetic sensibility was his main problem with the book.

"I wanted to write imaginative prose that did not strain for metaphorical brilliance," he said, "I spent time taking things out of my prose." The book came hard, he added, because separating words from rhythm was like "putting on a wooden overcoat."

He succeeded in delivering straightforward prose, though it carried strongly poetic overtones. Mr. Dickey's poetry, on the other hand, like that of many of his contemporaries, often appeared to be a typographer's nightmare. Reviewing his collection *The Strength of Fields,* in *The New York Times Book Review* in 1980, the critic Paul Zweig wrote admiringly:

> The poems in James Dickey's new book float down over-wide pages, contract to a single word, lapse into italics, skip over blank intervals. They are like richly modulated hollers, a sort of rough, American-style bel canto advertising its freedom from the constraints of ordinary language. Dickey's style is so personal, his rhythms so willfully eccentric, that the poems seem to swell up and overflow like that oldest of American art forms, the boast. Dickey is crowing, flooding his subjects with sheer style.

Mr. Dickey's favorite themes were commonplace: the

tongue-in-cheek poems, poems about fighter pilots and about his experiences in World War II, the animal poems, those about death and grief, and those about bow-and-arrow hunters and football players and running marathons.

In **"For the Death of Vince Lombardi,"** which immortalized the storied football coach, Mr. Dickey, with great relish, extolled the game for its "aggression meanness deception delight in giving pain to others," with such wholeheartedness that the game seems to stand for the onslaught of life itself. The poem reads in part:

> Around your bed the knocked-out teeth like hail
>   pebbles
> Rattle down miles of adhesive tape from hands
>   and ankles
> Writhe in the room like vines, gallons of sweat
>   blaze in buckets
> In the corners the blue and yellow bruises
> Make one vast sunset around you.

Among Mr. Dickey's volumes of poems were *Drowning with Others, The Eye-Beaters, The Zodiac, Scion, Puella* and *The Central Motion.* His critical works included *Babel to Byzantium* and *Sorties.*

Mr. Dickey's first wife, Maxine, died in 1976, and two months later he married Deborah Dodson, who was one of his students. He is survived by his wife; two sons, Kevin and Christopher, from his first marriage, and a daughter, Bronwen Elaine.

REVIEWS OF DICKEY'S RECENT WORKS

Lachlan Mackinnon (review date 10 May 1991)

SOURCE: "Mumbling and Clanging," in *Times Literary Supplement,* May 10, 1991, p. 22.

[*In the following excerpt, Mackinnon condemns Dickey's* The Eagle's Mile *as "a clanging, overweening collection."*]

[I]n the title poem, **"The Eagle's Mile",** in memory of Justice William Douglas, theoretically welcome as a public elegy and especially as one about such a man, Dickey invites the addressee to reappear in landscape and "power-hang in it all now, for all / The whole thing is worth: catch without warning / Somewhere in the North Georgia creek like ghost-muscle tensing / Forever, or on the high grass bed / Yellow of dawn, catch like a man stamp-printed by God- / shock, blue as the very foot / Of fire." All the words work like pistons in a museum engine, flailing, rhetorical and futile.

A quieter poem like **"The Olympian"**, in which Dickey races "the Olympian, / Now my oldest boy's junior / High school algebra teacher" round his garden, reads better. The teacher trips "and on a bloated blessed doughnut-ring / Of rubber rolled" and laughs in a way Dickey "maybe" hears "all over the earth, where that day and any and every / Day after it, devil hindmost and Goddamn it / To glory, I lumbered for gold." "Lumbered" merits the epical overwriting that precedes it, but such touches of poetic self-awareness are too rare to redeem a clanging, overweening collection.

William Pratt (review date Summer 1991)

SOURCE: A review of *The Eagle's Mile,* in *World Literature Today,* Summer, 1991, p. 489.

[*In the following review, Pratt discusses the language in* The Eagle's Mile.]

Having long ago charted his place as a leading American poet of flight, James Dickey makes flight the central theme of his latest collection of poems. He borrows his title from a line of William Blake, "The Emmet's Inch & Eagle's Mile," and like Blake he mixes the visionary with the actual, sometimes mounting on the powerful wings of eagles, sometimes on the delicate wings of butterflies, letting his imagination soar into space or, at other times, calling back images of aerial gunnery in the Pacific, from his service as a night-fighter pilot in World War II and the Korean War. There is no poem in **The Eagle's Mile** as sensational as his earlier famous **"Falling,"** which combines the exhilaration of flying, the erotic motions of a woman's body in space, and the inevitability of dying, but the brilliant colors of **"To the Butterflies"** offer a visual and descriptive feast to be enjoyed along with its imaginary flight.

Dickey has always been an experimentalist with form, never settling for casual or conversational free verse, but shaping his words in strongly patterned cadences, with frequent spaced pauses and marked accents in the manner of [Gerard Manley] Hopkins (suggesting that "The Windhover" is one of his models of poetic flight), producing staccato and crescendo effects that bear some resemblance to the vibrating movement of engines in human flight. Dickey has a fondness for the incantatory power of words which links him with [Edgar Allan] Poe, and as in Poe, the sounds of his words sometimes seem to take on more significance than their meanings, creating what Poe would have called an emotional "effect" more important than any meaning.

The title poem shows all the strengths, and the weaknesses, of Dickey's poetry: **"The Eagle's Mile"** is dedicated to the late Justice William Douglas of the U.S. Supreme Court, who

was an outdoorsman like Dickey and loved the Appalachian Trail that ran "from Springer Mountain [in Georgia] to Maine," as the poem remembers, describing hiking journeys along the trial and also envisioning flight above it, where you "like Adam find yourself splintering out / Somewhere on the eagle's mile." In a trick of ventriloquy, however, the poem addresses Douglas directly as if he were still alive, making it the sort of public performance which Dickey more and more favors (he was the Poet Laureate of Jimmy Carter's presidency, and in the new collection there is a poem for "a South Carolina inauguration of Richard Riley as governor"), and at times he strains for words like the hurdler he once was—"Douglas, power-hang in it all now, for all / The whole thing is worth"—so forcing his reader into collaboration with him in what seems a rhetorical act of celebration as much as a poem.

Dickey's poetry is a mixture of the visionary with the actual that sometimes soars and sometimes runs aground, splitting consciousness as he likes to split his lines, thus deliberately keeping any single poem from becoming a unified and harmonious whole, despite its often singing and moving uses of language.

Robert Kirschten (review date May 1993)

SOURCE: "Form and Genre in James Dickey's 'Falling': The Great Goddess Gives Birth to the Earth," in *South Atlantic Review,* Vol. 58, No. 2, May, 1993, pp. 127-54.

[*In the following essay, Kirschten analyzes the significance of the stewardess in Dickey's "Falling."*]

A quarter of a century ago, well before many current intellectual trends became mainstream, James Dickey reaffirmed the multicultural brotherhood of his own poetic vision with Native Americans, when, in **Self-Interviews,** he lamented

> the loss of a sense of intimacy with the natural process. I think you would be very hard-put . . . to find a more harmonious relationship to an environment than the American Indians had. We can't return to a primitive society . . . but there is a property of mind which, if encouraged, could have this personally animistic relationship to things. . . . It's what gives us a *personal* relationship to the sun and the moon, the flow of rivers, the growth and decay of natural forms, and the cycles of death and rebirth.

An exhilarating celebration of just those harmonious cycles, **"Falling"** is one of Dickey's best known and most spectacular poems. The lyric runs more than six full pages in page-wide lines with minimal punctuation to interrupt its accelerating whirlwind of energy while depicting the fatal fall of a twenty-nine-year-old stewardess from a commercial airplane over Kansas. Although this woman starts off as the victim of a tragic accident, her fall is exhilarating because she ends up as someone significantly different.

Critics have offered clues to this transformation. Joyce Carol Oates claims that the stewardess is "a kind of mortal goddess, given as much immortality . . . as poetry is capable of giving its subjects." Monroe Spears notes that she "becomes a goddess, embodiment of a myth." Joyce Pair, editor of *The James Dickey Newsletter,* observes that the stewardess is "a modern incarnation of the goddess of crops and fertility." Even Dickey himself says that the stewardess has a "goddess-like invulnerability." While these clues identify the stewardess as a goddess, there are few extended discussions of the poem that develop this premise. My own seven-page analysis, written in 1983 as part of a chapter on sacrificial victims in a book-length study of Dickey's poetry, concurs with these opinions to some degree, suggesting that "we may best read '**Falling**' . . . as a ritual reenactment of the primitive practice of killing a god of vegetation to ensure both the perpetuation of crops and the continuation of the human species itself." However, after more extensive reading in mythological literatures, I believe that my initial assessment undervalues the power and character of this woman and that a more detailed reading is in order. To say that the stewardess is merely a "sacrificial victim"—a term derived from Kenneth Burke and René Girard—renders her passive in a way that does not reflect her true dynamic and dramatic character. We need thus to trace more fully the process of empowerment (the "plot" or "form" of the poem) that the stewardess undergoes by looking at the kind of mythological activity (the "genre") this process resembles. By offering three analogies with goddesses from Native American, Asian, and Mesoamerican myths, we may best see "**Falling**" as an animistic, matriarchal, creation myth—in many ways, the emotional and cultural opposite of the patriarchal narrative in Genesis—whose particular rendering in Dickey's hands reveals further insights into his conceptions of women and nature. My claim is that "**Falling**" is Dickey's remarkable transformation of an airline employee into an analogue of one of the Great Goddesses of primitive seed-planting cultures, more specifically, Mother Earth, who, in the process of falling and dying, gives birth to herself and the earth.

First Analogy: Bird Woman (or Lady of the Animals) and The Woman Who Fell from the Sky

After the stewardess falls out of the plane, she panics at first, then experiments with her fall. Dickey says, "[S]he develops interest she turns in her maneuverable body / / To watch it." Not only does she begin to enjoy her fall, but she takes on the first in a series of new kinds of power, namely, the power of animals. At line 30, she changes from someone

merely performing "endless gymnastics" into what I will call her role as "Bird Woman," for she now can "slant   slide / Off tumbling   into the emblem of a bird with its wings half-spread." Whether in "**Reincarnation II**," where we find "There is a wing-growing motion / Half-alive in every creature," or in "**Eagles,**" where the poet says "My feathers were not / Of feather-make, but broke from a desire to drink / The rain before it falls," the empowerment of human beings through magical contact with animals is a long-standing commonplace in Dickey's work. This topic recalls two of Jungian psychologist Erich Neumann's observations when he discusses animals symbolic of ancient goddesses: first, that the "birdlike character of woman points primarily to her correlation with the heavens," and second, that in Creto-Aegean culture "The Great Mother as a nature goddess . . . was mistress of the mountains and of wild animals" and that "birds . . . symbolized her presence."

In "**Falling,**" Dickey's stewardess-goddess has "Time to live / In superhuman health" by so taking on the properties of bird flight and vision that she becomes a variation of what is called in Pali Buddhism "The great woman rich in creatures":

> Arms out   she slow-rolls over   steadies out
>   waits for something great
> To take control of her   trembles near feathers
>   planes head-down
> The quick movements of bird-necks turning her
>   head   gold eyes the insight-
> eyesight of owls blazing into the hencoops   a
>   taste for chicken overwhelming
> Her   the long-range vision of hawks enlarging all
>   human lights of cars
> Freight trains   looped bridges   enlarging the
>   moon racing slowly
> Through all the curves of a river   all the darks of
>   the midwest blazing
> From above.

By acquiring the "insight- / eyesight of owls" and "The long-range vision of hawks," the stewardess is not only rich in creatures but reenacts the role of a prehistoric goddess known as "The Lady of the Animals" who often appears in the form of a bird. Citing Marija Gimbutas's *The Goddesses and Gods of Old Europe,* Carol Christ tells us that Gimbutas found a

> pre-Bronze Age culture that was "matrifocal" . . .
> presided over by a Goddess as Source and Giver of
> All. Originally the Goddess did not appear with animals but herself had animal characteristics. One of
> her earliest forms was as the Snake and Bird Goddess, associated with water, and represented as a
> snake, a water bird, a duck, goose, crane, diver bird,

or owl, or as a woman with a bird head or birdlike posture. She was the Goddess Creatress, the giver of Life.

Known in classical mythology as "Aphrodite with her dove, Athene with her owl, [and] Artemis with her deer," the image of the Lady of Animals, Christ notes, goes back in history beyond Homer to the Neolithic and Paleolithic eras. In the Homeric Hymns (c. 800-400 BC), "The Lady of the Animals is cosmic power; she is mother of all; the animals of Earth, sea, and air are hers; the wildest and most fearsome of animals. . . . [She] is also earth: she is the firm foundation undergirding all life."

In **"Falling,"** Dickey's Lady of the Animals not only possesses the vision of hawks and owls but also their "fearsome" power over prey and, most importantly, their powers and instruments of flight. With "a taste for chicken   overwhelming / Her" and "The air beast-crooning to her   warbling," the stewardess arranges her skirt "Like a diagram of a bat" and thus "has this flying-skin / Made of garments." These diverse animal traits dramatically enable her to change both her activity and her character. Her fall becomes purposive, no longer the formless result of an unintended accident, but instead "a long stoop   a hurtling   a fall / That is controlled   that plummets as it wills." As the velocity of her fall accelerates, an effect conveyed brilliantly by Dickey's spectacular visual imagery, so too the stewardess' plummeting will-to-power increases. At one point, she alters the very laws of nature as she "Turns gravity / Into a new condition, showing its other side like a moon shining / New Powers." And shortly thereafter, she begins to become fully active by determining her own fate; that is, she will not "just *fall   just tumble screaming all that time.*" She will "use / *It*" (italics in original).

While magically connected to animals, yet still in her human form, Dickey's stewardess also resembles a goddess who experiences a similar fall in an Iroquois creation myth called "The Woman Who Fell from the Sky." From J. B. N. Hewitt's "Iroquois Cosmology" (as abridged and recast in Campbell's *World Mythology*) we learn that in "regions above," where "[s]orrow and death were unknown. . . ," a

> tree had been uprooted [so that] . . . a hole was left . . . opened to the world below. . . . [A] woman-being . . . fell into the hole and kept on falling through its darkness, and after a while passed through its length. And when she had passed quite through onto this other world, she . . . looked in all directions and saw on all sides about her that everything was blue. . . . [S]he was now looking upon a great expanse . . . of water. . . . On the surface of the water . . . were all sorts and forms of waterfowl. . . . [One of them] noticed her. . . . [T]hey sent up to her a

flight of numerous ducks of various kinds, which in a very compact body elevated themselves to meet her on high. And on their backs, thereupon, her body did indeed alight. So then slowly they descended, bearing on their backs her body.

Though the birds and animals in Dickey's poem do not bear the stewardess on their backs, they form an entourage of accompanying support that shapes the very contour of her fall. Her alignment with hawks, owls, and bats changes her fall from a "Tumble" to a fall like that of "sky-divers on TV," which, at least, hypothetically, offers her the hope that, "like a diver," she may "plunge" into "water like a needle to come out healthily dripping / And be handed a Coca-Cola." In addition to her birdlike motion, the Iroquois woman-being, like the stewardess, shares a similar creative relationship with the earth. When the Iroquois woman falls, there is no land below her, only water. To safeguard her from drowning, the ducks place her on the back of the Great Turtle. Beaver and Otter try to bring up mud from the bottom to fashion earth for her, but they die in the process. So does Muskrat. As he surfaces, however, mud is found in his paws, and this the animals place around the carapace of the turtle. When the woman awakes, she finds the mud, like Dickey's "enlarging" earth, transformed:

> [T]he earth whereupon she sat had become in size enlarged. . . . [S]he . . . saw that willows along the edge of the water had grown to be bushes. . . . [S]he saw . . . growing shrubs of the rose willow along the edge of the water. . . . [S]he saw take up its course a little rivulet. In that way, in their turn things came to pass. The earth rapidly was increasing in size. She . . . saw all kinds of herbs and grasses spring from the earth and grow . . . toward maturity.

Later in this legend, the woman-being gives birth to a daughter who in turn gives birth to a set of twins. The first twin, Sapling, tosses the sun and the moon into the sky and forms the race of mankind. The Woman Who Fell from the Sky is thus a kind of mother responsible for the creation of the cosmos, the earth, and humanity.

In **"Falling"** the stewardess gives birth to a special kind of "enlarging earth." After she determines to "use" her fall, the American landscape "enlarges" not only because she falls closer to ground; it becomes animated—animistic—and a tremendous source of revelation and energy for her. Dickey's earth is, in fact, created out of animated elements similar to those in Chinese and Babylonian creation myths in which reality is said to emerge out of original "chaos" when "all was darkness and water." When the stewardess falls out of a layer of clouds, she beholds a new world likewise issuing out of "chaos" and "darkness and water": "New darks   new progressions of headlights along dirt roads   from chaos / / And night   a gradual warming   a new-made, inevitable world of one's own / Country" with "its waiting waters." These "waiting waters," like those toward which the Iroquois woman falls, also come magically alive as the source of all life for Dickey's goddess. Even though, on a literal level, the stewardess stands little chance of diving safely into water, imagery of "The waters / Of life" is so pervasive that it constitutes a major element in the vast scenic receptacle of natural movement in the "new-made . . . world" that receives her. As she heads "Toward the blazing-bare lake," this world of water is "new-made" and life-giving because of its tremendous potential for burgeoning energy. Like a life-saving rope that cannot aid her, "The moon [is] packed and coiled in a reservoir," and in the agricultural and sexual worlds of fecundity that she will never know, "farmers sleepwalk . . . a walk like falling toward the far waters / Of life in moonlight . . . [t]oward the flowering of the harvest in their hands." As nourisher and transformer, water is the vessel of life in the womb; its nutrients make it a medium for growth, and, of course, the sea is the source of life, but also, tragically, the destroyer. Water thus unites heaven and earth in the "Great Round" of life and death. By entering so fully into this perpetual cycle, Dickey's stewardess is the great Egyptian heaven goddess Nut, who is, Neumann reminds us,

> water above and below, vault above and below, life and death, east and west, generating and killing, in one. . . . The Great Goddess is the flowing unity of subterranean and celestial primordial water, the sea of heaven on which sail the barks of the gods of light, the circular life-generating ocean above and below the earth. To her belong all waters, streams, fountains, ponds, and springs, as well as the rain. She is the ocean of life with its life- and death-bringing seasons. . . .

This realm is not the world of discursive consciousness. It is, rather, what Neumann calls "The primordial darkness" of "The Dark Mother," "The Nocturnal Mother," or more specifically, "The matriarchal world of the beginning" of the creative unconscious, which "the patriarchal world strives to deny." And with its "moon-crazed inner eye of midwest imprisoned / Water," Dickey's night-world is far less the real Kansas than it is D. H. Lawrence's Etruscan universe in which "all was alive. . . . The whole thing was alive, and had a great soul, or *anima.*"

Dickey's animistic conception of nature radically opposes that of the machine-world of the airliner with which the poem begins. In considering Dickey's animism, which reveals much about his main character, it is useful to recall Carol Christ's statement: "To the Old Europeans the Lady of the Animals was not a power transcending earth, but rather the power that creates, sustains, and is manifest in the infinite

variant of life forms on earth. Old Europe did not celebrate humanity's uniqueness and separation from nature but rather humanity's participation in and connection to nature's cycles of birth, death, and renewal." Speaking in a similar vein about natural "connection" in *Self-Interviews,* Dickey paraphrases Lawrence's statement to the effect that "as a result of our science and industrialization, we have lost the cosmos. The parts of the universe we can investigate by means of machinery and scientific empirical techniques we may understand better than our predecessors did, but we no longer know the universe emotionally." Dickey's poetic answer to technological alienation characterized by "The vast, sluggish forces of habit, mechanization and mental torpor" is to build a universe populated not only by what he has called, in an article so titled, **"The Energized Man,"** but, in this poem, what we may call the "Energized Woman." She is, among other things, a poetic adversary of contemporary commercialism. The Energized Woman is someone whose mind is "not used simply to sell neckties or industrial machines or to make cocktail conversation, but to serve as the vital center of a moving and changing, perceiving and evaluating world which . . . is that world of delivery from drift and inconsequence." She does not dwell in an earth filled with the deadening rhetoric of advertising; Dickey even parodies advertising slogans: when "*opening the natural wings of* [her] *jacket / By Don Loper,*" the stewardess shifts in the same poetic line from the world of fashion to the primitive world of movement "*like a hunting owl toward the glitter of water*" (italics in original). Rather, the Energized Woman lives in a world filled with the dynamic energy of "mana," which is, in Jane Harrison's description, "a world of unseen power lying behind the visible universe, a world which is the sphere . . . of magical activity and the medium of mysticism."

Commenting on the Iroquois myth, Joseph Campbell sheds further light on Dickey's energized "Sky Woman" and this magical, mystical power she possesses. The Woman Who Fell from the Sky is, Campbell says, "a North American example of . . . a universally recognized, early planting-culture mythology, wherein by analogy with the seeded earth, the creative and motivating force (*sakti*) of the world illusion (*maya*) was envisioned, and in fact experienced, as female (*devi*)." The Sky Woman is an "avatar from the Sky World to this earth, bearing in her womb the gift of a race of human beings, heavenly endowed to join in mutual regard the supportive animal population already present." She is also a Neolithic great moon goddess or moon-messenger. Gimbutas notes that the moon goddess was "essentially a Goddess of Regeneration, . . . product of a . . . matrilinear community. . . . [She] was giver of life and all that promotes fertility. . . ." Lamenting the fact that "[t]here's no moon goddess now," Dickey once stated that, from a scientific point of view, the moon is "simply a dead stone, a great ruined stone in the sky." And so it is, at the opening of **"Falling,"** that "[t]he states" are "drawing moonlight out of the great / One-sided stone hung off the starboard wingtip." As the stewardess acquires momentum, however, the ancient mythological connection between the moon and water comes magically alive, for the moon is transformed into "The harvest moon," "racing slowly / Through all the curves of a river" and into "a great stone of light in waiting waters." This all takes place beneath and above a moon-bride who falls from "The heavenly rapture of experienced non-duality. . . . [T]he woman's fall is at once a death (to the sky) and a birth (to this earth)."

Second Analogy: Mistress of All Desires and Joys; Or, Goddess Unchained

The role of the stewardess as Sky Woman continues throughout her fall, but at line 94, her "shining / New Powers" take on an even greater scope. Dickey provides a clue to this stage of change in **Self-Interviews** when he says that he tried "To think of the mystical possibility there might be for farmers in that vicinity." Not only farmers, we might add, but all who feel the influence of the moon goddess are drawn, as

> under her   under chenille bedspreads
> The farm girls are feeling the goddess in them
>   struggle and rise brooding
> On the scratch-shining posts of the bed   dreaming
>   of female signs
> Of the moon   male blood like iron   of what is
>   really said by the moan
> Of airliners passing over them at dead of midwest
>   midnight   passing
> Over brush fires   burning out in silence on little
>   hills   and will wake
> To see the woman they should be   struggling on
>   the rooftree to become
> Stars

At this passage, the stewardess acquires a pervasive sexual power that animates sexual instinct in all those, women and men, who fall within her range. This power accelerates in the following lines when, defiantly, "To die / Beyond explanation," the stewardess rids herself of the restrictive trappings of her airline uniform, "The girdle required by regulations," and "The long windsocks of her stockings." She is now Goddess unchained, and her flight is "superhuman" because her mystical, sexual power is even more comprehensive. She is

> desired by every sleeper in his dream:
> Boys finding for the first time their loins filled
>   with heart's blood
> Widowed farmers whose hands float under light
>   covers to find themselves
> Arisen at sunrise   the splendid position of blood

> unearthly drawn
> Toward clouds   all feel something   pass over
>   them as she passes
> Her palms over *her* long legs   *her* small breasts
>   and deeply between
> Her thighs
> (italics in original)

From lines 94 to 141 (just before she enters the ground and becomes the earth's creative force), the stewardess's procreative powers lead to a stage of empowerment at which we may call her the "Mistress of All Desires and Joys" or the "Great Maya." Speaking of the Buddhist "mother-goddess or earth-mother" who "signifies the triumph of the feminine principle over the masculine," Heinrich Zimmer says,

> The goddess, who "consists of all the beings and worlds" is herself the pregnant salt womb of the life sea, holding all forms of life in her embrace and nourishing them; she herself casts them adrift in the sea and gives them over to decay, and in all innocence rebuilds them into forms forever new. . . .

She is the agreeable side of the hideous Indian goddess Kali, who after she drinks blood, changes faces and becomes "The world mother"; she bestows "existence upon new living forms in a process of unceasing procreation." In "Hinduism," Zimmer says, "The male looks upon all womanhood . . . as the self-revelation of the goddess in the world of appearances." And "in the secret orgiastic ritual of the Tantras, reserved to the initiate, the erotic sacrament of the sexes stands above the enjoyment of meat and drink as the supreme intoxicant by which men can attain redemption in their lifetime." She has a "magic power, which fulfills and hallows, is embodied in everything feminine. . . . [A]ll [women] have a shimmer of superhuman dignity, as vessel and symbol of the supreme natural force (*sakti*) of the mother-goddess, to whom all things owe their existence."

Terms such as "The supreme intoxicant" and "orgiastic ritual" lead to further considerations about the erotic aspect of Dickey's poetic method. This method centers on an intoxicating, dreamlike ecstasy signaled early in the poem as the stewardess falls "with the delaying, dumfounding ease / Of a dream of being drawn / like endless moonlight to the harvest soil / Of a central state of one's country." Both nightmare and adrenaline rush, these dream-states run throughout **"Falling,"** suggesting [Friedrich] Nietzsche's Dionysian and Apollonian forces upon which art depends, "as procreation is dependent on the duality of the sexes, involving perpetual conflicts with only periodically intervening reconciliations." Insofar as Monroe Spears notes in *Dionysus and the City* that Dickey's poetry is at its best when "basic Dionysian preoccupations . . . operate in proper balance with the Apollonian elements," we would do well to take a moment to see how these two Nietzschean opposites—in "balance" and "perpetual conflict"—operate in **"Falling."**

The Apollonian or dream component of the poem can be found in the fantastic stream of explosive celestial images that flow about the stewardess as she falls and in the Olympian point of view from which she has a godlike scope of vision. Nietzsche claims that such dreamstates conduce to extraordinary modes of holistic consciousness, a philosophic topic that runs throughout Dickey's poetry and is incorporated in two oxymorons at the end of the elegiac **"The Eagle's Mile,"** where we find Justice William O. Douglas's "death drawing life / From growth / from flow" so that, in the poem's last line, he may "Splinter uncontrollably whole." Of this kind of ecstatic dream vision, Nietzsche says:

> In dreams, according to the conception of Lucretius, the glorious divine figures first appeared to the souls of men, in dreams the great shaper beheld the charming corporeal structure of superhuman beings. . . . [F]or Apollo, as the god of all shaping energies, is also the sooth saying god. . . . The higher truth, the perfection of [the inner world of fantasies] . . . in contrast to the only partially intelligible everyday world, ay, the deep consciousness of nature, healing and helping in sleep and dream, is at the same time the symbolical analogue of the faculty of soothsaying and, in general, of the arts, through which life is made possible and worth living.

In Dickey's poem, what is prophetic (and "healing") about the stewardess's visioning powers is not that she attains a truth that can be put in the form of an oracle or conceptual proposition but, rather, that the panoramic faculty of her eye and its streaming "openness"—that of Apollo, Nietzsche's "sculptor-god"—result in her "accessibility" to the Dionysian powers of the "more than human," to "metamorphosis and transfiguration." That is, though she faces certain death, the energy from her Apollonian rush of consciousness and its Dionysian content "prophesizes" (i.e., foretells and foreshadows) an ecstatic, life-affirming reversal of her fate; for, not only are "Her eyes opened wide by wind" so that she sees the earth approaching, but also she is "lying in one after another of all the positions for love / Making   dancing" in a vibrant Dionysian ecstasy.

The result of yet another of Dickey's monstrous combinations of poetic "good / And evil," the stewardess's drama explodes in power by representing her Nietzschean opposites in a "perpetual conflict" that produces a stunning kind of frenzy (or ecstasy). The dramatic method involved here is, as Nietzsche says, "The Apollonian embodiment of Dionysian perceptions and influences," which produces "enchantment" as a kind of reverse irony. Instead of the audi-

ence distancing itself from the central action by knowing more than the performing character, the end of this ironic frenzy is

> to see one's self transformed before one's self and then to act as if one had really entered into another body, into another character. . . . [H]ere we actually have a surrender of the individual by his entering into another nature. . . . In this enchantment the Dionysian reveller sees himself as a satyr, *and as satyr he in turn beholds the god. . . .* [In] his transformation he sees a new vision outside him as the Apollonian consummation of his state. With this new vision the drama is complete.

The stewardess becomes a goddess—as does the reader, participating emotionally with her—precisely through this Dionysian state of intoxicating new vision, itself a delirious peripety. Her frenzy is a "rapturous transport," a "narcotic potion," which, like certain varieties of mysticism, erases "all sense of individuality in self-forgetfulness," or, we might add, like a mystical transport that produces movement transfiguring the vulnerable self into a greater power, when, for example, one feels the sensation of being intoxicated by speed:

> She is watching her country lose its evoked master
>   shape   watching it lose
> And gain   get back its houses and peoples
>   watching it bring up
> Its local lights   single homes   lamps on barn
>   roofs   if she fell
> Into water she might live   like a diver   cleaving
>   perfect   plunge
> Into another   heavy silver   unbreathable
>   slowing   saving
> Element. . . .

Dickey's technical virtuosity in **"Falling,"** as seen in the long, Whitmanesque lines punctuated by caesura, his terraces of spectacularly ascending rhythm, his striking image groups conveying the impression of a free fall, produce in the reader the sensation that his Dionysian deity of motion, like Nietzsche's, is "on the point of taking a dancing flight into the air." Nietzsche continues: "His gestures bespeak enchantment. . . . [S]omething supernatural sounds forth from him: he feels himself a god." Of such frenzy, the German philosopher writes:

> The essential thing in all intoxication is the feeling of heightened power and fullness. With this feeling one . . . compels [things] to receive what one has to give. . . .
> One enriches everything out of one's own fullness:

whatever one sees, whatever one wills, is seen swelled, taut, strong, overloaded with strength. The individual in this state transforms things until they mirror his power—until they are reflections of his perfection.

The frenzy in **"Falling"** is not simple escapism; it is entrance into an archetypal mode of motion that features the cycle of desire and death (Eros and Thanatos) but transcends death by participating fully in this eternal cycle. Whereas Dickey's stewardess-goddess fills boys' "loins with heart's blood," she will also soon become part of "The loam where extinction slumbers in corn tassels thickly." This concept of life-in-death fits Nietzsche's conception of the "orgiastic," which underscores the fabulous life-affirming impulse of the stewardess even in the face of her own death:

> [T]he orgiastic [is] an overflowing feeling of life and strength, where even pain still has the effect of a stimulus. . . . Tragedy is . . . [the] repudiation and counter-instance [of pessimism]. Saying Yes to life, even in its strangest and hardest problems, the will to life rejoicing over its own inexhaustibility even in the very sacrifice of its highest types—*that* is what I called Dionysian. . . . [One does not experience tragedy] to be liberated from terror and pity, not in order to purge oneself of a dangerous affect by its vehement discharge—Aristotle understood it that way—but in order to be *oneself* the eternal joy of becoming, . . . that joy which included even joy in destroying. . . . Herewith I again stand on the soil out of which my intention . . . grows—I, the teacher of eternal recurrence.

In **"Falling,"** this Yea-saying Dionysian power features a matriarchal component that is reflected in Nietzsche's own metaphor; he claims that this is a world in which "nature speaks to us with its true undissembled voice: 'Be as I am! Amidst the ceaseless change of phenomena the eternally creative primordial mother, eternally impelling to existence, self-satisfying eternally with this change of phenomena!'"

This orgiastic power is not the power of domination or control. Rather, it is what Herbert Marcuse calls an erotic stance that reconciles Eros and Thanatos in "a world that is not to be mastered and controlled but to be liberated." In such a realm, the "opposition between man and nature, subject and object, is overcome. Being is experienced as gratification." The stewardess's shedding of her clothes is, thus, an enabling ritual or dance, designed to affirm a social "order without repression" and to amplify her basic bodily powers, as Dickey says, in a "last superhuman act" that defies the death of the body and expresses what Marcuse calls "a non-repressive erotic attitude toward reality." Instead of the functionary of a commercial airline, the stewardess is, in Marcusian

terms, "[n]o longer used as a full-time instrument of labor," for her body is "resexualized" such that "Eros, freed from surplus-repression, would be strengthened" and "[d]eath would cease to be an instinctual goal." This transforming dance and ecstatic vision of sexuality are not limited to gender. Dionysian rapture as a sexual mode of holistic motion transcending death also attracted Theodore Roethke, who reveals this account in his notebooks:

> . . . I got into this real strange state. I got in the woods and started a circular kind of dance. . . . I kept going around and just shedding clothes. Sounds Freudian as hell, but in the end, I had a sort of circle—as if, I think, I understood intuitively what the frenzy is. That is, you go way beyond yourself, and . . . this is not sheer exhaustion but this strange sort of a . . . not illumination . . . but a sense of being again a part of the whole universe. I mean, anything but quiet. I mean, in a sense everything is symbolical. . . . [I]t was one of the deepest and [most] profound experiences I ever had. And accompanying it was a real sexual excitement also . . . and this tremendous feeling of actual power. . . .

> The *real* point is that this business of the dance accompanies exaltation of the highest, the human thing, and it also goes into the Dionysian frenzy, which in modern life hardly anyone even *speaks* of anymore. . . . [W]hen Vaughan says, "When felt through all my fleshy dress, / Ripe shoots of everlastingness," well, *that's* the feeling. You feel . . . that you are eternal, or immortal. . . . [F]urthermore, death becomes . . . an absurdity, of no consequence.

That Dickey should feature this kind of movement in **"Falling"** comes as no surprise, for the "Delphic trance" and "world of perpetual genesis" are aspects of Roethke's poetic vision that Dickey has long admired.

Third Analogy: Maize Stalk Drinking Blood

It is precisely these Nietzschean opposites in orgiastic combination—joy and destruction, tragedy and inexhaustibility, power and pain—in **"Falling"** that lead to our third analogy. The stewardess's flight ends abruptly when she enters the earth with a tremendous impact, which Dickey does not show, but represents symbolically with pronouns, "This is it   THIS," and which is all the more powerful and tragic for that indirect symbolization. At first glance, this moment exhibits a cataclysmic reversal of the life-force of her flight, for immediately after she lands, she is, terrifyingly

                                                    impressed
   In the soft loam   gone down   driven well into

the image of her body
The furrows for miles flowing in upon her where
  she lies very deep
In her mortal outline   in the earth as it is in cloud

She continues to live for a time after the impact; at the end of the poem, some thirty lines later, her last words are given in capitals: "AH, GOD—." Though she dies, this final poetic space, approximately one-sixth of the entire lyric, exhibits her full goddesslike nature and power in a way more compelling even than her fall. It bears repeating that Dickey does not dwell here on a mutilated woman. It is not her death that is his focus but a circle (or cycle) much wider in scope. In addition to our natural compassion for her death, our feeling for her issues from a deeper recognition of the universal in Dickey's dramatization of the intermingling forces of life and death. For those who find her, the poet says,

                        can tell nothing
But that she is there   inexplicable   unquestion-
  able   and remember
That something broke in them as well   and began
  to live and die more
When they walked for no reason into their fields to
  where the whole earth
Caught her

At this point, this contemporary airline stewardess bears comparison to the great Mesoamerican mother of the gods, Maize Stalk Drinking Blood. In a painting from the Codex Borgia, Mexico (c. AD 1500), called "The Tree of the Middle Place," these striking images occur:

> Rising from the body of an earth goddess recumbent on the spines of the . . . alligator . . . of the abyss, the Tree, encircled by the World Sea, is surmounted by a quetzal bird of bright plummage. Two streams of blood pour into the goddess, and from her body rise two ears of maize, a yellow and a red. . . . Personifying the fertile earth, this goddess of life out of death is normally identified by a skull or skeletal jaw. . . . She is known as the Maize Stalk Drinking Blood. . . . As noticed by Jill Leslie Furst, treating this goddess in a monograph entitled *The Skull as Fertility Symbol:* "The . . . skeletal remains were . . . regarded as the seat of the essential life force and the metaphorical seed from which the individual, whether human, animal, or plant, is reborn. . . ."

This voracious image of death points to a different aspect of the stewardess and of Great Goddesses in many cultures, namely, their terrible power of destruction. As Erich Neumann says,

The Great Mother as Terrible Goddess of the earth and of death is herself the earth, in which things rot. The Earth Goddess is "The devourer of the dead bodies of mankind" and the "mistress and lady of the tomb." Like Gaea, the Greek Earth Mother, she is mistress of the vessel and at the same time the great underworld vessel itself, into which dead souls enter, and out of which they fly up again.

The power of this goddess, also called the "Terrible Mother," is double-edged, suggesting not only death and destruction but also new life, for out of the body of Maize Stalk grow two ears of corn, signs of regeneration and rebirth. Discussing the story of Demeter and Persephone in the Greek festival Thesmophoria, Joseph Campbell emphasizes this redemptive power in the Great Goddess when he notes that in certain primitive Indonesian cycles

> goddesses [are] identified with the local food plants, . . . the underworld, and the moon, whose rites insure both a growth of the plants and a passage of the soul to the land of the dead. In both the marriage of the maiden goddess . . . is equivalent to her death, which is imaged as a descent into the earth and is followed, after a time, by her metamorphosis into food. . . .

These redemptive and sexual powers constitute one phase of the cycle of life and death through which humankind passes. Dickey's Goddess is Mother Earth giving birth and death to herself, for the goddess of sex is the goddess of death. Campbell notes that "The death god, Ghede, of the Haitian Voodoo tradition, is also the sex god. The Egyptian god Osiris was the judge and lord of the dead, and the lord of the regeneration of life." And, commenting on the "primitive-village mythology" of certain New Guinea tribes that include the "death-feast" of a "divine maiden" who died by sinking "into the earth among the roots of a tree" to rise later in the sky as the moon, he discusses this dialectical pairing of sex and death:

> [T]he plants on which man lives derive from this death. The world lives on death. . . . Reproduction without death would be a calamity, as would death without reproduction. . . . [T]he interdependence of death and sex, their import as the complementary aspects of a single state of being, and the necessity of . . . killing and eating . . . —this deeply moving, emotionally disturbing glimpse of death as the life of the living is the fundamental motivation supporting the rites around which the social structure of the early planting villages was composed.

A considerably less violent figure than the goddess in "The Tree of the Middle Place" or the New Guinean moon-maiden, Dickey's stewardess nonetheless enters the earth in a way suggesting that she gives birth to a similar cycle of generation and decay and that her death is not, merely, the termination of a single, discontinuous individual:

> All the known air above her is not giving up
>   quite one
> Breath   it is all gone   and yet not dead   not
>   anywhere else
> Quite   lying still in the field on her back   sens-
>   ing the smells
> Of incessant growth try to lift her

By accretions of these cyclic moments of death-in-life, Dickey often builds his poems out of magical circles, poetic "mandalas" (Sanskrit for "circle"); **"Falling"** also suggests the transference (and continuance) of the stewardess's fertile powers in the comic totems of "her clothes" which, magically, are "beginning / To come down all over Kansas": "her blouse on a lightning rod" and "her girdle coming down fantastically / On a clothesline, where it belongs." Further proof that her "all-sustaining, all-nourishing" sexual power continues is that it is felt sympathetically in the lives and in the fields of local farmers who perpetuate and participate in her extraordinary energy when the erotic dream sequence impels them to

>   sleepwalk without
> Their women from houses   a walk like falling
>   toward the far waters
> Of life   in moonlight   toward the dreamed
>   eternal meaning of their farms
> Toward the flowering of the harvest in their hands

When **"Falling"** is read aloud, the poem's cumulative energy is so overwhelming by the end of the performance that—although the death of the stewardess is a necessary, realistic outcome of her accident—her death has in it the feeling of a beginning. This beginning resembles the tremendous burgeoning that Kenneth Burke sees as the "frantic urgency of growth" in Theodore Roethke's "greenhouse poems," where "Nothing would give up life: / Even the dirt kept breathing a small breath." What truly animates Dickey's earth is the stewardess's cyclone of energy that is magically transferred to the ground she enters. Rather than a death, her impregnation of the land is the beginning of a new cycle of growth and decay. At poem's end, this cycle has been put in full motion by the poet. The reader's or listener's poetic experience of the stewardess's death is not a sense of cessation but of transformation. Just as the form of the poem is the reversal of the journalistic narrative that begins the action by announcing the airplane accident, the stewardess is never more alive than when she dies into her new life. Yet one more variation on Dickey's favorite topic of poetic motion, the stewardess's death is, as Campbell notes about ritual

love-death, a "fresh enactment, here and now" of a "god's own sacrifice . . . through which . . . she . . . became incarnate in the world process"; she is a constant reminder to us that "sudden, monstrous death" is a "revelation of the . . . inhumanity of the order of the universe." Yet we are also reminded, as Zimmer says of the plague goddesses of southern India, that "[t]o see the twofold, embracing and devouring, nature of the goddess, to see repose in catastrophe, security in decay, is to know her and be saved."

Social and Political Ends of "Falling"

Because it involves an erotic component and the death of a woman, **"Falling"** has received a considerable amount of negative commentary. By way of completing an inquiry into the form, genre, and value of this poem, we may use the preceding analysis to address a number of statements about this poem and Dickey himself. Some of these statements assess not only **"Falling"** negatively but also Dickey's work in general.

First, there are the charges of sexual perversion and insensitivity to women. In *Thinking About Women*, Mary Ellmann states that Dickey's depiction of women is "unnerving":

> James Dickey's poem **"Falling"** expresses an extraordinary concern with the underwear of a woman who has fallen out of an airplane. While this woman, a stewardess, was in the airplane, her girdle obscured, to the observation of even the most alert passenger, her mesial groove. The effect was, as the poem recalls, "monobuttocked." As the woman falls, however, she undresses and "passes her palms" over her legs, her breasts, and "deeply between her thighs." Beneath her, "widowed farmers" are soon to wake with futile (and irrelevant?) erections. She lands on her back in a field, naked, and dies. The sensation of the poem is necrophilic: it mourns a vagina rather than a person crashing to the ground.

Ellmann's charge that Dickey is victimizing women requires some time to sort out. With regard to her claim that Dickey shows an "extraordinary concern with the underwear of a woman," there is little "concern" about underwear that is "extraordinary" at all in **"Falling."** The stewardess's underwear, mentioned only twice in a poem of more than 175 lines and even then quite briefly, with no detailed description of the garments or lingering preoccupation whatsoever, emphasizes the transformation of a rigidly and commercially clothed woman who is nonetheless a goddess. In the first instance where "The underwear of a woman" appears, it is mentioned briefly in four lines and is part of the stream of clothes shed by the stewardess not to titillate men but to animate the earth sexually as part of her ritual defiance of mortality so that she may "die / Beyond explanation." When the underwear is mentioned, it is treated comically: "absurd / Brassiere" and "The girdle required by regulations." In the poem's second reference to underwear, it appears in one line only and, once again, in a comic context, with the stewardess's girdle described as "coming down fantastically / On a clothesline, where it belongs."

Second, Ellmann's claim that the stewardess is "monobuttocked" misses the point. The passenger's view of her "monobuttocked" condition is never mentioned in the poem. We scarcely see the stewardess in the plane; she falls out at line 7, and there is not the slightest hint of her being "monobuttocked" until 118 lines later, when the girdle is "squirming / Off her." Rather than stressing the girdle's "obscur[ing], to the observation of even the most alert passenger, her mesial groove," the poem emphasizes the stewardess's act of removing the girdle and revealing herself as goddess. The poem says that the stewardess is "*no longer* monobuttocked" (italics mine). The poem does not "recall" the view that Ellmann derides; instead, the poem describes the stewardess's liberation from the unnaturally confining, "monobuttocked" condition.

Third, Ellmann offers a brief comment on the stewardess's running her hands over her naked body (while farmers below her have "futile" and "irrelevant" erections) then dying in a field when she lands. Based on this excerpted narrative, Ellmann makes the most astounding claim that "[t]he sensation of the poem is necrophilic; it mourns a vagina rather than a person crashing to the ground." As reductive an example of critical paraphrase as one is likely to find, Ellmann's summary, which most certainly does not conform to Dickey's poem, is the only evidence for her bizarre charge. Ellmann's rewriting of Dickey turns **"Falling"** into a narrative of punitive reparation for the stewardess's sexuality, independence, and strength, a narrative whose tendency runs totally opposite to the poem's true course; her paraphrase does not admit of the tremendous energy of the poem or the fabulous series of powers that the stewardess acquires. The key point Ellmann misses is, as noted earlier, that *Dickey's poem reverses the tragic journalistic narrative* (which begins the poem) by converting a mortal stewardess into an earth goddess who lives and dies in the perpetual, natural alternation of generation and decay. Ellmann's omission of the poem's subtext that reverses the "journalistic" text is a disastrous misreading that turns a goddess into an inanimate corpse. To say that the poem "mourns a vagina"— only one four-word phrase in the work, "deeply between her thighs," even remotely mentions this anatomical area—is perverse and preposterous.

Instead of mourning a dynamic woman unfairly reduced to a body part, we do better to conclude with questions centering on the social and political values of Dickey's poem and to address these issues with the ideas of four strong, intelligent women. Does **"Falling"** challenge our traditional conceptions of divinity as masculine, inherited from a Judeo-Christian religious history? What implications does the metamorphosis of a woman into an earth goddess such as one finds described in so-called "primitive" cultures have for a contemporary Western audience? What does the poem, as an enabling, matriarchal, creation myth with its distinctive conception of nature, say politically to both women and men? And, finally, does Dickey's mythological conception of woman impose any limit on feminine power?

First, with regard to conceptions of divinity as masculine, Carol Christ thinks that the idea of goddesses is revolutionary. Goddesses "are about female power. . . . This power is so threatening to the status quo that the word *Goddess* still remains unspeakable even to many of the most radical Christian and Jewish theologians." Joseph Campbell has a similar notion about this traditional image of female power: "There can be no doubt that in the very earliest ages of human history the magical force and wonder of the female was no less a marvel than the universe itself; and this gave to woman a prodigious power, which it has been one of the chief concerns of the masculine part of the population to break, control, and employ to its own ends." That Dickey's matriarchal creation myth in **"Falling"** is literally a revolution—a reversal or turning around—of our Western biblical tradition of Genesis and its concept of woman can be buttressed by further testimony from Campbell's comments on the Iroquois tale of the Woman Who Fell from the Sky:

> The . . . episode . . . of the flight of ducks ascending to ease the woman's fall; the earth divers in willing sacrifice of their lives preparing hastily a place upon which to receive her; Great Turtle becoming, also willingly, the supporting ground of a new earth, upon which . . . a new arrival from the sphere of Air, would rest . . . while the new earth took form around her . . . represents a point of view with respect to the relationship of man to nature, and of the creatures of nature to man, that is in striking contrast to that defined in Genesis 3:14-19, where man is cursed, woman is cursed, the serpent is cursed, and the earth is cursed to "bring forth thorns and thistles." . . . [T]he basic and sustaining sense of the relationship to mankind of the natural world and its creatures in this Native American origin myth, is of compassion, harmony, and cooperation.

Using language from Christine Froula's article "When Eve Reads Milton," we may say that Dickey's goddess is the opposite of Adam's God, "who is a *perfected* image of Adam: an all-powerful *male* creator who soothes Adam's fears of female power by Himself claiming credit for the original creation of the world."

The second question centers on current implications of the stewardess's divinity. Summarizing Rita Gross's article "Hindu Female Deities as a Resource for the Contemporary Rediscovery of the Goddess," Christ indicates five lessons that "The symbol of the Goddess" from "ancient mythologies" can "Teach modern Westerners." Analogues to these points can be found in our analysis of **"Falling":**

> First, the Goddess's obvious strength, capability, and transcendence validate the power of women as women that has been denied in Western religion and culture. Second, Goddess symbolism involves the coincidence of opposites—of death and life, destruction and creativity—that reminds humans of the finitude of life and points to its transcendent ground. Third, Goddess religion values motherhood as symbolic of divine creativity, but without limiting female power to biological destiny. Fourth, Goddess symbolism also associates women with a wide range of culturally valued phenomena, including wealth, prosperity, culture, artful living, and spiritual teaching. Fifth, the Goddess requires the explicit reintroduction of sexuality as a religious metaphor in a symbol system where God is imaged as both male and female.

Also addressing the meaning of a primitive goddess for a Western audience, Christ lists four reasons "Why Women Need the Goddess" (one of her chapters is so titled) that may serve us as descriptions of the social ends effected by the enabling, mythic drama in **"Falling":**

> First, the Goddess is symbol of the legitimacy and beneficence of female power in contrast to the image of female power as anomalous or evil in biblical religion. Second, the Goddess validates women's bodily experiences, including menstruation, birth, lactation, and menopause, and validates the human connection to finitude, which has been denigrated in Western religions. Third, the Goddess symbol in the context of feminist goddess worship values the female will, which has been viewed as the origin of evil in biblical mythology. Fourth, the goddess points to the valuing of woman-to-woman bonds[,] . . . which is celebrated in the story of Demeter and Persephone. . . . The symbol of Goddess . . . legitimates and undergirds the moods and motivations inspired by feminism just as the symbol of God has legitimated patriarchal attitudes for several thousand years.

Third, speaking of "The ritual poem in feminist spiritual circles," Alicia Ostriker offers a suggestive conception of "ritual" that articulates the kind of potential political effects we sense in Dickey's ritualized form:

For poet and reader-participant alike, ritual poetry implies the possibility of healing alternatives to dominance-submission scenarios. It suggests nonoppressive models of the conjunction between religion and politics, usually by re-imaging the sacred as immanent rather than transcendent, by defining its audience as members of a potentially strong community rather than as helplessly lonely individual victims, and by turning to nature (seen as sacred and female) as a source of power rather than passivity.

Finally, to those who argue that Dickey's treatment of the Great Goddess confines female power to maternity, we counterargue by offering a summarizing definition of the stewardess in terms of the active powers she employs. Ranging from emotional to athletic to perceptual, these capacities far exceed nourishing or bearing only. Her dramatic character may be briefly outlined in a series of gerunds that disclose the plot of her transformation from that of victim to Energized Woman: falling out of the plane; blacking out; screaming; despairing; developing interest in her fall; dreaming; slanting; tumbling; diving; flying, seeing, and tasting like a bird; controlling her fall; arranging her skirt like a bat and thus changing the shape of her fall; energizing and watching the earth magically grow below; being born out of "chaos"; planing superhumanly; using her fall; feeling the Goddess in her and other women emerge; affirming her fate; shedding her clothes "To die / Beyond explanation"; sexually animating herself and those below; landing; living into her dying; breathing "at last fully / . . . AH, GOD—"; and, finally, dying into a new round of living. In **"Falling"** Dickey's Energized Woman, like his "Energized Man," acquires, in his own words about the power of poetry, "an enormous increase in perceptiveness, an increased ability to understand and interpret the order of one's experience . . . bringing only the best of oneself: one's sharpest perceptions, one's best mind, one's most hilarious and delighted and tragic senses." Exchanging electrifying traits of goddesses from a plurality of cultures and religious traditions, **"Falling"** is James Dickey's exhilarating, mythopoeic celebration of tragedy transformed into delight and ecstasy, with a woman at the center of creation.

Greg Johnson (review date 19 September 1993)

SOURCE: "A Walk on the Dark Side," in *Chicago Tribune,* September 19, 1993, p. 5.

[*In the following review, Johnson asserts that Dickey's* To the White Sea *"is less ambitious and in some ways less accomplished than his previous novels."*]

Only a handful of writers have managed to excel at both poetry and the novel. The fiction of major poets—Sylvia Plath's *The Bell Jar,* for example—is often simply an autobiographical coda to their collected poems; and while such tireless novelists as John Updike and Joyce Carol Oates write an abundant quantity of poetry as well, the results are decidedly minor, at least when compared to their most important achievements in fiction.

Thomas Hardy, D. H. Lawrence and Robert Penn Warren are among the select group of writers who have produced, in both forms, undeniably first-rate work, and to this short list many critics would add the name of James Dickey. Long acknowledged as one of our finest contemporary poets, with **Deliverance** Dickey produced one of the most celebrated novels of its decade. Although his hefty second novel, **Alnilam,** garnered a mixed response, its ambitious scope and often dazzling use of language furthered his reputation as a novelist of considerable powers.

Dickey's new work of fiction, **To the White Sea,** probably will not harm that reputation, though it is less ambitious and in some ways less accomplished than his previous novels. The first-person account of an U.S. Army Air Force gunner forced to parachute into Japan during World War II, this book has the structure and pacing of an extended short story. It features a relatively meager plot, virtually no dialogue and a technique that depends largely on such poetic devices as symbolism and tone rather than the more prosaic conventions of narrative fiction.

To the White Sea does, however, have its antecedents in the novel form. The story of one man confronting an alien environment, it occasionally recalls such epics of survival as [Daniel] Defoe's *Robinson Crusoe.* Dickey's story, however, lacks the human element provided in that novel by the appearance of Friday; here the focus is almost exclusively on the hero, Muldrow, who gradually becomes one with his increasingly primitive surroundings.

Muldrow is an intriguing character, though few readers will find him sympathetic. Unreflective, wholly self-centered, he undertakes a violent journey out of war-ravaged Tokyo and toward Japan's northern wilderness. Along the way, he commits a series of killings: A woman who recognizes his nationality is quickly knifed to death; he shoots one man for his clothes, stabs another for his shoes.

Proceeding northward, Muldrow becomes a human chameleon: "If I took my time—and I had plenty of it—I should be able to fit the color of some of my situations—hillsides, fields, woods—and tune to them: tune myself to them by color."

But as he relishes the sensation of becoming one with nature, human beings keep getting in the way. Soon after he enters a populated valley, an old woman sees him: "I had the knife through her before she could even blink, and then pulled it out and put it through her again."

Dickey makes clear that Muldrow's conscience, his sense of human compassion, is not merely suspended because of the exigencies of war and survival; rather, he seems from the beginning a man without pity, a natural predator who has always been myopically focused on gratifying his own needs.

Even for an American male in the 1940s, Muldrow is notably sexist and racist. He recalls his American girlfriend, "a college girl from Kansas. . . . She was a good enough girl in some ways, strong and smart, with calves like a couple of kegs." As for the Japanese, they "love machinery, and they try their damnedest to be like white people, especially Americans. If it weren't for us they wouldn't have any factories, any cars, much less any airplanes."

Dickey's hero, and occasionally even his prose style, is clearly derived from Hemingway. Muldrow's identification with primitive nature comes directly out of Hemingway's Nick Adams stories, and his clashes with other people recall the self-centered, ironic posturing of other Hemingway heroes.

What is original in **To the White Sea,** however, is the intimate identification with natural creatures, a theme that often marks Dickey's poetry as well. Thus Muldrow's admiration for the fish he catches and eats along the way:

> A fish's eye cuts things into clean outlines and then lets them go back to being dim when he's through with them, when he goes on past. And there's always the feeling of slotting through, but you never touch the sides of the slot. As I say, there are a lot of good things about it, but hard to talk about.

The farther Muldrow progresses into the wilderness, the more his experiences seem a pleasure rather than a hardship. At one point he realizes he is "having fun": "There was no friend anywhere, only thousands of people who wanted to cut off my head, castrate me, do anything they could to me. But fun it was, anyway." He looks forward to his final trek up into the rugged mountain country "like I was going on a vacation."

Eventually the reader loses count of the people, mostly civilians, whom Muldrow runs through with his knife; he is no more bothered by these killings than are the predatory fisher martens and other wild creatures he admires so much in the Japanese wilderness. And unlike Crusoe, he never feels any longing for human companionship. Instead, he relishes his increasing primitivism ("Don't let anybody ever tell you blood is not good to drink").

Any reader approaching *To the White Sea* in the hope of finding a traditional war story or an adventure novel will be sharply disappointed. But the book will surely please admirers of Dickey's poetry and of his harsh, unsettling vision of natural savagery.

—*Greg Johnson*

Muldrow's final surge into the wilderness gives the poet in Dickey an opportunity for some climactic, apocalyptic passages of searing beauty. By the time it concludes, however, *To the White Sea* has ceased to be a novel, just as Muldrow is no longer a "character." The book has become a prose poem, celebrating the darker side of man in nature, with Muldrow as its disembodied lyric voice.

Any reader approaching *To the White Sea* in the hope of finding a traditional war story or an adventure novel will be sharply disappointed. But the book will surely please admirers of Dickey's poetry and of his harsh, unsettling vision of natural savagery.

Richard Wiley (review date 19 September 1993)

SOURCE: "The Fittest Survive, but Fit for What?" in *Los Angeles Times Book Review,* September 19, 1993, pp. 2, 8.

[*In the following review, Wiley discusses the main theme of Dickey's* To the White Sea.]

James Dickey makes novels out of ideas. In *Deliverance,* 23 years ago, the idea was to take four men, each representing various degrees of self-reliance, and see what happens to them when, during a canoe trip down a wild river, the laws of civilization break down. As it turned out, the toughest of those men, a character named Lewis who must have had a bomb shelter full of weapons and canned goods in his back yard, was the prototype for Sgt. Muldrow, the narrative voice driving James Dickey's new novel, *To the White Sea.*

As this new work opens it is early March of 1945, and Muldrow, a tail gunner, is preparing for one of the last missions over Tokyo before the great fire bombings that preceded the end of the war. Muldrow is a man of precise preparations, attention to every detail. He shaves before each mission so that his oxygen mask will fit more tightly on his face, he secures his survival kit to his abdomen under his

uniform, he conceals a bread knife down by his boot and he tapes one of the crew's parachutes to the inside wall of the airplane. It is because of this last preparation that Muldrow survives.

Almost as soon as the mission begins his plane is shot out of the air, unsecured parachutes and unprepared men fly out into the night, and while the plane is twirling through the air, Muldrow rips the one remaining chute from the fuselage, bullies himself into it, and floats down into wartime Tokyo unseen, where his parachute hangs up on a dockyard crane. The ongoing bombing allows Muldrow to get down off the crane and find a sewer in which to hide. He tells us, "The smell put my eyes out, I mean it hit my eyeballs like the worst light . . . but it was a hole and I could go into it if I wanted to. I took another match and lit it, though I knew that sewers could blow up. That would be something, I told myself. . . ."

Since Muldrow was raised on the slopes of the Brooks Range in Alaska and knows how to survive in freezing weather, he decides that he will make his way from Tokyo all the way up to Japan's northern island of Hokkaido, where, if he can find similar terrain to that of the Brooks Range, namely ice and snow, he knows he will be safe.

What a fine beginning this book has! It is exciting and precisely written. Lucky for Muldrow the fire bombing starts almost immediately after his descent, so he is able to take advantage of the wild confusion to begin his run. And his sense of observation is as detailed as his preparation had been. He notices that the Japanese walk bent over with their eyes on the ground so he blackens his face with ash from a burning wall and walks the same way. He is so wily and his senses are so well-tuned, in fact, that just watching him get out of Tokyo makes us understand that even Lewis from *Deliverance* would be dead in the first half-hour or so.

It is when the killing starts that Dickey shows us that this is no mere adventure novel. It is not about one man's escape from the land of his enemies, but is a kind of treatise on the nature of modern humankind. Muldrow kills a lot of people. He kills one man for his shoes and a couple of others for the clothing they wear. He kills a gentle man for the feathers of the swans he tends, and he battles an old blind Samurai for the food and other items that he might be able to find in the old man's house.

As the journey north progresses, however, we begin to see that the central question of the novel is not, "How will this man survive?" but "What kind of man is this who is surviving so well?" This is what Muldrow says about the rest of us: "I will tell anybody who hears me say this, look around you and be honest with yourself. For most of you fight is not in you, and never has been."

Fair enough. Most of us know that the ancient torch that il-luminated the cave wall and showed us the words, *survival of the fittest* written there has died within us. And Dickey uses great skill to keep us off balance where the nature of Muldrow's character is concerned. Each time he kills, the killing is arguably necessary. He shows absolutely no com-passion, except where animals are concerned, but he isn't gratuitously mean or overly violent either.

In one of his many dreams about the Brooks Range Muldrow says, "It was night now, another night. Snow again, a slope down to a long valley almost like a tunnel. Caribou were in it again, moving through the valley, but I was not one of them. I was on a hill with some others like me, watching them, waiting for the time to move . . . going down in twos and threes when the stragglers fell back, and when we knew enough."

Muldrow, then, is a wolf, a predator in Japanese clothes, and let loose in peace time, anywhere on the earth, he would surely have been a murderer, an animal with a calculating and uncompassionate mind.

When I began this book I expected that it would be about Japan, but it is not. Dickey could have set the book in a wide variety of places with the same result. And by the end of the book the questions concerning Muldrow are answered, the balance is broken—the break is right there in the story for us to find if we can—and I, at least, found myself not so much rooting for Muldrow's success, as for his failure, which would then leave room for the evolution of civilization and thus for ordinary people like me.

John Melmoth (review date 11 February 1994)

SOURCE: "A Man in the Wilderness," in *Times Literary Supplement,* February 11, 1994, p. 20.

[*In the following review, Melmoth calls Dickey's* To the White Sea *"a bitterly cold novel" that "is not for those of a nervous disposition."*]

To the White Sea is a bitterly cold novel that seals the outback gothic of **Deliverance** in a crust of permafrost. As in the earlier book, James Dickey's milieu is wilderness, his concern less with the struggle against the elements, more with the way men's relations with other men can deteriorate in extreme situations. At the same time as admiring the hu-man capacity for survival, it takes a dim view of human na-ture.

As if to pre-empt its being read as another allegory about the nasty, brutish and short thing we call life, the novel's

opening is clearly located in space and time: Tinian Island, March 8, 1945. Muldrow, a tail gunner in the US Air Force, preparing for a bombing raid over Tokyo, is preoccupied with his kit. It soon becomes plain that this is not going to be a standard-issue war story. Muldrow is a man alone, short on conventional emotional responses. His mother died when he was a child, his father the year before he joined up. He was raised in Alaska, on the north face of the Brooks Range, "which is away from everything". He never went to school—his father taught him to read and write, and also how to hunt. This is someone on whom civilization has made little im-pact: "Out on the Range . . . I had got where I was scared of the human voice."

Muldrow's plane is shot down, the rest of the crew killed, and he parachutes into the burning dock area, where the only place he can find to hide is in one of Tokyo's sewage out-lets. The city itself scarcely exists for him, reduced as it is to the accumulated filth that flows around him. His strategy is to head north and attempt to cross to the island of Hokkaido, where the snow and ice will be familiar territory.

To the White Sea tracks Muldrow on his journey and watches impassively while he kills without compunction for the things he needs—clothes, food, shoes. The longer his flight continues, the more complex his sense of self becomes. On the one hand, nothing is allowed to stand in the way of his continued existence; yet that personal essence which he will do anything to preserve is dwindling. He becomes taken up with camouflage, with blending in, becoming nothing. At one point, he dreams of walking in the snow—"my marks were like a ghost had made them". Success, in his eyes, is to move in silence and to leave behind not a suspicion of his passing.

Muldrow may represent some kind of bleak prelapsarian in-nocence, but he is far from comfortable. He is obsessed with death and killing, ponders endlessly the way the light catches the edge of his knife, alternating between a kind of dull pla-cidity and alarming surges of adrenalin. He comes to real-ize that "the most satisfying thing that ever happened" to him was killing a Japanese soldier by jumping on him from the roof of a truck. If he calmed down a bit, he might pass as a psychopath. He eventually makes it to the frozen spaces he has been imagining and, when not living with the forest people or tending to an old falconer, composes eulogies to life in the freezer, where the cold "threads down through your nose like steel that gives you life". Nevertheless, his "heart of ice" proves to be another heart of darkness. Things take an apocalyptic turn and end in a welter of blood and feathers.

The language of *To the White Sea* is poetic and highly charged. Dickey takes language as far as it will go and some-times overdoes it, even attempting to find words for things for which, Muldrow insists, no words exist. Some of the writing has an eerie brilliance; in one remarkable scene, Muldrow slaughters and plucks a flock of terrified swans in the moonlight, then gorges on raw flesh. "I was left with the long neck in my hands and the wings down limp: all that power, and the thing so light."

Like *Deliverance, To the White Sea* is not for those of a nervous disposition. Muldrow is so alarming because his instincts are so diametrically opposed to anything we think of as normal; he moves away from society, warmth and domesticity, and towards solitude, cold and having to kill for a living. Ultimately the reader's response to the book is likely to be determined by whether one believes that there is something of Muldrow in all of us, or that he is an isolated phenomenon, profoundly alienated, a freak.

William G. Tapply (essay date May 1994)

SOURCE: "Because It's There: James Dickey and *Deliverance*," in *The Armchair Detective,* Vol. 27, May, 1994, pp. 342-45.

[*In the following essay, Tapply argues that Dickey's* Deliverance *is among the great novels of American culture.*]

When my friend Mike McGill gave me a book for my thirtieth birthday in 1970, he said, "Don't be put off by the fact that the author's a poet. I think you'll like it. It's got bowhunting and white-water canoeing in it." I devoured *Deliverance.* James Dickey's prose swept me along the way the river in the story carried the four men in canoes. It accelerated as I read, tossing and twisting and tumbling me so that I could no more put down the book than Ed and Lewis and Bobby and Drew could step out of their canoes in the rocky rapids of the Cahulawassee River in the middle of the Georgia wilderness. When it finally ended, I was exhausted. It had been quite a ride. I couldn't remember reading a more gripping, suspenseful story.

I was vaguely aware, even while reading it for the first time, that *Deliverance* explored the Important Themes that I had been taught in Mr. Cheever's high school English class—Man versus Nature, Man versus Man, Man versus Himself. I knew that I identified with the characters in ways that I had never connected to fictional men before. I liked the fact that Dickey's writing submerged itself in the story. From an award-winning poet I had expected extended, self-conscious figures of speech, convoluted symbols, fancy language. Instead I got a story so smoothly and clearly written that I was unaware of a writer at work.

It was a helluva book, and there it might have remained in my memory, one of those stories you hate to see end—but it finally does—and then you go looking for another one to read. Except soon afterwards *Deliverance* became a film. Dickey wrote the screenplay, and Burt Reynolds played Lewis in his finest performance (perhaps the only fine performance of his career), and I decided to try the book again.

> Of all the books I have read, [*Deliverance*] is the one that makes me jealous. It's a perfect book. I wish I'd written it.
> —*William G. Tapply*

Normally suspense stories don't work the second time around. After all, the essence of suspense lies in not knowing what's going to happen. Yet this time through the book, even with the movie's faithful story line fresh in my memory, I had to work against being swept along again on the story's momentum. I began to notice the themes and meanings that were woven so naturally into the plot that they had eluded me the first time through. And when I finished this second read, I did something I had never done before: I turned back to the first page and read it again.

And I decided that *Deliverance* deserved to be ranked with *The Adventures of Huckleberry Finn* as one of the great novels our culture has produced. It was not, I believed, simply a genre book, an "adventure" or a "novel of suspense," anymore than *Huck Finn* was a "young adult." It should be read and studied and admired—for the quality of its writing, for the insights it gives us into human nature, for the American themes it explores, for the absolute seamlessness of the story line.

Of all the books I have read, this is the one that makes me jealous. It's a perfect book. I wish I'd written it.

Deliverance, like *Huck Finn* one hundred years earlier, proves that great literature need not be "literary." At the beginning of his masterpiece, Mark Twain penned a caution: "Persons attempting to find a motive in this narrative will be prosecuted; persons attempting to find a moral in it will be banished; persons attempting to find a plot in it will be shot." I read *Huck* as a kid and found it a rollicking good yarn. When I got older and reread and studied *Huck,* I risked the author's wrath by finding plenty of motives and morals in it.

It has always seemed to me that the morals and motives in books work best when they are so tightly entwined in the story line that we are unaware of them. But they stick with us. Most kids, with minimal prodding, can talk about what freedom meant to an abused boy and a slave, and how all of us at certain stages in our lives share Huck's and Jim's need to climb onto a raft and go floating down a river.

Go floating down a river is what the four middle-aged city men in **Deliverance** decide to do. All men, figuratively, long to do the same thing. Years before midlife crises became fashionable and males began to talk about "bonding," Dickey captured perfectly the angst of men at a certain age. Ed, the story's narrator, muses on his discontent:

> The feeling of the inconsequence of whatever I would do, of anything I would pick up or think about or turn to see was at that moment being set in the very bone marrow. How does one get through this? I asked myself. By doing something that is at hand to be done was the best answer I could give; that and not saying anything about the feeling to anyone. It was the old mortal, helpless, time-terrified human feeling, just the same.

The canoe trip is Lewis's idea. He understands how middle-aged men can find themselves sliding through life, trying to ignore their discontent, riding a placid river toward old age and death. "Sliding is living antifriction," he tells Ed. "Or, no, sliding is living *by* antifriction. It is finding a modest thing you can do, and then greasing that thing. On both sides. It is grooving with comfort."

Like the Mississippi in *Huck Finn,* the Cahulawassee River represents a kind of freedom for the four men, a brief weekend escape from the enslavement of middle class city life, what Robert Frost called "a momentary stay against confusion." The irony in **Deliverance** is that the river is being dammed. Within a few years the wild valley where white water flows will be buried under a man-made reservoir. So when Lewis says they must go down the river "because it's there," he is not speaking glibly. The men must go now—while the river still flows wild—and before their lives become so "grooved with comfort" that they will be unable to get away.

The Cahulawassee, like the Mississippi in *Huck,* is the frontier, the "safety valve" that has left its imprint on American history and American literature. Like all frontiers, it will close. The dam—the implacable force of American civilization—will destroy the river. Man will conquer Nature.

Ed, Lewis, Drew and Bobby are not close friends. They have not "bonded." They are middle-aged men, caught up in the private, deadening sameness and high-pressure demands of their day-to-day lives. But the challenges and dangers of the river force them together—not out of comradeship, but out of necessity. "I bound myself with my brain and heart to the others," says Ed. "With them was the only way I would ever get out."

They drive from the city into the hills, leaving civilization behind, and launch their canoes. At first the river flows placidly. Occasional rapids hint at its power, and the men feel exhilarated and liberated when they conquer them. The river carries them ever deeper into the wilderness. Then a violent confrontation with two mountain men transforms the story from a white-water adventure into a life-and-death struggle. Bobby is humiliated and brutally sodomized at gunpoint, and it's clear that when the hillbillies are done with the city boys, they will murder them. Lewis stalks the mountain men as if they were deer and kills one with an arrow, while the other flees into the forest.

The four canoeists are left with the question of what to do with the dead man's body. James Dickey, like John Locke and Thomas Hobbes, postulates a "state of nature," a condition without government or law. The men's dilemma forces them to consider age-old questions of right and wrong, man-made versus natural law.

Drew, who represents the voice of civilized reason, insists that they abide by man's law and "do the right thing" by bringing the body down the river with them and reporting the incident to the authorities.

> "We just ought to wait a minute," replies Lewis, "before we decide to be so all-fired boy scoutish and do the right thing. There's not any right thing."
>
> "You bet there is," says Drew. "There's only *one* thing . . . Lewis, I mean it. . . . This is not one of your fucking games."
>
> "It may be the most serious kind of game there is," answers Lewis, "but if you don't see it as a game, you're missing an important point."
>
> "I can't go along with this," insists Drew. "It's not a matter of guts; it's a matter of the law."

And Lewis, the man of nature, answers, "You see any law around here? We're the law. What we decide is going to be the way things are."

Bury the body, says Lewis, and all but Drew agree. The killing was a simple matter of survival. It was kill or be killed. Nature's law, not civilization's version of justice, applies in this wilderness. Bobby, the crudest and least sensitive of them and the victim of the incident, goes along simply because it's the only way to hide his shame. Ed, the narrator, is neither noble nor philosophical. He reduces the debate to his own self-interest. "I was ready to gamble," he tells us. "After all, I hadn't done anything but stand tied to a tree, and nobody could prove anything else, no matter what it came to. I believed Lewis could get us out. If I went along with concealing the body and we got caught it could be made to seem a matter of necessity, of simply being outvoted."

So what begins as a temporary escape from the pressures of family and business becomes an elemental struggle against the dual forces of a powerful river and a vengeful, lawless backwoodsman. Each of the four men must confront his own nature to find the limits of his strength and courage. Drew, inevitably, does not survive. The gentlest and most socialized of the four, he is shot by the surviving hillbilly from atop the cliff that borders the river. "The best of us," eulogizes Ed. "The only decent one; the only sane one." In the state of nature, Drew is the man who must die.

Lewis, on whose strength and courage the others have depended, fractures his leg when the canoe crashes in the rapids. Bobby remains weak and untrustworthy. "I ought to take this rifle and shoot the hell out of you, Bobby, you incompetent asshole, you soft city country-club man," thinks Ed.

With Drew dead, Lewis critically injured, and Bobby incompetent, it's left to Ed to save the three of them. He is an ordinary man challenged to perform extraordinarily, to climb a sheer cliff at night, to ambush an enemy on unfamiliar terrain with a primitive weapon, to steer a canoe through treacherous white water, to bring himself and his companions out alive, and to devise a coverup so that the law will not prosecute them for murder.

It's the stuff of adventure, suspense and mystery. Buried in the story's heart, however, is the complicated stuff of philosophy and religion.

When they finally return to civilization, one of the locals asks Ed, "How come you to be doing this, in the fust place?"

Ed's answer, which would have been the simple truth before the adventure, now drips with irony: "Oh," he says, "I guess we just wanted to get out a little. All of us work in the city, and it gets pretty tiresome, just sitting in an office all the time. . . . That's all. No really good reason, I suppose. Just boredom."

When I first read **Deliverance** I had not yet entered the difficult time that, I'm convinced, all men encounter at midlife, when we cannot avoid such questions as, "What does it all mean?" and "What am I doing here?" Ed, Lewis, Bobby, and Drew are four very different men. Each confronts the conflicts and disappointments of his own life in his own way. When I was thirty, the book spoke to the midlife crises that awaited me. As I reread it through the years, I gained understanding—though no simple answers—to what I was feeling. Each of the four characters represented contradictory pieces of me.

I've given **Deliverance** to women of my acquaintance. They agree that it's a gripping adventure story. "But there are no significant women in it," they tell me. "It's a guy's book." Maybe they're right, although I'm tempted to point out that *Moby Dick* and *Huck Finn* and *The Old Man and the Sea* are, by the same standard, "guy's books."

When I taught high-school English, I asked several times for permission to assign **Deliverance** to my classes. "I want to study this book with my kids," I pleaded. "They'll love it. It will make them like to read. It's beautifully written, and it's important, and it's got all the themes. . . ."

My superiors frowned. Few of them had read it. "That's the Burt Reynolds movie, right?"

"Yes. A good film. But the book's a masterpiece."

Alas. We cannot, I was told, assign high-school kids a book in which the plot pivots on a scene where a man is sodomized at gunpoint, in which the heroes "get away" with murder, in which verboten vocabulary words appear. We've got to think of our students' moral development. And what would their parents think? Better stick to *Ethan Frome* and *The Red Badge of Courage.*

I take small consolation from the fact that for years *The Adventures of Huckleberry Finn* was widely banned from schools and libraries. I remain hopeful that one day **Deliverance** will be recognized as an important novel, a classic. It may not be The Great American Novel. But it is a great novel, and distinctly American.

Ronald Curran (review date Autumn 1994)

SOURCE: A review of *To the White Sea,* in *World Literature Today,* Autumn, 1994, pp. 809-10.

[*In the following review, Curran states that Dickey's* To the White Sea *"becomes a quest for the pure ecstasy that identification with nature will grant Muldrow."*]

In the early going **To the White Sea** appears to be an adventure tale on the order of **Deliverance.** Ball-turret gunner's B-29 downed over Tokyo. The only survivor is Muldrow, a Lewis Medlock figure in wartime Japan instead of the north Georgia woods. His life as the son of a wifeless "loner of all loners" on the north face of the Brooks Range in Alaska provides the survival skills to escape from Tokyo to the northern island of Hokkaido. There he will find an environment comparable to where you encounter "cold that cleans out your insides like fire," the one he shared with Eskimos.

Once again Dickey is working a variation on the stock adventure novel's structure and dynamics.

Caught initially in the thrall of what happens next, the reader connects with the survival conflict and its complications. So positioned by the conventional trappings of the escape drama, he is engaged more by the personality of Muldrow, whose Alaskan metaphysics suggest a transcendent dimension that points beyond mere physical survival. Escape in *To the White Sea* then becomes an opportunity to identify with the animal adaptations on the tundra and to access a form of consciousness that involves the limbic system as much as it does the higher functions of the cerebrum.

The escape-to-Hokkaido narrative soon entwines the reader's attention in the web of a far more subtle tale. This collateral narrative breathes its way into the novel like an incipient "fairy tale." To me it suggested [Conrad] Aiken's "Silent Snow, Secret Snow" or [Hans Christian] Andersen's "Snow Queen." Like *To the White Sea,* both are journeys into kingdoms of snow and ice. In similar fashion, Dickey's novel suggests radical forms of retreat from society and the use of nature in the service of personifying states of purity, fulfillment, and transcendence. The novel's final scene portrays an ecstatic death reminiscent of the martyrdom of many Christian saints, although Dickey's perspective is purely secular.

Muldrow's predicament and the war encompassing it function more as fortuitous opportunities for an escape into nature. Their powerfully engaging concrete sides seem almost secondary. However, while the surviving gunner struggles with the logistics of his escape from the city as well as his survival in the countryside, the novel often digresses on equipment and technique more to pleasure hunters than the average reader. Its mystical element eventually supersedes the concrete struggle going on to the point that it competes with the narrative of transcendence and becomes potentially more intrusive than engaging.

Once the mystical level engages, the novel becomes a quest for the pure ecstasy that identification with nature will grant Muldrow. He can move through physical death and into a state of being beyond the corporeal. In that state human beings do not face the conventional Judeo-Christian options. Neither do they become part of the earth's memory, as Lewis Thomas conjectured shortly before his death. In Dickey's view, Muldrow becomes part of its weather immediately after identifying with a swan: "A voice in the wind: a voice without a voice, which doesn't make a sound. You can pick it up anytime it snows . . . or even just when the wind is from the north." How Muldrow gets to this point makes or spoils the novel. It ends with his execution in the mountains of Hokkaido. As he spins in a hailstorm of Japanese bullets, he is contained in a moment of joyous release and transfor-

mation. Having smeared himself with his own blood and that of his fellow mountain recluse, Muldrow then rolls in a pile of swan feathers. Riddled with the bullets of his pursuers like famous American criminals of the twenties and before, he recounts his last moments of life, saying: "In the wind the swan feathers fluttered on me, and I could have flown. I could have flown with the hawks and the swans."

The reader's appreciation of this final ecstatic moment relies heavily on the portrayal of Muldrow. In his development of the B-29 gunner Dickey could have shown the reader a source of human longing and transcendence that the myopia of social adaptation blurs for us all. He could have moved beyond the relational energies which bind the characters in *Deliverance* and which link them to the world of persons with whom they share present and future. But the main character in *To the White Sea* has hardly any emotional connection to anyone. He seems to be without any kinship libido whatever. Muldrow's detachment puts considerable strain on empathy. The reader must seek and love ice as much as he does: "I didn't belong anywhere, really, but above seventy degrees north." He is, in his father's words, "half snow goose and half wolverine," like a figure in the literature of the Old Southwest.

In Muldrow's pursuit of shoes, clothing, food, and invisibility, he blows people's heads off, slits throats, guts, decapitates, and, in one instance, removes and cracks the arm bone of an old man he has killed in order to smash it into splinters suitable for making sewing needles. To be squeamish about his killings seems precious—unmasculine even—given the conditions of war and the inevitable castration and decapitation he himself faces if captured. Still, his killings, however justified, turn ugly, as he stabs an old woman who accidentally catches sight of him near a water wheel. The wheel itself gives him a notion of what to do. He saws off her head and fits it into one of the revolving buckets as it comes past him on its circular route.

Whatever his motives or state of mind, Muldrow can begin to recede as empathy erodes in the face of his schizoid character that is alienated from everything but the mountains of Hokkaido, Alaskan animals, the ice, and the snow. At times it is difficult not to adopt the attitude of his fellow gunners: "Don't fool with him." Often it is hard to determine whether he is moving toward higher levels of human consciousness on the way to self-transcendence, or if he is simply going mad. However the reader conceives of Muldrow's musings about his adaptive identifications with animals or his eventual transcendence into weather itself, the success of *To the White Sea* depends upon whether or not empathic identification can be fostered. If not, authentic involvement can turn into a combination of natural curiosity and frustration over Muldrow's arctic hysteria and its intrusion into an otherwise engaging tale of adventure.

Robert Kirschten (essay date Spring 1995)

SOURCE: "The Momentum of Word-Magic in James Dickey's *The Eye-Beaters, Blood, Victory, Madness, Buckhead and Mercy*," in *Contemporary Literature*, Spring, 1995, pp. 130-63.

[*In the following essay, Kirschten asserts that Dickey's* The Eye-Beaters, Blood, Victory, Madness, Buckhead and Mercy *"constitutes one of the central transitional texts in Dickey's poetic canon."*]

In the late sixties, when he collected his first five books of poetry into one volume, James Dickey had reached such a considerable level of literary success that Louis Untermeyer claimed that *Poems 1957-1967* "is the poetry book of the year, and I have little doubt that it will prove to be the outstanding collection of one man's poems to appear in this decade." While Peter Davison and James Tulip ranked Dickey and Robert Lowell as the two major poets in the country, John Simon was even more enthusiastic when he declared, "I place Dickey squarely above Lowell." However, in 1968, with the appearance of Dickey's very next book, *The Eye-Beaters, Blood, Victory, Madness, Buckhead and Mercy,* critics seemed annoyed, even dismayed, at the new direction of his highly experimental collection of verse. Herbert Leibowitz noted that the "balance of pure abandon and meticulous observation breaks apart in Dickey's latest volume," and further, that a "stagy, unpleasant hysteria enters the poems." Benjamin DeMott charged that the "poet runs on unrestrainedly," giving "no shapely object to delight in, little refinement of feeling or subtlety of judgment, no intellectual distinction, no hint of wisdom." Even as staunch an early supporter as Richard Howard lamented that "The look of these poems on the page is disconcerting: forms are sundered, wrenched apart rather than wrought together." Howard then concludes with a statement of considerable strength: "The cost to [Dickey's] poetry is tremendous, for it has cost him poems themselves—there are not poems here . . . only—only!—poetry."

Despite the severity of these appraisals, *Eye-Beaters* contains at least seven of Dickey's major poems and constitutes one of the central transitional texts in Dickey's poetic canon. During this period, Dickey's experiments in two basic areas, form and diction, opened a number of technical, poetic doors that propelled him through his remarkable and controversial book-length poem *The Zodiac* in 1976 to major achievements in the eighties in *Puella* and *The Eagle's Mile,* two of his best volumes of verse. In *The Eye-Beaters,* Dickey still kept his eye at times on a classical sense of narrative—the story-based poem on which he built such a wide following of readers; however, he also began to highlight word groups that radically altered his techniques of telling and gained him especially dramatic entrance to the world of darkness and terror that strongly unsettled Leibowitz, DeMott, and Howard. These word groups reveal fundamental methods in Dickey's word-magic and the subsequent momentum of his poetic thought, which, to my mind, has been misrepresented by many of his negative critics. These critics look for intellectual or discursive thinking in a poet who is not understandable only to the rational mind, and, as a result, they find Dickey's poems lacking in elements that are completely irrelevant to his poetic program. Dickey's best poems in this book are not hysterical, unrestrained, unshaped, unsubtle, or wrenched apart but are intricately constructed forms generated by a mode of thinking that is rooted in anthropological and mythopoeic criticism, namely, contagious magic.

Presupposing an ancient, universal law of contact between animate and inanimate objects, even those which are geographically distant such as the moon and stars, contagious magic seems, at first primitive, simple, or scientifically mistaken. However, when developed through the complex combinations within his extraordinary diction, Dickey's version of this practical causal principle allows him to reinvent a world in which magic not only seems plausible but natural and even necessary. For out of his animated series of "natural" connections, Dickey constructs a diverse range of rituals, ranging from sacrificial rites to linguistic acts of creation, which, reflexively, depend on his magical ontology for their effectiveness. When properly constructed, these rites reveal special, therapeutic powers designed to bring some measure of human control to the catastrophic, real worlds of "blood" and "madness." The plausibility of Dickey's word-magic takes its authority from its appeal to deeper reaches of the human mind that are closed to more discursive modes of lyric action. Not "deep-image poetry" exactly, his poetry operates through archetypal images within a deeply appealing and personal mode that also engages and alters the social self, especially the self traumatized by war. While his verbal and formal magic has distinguished precedents in the work of Hart Crane, Dylan Thomas, Theodore Roethke, and even Samuel Taylor Coleridge, critics often fail to judge Dickey by those principles that have been used to canonize these writers. To establish critical criteria—especially those in a mythopoeic mode—more accurately attuned to Dickey's true poetic vision in *The Eye-Beaters,* we need to focus on a number of issues that preoccupied the poet at this point in his career: his construction of poetic form in relation to word-magic, the subsequent shift of formal momentum in his poetry from action to image, and the shaping elements in at least one of the historical genres in which he was writing.

To initiate his keynote speech to the South Atlantic Modern Language Association in November 1982, Dickey borrowed a distinction from the *Notebooks* of poet Winfield Townley Scott. Centering on two kinds of poetry, or, rather, two kinds of poetic diction, this distinction is simple enough yet reveals much about Dickey's own poetic practice. The first type of poetry is, according to Scott, literalistic and marked by its capacity for moving, external reference. It is "a commentary on human life so concentrated as to give off considerable pressure." Two of its central practitioners are [William] Wordsworth and [Thomas] Hardy, and it "is represented by [Edwin Arlington] Robinson's [line]: 'And he was all alone there when he died.'" The second and opposite type, less literal and more evocative in character, "is a magic gesture of language," among whose proponents are Poe and Rimbaud; this second type is illustrated by lines from Hart Crane's poem "Voyages":

> O minstrel galleons of Carib fire,
> Bequeath us to no earthly shore until
> Is answered in the vortex of our grave
> The seal's wide spindrift gaze toward paradise.

For Dickey, the key word in these lines is "spindrift," whose peculiar qualities place Crane among what Dickey calls, following Scott, the "Magic-Language exemplars" of poetry. Instead of a literal or essential component of the seal's manner of seeing, "spindrift" belongs less to the "reality-world" of animal vision than to the "word-world" of verbal association (or what Crane calls, in his well-known phrase, the "logic of metaphor"). Dickey explains that "'Spindrift' is sea-foam, wave-foam, usually wind-blown along beaches, and, though the seal's eyes may be wide, and his gaze toward Paradise, 'spindrift' is really not, cannot be, part of his vision: the word is word only, associational word, and in its way beautiful, but word."

Instead of inventing poems characterized by statements that have an empirical or external referential direction, the poets of word-magic work from inside a reverberating, self-generating world of linguistic interplay. According to Dickey, these writers are less interested in realistic narratives or personal anecdotes which convey maxims about the world of human action and ideas than in the evocative powers and suggestions of words themselves. This wordplay may be further understood by considering its opposite, namely, that kind of diction that belongs to poets whom Dickey calls "the literalists." Unlike the "magic-language practitioners," "literal-minded poets" believe "in words as agents which illuminate events and situations that are part of an already given continuum." For example,

> The Robinson line ... is simply factual. There are only plain words in it: a statement. Plain words in ordinary order; nothing unusual, much less exotic. The line puts the reader into contemplation of something that happened to someone, and the condition of the happening: it is the clear pane of glass that does not call attention to itself, but gives clearly and cleanly on a circumstance.

On the other hand, word-magicians do not give primacy to plot or to the discursive revelations of character, but to a dream mode or some kind of surrealistic space in which the powers of reason have little importance. Although Dickey's remarks were made with *Puella* in mind, the book with his fullest use of word-magic and to which this article is a preliminary study, these observations reveal much about his own magical approach throughout his poetry. This approach is evident as far back in Dickey's work as the opening poem, the magical chant **"Sleeping Out at Easter,"** in his first collection of poems, *Into the Stone.* Of word-magicians, Dickey said in 1982:

> For the Magicians, language itself must be paramount: language and the connotative aura it gives off. . . . The words are seen as illuminations mainly of one another; their light of meaning plays back and forth between them, and, though it must by nature refer beyond, outside itself, shimmers back off the external world in a way whereby the world—or objective reality, or just Reality—serves as a kind of secondary necessity, a non-verbal backdrop to highlight the dance of words and their bemused interplay.

However magical Dickey's interests became at this point, he never fully divorced himself from his commitment to literal-mindedness or his belief in the necessity of basic storytelling. For in the same essay, he criticizes purely magical poetry for its considerable limitations. In magical poetry divorced from public concerns, Dickey says, "the *world* is lacking, and the buzz of language and hit-or-miss-metaphor-generation is everything; the poem itself is nothing; or only a collection of fragments." Although he admits to being "profoundly interested" in "the absolute freedom" that the magical making of metaphors offers the poet, Dickey also wants lyrics "bound into one poetic situation, one scene, one event after the other." A further problem with the magical method, especially in the surrealistic school, is that it invents without discovering, as Wallace Stevens noted. It does not reveal the contents of the unconscious but mere phantasms. Nor does it have "*drama,*" for it "cannot *build.*" Of poems in this style, Dickey observes that they have no narrative, no logic, no idea development, no transformation, no "publicly available" themes.

If one wonders in which camp Dickey places his own poetic language, he provides what appears to be a decisive response earlier in his address. Although he greatly admires the best of them, he claims, "I am not of the party of the magic-language practitioners." At first glance, this self-classification seems true. Because so much of Dickey's early poetry depends on anecdotal narrative and extrinsic reference to topics and events from his own life (world war, family, animals, even a Southern Baptist preacher), he seems justified in placing himself among those poets whom he calls "literal-minded," for example, Robert Frost, Edgar Lee Masters, and Randall Jarrell. From a stylistic or linguistic point of view, however, Dickey's poetry also suggests an extremely strong magical orientation. In the mid and late sixties in particular, Dickey began to experiment with word groups bunched together by means of techniques such as the "block format" and the "split line." At this time, words themselves and their "connotative aura" became singularly featured on the pages of his lyrics. In **"May Day Sermon," "Falling," "The Shark's Parlor," "The Fiend,"** and to some extent in **"The Firebombing,"** he built "wall[s] of words" out of distinctive visual and semantic combinations that were not only striking to behold but, more importantly, approximated, as Dickey says, "the real way of the mind as it associates verbally. . . . in bursts of words, in jumps."

One major effect of the method (or "real way") of these mental word "bursts" and "jumps" is the construction of an emotionally immediate, if not obsessive, universe in which the magical contiguity of natural forms of life and death is conveyed by Dickey's imagistic contiguities. Dickey calls the semantic aspect of this magical contact "apparently unjustifiable juxtapositions" and "shifts of meaning or consciousness." These juxtapositions may be rationally "unjustifiable" but, from a poetic and emotional point of view, they enable the objects inside his visually bracketed word groups to exchange (or share) properties in an especially dramatic and vivid manner. These stylistically fused traits build scenes so rich in texture that they constitute the animating ground of the poem's action and thus possibility for Dickey's characters. **"May Day Sermon"** provides an especially vivid example of how the poet's word-magic "jumps" across the page with a stunning momentum that energizes the woman preacher who delivers the lines. This momentum also animates the objects of nature in Dickey's universe and reveals how he thinks magically through them:

>   Sisters, understand about men and
> sheaths:
>
> About nakedness: understand how butterflies,
>   amazed, pass out
> Of their natal silks   how the tight snake takes a
>   great breath   bursts
> Through himself and leaves himself behind   how
>   a man casts finally
> Off everything that shields him from another
>   beholds his loins
> Shine with his children forever   burn with the
>   very juice
> Of resurrection

In this section, Dickey's word-magic builds the poem's (and nature's) momentum by means of his striking grammatical strategies of predication, strategies that, as we will see, are also central to his magical method in **"Pine."** In the arrangement of word blocks in **"May Day Sermon,"** nouns such as "butterflies," "the tight snake," "man," and "his children" share the ejaculatory, universal motion of sheaths and nakedness which "pass out," breathe, burst, "shield," behold, "[s]hine," and "burn with . . . resurrection." This sharing is effected by an elaborate series of delayed predicates in parallel constructions in which the poet omits punctuation and connectives in favor of breath spaces. By keeping mechanical interrupters and conjunctions to a minimum, Dickey creates an oratorical and ontological momentum marked by "fluidity and flux" that is his own specification of William James's famous stream of consciousness. Dickey's poetic flow—more like a tidal wave in this poem—makes objects exchange attributes by making the mind "jump" between nouns and predicates such that a verb (and its textural traits) in one clause may be plausibly predicated of two or more preceding subjects. In the lines cited above, the subject of "burn" is "loins" but may as well be "children," for both "loins" and "children"—albeit in different modes—"burn with the very juice / Of resurrection." Dickey does not use this technique only for single terms. Because he begins his word blocks with dynamic verbs, gerunds, and present participles, he drives these blocks forward in a stream of sexual, natural, and grammatical motion while simultaneously allowing the eye to linger upon visually separated word groups so that entire groups of words appear to serve as nouns for several series of subsequent verbals. Several lines later in **"May Day Sermon,"** it is a trout which flows and slides upstream, but Dickey's spatial arrangement of his word groups makes it appear that the trout's "cold / Mountain of his birth" does the same, for the trout "heads upstream, breathing mist like water, for the cold / Mountain of his birth flowing   sliding in and through the ego- / maniacal sleep of gamecocks." The metaphysical mechanism behind these shared predicates is a mode of connection that Sir James Frazer calls "contagious magic" in *The Golden Bough,* namely, "that things which have once been in contact with each other are always in contact." In Dickey's poetic universe, these grammatical and ontological connections produce a magical animism, in which, to use Joseph Campbell's phrasing, "there is no such thing as absolute death, only a passing of individuals back and forth, as it were, through a veil or screen of visibility, until—for one reason or another—they dissolve into an undifferentiated ground that is not of death, but of potential life, out of which new individuals appear."

Not only objects and groups of objects are animated by mental word-magic in Dickey's world. Dickey's word-magic also drives the emotionally animating end of **"May Day Sermon,"** which is nothing less than the resurrection in springtime of nature, sexual instinct, and the vocalized anima (or soul) of the victimized daughter, all under the aegis of the oratorical triad of energized women: preacher, audience, and subject of the sermon (the daughter). The daughter of the abusive, backwoods, Bible-reading father is able to return from the dead each year precisely because, in Dickey's lyric universe, "there is," in Campbell's words, "no such thing as absolute death." Dickey's is a world in which life and death cyclically and magically dissolve into and out of each other and in which the animating power of the woman preacher's eternal logos—like "men" and "nakedness"—also "bursts," "[s]hine[s]," and "burn[s] with the very juice / Of resurrection." The daughter does not die for her sexual freedom but dies as a fertility goddess who transcends death each spring, like the earth itself, by riding the eternal continuum of decay, regeneration, and rebirth, empowered in Dickey's worldview by the words of women and the poet's magical modes of "resurrection." The very possibility of the daughter's archetypal transcendence is thus rooted in a magically empowered and conceived setting which eternally energizes her.

If the ritualized methods and the ground of action in Dickey's lyrics take on a special primitive power in the mid sixties, the effects of his word-magic and its reverberating linguistic momentum become even more pronounced in the late sixties and the early seventies. His magical diction is primarily effected through catalogues of tactile, concrete metaphors, hyphenated word combinations, and explosive, staggered groups of action-packed gerundives. When working in a distinctively surrealistic or hallucinatory dream mode, Dickey distances himself even further from his earlier formal strategies, realistic anecdotes, and the relatively sober revelations of romantic perception, in favor of an exuberant emphasis on magical imagery. For instance, in **"The Eye-Beaters,"** the narrator does not go inside the minds of blind children for internal revelation when he visits a home for the children in Indiana, but instead externalizes his imagined vision of what they see as he addresses himself:

> Smudge-eyed, wide-eyed, gouged, horned,
> caved-
> in, they are silent: it is for you to guess what they
>   hold back inside
> The brown and hazel   inside the failed green
>   the vacant
>   blue-
> eyed floating of the soul.

At first, there appears to be little here of what could be traditionally called a complicated plot which changes the fortunes of its characters. Neither the children nor the narrator can change. Try as he may, the speaker cannot alter the condition of the blind children who beat their eyes in frustration. In a sense, then, the animating end of this poem is the realistic failure of the poet's magical, elaborate techniques of animation. This failure, however, is only half the equation. After acknowledging the therapeutic limits of his poetry, the speaker frantically continues to build his fictional wall of mythic images for his own sake and for that of the real "vision" of the children. He argues rationally that in spite of their blindness, these children are still important, and that "what they see must be crucial / To the human race." Despite his claim to reason, Dickey's magic produces nothing more than a semihysterical nightmare of his own darkness and rage as the poet tries to see what is "under their pummeled lids."

His word-magic is thus closer to word-madness than magic. Yet this madness has its own peculiar visioning power. In **"May Day Sermon,"** while partially maddened by her belief system, by abuse to the farmer's daughter, and by Dickey's inflamed rhetoric, the woman preacher nonetheless effects an optimistic, mythopoeic reincarnation of the victimized girl. In *The Eye-Beaters,* Dickey's word-madness seeks a magic that at first appears ineffective. This magic is built out of nothing but the "sheer / Despair of invention" in the real world where the narrator's poetic powers cannot heal. However, what comes most alive in this world—even more than plot and character—is the poet's mental cave of magical images, that is, the cave of "perversity" and "madness," constituted by Dickey's wall of words. It is as if he has taken us inside Plato's cave of illusions or inside one of the Paleolithic caves at Montesquieu-Avantes in the Pyrenees and left us in the dark. In such a world, "Half-broken light flickers" briefly and shows us partial images of "ibex quagga . . . cave bear   aurochs   [and] mammoth." However, this is a mental world which is even darker and more claustrophobic, where the poet's "reason" has "gone / Like eyes," and only his primal images offer him solace. We thus come closer to experiencing the dark world of these children than we ever would have without Dickey's disturbing and dazzling poem, at the heart of which is yet another of his extraordinary, primitivistic exchanges. This exchange transforms speaker and reader by linking sighted readers to blind children, even though the mode of shared "vision" is only—or, to use Richard Howard's exclamation, "only!"—poetic.

As we trace the evolution of Dickey's use of magical language, what is important to note in **"The Eye-Beaters"**—as well as in **"Mercy,"** **"Victory,"** and **"Pine"** in the same volume—is that Dickey's walls of words are so powerful that their contagious, magical energy appears to displace plot, character, and revelation as emotionally central parts of his poetic action. These traditional shaping elements are, of course, still prominent in his work of this period. However, we may well be able to claim—using Dickey's own description of poetic word-magicians—that, in these boldly experimental poems, he has gone further than ever toward giving primacy to "language and the connotative aura it gives off." This new primacy of parts enables him to invent a new poetic "Reality [which] serves as a . . . backdrop to highlight the dance of words and their bemused interplay." To put it another way, Dickey's radically magical walls of reality establish settings which not so much displace thought and character as they take on the functions of character, revelation, and the solution (or opposition) to the protagonist's driving needs. In **"May Day Sermon,"** magical word groups not only create the physical setting but also the animating ground of change and motivation for the woman preacher. Yet they also constitute a formal revolution, what would in contemporary criticism be called a "deconstruction," in which Dickey's word-magic achieves a parity of power with the classic, Aristotelian elements of thought and action, and even becomes the central pattern of thought and action. By focusing on "[the] action of words upon each other, for whatever meaning or sensation they may throw off, evoke," Dickey uses these networks of "meaning or sensation" not to remain mired in sensation but to invent what is for him a new kind of poetic form. Insofar as his new diction produces a "connotative aura" that radically alters his speaker's fundamental mode of perception while also shaping and guiding the reader's point of view, Dickey's mythical language becomes both his poetic action *and* his basic method of representation. This collapse—or fusion—of analytic distinctions is true for all poetry insofar as poetry's shaping causes are synthesized within its verbal materials. But for Dickey, his distinctive change in emphasis yields especially vivid insights into a new way of thinking through words which themselves revolutionize his poetry.

If, in this middle period of his career, Dickey begins to think in a radically mytho-magical mode while quite consciously moving away from anecdote and narrative, we see yet another reason why his poetry upsets the Aristotelian causal hierarchy which privileges plot the way Dickey did in his early work. The very nature of thought manifested in Dickey's word-magic demands this formal shift. For, as Ernst Cassirer notes, "mythical consciousness . . . knows nothing of certain distinctions. . . . it lacks any fixed dividing line between mere 'representation' and 'real' perception, between wish and fulfillment, between image and thing." Further, by using a mode of thought which burkes classical logical axioms and assumes instead magical principles—such as "the part not only *stands for* the whole but positively *is* the whole"—Dickey confounded many critics in the late sixties and early seventies by inventing an "aura" that baffled them when they applied discursive or meditative criteria. For when Dickey's linguistic "aura" became a dominant force, it produced a dreamworld like that of the undifferentiated reality of primitive consciousness; thus many readers dismissed the poems in *The Eye-Beaters* as formless or poorly constructed. On the contrary, these poems are intricately constructed, and further, they are designed to convey the atmosphere of nightmares or dream consciousness, the very nature of which is cloudy or phantasmic.

One magical mode, the conversion of properties or attributes of objects into bodies, appears in the scenic imagery of **"Mercy,"** a nightmare poem about the narrator's lover Fay, a nurse at a hospital in "slum Atlanta," whom he picks up at the nurses' dormitory called "Mercy Manor." By mixing hypostatized, imagistic traits of love, mortality, blood, and banal pop culture in a dazzling scene of surrealistic transformation, Dickey converts Fay into a contemporary Persephone, macabre yet heroic. While "perfume and disinfectant battle / In her armpits," she straddles the worlds of life and death, goddess-like, when, in the poem's conclusion, the speaker imagines himself "Collapsed on the street," having a kind of heart (or love) attack: "I nearly am dead / In love." Herself a stark contrast in the colors of healing and of death, Fay leans over him as he calls for her kiss to silence the cry of mortality from his lips and to bear him safely from the world of darkness into the "mercy" of St. Joseph's hospital:

> She would bend
> Over me like this   sink down
> With me in her white dress
> Changing to black   we sink
> Down flickering
> Like television   like Arthur Godfrey's face
> Coming on   huge   happy
> About us   happy
> About everything   O bring up
> My lips   hold them down don't let them cry
> With the cry   close   closer   eyeball to eyeball
> In my arms, O queen of death
> Alive, and with me at the end.

If Fay, like Persephone, possesses a goddess-like power of healing and renewal, she does so because the poet rescues her from a convincing technical, pop cultural hell that enervates yet simultaneously animates her. As he does in **"The Eye-Beaters,"** Dickey builds another dynamic wall of words—this time, down the middle of the page—that makes the night world of hospitals come alive in a sensuously dark dream scene. This scene is not static. As the drama develops, the setting not only gains emotional power by means of the affective accumulation of Dickey's detail; it propels the action forward by providing an overwhelming opponent of "night" and "mortality" against which the speaker battles for "care" and "love." In the night world of this hospital, "love," if not life, has never felt more vulnerable. One cause of this vulnerability is the massive sense of indifference that the setting, indeed, the world, evinces toward the speaker. This anomie is reflected in Dickey's magical, imagistic hypostatization of Arthur Godfrey's smiling television face, whose mind-numbing, "happy" countenance benignly smiles over the night world of pain and death with the comic indifference of a plastic Halloween mask. Ernst Cassirer says that in magical thought, "The 'image' does not represent the 'thing'; it is the thing; it does not merely stand for the object, but has the same actuality, so that it replaces the thing's immediate presence." We do not confuse Arthur Godfrey with his image. Rather, Dickey so animates the banality of the image that its preposterous happiness becomes an oppressive, real, actual body. In this animated, surrealistic space, the poet turns a complex of cultural and technological relations into "a pre-existing material substance" in which, in Cassirer's words, "all mere properties or attributes . . . become *bodies.*" By magically making banality a substance, Dickey provides one element in the poisoned substratum of a contemporary, urban scene against which the energized passion of a goddess-woman offers temporary redemption from the speaker's hysterical "wail" and the dark, cold world of mortality and indifference.

In this stage of Dickey's poetic career—which may be labeled a magical period in which he makes a radical move from action to image—voice, points of view (reader's and speaker's), and plot seem less like specific, separable literary devices than undifferentiated aspects of the dreamy aura of his word selection. These strategically constructed word groups reveal the movement of his mind from linguistic block to block in modes of nondiscursive, non-analytical thought that Cassirer discusses in his chapter "Word Magic" in *Language and Myth:*

> mythic ideation and primitive verbal conception. . . . [involve] a process of almost violent separation and individuation. Only when this intense individuation has been consummated, when the immediate intuition has been focused and . . . reduced to a single point, does the mythic or linguistic form emerge, and the word or the momentary god is created. . . . the process of apprehension aims not at an expansion, extension, universalizing of the content, but rather at its highest intensification. . . . The conscious experience is not merely wedded to the word, but is consumed by it. Whatever has been fixed by a name, henceforth is not only real, but is Reality.

In the momentum of Dickey's thought in the best poems from *The Eye-Beaters,* objects and events are individuated through narratives that antagonize and separate agents. Things and acts are also individuated through strategic spatial separations (different from the split line but an off-shoot of it) and through emphases of the arrangement of words on the page. Dickey's word blocks isolate images in focused impressions that, when grouped in his distinctive series of sequences, give the sense that a name and its referent are magically connected—indeed, that reality is built out of momentary bursts of tangible, tactile names. These names not only share the properties of what they signify but feel as if

they are some essential part (or the whole) of their referents while simultaneously amplifying the emotional impact of those parts. At times, Dickey's focused images give us an animal's surrealistic, enlarged perspective of heads and eyes in word groups that themselves enlarge the objects represented. For example, in **"Madness,"** a family hound is bitten by a rabid female fox, and the experience of sound and pain is conveyed and enlarged in a poetic form marked by the isolation of intensified moments from the story:

> she bit down
> Hard on a great yell
> To the house being eaten alive
> By April's leaves. Bawled; they came and found.
> The children cried
>
> Helping tote to the full moon
> Of the kitchen   "I carried the head"   O full of eyes
> Heads kept coming across, and friends and family
> Hurt   hurt
> The spirit of the household, on the kitchen
> Table being thick-sewed

To no small degree, the basic representational device in this poem progressively becomes the form of the poem. That is, the strategic isolation of the names of fragments of events results in a magic pointillism that fixes as its primary patterned reality the surrealistic aspects of the core event that pattern depicts. Summarized under the title of **"Madness,"** the basic narrative is simple: a family dog is bitten, becomes rabid, is hunted down, then beheaded. However, the stylized, magical story is considerably more complex, primarily because of the way it is told: the conversion of a family hound into an energized, manic god of the hunt and kill, who, through a narrative of hallucinatory frenzy marked by the contagious, explosive escalation of sexuality and violence, dies a divine death as a nonretaliatory scapegoat; the humans in the poem project their own mimetic desire for violence upon this sacrificial monster who is expelled from the circle of domestic safety and then closes the poem's process of overflowing violence with his own execution. Dickey's verbal methods of separation, individuation, and amplification are essential to the monster-making process because they amplify the dog's bizarre and dangerous traits into monstrous proportions, so that his sacrificial death, dramatically mandated, purges the stable world that he himself has infected and threatened. One instance of this amplification process occurs after the dog is bitten. It is carried into the family kitchen, and the phrase "O full of eyes" floods the moment with what Dickey construes to be the animal's vision, yet also isolates that moment with an image in which eyes seem disembodied and bizarre, as would befit a being which is in the process of transgressing normal social boundaries. That the poem is so effectively disturbing and dark reveals that Dickey's vibrant word-magic makes fully tangible the traits of surrealistic monstrosity which the poem requires for its sacred drama.

Although there is none of the archetypal pairing of the intensely dramatic mythopoeic opposites of sex and violence in the three-page lyric **"Pine,"** this poem reveals several other aspects of Dickey's remarkable—and difficult—mode of magical meditation. Cast in a sequence of "successive apprehensions" (or "four ways / Of being"), with a fifth, concluding, single-word section ("Glory"), **"Pine"** examines a pine tree by means of four senses: hearing, smell, taste, and touch. At first glance, the poem's process of thought appears to be built out of compounds—or, to use Dickey's own term, "a dark / Flood"—of traits which the speaker is "Opening one by one." Each section features, though not exclusively, one sense which Dickey examines by means of a series of percepts, analogies, intuitions, and visceral experiences of the body. This flood of synesthetic experience combines to form a whole of some kind, when, at the end, Dickey claims:

> A final form
> And color at last comes out
> Of you alone putting it all
> Together like nothing
> Here like almighty
>
> V
>
> Glory.

To some extent, Dickey's mode of perception resembles the kind of accumulation that, according to Denis Donoghue, constitutes "the self" in Walt Whitman's lengthy catalogues:

> he begins by saying, Let x equal the self. Then x equals A plus B plus C plus D plus E . . . where each letter stands for a new experience contained and possessed, and the self is the sum of its possessions. This is the law of Whitman's lists. If you say that the self—x—is the sum of its possessions . . . then the more you add to the right-hand side of the equation, the more you enrich the left, and you do this without bothering about the "nature" of the x. You assume, as most Romantic poets did, that the self is not at any moment fixed, complete, or predetermined, and then you are free to develop or enlarge it at any time by adding to its experience.

The Romantic aspect of Dickey's poetic identity certainly coincides with the latter part of Donoghue's observation about flow and indeterminacy. However, Dickey's mental method of accumulation—and, consequently, his conception of his poetic "self"—does not depend on a mere unity that is the "sum of its possessions." Dickey does not build his perceptual objects out of discrete properties only, but, in-

stead, conceives a different kind of whole constituted by an empathic mode of consubstantiality. One may best see the method in his word-magic in the Melanesian concept of "mana," which is a general, undifferentiated power that appears in different forms and different objects in a sacred, rather than a profane, world. In such a realm, not every animate thing possesses "mana," only certain objects that evoke a sense of wonder and delight. Sacred wonder and delight in the world of physical sensation and magical things (especially animals and natural objects in motion) are constants in Dickey's lyric universe, the various elements of which are bound together by a principle of shared power that Cassirer calls the "law" of "concrescence or coincidence":

> Mythical thinking . . . knows such a unity neither of combination nor of separation. Even where it seems to divide an action into a number of stages, it considers the action in an entirely substantial form. It explains any attribute of the action by a specific material quality which passes from one thing in which it is inherent to other things. Even what in empirical and scientific thought appears to be a mere dependent attribute or momentary property here obtains a character of complete substantiality and hence of transferability.

Even though the major parts of **"Pine"** are divided by individual sense, Dickey builds the poem's progression out of a fluid "merging of properties" which is effected by collections of hyphenated compounds and jammed fragments of thoughts and feelings. These compounds—especially Dickey's phrase "sift-softening"—and his fragmented, syntactic shorthand recall the opening lines from the fourth stanza of Gerard Manley Hopkins's "The Wreck of the Deutschland":

> I am soft sift
> In an hourglass—at the wall
> Fast, but mined with a motion, a drift,
> And it crowds and it combs to the fall[.]

Hopkins's "soft sift / In an hourglass" serves to remind him that his body decays with time and that he can achieve redemption only by "Christ's gift" of eternal salvation, "proffer[ed]" in the gospel. In **"Pine,"** Dickey's "sift-softening" does not stand for the "motion" and "drift" of a heightened sense of personal mortality. Rather, "sift-softening" is one stage in his poetic process of rendering both sensible and transferable the motion of the wind through pine needles. If yet another mark of magical thinking is that substance and force are not sharply distinguished, then Dickey's fusion of force and thing demonstrates even more fully his mythopoeic mode of transforming relations between objects into tactile, living presences which he offers to perception. For instance, here is Dickey's flow of compounded properties that he unifies—or, in his own word, "assign[s]"—as he makes the force of the sound of pine sensuous and, therefore, substantial:

> Low-cloudly it whistles, changing heads
> On you. How hard to hold and shape head-round.
>   So any hard hold
> Now loses; form breathes near. Close to forest-
>   form
>   By ear. . .
>   . . . .
>   Overhead assign the bright and dark
> Heels distance-running from all   overdrawing the
>   only sound
>   Of this sound   sound of a life-mass
> Drawn in long lines in the air   unbroken
>   brother-saving
>   Sound merely soft
> And loudly soft just in time then nothing and then
>   Soft   soft and a little caring-for   sift-softening
>   And soared-to.

Because the form of the sound of pine is difficult to grasp—as Dickey says, "any hard hold / Now loses"—he hypostatizes the pine's "sound of a life-mass" by inventing a sequence of modes of motion, each of which is assigned a distinctive trait such as sifting, soaring, and whistling. By giving even the softest sound a tangibility, Dickey makes his own poetic process of perception—and thus his poetic form—substantial. What was "hard to hold" now has elements that can be held, and can be held in a discernible sequence or form. Further, by making sound a mode of motion shared among the fragments of his "apprehension," Dickey also makes these substantial traits transferable from one part of the apprehension to another, and thus to the whole percept. The form of the stanza is the flow of the traits of felt motion commingling and building toward a whole. This process of substantiation and consubstantiation begins to culminate in the phrase "O ankle-wings lightening and fleeing," which represents the magical fusion of the substantiated properties of the "sound" of pine; these properties include speed, lightness, evanescence, alternation, and texture. A few lines later, in its conclusion, the stanza reveals one whole, unified aspect of pine in terms of hearing. Pine's basic properties merge in the figure of "footless flight," which the reader understands can be heard yet is difficult to hear—like the sound of pine—for it is "coming and fleeing / From ear-you and pine, and all pine."

Another way to examine the poem's formal momentum is to think of Dickey's cataloguing and combining of properties as a mythopoeic mode of predication, that is, as a preliminary process of naming—and thus dividing—an undifferentiated subject into specific predicates from which he builds a differentiated reality. As an analogue of this pre-liminary, linguistic stage of cognition, Dickey's poem makes pine feel like "mana," in that it emerges through his word groups with what feels like its own mysterious energy and power. Like the Sioux conception of Wakanda ("Great Spirit," or world creator, or mystery, or grandeur, or sacredness—the term is nearly untranslatable in English), the spirit-force of pine grows magically through animated substances and, in Dickey's case, toward an ultimate, imaginatively conceived unity that differentiates it from its ground of perception. In his primitive predication of properties and in his conception of an animated whole, Dickey's poetic method is radically perspectival. As Cassirer notes, "for mythical thinking[,] the attribute is not one defining the aspect of the thing; rather, it expresses and contains within it the whole of the thing, seen from a different angle." Not only is each perceptual sense in each major part of **"Pine"** "a different angle"; each tangible attribute of each sense is also "a different angle." Further, as we saw, each "angle" reveals and incorporates the whole by means of Dickey's complex movement of concrete imagery. These new angles are themselves new views, new names of aspects of pine rendered plausible, determinate, and separable from the preconscious welter of sensation out of which pine reveals itself to consciousness.

In his verbal act of distinguishing perspectives, Dickey calls pine into being through the magical power of naming. With regard to this constitutive, predicative dimension, Dickey's perspectival form is a linguistic act of creation. Like the narrative thrust in many primitive creation myths, the direction of Dickey's mythic speech moves a differentiating human preconsciousness away from the chaotic condition of heaven and earth before things had names and thus could be verbally distinguished. What is magical and sacred about this naming is that, in Dickey's poem, names do not merely signify but convey the potential powers of the things named and thus symbolically created. In **"Pine,"** Dickey's series of imagistic potencies—for example, "Your skull like clover lung-swimming in rosin"—literally become the poetic essence of the identity of pine as the speaker's whole being, not just the rational component of the human mind, engages the world of nature and its emerging objects through his nascent language. No better description of the epistemological implications of Dickey's unity-effecting word-magic can be found than in an analogy between the primitive process of object formation and its relation to language, taken from the biblical narrative of creation. Cassirer recalls that after the word of God separated darkness from light to produce heaven and earth, the distinctively human element then entered the linguistic process of genesis:

> the names of earthly creatures are no longer directly given by the Creator, but have to wait their assignment by Man. . . . In this act of appellation, man takes possession of the world both physically and intellectually—subjects it to his knowledge and his

rule. . . . This unity, however, cannot be discovered except as it reveals itself in outward form by virtue of the concrete structures of language and myth, in which it is embodied, and from which it is afterward regained by the process of logical reflection.

Dickey's one-word conclusion to **"Pine"** thus signals his sacred finale to the linguistic process of inventing a "momentary god." In this kind of "holy" and "mythico-religious" atmosphere, the unity-effecting name and the god's nature (or power) are thus felt, however evanescently, to be one: "Glory."

Another formal achievement derived from the momentum of word-magic and magical thinking in *The Eye-Beaters* is the most dramatic aspect of Dickey's neo-Romanticism, namely, his reinvention of the ode of terror. To be sure, Dickey has explored the world of nightmares and dream consciousness from the very beginning of his work in poems such as **"The Vegetable King"** and **"The Firebombing."** However, in **"Mercy"** and **"Madness,"** his word-magic in this volume signals his fullest and most frightening contribution to a genre of poetry that was extremely popular in the late eighteenth and early nineteenth centuries. Represented on Coleridge's dark side by "The Rime of the Ancient Mariner" and "Dejection: An Ode," this genre took its criteria for excellence from Longinus's classic treatise "On the Sublime," especially that aspect of the sublime that focuses on "the most striking and vehement circumstances of passion." Because, in Edmund Burke's opinion, the sublime produces "the strongest emotion which the mind is capable of feeling," and because terror was felt to be an emotional corollary of the feeling of religious dread occasioned by nothing less in importance than "the supreme evil," the ode of terror was held by many to be the highest form of lyric. Although there is no explicit theodicean component in **"Victory,"** this historic genre—"so wildly awful, so gloomily terrific," as the eighteenth-century critic Nathan Drake enthusiastically put it—combined a number of traits that bear directly on Dickey:

> To excel in this species of Ode demands a felicity and strength of genius that has seldom been attained; all the higher beauties of poetry, vastness of conception, brilliancy of colouring, grandeur of sentiment, the terrible and the appalling, must combine, and with mysterious energy alarm and elevate the imagination. A lightning of phrase should pervade the more empassioned parts, and an awful and even dreadful obscurity, from prophetic, or superhuman agency, diffuse its influence over the whole.

"Terrible" and "appalling," with a "mysterious energy" that appears to issue from a "superhuman agency," **"Victory"** is Dickey's striking nightmare poem about one of the most "su-

preme evil[s]" of human experience: world war. The poem recounts the story of a GI in the Pacific theater who anticipates the surrender of the Japanese on V-J Day (September 2, 1945) two years before the actual fact. "[T]wo birthdays / / Back, in the jungle, before [he] sailed high on the rainbow / Waters of victory," the soldier drinks whiskey sent by his mother as a present, then explains to her—apparently, in a letter—how he later found himself drunk in a tattoo parlor in Yokahama, with "four / Men . . . bent over me," who tattoo his entire torso with a brightly colored snake that follows the contours of his body:

it was at my throat
Beginning with its tail, . . .
moving under
My armpit like a sailor's, scale
By scale. . . .

. . . .
I retched but choked
It back, for he had crossed my breast. . . .
. . . .
Oh yes and now he lay low

On my belly, and gathered together the rainbow
Ships of Buckner Bay. I slumbered deep and he
crossed the small
Of my back   increased
His patchwork hold on my hip   passed through
the V between
My legs, and came
Around once more   all but the head   then I was
turning   the snake
Coiled round my right thigh and crossed
Me with light hands

The soldier's experience with this all-devouring, demonic snake warrants immediate comparison with two turbulent moments from Coleridge's odes of terror. Dickey's snake-filled, nightmare world in **"Victory"**—especially "the dark side / Of the mind"—recalls Coleridge's "viper thoughts, that coil around my mind, / Reality's dark dream!" from "Dejection: An Ode." When Coleridge turns from these viperous thoughts to "listen to the wind," he hears, with greater terror, the "groans, of trampled men, with smarting wounds— / At once they groan with pain, and shudder with the cold!" Likewise, Dickey's world of war is filled with the pain of men, that of his living "buddies," "ready," as he is, "to sail . . . toward life / After death," along with the memories of "others long buried / At sea." Even more important, the retching and choking of Dickey's soldier in a time of war suggest the sixth stanza from "Ode to the Departing Year," which records Coleridge's rage and shock at human slaughter carried out in the name of liberty during the French Revolution and at the massacre of Ismail in 1770. After experiencing, "on no earthly shore," a nightmare vision of the Departing Year, whose past events and "robe [are] inscrib'd with gore," this Romantic poet awakes to find that his predatory dream continues to flood traumatically through his soul, to the same degree that World War II traumatically pervades Dickey's poetry and fiction (even half a century later in Dickey's best and most recent novel, **To the White Sea**). One has only to place sections from **"Victory"** and "Ode to the Departing Year" side by side to note the emotional frenzy and pain shared by the two writers. Here are Coleridge's words, still striking after two hundred years:

> Yet still I gasp'd and reel'd with dread.
> And ever, when the dream of night
> Renews the phantom to my sight,
> Cold sweat-drops gather on my limbs;
>   My ears throb hot; my eye-balls start;
> My brain with horrid tumult swims;
>   Wild is the tempest of my heart;
> And my thick and struggling breath
> Imitates the toil of death!
> No stranger agony confounds
>   The Soldier on the war-field spread,
> When all foredone with toil and wounds,
> Death-like he dozes among heaps of dead!

While terror signals the presence of an emotionally animating form in both poems and indicates the genre to which they belong, the method of closure in each differs considerably, and this difference sheds further light on the momentum of Dickey's word-magic. To be sure, both poems close with a suffocating terror that demands release. Each poet has worked his way through considerable psychological pain; however, to remain in a state of such dread is emotional, moral, and political paralysis. In short, the pervasive terror in the body of each ode demands the poet's return to action in his conclusion, lest the momentum in each piece remain mired in pathetic tragedy. This two-step process—stasis and renewal—occurs in Coleridge's ending when he warns England that it has been protected from the political terrors of the Departing Year primarily because of the military value of its geographic isolation. Threatened even as he closes, Coleridge hears "the Birds of warning sing," then personally resolves to be "unpartaking of the evil thing" and to remain alert, "Cleans'd from the vaporous passions that bedim / God's Image."

Dickey, also acutely aware of catastrophic evil in human nature, needs to be "Cleans'd" from his exposure to the atrocities of war, which, like Coleridge, he personifies in animal form. Although both poets subscribe to a harmonious pantheism that incorporates historical calamity as fully realistic material for the poetic imagination, Dickey postulates nothing like a divine providence—as does Coleridge when he "recentre[s]" his "immortal mind"—as a subsumptive or unifying principle to which he can appeal for relief. Instead, on a personal level, Dickey dramatizes an inferred, magical animism in which life and death are not exclusive opposites but shared moments in a cycle of perpetual motion. In a world in which life and death constantly emerge into and out of each other, Dickey's snake—unlike Coleridge's birds, "the famish'd brood of prey"—has a double nature. First, the boa constrictor-like coiling and physical mutilation of the snake constitute a "confrontation" or "death encounter" for the speaker, a poetic event that has an emotional analogy with his vast experience of death from war and simultaneously stands for his desire for the symbolic death of his mutilated war self. With what appears at first to be an "appalling" movement, the snake then enters its subject from behind, and an opposite movement begins, namely, the renewal of the soldier that is initiated in the poem's final line. Strangely enough, the motion of the snake alters—indeed, redeems—both serpent and host, for the snake acquires, in Drake's terms, a "mysterious energy" that transforms the soldier, Christ-like, into "the new prince of peace":

>   I felt myself opened
>   Just enough, where the serpent staggered on his
>   last
>   Colors   needles gasping for air   jack-hammering
>   My right haunch burned by the hundreds
>   Of holes, as the snake shone on me complete
>   escaping
>   Forever   surviving   crushing   going home
>   To the bowels of the living,
>   His master, and the new prince of peace.

As is the case with Dickey's animals in many of his poems, such as **"Approaching Prayer," "Eagles," "Reincarnation I and II,"** and **"The Sheep Child,"** the snake now functions redemptively by assuming the role of what is a shamanic commonplace in anthropological literature, namely, a power animal. In keeping with the classical, mythological character of a power animal, Dickey's snake acquires a "mysterious power" that is both malign and benign. On the one hand, as a cross-cultural symbol of the range of human evil (including war), the snake is a traditional object of terror. Joseph Campbell says, "in its threatening character, as a traveling aesophagus, the serpent is . . . an image of the consuming power of the . . . will [in nature], foreboding death to all that lives." On the other hand, Campbell notes, "The ability of the serpent to shed its skin and thus to renew itself, as the moon is renewed by sloughing its shadow, has recommended it, throughout the world, as an obvious image of the mystery of the [same] will in nature, which is ever self-renewing in its generation of living beings." This ancient mythological connection between snake and moon thus enables the serpent to play its double role by providing it with the "self-renewing" power that is passed on to the soldier. In **"Victory,"** as in **"May Day Sermon"** and **"The Eye-Beaters,"** Dickey establishes yet another magical setting in which his poetic agent is energized as he tries to overcome overwhelming odds. On the road of this momentous psychic journey, Dickey's soldier struggles forward to rid himself of war by acquiring traits of natural objects which are really rhetorical, self-animating aspects of his own mind. That nature should seem beneficent and helpful, rather than another debilitating oppressor, adds considerably to the momentum of the healing process.

Consequently, in Dickey's ritual scene, the moon is not static but carries with it a renewing, ancient, magical light. For example, in **"Victory,"** "two birthdays / Ago," when the soldier got drunk—drunkenness being another variation of the hallucinatory state of shamanic transition—he did so at night when "the moon burned with the light it had when it split / / From the earth." Dickey's soldier, like this moon, has been "split" by war from the human and emotional ground that he desperately requires. However, this moon retains the "light" or energizing possibility to split, then become something different and uniquely powerful, a possibility and process that bear direct analogy to the soldier's ritual journey of healing and self-empowerment. While expressing a dynamic relation between life and death, metaphors throughout the poem further bind the motions of snake and moon, suggesting once more that, in Dickey's world, there operates something analogous to Frazer's principle of a power-exchanging, contagious magic. When the soldier says, "I reached for the bottle. It was dying and the moon / Writhed closer to be free," the dying energy of whiskey's liberating hallucination gives rise to the snakelike motion of the moon, which sheds its animating light on the soldier's "smile of foreknowledge" that he will survive the war. Similarly, just before the visionary snake emerges from the bottle, the speaker indicates another, closer connection between snake and moon that images the archetypal movement of life out of death: "Had the Form in the moon come from the dead soldier / Of your bottle, Mother?" Finally, even during the tattooing process, the passive host gives himself over to the animating, magical motion of the snake. Earlier, he described the snake by saying, "the angel / Of peace is limbless." Yet as the snake covers his body, the soldier identifies with the shape and motion of this "dreadful . . . superhuman agency" (Drake's terms) and so takes on its sustaining and renewing moon-energy as he notes, "limbless I fell and moved like moonlight / On the needles."

Even though Dickey's poem suggests that the "Form in the moon" (which I read to be an incipient image of the "snakehead") comes from a masculine source (albeit from his mother: "the dead soldier / Of your bottle"), and though the form's shape suggests a phallocentric image, the serpent is, by no means, a universal sign of masculine power. As an instrument of self-revelation and transformation, the serpent is conceived in many cultures as a feminine totem that symbolizes modes of coming to consciousness that bear directly on central religious components in Dickey's poem. For example, Campbell notes that in "India's Kundalini Yoga . . . the energy of life—all life—is symbolized as . . . a female serpent." In this sect,

> The aim of the yoga is to wake this Serpent Maiden, coiled in upon herself, and bring her up the spine to full consciousness, both of herself and of the spiritual nature of all things. She is awakened by the sound of the energy of the light of consciousness (the sound of the syllable "om"), which is brought to her first on the rhythm of the breath, but fully heard only when she has uncoiled and ascended to the center of the heart.

As it does in this Indian ritual initiated through feminine power, the snake in **"Victory"** covers the soldier's body with a motion that constitutes a hypnotic, somatic meditation, a meditation that, like Dickey's poem, involves the total transformation and awareness of its participant. Examples of the movement of Dickey's snake warrant repeating here to confirm this striking analogy: "the snake . . . was at my throat / Beginning with its tail . . . moving under / My armpit. . . . He coiled around me . . . I turned with him side / To side . . . he grew. . . . I lay and it lay / Now over my heart. . . . and I knew that many- / colored snakeskin was living with my heart   our hearts / Beat as one."

In Campbell's citation, the symbolic purpose of the Indian snake is to unify all human emotional and psychic centers, whether at the lowest point in the genitals or at the higher reaches of the heart. This somatic concordance then leads each center along the "One Way Trail" to full consciousness at "the crown of the head." To carry the whole man—sensory and cognitive, conscious and unconscious—through a comprehensive healing process, Dickey's serpent enters the soldier's bowels with the ritual motion of the mythical ouraboros, the serpent eating its own tail in the eternally circular process of separation and return to an energizing source. When Dickey's serpent passes the navel (that part of the body that Campbell interprets as a mythological symbol of "[the] will to power, aggression") and enters the soldier, we may read this event as the poem's climactic moment, a culmination of the fully conscious, circular transformation of the aggressive, war-torn, and exhausted phallus into an instrument of peace and renewal. Thinking through the physical imagery of the male body, Dickey transcends the merely physical by concluding in the mystical tradition of T. S. Eliot in "East Coker." While we may see a pun equal to Kenneth Burke's wordplay in his essay on the bodily tropes, we also see a standard, religious oxymoron in Eliot's words that locates Dickey's poetic attitude in a well-documented series of theological traditions, namely, that "In my end is my beginning."

If one thinks that this kind of closural magic (or, indeed, the formal, snakelike movement of Dickey's poem down the page) is trivial or may be reduced to static, sensory experience, one needs only to examine similar forms of "religious" meditation in other cultures, ranging from that of the Hopi Indians to certain Oriental religions. Consistent with the world-views in many of these beliefs, Dickey's magical method in **"Victory"** is not a form of escapism but rather a nondualistic way of clearing the ego of earthly pain in order to stand outside dominating sensation and emotion, and thus to free oneself from their tyranny. In many ways, the animating emotional form of **"Victory"** is analogous to the utterance of the mythic syllable *om,* which carries its practitioner through levels of consciousness, beyond myriad mental opposites, to the infernal and celestial vision deep within one's own soul. Dickey's magical, religious method of closure is thus both ancient and cross-cultural; it is directed to an external narrative of traumatic historical events, yet also inner-directed to the most sensitive reaction to these events by the human body. That this method should involve a sexual component becomes even more intelligible when related to certain basic religious principles, shared by Buddhist and Hindu sects. As Campbell notes of the Sahajiya cult in the Pala dynasty from Bengal, between A.D. 700 and 1200:

> it was held that the only true experience of the pure rapture of the void was the rapture of sexual union, wherein "each is both." This was the natural path . . . to the innate nature (*sahaja*) of oneself, and therewith of the universe: the path along which nature itself leads the way.

> So we read . . . "This sahaja is to be intuited within." "It is free from all sounds, colors, and qualities; can be neither spoken of nor known." "Where the mind dies out and the vital breath is gone, there is the Great Delight supreme: it neither stands steady nor fluctuates; nor is it expressible in words." "In that state the individual mind joins sahaja as water water." "There is no duality in sahaja. It is perfect, like the sky."

> . . . One knows then: "I am the universe: I am the Buddha: I am perfect purity: I am non-cognition: I the annihilator of the cycle of existence."

"Victory" originally appeared in the *Atlantic Monthly* in 1968. Twenty-five years later, in fall 1993, Dickey dramatized yet again his paramount interest in mystical momentum by using word-magic to conclude his novel ***To the White Sea.*** Here, his hero-predator, the American tail gunner Muldrow, shot down over war-torn Japan, is killed by Japanese soldiers. As their bullets go through him, he does not exactly die but rather enters a desireless, objectless, bodiless world, like the Sahajiyaian realm of supreme rapture, in which "the mind dies out and the vital breath is gone," which "neither stands steady nor fluctuates," and in which there is "no duality," for "the individual mind joins [nature] as water water." This absolute, circular flow—the union of life and death, waking and dreaming, pain and the absence of sensation—then hypnotically transports him to a kind of waking trance beyond even these harmonious opposites. In the novel's final lines, Muldrow's predatory quest ends when he closes his eyes and the individuality of his speaking voice dissolves into a darkened silence, which Campbell calls the "fourth element" of *om,* "the sphere of bliss," described in the Mandukya Upanishad as "neither inward- nor outward-turned consciousness, nor the two together . . . neither knowing nor unknowing . . . the coming to peaceful rest of all differentiated, relative existence: utterly quiet: peaceful-bliss-ful." In the purity of his motionless motion, this soldier, like the soldier in **"Victory,"** is propelled by the momentum of Dickey's extraordinary word-magic into the ecstatic silence that is his and its own final form:

> When I tell you this, just say that it came from a voice in the wind: a voice without a voice, which doesn't make a sound. You can pick it up any time it snows, where you are, or even just when the wind is from the north, from anywhere north of east or west. I was in the place I tried to get to. I had made it in exactly the shape I wanted to be in, though maybe just a little beat up. But the main thing was that I had got to the landscape and the weather, and you can remember me standing there with the bullets going through, and me not feeling a thing. There it was. A red wall blazed. For a second there was a terrific heat, like somebody had opened a furnace door, the most terrible heat, something that could have burned up the world, and I was sure I was gone. But the cold and the snow came back. The wind mixed the flakes, and I knew I had it. I was in it, and part of it. I matched it all. And I will be everywhere in it from now on. You will be able to hear me, just like you're hearing me now. Everywhere in it, for the first time and the last, as soon as I close my eyes.

Martin Bidney (essay date Fall 1995)

SOURCE: "Spirit-Bird, Bowshot, Water-Snake, Corpses, Cosmic Love: Reshaping the Coleridge Legacy in Dickey's *Deliverance,*" in *Papers on Language and Literature,* Vol. 31, No. 4, Fall, 1995, pp. 389-405.

[*In the following essay, Bidney traces the influence of Samuel Taylor Coleridge's writing in Dickey's* Deliverance.]

"I like to work my mind, such as it is," said James Dickey to Francis Roberts in 1968, "to see what I can get out of it and put into it. As John Livingston Lowes revealed in that wonderful book on Coleridge, *The Road to Xanadu*, if these things are in your mind, Lord knows what amalgams you can get out of it." Two years later, in his 1970 novel *Deliverance*, Dickey demonstrated his capacity to produce not only a visionary "amalgam" of the sort he found laid out in Lowes but, more surprisingly, a richly suggestive pattern of allusions to the work of Coleridge himself. In what follows I would like to offer a brief "Road to *Deliverance*," exploring that neo-Coleridgean pattern and its (re)visionary implications.

Dickey has elsewhere made clear his fondness for Coleridge. It has been noted that the last line of the war poem **"Bread"** ("I ate the food I ne'er had eat") varies "It ate the bread it ne'er had eat" from "The Rime of the Ancient Mariner." And in 1965 Dickey expressed to an interviewer from *Eclipse* the ambition to produce in his own verse "a sense such as if you stumbled on the village idiot, and he began to mutter amazing things to you, and, like in 'The Ancient Mariner,' you could not help but hear. . . ." *Deliverance*, as the title of my essay implies, is firmly anchored in the thematic pattern of "Mariner." But "The Eolian Harp" and "Dejection" and "Kubla Khan" will be seen to play a role as well; Dickey has done many and varied things with the legacy of his wise but troubled mentor.

Daniel B. Marin, the one critic who refers explicitly to "Ancient Mariner" in the context of *Deliverance*, writes that the tone at the book's conclusion is "quiet and maybe even melancholy. I am reminded of Coleridge's Wedding Guest: 'A sadder and a wiser man / He rose the morrow morn,' though not exactly. Is it that the note of 'pure abandon' Dickey reaches so wonderfully in the poetry can never be sung here in the darklight, in the 'darkness visible' of *Deliverance*?" My own feeling about the contrast between the endings of "Mariner" and *Deliverance* is rather the opposite of Marin's: I find Dickey more disposed to conclude on a note of comradely reassurance. Coleridge's aged sailor must endlessly retell the tale of his crime in an immortal repetition compulsion that is rightly styled "Life-in-Death." By contrast, Dickey's narrator Ed Gentry is not possessed by the vision of his narrative; the story is *his* possession—not something he owns up to guiltily, but something he owns proudly: "The river and everything I remembered about it became a possession to me, a personal, private possession, as nothing else in my life ever had. Now it ran nowhere but in my head, but there it ran as though immortally."

This is no Life-in-Death but a far pleasanter kind of immortality. Ed Gentry tells us that his hero-friend, Medlock Lewis—likewise no guilt-ridden intrusive presence but comfortingly called "a human being, and a good one"—refers

to Ed confidentially as "U.C., which means—to him and me—'Unorganized Crime,' and this has become a kind of minor conversation piece at parties, and at lunch in the city with strangers." Unorganized Crime of this smoothed-over sort, when juxtaposed to the Mariner's paranoid guilt obsession, seems a fraternal joke, or a whimsical authorial wink at the visionary tradition: "U. C." = "You (and I) *see*."

Yet the sad wisdom invoked by Marin is deep-rooted in Dickey's book as well; indeed, the entire conflictual structure of the work is Coleridgean. Every reader of "Mariner" feels the unresolved tension between the explicit transcendent message of cosmic love and the punishing prophetic burden of the driven wanderer who is forced to preach it, the difficulty of separating divine revelation from cruel fate, heavenly truth from purgatorial reality. Dickey's two epigraphs epitomize a similar unresolved tension between metaphysical meaning and the sense of ungovernable chaos, as the biblical Obadiah reveals a meaningful moral order ("The pride of thine heart hath deceived thee") while the philosopher Georges Bataille blames the inescapable conditions of human life itself for our frustrations ("Il existe à la base de la vie humaine, un principe d'insuffisance").

This is the same tension or conflict that generally divides analyses of Dickey's book into two groups. Some critical accounts of *Deliverance* have emphasized the heartening messages apparently conveyed: "penetrating insights into the political values forged by the American experience" [Charles M. Redenius, "Recreating the Social Contract: James Dickey's *Deliverance*," *The Canadian Review of American Studies* 17 (1986): 285-99], "the alleviation of fears associated with the omnipotence of thought by making restitution for hostile, destructive wishes" [James W. Hamiltion, "James Dickey's *Deliverance*: Midlife and the Creative Process," in *American Imago* 384 (1981): 389-405], or the "discovery, *in extremis*, that the sole means of controlling anxiety is through the imposition of aesthetic order" and "the maintenance of civilized values" [Michail K. Glenday, "*Deliverance* and the Aesthetics of Survival," in *American Literature* 56 (1984): 149-61]. Other analyses have just as emphatically portrayed the overwhelming power of evil or "darkness visible" in *Deliverance*—the idea that the narrator's "being-beyond-himself is the result of an act of transgression" [Heinz Tschachler, "*Un principe d'insuffisance*: Dickey's Dialogue with Bataille," in *Mosaic* 20 (1987): 81-93], or the analogous potentials for evil revealed in both heroes *and* villains ("The 'countrified jerk' in the city who wants a girl's buttocks in his ad is a part of Ed himself, and his domain is deep in Ed's unconscious"; "The cat that claws the girl's panties in Ed's dream and the owl that rips the canvas of Ed's tent anticipate the bestial man who commands Bobby to 'drop them panties'" in the scene of sexual violence [Peggy

Goodman Endel, "Dickey, Dante, and the Demonic: Re-assessing *Deliverance*," in *American Literature* 60 (1988): 611-24]).

What the pattern of Coleridgean allusion accomplishes is to dramatize all these conflicting tendencies and thereby to heighten the visionary drama of **Deliverance.** We shall see that here, as in "Mariner," images of spirit-like bird and flashing water-snake each embody an ambivalence; juxtaposed, they create still further conflict. The motifs of multiple corpses and cosmic love, taken from Coleridge's enigmatic epos of terror and transcendence, are enlisted in the service of Dickey's equally vivid moral-metaphysical *chiaroscuro*. Additional themes—dulcimer and sacred circle from "Kubla Khan," wind-played musical instrument and dancing diamonds on the main from "The Eolian Harp," as well as the motifs of rottenness, water tracks, angels, fire-water unity and the moving moon from "Mariner"—give **Deliverance** a pervasively Coleridgean ambiance and make it a major neo-Romantic re-envisioning and revision.

"Revision" is the key word here, for it is not only the reassuring tonality of the ending that (as I have suggested) distinguishes **Deliverance** from "Mariner." Rather, this changed conclusion indicates a noticeable shift in concern—from the psychodynamics of persecution to the ambivalences central to (human) nature. Only through the extremely risky unleashing of a desire for violent victory does Ed attain the transcendent insights of pantheistic oneness. As Heinz Tschachler has shown, this is a troublesome dialectic traceable in part to Georges Bataille: in **Deliverance** as in the thinking of Bataille, only when the "principle of individuation" is put at risk (as a result of the individual's risking his life) are hidden continuities exposed to view and feelings of sacred merger briefly attainable. By strategic alterations and re-orchestration of Coleridgean motifs Dickey makes this thesis vivid and its *exemplum* ineffaceably present to the imagination.

As Lewis, with evangelizing fervor, outlines to Ed his project for a canoeing venture, the latter worries at one point that "he's going to turn this into . . . A lesson. A Moral"; here Ed shows the same discomfort with "morals" that Coleridge showed when responding to Anna Barbauld's complaint that "Ancient Mariner" lacked a moral, the poet famously countered that it had "too much" of one. Ed buys into the trip, mainly out of boredom induced by routine; when his wife asks, "Is it my fault?" he says no but thinks to himself that "it partly was, just as it's any woman's fault who represents normalcy." Ed likes his wife well enough; it's just that married life has the fault of being normal: in "Mariner" the Wedding Guest was obliged to direct his imaginative attention to something a good deal less normal than weddings, and in **Deliverance** the same priority is given to an extraordinary experience promised by a man. Lewis's surname,

"Medlock," has in fact a striking resemblance to "wedlock," but what Lewis offers in proposing his expedition for a group of four men is a venture in platonic male bonding, a male adventure trip that will temporarily replace the routine life Ed leads in *wedlock* (an idea hideously parodied, of course, in the eventual rape committed by the rural stranger). One may find a bit of misogyny in this humdrum picture of marriage, but if so, it is a problem Dickey shares with Coleridge.

The chief attraction of the trip for Ed, as sportsman, is not canoeing but hunting with a bow; only in the film version is a crossbow used, certainly an additional contribution to "Mariner" thematics. Allusions to the motif of the albatross are also oblique, but they are multiple, varied, and ingenious. The *alb*-syllable, an etymon for the whiteness of the white bird, appears, along with the birdlike motif of music, when the "*alb*ino boy" Lonnie plays banjo in a duet of magical beauty with Ed's and Lewis's co-traveler Drew. Playing with Lonnie makes even the back of Drew's neck express "sheer joy": the albino conveys a sudden and profound inspiration, like that suggested by Coleridge's quasi-supernatural white bird. Each of the albino's eyes is singular in its strange independence, as they focus in different directions; soon afterwards, another singular eye, the "glazed" and "half-open" eye of a chicken's head, appears to the travelers in a stagnant patch of river downstream from the poultry plant. So even if no albatross is killed in **Deliverance,** the singular eye of the bird-related albino appears to us soon in a metamorphosed form of death.

Bird allusions abound in the first part of **Deliverance**; for example, a certain Mr. Holley, Ed's subordinate in his design consulting firm, turns "one of [Georges] Braque's birds into a Pegasus," and Lewis Medlock himself rather strikingly resembles a bird, with his "face like a hawk," beakish "long-nosed" profile, and "whitish patch up toward the crown of his head." C. Hines Edwards, Jr. has specifically studied the prominent and recurrent owl-theme, noting the contrasts it embodies: the owl is at once bird "of prey" and "bird of wisdom," conventionally an "ill omen" and yet used in the book to suggest both nature and—in the form of the owl-shaped wind chime—civilization.

But two Coleridgean insights need to be added to this. First, the repeated mention of the "ringing of the owl on the other birds, in Martha's wind-toy at home" brings the bird motif together with the Aeolian harp motif, betokening Coleridgean inspiration: wind chimes are modern suburbia's answer to the Aeolian harp. Second, the owl that repeatedly visits Ed during the night—and whose frightening "stony toe" Ed even learns to touch without fear—resembles a familiar spirit, a haunting presence familiar yet uncanny in its incessant departures and returns: "All night the owl kept coming back to hunt from the top of the tent," just as the Coleridgean albatross, "every day, for food or play, / Came to the mariner's hollo!" In its quasi-supernatural uncanniness, in its friendly association with the wind-generated music favored by Coleridge, and in its ambivalent implications, Dickey's owl-symbol, like the musical albino, shares the enigmatic nature of the Coleridgean Mariner's albatross. Even in its size the owl is exceptional, closer to the ungainly dimensions of the Coleridgean bird—a "big night bird—surely it was very big, from the size of the nails and feet."

The ambivalent implications of both albatross and owl are in part covert: the Mariner has no way of suspecting that if he kills the albatross 200 sailors' deaths will result; and Ed, who spends the night pleasantly imagining the owl's hunting feats on its various flights, does not imagine that the huge "talons" which had so terrifyingly punctured the roof of his tent are foreshadowings of the *lex talionis,* the pitiless rule of retribution or Law of the Claw that will govern the latter part of the men's violent adventure. But in both the Coleridge and Dickey narratives, an atmosphere of nausea is quickly induced by the recurrent use of the theme of "rot" as the tales proceed. After the Mariner kills the bird, "The very deep did rot: O Christ! / That ever this should be!" After the rural villain commits his rape of Bobby, the adventurers find themselves "by a sump of some kind, a blue-black seepage of rotten water," and when Lewis kills the rapist and tries to bury the body, the earth has turned into sheer rot: "There was no earth; it was all leaves and rotten stuff. It had the smell of generations of mould." In both stories, intimations of unfathomably deep corruption overwhelm the soul and body.

Yet it is not long before the moon provides, for both Coleridge's and Dickey's protagonists, a moving emblem of visionary hope. Life-in-Death has won the Mariner's soul; Drew has been murdered by the rapist's cohort. Yet the Mariner, at least, has triumphed over Death itself; and Lewis and Ed have worked out their plans for both defense and retribution—they, too, can somehow glory in "pure survival." The moon, betokening hope, is evoked with strikingly similar language in the two works. Coleridge's marginal annotations describe a "silent *joy*" in the scene where "The moving Moon *went up* the sky, / And no where did abide: / Softly she *was going up* . . ." (emphases added). And Ed tells us his "heart expanded with *joy*" as he watched while "the moon *was going up and up* . . ." (emphases added). It will only take another moment, in both narratives, for the climactic water-snake epiphany to arise in moonlit glory.

Let us look first at the Coleridgean precedent, which Dickey will vary in a composite epiphany consisting of four brief episodes. In the light of the just-ascended moon, says the Mariner,

> I watched the water-snakes:

> They moved in tracks of shining white,
> And when they reared, the elfish light
> Fell off in hoary flakes.
> . . . .
> They coiled and swam; and every track
> Was a flash of golden fire.

> O happy living things! no tongue
> Their beauty might declare:
> A spring of love gushed from my heart,
> And I blessed them unaware. . . .

Traditionally cursed, the seeming symbol of evil is revealed as in its unfamiliar way wholly divine. Serpentine horrors can now be seen as inseparable from the life-power, the fertility and wisdom and immortality, that mythic traditions world-wide have rightly credited to the coiled *ouroboros.*

In Dickey's four-phase moonlit epiphany all the appearances of the water-snake are metaphoric. But they are overpoweringly real. And note the evocative borrowings already in phase one:

> Despite everything, I looked down. The river had spread flat and *filled with moonlight.* It took up the whole of space under me, bearing in the center of itself a long *coiling image of light,* a chill, bending *flame.* I must have been seventy-five or a hundred feet above it, hanging poised over some kind of inescapable glory, a bright pit. (emphasis added)

Coleridge's "fire" is Dickey's "flame"; the Mariner's snakes that flashingly "coiled" have become Ed's "coiling image of light"; moonlight fills the water in both scenes. Dickey wants no loss of symbolic ambivalence in the transfer: he insists on the image of the snaky abyss in his "bright pit." Inescapable glory is wedded to acceptance of the lowest.

In fact, a few pages later the light spreads out on the water "eternally, the moon so huge on it that it hurt the eyes," just as the Mariner speaks soon afterward of the blinding lightning descending from moon-level as "a river steep and wide." And when "angelic spirits" come down instantly to enter the bodies of the dead and one of these spirits even helps the Mariner as they pull together "at one rope," a precedent is set for a vivid metaphoric wording in Dickey's analogous multiphase epiphany: "The thought struck me with my full adrenaline supply, all hitting the veins at once. Angelic. Angelic. Is that what it means? It very likely does. And I have a lot of nylon rope. . . ." Coleridge writes of water-snakes and heavenly angels in the literal language of suspended disbelief, of high gothic dreamwork; Dickey's snakes and angels are metaphoric, observing the conventions of lyrical-psychological prose. But it is still visionary prose—vatic, and Coleridgean.

The third phase of the metaphoric water-snake epiphany returns to Coleridge's original depiction of the snakes:

> What a view, I said again. The river was *blank* and *mindless* with beauty. It was the most glorious thing I have ever seen. But it was not seeing, really. For once it was not just seeing. It was beholding. I *beheld* the river in its icy pit of brightness, in its far-below sound and *indifference,* in its *large coil* and *tiny points and flashes of the moon,* in its *long sinuous form,* in its *uncomprehending* consequence. (emphases added, except for "beheld," italicized by Dickey)

Words like "mindless" and "indifference" and "uncomprehending" recall the Mariner's blessing the snakes "unaware"; the "large coil" and "long sinuous form" make the serpent-image gloriously present in an emphatically Coleridgean way; the "tiny points and flashes of the moon" on the water clearly recall the "hoary flakes" of moonlight and the multiform "flash" of reflected moon-fire from Coleridge's sacred scene. Ed's experience is a visionary triumph—an act of not mere seeing but beholding—in itself. But reading it with Coleridge in mind heightens its vibrancy and reveals it as a worthy homage to a suitably complex and many-sided master.

The fourth and final phase of the neo-Coleridgean epiphany repeats and underlines the main motifs—awe, the life-force, the moon, the metaphoric snake, the visionary light:

> Fear and a kind of enormous *moon-blazing sexuality* lifted me, millimeter by millimeter. . . . I looked for a slice of gold . . . in the river . . . something lovable, in the *huge serpent-shape of light.*
>
> Above me the darks changed, and in one of them was a star. On both sides of that small light the rocks went on up, black and solid as ever, but *their power was broken. . . .*
>
> I was crying. What reason? There was not any, for I was really not ashamed or terrified; I was just there. . . . Lord, Lord. The river hazed and danced into the sparkle of my eyelashes, the more wonderful for being unbearable. (emphases added)

Ed's mysterious sense that the "power" of the rocks was "broken" by the visionary light makes us remember how "The spell begins to break" in Coleridge's marginal annotation to the line, after the water-snake epiphany, in which the Mariner finds himself finally able again to worship. "That selfsame moment I could pray," says the Mariner—the precedent for Ed's joyous, awed outcry, "Lord, Lord." The fact that the river "hazed and *danced* into the *sparkle* of [Ed's]

eyelashes" (emphases added) alludes to yet another epiphanic scene: recall the speaker in "The Eolian Harp," who stretches his limbs at noon "Whilst through my half-clos'd *eyelids* I behold / The sunbeams *dance,* like *diamonds,* on the main" (emphases added). Dickey has conflated two scenarios of Coleridgean glory.

Coleridgean revelation also sheds a closely related light on Ed's foolhardy but heroic adventurer-mentor, Lewis Medlock. For all his miscalculations and improvidence, Medlock is deemed worthy of transfiguration for a moment in a clever variant of the Mariner's water-snake reverie. We remember that when the water-snakes glided through the moonlit waves, "every track / Was a flash of golden fire": the tracks of the glorious creatures seem wondrously to unite the incompatible elements of fire and water. The same word, "track," the same motif of tracks in the water, and the same quasi-miraculous union of the fiery and the liquid ("red" for fire and "blue" for water) are motifs reworked in Ed's wonderstruck portrait of his mentor:

> Everything he had done for himself for years paid off as he stood there in his *tracks in the water.* I could tell by the way he glanced at me; the payoff was in my eyes. . . . The muscles were bound up in him smoothly, and when he moved, the veins in the moving part would surface. If you looked at him that way, he seemed made out of well-matched *red-*brown chunks wrapped in *blue* wire. (emphases added)

The "Mariner" variation is ingenious, unobtrusive, and effective. In the vivid and often coarse tale that constitutes **Deliverance,** Dickey has lost none of the delicate allusive subtlety that distinguishes him as lyric poet.

When Coleridge somewhat perversely insisted to Mrs. Barbauld that "Ancient Mariner" had too much of a moral—that it "ought to have had no more moral than the Arabian Nights' tale" of the merchant who, during a snack, tosses a nutshell aside and is accused of murder because a genie claims the shell has put out the eye of the genie's son—Coleridge was mistaken. The cosmic love moral, as we may call it—

> He prayeth well, who loveth well
> Both man and bird and beast.
>
> He prayeth best, who loveth best
> All things both great and small;
> For the dear God who loveth us,
> He made and loveth all

—is crucial to the poem's enduring fascination, which lies precisely in the tension between the Mariner's moment of transcendence and the immense, absurdly disproportionate price he has to pay for it. Such paradoxes afflict and bless and puzzle all of us. James Dickey's **Deliverance** likewise takes account of them, building on Coleridge's insights, not on his arbitrary or irked disclaimers.

There are many cosmic love or universal empathy passages in Dickey's narrative, suitably presented in the context of the four-phase water-snake epiphany: for example, as he moves up the steep escarpment, Ed begins, as it were, to "make love to the cliff"; as he inches upward he moves "with the most intimate motions of my body, motions I had never dared use with Martha, or with any other human woman." But the central, most striking passage of paradoxical empathy is the one in which Ed opens up to a strange transpersonal oneness with his enemy, precisely the man on whom he will wreak revenge with a bowshot for the murder of Drew:

> I had thought so long and hard about him that to this day I still believe I felt, in the moonlight, our minds fuse. It was not that I felt myself turning evil, but that an enormous physical indifference, as vast as the whole abyss of light at my feet, came to me: an indifference not only to the other man's body scrambling and kicking on the ground with an arrow through it, but also to mine. If Lewis had not shot his companion, he and I would have made a kind of love, painful and terrifying to me, in some dreadful way pleasurable to him, but we would have been together in the flesh, there on the floor of the woods, and it was strange to think of it.

This cosmic empathy feeling recurs repeatedly in ever-changing forms: a few pages later we read, for example,

> The needles were filling slowly with the beginnings of daylight, and the tree began to flow softly, shining the frail light held by the needles inward on me, and I felt as though I were giving it back outward.

Even after he has killed the offender, Ed feels that "His brain and mine unlocked and fell apart, and in a way I was sorry to see it go. I never had thought with another man's mind on matters of life and death, and would never think that way again." The precedent for these seemingly inconceivable unities disclosed in existential crisis may be found in "Mariner," but the Coleridgean revelation is elaborated and multiply varied in **Deliverance.**

It would not be easy—to say the least of it—for Ed "to get used to the idea that I had buried three men [the rapist killed by Lewis, then Drew, and finally Drew's murderer] in two days, and that I had killed one of them." But the neo-Coleridgean fascination of Ed's narrative would not exert its hypnotic force without both of the factors that constitute the book's reason-challenging antinomy, its tragic enlightenment: multiple corpses *and* cosmic empathy; deadly peril and lifegiving love—a quasi-mystical or pantheist transcendence that arises from an existential test, pushing aside the principle of individuation to reveal unimaginable continuities, unsuspected and not always gratifying oneness.

It is in the light of this antinomy, finally, that we should read the "Kubla Khan" and "Dejection" allusions in the earlier part of **Deliverance**—which I have postponed for separate treatment for that reason. These unmistakable allusions begin when Lewis tries to interest Ed in the folkloric riches of mountain music: "there are songs in those hills that collectors have never put on tape. And I've seen one family with a dulcimer." "If those people in the hills," retorts Ed skeptically, "the ones with the folk songs and *dulcimers,* came out of the hills and led us all toward *a new heaven and a new earth,* it would not make a particle of difference to me" (emphases added). In this wittily allusive interchange we not only hear an echo of Coleridge's "damsel with a dulcimer" but also an ironic reference to the "new Earth and new Heaven" which Imagination gives us by "wedding Nature to us"—as it does when Aeolian harps (which are wind-dulcimers, emblems of the harmonious unity of spirit/breath and world) function properly.

The Coleridgean irony grows into a dreadful grotesquerie after the villainous rapist, mortally wounded by Lewis's avenging arrow, goes into "convulsions" that resemble the visionary seizure of the shaman-figure depicted in "Kubla Khan":

> He took a couple of strides toward the woods and then seemed to change his mind and *danced* back to me, *lurching* and clog-stepping in a *secret circle.* He held out a hand to me, like a *prophet.* . . . (emphases added)

The verb "danced" and the "secret circle" make us think of Coleridge's "Weave a circle round him thrice"—a circle woven precisely through ritual dance; the "lurching" and "convulsions" of the dizzily dancing victim recall the "flashing eyes and floating hair" of the shamanistic seer in "Kubla Khan," his being possessed in a state of seizure, a fit—precisely the mad ecstasy of a "prophet," as Dickey says. All this relates with horrific irony but all-too-evident appropriateness—via the mountain "dulcimer" motif—to the evil archetype of the "demon-lover."

Yet there is a Coleridgean tragic tenderness, as well, in Dickey's final symbolic depiction of the criminal-victim's farewell: "He held out a hand to me, like a prophet. . . ." In a context of Coleridgean allusion, the word "prophecy" refers to no specific predictions or forecasts; rather, it points to some transcendent insight or awareness of ultimate value:

here, the prophetic insight acquired—even by a bestial villain—at the threshold of death is unspoken, perhaps unspeakable. The Ancient Mariner, too, was a prophet, though a reluctant one, like Jonah, or like Paul. It may, indeed, be best to end our comparative journey with this final instance of an epitomizing symbol of deep kinships that can never be fully articulated, a symbolic gesture that serves as testimony to a neo-Coleridgean seed of enlightenment arising from crisis and trial, a "bright pit."

Susanna Rich (review date Winter 1996)

SOURCE: "Dickey's 'The Firebombing,'" in *The Explicator,* Vol. 54, No. 2, Winter, 1996, pp. 110-13.

[In the following review, Rich asserts that Dickey's poem "The Firebombing" "can be shown to implicate the reader in the blame for the firebombing of Japan during World War II."]

Jacques-Louis David originally displayed his painting *The Sabines* facing a cartouched oval mirror. When patrons turned their backs to the painting to look into the mirror, they saw themselves flattened two-dimensionally into the midst of the battle of the Sabines against the Romans—either imprinted over the central figure of the woman with arms outstretched as if on a crucifix, or standing under her arms, as if under protective wings. With a slight shift, the viewer became imprinted over the figure of the naked invading Roman who has his back to us, a round shield covering him. David's unusual orchestration made a political statement at the time of the French Revolution: We are all involved and implicated in the struggle over freedom. The spectator may turn a back to it only to find herself or himself more fully reflected in it.

What David did with *The Sabines,* James Dickey does with his perhaps most controversial poem **"The Firebombing."** This poem, written sympathetically from the point of view of an ex-bomber pilot in World War II, has been described by Robert Bly as "gloating over power over others." He calls Dickey a "Georgia Cracker Kipling" for writing what Bly characterizes as "new critical brainwashing that doesn't wash." But **"The Firebombing"** can be shown to implicate the reader in the blame for the firebombing of Japan during World War II. Bearing out the experiences of many war veterans, this reading is sound on several levels. First, politically, by sanctioning a government that, in war, sends people into battle, Americans sanction the bloodshed that ensues. Soldiers follow orders that are, "on behalf of the American people." Second, psychologically, when the weight of guilt is too hard to bear, we pass it on to others to share it with us. Dickey, through the mirror of his craft, deftly reflects back into the picture those of us who deny complicity and disagree with the poem's message.

The poem begins with a rousing imperative, much like a pep talk given by a sergeant to his soldiers: "Homeowners unite"—a one-line, two-word stanza that looms larger because of the frame of white space around it. Dickey uses five of these one-line stanzas in the first three pages, and then, just when we become accustomed to them, stops. His stanzas vary in length, organization, and line length. Sometimes he begins the next line at the visual point where the previous line ends. We feel dropped. All this variation is unsettling, inviting us to grasp onto some comforting structure, impose it ourselves, just as a government imposes orders onto its military in the chaos of battle.

Unsettling, as well, is his shift to triple spacing between words, dividing verbs from adverbs, prepositions from their objects, verbs from their objects, nouns from their verbs. This invites the reader to try, albeit unconsciously, to pull the words back to comfortable regularity, thus including the reader in the shaping of the words on the page and, by implication, closing the distance between us as passive listeners and the speaker as active creator. In some places this spacing invites us to punctuate, as for example in these lines:

> Grocery baskets   toy fire engines
> New Buicks stalled by the half-moon
> Shining at midnight on crossroads   green paint
> Of jolly garden tools   red Christmas ribbons:

This invitation to punctuate is a haunting move, for dropping punctuation into written discourse as an afterthought, done by someone other than the author, is visually, and metaphorically, like dropping bombs into a landscape.

Dickey further unsettles us with stutterings:

> In a dark dream   that   that is
> That is like flying inside someone's head
> Think of this   this of this
> . . . .
> Letting go   letting go

As with any stutterer, we are tempted to say it for him just to stop the halting, get closure, be finished with it. And so we are drawn into the bombing, for these lines stutter the way a machine gun would. We want the words to empty out, the bombs to leave the bomb bay. With these and other unsettling moves Dickey makes us vulnerable, forcing us to look for some structure into which we can settle.

Dickey also draws us in with patterns such as anagramatic alliteration. For example, he often starts a series of lines with the same letters, as in stanza 3:

There are cowl flaps . . .
The shovel-marked . . .
The enemy . . .

or later:

Forever I do sleep . . .
For home that breaks . . .
From my wingtips . . .

Even his capitalization of first words offers the safety of return, and so we grab for the next line, and the next line, and are driven along to read more of the bomber's rapturous ode. Then there are visual and aural alliterations that link words in lines and across lines: the *b*'s in,

Break under the first bomb, around those
In bed, or late in public baths . . .

and the look and sound of *c*'s in,

Of Chicago fire:
Come up with the carp pond showing . . .

Whitmanesque catalogues of the landscape viewed from the cockpit name the elements of what is being bombed, like Adam's first naming and thus making conscious the parts of Paradise. We are drawn to this voice by its exuberance and power. We want to be part of a power that is not affected by moral strictures that seem, like the Japanese villages seen from the distance of an airplane, mere abstractions.

It would be easy for us to blame the pilot-speaker, to unburden ourselves of the guilt of having enjoyed this poem and of feeling the power of destruction. But there is the "Catch 22": If we blame the firebomber, we destroy what we have co-created, and if we do not, then we are co-pilots and guilty as well.

Dickey begins **"The Firebombing"** with an epigram taken from the Book of Job, "Or hast thou an arm like God?" Dickey offers us two alternatives: to be blameworthy by blaming the firebomber for his lack of guilt, or to be forgiven by forgiving: to damn like the devil, or to forgive with the sweep of God's arm, and thus, like David's spectator, become the Christlike Sabine with outstretched arms—the one taken in violence.

Keen Butterworth (essay date Spring 1996)

SOURCE: "The Savage Mind: James Dickey's *Deliverance*," in *The Southern Literary Journal,* Vol. XXVIII, No. 2, Spring, 1996, pp. 69-78.

[*In the following essay, Butterworth discusses the savage side of man portrayed in Dickey's* Deliverance *and analyzes how characterization structures the novel.*]

On the dust jacket of the first edition of James Dickey's *Deliverance* an eye peers out through a surrounding cluster of hemlock fronds. It is not the poison hemlock shrub of Socrates, but the benign water-loving hemlock tree (*Tsuga canadensis*) of our Appalachian forests. It would grow in abundance, probably in virgin stands, along the Cahulawassee, the fictional river on which most of the story of *Deliverance* takes place. The fronds provide the screen of Nature from which the eye looks out. The eye's blue iris is the color of the sky—or of clear deep pools of water. The white ball is the color of clouds—or of turbid falling waters. The skin around the eye has the green cast of deep forests. Is it the eye of the murderous mountaineer? The eye of the narrator Ed Gentry? Of some Nature spirit or pantheistic god? Is it the eye of the author? Probably it is all of these, for it is the eye of the book itself.

In lectures and readings Dickey often quotes the final statement of [Rainer Maria] Rilke's poem "Archaic Torso of Apollo": "You must change your life." (*Du muss dela leben andern.*) This, says Dickey, is what all important art demands, and certainly this is the effect that Dickey wants his work—poems and novels—to have on his readers. I am reminded of the warning Boehme gives at the outset of one of his books: he asks his readers to go no further unless they are willing to make changes in their lives that the book will call for; if they are not, then reading the book might be bad for them, even dangerous. Readers of *Deliverance* might heed a similar warning, for the novel records a harrowing descent into the abyss, the dark chasm of our own psyches; and the change Dickey calls for is in our understanding of ourselves as human animals whose genetic origins lie in a dark but certain past. Unless the reader understands the violence of the story as it relates to his own psyche, then the effect of the novel might indeed be dangerous.

"*Denn da ist keine Stelle, die dich nicht sieht.*" This assertion which precedes the final statement of Rilke's poem seems even more to the point: "There is no part that does not see you." We stand naked before the naked work of art. It sees us—and if we have the stomach for it, we see ourselves, through reflection and contrast—for what we are: flawed, incomplete creatures; and we must change, or, at least, accept the imperative to change.

Flawed certainly, but to say we are *incomplete* may be misleading: our incompleteness often results from our refusal to accept a part of ourselves, an innate part of our psyches, which we are afraid to claim. Under the intimidating light of modern civilization, we hide our shadow, our instinctual selves, not only because we distrust it, but also because John

Locke and the Enlightenment have convinced us that it does not exist. The Puritan Manichean ethos has taught us to project it conveniently elsewhere—as the devil, or on some darker complexioned race. Yet from time to time we feel the Aurignacian Man lurking just beneath our skins, and that scares the devil out of us; so we turn him out, or push him back deep into the recesses of our psyches, where we will not have to face his reality at close hand. To that subterfuge of modern man Dickey says his No—not in Thunder, but to the roar of mountain water. In the poem **"Falling"** the protagonist strips away her clothes, the integuments of civilization, to the roar of wind, as she falls from womb to grave, discovering—or inventing—in the process who she is. In *Deliverance* Dickey strips himself bare by breaking the psyche down into its component parts and testing them in a baptism, a trial by water, original water, near the source, not yet damped by the controls of civilization: the uterine font, launching the quarter of characters forth into a new life where only the fittest will prevail.

Dickey has discouraged symbolic readings of his novels and poems because he wants to emphasize the importance of story and storytelling, which he feels are too often devalued by modern theory and practice.
—Keen Butterworth

And so the eye of Dickey's book sees us: subdued creatures of an urban-industrial civilization, separated from Nature—save our own; and that nature-in-ourselves we cannot understand because of our isolation from the natural world which could furnish the analogies necessary for understanding. The rise of civilization, Carl Jung tells us, has been the history of the rational mind's successive gains against the instinctual, until we scarcely recognize ourselves as part of the natural world at all, but rather, in the Christian redaction, as separate creations altogether. The problems caused by this sublimation have been enumerated and analyzed by modern psychology. In *Deliverance* those problems, and perhaps a solution, have been dramatized.

Deliverance. From what? From the murderous mountain men? From the primordial dangers of the river? Certainly these are the most obvious referents of the title. But there is also the implication of a deliverance from the enslaving monotony of modern urban life. And, beyond that, to a deliverance from the parts of ourselves which also hold us in a kind of bondage, which thwart self-knowledge and consequently hinder our pursuit of vitality itself.

Dickey has discouraged symbolic readings of his novels and poems because he wants to emphasize the importance of story and storytelling, which he feels are too often deval-

ued by modern theory and practice. Whatever meaning, in the abstract sense, his work might suggest has grown out of narrative action. This is certainly a healthy corrective to synthetic theories deriving from Poe and tracing their development through the symbolists, T. S. Eliot's objective correlative, to the postmodern practices of the anti-novel, where effect (or idea) is the first consideration and the synthesis of materials to produce that effect second: narrative thus becomes tertiary—a means of effecting the synthesis, often by inventive but unnatural means. Dickey opts for Nature. He would agree, I think, with [Walter Savage] Landor's old philosopher: "Nature I loved, and next to Nature Art." For Dickey empirical experience is authentic, salutary. His mode is thus mimetic, but informed by the esemplastic imagination.

Form and metaphor, Dickey says, must grow out of the material. But then, too, we know that the imagination of the artist is attracted to those materials in which form and metaphor inhere. First, the basic structure of *Deliverance* is archetypal: Descent and Return—as old at least as *The Gilgamesh,* and tracing its lineage upward through *The Odyssey, The Divine Comedy, King Lear, Faust, Moby-Dick.* There are some who hold that it is the basic structure of all great narrative. It is certainly the emphasized structure of *Deliverance.* Then, there is the river—the great mystery and power of water: life-giving but dangerous, vitalizing, primarily feminine in its associations. American literature is obsessed with water, whether it be [James Fenimore] Cooper's and Poe's and Melville's oceanic expanses, or Twain's and Faulkner's rivers. Water is life—vast and deep in the collective oceans, flowing and inexorable in its journey from highlands to estuary. But Dickey's Cahulawassee differs significantly from Twain's and Faulkner's Mississippi. It is the river of origins, chaotic and primitive. The Mississippi has tremendous power, but it is a gathered power, belied by its placid surface. The Cahulawassee is anything but placid; it is too original and unsophisticated to disguise its energy as it plunges through the rapids and gorges of North Georgia. It represents life untouched by the civilizing hand of man, or even by the tempering forces of Nature itself. The river is raw and wild.

On the other hand, there is the opposing metaphor of the dam being built at Aintry, which will cause the submersion of the river as it floods the valleys and gorges through which the characters of the novel travel. The dam is a symbol of man's abstractions, of Bergson's geometric order. As an architectural structure, it is like man's laws, his mores, his religions, his arts, which he uses to subdue and control the wild and primitive vitality in himself. As the waters rise behind the dam, they will subdue the wild river, diffuse its power, and cover over the rugged landscape it has wrought. Finally, it will create a placid, monotonous surface, and the wild river will be only a personal memory of those who have experienced it, or a cultural memory of those who have heard or read the stories told by their forebears. Like the dam, the shaping forms of civilization do not so much create order as they effect a monotonous peace which allows man to go about his daily business without threat of disruption. Instinct and passion are sublimated for the sake of society and progress.

Dickey illustrates this monotonous peace in the first section of the novel. In this prologue entitled "Before," Ed Gentry, the narrator, goes through his daily routines as an advertising executive and suburban family man in Atlanta. By the standards of modern society, it is a good life, but dull and feminized: when Ed returns to his office from lunch, he realizes there is not a man, save himself, on the street, only a bevy of women. His business, though prosperous, is mediocre: it cannot even strive for excellence, lest it out-class the market and thus lose accounts. His wife Martha is a generous, sympathetic woman, but their sexual coupling indicates that romance and adventure have long since departed their marriage. The only excitement Ed experiences is caused by the gold fleck in the eye of a nearly nude model his agency has employed. The eye is different, mysterious—it seems to represent the flaw in humanity, in the human condition, which can be beautiful and fascinating, particularly when found in an object or person approximating perfection. It is a symbol of mystery and exotic possibility. Her eye seizes Ed's imagination, and its image comes back to him several times during the course of the novel; but it offers only a temporary relief from the general boredom of his life.

At an unconscious level, Ed seeks deliverance from the monotony and tedium of this urban-suburban life. Yet he hesitates to go on the trip his friend Lewis Medlock has planned down the Cahulawassee. Adventure seems hardly worth the trouble of disrupting the comfortable apathy of his life, just as a passionate pursuit of the girl with the golden eye would disrupt his impersonal business relations. But he goes nevertheless because of the contagious enthusiasm of Lewis: psychologically, it would be more difficult for Ed to refuse Lewis than to go along with him. Thus, in a way, even here, Ed is choosing a path of least resistance. He is seduced by Lewis's enthusiasm: when Lewis rolls the topographical map out on the table for Drew, Bobby, and Ed to see, he makes the trip sound like pure romance. The map, however, gives no more idea of what the actual terrain is like than a textbook in anthropology allows us to understand the life of an ice-age hunter. It is an abstraction, another of the reductions by which we separate ourselves from the concrete reality of things and events. There are only two ways of confronting and understanding that reality. Direct experience: the way of Ed Gentry. Or by an act of the imagination: the way of Dickey, the poet-novelist.

What happens to the characters during their ordeal on the Cahulawassee, and what they learn from that experience, is directly related to the personalities they reveal during the course of the narrative. Drew is a corporate executive with a highly developed sense of social and moral order. He is an organization man, but in the best, not the pejorative, sense of the term. He is also a family man with a strong sense of duty. His love of music, which has a mathematical order and logic, but also an emotional warmth, reflects these qualities in him. Even his last name, Ballenger, might suggest balance. Because of this highly developed sense of order and social morality, Drew is not able to cope with the chaos of the primitive drama in which he is forced to participate. Consequently, he is destroyed.

Bobby, on the other hand, is violated, but not destroyed. He is a social being also, but without the ideals of Drew. Whereas Drew is an executive with responsibility and position, Bobby is the salesman who has to sell himself, to please and win others, at whatever cost to his own integrity and pride. He also lacks discipline, as revealed by Ed's memory of his blowing up at a party. He is the softest, effeminate and porcine, and the quickest to complain. Thus, Bobby cannot protect himself from the violation of his being by gratuitous evil, represented by the two mountaineers, Stovall and Benson. But he does survive that violation, because his moral lassitude (some might call it flexibility) allows him to.

Lewis Medlock, the enthusiast and instigator of the trip, is quite different from either Drew or Bobby. He is a man of independent means, directly indebted to no one. He can develop his individuality at will—which he does, and thus comes to believe in his own invincibility. He has become expert at every athletic activity he pursues—archery, fly-casting, weight-lifting—and insists on doing everything his own way. He even believes that he can survive a nuclear holocaust, if it comes. As Ed says, Lewis thinks he is immortal. Perhaps Lewis is weakened by his overspecialization and hubris. In the course of the ordeal he is humbled by his experience and forced to realize his vulnerability and mortality. He is a changed and wiser man when he returns to Atlanta.

Ed is the most successful of the tour men in coping with his experience, probably because he is the best all around, and the least specialized. He also has more imagination, more of a power of empathy or negative capability, than the other three. He is able to understand moral relativity and adapt to the unexpected very quickly. He also establishes a rapport with nature in a short time, even though almost totally ignorant of her ways before this adventure. His flexibility allows him to enter into the drama of survival of the fittest and call on reserves deep inside himself to predict and destroy his enemy. As a result of his experience he realizes the violence that man, himself included, is capable of committing, but he can also take pride in his ability to enter the primitive world on its own terms and survive if not triumph over it. "Deliverance" at this level takes on a new meaning: it suggests that Ed has been delivered from the terror of his primitive ordeal and the realized savage in himself. When he returns to Atlanta, he has a new understanding of himself and an appreciation of the values and amenities of civilized life. His experience has indeed been a "recreation," in a way he could not have suspected when he drove north out of Atlanta with Lewis: it has been a "re-creation" of the life of his distant ancestry—tribal, or even pretribal, man. The routines, the manners, the trivialized human encounters of modern life—these are the price we pay for our deliverance from the terrors of primal chaos. But our realization and memory of that terror can give meaning, and poignancy, to the tedium of our daily lives. This is the lesson Ed Gentry has learned, and his memory will keep that lesson alive. Ed has, indeed, "changed his life."

Dickey's use of characterization to structure and inform *Deliverance* suggests other possibilities of interpretation as well. From a certain angle of vision, the four main characters appear to be four aspects of the author's own personality. In fact, they might be classified in psychoanalytic terms. Bobby has certain characteristics of the id: he is concerned with his own immediate comfort and gratification; he is impulsive, almost totally lacking in self-control: he is androgynous, undifferentiated, social without a social conscience. Because he lacks anything like a "higher" consciousness, we might say that he lives on an animal level, the level of instinct, much as the id operates within the psychic totality. (In this regard, the mountaineers, Benson and Stovall, who rape Bobby, probably murder Drew, and threaten to kill Lewis and Ed, might be seen as elements of the libido, an unchecked and undifferentiated sexual energy which is frightening and destructive until brought under control by the psyche.)

Lewis, on the other hand, can be seen as the ego: he is concerned with his own survival as an individual, not with the survival of society; he values his relative independence from the economic institutions of society; of all the characters he is the most in touch with external (physical) reality; he is disciplined, but only in activities related to his personal fitness for survival. Before the ordeal on the Cahulawassee he believes, as [Sigmund] Freud said of the ego, that he is "immortal."

Drew is like the superego: he is social-institutional man; his values are the internalized codes of his civilization; his reactions are not instinctive, but they are reflexive, because in him the internalization of values is so complete that they operate on an unconscious level. (I am avoiding here the question of how much of social consciousness is innate and how much learned. The modern science of ethology has indeed shown that a large part of what we might call "super-ego" is instinctual and present in many of the mammalian species. But for the purposes of the analysis here I am assuming that consideration irrelevant.) Drew places more value on corporate and social well-being than on his own. His highest allegiance is to the articulated principles, such as law, that make civilization possible. His love of music might seem an anomaly, but it is not. Music mediates and formalizes the instincts and passions through the orderly arrangement of tone and rhythm, and thus allows "civil" communication. It expresses our human interrelatedness: like the other arts it is one of the highest expressions of our sense of community.

Ed Gentry is the psyche: he takes charge over the other components of the personality, because none of them, by themselves, is adequate to meet the demands of the ordeal, which require the totality of self for survival. As narrator, Ed is the mediator between the other characters and the external world (represented by the reading public), just as the psyche must be the mediator between the various components of the personality and its environment. Ed is adequate to the task; thus, the self, though much battered and altered, prevails. An interesting development, however, is that Bobby (the id) disappears: although the id survives, the ordeal has dispatched it so that the psyche no longer has to deal with it directly. The id has been chastened and brought under control; it is sufficient only that the psyche remember that the id still exists.

On the other hand, Drew, the superego, does not survive. The implication here is that an automatic, reflexive code based on societal values cannot survive when it ventures beyond the protective boundaries of the civilization that evolved those values for its own preservation. In the primal chaos outside those boundaries, the superego is not only irrelevant; it is also a hindrance to survival. Thus it is destroyed. This does not mean that the superego is without value. As Ed says at the end of the novel, Drew was the "best" of the bunch of them. Because of the psychic violence of the ordeal, the superego cannot survive as an autonomous component of the self, but it can be valued in memory as a valuable principle.

Although this Freudian structure may not be immediately obvious, once discovered it seems too precise not to have been a consideration during composition. In my own conversations with Dickey, however, he has denied that he was conscious of this division of the Freudian paradigm among the four characters of the novel. If this is so, an interesting possibility is raised: Freudian metaphor has become so imbedded in modern thought that it often functions today at a subliminal level.

An indication that Dickey consciously intended the four major characters to represent aspects of himself is the distribution of his vocations and hobbies among them. The narrator Ed Gentry is an advertising executive in Atlanta: Dickey had been a highly successful advertising executive in Atlanta and New York during the late 1950s. Lewis Medlock lifts weights and is an expert archer: Dickey was an athlete who took his weightlifting seriously, and during the 1950s and 60s he became an expert field archer—an accomplishment he has been quite proud of. Drew Ballenger is a guitarist: Dickey's house is filled with guitars, both 6- and 12-stringed varieties; during the 1960s he practiced on the instrument religiously and became a technically proficient musician, and he still plays with much enjoyment today.

That leaves only Bobby Trippe to account for: he has no talents except his sociability; his name suggests the porcine and unsavory; his behavior is childish, cowardly, and embarrassing. It seems that Bobby represents that undisciplined and sometimes ludicrous part of the self that we all wish to be rid of. And that is just what Dickey does in the course of the novel: dispatch Bobby to regions where he will not be an embarrassment to Ed and Lewis.

If the four characters represent aspects of the author, the novel can then be seen as metaphor for Dickey's own life. He leaves the security of a good position in advertising and a comfortable middle-class family existence to enter the imaginative life of the poet. That life requires a descent into the abyss of being to find the sources of imaginative energy. Horrors lurk there, but discovery of the hidden self can be exhilarating. The poet finds in the depths and recesses of the conscious and unconscious mind the primitive well-springs of the poetic imagination. Support for this interpretation can be found in the sleep-dream motif of the novel. Before the adventure, Ed plunged deeply into sleep each night, probably to renew contact with the unconscious sources of vitality. But something has always kept him from remembering what he dreamed; his internal censor will not allow the dreams' contents to rise to consciousness. On the trip with Lewis to the Cahulawassee, Ed moves in and out of sleep, as though he is about to enter a dream. And indeed he does— a nightmare out of man's primitive past, violent and lawless. And this time he brings the dream back into the light of consciousness by telling us about it, just as the poet Dickey is objectifying and dramatizing, through metaphor, his descent into his own elemental self.

Deliverance is not an American *Heart of Darkness.* Unlike Marlow, the American hero does not beat a paranoiac retreat when he encounters the primitive aspects of his own psyche; rather he approaches those manifestations, with trepidation perhaps, but also with fascination and a desire to understand their meaning and value. Natty Bumppo, Ishmael, Huck Finn, Isaac McCaslin, R. P. McMurphy, all embrace their shadows. (Both [Nathaniel] Hawthorne and Henry James are primarily European in their attitudes toward

the shadow, and are thus exceptions to the generalizations I am making here.) The instinctual self turns out to be a source not only of vitality but also of some of man's most admirable traits. In *Deliverance,* however, there is no Chingachgook, Queequeg, Jim, Sam Fathers, or Bromden, because Dickey's vision has passed beyond the Puritan Manichean psychology that begot the shadow. Dickey's psychology is more modern, more complex, for the instinctual self rises from within when called upon to meet the challenge of survival. Projection is evident only in Ed's mildly paranoiac attitude toward mountain people in general, and in the symbolic projection of evil onto Benson and Stovall, in particular. Nonetheless, *Deliverance* stands in the tradition of Cooper, Melville, Twain, Hemingway, and Faulkner. It is also indebted to the primitivism of Jack London, particularly to *The Call of the Wild,* for which Dickey wrote the screenplay of a 1975 television production. The American work that *Deliverance* stands closest to, however, is Poe's *The Narrative of Arthur Gordon Pym.* Both are explorations of the modern psyche in similar motival and symbolic terms. The major difference between the two works lies in the authors' attitudes toward knowledge. Poe's residual transcendentalism takes for granted that ultimate knowledge lies outside the self, in a realm whose shadowy existence can be sensed only through the intuition. If for Dickey transcendental knowledge exists, it is not a concern of either his poetry or fiction. Knowledge in *Deliverance* comes from within, from the shadowy regions deep in the individual psyche. For Dickey, it would seem, the only access to that knowledge is through action, the recreation of archetypal experience, the realization of dream. The act may entail actual participation—or it may be realized in the creation of art. In both, the archetypal is externalized and made concrete.

For many of us, an opportunity to participate in archetypal experience like that described in *Deliverance* is unavailable or improbable. And if it were available, most of us would be unequal to the ordeal of confronting and absorbing its terror. Furthermore, unless we are writers of the order of Melville or Faulkner or Dickey, we shall never realize such experience effectively through imagination. That is why the artist is of extraordinary value to our modern culture: he has the imaginative power and will to break through the conventions that blind us to the nature of reality outside those conventions—and to the darker regions of our own psyche, which, again, convention urges us to suppress or ignore. The great writer is our Perseus who confronts and overcomes the bright Medusa of existence, the Gorgon which we all contain within ourselves—for the Medusa is the consummate Anima figure, in all her beauty and hideousness. The writer's mirror-shield is his art. In it he sees Life, he sees Us—thus inviting us to see ourselves. He also invites us to grasp, with him, the Sickle of Knowledge and slay the Gorgon. If we have the courage to accept that invitation and sever the petrifying head, then Pegasus flies free and our lives are changed. That is the only kind of knowledge that gives meaning to the tedium of our daily existence, and allows us to rise occasionally above it to perform a heroic action—or at least to understand the nature of heroism.

Laurence Lieberman (essay date Winter 1997)

SOURCE: "Warrior, Visionary, Natural Philosopher: James Dickey's *To the White Sea,*" in *The Southern Review,* Vol. 33, Winter, 1997, pp. 164-80.

[*In the following essay, Lieberman asserts that Muldrow, the main character in Dickey's* To the White Sea, *"serves as a kind of contemplative mouthpiece for the author and . . . embodies many of the wisdoms and lessons of Dickey's poetry."*]

To the White Sea, James Dickey's third novel, achieves perhaps as much a summing-up of the milestones and peak moments in its author's best poems as did Yeats's "The Circus Animals' Desertion," also written in late career. Within the work's horrific narrative labyrinth are numerous passages that offer a retrospective survey of Dickey's hard-earned poetic mythologies, his achieved personal mythos. The book links the poet's favorite creeds, lores, and mystiques for an advance into his autumnal grasp that both contains and soars beyond them. Further, in its grappling with the key myths of Dickey's major poems, this book's spiritual dimension pulls together the diverse strands of his pantheism, composing a religio-philosophic credo that recalls [William Butler] Yeats's formulation of his own mature (and occult) mythos in *A Vision.* Throughout *To the White Sea* the reader is struck by eloquent forays into homemade theories of optics, physics, and aesthetics and into the esoteric lore of icebergs and arctic predators . . . all of which, taken together, quietly adds up to a fascinating and innovative treatise of natural philosophy. True to his mentor Lucretius, Dickey in *To the White Sea* adorns naive scientific inquiry with painstakingly exact poetic image-making. His prose style never departs from the plain idiom of common speech—and yet he manages an uncannily precise descriptive power and a musical lyricism, both of these filtered through his secret amanuensis, Sergeant Muldrow, a character who serves as a kind of contemplative mouthpiece for the author and who embodies many of the wisdoms and lessons of Dickey's poetry. I take this aspect of Muldrow to be the source of his elation and, finally, of his abiding faith in survival.

Donald Armstrong, the heroic protagonist of **"The Performance,"** was Muldrow's earliest forerunner. Perfection of his acrobatics, high-spirited gymnastic tricks, gave Armstrong access to a sacred mind-space that enabled him to transcend the horror of his own beheading:

> Yet I put my flat hand to my eyebrows
> Months later, to see him again
> In the sun, when I learned how he died,
> And imagined him, there,
> Come, judged, before his small captors,
>
> Doing all his lean tricks to amaze them—
> The back somersault, the kip-up—
> And at last, the stand on his hands,
> Perfect, with his feet together,
> His head down, evenly breathing,
> As the sun poured up from the sea
>
> And the headsman broke down
> In a blaze of tears, in that light
> Of the thin, long human frame
> Upside down in its own strange joy,
> And, if some other one had not told him,
> Would have cut off the feet
>
> Instead of the head,
> And if Armstrong had not presently risen
> In kingly, round-shouldered attendance,
> And then knelt down in himself
> Beside his hacked, glittering grave, having done
> All things in this life that he could.

Armstrong's triumph over brutality is shared; he is secretly vindicated by the headsman's anguish. Contrarily, the only witness to Muldrow's final immolation and act of transcendence—his parading himself before a *de facto* firing squad in a suit of swan feathers pasted to his naked body with human blood—is the reader . . . hence his direct appeal to the reader as witness in the book's last pages.

Muldrow emerges, in the end, as an original antihero. I find him to be one of the authentic—if improbable and accidental—religious mystics in literature. How paradoxical, then, is his disavowal of *any* religious leanings to the expatriate American monk he meets in Japan. This denial comes from a total lack of intellectual pretense, but Muldrow *is* a believer, ever faithful to his vision. The essence of the religious philosopher is to risk everything, to be willing to live and die, each moment, in the spirit of his sacred idea; and what character in literature has more diligently labored through, in his life *and* thought, all the ramifications of his one brave, impossible theory? In this way Muldrow is in fact deeply committed, may even be seen in his final martyrdom as a kind of saint.

Amoral he is in most ways, yes, which frees him from angst and from doubt: his rare twinges of guilt occur only when he violates, transgresses, his own code. When he has slain the hunter whose tribe saved his life, a first, belated passion of guilt overtakes Muldrow. It is fleeting, but it comes as a saving hallmark of conscience: "... more than one time I was sorry I had killed the little bearded man who had hunted the goats at the same time as I did. I wish I hadn't done it, because in a way he had been a good friend, and he was a hunter, too. Too bad, but there was not anything I could do about it now." How, then, can he be dismissed as simply a "monster," as some of the novel's early commentators have proposed?

In the book's frequent visionary passages, Dickey's identification with his protagonist comes to seem pervasive; Muldrow is perhaps the most personally revealing of all his characters. Consequently, I find it difficult to reconcile the soldier's moments of high aesthetic passion with his brutality. Now and again I find myself wondering whether the lapses into needless viciousness have been thrown in to mislead us, to disguise the radical extent to which the author is incarnated in his character.

Once Muldrow escapes Tokyo and the drama of his voyage north is in full swing, we discover that he is a man compelled by two competing agendas: the Survival Kit and the Dream Life. From this point on, his psychic priorities may be viewed as shifting back and forth by turns. This seesawing between the warrior and the visionary, two rival identities vying for the seat of Muldrow's Being, reaches a marvelous climax during his most prolonged soliloquy, while kayak-paddling across the strait between Japan's two great islands, Honshu and Hokkaido:

> Nothing happened for four hours. I was into my rhythm, and deeper and deeper into it. I didn't have any notion as to how much distance I had made except by the time it took me to make it. My main worry was that I wouldn't be able to get all the way across in the dark. In daylight I would be a sitting duck for sure, with no cover and camouflage, and no scheme I could come up with would be good enough. But that was not the point. The point was that I was moving on the water, and that I was moving the water. But the thought kept coming back to me: what was I *doing* here, halfway between the enemy's two countries, something nobody could even have dreamed up? The water hit the sides of the boat as I kept up my rhythm. Who had a better right to it? But again, what was I doing here? The water was right, felt right, I could have been here on vacation and nobody would have said anything about it. But I was not fooling myself. I was where I was. But after a minute I didn't let myself think like that. Only for a second did I think like that,

but it was wrong. Only for a second: a flash, a night flash. Then, no more.

> But when the oars had come into my hands double-bladed, a kayak paddle now, something happened to the strait between Honshu and Hokkaido, something the place could never have imagined, that would never be there again. The snow came back, and the real cold, the gut-blue water and the long stretches and, above all, the ice. There was the glacier. The glacier was coming to me with every dig of the paddle, every stroke, every slant of the body to go with the paddle, left and right. I had seen it, and would see it again, the real pure thing, the pure color.... When I told you before that you wouldn't see this every day, I was right. It was the most intense, and the most pure, it was—well, you could say—secret, the best of it, the heart of ice, the heart you never had any idea was there, and when you saw it, knew had to be there.... But now it was the ice, the water and the ice, the white sea; what I said.

This great peroration, addressed to the reader-witness ("When I told you before that you wouldn't see this every day, I was right"), culminates in the sole recitation of the book's title image. The whole eloquent passage marks a beautiful crossover into the novel's dream empyrean, a crossover that parallels the crossing, at long last, of the strait. Now there will be no turning back from the fulfillment of Muldrow's dream agenda ... whatever the fleshly cost. The priorities have swung to psychic due North, once and for all: "Only for a second did I think like that, but it was wrong. Only for a second: a flash, a night flash. Then, no more."

Muldrow's vigorous dialectic, a quarreling with himself akin to the soliloquies of Hamlet or Lear, plumbs the depths of his soul and hurls accusatory questions at the sky. These are the big existential questions, though posited humbly enough: *Who am I, and what am I doing here?* For once, Muldrow resolves that survival must take a backseat to his exhilarating adventure in the spirit: "In daylight I would be a sitting duck for sure, with no cover and camouflage.... But that was not the point.... [W]hen the oars had come into my hands double-bladed, a kayak paddle now, something happened to the strait between Honshu and Hokkaido, something the place could never have imagined, that would never be there again."

Auspiciously, the rhythm of rowing—"The water rocked me; I rocked the water"—primes Muldrow for the great awakening and revelations that occur en route:

> You would have to be out there in a kayak, where it is quiet, no engines; where you lift your paddle

out of the water because there's not anything else you can do. The ice slides, you with your mouth open, slides down and falls . . . it was something else, something that the world said itself, that nobody could know except what said it. But there it was, right ahead of me, the shucked-out middle of the glacier. . . . When you were out in the kayak you started with some notion of walrus, of seal, of whatever you might find on the floe, even a polar bear. But when the glacier starts to calve, all animals go somewhere else; there is nothing but what is.

In this pilgrim-explorer's religion, then, the message must be exhaled, purely, by the world itself. There can be no mediation by church, Bible, or presiding ecclesiastic. Nature speaks directly to you, in flashes; you hear it or you don't. These ideas keep whirling about in Muldrow's mind, as if guided by a will of their own, or empowered by a spirit in the universe that has found in him just the right medium for their formulation.

Sergeant Muldrow, happily, is working through the terms of his pantheistic vision, improvising them as if for the first time. He is molding, under these extraordinary circumstances, a coherent worldview . . . fitting its parts together with the same grace and finesse he applied, earlier, to the obsessive inventory of his Emergency Survival Kit. The rhythm of double-bladed paddling keeps nurturing the higher mind that gives these ideas their final shape. Muldrow would never try to dignify this arduous process with the term *meditation,* but it is by means of the loftiest kind of meditative rigor that these ideas coalesce into a grand overview . . . into a system of natural philosophy.

At the outset of his migration through Japan, Muldrow's mastery of camouflage, a necessity for survival, may accidentally have set into motion the creation of his dream selves. The fugitive's whole visionary life may have sprung from his attempts at disguise. As he perfects the art of matching skin color to each new background, it's as though a second self, a spiritual other, is born, hiding in his body. His ghostly twin is begotten of the mystery of concealment:

> As the color of my face disappeared and went to another color, there was something inside me that changed, too. It moved, and then sat still. In my mind there was a shape I couldn't exactly make out, but it seemed to be in a crouch, pulled up into itself and ready, and that was the feeling I got from the soot, the stronger the more I put on.

The repeated process of finding the right soil, soot, or vegetation with which to render himself invisible—mimicking the strategies of his favorite arctic animals—brilliantly echoes Muldrow's constant shifting between two versions of

himself, alternate identities if you will: soldier and dreamer, warrior and visionary. Progressively, he trains himself to become a quick-change artist, a magician of self-vanishings. A supreme chameleon:

> My camouflage made a lot of difference in the way I was moving, like I had put on some other kind of dimension, you might say; that was the feeling of it. And because it was, the trees and bushes and pine needles and rocks that were on the slope were different, too. I used the trees in another way from what I was used to. When I came to a bare place the other dimension was stronger, like it even stood out from me, stood off me a little, and everything in me and on me got better.

When Muldrow perfects his camouflage, it's as if he is reinventing himself and becoming a new species of mammal. The "other dimension" in which he clothes himself is an *aura,* the raiment of invisibility. Something strange happens to the light around his body. "It stood out from me, stood off me a little." His psyche grooms its fluttering to participate in his body's vanishment, and this honing and refining of mental moves, of inner stillnesses, contributes as much to his invisibility as the skin-rubbings do: "everything in me and on me got better." Muldrow's alteration of his identity is so total and so powerful that he senses—believes—that his body transforms the "trees and bushes and pine needles and rocks" of the scene he glides through; his Being collides with and changes the environment.

Muldrow learned this magic of self-erasure from observing, at age ten, a rattlesnake in the hills near Greeley, Colorado:

> And then it moved again, like a wave of rock, coming to life and flowing, almost floating, over the other ground with the same marks. It was a big rattlesnake, the only one I ever saw, and when it quit moving again I got as still as it was, and took it in. We both stayed a long time, and then it started off again. *When it moved the whole canyon shifted a little.* [My italics.]

At the time Muldrow didn't fully comprehend what he'd seen, but the intense memory stayed with him. In the present of the novel, he goes back to that mystery-laden moment, and he now has the wisdom and insight to process the image, even to duplicate the snake's powers. What a rare discipline, this skill in dredging up recollected treasures from childhood for discovery-in-action today!

We follow with astonishment the early stages of Muldrow's development as a visionary thinker. That occult journey, the voyage of his dream-life, operates like a second narrative, an undercurrent, moving along by laws of its own just below the surface of the story of his northward flight. The second narrative line, though secret, half-hidden, is no less an ongoing story in its own right. The reader can trace the birth and wavelike growth of Muldrow's dream-cosmos: it lives out its own full lifespan—rising and falling, at intervals—to apocalypse.

The soldier's interior metamorphosis is progressive and cumulative. Oh, how well he knows he's building a vision! That vision becomes his life, his mission, supplanting all other goals. If necessary, he will gladly sacrifice his *mortal* life to its fulfillment. He guides his dream-life with coolly rational control, never losing any important link in its unfolding. As he inspects parts of his dream-composite, prepares them for use, he might as well be reviewing the tools in the kit he has taped to his chest. The same total focus and discipline abides, equivalently, in both worlds; Muldrow the craftsman, the superb technician in aircraft and gunnery, brings a tough-minded, punishingly austere concentration to his visionary world. An artist in his way, he fashions an *equipage,* an outfit, for survival of the spirit against all odds: it can stand up against—as he says—any trials his enemy can dish out.

Muldrow is enthralled by the beauty he encounters in nature. He takes pride in his power to behold such marvels as the hypnotic blue light discharged by a glacier's "heart" when massive sheets of ice calve off, sliding into the sea; or the amazing "red-orange box" that appears under a body of still water when the sun strikes its surface at a particular angle:

> The sun on top of water is one thing, but the sun *in* it—down somewhere under the surface where it makes a kind of box shape, you could say, a box that changes, that goes in and out like it's breathing—that's something else again, I'll tell you. This lake had that for me. It might have been my angle from it, or the angle of the sun, or maybe both, but I saw that gold box with the sides thinner than any paper, alive down there, alive with itself. It was big, too, the biggest yet; it would've had to be big for me to see it from that far. Then the box was gone, but I took it for a good sign, and knew I could go down and do whatever I wanted, near where it was.

These small miracles are offered up only to the alertest observer, and only at those rare moments when a unique set of variables comes together. When Muldrow stumbles upon such a treasure, he counts himself most blessed. He is among the chosen few ("I took it for a good sign"). He reminds us again and again that he need observe an event just once; the awe-inspiring image and the lesson received are indelibly carved into memory. "I had it," he says, confident that the image flashed before his eyes has become as much a per-

manent fixture in his repertory of available mental pictures as if he'd snapped it on film with a Nikon: "I had seen it from the hill, in a way that must be like you'd see a ghost, and that heart, that sun in a box, I had. It meant a lot to me. I kept thinking about it: the underwater cube, about half box and half diamond." Why is this cube of underwater light so important to Muldrow—what does it confirm? He is no materialist, but the *sun in a box* is a prize possession to him; he owns it, for all his life, and no one can take it from him. Such revelatory moments in nature sustain Muldrow. They uplift him, bolstering his high elation: they *are* his best life.

Hence it can be argued that Muldrow, though unschooled, has attained a highly sophisticated level of aesthetic receptiveness. He *lives* for beauty, for the beautiful in nature. Ah, what an appetite he has for it! (We note again and again that he is oblivious to beauty in women—if aggressively and willfully so.) Moreover, on occasion Muldrow seems to view himself as one of God's Elect. The universe speaks to him, gives him omens ("I took it for a good sign, and knew I could go down and do whatever I wanted, near where it was")—the spirit in nature wants to help him survive, wants to empower him: "Wait, I said; wait on the cold and the weather that would make a suit of feathers feel like it was something that God made just for you. Wait for the other island, I said. Or the full north of this one."

Both religious philosopher and aesthete, then, Muldrow is a man who can be gratified completely by his epiphanies. The physical world—the seasons, trees, animals, the white sea—gives him an aesthetic high equal to the one great books, paintings, sculpture, and music afford modern cognoscenti. *Primitive,* yes, this going back to art's and religion's origins in the splendor of nature:

> That was a new thrill every time I thought about it. I remembered the deep, pure interior blue of the iceberg, with Tornarssuk and I stopped beyond words, both paddles out of the water. What a thing that was: the only color in the world, a new color, with life in it, the life of the heart of ice, which came clear when everything between it and us tore off, slid, and fell.

Such images are the fabled gold at the end of the rainbow for Muldrow. He often returns to them in memory for solace, in the way many people revere their families. And whether he recognizes it or not, his reliance on these images to provide strength to face his predicament is *prayerful.* The profound spirituality of this activity is especially evident when we contrast it with, say, the tepid, passionless rituals of the American monk, which seem to lack any true investment of selfhood. The expat monk is hollowly simulating the moves of his Japanese peers, paying lip service to principles that are, for him, life-negating rather than life-affirming. Perhaps the real reason he betrays his countryman to the Japanese soldiers is that Muldrow's authentic happiness, his nature visions, challenge and threaten this Buddhist *manqué*. The "military" American holds up a mirror to his fraudulence, and he can't bear it.

Toward the climax of his journey, Muldrow suffers momentary lapses of faith when he fails in attempts to conjure up the images. The dream-pictures seem, unforgivingly, to be breaking apart; and the physical pain of being beaten by the soldiers who briefly hold him captive can't approach this psychic anguish. The reader may be surprised by the pathos and tragic amplitude in Dickey's writing about these crises. Not long before Muldrow's final capture, we find this heart-wrenching account of his failed efforts to revive his dream-vision:

> The road was rough. It bashed upward and bumped around a lot, and it seemed like every lick was aimed at my face. I felt around inside my mouth with my tongue, and I was missing three teeth, with another one loose. That was not going to kill me, though like I say, I was hurting pretty good. As quiet as I could make myself, I concentrated on the rope, but I couldn't get it loose behind my back no matter what I did. . . . I went back to the log train, and how good some of the riding had been, especially the night part when I could put out from my mind anything I wanted, overlay Japan with it, and watch the Brooks Range become everything in the world. . . . I couldn't do the same thing here, not like I had on the train. I tried hard, though: tried to see the line of deer heads in the snow, all pointed one way, the horns trued up like right dress on parade. Maybe it was because my face hurt so much, and now my ribs, that I couldn't get things to come right. The deer kept breaking formation, busting up out of the snow, when all I wanted was the heads. Maybe it was that I was hurting, and my eyes were still about half crossed, or maybe it was because the truck was headed in the wrong direction. I don't know, I really don't. But my hands were in front of me, and when the deer heads wouldn't line up I knew it was time. . . .

The passion evoked here is quite lovely, and given Muldrow's amoral—not to say criminal—nature, we are not prepared for his undoubted largeness of soul. At such moments he takes on a fully tragic stature.

The religious prodigality in Muldrow's spirit is most vividly revealed in the scene of his two-day stopover at the waterfall:

> A waterfall about fifteen feet high was there in front

of me, and I stood on my last big rock and looked at it with the low sun striking gold across that pure white: whiter than cloud, whiter than egg white, whiter than snow, whiter than an eyeball, whiter than anything. . . . I felt so comfortable and secure, with the waterfall standing like it was watching over me, looking out for me, that I made the decision I had been putting off. I would stay one more day, and two if I felt like it. . . . When I went out of there I wanted to feel like I could take on anything.

The beauty of those plunging whites, like the blues of the glacier's interior, reinvigorates him, restores his confidence. It is as if the falls, which loom protectively above, are a guardian angel; as if a beneficent universe, embodied in the blazing barrage of white tinged with the sun's gold, is opening its heart to its chosen one, spewing nourishment upon his brow. He need only recognize the beckoning hand and receive nature's gift: its spiritual succor and bodily sustenance, *transfusions* both, as he comes to call them.

Religious wakenings are often prompted by beauties in nature, and what could more compellingly bespeak such a change than Muldrow's bursts of playfulness as he sprints alongside the creek below the falls, racing leaves downstream?

> Before I left I knew every rock, from the waterfall to the lake, and the last afternoon I went up and down them twice, trying for some kind of personal record, running with the current and then against it, with the banks, and racing downstream with special leaves I set going. The leaves were dry, and there were some big ones, and I picked them by how much they curled up on themselves and rode high in the water, going through the rapids better than anybody'd have believed. These things happen, you know; all you have to do is watch.

He celebrates the beauty and wonder of these leaf dances. For Muldrow, as for primitive clans, objects in nature serve as emblems of the sacred. In that way, his pantheistic worldview may resemble the totemism or animism of ancient tribes. Thus, the leaves he chases may be conceived of as avatars, incarnations of the spirit; they embody the godhead, and Muldrow gets a charge of self-renewal from interacting with them. His joy, as purely instinctual as a child's or an animal's, reflects a deep reverence for life, despite his alienation from all but a few of his fellow humans. At his worst Muldrow is a misogynist and a violent misanthrope; but like Shakespeare's Timon of Athens, that titan of misanthropes, he proves that a vision that repudiates most of humanity can, finally, be healing and redemptive.

At times in his grueling passage north, Muldrow appears to

be on the brink of developing moral scruples, such as the tribute he pays to the aged samurai when he places the two-handed sword on his corpse with ritual tenderness ("I put some more silk over him, dark silk, and the sword on top of that, without the scabbard"); and in the nearly comic restraint he exercises when he teaches cat's cradle string tricks to a pair of Japanese infants who surprise him in the act of stealing rice and fish-heads from their family's storage crypt.

But Muldrow's emerging moral sense gets derailed by a series of betrayals and disappointments. During his convalescence from a severe puncture wound in his thigh, inflicted by a mountain goat, he grows fond of the tribe of bear hunters who nurse and befriend him. For a time he seems tempted to join this clan, this community.

> The village was the cleanest place I had ever seen men live in. It was very neat indeed; it was a pleasure to be there.

> I could walk around some now, and when I could do it without favoring my leg so much, it seemed like it made the whole village happy. I had never in my life seen such friendly people; even Eskimoes couldn't compare with them.

However, when he's just begun to risk a cautious love for these people, he is abruptly shocked and disaffected by their abuse of two bear cubs. Perhaps his nearest approach to a full-blown human conscience is the repugnance and loathing—a moral outrage, of sorts—that he feels on behalf of the assaulted creatures:

> They showed me two cubs in a wood cage, and I thought at first that they were being kept for pets, a couple of live ones in amongst all the pieces of dead ones; it was good to see a bear move around. But they were putting up little sticks around the cage, painted sticks with the top ends shaved down with the wood curling, and there was a lot of carrying on, with the women singing and dancing and now the men coming into it, too, and I knew they were going to kill one of the cubs, or maybe both, probably with a lot of noise and singing and speeches. I was never one for any of that. Whatever animal they decided on, they could have done this with. They could have done it with the lynx—if there had been any of them—with the arctic fox or the wolverine. I had been wrong. I had been dead wrong about them. No matter how friendly they were, these were men like all the others, and they did the same things as the others. They wanted bear meat and furs, and their guilt about it set up all that singing, to agree on it, to put it right; set up all that singing and dancing, and playing those twanging in-

struments that all sounded out of tune. I say screw that. The animals are a lot better than any such. Better, a lot better, than the people. My heart turned around and locked.

Muldrow is driven to a towering rage by this ceremony, though he keeps his anger under wraps, for now. Why such bitter scorn? It seems to him the tribe is making war on his closest kin, his family so to say, and he feels powerfully betrayed, the pain intensified by his initial affection for the villagers. The American soldier's Timonesque revulsion against his fellows has never been quite so intense as now, following his last-ditch effort to spring back from exile, to repatriate himself to the human community. But he feels violated in a new way, much more punishing to his sensibility than the thrashing he took as a prisoner. That was acceptable to his spirit; that was war. But these tribespeople fooled him. They *took him in.* Never before has he seen so clearly the polarization between the two families vying for him, human and animal. He is forced to choose, once and for all; and not surprisingly, he chooses the family that counts among its ranks his brothers-for-life, the lynx, the fisher marten, the snowshoe hare, the arctic fox, and the wolverine.

During this interlude, I found myself speculating that the persona of Dickey's poem **"The Eye-Beaters,"** now incarnated in Muldrow, has finally carried out his deep wish to go back to the world of primitive tribes and espouse their raw survival ethic. Subsequently he would become totally disillusioned, finding the natives no less barbarous and malevolent in their treatment of their animal kin than our modern civilized breed, thereby shattering any myth of the blameless, unspoiled savages.

When Muldrow slips away from the village and recommences his trek, he experiences a moment of profound arrival and exultation: he recognizes that in his exploits as a warrior he has achieved supremacy in both families, both worlds, human *and* animal:

> I kept traveling: three days, four. There were bigger trees than I had seen anywhere in Japan, and then there would be long open stretches. Open. Empty. I like empty. I also liked what I had come through to get where I was; I liked my knocked-out teeth and my thigh gored to the bloody bone. I had gone through it, and I carried the marks of it here. I had got here any way it took, and there was no human thing or animal thing that could stand against me.

The veteran soldier is now (any whiff of pride or egotism aside) taking stock of his accomplishments, tallying wins and losses on the field of battle. He carries off the recitation with dignity and honor, then unleashes a dance of ecstasy on his snowshoes, celebrating this happiest arrival:

> In the middle of one of the biggest bare places, one I could hardly see across, I stopped and put both feet together in the best of breathing in the sky, and the good, the great steel went down both nostrils and all over me, and if heaven has got anything better I don't want to know it. I can't know it, because heaven has not got it. Not yet. The clear cold was so wonderful that I damned near cried. I could stand in it, I could sleep in it, I could jump up and down in it. What I did was dance, danced on the snowshoes, as much as I felt like, which was plenty. Then I went on, still dancing a little.

Muldrow's dance revivifies the memory of his joyous snowshoe romps as a child in the Brooks Range in Alaska, and it also tacitly rebukes the mawkish, choreographed song and dance of the tribeswomen during the torture and killing of the bear cubs. Though this chantlike passage reeks of Muldrow's feeling of *victory,* we do well to recall that all he has ever wanted in the way of spoils, bounty, triumph, is to be free and alone, to survive purely by his own wits in the wilderness.

This scene is a prelude to the final sequence, in which Muldrow forms a partnership with a reclusive old falconer. In his work with the birds, he develops a great passion for throwing his spear across snowfields. We soon learn that while training his arm, Muldrow has been exercising his visionary reach as well. This rigor and discipline has gradually become his single-minded obsession. Freed of having to fend for himself by the ministrations of the caretaker birds, who provide the falconer and companion with an ample supply of rabbit, Muldrow turns his best energies to that other enterprise, the soaring beyond human limits of his visionary mind, a power he has been fostering throughout his adventure in Japan:

> My spear with the chipped head and the hawks. The hawk's view, which was beyond any man's. It was being able to see what you don't. It was being able to see into the snowbank, into the stone. To see beyond what any human, any man who has ever been born, could see. Like I tell you, out of the snowdrift, into the snowdrift, into the stone.

How far into this new frontier has Muldrow traveled by now? "Into the stone," he says. With his Stone Age spearhead, he has burrowed all the way back to prehistory. To before human time. To outside time. So at last he is ready, as never before now, to die or *not* to die into the realm "beyond explanation," the deathless *beyond* hinted at twenty-five years

before by the vision of the stewardess in Dickey's remarkable poem **"Falling."**

During setbacks, or when Muldrow has reached an impasse in his journey, he often boosts his flagging spirit by looking back at the obstacles he has surmounted:

> Maybe I had made it through the fire, through the fields and the terraces, through the fights, through my own blood and gone teeth, through the lakes and the creeks, through the stars, through the good times and the bad. If the ocean opened up in front of me, I didn't think there was anything I couldn't do. And if I could find a way to get to the other island, and into the cold country, the real country, the mountains and the isolation, and find just a little game, I believed there was not a person in Japan, or any bunch of them, who could stay in it with me.

Clearly it proves therapeutic to make such a periodic reckoning of the highs and lows, the watersheds, the whole linked chain of events in his vigil and passage north. When stalled, Muldrow rebuilds momentum by plotting out this survey. He calls this self-bolstering process his "plan."

But what began simply as a tactic for survival against great odds, a soldier's code, has gradually been amplified into a commanding life mission, into a visionary's blueprint for prevailing over limits of mind and body—for stretching the supposed boundaries of Being in nature. Muldrow's "plan" becomes a credo-in-action that would do the most ambitious and adventurous natural philosopher proud. As he faces the stiffest trials, Muldrow *develops,* grows in stature; he keeps exploring the new "possibilities" of existence that are revealed to him as if for the first time, though they are assembled, like collages, from scraps of insight he collected at random in his youth, scraps now coming together in an awakened and expanded consciousness. And this new-minted vision of existence leads him, stage by stage, to grand intellectual aspirations. He's at the frontier, the cutting edge if you will, of a novel experiment in lifemanship, a new gamble with the unknown:

> I hit my knees to the floor and rolled in the feathers, like I was rolling in the snow. I was close. I was very close.
>
> I walked out and knew I had found it, what I had been looking for all my life, in all the blood and the fucking and the right arm and the fast move, in everything I had done and everybody I had to deal with. I knew I had found it, but up till now I had never had the full thing. In the wind the swan feathers fluttered on me, and I could have flown. I could have flown with the hawks and the swans if I had

wanted to. But I didn't want to. I wanted to stand there.

Stepping off into those frontiers—oh, yes, a frontiersman he is—demands all his toughness, all the staunch discipline he's previously applied to fishing, hunting, gunnery, and survival in the enemy wilds . . . but turned now to other goals in the world of spirit. This mission has stolen his heart away, and engaged his unwavering steadfastness. He has been changed, utterly, healed in soul by the nobility of his task. And he will never again settle, whatever the cost, for less than his soul's fulfillment. What human drama, we might well ask, can so stringently demand our fullest possibilities—can be, at last, more heroic? If he—meaning, now, both Dickey and Muldrow—succeeds in his quest, what a feat of endurance he has brought off!

Additional coverage of Dickey's life and career is contained in the following sources published by Gale: *Authors in the News,* **Vols. 1 and 2;** *Concise Dictionary of American Literary Biography,* **1968-1988;** *Contemporary Authors,* **Vols. 9-12R and 156;** *Contemporary Authors Bibliographical Series,* **Vol. 2;** *Contemporary Authors New Revision Series,* **Vols. 10, 48, and 61;** *Dictionary of Literary Biography,* **Vol. 5;** *Dictionary of Literary Biography Documentary Series,* **Vol. 7;** *Dictionary of Literary Biography Yearbook,* **Vols. 82, 93, and 96;** *DISCovering Authors Modules: Novelists, Poets,* **and** *Popular Fiction and Genre Authors;* **and** *Major Twentieth-Century Writers.*

Michael Dorris

1945-1997

American novelist, short story writer, nonfiction writer, and author of books for children.

INTRODUCTION

One of the most renowned Native American writers, Dorris promoted understanding of the Native American community and awareness of its burdens through his award-winning books. *The Broken Cord* (1989), his best known and best-selling work, tells the story of his own adopted son's battle with fetal alcohol syndrome (FAS), a debilitating consequence of excessive alcohol consumption during pregnancy that was found to be disproportionately common among Native Americans. Granted the National Book Critics Circle Award for general nonfiction and made into a television movie, *The Broken Cord* garnered widespread accolades for Dorris's intimate storytelling and statistical accuracy, and attracted international attention to the problem of FAS. Dorris collaborated with wife Louis Erdrich, also a noted author, to produce *The Crown of Columbus* (1991), a novel about Christopher Columbus and his impact on the contemporary world, particularly on Native America. Dorris's other novels, generally concentrating on the quest for an authentic Native identity, include the best-selling *A Yellow Raft in Blue Water* (1987), which relates the experience of Native American women across three generations, and the enthusiastically received *Cloud Chamber* (1997), which traces the mixed-blood paternal family lines of Rayona, a character from *A Yellow Raft in Blue Water*. In his fiction for young readers, Dorris explored notable historical events from a juvenile Native American perspective, including Columbus's arrival in America in *Morning Girl* (1992) and the first American Thanksgiving in *Guests* (1995).

In an interview with Rick Lyman shortly after Dorris's death, Erdrich, who married Dorris in 1981, reported that she had known he was suicidal "from the second year of our marriage." He fought a constant battle with depression, although to friends he never failed to present a facade of happiness. His second suicide attempt succeeded on April 11, 1997, shortly after he learned that he was the subject of an investigation for the possible sexual abuse of one or more of his children. At the time of his death, Dorris and Erdrich were in the process of divorcing. Erdrich declined to discuss the case, stating, "I don't agree with trying a man in the press after he is dead and judging him guilty or innocent." A number of Dorris's friends spoke out against the charges, citing Dorris's reputation as an outstanding father and advocate of children's rights. Douglas Foster, former editor of *Mother Jones* magazine, reported that Dorris had told him the

charges were false but that he "didn't know how to fight without making things worse. And he had a realistic idea that no matter how baseless the allegations were, they were going to have a strong negative effect on his family and his work." Dorris held degrees from Georgetown University and Yale University and worked as a professor of English and anthropology at Dartmouth College. Perhaps his greatest achievement in the world of education was the Native American Studies department at Dartmouth, which he founded in 1972 and chaired until 1985. The Associated Press reported that Dartmouth President James Freedman said Dorris "was beloved by a generation of Dartmouth students, whose lives were touched with his humanity and his idealism. The Native American Studies program will stand as one of his enduring contributions to Dartmouth and to American higher education."

PRINCIPAL WORKS

Native Americans: Five Hundred Years After (nonfiction)

1977

A Guide to Research on North American Indians [with Arlene B. Hirschfelder and Mary Gloyne Byler] (nonfiction) 1983

A Yellow Raft in Blue Water (novel) 1987

The Broken Cord: A Family's On-Going Struggle with Fetal Alcohol Syndrome (nonfiction) 1989; also published as *The Broken Cord: A Father's Story,* 1990

Route Two and Back [with Louise Erdrich] (travel memoir) 1991

The Crown of Columbus (novel) 1991

Morning Girl (young adult fiction) 1992

Rooms in the House of Stone (essays) 1993

Working Men (short stories) 1993

Paper Trail: Collected Essays, 1967-1992 (essays) 1994

Guests (young adult fiction) 1995

Cloud Chamber (novel) 1997

The Window (young adult fiction) 1997

OBITUARIES

Associated Press (obituary date 14 April 1997)

SOURCE: "Fetal Alcohol Syndrome Author Michael Dorris Dies," in *Associated Press,* April 14, 1997.

[*In the following obituary, the writer summarizes Dorris's literary achievements.*]

Michael Dorris, who told the story of his adopted son's battle with fetal alcohol syndrome in his award-winning book *The Broken Cord,* has died, an apparent suicide, police said. He was 52.

The *Concord* [New Hampshire] *Monitor* reported that Dorris was found Friday afternoon in a motel room and said Dorris apparently suffocated himself using a plastic bag.

Police Lt. Paul Murphy confirmed the cause of death was apparent suicide, but would give no details.

Dorris and author Louise Erdrich, with whom he wrote the 1991 best-selling novel *The Crown of Columbus,* were divorcing.

Dorris, who held degrees from Georgetown and Yale universities, had been on leave as an English professor at Dartmouth College, where, as an anthropology professor, he founded the Native American Studies department in 1972 and headed it until 1985.

In 1971, Dorris, who was of part American Indian descent, became one of the first bachelors in the country allowed to

adopt a child. He later adopted two more children, and had three more children after his 1981 marriage to Erdrich.

His adopted son Reynold, whom he called "Adam" in his book, was born on a Sioux reservation to a woman who eventually died of alcohol poisoning.

The Broken Cord, published in 1989, detailed Reynold's struggles with incurable mental handicaps caused by his birth mother's drinking. The book helped spread understanding of the problem of fetal alcohol syndrome and won a National Book Critics Circle award in the nonfiction category.

In a 1989 Associated Press interview, Dorris said that even as a young adult, Reynold lived in a group home and had to be reminded to bathe, change his clothes, even eat.

Writing the book, he said, did not prove "cathartic. One of the problems with this book is that it does not have an ending."

"It keeps going on. It's like constantly opening doors into a dark room."

Reynold has since died, and more heartbreak was in store for Dorris in 1995, when another adopted son, Jeffrey, stood trial on charges he used threats to try to get Dorris and his wife to give him $15,000 and publish a manuscript he wrote. Jeffrey Dorris was acquitted of one charge and a second was dismissed when jurors deadlocked.

Dorris' other nonfiction works include *Native Americans: 500 Years After, A Guide to Research in Native American Studies* and *A Yellow Raft in Blue Water.* His latest book, *Cloud Chamber,* a novel, was published earlier this year.

His wife wrote *Love Medicine* and other acclaimed novels about American Indians.

Dorris was working on a follow-up to *The Broken Cord* called *Matter of Conscience,* scheduled to be published in 1998. The book is about fetal alcohol effect, a slightly less debilitating disease than full-blown fetal alcohol syndrome.

Dartmouth President James Freedman said Dorris "was beloved by a generation of Dartmouth students, whose lives were touched with his humanity and idealism."

"The Native American Studies program . . . will stand as one of his enduring contributions to Dartmouth and to American higher education."

Dorris was to have started working as a visiting professor at the University of Minnesota in Minneapolis on March 31, but canceled because of illness, said Leslie Cooney, coordinator of the English department's creative writing program.

Los Angeles Times (obituary date 15 April 1997)

SOURCE: "Michael Dorris; Chronicler of Fetal Alcohol Syndrome," in *Los Angeles Times,* April 15, 1997, p. A18.

[*The following obituary focuses on the legacy of Dorris's life and works.*]

Writer Michael Dorris, whose book about raising a brain-damaged child, *The Broken Cord,* brought international attention to the problem of fetal alcohol syndrome, has been found dead in a motel room, an apparent suicide, police said Monday.

Concord police said Dorris, 52, an author, anthropologist and founder of Dartmouth College's Native American Studies Program, apparently suffocated himself Friday with a plastic bag. An autopsy report is pending.

Dorris, who was married to best-selling novelist Louise Erdrich, co-wrote *The Crown of Columbus* with her in 1991 after a publisher agreed to pay the couple $1.5 million on the basis of a five-page outline.

Of Irish, French and American Indian ancestry, Dorris was the author of two novels, including the recently published *Cloud Chamber,* but was best known for *The Broken Cord,* his best-selling 1989 memoir of adopting an American Indian child who suffered from fetal alcohol syndrome.

Dorris, who was one of the first unmarried American men to legally adopt a child, told the story of his son Reynold (using a pseudonym in the book), who suffered brain damage as a result of his mother's heavy drinking. The youth died at 23 in a car accident in 1992.

"You can't undo the past, you can't unwish someone's life, and that's the real tragedy here," Dorris told *The Times* shortly after the book was published. "It was years before we accepted the fact that [Reynold] was not going to change. You never want to accept that about a child, but he was always the little engine that couldn't get over the mountain, no matter how hard he tried."

Reflecting later on the youth's short life, Dorris wrote in an article for the *Minneapolis Star Tribune,* "He lived for 23 years endured daily loneliness and confusion and hardship and frustration, and in all that time he never once did anything that was intentionally cruel or hurtful to another living creature.

"He was maddening in his inability to learn from experience, to grasp a larger picture. If only he had been able to learn how to cross the street in accordance with a green light."

Dorris' book drew international attention to the dangers children face if their mothers drink during pregnancy, and it led to moves in Congress to issue warnings about the risks.

The Georgetown- and Yale-educated Dorris adopted two other children, and had three more with Erdrich, whom he married in 1981. He had been working on a follow-up book to *The Broken Cord,* titled *Matter of Conscience.*

Rick Lyman (obituary date 15 April 1997)

SOURCE: An obituary for Michael Dorris, in *The New York Times,* April 15, 1997, p. B11.

[*Below, Lyman recounts Dorris's literary career and personal life, noting his relationship with Erdrich, his academic colleagues, and professional associations.*]

Michael Dorris, a prolific novelist, essayist, critic and educator who won the National Book Award in 1989 for *The Broken Cord,* about his adopted son's struggle with fetal alcohol syndrome, was found dead on Friday in a motel in Concord, N.H., where he had taken a room under an assumed name. He was 52.

Mr. Dorris was found in a room at the Brick Tower Motor Inn with a plastic bag over his head, the police said. Although the medical examiner's report was not to be completed until today, the police said he had apparently committed suicide. They said a note was found at the scene, but declined to give details.

Mr. Dorris's first success as a writer came with the publication of his first novel, *A Yellow Raft in Blue Water* in 1987. His greatest success, however, was *A Broken Cord* (1989), a work of nonfiction in which he chronicled the problems suffered by his son, Abel, who suffered from fetal alcohol syndrome. The book brought national attention to the issue and helped spur Congress to approve legislation warning women of the dangers of drinking while pregnant. Abel Dorris was struck by a car and killed in 1992, at 23.

Michael Dorris, who was part American Indian, earned degrees in English at Georgetown University and anthropology at Yale University before founding the Native American Studies Program at Dartmouth College in 1972.

He was separated from his wife, the novelist Louise Erdrich, and friends said divorce proceedings were under way.

Mr. Dorris, a tall and handsome man with a shock of light-brown hair and a commanding presence, had had an extraordinarily intense and cooperative relationship with Ms. Erdrich. They worked so closely that it was often difficult for them to explain which of them had written which parts of their books or decide whose name should appear on the cover as author. Ms. Erdrich won fame on her own with books like *The Beet Queen* and *Love Medicine.*

The couple met at Dartmouth, where she was one of the first women admitted, in 1976. As recounted in ***The Broken Cord,*** they renewed their acquaintance three years later at a poetry reading Ms. Erdrich gave at Dartmouth and eventually married.

When he was single, Mr. Dorris had adopted his son and two daughters, all of American Indian descent; after he married Ms. Erdrich, she adopted them as well. Together, they had three more daughters, who live with Ms. Erdrich in Minneapolis.

Early in Ms. Erdrich's career, colleagues said, Mr. Dorris acted as her editor and agent. Later, as his own writing career blossomed, they worked together, editing and reworking each other's prose.

"We have both been interviewed separately, at different times," Ms. Erdrich said in 1986. "But when it comes to our work, it is almost awkward to be alone. We do the work together; we do everything together."

Mr. Dorris had been on tour to promote his most recent novel, ***The Cloud Chamber,*** published earlier this year by Scribner & Sons. In recent days, though, he had canceled some long-standing commitments, including a book signing and an appearance at a three-day celebration of the 25th anniversary of the Dartmouth Native American Studies Program, which began on Thursday.

This month he was to have begun a one-semester stint as Winton Chair Scholar at the University of Minnesota, teaching a course called "Topics in Advanced Creative Writing: Building Character."

Leslie Cooney, a coordinator of the university's creative writing program, said that Mr. Dorris's assistant had called shortly before the course was to have begun to say that Mr. Dorris was ill and would not be able to assume the visiting professorship.

Charles Rembar, a New York City publishing lawyer who represented both Mr. Dorris and Ms. Erdrich, said that Mr. Dorris had been uncharacteristically out of touch in recent weeks, but that "it didn't seem remarkable" because of the writer's recent grueling work schedule.

Susan Moldow, Mr. Dorris's editor at Scribner's, said that his separation from Ms. Erdrich had been "a source of considerable pain to him."

For years, the couple had lived in a farmhouse outside Cornish, N.H., but in recent years had moved to Minneapolis. Among the things that drew them together, Mr. Dorris told an interviewer, was that they both came from mixed-race backgrounds, including American Indian blood.

"I think you have to watch things very closely when you are marginal," Mr. Dorris said. "One observes and imagines a lot of things. It's impossible sometimes not to wish you were absolutely one thing."

With Ms. Erdrich, Mr. Dorris wrote ***The Crown of Columbus,*** a novel about Christopher Columbus, in 1991, and ***Route Two and Back,*** a travel memoir, the same year.

He also published a collection of essays, ***Paper Trail,*** in 1994; a collection of short stories, ***Working Men,*** in 1993, and several children's books, including ***The Window,*** newly published. At the time of his death, he was under contract to write *A Matter of Conscience,* also about fetal alcohol syndrome.

In addition to his wife, he is survived by two adopted daughters, Sava and Madeline, both of Denver; three other daughters, Persia, Pallas and Aza; and his mother, Mary B. Dorris of Louisville, Ky.

"From a publisher's point of view, it was incredible the amount of time he put in working," Ms. Moldow said. "And he was out there until the very end. He was on the road."

David Streitfeld (obituary date 15 April 1997)

SOURCE: "The Writer's Cloudy Final Chapter," in *The Washington Post,* April 15, 1997, p. D1.

[*In the obituary below, Streitfeld relates the shock that greeted news of Dorris's death.*]

The literary world was shocked yesterday at the news that Michael Dorris, a novelist and nonfiction writer seemingly at the top of his game, had killed himself.

Dorris, 52, checked into a motel in Concord, N.H., under an assumed name. He used a plastic bag to suffocate himself, police said. His body was found on Friday but the news did not filter out to the media until late Sunday night.

A man of many talents, Dorris wrote novels for adults and

children, essays, short stories and nonfiction. One of his key works is the best-selling *The Broken Cord,* which chronicled the crisis of an adopted child with fetal alcohol syndrome. It became a hit ABC-TV movie in 1992. His novel *A Yellow Raft in Blue Water* has sold hundreds of thousands of copies; a second novel this past winter garnered strong reviews.

Friends said Dorris had first tried to kill himself on March 28, but had been interrupted. He was then hospitalized for a short time for "exhaustion."

"I'm not only a novelist but a psychologist, and I'm totally shocked," mystery writer Jonathan Kellerman said on hearing the news yesterday morning. "I saw him in October . . . I didn't see any sign of depression."

Bill Shinker, who had published three books by Dorris and had another under contract, said, "It's incomprehensible, totally incomprehensible. He was in the prime of life. It doesn't make sense from so many perspectives."

Dorris and his wife, the acclaimed novelist Louise Erdrich, 42, were in the middle of a divorce that was apparently very acrimonious. "He was devastated by it," Shinker said. "Who wouldn't be in that situation? It's a natural reaction." The couple, who lived most recently in Minneapolis, had three young daughters together.

"It doesn't compute," said Caroline Leavitt, a novelist for whom Dorris has been acting as agent. In e-mail communications with her, Dorris would sometimes say things like, "You don't know what's going on. You don't want to know the melodrama." She did, of course, but he would never be explicit.

"He was so determined that, although this was a terrible time, he would get over it and be happy," Leavitt said. "He wasn't going to live his life alone like his mother did. He was going to find someone else. He really didn't bear any animosity toward Louise."

His novel *Cloud Chamber,* published in January, included a dedication that, even in the midst of his despair, he did not wish to change. "For Louise," it said simply. "Who found the song and gave me voice."

One of Dorris's last messages to Leavitt, in February, said, "Pray for me."

Via her lawyer-agent, Erdrich issued a brief statement yesterday. "Michael did a great deal of good for the world. He is deeply grieved by his family and friends." She suggested that any donations in his memory go to the Seattle Foundation for Fetal Alcohol Syndrome.

In the early '70s, Dorris, who was part Modoc Indian, was widely credited with being the first single father in the country to adopt. The child was a Native American suffering from fetal alcohol syndrome. Dorris, who founded the Native American Studies Program at Dartmouth, later adopted two more children, also with FAS.

He recounted the experience of the eldest child, Abel, in *The Broken Cord* in 1989. The book won a National Book Critics Circle award for nonfiction and prompted thousands of letters to Dorris by people concerned about the problem. The story, however, ended in tragedy: Abel was killed in 1991 after being hit by a car.

Two years ago, the middle child, Sava, stood trial on charges of trying to extort $15,000 from Dorris and Erdrich. A jury acquitted him on one charge and deadlocked on a second, leading to its dismissal.

The mere fact that Dorris and Erdrich were splitting up was unbelievable to some. Their marriage, as several friends noted sadly yesterday, was one of the great literary love stories of the 1980s. They not only had brilliant careers but were very public about their esteem and passion for each other.

"I would not be writing if I were not working with her," Dorris said in 1987. The following year, Erdrich called Dorris "a spiritual guide, a therapist, someone who allows you to go down to where you just exist and where you are in contact with those very powerful feelings that you had in your childhood." She, too, said she would never be able to go on writing without him.

The dedications of their books made their feelings clear. "To Michael: Complice in every word, essential as air," said her 1986 novel *The Beet Queen.* "For Louise: Companion through every page, through every day. Compeer," said *A Yellow Raft,* which appeared in 1987.

While different names were on most of the books, the couple insisted in interviews that everything was done together. They compared their collaborative process to the Vulcan "mind meld" on "Star Trek."

In 1985, Dorris explained his role in the writing of Erdrich's novel *Love Medicine:* "We talked about the plots, the characterization, the conceptualization, the order, all that stuff, and then, as a draft or part of a draft is finished, Louise gives it to me, and I read it, and make suggestions and comments or reinforcements, as the case may be."

And then somehow, it all went wrong. Nevertheless, a friend said, "he said to me a number of times, their intention was to still work together."

His editor at Scribner, Susan Moldow, said, "I don't know what was going on, and I don't want to speculate. I don't think suicide is ever the result of any one cause."

In a front-page review in *The Washington Post Book World* three months ago, Alice McDermott lauded **Cloud Chamber** for "its vivid, intelligent portrayal of our perpetual, universal and mostly inextinguishable longing for both transcendence and (here's the rub) communion in love."

The book sold well for literary fiction, making bestseller lists in San Francisco, Boston and elsewhere.

As part of his book tour late last month, Dorris read here before about 350 people in PEN/Faulkner's literary series. He read from **Cloud Chamber** and a forthcoming children's book, both of which feature the teenager named Rayona who starred in **Yellow Raft.**

"Rayona's a character I can't let alone, or she won't let me alone," he told the crowd. "Somebody said that in my next life I will come back as a 14-year-old girl. I said, 'That's this life. Next life, I'll come back as me.'"

During the Q&A part of the program, he mentioned Erdrich once or twice. He never let on that they were getting divorced, nor gave any sort of tiny clue, even in retrospect, that he would try to kill himself within a week. He was practically bubbling over with projects for the future. Everyone lined up to have a book signed. Unlike many writers during lengthy autograph sessions, he was sweet and patient to the very end.

Afterward, he had enough energy to go to Blues Alley to hear Melba Moore. Lou Stovall, a member of the PEN/Faulkner board who went with him, said that "he referred to Louise only in the abstract—I knew he was feeling estranged from something—but there wasn't anything that didn't seem life-affirming about his whole demeanor."

Earlier that day, Dorris had visited a class at Cardozo High School under the PEN/Faulkner visiting writers program. Dorris particularly wanted to go to Cardozo because he had volunteered there when a student at Georgetown in the late '60s.

He talked to 30 advanced-placement English students. "It was just a great warm experience," said their teacher, Frazier O'Leary.

Yesterday, O'Leary had to break the news that Dorris had killed himself. He had the students write about their feelings, and then they read the essays aloud. "They were very upset. We talked about how they couldn't understand how someone with so much life, and who seemed to have so

much together, could do that," the teacher said. "This is definitely something they won't ever forget."

OVERVIEWS

Louis Owens (essay date 1992)

SOURCE: "Erdrich and Dorris's Mixed Bloods and Multiple Narratives," in his *Other Destinies: Understanding the American Indian Novel,* University of Oklahoma Press, 1992, pp. 192-224.

[*In the following excerpt of an essay devoted to Louise Erdrich's writings, Owens examines how Native American identity is constructed in Dorris's* A Yellow Raft in Blue Water.]

Despite the importance of N. Scott Momaday's Pulitzer Prize for *House Made of Dawn* in 1969, no American Indian author has achieved such immediate and enormous success as Louise Erdrich with her first novel, *Love Medicine.* A bestseller, *Love Medicine* not only outsold any previous novel by an Indian author, but it also gathered an impressive array of critical awards including the National Book Critics Circle Award for Fiction in 1984, the American Academy and Institute of Arts and Letters award for Best First Novel, the Virginia McCormack Scully Prize for Best Book of 1984 dealing with Indians or Chicanos, the American Book Award from the Before Columbus Foundation, and the *L.A. Times* award for best novel of the year.

Why such astounding success for an author writing about a subject—Indians—in which Americans had previously shown only a passing interest (and that predominantly in the romantic vein mined by non-Indian authors)? The answer to such a question delves into the heart of Louise Erdrich's achievement with *Love Medicine* as well as her very popular second and third novels, *The Beet Queen* (1986) and *Tracks* (1988). And to examine Erdrich's fiction closely is also to explore that of her husband/agent/collaborator, Michael Dorris, whose first novel, *A Yellow Raft in Blue Water* (1987), has also been received with enthusiasm by readers and critics.

. . . .

At the end of Michael Dorris's novel *A Yellow Raft in Blue Water* (1987), one of the book's three narrators and protagonists, Aunt Ida, is braiding her hair as a priest watches: "As a man with cut hair, he did not identify the rhythm of three strands, the whispers of coming and going, of twisting and tying and blending, of catching and of letting go, of braiding." The metaphor of braiding—tying and blending—illuminates the substance of this novel, for it is, like Erdrich's works, a tale of intertwined lives caught up in one another the way distinct narrative threads are woven to make a single story. Like Erdrich, Dorris—part Modoc and for many years a professor of Native American studies at Dartmouth College—constructs his novel out of multiple narratives so that the reader must triangulate to find the "truth" of the fiction. And like Erdrich and other Indian writers, Dorris makes the subject of his fiction the quest for identity through a remembering of the past.

The metaphor of braiding—tying and blending—illuminates the substance of [*A Yellow Raft in Blue Water*], for it is . . . a tale of intertwined lives caught up in one another the way distinct narrative threads are woven to make a single story.
—Louis Owens

Yellow Raft is told in three parts by three narrators—daughter, mother, grandmother, beginning with the youngest generation—so that as we move through the novel, stories are peeled off one another like layers of the proverbial onion as blanks are gradually filled in and we circle in both time and space from an unnamed Montana reservation to Seattle and back, and from the present to the past and back again. As in so many other fictions by Indian writers, the women in this novel live oddly isolated and self-sufficient lives, raising their children and keeping their stories intact without the aid of the alienated males whose lives intersect briefly with theirs. These intersecting lives are caught up in pathos rather than tragedy, and though most of the events of the novel take place on a reservation and involve characters who identify primarily as Indian, Dorris succeeds in highlighting the universality of tangled and fragile relationships. For those who want to pin down the precise setting of this novel, Dorris has said, "The action takes place on a reservation in eastern Montana. There are about five reservations in eastern Montana. We have discovered that it's easier if nobody thinks it's about them. It's not. None of these books is about real people." Though this book may not be about "real people," these characters suffer through many of the same confusions and conflicts, pleasures and pains that we might find in a Los Angeles barrio or a Chicago suburb. Like Erdrich, Dorris has succeeded in *Yellow Raft* in allowing his Indian characters to be human to escape from the deadly limitations of stereotyping.

The first narrator of *Yellow Raft* is Rayona, a young half-Indian, half-African American teenager with all the resiliency of the synthetic fabric for which she is named. Like most mixedbloods in fiction by Indian writers, Rayona is trying to comprehend her life, particularly her abandonment by her Black father and her strangely tenuous connections to her Indian mother, Christine. Unlike *Tracks,* with its opening and closing repetition of *We, Yellow Raft* opens with the singular *I* as Rayona describes her position in her mother's hospital room. Though Rayona does not realize it at the time, her mother, Christine, is dying, having destroyed her internal organs through drinking and hard living. With an intensely undependable mother and a mostly absentee father, of whom she ironically says, "Dad was a temp," Rayona is cast back upon the *I* that is the novel's first word and the dangerous antithesis of the communal identity central to Native American cultures. Relying mostly upon her self, Rayona has achieved a precariously balanced sense of self that straddles what the lecherous Father Tom calls her "dual heritage."

The closest thing to a secure community Christina can offer her daughter is a lifetime membership at Village Video. "It's like something I'd leave you," Christina says in a statement that offers a brilliant contrast to the legacies of tribal identity left to other characters in such novels as *House Made of Dawn,* [James Welch's] *Winter in the Blood,* or [Leslie Marmon Silko's] *Ceremony.* In somewhat the same way that the traditional stories permeate *Ceremony* and *House Made of Dawn,* video permeates *Yellow Raft,* to the extent that the old idea of an Indian "village" could be said to have given way to a more modern—and culturally bankrupt—"Video Village." Christine emphasizes this disturbing transformation when she looks at a videotape of *Little Big Man* and says, "I dated a guy who played an Indian in that movie." We are left to wonder if the guy was an Indian "playing" what Hollywood defines as Indian or if he was a white man playing an Indian. Either way, there is an unmistakable suggestion that "Indian" is a role to be played and identity something conferred by script and camera. Dorris will reinforce this video omnipresence throughout the novel, with characters constantly referring to movies and television to reaffirm their shifting senses of reality. In this world, surface has replaced the depth found in *Tracks,* trivialized aesthetics displacing the ethics of traditionally ecosystemic Indian values.

Even Aunt Ida, a character with a strong sense of self, seems an MTV caricature when we first encounter her wearing overalls, a "black bouffant wig" tacked on by shiny bobby pins, a dark blue bra, sunglasses, and Walkman speakers. Pushing a lawn mower that has no effect upon the grass, Aunt Ida is belting out, like a Stevie Wonder imitation in the wrong tune, the words to what should be considered the novel's theme song: "I've been looking for love in all the wrong places." For the rest of the novel, Ida will seldom be far from a television set, involving herself in the twisted lives of scripted characters of soap operas while living in virtual isolation from the rest of her family and tribe. And when Christine and Aunt Ida confront one another for the first time after many years, Rayona can only say, "I . . . watch as though I'm seeing this scene on an old movie and a commercial could come along any time." Christine, in turn, says, "I couldn't guess what Ray had in mind for a grandmother. Probably somebody from TV, Grandma Walton or even Granny from 'The Beverly Hillbillies,' but they were a far cry from Aunt Ida." These mixedblood characters suffer from a loss of authenticity intensified by an inability to selectively assimilate the words and images besieging them from the ubiquitous media. [Mikhail] Bakhtin suggests that the

> tendency to assimilate others' discourse takes on an even deeper and more basic significance in an individual's ideological becoming, in the most fundamental sense. Another's discourse performs here no longer as information, directions, rules, models and so forth—but strives rather to determine the very basis of our behavior, it performs here as *authoritative discourse,* and an *internally persuasive discourse.*

The characters in Dorris's novel, seemingly trapped in a dialectic that never moves toward *telos,* or resolution, incapable of dialogue and without significant community to aid them in developing a coherent sense of self, become comic reflectors for the monologic discourse of the privileged center beamed to them in their isolation. The result is poignantly funny, pathos pointing—like the narrator's frozen father in *Winter in the Blood*—toward cultural tragedy.

Despite her resiliency, Rayona is as lost between cultures and identities as any character in Indian fiction, truly a stranger in a very bizarre land. Father Tom, who is trying to convince Rayona to go back to Seattle and far from the reservation where she might tell about his sexual advances, says, "And you won't feel so alone, so out of place. . . . There'll be others in a community of that size who share your dual heritage." In a nicely ironic testimony to her dilemma, the lascivious priest offers Rayona a cheap, pseudo-Indian medallion he has been wearing, saying, "Wear this. Then people will know you're an Indian." Identity is all surface. The center is lost. With a medallion, Rayona may become Native American rather than African American. Rayona's predicament is underscored even more ironically when she stops beneath a sign that reads, "IF LOST, STAY WHERE YOU ARE. DON'T PANIC. YOU WILL BE FOUND." Rayona takes this advice and stays at Bearpaw Lake State Park, where the ladies' restroom "has a cartoon picture of an Indian squaw on the door." She doesn't panic, though she does attempt halfheartedly to appropriate the identity—rich family and all—of a popular, spoiled white girl, and she is found by Sky, a good-hearted draft-dodger who doesn't notice trivial details like skin color, and his tough-as-nails wife, Evelyn. Appropriately, Sky and Evelyn—Father Sky, Mother Earth—subsist in the "video village" of contemporary

America on TV dinners; and lying on their couch, Rayona muses upon her fragmented self: "It's as though I'm dreaming a lot of lives and I can mix and match the parts into something new each time." Indian identity is further undercut when the wealthy white parents of Rayona's coworker talk of their "adopted" Indian son who lives on a "mission": "When he writes to us now he calls us Mother and Pops just like one of our own kids." Such an image suggests the distantly marginalized voice, the "wilderness children" of McNickle's novels, writing back to the metropolitan center—"Pops," the white father—in a poignant imitation of the expected discourse.

Rayona returns to the reservation and her mother via an Indian rodeo, where she achieves a totally unconvincing bronc-busting triumph that reminds everyone of Lee, Christine's brother killed in Vietnam. And once she is back, the three strands of family begin to be woven into one thread. Rayona's mother, Christine, begins the second book of the novel by declaring, "I had to find my own way and I started out in the hole, the bastard daughter of a woman who wouldn't even admit she was my mother." In a novel in which identity is obscure at best, Christine is actually the daughter of Ida's father and Ida's mother's sister, Clara; she is the half-sister of the woman she thinks of as her mother. It is ironic that among many tribes, as we have seen in James Welch's *Fools Crow,* it was once common for a man to take his wife's sisters as additional wives, especially if his first wife was in need of assistance and one of her sisters, like Clara, needed a home. According to traditional tribal values, at one time there might have been nothing at all improper about Clara bearing the child of her sister's husband had the situation been handled correctly. But that world is long gone, and Clara's pregnancy is a potentially damning scandal. In spite of the fact that Christine has taught Rayona to speak "Indian" and Ida still knows how to dance traditionally, most values have been lost in the confusion of a reservation where young girls mouth the lyrics to "Poor Little Fool" ("I felt like a fool," Welch's *Winter* narrator says) while awaiting Armageddon, grandmothers wear black wigs and Walkmans, and a talented boy is labeled "the Indian JFK" and ridiculed by his sister when he speaks of "Mother Earth and Father Sky."

Christine's "brother," Lee, is the son of Ida and Willard Pretty Dog. A warrior, Willard has come home, like Russell in *The Beet Queen* and all the other soldiers in Indian fiction, with hideous scars and no hero's welcome, taken in like a refugee by Ida. Out of pride, Ida has ultimately rejected Willard and never acknowledged him as her son's father. Thus while Christine mistakenly believes Ida to be her mother and Lee her brother, neither Christine nor Lee can claim a father. Noting her differences from Lee, Christine says, "We were so different I wondered if we had the same father. . . . I studied middle-aged men on the reservation for a clue in their faces." At Lee's funeral, Christine observes, "A woman who was somehow related to us wailed softly," and of the crowd of men she says, "One of them was probably Lee's father, my father, but that was an old question that would never be answered." When Ida finally takes Christine to visit Clara as Clara lies dying in a hospital, Ida drags Christine away quickly, obviously afraid that Clara will confess that she, not Ida, is Christine's mother. Christine, with little time left to live, will never learn the truth of her biological mother, but she will by the end of the novel be accepted once again as a daughter by Ida.

In the third book of the novel, Ida tells her story, and the threads of relationships in the novel become more clear. It is in this book that relationships are also reforged. Christine, who jealously hounded Lee into the military and toward his death, is forgiven by Ida and forgives the bitter old lady in return. Dayton, Lee's best friend, both forgives Christine and is in turn forgiven. Rayona is reunited with Christine and taken in as a daughter by Dayton, the mixedblood with whom Christine lives out her final days. Father Hurlburt, silent witness and participant in all—who is vaguely part Indian and has learned to speak Ida's language—is there in the end to watch and approve. And most significantly, Ida becomes the novel's supreme storyteller, as befits the Indian grandmother. "I tell my story the way I remember, the way I want," she says, adding:

> I have to tell this story every day, add to it, revise, invent the parts I forget or never knew. No one but me carries it all and no one will—unless I tell Rayona, who might understand. She's heard her mother's side, and she's got eyes. But she doesn't guess what happened before. She doesn't know my true importance. She doesn't realize that I am the story, and that is my savings, to leave her or not.

With Ida's acceptance of her crucial role as the storyteller who holds the meaning of past, present and future within her words, Dorris moves his novel closer to the mainstream of Indian fiction. Ida becomes, like Nanapush in *Tracks,* the grandmother in *Winter in the Blood,* Francisco in *House Made of Dawn,* and all storytellers, the bearer of the identity and order that are so fragile they may perish in a single generation if unarticulated. Within Ida resides the power to abrogate the authority of that "other" discourse assaulting Indians from the media of Euramerica: she can take off her earphones and wig, turn off the television soap operas, and become a story-teller, leaving her "savings"—a recovered sense of self, identity, authenticity—to Rayona.

Though resolution and closure come with a somewhat unpersuasive rapidity and ease in this novel, *A Yellow Raft in Blue Water* moves energetically into Welch's Montana terrain to illuminate the lives of Indians who live on ves-

tiges of tribal identities and reservation fringes, bombarded by video and the American Dream. In choosing to write of a nameless tribe on a nameless reservation, Dorris deliberately emphasizes the ordinariness of these experiences for the great number of Native Americans who, in searching for a sense of self, must reach back even further and with much less hope of success than a Tayo or Abel or even the narrator of *Winter in the Blood.* Writing in a prose style that inundates the reader with an occasionally annoying plethora of incidental detail, Dorris forces his reader to share his characters' experience of incessant strafing by the foreign and the trivial. The world of permanence and significance, where every detail must count and be counted—the Indian pueblo/village community portrayed so effectively in *Ceremony* and *Fools Crow*—has given way to an Indian Video Village in which alien discourses assert a prior authority and resist, with their privileged cacophony, easy assimilation. The individual who would "be" Indian rather than "play" Indian is faced with an overwhelming challenge.

REVIEWS OF DORRIS'S RECENT WORKS

Patricia Guthrie (review date 30 July 1989)

SOURCE: "Alcohol's Child: A Father Tells His Tale," in *The New York Times Book Review,* July 30, 1989, pp. 1, 20.

[*In the following review, Guthrie asserts that "the alarming statistics and consequences of fetal alcohol syndrome are skillfully interwoven with the human story of one of its victims in* The Broken Cord.]

In 1971, Michael Dorris, 26 years old and unmarried, was living in an isolated Indian community in Alaska, doing fieldwork for his doctorate in anthropology. Realizing that "in a world of 'we,' I was an 'I'" he decided that he wanted to be a father. Lacking a partner, Mr. Dorris decided to try to adopt a child alone. Part American Indian himself, he asked for an Indian child, and his application was forwarded to a national adoption service. A few months later, as he was settling into a new teaching job in New Hampshire, a social worker called to tell him that a 3-year-old boy from a Sioux reservation in South Dakota was up for adoption.

Mr. Dorris was warned that the boy had been born almost seven weeks premature; his mother was a heavy drinker who neglected him; he "had not been toilet-trained or taught to speak more than a few words. He was diagnosed as mentally retarded." In the perfect abstraction of longing to be a parent, Mr. Dorris believed in the "positive impact of environment." He assured himself: "With me he'll catch up."

At their first meeting in the social worker's office the boy

Mr. Dorris calls Adam looked up from his toy truck and said "Hi, Daddy." It was the beginning of a bittersweet relationship that has gone on for 18 years, lovingly and painfully described in *The Broken Cord,* the story of a child afflicted by fetal alcohol syndrome and of Mr. Dorris's personal investigation of the condition that has blighted his son's life.

Despite the attention of the best teachers, countless examinations by medical doctors and psychologists and the constant, doting care of his father and family, Adam Dorris never shook his bad start. He struggled through the Cornish, N.H., public elementary school; at graduation in 1983, "he could not add, subtract, count money, or consistently identify the town, state, country or planet." He went on to high school in Claremont, a half-hour bus ride away. He was sent each day, but could not reliably get on the right bus going in the right direction to get home. He was transferred to a vocational education program at a school farther away. At the age of 20, he still could not count money or tell time. His I.Q. remained a steady 65.

In 1982, after Mr. Dorris had adopted a second son and a daughter and was on his way to having three more children with his wife, the writer Louise Erdrich, he learned at last what was really wrong with Adam. As head of Native American studies at Dartmouth College, Mr. Dorris was visiting a treatment center for chemically dependent teen-agers on South Dakota's Pine Ridge Sioux reservation when he saw three "uncannily familiar" boys who not only behaved like Adam but looked like him. He reached for a wallet photo of Adam to show the program director, who "nodded, and handed it back. 'FAS too'" he replied. It was the first time Mr. Dorris had heard the initials that stand for fetal alcohol syndrome.

"They come from alcoholic families, mothers who drank," the director told him. "Your wife too?" he asked.

"He's adopted," Mr. Dorris replied, "And, yes, his mother did drink." Alcohol, Mr. Dorris soon learned, had damaged Adam's brain while he was still in the womb. And the damage could not be undone.

In the next few years Mr. Dorris learned a lot about fetal alcohol syndrome, a condition that was being identified and explored by the international medical community in the 1970's, just when Adam's medical and learning disabilities were baffling his father.

Medical news doesn't always travel fast. While Adam was struggling to comprehend the simplest of tasks in elementary school, some doctors were still prescribing an occasional glass of wine to pregnant women for relaxation. But by 1981, the Food and Drug Administration was warning health professionals that pregnant women should drink no alcohol at all, that even small, casual doses had been linked to increased risk of low birth weight and spontaneous abortion.

The definition of fetal alcohol syndrome, Mr. Dorris writes, embraces individuals who share several recognizable characteristics: "(1) significant growth retardation both before and after birth; (2) measurable mental deficit; (3) altered facial characteristics; (4) other physical abnormalities; and (5) documentation of maternal alcoholism." By 1968 the "mental deficit" category had been refined to include "attention deficits," or the inability to concentrate on a single task; memory problems; hyperactivity; low I.Q.; and an inability, apparently connected to a defective grasp of cause-and-effect relations, to handle money, regardless of "sex, age, educational level or background."

For three years after he learned the name of Adam's condition, Mr. Dorris traveled the country, collecting the bleak stories of Indians dying from whatever alcohol product they could find; death by hair spray, death by antifreeze (the fate of Adam's natural mother). He also heard of the grim beginnings; babies born reeking of cheap wine, babies born with delirium tremens.

At the numerous medical conferences he attended, Mr. Dorris learned that thousands of children are born each year with full fetal alcohol syndrome—about 7,500 by one estimate. Thousands more suffer the lesser disabilities of fetal alcohol effect—feeding difficulties in infants, in older children marginal mental retardation, short memory span, emotional instability. These are afflictions that know no ethnic or class bounds, Mr. Dorris realized, although, as he writes, "historically and presently" it is a "major problem for American Indians." Drinking alcohol has long been a "venerable part of social culture" in many societies—for men. However, according to recent studies, the condition seems to be emerging around the world when "'modern' women, regardless of their class or ethnic background" begin drinking. As Adam had struggled, so many other children around the world struggled: to tie their shoes, to write their names, to remember to wear a coat when it is snowing outside. All because their mothers drank.

The alarming statistics and consequences of fetal alcohol syndrome are skillfully interwoven with the human story of one of its victims in *The Broken Cord.* Mr. Dorris's prose is clear and affecting: "Adam's birthdays are reminders for me. For each celebration commemorating that he was born, there is the pang, the rage, that he was not born whole."

The last chapter of the book is "The Adam Dorris Story by Adam Dorris." At his father's suggestion, the young man typed out his life memories, and to everyone's surprise he finished the project. With incurably misspelled words and hopeless punctuation, Adam lists stacking wood and pulling up burdock bushes as his biggest triumphs. "I might of not told you this before but stacking wood is one of my favorite hobbies. I don't really mind stacking wood at all. And my other hobby is mowing lawns. I don't have any other hobby besides those two right there."

Adam does not write about the first time he danced with a girl or about playing in his first baseball game, nor does he seem aware that he missed them. But his father knows what Adam is missing. And it is he, not Adam, who lives with this knowledge.

Mr. Dorris also raises and struggles with, but cannot answer, some Solomonic questions: what should communities do with pregnant women who insist on drinking? How can society possibly protect an unborn child against maternal behavior that is not only legal almost everywhere, but almost impossible to prevent anywhere? Should such women be incarcerated? Should mothers of fetal alcohol children be sterilized if they intend to keep drinking and reproducing? Can civil rights be abrogated for the protection of the unborn? Should liquor companies he held liable for these damaged children if adequate warnings are not on their products?

Those are abstractions, and worth consideration. Throughout his book, Mr. Dorris returns time and again to one real, haunting question: what if someone had stopped Adam's biological mother from drinking?

The Broken Cord should be required reading for all medical professionals and social workers, and especially for pregnant women, and women who contemplate pregnancy, who may be tempted to drink. At the very least, Michael Dorris's last comment should be prescribed:

> My son will forever travel through a moonless night with only the roar of wind for company. Don't talk to him of mountains, of tropical beaches. Don't ask him to swoon at sunrises or marvel at the filter of light through leaves. He's never had time for such things, and he does not believe in them. . . . A drowning man is not separated from the lust for air by a bridge of thought—he is one with it—and my son, conceived and grown in an ethanol bath, lives each day in the act of drowning. For him there is no shore.

Peter Lomas (review date 24-30 August 1990)

SOURCE: "Beyond Healing's Reach?," in *Times Literary Supplement,* August 24-30, 1990, p. 893.

[*In the following excerpt, Lomas reviews* The Broken Cord.]

Dorris's craving for fatherhood is so intense that he overcomes all obstacles to become the first single man in America to be granted an adoption. He is of mixed blood and the child is a three-year-old American Indian. The fact that the boy is said to be mentally retarded does not dismay him, and from the moment he sets eyes on "Adam" he is besotted—"How often in a four-day period can one person fall in love with another, each time as it is the first?"

Dorris brushes aside all difficulties until Adam has an epileptic fit and becomes gravely ill. But even though, at the time, Dorris is nearly driven mad with worry, he continues to rationalize all subsequent manifestations of illness and defect, seeing them merely as the consequences of a "slow start". He summons all his anthropological expertise to oppose any suggestion from medical experts that Adam has a serious impediment. However, the evidence accumulates, and it is soon clear that Adam's plight is due to his mother's excessive drinking during her pregnancy; his condition is known as Foetal Alcohol Syndrome, and finally it becomes impossible for Dorris to pretend otherwise.

Dorris then channels his anger and grief into a professional study of the disease and its social implications, and *The Broken Cord* is one product of that effort. His scholarly account of the ravages inflicted on American Indians is frightening in its implications, not only for the Indian reservations but for all women who consume alcohol, even in modest proportions. It is in order to give weight to his plea that he makes the story of Adam the centrepiece of the book. And in doing so not only has he succeeded in alerting us to some of the worst and least publicized dangers of alcoholism, but with courage and humour, he has reported an inspiring account of a father-and-son relationship.

The Broken Cord is introduced by the novelist Louise Erdrich, whom Dorris later married and who helped him to look after Adam and two other children whom he subsequently adopted. The final chapter is written by Adam himself, a surprising feat for someone so damaged and one which reveals the limitations of his imagination. This, for Dorris, is the greatest loss.

> Don't talk to him of mountains, of tropical beaches. Don't ask him to swoon at sunrises or marvel at the filter of light through leaves. He's never had time for such things, and he does not believe in them. He may pass by them close enough to touch on either side but his hands are stretched forward, grasping for balance instead of pleasure.

Kirsty Milne (review date 7 September 1990)

SOURCE: "Sins of Mothers . . . and Fathers," in *New Statesman & Society,* September 7, 1990, p. 44.

[*In the excerpt below, Milne reviews* The Broken Cord *and notes that Dorris "sees drinking as pre-natal child abuse."*]

When Michael Dorris adopted an enchanting three-year-old Sioux child, Adam, he knew the boy's mother had died of alcohol poisoning. He didn't know how that would blight his rapturous single parenthood.

Adam started having unexplained and frightening seizures. At five, he was still not toilet-trained; he could not count or tell colours apart. His frantic father harried hundreds of professionals and dared them to tell him Adam's backwardness was more than temporary. "To judge him lacking in innate ability, I darkly hinted, implied poor teaching, racism or a defeatist attitude."

After months of painful research, Dorris established that Adam was suffering from Foetal Alcohol Syndrome (FAS), caused by his mother's heavy drinking during pregnancy. This discovery prompted Dorris, who is Indian himself, to confront the taboo subject of alcoholism among native Americans. Health workers told him that on some reservations as many as one in four children had been damaged by alcohol while still in the womb.

Even now, at 22, Adam is unable to relate cause to effect. Unless reminded, he forgets to eat or take the medicine which stops him having seizures. He will go out in sub-zero temperatures wearing a T-shirt because he cannot foresee the consequences.

Faced with Adam's truncated potential, Dorris and his wife, the writer Louise Erdrich, have found their liberal convictions melting away like snow. They have come to believe that in the last resort, mothers of FAS children should be imprisoned to prevent them drinking their way through another pregnancy. (Some Indian reservations, which are entitled to make their own laws, have put this into practice already.)

Dorris sees drinking as pre-natal child abuse. Like other supporters of "foetal rights" [. . .] , he argues that the mother's civil liberties are less important than her child's chance of a normal life. If Adam's mother had smashed his skull with a baseball bat *after* he was born, society would have intervened. As it is, "because his mother drank, Adam is one of the earth's damaged."

Alice McDermott (review date 8 November 1992)

SOURCE: "The Girl Columbus Discovered," in *The New York Times Book Review,* November 8, 1992, p. 33.

[*In the following review, McDermott considers the family values extolled in* Morning Girl.]

Christopher Columbus is a mere postscript in *Morning Girl,* a lovely novel by the author of *A Yellow Raft in Blue Water, The Broken Cord* and, with Louise Erdrich, *The Crown of Columbus.* There is evidence of him only in the final pages, when a group of squat strangers who "had wrapped every part of their bodies with colorful leaves and cotton" approach a Bahaman island in a fat canoe. His name itself appears only in the epilogue: a brief excerpt from his diaries in which he mentions seeing only one "quite young girl" among the people who greet his ships.

It is this young girl, Morning Girl; her brother, Star Boy; their family, and the life of their people in 1492 that are the focus of the story. And although a reader may be well aware of the tale's historical context, it is testimony to Michael Dorris's graceful and engaging narrative that there is not a single moment when a reader, young or old, will pause to wonder just when Columbus will enter. He is simply not needed.

In alternating chapters, Morning Girl and Star Boy describe their daily lives on this beautiful, but not idyllic, island. They are typical cantankerous siblings, each amazed that the other could have sprung from the same source. Morning Girl is so called because she wakes early, "as soon as the light calls through the smoke hole in the roof." Star Boy prefers the night, when "you can be dreaming even if you're awake."

"I don't know how my brother came to see everything so upside down from me," Morning Girl tells us. "It's as though time is split between us, and we only pass by each other as the sun rises or sets. Usually, for me, that's enough."

And yet, typical siblings, they are also amazed at times to discover the depth of their affection. When their mother returns from Grandmother's house after a miscarriage, Star Boy wraps his arms around her and Morning Girl observes, "Seeing Mother and Star Boy like that was so right, so how it should be, that for a long moment I didn't wish it was me in her arms." At the feast that celebrates the end of a devastating hurricane in which he almost lost his life, Star Boy whispers a new name for his sister, one he will use from then on whenever they are alone together: "The One Who Stands Beside."

The children's mother, She Wins the Race, and their father, Speaks to Birds, are surely the most loving, wise, compassionate and patient parents to be found in recent literature, young adult or otherwise. There is a wonderful scene in which Morning Girl, anxious to discover what her face looks like ("Is it long and wrinkled, like Grandmother's, or round as a coconut, like Star Boy's?"), questions first her mother and then her father. Her mother tells her to close her eyes and trace with her hands both her mother's face and her own. Her father tells her to look into his eyes

> "Who are those pretty girls who live inside your head?" she asks him.

> "They are the answer to your question," he replies. "And they are always here when you need to find them."

Lest the modern reader begin to wonder if it was indeed 1492 when the world last saw such a perfectly *functional* family, the author drops a mention of Star Boy's friend Red Feather, who has been sent to live with an uncle because his parents "were arguing with each other again."

But despite this apparent nod to our modern sensibilities, despite the current fashion for Columbus bashing, ***Morning Girl*** is in no way a lesson in historical re-evaluation. It is a warm story full of real characters and situations, told in marvelous language that makes it a pleasure to read out loud. If it offers a larger lesson it is, perhaps, in perspective. The reader breaks the surface of the ocean with Morning Girl during her dawn swim and, with the sunlight and the water sparkling, catches the first glimpse of the fat canoe full of strange visitors. A curiosity, perhaps, but certainly not an essential dramatic moment for the story—not when Morning Girl has just discovered a perfect white conch shell to give to her brother, to begin anew the collection that he lost in the hurricane. Not when she has just discovered the right name for the sister who was never born, She Listens.

It is a lesson in perspective that will lend new meaning to Columbus's final words in the novel's epilogue: "Our Lord pleasing, at the time of my departure I will take six of them from here to Your Highnesses in order that they may learn to speak."

Ron Hansen (review date 7 November 1993)

SOURCE: "Importance of Everyday," in *Los Angeles Times Book Review,* November 7, 1993, pp. 2, 13.

[*In the review below, Hansen addresses aspects of the "ordinary" represented in* Working Men.]

Fiction writers have a natural fascination with ordinary jobs. Holed up alone in our offices, we gaze out windows with the left-out feelings of children kept after school, and fantasize, when our writing stinks, of friendlier ways of making a living. Michael Dorris's fascination takes the form of 14 varied but cohesive stories in this skillful collection [***Working Men***], each offering fresh perspectives on those faceless Americans who seem to have no definition beyond what they do, but whose hidden lives are full of poignance and complexity.

Whether male or female, Michael Dorris's characters are often powerless in love relationships, finding themselves subject to the whims and options of others. In **"Earnest Money,"** a feckless man who evaded the Vietnam draft by going to Canada, returns to Montana after his father's death, inherits $13,000, and finds himself turning it over to a scheming woman he's hastily married. "The thing was, I recognized her bossiness for what it was: the instruction booklet that up to then my life had been lacking. It was a relief for questions to come with the decisions already made, to have firm opinions to rub against. After passing so many fair days, Evelyn was a thunderstorm that knocked out all competing electricity."

In **"Anything,"** Aileen goes to a Burger King to form wedding plans with the dull man she's engaged to but doesn't love. She gets a phone call there from a pining former boyfriend and she jilts her finance for him. The former boyfriend changes his mind within hours, saying he'd fleetingly felt "empathy, complete, selfless love" for her, but then it just "switched off." And Aileen sees the bleak future she'd barely escaped—"stuck and wondering why"—in which she could have been married to either man "without ever actually choosing to do it."

And in **"Qiana,"** an oafish New Hampshire snowplow operator finds a fancy shirt at a yard sale and falls into an affair with the former wife of its owner. With his own wife, Irene, Normand had "the kind of arrangement a twin brother and sister might concoct, the kind where two people had read each other's minds so long they had lost interest in the novelty." With the divorced woman, Normand invites an identical disdain, so that "she found herself wishing that Irene still had the daily care of him, the cleanup chores, the small duties of praise and complaint, the silent dinners for two." And so he fuddles his way back to his wife.

But if they're helpless and confused by emotions, for the most part these ***Working Men*** are supremely confident and present in their jobs. In the "hatless, gloveless temperature" of autumn, Normand overhauls the snowplow's engine and slowly peruses the back roads that will soon be filled with snow, "alert for soft shoulders or runoff ruts that might catch a wheel. Alone on these reconnaissance trips, Normand regarded himself as a professional, an expert who saw what ordinary men might miss, and when he identified a loose bed or an unsupported erosion, he congratulated his keen eye and forgave himself his sins."

And here is an architect of ponds: "To start a job, you drive a nail into a peak of ledge, pound it deep, make it your benchmark, your one-hundred scale. The transit measures from that arbitrary point as you compute all distance in links and chains. Weather patterns can alter, crops grow, houses get built and collapse, but you can return in 50 years and position a tripod, rotate the dials of the spirit until the air bubble precisely crosses the hairline, then aim an alidade at that solitary, centering nail and be in business."

Easily the most affecting story in the collection is **"Jeopardy,"** about a shrewd Allied Pharmaceuticals salesman and seeming Lothario who is forced to wheedle and con his way past clinic receptionists in order to get to the doctors for a few minutes. "Sympathy's the key to Lisa's lock, as it is with a lot of them. You open your heart wide enough, she presses the buzzer under her desk and it's Hello Sesame." But he has not opened his heart wide enough to admit he has homosexual affairs with fellow salesman on the road, or that the father he loved has just died. When, in his grief, he calls a favorite receptionist at home, she interrupts him with thanks for an inhaler that seems to have saved her son's life. And he thinks, "There's purposes we don't suspect, side paths we don't venture but a few steps down, and yet there's a give-and-take that leads forward, a surprise when we don't even know we need it."

Whether he's writing comically about a high school football coach who fakes his way through his classes in French knowing little more than *oui*, or seriously about a postgraduate anthropologist in an Alaskan fishing village, Dorris's details are authoritative and apt, his voices distinct and persuasive. Even stories written in the first-person female have the feel of authenticity. And his writing is often stunning in its shorthand poetry: "Without Dad around, Mom was horsepower with nothing to move."

Michael Dorris is best known as the author of the novels *A Yellow Raft in Blue Water* and *The Crown of Columbus* (co-written with his wife, Louise Erdrich), and of the non-fiction account, *The Broken Cord*, winner of the National Book Critics Circle Award. *Working Men* features fiction previously published in *Mother Jones, Ploughshares, Northwest Review*, and other literary quarterlies, as well as four new stories. All are strikingly different, and are told with flair and efficiency and honed craftsmanship. *Working Men* is admirable not just for its mastery and variety, but for Michael Dorris's faith in the heroism and importance of ordinary American life.

Julian Ferraro (review date 2 December 1994)

SOURCE: "Vestiges of the West," in *Times Literary Supplement*, December 2, 1994, p. 22.

[*Below, Ferraro applauds the characterization, narration, and attention to detail he observes in* A Yellow Raft in Blue Water *and* Working Men.]

Michael Dorris's first novel, *A Yellow Raft in Blue Water* (1988), presents the interconnected stories of three women. It is divided into three sections, narrated in turn by Rayona (who would have been Raymond but is named instead after the label on her mother's rayon nightgown—"Didn't you ever hear of Ray for a girl?"), her mother, Christine, and her grandmother, the ruthless Aunt Ida. The action takes place in Seattle, on a Montana reservation and at a nearby National Park. This is a world of displacement and poverty; of hotel-rooms, mobile homes, bars, diners and the isolation of the reservation—the late twentieth-century vestiges of the American West.

The first section spans several months, beginning with fifteen-year-old Rayona visiting her mother in hospital and ending with their reconciliation on the reservation where Christine had spent her childhood and where she has returned to die. The second covers more than thirty years, opening with Christine herself at fifteen and ending by advancing the story just beyond the scope of Rayona's narrative. In the final section, Aunt Ida tells her story, culminating with the first incident related by Christine. It is only with Ida that the unspoken causes of the hurt and dislocation which permeates the previous accounts begin to be given a voice: "I have to tell this story every day, add to it, revise, invent the parts I forget or never knew. No one but me carries it all."

As each story is told and retold, actions and events are interpreted and reinterpreted, layers of significance are built up and layers of mystery are peeled away. Dorris's method—the way in which the stories are woven together, emphasizing both the separateness of the three women and, at the same time, the inevitable interdependence of their lives—is figured by the closing picture of Aunt Ida re-braiding her long black hair after Christine's failed attempt to perm it.

Dorris's descriptions blend the exotic or the poetic with the ordinary. Rayona's account of a moment of crisis early in the story—"My anger is nothing compared to hers. She's so mad she seems to light in the dark, but it's only a match flaring for her Kent"—is reformulated with a similarly controlled bathos in Christine's later recollection of the same incident: "I wanted to whirl, to fly like an unknotted balloon, to jack-hammer the road. I wanted to run into trees with my eyes closed, to set myself on fire. But all I did, once my breath came back, once I felt the ground under my feet, was reach back onto the dashboard, get a smoke, and light it." The book's imagery similarly blends extravagant flights of fancy with the mundane; just as characters' lives are painfully constrained by events beyond their power to control, so are their imaginations and their power to describe. Altogether Dorris creates a powerful sense of damaging, destructive experience, which are travestied, and at the same time made bearable, by the terms in which they are described—as Aunt Ida puts it: "I use the words that shaped my construction of events . . . the words that gave me power."

Working Men, Michael Dorris's most recent book, is a collection of short stories that makes a return to the approach to storytelling so successfully employed in *A Yellow Raft in Blue Water* after the departure of the self-consciously post-modern novel, *The Crown of Columbus* (1992), which was co-written with Louise Erdrich. These fourteen stories, which reveal an impressive range of register and subject-matter, all deal with love in one form or another, whether it is the love kindled between married and middle-aged Normand Pasco and divorced Marilyn Dixon by the purchase of "a shirt from a moment so precisely in the center of the 1970s that it might have been assigned a calendar date", or that between returning the draft dodger, Sky, and Evelyn, one of his mother's friends (characters already encountered in *A Yellow Raft in Blue Water*). The love with which these stories deal is seldom uncomplicated and often shadowed by loss, or the threat of loss. **"The Dark Snake"** tells the story of a woman who sacrifices the security of her surviving son to avenge the death of his younger brother. In **"Oui"**, one of the funniest pieces in the collection, Dwayne, a former high-school football star masquerading as a French teacher, allows his suspicions about Cecille's fidelity to run out of control until she is able to give an unexpected proof of her love.

Perhaps the best story in the book is **"Shining Agate"**, in which an ethnographer finds himself participating in the resolution of one of the mythical stories of the people he is studying. This is a beautifully wrought piece—the character of the narrator, the unfolding of his relationship with the inhabitants of Suscitna and the strange events with which the story closes are handled with sympathy and economy. Indeed, this story might serve as a paradigm for the strengths of both *Working Men* and *A Yellow Raft in Blue Water.* Dorris combines close observation of the small details out of which his characters' lives are constituted with an understanding, imaginative engagement with those lives, and this is an engagement that it is hard not to share.

Linda Perkins (review date 29 January 1995)

SOURCE: A review of *Guests,* in *The New York Times Book Review,* January 29, 1995, p. 20.

[*Below, Perkins offers a favorable assessment of* Guests, *noting that Dorris "weaves important moral themes—identity, responsibility, generosity—into his tale."*]

In his second novel for children [*Guests*], Michael Dorris steps into the life and mind of a young Native American boy named Moss as his clan prepares the traditional harvest feast. Moss's father has invited a group of hungry, strange-looking immigrants to join them. Despite the obvious contemporary parallels, the setting, though not specified, is probably 17th-century North America, and the scene bears a strong resemblance to the traditional Thanksgiving.

Moss wrestles with family traditions, questions his father's decision to invite the guests and observes the family tension surrounding the coming festival. He questions his older cousin Cloud about his "away time, a rite of passage into manhood, but the answer is always the same: 'You'll understand when the time comes.'" Angry and frustrated, Moss runs away.

Moss's distant relative Trouble has also run away. Inspired by the story of her grandmother's rebellious sister, she rails against family expectations and the traditional role of women. Her bruised, swollen face betrays a family violence she never mentions.

As in *Morning Girl,* his first work of fiction for children, Mr. Dorris writes lyrically of nature. The descriptions fill the senses, as when Moss sees "the shape of bark as it folded into gnarls" and smells "not just the ordinary musty odor of the forest, but many flavors—the tang of mint, the rot of logs, the sweet sing of water." His images are vivid, as when Moss walks through the forest: "The air was like a cave, cool and solemn, scratched by the brush of my legs as I wove between the short plants like a sewing bone."

There are tales within the primary narrative, as Moss and his family, after the boy returns to the celebration, entertain and instruct with animal fables and stories of headstrong ancestors. The story of the indulgent grandmother Can't Say No and her demanding granddaughter, Never Enough, adds humor and a certain sadness. Moss's father tells it to the strange-smelling guests to put them at ease and explain the common ancestry of humankind. In a nice touch of irony, Moss perceives the loud, ill-mannered visitors as descendants of the self-centered Never Enough.

The subtle, introspective quality of the story is best suited for able readers. Children unfamiliar with American Indian rites of passage such as the "away time" would benefit from background information, but it isn't needed to understand the story. There is ample fuel for discussion—the obvious but unstated resemblance to the Thanksgiving story, open-ended issues like Trouble's beating and even the fate of the American Indian.

Like the storytellers in Moss's family, Mr. Dorris weaves important moral themes—identity, responsibility, generosity—into his tale. He speaks through the voices of his characters. When Moss asks his father why they can't do only the things they want to do, his father explains: "Because we're not alone in the world. . . . We listen to need. We do what we are required." Earlier his mother had told him: "Hospitality isn't unusual, something you choose to do or not, it's ordinary. . . . It's like gathering wood so that you can have a fire when the snow comes. Like listening to good advice." Amen.

Stephen Lyons (review date May-June 1995)

SOURCE: A review of *Working Men* and *Paper Trail,* in *The Bloomsbury Review,* May-June, 1995, pp. 19, 21.

[*In the following review, Lyons observes "the breath and richness of contemporary American culture" in* Working Men *and* Paper Trail.]

In the current diminished relationship of literature and journalism, where the line between fact and fiction grows more incestuous with each tabloid headline and insta-book, it's a good thing we have the writings of Michael Dorris to show us the difference. No doubt exists as to which genre Dorris is writing for, whether he is reporting about world politics and hunger in *Rooms in the House of Stone* (1994), or tracing a life caught in the whirl of search in the novel *A Yellow Raft in Blue Water* (1987).

But it was Dorris' true story of his son's Fetal Alcohol Syndrome, *The Broken Cord* (1989), that most captured the nation's attention. The book was the National Book Critics Circle award for Best Nonfiction Book in 1989, the Heartland Prize, and the Christopher Award. (Even my battered hardback copy made the rounds of a school district in northeastern Washington, where teachers confront the horrific realities of both the syndrome and Fetal Alcohol Effect with each passing day. Alcohol remains the American West's version of crack.)

Curiously, it was *The Broken Cord* that I turned to most often during my five years as a single parent. For in a country where the card "deadbeat dad" is so often dealt, there are few havens for men to turn to for positive nurturing as fathers. It was in those eloquent chapters where I found confirmation—through Dorris' own courageous actions as a single parent—that it is indeed natural for men to nurture their children with passion and patience. You are not alone, Dorris told me.

For all of Dorris' shifting back and forth between styles, little quality is lost. The two recent books, *Working Men* and *Paper Trail,* are good evidence of Dorris' deft hand as literary stylist and storyteller. *Working Men's* 14 stories have a variety of voices, settings, and tones. Literary possibilities abound with characters reminiscent of those in Richard Ford's *Rock Springs* (1988). Like most of us, Dorris' characters sometimes manage to rise above ordinary situations for a moment of luminosity. They eat huckleberry pie at the Do-Re-Me, work for the railroad, live on Montana's Milk River, and, during the Vietnam War, spent time in Canada and Da Nang. They are Native Americans, like Dorris himself. They are gay. They are straight. If you look closely, you will see their eyes have "two-hundred-watt light bulb[s] lit behind them." Mostly life passes like the weather: constant and unpredictable.

Take Mrs. William Burke, in **"The Dark Snake,"** whose youngest son Andrew is killed on his very first day of working for the railroad. On that fateful day her hair turns from black to pure gold. She wants revenge even if it hurts her older son, also in the railroad's employ.

> All that week I went to daily Mass and remained kneeling when others stood or sat. The monsignor assumed that I prayed for Andrew and kept his eyes fixed on me during his blessings. . . . I used those hours of quiet to sort choices, to foresee the years that remained me. If I were to prevail, it would be through suffering.

Small ironies are evident. Whether to laugh or to cry is a delightful toss up. From, **"Earnest Money":** "'You want to shack up?' I asked, surprising myself. . . . 'You'll be sorry,' was all she answered." Characters are treated sympathetically, and their development is constructed from life's common threads. The personal becomes the public, and we are all better off for the tie.

Although there are too many articles and essays (more than 40) in the nonfiction collection *Paper Trail,* the reach and variety of the publications they were originally published in is impressive. How many writers can claim credits in *The Georgia Review* and *TV Guide*? With so many articles, it is difficult to connect with section themes, such as "Rites of Passage," and "Family Occasions." Fewer is always better with quality writers. Better still to be left wanting than saturated.

Still the effort is worthwhile. Dorris' prowess as a top-level cultural scholar shines in **"The Grass Still Grows, The Riv-**

ers Still Flow: Contemporary Native Americans." Dorris describes the destructive Dawes Act of 1887 as a set point in native culture.

> Thus, in one stroke of the pen, almost one-half of all the lands controlled by Indians in 1885 were declared "surplus" and passed out of native control.

Dorris' passion for children is evident in stories written from that tender reservoir he drew upon in **Broken Cord.** In the **"Power of Love,"** he tries to seek closure of his son Abel's death.

> Spontaneous and direct, love was his true power, the reaction he inspired in others, and love, for those who knew him or read about him or benefitted— without ever realizing the source—from the essence of his life, is his legacy.

Here, in the wise vision of one of our most compelling writers, you will find the breath and richness of current American culture, from children's rights to multiculturalism. As Dorris writes in **"Maintaining a Home,"** "In contemporary America, where we come from is rarely our ultimate destination."

Pam Houston (review date 16 February 1997)

SOURCE: "The Ventriloquist," in *Los Angeles Times Book Review,* February 16, 1997, p. 13.

[*In the following review of* Cloud Chamber, *Houston concentrates on Dorris's storytelling technique.*]

Michael Dorris' new novel, **Cloud Chamber,** confirms everything I suspected after reading **A Yellow Raft in Blue Water:** that he is one of the true masters of voice, of character and of storytelling in contemporary American literature. As comfortable in the voice of a consumptive teenage girl as he is in the voice of a black waiter in a German officers' club, as at home with the Irish landscape as he is with rural Kentucky and Montana's Great Plains, Dorris weaves five generations, at least that many ethnicities and three times that many locales into a cohesive and satisfying narrative— made all the more satisfying by its vastness and scope.

Cloud Chamber is a novel that begins in a pub in turn-of-the-century Ireland and ends up in a Kentucky Fried Chicken near Harve, Mont. Dorris moves the narrative from generation to generation and from place to place as smoothly and effortlessly as if he had a time machine. Each narrator's voice (there are eight in all) remains utterly distinct from the oth-

ers', most of them quite lovable, a few a little horrifying, each one fascinating, sympathetic and true.

> **Michael Dorris' new novel, *Cloud Chamber,* confirms everything I suspected after reading *A Yellow Raft in Blue Water:* that he is one of the true masters of voice, of character and of storytelling in contemporary American literature.**
> **—*Pam Houston***

The story opens in the voice of Rose Mannion, a fiery black-haired young woman from Roscommon County, Ireland, who fights on the side of the nationalists and calls herself a force to behold. Her mother dead from an English soldier's stray bullet, her father and brothers arrested before they can exact revenge, Rose falls in love with a leader in the movement called Gerry Lynch, and when he admits to her that he's a traitor, working on the side of the English, she makes love to him for hours, the next day gives him up to the nationalists, watches him hang and has a table made from the branch on which he hung.

That's just the first chapter, and in the chapters that follow, we hear the voices of all those whose lives Rose touches, all the lives she ruins to make up for the sadness in her own. First is Martin, the man Rose forces to marry her and take her away from Ireland and to Kentucky. Next is their son Robert, who marries a woman so like Rose that his only chance for escape is to get beaten so badly he loses his memory and then gets consumption ("I was being consumed," he says). Then Robert's wife Bridie speaks, and we hear about her plan to destroy him by the inconsistent denial of affection, making him settle each day for a little bit less.

Each of these characters, all of these places, come to life in the lovely precision of Dorris' prose. Rose describes Gerry Lynch in her door-frame—the stand of sunlight hair, the wild growth of reeds in a windstorm—and later, when she reveals Gerry's secret, Martin describes her: Her witness was unwilling, scraped out of her like a clam from its shell. Her pain was a living thing, embarrassing in its nakedness. When Bridie discusses her decision to marry Robert even though she is in love with his brother Andrew, the priest, she says of herself: "I would in 10 years find myself mired in a droning job, a woman forced to take pride in her appearance since no one else did, a woman who talked about her success with African violets, a woman standoffish, odd, furious. Alone with her secret memories."

Bridie's daughters, Marcella and Edna, take the story from there into the middle of the 20th century, into a racist South and into sanitariums, into convents and abortion clinics. They are as different, these two sisters, as their parents were from each other. Marcella lies on the sanitarium sun porch in her quilted satin robe flirting with the delivery boy and making a list called "Why I Am Nevertheless a Fortunate Person," while Edna faces her illness dead on and flirts only with the idea of a vocation. But by the thick and rich middle of *Cloud Chamber,* these sisters manage to come together in a way their parents and grandparents could never have hoped to, and with their love for life and each other they begin to turn their legacy of anger and hatred around.

Marcella and Edna pass the narrative on to Elgin, Marcella's only son, and he passes it on to Rayona, his only daughter, where it comes to rest five generations from where it started, near Harve, Mont., where part-black, part-Indian Rayona is about to take her Irish great-grandmother Rose's name, in a tribal naming ceremony that by her Aunt Ida's design breaks all the traditional rules.

Anyone who loved *A Yellow Raft in Blue Water* will be delighted by Ida and Rayona's return at the end of *Cloud Chamber.* Rayona is back and better than ever, and Dorris outdoes himself with her voice, which is precisely the right combination of hope and humor, of streetwise sarcasm and against-all-odds optimism, of a die-hard desire—intoxicating, free.

"The mountains are blue dreams, in a row of sideways right angles at the edge of the valley. The air smells green and yellow, and the only sound is the eight little wheels beneath me, whirling on their new Singapore bearings, standing at the asphalt. The sun is behind me so my shadow goes ahead, leading the way, and in a shadow I look good—graceful and long, bigger than myself, a shifting pattern on the grayness of the road. In shadow I could be anybody, fill-in-the-blank-anybody. In shadow I'm the dancing, flickering image of an overhead cloud whizzing across the lane, going anywhere fast, wherever the wind blows."

The characters in *Cloud Chamber* rise by degrees, each generation a little more free from the bitterness of the past, and though Rayona's life is no easier than Rose's, no freer of tragedy and pain, she has inside her every good thing her rainbow coalition of relatives has passed down to her, and in spite of everything, Rayona is going to be OK.

In *Cloud Chamber,* Dorris tells the American story of hard people leading difficult lives with as much courage, insight and allowance for complexity as anyone writing today. And when he turns those lives away from the darkness and toward all that is joyful, all that is redemptive, he does it so deftly, so softly and yet so completely that I am left speechless, cheering and crying at the same time.

Sandra Scofield (review date 2 March 1997)

SOURCE: "Michael Dorris Explores the Power of Family," in *Chicago Tribune,* March 2, 1997, p. 6.

[*In the review of* Cloud Chamber *below, Scofield comments on Dorris's vision of community.*]

Readers who remember the quiet power of Michael Dorris' novel, *A Yellow Raft in Blue Water,* will be delighted with this related but nonsequential follow-up [*Cloud Chamber*]. Dorris has gone back in time to trace the paternal family of one of the earlier characters, the half-Indian, half-black Rayona. The result is a story of five generations, beginning in beautiful, strife-torn West Ireland. It is a thoroughly absorbing novel remarkable for its lyricism, compassion, humor and thumping good story, all characteristics one has come to expect of the author's work. To my mind, *Cloud Chamber* is his best yet.

The novel is constructed in a fashion familiar to fans of Dorris and of his wife, Louise Erdrich. They have repeatedly explained that they view the concept of the "central character" as too constrained, and that family and community are the core interests of their work. Even their non-fiction has developed from this premise.

In Dorris' novel, then, we get a multivocal story that demonstrates that, despite betrayals of family, no one individual is truly independent. Even fourth-generation Elgin, the son of a white mother and black father, who seems to abandon his white past, is brought back to his mother's kin in a charming and moving ending to the novel. The last chapter tiptoes to the edge of sentimentality and laughs at it, as if to say: Somebody ought to envision unity in this deeply divided culture, and it might as well be fun.

The novel begins with Rose Mannion, a fiercely passionate Irish patriot. The force of her will transplants her and her new husband to Kentucky, where her bitterness and harsh loyalties set the whole family's future in motion. She is a wonderful character, deeply flawed, yet deeply sympathetic. Dorris gives us no one with whom we cannot empathize, because, I think, he cannot fail to empathize with anyone who is human.

Rose has two sons, one a priest—her favorite, and doomed—and one a railroad man who marries Bridie, as stubborn and withholding as her mother-in-law. Much of the book is devoted to their two daughters, Edna and Marcella, who contract their father's tuberculosis. Dorris shows us these girls in their youth as they tumble through infatuations that include Edna's sense of religious vocation (a thread that I found curiously cut without resolution, but this is a minor complaint). Marcella finds her great love, Earl Taylor, at the

TB sanitarium, to which he delivers groceries. He fathers her child, Elgin, then goes to war. Dorris gives us a sense of sweeping events, picking the story up and putting it down, switching narrators and decades with artful ease.

The opening chapters in Ireland are elegiac and epic. Then the voices subtly shift into more conventional telling, making the point that Rose Mannion's history is the mythic Genesis of a family tumbled about and bound together by circumstance and passion.

Each speaker has a unique voice, yet each is only part of a whole. Elgin, naturally, is the voice of a contemporary man, denied his black identity by the death of his father in wartime Germany. (All through his childhood, his aunt Edna takes him once a week for a few hours' visit with a black uncle's family. It is heart-rending.) The truth about the father's death is found in a totally unexpected, brilliant twist of narrative, yet once it is revealed, it seems inevitable.

This is a refreshingly moving, deeply decent, lovingly wise novel. Michael Dorris' vision of a new America is one to emulate; I hope he is richly rewarded by the embrace of readers.

Scott Bradfield (review date 16 May 1997)

SOURCE: "Ideals of Community," in *Times Literary Supplement,* May 16, 1997, p. 22.

[*In the following mixed review, Bradfield finds that* Cloud Chamber *"succeeds as a haunting reflection of Michael Dorris's humanitarian concerns; but as a compelling story about believable people, it does not."*]

Both in his work and in his life, Michael Dorris sought to establish whole families out of broken parts. He was one of the first single men in America to raise an adopted child. He consistently gave voice to the reservation-bound Indian culture that produced him. And in his award-winning book, *The Broken Cord,* he called public attention to the difficulties of bringing up a child with foetal alcohol syndrome, a pattern of addiction and abuse which can destroy a family long before it ever gets started. In everything he wrote, he was concerned with the ways people reach out to each other to make an intimate connection. Thus, Dorris's recent suicide robbed everyone (including his friends and children) of a staunch advocate of the ideal of community.

Dorris, like his wife and fellow-novelist, Louise Erdrich, grew up on an Indian reservation. And as with both William Faulkner and Toni Morrison, it was probably his deep sense of racial division that inspired him to write novels about the diffuse nature of American identity. *Cloud Chamber,* his second and last novel, begins in Ireland during the late nineteenth century, and concludes on a Montana Indian reservation more than a hundred years later. As the narrative progresses, a variety of immigrant and native cultures meet and intermingle. Races blend into one another—Black Irish and Afro-American, mulatto and Modoc Indian—until Dorris's vision of America becomes one in which everybody seems to be related to everybody else, whether they like it or not.

The novel's prime mover, Rose Mannion, is a young Connemara woman born into a season of political unrest, who decides to generate some additional turmoil of her own. After conceiving her first son, Andrew, Rose betrays the man she loves to "the Cause", then absconds with another man she doesn't love to America, where they produce a second, and less adored son, Robert. From the first pages, Rose proves one of those indomitable matriarchs who frequent multi-generational sagas. She runs her family with an iron hand, disdains the hard work and fidelity of her tame husband, and buries the memory of her forbidden Irish passion so deep in her heart that nobody else knows it exists.

In *Cloud Chamber,* buried passions run deep; it is only in the superficial world of bad jobs and dirty wars that people never manage to get along. Rose Mannion's descendants survive, endure, and sometimes even prevail, in a series of interwoven stories told from various first-person viewpoints. There is Bridie, the hardworking stenographer who marries Robert, and spends the rest of her life pining for Andrew. There are Bridie's daughters, Marcella and Edna, who while away their youth in TB sanitariums, until Marcella discovers a cure in a love affair with a black grocery-delivery man named Earl. Their son, Elgin, grows up in a house filled with Irish women who love him too much to tell him the truth about his parentage. Elgin departs for Vietnam in order to "find himself", and returns home to marry a Native American woman and produce yet another mixed-race child named Rayona (she is the protagonist of Dorris's first novel, *A Yellow Raft in Blue Water*). America is a big country, and Dorris tries to cover a lot of it.

The publicity surrounding Dorris's recent suicide has made it difficult to judge his last novel. For, while Dorris's intentions here are noble, and many of his passages eloquent and convincing, *Cloud Chamber* as whole doesn't come off. Primarily this is because all of its voices (from turn-of-the-century farm-girls to roller-blading contemporary teens) sound the same—earnest, vague and sentimental. Eventually, the entire narrative blends together into a rather indistinguishable murkiness, and too many potentially compelling scenes become mired in introspection. The novel succeeds as a haunting reflection of Michael Dorris's humanitarian concerns; but as a compelling story about believable people, it does not.

FURTHER READING

Biography

Lyman, Rick. "Troubling Death Brings Plea for Respect, not Sensation." *New York Times* (18 April 1997): A14.
Interview with Dorris's estranged wife, Louise Erdrich, who reveals that the author had battled with depression and suicidal thoughts for over a decade.

Streitfield, David. "Writer Was Suspected of Child Abuse." *Washington Post* (16 April 1997): D1.
Overview of Dorris's last years of life, including speculation as to the cause of his suicide and statements from friends defending him against child abuse charges.

Criticism

Flynn, Chick. Review of *Morning Girl,* by Michael Dorris. *The Bloomsbury Review* (October-November 1992): 23.
Flynn praises Dorris's *Morning Girl.*

Graham, Philip "Among the Professions" *Chicago Tribune Books* (24 October 1993): 6.
Review of Michael Dorris's *Working Men,* which Graham praises, describing it as an "honest, engaging collection."

Gundy, Jeff. "Can White Guys Write?" *The Georgia Review* XLIX, No. 2 (Summer 1995): 523-36.
Review of *Paper Trail,* admiring how Dorris "moves from the popular to the academic, from the intimate to the public, with an ease that makes him seem the sort of man we should cherish as an advisor, a teacher, even a friend."

Khader, Jamil. "Post Colonial Nativeness: Nomadism, Cultural Memory, and the Politics of Identity in Louise Erdrich's and Michael Dorris's *The Crown of Columbus.*" *Ariel: A Review of International English Literature* 28, No. 2 (April 1997): 81-101.
Investigates the "problematization of identity production" in *The Crown of Columbus.*

Lee, A. Robert. "Margins at the Center." *American Book Review* 16, No. 5 (December-February 1994-1995): 19.
Faults Dorris's storytelling techniques in *Working Men.*

Additional coverage of Dorris's life and career is contained in the following sources published by Gale: *Bestsellers,* 90:1; *Contemporary Authors,* Vol. 102; *Contemporary Authors New Revision Series,* Vols. 19 and 46; *DISCovering Authors Modules: Multicultural Authors* and *Novelists*; *Native North American Literature*; and *Something about the Author,* Vol. 75.

Allen Ginsberg

1926-1997

American poet, essayist, playwright, and nonfiction writer.

For further information on Ginsberg's life and career, see *CLC,* Volumes 1, 2, 3, 4, 6, 13, 36, and 69.

INTRODUCTION

A founder of the Beat movement, Allen Ginsberg is one of the most noted and popular poets of post-war America. His most famous poem, "Howl" (1956), is a post-modern classic. Born in Newark, New Jersey, in 1926, Ginsberg grew up in the same neighborhood as poet William Carlos Williams, who would later write the introduction to "Howl." Ginsberg's father, Louis, taught high school literature and published lyrical poetry. His mother, Naomi, a Russian immigrant committed to the Communist cause, suffered from mental illness. Ginsberg attended Columbia University where he met Jack Kerouac, William S. Burroughs and Neal Cassady, with whom he would later form the Beat movement. Ginsberg's social dissent began at this time and continued throughout his lifetime. In the 1950s he moved to San Francisco to take part in the counter-culture movement. In October 1955 Ginsberg gave a public recital of "Howl," impressing critics and establishing himself as a noteworthy voice of his generation. The poem became a success with the public after the government charged that it was pornographic; a judge ruled in favor of Ginsberg. In "Howl," Ginsberg established the traits which he would continue to develop throughout his lifetime: his candor, his focus on sexuality, particularly homosexuality, and his non-traditional writing style. One of Ginsberg's most famous poems, "Kaddish" (1958), centers on his mother's life and mental illness. Loosely patterned on a traditional Jewish prayer, the poem established Ginsberg as a Jewish writer. Critics often compare Ginsberg to Walt Whitman, largely because both poets emphasized the interdependency of political and sexual freedom. While some critics praised Ginsberg's unstructured form and controversial subject matter, others considered his skill overestimated, arguing that Ginsberg won his fame through his behavior, such as political protests, the advocacy of drug use and homosexuality, poetry readings, and collaboration with rock bands. Ginsberg continued to write until his death on April 5, 1997, in New York City.

PRINCIPAL WORKS

*Howl and Other Poems (poetry) 1956
*Siesta in Xbalva and Return to the States (poetry) 1956

Kaddish and Other Poems, (poetry) 1958-1960
Empty Mirror: Early Poems (poetry) 1961
The Change (poetry) 1963
Reality Sandwiches: 1953-1960 (poetry) 1963
The Yage Letters [with William Burroughs] (letters) 1963
Kral Majales (poetry) 1965
Wichita Vortex Sutra (poetry) 1966
TV Baby Poems (poetry) 1967
Airplane Dreams: Compositions from Journals (poetry) 1968
Ankor Wat (poetry) 1968
The Heat is a Clock (poetry) 1968
Message II (poetry) 1968
Planet News (poetry) 1968
Scrap Leaves, Tasty Scribbles (poetry) 1968
Wales—A Visitation, July 29, 1967 (poetry) 1968
For the Soul of the Planet is Wakening . . . (poetry) 1970
Indian Journals: March 1962-May 1963; Notebooks, Diary, Blank Pages, Writings (journals and diary) 1970
Notes after an Evening with William Carlos Williams (nonfiction) 1970
The Moments Return: A Poem (poetry) 1970

Ginsberg's Improvised Poetics (poetry) 1971

Bisxby Canyon Ocean Path Word Breeze (poetry) 1972

Iron Horse (poetry) 1972

Kaddish (play) 1972

New Year Blues (poetry) 1972

Open Head (poetry) 1972

The Fall of America: Poems of These States, 1965-1971 (poetry) 1973

The Gates of Wrath: Rhymed Poems, 1948-1952 (poetry) 1973

The Visions of the Great Rememberer (letters) 1974

Allen Verbatim: Lectures of Poetry, Politics, and Consciousness (lectures) 1975

Chicago Trial Testimony (nonfiction) 1975

First Blues: Rags, Ballads, and Harmonium Songs, 1971-1974 (poetry) 1975

Sad Dust Glories: Poems during Work Summer in Woods, 1974 (poetry) 1975

To Eberhart from Ginsberg (letters) 1976

Journals: Early Fifties, Early Sixties (journals) 1977

Careless Love: Two Rhymes (poetry) 1978

Mind Breaths: Poems, 1972-1977 (poetry) 1978

Mostly Sitting Haiku (poetry) 1978; revised and expanded, 1979

Poems All over the Place: Mostly Seventies (poetry) 1978

Plutonian Ode (poetry) 1982

Collected Poems: 1947-1980 (poetry) 1984

White Shroud: Poems, 1980-1985 (poetry) 1986

The Hydrogen Jukebox (play) 1990

Snapshot Poetics (poetry) 1993

Cosmopolitan Greetings: Poems 1986-1992 (poetry) 1995

Selected Poems 1947-1995 (poetry) 1996

*This work was also published in a revised edition as *Howl: Original Draft Facsimile, Transcript and Variant Versions* in 1986.

INTERVIEWS

Allen Ginsberg with Matthew Rothschild (interview date August 1994)

SOURCE: "Allen Ginsberg: 'I'm Banned from the Main Marketplace of Ideas in My Own Country.'," in *The Progressive,* Vol. 58, No. 8, August, 1994, pp. 34-39.

[*In the following interview, Ginsberg discusses censorship of his works, politics, and his reaction to fame.*]

I arrived at Allen Ginsberg's apartment on the lower east side of Manhattan at noon on April 15, two months before his sixty-eighth birthday. The Beat poet, icon of the 1960s counterculture, gay pioneer, had just published a new book of poetry, **Cosmopolitan Greetings,** almost forty years since he shattered the poetry scene with **"Howl."** I wanted to talk to him about his latest work and his current political views.

The narrow passageway leading into Ginsberg's small living room was clogged with equipment from a WGBH/BBC crew that was there to interview Ginsberg for a film on the history of rock-'n'-roll. I'd been told ahead of time that he'd be doing other interviews that afternoon, so I sat on a small squishy futon under the sole window and looked around. A framed and illustrated copy of Blake's "The Tyger" was at the entranceway. A large bookshelf stood against one wall, with an oversized volume about Lenin lurking on top. Poetry filled the top two shelves, and then nonfiction, including *Citizen Cohn,* and *J. Edgar Hoover,* and Edward Herman's and Noam Chomsky's *Manufacturing Consent.* Tapes of Bob Dylan and CDs of John Trudell, along with videos (*The Panama Deception*) gathered on another bookshelf.

After about half an hour, Ginsberg came out of his tiny bedroom. He was dressed in a deep blue shirt, gray slacks, black slip-on shoes, and a red-and-black tie. He introduced himself to me, and then engaged the film makers. They wanted his recollections of meeting Bob Dylan and John Lennon, so he dutifully performed in his kitchen through numerous takes as the film crew fidgeted with the sound and the light—a process that took about two hours. A framed, if slipping, portrait of Walt Whitman hung on one wall, along with a print of St. Francis in Ecstasy. On the refrigerator, next to low-fat food lists and Buddhist chants, was a leaflet: TEENAGERS! TIRED OF BEING HARASSED BY YOUR STUPID PARENTS? ACT NOW. MOVE OUT, GET A JOB, PAY YOUR OWN BILLS . . . WHILE YOU STILL KNOW EVERYTHING.

As the film crew was cleaning up, Ginsberg and I retreated to his bedroom for the interview, Buddhist shrine next to the bed, writing table nearby, and bookshelf of poetry at the front. Ginsberg was alternately impassioned and professional, even occasionally disputatious as he resisted being labeled a political poet. There was one magical moment when he took down an old hardback copy of Whitman and started to read passages he had marked up. Halfway through the interview, Ginsberg broke to go upstairs in his building to Philip Glass's apartment to work with the composer on a memorial for a mutual friend who had died of AIDS. When Ginsberg returned, we talked for two more hours, and I left exhausted at 6:30 in the evening.

[*Rothschild*]: *In* **Cosmopolitan Greetings,** *you have a phrase, "radioactive anticommunism." What do you mean by that?*

[Ginsberg]: Well, the bomb was built up beyond the Japanese war as a bulwark against communism. The extremist anticommunism went in for mass murder in El Salvador and assassination in the Congo, when we killed Lumumba and put in Mobutu. The military extremism was not much help in overthrowing communism, except maybe in bankrupting both sides, but that only left the communist countries helpless when they switched over to the free market.

But beyond that I think as much was done to subvert Marxist authoritarian rule by Edgar Allan Poe, blue jeans, rock-'n'-roll, Bob Dylan, the Beatles, modern American poetry, and Kerouac's *On the Road*—that was more effective in subverting the dictatorship and the brainwash there than all the military hoopla that cost us the nation, actually.

Why did these works undermine communism?

The authoritarian mind—Maoist, Hitler, Stalinist, monotheist, Ayatollahist, fundamentalist—shares a fear and hatred of sexual libertarianism, fear of free-association spontaneity, rigid control over thought forms and propaganda, fear of avant-garde and experimental art. The Stalinist word for this kind of avant-garde is "elitist individualism" or "subjectivism"; the Nazi word was "degenerate art"; the Maoist word was "spiritual corruption"; the fundamentalist word is "spiritual corruption and degenerate art"; the Jesse Helms argument is why should the average American taxpayer have to pay for this "elitist individualistic filth"? It's exactly what Stalin used to say: "Why should the Russian people have to pay for the avant-garde to display their egocentric individualism and immorality and not follow the Communist Party line?"

The whole authoritarian set of mind depends on suppression of individual thought, suppression of eccentric thought, suppression of inerrancy in the interpretation of the Bible, or of Marx, or *Mein Kampf,* or Mao's *Little Red Book* in favor of mass thought, mass buzz words, party lines. They all want to eliminate or get rid of the alien, or the stranger, or the Jews, or the gays, or the Gypsies, or the artists, or whoever are their infidels. And they're all willing to commit murder for it, whether Hitler or Stalin or Mao or the Ayatollah, and I have no doubt that if Rush Limbaugh or Pat Robertson or Ollie North ever got real power, there would be concentration camps and mass death. There already are in the police-state aspect of the "war on drugs."

In one of your new poems, you mention your frustration that Jesse Helms and the FCC have banned your works from the airwaves except during the wee hours of the morning. How did that happen?

As part of the totalitarian political-correctness mind-control movement on the fundamentalist Right, the makers of beer, Coors, funded the Heritage Foundation, which presented a position paper and the legal technical language for Jesse Helms, who is subsidized by the tobacco interests, to direct the FCC to forbid all so-called indecent language from the air twenty-four hours a day. It passed in October 1988 when the Senate was empty, and was signed by Reagan. I found out about it because there was a column in *The Village Voice* by Nat Hentoff in which the head of the Pacifica stations said they used to play my poetry quite a lot but now it was controversial—not that they didn't like it, not that it wasn't popular, but they were afraid it would be too expensive to defend in court. They couldn't afford an argument for free speech. So I helped organize a consortium of the Emergency Civil Liberties Committee, Harvey Silverglate, the then-head of the ACLU in Massachusetts, the Rabinowitz and Boudin law firm, and William Burroughs, myself, and the PEN club as friends of the court, and we helped bust the law.

You won?

Well, we won once. The FCC was directed to hold hearings as to whether or not it was legitimate to reduce the entire population of America to the level of minors, because the law was supposedly to protect the ears of minors. They agreed to define minors as eighteen, eliminating youth, teenyboppers—everybody's a minor now. The FCC came up with a homemade prejudiced thing, saying, "OK, the ban's not for twenty-four hours, it's only from 6:00 A.M. to midnight. And you can have sort of open passage, midnight to 6:00 A.M., when nobody is listening, for your art, your poetry, and your filthy books."

Then I participated in a roundtable discussion at an FCC lawyers' convention with James Quello, the oldest member on the FCC, and Quello pulled out a copy of **"Howl,"** and said, "This is a perfectly good poem you could broadcast on the air—all you have to do is eliminate a couple paragraphs." That was his idea of art! It was like a Soviet bureaucrat's statement. There's no difference between that Stalinist bureaucratic mentality and what's going on with these fundamentalist bureaucrats.

So we took it to court again. And the court said there was not sufficient proper scientific sociological investigation of when the kids were listening, but that it might be legitimate to protect their ears. So the FCC made it from 6:00 A.M. to 8:00 P.M. And that's being fought in court still on constitutional grounds.

How does this censorship affect you?

I'm a poet who specializes in oral recitation and performance. I am pleased that my work is good on the page—it should be solid on the page—but there is a dimension of sound, which Ezra Pound emphasized. I'm a specialist in that, I'm very good at vocalization, I'm famous for that around the world, and yet I'm banned from the "main marketplace of ideas" in my own country—radio, television, and God knows what they can do when the FCC gets a hold of the information highway. That means the entire brainwash is all under the control of the FCC so that "who got fucked in the ass by handsome sailors and screamed with joy" will be banned from electronic media. People don't read as much these decades but they hear. Like John Lennon heard my poetry on radio before he read it and was moved by it. That means that a main avenue that I would have for articulation of my own thinking, my own ideas, whether social or political or aesthetic, is closed off.

Do you see the Far Right gaining power in the United States?

They have power. They've got control of television now; they've censored television and radio. They already have power. You've already accomplished your censorship of the media, and intimidated them as well as legally censoring them. You got it. You have this organized gang of listeners who will write in at the drop of a hat—you know, they'll say, "Write in and denounce this or that politician, or this or that abortion, or this or that poem," then bam, you've got it. They mobilize all these relatively innocent people to be writing in denouncing art. It's demagoguery, and the media caved in to it.

One of my favorite poems in **Cosmopolitan Greetings** *is "After the Big Parade"—about the American public's reactions to Bush's Iraq war. Were you actually at one of those parades here?*

I was down in the parade with a tiny group of people protesting it in front of City Hall. There was a group of maybe ten people amid the millions that were out there under the confetti, and the bunting, and the bands, and the police.

How did the crowd respond to you?

They ignored us, or they threatened us. So I saw it first hand, the mob hysteria, as in the old Roman mob. And then within two days the entire enthusiasm had evaporated, and within a few months, people realized more and more that the Iraq war was one of the most successful instances of brainwashing ever turned out by Madison Avenue and Government— by control of the airwaves and mass-media censorship.

In hindsight, people realize that they were taken in, that alternative views weren't presented, and that in order to present this war as heroic, you had to ignore some very obvious things—like the fact that we were building up Saddam Hussein until the very day that we bombed him, and that we had played one gang against another in the Iran-Iraq war. In a way, we were responsible for the whole Middle East

situation. We had overthrown Mossadegh, as I've got in my poem, **"Just Say Yes Calypso."** Norman Schwarzkopf's father was directly involved in the overthrow of Mossadegh and the training of the Savak. People weren't aware of that. People thought Schwarzkopf was some sort of country bumpkin from the Midwest who got to be general rather than a sophisticated Persian-speaking son of a man who trained the Shah's secret police.

So it was some kind of American karma we were bombing, and people weren't really aware of the historical relevance of the land they were bombing, that this was the Garden of Eden we were bombing, the land of Ur and Abraham. And they didn't realize in a way that it was child molestation, because the average age of Iraqis at the time was only sixteen. The people being bombed were kids!

Trying to concentrate all that information into rhymed stanzas takes ingenuity, and interest, and curiosity. I think it's a really good poem because it's totally understated and it's a fact. "Have they forgotten the corridors of death?"—which was the boastful phrase that was used when we bombed the Iraqis. And "Will another hundred thousand desert deaths across the world be cause for the next rejoicing?" is a strangely sardonic compassionate touch—I don't know where I got that tone. It's not Pound; it might be Herman Melville's poetry. Melville has some thing like this in his poem, "On the Slain Collegians," who rushed into the battle and perished, "enlightened by the volleyed glare."

The specter of AIDS is in many of the poems in your latest work. How has the AIDS plague affected you?

There's this decimation of genius, particularly in theater and film and music and poetry. One of the greatest modern poems is called "Ward 7," written by Jim Dlugos, who was dying of AIDS. It's one of the most humane, heartfelt, sincere poems I've ever read. It's one of the great poems of this part of the century. So there's been a lot of loss.

My taste tends to be for young men and straight young men, so in a way in the early days of AIDS that sort of kept me a little bit safe. Now I'm very careful. It hasn't affected me all that much in terms of my love life, though lately I must say I'm getting older, I'm less successful in bedding young men and young straight men. And I like to be screwed, or screw, but I can't get it up anymore anyway (because of diabetes and other things that I mention in this book) unless there's a great deal of stimulation and rapport and real interest, so I'm not inclined to screw anybody because it's hard and I'd be a little scared to be screwed--though with people that I know real well and I know their situation and their history and have been tested, I wouldn't mind. But I don't know anyone that I like that well or that likes me enough to get it up.

Even in these days of AIDS, you're like the last apostle of desire. You still celebrate sex.

Safe sex is just as good as unsafe sex. And with safe sex you get something which I always liked anyway—you have these long pillow talks about what you're going to do with each other, how you're going to make love to each other, what you should do, and what you want to do, and who's going to be on top, and who's going to be on the bottom. You have a chance to talk it over if you're verbal at all, and that's fun because it's like opening up your secret recesses of desire to each other.

You seem to suggest that there's something not only human but liberating about sex.

I think it is. I always remember Kerouac saying, "Woe to those who deny the unbelievable joy of sexual love." The joy, the exquisite joy. I've found sexual communication to be one of the most thrilling and exquisite experiences in my life. With people I love, all shame is gone, everybody is naked, as Hart Crane said, "confessions between coverlet and pillow." And I think the best teaching is done in bed also, by the way, as did Socrates. It is an old tradition: transmission in bed, transmission of information, of virtue. I think Whitman thought so, Whitman pointed out that "adhesiveness" between the citizens was the necessary glue that kept democracy from degenerating into rivalry, competition, backbiting, dog-eat-dog. I think that's true. One of the problems of the Reagan-Bush era was the lack of cohesiveness, the competition, the rivalry, the Darwinian dog-eat-dog, which fed egocentricity, exploitation, and cruelty and indifference and left three million people out on the streets homeless.

Are you hopeful about the lesbian and gay rights movement in the United States?

Oh, sure. Everybody's gay in one way or another. "Everybody's got a big dong." Everybody's sexualized, and everybody's sex is somewhat repressed, and no one can really do any fingerpointing anymore. Everybody's a freak, so to speak, and I think people understand that. Certainly the younger generation does. I mean how long can you keep it secret that Cardinal Spellman was a flaming queen? How long can you keep it secret that J. Edgar Hoover was a transvestite blackmailed by the Mafia? How long can you keep it secret that Jesse Helms is overobsessed with homosexuality and is politically addicted to alcohol and tobacco interests? Even the press is sooner or later going to catch up with the hype.

What is the hype? The hype is hypocrisy, double standard, people coming on in public less intelligent than they are in private—say on something like marijuana. Everybody knows that marijuana is more or less harmless, but they won't say it in public. Everybody except maybe some crazed fundamentalists has smoked some grass or knows someone who's smoked some grass.

There's a schizophrenia between private knowledge and public knowledge. On sex, there's a schizophrenia between what people do in private and the way they talk in public. There's a schizophrenia about stimulants. A schizophrenia about politics: The contradictions are so big that it's a kind of public schizophrenia that people aren't in on what, say, the CIA in-group knows. The public never knows what the consequences of the hidden deals are. No one knows the ecological consequences or the political cause or consequences of an H-bomb, a Lumumba assassination, a Panama invasion—and the Government is supposed to be a democracy. That's schizophrenia.

Schizophrenia is no way to run a government or a society. You can't have a schizophrenic society without the results we're seeing: pollution of the air, pollution caused by conspicuous consumption, the very schizophrenia of thinking that we can continue to consume the vast amounts of raw material that we do disproportionate to our population, and saying everyone should aspire to be like us. If everybody were like us, the Earth would burn out overnight.

What's your assessment of President Clinton so far?

Bush was pretty much a sourpuss, a depressed and depressing person. I think Clinton is much more cheerful; I think that's always a help. I don't know that he can climb out of a pit that Reagan and Bush have dug in terms of national debt and exhaustion of national resources. But I like his attitude and I like his attempt to do something—I like his trying to do something about health, trying to do something about gays in the military. So I think he's a better person in terms of being more honest and inquisitive. At least he had the amusement to put a stick of grass between his lips. He's dealt with some real problems—like health, smoking, and ecology—which were being avoided or even subverted by Reagan and Bush.

In the book, you have a couple of criticisms of 1960s activists. New Leftists—"peace protesters angrier than war's cannonball noises," and you talk about "the scandal of the '60s"—people carrying pictures of Mao and Che and Castro.

It seems to me that the extreme one-dimensional politics of the New Left—which had no spiritual or adhesive element or direction but relied on "rising up angry" rage, which was considered by some to be the necessary gasoline or fuel for political action—was a great psychological mistake. Any gesture made in anger is going to create more anger. Any gesture coming from rage and resentment creates more rage and resentment. Any gesture taken in equanimity will create more equanimity. The 1968 Chicago police riot was, after all, to some extent provoked by the attitude, behavior, and propaganda of some of the members of the New Left, who had promised a Festival of Light but delivered an angry protest. The original Yippie idea, as announced, was to have a festival that would be cheerful, affirmative, ecologically sound, and generous emotionally sound, and generous emotionally so that it would outshadow the "Death Convention" of Johnson's war.

Before the Chicago thing, Jerry Rubin came over to my house, and I wanted reassurance that he didn't have any intention of starting a riot. I didn't want any blood. He swore, "not at this time." I should have suspected it then and there, but actually I do think unconsciously or consciously some wanted to precipitate an "exemplary" riot.

The result of the riot was to knock out Humphrey. And then many Leftists out of their hatred of Humphrey and their parents and their liberal middle-class background refused to vote and dropped out and so Nixon squeaked in by half a million votes. Millions of people didn't vote on the Left, angry at Johnson and his war, angry at Humphrey for going along (although everybody knew that Humphrey wanted to end the war, but it was just this totalitarian insistence on having it your way, the way you wanted to end the war, the method you wanted to end the war, rather than let the war decline in a way that was politically possible). In 1968, the Gallup Poll reported that 52 percent of the American people thought the war was a mistake. The question is, how come the Left could not lead America out of the war when the middle class was already disillusioned? I think it was because they were threatening the middle class with anger, because one motto was KILL YOUR PARENTS or BRING THE WAR HOME. They weren't leading the middle class, they weren't providing space for the middle class to change, they were threatening the middle class.

The Left, by not voting, let Nixon in. The Left, by discrediting the Democrats, let Nixon in. And once Nixon got in, the war got much worse—the bombing was escalated beyond the imagination of Johnson and Kennedy, the bankruptcy of the Treasury and the moral bankruptcy was escalated way beyond anyone's imagination.

It doesn't mean that the Left was wrong. The antiwar stance was correct. It's just that the method, which involved aggression and anger, was an unskillful means. The blood of the Vietnamese from 1968 on rests primarily on the right-wing conservatives and the Nixonites, but there is some blood on the Left for their ineptness in politics. That's what I meant by speeches "angrier than war's cannonball noises." It was

the mistake of waving a Viet Cong flag—and half the people who did it were FBI agents anyway. In New York City, I remember parades being taken over by extremists, who later turned out to be FBI provocateurs. People don't realize the enormity of the infiltration of the Left by the FBI in the form of extremist provocation, which the neurotics of the Left went along with thinking it was more macho, holier than thou, "more revolutionary than thou."

To what extent does your Buddhism contribute to this attitude of yours about the need for equanimity?

The original Beat idea was a spiritual change, an attitudinal change, a change of consciousness. Then, once having achieved some reform of one's own, begin with yourself and work outward. Not quite Buddhist, but Eastern thought and "Beatnik" thought is pacifistic.

Do you consider yourself a pacifist?

Well. I haven't found a war I liked yet.

You write in one of your new poems about being offended as a Jew at violent Zionists. What was your reaction to the Hebron massacre?

The extremism among the Jews refusing land for peace and insisting upon that piece of dirt being theirs—you know, fighting over a piece of ground—seems to me to be some kind of awful chauvinism, creating a karma that may never end, like the Irish-English fight. Who knows where it will end now? They've started a circle of violence that may never finish until Armageddon.

You say in one of the new poems that "all the spiritual groups scandal the shrine room."

That's true, especially the monotheist religions. By their very nature, the Jews, the Christians, and the Islamic people claim that they're talking for God. As a Buddhist I don't even believe in God, much less talking for Him if there were one. But all these guys have the *chutzpah* or the brass or the egocentric anthropomorphic totalitarian idea that they are the mouthpiece of God. The Ayatollah could tell Salman Rushdie to get killed, or the reactionary Israelis can say the Arabs are inferior, the Christians can create a holocaust. That's why I wrote "Stand up against governments, against God"—the monotheist domination of consciousness that insists on its own party line.

What is your assessment of the state of poetry, or political poetry, right now?

I myself don't believe in so-called political poetry. I think what a poet does is he "writes his mind." And like everybody else, his mind is concerned with sex, dope, and every-day living, politics included, whatever his experience is, so the personal experience of the poet will differ from the media representation of reality. As far as I'm concerned, my interest in poetry is in representing my actual mind as distinct from the official party line of the media, which is to say, *The New York Times, The Washington Post,* even *The Nation,* and from the official party line of the White House and the Establishment.

So, private experience is different from the way it's recorded in the newspapers and on television. We have our own real worlds, and then there's the pseudo-event of newspapers. As Pound says, "Poetry is news that stays news," which is our actual emotions, our feelings, thoughts—Kerouac said "the unspeakable visions of the individual."

The subject matter is the nature of my consciousness, and the texture of my consciousness, and what passes through my mind spontaneously, not what immediate effect can I have on PR or public politics or day-to-day polemics.

Yet more than almost any poet in the mid-century and the late-century, you've written in your poems about America.

It's not that I'm specializing in America. I've also written a lot about my sex life, I've also written about my family, and I've also written about food, and I've also written about meditation, and Buddhism—because those are the participating elements of my life, so I write about what I'm involved with. Which is not much different from anybody else. Maybe the Buddhism is a little more specialized and maybe the homosexual content is a little more specialized but everyone has their own sex lives.

There is a strain of contemporary poetry that is shorn of politics, that is hyper-private.

Who? Who? Mine is hyper-private, is what I'm saying. I'm just writing about what I think about privately. I'm amazed that more people don't write about what they actually think about privately, day after day.

I'm not trying to pigeonhole you into this little box called political poetry, which you don't want to be shoved into.

No. I don't mind that, but there's a distinction I'd like to make. I grew up in the '30s and '40s during the controversy between the socialists and the communists and the Trotskyites about political poetry. Now the theory that they laid down, both Stalin and the Maoists, and Hitler for that matter, is that poetry should serve the nation. And Jesse Helms and Pat Robertson also believe this; it's all the same, the dictatorial monotheists from Pat Robertson to Stalin. They all believe that poetry should be moral, defined in their own terms whether serving Christ, or the People, or the Central Committee of the Communist Party—that poetry is the vanguard of the revolution and since the will of the revolution and of the people is represented by the Central Committee of the Communist Party, therefore the poet should take his politics from what the Central Committee says is the proper party line, or what Pat Robertson says the Bible says.

You've got to remember the inheritors of that political Left tradition, the Students for a Democratic Society up to the Weathermen, the New Left, also first disapproved of psychedelics, also disapproved of rock-'n'-roll poetry, also disapproved of individual cock-sucking poetry—you know, and thought that "no, this was not advancing the cause."

The primitive notion of a one-dimensional political poetry, up through Abbie Hoffman, even, maintained dominance over the notion of political poetry, especially reinforced by the poetry of the anti-Vietnam war. So I think it's important to make a distinction between poetry which is (and should be, as far as I'm concerned) Ivory Tower, the politics of which come as a secondary reflection or concomitant potential but not as the central purpose, and the distinction between that and deliberate, intentional . . .

Polemical poetry?

Yeah, but what you're nice enough to call polemical was the basic idea of political poetry all along. "Why aren't you taking responsibility for writing about blah, blah, gays, the blacks, or women?" Still, political correctness, party line. "Is your poem politically correct, Mister Mayakovsky?" That's where that notion, that phrase, political correctness comes from originally, from old Stalinists and Maoists. That still has a minor voice in poetics now, both from the Right and the Left.

If you want to go to the root of things and move people's consciousness, you can't do it in that vulgar or blunderbuss way of the Stalinists of the Left and the Right.

I'm more in the lineage of Poe. Why is Poe interesting? He gives you this sense of paranoia, modern Twentieth Century world paranoia, world nausea, "The Pit and the Pendulum," "The Telltale Heart," "The Descent Into the Maelstrom." He's the first, you could say, psychedelic poet.

Now who was Poe? He was the most Ivory Tower, art for art's sake, beauty for the sake of beauty, isolated, unpolitical poet in the world, yet he penetrates everybody's consciousness all over the world and is the first maybe adult poet prose writer people read from Russia to China to England to America. He has more influence on people's consciousness, and individuating them, and making them conscious of their individuality and their isolation than any other writer, and yet he's the least political.

Dig? I'm addressing myself directly to your question. It turns out that the one who went for the jugular of pure aesthetic beauty is the most politically influential in certain ways in terms of individuating people, empowering people, and making them conscious of themselves as individuals as distinct from members of a mass under hypnotic mass control—whether television or Hitler or American co-optation.

So there is no real distinction between political and unpolitical poetry, and I would advise a poet to avoid politics and get to what is his or her most deeply felt perception or impulse—that's way more politically effective than writing sonnets about the Republicans.

In a way, you seem to claim yourself as Whitman's heir.

I don't claim myself as Whitman's heir. I'm inspired by Whitman, but I wouldn't be so presumptuous. I don't think I'm as good as Whitman at all. He's much more ample. In my last book the Whitman influence is not the famous Whitman of "Song of Myself," but his *Old Age Echoes,* the little gay poems, and the poems talking about "my aches and pains" and all that. Whitman wrote geriatric poems that were quite interesting. There's a poem from *Sands at Seventy:* "As I sit writing here sick and grown old, / Not my least burden is that, dullness of the years, querilities, / Ungracious glooms, aches, lethargy, constipation, whimpering *ennui* / May filter in my daily songs."

Whitman is a very good model for the glooms and the delights of growing old and being energetic, aware, and vigorous and going on toward death, looking back and looking forward.

"Garrulous to the very last," do you know that phrase? "After the supper and talk—after the day is done, / As a friend from friends his final withdrawal prolonging. / Goodbye and goodbye with emotional lips repeating. / (So hard for his hand to release those hands—no more will they meet. / No more for communion of sorrow and joy, of old and young, / A far-stretching journey awaits him, to return no more,) / Shunning, postponing severance—seeking to ward off the last word ever so little, / E'en at the exit door turning— charges superfluous calling back—e'en as he descends the steps, / Something to eke out a minute additional, shadows of nightfall deepening, / Farewells, messages lessening— dimmer the forthgoer's visage and form, / Soon to be lost for aye in the darkness—loth, O so loth to depart! / Garrulous to the very last." It's the last poem of *Sands at Seventy.* Isn't it charming?

In some passages in the latest book, you write that you're bored with fame. Do you ever get tired of being Allen Ginsberg?

No, there's no Allen Ginsberg. It's just a collection of empty atoms.

But in several of your latest poems, you seem to be wrestling with immortality.

No, I'm not wrestling. I'm saying, "Immortality comes later," by definition. It's a joke.

Well, in one poem, you say, "I missed my chance."

For salvation. Artistically I've got it made, but in terms of spiritual salvation, who knows? I certainly haven't taken advantage of all the good teachings I've been given, I must say. Otherwise, I wouldn't see anybody these days, and be on a three-year meditation retreat.

I can understand the need to feel that your life's work was worthwhile, but to feel the need that people will be reading you when you're gone I don't understand. You're not going to be around to enjoy it, anyhow. What's the big deal about immortality?

There's no total immortality. "The sun's not eternal, that's why there's the blues," as I wrote in a previous book. Even the sun goes out. There's "immortal as immortal is," which is temporary. However, it is important if you have the impulse of transmitting dharma or whatever wisdom you've got, writing "so that in black ink my love might still shine bright"—Shakespeare.

There is a Buddhist reason for fame and for immortality, which is that it gives you the opportunity to turn the wheel of dharma while you're alive to a larger mass of sentient beings and after you're dead that your poetry radio continues broadcasting dharmic understanding so that people pick up on it and the benefits of it after you're dead.

In a previous book, I wrote: "While I'm here I'll do the work. And what's the work? To ease the pain of living." You can ease the pain of living for people after you're dead through your art-work by creating a thing of beauty, like Poe, by creating a thing of political understanding, by creating a thing of psychological self-recognition like Walt Whitman, by making the ground safe for gays like Gore Vidal, Burroughs, and Jean Genet, by making the ground safe for straight people like Henry Miller and D. H. Lawrence.

Those works continue raying out wisdom even after the author's gone, and to the extent that your ambition is to relieve the mass of human sufferings, that can be accomplished with art, whether or not the planet survives. Even if it is in extremis, at the edge of death, as an individual or as a planet, there still is the consolation of insight and wisdom that you might get from a work of art that will ease the pain of passing from this life to whatever emptiness comes, and alchemize that sorrow into blissful recognition.

Allen Ginsberg with Gary Pacernick (interview date 10 February 1996)

SOURCE: "Allen Ginsberg: An Interview by Gary Pacernick," in *The American Poetry Review*, Vol. 4, July/August, 1997, pp. 23-27.

[*In the following interview, Ginsberg discusses inspiration and his role in American poetry.*]

[*Pacernick*]: *The tape is on now; this is the beginning.*

[Ginsberg]: "This is the forest primeval, the murmuring pines and the hemlocks, bearded with / moss . . ."

Allen, what have you found the hardest thing about being a poet?

Nothing particular. I mean—nothing particular. No hard part.

Okay.

Making a living at it. Making a living.

Well, what about inspiration? Has it always been easy?

Inspiration comes from the word spiritus. Spiritus means breathing. Inspiration means taking in breath. Expiration means letting breath go out. So inspiration is just a feeling of heightened breath or slightly exalted breath, when the body feels like a hollow reed in the wind of breath. Physical breath comes easily and thoughts come with it. Now that's a state of physical and mental heightening, but it's not absolutely necessary for great poetry. Though you find it's a kind of inspiration, a kind of breathing in Shelley's "Ode to the West Wind" or "Adonais" or Hart Crane's "Atlantis," or perhaps the Moloch section of **"Howl."** But for subject matter, which is what you mean, for ideas, ordinary mind and thoughts that occur every day are sufficient. It's a question of the quality of your attention to your own mind and your own thoughts.

Where does this breath come from that you find in the second part of "Howl," for example?

Well, it's a more excited breathing, longer breath, that you find in the examples that I cited which build sequentially as

a series of breaths until finally there's a kind of conclusive utterance. "Moloch whose name is the Mind."

You talk in the Paris Review *interview and other places about being inspired by Blake reciting "Sunflower."*

An auditory hallucination, hearing it, but that's a different kind of breath, completely. That's a quieter breath from the heart area. Like my voice now rather than the stentorian breath of "Atlantis" or **"Howl."**

So you're not talking about what we usually talk about in terms of prophesy, in terms of some divine voice.

Now wait a minute. You're switching your words now. We were using the word inspiration and voice. Now what are you talking about? What's your question, really?

What is a breath unit?

A breath unit as a measure of the verse line? Why, a breath unit as a measure of the verse line is one breath, and then continuing with the sentence is another breath. Or saying "or" is another breath, and then you take another breath and continue. So you arrange the verse line on the page according to where you have your breath stop, and the number of words within one breath, whether it's long or short, as this long breath has just become.

Okay now, you're talking about great poetry—.

No, no, I'm talking about how you arrange the verse lines on the page by the breath.

No, I understand, but when we were talking about inspiration you used the word breath again.

Because the word inspiration comes from the Latin word spiritus, which means breathing. So I was trying to nail down what the word inspiration means rather than have a vague term that we didn't know what we were talking about.

But to me, and obviously I could be totally off, it sounds like you're talking about poetry as a kind of series of breathing exercises.

Well it is, in a way, or the vocal part, the oral part, is related to the breath, yes.

What inspires the breath?

The breath is inspiration itself. Breath is itself, breath is breath: Where there is life, there is breath, remember? Breath is spirit, spiritus.

So every once in awhile this spirit breath visits you and other poets?

No, you're breathing all the time, it's just that you become aware of your breath. Every once in awhile you become aware that you're alive. Every once in awhile you become aware of your breathing. Or of the whole process of being alive, breathing in the universe, being awake, and so you could say that that's the inspiration or the key, that you become aware of what's already going on.

You probably didn't know this when you were sixteen, eighteen, twenty years old and first writing poetry.

Oh, well, pretty soon. A sort of latent understanding, yeah. That notion of awareness, conscious awareness.

Did Williams or Pound influence this?

Pound and Williams specialized in this. They broke the ground for this kind of thinking. Williams trying to write in vernacular speech and dividing it up into pieces, and dividing the verse line into pieces of vernacular speech, sometimes by counting syllables, sometimes by the breath stop, sometimes by running counter to the breath stop. Do you know what I mean by the breath stop?

You were in Dayton years ago and I was there with my wife and child, and I said to you, "What is a breath unit?" and you were sort of showing me with your hand as I spoke. Charles Olson talks about it. But Pound and Williams don't talk about breath, do they?

Well, it's implicit in what they were doing, because they were talking about actual talk.

I understand.

And measuring the measure—what Williams talks about was an American measure, a measure of actual speech.

Right.

And his disciples like Olson and Creeley drew from that the notion of projective verse or verse by breath or measuring the verse line by where the breath stops.

But we both know that your breaths in "Kaddish" and "Howl" and your other inspired poems are—

Different from somebody else?

Not only different, but so long.

Everybody's is different. Everybody's breath is different. Everybody, like Creeley's is short and minimal, in a way.

Well, it's beyond short and minimal. It's like one one-hundredth of what yours is in some of your longer lines.

Well, sometimes. But on the other hand the poems that are like those, too, like Williams or Pound.

Does that mean, since your line is the longest, that you're the most inspired?

Well, the deepest inspiration, probably, yes, the deepest breath.

So you are, you're literally equating poetic inspiration with breath.

That aspect of it. There's two kinds I said. There is the deep breath, but there is also, in the more common use of the word inspiration, i.e., where do you get your ideas, is also just ordinary mind and ordinary breath, and short breath, too. Ordinary mind means what passes through your mind while you're sitting on the toilet.

But in your poem "Kaddish" you're doing more than that.

But I'm saying there are different kinds of poetry. In "Kaddish" what I'm doing is a longer breath, yes. Then in other poems like in *White Shroud* the poem to William Carlos Williams, "Written in My Dream by W. C. Williams," it's a short breath.

Let's switch it a little bit, then maybe we can come back to that. In "Howl" you affirm the beat lifestyle.

You know, one thing is, you're fixated on poems of thirty, forty years ago. I don't mind talking about them, but in context of a whole curve of poetry up to the present. But go on.

Okay, fine. You affirm the beat lifestyle that often leads to madness and/or death.

I didn't use the word "lifestyle." That's a later sort of media term and I don't like you to use it. I think it's bullshit.

You said "Mad generation! down on the rocks of Time!" A lot of the people, most of the people have died.

Not so. Just the opposite, sir. Just the opposite. You've got it all wrong, inside out. Burroughs is alive at the age of eighty-three and just had a birthday. Huncke just had his birthday in February also, and he's eighty-one. Gary Snyder is in very good health in California and is a world-renowned influence in poetry. Philip Whalen is a Zen master now. I'm doing quite well at Naropa and Brooklyn College and writing poems. Michael McClure is touring with Ray Manzarek. So Kerouac died, Neal Cassady died, and Lou Welsh died. But on the other hand Gregory Corso is living across town. We're all in touch with each other. Ann Waldman has founded the Kerouac School of Poetics at Naropa and John Ashbery and everybody go there, and I go there between terms. So we have a better actuarial span than most insurance people. But you've got the stereotype I'm trying to get away from.

Let's go to "Howl" itself.

As I keep saying, you're fixated on images of that. Anyway, go on.

Well, those people are very unhappy, the people you portray in the poem.

Yes. They were young.

Okay. Let's just say you have survived.

And so have most of my friends.

Where do you draw your strength?

Oh, inspiration. I keep breathing. Also I never drank.

You never drank?

No. I never drank. And I was very moderate in my use of drugs. I was more interested in the politics than the drugs themselves.

But you have all those poems that are titled after drugs.

If you'll notice, it's about one percent of my poetry.

Okay. I'll go back and take a look.

You'll find a poem called **"Nitrous Oxide"** and another called **"Ether"** and another called **"LSD,"** another called **"Marijuana Notation,"** another called **"Mescaline"**. And that's about it. And your have Peyote for the central section of **"Howl"**—

The religious visions.

And a couple other things, then you have some stuff from the **"Yage"** and that's it. Out of about eight hundred pages, you've got about fifty pages of drugs.

All right, that takes care of that.

You have the media stereotypes you're dealing with.

Well, I don't know you.

Well, you don't have to. Just look at the texts. I've named all the texts that are on drugs.

In "Kaddish" were you responding to the Hebrew prayer in any particular way, or were you responding in a more general way to your grief over Naomi's death?

Both. You know, I had never heard the formal rhythms of the Kaddish before, pronounced aloud, or never consciously heard them. They sounded familiar. But all of a sudden I realized it was some kind of interesting, moving, powerful cadence.

You must have been to a service.

Yes. But I have never noticed or heard or consciously heard it, as I said.

But you have said it, though.

No. I've never said it. I don't read Hebrew. I wasn't Bar Mitzvahed. And I was kicked out of Hebrew school for asking questions. I don't know.

Were you being sentimental when you named it "Kaddish"?

No, 'cause I used the basic rhythm of the Kaddish and I quoted the Kaddish.

But you said you didn't know it.

I heard it that morning. Someone read it to me that morning.

The morning you wrote the poem?

Yeah, when I started writing it, or that evening. About 3 A.M. And I was impressed by the cadence and the rhythm and the depth of the sound, as it says in the very opening line, "rending the Kaddish aloud . . . the rhythm the rhythm—and your memory in my head three years after." It says exactly what it was. Mixed with "Ray Charles blues shout blind on the phonograph." With a similar rhythm, by the way. "I got a woman, yes indeed."

So—

A sort of repeated cadence that was right, like Ray Charles or the Kaddish.

So you're inspired by that prayer, you're inspired by mu-

sic, by the rhythm of the music. What about the image, though?

What's the image? Which one?

Williams and the emphasis on—

Minute particular details. Now the phrase that I am thinking of is "minute particulars." Do you know that phrase? Do you know where that's from?

"Minute particulars."

Yes. "Labor well the minute particulars. Take care of the little ones." That's from William Blake's "Jerusalem." Little ones, the little details. And Kerouac says, "Details are the life of prose." And Pound says, "The natural object is the adequate symbol." And Trungpa says, "Things are symbols of themselves."

Well let me ask you this—

So the image comes from, or the image is related to the following idea. If you want to give a mirror of your consciousness and you become aware of your consciousness, conscious awareness manifests itself sacramentally in the quality of the attention to clear-seeing focus on chance, minute, particular details that present themselves with charismatic vividness to author and to reader.

You do both that and hear music also? Simultaneously?

No. You have a picture in your mind, as Pound points out, in "Chinese Written Language as a Medium for Poetry," published by City Lights now. The Chinese is interesting as a poetic language because it consists in little pictographs. So you can't be vague and talk about beauty. You have to talk about something concrete and process. At the same time, the language has got a sonorous aspect or sound or vocal sound, so you hear it in your head sometimes. Sometimes you make the language up out of the picture. Sometimes the language itself has its own melodic part that comes up by itself. Like the other day I got up off the toilet, and I said, "That was good, that was great, that was important!" And stood up to pull the chain. And I heard myself saying that, and I noticed I had said that, and I said, that's fairly interesting, that's like a haiku. How many syllables was that? "That was good, that was great, that was important!" That's eleven syllables.

Maybe twelve.

Ending on the twelfth. "That was good, that was great, that was important!" No, that's eleven. "Standing up to pull the chain" adds another six, so that's seventeen all together. So, okay, I noticed the situation, that there was the visual ele-

ment, standing to pull the chain, the picture there, and there was what ran in my mind, so the picture gave the context for the interior utterance.

Okay, so the picture can sometimes inspire the music.

Not inspire! No, no, no! I hear you using that word over and over again, abusing it, using it out of its meaning. You're making it into oatmeal.

How would you say it? The picture induces?

The picture originates the poem or the origin or the flash. You flash on a picture, and you write it down. Or you flash on something you say to yourself, and you write it down.

And sometimes that can have music.

You can hear a tune. But the words "That was good, that was great, that was important!" have a rhythm. (Demonstration of rhythm.) That has its own cadence, you know what it's saying and the rhythm of the sounds are both the same.

It's not metrical obviously.

It is metrical. (Demonstration of rhythm.) That's a meter. That's an old classic Greek meter.

Anapest? Short, short long?

It's an anapest. Ta ta ta ta-ta. One, two, three, four, five. There's a Greek rhythm that is a four beat rhythm or a four syllable rhythm. I don't know what its called, maybe dithyrambic or something.

Do you know Greek?

No, but I know some of the Greek rhythms.

You're the prototype, I guess it's a stereotype, of the free verse poet, but you're saying you hear meters.

Yes, sure I hear meters. My father was a poet, it's a family business, and I grew up with a facility for rhyme and stanza from when I was very young, without even trying. I know yards and yards of poetry, like Edgar Allen Poe's "Bells" or Vachel Lindsay's "Congo," poems by Edna St. Vincent Millay and Elinor Wylie.

*But didn't you, I mean you've said many times you had to go beyond that in order to write **"Howl"** and **"Kaddish."***

Well, naturally, you know, but the point is those forms are appropriate, they're called lyric poetry or the shorter forms which have short stanzas, they're called lyric poetry. Now, what is the root of the word lyric?

Song, isn't it?

No, no. Think. What is the root, literally, of the word lyric? What instrument?

Lyre.

Right, right! And what was a lyre? It was a stringed instrument played by Homer or Sappho or the early poets, the Muse's lyre. So it's just like Bob Dylan or something, a stringed instrument, where you sing to stanza with rhyme and you have a melody that revolves around itself and has a recurrence, right? So because the melody has a recurrence, you therefore have a recurrence, a cadence for the stanza, and you use rhyme. When you stop using the stringed instrument and just write the form without the music, then it begins to degenerate and lose its muscularity and its variety and its syncopation. So when I came in in 1950, people were trying to write those lyric stanzas, but without music. And that was the complaint that Pound and Williams had. And so historically—and also Whitman—so they moved away from a fake lyric, that is to say a half-assed lyric that did not have the musical accompaniment, but just spoken language, but arranged as if it were a song. They moved away to the use of living language rather than a dead form and began rewriting the idea of rhythm and measure. And so Williams had the idea of an American measure rather than the old English lyric, which was being imitated in the twenties by Edwin Arlington Robinson and Elinor Wylie and Sara Teasdale and Edna St. Vincent Millay and all the minor poets of that time. He moved out into trying to isolate the rhythms of actual speaking and that led to my own generation of projective verse, writing in the living speech rather than in an imitation of an older English cadence. It didn't mean that there wasn't rhythm, it meant that the rhythms were the rhythms that you heard in speech, like "da dada da da dada dada." It didn't mean that there wasn't rhythm. That's a rhythm.

Frost supposedly hears a meter. There's meter in Frost as well as the rhythm. "Something there is that doesn't love a wall."

Okay, that's a metronomic meter, where it's recurrent. But you know, the classic meters of Greece were much more varied than the four or five, four usually, used in English. We have iamb, trochee, dactyl, and anapest.

Spondee.

And that's usually the range. Spondees are used less, but they

come in. So now there are the two syllable and three syllable meters. We have mostly the iamb and the trochee, but then there's also molossos, the three syllable meters. "Oh, good God!" Da da da. Or there is the bacchius meter, "Is God love? Believe me." Dada da, dada da. Then there are four syllable meters, like, oh, insistently. Dadadada dadadada dadadada dadadada. Insistently, insistently, insistently. Or the ionic A minor, which is "in the twilight" dadadada dadadada dadadada. Or delightfully, delightfully, delightfully. That's the second ionic. Or the epitritus primus, "your sweet blue eyes," "I hate your guts." So then there's the epitritus secundus. "Bite the big nut," dadadada, or "Give her a dime" dadadada. And then there are the five syllable ones. "I bit off his nose," da da da dada. Or the dulcimaic, which Hart Crane used, "Lo, lord, thou ridest!" Bom bom dadada. "Fall fruits and flowers." That's Ben Jonson. Dom dom dadada. Those were the ones we used as the climax of Greek plays, with the revelation of the moment. Bom bom dadada.

So there's a lot more, you're saying, than the simple two syllable foot.

So, and they could use these different feet like a Lego set and could build very various musicality, complex musical things, like Sappho? You know the Sapphic stanza?

No, I don't know much about it.

You know the the rhythm of it.

No.

Trochee, trochee, dactyl, trochee, trochee. Trochee, trochee, dactyl, trochee, trochee. Trochee, trochee, dactyl, trochee, trochee. Dactyl, trochee. (Demonstration of rhythm.)

So the first line of "Howl":—

No, I wasn't thinking of that, but I was so trained and I had all those in my bones. But the one that pointed out to me, many years later, that the Moloch section (demonstration of rhythm), "Moloch whose eyes are a thousand blind windows," was Ed Sanders, who's trained in classical prosody and versification. Then I got interested in what the names of these were.

Let me ask you something else.

Yes, well that's what you're doing.

Have you ever considered yourself a Jewish poet?

Yeah, I am a Jewish poet. I'm Jewish.

You are? You surprise me.

I'm Jewish. My name is Ginsberg. I wrote a book called **Kaddish.**

No, that's great!

My last book has a long poem called **"Why I'm Jewish."**

I'll have to take a look. I've got it.

It's called **"Yiddishe Kopf."**

Cosmopolitan Greetings?

Yeah, **"Yiddishe Kopf."**

I'll have to look it up. So you're a Jewish poet.

I'm also a gay poet.

I know that.

I'm also a New Jersey poet.

You're a Buddhist poet.

And I'm a Buddhist poet. And also I'm an academic poet, and also I'm a beatnik poet, I'm an international poet,—

What was the Jewish influence? Your mother, essentially?

No. My mother, my father, my grandparents were all Jewish. My whole family is Jewish and that's just the whole thing in my bones.

What about the Bible? Did that influence you?

Yeah, I read a lot of the Bible, sure. I read it all through, a number of times. But you know, like I know wherever the golden bow be broken and the silver cord be loosed wheel be broken at the cistern and so forth.

Is there a cadence—

The cadences of Ecclesiastes and the Psalms. The Song of Songs.

And you probably get some inspiration from the parallelism of the Hebrew prophets.

Oh, of course. But also, you know, indirectly. One of my great models as a poet, or for me a great model, is Christopher Smart.

Right, "Jubilate Agno."

Right. And he was a fantastic translator of the Bible, of Hebrew.

Of psalms?

Of psalms and everything like that. And his "Jubilate Agno"—I don't know if you've seen my annotated **"Howl"**?

I have, yeah.

Well, at the end you'll find a selection from Smart.

That's right. I remember that.

If you'll notice, it's done in the parallelisms of the Bible. And my own verse line in **"Howl"** and elsewhere is drawn from that. The Bible via Smart, as well as the Bible itself that I'm familiar with. You know, my father was a poet and so all this stuff, the Song of Songs, was part of the family heritage.

Are being Jewish and being gay connected in any way? I mean, being oppressed?

I've known gay Jews. Who was it, David and Jonathan? I mean, that's an old business. What is it, Jesus and young John?

Here's a chance to talk about the present. Because I started out interviewing Stanley Kunitz and Carl Rakosi, who are in their nineties.

Yeah, marvelous people. Rakosi, I love. I love Rakosi.

Well, I was in Maine and I talked to him a lot. I was in Maine when he did that reading with you.

And I saw him last summer at Naropa.

And I interviewed him in December in San Francisco, and he's great.

I think he is our greatest poet, Jewish or non-Jewish.

He told me you like Reznikoff even more.

No, I like both.

It's good that you like him.

I think Rakosi—you know, his *Collected Poems* is a great volume.

Yeah, I have that. I got it in Maine. I really fell in love with it.

Did you think I liked Reznikoff more?

Well, Rakosi said that. He said that when I saw him in San Francisco.

I discovered him earlier.

But he hasn't gotten enough attention.

He got a lot from me.

Most of the attention has gone to the other Objectivists: Zukofsky and Oppen.

Well, fortunately we pay a lot of attention to him at Naropa.

That's great.

And in Maine.

Are you going to go to Maine again?

I won't be able to this summer. It's there when I'm in Naropa.

I was there, I talked to you a lot. I'm going to England this time.

What's your business?

I teach creative writing and I write poetry and criticism.

Where?

At Wright State University in Dayton.

Where?

At Wright State University in Dayton.

I think I've been there.

Yeah, well, you were at the University of Dayton. You were with a poet named Herb Martin.

Long ago.

A long time ago.

Where is he now?

He's still there. He's become famous for his reading of Paul Laurence Dunbar.

He's doing Dunbar's work.

Right, he's doing a lot of that. Well let me ask you another line of questions. Let's go on. Does maturity give you any kind of new, fresh perspective?

Look at my new poems. **Cosmopolitan Greetings** is all about that. There's one particular poem, but you know there are lots of poems about being a senior citizen in there.

Yeah. That's right.

But there's one particular poem that begins, "At 66 just learning how to take care of my body." Do you know that?

I've got it right in front of me. I'll look at it.

Hold on. I'll get it.

The one I really like is the one where you've got the photograph.

"May Days."

And then you've got all the details about the apartment. There's great concentration of imagery, the minute particulars.

Yeah, that's a good one. That was translated, incidentally, into Hebrew by Natan Zach, a Hebrew poet.

Did you take the picture? "May Days 1988" with the New York Times *on the window sill.*

The new book has similar stuff, a thing called **"Charnel Ground,"** which is going out the window and looking around at the neighborhood. Anyway, there's poem called **"Autumn Leaves."**

It's also in **Cosmopolitan Greetings?**

"Autumn Leaves."

All right. How does one face death? You've written poems about death.

Every poet does. Shelley did when he was twenty-seven. Keats did when he was twenty-four.

Does poetry help?

Yes. I think poetry helps because you imagine your death, and you begin to blueprint and plan and realize mortality and then after awhile you become consciously aware of the fact that mortality is limited and then you begin to appreciate living more. As well as appreciate the great adventure of dying and then realize that it is part of the vast process and an occasion for lamentation and rejoicing and everything. The whole thing comes together. It's the great subject. Because, you know, without death there's no life. Without life there's no death.

So, sort of like "death is the mother of beauty."

I think in **"Kaddish"** I said, "death is the mother of the universe."

What about love?

Well, what about it?

That's not as big? Okay.

I think above death and above love, I would say, in a poem I did say, awareness encompasses love, death, and everything.

Awareness of mortality?

No. Awareness itself. Conscious awareness. It leads to, encompasses compassion, love, and awareness of death.

What has poetry taught you about language, words?

I don't know. What have words taught me about poetry? You could say that's the same thing.

Well, how about it?

It taught me not to bullshit. It taught me not to indulge in abstract language which is undefined, but to try and nail down any generalization with a "for instance." You know, like "give me a for instance." So it taught me that. "No ideas but in things," as Williams says. Or "The natural object is always the adequate symbol," says Pound. And again, I'll repeat, as Trungpa said, "Things are symbols of themselves."

Okay. I like that.

That's a great one.

I believe in all that. It's just that it's all being challenged today.

By whom?

The Language poets.

Well, they're saying that language is language. A word is a word.

But it doesn't symbolize anything. It's just a nonsense sound.

No, they're saying that it actually—there are conditions. Their angle on symbolization is something different, that the conditioning, the social conditioning is built into the use of the word. That the social conditioning outweighs the visual or the auditory meaning.

Well, they deconstruct or break down all the syntax and the meaning and you end up with nothing but sound.

But the purpose of the deconstruction was to break down the social conditioning associated with the sounds.

Right. And then you end up breaking down poetry, I think, as well.

Ah, I wouldn't worry about poetry. Poetry can take it. And sometimes it's interesting, like Burroughs's cut up aspect was very interesting. A deconditioning to conditioned language. A whole way of inventing new, interesting phrases like "wind hand caught in the door" which is a by-product of Burroughs's cut-ups. "Wind hand caught in the door."

Your poetry always makes sense to me. I mean you don't seem to try to distort—

Well, I try, and you know, I'm out of Williams. I come from the Williams lineage and Kerouac. Kerouac wrote spontaneously and wrote nonsense, but there was always this basic theme. Burroughs cut up his stuff, but there was always this basic theme. No matter how you cut it up, it's still Burroughs talking about authoritarian hypnosis from the state.

And you can always see that?

Yeah. It comes through no matter how you cut up his works.

Because when I read these language poets, it's more like Gertrude Stein. I don't know what they're talking about.

Stein is interesting in her own way, you know what I mean? Have you ever heard her record?

No.

There's a Caedmon record of Stein, and if you hear her once you really get the idea what she was after. Williams told me that she had one specific simple thing and it was really great and you know, if you get that then you get something. An inimitable voice. Speaking voice. A Yiddish voice, too.

A Yiddish voice. Not Stein! What place do you most identify with, in other words, what physical location, like Jersey or—

Living Lower East Side, probably.

Have you lived there much of your life, even though you've traveled all over the world?

Well, I've had this one apartment where I am now for twenty-one years.

I didn't know that.

And then before that I had—see, my mother, when she came to America, moved to about a mile from here on Orchard and Rivington. That was her first place of residence. Then they moved to Newark. So Orchard-Rivington is about a mile from where I am now.

So it's really your roots.

So, I'm really back where my mother's family—my father's family came to New York and then Newark. But before I lived here, I moved here in '75, I lived for five years or so on East 10th Street, a couple blocks away. And before that on East 2nd Street in the sixties. And in the fifties, where I took all those photographs, early photographs of Burroughs and Kerouac, that's East 7th Street.

You wrote a powerful poem about being mugged. It must have been down in one of those neighborhoods.

That was in 1972 on 10th Street, when I was living there. Two blocks from here.

And where are you now?

East 12th Street.

In the Village?

East Village. Lower East Side.

If you could do it again, what would you do differently, if anything?

There's a certain guy I was in love with when I was young who invited me to bed and I was too shy, because I was in the closet. And I've always regretted it. And I wrote a poem about it. I wrote about it in Sapphic verse. In **Mindbreaths,** something like that. One of the books. It's in my **Collected Poems**—1978 or so.

Helen Vendler sort of surprisingly to me wrote very warmly of you, I think, in her anthology.

Yeah, I was surprised.

Right, I was surprised.

She likes me and Snyder and she has no reaction at all to Creeley or Corso or Kerouac's poetry or anyone else.

Maybe it was another critic I was reading, and she talks about what must have been the great difficulty for you, especially as a young Jewish man being gay. I thought that was a sensitive remark.

I didn't think it was that difficult, you know? I was in the closet until I was about seventeen. But then I had such nice company, with Kerouac and Burroughs, who were themselves so far out and Burroughs was gay. Kerouac was very straight, but none the less—

He wasn't gay or bisexual?

I wouldn't say so.

What about Neal Cassady, whom you're always writing about?

Cassady was a lady's man, but he was sort of pan-sexual. I made out with him, but I was one of the few people he made out with. Maybe he hustled as a younger kid, as a young orphan.

In a sense, you always had a family.

Yeah. I had my regular family. I was pretty close. And also an alternative family.

I mean a family of brothers. Because I've thought over the years that poets like Roethke and Berryman and Lowell, they were alone, even though they were straight.

They did have that community. Berryman, Lowell, they were all part of that southern agrarian second generation, from Ransom and Robert Penn Warren and Allen Tate. But the people who were their elders were such puritanical, such mean people, like Allen Tate was an alcoholic, and he kept putting down Hart Crane for being gay, and drank himself to death. Or drank too much.

I think he smoked too much, too.

Or smoked. And then I remember when *Big Table* was going to have a post-Christian issue, they invited him and Burroughs and myself and others to contribute, and he said he wouldn't appear in a magazine with Burroughs. So what kind of model is that for those guys? No wonder they didn't have a sense of family. Sort of intolerant snobs.

Well, I think in certain ways maybe it worked for you to have those people you mentioned.

Yeah. The funny part was that I had also connections with that *Kenyon Review* crowd through Lionel Trilling.

Now, when you say Kenyon Review *crowd, you don't mean Ransom and—*

Yes, I knew Ransom later, but Trilling was one of the major icons of the *Partisan Review.*

Were you published in the Kenyon Review?

No. Yes, later on, yes. It's now under the hands of a lesbian editoress.

I don't think she is editor anymore. I know whom you mean, Marilyn Hacker?

Yeah. She's a nice girl. Nice woman.

What is the most amazing thing about life?

Oh, the fact that it's here at all, and that it disappears.

What's the most amazing thing about your life?

I'm pretty dumb, quite stupid in a way. Even backward. I don't know how I got where I am now, to be like a kind of great poet of some kind. And I don't understand how it happened.

Well, from what you told me at the beginning, it had to do with breath.

Breath, but also the other quality was because I ran into Kerouac and Burroughs when I was sixteen and seventeen. I suddenly realized how provincial and dumb I was, and I resolved, rather than asserting myself constantly and arguing and being argumentative, which would have been my normal nature, I should shut up and listen and learn something. So I always took a kind of back seat and listened to my elders. I always had teachers and gurus, you know, from the very beginning. So actually I learned a lot from other people and had the quality of attention, to listen to Burroughs and serve him, in a way. You know, like work with him and be his amanuensis or his agent or work with him and encourage him and listen to him and do what I could to make his life workable, and I learned a lot that way. And I have relations, had relations like that with Chogyam Trungpa, the Tibetan lama, and Gelek Rinpoche right now, since Trungpa did, a Tibetan lama. And so I've always had teachers and I've always listened to them. And I think that's really delivered me to some kind of workable, practical self-confidence.

But you wrote "Howl," no one else did. I think that's what made you famous.

Yeah, but you know, I was trying to imitate Kerouac.

That's interesting.

I was a student of Kerouac's, Kerouac broke ground, and I moved in on that territory. And he said, "You guys," me and Gary Snyder, "you guys call yourselves poets. I'm a poet, too, except that my verse line is longer than yours. I write verses that are two pages long!" Like the opening sentences in *The Subterranians.* Which are beautiful, poetic sentences, you know.

I'm pretty dumb, quite stupid in a way. Even backward. I don't know how I got where I am now, to be like a kind of great poet of some kind. And I don't understand how it happened.
—Allen Ginsberg

He was the key influence, then.

Yeah. I would say him and Burroughs. He was the key vocal influence or verbal, and Burroughs the key intellectual.

And then, of course, as everyone's written about, also Blake and Pound and Whitman and Williams.

Well, I had a good education, I had a regular Columbia education, but I also had the advantage of an education through Kerouac and Burroughs and the books they suggested, but also through my father, who was very well cultivated in poetry.

And wrote in a very, very traditional lyric style.

Yeah, well, you know, he would stomp around the house, not stomp, walk around the house reciting Milton and Shakespeare and Poe, "The Bells," "The Raven," "Annabell Lee." I memorized those when I was a kid. When I was eight years old I could recite a lot of "The Bells."

Your parents are in the poem "Kaddish," which to me is probably the most powerful one. Did Naomi actually speak about the key in the window?

Yes, she did speak. No. After she died, a day or so after I got a telegram saying she was dead, I got a letter from her that had been posted just before she died of a stroke. And I'm quoting that letter, yeah.

And then that wonderful talk in there, that Yiddish talk, where she's talking about soup. That's pretty much what she sounded like?

She likes lentil soup. That's literal. Now that I look back, I said, how come she said that? How come I didn't ask her what she meant? That I wasn't more persistent. It was so vivid but I was a little shy of pursuing the subject. For fear that she was completely nuts rather than discovering that she had a good sense of humor.

You put more of the personal into that poem than just about anyone I can think of. I mean of that kind of material. And your father comes off, to me, as a very sad man.

In that poem.

But he wasn't that sad?

Then, but a little later on he and I read a lot together and we got closer and closer. We went to Europe together, and he blessed me on his deathbed, and I blessed him.

He remarried, I gather, at some point.

He remarried a very nice woman who was a very good influence on him, and brought us together quite well, and just had her ninetieth birthday this week.

A Jewish woman?

Yeah, yeah, Edith Ginsberg. She just survived, at the age of eighty-nine, two valve transplants. A pig valve and a sheep valve, so she says, joking, she's no longer kosher.

Let me ask you one—

I don't know if you know this, about a little film, *The Life and Times of Allen Ginsberg*?

I saw it.

She's in there. Very nice.

I'd have to see it again. I saw it in Yellow Springs, Ohio. Have you ever been to Yellow Springs, Antioch College?

Yeah, sure. Long ago, though.

I saw it there. It was too short, almost.

Well, enough for me. But mainly family oriented, in a way.

How do you see your place in American poetry?

Well, I have a poem called **"Ego Confessions,"** which is sort of like a grandiose vision. Take a look at that. Because I want to be known as the most intelligent man in America. Worst case scenario of megalomania. But the whole point of poetry is not to be afraid of worst case neurosis, but to reveal it, go right into the wind rather than being afraid of admitting it.

Well, you certainly showed us that.

So I'd like to be remembered as someone who advanced, actually advanced the notion of compassion in open heart, open form poetry, continuing the tradition of Whitman and Williams. And part of the honorific aspect of the whole beat generation.

You seem to have accomplished a lot of that.

Well, not really, because you know my major poems that we're talking about are banned from the air, from radio and television now, with a law suggested by Jesse Helms. He directed the FCC to ban all so-called indecent language off the air, I think it's between 6 A.M. and 10 P.M. And the Supreme Court just affirmed that by refusing to hear our appeal. And that's just been extended to Internet. So it may be that the text of **"Howl"** or **"Please Master"** or **"Kaddish"** or **"Sunflower Sutra"** will be soon inadmissible on Internet because of foul language that might offend the ears of minors. So the right wing is reimposing the same kind of censorship on the electronic media that we overthrew in the written, printed media '58 to '62.

That was the famous Berkeley trial?

Yeah. Well, that, and also the trials of Henry Miller, D. H. Lawrence, Jean Genet, up to *Naked Lunch* in 1962, which liberated literature.

So, we're back there.

No, on a more grand, international scale, we're back with censorship in the electronic world, but not in the written book world.

Are we at the end of the long journey of poetry, then?

What do you mean?

I mean—let's put it this way. What can a late twentieth-century poet, given what you've just told me about Jesse Helms and all that what can a late twentieth-century poet hope to accomplish?

Oh, the poetry doesn't depend on electronic media. You could pull all those plugs and it wouldn't affect poetry. Or plug them all in. Poetry is an individual thing that gets around by word of mouth. It's an oral tradition, as well as a written, printed tradition, as well as a spoken tradition. So it'll get around. Anything really good will get around.

You have that faith.

Well, it's experience. I mean, when **Howl** was on trial, I didn't care one way or the other. Well, I mean, I cared, but I realized if I lose the trial, I'll be a big hero and everybody will want to read my book. All the police did was do me a big favor by publicizing my poetry. They always do that. They're so dumb. Like, do you think Mapplethorpe would be so famous if it weren't for Jesse Helms trying to quash him or something. It's amazing!

Well, they made you famous.

They made Mapplethorpe famous. They're going to make Michelangelo famous when they start censoring his statues of Bacchus or the Slaves. They're already censoring his David.

Oh, you're kidding me.

Yeah, you can't put that on the Internet, because its got a big dick that minors might see. Frontal nudity. (Laughter.) So they just make people more conscious of the censorship and of the restrictions and of the mentality and mindset and then they'll cause a counter-reaction.

One base we haven't touched: How has Buddhism helped you?

Oh, it's made me more aware of the fact that everything can be done 'twixt earnest and joke. Things are completely real and simultaneously and without any contradiction, they are also completely empty and unreal. Just like a dream.

Both?

Both at once. Without contradiction, i.e., a dream is real while you're dreaming but when you wake up it vanishes. There's no inherent permanence. Life is real while you're alive, but then when you die, it vanishes. It has no inherent permanence. So it's like—so it's real, but it also simultaneously has that aspect. One aspect is the reality, the other aspect is the transitoriness or mutability, as Shelley said.

And you see both?

Well, everybody sees both. So it's the ability to see both simultaneously that gives life its sort of charisma and glamour and workability. You're never stuck. There's no permanent Hell. There's no permanent Heaven.

So that liberates you.

Sure! It liberates you from the nightmare of thinking, "Oh god, I'm stuck, I'm gonna die, blah, blah, blah."

You're not afraid?

What's there to be afraid of? It's like being in a dream and realizing it's a dream, so then you're not afraid anymore.

And where do you end up? In the dream, just an extension of the dream?

Well, you end up waking up somewhere else. I guess. Or maybe you don't wake up. Maybe you just go to sleep and that's the end of it.

May be that wouldn't be so bad.

Well, have you ever been in a dentist's chair with nitrous oxide?

Yeah.

Have you ever been put out? Okay, so what's the last thing you hear? Or what's the last sense that disappears? To me, it was sound. The music, the Muzak. So what if the last thing to go is the end of the symphony? Like, the pain is gone, physical feeling is gone, sight is gone, taste is gone, smell is gone, the only thing left is sound. The sound is the music, then you hear the last note of the symphony and—

Well that's a nice one. But then there's all the folks during the Holocaust who were butchered every second by the Nazis.

Yeah, but on the other hand, the last thing they heard was the sound of a scream and then the scream ended. And there was nice, peaceful—

Let's hope.

Well, unless they were reborn. Do you think they went to hell or something?

I don't believe that.

They wouldn't have gone to hell. Do you think they went to heaven?

I don't think so.

I don't think there's a heaven. So therefore where did they go? They certainly went to a peaceful place.

I hope so.

Well, where else?

I think you're right!

Can you imagine anywhere else? Can you even imagine someplace that wasn't peaceful?

I'm Jewish. I'll have to go with that.

The Sheol, or maybe Sheol.

Sheol. Okay.

The Buddhists might give the worst case, that they get reborn to go through it all over again. Reborn as Nazis. Reborn in Israel and persecuting the Palestinians.

That would be hell.

Okay. I gotta stop.

OBITUARIES

Wilborn Hampton (obituary date 6 April 1997)

SOURCE: An obituary for Allen Ginsberg, in *New York Times,* April 6, 1997, pp. A1, A42.

[*In the following obituary, Hampton eulogizes Ginsberg, providing a review of his life and work.*]

Allen Ginsberg, the poet laureate of the Beat Generation whose **"Howl!"** became a manifesto for the sexual revolution and a cause célèbre for free speech in the 1950's, eventually earning its author a place in America's literary pantheon, died early yesterday. He was 70 and lived in Manhattan.

He died of liver cancer, Bill Morgan, a friend and the poet's archivist, said.

Mr. Morgan said that Mr. Ginsberg wrote right to the end. "He's working on a lot of poems, talking to old friends," Mr. Morgan said on Friday. "He's in very good spirits. He wants to write poetry and finish his life's work."

William S. Burroughs, one of Mr. Ginsberg's lifelong friends and a fellow Beat, said that Mr. Ginsberg's death was "a great loss to me and to everybody."

"We were friends for more than 50 years," Mr. Burroughs said. "Allen was a great person with worldwide influence. He was a pioneer of openness and a lifelong model of candor. He stood for freedom of expression and for coming out of all the closets long before others did. He has influence because he said what he believed. I will miss him."

As much through the strength of his own irrepressible personality as through his poetry, Mr. Ginsberg provided a bridge between the Underground and the Transcendental. He was as comfortable in the ashrams of Indian gurus in the 1960's as he had been in the Beat coffeehouses of the preceding decade.

A ubiquitous presence at the love-ins and be-ins that marked the drug-oriented counterculture of the Flower Children years, Mr. Ginsberg was also in the vanguard of the political protest movements they helped spawn. He marched against the war in Vietnam, the C.I.A. and the Shah of Iran, among other causes.

If his early verse shocked Eisenhower's America with its celebration of homosexuality and drugs, his involvement in protests kept him in the public eye and fed ammunition to his critics. But through it all, Mr. Ginsberg maintained a sort of teddy bear quality that deflected much of the indignation he inspired.

He was known around the world as a master of the outrageous. He read his poetry and played finger cymbals at the Albert Hall in London; he was expelled from Cuba after saying he found Che Guevara "cute"; he sang duets with Bob Dylan, and he chanted "Hare Krishna" on William F. Buckley Jr.'s television program. As the critic John Leonard observed in a 1988 appreciation: "He is of course a social bandit. But he is a nonviolent social bandit."

Or as the narrator in Saul Bellow's "Him With His Foot in His Mouth" said of Mr. Ginsberg: "Under all this self-revealing candor is purity of heart. And the only authentic living representative of American Transcendentalism is that fat-breasted, bald, bearded homosexual in smeared goggles, innocent in his uncleanness."

J. D. McClatchy, a poet and the editor of *The Yale Review* said yesterday: "Ginsberg was the best-known American poet of his generation, as much a social force as a literary phenomenon.

"Like Whitman, he was a bard in the old manner—outsized, darkly prophetic, part exuberance, part prayer, part rant. His work is finally a history of our era's psyche, with all its contradictory urges."

Allen Ginsberg was born on June 3, 1926, in Newark and grew up in Paterson, N.J., the second son of Louis Ginsberg, a school-teacher and sometime poet, and the former Naomi Levy, a Russian émigrée and fervent Marxist. His brother, Eugene, named for Eugene V. Debs, also wrote poetry, under the name Eugene Brooks. Eugene, a lawyer, survives.

Recalling his parents in a 1985 interview, Mr. Ginsberg said:

> "They were old-fashioned delicatessen philosophers. My father would go around the house either reciting Emily Dickinson and Longfellow under his breath or attacking T. S. Eliot for ruining poetry with his 'obscurantism.' My mother made up bedtime stories that all went something like: 'The good king rode forth from his castle, saw the suffering workers and healed them.' I grew suspicious of both sides."

Allen Ginsberg's mother later suffered from paranoia and was in and out of mental hospitals; Mr. Ginsberg signed an authorization for a lobotomy. Two days after she died in 1956 in Pilgrim State Mental Hospital on Long Island, he received a letter from her that said: "The key is in the window, the key is in the sunlight in the window—I have the key—get married Allen don't take drugs. . . . Love, your mother."

Three years after her death, Mr. Ginsberg wrote "**Kaddish for Naomi Ginsberg (1894-1956)**" an elegy that many consider his finest poem.

> Strange now to think of you, gone without corsets & eyes, while I walk on the sunny pavement of Greenwich Village, downtown Manhattan, clear winter noon, and I've been up all night, talking talking, reading the Kaddish aloud, listening to Ray Charles blues shout blind on the phonograph the rhythm, the rhythm—and your memory in my head three years after

"**Kaddish**" burnished a reputation that had been forged with the publication of "**Howl!**" three years earlier. The two works established Mr. Ginsberg as a major voice in what came to be known as the Beat Generation of writers.

Mr. Ginsberg's journey to his place as one of America's most celebrated poets began during his college days. He first attended Montclair State College. But in 1943, he received a small scholarship from the Young Men's Hebrew Association of Paterson and enrolled at Columbia University. He considered becoming a lawyer like his brother, but was soon attracted to the literary courses offered by Mark Van Doren and Lionel Trilling, and switched his major from pre-law to literature.

At Columbia he fell in with a crowd that included Jack Kerouac, a former student four years his senior, Lucien Carr and William Burroughs, and later, Neal Cassady, a railway worker who had literary aspirations. Together they formed the nucleus of what would become the Beats.

Kerouac and Carr became the poet's mentors, and Kerouac and Cassady became his lovers. It was also at Columbia that Mr. Ginsberg began to experiment with mind-altering drugs like LSD, which would gain widespread use in the decade to follow and which Mr. Ginsberg would celebrate in his verse along with his homosexuality and his immersion in Eastern transcendental religions.

But if the Beats were creating literary history around Columbia and the West End Cafe, there was a dangerous undercurrent to their activities. Mr. Carr spent a brief time in jail for manslaughter, and Mr. Ginsberg, because he had associated with Mr. Carr, was suspended from Columbia for a year.

In 1949, after Mr. Ginsberg had received his bachelor's degree, Herbert Huncke, a writer and hustler, moved into his apartment and stored stolen goods there. Mr. Huncke was eventually jailed, and Mr. Ginsberg, pleading psychological disability, was sent to a psychiatric institution for eight months. At the institution, he met another patient, Carl Solomon, whom Mr. Ginsberg credited with deepening his understanding of poetry and its power as a weapon of political dissent.

Returning home to Paterson, Mr. Ginsberg became a protégé of William Carlos Williams, the physician and poet, who lived nearby. Williams's use of colloquial American language in his poetry was a major influence on the young Mr. Ginsberg.

After leaving Columbia, Mr. Ginsberg first went to work for a Madison Avenue advertising agency. After five years, he once recalled, he found himself taking part in a consumer-research project trying to determine whether Americans preferred the word "sparkling" or "glamorous" to describe ideal teeth. "We already knew people associate diamonds with 'sparkling' and furs with 'glamorous,'" he said "We spent $150,000 to learn most people didn't want furry teeth."

The poet said he decided to give up the corporate world "when my shrink asked me what would make me happy." He hung his gray flannel suit in the closet and went to San Francisco with six months of unemployment insurance in his pocket. San Francisco was then the center of considerable literary energy. He took a room around the corner from City Lights, Lawrence Ferlinghetti's bookstore and underground publishing house, and began to write.

During this period, Mr. Ginsberg, also became part of the

San Francisco literary circle that included Kenneth Rexroth—an author, critic and painter—Gary Snyder, Michael McClure, Philip Whalen, Robert Duncan and Philip Lamantia. He also met Peter Orlovsky, who would be his companion for the next 30 years.

His first major work from San Francisco was *Howl!* The long-running poem expressed the anxieties and ideals of a generation alienated from mainstream society. *Howl!* which was to become Mr. Ginsberg's most famous poem, was dedicated to Carl Solomon, and begins:

> I saw the best minds of my generation
>   destroyed by madness, starving
>   hysterical naked,
> dragging themselves through the negro
>   streets at dawn looking for an angry
>   fix,
> angelheaded hipsters burning for the
>   ancient heavenly connection to the
>   starry dynamo in the machinery of
>   night. . . .

Mr. Ginsberg read the poem to a gathering arranged by Mr. Rexroth, and those present never forgot the poem, its author and the occasion.

Mr. Rexroth's wife privately distributed a mimeographed 50-copy edition of **"Howl!"** and in 1956, Mr. Ferlinghetti published **"Howl!"** and Other Poems in what he called his "pocket poets series."

With its open and often vivid celebration of homosexuality and eroticism, **"Howl!"** was impounded by United States Customs agents and Mr. Ginsberg was tried on obscenity charges.

After a long trial, Judge Clayton Horn ruled that the poem was not without "redeeming social importance."

The result was to make **"Howl!"** immensely popular and establish it as à landmark against censorship. The outrage and furor did not stop with the sexual revolution. As late as 1988, the radio station WBAI refused to allow **"Howl!"** to be read on the air during a week long series about censorship in America.

There were almost as many definitions of Beatniks and the Beat movement as there were writers who claimed to be part of it. As John Clellan Holmes described it, "To be beat is to be at the bottom of your personality looking up." But if the movement grew out of disillusionment, it was disillusionment with a conscience.

Mr. Ginsberg tried to explain the aims of the Beats in a letter to his father in 1957: "Whitman long ago complained that unless the material power of America were leavened by some kind of spiritual infusion, we would wind up among the 'fabled damned.' We're approaching that state as far as I can see. Only way out is individuals taking responsibility and saying what they actually feel. That's what we as a group have been trying to do."

On another occasion, he described the literary rules more succinctly: "You don't have to be right. All you have to do is be candid." Mr. Ginsberg was nothing if not candid.

As he wrote in **"America,"** another 1956 poem, which took aim at Eisenhower's post-McCarthy era:

> America I've given you all and now I'm
>   nothing
> America two dollars and twentyseven
>   cents January 17, 1956
>
> America this is quite serious
> America this is the impression I get from
>   looking in the television set
> America is this correct?

Mr. Ginsberg claimed that the poets who formed the prime influence on his own work were William Blake, Walt Whitman, Ezra Pound and William Carlos Williams. He declared he had found a new method of poetry. "All you have to do," he said, "is think of anything that comes into your head, then arrange in lines of two, three or four words each, don't bother about sentences, in sections of two, three or four lines each."

His disdain for poetry's traditional rules only gave ammunition to his critics. James Dickey once complained that the "problem" with Allen Ginsberg was that he made it seem as if anybody could write poetry.

Mr. Ginsberg used the celebrity he gained with *Howl!* to travel widely during the next two decades. He went to China and India to study with gurus and Zen masters and to Venice to see Pound. On his way home, he was crowned King of the May by dissident university students in Prague, only to be expelled by the Communist Government. He read his poetry wherever they would let him, from concert stages to off-campus coffeehouses.

He was in the forefront of whatever movement was in fashion: the sexual revolution and drug culture of the 1960's, the anti-Vietnam war and anti-C.I.A. demonstrations of the 1970's, the anti-Shah and anti-Reagan protests of the 1980's. In 1967 he was arrested in an antiwar protest in New York City, and he was arrested again, for the same reason, at the

Democratic National Convention in Chicago in 1968. He testified in the trial of the so-called Chicago Seven,

Through it all, he kept writing. After *Kaddish* in 1959, major works included *TV Baby* in 1960, *Wichita Vortex Sutra* (1966), *Wales Visitation* (1967), *Don't Grow Old* (1976) and *White Shroud* (1983).

In a celebrated career, Mr. Ginsberg received many awards, including the National Book Award (1973), the Robert Frost Medal for distinguished poetic achievement (1986), and an American Book Award for contributions to literary excellence (1990).

In 1968, Neal Cassady died of a drug overdose. Kerouac died of alcoholism the next year. By the mid-1970's, Mr. Ginsberg had helped start the Jack Kerouac School of Disembodied Poetics of the Naropa Institute in Boulder, Colo., a Buddhist university where he taught summer courses in poetry and in Buddhist meditation. He also was becoming one of the last living voices of the Beat generation and the keeper of the flame.

In 1985, Harper & Row published Mr. Ginsberg's *Collected Poems,* an anthology of his work in one volume that firmly established the poet in the mainstream of American literature. The poet again made tours, showing up on television shows, but this time he was in suit and tie offering a sort of explanation of his work.

"People ask me if I've gone respectable now," he said to one interviewer. "I tell them I've always been respectable."

During another interview, he confessed: "My intention was to make a picture of the mind, mistakes and all. Of course I learned I'm an idiot, a complete idiot who wasn't as prophetic as I thought I was. The crazy, angry Philippic sometimes got in the way of clear perception.

"I thought the North Vietnamese would be a lot better than they turned out to be. I shouldn't have been marching against the Shah of Iran because the mullahs have turned out to be a lot worse."

But despite his suit and tie, the censors continued to look over Mr. Ginsberg's shoulder. During the interviews, David Remnick, then of *The Washington Post,* accompanied him to CBS's "Nightwatch." A producer, unfamiliar with the poet's work, asked if he would read something on the show.

> "How about reading that poem about your mother?" she suggested.
>
> "'**Kaddish,**' yes. *Time* magazine calls it my masterpiece," Ginsberg replied. "But I don't know. . . ."

The poet pointed to a word in the poem he doubted would make prime time. As Mr. Remnick reported, the producer's eyes glazed over and there was a long silence.

"Your mother's . . . ?" the producer said in horror.

"Couldn't we just bleep that part out?" the poet offered, always helpful.

"No," the producer said.

"It's O.K.," the poet replied. "I've got other poems."

London Times (obituary date 7 April 1997)

SOURCE: "Allen Ginsberg," in *London Times,* April 7, 1997, p. 23.

[*In the following obituary, the critic discusses Ginsberg's role as a voice of protest and his contribution to the Beat movement.*]

Whether as a prophetic bard or a pretentious beatnik, Allen Ginsberg has survived for four decades as an icon of American counterculture. He was one of the last survivors of the Beats, a cool cabal of mid-Fifties writers who, centering on Jack Kerouac, sought to rebel against staid, middle-class convention.

"Hold back the edges of your gowns, Ladies, we are going though hell," wrote William Carlos Williams in his introduction to Ginsberg's 1956 poem *Howl.* A court case ensued in which the publisher was, unsuccessfully, prosecuted for obscenity. *Howl* at once became one of the most widely circulated books of the time; a bible for a beatnik youth. Its opening lines remain one of the most notorious passages in postwar American poetry. "I saw the best minds of my generation destroyed by / madness, starving hysterical naked, / Dragging themselves through the negro streets at dawn / looking for an active fix".

It was never quite clear what exactly the Beats stood for. Jack Kerouac had coined the name, playing with its punning overtones of "beaten down" and "beatified". But broadly speaking, its key writers—Kerouac and Ginsberg, William Burroughs and Gregory Corso—aimed to cast aside the proprieties of English prosody and to play with the rhythms and improvisations of American jazz, instead. Their work had a dramatic immediacy.

To his admirers Ginsberg was seen to have liberated American poetry, in the same way as John Osborne revitalized English theater with *Look Back in Anger*. He recorded the rhythms of voices around him and conveyed his most vivid feelings in the long tumbling lines which became his trademark style. His work has now become mainstream. It is found on university syllabuses all over the world.

Yet Ginsberg never won a major literary prize. And there is another school of thought which finds his work freewheeling and shallow—the rantings of a drug-befuddled mind. Ginsberg did, indeed, experiment with a bewildering array of narcotics from mescaline to morphine, from dope to LSD. Bob Dylan, with whom he collaborated for some time, once described him as a "con man extraordinaire"; while John Giorno, the poet and former lover of Andy Warhol, described him as "the founding father of bullshit liberals".

But, whatever the criticisms, Ginsberg was, as one of his biographers put it, "the most practically effective drop-out around". He was the model non-conformist, the archetypal gay rights activist, the classic campaigner against censorship. And in later age he would hold forth on any of these subjects in lengthily repetitive monologues. He virtually invented "flower power" and the fashion for bald, bearded men in home-stitched sandals.

He became something of an institution, renowned for such declarations as "poetry is best read naked" and such outlandish feats, as the time he removed all his clothing at a party, except for his underpants which he balanced on his head. A "please do not disturb sign" was suspended from his penis. At one point he spent some time learning to dance like a kangaroo from an aboriginal instructor.

Yet if his exploits sometimes appeared ludicrous, Ginsberg proved an adroit survivor. He outlived most of his enemies including J. Edgar Hoover, who declared covert war on the Beats, and McCarthy and his witch-hunters. And if he saw one generation grow out of his work, a new one arose to show themselves interested. In later years he collaborated with such bands as The Clash, Sonic Youth and, most recently, Bono of U2.

Allen Ginsberg was born in New Jersey, the son of Russian Jewish immigrants. His father, Louis, was a schoolteacher, and a poet of modest repute. He and his wife Naomi—in her youth an articulate and idealistic Marxist—were enthusiasts of naturism. But as a boy Allen led a disturbed life. Few visitors came to the house for, as his mother's periodic bouts of schizophrenia intensified, she routinely walked about naked crying out that her mother-in-law was trying to kill her with poison gas.

At the age of five Ginsberg watched from his cot as his mother set fire to the house and when he was nine he was standing outside the bathroom door while she, locked inside,

slashed her wrists with a knife. His second major poem *Kaddish* (1960) was inspired by a memory of his mother cooking him supper while she told him of her meeting with God: "the Charity of her hands stinking with Manhattan, madness, desire to please me, cold undercooked fish—pale red near the bones. Her smells—and oft naked in the room, so that I stare ahead, or turn a book ignoring her." In 1947—long after the divorce of their parents—Allen Ginsberg and his elder brother Gene were finally to sign consent for their mother to be lobotomized.

Ginsberg was educated in Paterson, New Jersey, and went on to Columbia University intending to become a lawyer. Although he proved himself extremely bright, he was suspended for writing obscene graffiti on the dirty windows of his dormitory. Eventually allowed to resume his studies, he graduated in 1948.

In the interim, however, Ginsberg had already started on his unofficial education. He had worked several short stints as a messman in the Merchant Navy and had his first homosexual encounter with a middle-aged sailor. He had fallen under the influence of William Burroughs who, 12 years his senior, had a flat nearby. Burroughs had not yet written a book; it was to be Ginsberg who eventually persuaded him to do so. He had also been in trouble with the police after his flat was used as a base for a robbery. "Genius Columbia Student, Master of Crime Ring," read the headlines of the local paper.

To avoid prosecution as an accomplice, Ginsberg pleaded insanity and spent eight months in a mental hospital. But perhaps he was not altogether unsuited for the place. He had been using hallucinogens heavily-God had spoken to him while he was reading Blake, he said. He met Carl Solomon in the asylum, to whom he later dedicated *Howl.*

On his discharge Ginsberg found desultory employment: on a magazine, in a ribbon factory in New Jersey and as a market research consultant in San Francisco. But then in 1954 he met Peter Orlovsky who was to remain his lifelong companion. And in that year he finally decided to dedicate himself to "Blake, smoking pot, and doing whatever I wanted to do". He never looked back.

Drawn to San Francisco by what he called "its long tradition of Bohemia", he met and mixed with such San Francisco poets as Robert Duncan, Gary Snyder and Lawrence Ferlinghetti. It was the last who, in 1956, published the poem *Howl.* Ferlinghetti was charged with obscenity and Ginsberg's reputation was made.

He went on to publish some ten more volumes of poetry as well as copious journals. He also made a number of "spontaneous films". During the 1960s he traveled extensively, including to India to study Buddhism, to Cuba where he publicly attacked the Castro Government for its repression of homosexuals, and to England where he accompanied Bob Dylan on his *Don't Look Back* tour. In London he performed at the Royal Albert Hall, accompanying himself on the harmonium. He and his friend, Gregory Corso, took the opportunity to visit W.H. Auden in Oxford. Corso attempted to kiss the turn ups of Auden's trousers. During another encounter with a famous poet, the 82-year-old Ezra Pound, Ginsberg played him the Beatles *Yellow Submarine.* "He seemed to like it," he said. "He tapped his stick."

All over America, Ginsberg gave countless poetry readings and held "office hours" at universities. He was a presence at everything from "be-ins"—mass outdoor festivals of chanting costumes and music—to anti-war protests. He spoke out at first, for the legalization of drugs, although gradually he came to regret his involvement in the drugs scene and toured universities instead preaching the superiority of yoga and meditation over narcotic abuse—although he still claimed that LSD had enabled him to pray for President Lyndon Johnson instead of hating him.

For the last 20 years of his life Ginsberg devoted much of his time to a Buddhist college, the Naropa Institute in Colorado, where he taught poetry. His principal guru Chögyam Trungpa, whose nirvanic state never quite overcame his earthly passions for women, cars and cannabis, died in 1987. But Ginsberg continued to defend him and his somewhat unconvincing habits—which included staffing his house with devotees rigged out as English butlers and teaching his students Oxonian English "so that they would be conscious of speech as a formulated aesthetic act like flower arranging".

Ginsberg suffered from diabetes and in later years from heart problems and hepatitis. In 1970 he contracted Bell's Palsy. The disease affected his eyes which were left, as *Time* magazine unkindly put it, "one wide and innocent, gazing at eternity; the other narrow and scrutinising, looking for its market share". Perhaps this was unfair. Ginsberg gave large proportions of his money to a charity he set up in aid of struggling poets. He lived in a run down-flat on New York's Lower East Side where he ate macrobiotically and meditated daily. He always resisted being lionized as poet. Yet today his work sells more copies than it did even in the Sixties.

He leaves no survivors.

OVERVIEW

Allen Grossman (essay date Fall 1962)

SOURCE: "Allen Ginsberg: The Jew as an American Poet," in *Judaism,* Vol. 11, No. 4, Fall, 1962, pp. 303-08.

[*In the following essay, Grossman discusses Ginsberg's contribution to Jewish poetry, focusing particularly on* Kaddish.]

The Jew, like the Irishman, presents himself as a type of the sufferer in history. At a mysterious moment near the end of the nineteenth century the Irish produced a literature of international importance without having previously contributed a single significant poem in English. The Jewish poet in America today resembles the Irishman in England during the 1890's. From a literary point of view, he is emerging from parochialism into the mainstream of writing in English, and he is bringing with him a cultural mystery arising out of his centrality in history as a sufferer, and also out of his relation to a vast body of literature in another language. The Irish at the end of the nineteenth century discovered rather suddenly that their political experience had a symbolic relation to modern history as a whole, and that their ancient literature provided an inexhaustible resource of mythology by which to interpret that history. The Jewish poet in America at this time is engaged in the attempt to express the meaning of his own historical centrality, and he too possesses a vast body of literature in another language—the *Zohar,* for example—which constitutes a symbolic resource as yet unworked in terms of English literature.

None of the Anglo-Irish poets of the Celtic renaissance began as celebrants of the Irish subject matter, or practitioners of a style which might be called peculiarly Irish. They, all of them, "went Irish" when it became professionally useful for them to do so. Similarly, there is a tendency at the present for Jewish poets, whose work appeared at first under culturally neutral auspices, to present their work again (Karl Shapiro is the most obvious example) as *Poems of a Jew.* In the case of Allen Ginsberg, the development is quite clear. His earliest poems (reprinted as **Empty Mirror,** Totem Press, 1961) are culturally anonymous. His first published volume of poems (**Howl,** the Pocket Poets' Series, 1955) draws its title from Blake, and presents itself as part of a completely formed artificial subculture called "Beat" which takes the place of the lost real ethnic and political subcultures which in the past succored and gave identity to the outcast by forming a community of outcasts. Ginsberg's most recent volume, **Kaddish,** is presented under an aggressively Jewish title despite the fact that it is in no simple sense a Jewish book.

The Beat movement, which is now more or less done with, is antinomian and predominantly mystic in substance, and Ginsberg, though still from a position within the movement, is quite clearly invoking the Jewish cultural mystery as a new ground for poetic identity beyond the disintegrating coterie which first gave him notoriety and a language.

Ginsberg's poetry belongs to that strange and almost post-humous poetic literature which began to be produced in America after World War II, and in which the greatest figure is the spoiled Calvinist (Catholic), Robert Lowell. The characteristic literary posture of the post-war poet in America is that of the survivor—a man who is not quite certain that he is not in fact dead. It is here that the Jew as a symbolic figure takes on his true centrality. The position can be stated hypothetically from the point of view of a European survivor who has made the Stygian crossing to America: "Since so many like me died, and since my survival is an unaccountable accident, how can I be certain that I did not myself die and that America is not in fact Hell, as indeed all the social critics say it is?" Ginsberg's poetry is the poetry of a terminal cultural situation. It is a Jewish poetry because the Jew is the prime symbolic representative of man overthrown by history.

It must be remembered that the image of the Jew in America as it underlies the poetry of Ginsberg is not in any sense the same as the image of the Jew in Europe, such as we find, for example, in the poetry of Eliot. Eliot's Jew is a familiar figure resembling Shylock and the Ugly American. Eliot's Jew is the phantom of a dead cultural situation. Ginsberg's Jewish protagonist is the apotheosis of the young radical Jewish intellectual, born out of his time and place, possessing now neither social nor political status. Having exhausted all the stratagems of personal identity, sexual and ethnic, he is nonetheless determined to celebrate his state of being and his moment in history.

From a general point of view, what Ginsberg says in *Kaddish* is that there is no longer any wisdom in experience. In a conversation not long ago with another poet of the "Beat scene," I was astonished to learn that Ginsberg is regarded as a "Dionysian" writer. One must hope that the Dionysian man has more joy in his ecstasy. Certainly the opposite is the case. *Howl,* Ginsberg's only major poem, is a lament for the passing of experience as a resource for wisdom. In Ginsberg and the Beat writers generally the word "wisdom" is an important technical term. If there are two traditions of wisdom-education, the first proposing that the greatest wisdom arises from the most intense transaction with experience, as exemplified, for instance, in the career of Oedipus; and the second, that wisdom arises from the least transaction with experience, Socrates and Jesus being the examples—then Ginsberg represents a culture that has exhausted the first of these resources and that has turned, with hardly more certitude than the mere assertion, to the second. Ginsberg represents himself as the last wise child in a secular culture, whose mission it is to reconstitute the relation of the world and its soul.

The symbol of the ultimate transaction with experience for Ginsberg, as for Sophocles, is possession of the mother.

Nothing, needless to say, could be more predictable from the point of view of the popular sociology of the Jewish family. But what represents Ginsberg's point of view as so entirely desolating is that he documents the death of the mother, and therefore of the ground of experience itself, as a source of value. At the end of the great sentence which constitutes the first 150 lines of *Howl,* the speaker has reproduced the crime of Oedipus, and found guilt without transformation. The New York of Ginsberg is a kind of Thebes through which the poet wanders like a king become prophet by some terrible and inappropriate transformation; but beyond Thebes there is no Colonus where the prophet becomes a king once again outside of life. In *Kaddish* Ginsberg laments the death of the mother herself, the ground of all being both physical and ethnic. In *Kaddish* the archetypal female is a mutilated and paranoid old woman ("scars of operations, pancreas, belly wounds, abortions, appendix, stitching of incisions pulling down in the fat like hideous thick zippers . . .") haunted by the image of Hitler and dying, obscene and abandoned, in a sanatorium.

This is Ginsberg's version of the Jewish mother and, simultaneously, of the *Shechina,* the wandering soul of Israel herself. Ginsberg is the last dutiful son of Israel reciting *kaddish* at the grave of his mother and of the symbolic image of his people. The mysticism of Ginsberg is peculiarly Jewish in the same sense that the *Zohar* is Jewish. As Gershom Scholem has recently shown, the origins of Zoharistic mysticism lie deeply embedded in Christian Gnosticism. For Ginsberg, as for the Jewish mystic in general, the gnostic attitude represents the attempt of the Jewish mind to reconstitute itself outside of history. The Jewish mother in *Kaddish* phantasies herself hunted by friend and enemy alike, by her own mother, by her husband, by Roosevelt, Hitler, by Doctor Isaac, by history itself. She possesses an insane idealism of which her son is heir, and in the end she dies in a fashion so ignominious as to be obscene. Ginsberg erects on her grave an image which is no longer ethnic and which therefore is no longer obsessed by the mystery of the Jewish people in history. To Naomi dead he cries out:

> O glorious muse that bore me from the womb, gave suck first mystic life & taught me talk and music, from whose pained head I first took Vision—

> Tortured and beaten in the skull—What mad hallucinations of the damned that drive me out of my own skull to seek Eternity till I find Peace for Thee, O Poetry—and for all humankind call on the Origin,

> Death which is the mother of the universe!—Now wear your nakedness forever, white flowers in your hair, your marriage sealed behind the sky—no revolution might destroy that maidenhood—

O beautiful Garbo of my Karma—

In his poetry Ginsberg attempts simultaneously to document the death of history itself, of which the Jewish people personified by his mother Naomi is the symbol, and to erect a new ground of being beyond history of which his own poetry is the type and of which the symbol is the mother, or Israel, transformed as Muse.

Curiously enough, Ginsberg finds a tradition for his peculiar form of Jewish Gnosticism in the history of American stylistics. Ginsberg, and to some extent the Beat movement in general, regards himself as the heir of the American transcendentalist rhetoric. He himself refers to his style as "Hebraic-Melvillian." The transcendentalism of Emerson, founded as it is on the *Metaphysics* of Leibnitz rather than on the *Ethics* of Spinoza, provides a national strain upon which Ginsberg, who is at once casual and profoundly serious about his references to history, attempts to graft his "Angelical Ravings." This mixture of nationalism and ethnicism represents the peculiar position of the American Jewish poet who regards himself as simultaneously native and, in the special sense which always pertains to the Jew, alien.

Significantly, Ginsberg's attempt to trace his particular form of transcendental ambition to Whitman is, in all but the grossest sense, absurd. The Whitmanian style is founded upon the celebration of the secular world as an inexhaustible resource of sensation and identity. The world of Ginsberg, on the other hand, is the world of the ruined mind presiding over the death of its physical being and attempting to refound itself in a new reality. The culture of Ginsberg's poems, despite its attempt to naturalize itself, is fundamentally an international culture, as the mind of the Jew is fundamentally an international or extranational phenomenon. *Kaddish* opens with a neo-Platonic reference to Shelley's *Adonais,* a prophetic memory of the Hebrew anthem, and echoes of Christian apocalypse. His style recalls successively Yeats, Hart Crane, William Blake, the Jacobean prose of the Authorized Version, the ecstatic prose of *Moby Dick,* the translations from the Thirties of the Chinese wisdom literatures. Whereas the national image in Whitman is a stable symbol of an ideal form of the self, Ginsberg's reference to America is an effort to naturalize a fundamentally alien consciousness. For Ginsberg the poetic identity must supersede the ethnic identity if the poet is to survive.

Ginsberg's poetry, insofar as it is American poetry, represents an attempt to refound moral culture from a point of view outside any given tradition. The form of his poetry— that of the enormous unifying syntax of the single sentence— is proposed as a model or archetype of some new language of personal being. Like the Jewish Kabbalist, Ginsberg regards his words and indeed the letters of which they are composed as living things which in their form represent the

recreation of "the syntax and measure of poor human prose." The ideal of unity in the self, which represents a legitimization of both the body and the soul in terms of one another, finds its source in the English poetic tradition in William Blake. Blake himself drew on Swedenborg, Law's translations of Boehme, Milton and other sources many of which are themselves identical with the culture out of which Jewish mysticism arises. Ginsberg gathers together in his peculiar way all these ancient cries of ecstatic being, and lays them down on the page as a kind of epitome of failed hopefulness.

The enemy in Ginsberg is Moloch, who is quite simply the image of the objective world of which the economic culture of America is the demiurgic creator. Moloch, or Capitalism, destroys the soul and drives the "angel" to a frenzied search for new worlds. Similarly, in the Jewish mystical tradition the neophyte attempts to uncreate himself and to return turn back along the developmental continuum to the womb and primal substance in which he had his origin. Curiously, the symbols which Ginsberg employs to identify the moral enemy are in part the symbols by which the Jewish role in culture is traditionally defined. Throughout Ginsberg's writing there is an ambivalence towards Jewishness which should be recognized, as it seems to be an emphatic part of his public statement.

The death of the Jewish mother in Ginsberg's *Kaddish,* and the succession of cultural generations implied in the burden of identity laid by the mother on the son, is unquestionably the most momentous record in English of the problem of the passing of the older sociology and meaning of the Jewish family-centered culture in America. But the mysticism with which Ginsberg faces the problem of the death of Israel is, perhaps, less momentous than the poetry which he makes the vehicle of that problem. There is, as I stated at the outset, no major tradition of Jewish poetry in America, as there was before Robert Lowell no major tradition of Catholic poetry, or as there was before Yeats no major tradition of Irish poetry in England. On the one hand Ginsberg uses his Jewishness as a way of representing the general condition of the culture of value in America without relying on meaninglessly familiar symbols. On the other hand he represents himself as the only surviving son of a Jewish universe which died with the death of his mother. We may note that the Jewish symbology becomes available in American poetry just at the point at which the Jewish poet finds it necessary to document the death of the Jewish cultural fact.

The earlier poetry of Ginsberg, that represented primarily by the volume entitled *Howl,* is a great deal more buoyant than the poetry which we are here considering. Between *Howl* and *Kaddish* Ginsberg has lost his humor and gained a kind of horror which even he cannot accommodate to the necessary reticence of the poetic mode. Ginsberg's chief artistic contribution in *Kaddish* is a virtually psychotic candor which effects the mind less like poetry than like some real experience which is so terrible that it cannot be understood. In America, which did not experience the Second World War on its own soil, the Jew may indeed be the proper interpreter of horror.

Allen Ginsberg himself was too young to experience the Second World War either as a soldier or civilian. For him, as for other American poets in this decade, the extreme situation, the American analogy of the bombed city and the concentration camp, is mental illness and the horrors of private life. In this sense the Jewish family, as Ginsberg represents it, becomes the type of the private suffering of the American soul. The tendency of recent American poetry to represent the terrors of history in terms of purely mental agony is almost universal. This is the subject of Snodgrass' *Heart's Needle,* Sexton's *To Bedlam,* and, most recently, Dugan's *Poems.* Ginsberg's image, however, is more extreme than any of these, and I am inclined to think that it is the Jewish mystery which makes that stern agony possible.

> **Ginsberg's chief artistic contribution in *Kaddish* is a virtually psychotic candor which effects the mind less like poetry than like some real experience which is so terrible that it cannot be understood.**
> **—Allen Grossman**

Now I should like to return to the general problem of Jewish poetry in America with which I began. It is clear that Ginsberg uses Jewishness as a way out of the cultural *cul de sac* of the Beat style, and as a way into the soul of the American intellectual. It is clear also that Ginsberg can entertain the Jewish subject matter only as it is in the process of being transformed into something else. Quite possibly the documentation of the death of Judaism is, and will always be, the characteristic Jewish subject. However that may be, Ginsberg has had the sense to perceive that the only significant Jewish poetry will also be a significant American poetry in the sense that its style will be dictated by the universe of recognition formed by the discourse of American poetry as a whole, and not by the universe of recognition constituted by the parochial concern to which the typical Yiddish-American writer addresses himself.

The basic criterion for an American poetry which is also Jewish is an intimate commitment to the stylistic canons of the English and American literary community. It is only under the stylistic auspices of the great literary tradition of the English-speaking peoples that Jewish symbols and Jewish historical attitudes will become significant poetic subjects in America. The fact that Ginsberg seems to be a Jewish poet

less by design than by the habitual candor of his nature is the sanction for such Jewish meaning as truly exists in his verse. What is happening in Ginsberg is that a sense of the disintegration of past cultural identities has led to a return to even more ancient symbols of moral being, such as those embedded in the matrix of medieval Jewish mysticism. The death of the mother in *Kaddish* represents the death of parochial culture, and the poem emerges at the point when it is necessary to lament that loss and to refound the sense of identity on more essential and less time-limited images.

Judaism is an a-historical religion and the entry of its symbols into the English and American literary community at large has been prevented by a perverse commitment to history which is represented by cultural and linguistic parochialism. There is more essentially Jewish mystical symbolism in the use of Kabbalah by Yeats and the French Symbolists than there is in the current Jewish poetry which is presently appearing in the periodicals. Ginsberg represents a brilliant though uncertain invasion of the American literary community by the Jewish sensibility in the process of transcending parochial definitions. It is an irony, though not necessarily an unproductive one, that the *kaddish* which is recited for the death of the archetypal Jewish mother should be embedded in the language of Yeats and Whitman.

Paul Zweig (review date 10 March 1969)

SOURCE: "A Music of Angels," in *Nation,* Vol. 208, No. 10, March 10, 1969, pp. 311-13.

[*In the following review of* Planet News, *Zweig argues that Ginsberg pushes poetry forward in subject matter and style.*]

Communicating vases: so the French sur-realists described them. Between the inner and the outer vase, a boil of suffering: memories churning over the psychic obstacles, on their way to be captured in the nets of grammar and consecutive statement. If there is one man who has helped us to believe in and to practice the mystery of these communicating vases, it is Allen Ginsberg, whose new book, *Planet News* contains some of his finest poems. Between the planet earth and the planet Ginsberg, a banter of loves and disasters has been carried on; between this aging space of ecstasies, who insists aloud:

> I am that I am I am the
>   man & the Adam of hair in
>   my loins This is my spirit and
>   physical shape. I inhabit
>   this Universe

and that other jet-diminished globe, riddled with places.

Warsaw, New York, Calcutta, Wales ... titles of so many personal, gritty moments from which poems arise.

What Ginsberg forced us to understand in *Howl,* twelve years ago, was that nothing is safe from poetry. His argument was not for new poetic subjects, for speech rhythms, for more emotions, or for mysticism. Argument in fact, is not the word for the unsettling spell Ginsberg-as-shaman chanted, suffered and danced in *Howl.* In life, as in poetry, the shaman does not argue. He climbs the psychic hill, beyond the last familiar stone, and then disappears. Later the wind will blow disquieting noises back to us. Morality has pursued him like a clean razor and dismembered his body; his spirit has been assaulted by righteous chancres; rumors abound that he has been nailed to a tree, where the animals will play upon his bones forever, like a harp. But then the poet-shaman reappears, carrying the sick soul he had gone to save: anyone and everyone's soul, his own too, for the shaman must have suffered from all the ills he can cure. He comes back, but he is changed, for he has seen, played before him, all the fantasies of the hidden psyche, and all the possibilities of the will. He has learned the demanding truth that Montaigne discovered in his tower: "I am a man, and nothing human is foreign to me." Here, I think, lies the generous fantasy of *Planet News.* Ginsberg has brought back the sick soul—his own, mine, yours. In payment, he has received the gift of love. Now nothing human is foreign to him.

We know how much what we are is bound up in what, and how, we remember. Our character, and therefore what we do, depends upon—and is—the style of our remembering. I insist upon the word "style," for quantity, the sheer bulk of what we have been, has nothing to do with it. It is like stringing beads out of a huge box of beads. I work in reds, you in shades of green, and you in sharp edges. The "I" is selective, distrustful. And when, beguiled by travel, drugs or women, I recklessly string a rainbow stone, or a piece of turd, that too is part of the pattern. I have learned to be selectively reckless. On principle I open a certain third eye, let it flicker on the marvel of endless possibility, and then hurry it shut, afraid I will be convicted of "too much."

Ginsberg has made "too much" the affair of his life. Like Whitman, Blake, Traherne, Rabelais, he has enacted what it means to say: "I am the greatest lover in the universe." It is the mystery of seeing, and not judging, of understanding, and not discriminating. If such a life can have a program, then Whitman formulated it:

> This is the meal equally set, this the
>   meat for natural hunger.
> It is for the wicked just the same as for
>   the righteous,
>   I make appointments with all,
> I will not have a single person slighted

> or left away,
> The kept-woman, sponger, thief, are
>   hereby invited,
> The heavy-lipp'd slave is invited, the
>   venerealee is invited;
> There shall be no difference between
>   them and the rest.

In *Planet News,* the quintessential poem of "too much," is **"Television Is A Baby Crawling Toward That Death Chamber."** It is a poem which, like electricity, is sustained by its own movement. And the movement arises from Ginsberg's magical ability to know all the beads, and yet select none, for he selects all. Here as elsewhere, Ginsberg opens a hot line to every recess of his roomy, endless body. Like the infinite interconnection of all phenomena in the physical world (when I spit into the ocean, it rises; when I blow, the wind changes direction), the tangled relationships of everything with everything speak in Ginsberg's poem. He has faith that this is so; that all fishing in the dark water is successful. When Ginsberg is at his best, his mad leaps of association are perfect; they imitate the ideal knowledge of a Monad linked, lovingly, to the whole planet: even to cat vomit, Peruvian skulls, disappointed old body, or LSD pastoral worships:

> That's what I came here to compose,
>   what I knocked off my
> life to Inscribe on my grey metal
>   typewriter,
> borrowed from somebody's lover's
>   mother got it from Welfare,
> all interconnected and gracious
>   bunch of Murderers
> as possible in this Kalpa of Hungry
>   blood-drunkard Ghosts—

The shape of **"Television ..."** is the shape of "too much", which is to say that it works against the very idea of poetic form. And yet, by creating the experience (or enchantment) of "too much," it claims for itself all the privileges of form, i.e.: the privilege of being this irreplaceable, absolutely achieved word-vision. Ginsberg, like Whitman, does not forget the place he occupies in the spectrum of cultural forms. He has the pleasure of knowing, from some shy Victorian refuge in his own psyche, that he is being a bit ridiculous. And so he acts out for us our temptation to judge his "too-muchness", and to contain it. What I mean is that Ginsberg, like his spiritual godfather, Walt Whitman, has a sense of comedy. He is an American humorist:

> Dusty moonlight, Starbeam riding its
>   own flute, soul
> revealed in the scribble, an ounce
>   of looks, an invisible

Seeing, Hope, The Vanisher betokening Eternity
one finger raised warning above his
   gold eyeglasses—and
Mozart playing giddy-note an hour
   on the Marxist
gramophone—

. . . .

The Bardo Thodol extends in the millions
   of black jello for
every dying Mechanic—We will
   make Colossal movies—
We will be a great Tantric Mogul &
   starify a new Hollywood
with our unimaginable Flop—
   Great Paranoia!

The humor is part of the generosity of *Planet News.*
Ginsberg, in his expansive way, is trying to convince us to
wade out from the moralizing beaches where we have
learned too well to string our beads. The water is fine, he
says. If only we could stop judging and disdaining, we would
realize how simple it is to paddle around in the world (and
in ourselves).

Often *Planet News* modulates from the glutted, sexual fantasy of "too-muchness," to a quieter, more intimate vision.
When the Kalpas of extended space collapse momentarily,
Ginsberg remembers himself: the citizen of an aging body,
uprooted, humanly unhappy, and yet far from lament, for—
and this is the peculiar strength of these moments—he has
learned to love even his own aging despair:

Allen Ginsberg says this: I am
   a mass of sores and worms
   & baldness & belly & smell
   I am false Name the prey
   of Yamantaka Devourer of
   Strange Dreams . . .

. . . .

and I lay back on my pallet contemplating $50 phone bill,
broke, drowsy, anxious, my heart
   fearful of the
fingers dialing, the deaths, the
   singing of telephone
bells

Ginsberg, in *Planet News,* has given us a music of angels.
Not Christian holy angels, but the angels of which Rilke
spoke: "those almost deadly birds of the soul." They are almost deadly, because they ask what is most difficult to do:
to love even what is not lovable, to serve up the meal for
everyone, to love fate while seeing with intelligent, discriminating eyes what fate is.

I have insisted on evoking the ancestry of Ginsberg's vision
because there is in this poetry of "too-muchness" a tradition
and a genre which deserve to be noticed. In **"Journal Night
Thoughts,"** for example, Ginsberg echoes a conventional
form and uses it, with humor, to express his continuous fantasy. It is a poem of night images, traveling a path of the
mind's peregrinations in New York. One thinks, inevitably,
of Young's "Night Thoughts," of Whitman's lovely poem,
"The Sleepers." Ginsberg has confidence that form, once
rhetorical shapes have been discarded, can arise from life
itself, referring backward and forward, in the fashion of a
psychic genre, to a larger shape of human experience. Here
Ginsberg writes the "night-ode" or whatever name we give
it: a form more ample for our total needs than sonnet, epic,
or other hanger for old clothes.

Thomas Parkinson (essay date Spring 1969)

SOURCE: "Reflections on Allen Ginsberg as Poet," in *Concerning Poetry,* Vol. 2, No. 1, Spring, 1969, pp. 21-24.

[*In the following essay, Parkinson considers whether
Ginsberg is truly a poet, centering his discussion on* Planet
News.]

Allen Ginsberg is a notoriety, a celebrity; to many readers
and non-readers of poetry he has the capacity for releasing
odd energetic responses of hatred and love or amused affection or indignant moralizing. There are even people who
are roused to very flat indifference by the friendly near-
sighted shambling bearded figure who has some of the qualities of such comic stars as Buster Keaton or Charlie Chaplin.
And some of their seriousness.

His latest book *Planet News* grants another revelation of his
sensibility. The usual characteristics of his work are there,
the rhapsodic lines, the odd collocations of images and
thoughts and processes, the occasional rant, the extraordinary tenderness. His poetry resembles the Picasso sculpture
melted together of children toys, or the sculpture of drift-
wood and old tires and metal barrels and tin cans shaped
by enterprising imaginative young people along the polluted
shores of San Francisco Bay. You can make credible Viking
warriors from such materials. Ginsberg's poetry works in
parallel processes; it is junk poetry, not in the drug sense of
junk but in its building blocks. It joins together the waste
and loss that have come to characterize the current world,
Cuba, Czechoslovakia, the Orient, the United States, Peru.

Out of such debris as is offered he makes what poetry he can.

He doesn't bring news of the earth but of the planet. Earth drives us down, confines, mires, isolates, and besides there is less and less earth available to perception and more and more artifice. The late C. S. Lewis might not have enjoyed having his name brought into this discussion, but his great trilogy that begins with *Out of the Silent Planet* and ends with *That Hideous Strength* demonstrates the same concern with the planet as Ginsberg's new book. Both of them see Earth as a planet, part of a solar system, part of a galaxy, part of a universe, cosmic. But where Lewis wrote out of hatred, indignation, and despair at the destruction of tradition by mindless technology, Ginsberg writes from sad lost affection. I think Ginsberg is our only truly sad writer, sad with a heavy, heavy world, and somehow always courageous and content to remain in the human continuum with all his knowledge of human ill and malice clear. He persists.

But is it poetry? This question is so often asked that it does require answering not only within the confines of Ginsberg's work but generally. I am not entirely sure what the question means, since it could legitimately be asked of Whitman or Hart Crane, has been asked of them. What Ginsberg's work represents is an enormous purging and exorcising operation; it is in the area of religious and spiritual exploration rather than that of aesthetic accomplishment. In the dispute between Whistler and Ruskin over the concept of artistic "finish," Ginsberg's poetry would stand with Whistler's painting. He tends to use the term "poet" not as "maker" but revealer at best; at worst he accepts the notion that makes "poets" out of all confused serious persons who are genuinely unquiet about their souls and the condition of the planet. This is a widely embracing category. What troubles many readers of Ginsberg's work, if they are frank about it, is the continuous and consequently tedious reference to semen, excrement, masturbation, buggery, fornication, and the limited series of variations on such substances and processes. Who needs all the soiled bed-sheets? The only proper answer is that Ginsberg does—or did. They were reminders of the shame, guilt, and disorder that apparently afflicted his sexual life and obsessions; they needed to be purged and declared innocent, and the poems attend seriously to that very problem. To some readers they are frank, courageous, out-spoken; others find them violations of the artistic principle of reticence. Both arguments seem to me trivial, having to do with civil rights or social formalities. What occurred in Ginsberg's work seems to me at once more rational and more historically determined than many readers seem willing to admit.

If Ginsberg is nothing else, he is a large contributor to the *Zeitgeist.* Legally and linguistically, he not merely reflected the drift of his time but diverted and channeled it, not out of any sensational interest in so acting but out of the neces-

sities that his being exacted from history. The co-incidence of his particular hang-ups and there is no other way to describe them—with the taboos of the society generated a freely inevitable kind of writing. For in addition to the concern for his own troubled being, he was involved in liberating his body and liberating his mind so that both could function properly: spontaneous me. I sing the body electric. In their most considerable work, both Whitman and Ginsberg are intent on destroying those cerebral bonds that impair their sympathy with their bodies and with others. For others appear only in the body. The irony in both writers is that their most rationally ordered poems are those that argue against the rational faculties. In fact, their real quarrel is with the misuse of cerebral power; they share this sense of imbalance with Blake and Lawrence. And there must be moments when Ginsberg would ruefully agree with Lawrence who answered a correspondent who questioned his intellectual fulminating against the intellect by saying, in effect, that yes, he reminded himself of Carlyle who once said that he had written fifty books on the virtue of silence.

> **If Ginsberg is nothing else, he is a large contributor to the *Zeitgeist.* Legally and linguistically, he not merely reflected the drift of his time but diverted and channeled it, not out of any sensational interest in so acting but out of the necessities that his being exacted from history.**
> —*Thomas Parkinson*

When such paragraphs as the preceding one place Ginsberg in the realm of Whitman, Blake, Lawrence, and Carlyle, a certain uneasiness might justly prevail. I think that this is more a matter of habit than of perception. When the Epstein statue of Blake was placed in Westminster Abbey, I felt slightly miserable it seemed that the British talent for retrospectively accepting the eccentric had over-reached itself. I don't want to see Ginsberg canonized because it would take the edge off his work. With contemporary poets, all question of relative evaluation with the mighty dead is impertinent. Some years back an acquaintance of mine was bad-mouthing Robert Frost and ended with what he took to be an unanswerable question, "Will he last?" and I tried to bring him back to biological reality by murmuring, "None of us will." What we can ask from our writers is a willingness to face up to the troubled planet.

Returning again to the sexuality of Ginsberg's work, I find that in this book, arranged chronologically, there seems to be a steady diminution of concern with the vocabulary and processes that bother many otherwise sympathetic readers. Several of the poems are among his very best work: **"Kral**

Majales"; "Who Be Kind To"; "Wichita Vortex Sutra"; "Wales Visitation." I can't imagine Ginsberg ever solving to his satisfaction the problems that have troubled his being for so many years; but he does seem to have undergone some profound religious experiences during the past five years that give his work a new density and fullness. He is one of the most important men alive on the planet. We should all be grateful for his presence.

But is he a poet? Again I find the question meaningless. He has written over a dozen first-rate poems; he has brought back to life, through his studies in French and Spanish verse, the Whitman tradition and informed it with a new pulse; he has served as a large part of the prophetic conscience of this country during its darkest period; he has been brave and productive. He has gone off on side-tracks; he has indulged himself publicly in some poems that seem better confined to note-books. But when a man liberates the sense of prosodic possibility and embodies in his work a profoundly meaningful spiritual quest that is compelling and clarifying to any reasonably sympathetic reader, well, yes, he is a poet. Only envy and spite could deny the title.

Gregory Stephenson (excerpt date 1990)

SOURCE: "Allen Ginsberg's 'Howl': A Reading," in *The Daybreak Boys: Essays on the Literature of the Beat Generation,* Southern Illinois University Press, 1990, pp. 50-58.

[*In the following excerpt, Stephenson argues that Ginsberg's focus in "Howl" is transcendence in contemporary life.*]

In the quarter century since its publication by City Lights Books, Allen Ginsberg's poem "Howl" has been reviled and admired but has received little serious critical attention. Reviewers and critics have generally emphasized the social or political aspects of the poem, its breakthrough use of obscenity and its allusions to homosexuality, or its long-line, free-verse, open form. For these reasons "Howl" is already being relegated to the status of a literary artifact. I want to consider "Howl" as essentially a record of psychic process and to indicate its relationship to spiritual and literary traditions and to archetypal patterns.

The concept of transcendence with the inherent problems of how to achieve it and where it leaves us afterward is central to romantic literature. This complex has its antecedents in Orphism, Pythagoreanism, Platonism, heterodox Judaism, Gnosticism, and the mystical tradition. "Howl" expresses a contemporary confrontation with the concept of transcendence and examines the personal and social consequences of trying to achieve and return from the state of transcendence.

Transcendence and its attendant problems may be summarized in this way: the poet, for a visionary instant, transcends the realm of the actual into the realm of the ideal, and then, unable to sustain the vision, returns to the realm of the actual. Afterwards the poet feels exiled from the eternal, the numinous, the superconscious. The material world, the realm of the actual, seems empty and desolate. (Poe, in *The Fall of the House of Usher,* describes this sensation as "the bitter lapse into everyday life, the hideous dropping off of the veil.") The poet (like Keats' knight at arms) starves for heavenly manna. This theme of transcendence is treated in the work of Coleridge, Wordsworth, Keats, Shelley, Nerval, Rimbaud, and many other poets and writers. "Howl" describes and resolves the problems, using as a unifying image the archetype of the night-sea journey.

The night-sea journey (or night-sea crossing) is perhaps the earliest of the sun myths. "The ancient dwellers by the sea-shore believed that at nightfall, when the sun disappeared into the sea, it was swallowed by a monster. In the morning the monster disgorged its prey in the eastern sky." Carl Jung discusses the myth in his *Contributions to Analytical Psychology* and Maud Bodkin applies it to "The Rime of the Ancient Mariner" in her book *Archetypal Patterns in Poetry.* The essential situation, in one form or another, may be found in a number of myths, legends, and folktales, and in literature.

For Jung and Bodkin the night-sea journey is a descent into the underworld, a necessary part of the path of the hero. It is "a plunge into the unconscious . . . darkness and watery depths. . . . The journey's end is expressive of resurrection and the overcoming of death." The swallowing of Jonah by a great fish in the Old Testament, the *Aeneid* of Virgil, and the *Inferno* of Dante are records of night-sea journeys.

The movement of "Howl" (including "Footnote to Howl") is from protest, pain, outrage, attack, and lamentation to acceptance, affirmation, love and vision—from alienation to communion. The poet descends into an underworld of darkness, suffering, and isolation and then ascends into spiritual knowledge, blessedness, achieved vision, and a sense of union with the human community and with God. The poem is unified with and the movement carried forward by recurring images of falling and rising, destruction and regeneration, starvation and nourishment, sleeping and waking, darkness and illumination, blindness and sight, death and resurrection.

In the first section of "Howl," Ginsberg describes the desperation, the suffering, and the persecution of a group of outcasts, including himself, who are seeking transcendent reality. They are "starving" and "looking for an angry fix" in a metaphorical more than a literal sense. Both metaphors suggest the intensity of the quest, the driving need. (William S. Burroughs uses the phrase "final fix" as the object of his quest at the end of his novel *Junkie.*) The metaphor of narcotics is extended by their search for "the ancient heavenly connection." (Connection suggests not only a visionary experience in this context—a link to or a union with the divine—but also refers to the slang term for a source of narcotics in the 1940s and the 1950s.) These seekers are impoverished, alienated, arrested, and driven to suicide both by the hostility of the society in which they pursue their quest and by the desperate nature of the quest itself, by its inherent terrors and dangers.

Ginsberg's "angelheaded" seekers follow a sort of Rimbaudian "derangement of the senses" to arrive at spiritual clarity; they pursue a Blakean "path of excess to the Palace of Wisdom." They "purgatory" themselves in the manner of medieval flagellants with profligate and dissolute living (alcohol, sexual excess, peyote, marijuana, benzedrine). And through these means they achieve occasional epiphanous glimpses: angels on tenement roofs, "lightning in the mind", illuminations, brilliant insights, vibrations of the cosmos, gleanings of "supernatural ecstasy," visions, hallucinations; they are "crowned with flame," tantalized when "the soul illuminated its hair for a second," "crash through their minds," receive "sudden flashes," and make incarnate "gaps in Time & Space"; they trap "the Archangel of the soul" and experience the consciousness of "Pater Omnipotens Aeterna Deus." For such sensualized spirituality and for their frenzied pursuit of ultimate reality, they are outcast, driven mad, suicided (as Artaud says) by society, driven into exile, despised, incarcerated, institutionalized.

Ginsberg has phrased the issue in the first section of the poem as "the difficulties that nuts and poets and visionaries and seekers have.... The social disgrace—*dis*grace—attached to certain states of soul. The confrontation with a society ... which is going in a different direction ... knowing how to feel human and holy and not like a madman in a world which is rigid and materialistic and all caught up in the immediate necessities...." The anguish of the visionary in exile from ultimate reality and desperately seeking reunion with it is intensified by a society which refuses to recognize the validity of the visionary experience and maintains a monopoly on reality, imposing and enforcing a single, materialist-rationalist view.

A number of the incidents in the first section are autobiographical, alluding to the poet's own experiences, such as his travels, his expulsion from Columbia University, his visions of Blake, his studies of mystical writers and Cézanne's paintings, his time in jail and in the asylum. Some of the more obscure personal allusions, such as "the brilliant Spaniard" in Houston, may be clarified by reading Ginsberg's *Journals.* Other references are to his friends and acquaintances—Herbert Huncke, William S. Burroughs, Neal

Cassady, William Cannastra, and others. (Certain characters, incidents, and places in **"Howl"** are also treated in Jack Kerouac's *The Town and the City,* John Clellon Holmes' *Go,* and William S. Burroughs' *Junkie.*)

Ginsberg presents not only the personal tragedies and persecutions of his generation of seekers but alludes back to an earlier generation with embedded references to Vachel Lindsay "who ate fire in paint hotels" and Hart Crane "who blew and were blown by those human seraphim, the sailors." And for the poet, the prototype of the persecuted and martyred visionary is his own mother, Naomi Ginsberg, who is twice mentioned in the poem and whose spirit provides much of the impetus for the poem. "'Howl' is really about my mother, in her last year at Pilgrim State Hospital—acceptance of her later inscribed in **Kaddish** detail."

The personal nature of the references in **"Howl"** do not make it a poem *á clef* or a private communication. Nor is the poem reduced or obscured by its personal allusions. To the contrary, as images the persons, places, and events alluded to have great suggestive power. They possess a mythic, poetic clarity. We need know nothing of Ginsberg's experiences at Columbia University to understand the poetic sense of the lines

> who passed through universities with radiant cool
>   eyes hallucinating Arkansas and Blake-light
>   tragedy among the scholars of war,
> who were expelled from the academies for crazy &
>   publishing
>   obscene odes on the windows of the skull.

And we do not have to know that the line "who walked all night with their shoes full of blood. . . ." refers to Herbert Huncke before we are moved to pity and terror by the picture. For Ginsberg, as for Whitman, the personal communicates the universal. The images are ultimately autonomous and multivalent engaging our poetic understanding by their very intensity and mystery.

Ginsberg was not alone in lamenting the destruction of a generation of frenzied, Dostoyevskian questers. In an early article on the Beats, Jack Kerouac mourned "characters of a special spirituality ... solitary Bartlebies staring out the dead wall window of our civilization. The subterranean heroes who'd finally turned from the 'freedom' machine of the West and were taking drugs, digging bop, having flashes of insight, experiencing the 'derangement of the senses,' talking strange, being poor and glad, prophesying a new style for American culture ... [but who] ... after 1950 vanished into jails and madhouses or were shamed into silent conformity." Ken Kesey, in his novel *One Flew over the Cuckoo's Nest,* also treats the issue of the imposition of a false, shallow, materialist-rationalist reality on the human spirit and the consequent persecution and oppression of those who cannot or will not accept the official reality.

Several lines near the end of the first section (from "who demanded sanity trials" to "animal soup of time—") describe the exploits and sufferings of the dedicatee of the poem, Carl Solomon, the martyr in whom Ginsberg symbolizes his generation of oppressed celestial pilgrims. Ginsberg's statement of spiritual solidarity with Solomon—"ah Carl, while you are not safe I am not safe"—presages the climactic third section of the poem. This compassionate identification with a fellow quester-victim is very similar to the Bodhisattva vow in Buddhism and anticipates the poet's later interest in Buddhist thought.

After a statement on the technique and intention of the poem, the section ends with strong images of ascent and rebirth and with a suggestion that the martyrs are redemptive, sacrificial figures whose sufferings can refine the present and the future.

The second section of the poem continues and expands the image of pagan sacrifice with which the first section concludes. To what merciless, cold, blind idol were the "angelheaded" of section one given in sacrifice?, Ginsberg asks. And he answers, "Moloch!" Moloch (or Molech), god of abominations, to whom children were sacrificed ("passed through the fire to Molech"), the evil deity against whom the Bible warns repeatedly, is the ruling principle of our age. To him all violence, unkindness, alienation, guilt, ignorance, greed, repression, and exploitation are attributable. The poet sees his face and body in buildings, factories, and weapons—as Fritz Lang saw his devouring maw in the furnace of *Metropolis.*

Ginsberg presents a comprehensive nightmare image of contemporary society, an inventory of terrors and afflictions that is as penetrating as Blake's "London." And like Blake in "London," Ginsberg places the source of human woe within human consciousness and perception. Moloch is a condition of the mind, a state of the soul: "Mental Moloch!"; "Moloch whose name is the Mind!" We are born, according to Ginsberg, in a state of "natural ecstasy," but Moloch enters the soul early. (See Blake's "Infant Sorrow.") We can regain that celestial, ecstatic vision of life ("Heaven which exists and is everywhere about us!") by emerging from the belly of Moloch, the monster that has devoured us, who "ate up . . . [our] brains and imagination." We can "wake up in Moloch!"

The remainder of the second section returns to a lament for the visionaries of section one. American society is seen as having consistently ignored, suppressed, and destroyed any manifestation of the miraculous, the ecstatic, the sacred, and the epiphanous.

In the pivotal section two of **"Howl,"** Ginsberg names Moloch as the cause of the destruction of visionary consciousness and describes the manifestations of this antispirit, this malevolent god. Ginsberg also indicates that the Blakean "mind forg'd manacles" of Moloch can be broken and that beatific vision can be regained. In this section the poet has also made clear that transcendence is not merely of concern to poets and mystics but to every member of the social body. Ginsberg has shown the effects of a society without vision. Commercialism, militarism, sexual repression, technocracy, soulless industrialization, inhuman life, and the death of the spirit are the consequences of Mental Moloch.

The third section of the poem reaffirms and develops the sympathetic, affectionate identification of Ginsberg with the man who for him epitomizes the rebellious visionary victim. The section is a celebration of the courage and endurance of Carl Solomon, a final paean to the martyrs of the spirit, and an affirmation of human love.

The piteous and brave cry of Solomon from the Rockland Mental Hospital is the essence of the poem's statement; his is the howl of anguished and desperate conviction. "The soul is innocent and immortal it should never die ungodly in an armed madhouse." The image of the "armed madhouse" is both macrocosmic and microcosmic. Each human soul inhabits the defensive, fearful "armed madhouse" of the ego personality, the social self, and the American nation has also become "an armed madhouse." (Kesey also uses the madhouse as metaphor in his novel *One Flew over the Cuckoo's Nest.*) The psychic armor that confines and isolates the individual ego selves and the nuclear armaments of the nation are mutually reflective; they mirror and create each other. At both levels, the individual and the national, the innocent and the immortal soul is starved, suffocated, murdered.

The imagery of crucifixion ("cross in the void," "fascist national Golgotha") reemphasizes Ginsberg's view of the visionary as sacrificial redeemer. Such images culminate in the poet's hope that Solomon "will split the heavens . . . and resurrect your living human Jesus from the superhuman tomb." I understand this to mean that Solomon will discover the internal messiah, liberate himself from Mental Moloch ("whose ear is a smoking tomb"), and attain spiritual rebirth.

The final images of **"Howl"** are confident and expansive, a projected apocalypse of Moloch, the Great Awakening "out of the coma" of life-in-death. Confinement, repression, alienation, and the dark night of the soul are ended. The "imaginary walls collapse" (walls of egotism, competition, materialism—all the woes and weaknesses engendered by Mental Moloch), and the human spirit emerges in victory, virtue, mercy, and freedom. The "sea-journey" of Solomon and of the human spirit is completed.

"Footnote to Howl," originally a section of "Howl" excised by Ginsberg on the advice of Kenneth Rexroth, extends the poet's vision of Blake's phrase "the Eye altering alters all" in "The Mental Traveller." The poem is a rhapsodic, Blakean, Whitmanesque illumination of the realm of the actual, the material world. If we accept and observe attentively, if we see, Ginsberg tells us, then all is reconciled and all is recognized for what it in essence truly is: holy, divine.

The eye can become discerning in the deepest sense. Perceiving the inscape of each object, each event and life, we can perceive the divine presence. We can see the angel in every human form; we can see "eternity in time"; we can even see "the Angel in Moloch." Perception is a reciprocal process. You are what you behold; what you behold is what you are. ("Who digs Los Angeles IS Los Angeles"—i.e., we can see either the dirty, lonely city of woe and weakness or the City of the Angels.) The essence of everything, of every being, is holy; only the form may be foul or corrupted; therefore, "holy the visions . . . holy the eyeball." In this way Ginsberg's earlier assertion that "Heaven . . . exists and is everywhere about us" is extended and fulfilled. If we can wake up in Moloch, we can awake out of Moloch.

The acceptance of the body is essential for Ginsberg, for the senses can be a way to illumination. The body is where we must begin. Throughout *Howl* sexual repression or disgust with the body or denial of the senses have been seen as forms of Mental Moloch: "Moloch in whom I am a consciousness without a body!"; "where the faculties of the skull no longer admit the worms of the senses." That is why the "**Footnote**" proclaims: "The soul is holy! The skin is holy! The nose is holy! The tongue and cock and hand and asshole holy!" Body and spirit are affirmed and reconciled.

Heracleitus taught that "the way up and the way down are the same way." For Ginsberg, in his night-sea journey, the path of descent described in the first two sections of "Howl" has become the path of ascent, of victory and vision, as presented in section three and in "Footnote to Howl." "Howl" records a solstice of the soul, a nadir of darkness, and then a growth again towards light. The poem exemplifies Jack Kerouac's understanding that to be Beat was "the root, the soul of Beatific."

For many of the romantic writers the loss of vision and the return to the actual was a permanent defeat: their lives and their art became sorrowful and passive; they languished and mourned; their behavior became self-destructive, even suicidal. Ginsberg transforms his season in hell into new resolve and purpose. Like Coleridge's ancient mariner, he has returned from a journey of splendors and wonders and terrors and intense suffering with a new vision of human community, a new reverence for life. Like Blake's Bard, his is a voice of prophetic anger, compassion, and hope. Implicit in

Ginsberg's vision in "Howl" of human solidarity and ultimate victory is the Blakean vow as expressed in "A New Jerusalem": "I shall not cease from mental fight . . . till we have built Jerusalem. . . ."

Ginsberg's sense of our common human necessity to redeem light from darkness, to seek vision and to practice virtue, is communicated in verse by the breath-measured, long-line, chant rhythm of "Howl." Andrew Welch observes that:

> The chant rhythm is a basic use of language that both reflects and directs social action toward community goals, a force that seems never to be far away when this rhythm enters poetry. In the Eskimo dance song, in the Navaho and Australian chants, in the prophecies of the Ghost Dance and of the Maya poet Chilam Balam, and in the poems of Ginsberg and Baraka, there is rhythmically and thematically a strong sense of movement and action, a communal rhythm enforcing communal participation and communal identity.

In this way, "Howl" is linked not only to the romantic tradition but also to the preliterary, oral, magic incantations of the universal shamanist tradition.

"Howl" not only invokes and participates in the tradition of vatic poetry but significantly contributes to and furthers that tradition. The poem's considerable achievements, by Ginsberg's use of myth, rhythm, and prophetic vision, are the resolution of the problems associated with transcendence and the embodiment in verse of a new syncretic mode of spiritual awareness, a new social consciousness. A quarter of a century later, "Howl" is still on point, still vital and still pertinent. Rather than a literary artifact, the poem is likely to become a classic.

Alexander Theroux (review date 11 June 1995)

SOURCE: "Bits from a Beat," in *Chicago Tribune Books,* June 11, 1995, p. 5.

[*In the following review of* Journals Mid-Fifties, *Theroux argues that the journals are often dull and reveal little of Ginsberg's life.*]

A pile of pages, scribbled odds and ends, Allen Ginsberg's *Journals Mid-Fifties (1954-1958),* the thoughts and observations of a young would-be poet between ages 28 and 32, are nothing like the polished records of Virginia Woolf, James Boswell or Anais Nin, certainly nothing like the studied and deliberate journals of Hawthorne or Henry James.

"The instigation for getting things together, finding all these old notebooks," writes Ginsberg, who back in the early '50s "thought it would be a good idea to keep track of it all"—the social foment, new consciousness and hip restlessness of the "Beat" movement—"was the advantage of having apprentices at Naropa during the mid-seventies, late seventies, and early eighties, who were beginning to type the whole mass of material up." Forgive me if I find it difficult to picture a Beat poet with typing "apprentice," never mind that being the occasion, formally stated, of publishing a book. In any case, Ginsberg had his pages. He had his typists. And he had his editor. He had his ducks in a row.

Gordon Ball has spent 12 years unearthing, sorting through, Ginsberg's breast-pocket spirals, manuscripts, letters, visual sketches, photographs and materials relating to this period in the poet's life. The third collection of Ginsberg's journals, following **Journals Early Fifties Early Sixties** (1977) and the earlier **Indian Journals** (1962), this new volume represents the period from his entering the Bay Area, where he would write **"Howl,"** through his first trip through the Arctic and to North Africa and Europe, where he made notes that would lead to **"Kaddish"** several years later.

This is a true potpourri, an agglomeration of personal notes, booklists, dreams—he dreamt a good deal about Kerouac, Brando, Truman, his mother Naomi, fumbling young men and fellatio—reveries of childhood, pages of porno, fragments of poems, fantasies, stories of pickups and the general complications of love and friendship.

It is in places desperately confessional ("I'm consumed with envy of Jack's holiness & devotion to single-minded expression in writing") and at times monstrously self-deluded ("I'm the greatest poet in America I know it and others know it too") and almost always utterly humorless.

Ginsberg writes in one entry, "I myself write nothing and am sick of fragment sketching. The poems I build out of them are fragmentary, slight." In another "Tiring of the Journal—no writing in it—promotes slop—an egocentric method."

What we do find to a degree in these pages is passion. Ginsberg develops intense feeling—often, it seems, born of insecurity and the need to belong—in the case of both friends and lovers. An intense yearning for an erotic encounter with Neal Cassady—the prototype for Dean Moriarty in Kerouac's *On the Road*—at last comes true, and when he is discovered in bed with Neal, Carolyn, Neal's wife, boots him out.

Ginsberg's expectations are always huge. In 1955 he meets Peter Orlovsky, 21 years old and recently discharged from the Army, and his journal entries are aflame—not only with considerable pangs of love for Orlovsky but also with his own trip through the "karma" of the whole complex situation.

He has a constant admiration for, competition with and jealousy of Kerouac, Lenin to his Trotsky. ("The droppings of the mind on the page," he grumpily writes of Kerouac's poems at one point. And later, "I didn't realize that Jack's self-pity was so akin—so imitative—of Wolfe's . . . Even to the very language of brooding, mysterious swirls and red October afternoons.")

A considerable passion in Ginsberg's life was his mother, Naomi. When she died, on June 9, 1956, he wrote: "Tenderness and a tomb—the world is a tomb of tenderness. Life is a short flicker of love. Went out into the grass knelt down and cried a little to heaven for her. Otherwise nothing."

It is Ginsberg's feeling that his childhood disappeared when she died—and his memory. The intermittent entries on Naomi constitute perhaps the most "felt" and sincerely committed motif in these pages and serve as first drafts towards the elegy that he eventually wrote, **"Kaddish."**

What sort of personality emerges in **Journals Mid-Fifties**? A tourist, an observer, a lonely gay man who is steeped in poetry and who loves poetry and who in studying past models, especially Christopher Smart, William Blake, Walt Whitman, William Carlos Williams, is himself trying to grow.

Ginsberg's search for guidance takes its cue, on several levels, especially from Whitman. "I Allen Ginsberg Bard out of New Jersey take up the laurel tree cudgel from Whitman." And all the rant and cant and chanting of the Square Deific we've come to know Ginsberg by—"America, when will you be angelic? / America when will you take off your clothes and be human? / America when will you give me back my mother? / America when will you give me back my love?" etc.—owes a lot to his immersion in the Good Gray Poet. He trembles with the same ecstasy—one of Ginsberg's favorite words—raids the same vocabulary and, with the same insistence on taking a national overview, ransacks the same chaos.

Sadly these pages are often remarkably dull and rarely original and insightful. Readers seeking more, and wider details of Ginsberg's life at his period are better referred to the biographies by Barry Miles and Michael Schumacher and to the forthcoming edition of Ginsberg's selected letters edited by Miles. When midway through the pages of **Journals Mid-Fifties 1954-1958** you come across these lines. "The notebook is holy the poem is holy. The voice is holy the audience is holy the typewriter is holy,"—my advice is, don't believe it.

Brian Docherty (essay date 1995)

SOURCE: "Allen Ginsberg," in *American Poetry: The Modernist Ideal,* edited by Clive Bloom and Brian Docherty, St. Martin's Press, 1995, pp. 199-217.

[*In the following essay, Docherty compares Ginsberg's work with that of Walt Whitman, arguing that they are similar in subject and philosophy but not style.*]

Allen Ginsberg nowadays looks like a successful Jewish dentist since he cut his hair and beard and donned suit and tie at the instigation of his Guru Chögyam Trungpa Rinpoche. As the half-title page of his **Collected Poems** notes, he is a 'Member of the American Institute of Arts and Letters and co-founder of the Jack Kerouac School of Disembodied Poetics at the Naropa Institute' and he describes himself gleefully in an interview with Jim Burns as 'a most respectable figure'. A founder member of the Beat Generation, along with Jack Kerouac and William Burroughs, circa 1944, Ginsberg is still best known for **Howl, Kaddish** and the poems of his first ten years or so as a public figure. (The early poems written from 1945 to 1952 did not appear until 1972 as **Gates of Wrath,** since the 'ms was carried to London by lady friend early fifties, it disappeared and I had no complete copy till 1968 when old typescript was returned thru poet Bob Dylan—it passed into his hands years earlier'.) Although Ginsberg clearly belongs to that neo-modernist grouping which derives its poetics from Ezra Pound and William Carlos Williams, he is a more social and political poet than either. He also derives parts of his poetics from William Blake, from the eighteenth-century poet Christopher Smart, the French Surrealists, Cézanne (whom he studied at Columbia with Meyer Shapiro), Herman Melville, Céline, and fellow Beats Kerouac and Burroughs. Another influence was his father Louis, a traditional lyric poet who appears in anthologies, such as *May Days* and *Unrest,* of radical poets of the 1920s and 1930s. He read his parents' magazines, such as *The New Masses* which published Mike Gold and Arturo Giovanitti, who used the long line and declamatory style of Walt Whitman and Carl Sandburg. Ginsberg also states that 'the poem from that period that had a big effect on me was Ben Maddow's *The City.* That influenced me a lot when I was writing **"Howl"**'.

Along with the radical politics, and the complex matrix of literary influences, there is also the transcendentalist philosophy of Thoreau, Emerson and Whitman. According to John Tytell, 'the Romantic militancy of the Beats found its roots in American transcendentalism . . . the Beats' spiritual ancestors were Thoreau, Melville and Whitman optimistically proclaiming with egalitarian gusto the raw newness and velocity of self renewing change in America while joyously admiring the potential of the common man'.

I would argue that the influence of Whitman has been most important to Ginsberg, and this essay will focus on Ginsberg's relation to Whitman, and the conjunction of sexuality and politics which informs their writing. There are, of course, several competing views of Whitman to be found and the view expressed in this essay does not aim to be full or complete. Whitman, of course, embraced contradiction and diversity and had no doubts about the value in social and political terms of an American poetry. Ginsberg, too, has from the start had a messianic faith in his ability to be a spokesman and chronicler, as set out in the opening line of **Howl:**

> I saw the best minds of my generation destroyed
> by madness, starving hysterical naked.

Nakedness; physical, emotional, psychological, was to become a recurrent theme of Ginsberg's poetry. This openness to life and experience is characteristic of the Beat project, and would in itself be enough to mark it as an oppositional tendency in the late 1940s and 1950s without the spirit of protest and revolt picked up on by most critics when **Howl and Other Poems** appeared in 1956. The shift in post-war values to Cold War hysteria and McCarthyite repression is well documented; the enemy without became the enemy within and the prosperity brought by the military-industrial complex had its accompanying tensions. Significantly, the major establishment poet of the fifties, Robert Lowell, talked of 'the tranquillized fifties', reflecting the Confessional poets' (Lowell, Berryman, Sexton *et al.*) obsession with interiority and public exorcism of private demons. Ginsberg's work has some superficial similarities with these poets, but it is always firmly grounded in the social and political as well as employing fundamentally different strategies (i.e. the ideogrammatic method of Pound rather than the procedures authorized by the New Criticism of Allan Tate and John Crowe Ransome).

Lifestyle and sexuality are celebrated, even paraded, in Beat writing, and their tender nakedness is quite different from, say, John Berryman's use of the poem as public psychoanalyst's couch. Since Ginsberg could be more open that Whitman, and was temperamentally inclined to be so, it quickly became apparent that this nakedness was offered as visions of the unspeakable individual, the homosexual. The love that dared not speak its name had not only come out of the closet, but followed Whitman's recommendation to 'unscrew the doors from the jamb' in a democratic gesture of inclusiveness, at least as far as men were concerned. There were, of course, other poets in the 1950s writing as gay men, notably Robert Duncan and Frank O'Hara, but Ginsberg is the pioneer closet dismantler. Whitman, however, is the American trailblazer.

It is in the 'Calamus' poems, even more than in the 'Children of Adam' poems, that Whitman's enduring quality as an American original resides. The first edition of *Leaves of Grass* makes clear Whitman's views on democracy and liberty, and many readers will consider that being the great poet of democracy is a sufficient claim to originality. We must look for more in a great poet, and I would argue that the open celebration of physicality and homosexuality, linked to democratic politics, constitutes Whitman's distinctive claim to be regarded as one of the major figures in world literature. This characteristic pluralism of expression, both personally and politically, represents the Whitmanian legacy to future writers, although the next generation, the poets of the 1890s such as Edwin Arlington Robinson, mainly conventional and conservative, turned away from Whitman's poetics. Even the arch-revolutionist of poetry, Ezra Pound, only came to terms with Whitman reluctantly, describing him as an exceeding great stench. Pound, in many ways a generous supporter of other poets, could also be a cantankerous bigot on occasion, and his remarks on homosexuality in *The Cantos* are in his cracker-barrel fascist mode. William Carlos Williams recognized Whitman as an innovator and major poetic force and resource, but he believed that Whitman had not succeeded in the search for a distinctive American vernacular which would form the basis of a specifically American poetry that owed nothing to Europe. Vachel Linsday, Robinson Jeffers and Carl Sandburg were virtually alone in pursuing a parallel course to Whitman in terms of a long-breathed line, and, of the three, only Sandburg's early works have much in common with Whitman. Lindsay's populism is that of the music hall and tent show while Jeffers's iconoclasm and 'inhumanism' are a severe corrective to Whitman's effusive optimism.

Whitman's qualities were undervalued or misunderstood by the 'New Critics', and were contrary to the prevailing spirit of the 1950s, characterized by Ginsberg as 'the syndrome of shutdown', so it was perhaps natural, even inevitable, that Ginsberg should have reached back past Williams and Communist versifiers such as Mike Gold to Whitman as a source of inspiration. He must indeed have screamed with joy reading Whitman for himself, since Ginsberg has characterized the way Whitman was taught at Columbia as stupidity and ignorance. Whitman also provided a way out of the psychic impasse induced by his earlier Blake fixation. Whilst a student at Columbia in June 1948, he had a mystical experience as a result of simultaneously reading Blake's 'Ah! Sunflower' and masturbating. Ginsberg heard a voice he took to be Blake's and, as Paul Portugés notes, 'suddenly he felt with Blake's voice guiding him that he could penetrate the essence of the universe. He felt himself floating out of his body and thinking that heaven was on earth.' Soon afterwards he heard Blake's voice chanting 'The Sick Rose,' then a third experience of Blake chanting 'The Little Girl Lost'. Ginsberg gained a new sense of purpose from this experience, feeling that everything which had happened in the past

few years, such as problems in his relationship with Neal Cassady, and the illness of his mother, had been some sort of preparation for the vision. Following this, Ginsberg, in an exalted state of mind, attempted to communicate his experience to his tutors, who doubted his sanity. During this period he had the opportunity of reading a collection of religious and mystical texts belonging to Russel Durgin, left in the flat where he was living. As well as Blake, he was reading Marvell, St Teresa of Avila, Plotinus, Martin Luther, St John of the Cross, Plato and St John Perse.

An intense reading of authors such as these is undoubtedly conducive to mystical events, and Ginsberg had two further episodes, one in the university bookshop, one in the field near the library. After this he felt compelled to tell everyone he met, with the result that people thought he was either lying or on the verge of a nervous breakdown. Even Jack Kerouac failed to take him seriously. About a year later, Ginsberg was committed to Columbia Psychiatric Institute, but this was the result of an incident where a gangster living in his apartment managed to crash a stolen car full of stolen property. Ginsberg, who was in the car but not party to the robbery, was arrested but later escaped prison through the influence of his tutors at Columbia. *Howl* resulted from his stay in hospital, but, perhaps more importantly, his Blake experiences gave him a direction and role as a poet, that of visionary prophet. He spent the years from 1950 to 1953 mostly in his father's house in Paterson, and the poems of this period, collected in *Empty Mirror* and *Gates of Wrath* are largely a sustained attempt to record his experiences.

Ginsberg's voice, manner and tone are quite distinct from Whitman's and their affinity lies in their affirmative responses to life, their proclamation of the physicallity of life, and the insistence on the link between sexual freedom and political freedom.

—*Brian Docherty*

These early poems are mostly archaic and derivative, densely packed with mysticism and abstraction, although a few fine poems, such as **"The Bricklayers' Lunch Hour"**, show the influence of Williams. The influence and example of Williams was decisive, turning Ginsberg towards a poetry packed with closely observed detail from the everyday world, concerned with literal accuracy and less with expressing ideas or abstract concepts. Prose journals supplied the basic material for the new work, organized by the physical breath, not by literary rules. Ginsberg derived a theory of the poetic line from his understanding of William's practice. One breath equalled one line of spoken poem and the poems were transcribed to show this on the page. Williams, who was in his sixties by this time, had a somewhat sparer line than the rhapsodic young Ginsberg, who started to write a long Whitmanian line as well as the more 'controlled' short-line poems. Ginsberg's poetry has always been more varied than *Howl,* of course, and he has been a keen student of Pound's and Charles Olson's use of the facilities of the typewriter to provide a score for the reading voice.

Ginsberg's voice, manner and tone are quite distinct from Whitman's and their affinity lies in their affirmative responses to life, their proclamation of the physicality of life, and the insistence on the link between sexual freedom and political freedom. As Tytell remarks, 'Ginsberg is feared in America just as Whitman was feared: to believe in democracy is the first step toward making it possible, and such seriousness is dangerous.' The extent of this fear became apparent in 1957 when Lawrence Ferlinghetti and Shigeyoshi Murao were prosecuted under Section 305 of the Tariff Act 1930, for allegedly selling or publishing obscene writings, namely ***Howl and Other Poems*** and issue 11/12 of *The Miscellaneous Man* (*The Miscellaneous Man* was actually published by William Margolis in Berkeley so this charge was dropped). Ferlinghetti and Murao (City Lights Bookshop Manager) were defended by three formidable lawyers as an ACLU test case, supported by testimony on the book's literary qualities from a variety of eminent critics and writers including Kenneth Rexroth, while the prosecution produced one tutor from a Catholic University and one private elocution teacher who proved totally inept. Hardly surprisingly the case was dismissed, but the judge established an important principle, namely that if a text could be demonstrated to have some literary value or worth, then the test of 'obscenity' could not be applied no matter what form of words was employed. It will not be forgotten that Whitman lost his job because of official disapproval of *Leaves of Grass,* and that in April 1882 his publisher James R. Osgood withdrew the 1881 edition after the Boston District Attorney ruled that certain poems were obscene. Whitman found another publisher in Philadelphia, and the publicity arising from this official censorship stimulated sales to the extent that he earned $1439.80 royalties that year, much more than in previous or subsequent years. Thus, in both cases, the state achieved exactly the opposite effect from what had been intended. Ginsberg's book sales run into millions world wide, he is probably the best selling poet ever.

It is clear that this last failed attempt at McCarthyite repression is a reflex of the corporate state's inability to deal with social criticism, and a recognition that Ginsberg stands in a long line of poets who have dissented publicly from the dominant values of their society or culture; and that, as Tytell reminds us, 'Ginsberg's most significant relation to Blake has been ideological—a sympathy with social concerns, a desire to transform consciousness to use poetry as an instrument of power or as sacramental invocation.' This of course

applies equally to his relationship with Whitman. The rejection of American values, or at least the bourgeois values of the post-World War II era, is clearly expressed in the 1949 poem **'Paterson.'**

The rejection of bourgeois values, whether the 'protestant work ethic', the immigrant (e.g. Jewish and Italian) drive for business success and suburban respectability, or the 'cleanliness is next to Godliness' ethos, contributed to the public perception of the Beats which saw them labelled as 'beatniks' or 'the great unwashed', and users of 'dangerous drugs'. The poem's second section features Ginsberg's vision of himself as a crucified and persecuted Christ figure, an expression of a desire for death or annihilation which is a recurrent characteristic of his poetry between 1948 and 1963, the year when Ginsberg finally rejected the influence of his Blake experiences, although Blake remained important in other ways. Nevertheless, in spite of the negativity of this poem it is clear that Ginsberg's poetry, as much as Kerouac's novels, epitomizes the Beat desire *to be,* and that it is affirmative, if at times a rather grim celebration of existence as a positive value in an era of apathy and dull conformity. The poem's insistent anaphoric 'rather' does express a positive choice, a claiming of the freedom to live life to the full, to experience everything and reject nothing. Thus the Beats were able to claim saint-like status, and ascribe 'beatitude' to their way of life.

Living life to the full meant accepting all aspects of sexuality and refusing to be limited by heterosexuality and monogamous pair-bonding. In practice, as far as Ginsberg was concerned, this meant homosexuality or bi-sexuality. As in all the best American movies, the Beat story was very much a 'buddy' story, with women featured only as 'minor characters'. Neal Cassady was the central figure in the drama, hero of *On the Road* and *Visions of Cody* and man of action who lacked Kerouac's Catholic inhibitions. Although basically heterosexual, he was capable of intimate relationships with men, including Ginsberg, who fell in love with him at first sight. The many poems to or about Cassady make it clear that Ginsberg virtually worshipped him. Marriage, first to Luanne, and then to Carolyn Cassady, did not restrain Neal Cassady, as the 1954 poem **'Love Poem on a Theme by Whitman'** makes clear. This poem is in Ginsberg's most Whitmanian manner, yet there are clear differences in tone and style. The announced 'theme' is based on Whitman's own poem 'The Sleepers', particularly lines 11-20

> The married couple sleep calmly in their beds, he with his
> palm on the hip of the wife, and she with her palm on the
> hip of the husband,
> The sisters sleep lovingly side by side in their bed,
> The men sleep side by side in theirs,

Another mother sleeps with her little child
  carefully wrapt

. . .

I go from bedside to bedside, I sleep close with the
  other sleepers
each in turn

—Leaves of Grass

I roll myself upon you as upon a bed, I resign
  myself to the dusk

—Leaves of Grass

The poem can be read as a celebration of homosexual love and companionship and a rejection of monogamy, and the 1855 edition contained a passage excised from subsequent editions, perhaps to avoid prosecution:

The cloth laps a first sweet eating and drinking,
Laps life-swelling yolks . . . laps ear of rose-corn,
  milky and just ripened:
The white teeth stay, and the boss-tooth advances
  in darkness,
And liquor is spilled on lips and bosoms by
  touching the glass, and the best liquor afterward

It seems clear that Whitman is describing the act of fellatio, probably by another man; Martin takes the view that nineteenth-century women were unlikely to indulge in fellatio, and that Whitman wrote "The Sleepers" as an example of 'the role of sexuality in the establishment of a mystic sense of unity'. This is close to Ginsberg's approach to sex, in so far as he views buggery as a means of achieving religious ecstasy and union with the godhead. Whitman's poem is structured as a vision, while Ginsberg enters unambiguously into the bedroom to interpose himself between the married couple.

Ginsberg is more explicit and less mysterious than Whitman, but the poem gains from its directness, whilst having a strong rhythm and a solidity of expression which make it one of the best of the pre-**'Howl'** poems. Ginsberg's literary relationship, in the sense of writing poems to or about Whitman, is made plain in **'A Supermarket in California',** which addresses Whitman directly as both a father figure and a lover. The poem is both funny and poignant, yet critics often describe Ginsberg's work as neurotic and joyless, usually failing completely to appreciate its moments of humour. Ginsberg speaks to Whitman man to man, but he also speaks poet to poet, inviting Whitman to share his view of modern America, where monopoly capitalism has turned the entire nation into a supermarket, where art and sex are commodities to be sold alongside the other 'frozen delicacies'.

One of Ginsberg's recurrent themes is that of bodily ageing and death, and it is significant that he imagines Whitman not as the brawny vigorous thirty-seven-year-old portrayed in section nine of 'I Sing the Body Electric', but as a 'lonely old grubber poking / among the meats in the refrigerator and eyeing the grocery boys'. His sad old man is, however, funny rather than pathetic as he cruises the aisles with manic determination, accosting the grocery boys. Ginsberg does not mock Whitman, but rather uses the humour to offer an ironic critique of a mercenary society where a lonely old man whose desires are undiminished is no longer able to obtain sexual satisfaction. Ginsberg's own appetite for juvenile flesh is well documented in his writing, and it may be that he is expressing his own fear that as he grows older he will no longer be able to compete successfully in the sexual marketplace. His imaginative compensation of 'possessing every frozen delicacy, and never passing the cashier' is disturbed, but not prevented, by the figure of repressive authority, the store detective.

However, Whitman's expansive confidence and his faith in America's ability to achieve an egalitarian democracy where adhesive love would be the norm, is not available to Ginsberg. His America, even the golden state of California, is a place where 'we'll both be lonely.' 'The lost America of love' has been replaced by 'blue automobiles in driveways', the suburban conformity which the Beats set out to subvert. For Ginsberg, Whitman is surrogate parent and teacher, the figure of liberation his own father Louis could not be. The affection for Whitman, and the recognition of his indebtedness, is clear in Ginsberg's poem, but it is also clear that the America of 1956 is not the America of 1856. The corporate state, dominating every aspect of people's lives, is a powerful and oppressive force in Ginsberg's poetry, just as it is absent in Whitman. The great industrial empires of such capitalist 'übermenschen' as Carnegie, Rockefeller, and Pierpont Morgan are not dealt with in Whitman's poetry, even though the various monopolies were well established by the time the later editions of *Leaves of Grass* were published. Instead he describes American working men as craftsmen and small masters, picturing them in heroic terms. Ginsberg, by contrast, grew up with the organized militant working class, taken to political meetings as a child by his mother. In **'America',** one of his finest fusions of Jewish humour and social comments, he describe his cultural heritage. He grew up surrounded by the rich Jewish, Communist, and Anarchist political traditions and this background should not be forgotten even though poems like **'Kral Majales'** show a demonstrable disenchantment with Communism in its Eastern European formulations.

'Kral Majales', written on 7 May 1965, is one of the texts where sexuality intersects with politics in Ginsberg's writing. He returns to the insistent anaphoric technique of *Howl* to document his outrage at his treatment by the Czechoslovakian bureaucracy and its police henchmen. In Ginsberg's hands, the anaphora gives the impression that the poem has started in mid-sentence or mid-stanza. It gives the effect of a television news interview where what is transmitted is obviously an excerpt of the complete interview or statement. Geoffrey Thurley describes Ginsberg as 'the public dropout, the guru, the subterranean jet-setter, the King of the May', a sneer which imputes a lack of sincerity of Ginsberg's past. Thurley is, however, correct to point out the public stance of poems such as **'Kral Majales',** as demonstrated by p. 355 of the *Collected Poems,* which is a reproduction of a broadsheet, with art by Robert La Vigne, showing the poem's text flanked by two silhouettes of a naked Ginsberg in tennis shoes, with six hands and finger cymbals. Each figure is enclosed in a large penis column. This broadsheet provides a conclusive answer to those critics who claim that Ginsberg's work is formless: form and content are perfectly fused in a gesture which not only illustrates his underlying principles, but also functions as a definitive reply to the Czechoslovakian authorities.

The poem condemns both State Communism and capitalism, and notes Ginsberg's dismay at discovering that the Communist State has a backward and repressive attitude towards homosexuality. Most of the poem, though, is a gesture of triumph, the personal being privileged over the narrowly political—'And I am the King of May, which is the power of sexual youth' . . . 'and I am the King of May, naturally, for I am of Slavic parentage and a / Buddhist Jew.' "**Kral Majales**" ends with the political reality, a Kafka-esque note of repression by the all-powerful and unaccountable bureaucratic state. The poem has a powerful symbolic force, because although Ginsberg has been beaten up and deported, he has turned the occasion into a ringing statement of his personal beliefs which invites comparison with Whitman's optimism. Whitman was never faced with this sort of state power, and indeed writes as if the state did not exist. The state cannot censor poems such as "**Kral Majales**" and cannot prevent Ginsberg acting as witness to the change in consciousness he is helping to bring about. Twenty-five years after he was thrown out of Prague, Ginsberg returned to recover the notebooks confiscated by the secret police and reclaim his crown. Ginsberg was the last King of the May to be elected. In the new democratic Czechoslovakia, where the president is a former dissident playwriter (Vaclav Havel), his crown is 'ceremoniously handed back to him by the Major of Prague ("who just happens to be the Czech translator of Gary Snyder's poetry", Ginsberg adds to stress how the Beat poets were admired in Eastern Europe)'. Poems such as this reached a huge audience and helped to radicalize attitudes, and give people the strength to start the process of changing their lives. Sexual liberation and political liberation are inseparably linked, and Ginsberg's poetry was an important part of delivering that message in the 1960s. The long Whitmanian line was essential to carry the stream of energy which flowed out as Ginsberg combined 'the rhetorical voice of American populist tradition with a passionate, personal intelligence and wit'. However, as Ginsberg explains to Jim Burns, the reactionaries are fighting back.

> 'It's similar to McCarthyism', Ginsberg insists, and you can also draw parallels with Nazi book burning and Stalinist attacks on intellectuals broadcasting *Howl,* not to mention work by Kerouac, Genet, Henry Miller, and many others. Ginsberg sees it as part of a pattern which includes censorship of student publications, restrictions on press reporting of certain events, FBI surveillance of libraries and a long list of similar activities. 'It's an attack on language' he claims, and an attempt at thought control. 'Much of my poetry is specifically aimed to rouse the sense of liberty of thought and political social expression of that thought in young adolescents. I believe I am conducting spiritual war for liberation of their souls from mass homogenization of greedy materialistic commerce and emotional desensitization. Pseudo-religious legal intolerance with my speech amounts to setting up a state religion much in the mode of intolerant. Ayatollah or a Stalinoid bureaucratic party line'. The interesting thing is, Ginsberg points out, that the neo-conservative and religious fanatics who are behind much of the drive for censorship are the types who, a few years ago, would have been in the forefront of anti communist agitation. Now they use the same tactics as their one time opponents 'to enforce the authority of their own solidified thought police and ethical systems'. And is it strange that this should happen? 'No', answers Ginsberg, 'Blake put his finger on it when he said "They became what they beheld".'

Ginsberg also tells Jim Burns that although he has not written much poetry since *White Shroud* he is working on a collection of photographs and that his opera *Hydrogen Box,* written with Philip Glass, has been performed at the Spoleto Festival in Italy. It is to be hoped that the enemies of free speech, so intent on denying Ginsberg's constitutional right of free speech and thought, are suitably dismayed (or enraged) to note that in 1990 Ginsberg has a new recording of poetry and music (*The Lion for Real* on Antilles Records) and still draws audiences of thousands for public readings in London and elsewhere. The message of Blake and Whitman is still being carried to all corners of the world in person and on compact disc.

One of the ways in which Ginsberg differs from Whitman

is in the personalized nature of his poems. Whitman of course was not in a position to write openly to, or about, Peter Doyle, or to dedicate a volume to him, because of the enormous social pressure which made absolute discretion imperative. The year after Whitman died, another notable homosexual, the Russian composer Tchaikovsky, was forced to commit suicide. Ginsberg, writing one hundred years later, and more concerned with recording his full experience openly and honestly, rejected all constraints. There are many beautiful passages depicting male intimacy in Whitman, but nothing resembling Ginsberg's **'Many Loves'**. Appropriately, the poem has an epigraph from Whitman, 'Resolved to sing no songs henceforth, but those of manly attachment'. Taking this as a starting point, **'Many Loves'** is the first of a number of poems about Ginsberg's relationship with Neal Cassady. It is explicit without being pornographic, and answers the old question, 'what do homosexuals do in bed?.

The poem details the physical pleasures of lovemaking with a man as well as giving a potted biography of Cassady's youth in Denver, and describes him in heroic terms. The emphasis on Cassady's juvenile career as a car thief, and on his physical beauty, no doubt contributed to the myths surrounding Cassady, and to an underestimation of his talents, and his influence on the writing of Ginsberg and Jack Kerouac. In May 1968, Ginsberg wrote **'Please Master'**, another love poem to Cassady, but in a different mode. In **'Many Loves',** Ginsberg writes that his 'first mistake' was to make Cassady his 'Master', a statement which a reading of their correspondence will bear out. **'Please Master'** places Ginsberg in the position of acolyte, anxious to please even by acts of self-abasement. The tone is pleadingly submissive, expressing 'a desire to be fucked, a desire which one supposes is the equivalent to the poet's desire to be fucked by the universe, to be overcome by its sensations'.

As Martin points out, this is a long way from anything in Whitman, where the sexual act is mutual and reciprocal, but he notes that **'Please Master'** is a 'necessary political—sexual statement of the need to admit openly one's desire for anal intercourse'. He goes on to make the curious statement that 'Ginsberg's master is unnamed, undescribed, totally anonymous; he is the coming to life of a statue, a fantasy embodied', which suggests that his reading of Ginsberg has been somewhat cursory. It would be clear to anyone who had followed the careers of Ginsberg and other Beat figures, and who had read the poems, journals and letters attentively, that it is Cassady who is being addressed. Martin was also presumably unaware that Neal Cassady had died in miserable circumstances only four months before the poem was written. It was printed in *The Fall of America* as part of Section III, 'Elegies for Neal Cassady'. The first of these elegies is dated 10 Feb 1968, making it clear that Ginsberg was mourning the death of a friend and former lover. This knowledge gives the elegies a real poignancy, and

point to the difficulties involved in coming to terms with the death of someone you have known for over twenty years.

Another important difference between Whitman and Ginsberg lies in their respective attitudes to women. Whitman believed in social and political equality for women, and he urged women to be open, frank, and active in their relationships. He was opposed to nineteenth-century concepts of femininity, and believed that his own greater openness about sex might make a contribution to women's emancipation by encouraging similar openness in women. In Section 5 of 'Song of Myself', he declares that all 'the women are my sisters and lovers', and in Section 21 claims

> I am the poet of the woman the same as the man,
> And I say it is as great to be a woman as to be a
>   man,
> And I say there is nothing greater than the mother
>   of men.

> —*Leaves of Grass*

In "A Woman Waits for Me", he states 'all were lacking if sex were lacking' and

> Now I will dismiss myself from impassive women
> I will go stay with her who waits for me, and with
>   those
> women that are warm-blooded and sufficient for
>   me

> —*Leaves of Grass*

However, although Whitman wanted American women to be 'warm-blooded', like most nineteenth-century men (and twentieth-century men?) he had a blank spot regarding female sexuality. 'Adhesiveness' was a male preserve, and active female desire, especially for other women, does not feature in Whitman's view of women's capacities. He may not have appreciated that a positive, active, emancipated woman might well be a lesbian. Apart from this limitation, Whitman's attitudes to women are considerably more progressive than most male writers. Ginsberg's attitudes in many respects form a sorry contrast, especially for a poet committed to Gay Liberation. The attitude of fear and disgust encountered in his poetry may derive in part from his reaction to Naomi Ginsberg's behavior after her breakdown, but negative attitudes to women are commonplace among Beat writers. Burroughs, in particular, exhibits a particularly unpleasant brand of misogyny, and it is perhaps fortunate that it was not Burroughs who became the 'public guru' of the 60s counter-culture. Gary Snyder, although weak in his understanding of sexism, is one of the few Beat figures who actually likes and respects women.

The first poem the reader encounters in the *Collected Poems,* **'In Society'**, is dated Spring 1947, and the second stanza is an ugly tirade against a woman who says she doesn't like the speaker of the poem. In **'The Blue Angel'**, Marlene Dietrich is portrayed as a 'life sized toy' who needs 'a man / to occupy my mind'. Women, for Ginsberg, are machines with no life of their own until they can capture a man, from whom they will drain the mental and emotional energies. This concept perhaps owes something to the Jewish idea of the 'golem'. Woman is seen as an object, the 'other' to be avoided by men if they wish to remain alive and independent, a view strikingly at variance with Whitman's. In 'How Come He Got Canned at the Ribbon Factory', a male apprentice intrudes into the female sphere of operations, and is perceived as 'this character', inadequate and incompetent, and dismissed by the women as 'not a real man any way but a goop'. Relations between men and women are clearly problematic for Ginsberg and it is significant that he needed Whitman's guidance and example to write **'Love Poem on Theme by Whitman'**. Neal Cassady and Jack Kerouac were both bisexual to some extent, and even Burroughs fathered a child by the wife he shot in Mexico City, but Ginsberg celebrates the exclusivity of sex with younger (blond) men, as the opening two poems in Section III testify. Ginsberg's partner for many years from 1954 on was Peter Orlovsky, and **'Malest Cornifici Tuo Catullo'** presumably records the start of this relationship. **'Dream Record: June 1955'** records the stereotype of casual relationships and drunken sex, a paradigm of pre-AIDS innocence. Versions of this poem, such as **'Sweet Boy Gimme Your Ass'** are scattered throughout the *Collected Poems* and *White Shroud.*

'Kaddish', Ginsberg's elegy for his mother, written after her death in 1956, is in some senses an antiphon to **'Howl'** and necessary to an understanding of the pressures which inform **'Howl'**. It is a true epic in that it includes history; the history of Naomi Ginsberg's life in America, the history of her relations with her family, the history of her breakdown and treatment, the history of political radicalism in twentieth-century America, and the history of her troubled relationship with Allen. It is a complex occasion, and one of the few instances where Ginsberg actually makes use of his Jewish heritage, rather than merely referring to it. The response by Jewish literary critics was divided, with one critic denying the poet's right to use the ritual term 'kaddish', claiming that the use of tradition was illegitimate. Other critics were able to be more positive, and respond to the personal and historical imperatives of the poem. A selection of these responses to **'Kaddish'** can be found in Lewis Hyde's invaluable compendium of Ginsberg criticism.

The physical decline which accompanied Naomi Ginsberg's mental breakdown is graphically described, with the poet's attitudes to his mother portrayed as a mixture of disgust, compassion, indifference and Oedipal fascination. Nothing is withheld. Although, according to the poem, her first breakdown occurred in 1919, the poem is mainly concerned with events from the mid 1930s to the late 1940s, the years of Ginsberg's adolescence and early manhood. Whitman demonstrated that male homosexuality could be compatible with positive attitudes to women, and Ginsberg's attitudes cannot be ascribed to his gayness. However, given the traumas of his family life as related in **'Kaddish'**, his views are understandable although not excusable. The contradictions in his position are revealed in **'This Form of Life Needs Sex'**, a poem which mixes fear of women with wry humour, and a knowledge of mutability. It starts out 'I will have to accept women / if I want to continue the race' and goes on to talk about 'ignorant Fuckery' asking 'why have I feared' the 'one hole that repelled me 1937 on'. He can still, however, be wryly funny about both the joys and limitations of homosexuality.

His 'situation' is that the sexual revolution and the accompanying revolution of consciousness has no place for women, since Ginsberg has difficulty seeing women as people, human beings in their own right. Given these attitudes from someone perceived as a leader of the American radical movement it is now clear why there was a feminist backlash from about 1968 onwards. I do not wish to caricature the complex history of Women's Movement, but that history is outside the scope of this chapter. However, as Gloria Steinem has said, 'the sexual revolution was not our revolution'. Yet according to John Tytell, the Whitmanian adhesiveness which inspired Ginsberg was 'his feeling of Kinship with all classes and kinds of people'. The Women's Movement was obliged to work out its own version of adhesiveness, often in angry rejection of men and male sexuality, but it may be that attitudes towards women encountered in Beat writing, and in Beat-influenced songwriters such as Bob Dylan, provided a necessary catalyst for the development of modern feminism.

In 1968, Ginsberg provided an eloquent definition of adhesiveness, in testimony before Judge Hoffman at the 'Chicago Seven' trial. In reply to a question by prosecutor Foran on the religious significance of **'Love Poem on Theme by Whitman'**, he replied:

> Whitman said that unless there was an infusion of feeling, of tenderness, of fearlessness, of spirituality, of natural sexuality of natural delight in each others bodies, into the hardened materialistic, cynical, life denying, clearly competitive, afraid, scared, armored bodies, there would be no chance for spiritual democracy to take root in America—and he defined that tenderness between the citizens as in his words, an 'Adhesiveness', a natural tenderness, flowing between all citizens, not only men and women, but also a tenderness between men and men

as part of our democratic heritage, part of the Adhesiveness which would make the democracy function: that men could work together not as competitive beats but as tender lovers and fellows. So he projected from his own desire and from his own unconscious a sexual urge which he felt was normal to the unconscious of most people, though forbidden for the most part.

The obvious question must be, where are the women in all this, except as adjuncts to men? Ginsberg's 'demos'—the people—appears to be men only. No wonder Joyce Johnson called her book *Minor Characters,* an accurate reflection of the importance of women in the lives of the Beat writers, and of the part women were allowed to play in the counter-culture revolution. If that revolution was a failure, it was because any revolution which incorporated the oppression of women into its structure (as well as alienating the working classes) could not succeed. Nevertheless there were significant gains, and Ginsberg and the Beat writers achieved a great deal in terms of sexual liberation and personal liberation, and helped to bring about a change of consciousness which cannot be reversed. As Kenneth Rexroth, who supported some aspects of the counter-culture noted, the contempt for women and the Beat practice of 'treating a girl exactly as one would treat a casual homosexual pick up in a public convenience' cannot be ignored or glossed over. Rexroth also points out that

> it is pretty hard to dismiss anyone who can fill the largest auditorium in any city he chooses to appear in like Joan Baez, Bob Dylan, or the Beatles—and who has produced thousands of followers, in all the civilized and many uncivilized languages.

Rexroth, who as both a major poet and a trenchant critic was perhaps uniquely qualified to comment on the development of American poetry, places Ginsberg as 'one of the most traditionalist poets now living. His work is an almost perfect fulfillment of the long Whitman, Populist, social revolutionary tradition in American poetry. . . . Ginsberg meant something of the greatest importance and so his effects have endured and permeated the whole society. Rexroth was the master of ceremonies at the historic Six Gallery reading which launched the Beat Generation as a public phenomenon, and in the 1950s acted as Godfather to the San Francisco poets. Although his initial enthusiasm waned, his judgement recorded here must have been gratifying recognition, especially after some of the things written by critics and academics, who have largely failed to recognize the value of the Beat project. But then, Ginsberg expressed his attitude to Norman Podhoretz and other critics in *Notes for Howl and Other Poems:*

A word on Academics; poetry has been attacked

by an ignorant & frightened bunch of bores
who don't understand how its made, & the trouble
with these creeps is that they wouldn't know
  Poetry
if it came up and buggered them in broad daylight

Appropriately, this statement is dated Independence Day, the occasion of the celebration of the American Revolution.

Helen Vendler (essay date 1995)

SOURCE: "The Reversed Pietà: Allen Ginsberg's 'Kaddish'," in *Soul Says: On Recent Poetry,* Belknap Press, 1995, pp. 9-15.

[*In the following excerpt, Vendler discusses Ginsberg's use of traditional Jewish prayer, the influence of other writers, and his observations on his mother in the poem* "Kaddish."]

The poem **"Kaddish,"** now thirty years old, appeared in 1961 with two manifestos by Ginsberg bracketing it. The first, on the copyright page of the volume *Kaddish,* announced that "the established literary quarterlies of my day are bankrupt poetically thru their own hatred, dull ambition or loudmouthed obtuseness," and, in acknowledging previous appearances of the poems in journals, remarked that two of those publications were begun by "youths who quit editing university magazines to avoid hysterical academic censorship." This Ginsberg manifesto is one of irritated satiric energy; the other, appearing on the back cover of the volume, abounds in passionate phrases like "broken consciousness," "suffering anguish of separation," "blissful union," "desolate . . . homeless . . . at war," "original trembling of bliss in breast and belly," "fear," "defenseless living hurt self," and "hymn completed in tears." Things that are separate in the manifestos—satire and pathos—come together in Ginsberg's great elegy for his mother. Though **"Kaddish"** will always remain a son's poem, a poem which we enunciate in the position of a mourning child, it is now more than ever Naomi Ginsberg's poem, too—a poem bringing into representation, with both tragic and comic energy, a woman's hideously afflicted life. In this reversal of the cultural icon we call the pietà, we see not the mother holding the broken body of the son, but the son holding the broken body of the mother. "I saw my self my own mother and my very nation trapped desolate," says Ginsberg in his manifesto; but it is his mother that is the chief icon of the trappedness.

"Kaddish" declares its descent from classical elegy in its epigraph from Shelley's Hellenizing "Adonais"—"Die, / If thou wouldst be with that which thou dost seek!" Personal extinction becomes real at the death of the sheltering parent; and Ginsberg, through his own resistance to death, has to find a way to the identity of idealization and dissolution understood by Shelley.

"Kaddish" is chiefly an elegy of the body—the physical body and the historically conditioned body of Naomi Ginsberg. Is it the first such elegy of the body (rather than the transcendent self) of another? *Leaves of Grass* was the first American book to expose at length the physical and historical body, but that body was Whitman's own; in "Kaddish" it is Naomi's body that is born, grows, gives birth, is scarred in flesh and brain, rots in a living death, dies, and is buried. The absence of a developed Jewish doctrine of the afterlife may in part explain why this poem—named so defiantly with a title foreign to non-Jews—is a poem of the body. The biblical history internalized as the history of the Jewish people may explain why it is also so much a poem of history. Finally, besides being a poem of the body and a poem of history, it is a poem of balked prayer. The prayer of the Kaddish, quoted in the second part of the poem, forms, as Ginsberg has said, "the rhythmic substrate" of the poem: "Yisborach, v'yistabach, v'yispoar, v'yisroman, v'yisnaseh, v'yishador, v'yishalleh, v'yishallol. . . ." Ginsberg, in California when his mother died, missed her funeral, where (as Ginsberg's brother wrote him) there were not enough people present to form a minyan, so Kaddish could not be said for her. Several years later, Ginsberg wrote his own "Kaddish" to repair the lack. The rhythm of the Hebrew Kaddish shows itself chiefly at the end of the first part of the poem, the elegy proper: "Magnificent, mourned no more, marred of heart, mind behind, married dreamed, mortal changed . . . / almed in Earth, balmed in Lone"; and, a moment later, "This is the end, the redemption from Wilderness, way for the Wonderer, House sought for All . . . Death stay thy phantoms!"

A poem of the body, then; and a poem of history; and a balked rhythmic prayer or hymn. "Kaddish" has five numbered parts, and one extra-numeric "Hymmnn" between Parts II and III. Part I is a lyrical overture addressed to Naomi, sounding the themes that will follow. Part II is a history—a recapitulation of Naomi's life intertwined with that of her son; in it, Naomi is alternately addressed in the second person and described in the third person, so that this part of the poem is both a colloquy with her and a history of her life. This is the part that is savagely comic—stucco'd (as Whitman might say) with birds and quadrupeds all over. In the "Hymmnn" of chanted blessings (imitating the recital of blessings in the Kaddish) that follows Part II, Naomi is both a living "you" and a dead "Thee." Part III is a prayer against forgetting—"Only not to have forgotten"—followed by a summary historical list of the insults to Naomi's body. Part IV is a litany with the refrain "Farewell." And Part V is a fugue in which the idealizing voice of prayer is repeatedly mocked with the crow's voice of mortal dissolution— "Lord Lord Lord caw caw caw."

In the Part I overture, the poet calls himself hymnless and Heavenless. How then does he arrive, many pages later, at his heavenly "Hymmnn" of blessings? It is Part II that lies between, the unbearably graphic, scandalous, farcical, and horrifying narrative of events in Naomi's life. "How can he write such things about his mother?" I was asked by one shaken student. Ginsberg spares us nothing of the maternal body: "Convulsions and red vomit coming out of her mouth—diarrhea water exploding from her behind—on all fours in front of the toilet—urine running between her legs— left retching on the tile floor smeared with her black feces— unfainted." In Ginsberg the Jewish immigrant novel meets lyric existentialist farce: "We're all alive at once then—even me & Gene & Naomi in one mythological Cousinesque room—screaming at each other in the Forever." The son, in the moment in which the poem looks satirically at its own parallel doings in life, tries to hold back madness with words: "I pushed her against the door and shouted 'DON'T KICK ELANOR!'" And at the moment in which the poem looks most tragically at its own doings, the mother does not recognize the son: "You're not Allen—." Can a poet elegize someone who no longer recognizes him? Can words, futile against madness in life, conquer madness after death?

In expanding elegy to take in such "un-English" details as Camp Nicht-Gedeiget, quotations from the Hebrew Kaddish, scenes in the Bronx and Newark, and Naomi's half-delusional list of enemies including "Hitler, Grandma, the Capitalists, Franco, Mussolini," Ginsberg wrenched the form away from its classical gravity and taught his contemporaries a lesson in American colloquiality (as Robert Lowell later acknowledged while loosening his own style). The poem is Ginsberg's own story as well as his mother's story, and it inserts into American lyric the self-conscious and alienated Jewishness of at least one of its poets, a Jewishness that Ginsberg's father, Louis, in his more innocuous "assimilated" poetry, had been unable to voice. The androgynous nature of "Kaddish," as the son-poet becomes stronger than his father by defining his own life as half Naomi's life, recalls the way the poet John Berryman eventually found his own voice through appropriating the sensibility of Anne Bradstreet as he imagined it. Ginsberg's "Kaddish" is not so much an incorporation of woman as a capitulation to her: she is "Naomi, from whose pained head I first took Vision." The Muse, so helpless in "Lycidas"—"Nor could the Muse herself defend her son"—has moved into a position of power here, appearing as a "Communist beauty, Russian-faced" (in defiance of American fears in the fifties of both Russia and Communism). But Naomi's eventual collapse into madness makes the Orphic son-poet wonder whether he can defend his mother.

The dignity of "Kaddish" is not compromised by, but is rather constituted by, its shameful and embarrassing disclosures, as well as by its hysteria, argot, and theatricality—all

"Jewish" qualities by conventional English and American Protestant standards, qualities largely suppressed in earlier immigrant Jewish poetry in deference to those standards. The madness of Naomi—and the consequent diction of the poem, which has to match her weird sublimity and hyperbole with its own—are clearly shown to be overdetermined phenomena; there are so many cultural and historical causes erupting into madness and poetry that it is impossible to list them all, though the extraordinary litany of Part IV makes the attempt.

This litany requires some explanation. It seems to resume much that the first three parts—the overture, the life history with its hymn, and the memorial recapitulation "Only not to have forgotten"—have already described. And at first the litany seems merely an extension of the Part III memorial that preceded it ("Only not to have forgotten") in its opening, "O mother / what have I forgotten." But it then modulates from a farewell into an undaunted physical inventory of Naomi's body—its appearance and its history. We can, perhaps, see the first half of this section as the elegiacally conventional, but always shocking, ritual viewing of the corpse before burial. The poet's steady gaze passes without flinching to each body part in turn, in a posthumous blazon disarticulating the once unified parts from each other. But then this section of the poem comes to a halt on, and remains fixated on, the least physical of body parts, Naomi's eyes. It dwells on them for twenty-eight lines, while they painfully fill to overbrimming with the physical, mental, familial, and political sufferings of Naomi's history—Russia, no money, false China, Aunt Elanor, starving India, pissing in the park, America taking a fall, failure at the piano, Czechoslovakia attacked by robots, killer Grandma—all the way down to the surgical attacks on the body itself—pancreas removed, appendix operation, abortion, ovaries removed, shock treatment, lobotomy—and the last crippling blows (one inner, one outer), divorce and stroke. It is an extraordinary passage, acting out to extremes and beyond Keats's words, "Do you not see how necessary a World of Pains and troubles is to school an Intelligence and make it a soul?" The blank eyes of the Russian child Naomi, arriving as an immigrant in the New World, gradually fill with consciousness through pain, and then move from consciousness to Vision—till they decline from Vision to madness. As they fill with experience, they become repositories of all sorrowful human awareness. They finally stand alone as spiritual wells of knowing:

> with your eyes alone
> with your eyes
> with your eyes
> with your Death full of Flowers

The flowers recall Ginsberg's Blakean talisman the Sunflower, which, whatever the cost, follows the light of reality, which Ginsberg here calls "Sun of all Sunflowers"; and

they recall the apotheosized Naomi before madness, her "long black hair . . . crowned with flowers."

The ascent to the eyes crowned with flowers counters, while not eradicating, the horror of Naomi Ginsberg's end in the lunatic asylum, and reasserts Ginsberg's belief—or hope—that somewhere behind schizophrenia and lobotomy lingered Naomi's early saner self, a belief vindicated by the consoling letter he receives after her death, in which Naomi once again knows him: "Get married Allen don't take drugs." The letter releases the son, too, from his last visual image of his mother in the locked ward of the state asylum, as it says, "The key is in the sunlight at the window—I have the key."

What would **"Kaddish"** be without the miraculous posthumous letter, the reprieve from despair? The letter stands as the crowning spiritual apotheosis of Naomi as mother and visionary, and is paired, thematically, with her physical apotheosis as a young Communist Muse with a mandolin. A traditional Western elegy would end with the double apotheosis. But Ginsberg goes beyond the consoling letter and gives his elegy a less transcendent Buddhist end, in which human experience, however full, is finally both spiritually and physically obliterated: "Naomi underneath this grass my halflife and my own as hers . . . / my eye be buried in the same Ground where I stand in Angel." Naomi's tear-suffused eyes and the poet's eye will both be buried in her grave. The only eye that remains at the close is that of the Universe: "Lord Lord great Eye that stares on All and moves in a black cloud." Against the impersonal, dark, and staring Eye of Necessity, Ginsberg sets the brief claim of lyric voice, "my voice . . . / the call of Time . . . an instant in the universe . . . / an echo in the sky the wind." He is remembering Hart Crane's "The Broken Tower":

> And so it was I entered the broken world
> To trace the visionary company of love, its voice
> An instant in the wind (I know not whither hurled)
> But not for long to hold each desperate choice.

The end of **"Kaddish"** is almost a standoff, as the ravens of unresting thought (Yeats's phrase) beat back the son's prayer in the desolate cemetery on Long Island. As Part V being, the crows' "Caw caw caw" antiphonally counters the son's "Lord Lord Lord," and at first the competing chants are held to a single anaphoric position at the beginning of each line. In the penultimate line, the standoff breaks down, and the crows begin to shriek after every halting broken phrase, phrases that summon up the poet's life or his mother's or father's—

> caw caw all years my birth a dream caw caw New
>   York the bus
> the broken shoe the vast highschool caw caw

At this point, the poet summons up all his Blakean force and cries out to the crows that these horrors are nonetheless "all Visions of the Lord." With that, the crows, though persisting, are balked of ultimate victory; the last line begins and ends with "Lord":

> all Visions of the Lord
> Lord Lord Lord caw caw caw Lord Lord Lord caw
>   caw caw
> Lord

The necessitarian Lord here invoked is the Eye in the black cloud, the Eye that only "stares" (a Yeatsian stare remembered perhaps from "Lapis Lazuli"—"On all the tragic scene they stare"). This Eye does not mark the fall of the sparrow. It is observational, not providential. The tenderness of **"Kaddish,"** which creates in some of its moments a "death full of Flowers," is not allowed finally to govern the poem. And of those two manifestos bracketing the **Kaddish** volume with which I began, the one on the back cover summing up the "broken consciousness of mid twentieth century suffering anguish of separation from my own body" is the one that relates most truly to the title poem. The irritable front-cover manifesto recalling the literary wars of the fifties between the university quarterlies and the Best poets tends to fade in memory, while the backcover testimony lasts. Though the topical quarrel is true, and lively, and worth remembering in literary history, the poem recalls itself to us now chiefly as memorable rhythmic speech. The monumental quality of **"Kaddish"** makes it one of those poems that, as Wallace Stevens said, take the place of a mountain. The eventual power of poetry always exists on an "exquisite plane," as Stevens said, beside which reality—even a reality as transfixing as the life of Naomi Ginsberg—is only, as Stevens concluded, "the base." "Reality is only the base," he wrote. "But," he added, "it is the base." In terms of literary history, we might say the same about the conventional elegy as we knew it in the past—with its Muse, its singer, its flowers, its eulogy, its dirge, its apotheosis. It is only the base of **"Kaddish,"** but it is the base. And on that classical base Ginsberg created the most nonclassical poem in the American elegiac canon, the immigrant elegy that seemed waiting in the air to be written, as we found to out astonishment when we first read it thirty years ago.

Helen Vendler (review date 4 November 1996)

SOURCE: "American X-rays: Forty Years of Allen Ginsberg's Poetry," in *New Yorker,* November 4, 1996, pp. 98-102.

[*In the following review of* Selected Poems 1947-1995, *Vendler argues that Ginsberg's poems raise consciousness.*]

In a poem to Allen Ginsberg, Czeslaw Milosz wrote:

> I envy your courage of absolute defiance,
>   words inflamed, the fierce
>   maledictions of a prophet. . . .
> Your blasphemous howl still resounds
>   in a neon desert where the human tribe
>   wanders, sentenced to unreality. . . .
> And your journalistic clichés, your
>   beard and beads and your dress of a
>   rebel of another epoch are forgiven.

Allen Ginsberg, at the beginning of his **Selected Poems 1947-1995,** gives his own definition of his "absolute defiance": "I imagined a force field of language counter to the hypnotic force-field control apparatus of media Government secret police & military with their Dollar billions of inertia, disinformation, brainwash, mass hallucination."

Ginsberg's "force field" came to public notice with the publication of **Howl and Other Poems,** in 1956, when Ginsberg was thirty years old. The title poem of the volume cried out against an America that devoured its young as the pagan god Moloch had devoured the children sacrificed to him. Ginsberg had seen his mother, Naomi—an immigrant from Russia—decline into persecution mania and eventual institutionalization; and he himself, after an apparently successful transition from Paterson, New Jersey, to Columbia University, fell in with the petty criminality of friends, was briefly hospitalized in lieu of serving a prison sentence, and eventually left New York for San Francisco. Like his father, Louis, who was a high-school English teacher, Ginsberg wrote verse; but, while Louis's poetry was conventional and high-minded, his son's was tormented and ecstatic. In San Francisco, Ginsberg and others (Kenneth Rexroth, Jack Kerouac, Gary Snyder, Robert Duncan) emerged as the Beat movement, which in its frankness and its commitment to social and erotic reform provoked a storm in the world of writing. United States customs impounded as obscene copies of *Howl* printed in England, and the San Francisco police sent two officers to the City Lights bookshop, where the first edition was for sale, and arrested the publisher, the poet Lawrence Ferlinghetti. At the subsequent trial, the judge pronounced *Howl* not obscene, and declared Ferlinghetti not guilty; the attendant publicity made both *Howl* and Ginsberg famous.

Howl was followed by other remarkable books, of which the most notable was **Kaddish and Other Poems,** in which the title poem, a long elegy for Ginsberg's mother, widened the sympathies of the American lyric by incorporating into it the vernacular anguish of the Jewish immigrant experience. Ginsberg later, with some grandeur, called two of his volumes **Planet News** and **The Fall of America.** William Carlos Williams had written, "It is difficult to get the news from poems," but Ginsberg put the news of the day into poetry in a bold and irreverent way. The F.B.I., the C.I.A., the Vietnam War, gay life, urban decay—all appeared regularly in Ginsberg's bulletins. Yet Ginsberg's remarkable poetic powers have been less extensively commented on than his many charities, his indefatigable political investigations, his support of other writers, his thronged readings (accompanied by finger cymbals, harmonium, chants), his world travel, his theatrical protests, his moral injunctions (against the hydrogen bomb, against political lies, against eco-destruction). These actions make him a significant cultural figure, but it is the poetry that makes him a significant literary figure.

Against the high odds of fame, over-occupation, and aging, Ginsberg has continued to write poetry; and every one of his books has had its memorable pieces. But that success has also been perennially threatened, and at times undone, by his two opposing neurotic temptations, which are paranoia and emotional withdrawal, and by his two poetic temptations, which are populism and "spontaneity." In his best poems, the ever-flickering paranoia is tempered by self-irony, humor, wisdom, or sheer curiosity about being; and the Buddhist quietism that would turn every phenomenon into illusion is revoked, just in time, by an eddy of feeling. If Ginsberg's populism craves a platinum record, it is checked by a scruple of art; and the spontaneity that records bus voice-overs on his travels is corralled by a sense of shapeliness. (When the balance of powers fails, the poems become either rant or sermon, rock lyric or journal notes.) Taken all together, Ginsberg's poems are X-rays of a considerable part of American society during the last four decades.

> **Ginsberg differed from his apolitical contemporaries not only in that his political education had begun early (through his mother) but in that his own marginality as a homosexual made resistance to the status quo necessary for self-respect.**
> —*Helen Vendler*

Ginsberg's dark sense of social evil must stem in part from his imaginative symbiosis with his paranoid mother, "from whose pained head," he says in **"Kaddish,"** "I first took Vision." On the other hand, the America in which he came of age defined homosexual acts as crimes, pursued undeclared wars in Korea and Vietnam, ran puppet governments in South America and elsewhere, was undisguisedly racist, had unsavory dealings with the drug trade, and spied shamelessly on its citizens through the F.B.I. Ginsberg differed from his apolitical contemporaries not only in that his political education had begun early (through his mother) but in that his

own marginality as a homosexual made resistance to the status quo necessary for self-respect. He differed from many activist poets in eventually coming to recognize that all bureaucracies are much the same: he was as unwelcome in Communist police states (Czechoslovakia and Cuba both threw him out) as he was in the United States. And he was aware (as most reformers are not) that the underlying cause of his zeal was aggression within himself, which was projected outward as suspected aggression in others. The rage and despair in Ginsberg's early poems were as much a product of self-loathing as of objective criticism of the world. Yet his own crises of feeling enabled his violent insights into the suffering inflicted by a repressive society on its young,

> who were expelled from the academies
> for crazy & publishing obscene odes
> on the windows of the skull . . .
> who got busted in their pubic beards
> returning through Laredo with a
> belt of marijuana for New York . . .
> who howled on their knees in the
> subway and were dragged off the roof
> waving genitals and manuscripts.

Ginsberg was saved from suicidal depression by what he called an "auditory vision," in which he heard a voice—he took it to be that of William Blake—reciting poetry. Since Ginsberg's own poetry has always been scored for the audible voice—endorsing orality over the inhibitions of literacy—it is no surprise that the vision was an auditory one. And, since Blake is the greatest English poet of disinhibition—as Whitman is its greatest American poet—it was Blake who would be the instigator and Whitman the guru of Ginsberg's early verse. Whitman's "Unscrew the locks from the doors! / Unscrew the doors themselves from their jambs!" was the epigraph for *Howl;* and—to complete the revolutionary triad of precursors—Shelley's "Die, / If thou wouldst be with that which thou dost seek!" was the epigraph for *Kaddish.*

Blake and Shelley and Whitman were, on the whole, better poetic models for Ginsberg's verse than Buddhist sutras. Ginsberg's path resembles that of T. S. Eliot: both possessed exceptionally high-strung sensibilities, which when exacerbated plunged them into states alarmingly close to madness; both had breakdowns; both sought some form of wisdom that could ameliorate, guide, or correct the excesses of their reactions; and what Eliot found in Dr. Vittoz's Lausanne sanatorium ("Give . . . Sympathize . . . Control," words from an Upanishad quoted in "The Waste Land") Ginsberg found in Buddhist mantras and meditative practice.

Ginsberg's Buddhism seems to me to have had roughly the same effect on his lyrics that Eliot's Anglo-Catholicism had on his: a tension goes out of the poetry, and didacticism replaces it. In taming the uncontrollable, in regulating the nerves, the flinching person is made able to live; one cannot dispute the wisdom, in life, of staying out of the asylum. Yet the analysis of unregulated and baffling pain is a deep source of powerful lyric expression. The discipline that is taken up to regulate such pain is, of course, in itself a source of a different kind of deep pain—the pain of self-mutilation. Though the Eliot of "Four Quartets" recognizes this, Ginsberg is not very much interested in it. He finds consolation, rather than pain, in the atheist emptiness of his Buddhism.

The new *Selected* is not entirely satisfactory. Many wonderful poems—from **"American Change"** to **"Chances R,"** from **"Ecologue"** to **"Black Shroud"**—have been omitted so that some sixty pages of Ginsberg's songs (none of which appeared in the 1984 *Collected Poems*) could be included. The songs may be convincing in performance, but they don't survive cold print, and Ginsberg's association with Bob Dylan is recalled rather too buoyantly: "I'm pleased with this intergenerational exchange of influence which confirms old traditions of artistic & spiritual transmission." Hardly an accurate interpretation: what of Ginsberg will enter the matrix of tradition is least likely to be the song lyrics imitating Dylan. But a truer statement follows: "The original task was to 'widen the area of consciousness,' make pragmatic examination of the texture of consciousness, even somewhat transform consciousness." That seems a fair summary of what Ginsberg's work has, in fact, done. Of course, his public appearances and his political activities have in their own way helped to "widen the area of consciousness," just as have Czeslaw Milosz's and Adrienne Rich's essays. But poetry has its own means, and they are not the same as marching in parades or writing persuasive prose.

Ginsberg's poetry gains much of its power from a cinematically detailed immersion in present-tense immediacy. You are there (as in any Ginsberg poem) when, in **"Manhattan May Day Midnight,"** Ginsberg goes out at night to buy the newspapers and sees workmen tracking down a gas leak. He notices the bullet-shaped skull of the man in the manhole, he remarks the conjunction of asphalt and granite, he registers the presence of an idling truck:

> At the Corner of 11th under dim
>   Street-light in a hole in the ground
> a man wrapped in work-Cloth and
>   wool Cap pulled down his bullet skull
> stood & bent with a rod & flashlight
>   turning round in his pit halfway sunk
>   in earth
> Peering down at his feet, up to his
>   chest in the asphalt by a granite Curb . . .
> Yes the body stink of City bowels,
>   rotting tubes six feet under

> Could explode any minute sparked by
>   Con Ed's breathing Puttering truck
> I noticed parked.

What is agreeable here is that there's no agenda. We are not asked to sympathize with the proletariat or to feel ecologically alarmed by the gas leak. Ginsberg's invincible interest in the real liberates us into a participatory disinterestedness. And his mind roams widely, in unpredictable ways. In another poem, the gas scene might have led to Ginsberg's own gas stove, or to comparable workers he had seen in India, or to the lure of night walking. In this case, his mind turns unexpectedly to Ancient Rome and Ur:

> I passed by hurriedly Thinking Ancient
>   Rome, Ur
> Were they like this, the same shadowy
>   surveyors & passers-by
> scribing records of decaying pipes &
>   Garbage piles on Marble, Cuneiform,
> ordinary midnight citizen out on the
>   street looking for Empire News.

One can't widen consciousness in poetry by having it follow a programmed path (as most ideologically committed poetry does). However noble its intentions, a programmed path *narrows* consciousness. Ginsberg, at his best, is alert, unprogrammed, free.

To examine "the texture of consciousness" means to find the million places existing in the interstices between our coarse terms for the activities of consciousness: "planning," "remembering," "memorizing," "grieving," "hoping." The texture of consciousness has had such marvelous explorers in our century (Joyce and Woolf in the novel, Eliot and Stevens in poetry) that it might seem that the task has already been accomplished. But Ginsberg has added something new. This has generally been thought to be the unspeakable (his mother's vomiting and defecating in the bathroom in **"Kaddish,"** his own sexual grovelling in **"Please Master,"** his embarrassment at the effects of Bell's palsy in "What You Up To?"). But, though Ginsberg has tracked shame and humiliation with great thoroughness, he has equally been the "Curator of funny emotions to the mob"—to borrow the title he bestowed on Frank O'Hara.

The comedy of consciousness was not the stock-in-trade of Eliot or Stevens, but it occurs with brio in Ginsberg, whose satiric eye is always ready to pick up a new contemporary genre—the **"Personals"** ad, for instance—and use it for a CAT scan of his own psyche:

> Poet professor in autumn years
> seeks helpmate companion protector
>   friend . . .

to share bed meditation apartment
     Lower East Side,
help inspire mankind conquer world
     anger & guilt,
empowered by Whitman Blake
     Rimbaud Ma Rainey & Vivaldi . . .
Find me here in New York alone with
     the Alone.

Which of us, Ginsberg's poem suggests, has not read the "Personals" ads and mentally composed one? Which of us has not recognized the intrinsic absurdity of self-description? The very levels of consciousness that exist to be explored are mocked by their jockeying for place in Ginsberg's ad: the tabloid self-epithet, "poet professor"; the helpless stock of cliche, "autumn years"; the archaic reversion, "seeks"; the casting about for names for homosexual partnership, "helpmate companion protector friend." (The writer's mental state alters slightly with each of these: from the Biblical "helpmate" to the euphemistic "companion" and on to the feudal "protector" and the longed-for "friend.") The impossibility of enumerating all the levels of consciousness shows up in the forced coexistence on a single line of Rimbaud and Ma Rainey; and Ginsberg's self-silhouetting—the last line echoes Lionel Johnson, who wrote, grandly, *Lonely, unto the Lone I go; / Divine, to the Divinity*"—shows his determination not to forsake the (parodic) sublime.

In lyric poetry one transforms the consciousness of others solely by transforming one's own. Ginsberg's self-transformations (rather like Whitman's) license his readers to go and do likewise. **"Sunflower Sutra"** is one of the famous rhapsodic self-transformations ("You were never no locomotive, Sunflower, you were a sunflower!"), but there are also satiric ones, of which the most outrageously cheerful is the famous **"Pull My Daisy"**:

Pull my daisy
tip my cup
all my doors are open
Cut my thoughts
for coconuts
all my eggs are broken.

It's hardly possible to say this without losing a lot of pompousness (if one happens to be harboring any). To become Ginsberg as one reads his poems is to undergo a powerful, if transient, alteration of consciousness. Under his spell, one is both more excited and more noticing, more tender and more mocking. As humor bests aggression, and curiosity bests xenophobia, the world improves.

Finally, Ginsberg's ever reliable means of consciousness-raising is his rhythmic momentum, expressed by his long lines rolling in like breakers. Its urgency—at times strained,

when Ginsberg is forcing the issue, but often genuine—means that some portion of life is demanding its place in the museum of history. If Ginsberg had not been mugged in New York, we would not have had the unstable rhythms of **"Mugging"**:

I went down shouting Om Ah Hum
     to gangs of lovers on the stoop watching
slowly appreciating, why this is a raid,
     these strangers mean strange business
with what—my pockets, bald head,
     broken-healed-bone leg, my softshoes,
     my heart—
Have they knives? Om Ah Hum—
     Have they sharp metal wood to
     shove in eye ear ass? Om Ah Hum
& slowly reclined on the pavement,
     struggling to keep my woolen bag
     of poetry address calendar & Leary-
     lawyer notes hung from my shoulder.

Ginsberg's nonresistant chanting drives the muggers crazy— "Shut up or we'll murder you"—and the poet concludes that it's easier to transform your own consciousness than that of the man in the street. Yet, though the poem descends from its idealist hopes, and closes ruefully in the realm of the real, it does not dismiss the premise that nonviolence as a response to violence is the only alternative to an endless chain of aggression. The new generation reading Ginsberg's *Selected* will find in such poems that Ginsberg's "force field of language" still exerts a powerful imaginative pressure.

Alicia Ostriker (essay date July/August 1997)

SOURCE: "'Howl' Revisited: The Poet as Jew," in *The American Poetry Review*, Vol. 4, 1997, pp. 28-31.

[*In the following essay, Ostriker argues that while Ginsberg rejected elements of his Jewish heritage, it still influenced his writing.*]

I have reverenced Allen Ginsberg—man and poet—for three decades and see no reason to stop now. The first time I met Allen I was amazed, as this essay suggests, by his voice: the power and sweetness and humor of it. His breath, I thought, was the breath of the spirit. The last time was the same but more so. We were at the Dodge Poetry Festival in Waterloo, N.J., in the soft weather of early fall, 1996. At dinner I told him I had written an essay about him as a Jew, that he would probably disapprove of, and he shrugged this off and talked about his new apartment. He was looking ailing and frail. He was ailing and frail, until he went on stage, seated with his harmonium, and then—what can one say except that

Allen's voice was channeling huge quantities of spiritual energy, joy, pain, love, hope, laughter, from the Great Beyond, or wherever that stuff comes from, and spraying it like a cosmic fire hydrant into the big tent and out into the warm night. For forty-five minutes he hosed us up and down, and we all rode the billows of delight. I imagine he is having a fine time now, in the holy company of Whitman, Blake, Williams, and the Prophet Jeremiah.

i Ginsberg the Yid

It was the best of times; it was the worst of times. It was 1966. We were in Vietnam but thought in our antiwar innocence that we might be out soon. Medgar Evers and Malcolm X were dead but Robert Kennedy and Martin Luther King were still alive. The Chicago riots, the invasion of Cambodia, the killing of four students at Kent State hadn't happened yet. Allen Ginsberg was giving a reading at Princeton University with Gary Snyder. In Princeton I lived at that time disguised as a young faculty wife and mother of two. Simultaneously at Rutgers University I went to work disguised as a promising young scholar of late eighteenth and early nineteenth-century poetry and prosody. Officially I was a Blakean. My own poetry remained in the closet during the years of my assistant professorship; had my colleagues known of my folly I would probably not have gotten the job, since most of them considered creative writing the equivalent of basket weaving, an activity for the retarded. Also in the closet were my two daughters in diapers. One did not discuss family in my department, where my senior colleagues were witty and charming men who all looked and behaved as if they had never in their lives laid eyes on a diaper.

I had already heard Allen once, at Rutgers, where he took off the top of my head in the standing room only vault of Voorhees Chapel by introducing as his opening act, of all people, his father Louis Ginsberg. Louis, with considerable self-importance, read some of his own poetry—rhymed, refined, culturally anonymous lyrics—as if to say this is how it should be done, here's the real thing, now you can listen to my son. Louis's condescension was not a joke, it was real. Equally real was Allen's affectionate graciousness toward his dad. As the daughter of a mother who also wrote rhymed poetry, of the same vintage as Louis's, I was overwhelmed. I couldn't *dream* of doing a reading with my mom. Embarrassing! Impossible! Couldn't dream of achieving the spiritual state that would make such openness possible for me. . . . But what if . . . ? And indeed, a mere twenty years later, I found myself able to do it, give readings with my mother. Not often, not easily, but with a certain amount of grace which would have been impossible for me without that distant model.

In Princeton Allen read **"Please Master,"** and I was scandalized. But I had a question to ask him and at the post-read-

ing party I fought my way through the crowd of adoring boy undergraduates to ask it. It concerned his voice. That sonorous, sweet, deep, vibrant, patient baritone seemed to emerge from some inexhaustible energy source, manifesting the double sense of *spiritus* as simultaneously breath and spirit. But I had listened to an early recording of **"Howl"** in which, far from having the long lines express the poet's "natural" breath units as he so often claimed, the voice was high-pitched and short-breathed—entirely *un*equal to the long lines. What about it? Did he really develop the voice to go with the lines, and not the other way around? Yes, he cheerfully agreed, he had written the lines to go with his *potential* voice. And how, I asked—for this was what I wished to learn—did he train his voice to do what it did now? Could I do that? Allen smiled and suggested filling the bathtub and lying in the water face down reciting poems. Then he took another look at me and said: It's not so hard. Just do the breathing exercises you learned in childbirth classes.

The breathing exercises I had learned in childbirth classes. How did this gay guy, who knew nothing about women, know at a glance that the shy chick in front of him had taken childbirth classes? How did he know that pregnancy and childbirth had been, for her, peak spiritual experiences? I wanted to kiss his sandals. I watched him then with the flock of Princeton boys and saw how he listened to each one with the same focused attention, responding to each according to his need. It occurred to me that he didn't just want to sleep with them. He wanted to love them.

There is a word in Hebrew for a virtue at the core of Ginsberg's character and his writing, a virtue that has been noticed by infinite numbers of people—*chesed*. It means kindness, or loving kindness. *Chesed* is one of thirteen attributes of God according to Maimonides (who gets it from Exodus 34.6); it is, in addition, a quality of Torah (a Jew expresses gratitude each day to the God who has given us a Torah of life, and loving kindness, and righteousness, and compassion, and peace); it is a quality highly regarded among traditional Jewish men, whom Talmud praises as "compassionate sons of compassionate fathers."

In no way could the young Allen Ginsberg have *known* any of this in the secular family in which he grew up, which was not merely secular but adamantly atheist. And yet these ideals would have saturated the air he breathed, for Jewish atheism in its Eastern European sources is fueled by the dream of social justice which is also a dream of human kindness. In the classic East European Yiddish literature whose shtetl ethos was the mulch from which Louis Ginsberg's socialism and Naomi Ginsberg's communism fed, Irving Howe describes what he calls the value of "sweetness," "the tone of love . . . with which such masters as Sholem Aleichem and Peretz faced the grimmest facts about Jewish life." Howe's further remarks on the fictions of Mendele and

Scholem Aleichem, Peretz, Singer, and Jacob Glatstein, might well describe **"Howl"**: "The virtue of powerlessness, the power of helplessness, the company of the dispossessed, the sanctity of the insulted and injured—these, finally, are the great themes of Yiddish literature" in which, as well, we find the humor (self-mocking, buffoonish, absurd), the acerbity, the irremediable pain and melancholy a millimeter below the surface, which we find also in Allen Ginsberg.

Sholom Aleichem's village of Kasrilevke and Greenwich Village? Singer's saintly Gimpel the fool and Ginsberg's angelheaded hipsters? Or, still more appallingly/appealingly, a "chosen people"—chosen for persecution, for pogroms, for the chimneys—reincarnated as "the best minds of my generation"? Like the Jews of Europe, Ginsberg's "best minds" suffer for a stubborn adherence to their faith. Yiddishkeit and Ginsberg? A mere generation of partial American assimilation divides them. Ginsberg in **"Howl"** will record, in veiled fashion, the humiliation and crippling of a population of immigrants to shores which promised hope and produced despair. He will gather the threads dropped by the revolutionary poetry of the thirties, left dangling in the winter of McCarthyism. He will *schpritz* shamelessly alongside Henny Youngman and Lenny Bruce. Think of his extraordinary language. Ginsberg's beat lexicon, his determination to write a *low* dialect opposed to the literary diction promoted by his onetime mentor Lionel Trilling, may have been supported by William Carlos Williams. But it is also a tribute to his Yiddish-speaking ancestors and the obscure longevity of their gift for juicy emotional tragicomedy.

ii Ginsberg the Prophet

"People have been comparing me to Whitman, and although I love and adore and am a child of Whitman, both of us come from the Bible . . . We are talking about the endless quarrel between the establishment and the prophets, and I hope to be forever on the side of the prophets."

That is not Allen Ginsberg, it is Muriel Rukeyser, a poet a generation earlier, sprung from an assimilated Jewish family of quite another class from Ginsberg's; but one feels it *might* be Allen. Here, I want to argue, is the second area of the poet's Jewishness: if his personal style is an American incarnation of the Yiddish personality, his moral power descends in a direct line from the power of Hebrew prophecy. Certainly "prophet" and "prophetic" are terms that are freely used about his work, and that he often uses himself. Describing his 1948 Blake-inspired visions, "he realized," Paul Portugés tells us, "that his visionary experiences were not unlike the calling forth of the Hebrew prophets by their Creator" and that his task as a poet would be to recreate "prophetic illuminative seizure." But the notion of the poet as prophet is a loose one. From the Greek *prophets,* interpreter or proclaimer, or one who speaks for a deity, the term has

been used in the English tradition since the late eighteenth century to denote a variety of sublimities opposed to neoclassic rationality. Jean Wojcik and Raymond-Jean Frontain define a "prophetic" stance in Western art as implying private vision, an insistence on the righteousness of the prophet and the corruption of his society, passionate and hyperbolic language, social radicalism, stylistic obscurity or incoherence, and "obsession, fine or frenzied," as "with every technique of language he can muster, the prophet delivers a message that never arrives." Herbert N. Schneider proposes a definition of the prophet as one who forces people to "look at their culture and see a myth . . . they can no longer believe in, for it is a living lie."

In his 1967 *Paris Review* interview, Ginsberg describes the genesis of **"Howl"**: "I thought I wouldn't write a *poem* but just write what I wanted to without fear, let my imagination go, open secrecy, and scribble magic lines from my real mind." Beginning Part I he found himself composing "a tragic custard-pie comedy of wild phrasing, meaningless images for the beauty of abstract poetry of mind," and got excited and went on, "continuing to prophecy what I really know, despite the drear consciousness of the world." In Ginsberg's 1971 *New York Quarterly* interview with William Packard he remarks of **"Howl"** that "The poetic precedent for this situation is like Ezekiel and Jeremiah and the Hebrew prophets in the bible who were warning Babylon against its downfall . . . they were talking about the fall of a city like Babylon, or the fall of a tribe, and cursing out the sins of a nation." Now, what is wrong with this picture is that it suggests a view of the Hebrew prophets which charity might call at best sketchy. Jerusalem, not Babylon, for example, is the city warned and mourned in by Ezekiel and Jeremiah. The degree to which Ginsberg nonetheless reproduces not merely the King James cadences and rhetoric but the essential contradictions of Hebrew prophecy (as against Christian adaptations) is all the more starting. I want to argue here that the "prophetic" work **"Howl"** most resembles is the Lamentations of Jeremiah.

Extremity is the ground note of prophecy. Condemnation and warning dominate pre-exilic prophecy, eschatological promises dominate post-exilic. But where Isaiah and Ezekiel are inspired by and speak for the God of the Covenant, the voice of Lamentations howls in a void: God is terrifyingly present as an agent of destruction, yet terrifyingly absent from discourse. Invoked and prayed to out of the depths, he does not reply. But it is precisely the failure of divine response which has produced, as Alan Mintz argues, a literature of catastrophe which itself is an agent of survival:

> Jewish society . . . has had many massive individual catastrophes visited upon it and still survived; and in each case the reconstruction was undertaken in significant measure by the exertions of the Hebrew

literary imagination. . . . It is the story of the transcendence of the catastrophe rather than of the catastrophe itself which is compelling.

The City of Jerusalem was sacked, its temple destroyed, in 587 B.C.E. Most of the population sought exile; those who remained suffered famine. If the witness of the Book of Lamentations is to be believed, some of those who remained fed on the bodies of dead children. Emerging from a prophetic paradigm according to which "destruction is . . . a deserved and necessary punishment for sin," which "allows a penitent remnant to survive in a rehabilitated restored relationship to God," Lamentations deviates from the paradigm in that confession of sin in this poem is vastly secondary to "the experience of abandonment and the horror of destruction." The task of the poet is "to find adequate language for the horror." Crucial to Lamentations—and to the genre which will succeed it—is first of all that God, and not a mere human adversary, is the ultimate destroyer, and second that "God remains silent . . . but the sufferer's emergence from soliloquy to prayer enables him at least to recover God as the addressable other" and not merely as a brutal enemy.

Between Lamentations and **"Howl"** the parallels are numerous and uncanny, commencing with the one-word title promising a discourse in the semiotic register of meaningless sound. Outside, or prior to, the Law: the lament. Beyond or before the symbolic register, a howl. A language of vowels. A memory between or among the lines, of the universal inconsolable infant for whom the umbilicus to the Absolute is broken. The infant without boundaries, the I who is Other, or infinite, or zero, witness and victim, betrayed by the word, unable to speak a word. The shriek of the powerless feminized male child.

In both poems the voice is exclamatory, impassioned, hyperbolic, intensely figurative, and virtually impossible to pin down, to locate, to identify. In both, the speaking or shrieking or wailing "I" oscillates between the individual and collective identity. In the first chapter of Lamentations the baffled third person lament—"How doth the city sit solitary, that was full of people How is she become as a widow!" slides without warning, in mid-verse, into first-person: "All her people sigh, they seek bread; they have given their pleasant things for meat to relieve the soul: see, O Lord, and consider; for I am become vile." Note that "pleasant things" in this passage is a euphemism for sexual organs; the image is of a starving woman prostituting herself. And again, "Is it nothing to you, all ye that pass by? Behold, and see if there be any sorrow like unto my sorrow which is done unto me, wherewith the Lord hath afflicted me in the day of his fierce anger." Is this "I" the defiled and deserted Jerusalem speaking? Or a narrator identifying with her? Impossible to say, and the whole opening chapter refuses to differentiate. Chapter 2 is inhabited by a voice recounting, with horror, the unthinkable hostilities of the Lord against his own people and artifacts: "The Lord was an enemy, he hath swallowed up Israel, he hath swallowed up all her palaces, he hath destroyed his strongholds . . . And he hath violently taken away his tabernacle . . . he hath destroyed his places of the assembly". But the voice shifts into first person to exclaim, "Mine eyes do fail with tears, my bowels are troubled, my liver is poured out upon the earth, for the destruction of the daughter of my people" and then to bewail the impossibility of metaphor or comfort. "What thing shall I liken to thee, O daughter of Jerusalem? What shall I equal to thee, that I may comfort thee . . . For thy breach is great like the sea; who can heal thee?" In 3.1 an "I" witnesses distinctly: "I am the man that hath seen affliction"—it is this line which produces Whitman's "I am the man, I suffered, I was there"—and almost immediately *is* afflicted: "My flesh and my skin hath he made old; he hath broken my bones." Toward the close of Lamentations 4 and throughout 5 the pronouns shift again, toward a first-person plural, a "we."

In the first moment of **"Howl,"** "I saw the best minds of my generation destroyed by madness, starving hysterical naked, / dragging themselves through the negro streets at dawn looking for an angry fix," and the voice dissolves into what is seen. The "I" releases itself or is released into its surge of empathic madness. In Blakean terms, Ginsberg becomes what he beholds, an anaphoric catalogue of self-destructive souls whose search for the "ancient heavenly connection" which is simultaneously revelation and drug dealer, fails to find the "fix" which would be simultaneously a practical repair and a drugged ecstasy. No further "I" enters the poem until the middle of Part II, where Ginsberg briefly interrupts his invocation / exorcism of the sacrificial deity of industrial capitalist rationality, "Moloch whose name is the Mind," with a spurt of self—"Moloch in whom I sit lonely! Moloch in whom I dream Angels! Crazy in Moloch! Cocksucker in Moloch! Lacklove and manless in Moloch!"—and almost immediately disappears from his own text again. Only in Part III, with the intimate and affectionate address to a friend which parallels the "we" of Lamentations chapter 4, and the refrain "I'm with you in Rockland," does the poem at last imagine a possibility of coherent identity, an "I" in relatively stable relation to a "you." In the "Footnote," personal identity is again transcended; no "I" interrupts the absurd utterance of ecstasy.

The importance of geography in both Lamentations and **"Howl"** is likewise central and likewise paradoxical and contradictory. In both poems, identity is not only collective but requires rootedness in place. The city, Zion, the daughter of Zion, Jerusalem, the cities of Judah. Hallucinating Arkansas, poles of Canada and Paterson, Battery to holy Bronx. In both, the connection of place and people has been ruptured—by starvation literal and figurative, by conquest and exile: place does not *sustain* what should be its people, and hence *identity* is impossible.

The rhetoric of both poems relies on sexual figures and on body images, especially images of sexual humiliation and public disgrace. The pain of Jerusalem is also shame: "The adversaries saw her". "They have seen her nakedness". "Her filthiness is in her skirts". "The adversary hath spread out his hand upon all her pleasant things . . . the heathen entered into her sanctuary". "Jerusalem is as a menstruous woman". The male speaker experiences God as fire in his bones, a net for his feet, a yoke on his neck. In 2.11, "Mine eyes do fail with tears, my bowels are troubled, my liver is poured out upon the earth for the destruction of the daughter of my people." In 2.16, Zion's enemies "hiss and gnash the teeth." In 3.4, "my flesh and skin he hath made old, he hath broken my bones." In 3.16, "he hath broken my teeth with gravel stones." Likewise in Ginsberg Part I, the body is constantly at issue and the issue is commonly exposure, humiliation, deprivation: "starving hysterical naked" comrades "bared their brains to Heaven under the El," "got busted in their public beards," "purgatoried their torsos," "broke down crying in white gymnasiums naked," "were dragged off the roof waving genitals and manuscripts," "let themselves be fucked in the ass by saintly motorcyclists, and screamed with joy," "walked all night with their shoes full of blood on the snowbank docks," "cut their wrists three times successively unsuccessfully," and so on. Extremity of spirit is enacted through bodily extremity, the crowning image of which in both poems is cannibalism. In a moment of climactic horror after describing famine in the city, and accusing God of causing it, Lamentations asks, "Shall the women eat their fruit, and children of a span long?" At the close of **"Howl"** Part I, Ginsberg evokes "the absolute heart of the poem of life butchered out of their own bodies good to eat a thousand years."

What Lamentations and **"Howl"** share most crucially is the anguished and intolerable sense of a divine power which thwarts, punishes, and destroys, which seems absolutely cruel rather then merely indifferent to human suffering, which cannot be appealed to and which remains silent, and yet which must be appealed to because it *is* God. It is ultimately God who is cannibalistically gorging on the bodies of babies in Lamentations, as the poem makes clear in its images of mouth and hand. "The Lord hath swallowed up all the habitations of Jacob, and hath not pitied . . . he hath bent his bow like an enemy . . . he hath not withdrawn his hand from destroying". The horrifying sublime prepares for, explains and contains the horrifying pathetic: "The hands of the pitiful women have sodden [i.e. boiled] their own children; they were their meat in the destruction of the daughter of my people. The Lord hath accomplished his fury". Ginsberg's generation has likewise been swallowed up by a more than human

force, as the figurative conclusion of **"Howl"** I—the butchered heart of the poem of life "good to eat a thousand years" is literalized in the opening line of Part II: it is likewise a God who "bashed open their skulls and ate up their brains and imagination."

A pause here for Ginsberg's "Moloch," that sublimely elaborate invention of Part II:

> Moloch! Solitude! Filth! Ugliness! Ashcans and
> unobtainable
>   dollars! Children screaming under the stair-
> ways! Boys
>   sobbing in armies! Old men weeping in the
> parks!
> Moloch! Moloch! Nightmare of Moloch! Moloch
> the loveless!
>   Mental Moloch! Moloch the heavy judger of
> men!
> Moloch the incomprehensible prison! Moloch the
> crossbone
>   soulless jailhouse and Congress of sorrows!
> Moloch
>   whose buildings are judgment; Moloch the vast
> stone
>   of war! Moloch the stunned governments! . . .

The name is derived from the Canaanite God of fire, Molech, to whom children were offered in sacrifice and whose worship by the Israelites is condemned in Leviticus, 1 and 2 Kings, Jeremiah, Amos and Ezekiel: "Moreover thou hast taken thy sons and daughters whom thou hast borne unto me, and these thou hast sacrificed unto them to be devoured. Is this of thy whoredoms a small matter, that thou hast slain my children and delivered them to cause them to pass through the fire for them?" (Ezekiel 16.20-21). Israelite society for several centuries intermittently practiced human sacrifice which in theory it rejected. America, **"Howl"** Part II tells us, does the same. William Blake's Moloch represents the obsessive human sacrifice of war, especially as connected with perversely suppressed sexuality. Ginsberg's mind-forged Moloch likewise has this aspect, and is a broadly Urizenic figure for the oppressiveness of a modern industrial and military state, exuded from Reason. Ginsberg's Moloch is also the modern version of Mammon, the capitalism of "Unobtainable dollars . . . running money . . . electricity and banks!" But although you cannot worship both God and Mammon, Moloch is not an alternative to God, Moloch *is* God: "heavy judger of men . . . endless Jehovahs . . . They broke their backs lifting Moloch to Heaven!" Inorganic, abstract, Moloch is simultaneously within us and without us, incubus and whale's belly: "Moloch who entered my soul early! Moloch in whom I am a consciousness without a body!" Inescapable Moloch parallels the God of Lamentations.

The contradiction of a God who is also an enemy leads to a deeper contradiction central to the genre of lamentation and, it has been argued, to Jewishness itself. Chapter 3 of Lamentations, its longest chapter, centers on a fusion of despair and hope: "He hath turned aside my ways, and pulled me in pieces" turns itself inside out with "The Lord is my portion, saith my soul; therefore have I hope". "Out of the mouth of the Most High proceedeth not evil and good?". As literature and as consolation, the poem of lamentation "must communicate its own inadequacy. Its success, in a sense, depends on its failure." When Ginsberg's manic **"Footnote to Howl"** announces the holiness of everything, it produces an absurd, irrational, extravagant inversion of Part I. Like the hope of the author of Lamentations, Ginsberg's celebration is not logical but willed:

> Holy! Holy! Holy! Holy! Holy! Holy! Holy! Holy!
> Holy!
> Holy! Holy! Holy! Holy! Holy! Holy!
> The world is holy! The soul is holy! The skin is
> holy!
> The nose is holy! The tongue and cock and
> hand
> and asshole holy!
> Everything is holy! everybody's holy! everywhere
> is
> holy! everyday is in eternity! Everyman's an
> angel!

This ecstatic revelation has its literary source in the "Holy, holy, holy" shout of the seraphim praising God in Isaiah 6.3, but as in Blake's "Marriage of Heaven and Hell," which is clearly one of Ginsberg's most important models here, "everything that lives is holy." Whitman, too, had claimed "Divine am I inside and out, and I make holy whatever I touch or am touched from; The scent of these arm-pits is aroma finer than prayer." Further, as "Holy" inverts "howly," what has previously been interpreted as monstrous by the poet himself may now be re-interpreted:

> Holy the solitudes of skyscrapers and pavements!
> Holy
> the cafeterias filled with the millions! Holy the
> mysterious rivers of tears under the streets!

in a spurt of hilarity, even Moloch can and must be included:

> Holy time in eternity holy eternity in time holy the
> clocks in space holy the fourth dimension holy
> the fifth International holy the Angel in
> Moloch!

And finally

> Holy the supernatural extra brilliant intelligent

kindness of the soul!

Kindness again. That almost imperceptible Yiddish kindness. It is perhaps of interest that Ginsberg apparently thought the poem finished after Part III, and mailed copies to numerous friends and critics, including Richard Eberhart to whom he wrote an extended formal discussion of the poem without the footnote on May 18, 1956; and including his father. He received a letter from Louis dated February 29, 1956; "I am gratified about your new ms. It's a wild, rhapsodic, explosive outpouring with good figures of speech flashing by in its volcanic rushing. . . .It's a hot geyser of emotion suddenly released in wild abandon from subterranean depths of your being." Louis insisted, however, "there is no need for dirty, ugly words, as they will entangle you unnecessarily in trouble," and added his anxiety that the poem "is a one-sided neurotic view of life, it has not enough glad, Whitmanic affirmations." Sweet, embarrassed, embarrassing Louis. And did Allen perhaps compose the footnote under the invisible pressure of his father's admonition?

iii It Occurs to Him That He Is America

> To be a Jew in the twentieth century
> Is to be offered a gift. If you refuse,
> Wishing to be invisible, you choose
> Death of the spirit, the stone insanity.
> Accepting, take full life. Full agonies:
> Your evening deep in labyrinthine blood
> Of those who resist, fail and resist; and God
> Reduced to a hostage among hostages.
>
> The gift is torment. Not alone the still
> Torture, isolation; or torture of the flesh
> That may come also. But the accepting wish,
> The whole and fertile spirit as guarantee
> For every human freedom, suffering to be free,
> Daring to live for the impossible.

That is of course Rukeyser again, the Rukeyser of "Letter to the Front," published in 1944, stylistically a world away from **"Howl,"** chronologically a decade away, morally shoulder to queer Jewish shoulder. How Jewish then is the Ginsberg of **"Howl"**? I have been attempting to suggest both a low Yiddish element and a high Hebraic element in that poem, notwithstanding what must also be spoken of: the poet as a "Jew in flight from Judaism," or what Isaac Deutscher called "the non-Jewish Jew."

His ethnicity was never exactly invisible to others. "Naive, he was incredibly naive," recalled Lucien Carr of his fellow student at Columbia. "He was just an eager young Jewish kid from Paterson who wanted to know everything about books and writers and art and painting." Kerouac fictionalizes the young Allen in *The Town and the City* (1946):

"Levinsky was an eager, sharply intelligent boy of Russian-Jewish parentage who rushed around New York in a perpetual sweat of emotional activity." And in *The Vanity of Duluoz:* "I was sitting in Edie's apartment one day when the door opened and in walks this spindly Jewish kid with horn-rim glasses and tremendous ears sticking out, 17 years old, burning black eyes, a strangely deep voice." Introducing **Empty Mirror,** William Carlos Williams calls Ginsberg "this young Jewish boy," before going on to compare him with Dante and Chaucer, but then comes around to paralleling him with the prophet Jeremiah." Richard Eberhart, describing Ginsberg's performance of **"Howl"** at the Six Gallery reading for the September 2, 1956 *New York Times Book Review,* writes, "My first reaction was that it is based on destructive violence. It is profoundly Jewish in temper. It is Biblical in its repetitive grammatical buildup. It is a howl against anything in our mechanistic civilization which kills the spirit. . . ." M. L. Rosenthal reviewing **"Howl"** in *The Nation* in 1957 wrote that the poem had "the single-minded frenzy of a raving madwoman" (brilliant guesswork, one might say; Naomi *is* that madwoman, for it can be argued that **"Howl"** ventriloquizes her voice just as the speaker of Lamentations ventriloquizes Jerusalem's, although **"Kaddish"** has not been published yet) but that some of Ginsberg's early poems at the back of the book "have a heavy Yiddish melancholy." (Rosenthal in conversation with me called the "madwoman" a "typo" which he feared was insulting to both women and homosexuals and later changed to "madman," but I would say he guessed better than he knew.) Edward Albee remembers Allen in the late fifties as "you young, a young old testament prophet." For Hayden Carruth he is "mindpetal, spectre, strangest jew, cityboy." Yevgeny Yevtushenko, who with a charm equal to Allen's own calls him the "Omm-issar of American Poetry," remembers the beats as "the uprising of the garbage dumps of the suburbs. . . . And riding bareback on a garbage can, careering wildly past the Plaza and the Hilton, like a Jewish Mowgli of the concrete jungles, came Allen Ginsberg, prophet of the outpouring."

As to Allen's own testimony, "At 14 I was an introvert, an atheist, a Communist and a Jew, and I still wanted to be president of the United States." His family listened to Eddie Cantor on the radio, and "It was a . . . high point of the week. I guess because he was Jewish and a national comedian and everybody in the family identified with him." In the last year of high school Ginsberg vowed to devote his life to helping the working classes if he got into Columbia University. The simplicity of these identifications and that identity failed to outlast his crossing the river to Columbia and his immediate attraction to the bohemian likes of Lucien Carr, Jack Kerouac, William Burroughs, Neil Cassady, all non-Jews, apolitical, amoral. What was a nice Jewish boy doing with these types? Poor Louis kept asking. What did he have in mind by writing "Fuck the Jews" accompanied

by a skull and crossbones on his dusty dorm window? Ginsberg's biographer Barry Miles takes Allen's word at face value that his little naughtiness was to catch the attention of an Irish cleaning woman he suspected of being anti-Semitic. "Trilling and his wife were utterly unable to accept that Allen was simply goading the anti-Semitic Irish cleaner, and years later Diana Trilling was still using the incident as an example of Ginsberg's 'Jewish self-hatred.'"

A few chapters later Barry Miles observes that Ginsberg "was unable to relate to his Jewish heritage." How very Jewish. Carl Solomon, the dedicatee of **"Howl,"** publishes his "Report from the Asylum: After-thoughts of a Shock patient" under the name Carl Goy. Allen's brother Eugene changes his surname to Brooks when he becomes a lawyer. It would be years before Allen started identifying himself humorously as a Jewish Buddhist. When Ginsberg cites the sources and precedents for **"Howl,"** he includes Blake, Shelley, Whitman, Christopher Smart, Charlie Parker, Cézanne, Wilhelm Reich, Leadbelly, William Carlos Williams, Rimbaud, Céline, Brecht, Jean Genet, Hart Crane, and Tristan Corbière, to name a few. He names no Jewish source, and commenting on the phrase "bop kabbalah" distances himself from it as a bit of "mystical name-dropping" and says he had read "little on kabbalah."

Two interesting essays by fellow poets touch on this matter of Ginsberg's reluctance to identify with Jewishness—his wish to "pass" as an unmarked member of the Euro-American avant-garde—through meditating on the ancient heavenly connection of Allen-Naomi. To Clayton Eshleman, Ginsberg's "visionary panic over the destructiveness of North American society, the way it titillates the self and then cold-cocks it," derives from how "on a very personal level, North America had done the same thing to his mother . . . it is the agony of the son who escorted his mother when he was twelve to the asylum . . . that flows through the magnificent first movement of *Howl.* . . . Ginsberg would save Mankind since he was unable to save Naomi." This seems to me entirely correct. Supporting Eshleman's intuition we might notice that the nominal "secret hero" of Part I may be Neil Cassady, "N. C. . . . cocksman and Adonis of Denver," but toward the close of Part I comes a set of lines whose reference is Carl Solomon, and in its midst "the mother finally ******" and the yellow paper rose twisted on a wire hanger in the nameless Naomi's madhouse closet. In a letter to John Hollander Ginsberg calls the **"Footnote"** "too serious a joke to explain," and then explains it by saying its real dedicatee is "my mother who died in the madhouse and it says I loved her anyway." Having said this, the letter then hastens to return to technical talk about "open prophetic bardic poetry." Allen Grossman, in a partially skewed essay on Ginsberg, "The Jew as American Poet," argues that "the Jew, like the Irishman, presents himself as the type of the sufferer in history" but that for Ginsberg the beat subculture "takes the place of the real ethnic and political sub-cultures which in the past succored and gave identity to the outcast by forming a community of outcasts". "In **'Kaddish,'**" Grossman continues, "the archetypal female is a mutilated and paranoid old woman ('scars of operations, pancreas, belly wounds, abortions, appendix, stitching of incisions pulling down in the fat like hideous thick zippers') haunted by the image of Hitler and dying, obscene and abandoned, in the sanitarium. This is Ginsberg's version of the Jewish mother and, simultaneously, of the shechina, the wandering soul of Israel herself." Surely this is correct and surely what is expressed in "Kaddish" is repressed but powerfully latent in **"Howl"**—so much so that one may almost feel the son's voice to be that of the mother. Does he speak for her, or is she speaking through him? This is as impossible to decide as it is to identify the voice of Lamentations as witness *or* victim. And if Naomi is the invisible mother/matter of Ginsberg's first great poem, there is an uncanny connection between this mother who almost devoured her son and the mothers who cannibalize their infants in the streets of Jerusalem. Grossman goes on, however, to claim that Ginsberg "erects on [Naomi's] grave an image which is no longer ethnic and which therefore is no longer obsessed by the mystery of the Jewish people in history," and to remark that "throughout Ginsberg's writing there is an ambivalence toward Jewishness which should be recognized as it seems to be an emphatic part of his public statement." Grossman is implying, I think, that Ginsberg is somehow or other not a *real* Jew because of this.

Yet ambivalence toward Jewishness, like pepper in the stew, is a key ingredient of post-Enlightenment Jewish writing. Alan Mintz, tracing "responses to catastrophe in Hebrew literature" from Lamentations to the post-Holocaust era, stresses four historic stances: First, there is an early rabbinic theme of *shame* at Israel's humiliation before the nations, quite apart from the insistence on Israel's sinfulness. During the late medieval period, in response to arbitrary Christian massacres of Jews, there develops an exaltation of suffering as "an opportunity awarded by God to the most worthy for the display of righteousness." In the early modern period, from the 1880's to the early 1900's, writers like Shalom Abromowitsch, Saul Tchernichevsky, and Chaim Nachman Bialik respond to the devastating pogroms that swept Russia and Eastern Europe with a literature of profound and bitter ambivalence toward the masses of Jewish people—part pity, part contempt. And in the Palmach generation of Israeli writers the dominant stance toward the European victims of the holocaust was indeed contempt.

To be a Jew in diaspora is to be ambivalent. It is commonly also to take on the colors of the host culture. To be more German than the Germans, like Heine; more French than the French, like Dreyfuss, Sartre, and Simone Weil; more English than the English, like Disraeli; more Russian than the Russians, like Isaac Babel, who rode with the Cossacks. Would someone named Bobby Zimmerman have had the extraordinary effect on American youth wielded by someone named Bob Dylan? To believe in the host culture's own ideals about itself, and then to write as an indignant social critic when the host nation fails (of course) to embody those ideals: this is all normal for the Jewish writer.

Yet Allen as Jew remains a good son. From his father's socialism, that tenderhearted materialism, Allen keeps and intensifies the tenderness while questioning the materialism. Of his mother's communism—her paranoid idealism—Allen tries to exorcise the paranoia (everything's holy, Moloch is holy, breathe deep and say Om) while holding fast to the idealism, free love and all, physical and emotional nudism and all. From Louis's poetry he retains a devotion to form. From Naomi's madness he retains the outrageousness and outgrows the self-destructiveness.

From America Allen takes Whitman. The manly love of comrades, the open road, the democratic vistas stretching to eternity, and also the eyes of America taking a fall, which he plants, later, in his mother's head. America will always be, for him, infinite hope and infinite disappointment. That's very Jewish.

And from Judaism he takes the universal compassion and rejects the tribalism. Instead of professing victimization as Jew, his writing projects victimization onto the world, and in the same moment proposes, through the mystery of rhetoric, to save it. The power of prophetic rhetoric in the genre of Lamentation is that it must wring cosmic affirmation out of despair. God is your enemy, and you must trust him. Moloch whose eyes are a thousand blind windows eats his children, but you must declare him holy. A decade after completing **"Howl,"** Ginsberg at the climax of **"Wichita Vortex Sutra"** calls "all the powers of the Imagination" to his side and declares "the end of the War." Ridiculous, absurd, foolish, impossible. Daring to live for the impossible.

FURTHER READING

Criticism

Bawer, Bruce. "The Phenomenon of Allen Ginsberg." In his *Prophets & Professors: Essays on the Lives and Works of Modern Poets,* pp. 193-214. Brownsville, Oregon: Story Line Press, 1995.

Reviews Ginsberg's career and concludes that his poetry is banal and his fame is the result of his flamboyant lifestyle.

Beam, Jeffrey. Review of *Cosmopolitan Greetings,* by Allen

Ginsberg. *Lambda Book Report* 4, No. 6 (September/October 1994): 34-5.

Reviews *Cosmopolitan Greetings* favorably.

Berkson, Bill. Review of *Planet News,* by Allen Ginsberg. *Poetry* 114, No. 4 (July 1969): 251-56.

Argues that *Planet News* marks an improvement in Ginsberg's writing.

Everett, Nicholas. "Pushing Seventy." *Times Literary Supplement* (10 February 1995): 22.

Argues that while Ginsberg's form has not changed, he is tackling new subjects in *Cosmopolitan Greetings.*

Goldberg, Danny. "Allen Ginsberg Remembered." *Tikkun* 12, No. 3 (1997): 78-80.

Presents anecdotes from Ginsberg's life.

Haines, John. "Poetry Chronicle." *The Hudson Review* XLVIII, No. 4 (Winter 1996): 668-69.

Reviews *Cosmopolitan Greetings* and argues that the poetry offered is of mixed quality.

Nathan, Jean. "The forty-year Howl." *New York* 28, No. 45 (13 November 1995): 84.

Discusses the resurgence of the Beat movement in the 1990s.

Oppen, George. Review of *Kaddish and Other Poems,* by Allen Ginsberg. *Poetry* 100, No. 5 (August 1962): 329-30.

Praises "Kaddish" but finds the rest of the volume uneven.

Rosenberg, Harold. "Six American Poets." *Commentary* 32, No. 4 (October 1961): 349-53.

Reviews *Kaddish* and praises Ginsberg as an innovator.

Stein, Charles. Review of *T.V. Baby Poems,* by Allen Ginsberg. *Nation* 208, No. 7 (17 February 1969): 217.

Favorably reviews the collection and singles out "Television Was a Baby Crawling Toward That Death Chamber" for praise.

Trilling, Diana. "The Other Night at Columbia: A Report from the Academy." *Partisan Review* XXVI, No. 2 (Spring 1959): 214-30.

Remarks on incidents in her contact with Ginsberg and her efforts to understand him.

Tucker, Ken. "From Beat Poet to Pop Chic." *New York Times* (25 September 1994): 34, 39.

Favorably reviews a four-CD collection of Ginsberg's poems and songs.

Interview

Ganguly, Suranjan. "Allen Ginsberg in India: An Interview." *Ariel* 24, No. 4 (October 1993): 21-32.

Interview in which Ginsberg describes his visit to India and the influence of the Baul sect on his poetry.

Additional coverage of Ginsberg's life and career is contained in the following sources published by Gale: *Authors in the News,* **Vol. 2;** *Contemporary Authors,* **Vols. 1-4R;** *Contemporary Authors New Revision Series,* **Vols. 2 and 41;** *Concise Dictionary of American Literary Biography 1941-1968; DISCovering Authors; DISCovering Authors Modules: Most-studied Authors, Poets; Dictionary of Literary Biography,* **Vols. 5, 16, and 169;** *Major 20th-Century Writers; Poetry Criticism,* **Vol. 4; and** *World Literature Criticism.*

James A. Michener
1907-1997

American novelist, short story writer, nonfiction writer, essayist, memoirist, and art historian.

For further information on Michener's life and career, see *CLC*, Volumes 1, 5, 11, 29, and 60.

INTRODUCTION

With forty best-sellers to his name, Michener was thought to be one of America's most popular and prolific novelists of the twentieth century. Considered a master of epic narrative, he started life as an orphan and did not begin to write in earnest until he was in his forties. Michener became an avid reader as a child Doylestown, Pennsylvania, where he was raised by a poor Quaker widow. He graduated summa cum laude from Swarthmore College in 1929 with a degree in English literature, after which he taught social studies until 1931 when he won a fellowship to study in Europe. In 1940 he served as a visiting professor of history at Harvard's School of Education and published several scholarly articles for professional journals. While in the Navy in World War II, he was assigned as naval historian in the South Pacific. Later he submitted short stories he'd written during the war to Macmillan publishing house. These were published in 1947 as *Tales of the South Pacific.* Although not a commercial success, the book won a Pulitzer Prize in 1948 and became the basis for the hit musical *South Pacific.* Michener continued to write travel articles, essays, and novellas, but became best known for monumental sagas that dramatized the social and political development of nations and regions spanning several generations. Critically acclaimed *Hawaii* (1959), was the first of these, and his first best-seller. *The Source* (1965), *Centennial* (1974), and *Chesapeake* (1978), were just a few of his other blockbuster successes. Michener imbued his protagonists with patriotism, frugality, common sense, and courage, qualities admired by his wide readership but considered trite to some critics. Some of these reviewers criticized his novels for their casual blending of fact and fiction, predictable plots, moralizing, and digression. Other critics, however, praised his ability to transport his readers to another time and place, and to expertly document historical events while entertaining them.

PRINCIPAL WORKS

Tales of the South Pacific (short stories) 1947

The Fires of Spring (novel) 1949
The Bridges at Toko-Ri (novel) 1953
Sayonara (novel) 1954
The Bridge at Andau (novel) 1957
Hawaii (novel) 1959
Caravans (novel) 1963
The Source (novel) 1965
The Drifters (novel) 1971
Centennial (novel) 1974
Chesapeake (novel) 1978
The Covenant (novel) 1980
Space (novel) 1982
Poland (novel) 1983
Texas (novel) 1985
Legacy (novel) 1987
Alaska (novel) 1988
Caribbean (novel) 1989
Journey (novel) 1989
Mexico (novel) 1992
The World Is My Home (memoir) 1992
Literary Reflections (nonfiction) 1993
Recessional (novel) 1994

OBITUARIES

John Omicinski (obituary date 16 October 1997)

SOURCE: "Writer James Michener Dies at 90," in *USA Today,* October 16, 1997, p. 4A.

[*In the following obituary, Omicinski lauds Michener's life and works.*]

James Michener's novels are hard to put down.

Indeed, some are difficult to pick up, too.

Michener, who last week ordered doctors to remove him from life-sustaining kidney dialysis, died Thursday in Austin, Texas. He was 90.

Millions who have read Michener's engrossing and best-selling doorstopper sagas like *Hawaii, Chesapeake* and *Poland,* find them uplifting as well as arm-testing experiences.

For 50 years the social-studies-teacher-turned-novelist delivered the goods in plot, history, writing and heft. His maze-plotted novels—peopled by dozens of characters in exotic faraway places readers might never see except through his eyes—spilled Niagaras of fact and fable.

One biographer called him "a master reporter of his generation."

Readers loved it, scooping up more than 75 million Micheners.

Having read him, readers felt they understood complex societies like South Africa (*The Covenant*), Hungary (*The Bridge at Andau*), Colorado (*Centennial*) and Israel (*The Source*).

Michener's secrets were his essential sympathy and a drive to write as if his life depended on it. He never stomped on his characters, even the evil ones, and his unalloyed gee-whiz quality never flagged through more than 40 books and novels.

Michener also didn't intimidate readers.

"I tried to create an ambience that would both entertain and instruct the reader," he said, and "to invent characters who were as real as I could make them," giving them "only such heroics as I myself had experienced or found credible."

That patrician intellectuals berated his plebeian popularity

didn't seem to bother Michener; Main Street's adulation and sales more than made up for it.

"I have always remained out of the literary mainstream," he once wrote, " . . . as an act of conscious policy."

Michener was harsh in his judgments of himself.

He once called himself no example for young writers. "I certainly do not recommend either my behavior or my writing to them. I am a loner to an extent that would frighten most men," indicating he paid a penalty for his wealth and fame in hard work and enforced solitude.

Michener admitted, too, that his understated, often elliptical writing often missed its mark.

"I . . . am aware," he wrote in a personal memoir titled *The World Is My Home,* "that I frequently fail to make my point with the average reader. Thousands of people read *Hawaii* without recognizing it as a strong statement on race relations, and this same failure to understand has happened with several of my other books, notably *The Source* and *The Covenant.*"

Yet reviewers credited him with "perfect best-seller pitch: enough intrigue to make life exciting, enough chronological and geographical distance to make the thrills thrilling, not threatening."

Perhaps equally as important, Michener never talked down to his audience.

His sweeping literary dioramas took readers from primordial time to the day before yesterday. One critic called Michener's work "more truth than fact" with history slightly skewed to fit plots.

Hawaii is about imperialism, noted one reviewer, but the reader never noticed or cared while turning 1,140 pages that held down many beach towels in 1959. No matter what the formula was, Michener stories were simply too good to put down.

If they didn't remember many of Michener's characters after *South Pacific,* readers remembered that they liked the books.

But Michener—though a teacher at heart—didn't get lost in ancient history.

Several books—notably his 1961 *Report of the County Chairman* and his 1971 *Kent State: What Happened and Why*—were literally deadline reports on contemporaneous events. His 1971 *The Drifters,* a novel concerning six disenchanted young people touring Spain, was one of the first serious efforts to examine the '60s counterculture.

Whether they knew it or not, readers also were getting from Michener a not-so-subtle sociological education—which he once taught at Harvard—as well as a ratification of the Christian ethic, wrapped up in richly painted characters and cliff-hanging plots.

James Albert Michener wrote superlong. His manuscripts were so beefy there usually was enough surplus to make another book or two.

Leftovers from the 1,000-page *Alaska* of 1988 became *Journey,* a tale of the 19th-century gold rush to the Klondike. Notes from the 1985 blockbuster *Texas* were enough to write the 1990 *The Eagle and the Raven,* which was essentially twin portraits of General Santa Anna and Sam Houston.

One reviewer called him the "literary world's Cecil B. DeMille."

Michener was the consummate showman who knew what his audience of middle-class Americans wanted to see, hear and feel, and who gave them plenty of it. Teams of researchers helped him write his books in projects as well-organized as military operations. He used 15 local researchers on the 1983 *Poland* and made eight visits behind the Iron Curtain himself.

If his work resembled DeMille, Michener's personal life was more like Huckleberry Finn's.

An adopted orphan who spent time in poorhouses when his mother ran out of food, he once told an interviewer "We never had a sled, never had baseball gloves, never had a bicycle, never had a wagon. Nothing."

Friends remembered him as the brightest boy in grade school, and that his toes stuck out of his threadbare sneakers. Like Huck, he lit out for the territory at 14 from Doylestown, Pa., got a job in a traveling show and never looked back, hitchhiking through 45 states.

After Swarthmore College and teaching—including a 1939 stint as a Harvard lecturer in sociology—Michener's first effort at writing was a professional study called *The Future of Social Studies.*

Like so many men and women of his time, Michener's life was transformed by World War II. It was as a naval historian, gathering data on Pacific sea operations from an island in the New Hebrides (now Vanuatu) named Espiritu Santo, that Michener turned into a writer of fiction.

Michener's wartime scribblings in damp little notebooks became post-war short stories in *The Saturday Evening Post,* then a small 1947 book called *Tales of the South Pacific.*

Those stories, hammered out in a Pacific island quonset hut, won the 1948 Pulitzer Prize. They became the script for the landmark Broadway musical that gave the world All-American nurse Nellie Forbush, scam artist Luther Billis, matchmaker Bloody Mary and unforgettable songs like *There is Nothin' Like a Dame* and *I'm Gonna Wash That Man Right Out of My Hair.*

The author said he never wrote a better character than Nellie.

Michener visited 49 islands while working on naval histories, discovering in the French owner of a copra plantation named Aubert Ratard the makings of Emile De Becque of *South Pacific*'s "Some Enchanted Evening."

On the island, as well, was an overweight worker nicknamed "Bloody Mary."

He found the intriguing name "Bali Ha'i" on a signboard in "the most miserable Melanesian village I would ever see" and transformed it into a synonym for earthly paradise.

His own Bali Ha'i, he said, was Bora Bora, calling it the most beautiful island on Earth.

He recast the story for children in a 1992 book called *South Pacific,* as told by James A. Michener. Later in life he had this advice for aspiring writers: "Be sure your novel is read by (Richard) Rodgers and (Oscar) Hammerstein," who wrote the musical.

Dirt-poor Michener was supposed to get a measly 1% of the profits from the Broadway show, but on opening night—when it was obviously going to be one of the biggest hits of all time—Hammerstein loaned him $5,000 to invest in the show on the spot.

The $5,000 helped make him a fortune.

The *Pacific* tales and *South Pacific* royalties launched former Pennsylvania poor boy Michener on an author's life. A literary King Midas, virtually everything he wrote turned to gold and allowed Michener to give more than $100 million to charities and museums.

Pacific led him into a series of books and novels on Asia— *The Voice of Asia, The Floating World, Sayonara, The Bridges at Toko-Ri, Hawaii* and *Caravans,* the latter a romance-adventure set in Afghanistan.

From there, his novels toured the globe with special attention to North America, where he set six blockbusters including the 1978 *Chesapeake,* which sold 900,000 books.

Michener regarded 1965's *The Source* as his best-written book because the story was so complicated. But some reviewers saw Michener's 1974 *Centennial*—a story of Colorado—as his most accomplished.

Toward the end of his life, Michener said he regretted producing no short stories and failing to write a South American historical saga. (A short story for Michener may have been anything less than 500 pages.)

A man who had literally seen every nook and cranny on the globe, Michener said the Incan ruins of Peru's Machu Picchu was the one locale that had somehow eluded him for his 90 years.

Tightly wrapped and dedicated to work, Michener married three times but said few people really knew him. "I doubt it," he ruefully told an interviewer.

Michener, soaking up as much of a place as he could, usually lived in areas he was writing about.

Perhaps echoing Thomas Wolfe's "You can't go home again," Michener never wrote a big novel about his boyhood home of Doylestown or surrounding Bucks County. That was an area well-mined by John O'Hara, a novelist who Michener admired and who also cranked out big mass-market novels loved by readers but snubbed by Fifth Avenue literati.

To write about Bucks County, he said, he would have to go back and live there, read the newspapers, watch the sun set, attend meetings and interview parsons and principals.

Bart Barnes (obituary date 17 October 1997)

SOURCE: "Epic Novelist James Michener Is Dead at 90," in *The Washington Post,* October 17, 1997, p. A01.

[*In the following obituary, Barnes gives an overview of the author's works, calling him a "gifted storyteller, with a panoramic vision."*]

James A. Michener, a prolific author whose best-selling works ranged from poignant and compassionate stories of men and women in love and war to weighty novels spanning centuries and millennia while combining fiction and historical fact, died yesterday of kidney failure at his home in Austin. He was 90.

Michener was 40 before he wrote his first book, *Tales of the South Pacific,* but it made an immediate and lasting impact. It won the 1948 Pulitzer Prize for literature and became the basis for the hit musical *South Pacific,* by Richard Rodgers and Oscar Hammerstein II. The show, starring Mary Martin and Ezio Pinza, ran on Broadway for more than five years beginning in 1949, and it included some of the most popular music of the post-World War II era.

Michener also wrote travel articles, essays, novellas and short stories. But he became best known as a specialist in narrative epics that dramatized the social and political evolution of nations and regions as experienced over generations by real and imaginary participants, a technique he first developed with his 1959 bestseller, *Hawaii.*

In that novel, Michener traced the history of the Hawaiian islands from their earliest geological formations through the arrivals of diverse immigrants from Polynesia, Japan, the Philippines, the Asian mainland and the United States.

Published only months after Hawaii was granted statehood in August 1959, the book was praised by reviewers as a superlative account of the amalgamation of dissimilar people into an integrated society. It also provided Michener with a formula that he followed to varying degrees with such subsequent bestsellers as *The Source,* a 1965 novel covering 12,000 years of successive civilizations in Israel; *Centennial,* a 1974 novel about Colorado; *Chesapeake* (1978); *Poland* (1983); *Texas* (1986); *Alaska* (1988); and *Caribbean* (1989).

Those books and others earned Michener a reputation as a gifted storyteller with a panoramic vision, an eye for detail and a capacity for painstaking research. He was a solid craftsman but not an eloquent literary stylist, and some critics said his characters lacked dimension. He was, nevertheless, one of America's all-time best-selling authors, with more than 50 million books in print.

It was his World War II experience in the Navy that gave Michener the idea for *Tales of the South Pacific,* a collection of 18 loosely linked stories about U.S. Marines, Seabees, nurses and native islanders of the South Pacific during the war. Royalties from the Broadway musical and a 1958 film adaptation of his story made him independently wealthy and permitted him to devote himself full time to writing.

"I have only one bit of advice to the beginning writer: Be sure your novel is read by Rodgers and Hammerstein," he later told a friend and colleague, A. Grove Day.

His second novel, *The Fires of Spring,* published in 1949, was a critical disappointment, partly because of the high level of expectation after *Tales of the South Pacific.* It told the story of a creative artist's search for identity and included many autobiographical details, including attendance at a Quaker College and traveling with a tent show.

After a series of short stories and essays combined in a 1951 book, *Return to Paradise,* as well as travel articles and features about the Pacific and Far East, Michener wrote an immensely popular novella, *The Bridges at Toko-Ri,* which later became a hit movie starring William Holden. Initially, the story appeared in *Life* magazine in the summer of 1953, and it later was released in book form. It was about a Navy jet pilot and his family during the Korean War. The pilot is killed after completing a mission to destroy four vital bridges.

Michener's next book, *Sayonara,* published in 1954, was a tender and compassionate story of the ill-fated love of a U.S. Air Force officer for a beautiful young Japanese woman during the Korean War. It, too, became a popular movie, starring Marlon Brando.

Among Michener's other works adapted for film were the short stories "Until They Sail" and "Mr. Morgan" (from *Return to Paradise*). His novel *Hawaii* was made into two films, *Hawaii,* and *Hawaiians,* both released by United Artists. *Centennial* was adapted for television in the 1978-79 season. *Space,* Michener's best-selling 1982 novel about the U.S. space program, became a television miniseries in 1985.

Born on Feb. 3, 1907, in New York, Michener was taken as an infant to an orphanage in Bucks County, Pa., where he later was raised by Quaker foster parents, Edwin and Mabel Michener, whose surname he took. He was an avid reader as a youth, and at the age of 15, he hitchhiked and rode boxcars across the United States.

He won a $2,000 scholarship to Swarthmore College, where he graduated summa cum laude in 1929 with a degree in English literature. In 1984, declaring that he had always considered the scholarship "a loan against future earnings," Michener gave Swarthmore $2 million as repayment.

After college, he taught for two years at the Hill School in Pottstown, Pa., then in 1931 won a fellowship to study and travel in Europe. In this period, he worked as a chart corrector aboard a coal carrier in the Mediterranean, studied at St. Andrews University in Scotland, spent a winter in the Outer Hebrides collecting folk songs and studied Italian art in Siena and at the British Museum in London.

In 1933, Michener returned to the United States, taught three years at the George School in Newtown, Pa., then taught for five years at Colorado State College of Edu-

cation at Greeley. In 1940, he served as a visiting professor of history at Harvard's School of Education.

He wrote several scholarly articles for professional journals, work that he found unrewarding, he would later say, except that it taught him what many authors never learn, "how to explain something so that somebody else can understand it."

When the United States entered World War II, Michener was working as an editor in the education division of the Macmillan publishing house in New York. He enlisted in the Navy and was assigned to the South Pacific, initially as a keeper of records on naval aircraft maintenance and later as a naval historian. Both assignments required travel from island to island, and he recorded his impressions as he went.

Near the end of the war, Michener went off by himself to one of the smaller islands, where he began writing fictional vignettes based on his experiences. He offered his manuscript to Macmillan after leaving the Navy, and the stories were published as *Tales of the South Pacific* in 1947.

During the 1950s and into the early 1960s, Michener continued to set much of his writing in the Pacific and Far East. He lived in Hawaii for much of this time, accumulating material for *Hawaii,* but he also traveled extensively. He went to Europe at the time of the Hungarian uprising in the fall of 1956, and a year later, he published *The Bridge at Andau,* a dramatic account of the escape of 20,000 Hungarian refugees across the bridge at Andau, Austria, during the uprising.

He became involved in national politics during the 1960 presidential campaign of John F. Kennedy, then wrote about his experience in *Report of the County Chairman,* an account of national politics at the local level and of Michener's work as manager of the Kennedy campaign in Bucks County, Pa.

Americans and their experiences in far-off and exotic lands were among Michener's favorite subjects. He wrote about them in *Caravans,* a 1963 novel based on a trip to Afghanistan several years earlier; *The Drifters,* a 1971 novel about the wanderings and lifestyles of six alienated young people, three of them from the United States; and *Iberia: Spanish Travels and Reflections,* a 1968 book based upon Michener's own many visits to Spain since his student days of the 1930s.

With the aid of a large staff from *Reader's Digest,* he wrote about the killing of four students by Ohio National Guardsmen during a 1970 anti-war protest, *Kent State: What Happened and Why* (1971). A 1980 novel about the history and development of race relations in South Africa, *The Cov-*

enant, was criticized as lacking the crispness of some of his earlier work.

"I don't think the way I write books is the best or even second best," Michener once said. "The really great writers are people like Emily Bronte, who sit in a room and write out of their limited experience and unlimited imagination. But people in my position also do some very good work."

Michener's marriages to the former Patti Koon and Vange Nord ended in divorce. In 1955, he married Mari Yoriko Sabusawa. She died in 1994.

Juan B. Elizondo Jr. (obituary date 17 October 1997)

SOURCE: "Writer James Michener Dies at 90," in the *Atlanta Journal and Constitution,* October 17, 1997, p. A16.

[*In the following obituary, Elizondo calls Michener's works entertaining and inspiring.*]

James Michener's second novel tells of a poor Pennsylvania boy who becomes a writer—an autobiographical touch from the Pulitzer Prize-winning author who went from the Bucks County Poorhouse to the far reaches of the globe.

He spent decades wandering from Japan and Korea to Hungary, Hawaii, Afghanistan, Spain, South Africa, Colorado, Israel, Chesapeake Bay, Poland, Texas, Alaska and the Caribbean.

Every step of the way, through 40 best-selling novels, Michener's readers were entertained and inspired as he argued for universal ideals: religious and racial tolerance, hard work and self-reliance.

Michener, who once admitted that he wasn't very good at composing dialogue but he sure knew how to hold the reader's interest with a good narrative, died of kidney failure Thursday at age 90.

"Jim Michener was America's storyteller," said Harold Evans, president and publisher of the Random House Trade Publishing Group. "He enlightened millions of people around the globe with the fruits of his labor during his stunning 50-year writing career."

His death came less than a week after he ordered doctors to disconnect him from life-sustaining dialysis treatments.

Michener was born Feb. 3, 1907, in New York City, and was

taken as an orphan to the poorhouse in Doylestown, Pa., where he was adopted by a Quaker widow, Mabel Michener.

His childhood was not one of privilege, "so that accounts for my social attitude—I'm a fiery liberal," he once said.

"I've never felt in a position to reject anybody," he said in a 1972 interview. "I could be Jewish, part Negro, probably not Oriental, but almost anything else. This has loomed large in my thoughts."

Michener's heralded writing career began in 1947 when he was 40, with *Tales of the South Pacific.* The book, written during his tour of duty with the Navy in World War II, won the Pulitzer Prize in 1948 and was the basis for *South Pacific,* a Broadway musical later made into a motion picture.

Michener wrote historical-geographic blockbusters, living in and absorbing the culture of the places about which he wrote.

In *Voice of Asia* in 1951, he presented a variety of points of view gathered from interviews in Japan, India and other countries of the Orient. *The Bridges at Toko-Ri* (1953) and *Sayonara* (1954) were based on the Korean war, and in 1955 Michener produced *The Floating World,* a history of Japanese prints.

During the Hungarian revolt in 1956, Michener was in Austria where some 20,000 refugees crossed to the West. He assisted dozens to safety, writing about the experience in 1957's *The Bridge at Andau.*

By that time, Michener was living in Hawaii, where he worked seven years to produce *Hawaii.* The novel appeared in 1959 as the islands became the 50th state.

Then Michener was in Afghanistan to write *Caravans* (1963); in Israel for *The Source* (1965); in Spain for *Iberia* (1968) and *The Drifters* (1971).

Between trips during the 1960s, Michener again was based in Pennsylvania, where he worked as chairman of the Bucks County Citizens for Kennedy Committee. He wrote about that experience in 1961's *Report of the County Chairman.*

In 1971, he wrote *Kent State: What Happened and Why,* a sympathetic account of the tragic student protests at Kent State University.

In 1974, he completed *Centennial,* an epic tale of Colorado. It became a 26-hour television miniseries, the longest ever.

Then his attention shifted to the East Coast for *Chesapeake* in 1978, to South Africa and *The Covenant* in 1980, *Space* in 1982 and *Poland* in 1983.

"James Michener wanted to enlarge his readers' horizons and he did so in a wonderful way," said Texas Gov. George W. Bush. "His vast works taught us, entertained us and inspired us."

Former Texas Gov. Bill Clements invited Michener to profile his state in 1981, and offered the author a staff position at the University of Texas to help him. Michener made *Texas* his biggest book at 1,096 pages, and Austin his final home.

Michener never quit working, saying "as long as the old brain keeps functioning, I know the desire will always be there."

He released his latest book, *A Century of Sonnets,* earlier this year and reportedly was working on a book about his illness.

"I'm not a stylist," Michener once said of his writing. "There are a whole lot of things I'm not good at. I'm not hard in dialogue; I don't have that wonderful crispness. I don't think I'm good at psychology. But what I can do is put a good narrative together and hold the reader's interest."

Before the Navy and his writing, Michener taught at a prep school for two years, then won a two-year grant for study and travel in Europe. He did graduate work at the University of St. Andrews in Scotland, studied art in Siena, Italy, and in London, and spent a winter in the Outer Hebrides collecting folksongs.

He graduated with highest honors in English from Swarthmore College in suburban Philadelphia in 1929.

From 1933 to 1941, Michener taught English at various schools including Harvard University, taking time out to earn a master's degree. He worked as an editor of educational books at Macmillan publishing company in New York from 1941 until his enlistment in the Navy the following year.

He taught part-time well into his 80s, at the University of Texas and at Eckerd College in St. Petersburg, Fla.

His first two marriages, to Patti Koon in 1935 and Vange Nord in 1948, ended in divorce. In 1955, he married Mari Yoriko Sabusawa. She died in September 1994.

His work made Michener wealthy. Gifts from Michener and his third wife to the University of Texas over the years totaled $44.2 million, including a $15 million donation in 1992.

In 1996, *Fortune* magazine ranked him among the nation's top 25 philanthropists, estimating he gave away $24 million

in that year alone. Other donations included $1 million to a Bucks County art museum that bears his name.

Michener will be cremated and buried alongside his wife, said John Kings, Michener's longtime friend and assistant.

A funeral service will be held Tuesday in Austin.

Albin Krebs (obituary date 17 October 1997)

SOURCE: "James Michener, 90, Pulitzer-Prize Winning Author," in *The New York Times,* October 17, 1997, p. B8.

[*In the following obituary, Krebs discusses Michener's work and comments on his expert documentation and narrative ability.*]

James A. Michener, who survived a Dickensian childhood to win the Pulitzer Prize with his very first book, published when he was about 40, and then became one of America's favorite storytellers with grand-scale novels like *Hawaii, The Source* and *Texas,* died in his home in Austin, Texas, on Thursday. He was about 90.

Michener chose to discontinue life-saving kidney dialysis treatment earlier this month and died of complications following renal failure, according to John Kings, a longtime friend and assistant of Michener's.

"He felt he had accomplished what he wanted to accomplish in terms of his life's work," Kings said. "He did not want to suffer a long series of complications."

Michener's entry in *Who's Who in America* says he was born on Feb. 3, 1907. But he said in his 1992 memoirs that the circumstances of his birth remained cloudy and that he did not know just when he was born or who his parents were.

Tales of the South Pacific, a collection of stories he began while he was in the Navy during World War II, was his first published fiction and won the Pulitzer Prize in 1948. Although it later became a classic Broadway musical by Richard Rodgers and Oscar Hammerstein and a successful film, it was not a best seller at first.

It was not until Michener moved from his brief tales of people to his monumental sagas of places—beginning with *Hawaii* in 1959—that he became one of those rare writers whose books are snatched up by the book clubs and become almost automatic best sellers even before they hit the book stores. As of late 1992, he was one of only eight authors who had written six or more No. 1 best sellers in the half-century history of the weekly *New York Times* best-seller list.

And just the mention of his name was enough to gain *Time*'s best-seller list. And just the mention of his name was enough to gain movie or television interest.

In the years after *Hawaii,* Michener was often scorned by critics even as he achieved a huge and appreciative following. Expertly applying his tried-and-true formula, he wove big, old-fashioned narratives involving generations of fictional families as they moved through expertly documented events in history. As a writer, he liked to celebrate the all-American virtues of patriotism, frugality, common sense, and courage and to enrich his episodic, educational fiction with such details as the geological origins and prehistory of the territory he staked out as his subject.

> **As a writer, [Michener] liked to celebrate the all-American virtues of patriotism, frugality, common sense, and courage and to enrich his episodic, educational fiction with such details as the geological origins and prehistory of the territory he staked out as his subject.**
> **—*Albin Krebs***

To gather information for his books, Michener often moved to the place he wanted to write about, soaking up atmosphere and collecting detailed information. In 1981, for example, he accepted an invitation from Gov. William P. Clements Jr. to write about Texas. He moved to the state from Maryland, where he had passed several years researching and writing *Chesapeake* (1978). Working out of Austin, he and a hired staff traveled extensively to gather research and interview Texans for the novel, which dealt with the state's history and culture and the people who lived there from early times to the present.

When *Texas* appeared in 1985, its 1,096 pages made it heftier than any previous Michener work, and its publisher, Random House, said that the first printing of 750,000 copies was the largest in the company's history. Michener was about 78 when *Texas* came out, and his health was becoming precarious, but he immediately took on another huge subject for his next book.

He and his wife had decided to settle near Austin, where the University of Texas had named him a professor emeritus, but they spent part of 1985 in Sitka, Alaska, to do research for his panoramic 1988 historical novel, *Alaska,* which swept from the mastodon era to modern times. He followed *Alaska,* the next year with *Journey,* a novel about four men on a trip from England to the Klondike during the 1897 gold rush.

"Storytelling came naturally to me," he said. It was a gift

that made him a multimillionaire, for in addition to the phenomenal total sales of hardcover and paperback editions of his 40-odd books, a number were sold to the movies and television—including *Centennial* (1974), encompassing Colorado's history, *Space* (1982), about the space program, and *Texas.*

Typical of the critics' response to most of Michener's work was that of Orville Prescott of *The New York Times,* who wrote of *Hawaii* when it was published in 1959: "It may never make literary history, but for some time it has been making publishing history." The 450,000-word novel was selected by the Book-of-the-Month Club and the *Reader's Digest* Condensed Book Club, and it was sold for $1 million for a movie that starred Julie Andrews, Max von Sydow, Richard Harris, and Gene Hackman.

The Micheners had lived in Hawaii for some years, and in his novel Michener sought to show that the islands had been able to harmonize different cultures and races and to set an example that could benefit the rest of the United States. However, two years after the publication of *Hawaii* and after it had been at the top of the best-seller lists for 70 weeks, Michener and his wife, Mari, the daughter of Japanese immigrants, left the islands.

"On the day-to-day operating level at which my wife and I lived," he said at the time, "we met with more racial discrimination in Hawaii than we did in eastern Pennsylvania, where we had previously lived."

The Covenant, Michener's 1980 novel depicting the rise and triumph of the Dutch settlers in South Africa, was banned in that country two months before its publication. The novel's time span was, for Michener, relatively brief—from 1647 to the present. His previous epic, *Chesapeake,* used the stories of his characters to trace the development of the Chesapeake Bay area from the 16th century to the 1970s.

James Albert Michener, a mild-mannered, spectacled man who could have been mistaken for the small-town teacher he once was, was born in New York City, according to his entry in *Who's Who.* But in a 1985 interview with Caryn James of *The New York Times,* he indicated that he had no definite information about his birth. "I have no idea who I am," he said. "I know what I was told, that I was a foundling."

According to his 1992 autobiography, *The World Is My Home: A Memoir,* he was taken in by Mabel Haddock Michener, a poor young widow, and raised alongside other children who came and went from her home in Doylestown, Pa. "My mother made her living by taking in orphaned children and doing other families' laundry," he wrote. "The family I was reared in usually had four or five and sometimes as many as six other children."

He recalled that in later years he had sought out more specific information about who he was because he lacked the birth certificate needed to obtain a passport. "In such circumstances," he wrote, "it is common to hire a lawyer who will interrogate neighbors to establish the earliest possible date at which the child was known to have been in the community."

And so, he recounted, he engaged a lawyer in Doylestown "who proved that I had lived in that town since the age of 2." In addition, Michener reported, "It was generally believed that I had been born in New York and had arrived in town when I was about two weeks old." He wrote that he had fallen into Mrs. Michener's home "one way or another."

Despite his childhood poverty, he said he felt loved and inspired by Mabel Michener, a Quaker who read aloud to him from 19th-century novels, especially Dickens. Michener wrote movingly about the experiences of his childhood in his second, highly autobiographical novel, *The Fires of Spring* (1949).

He was a footloose youth. "As a kid of 14, I bummed across the country on nickels and dimes," he recalled. "Before I was 20, I had seen all the states but Washington, Oregon, and Florida. I had an insatiable love of hearing people tell stories, and what they didn't tell I made up."

At Swarthmore College, on a scholarship, he majored in English and history, receiving a bachelor's degree with highest honors in 1929.

It was also at Swarthmore, he recounted, that he learned from an acquaintance for the first time that he was adopted. John P. Hayes, in a biography of Michener, maintained that he was, in fact, Mabel Michener's illegitimate son. Asked about that possibility, Michener told *The New York Times:* "I don't know whether it's true or not. I have no idea who I am."

He went on to teach for two years at the Hill School in Pottstown, Pa., and to spend two years in Europe on a traveling grant. Later, he taught at the George School in Newtown, Pa., where a friendly Quaker woman who was on its board gave him advice that he said helped him form his philosophy of education. He quoted her: "Thee is too conservative. Thee has these children only a few years of their lives. Thee must tell them more."

"I recall that advice with pleasure when I hear others lament the stupidity and conservation of American education," Michener said. For his own part, he became what he called "a specialist in teaching others how to teach, serving with

several educational groups writing and publishing research papers" on teaching. He did some education research at Harvard.

Soon after he joined Macmillan Publishing Co. in New York as a textbook editor in 1941, Japanese military forces attacked Pearl Harbor and, he said, "I waived my Quaker principles and volunteered for service." He began as a Navy enlisted man, but he soon became an officer and was made a "super-secretary" to an aviation maintenance unit in the Solomon Islands.

It was mostly humdrum duty, Michener said. To pass the time in the afternoon, he drafted the outlines of "some stories that disturbed me." At night, he turned the outlines into the short stories that became *Tales of the South Pacific,* published in 1947.

By then, Michener was back at his job at Macmillan, but not for long. The hardcover edition of *Tales of the South Pacific* had only modest sales—25,000 copies, despite the Pulitzer Prize—but the wildly popular 1949 musical *South Pacific,* based on the Michener stories, turned the paperback version of the book into a runaway best seller of more than 2 million copies. The musical, which starred Mary Martin and Ezio Pinza, won another Pulitzer Prize, ran for 1,925 performances, and was made into a popular movie in 1958. Michener liked to advise struggling writers on the key to success: "Make sure Rodgers and Hammerstein read your first book."

Michener was around 40 when his first book was published. Several years later, he said that if an aspirant "hasn't published a book by the time he is 35, he's not likely ever to amount to anything as a writer," adding that the "accident of the war may have delayed me." He continued: "Writing is hard for me. I'm weak on style, plot, and form—all the things you're supposed to be good at. My first drafts are pretty terrible. Also, I start a great deal that I don't finish. But I always have a great backlog I want to write about. I can't ever conceive of running out of ideas. They crowd me."

After his initial success, his name reappeared on best-seller lists again and again, decade after decade, on into the 1990s. Among the books that followed *South Pacific* were *Return to Paradise,* a collection of travel writings and short stories, and *The Voice of Asia,* both published in 1951; *The Bridges at Toko-Ri,* 1953; *Sayonara,* 1954; *Floating World,* 1955; *The Bridge at Andau,* 1957; *Caravans,* a novel set in 1946 in Afghanistan, 1963; *The Source,* a novel, covering 12,000 years of history, about life in and around what became an Israeli town, 1965; *Iberia,* a highly regarded travel book on Spain and Portugal, 1968; *Kent State,* 1971; *Sports in America,* 1976; *Poland,* 700 years of history in novel form, 1983; *Legacy,* a brief novel about an Army major called to testify at the Iran-Contra hearings and about his patriot fore-bears, 1987; *Caribbean,* a novel recounting Caribbean history, 1989; *The Novel,* a fictional study of book publishers and kindred souls, 1991; *Mexico,* a novel in which an American journalist learns Mexican history, 1992; *Literary Reflections,* a collection of Michener's occasional writings, 1993; and *Recessional,* a 1994 novel that addressed issues linked with aging in America.

His last fictional work appeared in 1995, a short novel of the supernatural called *Miracle in Seville,* set in the Spanish bullfighting world. Allen Josephs, writing in *The New York Times Book Review,* called it "a vintage demonstration of Michener storytelling." A nonfiction work about his vision of the United States, *This Noble Land,* was published in 1996.

Resourcefully, Michener also drew on his experiences in politics during the early 1960s. Having returned from Hawaii to live near Doylestown, he became an avid campaign worker for the election of John F. Kennedy to the presidency in 1960. In 1962, he ran for Congress as a Democrat, seeking to unseat Rep. Willard S. Curtin, the Republican incumbent from the House district embracing Doylestown. He was unsuccessful.

"If I were found worthy to participate in the government of my nation I would be happy indeed," Michener said. "I would consider the work more important than the writing of another book."

He wrote about his 1960 electioneering in *Report of the County Chairman* (1961) and he turned out a thoughtful book on how Americans choose their president, *Presidential Lottery,* in 1969.

Michener suffered a serious heart attack in 1964, but his recovery was excellent and he continued writing. He did ease his workload by employing researchers and an editor to take care of much of the detail work he had previously done himself.

His reaction to his monumental success as an author has been described by friends as "humble." He remained haunted by his years of poverty in the Depression. He told Ms. James: "They have a deeper impact on someone like me than people realize. It makes you more dour, more tightly ingrained. It inhibits you. . . . I live as if I had stayed on my job and retired on a small pension and some savings and security."

Michener gave much of his money away and was generous to young writers. The Associated Press reported late in 1994 that his wife, Mari, had played a major role in directing donations by him that had totaled more than $100 million. The beneficiaries included Swarthmore College, the University of Texas, the Writers' Workshop at the University of Iowa, and The Authors League Fund.

By 1992, the Micheners had given more than $37 million to the University of Texas—the most ever given to that university by a single donor. The university exhibits a collection of 20th-century American art valued at several million dollars donated and lent by the Micheners along with an endowment to acquire more. The Micheners' collection of more than 1,500 Japanese prints has gone to the University of Hawaii. In February 1996, he pledged $5.5 million to the art museum in Doylestown that bears his name and to other cultural institutions in Pennsylvania. Earlier this month, it was announced that the University of Northern Colorado in Greeley, where he received a master's degree in 1937, would be the only recipient of his manuscripts, personal documents, notes, and other items totaling 60,000.

Michener's 1935 marriage to Patti Koon ended in divorce in 1948, and his 1948 marriage to Vange Nord ended in divorce in 1955. Later that year, he married Mari Yoriko Sabusawa, an editor, who, as the American daughter of Japanese parents, had been in a detention camp in World War II. She died in 1994. Michener had no surviving children.

Despite the scope of his philanthropy, he described himself in a 1989 interview simply as "a storyteller." He added: "I'm sure that in the dawn of civilization, I would have gone out with the hunters, then stayed behind a safe tree and at night explained how it all happened."

Stephanie Simon (obituary date 17 October 1997)

SOURCE: "Blockbuster Author Michener Dies," in *The Los Angeles Times,* October 17, 1997, p. 1.

[*In the following obituary, Simon discusses Michener's amazing success and popularity with his readers, despite the criticism of reviewers.*]

James A. Michener, the extravagant storyteller who delivered whole states, whole nations—indeed, whole epochs—to an adoring international audience by wrapping historical fact in sweeping fiction, died Thursday. He was 90 and died at his home in Austin, Texas.

The author of such blockbusters as *Hawaii, Texas, Centennial* and *Iberia*—which sold in incredible volume, despite their imposing length—Michener died of renal failure.

He had been in frail health in recent years, undergoing a quadruple bypass and hip surgery. Though he continued to work, his need for kidney dialysis three times a week forced him to stay close to his modest home in Austin.

His condition had deteriorated to the point where he ordered his doctors to take him off the dialysis unit last week, and his death had been imminent since.

Michener leaves behind fans all over the globe, readers who grabbed every book he wrote regardless of the topic, certain he would carry them away with his broad narratives while teaching them history, geography, botany and more.

Los Angeles Times book editor Steve Wasserman said: "James Michener's death diminishes American letters. He was the most democratic of authors, believing passionately in the promise of America, with a profound love of its people."

"His generosity of spirit was palpable in the books he wrote, which gave pleasure to millions the world over."

Michener did not write his first manuscript until he was 40. But that book—*Tales of the South Pacific,* typed out in a Navy Quonset hut by the glow of a foul-smelling lantern— won him the Pulitzer Prize in 1948.

From then on, he wrote, and wrote, and wrote.

Forty-seven books. One hundred million copies sold. Movie, theater and miniseries spinoffs. Translations into at least 50 languages.

The Michener Phenomenon, publishers called it.

To be sure, Michener did much else in his long life besides pump out bestsellers. He was a philanthropist who donated a fortune to education. He was a sought-after teacher, too. And an art collector who wrote two books on Japanese prints. He won the Presidential Medal of Freedom, this country's highest civilian honor.

Proud to be called a knee-jerk liberal, Michener was also passionately political; he even ran for Congress himself. He spoke out against McCarthyism. He lobbied for the right to die. He chaired President John F. Kennedy's Food for Peace Program. He served on a committee that recommended worthy figures to adorn U.S. postage stamps.

But his true love—and his true gift—was telling stories.

He approached his craft with methodical, journeyman style. As he told a radio interviewer in 1992: "My job is to be a hard-working man who sits at a modern typewriter and tries to write books that a lot of people will want to read."

By that measure, he succeeded in the grandest possible style.

Critics might call Michener's fiction flat, might carp about his cardboard characters or his dreary dialogue. Fellow novelists might grumble that he moralized too much, used too many cliches, digressed too often. His readers didn't care. They knew they could count on Michener to transport them to another time, another place—to enlighten even as he entertained.

He wrote about space, and they bought it. He wrote about sports, and they bought that, too. He wrote about presidential politics, racial discrimination, South Africa, the Caribbean, nursing homes.

They bought it all.

Indeed, the devotion of Michener's readers was legendary.

They dreamed up plots to secure advance copies of upcoming books. They wrote him that old aunts, wasting away on deathbeds, had asked for his novels to be read aloud. They even named their children after his characters.

One reviewer summed up the appeal this way: "Michener's are the beach books that, unlike most other beach books, leave you smarter than you were when you started reading. Each delivers the product of all that research, doled out to the reader at just the right rate. You know right away who the bad guys are—the petty ones, the stingy ones. The heroes are generous and energetic and smart and, above all, unprejudiced."

Despite his roaring commercial success, Michener never took a vacation. He worked seven days a week. He rarely treated himself to luxuries. And he never thought of himself as a bona fide author.

"I think the word 'author' ought to be reserved for those figures that used to appear in our classrooms in America years ago, people from the last century, always with beards, always with three names—James Russell Lowell, Ralph Waldo Emerson," he once said.

To another reporter, he commented: "I'm not a brilliant mind. I'm more Germanic. I'm the guy who can see the thing through. I know how to organize material. That's different than the sheer brilliance of a Norman Mailer or a Truman Capote."

But his fans would say he had his own brand of brilliance.

. . . . .

James Albert Michener knew next to nothing about his origins.

Like adventure novelist Harold Robbins, who died Tuesday and who surpassed Michener in copies sold but not in critical praise, Michener was an abandoned child.

Born Feb. 3, 1907, probably in New York City, he was a foundling, as he called himself. A Quaker woman named Mabel Michener took him into her home in rural Doylestown, Pa., and raised him as her own.

The family was poor. Young James sometimes went hungry. He always wore castoff clothes. For a few bleak periods, he was forced to return to the orphanage because Mabel Michener could not afford to feed him. Still, he remembered some happy times. Mabel read him the classics, especially Dickens. She imbued him with a strong Quaker faith, which propelled his lifelong commitment to fighting discrimination. And he was able to indulge his itch for travel one year by hitchhiking through 45 states.

When, as a teenager, Michener learned that Mabel was not his biological mother, he said he "had a bad three days." But he resolved not to think of it again. He also vowed not to attempt to track down his birth parents. From then on, Michener rarely revisited the subject of his childhood, not even while writing his curiously detached 1991 memoir, *The World Is My Home.*

"It has not mattered in my life, not even one-tenth of one percent," he once said.

A skilled athlete and excellent student, Michener attended Swarthmore College on a scholarship (over the objections of his high school principal, who feared he would shame the school by flunking out). The principal suggested Michener become a plumber. Instead, he went to Swarthmore—and graduated summa cum laude in 1929.

After a brief stint teaching in a local school, Michener won a fellowship to travel abroad—and embarked on an adventure of the kind he would later learn to put in prose. He toured with Spanish bullfighters, worked on a cargo ship in the Mediterranean, explored folk legends on islands off the coast of Scotland.

But though he collected color wherever he went, Michener did not try his hand at writing. Not yet.

Instead, he returned to teaching social studies for a time, then accepted a post as associate editor with Macmillan Co. in New York. The experience, he later said, proved to be excellent grounding for his writing career. "I learned what a great many people never learn," he said. "I learned how to write a sentence and how to write a paragraph."

Michener turned those skills to good use as he wound down his tour of duty as a lieutenant commander in the U.S. Navy during World War II. Setting up a typewriter in a musty Quonset hut, he tapped out the series of short stories that became *Tales of the South Pacific.*

Though some critics complained that the stories were too long, *Tales of the South Pacific* won praise for its texture, its drama, its originality. "Romantic, nostalgic, tragic—call it what you will—this book seems to me the finest piece of fiction to come out of the South Pacific War," one reviewer proclaimed.

Even when honored with the Pulitzer Prize, however—beating out novels by John Steinbeck and Sinclair Lewis—the book did not become a bestseller. Michener did not make real money off it until Richard Rodgers and Oscar Hammerstein II adapted it into the musical *South Pacific.* ("I have only one bit of advice to the beginning writer," Michener said years later. "Be sure your novel is read by Rodgers and Hammerstein.")

Royalties from the musical allowed Michener to pursue his writing career full-time.

Later, of course, his other books made him a very rich man, and his official biography notes that he donated more than $100 million to charity over the years. His donations to University of Texas at Austin topped $37 million, including $15 million for a writers' program. Michener also gave away his impressive collections of Japanese and American art. And he put dozens of students through college.

Michener's financial success really started with *Hawaii,* published by Random House in 1959. By then he had married his third wife, Mari Yoriko Sabusawa, a librarian who would stay at his side until her death in 1994 after 38 years of marriage. (He will be cremated and buried beside her Tuesday in Austin.)

Hawaii was an instant hit.

The novel's scope was audacious, its approach striking. In it, Michener swept through hundreds of years of history by creating fictional families and then tracing their lives through generations.

His characters were not subtle; psychological insight was not the point. Michener was not even particularly concerned with plot. His goal was to use his fictional families to illuminate sociological issues and moral concerns and, of course, as a vehicle for reviewing history.

The formula proved wildly successful. And it established Michener as a brand-name, bankable author. "I stumbled on the device of the long novel," he said in 1996, "and the crazy things sold unbelievably."

Indeed, after *Hawaii,* Michener would use the same format for many of his most famous books, including *The Source* (about Israel), *The Covenant* (about South Africa), *Iberia* (Spain) and *Centennial* (the American West).

Michener churned out these regional tapestries with astounding speed.

He produced *Space* in 1982, *Poland* in 1983, *Texas* in 1985. He broke from the tried-and-true format to write *Legacy,* a novel based on the Iran-Contra scandal, in 1987. But the slim novel was panned by critics, and Michener returned to his familiar heavy tomes with *Alaska* in 1988, *Caribbean* in 1989 and *Mexico* in 1992. (He had actually started *Mexico* 30 years earlier, but lost the manuscript; when a relative found it in a neglected cupboard, he freshened it up and finished it.)

Though his prolific pace made it hard to believe, Michener always insisted he did all his research himself, aided only by his longtime assistant John Kings.

Michener made repeated visits to each place he wrote about, sometimes living there for months or even years to steep himself in the atmosphere before memorializing it in print. Lodged for a time in Maryland, say, or Colorado, he would make every effort to think like a local. He would badger his wife to haunt the supermarkets and bring him word of the chit-chat she heard. He would listen to the weather reports, attend the sporting events, interview residents from all walks of life.

"He knows everybody from the Pope on down. He'll talk to a plumber just as he'll talk to Bill Clinton," Michener's secretary, Theresa Potter, recounted.

He also read incessantly. According to Kings, he went through 200 to 300 books in preparation for each novel.

Michener took tremendous pride in his ability to synthesize all that information and turn even the dullest facts into an appealing story. "If I try to describe a chair," he once said, "I can describe it so that a person will read it to the end."

Still, some critics called his works interminable. "He begins with the first faint primordial stirring on the face of the deep and slogs onward through the ages until he hits the day before yesterday," scoffed one reviewer for Time. A Los Angeles Times reviewer added that Michener wrote "at a pace any glacier would enjoy."

A Washington Post critic took issue as well with Michener's casual blending of fact and fiction. Writing about *The Covenant,* he complained that Michener mentioned many well-known South African figures but attributed their actions to his fictional creations. "Imagine a novel prominently featuring Abraham Lincoln but attributing the Gettysburg Address to a fictitious minor character," the reviewer huffed.

But other critics found value in the historical panoramas, however long, and praised Michener's ability to bring alive events that "would otherwise be dry as dust."

While Michener is best known for his fat historical novels, he returned again and again through his long career to social, political and religious themes.

A lifelong Democrat, Michener had a strong sense of social justice that shone through nearly all of his writing, from his admiration for Hawaii's multiracial society to his indignation at Texas' shabby treatment of Mexican Americans.

"No other American writer has made the world the subject of his writing with such sympathy for the universal nature of people everywhere," a reviewer wrote in an appreciative look at Michener's memoir.

Michener was also an avid student of the American political system. He chronicled his work campaigning for John F. Kennedy in one nonfiction book called *Report of the County Chairman.* In another, *Presidential Lottery,* he set out arguments for reforming the electoral system.

He used his novel *Space,* published while he was serving on a NASA advisory council, as a platform for advocating scientific research. In several books, he chastised Americans for ignoring public education and the arts. And he explored the issue of doctor-assisted suicide for the terminally ill—a cause he passionately believed in—in *Recessional,* set in a Florida nursing home and published in 1994.

Over the years, Michener also served on various government committees, including the International Broadcasting Board and the State Department's Advisory Committee on the Arts.

He received numerous awards, most notably the Medal of Freedom in 1977. He taught and lectured all over the world. And he always supported programs for young writers. (He had no children of his own. Though he and his second wife adopted two children, they gave them up after their divorce.)

When speaking to aspiring authors, Michener always emphasized that writing was not as easy as he made it seem.

Even after four decades of success, he said he still woke up in the middle of the night, sweating and fretting about his current project. And he acknowledged a habit of writing out of sequence, taking the easy parts first.

"In the middle of every book, I get panic stricken," Michener told The Times in 1991. "I think, 'Who's going to read this?' Then I think, 'Well, there's nobody on this block who could tell this story any better than I could.'"

REVIEWS OF MICHENER'S RECENT WORKS

Bill Barich (review date 12 January 1992)

SOURCE: "Sing along with Michener," in the *Los Angeles Times Book Review,* January 12, 1992, p. 4.

[*In the following review, Barich praises Michener's memoir,* The World Is My Home, *as a "Horatio Alger story," both entertaining and touching.*]

In his new memoir, **The World Is My Home,** James Michener puts to rest the idea that there are no second acts in American lives. As the old saying goes, his life really began at 40, when, during World War II, he sat down in a Quonset hut on Espiritu Santo Island, lit a smoky lantern, and turned out the linked stories that became **Tales of the South Pacific,** which won him a Pulitzer Prize in 1947. This stroke of luck helped to transform him into James Michener, the best-selling phenomenon, and he has continued to live on the grand scale ever since, becoming in the process America's "best-loved" writer.

Michener's reminiscences don't have much in common with the usual literary fare. There are no drunken brawls, no brilliant seductions, no drugs, and precious little animosity. Vice for Michener consists of an addiction to the fine arts. When he discusses writing, he often does it with an eye toward the business end of things, offering cautionary advice to beginners. Above all, he comes across as a practical person, and his book has the flavor of another, pre-Elvis era, when issues of complexity could be mastered through grit, hard work and positive thinking.

In choosing to call **The World Is My Home** a memoir rather than an autobiography, Michener alerts us at the start that he will not be terribly forthcoming about himself. We must ferret out the salient facts from chapters that are arranged according to subject—Travel, People, Health and so on—not chronologically. He jumps backward and forward in time, and while this allows him the leisure to dwell on his strongest concerns, it opens gaps in the narrative that leave a reader scratching his head over the missing parts of the puzzle.

Michener had a difficult, scarring, Dickensian childhood. Orphaned at birth, he grew up in Pennsylvania, bouncing from one foster home to another. The homes were run by Mabel Michener, a caring, intelligent woman who took in the wounded and the abandoned. Others in the Michener clan were not so kind and put it to young James that he was not a true Michener, and this gave him an independence of spirit, as well as an emotional armoring, that molded his character. He became a Quaker and has always had the sturdy, unshakable values of the Pennsylvania Dutch.

In his teens, Michener took to the road, hitchhiking around the country and developing a love of exploration and adventure that never left him. As a scholarship student at Swarthmore, he was a classic high achiever. He enjoyed painting, poetry and music, especially opera, but he showed no predisposition toward writing. Eventually, he went to work in publishing, and as his 40th birthday approached he found himself about to be drafted into the Army. He enlisted in the Navy instead and was stationed in the South Pacific, where the life-changing episodes began.

The chapters that deal with Polynesia are the stars of **The World Is My Home.** Michener's recollections are sweetly nostalgic and have a simple human happiness that is sometimes missing elsewhere in the book. He fell into an island paradise that was far enough removed from the war theater to pose no serious threat, and he was soon gifted with a writer's most precious possession—wonderful material. There were honky-tonks, colorful characters, a surpassingly beautiful landscape, and just enough weirdness around the edges to keep everybody on his toes.

Michener admits to being a bit of a Boy Scout, but the South Pacific seems to have loosened him up a little. In a distant, Victorian way, he describes the sexual dreamland in which many American GIs were living, invited by their hosts to take up residence with the most gorgeous young girls of the islands. So lubricious was the scene on Bora Bora that soldiers often didn't want to return to the states. Michener makes Polynesia sound like the Playboy Mansion, but he plays his cards so close to the vest that it's impossible to tell whether he was only an observer, someone who liked to admire the naked bodies of the natives when they went skinny-dipping at twilight.

Observation has always been central to Michener's work. He has a vast curiosity, and research and reporting provide the substance for his novels. Yet, by his account, he might never have written a word if he hadn't almost died in a plane crash while landing at Tontouta Air Base. His brush with death gave him the willies, and during a long night of soul-searching he realized that he was dissatisfied with himself. "As the stars came out and I could see the low mountains I had escaped," he says. "I swore: 'I'm going to live the rest of my life as if I were a great man.'" It's the *as if* that matters here, for Michener is essentially a modest soul. From that moment on, though, he would ask the best of himself.

It takes an idealist to make such a vow, and Michener is idealistic to the core. He confesses that he would have made a good minister if he had had more religion. But it was his fate to hole up in his Quonset hut and transcribe as accurately as possible his vision of the South Pacific. When the manuscript was finished, he submitted it anonymously to Macmillan, where he had gone back to work as an editor, and the company published it to scant critical praise and indifferent sales. The cheap, ugly dust jacket remains an object of scorn to Michener. On the basis of his reception, he had no intention of quitting his job, but then, out of the blue, he won the Pulitzer, and his transformation was complete.

Well, not quite. *Tales* went on to sell many copies, but Michener earned his first megabucks from the Broadway adaptation, *South Pacific,* a Rodgers and Hammerstein collaboration. For a time after his success, he struggled with his identity as a writer until he hit on the sort of formulaic "big book" that has become his stock-in-trade. The formula allowed him to travel widely, and Random House provided him with a well-oiled editorial machine geared to getting his manuscripts in shape and between covers in a timely way. Michener views himself as an old-fashioned storyteller and claims not to be affected by critics—a claim his fellow writers might doubt. But there is no doubting another claim of his, that he has pleased a huge international audience.

In a crucial sense, the ability to please readers is only half the battle of literature. To be "best-loved" at anything, you have to dance around the darkness. In *The World Is My Home,* it is the darkness that Michener avoids, seldom delving below the surface.

He doesn't seem comfortable with intimacy or emotions, and one suspects that this must go back to his earliest days as an orphan, when he had to steel himself against the world rather than embrace it. Although he has gone through two painful divorces, he mentions them only in passing. His current wife is barely alluded to, and we get so little information about their relationship that we wonder at the intensity of Michener's privacy.

His public adventures are much more fully recounted. We are offered glimpses of Michener as a liberal politician, as a goodwill ambassador for the United States and as a fortune-teller whose prescience astounds the residents of Doylestown. He sprinkles the book with famous names, but there is seldom anything revealing in the anecdotes, and we must be content to learn that he has palled around with singer Ezio Pinza, Walter Cronkite and Art Buchwald, and that he

lobbied to get Robin Roberts, the old Phillies' pitcher, into the Hall of Fame.

The portrait Michener draws of himself shows us an honorable, driven, high-minded man who hangs onto his optimism at all costs. His generosity to universities and to other writers is well-known, and he may have no peer as a knee-jerk liberal—to Michener, that's a term of praise. Where his work will ultimately land is up to posterity, of course, but he has a right to be proud of his output, since writing one book, much less 34, demands a certain respect. In contrast to most immensely popular novelists, he has picked themes and topics that are challenging and sometimes politically sensitive, and he has never indulged in the cheap shot.

In the end, *The World Is My Home* most resembles a Horatio Alger story, in which all the traditional American virtues lead to a triumph on the grand scale. It is an entirely American document that could not have come into existence without being nurtured by the Puritan taproots of the country. Michener's memoir is high-strung, entertaining, occasionally funny, and curiously touching in what it omits. We admire the passion and the energy he brings to the task, especially at the age of 85.

Michener fans will surely be delighted, while other readers will find enough interesting material to keep the pages turning.

Reeve Lindbergh (review date 16 October 1994)

SOURCE: "James Michener's September Song," in *Washington Post Book World,* October 16, 1994, pp. 1, 18.

[*In the following review, Lindbergh faults Michener's* Recessional *for its two-dimensional characters and predictable plot.*]

The trouble with James Michener's latest novel may be that it is too true to its title. It seems odd to say this, because Michener's strength as an author so often lies in his faithful representation of whatever it is his titles tell us he has written about: *Hawaii, Poland, Chesapeake.* Most of his books concern themselves with specific pieces of geography, places one can find on the map. There is something both heartening and encompassing in sharing James Michener's view of life. We have a sense of taking in whole continents, and entire cultures, as well as the minutiae of one meadow in eastern Europe, or the awkward absurdity of a pelican in the Florida Everglade. Reading Michener at his best is like going on a field trip with God. His landscapes are as rich as fine loam with the physical truths of this earth, and because of this they are often unforgettable.

But this book deals with old age, and age is not a landscape. It is not a place on the map, and it is not exactly a "recessional," either; as the frontispiece of this book defines the word: "A hymn or other piece of music played at the end of the service while the congregation is filing out." The last years of life cannot be measured realistically by the steady, even tread suggested here, an orderly parade toward finality. Old age is as passionate and varied as any other time in life, and human beings generally do not "file out" of existence any more than they "file in."

The central character in the story is not, in fact, an old man but a young one: Dr. Andy Zorn, formerly of Chicago. He has been recruited by James Taggart of the mammoth "Taggart Enterprises," to salvage The Palms, one of the many retirement centers the corporation operates. The Palms is suffering from economic instability, and needs new management. Zorn has a bit of salvaging of his own to do, with a failed marriage and two malpractice suits (fraudulent, but damaging) behind him. Still, Zorn's character is solid and his managerial skills impressive, and he sets to work turning things around.

Most of the novel focuses upon the people he meets during this process, including the staff and elderly residents of the retirement center, and their families. The pace and rhythm of the book make it impossible to stay with anyone for very long, though, and we are left with snapshots of each person as he or she passes by. The problem is compounded because these people, like so many Michener characters in other books, tend to come across to us as types rather than individuals: The Society Beauty (now an Alzheimer's patient); her devoted husband, a burly, gruff-voiced factory owner whom our grandmothers surely would have labeled a Rough Diamond; The Retired Judge; The Famous Baseball Player; The Senator; The Ambassador; The Colombian Exile. People even talk about themselves—and sometimes each other—in a kind of representative voice, avoiding what is personal and particular to each human being. A woman says "I was the headmistress of an elite private girl's school," but fails to tell us which one. A fax comes in from a newspaper editor intending to publish a story about The Palms. He promises to send "our world-famous Austrian photographer," a man who appears to have no proper name. Zorn himself, during his initial job interview with the tycoon Taggart, describes himself in terms of his family background, this way: "Mother's a sentimental Irish Catholic from County Kerry. Dad's a tough-minded German Lutheran from Swabia."

At this point, a reader may wish to be transported to one of these places, where surely Michener would ground our wandering attention in ethnic and geographical information. It is hard to stay interested in the well-meaning but faceless Zorn.

Sometimes the portraits of individuals through the young doctor's eyes are acute and moving, even in such quick takes as we get before the procession continues. Zorn muses while watching Marjorie Duggan, the woman with advanced Alzheimers: "How beautiful she was, how extraordinarily fragile, as if her head were made of some exquisite Chinese ceramic that allowed the veins to peek through." But in another place a description will surrender meaning to generality: A resident's granddaughters are so attractive "they could have posed for ads for expensive soaps."

We do meet some engaging personalities in this book, and after a while we yearn to concentrate upon one of them, forgetting Zorn and his past problems, present responsibilities, and mild-mannered romance. (A beautiful amputee comes to The Palms for physical therapy and rehabilitation, then with encouragement from kindly residents and staff, captures the doctor's heart.) There is the head nurse, Nora Varney, who combines common sense with sensitivity, and shows Zorn her vision of "the other side of medical practice," an AIDS hospice in the back streets of Tampa. There are "the dancing Mallorys," a genial, spirited old couple who enjoy life so much that their children take them to court for spending too much money on themselves. At the other end of the spectrum is Berta Umlauf, struggling to prevent her failing health from becoming a long-term financial and emotional burden upon her family.

My favorite character in ***Recessional*** is not a person at all, however, but a rattlesnake. He is a neighbor of The Palms, not a resident, living where he has lived for many years, deep in the cypress swamps and under the low bushes of what remains of the wilderness area surrounding the retirement center. He eats frogs, squirrels, and baby herons, and resents the encroachment of all condominiums. He is a reptilian curmudgeon, refusing to be part of anybody's parade. He is not a mover or even a shaker, retired or otherwise. He is a Rattler, a creature much more primordial, and he stays put.

The Rattler also bites, once in a while. He is just about the only character in the book who does, though there is some fairly nasty potential in a man called Clarence Hasselbrook, a kind of 1990s style Inquisitor in a cheap suit. Hasselbrook infiltrates The Palms on behalf of a nationwide organization bent on banning the execution of Living Wills, and he quickly introduces his own brand of venom into this tale—a nice touch. Michener has always been a good storyteller, and the smaller stories in the book are told well. The novel itself, overall, would be better for a little less evenness and predictability, and perhaps a few more rattlesnakes, as well.

Hilma Wolitzer (review date 16 October 1994)

SOURCE: "Death Before Dying," in *The New York Times Book Review,* October 16, 1994, p. 20.

[In the following review, Wolitzer finds that Michener's melodramatic Recessional *pales in comparison to his poignant* The World Is My Home.]*

James A. Michener seems to heed the old dictum to "write about what you know," which in his case is hardly limiting. In more than 40 books, published over the past 47 years, he's covered such diverse topics as wartime in the South Pacific, Alaska's social development and the space program. These heavily researched, fact-filled works are enormously popular, especially with readers who prefer their history and geography in the guise of fiction.

Now, in *Recessional,* Mr. Michener, who was born in 1907, addresses the complex issues associated with aging in America. He has chosen to present what must be an intensely personal subject through the perspective of his novel's idealistic young hero, Dr. Andy Zorn. After enduring some nasty malpractice suits and a divorce in Chicago, the 35-year-old Zorn has abandoned his medical practice to become general manager of the Palms, a flagship facility in Tampa, Fl., for people too old and infirm to live independently.

At the Palms, terms like "nursing home," "hospital" and "hospice" are forbidden. Instead, residents are discreetly moved from the "Retirement Area" to "Assisted Living" to "Extended Care." Euphemisms and ironies abound. The book's epigraph explains that a recessional is "a hymn or other piece of music played at the end of a service while the congregation is filing out." And as Andy Zorn drives through Tampa, he notes a welcoming sign: "You are now entering God's Paradise. The O'Neill Crematorium. Complete Services $475."

Mr. Michener, whose own views (like Zorn's) on medical ethics appear to be liberal and humanistic, allows some of his characters to offer more conservative opinions. (Of the system of triage created by managed care, one man notes: "The budget, inescapable from the moment of birth till the instant of death, will have dictated the value decisions." Replying to the idea of a "therapeutic abortion" done, as a character explains, "to correct nature's accident," another responds that "God does not make mistakes.") In fact, *Recessional* provides a thoroughly informed overview of what happens to the elderly in this country (along with a survey of numerous other matters, from religion to politics), mostly through the impassioned discussions of a four-member *tertulia,* or informal debating society, that regularly convenes in the dining room at the Palms.

Unfortunately, the prose style and dialogue in this issue-driven novel are too often stilted and expository. Characters tend to speechify rather than speak, and even Andy Zorn's thoughts are rendered in unnaturally formal, coherent blocks of prose that halt and summarize the action. "Here I sit," he remarks early on, when informed of the Florida laws that regulate the Palms, "a certified doctor with these handsome facilities at hand, and I'm forbidden to use either my own skills or these wonderful lifesaving machines. I've thrown myself into a weird world."

The world of old age is indeed weird, and terrifying, as autonomy diminishes along with physical and mental well-being. Among the villains here (aside from nature) are greedy children, ambitious doctors and medical science itself, which manages to prolong life without sustaining its quality, "so the loved one who has died without dying lives on and on."

The best moments in the novel occur when the characters disclose what's in their hearts and minds with rueful, snappy humor. One Palms resident succinctly complains. "Television six hours a day, and the yogurt machine is never working." Another quips, "The two sorriest days in a man's life in this joint is when his wife dies and when he has to give up his driver's license. Not necessarily in that order." There are also some genuinely poignant passages. An articulate member of the *tertulia* finds himself mysteriously unable, one morning, to knot his own necktie. And an Alzheimer's patient who manages to elude her warders by wandering outdoors discovers "what she had sought from the moment she climbed out of bed, the freedom of the open air, escape from nurses and bells, the joy of striding along as the sun began to display its power in the east."

But the wordiness and melodramatic subplots of *Recessional*—including Andy Zorn's romance with a beautiful young double amputee, the comings and goings of a mysterious Kevorkian-like figure at an AIDS hospice and the infiltration of the Palms by a spy from a fanatical organization called Life is Sacred—eventually swamp the essential drama of old age and how we deal with it. James Michener's own remarkable career, as it is intriguingly revealed in his 1992 memoir, *The World Is My Home,* not to mention his continuing vigorous engagement with that infinite world, makes a much stronger argument against the isolation and disenfranchisement of the elderly.

FURTHER READING

Bibliography

Groseclose, Karen and David A. *James A. Michener, A Bibliography.* State House Press: Austin, 1996.
     Provides a detailed chronology of Michener's life and career.

Criticism

Baker, John. "A Novel Approach." *Chicago Tribune Book Review* (21 April 1991): 3, 5.

> Praises Michener's *The Novel* for its candid look at writing and the publishing industry, but gives mixed reviews of its artistry.

Galloway, Paul. "Author James A. Michener, 90, Dies After 50-Year Writing Saga." *Chicago Tribune* (17 October 1997): 3.

> Summarizes Michener's life and works, acclaiming him as a master storyteller.

Irving, Clifford. "The Long Love Affair of a Tough Old Bird." *New York Times Book Review* (20 December 1992): 8-9.

> Favorably reviews Michener's *Mexico,* an epic novel, and *My Lost Mexico,* which relates the former's "genesis, abandonment, and resurrection" thirty years later.

Review of *Miracle in Seville,* by James A. Michener. *Kirkus Reviews* (1 August 1995): 1051-52.

> Negative review of *Miracle in Seville,* a novella about a Spanish rancher of fighting bulls.

> **Additional coverage of Michener's life and career is contained in the following sources published by Gale:** *Authors in the News,* **Vol. 1;** *Bestsellers,* **1990: 1;** *Contemporary Authors,* **Vols. 5-8R;** *Contemporary Authors New Revision Series,* **Vols. 21 and 45;** *Dictionary of Literary Biography,* **Vol. 6;** *DISCovering Authors Modules: Novelists* **and** *Popular Fiction and Genre Authors;* **and** *Major Twentieth Century Writers.*

Mike Royko

1932-1997

American newspaper columnist and biographer.

INTRODUCTION

Royko was a widely-admired Chicago newspaper columnist whose work appeared in newspapers nationwide; several hundred of his columns were collected and published in book form. The winner of many journalism awards and the 1972 Pulitzer Prize for commentary, Royko's writings on politics, institutions, and everyday life were often biting, barbed, and full of humor. His biography *Boss: Richard J. Daley of Chicago* (1971) is regarded as a classic study of machine politics and political bosses. Royko often attributed his working-class voice and point of view to fictitious characters named Slats Grobnik (a perennial bar-stool occupant) and Dr. I. M. Kookie (who knew everything), but both simply reflected his own background. Royko's father was a Ukrainian immigrant who worked as a milkman before purchasing a saloon in a Polish neighborhood on Chicago's northwest side. As a teenager tending bar, Royko's responsibilities included Saturday-morning payments to the local police, whom he later wrote about as "The Burglars in Blue." He also learned about barroom brawls and toughness. After a brief attempt at college, Royko joined the Air Force and spent three years as a radioman, part of it in Korea. His writing career began in 1955 when he was transferred to the military base at Chicago's O'Hare Field. He claimed to have experience as a newswriter and was assigned to the base newspaper. After a two-year post-service stint with the Chicago News Bureau, Royko was hired as a reporter by the *Chicago Daily News.* His first weekly columns on county government impressed the editor, who gave him the freedom to write on any subject. He became a full-time columnist in 1964. For the next thirty-three years, for three successive Chicago newspapers, Royko wrote over 8,000 columns, generally at the rate of five per week. It has been said that Royko's columns boosted his paper's circulation by 100,000 copies. Royko was of the finger-in-the-eye school of columnizing. His sarcasm was an equal-opportunity spear; poking holes in people and institutions at will: the mayor, city aldermen, the police, the Chicago Cubs. He wrote on behalf of Bungalow Man, the disappearing working class with its "traditional values of work, family, and male supremacy." Royko once said, "like many Chicagoans, I grew up with a distrust of most things and creatures," but his persona was never in doubt: "As for myself, I haven't had an identity crisis. I have always known who I am, which, while deeply depressing, saved me a lot of running around looking for me." He wrote about such diverse topics as dieting,

driving, digital watches, draft evasion, dogs, sexual promiscuity, gun control, xenophobia, sticky ice cube trays, bureaucratic pettiness, and yuppies, but, as a *Washington Post* writer stated, "the persona looms larger than the writing." At various times he pretended to be a police officer, a social worker, a teacher, or a deputy coroner in efforts to gain material for his columns. He staged events to mock people and practices—a children's dog show for mutts, the winner being the entrant whose dog most resembled Royko's publisher; a penny-pitching contest, after Chicago police had charged penny-pitching elementary school children with gambling. When Tampa, Florida, tried to acquire the Chicago White Sox, he urged readers to send their dirty socks to Tampa officials. Royko showed a serious side in his writing as well: when he wrote about a Vietnam veteran whose face was so shattered he could only take nourishment with a syringe, President Nixon ordered slow-moving bureaucrats to hospitalize the man for treatment. Royko moved readers to anger—one wrote, "You should be arrested for defacing a public newspaper"—and he could move them to tears, as he did with his 1979 column about his first wife, Carol's death, at age 44. "We met when she was 6 and I was 9. Same neighborhood street. Same grammar school. So if you ever have a 9-year-old son who says he is in love, don't laugh at him. It can happen. . . . If there's someone you love but haven't said so in a while, say it now. Always, always, say it now." In addition to the Pulitzer Prize, Royko received the Ernie Pyle Memorial Award, the Heywood Broun Award of the American Newspaper Guild, and the first H. L. Mencken Award ever presented by the *Baltimore Sun.* Studs Terkel asserted that Royko was "an investigative reporter of the highest rank"; Jimmy Breslin called him "the best journalist of his time"; and *Esquire* magazine labeled him as "The Man Who Owns Chicago." His biting sarcasm and blunt opinions caused many readers to dislike him. Near the end of his career, several of Royko's targets criticized him for statements made in his columns—blacks, Latinos, feminists, homosexuals, and other groups often found his views racist and offensive. However, millions of readers felt that his voice effectively represented the urban Everyman, and he has been compared to humorists such as James Thurber and Robert Benchley. After Royko's death, his *Chicago Tribune* editor said, "He was the best journalist, period. There probably will never be another one like him."

PRINCIPAL WORKS

Up Against It (journalism) 1967
I May Be Wrong, but I Doubt It (journalism) 1968
Boss: Richard J. Daley of Chicago (unauthorized biography) 1971
Slats Grobnik and Some Other Friends (journalism) 1973
Sez Who? Sez Me (journalism) 1982
Like I Was Sayin' . . . (journalism) 1984
Dr. Kookie, You're Right (journalism) 1989

OBITUARIES

Jerry Crimmins and Rick Kogan (obituary date 29 April 1997)

SOURCE: "'Quite Simply the Best', Legendary Columnist, the Voice of Chicago for Decades, Dies," *The Chicago Tribune,* April 30, 1997, p. 1.

[*In the following obituary, Crimmins and Kogan offer a full appreciation of Royko's life and career.*]

Mike Royko, a self-described "flat-above-a-tavern youth" who became one of the best-known names in American journalism, wrote with a piercing wit and rugged honesty that reflected Chicago in all its two-fisted charm.

His daily column was a fixture in the city's storied journalistic history, and his blunt observations about crooked politicians, mobsters, exasperating bureaucracy and the odd twists of contemporary life reverberated across the nation.

It was Royko's inimitable combination of street-smart reporting, punchy phrasing and audacious humor that set his column apart, along with his remarkable durability in facing daily deadlines for more than three decades.

Royko, who was 64, died at 3:30 p.m. Tuesday of heart failure in Northwestern Memorial Hospital. A statement issued by the hospital read in part: "The family has asked us to express their deep gratitude for the outpouring of affection and concern during this period."

Royko was admitted to Evanston Hospital on April 22 after experiencing chest pains at his Winnetka home and later underwent surgery at Northwestern Memorial for an aneurysm. He had become ill in March while vacationing with his family in Florida.

"Mike was Chicago," said his longtime friend, author Studs Terkel. "He did it all and who was ever better about writing about the real Chicago, the Chicago of two-flats and the working man? He was an investigative reporter of the highest rank but also wrote with great humor. Some day in the future, when people are trying to understand the city and the meaning of political power, they will have to turn to Mike. He knew the turf better than anybody."

Royko, whose column appeared on Page 3 of the *Chicago Tribune* and was syndicated to more than 600 newspapers nationwide, had won nearly every journalistic prize available, including the 1972 Pulitzer Prize for commentary; the Ernie Pyle Memorial Award, named for the famed World War II war correspondent; the National Headliner Award; the Heywood Broun Award of the American Newspaper Guild; and the first H. L. Mencken Award presented by the *Baltimore Sun* in the name of its legendary columnist.

"From the time I first met him at the *Chicago Daily News,* I knew he was quite simply the best," said Jack Fuller, executive vice president of Tribune Publishing Co.

"Mike was more than the best columnist of his time," said *Tribune* Editor Howard Tyner. "He was the best journalist, period. There probably will never be another one like him."

Royko was indeed an original, a writer with a poet's sensibilities and a working-man's plain language. For more than 30 years, his column gave voice to the disenfranchised and offered a platform for skewering hypocrisy and pretension and for examining contemporary fads and foibles. The column could be sarcastic, funny and nostalgic, funny and cynical, funny and informative, occasionally very serious, and sometimes heart-rending.

Esquire magazine once called Royko "The Man Who Owns Chicago," but he was never one to act the big shot, though to some it seemed that way. His gruff exterior hid a soft soul. He most enjoyed listening to Beethoven, Brahms and Mozart, the blues and jazz, and was something of a self-proclaimed "fine cook." He could often be found, in his younger years, rubbing elbows at Billy Goat Tavern, pitching on one of the city's softball diamonds or ambling across a golf course. He was a lifelong Cubs fan who disdained those who said they wished both Chicago baseball teams would do well.

Though Royko didn't invent the word "clout," he defined its special backroom nature in Chicago like no other. And, in a way, he had it himself. More than a few politicians and judges found their fortunes influenced by Royko's opinions—and, if they were particularly unlucky, in more than one column.

A demon in print, he could appear to be a grizzly bear in public (or in the office), seemingly remote when meeting strangers. Those who knew him well, however, saw this sometimes gruff exterior as a necessary shield for a shy and sensitive man in a very sensitive and public position.

"I am the victim of the Frank Sinatra syndrome," he once told a reporter. "Whenever Frank Sinatra goes somewhere, somebody tries to pick a fight. It's the same with me, only the reasons are different. People want to hit Sinatra to get their names in the papers. People want to slug me because I make them angry."

He made plenty of readers angry. His column, forthright and with an uncanny instinct for the unpopular position, courted controversy and ire. In recent years, he ruffled a lot of feathers and riled some African-Americans and members of the gay community who took exception to some of his views. In March 1996, some 1,000 protesters gathered outside Tribune Tower demanding that Royko be fired for what they said were insulting portrayals of Mexicans in his column.

One of his principal critics was the writer and Catholic priest Rev. Andrew Greeley, who once described the content of Royko's columns as "crudity mixed with resentment." A dissatisfied reader, one of many whose letters Royko almost gleefully printed in his column, wrote, "You should be arrested for defacing a public newspaper. Your column is like an ugly time warp."

The man who was called by New York columnist Jimmy Breslin "the best journalist of his time," and whom Terkel called, "pound for pound . . . the best journalist in America," was born Sept. 19, 1932, in St. Mary of Nazareth Hospital at Division and Leavitt Streets on the Near Northwest Side, the third of four children and the first boy.

His father, also Michael, had immigrated to the United States at age 9 from the town of Dolina in Ukraine. His mother, Helen, whose maiden name was Zak, was born in America, the child of Polish immigrants from Warsaw.

At the time of Royko's birth, his father was a foreman and milkman for the Pure Farm Dairy and, for a time, the family lived in a basement apartment behind a store where his mother operated a cleaning and tailoring business.

In 1938, his parents bought a tavern at 2122 N. Milwaukee Ave., setting the stage for the young Royko's early immersion into the social, political and cultural life of middle-and working-class Chicago. This immersion formed the foundation of his writing and reporting. The Royko family moved into the flat above the tavern, and he became, in his description, "a flat-above-a-tavern youth."

Royko said his mother had about two years of high school, but was well read. His father "never had one day of school" but taught himself to read and write and do his own accounting.

His father also "read all the newspapers," Royko said. "Tavern keepers have a lot of down time to sit around and read." The father often sent the son down to the newsstand to pick up the papers when they came out, including the Polish language *Daily Zgoda.*

(Royko's sister Eleanor Cronin contended their father for the most part could not read and would ask his children to read to him, saying he had forgotten his glasses.)

After a checkered academic career—he spent much of his homework time tending bar in his dad's tavern—Royko abandoned college and joined the Air Force, where he was trained as a radio operator. First stationed in Washington state—where some bumpy plane rides gave him a lifelong aversion to flying—he later served for a time near Seoul during the Korean War. He returned to the U.S. and was stationed at O'Hare Field, then a military base. In 1955, to avoid becoming a military policeman, he applied for a job on the base newspaper.

"It struck me that any goof could write a newspaper story," he recalled years later.

Royko told the base public information officer that he had been a cub reporter for the *Chicago Daily News* before his enlistment, which was a lie, and flimflammed his way into running the base paper. After two weeks, he was joined by another young Air Force man who had been a reporter for United Press International.

Royko recalled that one morning the man said, "Don't con me. You never worked for a newspaper, did you?"

Whereupon Royko confessed and promptly assigned himself a column called, **"Mike's View."** His first in the paper made fun of the American Legion for supporting the Communist-hunting U.S. Sen. Joseph McCarthy.

"The next column was one I took great pride in," he recalled.

In it Royko rebuked the officers' wives for coming onto the base with their hair in curlers and wearing sloppy clothes, while their husbands had to go around starched and neat. The women's appearance, the column said, was bad for morale.

The reaction was swift. Three wives burst into the public information office demanding to see Royko. In an era before name tags, Sgt. Royko told the wives, "He just left on a 30-day leave."

He was at the time married to his childhood sweetheart, Carol Duckman, who had become his wife in 1954 and with whom he would have two sons, David and Robert.

After his discharge from the Air Force, Royko worked briefly as a reporter with the Lincoln-Belmont Booster, a twice-a-week paper belonging to the Lerner chain.

After six months, he joined the City News Bureau, a legendary training ground for journalists. He recalled that he made his first mark reporting on the police investigation into the death of the Grimes sisters, Patricia, 15, and Barbara, 14, who were found frozen and naked in a ditch near suburban Willow Springs on Jan. 22, 1957.

The case, which has never been solved, was front-page news for a month, and Royko said he got many scoops through doggedness and through such techniques as eavesdropping on the police from an adjacent office and interviewing people while pretending to be an undersheriff.

In February 1957, Royko interviewed at the *Daily News* but felt "overwhelmed . . . looking around this room at all these great reporters." He surprised acting city editor Maurice "Ritz" Fischer, by refusing a job offer.

"Mr. Fischer, I don't think there's any point in continuing this interview," Royko recalled saying. "I don't think I can do it. I just don't have enough experience. I'm going to fall on my face."

A year and a half later, when Royko finally thought he was

ready, he said the *Daily News* city editor was no longer interested in him; the *Tribune,* the *Sun-Times* and the *Chicago American* turned Royko down for lack of a college degree.

Casting about, Royko auditioned for a job as a combination news director, reporter, writer and anchorman for a television station in Ft. Wayne, Ind., but flunked the TV version of the screen test for "failure to project."

In 1959, he was hired as a reporter at the *Daily News,* starting with "lightweight stuff" on the day shift before moving to nights. During the day, he sold tombstones over the phone and through home visits to supplement his income.

Back on the day shift, Royko got his first very modest chance at column writing when he was asked to write a once-a-week County Building column.

Royko decided to make his column "a little different," he said. The first one was about "how much it costs the taxpayers to have an unofficial holiday on St. Patrick's Day" for local government workers.

It caught the attention of the paper's new editor, Larry Fanning, who asked Royko, "What would you like to do? Where would you like to go in this business?"

Royko recalled: "When he asked me that question, it just sort of clicked together. I said I'd like to be a local columnist."

Royko said he had in mind a column with "a strong Chicago flavor. I said I'd use satire. There's a lot of things people have never been told. Straight reporting doesn't tell it. I felt nobody had ever really described what a City Council meeting was like, what aldermen were like, what a County Board meeting was like."

He started as a full-time columnist in January 1964. He was an early champion for civil rights and consistently went after bigots, fat cats, politicians and greedy corporate officials.

"Royko has always been an angry man," syndicated columnist Art Buchwald once commented. "But he's so funny that his anger isn't obnoxious."

One of the most effective tools for that humor was the character Slats Grobnik, a tough neighborhood guy who many took to be Royko's alter ego and who the columnist employed, much like the Mr. Dooley character created by the great turn-of-the-century columnist Finley Peter Dunne, to provide commentary on life. In later years, as contemporary life became wackier, Royko created Dr. I. M. Kookie, an expert in almost everything, for the same purpose.

With a prodigious output—five columns a week for most of

his career—Royko made it look easy. But on the rare occasions when he would talk about how he did it, he said, "Blood drips out of my fingers every time."

In the late '60s, he acquired his first "legman," a reporter who worked exclusively for him. At the end, there had been 16 of them.

At a party at his house to celebrate the publication of one of his books, Royko ordered leatherbound copies for each of the "legs" embossed with their names on the cover. The book had been dedicated to them.

In every book, Royko had written, "You were the best. Don't tell the others."

When the circumstances warranted, Royko's pen could be deadly serious. In 1968, he won the Broun Award for his coverage of the Democratic Convention in Chicago that year and the police attacks on demonstrators and the media.

His principal nemesis during this time was the city's mayor, Richard J. Daley.

"It was inevitable," the columnist said. "If you were a mountain climber, you'd go climb Mt. Everest if you could. It was not just Daley, but the machine. It was a natural."

In 1971, Royko delivered a devastating blow in the form of the non-fiction book *Boss,* an incisive look at machine politics as practiced by Daley.

It was a best-selling sensation and received glowing reviews. However, the *Tribune* panned the book for treating Daley as a "two-dimensional villain."

"What Daley did that was good, I credited him for," Royko said years later. "He was a great public works guy, a family man. He had the old-fashioned virtues. He harnessed the machine for some good things."

The one subject on which Royko relentlessly hammered Daley in the book was his treatment of blacks.

Fifteen years after the book was published, after three other mayors had been in office, Royko was asked if his views on the late Mayor Daley had changed any.

"I might have been a little more understanding of him," Royko said.

"I wouldn't have been any more approving of him. Maybe he didn't have as many choices as I thought he did. . . . Maybe he didn't have the capacity to understand race problems and what could be done. Maybe what I was asking of

Daley was like asking somebody who's never done calculus to do calculus."

One of Daley's sons, Mayor Richard M. Daley, said of Royko: "The heart and soul of the community showed in the way he wrote. He had a style of writing—his wit and the ways in which he looked at an issue.

"He had a better understanding than most people ever realized. I think he broke barriers between a lot of people."

In 1972, Royko was awarded the Pulitzer Prize for his newspaper column (judges described him as "having a flair of an old-time Chicago newspaperman in the Ben Hecht tradition"), and the next year, he flirted with the idea of moving himself and his column to Washington, D.C.

"I was offered jobs by the *Washington Post* and the *Washington Star,*" and some negotiations took place. "(But) my wife didn't want to go to Washington. My kids didn't want to go to Washington. I didn't want to sell my house. . . .

"I said, 'Wait a minute. Do I need the *Washington Post* to give me an identity?'

"I said, 'Let's forget the whole thing.'"

Royko laughed recalling this episode. "All I got was a big ego job," he said.

Often badgered by publishers to write more books, Royko was content to periodically issue a collection of his columns or graciously contribute introductions to books by colleagues and friends. Ever turning down speeches or public appearances—and the larger fees that went along with them—he did dabble in television, often showing up to provide expertise during local stations' election coverage and, in 1981, hosting an hourlong interview show set in a saloon and called *Royko on Tap.*

He was comfortable in barrooms, whether the Billy Goat or the more rarefied Acorn on Oak, where he would sit deep into the mornings listening to his favorite piano player, Buddy Charles. His nocturnal habits added colorful splashes to his reputation. But there were darker sides too: Once he was locked up after a saloon scuffle and in 1994 was arrested and charged with driving under the influence.

This is how he addressed his reputation for a reporter: "You show me a man who can go to work every day, turn out five columns a week of consistently good quality, raise a family and still be a legendary drinker and I'll show you a bionic lush."

When the *Daily News* ceased operation in 1978, Royko and

his column moved to the surviving Field paper, the *Sun-Times;* but some of the fire was gone. "I work for the *Sun-Times,*" he said, at the time, "and I have no role in the paper other than my column. . . . It's more of a job to me now than it used to be."

His depression was intensified the following year with the death of his wife, Carol. She suffered a cerebral hemorrhage at age 44, and Royko went into a personal tailspin, which he characterized later as "a period of disintegration."

He stopped writing his column for several weeks with the exception of one brief column published on Oct. 5, 1979, more than two weeks after his wife's death: "We met when she was 6 and I was 9. Same neighborhood street. Same grammar school. So if you ever have a 9-year-old son who says he is in love, don't laugh at him. It can happen."

The column, which readers have always remembered, ended, "If there's someone you love but haven't said so in a while, say it now. Always, always, say it now."

He joined the *Tribune* in 1984, after resigning from the *Sun-Times* when it was sold by Field Enterprises to a conglomerate headed by Australian media baron Rupert Murdoch, who Royko derisively referred to in print and public as "The Alien." He added: "From what I've seen of Murdoch's papers in this country no self-respecting fish would want to be wrapped in them."

"Mike was not only the best reporter I've ever known but the best writer on any American newspaper," said Lois Wille, a close friend and a colleague at the *Daily News, Sun-Times* and *Tribune.*

In 1986, Royko married Judy Arndt, who had worked as the head of the *Sun-Times'* public service office and as a tennis instructor. He sometimes referred to her playfully in his columns as "the blonde." They lived for a time on the Northwest Side and later in the DePaul area before moving to the North Shore. They had recently purchased a condominium in Florida, in anticipation of vacations filled with golf (he held a solid 10 handicap, with ambitions to become a 7) and fishing (he claimed to be a "better fisherman than a writer").

Over the last few years, he spent less and less time in his office at the paper, doing much of his writing at home in a room filled with computers, books and oddly mismatched furniture.

That room is in a lovely house made of wood, with a wide and rolling back yard where Royko would play with his young children, 9-year-old Sam and 4-year-old Kate. That was one of the reasons he didn't come downtown that much anymore: the kids. And in the afternoons, he would trudge

upstairs to his office, a twinkle in his mind, and do what he has done more than 8,000 times before: write his column.

"It never occurred to me to do anything else," he said.

Howard Kurtz (obituary date 29 April 1997)

SOURCE: "Mike Royko: Columnist, Curmudgeon, Character," *Washington Post,* April 29, 1997, pp. C1, C4.

[*In the following obituary, Kurtz observes that while times changed, Royko remained the same—except for his house in the suburbs and country club membership.*]

He was cantankerous, soft-hearted, infuriating, earthy, bull-headed, funny. He was loved. He was hated. He was read.

Mike Royko, who died Tuesday at 64, was more than a Chicago legend, more than a throwback to the days when columnists smoked, drank, hired legmen and chased dames. He was a writer who made people mad, a rarity in today's buttoned-down, ironically detached, cappuccino-sipping journalistic culture.

For me, the shock a couple of years ago was visiting Royko in his airy third-floor study, not on the gritty Windy City streets where he made his name but in the leafy suburb of Winnetka. There were backporch swings and deer playing on an endless lawn that overlooked a ravine. He belonged to a country club, fer cryin' out loud.

Was this the same Royko, the shot-and-a-beer guy who hung out at Billy Goat's Tavern? The alter ego of his fictional everyman Slats Grobnik? Or was he just playing the character he had once been? A few hours of salty conversation made clear he was still mad at the world, even if time had transformed him into the sort of wealthy suburbanite he had once scorned.

Royko wore his success like an ill-fitting windbreaker, and his last years were rough. There were a couple of drunken-driving run-ins with police. He had been writing a column since 1963, and he was clearly tired of it. He said he kept going to support his two small children with his second wife, Judy (his first wife died years ago). But if Royko had a "symbiotic relationship" with Chicago, as his friend Studs Terkel put it, he increasingly seemed a man out of his time.

The persona looms larger than the writing in the haze of history, but the writing could sparkle. We know this not just from the honors, such as the Pulitzer Prize he won in 1972, but from the detractors, all the people and groups he kept ticking off. Royko was the one who stamped Jerry Brown with the moniker "Governor Moonbeam," who dissed Indianapolis as "the dullest large city in the United States." As for feminists, well, he wondered whether his fellow men would prefer "dropping a 40-foot putt, landing a 6-pound bass, bowling a 230 game, seeing the Sox or Cubs win a pennant or seeing your wife waddle across the room in a negligee. . . . Nobody ever asks us about our needs, our frustrations, our longings and yearnings. It's always, 'Madam, do you have your quota of orgasms?'"

During my visit, the gravel-voiced Royko showed me the former home of the Blue Sky Lounge, run by his father, a Ukrainian immigrant. The family lived over the tavern, and Royko, who tended bar, learned early how to pay off the cops to overlook infractions. He joined the Air Force at 19, served in Korea and later became a night police reporter for the *Chicago Daily News.*

Royko routinely did things that would be journalistic felonies today, carrying a counterfeit badge and impersonating cops, teachers and social workers. He exposed miscreants and bribe-takers and became the chief nemesis of Mayor Richard Daley. (Years later, ironically, he became pals with the younger Richard Daley, the current hizzoner.)

Once, in response to a critical letter, he wrote: "Basically, I have contempt for people like you. You live in a wealthy, pampered, trouble-free suburb in Glenco. I live in a corrupt, troubled city like Chicago. . . . What in the [expletive] do you worry about? Your crabgrass? Getting invited to a neighbor's brunch? . . . Shove your 15 cents in your ear."

Royko moved to the *Sun-Times* after the *Daily News* folded. When Rupert Murdoch bought the paper, Royko announced that "no self-respecting fish" would be wrapped in it and signed with the *Chicago Tribune.* He turned down job offers from Ben Bradlee at *The Washington Post,* fearing he would become one of those stuffed-shirt pundits who talks about the deficit. He was what he had always been, a Chicago scribe who settled scores with his typewriter.

Critics, rarely speaking for attribution, described him as a tyrant, an unpleasant bully. He remained a forbidding figure for many of his younger *Tribune* colleagues, sticking to his remote office, the only one where smoking was allowed.

The last time I talked to Royko was last year, when he had landed in some hot water. He returned the call even though he knew he would be hammered. He had written a diatribe about a woman named Maurica Taylor whose name landed her in a bureaucratic mixup. "Some black names defy explanation," Royko fumed, openly pining for the likes of Jane, Mary, Dorothy and Helen.

Royko-haters went wild. Blacks called him a racist. And,

under pressure from *Tribune* management, Royko publicly apologized. But he told me he had mixed feelings. "What's off-limits because of my race?" he asked. Some loyal readers, he admitted, were "disappointed that I apologized."

Mike Royko, saying he was sorry? What about his reputation for cursing out critics? "That reputation has been diminished somewhat this week," he told me wistfully.

His larger reputation will live as long as journalists value the old finger-in-the-eye school of columnizing. No graduate school can teach what Royko did; he amplified the workingman's grievances because he was one of them. But he learned in his final years that making fun of blacks, gays, feminists and vegetarians had become dangerous sport in a culture that barely resembled the tobacco-stained city rooms of yore.

Steve Marshall (obituary date 30 April 1997)

SOURCE: "Chicago Columnist Mike Royko Dies at 64," *USA Today,* April 30, 1997, p. 3A.

[*In the following brief obituary, Marshall looks at recollections of Royko by some of his early associates.*]

Mike Royko, who skewered everyone from mayors to yuppies in his gritty newspaper columns, died Tuesday in Chicago, the city many say he helped rule with his commentary.

Royko, 64, a Pulitzer-winning Chicago columnist syndicated in more than 600 newspapers, died at a hospital where he had undergone surgery last week for a weakened blood vessel in the brain.

"Through the years my family filed many of his columns, some critical and some supportive, but whether you agreed with him or not, you had to respect his honesty and his love for the city," said Mayor Richard M. Daley, whose late father, Mayor Richard J. Daley, had long tangled with Royko.

The elder Daley ruled Chicago from 1955 until his death in 1976.

Royko never hesitated to take on those outside of the Windy City's boundaries, either. Frank Sinatra, so infuriated over a Royko jab, once referred to him as "Jerk" at a Chicago benefit concert.

"When he wrote, nobody could touch that guy and I think he wrote for all of us," said Jon Hah, a columnist at the *Seattle Post-Intelligence,* who worked with Royko at *The Chi-*

cago *Daily News,* an afternoon daily home to literary great until its demise in 1978.

A frequent Royko companion in print was his fictional buddy, Slats Grobnik. "He wrote for the Slats in all of us," Hahn says.

Royko joined *The Daily News* in 1959 as a reporter and won the Pulitzer for commentary in 1972. He moved to the *Chicago Sun-Times* in 1978, then jumped to the rival *Chicago Tribune* in 1984, citing Rupert Murdoch's acquisition of the *Sun-Times.*

Royko's books included the 1971 best-seller **Boss: Richard J. Daley of Chicago.** It was so critical of the late mayor that Daley's enraged wife, Eleanor, launched a campaign to keep it off supermarket shelves.

The gravel-voiced, curmudgeonly columnist never strayed far from the city of his birth, though he had offers from *The Washington Post* after *The Daily News* folded.

Born in Chicago on Sept. 19, 1932, his childhood was anything but idyllic. "I grew up in taverns," he said. "I was a bartender at 12 or 13 . . . I had one foot in reform school."

He tried military school, but "was a rebel at that point and never fit in," says *Post-Intelligencer* writer Art Gorlick, who knew him at that academy.

After serving four years in the military, three of them in Korea, Royko became a reporter for a chain of Chicago neighborhood weekly newspapers, then moved on to the City News Bureau, a local Chicago wire service from which Royko later hired his "legmen," positions guaranteed to lead to promotions.

Author and radio commentator Studs Terkel, a Royko friend for 35 years, said Royko "covered the city like no one ever covered a city. He celebrated the uncelebrated."

Royko is survived by his wife, Judy, a 9-year-old son, Sam, and 4-year-old daughter, Kate, as well as two sons from his first marriage, David and Robert, and four grandchildren. His first wife, childhood sweetheart Carol Duckman, died in 1979.

Judy Pasternak (obituary date 30 April 1997)

SOURCE: "Mike Royko: Chicago Newspaper Columnist," *Los Angeles Times,* April 30, 1997, p. A18.

[*In the following obituary, Pasternak focuses on Royko's orneriness and some of the backlash it brought him.*]

Mike Royko, the ornery chronicler of an often ornery town, died Tuesday at Northwestern Memorial Hospital of complications following a brain aneurysm. He was 64.

Royko had suffered a stroke in early April and last week underwent surgery for the aneurysm, a rupture or weakening of a blood vessel.

In nearly 34 years as a columnist at one or another of Chicago's daily newspapers, Royko represented in print the views of the lunch-bucket white ethnic, long after he'd moved his own family to the wealthy northern suburb of Winnetka. He managed to continue offending powerful politicians, police, feminists, gays, blacks, Latinos and a certain veteran local television anchor, to list just a few.

In the process, he won the 1972 Pulitzer Prize for commentary and national acclaim for **Boss,** his biography of Chicago Mayor Richard J. Daley, who had refined machine politics to an art. Despite Royko's Chicago identity, his column was nationally syndicated, running in about 500 papers.

The words Royko wrote about Daley the day after the pugnacious mayor died in 1976 could have applied just as well to himself: "He wasn't graceful, suave, witty or smooth. But, then, this is not Paris or San Francisco. He was raucous, sentimental, hot-tempered, practical, simple, devious. . . . This is, after all, Chicago."

Daley, of course, had regarded Royko as a nemesis. The columnist regularly lampooned the mayor at a time when the rest of the press was considerably more respectful. Once, Royko recalled, the mayor shook his hand by rote in a receiving line, then realized whose hand he was gripping and let go hastily like he'd been holding "a snake."

But the columnist was merely following a long Chicago tradition of journalistic like-it-or-not bluntness, from Finley Peter Dunne's column about the opinionated bartender, Mr. Dooley, to Nelson Algren's love/hate letter to his town, a book called *City on the Make.*

Like them, Royko wrote words refracted through the lens of the guy just a bar stool away. Sometimes he gave the guy a name, Slats Grobnik. Sometimes he played off an equally fictional psychiatrist, Dr. I. M. Kookie. Most often, though, he dispensed with the alter egos and simply presented himself.

He certainly had solid urban blue-collar credentials, having grown up the son of a Ukrainian immigrant who ran the Blue Sky Lounge on Chicago's west side. The family lived upstairs. As a teenager, Royko's chores included tending bar and paying off the police sergeant every Saturday morning.

He joined the Air Force at 19, serving as a radio operator. When he was transferred to Chicago's O'Hare Field, there were no openings for radio men. He wanted to escape being assigned to MP or KP duty, so he talked his way into editing the base newspaper.

After the military, he worked for a group of neighborhood newspapers in Chicago and then for City News Bureau, a local wire service.

In 1959, he joined the *Chicago Daily News* as a police reporter, entering a world that hadn't changed much since Ben Hecht's *The Front Page*. Royko has admitted in interviews that he joined his freewheeling colleagues in gaining information by pretense.

"I posed as a deputy coroner," he told the *Washington Post.* "I once posed as a female high school principal, in a falsetto voice over the phone."

In 1962, he began a weekly government column called "County Beat." In 1963, the *Daily News* gave him regular space for his own thoughts on whatever subject he chose.

In 1978, the paper folded.

Royko didn't have to move far for his next job, at the tabloid *Sun-Times* in the same building. But in 1984, when Rupert Murdoch bought the *Sun-Times,* he proclaimed that "no self-respecting fish" would be wrapped in something published by the new owner. He landed at the *Chicago Tribune.*

By this time, he was a Chicago institution, having both called the Boss a racist and been called one by the city's first black mayor, Harold Washington.

The columnist also would spin sob stories about underdogs in trouble. But mostly he wrote tough, and acted tough too.

Royko threw fists in a bar brawl or two. He smoked, and snarled at colleagues. He was convicted twice of drunken driving—most recently in 1995, when his guilty plea brought a fine of $1,600, two years' probation and 80 hours of community service.

Royko drew plenty of blood. Last year alone, he set off uproars in the black and Latino communities here.

He wrote about a woman named Maurica Taylor who was falsely accused of being a father negligent in child support payments; the true suspect was named Maurice Taylor. The column started out sympathetic to the woman, but then Royko announced, "I put the blame on Ms. Taylor's mother. She is the one who decided to name her child Maurica. Some black names defy explanation."

He went on to muse that "a personnel officer at a corporation might be inclined—all things being equal—to lean toward hiring an accountant named Arthur Smith rather than one named Wanakumba Smith. It just looks neater on a business card."

He wrote a rare apology for that one.

Later in the year, he decided to explain to readers that "there is no reason for Mexico to be in such a mess except that it is run by Mexicans." He issued a challenge: "Just name one thing that Mexico has done this century that has been of any genuine use to the rest of this planet. Besides giving us tequila."

Mexican Americans called for a boycott of the *Tribune* and its Spanish-language *Exito,* a free weekly. More than 1,000 protesters rallied at the Tribune Tower.

The speakers gave as good as they'd gotten. "We are protesting against this little man who is nothing more than a drunk and a degenerate," said the leader of a Mexican students' group.

The *Tribune* defended its columnist, releasing a statement that read in part: "It was well within the confines of irony. Anyone who has read Royko over the past 30 years knows that he is not reluctant to speak sharply and sarcastically."

Royko is survived by his wife, Judy, three sons, a daughter and four grandchildren. His first wife, Carol Duckman, died in 1979.

Richard Pearson (obituary date 30 April 1997)

SOURCE: "Famed Chicago Columnist Mike Royko Dies at Age 64," *Washington Post,* April 30, 1997, p. B9.

[*In the following obituary excerpt, Pearson recounts some of the "events" Royko staged as part of his career-long campaign to deflate Chicago institutions and practices.*]

Mike Royko, 64, the *Chicago Tribune's* classically caustic, cantankerous columnist who spent 30 years lampooning the words and actions of the Windy City's high and mighty while serving as champion of such underdogs as the "common man" and the Chicago Cubs baseball team, died April 29 at a hospital in Evanston, Illinois.

He had a stroke while vacationing in early April in Florida and had undergone surgery for a brain aneurysm last week.

Mr. Royko, a lifelong Chicagoland resident, became something of a city monument, the king of newspaper columnists in a city where the craft has long been appreciated. He eventually wrote for three of the four major Chicago daily newspapers of his day, often making headlines when he switched papers.

His column was syndicated in more than 200 papers across the country. He was awarded the 1972 Pulitzer Prize for commentary and the 1995 Damon Runyon Award, and he was the author of the 1971 bestseller **Boss: Richard J. Daley of Chicago,** a biography of the legendary mayor.

Mr. Royko's influence was greatest in his home city. It had been estimated that his column, which appeared on Page 3 of every paper he wrote for, was worth 100,000 copies of circulation.

He was known for the enemies he made. Those included mob thugs, Daley, a legendary Chicago fire commissioner, fellow reporters, his readers, and his own editors and corporate bosses at all three papers.

At his first paper, the *Chicago Daily News,* he started a "mongrel dog show" in the early 1970s. The paper's publisher and the publisher's wife were "society" leaders who loved to see their pictures in their paper and had a yearly social triumph as sponsors of an exclusive Chicago dog show.

Mr. Royko announced that he was hosting a Chicago dog show that would be open only to children and their mutts. He promised Chicago's gigantic Soldier Field (home of the Chicago Bears) as the site. When the publisher balked at the rent, the columnist threatened to quit. The show was held.

Chicago aldermen were judges—they had agreed to be frisked to demonstrate that they had not been bribed—and the grand prize went to the dog that most resembled Mr. Royko's publisher. Mug shots of the two ran side by side in the extensive coverage the *Daily News* gave the event.

Other "happenings" included his 1968 column endorsing candidates for political office who somehow were the opposite of candidates endorsed by his paper on its editorial page.

He also hired one of the city's leading criminal lawyers to defend several elementary school children who had been arrested by suburban police for "penny pitching," a Chicago sport, and charged with gambling. Mr. Royko celebrated their mass acquittal by hosting a penny-pitching tournament in his paper's parking lot.

After the invasion of Afghanistan, he wrote memorable columns pondering the question of whether the United States should go to war with the Soviets if they occupied, say, Indiana. Upon reflection, Mr. Royko—who was not popular in the Hoosier state—decided that the United States should not fight.

Mr. Royko grew up above the Armitage Avenue tavern that his father, a Ukrainian immigrant, owned. the future columnist tended bar as a teenager. He once told a *Washington Post* reporter just how things worked in Chicago"

"You gave the police sergeant money every Saturday morning. If there were any fights, they'd respond quickly. You were making book, you were taking bets on horses, and they would ignore that. The sergeant would come around and I'd give him the envelope."

That may have led to his longtime campaign to change Chicago's motto from "Urbs in Horto" (a City in a Garden) to "Ubi Est Mea" (Where's Mine?).

Mr. Royko attended college only in the loosest sense, and he found his profession while serving in the Air Force in Korea. He ran the base newspaper, finding that enlisted men can ask more pointed questions as a "reporter" than in normal guise.

After the service, he worked for the Chicago City News Bureau, something of a news cooperative for the dailies that is largely staffed by beginning reporters. In 1959, he joined the *Daily News* as a police reporter. He began his column in 1963. When the *Daily News* folded in 1978, he moved to its sister publication, the *Sun-Times.* In 1984, he jumped from that paper to the rival morning paper, the *Chicago Tribune,* a publication he had always reviled in print.

Rupert Murdoch had bought the *Sun-Times,* and Mr. Royko announced to the world that "no self-respecting fish" would want to be wrapped in a Murdoch paper and that he was quitting.

Outside Chicago, he probably will be best remembered for his biography of Daley, the story of a quintessential figure who served as mayor from 1955 until his death in 1976. The media, aside from Mr. Royko, were well-nigh worshipful toward hizzoner. When the biography came out, Daley's wife persuaded one of the city's leading book chains not to carry the book. The book also was unavailable at Chicago's O'Hare International Airport—where even bookstores listen to the city government.

In recent years, Mr. Royko had lost his old machine targets, whom he had attacked as racist, lazy and more than a little crooked. He had become something of a target himself, coming under attack at different times by blacks, Latinos, women, gay men and lesbians, and even fellow journalists.

His image was also shaken by his convictions for driving under the influence of alcohol and perhaps most shaken by the fact that the chain-smoking, beer-drinking man of the people, creator of the legendary news source Slats Grobnik, drove a Lincoln Continental.

MSNBC News Services (obituary date 30 April 1997)

SOURCE: "Columnist Mike Royko Dies at Age 64," *MSNBC New Services,* April 30, 1997.

[*In the following excerpt, the author discusses Royko's death and relates some of the columnist's famous quotations.*]

Many of America's newspapers have lost one of their most popular voices.

Mike Royko, the Pulitzer Prize-winning newspaper columnist whose biting sarcasm and empathy for the common man captured the gritty essence of Chicago for more than three decades, died Tuesday. He was 64.

The *Chicago Tribune* announced Royko's death on its World Wide Web site.

Royko, whose *Chicago Tribune* column was syndicated to more than 600 newspapers nationwide, died at 3:30 p.m. at Northwestern Memorial Hospital. He underwent surgery there last week for an aneurysm, a rupture or weakening of a blood vessel.

Royko's column was a cornerstone of the daily newspaper for generations of Chicago readers, first in the now-defunct *Chicago Daily News,* alter with the Chicago *Sun-Times,* and since 1984 with the *Tribune.* For most of his career he wrote five days a week. He gained stature as a critic of the late Mayor Richard J. Daley at a time when most prominent Chicagoans treated Daley with cautious respect. Royko's 1971 biography, ***Boss: Richard J. Daley of Chicago*** portrayed Daley as a shrewd, autocratic politician who tolerated racism and corruption.

The book so infuriated the Daley family that the mayor's wife persuaded a grocery-store chain to remove the book from its stores.

After Royko's death, Richard M. Daley—the mayor's son, said: "Through the years, my family filled many of his columns, some critical and some supportive, but whether you agreed with him or not, you had to respect his honesty and his love for the city."

Royko tempered his political commentary with wry observations on news, social trends, his beloved Chicago Cubs and the foibles of everyday life. Many were presented in imagined conversations with Slats Grobnik, Royko's fictitious, blue-collar alter ego from the Polish neighborhood where Royko grew up.

Known for his gruff, often sarcastic tone, Royko's scorn could be withering.

In 1992, a woman called him to complain. She had found a 2,000-year-old Roman coin on the floor in her bank and returned it. To her dismay, she was not offered a reward.

"If you don't at least try to return it, you're a thief," Royko wrote. "So should we hold parades for people because they aren't thieves?"

He had no use for yuppies, as a column on buying practical gifts for spouses made clear:

"Many men love tools. Even those who don't know how to use them. I know one yuppie male who was thrilled when he got a set of screwdrivers. He said: 'Oh, these will be perfect for prying open shellfish.'"

When Tampa, Fla., tried to lure the White Sox away from Chicago in 1988, he urged city baseball fans to send their dirty socks to Florida officials. In return, Royko received citrus seeds from Florida fans.

But others didn't take the jibes so lightly, and in later years some readers wondered whether Royko was going too far. Where once his venom was reserved for politicians, he had begun to write more about ethnic minorities and gays, to the pleasure of neither.

Twice in March 1996, Hispanic protesters gathered at the Tribune Tower to demand an apology for remarks in his columns. Royko had written that tequila is the best thing Mexico has offered this century. Another column took a jaundiced view of anti-Castro Cubans. The protesters said Royko perpetuated stereotypes.

Royko himself got into legal trouble because of alcohol. In 1995, Royko pleaded guilty to drunken driving and resisting arrest after a traffic accident near his Winnetka home. According to court testimony, Royko had begun treatment for alcoholism a month before the accident and had enrolled in an after-care addiction program.

.In October 1995, Royko received the Damon Runyon Award, given annually to the journalist who best exemplifies the style that made Runyon one of the best columnists of his day.

In his acceptance speech, Royko reflected on how the newsroom had changed during his years in journalism.

"Forty years ago, we were on the tail of the *Front Page* era," Royko said. "There was a different point of view. Reporters and editors were more forgiving of public people. They didn't think they had to stick someone in jail to make a career."

OVERVIEW

William Howarth (review date 28 March 1971)

SOURCE: "October Nonfiction," *Washington Post Book World,* March 28, 1971, p. 8.

[*In the following excerpted review, Howarth discusses Royko's substance and style in* Like I Was Sayin'.]

No such modesty deters Mike Royko, whose *Like I Was Sayin'* . . . gathers 100 of his columns from the last two decades. Known in Chicago as a fearless battler of Mayor Daley, Royko has a style that runs to short graphs, heavy on the slang and sarcasm, fast with regional slurs. In his estimate, New Yorkers are rude, Californians weird, Texans "the world's tallest midgets." The tone is barroom banter, with all the subtlety of an ad for Lite Beer.

Yet below this style lies plenty of substance. Royko is a tough reporter. He runs down sources and asks hard questions, exposes fools or crooks with an impartial hand. His hero is the fabled "little guy," who lives today in a dwindling region between Chicago's affluent suburbs and high-rise lakeshore. This Bungalow Man, as Royko styles him, holds to the traditional values of work, family, and male supremacy: "We're in the age of wimps. It is nothing to be ashamed of."

Actually, Royko is only mock macho; he likes to pound his readers both left and right. After a harangue against draft evaders and permissive judges, he turns on the "hallelujah-peddlers" who want prayer back in school. The column on "King Ron," our affable chief executive, should be required reading for voters this year.

A cynic with a heart, Royko reflects the anger of many Korean War vets who have watched their country slide into venality and "pasta chic." A spiral seems to have caught his own career, which began with the liberal *Daily News* and now emanates from the Republican *Tribune.* Royko is there by choice, evading the Australian who owns Chicago's other paper.

Times Literary Supplement (essay date 12 November 1971)

SOURCE: "Chicago's Machine-Minder," *Times Literary Supplement,* November 12, 1971, p. 1413.

[*The following essay gives a British reviewer's opinion of Royko's 'unsympathetic' treatment of Chicago mayor Richard J. Daley in* Boss.]

The boss in politics is largely an American phenomenon. There have been bosses around the world—Chamberlain in Birmingham, Daferre in Marseilles—but the boss has flourished most against the tightly knit ethnic background of American cities. Richard Joseph Daley, the Democratic mayor of Chicago, is the finest and, perhaps, final flowering of the Irish-American boss, one with Curley of Boston and Murphy in New York.

Mike Royko's portrait is unsympathetic. Few Chicago newspapermen admire Daley, although their editors and publishers, even if they don't love the Boss, are able to get along with him. But, unsympathetic, biased as it is, his book is a marvellously detailed analysis of what makes a boss tick; his strengths and weaknesses.

First, the man. Daley is an unfamiliar type to those whose views of American politics have been formed by the cinema or television. He lives a quiet, sedate, pious life. He is not interested in the trappings of power; his home, his life-style are resolutely lower-middle-class. His interest is power. And, because he has the secret of holding power, he has attracted support from outside his normal constituency. "Even Republican businessmen contribute money to the [Daley] Machine", Mr Royko notes, "more than they give to Republican candidates. Republicans can't do anything for them, but Daley can."

The man, his love and exercise of power, reached their zenith, for non-Chicagoans at least, during the Democratic National Convention of 1968. This was *his* convention. As a henchman put it, delegates must be impressed "that they are not just visiting Chicago, but Mayor Daley's Chicago". That Chicago, events demonstrated, was one of unbridled police ferocity. Demonstrators and reporters were beaten up. There were mass clubbings on Michigan Avenue. People, many of them innocent spectators, were shoved through plate-glass windows. Police chased others into the lobby of the Hilton Hotel and pummelled them.

There were at the time, there still are, a few who sought to justify the police action. There can be little doubt that the police were sorely tried. Many of them saw in the demonstrators a force dedicated to the overthrow of their, the police's, way of life. The police, in Chicago or New York or Los Angeles, it should be remembered, are just as American as those who assault them and their values. Yet, on balance, three years after the event it is clear that the police, with the support of their superiors, including Richard J. Daley, ran amok that night. Of course, that was three years ago. A visitor to Chicago recently found that natives of that city have either forgotten the affair or, as one said blame it on "those Eastern television and newspaper people".

Bosses, and the machines they control, have a facility for overcoming problems raised by such things. Tammany reigned for sixty years after the New York draft riots in the Civil War. Daley's explanation was at least novel. The massive show and use of police force, he explained, was due to "reports and intelligence on my desk that certain people planned to assassinate the three contenders for the presidency". Oddly enough, this explanation, never supported by the FBI, sufficed for millions of the faithful in Chicago and the Middle West.

Daley got away with it. Why? Because he has built up a loyal machine. It is not a matter of money and jobs alone. There is the personal touch; attendance at wakes, very important in the Irish-American community; the instant, wolfishly jovial recognition of old friends, the ruthless discarding of those who have failed the Machine, if not Chicago. Daley's private life is spotless. He does not want philanderers and drunks around him, although he has played politics all his life with the forces that control gambling, vice and protection.

There is graft there, as Mr Royko shows: in insurance, in building contracts. For all Daley's professed sympathy for the Negro, Chicago's Black slums appal the visitor. Like most politicians who have emerged from a White, ethnic background—Irish, Polish, German, or Italian—Daley has little understanding for and less sympathy with the Black community's needs.

Daley and his kind are the true subversive influences in American life, far more dangerous than the Birchers or the innocents of the New Left. They will last as long as the White, blue-collar workers dominate the inner cities of America. When these workers move to the suburbs, the Daleys will go, to be replaced by Negro bosses of about the same levels of intelligence and integrity.

Paul P. Somers Jr. (essay date 1983)

SOURCE: "Mike Royko: Midwestern Satirist," *Midamerica X,* Vol. 10, 1983, pp. 177-86.

[*In the following essay, Somers assesses Royko's talents as a satirist.*]

Mike Royko is a nationally syndicated newspaper writer whose columns first appeared in the *Chicago Daily News* in 1966 and continued there until the paper's demise in 1978. They are now featured in the Chicago *Sun Times.* Selected columns have been reprinted in three books: *Up Against It* (1967), *I May Be Wrong, But I Doubt It* (1968), and *Slats Grobnik and Some Other Friends* (1973). Although his 1971 book, *Boss: Richard J. Daly of Chicago,* was widely acclaimed—outside the mayor's office—this study will concern itself with Royko's reprinted columns, considering him as a Midwesterner, an American humorist, a satirist, and, finally, as a moralist who is outraged by the world as he sees it.

Writing within the confining genre of the daily—thrice weekly during most of his years at the *Daily News*—newspaper column, Royko has created some memorable characters, especially Slats Grobnik, whom we'll discuss later. Royko's persona is not rural, like Kin Hubbard's Abe Martin, and, while it is emphatically urban, neither is it ethnic like Finley Peter Dunne's Irish Mr. Dooley. As a matter of fact, Royko doesn't seem to have had to create a persona at all. From all accounts, he really *is* overworked and irascible, and he has been aging ungracefully for the past ten years. In the introduction to *Up Against It,* Bill Mauldin wrote: "Royko is like his city. He has sharp elbows, he thinks sulphur and soot are natural ingredients of the atmosphere, and he has an astonishing capacity for idealism and love devoid of goo." Royko himself affirmed: "like many Chicagoans, I grew up with a distrust of most things and creatures."

The following reply to a letter from "A Good Teen-ager" succinctly identifies Royko's point of view, which he had established as early as 1967, two years before this column appeared:

Dear Good Teen-ager:

I received another one of your letters today. You are getting to be a pain in the neck. I wish your mommy and daddy would take your personalized stationery away from you.

After asking why Good Teen-ager doesn't thank him for being a Good Adult, working and paying the taxes for Good-Teen-ager's schools, Royko concluded:

And don't try that other tricky one on me—that business of the Good Teen-agers being the Generation of the Future. I used to be a Generation of the Future myself. And now I've got a thirty-seven-inch waist and a couple of kids who think it's funny to punch me in it.

As for his own generation, "the group that was born just before and after the Depression began," Royko can't even give it a name. In **"Who Actually Creates Gaps?"** he wrote: "Half the kids born in my generation were accidents. That's a hearty welcome for you." His generation's war had been Korea: "Coming back from Korea, and expecting people to be interested, was about like coming back from a Wisconsin vacation with color slides." He did, however, rally to claim for his generation Martin Luther King, Jr., Robert Kennedy, Lenny Bruce, and Malcolm X.

In a *Playboy* poll, Royko was one of twenty celebrities asked: "Has your sex life been affected by women's liberation?" Expressing fatigue and resignation rather than self-righteousness, he replied: "Well, I'm a married man, so I don't even think about things like that. I don't even have lust in my heart."

In **"Acute Crisis Identity,"** he made fun of those who question their role in life: "As for myself, I haven't had an identity crisis. I have always known who I am, which, while deeply depressing, saved me a lot of running around looking for me."

It is essential that a satirist know who he is, and, as he stated above, Mike Royko certainly does: he is the everyday, working citizen, living in a far from perfect urban society. It might be stretching matters to describe him as a cracker barrel philosopher, but he definitely represents common sense and the common man, the shot and beer bunch as opposed to the manhattan or martini set.

His identity is Midwestern, too. Although Jimmy Breslin praised **Boss,** Royko's collections don't receive much attention nationally, for reviewers tend to label, perhaps dismiss him as "regional." His life and career are bound inextricably with Chicago, and at times he takes on a big-city callousness, as in his 1968 column, **"Shock Proof,"** in which he scoffed at the notion that the hippies would be able to shock Chicago.

"Shocked? A city that has had Capone and Accardo, dead bodies and dead alewives, Calumet City and Marina City, Lar Daley and Mayor Daley, beer riots and race riots, isn't going to be fazed by a horde of kids with long hair and beads." And, by the time the city's "jackrollers and assorted creeps," not to mention its teen-age gangs, get through them,

"all that will remain of the sweet young things is a tuft of hair and a bead or two."

Royko's ruthlessness, even brutality, here is appropriate to a citizen of the Hog Butcher to the World.

Indeed, in a column from the same period, **"San-Fran-York on the Lake,"** he lashed his city and its citizens for turning soft, scornfully contrasting the brawling Chicago Sandburg had praised to the pampered metropolis of today:

CHICAGO

Hi-Rise for the World
Partygoer, Stacker of Stereo Tapes,
Player with Home Pool Tables and the Nation's
Jets;
Dapper, slender, filter-tipped-
City of the Big Credit Card:

                        . . .

And having answered so I turn once more to those
who
sneer at this my city, and I join in the sneer and
say to them:
Come and show me another city with razor-cut
head
singing so proud to have a Mustang and a white
turtle neck and reservations for dinner.
Fierce as a poodle with tongue lapping for dog
yummies.

Giggling!
Giggling the silly giggle of the fourth martini
at lunch; half naked, but not sweating, and if
sweating, not offending; Proud to be Hi-Rise
for the World, Partygoer, Stacker of Stereo Tapes,
Player with Home Pool Tables and Jet Handler to
the
Nation.

His satirist's blood has been heated to the boiling point by the sorry spectacle of the Midwest's greatest city giggling as it emulates the effeminate decadence of the East and the West coasts.

If Royko is identified with the Midwest and with Chicago, he also exhibits many characteristics of American humorists in general: he plays the Innocent Abroad; he exaggerates and boasts; he deflates the pretentious and brings us back to reality.

As the Innocent Abroad, he entered a Munich beer hall: ". . . it sounded as if a basketball game was in progress, with everybody shouting and cheering. As far as I could tell, they were cheering themselves for being drunk. . . . Some say it is beneficial for Bavarians to remain indoors and groggy because that makes them less likely to march across somebody's border."

In Paris, he greeted the maitre d' at Maxim's with a "hiya," and, the classic provincial, asked the waiter if he had ever tried the whipped cream at the Buffalo, at Pulaski and Irving in Chicago. The waiter was disdainful, but our Midwestern traveler had the last laugh: he didn't leave a tip.

Of the famous Casino in Monte Carlo, he observed: "I've seen more action at church carnivals on Grand Av. The famous Monte Carlo Casino is a dump."

The only place he really liked was Oberammergau, as described in **"Rumble in Bavaria."** A confrontation between some old men with a German Shepard and several young motorcyclists whom Royko immediately identified as "punks" was broken up by the sound of police sirens. " . . . I decided I liked Oberammergau. It's a place where a Chicagoan won't feel homesick."

Like most urban comedians, he occasionally portrays himself as the "little man" popularized by such humorists as James Thurber and Robert Benchley. Even though he made fun of Monte Carlo, Royko compared himself to James Bond in *Casino Royale:* "whereas 007 has slipped on his light chamois shoulder holster and .25 caliber Baretta automatic, Agent Royko slipped his Dr. Scholl arch supports into his shoes."

His column, **"Bugs in the Bug,"** began: "My car hates me. It is trying to destroy me and has been doing so for at least three years." This saga of man's uncontrollable mechanical "servant" ended with the demonic vehicle sprouting deadly toadstools with six-inch stems from its front seat. Royko subdued them with his shoe and took the bus to work.

He also utilized comic exaggeration, a typically American device going back to the frontier, to Mike Fink and Davy Crockett. In **"Has Pinochle Lost Its Whack?"** he lamented a pinochle tournament which had too little knuckle-whacking and too much politeness. In this tale tall enough for a riverboatmen, he averred: "The proper competitive spirit in pinochle was epitomized by a man I read about who was in a game in a Gary tavern one hot night. His partner made a serious mistake, so he leaped up, shouted: 'You should have led him in trump,' and shot him."

Even in a story about a penny-pitching tournament, Royko made a boast becoming a native of the City of the Broad Shoulders: "Being champion of Chicago is as good as being champion of the world."

"In some endeavors such as groin-kneeing, eye-gouging, ear-biting, dollar-hustling, or penny-pitching, being champion of Chicago is being champion of the world. New York is a rube town in such sports."

Comic exaggeration is a good classification under which to consider Slats Grobnik, Royko's most popular character. The Huck Finn of the alleys, Slats is a juvenile anti-hero, the boy your mother didn't want you to play with, an unwashed, untanned street kid. Before Slats' baby brother, Fats, swallowed his shooter, Slats used to be a champion at marbles. He exercised until his thumb muscles got bigger than his biceps. In the finest tradition of the Ring-tailed Roarer, Slats, upon hearing the story of David and Goliath, shrugged and said: "I could of done the same thing with a marble."

Slats excelled at sports like knuckle-cracking: "The first time Slats Grobnik cracked one of his knuckles, dogs all over the neighborhood began barking, and a squad car came to see who had been shot."

The Grobnik family itself is a link with an older, ethnic America. Mrs. Grobnik offered this bit of old-country wisdom about banks: "A good bank should look like a jail, except the bank's walls should be thicker." Watching the movie *Frankenstein,* she saw the mad scientist constructing the monster and said: "See? Doctors, they're all the same." Mr. Grobnik, meanwhile, had identified with the monster.

In addition to his comic exaggeration, another thing Royko does that American humorists have always done is to recall us to reality, to deflate the over-inflated. An uncollected column from 1978 pointed out the hypocrisy of Jane Fonda's lament that the trouble with Hollywood is that its writers are too money conscious—they should be willing to work for $100 a week. He suggested this is unappropriate coming from an actress about to make one million dollars for appearing in a movie written by that "capitalistic running dog" Neil Simon.

When we consider Royko as a bubble-burster, we run into several anti's; he is anti-sentimental, anti-romantic, and anti-intellectual. His anti-sentimentality often has an urban slant, as he works variations on the "tough childhood" theme, (often sentimental itself), of so many urban comedians, from Sam Levinson to Rodney Dangerfield to Richard Pryor to David Brenner.

Young Slats recalls us to reality with his observation about the Easter bunny: "No rabbit would come in this neighborhood, he'd be run over by a beer truck. . . . Anybody who can get in and out of that many houses without being seen is going to take stuff, not leave it." We laugh because we know that, alas, Slats is right.

And Christmas with the Grobniks is not exactly material for Currier and Ives: "In the morning the stockings would be loaded to the brim, and by the time they sat down to Christmas dinner, so would Mr. Grobnik." (Slats' father is one step removed from Royko's—and our—father, so he can write and we can laugh.) Slats catches his dad putting out the presents and immediately assumes he is stealing them.

Royko elsewhere mocks the sentimentalization of family ties, as in the time Mr. Grobnik ran amok and struck Slats and his mother with Slats' cymbals. Mrs. Grobnik took the children and left. "At first, Mr. Grobnik could not believe they were really gone. To make sure, he changed locks." This reversal of expectations is not at all unexpected to anyone who knows the Grobniks.

At times Royko goes beyond anti-sentimentality, as in the gleeful cruelty of **"Save a Kitty from Extinction."** To get rid of an unwanted cat, he threatened to drop it into a tank of piranhas unless children reading the article tell Mommy and Daddy to "do something to save the nice little calico kitty from the mean man in the newspaper." Otherwise, it will be "snap, snap, gobble, gobble, right down to his curly tail."

This is perhaps an understandable reaction to the sentimental excesses of Walt Disney. Nevertheless, it is mild compared to some examples from the *Tribune Primer,* written by Eugene Field in 1882 for the *Denver Tribune.* Field urged children to drink concentrated lye, play with lobsters and loaded guns, and kill a cockroach by biting it in two. Later he, like Royko after him, would become identified with Chicago.

Of course, romantic love is too fat a target for Royko to pass up. What could be more ludicrous than the spectacle of Slats in love? **"The Day Slats Fell for a Girl"** began: "Valentine's Day was never one of Slats Grobnik's favorite events. He was just a toddler when he saw a card with a drawing of a heart, pierced by an arrow, but his reaction was 'Good shot!'"

Using his own voice in **"Marriage No Field of Daisies,"** Royko wrote: "For every young fool who runs through high humidity in a field of daisies, you'll find fifty wise older men in air-conditioned bars."

Others of Royko's assaults on pretension come under the banner of anti-intellectualism, as he usually honors his alliance with the shot-and-beer crowd. "It is a strain for local newsmen, being interviewed by visiting writers, especially the scholarly ones. They always ask if the mayor has charisma. In the mayor's neighborhood, they could get punched for talking dirty."

When *Time* referred to a yellow two-piece bathing suit connected by a gold-link chain as "anything but deja vu," Royko scratched his head and wrote: "I don't know what deja vu means, but when a writer is afraid to say something in English, that's always a tip off that it's pretty wild."

A related element of humor in our democracy has been anti-respectability, slob appeal if you will. And what better spokes-person than that "well known social arbiter, Slats Grobnik," who, according to Royko, was the author of the best selling book, *My 30 New Year's Eves Without an Arrest*? Here are samples of Mr. Grobnik's advice:

> What to drink: Select one favorite beverage and stay with it all evening, and all the next day if you wish. I recommend the always-festive boilermaker. (Recipe: Pour one shot of whiskey down your throat. Follow with one glass of beer.) After midnight, the ingredients can be mixed in a glass, vase, or pot.

> At midnight, the traditional drink is champagne. But remember, never drink it straight from the bottle unless the hostess does so first.

While we must grant that there is some narrative distance between Royko and the low brow advice of Slats, grown here to a disreputable maturity, the opening line from **"Mrs. Grobnik a Checker-Upper"** is worthy of Archie Bunker: "A Chicago bank has hired a creature named Gucci to design arty new checks and checkbooks." "A creature" veritably drips contempt.

Deflation and bubble-bursting are, of course, expected of the satirist, and Royko often uses his wit to point out the folly of human nature, and, most frequently, the folly, the injustice, the corruption of the Daley Machine, which has been his Moby Dick. In his *Glossary of Literary Terms* M. H. Abrahams defines satire as "the art of diminishing a subject by making it ridiculous and evoking toward it attitudes of amusement, contempt, indignation, or scorn." This Royko does frequently.

On the subject of human nature, he told of Slat's uncle, Beer Belly Frank, who held an annual garage sale of merchandise his relatives and neighbors thought was stolen. When they eventually learned he had purchased it legally, they were angry at him for only pretending to be shady.

And then there was the theater owner who, in response to great public outcry, switched from X-rated movies to family films. He soon had to return to pornography, however, for so few decent citizens patronized his decent movies that he was going broke. "What do people want? I think they want you-know-what," Royko commented sardonically.

Moving on to Royko's nemesis, the Daley Machine, let's consider Leonard Feinberg's assertion in *Introduction to Satire* that "satire appeals to the sense of superiority." Many of Royko's columns are devoted to Mayor Daley and his minions, and it is gratifying to the reader to be able to feel superior to them. In **"Alinsky Not in Their League,"** for example, Royko wrote: "The City Council paid a great tribute to the late Saul Alinsky a few days ago. It refused to name a park after him." He then went on to tell of the notable public servants after whom parks *had* been named, men such as former sheriff William Meyerling, who was the guardian of Cook County's law and order in the days when Al Capone was its most famous citizen.

Other columns tell of the vice squad's heroic raid on a senior citizen's penny ante poker game, a peddler who was harrassed even though he has a permit, and so forth. Not surprisingly, Slats Grobnik's hero was a certain Chicago alderman, because he had heard Mrs. Grobnik say he had never worked a day in his life.

It has been said that satirists seldom if ever succeed, and Royko would be the first to concede that Richard Daley was Mayor of Chicago until he died, and that his Machine lives on. [In a front-page question and answer column in The Detroit *Free Press* for July 9, 1979, Royko admitted "I suppose I miss Daley."] According to Feinberg, one reason for satirists' failure to achieve important results is that they rarely attack the fundamental political and economic structures of their societies. Royko certainly doesn't suggest that Chicago be reorganized under Marxist principles.

Perhaps Royko's most admirable characteristic is his sense of outrage. In **"Laugh? I Thought I'd Die,"** he told of going to see a movie the day after Robert Kennedy was shot. Inside, some 300 ordinary, middle class men were watching an exploitatively violent film and laughing at the murder and the torture.

Outside, people were asking what is wrong with this country, why it kills the way it does. The world was asking if the United States is that sick and corrupt.

Inside the United Artists, and in theaters across the country, guns were barking, blood was flowing—and people were laughing.

They laughed and laughed and laughed. And by then the plane carrying the Senator's body had landed. Now, his family would bury him.

Similarly, he abandoned satire in his outrage and dismay at the assassination of Martin Luther King. In **"Millions in His Firing Squad,"** he wrote: "We have pointed a gun at our own head and we are squeezing the trigger. And nobody we elect is going to help us. It is our head and our trigger."

Thus, we have seen that Mike Royko is firmly anchored in his city, his region, his nation, and his generation (even if it doesn't have a name). He utilizes many of the devices typically associated with American humorists and emerges as a rather grumpy urban Everyman. Occasionally satire fails him as a weapon against human folly and the Daley Machine, and it is at these times when he is most effective: If his writing can't change this world, at least it will remind us that justice and decency exist and that they should be heeded.

Jerry Griswold (review date 2 January 1983)

SOURCE: "Royko Re-bound: Buying into a Journalistic Stereotype," *Los Angeles Times Book Review,* January 2, 1983, pp. 3, 7.

[*In the following review, Griswold, a California writer, praises Royko's book* Sez Who? Sez Me!]

Chicago is most often called the Second City by people prepared to drive six hours rather than spend a weekend in their own part of the Midwest. Chicago also is a city where holding opinions is confused with intelligence, contrariness is taken as proof of individuality, and the metropolitan style seems hopelessly frozen in an era when everyone wore hats.

As proof of this last observation, consider how Mike Royko is presented by his publishers in this recent collection of his columns: cigarette butts spilling out of an ashtray, filthy coffee cups everywhere, a ratty cubbyhole they call an office, and a newspaperman in a crumpled shirt hunching over an old Remington typewriter. His beat is Chicago, and he knows more about barroom hangouts, backroom politics and bureaucratic pettiness than any palooka on the street. He has a heart of gold, a ready hand for the Little Guy and the love of a whole city.

Come on, I find myself saying, this is beginning to sound like a Bogart movie called "Dead Men Don't Eat Quiche." Nonetheless, mention soon is made of the stockyards, the old neighborhood, Nelson Algren, Ben Hecht, and all the rest—so tiresomely familiar that one can only blush when Studs Terkel is dragged out to say that Royko is "like a famished alley mutt; he digs away at the bone of truth."

To be sure, Royko acts the part, too. Consider: "So, I urged him to go back to his native Greece and find a nice girl who knows nothing of checking accounts, Bonwit Teller, property laws, Gloria Steinem, and tennis clubs." Or "It was said that if Duke (a barroom dog) licked your hand, you could die of blood poisoning." Or "Her late husband died of a sudden stroke some years earlier while moving furniture. A night watchman in the furniture store had surprised him, and during the tussle he gave Billy Tom a terrific stroke on the brow with his club."

On my part, I confess an uneasy suspicion of individuals who have bought into a stereotype, whose lives so lack flexibility that it is impossible to envision them outside their chosen cliché. And it is impossible to imagine, say, Royko transported to California, stripped of his cigarettes and rumpled shirt, put into jogging clothes and pushed into the sunshine, and happy. To a certain extent, that was the point of the movie *Continental Divide,* where a Royko-like character was played by the late John Belushi (another Chicagoan).

Now with all my gripes and reservations on the table, and despite them, let me tell you that I loved the book and have not had such good laughs in years. I spent a long summer weekend trying to pry the book away from three friends.

One woman woke everyone at 7 a.m. by laughing in bed at Royko's column on practical jokes (**"Laugh and Learn"**). A Connecticut journalist drank coffee the entire time he read the book and concluded that Royko was the only person to understand the admiration/hatred/disappointment liberals felt about John Wayne. A public-relations specialist from New Mexico, who suffered from periodic spasms of titters, claimed that the best piece was a sports column Royko imagined Nixon might write. (**"A Perfectly, Clear View of Baseball"**).

On my part, as a result of reading this book, I now know: 1) what to do if arrested for negligent driving while passing through a carwash; 2) what folks in Chicago think of those in L.A. ("sleepy-eyed men who wear shirts open to their belly buttons"); 3) how to avoid a hangover ("stick with the drink you started with . . . if you started the evening drinking champagne, beer and frozen daiquiris, stick with champagne, beer and frozen daiquiris the rest of the evening").

By the end of this book, one can only conclude that Royko is too good for Chicago. As a result, I propose that readers write to Royko indicating that if he came to California he would not have to act like a cranky ethnic or wear wrinkled clothes in smoke-filled rooms, unless he really wanted to.

David Shaw (review date 23 September 1984)

SOURCE: "Columns of Grumpy Gems," *Los Angeles Times Book Review,* September 23, 1984, p. 5.

[*The following review contains praise for Royko's writing on the vicissitudes of everyday life in* Like I Was Sayin'.]

Mike Royko, the Pulitzer Prize-winning Chicago newspaper columnist, is such a delight to read that the all-but overwhelming temptation in reviewing his new book is to say:

"This book is a small sampling of some of Mike Royko's best columns from the past 18 years.

"Herewith is an even smaller sampling of some of Mike Royko's best lines from those columns."

Then I would quote extensively (but selectively) from the 100 columns reprinted in the book and figure that if you found them sufficiently amusing, insightful or provocative, you'd buy the book; and if you didn't, you wouldn't.

But Royko's columns are small jewels, not easily appreciated when chipped apart; besides, book review editors (and book review readers) expect more for their money (and their time) than that. So I should tell you that in this collection of his columns, Royko writes about every human activity from dieting to driving, about every social phenomenon from digital watches to draft evasion and about every political issue from feminism to racism. Moreover, Royko is almost always as entertaining as he is thoughtful, and unlike virtually every other newspaper columnist I read, even when he misses the mark—most egregiously in a column on capital punishment—there is always something to make you think or laugh (or both).

Royko writes with wit and style on matters large and small, writing as easily and as entertainingly on sexual promiscuity, xenophobia and gun control, for example, as he does on the hoarding of pecans in a corner of one's mouth while eating butter pecan ice cream. In this particular collection, however, Royko is generally best when writing about the vicissitudes of everyday life. I was particularly amused by his column in response to a woman who had asked his advice on removing a "starch build" from her iron and on coping with sticky, cloudy ice cubes:

"The sticking could be caused by several things," Royko wrote, "but the most common is water that is sticky. You might call the water commissioner . . . and demand to know if he is providing sticky water, and if so, why."

Royko also suggested the woman might try "the old fashioned method of rapping the tray against something to pop the cubes loose. The edge of a sink or the brow of an unruly child works fine."

As for her cloudy ice cubes, Royko said, "somebody is

creeping into your kitchen and pouring goodness knows what into your ice cube trays." Since Royko had no solution for the "starch build" on her iron ("Frankly, I don't know what a 'starch build' is"), he recommended she throw the iron out the window. "If you are lucky" he wrote, "it will land on whoever has been putting a foreign substance in your ice cube trays, thus solving two pesky problems with one iron."

Royko is especially funny/grumpy when he is writing about the hapless (until this season) Chicago Cubs. Here is Royko on the 1960 Cubs, a team filled with men who "had big biceps . . . They could hit home runs. The trouble was, most of them had big biceps in their arches, too, and the old ladies behind the concession counter could run faster."

By 1969, Royko wrote, the team had improved considerably: "For the first time in three decades, the players were better athletes than the grounds crew." Later in the same column, Royko complained that the Cubs had traded Jose Cardenal, "the only player I saw who could sleep between innings. In fact, Jose could sleep between pitches. With his potential, I had hoped he would remain in Chicago and someday become a distinguished alderman."

This blend of humor and cynical political commentary is what helped make Royko's early reputation in Chicago. In fact, righteous indignation—seriously expressed, on matters both political and personal—has often been as important a device as *bon mots* for him. Witness a 1982 column, reprinted in this book and originally published in response to a 30-year-old reader who had written Royko to say he was going to kill himself because he could not find work. Rather than "plead with you not to kill yourself," Royko wrote to the man about all the "rougher things in life than being unemployed" and suggested the man was "more coward than victim. . .

"If your kids don't have winter boots while you are alive, how is your being dead going to make their feet warmer?" Royko asked.

Royko concluded his column by suggesting that the man "give it a little more time," and then said:

"But if you must do it, go somewhere isolated and do it quietly. Your wife will have enough problems without cleaning up after you one last time."

Charles Monaghan (review date 14 October 1984)

SOURCE: "The Daley Question," *Washington Post Book World,* October 14, 1984, p. 8.

[*In the following review, Monaghan praises the writing and pacing of* Boss, *but notes that Royko's portrait of Mayor Richard Daley is only two-dimensional.*]

Mike Royko is a witty and widely respected columnist for the *Chicago Daily News,* long an outspoken foe of Mayor Richard Daley. Now he has given us a book on His Honor—neatly written, energetically paced, and full of marvelous stories sure to please lovers of urban politics. But ultimately it is a disappointment because it doesn't tell us what makes Daley tick.

If a writer is going to devote a book to one man, he should try at some point to look at the world through his protagonist's eyes. Royko, however, has only a thorough, steely contempt for his subject—he doesn't want to spend a moment in Daley's mind. As a result, his mayor is a two-dimensional villain, a man of bad will, bad manners, bad grammar, and—one feels certain by the end—bad breath.

For instance, Royko devotes one sentence to the fascinating fact that Daley's first political memories are of attending women's suffrage marches with his mother, but two pages of arrant speculation to Daley's association with the 1919 race riots. Royko never probes things that might add another dimension, such as the mayor's insistent identification with the common man. "The party permits ordinary people to get ahead," Royko quotes Daley as saying:

> Without the party, I couldn't be mayor. The rich guys can get elected on their money, but somebody like me, an ordinary person, needs the party. Without the party only the rich would get elected to office.

Royko properly details Daley's centralizing of political and administrative power and his monsignor-like dedication to bricks and mortar (though I would like to have seen more about how he wields power through his staff of "whiz kids"). But Royko doesn't pull the elements together into a coherent theory of the man.

The identification with the underdog, the view of ethnic blocs as the key to political power, the centralization, the emphasis on building things, the stress on administrative action—doesn't it all fall into a pattern? Isn't it reminiscent of the set of ideals surging in the heads of those young men who flocked to Washington in the Thirties to shape the New Deal? Daley may have been sitting in the Illinois legislature in the late Thirties, but his political mind was being formed by what was happening in the nation's capital. Today, he seems the quintessence of the New Deal politician-administrator.

Which is also the source of his troubles. Civil rights, for instance, was never the strong suit of the New Deal. The theory was then, and seems to be Daley's now, that induced prosperity is the best road to helping the underdog and assuring equality. But civil rights dissenters—not to mention ecology groups—often think that the goal of prosperity clouds more important issues. As for politics, the New Deal was the product of a coalition of big-city machines and Roosevelt could not have cared less what was happening to insurgents back in the Bronx, Kansas City, Memphis or Chicago. The important thing was that the Depression be broken, that prosperity return, and that the government run smoothly. Daley matches Roosevelt in his ardor for open politics.

There's something of a feeling of anachronism about Daley, a feeling that he is a man of another age, and I think it is because his style and world view lie back there thirty-five years ago. His ideals do too and there's bound to be a clash with other ideals now being put forward, such as participatory democracy and decentralization of government. But so far Chicago's voters don't seem to care too much about the difference.

Additional coverage of Royko's life and career is contained in the following sources published by Gale: *Contemporary Authors,* Vol. 157; and *Contemporary Authors New Revision Series,* Vol. 26.

Obituaries

In addition to the preceding authors, the following notable writers died in 1997:

Kathy Acker
April 18, 1948—November 30, 1997
American novelist, essayist, and short story writer

A controversial avant-garde writer and cult figure of the punk movement, Kathy Acker was considered among the most significant proponents of radical feminism and the postmodern literary aesthetic. Associated with the discordant, irreverent music of punk rock, Acker's iconoclastic metafiction—an amalgam of extreme profanity, violence, graphic sex, autobiography, fragmented narrative, and plagiarized texts—rejects conventional morality and traditional modes of literary expression. Her best known works, including *Great Expectations, Blood and Guts in High School,* and *Don Quixote,* feature female protagonists whose psychosexual misadventures—involving rape, incest, suicide, and abortion—underscore their individual struggles to discover meaning and identity in deconstructed patriarchal language and sexual masochism. She believed it is through the body that people come to their deepest meanings, pleasures, and agonies. Acker was the author of the screenplay *Variety,* and her later works included *Bodies of Work,* a collection of essays, and *Eurydice of the Underworld,* a book of short stories.

Robbie Tilley Branscum
June 17, 1937—May 24, 1997
American children's author

Branscum's stories for children mirrored the environment in which she was raised, and focused on the hardships and joys of country life. She grew up in Big Flat, Arkansas, dropped out of school in the seventh grade, married at age fifteen, divorced at age twenty-five, and after that worked on dirt farms. She was an avid reader and decided to try writing when a Southern Baptist newsletter accepted her essay "Men Who Walked with God." During her writing career she won many awards, including a Friends of American Writers Award in 1977 for *Toby, Granny, and George* and an Edgar Allan Poe Award in 1983 for *The Murder of Hound Dog Bates: A Novel.* Branscum wrote about rural America in her fiction, including topics such as moonshine, berry picking, and fried chicken. She frequently toured colleges and library associations to speak about her life and the trials of being a writer whose education had ended with the seventh grade.

Leon Edel
September 9, 1907—September 5, 1997
American biographer and professor

Best known for his five-volume biography of Henry James, Edel spent most of his life completing research for this work. It was while he was living in Paris that his interest in James was aroused, leading to his in-depth research. Edel talked to people who had known James, tracked down letters written by James, and had sole unrestricted use of thousands of manuscript letters at Harvard and elsewhere. He wore a ring that had belonged to James and, according to a *London Times* reviewer, colleagues teased Edel, telling him that he wasn't just researching James but was, in truth, married to his work. Edel taught at New York University from 1953 to 1978. He then moved to Hawaii, and continued to teach at the University of Hawaii. Edel received a Pulitzer Prize and the National Book Award in 1963 for the second and third volumes of *Henry James.* Edel also wrote biographies on Willa Cather, Henry David Thoreau, and James Joyce.

Percy Granger
August 8, 1945—March 10, 1997
American playwright, screenwriter, and actor

Granger, a magna cum laude graduate of Harvard University, was a founding member of Manhattan's Ensemble Studio Theater. He made his Broadway playwrighting debut in 1982 with *Eminent Domain.* An active part of the theatre, he started producing plays in 1972 with *The Complete Works of Stud Edsel,* a semi-autobiographical work about an idealistic law student who flees to Canada to escape the draft. Granger was also the author of the plays *Scheherezade, The Dolphin Position,* and *Vivien,* and the screenplays *My Brother's Wife* and *The Comeback.* He was one of the creators of the daytime television soap opera *Loving,* and contributed to the soap *As the World Turns.*

Helene Hanff
April 15, 1916—April 9, 1997
American playwright, screenwriter, and author

Hanff was an unheard-of freelance author, writing for television shows like "Playhouse 90," "The Adventures of Ellery Queen," and "Hallmark Hall of Fame" before the release of her book *84, Charing Cross Road* in 1970. Called charming by reviewers, the book is actually an epistolary memoir containing letters written between Hanff, in New York City, and Marks & Co bookseller Frank Doel, in London. Hanff, self-taught and a voracious reader, started writing to the used bookstore in 1949 when she began her life-long quest as a book collector. Although the letters from Doel were originally very succinct and business-like, by the time Doel died, he and Hanff were fast friends, and Hanff had been invited to visit him in London several times. It wasn't until after Doel's death, when Hanff published *84, Charing Cross Road,* however, that she raised enough money to finally visit London. After her visit, where she met Doel's wife, she published *The Duchess of Bloomsbury Street.* Later books were *Underfoot in Show Business* and *Letter from New York.*

Charles Kuralt
September 10, 1934—September 4, 1997
American journalist and writer

The recipient of three Peabody Awards and twelve Emmys, Kuralt worked for CBS for thirty-seven years as a journalist. At twenty-five he became the youngest correspondent for CBS, covering the Vietnam War and reporting from many Latin American countries, as well as becoming the anchor on "CBS News Sunday Morning." He was the author of over a half dozen books, including *The Perfect Year* and *Dateline America,* but his real fame came from his "On the Road" reports written over a period of thirteen years, from 1967 to 1980. Traveling around the country in a motor home, Kuralt covered stories that other reporters found unimportant. He did pieces on the wonders of nature and everyday miracles like the sharecropper in Mississippi who managed somehow to put nine children through college. Kuralt inherited his love of travel, he said, from his father, who used to take him on his social work supervisory trips, telling him history tidbits about the areas through which they were passing to keep him entertained. In

1981 Kuralt received the George Polk Memorial Award, and in 1985 he was named the Broadcaster of the Year by the International Radio-Television Society.

Judith Merril
January 21, 1923—September 12, 1997
American science fiction writer

Merril was one of the first female writers to enter the science fiction genre. Known as a pioneer of feminist ideas, her first science fiction story, about a mother's devoted love for a child deformed by radiation, was published in 1948 in *Astounding Science Fiction* magazine. Along with Isaac Asimov, James Blish, C. M. Kornbluth, and Frederick Pohl, she was associated with a group of science fiction enthusiasts called the Futurians. She was the editor of several anthologies of the best science fiction stories, widening the horizons of what was accepted as science fiction by her choice of stories published outside the usual magazines. Her 1950 novel about nuclear war, *Shadow on the Hearth,* was made into the film *Atomic Attack.* She later donated her collection of science fiction books to the Toronto Public Library, forming the Merril Collection of Science Fiction, Speculation, and Fantasy, one of the largest research centers for science fiction in the world.

Ann Petry
October 12, 1908—April 28, 1997
American educator and writer

Petry was best known for her first novel, *The Street,* the first major literary novel about life in Harlem. Petry grew up in Old Saybrook, Connecticut, a member of one of the few black families in the area, and was only exposed to Harlem for a nine-month period in which she worked in a Harlem experimental after-school program. However, she was considered a woman of great empathy and imagination, and her book about Ludie Johnson and Ludie's eight-year-old son Bub became an instant success upon its release in 1946. She wrote two other novels—*Country Place,* 1947, and *The Narrows,* 1953— but neither received the acclaim of her first novel. Petry later wrote books for young adults and children, including *Tituba of Salem Village* and *Harriet Tubman: Conductor on the Underground Railroad.* After 1970 she limited herself to writing articles for college journals.

V. S. Pritchett
December 16, 1900—March 20, 1997
British author, reviewer, biographer, and journalist

Pritchett was a writer whose optimistic portrayals of everyday life gave him a career writing reviews and essays for the *Christian Science Monitor,* the *New Statesman,* and the *Nation,* as well as some forty books of short stories, essays, literary criticism, novels, biographies, and travelogues. Best known for his short stories, including "When My Girl Comes Home," "A Sense of Humor," "The Camberwell Beauty," and "The Fly in the Ointment," he was knighted in 1975 for his services to literature. Gore Vidal, the well-known American author, said of Pritchett, "I reviewed a book of his essays about twenty years ago. I said I thought it would be very nice for literature if he lived forever." In the first volume of his autobiography, *A Cab at the Door,* Pritchett describes his early childhood, punctuated by constant moves to escape his father's creditors. It was this, he relates, that led to his love of travel and to such books as *Dublin: A Portrait.* Pritchett was also known for his sensitive biographies, among them *Balzac, The Gentle Barbarian: The Life and Work of Turgenev,* and his most famous, *Chekhov: A Spirit Set Free.*

A. L. Rowse
December 4, 1903—October 3, 1997
British historian and writer

Rowse, the author of one hundred books of history, poetry, literary criticism, biography, and autobi-ography, was known as an expert on the Elizabethan Age. He was a fellow at All Souls College, Oxford, and in 1996 was made the Companion of Honor, a coveted royal honor bestowed for "con-spicuous national service." He is best known for his *The Elizabethan Age,* a four-volume set of books exploring Elizabethan history, that received nearly universal acclaim for being historically accurate and vividly written. He is also credited with discovering that the "Dark Lady" in Shakespearean sonnets was Emilia Bassano Lanier. His comment to London's *Daily Telegraph* about those who didn't believe his evidence in support of this discovery was, "You imagine the impudence of these people answering me back over the Dark Lady. If they haven't the sense to see that I am the greatest authority on the Elizabethan Age, then I've no objection to telling them." Famous for being acerbic and brutally honest, Rowse, in an interview with the London *Times* in 1983, summerized his reasons for studying British history in one sentence: "This country's past is infinitely more fascinating than its future."

Topic in Literature: 1997

Memoirs of Trauma

INTRODUCTION

Last year, a number of reviewers noted an increase in the publication of memoirs, particularly memoirs of crises or traumatic incidents in the lives of the authors. "True torment sells," Doreen Carvajal wrote. "In an anxious and flat sales environment, publishers are buying the real life memoirs of private men and women with names that would not sell an American Express card, but traumas that will get them a talk show slot." Several articles analyzing the trend and its import to readers, modern literature, and society were published recently, with some critics asserting that the rise in popularity of memoirs is akin to that of the voyeuristic appeal of tabloid talk shows and indicates a lowering of standards in modern publishing. Others welcomed the increase in memoir publishing, seeing it as a healthy way for writers to exorcise their demons that is neither voyeuristic nor damaging to the literary sensibilities of readers. There is one element of the debate over which there can be no argument: true-life drama sells. Memoirs are now a staple of best-seller lists, and the National Book Critics Circle is considering adding a separate category for memoir to its prestigious annual awards.

Critical reaction to the books themselves has been mixed, and at times contentious. Tobias Wolff and Jonathan Yardley, both well-known and respected authors and critics, engaged in a printed sparring match over Kathryn Harrison's *The Kiss,* the story of her four-year affair with her father which began when she was 20. In the book, perhaps the most controversial publication of the year, Harrison describes being unable to resist her father's advances, unable to wrench herself free of the psychological imprisonment that she learned later to understand. Wolff defended the author while castigating other critics, declaring, "The reviews of Kathryn Harrison's *The Kiss* are enough to make you think she had committed a crime in writing about her seduction by her father and the bitter sexual entanglement that followed." Wolff further contended that, in their negative reviews, Yardley and several other critics used Harrison "as a target of convenience for their animus against the genre she's working in— the memoir." Yardley responded with the assertion that *The Kiss,* regardless of its genre, is "an irredeemably rotten book." Noting that Harrison's published fictional works deal with much of the same subject matter, some accused her of telling the same story again, but this time calling it autobiography, to further her career. "It might be better if this woeful memoir had been a novel; its tone of hysterical self-obsession might pass as fiction," Martha Duffy proclaimed. "But Kathryn Harrison has already drawn on the theme of adult incest in her 1991 novel, *Thicker than Water,* to no great reverberance, so in *The Kiss* she tries the currently fashionable route of confession." For the shock it has elicited from critics and readers, *The Kiss* has been compared to Vladimir Nabokov's *Lolita,* the fictional story of a man's incestuous relationship with his stepdaughter. "But if her father is a Humbert," James Wolcott asserted, "his daughter is no Lolita. The shock revelation in *The Kiss*—and, presumably, its selling point—is that the father-daughter incest it recounts is not childhood exploitation, but a consensual act between two adults."

Critical opinion of Frank McCourt's *Angela's Ashes,* the Pulitzer Prize-winning story of the author's desperately poor childhood in Limerick, Ireland, was resoundingly favorable. The oldest child of Angela and Malachy McCourt, Frank recalls beginning his life in a New York slum, then moving to his parents' homeland where they hope to find a better life but instead become hopelessly mired in an even more grievous existence. As the family grows, Malachy's drinking worsens: during the few-and-far-between times when he holds a job, his paycheck ends up in the hands of the local barkeeps. Food is scarce and proper clothing, shoes, and bedding never enter the grim reality of the McCourt household. The house itself is an unheated rental next to the neighborhood latrine; when it rains the downstairs floods with rainwater and overflow from next door. Over everything hangs the poisonous pall of the River Shannon, feared as the source of the respiratory ailments which plague the residents of Limerick. Frank survives; one sister and two twin brothers do not. His survival is more than corporeal, however: critics describe *Angela's Ashes* as evidence that, despite the grim facts of his first nineteen years, McCourt retained love for his family, an exceptional storytelling ability, and an abiding wit. "McCourt relives [his] childhood with tenderness and, above all, humor," Trudy Bush observed.

While *Angela's Ashes* occupied one end of the critical spectrum and *The Kiss* held the other, many more memoirs drew the interest of critics and readers in 1997. Like *Angela's Ashes,* Agate Nesaule's *A Woman in Amber* and Rick Bragg's *All Over but the Shoutin'* also portray traumatic childhoods, hers in wartime and his in poverty. In *Autobiography of a Face,* Lucy Grealy allows readers a glimpse of life within a deformed body. Linda Katherine Cutting (*Memory Slips*), Gillian Helfgott (*Love You to Bits and Pieces*), and David Pelzer (*A Child Called 'It'*) relate stories of childhood abuse and its residual affects in adulthood.

With *Darkness Visible,* novelist William Styron exposes the impact of a depression that slowly enveloped his life. *My Mother's Keeper* (Tara Elgin Holley), *Imagining Robert* (Jay Neugeboren), and *Mad House* (Clea Simon) explore the challenges of living with a mentally ill relative. The short stories collected and edited by Laurie Stone (*Close to the Bone*) and Kathryn Rhett (*Survival Stories*) offer a variety of autobiographical sketches.

REPRESENTATIVE WORKS DISCUSSED BELOW

Bragg, Rick: *All Over but the Shoutin'* 1997
Cutting, Linda Katherine: *Memory Slips* 1997
Diski, Jenny: *Skating to Antarctica* 1998
Friedman, Sally: *Swimming the Channel* 1996
Grealy, Lucy: *Autobiography of a Face* 1994
Helfgott, Gillian (with Alissa Tanskaya): *Love You to Bits and Pieces* 1997
Holley, Tara Elgin: *My Mother's Keeper* 1997
Nesaule, Agate: *A Woman in Amber* 1995
Neugeboren, Jay: *Imagining Robert* 1997
Pelzer, Dave: *A Child Called 'It'* 1995
Rhett, Kathryn (editor): *Survival Stories* 1997
Simon, Clea: *Mad House* 1997
Stone, Laurie (editor): *Close to the Bone* 1997
Styron, William: *Darkness Visible* 1992

OVERVIEW

Doreen Carvajal (essay date 5 April 1997)

SOURCE: "Book Publishers Are Eager for Tales of True Torment," in *The New York Times,* April 5, 1997, pp. 1, 37.

[*In the following essay, Carvajal surveys the upswing in publication of memoirs in recent years and provides an overview of a number of titles.*]

The line is swelling for literary confession and Ira Silverberg is a somewhat reluctant confessor. His authors are freely spilling ink and intimacies, tales of brother-sister incest and cross-dressing seduction, and the travails of a man stalked by a scorned woman who demanded more vigorous beatings.

But he is feeling uneasy about one writer's proposed sequel to a harsh memoir of drug addiction. "I passed on his version of being a sexual compulsive," said Mr. Silverberg, the editor in chief of Grove Press, an imprint of Grove Atlantic. "It was lacking the depth of self-revelation that works."

True torment sells. In an anxious and flat sales environment, publishers are buying the real life memoirs of private men and women with names that would not sell an American Express card, but traumas that will get them a talk show slot.

A retired high school teacher's memoir of his impoverished Irish childhood is No. 1 on the New York Times best-seller list, and publishers are still recovering from a fierce bidding battle over rights to a Kansas grandmother's homespun book about Midwestern life and an alcoholic husband.

By the frantic fall season—prime time for bookstore traffic and publishing profits—the nation's publishers are preparing to release a torrent of confessionals that offer competing visions of anxiety. Rape, downsizing and disease. Depression and blue huckleberry jelly recipes. The "cellular memories" of a heart and lung transplant recipient who mysteriously developed her donor's zest for beer and fried chicken.

Anorexia is a particularly high-fashion literary theme; at least three young authors are reminiscing about self-imposed starvation with advances from several major publishing houses. Earlier last year, Disney's Hyperion purchased Lori Gottlieb's adolescent diary, "Stick Figure," for six figures amid sniping from rivals that the 11-year-old anorexic diarist seemed rather poised.

"My second book will be about me at age 30," said Ms. Gottlieb, who would not reveal more. "I don't know if I will continue to write about myself after that because I don't want to exploit it. At a certain point, people start to ask, what makes you so interesting?"

> **Lonely readers . . . are yearning for truth and the intimacy of reality literature, which has become so plentiful that the National Book Critics Circle is debating whether to create a separate award category for memoir.**
> **—*Doreen Carvajal***

If this all sounds like the print version of the television anxiety show circuit, some writers and publishers gamely credit the programs for creating a tolerant climate for revelations.

Lonely readers, they say, are yearning for truth and the intimacy of reality literature, which has become so plentiful that the National Book Critics Circle is debating whether to create a separate award category for memoir. In turn, publishers want to sign memoirists because they make the most effective salespeople. With the right mix of charm, insight and writing talent, a first-time author like Frank McCourt has been able to nurture his memoir, *Angela's Ashes,* from a modest printing of 27,500 to the top of the New York Times best-seller list.

So many confessionals are in the works that on Tuesday the Authors Guild will be host to a quintessential New York debate that poses the question "The Memoir Explosion: Novel of the 90's or Just Another Brand of Therapy?"

Come fall, readers will be able to plunge into the first person universe of a man growing up gay in the "aluminum sided wilds" of Little Falls, N.J., or a woman growing up gay in the strict, blue-collar, Roman Catholic atmosphere of an unnamed New England town. There are helpful recipes for kosher latkes—the inspiration for a writer's exploration of her Jewish heritage—and for jam as the antidote to Debby Bull's heart wreck in *Blue Jelly: Love Lost and the Lessons of Canning.* There are fill-in-the-blank memoirs (*The Book of Myself: A Do-it-Yourself Autobiography in 201 Questions*) with ample space for regrets and natural hair color.

Even the art book publisher Harry N. Abrams is offering an illustrated memoir, *Out of My Mind: An Autobiography* by Kristin Nelson Tinker, the former wife of the late singer Ricky Nelson. Among the paintings is a courtroom battle scene with her brother, the actor Mark Harmon, who sought custody of her youngest son after forcing her into drug rehabilitation.

In publishing, success creates imitators and many editors contend that the current wave of reality literature dates back to the publication of *The Liars' Club: A Memoir,* a 1995 best-selling tale of the poet Mary Karr's East Texas childhood and "terrific family of liars and drunks." Since then other confessionals have climbed the best-seller lists such as Caroline Knapp's *Drinking: A Love Story* and Kathryn Harrison's *The Kiss,* a raw account of her incestuous affair with her minister father.

Celebrities and chief executive officers once dominated the field, but partly because of high-priced flops there is more ample room in the genre for talented amateurs, seasoned novelists and poets accustomed to using "I".

"It seems to me that what's happened is that we're looking for some sort of moral compass," said Ms. Karr, who is at work on a sequel. "We're somewhat alienated and it's hard to know how well you're doing."

The new memoir writers actually have more in common with 18th-century Puritan writers, who were captured by Indians and survived to pen tales of adversity and triumph that were the first nonfiction best sellers in North America. Memoir writers chronicled slavery, the opening of the West and missionary quests. But what's unique about the new wave is psy-

chological introspection, according to Patricia Willis, curator of the Yale Collection of American Literature.

Authors still write about adversity and triumph, but the themes are family traumas, compulsion and identity. The advances are also more generous. Jesse Lee Brown Foveaux, the Kansas grandmother, sold her bittersweet memoir to Warner Books for more than $1 million despite grumbling that the most interesting passages explored laundering techniques.

The contemporary genre can be divided into two categories, victim stories and shame narratives, according to Laurie Stone, the editor of an anthology of memories, called *Close to the Bone,* which will be published by Grove Press in the fall. What matters, she said, is the degree of insight and drama: "The whole point is not just to flash perversity, but that the writer has a story to tell, that they are using the self as a sort of lab rat."

The hunger for insight is evident at the bookstore appearances of Mr. McCourt, who took almost three decades to write the first volume of his life, *Angela's Ashes,* and is now at work on a sequel. A crowd of 400 gathered recently among the book-stacks at Borders in San Francisco to listen to Mr. McCourt reminisce about growing up in Limerick, Ireland. ("Worse than the ordinary miserable Irish childhood is the miserable Irish childhood, and worse yet is the miserable Irish Catholic childhood.")

Mr. McCourt, 66, said he had struggled to write a novel, but "my own life kept intruding into my miserable little fiction." He went on: "It was stronger in the long run. I was trying to create a story about growing up in the slum in Limerick and the characters were already there. I was hanging fantasy on them and it just didn't work. The voices were false."

Truth is the muse most often cited by new-wave memoirists who feel no particular need to hide behind fiction or even to warn their real-life characters about literary exposure. Yet the subjective use of memory does raise issues about authenticity.

"There's always a question of verity involved and I'm not casting any aspersions," said Art Winslow, the president of the National Book Critics Circle. "In the first-person memoir, you only have other members of a person's nuclear family with the authority to say, yes this is true or no it is not. It's in their interest to have dramatic tension in the work. There's a danger that could be exaggerated."

Elaine Marr, 30, is a poet and a first-time author who signed with HarperCollins to publish *Paper Daughter,* an account of her Denver childhood that explores her anorexia and suicidal tendencies along with a failed romantic relationship and her ambivalence about her Chinese-American heritage. She said the revelations would probably not have much of an impact on her parents because they did not speak English.

"We talked about changing names and using pseudonyms, but unless HarperCollins says this is a concern, I am not going to do it," she said. "I just want to be honest. When you write a novel, even thinly disguised, people know what you're doing. The process of standing up and talking about who you are is a little like coming out sexually."

Still, brutal candor troubles writers like Mr. McCourt, who contends that certain secrets should remain protected until family members are dead. He has reservations about the recent work of Kathryn Harrison, a seasoned novelist who turned to the memoir for the first time with the account of an affair with her father that began when she was 20.

"I thought she should have waited till he was dead, and even then I balk at the idea, especially if the person is vulnerable," Mr. McCourt said. "In some ways, there's a feeling of a subconscious vendetta and it makes me queasy."

Mrs. Harrison does not name her father in her memoir. And as a condition of interviews, she asks that no attempt be made to reach him.

"I went to a great deal of trouble to strip away any indicator; I didn't want to expose him," said Mrs. Harrison, who added that as a writer she felt a "great compulsion" to confess. "I wanted to show the workings of the relationship, to really vivisect myself."

Like Mr. McCourt, she is also at work on a sequel, a story of her grandmother, a dominant force in her family.

The sequel will be "kind of a hybrid; the memoir aspect will be the first 30 years of my life," Mrs. Harrison said. "She is the woman who raised me, of which I know early pieces, and I will have to reconstruct or invade her life."

Her first memoir offers a few early hints of the character to come. Her description sketches her grandmother's talent for screaming—"the shriek of a scalded infant, the cry of a young woman raped in the woods, the long howl of the werewolf who catches her scent, who finds and devours what's left of her."

Tobias Wolff (essay date 6 April 1997)

SOURCE: "Literary Conceits," in *The New York Times,* April 6, 1997, sec. 4, p. 19.

[*In the following essay, Wolff defends memoirists as undeserving of the harsh criticism that they often receive from reviewers.*]

The reviews of Kathryn Harrison's *The Kiss* are enough to make you think she had committed a crime in writing about her seduction by her father and the bitter sexual entanglement that followed. Michael Shnayerson suggests in *Vanity Fair* that her motive in telling her story was not, as she herself says, a matter of personal and artistic necessity, but a squalid grab for publicity and sales. The *Washington Post*'s Jonathan Yardley dismisses the entire book as "trash . . . not an artful word in it"—contrived "for personal gain and talk show notoriety."

James Wolcott, in *The New Republic,* brings the author up on charges of being not only a hack, but also a mercenary opportunist, a liar and a bad mother, a *wicked* mother, whose autobiographical writings "constitute a narcissistic act on Harrison's part intended to invite misery and humiliation upon her children, especially the daughter, as misery was visited upon her."

I've never met Kathryn Harrison, but I have read her book, thought it remarkably courageous and well-told and have been happy to recommend it. Certainly there's nothing in it to explain the rage "visited upon her" by these critics.

The truth is that they are using her as a target of convenience for their animus against the genre she's working in—the memoir. All of them preface their attacks on her with expressions of suspicion or downright contempt for the personal writings that have recently found favor with readers. They want to be seen as bucking the trend, when of course they could not be more au courant, for it is now entirely the fashion with our self-deputized Border Patrol to mew in dismay at the wistful appearance of any new memoir at the gate of Literature.

Are these books so bad? From my own fairly extensive reading in the field, I'd say this: Some are indeed dreadful; most are mediocre; a few are good; a very few are superb. In other words, they correspond in quality to the new novels I read, and the new stories, and poems. Robert Frost is supposed to have said that there haven't been 500 poets in the world since Homer. We could probably make a case for opening up a few more positions, but the fact remains that at any given time there isn't a whole lot of work out there of the first order, and the contemporary work we do praise in those terms will, if past is portent, mostly pass into oblivion.

That holds true for every genre and form. The novelist, the historian, the poet and the memoirist all labor under the virtual certainly of being forgotten, yet all share equally in the hope of escaping that fate with a book like *A Good Man Is*

Hard to Find or *The Oregon Trail* or *Life Studies* or *Memories of a Catholic Girlhood.*

A memoir is not bad because it is a memoir, but because it is a bad memoir. Of course it's true that many autobiographical writers have made ruthless use of their histories, exploited those who trusted them, betrayed intimacies, displayed their wounds in the marketplace. Robert Graves was accused of doing exactly those things when *Goodbye to All That* was published.

But when I came to write my own account of wartime service I was guided more by his memoir of World War I than by any of the Vietnam histories I'd been reading to put myself back in the picture. Though we were very different, his trials much harsher than mine and his record infinitely more distinguished, I learned from him. He did not impose global understandings and sympathies on the rather narrowminded young man he was then, whose area of greatest concern was, after all, the patch of ruined ground just in front of his trench; he treated his younger incarnation with neither condescension nor flattery, but with an objectivity that didn't flinch from revealing the juvenile priggishness, sexual confusion and self-importance to which he was subject, or the courage of which he was capable.

Without false apologies or exhibitions of right-mindedness he made me feel something of what it was like for one particular person to be drawn into that war, submit to its logic, then reject it utterly while somehow continuing to fight. I wanted to know how a man of flesh and blood, not of fiction, made sense of what had been done to him, and of what he had done. It is this sort of curiosity that draws people to memoirs, and it is a legitimate curiosity.

"To have written an autobiography," William Gass wrote in *Harper's* magazine three years ago, "is already to have made yourself a monster." His point was that the autobiographer is bound to puff himself up, to lie, to take revenge, to hide the greater sin by confessing the lesser, to crown herself with a halo. If this is true, it is no more true of memoirists than of other writers. What is the novelist's sentimentality (whether expressed in desperate cheer or easy cynicism) but a lie of the heart, and the conceit that nobody else is smart enough to see through it? Do poets not take revenge? Read your Catullus. As for halos, isn't Mr. Gass wearing one here?

Writers of all kinds are prone to self-idealization. But the best memoirists have an astonishing capacity for seeing themselves in the round, fully implicated in the fallen creation of which they write. Think of George Orwell's "Shooting an Elephant." There's no conceit here, no halo, no getting even with an unkind world, only the absurd helplessness of a man taken prisoner by his own spurious authority.

We see the same honesty at work in Susanna Kaysen's description of going to an ice cream parlor with her fellow lunatics in *Girl, Interrupted,* Frank Conroy's obsession with the yo-yo in *Stop Time,* Mary McCarthy's account in *Memories of a Catholic Girlhood* of how, by pretending to lose her faith, she *actually* lost her faith, Mary Karr deviling her legless grandmother in *The Liar's Club.*

We demand this sort of personal reckoning from the memoirist, and then we demand everything else: a sense of story, formal mastery, moral consciousness, the gift of bringing others to life in words, music. Auden said it all:

> Time that is intolerant
> Of the brave and innocent
> And indifferent in a week
> To a beautiful physique,
> Worships language and forgives
> Everyone by whom it lives.

Even memoirists.

Jonathan Yardley (essay date 14 April 1997)

SOURCE: "Thanks for the Memoirists," in *The Washington Post,* April 14, 1997, p. D2.

[*In the following essay, Yardley rebuts Tobias Wolff's defense of memoirists, particularly Kathryn Harrison, asserting that he objects to Harrison's* The Kiss *not because it is a memoir but because it is "an irredeemably rotten book."*]

Apologies at the outset on two counts: (a) for raising once again the subject of that odious book *The Kiss* and (b) for doing so with frequent use of the first person singular. Neither is to my taste, but like the maiden in an ancient two-reeler, I find myself called upon to defend my virtue—such of it as may still remain—and must do so under those conditions.

This arises because last week the novelist, memoirist and writing-school guru Tobias Wolff was granted a prestigious position on the op-ed page of the *New York Times* to defend Kathryn Harrison, author of *The Kiss,* and to attack those who have taken exception to that book. Yours truly is high on Wolff's list of malefactors. Along with Michael Schnayerson, writing in *Vanity Fair,* and James Wolcott, in the *New Republic,* I am accused by Wolff of inflicting "rage" upon Harrison. This leads him to a spectacular exercise in mind-reading and sweeping generalization:

> "The truth is that they are using [Harrison] as a target of convenience for their animus against the

genre she's working in—the memoir. All of them preface their attacks on her with expressions of suspicion or downright contempt for the personal writings that have recently found favor with readers. They want to be seen as bucking the trend, when of course they could not be more au courant, for it is now entirely the fashion with our self-deputized Border Patrol to mew in dismay at the wistful appearance of any new memoir at the gate of literature."

What, pray tell, has that man been smoking? Speaking only for myself, I can say with absolute confidence that not a single word in that paragraph is true. I have anything except "animus" against the memoir. I made no statement "of suspicion or downright contempt" for—I love this smarmy, oleaginous phrase—"the personal writings that have recently found favor with readers"; I said only that Harrison was "exploiting the current infatuation with confessional memoirs." I have no interest in running with any crowd, whether it be the fashionable memoirists whose cause Wolff embraces or some hobgoblin "Border Patrol" that he has invented.

Wolff is certainly entitled to know little or nothing about my opinions or published work, but if he is going to put thoughts in my head and words in my mouth, he has an obligation to those who publish and read him to be accurate. Had he bothered to make even the most cursory of inquiries, he would have found that not merely am I tolerant of, indeed receptive to, memoirs, I flat-out love them.

How else is one to explain two rather important aspects of my 3 1/2-decade writing career, if anything about it can be said to have any importance? The first is that of the five books I have written, the one of which I am proudest is a combination of family history, biography and personal memoir the subjects of which are my own parents. The second is that the fifth of these books, to be published later this year, is a biography of a writer whose main claim upon our attention is the "fictional memoir" he published three decades ago, a book that, I argue, is one of the monuments of postwar American literature.

How, precisely, could someone laboring under an "animus" against memoirs stand to expend so much time and effort on undertakings such as these? How, for that matter, could that same person have called Mary Karr's *The Liar's Club*—a book, FYI, extravagantly blurbed by Tobias Wolff—"a work of genuine originality and merit," one that, along with others of similar quality, suggests "the memoir may well be our most important literary form by the turn of the millennium"? Indeed, how could I somehow have managed to have cast forth, within the past year, favorable reviews of memoirs by so disparate a bunch as Gore Vidal, Neil Simon, Peter O'Toole, Jeffrey Simpson,

Marrie Walsh, Walter Bernstein, Claire Bloom and Jan Wong?

Ah, Wolff doubtless would say—yes, I am putting thoughts in his head and words in his mouth—many of those are conventional memoirs by conventional memoirists, i.e., people of some years whose lives arouse a measure of gossipy curiosity. By contrast, the memoirists whom Wolff defends are younger and relatively, in many cases totally, unknown. These people, he says, bring "personal reckoning" to their memoirs, and "everything else: a sense of story, formal mastery, moral consciousness, the gift of bringing others to life in words, music."

Them's pretty words, all right, but anyone who thinks that any of the above is to be found in *The Kiss* is either a fool or utterly devoid of literary taste. The truth, as opposed to Wolff's self-serving fantasy, is that my objections to *The Kiss* have absolutely nothing to do with its being a memoir per se, or even with its being one of those "personal writings that have recently found favor with readers." My objections are based entirely and exclusively in the simple, inescapable reality that *The Kiss* is an irredeemably rotten book. Per se.

Precisely why Wolff cannot understand this distinction is for him to explain. Whatever the reason for it, Wolff's failure to comprehend the difference between disliking a specific memoir and disliking memoirs generally is of a piece with the sentiments expressed by a recent contributor to the letters columns of this newspaper, who complained that my review of *The Kiss* was irresponsible because I failed to express disapproval of incest, the ostensible subject of *The Kiss*.

These folks just don't get it. The job of a reviewer is to pass judgment on specific books, not to issue blanket endorsements of literary genres or to indulge in psychotherapy. Just because I think *The Kiss* is meretricious trash doesn't mean that I think all memoirs are meretricious trash; the same line of reasoning would lead one to conclude that since I think Alexandra Ripley's novel *Scarlett* is, well, meretricious trash, obviously I think all novels are, uh, meretricious trash.

The self-evident truth is that among legitimate literary genres, there's no such thing as a "bad" one. There are only bad books, or, more frequently, mediocre books. Some books are better than others; it is a lamentable but inescapable fact of the lit'ry life. Eight years ago, reviewing a memoir called *This Boy's Life*, by Tobias Wolff, I called it "modest and charming and exact," but said it "cannot escape comparison" with *The Duke of Deception*, by his brother Geoffrey. The latter memoir, I said, "is the darker, deeper and—yes—funnier of the two."

That was my judgment in 1989; I stand by it today. But as

is the case with my judgment of *The Kiss,* it has everything to do with the merits of the books in question, nothing to do with some "animus" against memoirs.

Bob Minzesheimer (essay date 16 April 1997)

SOURCE: "Suddenly, Family Stories Are Selling Like Pulp Fiction," in *USA Today,* April 16, 1997.

[*In the following essay, Minzesheimer comments on the trend toward memoir writing and discusses both public and critical response to books including Frank McCourt's* Angela's Ashes *and Kathryn Harrison's* The Kiss.]

If Angela McCourt were still alive, her son Frank says, he couldn't have published *Angela's Ashes,* the memoir of childhood squalor that won him a Pulitzer Prize last week.

"My mother wouldn't have liked the book," McCourt says. "It was too revealing. She was ashamed of our past. Now we're ashamed of being ashamed."

Kathryn Harrison's father is still alive. But when she's asked about her memoir, *The Kiss,* about father-daughter incest, she replies, "All's fair in love and war." She pauses. "Or nothing is fair."

Both books are best sellers, leading a burst of first-person writing that's turning the phrase "a memoir" into publishing's favorite subtitle. *Angela's Ashes* has been on *USA TODAY*'s best seller list for 20 weeks—this week as the top hardcover and No. 2 overall.

Nothing is more popular than "memoirs of crisis." Publishers, like TV talk shows, are learning that agony sells, especially when touted as a true story.

"Books that once would have been written as novels are now written as memoirs," says Villard publisher David Rosenthal. "Things that once were taboo aren't anymore. We talk about our sex lives, we talk about our addictions. It's like one big 12-step meeting out there. 'Hi, my name is David and I wrote a memoir.'"

For those who take books as seriously as life itself, that's prompting questions. Is the memoir the novel of the '90s, a newly dominant and more authentic literary form? Or is it merely a marketing fad, a literature of solipsism by writers obsessed with themselves, exploiting family dysfunction to sell books? Has it become quaintly Victorian to suggest that some family secrets—say, incest—should stay secret?

Either way, says J. Anthony Lukas, historian and Authors Guild president, the conventional wisdom that only novelists "touched by heavenly fire could transmute the prosaic stuff of life into art" is dead.

Not that memoirs are new. Long before recovery programs, St. Augustine wrote his *Confessions.* Memoirist Kathryn Rhett turns to the Old Testament to ask, "What was the Book of Job but a memoir of crisis?" She has edited an anthology, out in August, called *Survival Stories: Memoirs of Crisis.*

Celebrity autobiographies have long had their niche in bookstores. But never have so many memoirs, often by unknown writers sharing impressions of a slice of their lives, been published and aggressively marketed.

The book world is still buzzing about last month's bidding war over the private memoirs of a great-grandmother in Manhattan, Kan., with an alcoholic husband. At 98, Jessie Lee Brown Foveaux signed her first book contract—for $1 million—with Warner Books.

Editor Clair Zion calls Foveaux's tale an "emotionally powerful story" of an everyday heroine. "We in New York try to sit here and think what the country is thinking. This is Kansas talking."

Memoirs to come include Claire Sylvia on surviving a heart transplant, David Gelernter on surviving the Unabomber and Julia Sweeney on surviving cancer.

Novelist Thomas Mallon, author of *Dewey Defeats Truman,* quips that he enjoyed "a happy childhood so damaging to a writer," and decries "the 20th century disease"—the view that "negative experiences are more authentic than positive ones."

While acknowledging "some wonderful memoirs," he says novels can be about "a big truth," but memoirs are about an "individual truth."

Frank Conroy, director of the University of Iowa Writers' Workshop and author of the classic adolescent memoir *Stop-Time,* says memoirs that work as literature go beyond individual situations and are "about the world. . . . The 'I' is merely a trick, a device."

The recent memoir rush began in 1995 with the critical and commercial success of *The Liars' Club,* poet Mary Karr's wickedly funny account of her East Texas childhood with a "terrific family of liars and drunks."

Karr's editor at Penguin, Courtney Hodell, credits Karr's writing and "message of redemption," and says memoirs capture the "chaos of ordinary life, not as plotted as novels. . . . It's exciting and reassuring to read about real lives."

Fritz McDonald, who's teaching a summer workshop in memoir-writing at Iowa, says memoirs are "more accessible and less daunting than fiction. Go into a bookstore and look at the blurbs on novels: Highfalutin' literary terms like, 'Has a wonderful sense of observation.' Memoirs say, 'Here's a story you can relate to.' There's a huge appetite for looking at other people's lives. It's what drives half of TV."

Justin Cronin, who teaches writing at La Salle College in Philadelphia, adds: "We live in a very confessional culture. We're saturated by the most embarrassing admissions, shouted from the town square, which has as much to do with TV as publishing."

Rhett, whose memoir *Near Breathing,* about her newborn daughter's brush with death, comes out next month, disagrees. Talk-show confessions, she says, put "a great distance between who's watching and who's watched. A good memoir draws readers into another world. . . . The appeal is not in the subject but in its articulation."

Still, Cronin says, memoirs can "blur the distinction between what's really happening and what's constructed. . . . A memoir is not a record. It's a memory. And what's the difference between memory and imagination? That's pretty slippery territory."

McCourt, a 66-year-old retired New York high school teacher, tried and failed to write a novel about the misery of his Irish childhood during what he calls "my James Joyce period. All the characters were too dramatic, too traumatic. It was awful."

In writing a memoir, he says, "I found my voice," but struggled over whether to include the scene where his desperate mother had sex with her cousin to help keep a roof over her family's head. He thought of cutting it, but he says his brother, actor Malachy McCourt, convinced him it was "a turning point."

Angela's Ashes has been praised by critics from *Entertainment Weekly* to *The New Yorker.* But Harrison's stark account of consensual incest that started when she was 20 triggered a war of words. "Harrison's book was not treated like a book at all," says *New York Observer* columnist Anne Roiphe, "but rather like an alarming social faux pas."

Harrison's first novel, *Thicker Than Water,* which did better among critics than among book buyers in 1991, was about a woman having an affair with her father. But Harrison, 36, says that character was "younger, more passive, sweeter and more of a victim than I." It was a book "I wanted to dis-

own. I betrayed my own history." She wrote *The Kiss,* she says, "not to expose my father," who's never mentioned by name, but "to face up to myself."

And while others debate what it all means, the memoirists keep writing. McCourt, Harrison and Karr all are working on sequels.

Suzanne Moore (essay date 15 August 1997)

SOURCE: "How Was It for Me?," in *New Statesman,* August 15, 1997, pp. 44-5.

[*Below, Moore expresses apprehension over the current popularity of memoir-writing but concludes, "Despite the excesses, I still feel that this has been a good thing, because those who resent it most are usually the most powerful." She also remarks on three publications, Sally Friedman's* Swimming the Channel, *Kathryn Harrison's* The Kiss, *and Jenny Diski's* Skating to Antarctica.]

The subject that obsesses us at the end of this long century is subjectivity itself. "How was it for me?" we continually ask ourselves. Such navel-gazing could be attributed to the fragmentation of modern life, the end of ideology, the collapse of the grand narratives or any postmodern, premillennial panic that you care to theorise. We cannot know or be certain of anything outside ourselves; it is all just too confusing. As the grand narratives shatter into millions of smaller ones, all crying "me, me, me", myriad voices whisper: "I may not be a novelist but I know what I'm like."

This belief in the subject as the only viable subject, the self as both author and authored, is not a purely literary phenomenon. Television likes authored documentaries in which quirky presenters give their entirely personal views. The art world likes self-revelatory bad girls such as Tracy Emin and Sam Taylor Wood; newspapers are brimming with the "new solipsists" who write of nothing but themselves, or just of nothing; music loves its self-made stars such as Liam Gallagher, who acted like a pop star long before he ever was one. We are in thrall to "attitude," whatever that means.

It is possible to read all this as incredibly liberating, allowing a plurality of voices that have not been heard before. Or it is possible to see it as the symptom of a supreme crisis of confidence in which no one can speak for anyone outside themselves, in which everyone emotes but no one thinks any more.

The memoir is hardly a new form, but at the moment it seems as though everyone who has had any experience of anything from cutting their toenails to giving birth feels compelled to write one. There is an element of undergoing therapy in public in much of what is published. These are the true self-help books. In the age of Oprah we know that speaking up, spitting it out, will help us "come to terms" with our pasts. But there is also the voyeuristic thrill of watching others who not only wash their dirty linen in public but also point out filthy stains of particular interest. A psycho-babbling culture, combined with media intrusion, has made a mockery of the old divide between private and public.

Despite the excesses, I still feel that this has been a good thing, because those who resent it most are usually the most powerful—and power rests, as we know, on a ruthless separation of the personal from the political. Whether this always makes for good writing is another issue. I have read too many dire feminist novels involving incest or eating disorders in my time and I think that much of this stuff would be better left unpublished. Writing it down may well do the author good but inflicting it upon others is an act of sadism by committed masochists. Anyway, these days the people making money out of rewriting their pasts are the boys, who just seem so much jollier than we do, perhaps because they get a round of applause for merely admitting that they have emotions at all.

So I wasn't overjoyed at the prospect of reading a bunch of memoirs by women. Sally Friedman's *Swimming the Channel* is subtitled "a memoir of love and loss." What memoir isn't about these things, one wonders? Friedman is an obsessive long-distance swimmer, a bit of a loner who falls head over heels in love with Paul and marries him. He encourages her to swim the Channel but is killed a few days before they are due to make the trip. This is a book about the two loves of her life, swimming and her late husband, and I suppose eventually it is about grieving and that horrible word "healing." It is as brave, honest and painful as these things are meant to be, but for me strangely unmoving, probably because I share neither of her obsessions—swimming or her husband. That may seem unkindly subjective, but the thing about the laying bare of personal pain is that you have to like or want to connect with the person displaying their life before you.

This was also part of my difficulty with Kathryn Harrison's book *The Kiss,* which is an easier book to admire than to like. It is the beautifully written tale of the affair Harrison had with her father when she was 20. Never feeling good enough for her narcissistic mother, she ends up seduced by her monstrous father. With chilling intensity she describes how the destruction of his internal barriers destroyed hers, and how the affair was a way of trying to penetrate her mother by using her father. In the jargon Harrison is the victim, yet there is something about this memoir that suggests a need to exonerate herself. Is she not culpable? Does an unhappy childhood or even the obvious psychoanalytic in-

terpretation excuse what she has done? Does the quality of her writing cover up the narcissism she has inherited from both parents?

Jenny Diski's *Skating to Antarctica* shows precisely what can be done with the form in the hands of a writer who is more interested in the world than in herself. Exploring her genuinely horrific childhood and the strangeness of Antarctica, Diski, an immensely cool writer, unravels both with superb understatement. Her seeking of oblivion, a denial of self, means that she has the writerly ability to distance herself from her own pain so that even in her darkest hours she can be wry. If for a true solipsist others exist only as an idea, Diski is no such creature. In writing about herself she is writing of many other lives, too. She trusts neither experience nor memory to reveal the whole truth. As she says: "There are infinite ways of telling the truth, including fiction. There are infinite ways of evading the truth, including non-fiction."

In between the mountains of self-obsession and self-deception that pass for heavily marketed "honesty" these days, that finally might be as much as we can ever know about ourselves, or anyone else for that matter.

Michiko Kakutani (essay date 21 October 1997)

SOURCE: "Woe Is Me: Rewards and Perils of Memoirs," in *The New York Times,* October 21, 1997, p. E8.

[*In the following essay, Kakutani remarks on the process of memoir-writing, asserting that "the current memoir craze . . . has encouraged the delusion that candor, daring and shamelessness are substitutes for craft, that the exposed life is the same thing as an examined one," and analyzes two collections: Laurie Stone's* Close to the Bone *and Kathryn Rhett's* Survival Stories.]

In her 1995 memoir *Dreaming,* Carolyn See described her father and stepmother's participation in Alcoholics Anonymous meetings: "Those people in A.A. in the late 40's and early 50's can be said to have reinvented American narrative style," she wrote. "All the terrible, terrible things that had ever happened to them just made for a great pitch."

Although the last few years have witnessed the publication of memoirs like Mary Karr's *Liars' Club* and André Aciman's *Out of Egypt,* which are masterpieces of the genre, it has also witnessed a flood of self-pitying, exhibitionistic and poorly written pitches that belong on afternoon television, not between the covers of a book. The current memoir craze has fostered the belief that confession is therapeutic, that therapy is redemptive and that redemption equals art, and it has encouraged the delusion that candor, daring and shamelessness are substitutes for craft, that the exposed life is the same thing as an examined one.

Both the perils and rewards of memoir writing are on display in two new anthologies: *Close to the Bone,* edited by Laurie Stone, and *Survival Stories,* edited by Kathryn Rhett. The big problem with these books stems from their self-important subtitles (respectively, "Memoirs of Hurt, Rage and Desire" and "Memoirs of Crisis"), subtitles that suggest a kind of literary ambulance-chasing, a "Hard Copy" set of mind. What you're getting with these books, the subtitles suggest, are stories about people in extremis, people who have suffered horrific violations, committed awful crimes or survived terrible odds.

"For *Close to the Bone,* I solicited writers energized by the new wave of candor and willing to cut as deep," Ms. Stone writes in her introduction. "As far as specific subject matter was concerned, I didn't want to be prescriptive. Everyone's pornography is their own. At the same time, I was looking for material relatively unexplored in literature." That material includes a girl's incestuous longings for her brother ("Brother," by Jane Creighton), a boy's sexual violation by his mother's boyfriend ("Baby Doll," by Terminator) and a middle-class drug addict's flirtation with inner-city crack dealers ("Pipe to the Head," by Jerry Stahl). Though each of these narratives is written in the first person, they all have the faintly stylized feel of fiction; indeed in another age—even five years ago, say—such works would have probably been published as short stories.

Close to the Bone also includes more conventionally written memoirs: Lois Gould's wistful but unsentimental portrait of her absent father ("Businessman"): Phillip Lopate's meticulously detailed meditation on his father's life ("The Story of My Father") and Catherine Texier's moving account of her 40-odd years searching for her absent father ("My Father's Picture"). These three contributions could each stand alone as small, finely hammered examples of the autobiographical essayist's art. For that matter, *Close to the Bone* as a whole turns out to be a far more substantial collection than its melodramatic title suggests: engaging, often powerful writing is its common denominator, not therapeutic or shock-the-reader revelations, as its publisher would have us believe.

The same, unfortunately, cannot be said of *Survival Stories,* a decidedly more uneven volume that conflates literature and therapy, genuine tragedy and self-dramatizing shame. In this volume, Ms. Rhett plucks excerpts from books by writers like William Styron and Jamaica Kincaid, pulling her selections out of context to italicize already extreme emotions. She lumps stories about cancer and physical disfigurement together with stories about adultery and divorce, and she uniformly refers to her contributors—even those who simply worked at a blue-collar job or confessed to an illicit affair—as "survivors," a term once reserved for people who lived through wars or famines or the Holocaust.

Although there are some affecting, beautifully written pieces in *Survival Stories*—most notably Rick Moody's impressionistic portrait of his late sister and Frances Mayes's fiercely observed account of her Gothic childhood in Georgia—all too many of the entries reflect the collection's therapeutic ethos. Ms. Rhett writes in her introduction that the book grew out of a workshop she taught at the Iowa Summer Writing Festival on the "memoir of crisis," and out of her own wish that "there were a section in bookstores for memoirs about bad times."

"You had to search through biography in most stores," she writes, "and then sometimes under subjects; the unhealthy baby stories, for example, were mixed in with all the parenting and baby-care books. My reading desires were not restricted by subject—I wanted to read about people at jarring moments in their lives, and cared more about quality of thought and writing than about topic." Reading other people's "crisis memoirs," Ms. Rhett writes, helped her cope with the difficult birth of her own daughter and made her feel "befriended."

No doubt writing can serve a therapeutic, even cathartic function. No doubt first-person accounts of living with cancer, losing a child or coming to terms with sexual abuse can provide solace to readers coping with similar problems. To go further, as Ms. Rhett does, however, and suggest that "the crisis memoir" is a form of literature, that it has a distinctive esthetic, is to succumb to sentimental pretension. In fact, for all Ms. Rhett's protestations that crisis memoirs do not resemble talk shows or support groups in "purpose, method and effect" many selections in this volume sound uncannily like stories recounted on Oprah and Geraldo.

Floyd Skloot writes about chronic fatigue syndrome in terms of balancing "the quest for understanding my illness with the quest to lead a rich life despite my illnesses' inexorable presence." Nancy Mairs talks about her husband's adultery in terms of her work of "reclaiming human experience, insofar as I can find it embodied in my own experience, from the morass of secrecy and shame into which Christian and pre-Christian social taboos have plunged it." And Laura Philpot Benedict speaks about overcoming the guilt she felt over an adulterous affair by going into therapy and beginning "a process of self-discovery" that she has "cultivated and developed continuously since."

By lumping such shapeless, psychobabble-filled pieces together with the polished works of writers like Rick Moody and William Styron, Ms. Rhett does a disservice to the reader. She suggests, absurdly, that you do not need craft or artistry to become a writer: you need only a crisis. In doing so, she assumes that the memoir and the pitch are one.

CRITICISM

Karl Miller (review date 21 March 1991)

SOURCE: "Literary Supplements," in *London Review of Books,* March 21, 1991, pp. 6-7.

[*In the following excerpt, Miller discusses William Styron's memoir,* Darkness Visible, *finding that it makes clear many truths of the author that have been alluded to in his novels. Miller remarks: "His novels, with their stress on suicide and gloom, could be said to find their afterword in the memoir."*]

The American novelist William Styron has written a short book which describes how he came to grief at around the age of sixty, falling into a depression which nearly cost him his life. He felt, in romantic-confessional style, that he had to write it, and it is good to have it. I hope that it is not a disorder of the liberal conscience to suppose that the voices of those who have been through spells or seasons of mental trouble can now, with or without the sponsorship of romance, be heard with respect if they choose to write down what happened to them. Styron's account has several interesting features. His father had suffered from the same illness, and he lost his mother when he was 13. Throughout his life he had been dependent on alcohol, to which he here pays startling tribute: 'I did use it—often in conjunction with music—as a means to let my mind conceive visions that the unaltered, sober brain has no access to. Alcohol was an invaluable senior partner of my intellect, besides being a friend whose ministrations I sought daily—sought also, I now see, as a means to calm the anxiety and incipient dread that I had hidden away for so long somewhere in the dungeons of my spirit.' Then quite suddenly he took a dislike to drink, and this threw him into a downward spiral, which was to be violently assisted by a psychiatrist's overprescription of the drug Halcion. Worries about his work—worries to which it is courageous of him to refer—made things worse, or were there at the start of his depression: part of the trouble could be termed writer's block writ hideously large. Last, but perhaps not least, he was brought round by being removed from his domestic surroundings, and from that lavish psychiatrist of his, and being placed in the seclusion of a hospital. Electro-convulsive therapy may have been mooted, but was avoided.

Darkness Visible has many vivid moments (one of which is Milton's). Two depressive onsets in particular lodge in the mind. On one occasion he is being awarded a prize in Paris. The ceremony is over, and he is counted on for lunch with the prize-giver's queenly widow and members of the Académie Française, at which point he tells this woman that he has to have lunch with his publisher. '*Alors*!' exclaims the queen as she turns her back on the author of *Lie Down in Darkness: 'Au revoir*!' This yields the black humour of certain depressive illnesses, whose lightnings have a tendency to strike at literary parties. On another occasion he was seized with dread in a place where he had always felt at home: 'One bright day on a walk through the woods with my dog I heard a flock of Canada geese honking high above trees ablaze with foliage; ordinarily a sight and sound that would have exhilarated me, the flight of birds caused me to stop, riveted with fear. . . .'

There are passages in the book which might have been written in the 19th century—some of them, give or take a word or two, by Poe: 'It may be more accurate to say that despair, owing to some evil trick played upon the sick brain by the inhabiting psyche, comes to resemble the diabolical discomfort of being imprisoned in a fiercely overheated room. And because no breeze stirs this cauldron, because there is no escape from this smothering confinement, it is entirely natural that the victim begins to think ceaselessly of oblivion.' Styron write of the 'dungeons' of his 'spirit', of a 'long-beshrouded metaphysical truth'—language that belongs to the Gothic strain of certain of his fictions. To make remarks about the sometimes laboured and allusive style of the book feels like complaining in some pursed way of the 'more's' and the 'lessnesses' in the desolation-commemorating passage: 'I had suffered more and more from a general feeling of worthlessness as the malady had progressed. My dank joylessness was therefore all the more ironic because. . . .' But to do so can hardly be beside the point; the book runs the risk of such objections, in the course of producing a style for the malady it recalls. This is a highly literary text, which is charged with references to other people's literary texts. The very name of his treacherous drug, Halcion, takes effect as an ironic allusion to the literary past. His novels, with their stress on suicide and gloom, could be said to find their afterword in the memoir, and the memoir abounds with references to other writers who suffered as he did—suicides and possible suicides, some of them his friends. Poe's pit and pendulum, Wordsworth's despondencies and madness, those enemies of promise, have shown up in Maine and Connecticut, as the lineaments of a present pain. Who would want to say that Styron is wearing a literary hat or a romantic mask, and who says they don't have dungeons in America any more?

World Literature Today (review date Summer 1991)

SOURCE: A review of *Darkness Visible,* in *World Literature Today,* Summer, 1991, p. 108.

[In the following review, the critic discusses William Styron's Darkness Visible, *noting that in the memoir the author offers many self-diagnoses.]*

William Styron's essay meanders through his experience of depression in a somewhat crotchety style, one which pulls the facts along like loose seaweed emerging through the surf. It is a wandering and poignant memoir that catalogues his *thinking* on depression.

So much has been written about this disorder. The 1980s (and now the 1990s) are the "ages" of depression, as the 1950s were the age of anxiety and the 1960s and 1970s were those of narcissism and borderline personality (Kohut, Kernberg, and Masterson). So I read *Darkness Visible* expecting a major footnote in the history of this disorder from the pen of an artist, not a clinician. To my surprise, the essay tends to relate the history of Styron's depression with an odd clinical detachment. He details his ambivalence toward pharmacological psychiatry, taking a more powerful stab at the etiology of depression than at allowing the reader into his experience of the madness it fosters.

The memoir begins with a clinical differentiation of the author's particular type of depression in psychiatric discourse: "At a later stage my entire mind would be dominated by anarchic disconnection . . . there was now something that resembled bifurcation of mood." In this early going Styron does a creditable job of detailing the particular symptomatology of his variety of depression. In the process he assembles an impressive community of literary colleagues with the same disorder—Albert Camus, Romain Gary, Abbie Hoffman, Randall Jarrell, Hart Crane, Cesare Pavese, Ernest Hemingway, Anne Sexton, and others.

Styron dates the onset of his depressive mood from the beginning of his intolerance for alcohol, a substance he had abused. For forty years alcohol had been "the magical conduit to fantasy and euphoria," "the enhancement of the imagination," "the invaluable senior partner." The deprivation arising from his sudden intolerance of alcohol made him feel "emotionally naked, vulnerable as [he] had never been before." Building on this mixture of biochemistry and folk wisdom, Styron folds his own quasi-medical analysis into the official cant: "Such madness is chemically induced amid the neurotransmitters of the brain, probably as the result of systemic stress, which for unknown reasons causes a depletion of the chemicals norepinephrine and serotonin, and the increase of a hormone, cortisol."

Once launched on the biochemistry of the disorder, Styron calls his psychiatrist, Dr. Gold, to [task] for not knowing his *Physicians Desk Reference* well enough to be aware of the pitfalls of Halcion and to prescribe the proper drug. From about midpoint to the conclusion *Darkness Visible* tends to weave in and out of biochemical and psychoanalytic models of explanation. So, while Styron feels that "psychiatry must be given due credit for its continuing struggle to treat depression pharmacologically," he praises cognitive therapy in the early stages, and he also acknowledges the psychoanalytics of objective relations when he claims "that devastating loss in childhood [his mother died when he was thirteen] figured as a probable genesis of my disorder." Alcohol, uninformed drug prescription, failed psychiatric therapy, loss and abandonment, turning sixty, vague dissatisfaction with work, and genetics (his father had it) are all singled out. He discovers the early warnings of his depression in his fiction: "Suicide had been a persistent theme in my books."

A. G. Mojtabai (review date 25 September 1994)

SOURCE: "I Was Too Ugly to Go to School," in *The New York Times Book Review,* September 25, 1994, pp. 11-12.

[Below, Mojtabai offers a positive review of Lucy Grealy's Autobiography of a Face, *praising the author's first published work as an account that "struggles from outer to inner to inmost senses of "face" as it charts the difficulties encountered in trying to carve a face for oneself from the inside out."]*

You should begin *Autobiography of a Face,* a poet's memoir in which no words are approximate or unfelt, by pausing to give its title due weight. All that is to follow is packed into the substitution of "face" for "person," "self" or "soul." The suggested equivalency is startling—yet not foreign, not utterly strange.

Consider your relationship to your own face, how deeply internalized it is and, at the same time, how dependent on mediation—reflection in mirrors, or the eyes of others. Our idioms fall out accordingly, on either side of a doubleness. We use the word "face" to mean appearance, outward show, a surface or facade, as in "on the face of it, it seems," or "prima facie evidence," or "putting the best face on" a failure. We also use "face" to stand for the reality, dignity or integrity, or even the inmost essential aspect, of a person or thing. We speak of looking the evidence in the face, of saving or losing face, of being faceless, of now seeing through a glass darkly, but then face to face.

Autobiography of a Face struggles from outer to inner to inmost senses of "face" as it charts the difficulties encountered in trying to carve a face for oneself from the inside out. It's a young woman's first book, the story of her own life, and both book and life are unforgettable.

The facts are these: At the age of 9, the author, Lucy Grealy, was stricken with a rare form of bone cancer called Ewing's sarcoma. Thanks to radical surgery involving the removal of half her jaw, and years of radiation and chemotherapy, she recovered from her disease, despite its low survival odds. But the physical pain she suffered turned out to be far easier to endure than her sense of disfigurement and her isolation from other children. Donning a witch's mask at Halloween bought her a few hours of childhood freedom, but this happened only once a year.

Growing up in Spring Valley, N.Y., as one of five children in an Irish immigrant family was tense and complicated enough. There were the pains of cultural dislocation, not experienced directly by Ms. Grealy, who made the journey from Dublin when she was 4, but felt keenly by her parents and her teen-age brothers. There were continual economic difficulties, for which she felt responsible. "Cancer is an obscenely expensive illness," she notes. "I saw the bills."

Although entitled to it, Ms. Grealy is not given to self-pity. At the most hurtful moments, her prose has a certain terseness, a crisp matter-of-factness: "Without bone to shape it, the right side of my face was starting to sink in." Later: "I was too ugly to go to school. I pretty much stopped going to the seventh grade."

In high school, Ms. Grealy's worst fears came true. To the usual woundings of adolescence were added stares, pointed avoidance of gaze and taunting from male students so relentless that she sought refuge in her guidance counselor's office, eating lunch alone. Sadly, the deepest wounds were self-inflicted, and salted with self-blame, with a conviction "that my ugliness was equal to a great personal failure."

Hers was a shadowy existence; she only "brushed against" other people's lives, shrinking and cringing, hiding behind a curtain of hair. "If it were possible," she reflects, "I would have stood behind that curtain forever, my head bent in an eternal act of deference. I was, however, dependent upon my audience. Their approval or disapproval defined everything for me, and I believed with every cell in my body that approval wasn't written into my particular script."

There was, at least, the merit of simplicity in this way of dealing with the world: "This singularity of meaning—I *was* my face, I *was* ugliness—though sometimes unbearable, also offered a possible point of escape. It became the launching pad from which to lift off, the one immediately recognizable place to point when asked what was wrong with my life. Everything led to it."

Wondering, as a young adult, whether to go through with another series of corrective operations after repeated reabsorption of grafts of skin and bone, the author reflected:

"How could I pass up the possibility that it might work, that at long last I might finally fix my face, fix my life, my soul?" Each subsequent operation intensified her single focus. Repeatedly, she promised herself: "*When my face gets fixed, then I'll start living.*"

Despite its unblinking stare at an excruciatingly painful subject, this is not a dour book. Ms. Grealy had intimations of what happiness might look like from the very beginning. In her brief reprieves from chemotherapy, she caught a glimmer of a happiness that "wasn't acquired through effort." It was something she already possessed "deep and sonorous inside of me," something that depended for its release on "removing the walls of pain around it."

Reading and writing poetry became a way of opening herself up to joy, a way of entering the world. At Sarah Lawrence College, where she was surrounded at last by friends and a supportive atmosphere, "poetry became a religion for me. . . . I'd pull people into a corner and say, without any sense of irony, 'You have to hear this, it will change your life.' I'd recite anything from Rilke to Ashbery, certain that the deep wonder and awe I felt from these poems would be immediately apparent. I recognized this wonder and awe as intimately connected to the feelings I'd discovered while recovering from chemotherapy sessions, when to simply 'be' was reason enough for joy. Now I knew that joy was a kind of fearlessness, a letting go of expectations."

Humor, too, had been breaking in from time to time, shattering her frame of expectation. Even way back in the early stages: "Bizarrely," she observes, "after they removed half my jaw, I limped." Later, in one of the darkest periods of her life, after an operation that grafted from hip to chin, and left in place, a strip of skin a foot and four inches long, she was forced out of hiding by a friend with a more urgent problem: "When I opened the door, I expected to have to go into a long explanation about why I looked the way I did, but before I could start Steven announced we were going dancing that night. Dancing? Was he serious? He was. He had only just come out as a homosexual, and he told me I was the only one he trusted enough to accompany him to the gay clubs. It was important, be said: he was counting on me to support him."

And dancing they went.

Finally, after "18 years and almost 30 operations," one succeeded. When congratulated on her new face, Ms. Grealy found herself reluctant to examine it in the mirror. For her, the transformation was a curiously mixed blessing—a death as well as a rebirth. For so much of her life she had handed herself over to others, for definition, for judgment, in hopes of remedy and ratification, that her first feelings were those of emptiness, facelessness. "Without another operation to hang all my hopes on," she reflects, "I was completely on my own. And now something inside me started to miss me."

Autobiography of a Face is a book about many things: sickness and health, body and soul, gender and social expectation. It is, importantly, a book about image, about the tyranny of the image of a beautiful—or even a pleasingly average—face. In the end, this tyranny is not so much overthrown as shrugged off. Ms. Grealy notes almost in passing: "As a child I had expected my liberation to come from getting a new face to put on, but now I saw it came from shedding something, shedding my image."

Some readers will be disappointed that the author's new face is never described: I was not. Her photograph on the cover flap strikes me as an irrelevance, at best. Long before the final operation, the text created a face for this reader, sculptured it down to the deeper-than-bone depths of character, a face that is taut, bright-eyed, fierce with intelligence and feeling—complete.

Sonia Jaffe Robbins (review date March 1995)

SOURCE: "Staring Pain in the Face," *London Review of Books,* March, 1995, p. 16.

[*In the following review, Robbins asserts that in* Autobiography of a Face *Lucy Grealy "has created a beautifully written re-creation of and meditation on her illness and treatment, growing up, love, and the years spent* being *her face."*]

At the age of nine, Lucy Grealy learned she had Ewing's sarcoma. An operation removed the tumor along with half of her jaw, and was followed by two years of radiation treatment and two and a half years of chemotherapy. Her chances of survival were around five percent.

I had my own preconceptions of what Lucy Grealy's account of her illness and its effect on her life would be. Eleven years ago I could have been sitting with Grealy's mother in the hospital. My daughter wasn't ill—she had been hit by a car just before her eleventh birthday. For thirteen days she was in a coma; she had a broken leg, cracks in her pelvis, bruised nerves in her neck that paralyzed her left arm. Now she is completely recovered. She graduated from college this year, has a job, her own apartment. The pain of those weeks in the hospital and years of recovery has never really been assimilated. But I confront that pain as a parent, who is supposed to protect her child from such destinies as car accidents or serious illness. Lucy Grealy confronts that pain from the perspective of the child, and the poet she has become, and has created a beautifully written re-creation of and

meditation on her illness and treatment, growing up, love, and the years spent *being* her face.

Grealy and her twin sister were the youngest of five children of an Irish broadcast journalist. The family emigrated to the United States when Grealy was four. Despite her father's initial success on network television, the family always had money problems, her mother suffered from depression and fits of anger, and her oldest brother eventually was diagnosed as a schizophrenic. When Grealy was sixteen, her father died of pancreatitis. Despite these elements of "dysfunctional" family, Grealy's account of her cancer, the treatment and the years of operations to "fix" her face never slips into melodrama. Indeed, her lucid evocation of events many would want to forget illuminates far more than her own reality.

Grealy tells two stories, of her illness and her appearance, and it is the latter one that will no doubt touch most readers. What teenage American girl, after all, hasn't thought at some moment that she was ugly? But Grealy's experience was on a different level; people really did stare, classmates were extremely cruel. To survive, Grealy developed a series of defenses, which she elucidates in fine detail.

Grealy was still a child and proud of her "tomboy heritage" when the cancer struck, and at first she ignored the changes in her appearance from surgery and treatment. But eventually her appearance became her defining nature: "This singularity of meaning—I was my face, I *was* ugliness—though sometimes unbearable, also offered a possible point of escape . . . the one immediately recognizable place to point to when asked what was wrong with my life."

Her mother gave her a sailor hat to cover the baldness from chemotherapy, and she clung to it as a barrier against people's stares. She had already felt a chasm open up between herself and her family, when her mother's Orthodox Jewish colleagues at a nursing home had offered her discarded wigs. At first the wigs had been a family joke with everyone, but when Grealy and her mother went to a custom wigmaker—and Grealy realized her mother might actually spend scarce money for one—she was appalled. Grealy thought the wigs made her look ridiculous, was amazed that her mother didn't think so too, and equally amazed that she didn't know Grealy's true feelings.

When her hair grew back, she almost unconsciously adopted a posture in which it hung down to cover her face. At first she met the teasing of other children with sarcastic retorts of her own; but as time went on, and especially when she reached junior high and high school, she tried to overcome the insults and teasing, primarily from boys, by training herself to believe that true beauty had nothing to do with looks, or by trying to forgive her taunters:

I thought that if I could do this, the pain they caused would be extinguished. Though I had genuine glimpses of what charity and transcendence meant, I was shooting for nothing less than sainthood; often, after my daily meeting with them, I only ended up hating myself instead.

She still had girlfriends, whom she now thought of as from her life "Before"—as well as friends she met on the children's ward at the hospital, in the life she labeled "After." Answering the questions of her friends from Before was in part an exercise in storytelling, even as she believed "they'd never understand what it was really like." Among her friends at the hospital, however, she and they could "redefine for each other what it was like to be sick."

When her doctors began talking about reconstructive surgery, she felt relief—"Maybe this wasn't my actual face at all but the face of some interloper . . . and my 'real' face, the one I was meant to have all along, was within reach"—followed by perplexity:

> I had put a great deal of effort into accepting that my life would be without love and beauty in order to be comforted by Love and Beauty. Did my eager willingness to grasp the idea of "fixing" my face somehow invalidate all those years of toil?

Only at Halloween, when she could cover her face with a mask along with everyone else, did she feel the freedom she believed others felt all the time. But the years of reconstructive surgery raised and dashed hopes so many times that when she finally had a face others considered hers, she felt empty, "without the framework of *when my face gets fixed, then I'll start living.*" It took her almost a year to learn to see herself, both literally and figuratively, and her insights into learning to treat herself better are flashes of intuition we can all use.

What most moved me, however, were Grealy's confrontations with illness, hospitals, pain and their reverberations on her relationships with others. At first she was excited by the attention and medical trappings. Her favorite television shows were *Emergency!* and *Medical Center,* and her first two operations rescued her from unfinished homework assignments. Later, hospital stays were times when she felt cared for, though at the same time ashamed—"Was there something wrong with me that I should find such comfort in being taken care of so? Did it mean I *liked* having operations and thus that I deserved them?"

She describes the hierarchy among hospitalized children: "The truly sick were at the top, but of course being too sick worked against you as you couldn't enjoy the status." She remembers her confusion on realizing that the almost three years of chemotherapy and radiation treatment were done: "As hard as it was to admit this to myself, I was afraid of it ending, of everything changing. I wouldn't be special anymore; no one would love me." At the same time, she resisted others' pity and felt intense embarrassment when, at her elementary school graduation, the vice-principal praised her bravery.

Coping with pain became one way Grealy tried to build up her self-esteem.

> It gave me pleasure to think that the boys who teased me openly at school and the adults who stared at me covertly elsewhere would never be able to stand this pain. . . . My whole body was tense and my stomach upside down, but I was convinced that because I did not admit these things, did not display them for others to see, it meant I had a chance at *really* being brave. . . .

But what really helped her through adolescence was horses. She loved animals and at fourteen got a job at a stable. Caring for the horses made her feel cared for; the animals didn't care what she looked like, only what she did for them.

In one episode Grealy shows how a child takes a parent's remark and turns it into an axiom of life. After her first chemotherapy session, when she cried before the injection, her mother tried to reassure her that crying was only from fear, she shouldn't be afraid, there was no need to cry. At nine, Grealy only partly understood. As she reflects now:

> My mother didn't know how to conquer *what* I was afraid of, nor could she even begin to tell me how to do it for myself. Instead, out of her own fear, she offered her own philosophy, which meant in this instance that I should conquer the fear by not crying. . . . I resolved to never cry again.

It was a resolve she could not meet, and she hated herself for not being strong enough. Some months later, when she noticed her mother's eyes filled with tears, she understood for the first time that her mother "was suffering not just because of, but also for, me."

Her relationship with her father seems simpler yet more poignant. Her mother's presence forced Grealy to take her into account as she suffered through the treatment sessions. But when her father took her, he couldn't bring himself to stay, thus leaving her at least "free to respond as *I* chose."

Grealy's writing is so marvelous that the gaps in her story are well hidden. The relationship with her twin, Sarah, for example, is barely touched on: Grealy doesn't even say whether she is an identical twin, and we're left to wonder whether Sarah had the face Grealy thought was her own "real" face. We hardly know how her siblings reacted to her illness—though she makes it clear that her family doesn't talk easily about emotions—or how much they might have contributed, even unwittingly, to her sense of ugliness or isolation. That it was her older sister, Susie, who put her in touch with the surgeon who finally succeeded in remaking her face might indicate both effort to help and concern about appearance.

But in the end these gaps do not damage Grealy's story so much as they illuminate it. Illness of this sort is isolating, no matter how much people love you or try, however ineffectually, to help. Grealy's descriptions of her attempts to confront that isolation also testify to isolation's numbing aspects. Her father's fatal illness was brief and came just months after the horse she loved died—yet grief at her father's death didn't seem to hit her until more than a year later. As she attempted to reconstruct his presence, the few details she could remember served only to underscore how little she knew him.

Grealy's memoir of living through and growing up with hardship is full of moments that both warned and chilled me. Illness—or injury—reveals how impotent parents are to protect their children, and also how difficult it is for parents or children to understand each other. If I were Grealy's mother, I would be immensely proud of her for writing this marvelous book; yet I probably couldn't bear to read it myself.

Mary Beth Loup (review date Spring 1995)

SOURCE: "Facing the World," in *Belles Lettres,* Spring, 1995, p. 53.

[*In the following positive review, Loup relates her reticence as a cancer survivor at reading Lucy Grealy's* Autobiography of a Face, *but finds that "Grealy learns to look in the mirror and accept what she sees: the reader privileged to have shared her mirror can do no less."*]

Unlike many readers who anticipated the appearance of Lucy Grealy's *Autobiography of a Face* after first reading her article "Mirrorings" in *Harper's,* I read the book first. Knowing only that the memoir deals with the author's facial disfigurement following cancer treatment as a child, I approached it cautiously. With my own cancer treatment so recently behind me, I feared that if Grealy's work were shallow, shoddy, sensational, or in any other way mediocre, it would, at the very least, disappoint by its lack of insight and, at worst, could even debase by banalization the very experience it set out to chronicle.

So, rather than plunge, I waded in thoughtfully. The title *Autobiography of a Face* can imply a multiplicity of meanings: its documentary tone, which mimics the detached observations of medical reports; the suggestion that a face, as separate from an integrated personality, is somehow able to relate its own story; and perhaps most obviously, the implied universality in the word choice of "a" face as opposed to "my" face.

Fortunately for the reader, not just any face inspired this work, but the face of a poet, Lucy Grealy. In the early 1970s at the age of nine, she submitted to the first of many operations: first to remove a sizable portion of her jaw to prevent the spread of cancer, and later to restore some semblance of normality to her appearance through plastic surgery. In between were radiation treatments and chemotherapy. Grealy's almost lifelong struggle with pain, suffering, and humiliation, on such a staggering scale that it defined and shaped her childhood universe, could well have brought her beyond the brink of psychic annihilation. Consider the traumatic consequences of her overwhelmed mother's impossible demands for bravery:

> There was no way to escape the pain. Yet with each successive visit to Dr. Woolf's examining room, my feelings of shame and guilt for failing not to suffer became more unbearable. The physical pain seemed almost easy in comparison. Was this how my body dealt with the onslaught, veering the focus away from itself, insisting that its burden be lessened by having my mind take on more than its fair share? Whatever the process was, it worked—worked in the sense that I became adept at handling my pain, deft at addressing its various complaints and demands for attention.

The miracle is that Grealy combines the unbearable sensitivity of a poet with the relentless observation of a journalist, and having survived these very attributes, which undoubtedly intensified her suffering, uses them to break free of the prison of her own suppressed fears. Her resulting memoir evokes with near total recall and absence of self-pity the world of a child whose happiest memory was of Halloween: "I walked down the streets suddenly bold and free: no one could see my face. I peered through the oval eye slits and did not see one person staring back at me, ready to make fun of my face." In prose that is both lilting and precise, Grealy lets the reader look both into her mask and out at the world from her own "oval eye slits." The view is not all-encompassing: her siblings, even her twin sister, are peripheral figures, and her parents seem to exist only in their relation to their daughter. This does not strike me as a weakness, but rather as a necessary narrowing of focus to increase the memoir's sharpness.

So completely did I embrace Grealy's point of view that I felt the stings of cruel taunts (this book should be required reading for all preadolescent boys), and I rejoiced in her eventual epiphany:

> And then I experienced a moment of the freedom I'd been practicing for behind my Halloween mask all those years ago. As a child I had expected my liberation to come from getting a new face to put on, but now I saw it came from shedding something, shedding my image.

Lucy Grealy learns to look in the mirror and accept what she sees: the reader privileged to have shared her mirror can do no less.

Carolyn Polese (review date December 1995)

SOURCE: A review of *A Child Called 'It,'* in *School Library Journal,* December, 1995, pp. 139-40.

[*In the following mixed review, the critic describes David Pelzer's* A Child Called 'It' *as "unforgettable," but faults the author's writing style and suggests that the book is not a good choice for young readers.*]

This autobiographical account charts the abuse of a young boy as his alcoholic mother first isolates him from the rest of the family; then torments him; and finally nearly kills him through starvation, poisoning, and one dramatic stabbing. Pelzer's portrayal of domestic tyranny and eventual escape is unforgettable, but falls short of providing understanding of extreme abuse or how he made his journey from "Victim to Victor." It takes some work to get past the poor writing and the self-aggrandizing back matter, but the book tries fervently to provide a much-needed perspective. One of the greater obstacles to healing for males is admitting that they have been victims, especially if their perpetrator is a woman. This author has overcome that obstacle and succeeded in life by such masculine norms as joining the Air Force and receiving awards for his volunteerism. However, while personal accounts of child maltreatment provide crucial information about the realities of childhood, youngsters need insight and hope in order to digest the raw material of abuse. James Deem's *The 3 NBs of Julian Drew* (Houghton, 1994) is a well-crafted, fictional work that effectively covers much of the same ground.

Los Angeles Times Book Review (review date 16 September 1996)

SOURCE: A review of *Darkness Visible,* in *Los Angeles Times Book Review,* September 16, 1996, p. 6.

[*In the following negative review of William Styron's* Darkness Visible, *the critic asserts that "there's nothing here that hasn't been said better elsewhere."*]

A law professor once said that legal scholarship had two problems—one its style, the other its content. I have a similar reaction to William Styron's new book, and say so reluctantly because it touches on a serious subject: depression, which brought the novelist to the edge of suicide.

Darkness Visible is not, in fact, about depression, since Styron says his bout was essentially beyond description; nor is it about his depression's effect on other people, family and friends making but cameo appearances; nor does it concern the medical world's understanding of the disease, Styron limiting himself to writing, in essence, that his doctors couldn't do much. He does touch on the connection between depression and creativity, citing Camus, Randall Jarrell, Primo Levi, Virginia Woolf and so on, but there's nothing here that hasn't been said better elsewhere.

It's a major stretch to think that a modest speech given at a medical school (Johns Hopkins), then adapted as a magazine article (Vanity Fair), could happily find a third life between hard covers.

John Blades (review date 22 October 1996)

SOURCE: "McCourt's Memoir Awash in Tales of Ireland, Booze," in *Chicago Tribune,* October 22. 1996, pp. 1, 3.

[*In the following review of Frank McCourt's memoir,* Angela's Ashes, *Blades relates the author's account of how the book came to be and what happened after the point at which the narrative ends.*]

If ever a man could personally testify to the evils of drink, it's Frank McCourt. As a survivor of what he calls the worst kind of "miserable childhood . . . the miserable Irish Catholic childhood," McCourt traces most of that misery to the demons rum, stout and whiskey, which were consumed in profligate quantities by his father, a stereotypically "shiftless loquacious alcoholic" Irishman.

Every page of McCourt's new memoir, *Angela's Ashes* (Scribner), seems to reek of strong drink, and worse, as McCourt recalls in comically agonizing detail his father's marathon benders. The book is so full of dispiriting tales about his down-and-out boyhood in Limerick, concluding with his father's "Irish divorce" (abandoning his wife and four sons), that it could easily serve as a temperance manual.

And yet here was McCourt, cheerfully partaking along with the other guests at a recent Chicago sendoff for his memoir, which was held not in a bookstore, library or any traditional literary forum but in Cullen's Bar & Grill, 3741 N. Southport Ave. Having set down so many sobering memories on paper, the author allowed that the pub party was indeed a contradiction as was his own reluctance to take the pledge of abstinence.

McCourt blithely dismissed that possibility, explaining, "I feel a great responsibility to the children of employees of breweries and distilleries." Then he added: "I should run a mile from the stuff, but I can take it in moderation."

According to reports out of New York, where McCourt has lived since coming to America in 1949, he's been a fixture at the Lion's Head Pub, part of a two-fisted typing and drinking fraternity whose membership over the years has included Jimmy Breslin, Norman Mailer, Pete Hamill and Joe Flaherty. As a teacher in the New York public schools, McCourt said be always felt "like the downstairs maid" among the journalists and novelists. But after being doubly blessed by *Angela's Ashes*—with critics' cheers and instant best-sellerdom—he's no longer just the "fellow with the odd manner" around the Lion's Head, but at the age of 66, "one of the boys."

Like McCourt himself, *Angela's Ashes* is a bundle of contradictions, as uproarious as they are grievous, whether the young Frankie is pushing his baby brother around Limerick, dumping loose coal and turf into his pram; his "pious, defeated" mother is begging a sheep's head for their Christmas dinner; or his soused father is rousing the boys in the middle of the night to sing "Kevin Barry" and other patriotic Irish songs.

When he took the stage of the Mercury Theater, adjoining Cullen's pub, to recite from *Angela's Ashes,* McCourt was accompanied by a bagpiper and drummer playing "Gary Owen." He read with tragicomic gusto from his memoir, recalling the misery of growing up in Limerick not only with a drunken father but "pompous priests," "bullying schoolmasters" and "the odor of piss wafting in from the outdoor jakes where many a man puked up his week's wages."

Though this was McCourt's literary coming-out party in Chicago, he'd been a familiar figure on local stages during the '80s. Billing themselves as "A Couple of Blaguards," he and his younger brother, Malachy, re-enacted their Limerick boyhood in story, song and verse for audiences at the Royal George and other theaters.

McCourt's book, like the brothers' autobiographical revue, has been almost universally greeted by reviewers as "lyrical and charming," McCourt said. "Always *lyrical* and *charming,*" he repeated, derisively. "That's how they like to describe Irish writers. It's like poor old Sam on the plantation, simple-minded and very musical, singing 'Old Man River.' But what gives Irish writing its distinctive flavor is not the charming stuff but the darkness."

Despite its associations with cheerful, bawdy Irish verse, Limerick was no Glocca Mora, an idyllic village in the midst of an emerald landscape, but a "gray place with a river that kills," McCourt said of the foul and poisonous River Shannon.

As much as anyone else, McCourt added, it was probably John Ford and his Hollywood stock company who cast the Irish in such a false and deceiving light. Even more misleading were Bing Crosby and Barry Fitzgerald as Fathers O'Malley and Fitzgibbon in *Going My Way,* which he also saw as a boy in Limerick. "We were always taken by the sweetness of American priests," said McCourt, whose gray hair, melodic accent and beguilingly gruff manner would easily qualify him for the Hollywood holy order. "We could never imagine a priest like Bing Crosby in Ireland, somebody who would get out and play ball with the boys and sing at Christmas."

McCourt was born in Brooklyn, but his parents returned to the old country when he 4. His sister had died in infancy and his father was unable to find work because of the Depression and his incorrigible drinking. If anything, however, Ireland was even more depressed, and depressing, than America. The McCourts lost two more children, twin brothers, and when his father found work, which was rarely and briefly, he'd spend all his wages in the pubs.

"It was the culture," McCourt said of the Irish dependence on fermented spirits. "For the men in our economic class, there were only two outlets, sports and the pubs. If a man drank too much, it was what was called a good man's failing. That was the one thing the church never denounced in Limerick. They denounced sex, dancing and Hollywood movies, but I never heard a priest get up and denounce drinking."

McCourt's mother, Angela, is the nominal heroine of his memoir, eternally on the dole, pathetically trying to clothe and feed her sons. But it's the blackguard father, also named Malachy, who obsesses McCourt, and who commandeers center stage in his memoir, long after he's abandoned his wife and family.

McCourt was 11 when his father left Ireland for England, during World War II, to look for work, and he didn't see him again until 1963. His father showed up in Brooklyn, where the family was then living, McCourt recalled, "saying he hadn't had a drink in three years. But as soon as he arrived, he went wild, boozing all over Brooklyn and destroying any hope of reconciliation with my mother. . . . He died in 1985, and I went to all the time and expense of going back to Belfast for his funeral—don't ask me why."

McCourt's memoir ends with him landing in the U.S. when he was 19. Quickly bringing his expatriate saga up to date, he said: "I got a job as a houseman at the Biltmore Hotel, going around with a mop and broom. Then the Korean War broke out, and I was drafted and sent to Germany for two years, training dogs. When I got out, I had the GI Bill but no high school education, but I managed to talk my way into NYU." After college, he taught in New York schools for 26 years, until his retirement in 1988.

An English teacher, McCourt said he was learning how to write along with his students. "As they were writing about their families and lives, I started writing about mine. There was an accumulation of material in my drawer, and in '94 I had to get it out of my system. It was seared into my memory, festering and gestating. If I hadn't finished it, I would have died howling with despair."

Eugenia Zukerman (review date 2 February 1997)

SOURCE: "Overture to a Recovery," in *The Washington Post Book World,* February 2, 1997, p. 5.

[*In the following review of Linda Katherine Cuttings'* Memory Slips, *Zukerman finds that the author "manages to write with simple candor and elegant prose about" her abuse as a child, "a subject that is too often sensationalized."*]

For most of her life, Linda Katherine Cutting was ordered to apologize and to keep silent. "If you tell you'll burn in hell," she was admonished by her minister father. Remarkably, Cutting grew up to become a successful concert pianist, but her performances came to a halt when memory lapses at the keyboard jolted memories muted since early childhood. Her subsequent breakdown and her climb back from suicidal despair are recorded in *Memory Slips.*

Family violence, sexual abuse, the suicides of both of her brothers, her cruel and hypocritical father, her passively complicit mother—Cutting's book is a testimony to the power of music and to the courage of a gifted and deeply wounded woman.

Two narratives, 10 years apart, alternate throughout the book

because, as the author explains, "Time is never strictly chronological in the way it is lived. Musicians know this. Anyone who has suffered grief, loss, or a broken heart knows this, too." This alternation affords the reader a necessary emotional rubato; her story is too harrowing to be told at a fast tempo. The narrative slips back and forth between 1982-83 and 1992. In the earlier years, when Cutting was performing with such orchestras as the Boston Pops, she was already experiencing recollections that troubled her. But it was not until 1992 that she was admitted to the National Center for the Treatment of Trauma and Dissociation. There, with the help of compassionate professionals, she began to put the pieces of her life back together.

Not only had she been abused by her father since the age of 6, but when she confronted her mother, she was met with total denial. "When I told her my father had molested me at home and at church, regular as his Sunday sermon," Cutting writes, "[Mother] assured me she didn't know about it. She also told me, 'If it were my father I'd never forgive him,' then, 'You've got to forgive your father' and finally, 'My husband would never do that'." Linda Cutting is never self-pitying. She bravely faces the truth and even asks herself difficult questions, such as, "What does it mean to honor your parents? To pretend that these things never happened or to love and forgive them in spite of knowing? Forgiveness starts with confessing your sins. But they have never asked my forgiveness. I was always ordered to ask my father's forgiveness, and for most of my life, I did. I was also ordered to keep silence. For most of my life, I did that, too."

For most of her life, Cutting also had music as her rampart, and it is music that is at the heart of her recovery. As she writes, "Without the music there would only be the quicksand. . . ." Cutting uses music both to mitigate her story and to tell it: "Scriabin, B-flat minor Prelude. It's spooky in the beginning, hushed, like someone is sneaking into your room late at night." The piano, we are told, "was sacred. . . . No one would touch me there. I was allowed to practice for hours." It was her father who encouraged her to practice, but it was also her father who did more than touch her. "Every Saturday night my mother typed my father's sermons. I remember lying in my bed hearing the metal letters strike the platen and the bell preceding each carriage return. I wondered how many bells before my father would enter my room."

Images of her father's midnight visits put a fermata on Linda Cutting's life. Breaking the silence enabled her to begin to heal and to finally play the piano again. Her brothers were not so fortunate. One hanged himself, the other shot himself "in a motel room in West Palm Beach. A three-fifty-seven magnum and two suicide notes were found next to him."

Cutting manages to write with simple candor and elegant prose about a subject that is too often sensationalized. She can even be kind to the man who tormented and betrayed her: "What I feel for my father in this moment is compassion. I watch him turning the pages of his past, see a sadness in his eyes, in his hands, in the slowness of his movements, a sadness that he has never let me close to." She writes lyrically about performing and about the process of learning and making music—"In the slow movement [of the Mozart Piano Concerto, K. 488] there is the stillness of a sleeping baby. I play the second theme more and more quietly until there is almost no sound. I hear my own breath, and feel that the audience breathes with me. . . ."

Performance involves personal risk and public trial, but when, in the Treatment Center, Cutting finally plays for her fellow patients, it is an act of pure generosity: "The whole room is quiet and I know I need to remember Schumann's 'Scenes from Childhood'—not just for my self, but for every woman here who has lost hers."

Linda Cutting returned to the concert stage in 1995 at the age of 41. *Memory Slips* is her memoir of music and healing; it is poetic and poignant. She has created a powerful piece from the dark melodies and painful dissonances of her lost childhood.

Frederick Busch (review date 9 February 1997)

SOURCE: "My Brother, Myself," in *New York Times Book Review,* February 9, 1997, p. 10.

[*In the following positive review of* Imagining Robert, *by Jay Neugeboren, Busch distinguishes between Neugeboren's roles as author and as brother, offering sympathetic opinions of both.*]

The novelist Jay Neugeboren would not agree that a discussion of his powerful story—his brother's battle for more than 30 years with mental illness—centers on him, the writer. He would insist that his brother is the heart of the matter. His belief is part of the appeal of his memoir, *Imagining Robert.*

But he is the writer, and it is he who has found the language and he who has fought exhaustion and despair and disorder, as much on his brother's behalf as on his own. So we might start by considering this story at the farther end of its awful arc: Robert Neugeboren, a 50-year-old man, has yet another breakdown and he is put in isolation in a psychiatric center. It is approximately the 50th time that he has been so hospitalized. The medicines to which he has finally become accustomed, and which seemed to do him a little good, are

changed. The psychiatrist who, when he saw Robert, at least did no harm is changed. Soon the dosages of his new medication are, predictably, increased. Jay, the older brother, who has cared on his own for his children since his wife left the family in 1986, has flown to Athens, Ohio, because his son, in college, is recovering from a bad LSD trip and has had strong suicidal impulses. Upon his return, Jay begins to receive calls from Florida concerning his mother, who left for the South after telling her older son, about Robert, "You be in charge from now on, Jay—I just can't handle it anymore." Jay is told that she has begun to wake in the middle of the night, to run onto roadways and highways, endangering herself and others. Jay's other college-age son returns to live at home with him, bringing anger and disorder. Robert deteriorates. And Jay wonders how to survive, and how to help his brother survive.

Jay Neugeboren lives, unsurprisingly, in a state of exhaustion, like the families of so many victims of schizophrenia and manic-depressive disorder. The patients are locked in cycles of careless and inattentive, often cruel, treatment, which can offer them and their families little hope. Over the years, Robert has participated in "group therapy, family therapy, multifamily group therapy, Gestalt therapy, psychoanalytically oriented psychotherapy, goal-oriented therapy; art therapy, behavioral therapy, vocational rehabilitation therapy, milieu therapy, et al." But, Mr. Neugeboren points out, the more chronic his brother's condition grew, the less therapy he received and the more drugs:

> "He was schizophrenic when enormous doses of Thorazine and Stelazine calmed him; he was manic-depressive (bipolar) when lithium worked; he was manic-depressive-with-psychotic-symptoms, or hypomanic, when Tegretol or Depakote (anticonvulsants), or some new antipsychotic or antidepressant—Trilafon, Adapin, Mellaril, Haldol, Klonopin, risperidone—showed promise of making him cooperative; and he was schizophrenic (again) when various doctors promised cures through insulin-coma therapy or megadose-vitamin therapy or Marxist therapy or gas therapy. At the same time, often in an attempt to minimize side effects, other drugs were poured into him: Artane, Benadryl, Cogentin, Kemadrin, Symmetrel, Prolixin, Pamelor, Navane."

So, since the mid-1960's, a bright, possibly brilliant young man has been shunted from harassed social worker to exhausted clinic psychiatrist, from 10-minute sessions billed as hourlong sessions, from beatings at the hands (and feet) of orderlies, from straitjackets and wet sheets to halfway house to isolation in a psychiatric center again, and from drug to drug to drug, from dysfunctional household to his brother's more tender care and back to isolation again, from quack to paper-pusher—and from breakdown to breakdown. He has been abandoned by his mother, his father has died, and the psychiatric profession as organized by New York State for its dependent citizens has moved its heavy haunches essentially to keep Robert Neugeboren quiet and out of the way. When he shows symptoms, he is punished—though "treatment" would be the word on his chart—with isolation and more drugs for the crime of "non-compliance."

Meanwhile, Jay Neugeboren, caring for his children, working at his craft and at teaching the students at the University of Massachusetts, Amherst, seems to live on the go and on the phone, trying to coordinate the nightmare "care" his brother receives so that Robert can be more than the sum total of his symptoms—so that he might have a functioning self.

As is so often the case in a crazy household—and Mr. Neugeboren's was: the climate was shaped by a sad, ineffectual father, an often cruel, seductive mother—guilt becomes a leitmotif. After he has moved his mother from a retirement community to a nursing home, Mr. Neugeboren wonders whether he is more comfortable being responsible for his mother than with loving her, or whether he has ever loved her. And he asks himself whether, in caring for her and for Robert and even his children, he is "merely trying to prove (to her? to myself? to the universe?) yet again that I am not the mean and selfish boy she always told me I was." This kind of honesty characterizes *Imagining Robert.* Such self-examination is woven into the narrative of mistreatment and malpractice, and guilt provides too tempting an invitation for Mr. Neugeboren to decline. He must consider it in terms of his own need for expiation or exorcism or (at least) self-analysis. Inevitably questions of guilt become questions of narrative: Why do I tell this tale? Do I serve, or use, my brother? Does my interest in telling the tale overwhelm my interest in serving my loved one?

Every writer serves his selfish needs. But in the case of this memoir, we deal with a writer who serves himself and who goes on to serve his brother for his brother's sake. He finds him in memory and presents him to us as an infant, as a child, as a clever adolescent. (It is in his teen-age years, when Jay goes to college after the boys have shared the same room and true affection for each other, that Robert begins to disintegrate.) Robert is a person here, and not a case history. Mr. Neugeboren finds his brother's noble moments, his triumphs of wit, the true Robert locked behind the trembling hands, the speeding talk, the frightening outbursts. Jay finds Robert by using his art: he imagines him for us, he makes his incoherent journey into a narrative that is organized and useful. He tells Robert's story, and so, at least in a small and permanent way, he frees him.

At the same time, he frees himself "by acting as if there were two Roberts: the brother I grew up with, and the brother who was now hospitalized." This act of the imagination makes it possible for Mr. Neugeboren to "spend time with Robert without making him feel that he (or I!) was somehow to *blame* for his fate." So, among the many enlightenments this book offers, there is a double lesson about the imagination and illness. The writer is spurred by a loved one's illness to order the chaos of his experience through writing. But the Jay who is a brother before he is an author is spurred by Robert's illness to re-create his brother—to invoke the imagination on behalf of sanity itself. And Jay Neugeboren therefore must contend with two kinds of guilt—with matters of his daily battle with Robert's illness and Robert himself, and with a writer's guilt about what (and whom) he has written.

The author finds his brother, through daily contention and through his writing. And he finds himself in his love for his brother. Coping with Robert's illness, Mr. Neugeboren himself almost succumbs—he is always shaken by stress and fear, and he comes close at several points to suicide—yet he does endure, and so, remarkably, does Robert. Each man seems to me heroic, in part because I know so much about each in his extremity. Mr. Neugeboren concludes that "knowledge and love often prove to be one." It is a writer's knowledge: he knew what he knew, and then, to save his life and his brother's, he imagined the rest of the truth.

> 'Oh, Robert,' I say then, 'how did we ever live together in that one small room for all those years?'
>
> 'Maybe,' Robert answers, 'we were the same person.'

Margaret Moorman (review date 9 February 1997)

SOURCE: "Fugue State," in *New York Times Book Review,* February 9, 1997, p. 18.

[*Below, Moorman offers a positive review of Linda Katherine Cutting's* Memory Slips, *describing the book as dignified and eloquent.*]

In 1989, Linda Katherine Cutting, a young, widely praised concert pianist, suffered a memory slip on stage. "I heard footsteps. Suddenly I was in the wrong key. . . . The footsteps came nearer to the piano. . . . I had to make sure it wasn't him." Six and a half bars into the opening of a Beethoven sonata, she stopped playing. "It was only a latecomer taking his seat," she writes in her extraordinary book, *Memory Slips.* She began again and mercifully made it through to the end of the piece.

This small lapse in Ms. Cutting's professional life signaled the intrusion of childhood memories that would soon overwhelm her. Only after a serious suicide attempt was she able to put past and present back together again during a hospitalization at the Center for Trauma and Dissociation, in Denver.

Ms. Cutting's trauma was intricately, almost eerily connected with her music. She describes sitting at an old upright piano in the hospital's cafeteria and beginning, tentatively, to play. Her fingers "suddenly remember one of Schumann's 'Scenes From Childhood.'" More of the Schumann comes to her, including two parts called "Frightening" and "A Child Falling Asleep." Suddenly she can't remember the next chord. "Where am I? What age? Five. I am 5 and I can't fall asleep. . . . Daddy's coming to tuck me in. Please, God, don't let him play those bad games. . . . I can't breathe. I'm frozen."

Ms. Cutting resolutely uncovers what she describes as memories of her minister father's sexual molestation of her, "regular as his Sunday sermon"; his sadistic whippings of her and her two brothers, both of whom killed themselves in young adulthood (a younger sister seems to have grown up unscathed); and her mother's utter failure either to protect or to comfort. The charges in this book are savage, yet she tells her story with restraint. It is a testament to her careful writing and to her humanity that in the end we are sure of our sympathy to her parents, even after all we know about them.

Ms. Cutting describes her memories of incest and violence through carefully chosen details—sticky hands, the stripes on her father's seer-sucker pajamas, his belt coming out of its loops. We also see Ms. Cutting's adult responses—her weight loss, her despair and her dependence on music to help her focus her mind and emotions. The slant of Ms. Cutting's descriptions protects readers from a sense of voyeurism and allows them to join with her as she struggles to remember what she was commanded to forget, to analyze its effects on her life and, steadily, to recover.

Subtitled "A Memoir of Music and Healing," the book is in part a beautifully written meditation on the composers, teachers and piano pieces Ms. Cutting loves. For the child Linda, music was a bribe: "If I don't talk back or tell anyone what goes on in our house, my father will buy me the piano. There, I can make all the sounds I want . . . and no one will know it is animal pain coming out as music." By the time the grown-up Linda finds "the words for this pain" she must also find a new path to the music that has always been her mainstay.

Writing *Memory Slips* was part of that rapprochement; Ms. Cutting even organizes the book musically, with strains of narrative revisited like melodies, in a cyclical rendering.

"Time is never strictly chronological in the way it is lived," she writes, and this may be especially true where memory plays such a large part. I was sometimes confused, however, about where we were in time.

Eventually, Ms. Cutting reported her father to the director of pastoral relations at the National Association of Congregational Churches, whose chilling reply was, "At this point, what you are saying is nothing but hearsay." Ms. Cutting's courage will lend great strength to other sufferers whose memories have met with such willful disbelief, for she has built a persuasive indictment with this dignified, eloquent book.

Martha Duffy (review date 10 March 1997)

SOURCE: "Taboo Time," in *Time,* March 10, 1997.

[*In the following negative review of Kathryn Harrison's* The Kiss, *Duffy concludes that "one hesitates to question the veracity of a book labeled a memoir," but proclaims the book "more a purple tale than a glimpse of truth."*]

It might be better if this woeful memoir had been a novel; its tone of hysterical self-obsession might pass as fiction. But Kathryn Harrison has already drawn on the theme of adult incest in her 1991 novel, *Thicker than Water,* to no great reverberance, so in *The Kiss* she tries the currently fashionable route of confession. Hers: an affair with her father.

Harrison's preacher father was kicked out of the house by her mother and grandparents when she was tiny, and she had almost no contact with him until she was 20. The household was grim. Grandmother would scream like a "scalded infant"; mother, who lived elsewhere most of the time, beat her daughter with a hairbrush. The child herself was unlikable. There is an unintentionally risible passage where she pries open the eyes of newborn kittens. The teenage years are marked by anorexia ("the dizzy rapture of starving") and bulimia ("I never taste what I eat. Sometimes I don't even know what it is until I throw it up.").

In short, she is a disaster waiting to happen when her father re-enters her life, and they become mutually obsessed. The actual affair does not begin until a gloomy courtship by letter, tape and phone call has worn thin. The carnal phase is really an epilogue. Soon the father has shed religion in favor of breeding attack dogs, and the daughter has decamped for New York City to write "a post-modern novel." One hesitates to question the veracity of a book labeled a memoir, but Harrison's overheated prose and her sketchy characters and settings make this more a purple tale than a glimpse of truth.

Mim Udovitch (review date 17 March 1997)

SOURCE: "The Evil Dads," in *New York,* March 17, 1997, pp. 57-8.

[*In the following excerpt, Udovitch asserts that Kathryn Harrison brings to* The Kiss *"a mannered, accomplished technique, which . . . is executed with precision and grace. What she fails to bring is any sense of rigorous engagement with her material."*]

Okay, let it first be said that if Kathryn Harrison, whose memoir *The Kiss* tells the story of the incestuous relationship she had with her father between the ages of 20 and 24, wants to make this experience the centerpiece of her published work, be it fictional, nonfictional, pictographic, or a series of rhyming billboards on the Garden State Parkway, the emotional, moral, and financial implications of this decision are nobody's business but hers. She has in fact told virtually the same story in fictional form with her debut novel, the pleasantly readable *Thicker Than Water,* as well as a variation on the theme in her second, the abrasively unreadable *Exposure.* (In her third book, a historical novel called *Poison,* the narrator sleeps with a priest, a father of a different kind.)

> *The Kiss* **is a book that seems destined to be received mostly for its extraliterary entertainment value, perhaps because it is a rather pallid piece of work.**
> —*Mim Udovitch*

But mine is a minority opinion, if the several prominent prepublication dissections of the author's possible motives for writing this book are any indication of consensus. There's been a lot of hand-wringing about the impact *The Kiss* might have on Harrison's children and while no one has gone so far as to suggest outright that Harrison had sex with her father in her twenties in order to advance her career at a later date, this was definitely the subtext of at least one editorial on the subject. That the publications in which these chastisements appeared themselves routinely tell stories as scandalous as Harrison's raises a very nineties question: Who controls the narrative? Well, Oprah. Let's move on.

So, *The Kiss* is a book that seems destined to be received mostly for its extraliterary entertainment value, perhaps because it is a rather pallid piece of work. Harrison is the child of teenage parents who separated in her infancy. She was raised primarily by her maternal grandparents and had just enough involvement with her negligent, seductive mother to establish a longing for more that must have amounted to a permanent low-boil torture. Although she saw her father on

two or three occasions in childhood, they were more or less estranged until the author was 20, when the titular kiss, involving tongue, occurred.

The period of sexual involvement that followed was in many ways typical of father-daughter incest, with the emotional coercion made possible, despite Harrison's nominally having reached an age of independence, by the profundity of her parentless neediness. (And, I think it fair to say—since the sex ended with the death of her mother, who suspected the affair—by the extremity of her anger at her other parent.)

This is obviously an awful story in life; but in art, even gothic and dreadful pain is only as interesting as what the artist brings to it. Harrison brings a mannered, accomplished technique, which, though not my cup of tea, is executed with precision and grace. What she fails to bring is any sense of rigorous engagement with her material.

This is partly because of the remote, almost somnambulant tone I imagine she's intentionally employing to convey her then-state of mind. But *The Kiss* is also padded with questions that are not really questions, anecdotes that are burnished to a little too high a literary gloss to retain their human complexity, and artful, thoughtless writing. "I'm always trudging after him over expanses of stained carpet and dull linoleum" goes one typically ominous example. "The walls around us warn of illegal transport. Arrows point to baggage claims and taxi stands. Everywhere there are small blue signs bearing international symbols for food, first aid, toilets." This is an awful lot of breath to waste unless your subject is the trauma to which you were subjected in your youth by an airport. Harrison has said that this book came out quickly because she'd been writing it in her head for years, and that's finally how it reads. It has all the facility, in both its positive and negative connotations, of (to cop a line from Joan Didion) a story you tell yourself in order to live.

James Wolcott (review date 31 March 1997)

SOURCE: "Dating Your Dad," in *The New Republic,* March 31, 1997, pp. 32-6.

[*In the following review, Wolcott gives an extensive analysis of Kathryn Harrison's* The Kiss. *In comparing it to her other works and to her statements in interviews, Wolcott questions whether* The Kiss *is fact or fiction.*]

Remember when it took some digging to unearth secrets? When guilt and repression were still powerful enforcers? In the aftermath of Freud and Jung, the unconscious seemed like a rich treasure bed, a sunken Atlantis of racial myth and murky memories, a crumbling Edgar Allan Poe estate choked with moss. To read one of Freud's case studies is to descend a spiral staircase where steps are broken or missing, dreams contain puns, and puns yield clues to primal events, usually involving some sexual eye-popper. However mistaken Freud's treatment may have been of "Dora" and the "Wolf Man," his case studies survive as detective literature, owing to the ingenious brainwork that he lavished against his patients' resistance. An element of play, a dogged glee, peeps through his struggle to free them of their fetters. In his analysis of "Dora," Freud modestly denied that he employed magical technique. Unlocking secrets was mostly a matter of being receptive, he claimed.

> He that has eyes to see and ears to hear may convince himself that no mortal can keep a secret. If his lips are silent, he chatters with his fingertips; betrayal oozes out of him at every pore. And thus the task of making conscious the most hidden recesses of the mind is one which it is quite possible to accomplish.

Now the problem is the opposite: getting people to put a cork in it. What was once quite possible to accomplish has become impossible to stop. Since the 1970s, the deluge of pop-psych best-sellers, celebrity confessionals and tabloid talk shows has made Freud's intellectual heavy-lifting seem as antiquated as washing by hand. Even our deepest, darkest secrets seem shallow now—easy pickings. Our once-hidden shames have become publicity hounds. It's as if our psyches are no longer labyrinths or flooded basements, but well-lit TV studios where we swivel in the guest chair, awaiting our cue. The recent rash of personal memoirs and autobiographical novels (*Bastard Out of Carolina, The Liars' Club, Drinking: A Love Story, The Blue Suit, Prozac Nation, Autobiography of a Face*) bear witness to this desire to shop one's pain in plain sight. Some memoir-writers are legitimately trying to clarify for themselves and the reader the experience of a cruel upbringing or an unfortunate twist of fate; others are simply peddling their stories for fame. Either way, we're approaching saturation—agony overload. I have three writer-friends currently working on memoirs. This summer the Iowa Writing Series is offering a weeklong workshop in "the powerful form of crisis memoir," in which students are asked to bring manuscripts of their own "survival stories."

With so many memoirs covering so many addictions and afflictions, the confessions have gotten kinkier and more gossipy, as writers add extra salsa to stand out from the growing herd. In the last few years we've had Michael Ryan confess to molesting the family dog in *Secret Life,* Daphne Merkin getting spanked in *The New Yorker,* the English writer Blake Morrison describes getting an erection while putting his young daughter to bed in *As If* (her rounded buttocks, etc.);

and soon we will have Naomi Wolf's *Promiscuities: An American Girlhood* and Katie Roiphe's memoir about her sister and drugs. But no crisis memoir has attracted more fireflies than Kathryn Harrison's *The Kiss.* Prefaced with a quotation from François Mauriac (classy dead French writer), this is a book that gift wraps its sordid secret in a Tiffany box. It's incest with a twist, trash with a capital "T."

Harrison is the author of three novels, *Thicker than Water, Exposure* and *Poison,* along with numerous magazine articles about herself for *Vogue.* For one of the *Vogue* pieces, a testy complaint about being treated as a bimbo just because she happens to be blond ("as if . . . in demonstrating both intelligence and blondness, I had broken some unspoken rule"), Harrison posed in fishnet stockings and a tacky dress slit thigh-high. The irony seemed lost on her. Her husband, Colin Harrison, is an editor at *Harper's* and the author of a breathless literary thriller called *Manhattan Nocturne.* He has also signed a reported million-dollar two-book deal. Their star-quality as a literary couple has made them attractive bait in the piranha tank of pop journalism.

No crisis memoir has attracted more fireflies than Kathryn Harrison's *The Kiss.* Prefaced with a quotation from François Mauriac (classy dead French writer), this is a book that gift wraps its sordid secret in a Tiffany box. It's incest with a twist, trash with a capital "T."
—James Wolcott

Before the publication of *The Kiss,* Harrison granted interviews to *Mirabella* and *The New York Observer* and refused to talk to *Vanity Fair,* which ran an unsympathetic piece by Michael Shnayerson. Then the English press got into the act. Nearly every article mentioned that an excerpt from *The Kiss* was due to run in *The New Yorker,* a bona fide indicator of the book's "buzz" value. But then the excerpt was aborted, an ominous sign. All this preliminary fuss has made the Harrisons understandably wary, and not just because they seemed to have lost control of the hype.

"Literary" writers such as the Harrisons often grumble that in the current showbiz climate they are reviewed not for the content of their work or the craft of their prose, but on the basis of sidebar issues: the size of their advances, the parties they attend, even their looks. (In the '80s, Gordon Lish seemed to be running a modeling school out of Knopf.) Writers now have to fret about being fashionable enough for the fickle press, but not so trendy that they provoke a backlash. And, given the touchy subject matter of *The Kiss,* the Harrisons had even more cause to feel targeted. "Colin and Kathy understood from the beginning that the book was going to be a magnet for a lot of small-hearted speculation," the novelist Bob Shacochis told the *Observer*. So many meanies out there! Since we don't wish to appear small-hearted, let's humor Colin and Kathy (and Bob). For the first half of this review, let's make our minds a perfect blank and focus on the book itself, on the text. Let's pretend we stumbled on the work unawares.

The first thing that strikes one about *The Kiss* is how airbrushed the writing is, how fadeaway. Its sentences leave wistful little vapor trails of Valium. The opening chapter, a brief flash-forward that finds Harrison and her father journeying together out West, has the mock-simple rosary-bead rhythm of a Joan Didion litany. "We meet at airports. We meet in cities where we've never been before. We meet where no one will recognize us." The tourist spots that they visit have a movie-location desolation that's also Didionesque.

> Increasingly, the places we go are unreal places: the Petrified Forest, Monument Valley, the Grand Canyon—places as stark and beautiful and deadly as those revealed in satellite photographs of distant planets. Airless, burning, inhuman.

Posed in front of these supersized postcards from perdition, these two are ready for their close-ups: "Against such backdrops, my father takes my face in his hands. He tips it up and kisses my closed eyes, my throat." Back in the car, they quarrel and weep, going from motel to motel, lovers on the lam, worming through the dusty soul of America.

But if her father is a Humbert, his daughter is no Lolita. The shock revelation in *The Kiss*—and, presumably, its selling point—is that the father-daughter incest it recounts is not childhood exploitation, but a consensual act between two adults. It began when Harrison was 20, and old enough to know better. Harrison's father, a preacher, left home when Kathryn was only 6 months old, insisting later that he was driven away. (He remarried and started another family.) Kathryn was raised mostly by her mother's parents. It was tense around the house; when her mother went out on dates, her grandmother howled like an animal. When Kathryn was 6, her mother moved out of the house to a nearby apartment, depriving her of the presence of both parents. The anger and the resentment that Harrison feels toward her wayward mother is later manifested as anorexia.

> An uneasy relationship with food is the standard example in cases such as my mother's and mine. At fifteen, when I stop eating, is it because I want to secure her grudging admiration? Do I want to make myself smaller and smaller until I disappear, truly becoming my mother's daughter: the one she doesn't see?

Her father does see, and how. He sees from the depths of his muddled being. At the age of 20, Kathryn meets the father whom she has barely known in an awkward family reunion of which mother makes three. Her slatternly mother being chronically late, Kathryn meets her father alone at the airport terminal.

> "Don't move," he says. "Just let me look at you."

> My father looks at me, then, as no one has ever looked at me before. His hot eyes consume me—eyes that I will discover are always just this bloodshot. I almost feel their touch. He takes my hands, one in each of his, and turns them over, stares at my palms. He does not actually kiss them, but his look is one that ravishes.

Training his personal high-beams on her, his eyes "burn like no other eyes I've ever seen before or since. Burn like a prophet's, a madman's, a lover's." Shades of Fu Manchu! "Always shining, always bloodshot, always turned on me with absolute attention. Intelligent eyes, enraptured eyes, luminous, stricken, brilliant, spellbound, spellbinding eyes." Alright, already!

The affair begins days later, with their goodbye kiss at the airport terminal—a kiss that begins as a proper one on his part but becomes a Roto-Rooter tongue probe, "wet, insistent, exploring, then withdrawn." Stunned, she watches his plane take off, "the thrust that lifts its heavy, shining belly into the clouds," an image that you don't need to be Freud to figure out. He bombards her with phone calls and letters, pleas to meet him. She shouldn't, she mustn't, but she must, she does. Soon they are saying goodbyes at different airports, which are yet all the same in their antiseptic dolor.

> Our protracted good-byes are consumed along with magazines and junk food by the weary, bored travelers who surround us, slumped in molded plastic chairs.

> Do we resemble each other enough that people suspect we're father and daughter? Do we sit too close to one another? Does his hand on my arm betray his intent? And why do we cling so, as if our parting will be as final as death?

At first surmise, Harrison's lapsing into an affair with her father seems a desperate attempt to sunbathe in the attention always denied her by her mother. ("Her eyes, when they turn at last toward me, are like two empty mirrors. I can't see myself in them.") It's also a sexual cat fight. When Harrison was in college, according to *The Kiss,* her mother insisted that she be fitted for a diaphragm and accompanied her to the gynecologist's examining room. The doctor informs them that the hymen needs to be broken before the fitting can be done. "You don't want me to do that, do you?" he asks. Yes, the mother says. And so, writes Harrison, "This doctor deflowers me in front of my mother," inserting one green dildo after another until there's blood.

It was the doctor's hand, but her mother's decision—her mother took her virginity. Thus Kathryn's affair with her father is a form of retaliation—a return jab. "Through my father I have begun at last to penetrate my mother, to tear away the masks that divide us." Her father is a stand-in for her mother; he has "disconcertingly visible" breasts and lovely feet. Though he may need one of those male bras from "Seinfeld" ("the mansière"), he's quite comfy in his flesh. Harrison: "For women like my mother and myself, careful listeners to society's normative messages of beauty and gender, a body such as my father's and his utter lack of self-consciousness over it are as subversive and disquieting as is his readiness to weep."

Bordering on camp, *The Kiss* is the oddest piece of kitsch, going from melodrama about hypnotic burning eyes to women's-magazine pap about "society's normative messages," from overblown omens ("every day the sun rises and sinks over the Grand Canyon, each time filling it with shadows the color of blood") to cardboard dialogue out of a drawing-room drama: "When I look at you," Harrison's father tells her, "I wonder if I, too, must not be handsome." (Take off your gloves, Count, and stay awhile.) Harrison's sentences carry a high instep as she treads through the fallen petals of her past. "The dizzy rapture of starving. The power of needing nothing. By force of will I will make myself the impossible sprite who lives on air, on water, on purity." It's bad Sylvia Plath.

Perhaps the passage that best captures the book's weird precocity comes when Harrison visits her grandfather (her father's father), and he, too, makes a pass at her. His pass deflected, gramps takes her on a tour of his greenhouse:

> The small glass structure is filled with color, as if every hue in this dry, gray city has been drawn into the vibrant box. In it, my grandfather is a magician, and his smile tells me he knows this. As I walk behind him and watch his hands gently turn a beautiful bloom toward my notice, do I remember the linguistic connection between orchids and male genitalia? Do I say the word silently to myself, *orchideclomy,* and define it as a surgical term for the removal of the testicles? I think, actually, that I do.

This book is so self-consciously writerly that when Harrison traps a cockroach under a glass we instantly grasp that this is no ordinary house bug, this is a metaphor for her condition. "I watch how it must relentlessly search for the seam, the tiny ridge or rill in the glass that might offer some hope of climbing, penetrating, escaping. But there is nothing about the glass that it understands." She, too, feels bewildered and trapped by transparent forces.

But it's one thing to be a small child at the mercy of adults, and another thing to be an adult participant yourself. Her father may have peppered her with wheedling phone calls and letters, but he wasn't looming at her bedroom door, taking advantage of his size and his age. Their affair wasn't a sordid domestic situation, it was a complex operation. She had to make travel arrangements to bunk with dad, then cover her tracks with lies. The conscious upkeep required for this relationship gets lost in the mental haze that Harrison maintains on the page. She sets the psychological framework for the incest, but she absents herself from the activity itself, depicting herself as a somnambulist, a white zombie.

When her father lifts her nightgown to perform cunnilingus (about as explicit as the book gets), Harrison disassociates from her body as the scene unfolds like some primitive rite. "Neither of us speaks, not even one word. The scene is as silent, as dark and dreamlike as if it proceeded from a fever or a drug." Over time, her mind erases the tapes. "In years to come, I won't be able to remember even one instance of our lying together. I'll have a composite, generic memory." It is true that childhood victims of sex abuse often reflect a mind-body split as a method of dealing with the trauma, but in this case you feel Harrison is doing an astral float in order to preserve some core of innocence. After all, if you're the glassy-eyed victim of a fever or a drug, you're not truly responsible for your actions; you're the victim, the pawn of outside agents. But Harrison speaks of "enchantment" and "enslavement," as if she were a fairy princess. The very title of *The Kiss* suggests that this is a Sleeping Beauty story—except in reverse, in which the kiss is not awakening but dumbfounding.

As the shame-spiral deepens, the sex becomes riskier, stagier, a sacred mortification of the flesh, with Kathryn and her father copulating on the floor of his church office. "I tell myself that if I give myself over to him to be sullied, then by the topsy-turvy Christian logic that exalts the reviled, I'll be made clean. I will if I can just do it willingly, trusting in the ultimate goodness of God, and the way in which he sometimes takes unexpected and even repugnant forms, like beggars and lepers, like Saint Dymphna's father. How could she have been martyred without him? How could she have been glorified?" The questions she ought to be asking at that moment are, "Suppose somebody catches us? How are we going to explain this?"

Real-life complications seldom impinge on the book's bummed-out fairy-tale trance. I found myself pondering the awful possibility of her becoming pregnant by her father, something right out of *Chinatown* ("my sister," *slap,* my daughter"). Like John Huston in the film, her father is a monster—angry, bullying, hypocritical—but he isn't a recognizable monster. He doesn't take shape on the page as anything but a toxic blob. To obscure his identity, and perhaps to make him more universal, Harrison doesn't even furnish us with his first name, or make up a new one for him. (Did she call him "Dad" in bed?) There's never an offhand, clinching anecdote about their meals and trips together, or a realistic scrap of conversation. He speaks only in rhetoric. "Is it possible that you don't realize my devotion? You say I'm disrupting your studies, but don't you see you've wreaked havoc in my heart!"

Common to narratives of dysfunctional life is the revelatory moment of hitting bottom. After having sex on the office floor and in her grandmother's house, after having dropped out of college, fallen ill and pondered suicide, Harrison hits bottom when she and her father meet at a welfare hotel in Brooklyn where they have sex and he takes nude Polaroids. "I feel that in my own story I've at last arrived in the dirty place I belong," she says of this Tarantula Arms. After her grandfather dies, she kneels by his corpse in the morgue and kisses his cheek, a kiss that "begins to wake me, just as my father's in the airport put me to sleep." (What symmetry!) Sleeping Beauty finally snaps out of her coma when her mother dies of cancer, and she pays vigil by her corpse, caressing the dead body as an erotic object and realizing at last that "the spell is broken, her death has released me." No longer needing her father to get at her (defunct) mother, Harrison finally ends the affair, her father fading shabbily into the ether.

In the years that follow, Harrison will be able to achieve some perspective and get past the blight. She marries, has children.

> In our marriage we've made a place for my father and what happened between me and him. It's a locked place, the psychic equivalent of a high cupboard, nearly out of reach.

> My children touch my face, my hair. They kiss me. To them I am perfect and beautiful.

But one has to step back from this happily-ever-after tableau and ask: Is the publication of *The Kiss* a responsible act? Does it truly provide Harrison with "closure" and end the cycle of misery? Or might it perpetuate another round?

The rationale given for writing *The Kiss* is that the incestuous affair between Harrison and her father so clouded and dampened her psyche that only directly addressing the issue would do. Her agent told *The New York Observer* that she advised Harrison to put aside the family saga novel that she was writing and tackle this obstruction as nonfiction. "It was my feeling that ... she needed to exorcise what happened with her father. Not that it was blocking her, but it was preoccupying her." Having been granted permission to say the unsayable, Harrison could hardly rein the words in her head, writing *The Kiss* "in one of those strange periods of white heat." *The Kiss* reads more like dry ice than white heat, but never mind. The point is: just because she wrote it doesn't mean she had to publish it.

It is certainly true that opportunism oozes from every pore of *The Kiss* and its launch.
—*James Wolcott*

It is assumed today that all secrets are bad, that withholding them is unhealthy; secrets denied the clean light of day will only fester. Yet the celebrities and near-celebrities who write or dictate tell-all books seldom find themselves purged and at peace. Instead, like Roseanne and Patti Davis, they feel compelled to toss out more red meat in even gaudier sequels. The truth is that some secrets may have a healthy purpose, providing a buffer zone or guardrail against a careless and uncaring all-impinging world. Secrets are an integral part of privacy, a personal identifying mark or a family bond. "Deeply experienced people—this continually impresses me—will keep things to themselves," the narrator of Saul Bellow's novella *The Bellarosa Connection* remarks.

For a writer, secrets are more than material; they are intellectual capital that accrues power and interest by being nursed in solitude. (Bellow's narrator speaks of secrets being converted into burnable energy.) To fling them out too freely is to vulgarize them, and to risk injuring those most intimately involved. There is a big difference between getting something out of your system and putting it on the market. Harrison herself claims, "I was never trying to figure out what I was going to get from this book. Really, I just wanted to write it." Why not wait, then, and give the manuscript time to cool?

It's not as if she hasn't broached the subject before. As Michael Shnayerson damagingly documented, some of the big set pieces in *The Kiss* (an incident involving kittens, the gynecological deflowering) are reprised from Harrison's first novel, *Thicker than Water.* Shnayerson concluded that "this is not a case of a novelist taking some bit from her past that appears in one book and re-examining it in the next. This is a wholesale lift." And the scenes in which her father takes photographs of her on the road recall her second novel, *Exposure,* which also featured a hovering, seductive shutterbug. Tonally, *The Kiss* is the same as *Thicker than Water* and *Exposure.* Harrison isn't following the lead of Philip Roth and saying, in effect, "You've read the novels—now for the facts behind the fiction." *The Kiss* doesn't read as a tonic antidote or a frank revision. It reads as yet another costume jewelry display of rapt sensibility. Shnayerson speculated that the reason Harrison chose to publish is one of expediency: she wanted to make a killing, to cash in on her catharsis. "Literary fiction" has become a dread phrase in publishing, and the sales of Harrison's novels have only been so-so; but a juicy memoir is where the money is. It is certainly true that opportunism oozes from every pore of *The Kiss* and its launch.

But I think that Harrison's decision to publicize her past is animated by something more, and even worse, than the desire for a best-seller. It's an acting-out unconsciously intended to inflict discomfort closer to home. For Colin and Kathryn Harrison have two children, a son and a daughter. It is the daughter, Sarah, on whom she dotes in print. In articles for women's magazines, Harrison stresses how beautiful her daughter is. In *Vogue,* she recalled sitting with another mother and watching their daughters play. "They are only six, but already we know that mine will spurn and hers will suffer." Last summer Harrison wrote her most intimate article concerning her future heartbreaker of a daughter. It was called "Tick," and it appeared in *The New Yorker.*

In retrospect, "Tick" served as an ugly little appetizer for *The Kiss.* It concerned an incident at the Harrisons' summer house, when the daughter was 5. Harrison is brushing Sarah's hair. "I brush longer than I need to. The tangles are out and the brushing soothes me with its repetitive motion, like sewing or sweeping or fucking, late-night, too-tired-to-fuck fucking." When I originally read this passage, I was puzzled as to why Harrison had sexualized the prosaic act of brushing her daughter's hair, and disturbed by how she had sexualized it in language that suggested joyless, slugged grinding.

Now, in *The Kiss,* we read how Harrison would sit at the vanity table as her mother brushed her hair. Harrison's long blond hair was a source of great pride to her: "a symbol of *me,*" "an obvious symbol of sexuality." Her hair is the first feature her father fawns over when he sees her after all those many years. When her mother falls ill, Harrison decides to have her Rapunzel locks chopped. "Within the haircut are, of course, love and anger: a hostile capitulation. I make my hair a sacrifice to my mother's vision of the daughter she wanted, a relic of the girl who lived to please her mother. . . ." (Harrison scholars should note that she told the same anecdote in an article in *Vogue,* September 1994. No one can say she doesn't recycle.) Sarah's hair, her "beautiful braids," is a living talisman, a seductive snare. Just as Harrison displaced her mother in her father's bed, she is destined to be sexually upstaged in time by her own beautiful daughter.

The hard brushing that she gives her daughter's hair suggests the resentment that she feels; and this amorphous resentment sharpens into focus when Harrison discovers a tick in her daughter's hair. The tick is pale and engorged. Using tweezers to extract the tick by its head, Harrison, repulsed yet fascinated, doesn't dispose of the parasite in the toilet, as most people would do. She decides to torture it, searching for steak knives like some backyard barbecue Lady Macbeth, but settling for an odd implement that looks like a nut pick. With ruthless precision, she amputates the tick's legs, studying its defensive posture and marveling over its determination to live; then locates the steak knives and really goes to town, debating whether to aim "for that tiny anus or whatever that little hole is," or run the point of the blade straight through the sucker.

Harrison's reaction to the tick is so extravagantly fierce, fanatical and steel-edged that it's clear this is no average tick. This is a symbolic insect, like the cockroach in *The Kiss.* Residing in the nest of sexuality, the tick is the embodiment of lurking evil. Harrison's true mission surfaces when she confides that her real purpose in poking holes into the tick is to pop it open and release her daughter's blood. "The reappearance of my daughter's stolen life will qualify as redemption," she claims, fatuously. But whose redemption? Her daughter is bawling somewhere in the house; redemption isn't on her agenda. Stolen life? All the tick drew was blood.

No, it was Harrison's life which was stolen, by her abandoning parents. And in going after that bulb of blood that the tick has become, Harrison is out to break her daughter's hymen, as her mother broke hers. She's left frustrated as the tick refuses to cooperate. Only when she pulps the tick's body does she realize that "Sarah's blood has turned to excrement." The unspoken lesson of "Tick" is, eros ends in shit.

Not only did Harrison write about her daughter within such a graphic, mad-scientist scenario, she also denied her daughter the decency, the solace, of anonymity. Accompanying Harrison's article, *The New Yorker* published a photograph of Sarah Harrison on her mother's lap. She looks unhappy in the shot, squirming, pouty, perhaps about to cry. Surely such a gross invasion of the child's privacy wasn't necessary. Rereading "Tick" after reading *The Kiss,* however, I can't help but feel that these two productions constitute a narcissistic act on Harrison's part intended to invite misery and humiliation upon her children, especially the daughter, as misery was visited upon her. (Narcissistic, because Harrison craves the public spotlight as deeply as she did her father's heat-seeking eyes.)

Discussing the possible impact that *The Kiss* and its resultant publicity might have on her children, Harrison has resorted to weasel words. She told *The New York Observer* that "my life as a writer is quite separate from my life as a mother, and I know this is an issue I'm probably going to have to address with my children, and I'm waiting for my cue from them." *Probably* have to address? You mean, as if this were a storm that might blow out to sea?

Similarly, she told *Mirabella* that "I would like them to be as little aware of it [the incest] as possible. . . . I don't want it to be thrust on them when they're not ready." Well, publishing a book and giving interviews to *Mirabella* and the *Observer* isn't exactly a protective-bubble policy. If Harrison is so concerned about her children being "ready," why not wait and publish the book when they are older, and better able to absorb the news? Why, in short, would you tell the entire world something before you tell those whose happiness and well-being matter most? She is the one doing the thrusting. And she may not even be telling the truth now. In the *Mirabella* interview, Harrison admits that "I wanted my father, let's just say that. And I got him." It is a statement of intent and initiative completely at odds with the narration and the tenor of *The Kiss,* where she is a meek passive vessel adrift and her father the pirate who boards her. No seduction is ever truly one-sided. Harrison's remarks in *Mirabella* suggest that *The Kiss* may be another form of fiction.

In the days of Dick Morris, we should hardly be surprised to see content providers sacrificing personal considerations to further their cockamamie careers. Colin Harrison, for his part, has written an article for *Vogue* on what it's like to be married to a woman who had incest with her father. Of course, when you have something intimate and painful to share, what better venue than *Vogue*? It didn't take much arm-twisting, a *Vogue* editor informed *Mediaweek:* "Colin was willing, and he wrote something that is quite beautiful and sturdy. Colin himself told *Mediaweek* that "this is the first piece of journalism I've written about her, ever. But it wasn't a hand-wringing situation by any means, because I'm extraordinarily proud of her. That's my overriding emotion in her—pride." The combined smarm of Colin and Kathryn Harrison is enough to drive one backwards. *The Kiss* will be soon forgotten, but the Harrisons have secured their place as the Sonny and Cher dysfunction.

A final note. Among the luminaries bestowing a blurb on *The Kiss* is the pyschologist and saint Robert Coles, author most recently of *The Moral Intelligence of Children.* The Harrisons don't know any better, but doesn't he?

Conan Putnam (review date 6 April 1997)

SOURCE: "Fear of Father," in *Chicago Tribune Books,* April 6, 1997, p. 3.

[*Below, Putnam reviews Linda Katherine Cutting's* Memory Slips *and Gillian Helfgott's* Love You to Bits and Pieces, *both memoirs of trauma in the lives of accomplished pianists. In considering Cutting's autobiographical piece, Putnam asserts that the author would have been more successful in reaching "deeper introspection" had she employed a more conventional narrative style. Putnam also praises* Love You to Bits and Pieces, *Gillian Helfgott's account (written with Alissa Tanskaya) of her life with piano prodigy David Helfgott and his battle to overcome "a cruelly damaging relationship with his father," finding the book "told with sensitivity, wit and great self-assurance."*]

"I think of my father, how bow-legged he was, how he wore down the outside soles of his shoes. What traumatized him? The war? He fought in the Battle of the Bulge, a sergeant in Patton's Third Army. Is that what made him violent?" writes Linda Katherine Cutting in her journal after listening to a lecture on trauma theory during her stay at the National Center for the Treatment of Trauma and Disassociation in Boulder, Colo. "I am looking and looking for some way to preserve the good father, to forgive the bad one."

Cutting's new book, *Memory Slips: A Memoir of Music and Healing,* is a kind of meditation on the theme of the destructiveness of the father. In journal-entry style, Cutting, a teacher at the Longy School of Music in Cambridge, Mass., and once a busy concert pianist, recounts her departure from the concert stage to retrieve long-buried memories of sexual abuse and the painfully slow healing process that this entailed.

"There are three kinds of memory slips" when performing music, Cutting tells her students. "One, when memory slips but you find your way back without losing a beat. Two, when you don't find your way back until the downbeat. Three, when you don't find your way back in time and must stop and restart the music."

In July 1989, 6 1/2 bars into a Beethoven sonata, Cutting experienced a memory slip that touched off a 10-year search for an explanation as to why the sound of footsteps caused her to freeze on stage, forgetting the piece she was playing. "I had to make sure it wasn't him," Cutting writes. "I stopped, put my hands in my lap, and looked out at the audience. It was only a latecomer taking his seat." Several seconds later, having recovered her poise, Cutting restarted the piece and continued on through a program that included, in addition to the Beethoven, a Bartok sonata and Schumann's Fantasy in C.

Two narratives alternate throughout the book. One spans Cutting's year at the trauma center, the other a period of time 10 years prior to her stay there, detailing her life as a concert pianist jetting from one performance to another as the cracks in her marriage and her shaky sense of self begin to show. By telling her story in this way, Cutting says, she hopes to "mimic the way time is experienced in the first movement of Beethoven's Sonata, op. 109. . . . In the 1982-83 sections, time is moving quickly, even rushing by. In the 1992 sections, time slows down, almost to a standstill."

This is an ambitious goal, and if performing a sonata were in any way similar to writing a memoir, Cutting might have pulled it off. Unfortunately, it turns out to be a jumpy, self-conscious strategy that tries the reader's patience and renders it nearly impossible to piece together either Cutting's story or the part music played in her healing.

"Today is my first journal group," Cutting writes from the trauma center. "Strange, to be joining a group to write. I can't imagine joining a group to practice the piano—the cacophony of sound would be terrifying. Practicing the piano and writing are lonely acts. They are meant to be done in private. And yet they are the very acts that keep me from feeling entirely alone." A few moments later, after informing the leader of the group that she is already a writer, having written in journals for most of her life and having completed a novel, she states: "I have, after all, lost most of my dignity in this place. Writing, for me, is an embodiment, a second skin. It covers the vulnerability and still exposes what needs to have light. Along with practicing the piano, writing is the thing that's kept me alive."

What is the reader to make of this kind of vague, circular writing?

> **One can't help but wonder if a more conventionally patterned narrative might have helped [Katherine] Cutting gain the authorial distance so clearly needed to engage in the deeper introspection that a book-length memoir of this type demands.**
> **—*Conan Putnam***

Whether Cutting is describing the landscape in Colorado ("The sky is bigger here. It's hard to explain. You only know it if you've spent time out west.") or how she feels, waiting for news of her brother David, missing for three days ("I've been climbing the walls at home. I can't sit at the piano for more than ten-minute intervals. I pace from room to room like a caged animal.") the core of her remembered experience and what it means to her remain a mystery.

After many pages of sketchy, impressionistic ruminations, the picture that emerges is of a young woman so shattered by the past that she finds it impossible to see her grownup self as separate from the victim of her childhood trauma. One

can't help but wonder if a more conventionally patterned narrative might have helped Cutting gain the authorial distance so clearly needed to engage in the deeper introspection that a book-length memoir of this type demands.

. . . . .

"You shouldn't have a 'father' thing. Just break out of it! Just break free!" was David Helfgott's advice to a young friend so tormented in childhood by an abusive father that it nearly derailed her musical career in later life. Helfgott, a piano prodigy who survived more than one nervous breakdown and years of exile from the concert stage, has, as many already know from seeing the biographical movie *Shine,* made an impressive recovery from a cruelly damaging relationship with his father. His healing process is energetically described by his wife, Gillian Helfgott, in her memoir (written with Alissa Tanskaya) *Love You to Bits and Pieces.*

Gillian, an astrologer, met David in the early '80s when he was living in a boarding house in Perth, Australia, swimming like a fiend by day in a friend's pool and playing the piano in Riccardo's, a wine bar, by night. At their first meeting, he invited her to come hear him play.

> "Riccardo's was by no means situated in a trendy part of town," Gillian writes. "Above the wine bar was a backpackers' hostel, and the bar itself had a '50s look with dark walls, chrome chairs and no windows. . . . As we entered, one could feel the audience's anticipation. . . .

> "David's fingers gently touched the keys and from the first sounds I could sense the crowd being drawn towards him. A change had come over David. The gangling, maniacally noisy creature, seemingly so insecure, became another person, completely absorbed and confident in his craft."

During a break, Gillian asked David to name his favorite piece. "Rak 3, Serge's Rak 3," he replied. He then went straight back to the piano and played Sergei Rachmaninoff's Piano Concerto No. 3 in its entirety while a "spellbound" Gillian marveled at his "majesty and passion." Nine months later, after consulting their astrology charts to make sure the planets were favorably aligned, Gillian married David.

Gillian's account of how she and others helped David rebuild his career as a concert pianist is told with sensitivity, wit and great self-assurance. Laying to rest rumors of his inability to hold up under the strain of regular performances required shoring up David's fragile sense of self as well as regular exposure of his talent in venues more suitable to classical piano than the wine bar. To these and countless other rehabilitative tasks Gillian applied herself with gusto. After cutting David's cigarette, coffee and gum consumption to near zero during performances, she set to work discouraging his incessant muttering while playing.

"Sometimes he sang away and muttered, and sometimes he didn't," she writes, "and to this day one can never predict what he will do when left alone on a stage."

As Gillian points out, David's muttering acts as a kind of self-protection ritual to ward off the cloud of negativity implanted in his psyche early on by his father's violent outbursts and the obsessive, perfectionist demands he placed on his son's gifts. Throughout the book there are references to "the fog," David's term for the swirl of chaotic, rambling thoughts and painful recollections that prevented him for many years from developing his talent in the disciplined, structured way that a successful career as a concert pianist requires.

"The fog" first appeared in London in the summer of 1969, when, at age 22, after successfully performing his beloved "Rak 3" before an adoring audience at the Royal College of Music, David failed to follow his strong inclination to return home to Australia to nurture his talent in less-stressful surroundings. Instead, he remained in London, where, under the influence of intense competition at the school and problems with alcohol and medication to tamp down ever-present feelings of panic and fear, he suffered his first breakdown.

"After the Rak it all went chaos," he told Gillian. "It all went absolutely foggy and misty, foggy and misty."

David's struggle to permanently dispel "the fog" continues, as does Gillian's push to see him gain the recognition she feels he missed as a result of being kept so firmly under his father's thumb when his career could have been taking off. Whether they will be successful depends on many variables, not the least of which is David's fragile temperament. Add to that the maw of the celebrity machine in which they are now caught as a result of *Shine* and the strenuous concert tour the couple is racing to complete, and you have enough material for a sequel to *Love You to Bits and Pieces.*

Joanne Kaufman (review date 20 April 1997)

SOURCE: "Novelist Kathryn Harrison's Memoir of Her Affair with Her Father," in *Chicago Tribune Books,* April 20, 1997, p. 2.

[*In the following review of Kathryn Harrison's* The Kiss, *Kaufman notes that "the reader wants, needs, what feels spontaneous; the reader gets something studied, carefully literary." She compares* The Kiss *to Harrison's other works and finds them similar, concluding that "perhaps* The Kiss *will serve as the means by which Harrison can finally exorcise her demons and begin to broaden the terrain of her fiction."*]

There are lots of really swell ways for authors to market their works these days: Concoct an elaborately clumsy piece of fiction but swear on a stack of *Publishers Weekly*s that it's non-fiction (check out *Sleepers* by Lorenzo Carcaterra). Slap between covers what is essentially non-fiction, call it fiction and credit it to Anonymous (Joe Klein's *Primary Colors*). Give potential customers something extra for their money by outfitting the book with a CD—it's got a good beat and you can read to it (a la Joyce Maynard and Laura Esquivel)! Or (with, perhaps, a certain amount of cynicism) put forward a memoir that traffics in the salacious and/or sensational, and become the subject of magazine and TV feature stories, in the manner of critically acclaimed novelist Kathryn Harrison.

The Kiss chronicles the affair, 16 years ago, between Harrison, then a college student, and her minister father. The product of a perfervid romance between two 17-year-olds who married in shotgun-wedding haste and divorced with dispatch, Harrison was raised mostly by her grandparents, Mom having decamped to live her own life, Dad, whom Harrison saw only twice during her childhood, having been summarily forced out of the picture. "It was in the garden . . . that my grandfather told my father that it was over between him and my mother. . . . My grandparents thought they could end it, erase my mother's unfortunate mistake. There was the baby, of course, the life that sprang from my mother's rebellion . . . there was me to consider, but I was a cost they'd accept. He, however, had to go."

Unsurprisingly, perhaps, Harrison had a troubled childhood and adolescence—nightmares, anorexia, bulimia. It was a landscape bordered by her narcissistic grandmother, her self-centered, withholding mother, a sometimes-endearing grandfather who became increasingly uncomfortable with Kathryn as she passed through puberty, and by her shadowy, letter-writing father. When she sees him at 20 for the first time in 10 years, "my once-bobbed hair long, and my flat chest filled out, my father's eyes are fixed on me; he tears his gaze away with reluctance. This kind of besotted focus is intoxicating, especially for a girl schooled in self-effacement and taught that virtue believes more in its ugliness than in its beauty. . . . I don't know it yet, not consciously, but I feel it: my father, holding himself so still and staring at me, has somehow begun to *see* me into being."

He has bloodshot eyes, he's overweight, he sleeps with Harrison's mother the first time all three of them are together (despite the fact that he is remarried with children), then, talks about it in most ungallant terms with Harrison. "'I didn't do it because I wanted to,' he says. Humiliated on behalf of my mother, and shocked that he would betray her this way, I look not at him but at my plate."

Unfortunately, *The Kiss,* which reads rather like a fever dream, doesn't probe as deeply or as far as Father's tongue.
—*Joanne Kaufman*

That indiscretion doesn't begin to prepare Harrison for the indiscretion at the airport as her father prepares to return to his other family. He "pushes his tongue deep into my mouth: wet, insistent. . . . In years to come, I'll think of the kiss as a kind of transforming sting, like that of a scorpion: a narcotic that spreads from my mouth to my brain. The kiss is the point at which I begin, slowly, inexorably, to fall asleep, to surrender volition, to become paralyzed. It's the drug my father administers in order that he might consume me. That I might desire to be consumed."

What draws the two of them together in this unholy alliance is "her," Harrison's distant mother, her father's elusive former wife; they are united in their love for a woman who can't, won't love them back. The affair, which is preceded by countless fulminations by Harrison's father that "God gave you to me," is played out at scenic points of interest and truck-stop motels across the Southwest, and it ends only with the death of Harrison's mother due to bone cancer.

Unfortunately, *The Kiss,* which reads rather like a fever dream, doesn't probe as deeply or as far as Father's tongue. While the story is set forth in the present tense, accruing to it an unsettling immediacy, Harrison has (understandably) so distanced herself from the events she recounts that the book's impact is greatly blunted. The reader wants, needs, what feels spontaneous; the reader gets something studied, carefully literary.

More problematic, *The Kiss* is told as though through a scrim; innuendo rather than specifics is the coin of the realm here. In so saying one feels like a greedy voyeur (of course, one feels like a voyeur by the very act of opening the book), but the fact is, if you're going to commit to telling the story Harrison has chosen to tell, either tell it and tell it in detail or don't publish it.

What this memoir confronts as fact has utterly informed Harrison's three novels. *Thicker Than Water,* which at the time the author insisted was purely a product of her imagination, covers precisely the same ground as *The Kiss,* if in more textured, graphic fashion. The potent *Exposure* deals with a woman haunted and almost undone by the erotic pictures taken of her in childhood by her celebrated photogra-

pher father. *Poison* is about a woman who has an affair with a priest (a different sort of father). Perhaps *The Kiss* will serve as the means by which Harrison can finally exorcise her demons and begin to broaden the terrain of her fiction. If so, it will have been worth it for the reader, certainly for Harrison.

Carolyn Alessio (review date 27 April 1997)

SOURCE: "Dark Angels," in *Chicago Tribune Books,* April 27, 1997, p. 3.

[*Below, Alessio reviews three memoirs examining the effects of mental illness on families: Tara Elgin Holley's* My Mother's Keeper, *Clea Simon's* Mad House, *and Jay Neugeboren's* Imagining Robert.]

The modern world recklessly equates mental illness with art. Consider the current world tour of Australian pianist David Helfgott, the subject of the popular film *Shine.* Despite reports of his abysmal technique, Helfgott plays to sold-out audiences, while his CD ranks as a best seller on classical music charts. Famous disturbed artists whose work did succeed, like Vincent Van Gogh and Robert Lowell, nurture the illusion that the insane are intermediaries from a mysterious aesthetic realm. As if the mentally ill did not have enough to contend with, recent books such as Arnold Ludwig's *The Price of Greatness: Resolving the Creativity and Madness Controversy* saddle their condition with the expectation of artistic greatness.

Romanticization of mental illness is best refuted by the relatives of the mentally ill. In three new memoirs, the loved ones of four schizophrenics explore the vagaries of caring for their relatives, from practical concerns like finding suitable halfway houses, to more profound issues of responsibility, anger and betrayal.

Ironically, two of these authors are artists—Jay Neugeboren, a novelist, and Tara Elgin Holley, a musician. Neugeboren and Holley, along with journalist Clea Simon, credit their mentally ill relatives with affecting the direction of their work, negatively and positively. Their aesthetic perspectives suggest an overlooked aspect of the relationship between art and madness: the artistic effect of madness on the family observer.

In the U.S. alone, 2.5 million people are diagnosed schizophrenics, about 1 percent of the population. According to the Diagnostic and Statistical Manual of Mental Disorders, schizophrenia is a disturbance that lasts at least 6 months and includes two or more of the following: delusions, hallucinations, disorganized speech, grossly disorganized or catatonic behavior, and loss of normal emotional functioning.

Not only is the nature of the illness fundamentally unpredictable, but so is the care, and the relatives of schizophrenics are often called upon to be creative with their skills and resources. In 1994, Neugeboren wrote a desperate letter to New York Gov. Mario Cuomo about Neugeboren's younger brother, Robert, who had suffered from mental illness for the last 32 of his 50 years. Robert had been asymptomatic for more than 6 months and was eager to move to a halfway/recovery house, but bureaucratic delays kept him on a locked ward at Staten Island's South Beach Psychiatric Center.

When Neugeboren consulted Robert's state-appointed psychiatrist about moving his brother, the psychiatrist snapped, "Talk to the governor." Cuomo responded, at least in part. When the psychiatric center's staff received a copy of the letter from the governor's office, it chastised Neugeboren and further complicated Robert's situation. Once again, Neugeboren was back where he started.

Imagining Robert: My Brother, Madness, and Survival rose out of 32 years of Jay Neugeboren's frustration with the ways in which the medical community and the outside world treated his brother. Neugeboren, author of 10 novels and nonfiction books, is a master chronicler of lives. In this ponderous and unsparing memoir, he relentlessly scours his own family's history for possible origins of his brother's illness. Though he pinpoints manic-depressive characteristics in his mother, Neugeboren hesitates to blame his brother's illness on pure heredity. A focus on genetics may someday lead to a cure, but his immediate interest is in day-to-day care issues.

Neugeboren candidly admits to some exasperation with his brother, who long has relied on him for comfort and support in the midst of repeated breakdowns. The book includes snippets of many disturbing, late-night phone calls and publicly humiliating scenes. But Neugeboren also depicts Robert's intellect and idiosyncratic humor, qualities that Neugeboren admits he relies on his brother to provide. In one scene Neugeboren asks Robert why he has survived his breakdowns and hospitalizations when so many of his mentally ill cohorts have completely deteriorated or committed suicide.

"First of all," Robert quips, "I realized that God is black and that she loves me." But when Jay presses him for a more serious answer, Robert says, "I just wanted to survive and persist. . . . [I]t's like Faulkner said in the speech he made, for the Nobel, remember?—I wanted to *endure* somehow."

Whereas Neugeboren gradually assumes a parental role in

caring for his brother, Tara Elgin Holley takes responsibility for her schizophrenic mother when Holley is in her late teens. Holley, who writes with her husband, journalist Joe Holley, traces her early maturity and love of music to her mother.

In 1951, Big Band singer Dawn Elgin was establishing herself in Hollywood, considering an offer from RCA Victor. There was talk, too, of a movie role for the aspiring 21-year-old actress, but suddenly Dawn departed for New York.

For months, her family in California heard nothing from their daughter. Then they received a telegram from Bellevue Hospital: "Your daughter is acute paranoid schizophrenic. Needs hospitalization." The telegram failed to mention that the unmarried Dawn had recently given birth to a daughter, whom she named Tara.

The only real information that remains about this period is that during Dawn's pregnancy, she began to dream of a dark angel. She continued to experience visions and dreams, mixed with bouts of rage, and soon her previous lifestyle eroded. Tara was raised primarily by relatives.

My Mother's Keeper is the brutal, insightful story of Tara Elgin Holley's attempt to decipher her mentally ill mother's relationship with the world. As a result, Holley discovers the unconventional ways in which her mother shaped her own identity.

By age 21, Holley had assumed full responsibility for her mother's hospitalizations, medications and transitional housing. This was no simple task for a college music student who also held two jobs, but she managed to keep vigil over Dawn, who wandered the streets of Austin, Texas, unkempt and often disoriented. Despite Holley's attempts to locate the most sympathetic doctors and hospitals, Dawn claimed to be happiest when she roamed the streets.

And despite Holley's strident loyalty to her mother, she admits to a moment or two of denial. In one painful scene, Holley is walking with a professor when she sees her mother in the distance, clad in urine-stained clothes. Holley panics, telling her professor she has to stop at the co-op, and ducks into a doorway. As her mother passes, Holley notes that her mother's fingernails are bitten off to the quick; blood has dried around the cuticles.

The moments of connection with her mother remain few but precious to Holley, who describes happily singing classical music for Dawn. But Dawn's enthusiastic response provoked both joy and guilt in Holley, who wondered why she and not her mother was allowed to pursue a musical career unhampered by mental illness. This complicated emotion haunts Holley later in her life, especially when she further hones her art and starts a family of her own. Dawn's crises never quite abate, regardless of new doctors and medications, and neither do Holley's (self-admittedly) improbable hopes that her mother will truly return.

For Clea Simon, the effect of mental illness on her family was doubly devastating; both her siblings were schizophrenic. By the time Simon was 12, her older brother and sister had been in and out of numerous hospitals, institutions and half-way houses. Simon was left to interpret her siblings' bizarre rages and periods of withdrawal and, later, to identify their effect on her own development. To corroborate her experience, Simon turned to other relatives of the mentally ill, members of the National Alliance for the Mentally Ill, and to experts such as Dr. E. Fuller Torrey, author of *Surviving Schizophrenia: A Manual for Families, Consumers, and Providers.*

There is comfort in talking to fellow siblings of the mentally ill, Simon says [in her memoir, *Mad House*], an undeniable need for peers among the perpetually disconnected. Simon, a journalist for the *Boston Globe,* blends interviews and medical information in this instructive but disturbing memoir.

"As siblings who have watched our brothers or sisters 'go mad,' lost our peers to psychosis, we share a unique experience: Our brothers and sisters are the ones we were supposed to have played with, learned to get along with, emulated if they were older or taken care of if they were younger, the people with whom we should have navigated the shoals of growing up. But instead they broke down."

Beyond identifying common characteristics in the relatives of the mentally ill—dread, guilt, a fear of succeeding in one's own career and relationships—Simon admits to fearing the obvious, genetic legacy. Simon, 36, writes from a slightly younger perspective than Neugeboren and Holley, and she brings a wary immediacy to her story; she has not yet had children herself. She and her partner have consulted a genetic counselor, who said a child of Simon's would have a 7 to 8 percent chance of developing schizophrenia. Beyond the genetic fears, Simon worries that she would be overly vigilant as a mother, and that she would somehow damage her child by transmitting her old feelings of guilt and unworthiness. Though she has worked extensively with therapists, her memories and dreams often take her back to childhood scenes in which her siblings frightened her, as when her sister killed Simon's hamster by slamming the piano lid down on it.

Simon says her anxiety was compounded by her parents' sporadic denial of their children's illnesses. When Simon was a freshman entering Harvard, she overheard her mother saying that Clea was her only child. Several years later, Simon's parents would tell her that her 30-year-old brother died in an accident. Later she would learn that he had committed suicide.

Confronting her siblings' illnesses is a lifelong process, according to Simon. "As family members of the mentally ill so often point out," she says, "we have mourning without resolution."

Susie Linfield (review date 11 May 1997)

SOURCE: "Les Liaisons Dangereuses," in *Los Angeles Times Book Review,* May 11, 1997, p. 8.

[*In the following positive review, Linfield praises Kathryn Harrison's* The Kiss *and rebuts the negative appraisals of several other critics.*]

Every now and then a book comes along that disturbs, disrupts and polarizes the public in new ways. Vladimir Nabokov's *Lolita* was such a book, as was Hannah Arendt's *Eichmann in Jerusalem,* William Styron's *The Confessions of Nat Turner,* Phillip Roth's *Portnoy's Complaint* and Charles Murray and Richard Herrnstein's *The Bell Curve.* (This used to happen with films, too—*Bonnie and Clyde, Last Tango in Paris, Shoah*—but that, alas, seems to be a thing of the past.) In such cases, it is not just the work itself but the author too—and, in particular, his motives, integrity and moral vision—that are scrutinized and interrogated. The debates over such books can turn highly unpleasant, yet they are, generally speaking, a good thing, for they force readers and critics to confront their most cherished ideas and even, sometimes, develop new ones.

Kathryn Harrison's *The Kiss,* a memoir of her incestuous relationship with her father, is the latest, and perhaps the best, example of such a polarizing work. To call it controversial would be a laughable understatement; it has been the object of almost apoplectic fury. The *Washington Post*'s Jonathan Yardley, who is one of the country's most prominent book critics, has written three vitriolic pieces on *The Kiss,* calling it "slimy," "repellent," "revolting" and "shameful"; Liz Smith, who is one of the country's most prominent gossip columnists, has also weighed in with a somewhat more concise, if no more restrained, "Yuck!"

Between Yardley and Smith, a wide range of critics (often, though not always, male) has damned the book, while several, such as novelists Francine Prose and Susan Cheever, have praised it. Harrison has been accused of dishonesty, opportunism, careerism, greed, exhibitionism, narcissism, selfishness, coyness, self-plagiarism and—the ultimate insult—bad mothering. (In olden days, one suspects, she would have simply been called a whore and a witch and promptly dispatched to the nunnery or the stake. Apparently, though, such words—and such solutions—are no longer feasible.)

Harrison's harshest critics—who have included Michael Shnayerson in *Vanity Fair* and James Wolcott in the *New Republic*—almost always cite her book as an example of the tacky, tell-all, television-based culture that, they fear, is engulfing us. A "growing number" of women memoirists, Shnayerson warned, are "baring the kind of behavior once kept secret even from close girlfriends"; even the best are "as of-the-moment as this afternoon's 'Oprah.'" But the question of how much women should tell about their emotional and sexual experiences—and of the appropriately Olympian tone to use when they do—is only tangentially related to the emergence of talk shows or tabloids; such questions are, in fact, far older—and more volatile.

> What makes *The Kiss* a very good book is the spare lyricism of its prose, the emotional authenticity of its narrator, its unblinking look at some horrible (but not, I would argue, inhuman) things and the undeniably fascinating story it tells. . . . It is an ugly tale, beautifully told.
> —*Susie Linfield*

Charlotte Bronte, for instance, was criticized for the unseemly, revelatory emotion of her work. As the literary scholar Carolyn G. Heilbrun noted almost a decade ago, "When Matthew Arnold disliked *Villette* because it was so full of hunger, rebellion, rage, he was at the same time identifying its strengths, but these were unbearably presumptuous in a woman writer." And although now generally respected as part of the canon, the work of such poets as Adrienne Rich, Sylvia Plath and Anne Sexton was often regarded as too confessional, too personal, too angry, too sexy and too disgusting when it first appeared. (And a poem like Plath's "Daddy" is still a shocker, even today.) Doris Lessing advised Kate Millett that "you cannot be intimidated into silence" when writing about the sexual truth of your life, but few writers are as sensibly courageous as Doris Lessing. The irony, of course, is that it is precisely when women reveal their most intimate experiences that they risk being viewed as unfeminine:

". . . consider the fate of women. / How unwomanly to discuss it!" the poet Carolyn Kizer wrote. So when *Wall Street Journal* critic Cynthia Crossen admonished Harrison to "hush up," she was hardly suggesting something new. Crossen, Shnayerson, Wolcott, Yardley, et al. have simply taken the well-worn, if not quite venerable, demand that women writers be decent, tactful, dignified, protective and discreet—that is, silent, secretive, deceptive, frightened and reassuring—and put a modern mediaphobic spin on it.

Still, the fact that some very good books (and poems) have been attacked for the same reasons—although, I suspect, with less venom—as *The Kiss* does not make *The Kiss* a very good book. What makes *The Kiss* a very good book is the spare lyricism of its prose, the emotional authenticity of its narrator, its unblinking look at some horrible (but not, I would argue, inhuman) things and the undeniably fascinating story it tells. Reading it, however, is neither easy nor pleasant; its harshness makes you recoil even as its vortex of emotions draws you in. It is an ugly tale, beautifully told.

The actual story is simple; the emotions are anything but. Harrison is raised in a volatile yet loveless home from which her father is virtually absent; when she meets him at age 20 (for only the third time in her life), he begins to pursue her with a demented intensity. She is the good girl who has spent her life desperately, and quite unsuccessfully, seeking the affections of her mother: Their joint project is "trying to make me into the child she can admire and love." Sadly, Harrison is a smart girl, and she has learned her lessons—that love is evasion, self-denial, enslavement, capitulation—all too well. Now caught between a mother who snarls don't-touch-me! and a father who demands touch-me!, she chooses the latter, exchanging one tyrant for another and regarding this, she dryly explains, as "an existential promotion." What is so horrifying about *The Kiss* is not that we can't understand this so-called choice but that, given the devastating clarity with which Harrison charts her emotionally parched landscape, we can.

And here, I think, is the source of much of the fury that has been directed against *The Kiss*. Jean-Paul Sartre has written that literature is a collaboration between author and reader; *The Kiss* turns us into collaborationists in the worst way. Harrison implicates us in grisly truths we don't want to know (but we do, we do): How rage can parade as love; how heartbreakingly hopeless, yet entirely inevitable, are all attempts to transcend loss; how deep sorrow so often transmogrifies into deep viciousness, instead of deep compassion; how those who are most damaged by their parents are the least able to walk—or even crawl—away from them. (And how the gods must chuckle over that one!) *The Kiss* is Freud's family romance played out with a vengeful literalness, and although the actions are certainly extreme, the emotions that underlie them are hardly unique. How, though, can we love a writer who brings us ever closer to—as Elizabeth Hardwick wrote of Sylvia Plath—her "infatuation with the hideous"? By making us, forcing us, to understand (which, it seems necessary to add, is not synonymous with "approve" or "condone"), Harrison blurs the boundary between her perversion and our normalcy.

In her life, too—a life that has received an extraordinary amount of (sometimes speculative) attention since the publication of *The Kiss*—Harrison smudges this line, and that also seems to enrage. Wolcott, for instance, spent much of his long, witty, nasty review of *The Kiss* insisting, rather astonishingly, that Harrison is a lousy mother—precisely, in his view, *because* she has written this memoir. There is no doubt that if Harrison were a hermit, a bag lady, a drug addict, a prostitute, a nun or, best of all, a suicide—that if, in short, she had been permanently and obviously ruined by her transgressions or was spending her life atoning for them—the reaction to *The Kiss* would be far different. Of course, she *may* be a psychological wreck (there is no way for an outside critic to know), but she at least appears to be doing quite well, thank you: There's the flourishing career, the successful husband, the two lovely children, the home in yuppie-heaven Park Slope. Inexplicably—audaciously!—Harrison's life looks quite a lot like those of her critics, especially in her creation of a seemingly normal family. The emotional turf that was supposedly reserved for "nice" people has been invaded; the Maginot Line of respectability has not held. There goes the neighborhood!

> **It is Harrison's bottomless anger—and her ruthlessness, her eagerness for revenge, her scorched-earth policy—that have, I suspect, so frightened certain critics.**
> *—Susie Linfield*

Although *The Kiss* is certainly about incest, its central relationship is the one between Kathryn and her mother. (In fact, the affair is not actually consummated until fairly late in the book, although we know of it from the start.) And the maternal relationship depicted here is almost as disturbing—if not quite as transgressive or deranged—as the paternal one. Harrison's mother (who, like her father, is never named) is an unfortunate, and dangerous, combination. In part, she is negligent (she moves into her own apartment when Harrison is 6, leaving her daughter, who is then raised by grandparents, to gaze at a beautiful frock and wonder, "If a dress like this was not worth taking, how could I have hoped to be?"); in part, she is cruel (she has Harrison deflowered by a gynecologist—while she watches). Not surprisingly, her daughter grows into an equally unfortunate, and no doubt more dangerous, mixture of obsequiousness—she is "the thin girl, the achiever, the grade-earner, the quiet girl, the unhungry girl, the girl who will shape-shift and perform any self-alchemy to win her mother's love"—and rage. Harrison makes clear that she enters the relationship with her father in part to get back at her mother, to break both her mother's heart and will. And it works. The book, and the affair, end with her mother's death from cancer at age 43.

This is not the self-portrait of the author as a nice person. It is, in fact, every mother's—every woman's—nightmare. When it comes to her mother, Harrison is the owner, in her own words, of "a fury so destructive that I would take from her what brief love she has known, because she has been so unwilling for so long to love me just a little." It is Harrison's bottomless anger—and her ruthlessness, her eagerness for revenge, her scorched-earth policy—that have, I suspect, so frightened certain critics. Her stance toward the reader, too, is boldly unapologetic—she is not ingratiating, or even particularly likable, not, apparently, interested in being one of those "close girlfriends" of whom Shnayerson writes.

Even scarier than Harrison's skill in betraying her mother is her ability to betray herself. Her mother's cruelty and her father's craziness may seem foreign, bizarre, unbelievable to some readers, but Harrison's capacity as a young woman to blur her own vision, deny her own feelings, negate her own needs and disavow her own knowledge will seem eerily, creepily, sickeningly familiar to many. Harrison herself recognizes that this is her fatal flaw, the *sine qua non* of her tragedy, the origin of her sin. "Years later," she writes, looking back on a suicide attempt, "what will strike me as more damning than my self-destructiveness is my capacity for secrecy, my genius at revealing so little of my heart—and thus the risk that I, too, could end up a woman as trapped within herself as my mother."

Although its subject matter is certainly shocking, *The Kiss* is an essentially old-fashioned book. It is not particularly smart, analytic, clever or fun; its pain is unalleviated by either the sweetness of redemption or the anesthesia of irony. "*King Lear* is almost intolerable, if it's done well," film critic Pauline Kael once observed; one might say *The Kiss* is done all too well. Far from conveniently plugging into the *Zeitgeist,* its unalloyed wall of anguish is pre-modern, not post.

Several critics have voiced the belief—which, in their case, is really a hope—that *The Kiss* is too far outside normal experience to attract many readers. (Similarly, throughout the book, Harrison expresses the fear that what she has done is "unspeakable.") They may be right, though I doubt it. This is the story of a young girl with a fifth column lodged firmly in her heart and of the terrible places it leads her. Precisely for that reason, I suspect, it will be read by women of all ages—and their mothers and their daughters of all ages, too—long after "Oprah" is off the air, and long after Harrison's sputtering critics have hushed up. Like all good literature, *The Kiss* illuminates something that we knew already, while also teaching us things we had not even suspected.

Trudy Bush (essay date 21 May 1997)

SOURCE: "Putting a Life in Order," in *Christian Century,* May 21-28, 1997, pp. 519-23.

[*Below, Bush discusses the current state of memoir-writing and reviews three works: Agate Nesaule's* A Woman in Amber *and Frank McCourt's* Angela's Ashes, *which she describes as "two of the best of the recent memoirs," and Kathryn Harrison's* The Kiss, *which she considers "one of the worst."*]

My mother is our family's storyteller, and an eventful life has given her great material. Born in the U.S. to immigrant parents who couldn't decide whether they preferred to live in America or Europe, she divided her childhood between Batschka Jarak, a small ethnic German village in what was then Yugoslavia, and Cleveland, Ohio. The frequent moves between continents and vastly different cultures disrupted her schooling and friendships and sometimes left her wondering who she was. Shortly before the outbreak of World War II, she married one of the village schoolteachers in Jarak and remained behind when her parents returned to the U.S.

Many of my mother's stories are about the people and customs of that long-ago village, customs that seemed strange and outlandish to her when she first encountered them but which she now recounts with affection and humor. But the great narrative of her life, repeated again and again, is the story of our horse-and-wagon flight from Yugoslavia in the last year of the war, our time in refugee camps in Germany, and our emigration to the U.S.

My mother's stories of even the worst of times are comforting because their subtext is always that we are tough people who survived; our ability to live productively and with zest was threatened and wounded, but we recovered. I know that a great deal of selectivity and even fictionalizing has gone into my mother's account of the past, but I'm glad that she has chosen to give her stories a positive, even triumphalist edge. My mother agrees with the poet and novelist May Sarton that "we have to make myths of our lives. It is the only way to live without despair."

The strength of this desire to tell one's story and create one's myth—and the appeal of this genre to readers—is evident in the flood of memoirs now pouring from publishing houses. It is a boom time for autobiography, especially of the confessional kind. A sign of the times is the report that a previously unpublished Kansas grandmother received more than $1 million for her manuscript about life with an alcoholic husband.

Why are memoirs so popular? Presumably because they offer truthful encounters with another self—encounters that are more authentic than what novels can provide. But memoirs are not necessarily more truthful or authentic than fiction.

In fact, all engaging memoirs have the artistry of good fiction. The writers imaginatively shape and recreate dialogues and scenes. Like my mother, they select from the multitude of their experiences those that will form a satisfying pattern. Through memoir, a writer gives a meaningful shape to her life and presents herself as she wishes to be seen.

Margot Peter's recent biography of May Sarton demonstrates the extent to which the life Sarton depicted in her journals—especially in *Plant Dreaming Deep*—was a literary artifice. Sarton presents herself as a woman alone, bravely and cheerfully establishing a home and garden, enjoying the adventures of solitude. She left out of her journal her many and stormy lesbian love affairs, her loneliness and rage, her difficult relationships with her neighbors and her inability to tolerate solitude for more than a few days at a time.

Nevertheless, despite the artifice, the critic Carolyn Heilbrun, who knew Sarton well, continues to value *Plant Dreaming Deep* as an "account of how solitude can be shown to be a possible life for women." Sarton's memoirs also are valuable because they present, Heilbrun writes, "that rare being, a unique person," one whose life "veered sharply from mine, granting her experiences I could never have imagined, let alone undertaken. . . . [She had] a kind of gaiety, an ability intensely to experience every moment and to convey that intensity in such a way as to enrich the lives of more sober folk."

Memoirs, then, are valuable not because everything in them is literally true, but because they present inner truths that inspire and provoke thought; they present a vision of life's possibilities. A good memoir makes us feel that we can find and articulate the significance of our own lives. In looking at memoirs, then, we should ask not whether a memoir is literally true but how well the writers have created a pattern of meaning out of the events of their lives, how vividly and convincingly they have conveyed that pattern, and whether, finally, that pattern has moral and spiritual worth.

According to these standards, two of the best of the recent memoirs are Agate Nesaule's *A Woman in Amber* and Frank McCourt's *Angela's Ashes* (which tops the *New York Times* best-seller list and won the Pulitzer Prize). One of the worst is Kathryn Harrison's *The Kiss,* an account of her incestuous relationship with her father.

Nesaule's memoir, like many contemporary examples of the genre, was born as an act of therapy. Her therapist told her, "You must write it, not just for yourself, but for others too. That is what *you* can do for others. Stories can change the human heart." She had been haunted by a sense of shame that she believed stemmed from her childhood experiences and from her immigrant family's stress on maintaining respectability.

Nesaule was born in Latvia several years before the outbreak of World War II and escaped with her family just before the Russian army occupied the country. She vividly recreates the wartime experiences that she believes cast a pall over her life and irreparably harmed her relationship with her mother.

Two of the most vivid scenes are Nesaule's description of her loss of faith—first in God, then in her mother. Both happen when she is seven years old. Forced to watch the execution of Pastor Braun, a German minister who had tried to help the refugees, Nesaule stops praying. "Prayer seemed pointless. No one was listening, no one was helping, no one would." Her estrangement from her mother begins when her mother, thinking all the women and children have been lined up to be shot, tries to pull her children to the front of the line so the three of them can die together without having to witness the deaths of the others. To Agate, this seems an ultimate betrayal: instead of protecting her, her mother wants her to die.

Both breaks are irrevocable. Nesaule will never again believe in a God who helps or cares, and she will not be able to break down the barrier between herself and her mother during her mother's lifetime. "The whole universe was motherless during the war and remained that way for me long afterwards."

When she remembers the starved child she once was, begging food from Russian soldiers who taunted her, she remembers becoming convinced that she was not worth feeding. When, as a teenager in Indianapolis, she had to testify in court against a man who tried to molest her, her mother angrily accused her of having shamed the family. Telling her story is for Nesaule a way of overcoming the feelings of shame and worthlessness.

Nesaule detects in her life a repeating pattern. She married a man who subconsciously reminded her of the soldiers who had demeaned and raped the Latvian refugees in Europe. In America the Latvian immigrants worked hard, educated themselves, and became prosperous, but one after another succumbed to depression, alcoholism or suicide. She concludes that experiencing the brutalities of war and dislocation, especially when young, permanently damages people. And her book is designed to illustrate that thesis. Consequently, Nesaule tells little about her achievements—about getting a Ph.D., establishing a women's studies program and becoming an excellent teacher, or forming satisfying friendships with other women. And she says almost nothing about her father, who she briefly tells us "kept alive his strong faith in God, his optimism and his compassion."

The book would seem reductive, too narrowly focused on only the dark aspects of life, even self-pitying, if it were not also a story of forgiveness and new beginnings. Nesaule finds the courage to break the destructive patterns, first by leaving her cruel and manipulative husband, and then by thinking about and telling the story of her life. While her mother is alive she is unable to break down the barrier between them. But as Nesaule begins to find sympathetic listeners, she recreates the story of her mother's life as well as her own, and thus is finally able to understand and forgive. She concludes by asserting that telling her story has indeed changed her life. "Gradually the silent oppressive images inside me have become words. The past takes on meaning and shape, loses its power to paralyze, silence and shame."

Her story, Nesaule realizes, is only "a tiny stinging particle of ice" in the "driving, cruel blizzard" of human suffering. But, she concludes, "We have to believe that dreams are meaningful, we have to believe that even the briefest human connections can heal. Otherwise life is unbearable." Her memoir is a kind of conversion story, telling first of the loss of faith in mother, life's goodness and God, and then the regaining of a trust in people and life (though not in God).

Frank McCourt's childhood was almost as grim as Nesaule's. "When I look back on my childhood I wonder how I survived at all," he begins. "It was, of course, a miserable childhood: the happy childhood is hardly worth your while. Worse than the ordinary miserable childhood is the miserable Irish childhood, and worse yet is the miserable Irish Catholic childhood." A retired high school English teacher, McCourt relives that childhood with tenderness and, above all, humor.

> **The story of Frank [McCourt]'s childhood . . . is a Dickensian series of adventures, seemingly with no purpose other than to tell a good story and create memorable characters. But underneath, [*Angela's Ashes*] deals with an important subject: How can children living in great poverty nevertheless grow up intelligent and good?**
> **—*Trudy Bush***

Growing up in the Limerick slums, McCourt had a father who rarely held a job and who drank up his wages when he did, and a mother who struggled to feed her children—three of whom died—on what little support she could get from Catholic charities. But in describing his father, McCourt depicts not only a man who allowed his children to go hungry, but one who also lit the fire, made the children's tea in the mornings, read aloud to them from the newspapers, and told them Irish legends and wonderful stories.

To McCourt, his father is "like the Holy Trinity, with three people in him, the one in the morning with the paper, the one at night with the stories and the prayers, and then the one who does the bad thing and comes home with the smell of whiskey and wants us to die for Ireland. . . . I feel sad over the bad thing but I can't back away from him because the one in the morning is my real father . . . ." This kind of resilience and ability not to let go of the good in people and in life marks McCourt's memoir.

The story of Frank's childhood, from age four, when his family makes the mistake of going from New York back to Ireland, until age 19, when he has finally amassed the boat fare to return to the U.S., is a Dickensian series of adventures, seemingly with no purpose other than to tell a good story and create memorable characters. But underneath, the book deals with an important subject: How can children living in great poverty nevertheless grow up intelligent and good?

Somehow, the McCourt children do both. They have no toys, no television, no adults focused on giving them enriching experiences. But Frank is surrounded by talkers who, even without much education, have a richly expressive language. As a child, he collects stories, poems and colorful expressions the way another child might collect teddy bears or toy cars. He takes the story of Cuchulain, the hero of Irish legend, as his own and fights another child who he thinks is trying to steal the story from him. He adds the phrase "the rich wouldn't give the poor the steam from their piss" to his colorful collection of memorable sayings. Later, he memorizes poems and lines from Shakespeare. And he studies people and notes their eccentricities. Neighbors, schoolmates, teachers, relatives, whether mean or kind—all are vivid characters to Frank and vividly realized on the page.

Perhaps because he continued to love and feel loved by his reprobate father, McCourt's characterizations of other people are almost always charitable. Even fat, lazy Aunt Aggie, who demeans children and grudges them every mouthful of food she gives them, is remembered for a glowing act of charity. Unbidden, she surprises Frank by buying him new clothes and shoes so he can begin his first job with self-respect. The bond Frank has with his brothers—his mother has always stressed that they should look after each other—helps him to grow up with a sense of responsibility for others.

McCourt isn't sentimental. In the worst of times, the children steal in order to eat. Frank earns his money to get back to America by helping someone who he knows is preying on the poor. Still, he keeps a clear sense of right and wrong.

McCourt's story includes a good share of unpleasant and disillusioning encounters with the church, but he doesn't lose his faith in God or the church. Shortly before he leaves Ireland, tormented by his sins and afraid to go to confession, a Franciscan priest comforts him and assures him of God's forgiveness. The book renders the encounter with a humor and

restraint that is profoundly touching—as is the kindness and decency many people retain even in terrible circumstances.

The Kiss has been called a powerful and courageous memoir. Like Nesaule's book, it is about a daughter's estrangement from her mother—another story of evil, betrayal and recovery. Like Nesaule, Harrison seems to believe that writing the book, telling the "truth," is necessary for herself and a gift to others. Both books are written in the present tense, giving them a hypnotic immediacy. Both conclude with a dream in which mother and daughter are reconciled.

Some critics have attacked [*The Kiss*] on the grounds that it ignores the hurt that these revelations will cause to [Kathryn] Harrison's children and to her father's other children. But *The Kiss* is irresponsible on a deeper level: Harrison evades all responsibility for what she has done.
—*Trudy Bush*

But Harrison's book raises serious questions about our culture's enthusiastic acceptance of the confessional memoir. Harrison does not directly tell readers why she felt compelled to tell the story of the four-year affair with her father that began when she was 20, but she hints that the motive is revenge. When she tells her father that she wants to end the affair, that she would like a normal life with a husband and children, he tells her, "It's too late for you . . . you'll never be able to have anyone else, because you won't be able to keep our secret. You'll tell whoever it is, and once he knows, he'll leave you."

Now married and the mother of two children, Harrison presents her memoir as public testimony that she has defeated her father. Though he wished her ill, she has survived and prospered. The implication for readers seems to be that they, too, can overcome even the most dark and shameful things in their lives by being open and accepting about them. But Harrison's father is still alive, a retired pastor with a wife and other children. She claims to have carefully removed from the book all clues by which anyone could identify him, but she must have known that someone surely would track him down—as someone has.

Some critics have attacked this memoir on the grounds that it ignores the hurt that these revelations will cause to Harrison's children and to her father's other children. But *The Kiss* is irresponsible on a deeper level: Harrison evades all responsibility for what she has done. She gives the story the disarmingly simple structure of a fairy tale. When Harrison was little, her mother hid from life by sleeping many hours each day. During her affair with her father, Harrison is the sleeper. The relationship begins when Harrison's father, who has not seen his child for many years, visits her and kisses her on the lips. "In years to come," she writes, "I'll think of that kiss as a kind of transforming sting, like that of a scorpion: a narcotic that spreads from my mouth to my brain. The kiss is the point at which I begin, slowly, inexorably, to fall asleep, to surrender volition, to become paralyzed."

She drops out of college, gives up all but one or two of her friends, meets her father in airports in towns where no one will know them, and allows herself to be devoured. She feels nothing when she embraces her father, she writes, and after the affair ends she remembers nothing about what they did in bed. She is a sleepwalker, and sleepwalkers are not responsible for what they do. When she finally awakens and ends the affair four years later, she still presents herself as passive. The affair ends with another kiss, this time the one she gives her dead grandfather. Her mother's death follows soon after. These two deaths, not any action on her part, free her from her enchantment and allow her to leave her father.

Harrison claims that the story is really about her mother—a mother who emotionally deserted and betrayed her child. That betrayal was sexual: Harrison lost her virginity in a gynecologist's office, where her mother insisted she be fitted with a diaphragm before going off to college. The daughter reciprocates by betraying her mother sexually—taking from her the man she still loves.

It's not surprising that Harrison's book is on the bestseller list. It has a sensational subject matter and is a quick and easy read. The lyrical style and fairy tale plot make the book hypnotic, and its intense emotional tone involves the reader. The narrative also vicariously satisfies the desire for revenge that at some point marks nearly everyone's daydreams.

The problem is that Harrison presents herself as a complete victim: she wasn't awake enough to make moral choices, and thus is not responsible for what she has done. There is no price to pay for incest, not even shame.

Memoirs are not necessarily true, but the shape people give to their lives tells us a lot about who the authors are. The stories we tell about ourselves may reveal that we are self-serving and self-deceived, as I believe is true in Harrison's case. Or they may reveal courage, and an ability to find humor and strength in the worst of circumstances. Those are the kind of memoirs that help us live.

Kirkus Reviews **(review date 1 June 1997)**

SOURCE: A review of *Survival Stories,* in *Kirkus Reviews,* June 1, 1997, p. 857.

[*Below, the critic offers a positive review of* Survival Stories, *edited by Kathryn Rhett.*]

Twenty fine essays, some never before published, mark episodes of life-changing loss or illness and the redemptive movement toward reconciliation.

Developed from Rhett's course in crisis memoir—or survival stories—at the Iowa Summer Writing Festival, the anthology features works that encompass the distinctive elements of the form: the "inclusion of present and past, narrative and digression," and an "urgency" that the work be written, which reveals itself in a sense of discovery for both writer and reader. The contributors include both well known writers, such as Lucy Grealy, Natalie Kusz, and William Styron, and newer voices, including Patton Hollow and Laura Philpot Benedict. Subjects span family deaths, abuse, illness, divorce, infidelity, physical disfigurement—all the sadder stuff of life. The events themselves are rendered dramatically or elliptically, as needed. But it's the observations that linger in the memory: Richard McCann's glimpse of a bereaved mother examining old photos, Alan Shapiro's vision of death, Nancy Mairs's encounter with grace. Steering clear of the potential dangers in the single-subject anthology, *Survival Stories* sustains interest with its variety of emotions and its many kinds of resolution. Years after his cancer, Reynolds Price analyzes his handwriting and his life and finds both "taller, more legible, with more air and stride." Months after her death, William Loizeaux awaits the consolation of the sudden presence ("the strange sense of proximity, the smell of her skin in the air") of an infant daughter; such moments, he has read, happen for those who grieve, but it does not come for him. Most important (and surprising), the immediacy and artistry of these works also inspire understanding, or at least companionship, though those seeking a religious dialogue or presence will for the most part need to look elsewhere.

Measured and full of affecting essays, this is ideal for readers itchy to read beyond the *Best American Essays* collections and sustaining to those in hard straits themselves.

Donna Seaman (review date July 1997)

SOURCE: A review of *Survival Stories,* in *Booklist,* July, 1997, p. 1778.

[*In the following highly positive review, Seaman recounts the process by which* Survival Stories, *edited by Kathryn*

Rhett, came to be, concluding that the essays in the collection "transcend all criticism."]

Rhett noticed that the most arresting essays written for the memoir-writing workshops she taught were about surviving crises. This observation inspired her to create a crises memoir course, in spite of her fears that such an intense focus could turn her classes into group therapy sessions. A real pro, Rhett was able to concentrate on the writing itself, thus helping her students develop the formal structures needed for telling their highly personal stories. Rhett scouted out stellar examples of the form and now has gathered together in a powerful anthology 20 indelible tales of death, illness, divorce, betrayal, depression, and unemployment by writers such as Rick Moody, Lucy Grealy, Nancy Mairs, and Christina Middlebrook. Each essay reflects points Rhett makes in her insightful introduction about how stories of survival illuminate "the connection between an old self and a new one" and about how the articulation of private traumas is a "step toward collective feelings." The memoir is as maligned as it is treasured, but these essays transcend all criticism.

Kirkus Reviews (review date 1 July 1997)

SOURCE: A review of *All Over but the Shoutin'*, in *Kirkus Reviews*, July 1, 1997, p. 995.

[*Below, the critic gives a positive review of Rick Bragg's* All Over but the Shoutin'.]

A celebrated Pulitzer Prize-winning *New York Times* reporter turns his investigative attention to his own past: growing up poor and making his way from rural Alabama to the top of his profession.

[Rick] Bragg, who was born in 1959, is poetic and convincing on his family's poverty and how it chipped away at their dreams "to the point that the hopelessness show[ed] through." His father, violent and an alcoholic, figures here, as do his siblings, but this is above all a son's story of love and respect for a mother who picked cotton, cleaned houses, and took in washing and ironing, determined to secure for her children the chance at a successful life that poverty had denied her. Bragg explores the ambivalence he felt about leaving home and his growing awareness that such choices will allow him to achieve at a level he's scarcely imagined. His labors lead eventually to a job at the *St. Petersburg (Fla.) Times,* and then to Harvard in 1992, when he receives a Nieman Fellowship that allows him to make up in reading and coursework some of what he'd missed by having left college early. Bragg won his Pulitzer in 1996 for his human interest stories, profiles of such figures as a courageous bodega owner, defying robbers, and of the 87-year-old Mis-

sissippi washerwoman who donated her life savings to a university. He realizes a long-cherished plan when he has enough money to buy a home for his mother. Says Bragg, "you do the best you can for the people . . . you love with all the strength in your body, once you finally figure out that they are who you are, and, in many ways, all there is."

Bragg, who now lives in Atlanta, has a strong voice and a sweeping style that, like his approach to newspaper writing, is rich, empathetic, and compelling. His memoir is a model of humility combined with pride in one's accomplishments.

Bret Lott (review date 11 September 1997)

SOURCE: "Up from Southern Poverty, into a Wider World," in *The New York Times Book Review,* September 11, 1997, p. C16.

[*In the following review, Lott describes Rick Bragg's writing in his memoir,* All Over but the Shoutin', *as self-conscious, asserting that the work "suffers from precisely what has made him such a fine reporter: the book reads as though it were a feature.*]

Regular readers of *The New York Times* know the work of Rick Bragg, the Pulitzer Prize-winning reporter whose piercing snapshots of Americans, from the Susan Smith murder trial in South Carolina to the Oklahoma bombing to street life in Harlem, have graced *The Times*'s pages since 1994.

But Mr. Bragg's memoir, *All Over but the Shoutin',* suffers from precisely what has made him such a fine reporter: the book reads as though it were a feature. Obviously the form has served him well for writing that is measured in column inches, but here it grows weary and, paradoxically enough for a memoir, awfully self-conscious when run into the hundreds of pages, and when the focus is himself.

At once a tribute to his long-suffering mother and a chronicle of his rise from profound poverty in his native Alabama to his present post as a national correspondent for *The Times,* Mr. Bragg's first book of nonfiction affords us few glimpses into the inner life of the man that aren't jampacked with a kind of cocky, colloquial imagery, the effect being that he doesn't seem to trust the bare truth of his material—his own life—to be moving enough, instead defaulting to heavy-handed writing that draws attention to itself rather than to the matter at hand.

Of his dying father's belated interest in eternal salvation, Mr. Bragg writes that "as the sickness squeezed his lungs he began to hope that Jesus was more than just a 50-cent mail-order picture enshrined in a dime store frame on the hallway wall, that salvation was the trick card he could play right at the end and stay in the money." Of his desire to work the Miami beat for *The St. Petersburg Times,* he observes that it was "a reporter's nirvana, a place where smash-and-grab robbers stalked tourists with chunks of concrete, where whole skyscrapers stood on foundations of drug money, where the Tontons Macoute of Haiti reached across the Florida Straits to kill political enemies, and old men with hatred infusing every cell of their bodies played soldier in the Glades, dreaming of the day they could kill Castro." At the sentence level the punchy tone and shiny litanies work fine, but line up too many of them on too many pages, and one finds the need for room to breathe, to look simply and deeply at a moment or desire in search of its heart, its portent.

> **[Rick] Bragg's first book of nonfiction, [*All Over but the Shoutin',*] affords us few glimpses into the inner life of the man that aren't jampacked with a kind of cocky, colloquial imagery, the effect being that he doesn't seem to trust the bare truth of his material—his own life—to be moving enough, instead defaulting to heavy-handed writing that draws attention to itself rather than to the matter at hand.**
> **—Bret Lott**

This is because much of the story is compelling in and of itself, and worth hearing. The first half of the book portrays Mr. Bragg's mother as a beautiful and heartbroken woman whose life is spent picking cotton and ironing others' clothes, and who has been left to raise her three sons alone save for those few instances when her husband suddenly appears, sometimes sober, sometimes not, but always for the worse.

Here some of the most tender scenes appear, scenes in which the writing is momentarily stripped of itself, letting breathe beautiful, if brief, instants of perfect clarity and depth. "She would pick May Pops for us," he writes of his mother and her efforts to entertain the boys with the available world, "and show us how the tiny stem inside looked just like a woman dancing if you twirled it between your fingers. She taught us that the hooting of owls and the cries of night birds are bad luck, and showed us how to find the best worms for fishing by looking under rotten planks."

The image that emerges is of a proud, determined and basically happy family held together by their staid and devoted mother, even in the face of an economic misery so deep that the black people down the road stop by now and again with the gift of leftover corn, this in a time and place overshadowed by the larger-than-life countenance of George Wallace.

The second half of the book kicks in, and this sense of self-consciousness—ofwriting about yourself as though you were the subject of a feature story—takes over with a vengeance. With the exception of a few backward glances, including the genuinely moving account of taking his mother from Possum Trot, Ala., to the Pulitzer Prize awards luncheon in Manhattan, Mr. Bragg spends much of the rest of the book regaling us with stories of his adventures in the paper trade, from his scrappy days reporting on stock car races and hometown football games, to various beats with various Southern newspapers, then to his prestigious Nieman fellowship year at Harvard, finally winding up with that Pulitzer at *The New York Times.*

But perhaps what seems most self-conscious about this end of the memoir is that the book becomes increasingly a kind of Rick Bragg reader, the author lifting lines, even whole pages, from various articles he has written through the years, holding them up to the reader like trophies. Of his first trip to Haiti to report for *The St. Petersburg Times,* in 1991, he writes: "The more I read about Haiti's history, the more fascinated I became. I learned that Haiti was rich once, a lush French colony with 95 percent of its people in chains. 'In 1791,' I wrote, 'a voodoo priest named Boukman drank the blood of a sacrificed pig. . . .'"

Mr. Bragg then goes on for much of the next two pages giving a pocket history of Haiti from no more impeccable a resource than himself. It's as if, finally, the articles he has written serve as stand-ins for his own life, leaving the core of the book—who is this man?—strangely insular and hollow at once.

At one point during Mr. Bragg's year at Harvard, his mentor, Bill Kovach, a former editor at *The New York Times,* gave him some prudent advice. "He told me I had a gift," Mr. Bragg writes, "which I guess anyone wants to hear even if it ain't noways true, but he also told me, more or less gently, that I could use some work. He told me I crowded too many pretty lines into my stories, that I needed space between them."

Though Mr. Bragg admits in the next line to trying to fix this problem, he still hasn't whittled away enough—at least for a memoir, a form in which the words that make the man must be stripped away by none other than the man himself to reveal the soul therein. Curiously enough, the missing figure in this entire endeavor is Rick Bragg, too shrouded in his craft to let us see inside.

Gloria Emerson (review date 14 September 1997)

SOURCE: "Dirty Laundry," in *Los Angeles Times Book Review,* September 14, 1997, p. 9.

[*Below, Emerson offers a positive review of Rick Bragg's* All Over but the Shoutin', *noting that she wished he had included more excerpts of his articles previously published in the* New York Times.]

The idea of a journalist born in 1959 writing his memoirs, with no great wars or historic events to report, is surprising. But what Rick Bragg gives us in *All Over but the Shoutin'* is his own story, a record of a life that has been harrowing, cruel and yet triumphant, written so beautifully he makes the book a marvel. "This is not an important book," he writes. "It is only the story of a strong woman, a tortured man and three sons who lived hemmed in by thin cotton and ragged history in northeastern Alabama. . . ." He put off writing *All Over but the Shoutin'* for 10 years because "dreaming backwards can carry a man through some dark rooms where the walls seemed lined with razor blades."

It is still a mystery why some children, bent by suffering, can transcend all the horror and hardships while others are doomed. Surely in Bragg's case, it was the love of his mother and her family that saved him as a boy. Scarred and driven, he has almost willed himself to become an astonishing writer who, as a *New York Times* reporter, won a Pulitzer Prize for feature writing in 1996. He is still not a peaceful man, but he no longer needs to wear "that chip on [his] shoulder like a crown."

Rising from so much suffering, he is a master at describing it. When he was barely 16, his mother asked him to go see his father, the "monster of my childhood," who had so often abandoned her and the children, leaving them penniless. He found his father in a dismal room where the older man looked "damaged, poisoned, used-up, crumpled up and thrown in a corner to die." There were gifts for the son: a Remington rifle and three cardboard egg cartons of books which the father had never read. The father just thought they looked pretty, like the books the rich would own.

"It's all over but the shoutin' now, ain't it, boy," he said.

The son asked the father to tell him about the war in Korea; he was refused, and then the drunk man picked "the lock on his past and tugged me inside," Bragg writes. It was the last story, and the father did not use it as an excuse for his behavior or the way he drank.

This is how Bragg tells it:

> The dead waved from the ditches in Korea. The arms of the soldiers reached out from bodies half in, half out of the frozen mud, as if begging for help even after their hearts had cooled and the ice had glazed their eyes.

And then:

> The ones who were shot were shot through five layers of clothes so sometimes the hurt and blood didn't show. It looked like a whole platoon of men had just gotten weary and laid down to sleep.

His father had never felt such cold until Korea.

Bragg, much too fine a writer to use the popular cliché "post-traumatic stress disorder," puts it this way: "I believe . . . that there, in that wretched place where the ground blows up under your feet and dead men motion to you from the sidelines of war, a boy with thin blood was rearranged. I believe it. I want to. I have to."

There is a snapshot of Bragg's mother's lovely face in the book before she was damaged and exhausted in so many ways. The older boys were still too small to protect her from her husband's beatings. She picked cotton when that was still done by hand and at night ironed other people's clothes. She stripped sugar cane. She stood in line at the welfare office and in line for government cheese because she had no choice. She would often not eat supper if there wasn't enough food for the children, as her own mother had done. Finally she went back to live with her mother, and the family was safe from the father, although just as poor.

The child did not know there was a Southern gentry or what privilege it bestowed until he went to school. The poshest place he had ever been was the dime store on the old courthouse square. A caste system divided the first grade: The Cardinals were the children of the well-to-do who studied from nice books, and the Jaybirds were the poor or those considered backward. He could read, but his teacher kept him in the Jaybirds so he would be with his own kind. "May she rot in hell," Bragg writes.

His portrait of the rural, violent Appalachian South, where people were kept crouching as they worked themselves to death, is stunning and sickening: "There was . . . a world of pulpwooders and millworkers and farmers, of men who ripped all the skin off their knuckles working on junk cars and ignored the blood that ran down their arms. In that world, strength and toughness were everything, sometimes the only thing. It was common, acceptable, not to be able to read, but a man who wouldn't fight, couldn't fight, was a pathetic thing. To be afraid was shameful."

He grew up, as did all the others, with the Protestant church pumping into his veins like an implanted IV. Warnings of damnation came from churches and radio stations "in a place where total strangers will walk up to you at the Piggly Wiggly and ask if you are Saved," he writes. It was a time of the Klan, the beatings of black men, the burnings of houses and the voice of the champion of segregation, George Wallace, working his voodoo on so many whites.

That South and its degrading poverty and viciousness has greatly changed, but Bragg bears its imprint. All these years he has been haunted by his mother's suffering and wanted to make it up to her, to fix things. She stopped going out of the house because she didn't want people wondering where her husband was, because she wore castoffs and torn sneakers. She prayed at home, eyes closed, lips moving, both hands on top of a second-hand television set as a young Oral Roberts preached. Most of all, she feared her sons would be ashamed of her in public.

After Bragg was rounded up and questioned by the police in a murder investigation because he looked like a poor teenage boy, his notion of survival became very clear: He wanted power "not so much to do a thing as it was of having power to stop things from being done to you." He enrolled in one class at Jackson State University, in feature writing, taught by Mamie B. Herb, who, after his first assignment, told Bragg he had talent and promise. That praise swung him into a new life. He slowly went from small newspapers to the bigger ones, never dreaming where it would end, how he "would run through the dark, twisting tunnels of other people's nightmares, that I would choose to do it that way because in a foolish and romantic way, I believed I knew the way."

At one newspaper, a friend called him "the misery writer," and others warned that those sorrowful stories would do him in. He did not listen and twice was sent to Haiti, where "the cruelties were still off the scale of sanity." He thought he had never seen misery like this.

Excerpts of some of his stories for the *New York Times* are included in the book, and I wished for more. "I was slowly beginning to realize that the only thing that was worth writing about was living and dying and the trembling membrane in between," Bragg writes. But there was one story of the noble spirit of an 87-year-old black washerwoman in Hattiesburg, Miss., who gave her life savings to the local university as an endowment for scholarships for poor students. She had lived by washing and ironing and put aside $150,000. Bragg remembered his mother amid all her piles of laundry, and some people thought it was the best story he had ever done.

Bragg no longer needs to get even with life, in his words. He finally did buy his mother a house of her own and insisted that she come to be with him at the Pulitzer lunch. The courageous woman, who had never been in an airplane or an elevator or on an escalator, never been in any city at all, overcame her immense fear and ended up having a fine time.

After a writing seminar he gave, a woman told Bragg that he had inspired her, and that she, born so poor, could use her own suffering and not try to always conceal it. It was what he had done.

"Like a weapon, yes," Bragg writes. He wanted to call her with a warning. "I've been meaning to tell her not to look for some well-defined finish line, that sometimes you run right past it and don't even know it's there, like fenceposts in the dark."

He tells us he will call the woman and that they might meet. But he worries that looking at him would reveal too much for her: the old anger and resentment etched in his face. This reader hopes he does and now knows he is not a marked man anymore.

Anthony Walton (review date 14 September 1997)

SOURCE: "The Hard Road from Dixie," in *New York Times Book Review,* September 14, 1997, p. 13.

[*In the following review, Walton praises Rick Bragg's* All Over but the Shoutin', *describing the memoir as "the kind of book that causes us to see ourselves more clearly because it corrects and heightens our vision."*]

There is an old saying among African-Americans to the effect that any white man who lives in poverty does so by choice. This saying is based on the premise that being born with white skin is so great an advantage as to determine a successful life. The colloquialism for disadvantaged Caucasians, "white trash," indicates that the nation as a whole holds these people responsible for their station as well. "Trash" means something without value, something unworthy of our attention and barely worthy of our contempt.

In his sad, beautiful, funny and moving memoir, *All Over but the Shoutin',* Rick Bragg gives us a report from the forgotten heart of "white trash" America, a sort of *Pilgrim's Progress* or *Up From Slavery* about how a clever and determined young man outwitted fate. The story he tells, of white suffering and disenfranchisment, is one too seldom heard. It is as if a descendant of one of the hollow-eyed children from *Let Us Now Praise Famous Men* had stepped out of a photograph to tell his own story, to narrate an experience that even Agee could not penetrate because he was not himself "trash."

Bragg, like the boys and girls around him in isolated and impoverished northeastern Alabama, did not choose to be poor. Along with them, he was intended in the rigid hierarchy of American life to be a logger, or to work in a pulp mill, or to drink and carouse and engage in the sort of small-scale criminal activity that leads to a fair portion of your life being spent behind bars. Instead he became, by his mid-30's, a Pulitzer Prize-winning correspondent for *The New York Times*. *All Over but the Shoutin'* is the story of that rise.

There is an early picture in the story that serves as an imaginative metaphor for the whole: Bragg recalls sitting on a gunny sack at the age of 2 or 3 and being dragged through a field by his mother. It is only years later that he realizes she had been working, picking cotton—degrading and back-breaking labor that could only have been made more onerous by the presence of a toddler. "The tall woman is wearing a man's britches and a man's old straw hat, and now and then she looks back over her shoulder to smile at the 3-year-old boy whose hair is almost as purely white as the bolls she picks, who rides the back of the six-foot-long sack like a magic carpet." Turning hard scrabble into a pleasant memory was something Margaret Bragg would do for her boy again and again as he grew.

Her sacrifice and suffering form the core of Bragg's experience and so of this book. How did she let him dream in the face of such discouragement, how did she protect his spirit from being broken, as so many others were? The father of the family, a hard-drinking and violent ne'er-do-well, is never more than intermittently involved in Bragg's life, and is gone for good by the time the boy is in elementary school. His brothers grow up to lives very different from his: Sam, several years older, is forced by circumstance to leave school early and begin what will be a life of working with his hands and back to try to make up, economically, for the absence of the father (Bragg relates, heartbreakingly, how Sam was made to "work off" Federal entitlements like school lunches by callous teachers and school administrators); his younger brother, Mark, falls into the pernicious Appalachian life style of alcoholism, making illegal liquor and being permanently situated on the wrong side of the law. This is the psychological and emotional landscape Bragg looks back on as he reconstructs his life.

Bragg is painfully honest about his feelings of insecurity and inadequacy as he moved among his "betters"—"the old-money white Southerners who ran things, who treated the rest of the South like beggars with muddy feet who were about to track up their white shag carpeting." He writes of a thwarted school love affair: "They named the sections of the divided classroom after birds. She was a Cardinal, one of the children of the well-to-do who studied from nice books with bright pictures, and I was a Jay-bird, one of the poor or just plain dumb children who got what was left after the good books were passed out. . . . The teacher—and I will always, always remember this—told me I would be much more comfortable with my own kind. I was 6, but even at 6 you understand what it means

to be told you are not good enough to sit with the well scrubbed."

In a time when Bragg's family was at rock bottom, without food, a black boy from down the road brought them some corn his mother had sent over. "In the few contacts we had with them as children, we had thrown rocks at them . . . I would like to say that we came together after the little boy brought us that food, that we learned about and from each other, but that would be a lie." In the brutal realities faced by those like Bragg who were not "white," not really, poor whites chose not to band together with blacks but to instead live in "two separate, distinct states." One would have liked to see even more commentary on this critical topic from so honest and thoughtful an observer.

After very limited college experience and very good luck (Bragg, at the age of 18, gets a job at a local paper when the first choice decides to remain employed at Kentucky Fried Chicken), he commences a rapid climb through the ranks of the newspaper trade, starting as a sports reporter in small towns in Alabama and getting a steady succession of better jobs through his plucky Ragged Dick combination of large talent and sheer will. Bragg moves to a new city just about every year for 10 years, moving ever farther away from the strict but sure comforts of his family back home and ever farther into "enemy territory," the polite and at best indifferent precincts of the white middle and upper classes.

From the vantage point of adulthood, Bragg contemplates "how I got over" the extent of his mother's accomplishment in not letting him be broken. He spends much of his rise scheming and saving to buy her a house. Gradually the reader becomes aware that what Bragg is really trying to buy for her is a place in the world, a place from which she doesn't have to move, a place where Mrs. Bragg can, for once, sit still, and be unconcerned with practical exigencies, be insulated from whatever random difficulties and humiliations the given day may bring. It is this sort of life-or-death urgency that gives his tale its majesty and power.

Bragg is showing us a place we have not seen before, not quite like this. And he is joining an elite group of American writers who have used the literature of childhood to affect our understanding of our society, standing in the tradition of Huck and Tom, Holden Caulfield and Dorothy Allison's Bone Boatwright, of Richard Wright and Harry Crews, those hard-headed but bighearted malcontents who ricochet through the land making trouble and keeping the rest of us honest.

There are books that let us see clearly a time and place; there are books that allow us to feel that we are experiencing with truth and accuracy the life of another person. Rick Bragg has written the kind of book that causes us to see ourselves more clearly because it corrects and heightens our vision, and through this vision we see for the first time the humanity of others and are able to imagine, if only for a moment, that unbridgeable divides can somehow, because of what we have learned we have in common, be surmounted.

Rick Bragg (essay date 18 September 1997)

SOURCE: "If the Doorbell's Ringing, It Must Be Home," in *The New York Times,* September 18, 1997, p. F20.

[*In the following essay, adapted from his memoir,* All Over but the Shoutin', *Bragg relates his mother's lifelong yearning for a home of her own.*]

All her life my momma had lived in other people's houses. Sometimes through cheap rent, sometimes through charity, she had lived beholden. The closest thing we had ever had to a home of our own was a small trailer we lived in for only a few months, when I was a boy.

Through it all, my mamma never said she wanted a house. She never even hinted. But if you could have seen her face when we rode down the rural roads of Calhoun County, Ala., heard her talk about how this house is an A-frame and that one is a Victorian, about how this one will need painting in a few years and that one has just got a new covering of aluminum siding, you would know.

She is the daughter of a carpenter, after all, a man who lived his whole life building other people's houses and never owned one of his own. I guess she never expected to own one, either.

When I was a teen-ager, she used to order catalogues from the Jim Walter Company, which was famous for building "affordable housing." These were neat, nice, small real-wood houses, usually white, with porches. She would flip through the pages like a child flipping through a toy catalogue, wishing. But there was no money for land, even if we could have ever saved enough to build anything bigger than a doghouse. You can dream on welfare. You can hope as you take in ironing. It is just less painful if you don't.

We all try to buy our way into heaven, one way or another. Some use the genuine currency of faith. Others, like me, try to barter, as if the great Hereafter were a swap meet in the clouds. Me, I'd always figured that if I did right by my momma, I had a shot.

I kept my promise to her on Nov. 2, 1996. I bought her a good four-bedroom house, the first thing of any real value she has ever owned. She never had a wedding ring, or a de-

cent car or even a set of furniture that matched. But now she had a house.

Made of beige brick with dark green shutters, it sits on top of a hill—she has always wanted to live on a hill—but it is not so steep that she will have a hard time walking down to the mailbox every afternoon. It has a porch on the front, and in the summertime she can sit there in the cool of the evening and snap beans or just wave at the cars.

It has 13 acres, with room for squirrels and ugly dogs and family. If it had been up to me, I would have bought her a white Victorian in town, one of those homes where she used to scrub floors. I would have done it for the pure poetic justice of it. But she wanted nothing to do with town. She wanted to walk in the pines and smell the wood smoke and plant rose of Sharon. She wanted her dog, the remarkably unattractive Gizzard, to live out his last, limping days in the country. She wanted to live as she had always lived, with room for a small garden and space to pace away her troubles, only on her own ground.

She picked out the house because she thought it was pretty, because it was close to my brother Sam's house and my other kinfolk, because the hill would always have a good breeze on it. We went to look at it, scuffed along the wall-to-wall carpet, opened the oven in the nice, roomy kitchen where she would can her jellies and peppers and green tomatoes. We flushed the toilets in all three bathrooms, walked down into the full basement and the "family room," twisted the dial on the thermostat to hear the heat pump click on. I saw her reach up to feel the cool air rush in and saw her smile.

"I won't run it 'cept on the real hot days," she told me. In the basement family room there is a fancy new wood heater with a rock fireplace, which she said she would use sometimes. I made it plain to her that the reason for buying this house was so that she could grow old in some comfort, that she wouldn't have to tote wood anymore to stay warm. She pretended not to hear me—there is no arguing with my momma's back—and went on talking about how the wood heater would heat that whole house, if she blocked off the space she didn't need.

She kept wandering back to the kitchen, with so many cabinets, so much space, such nice, clean space. "It's a lot of house for one woman," the real estate agent said, but I told him no, it was just right.

Then he told me what he was asking for it, and I saw my momma's eyes drop and her dream snap closed, because to a woman who had lived with next to nothing, that very reasonable price seemed impossible. She walked outside and stood in the yard, and wouldn't talk about it much, after that. Now and then she would slip in conversation and call it "my house." She drew pictures of it, but she never asked for it again.

It took a few months to close, until the November day when I showed up at her door unannounced, and told her she owned it. She smiled, as wide as I have ever seen her smile, and the tears pooled in her eyes. She asked me if we could afford the mortgage payments, and I told her there were none. It was hers.

My brother Sam went to work on it, fixing all the little things it needed, making a pretty house much prettier. He sawed down unwanted, spindly trees and crawled over it and under it, with a hammer in his hand and nails in his teeth, to make it perfect.

One night we sat in his living room, trying to decide between tan and off-white for the trim, and it struck us how odd that was. "Did you ever think we'd be doing this?" I asked him, and he shook his head. But there was no celebrating.

You celebrate winning, not just catching up.

"Did you know it had a doorbell?" my momma asked me. "I never had a doorbell." I asked her if the sound of it bothered her, and she shook her head. "I kind of like it."

Some weeks later I was talking to Sam on the telephone. He told me he was a little worried about one thing. "She rings her own doorbell," he said.

I told him to let her ring it till she wore it out.

There wasn't much to move, really, and memories don't weigh nothin'. She took a chrome and vinyl couch and chair, leftovers from some doctor's office, and took her washing machine, which she had nicknamed "Old Smokey," because a fire had blackened the white paint. Smokey didn't look like much and was prone to dance across the floor, as if possessed by demons on the spin cycle, but you couldn't kill him with a gun. "Still runs; don't leak," Momma said, refusing to let us get her a new washer.

The night after my momma's first full day in her new house, my little brother came to see her. Mark was drinking, a little bit. We had all asked him not to come there.

I don't know what right we had to say that or expect him to comply.

My big brother, Sam, drove up at about the same time, just to check on her. They faced off in the yard.

I guess Sam and Mark had to fight. They had to, because of who we are.

Sam fought because he believed he was protecting her. Mark fought because he felt he was being pushed away, which I guess is about the worst feeling in the world.

So, on my momma's second night in her new house, a 40-year-old man and his 33-year-old brother are fighting mean and earnest in the front yard of the very symbol of our new beginning. My momma introduced herself to her new neighbors not by taking them a jar of homemade jelly, or some pickled banana pepper, but by running to them for help.

Finally, they broke apart and it was just over. Sam only did what he believed I would have done. He did it to keep something good in her life from being tarnished.

But of course Momma didn't see it that way. She has tolerated drunks all her life; she is good at it. She expects it, like she expects the sun to rise in the morning. Instead of being angry at my little brother, her baby, she was mostly mad at Sam.

So, instead of fixing anything, I only built a stage, a prop, for another sadness. Even though I couldn't make everything right with the simple purchase of a house, I wanted to believe it would at least be someplace fresh, free for a while of that lingering aroma of dusty pain. And then I knew that maybe I had bought this house more to redo the past than to make her dreams come true.

It got better, of course. By Thanksgiving, Sam and Momma were working side by side again. She held the ladder for him, passing him nails and cooked him biscuits.

We had Thanksgiving dinner with Sam and his family, my Aunt Jo and Uncle John. Momma used every rack in the oven. And there were biscuits and dressing and mashed potatoes and pinto beans with a hambone as big as my fist, and a turkey that fell off the bone. For the first time ever we all sat in the same room and ate, because it was the first time we had ever had a room big enough to gather in. We tried hard not to notice the empty chair.

We started painting the wood trim and concrete block portions right after Thanksgiving. My momma paints as high as she can reach, and Sam paints the rest. It doesn't bother her at all that the wooden part of the house is forest green in some places and "ivory" in others. She isn't like me, as I said.

In the guest bathroom, I noticed that the towel said "Emory Hospital" on it. Stolen, no doubt, and given to my momma in one of those boxes of donated clothes. Just on a hunch I went to the next bathroom. The towel there said, "Peninsula Medical Center," and I started to laugh.

Of course, you can't buy respectability with a house. I had wanted her to have a place where she could be more comfortable, where she could enjoy the good times in her life and tolerate the bad. And she has exactly that. But I had set my hopes on something higher. I wanted to redo the past, feel that we had won, after all.

Well, we have.

She has a split-level castle with stolen towels.

She has a four-bedroom, brick-facade mansion with vinyl furniture scavenged from a closed-down doctor's office.

She has a home.

"The thing we got to remember," I told her, "is that we ain't gonna be any different here. We just got a little bit better place to be us in."

The squirrels have been raiding the old hickory nut tree in the neat, green front yard, leaving a carpet of dark hulls on the lawn. It is a good sign, that tree. It is hard to be lonely with a yard full of gray squirrels.

This summer, Momma has smothered the house in flowers.

But it being us, the yard may just blossom with junk cars, too.

"No, it ain't going to be that way," she insisted. "It's going to be real purty."

It may be somewhere in between. And we will live with that.

FURTHER READING

Criticism

Ackerman, Felicia. "Volte Face." *American Scholar* (Winter 1996): 142.
    Review of Lucy Grealy's *Autobiography of a Face.*

Berry, Jason. "Moving On." *Chicago Tribune* (19 October 1997): sec. 14, p. 4.
    Review of Rick Bragg's *All Over but the Shoutin'.*

Rose, Lloyd. "Hearts of Darkness." *Voice Literary Supplement* (November 1990): 12-14.
    Examines depression as a topic in the writings of William Styron, Oliver Sacks, Susan Sontag, and others.

□ Contemporary Literary Criticism

Indexes

Literary Criticism Series
Cumulative Author Index
Cumulative Topic Index
Cumulative Nationality Index
Title Index, Volume 109

How to Use This Index

The main references

Camus, Albert
1913-1960 ...... **CLC 1, 2, 4, 9, 11, 14,
32, 69; DA; DAB; DAC; DAM DRAM,
MST, NOV; DC2; SSC 9; WLC**

list all author entries in the following Gale Literary Criticism series:

BLC = *Black Literature Criticism*
CLC = *Contemporary Literary Criticism*
CLR = *Children's Literature Review*
CMLC = *Classical and Medieval Literature Criticism*
DA = *DISCovering Authors*
DAB = *DISCovering Authors: British*
DAC = *DISCovering Authors: Canadian*
DAM = *DISCovering Authors Modules*
  DRAM = *dramatists;* **MST** = *most-studied
  authors;* **MULT** = *multicultural authors;* **NOV** =
  novelists; **POET** = *poets;* **POP** = *popular/genre
  writers;* **DC** = *Drama Criticism*
HLC = *Hispanic Literature Criticism*
LC = *Literature Criticism from 1400 to 1800*
NCLC = *Nineteenth-Century Literature Criticism*
PC = *Poetry Criticism*
SSC = *Short Story Criticism*
TCLC = *Twentieth-Century Literary Criticism*
WLC = *World Literature Criticism, 1500 to the Present*
WLCS = *World Literature Criticism Supplement*

The cross-references

See also CA 89-92; DLB 72; MTCW

list all author entries in the following Gale biographical and literary sources:

AAYA = *Authors & Artists for Young Adults*
AITN = *Authors in the News*
BEST = *Bestsellers*
BW = *Black Writers*
CA = *Contemporary Authors*
CAAS = *Contemporary Authors Autobiography
Series*
CABS = *Contemporary Authors Bibliographical
Series*
CANR = *Contemporary Authors New Revision Series*
CAP = *Contemporary Authors Permanent Series*
CDALB = *Concise Dictionary of American Literary
Biography*
CDBLB = *Concise Dictionary of British Literary
Biography*

DLB = *Dictionary of Literary Biography*
DLBD = *Dictionary of Literary Biography
Documentary Series*
DLBY = *Dictionary of Literary Biography Yearbook*
HW = *Hispanic Writers*
JRDA = *Junior DISCovering Authors*
MAICYA = *Major Authors and Illustrators for
Children and Young Adults*
MTCW = *Major 20th-Century Writers*
NNAL = *Native North American Literature*
SAAS = *Something about the Author Autobiography
Series*
SATA = *Something about the Author*
YABC = *Yesterday's Authors of Books for Children*

Literary Criticism Series
Cumulative Author Index

Abasiyanik, Sait Faik 1906-1954
See Sait Faik
See also CA 123

Abbey, Edward 1927-1989 .... CLC 36, 59
See also CA 45-48; 128; CANR 2, 41

Abbott, Lee K(ittredge) 1947- .... CLC 48
See also CA 124; CANR 51; DLB 130

Abe, Kobo 1924-1993CLC 8, 22, 53, 81; DAM NOV
See also CA 65-68; 140; CANR 24, 60; DLB 182; MTCW

Abelard, Peter c. 1079-c. 1142 ...... CMLC 11
See also DLB 115

Abell, Kjeld 1901-1961 .... CLC 15
See also CA 111

Abish, Walter 1931- .... CLC 22
See also CA 101; CANR 37; DLB 130

Abrahams, Peter (Henry) 1919- .... CLC 4
See also BW 1; CA 57-60; CANR 26; DLB 117; MTCW

Abrams, M(eyer) H(oward) 1912- ... CLC 24
See also CA 57-60; CANR 13, 33; DLB 67

Abse, Dannie 1923- ... CLC 7, 29; DAB; DAM POET
See also CA 53-56; CAAS 1; CANR 4, 46; DLB 27

Achebe, (Albert) Chinua(lumogu) 1930-C L C 1, 3, 5, 7, 11, 26, 51, 75; BLC; DA; DAB; DAC; DAM MST, MULT, NOV; WLC
See also AAYA 15; BW 2; CA 1-4R; CANR 6, 26, 47; CLR 20; DLB 117; MAICYA; MTCW; SATA 40; SATA-Brief 38

Acker, Kathy 1948-1997 .... CLC 45
See also CA 117; 122; 162; CANR 55

Ackroyd, Peter 1949- .... CLC 34, 52
See also CA 123; 127; CANR 51; DLB 155; INT 127

Acorn, Milton 1923- .... CLC 15; DAC
See also CA 103; DLB 53; INT 103

Adamov, Arthur 1908-1970CLC 4, 25; DAM DRAM
See also CA 17-18; 25-28R; CAP 2; MTCW

Adams, Alice (Boyd) 1926-CLC 6, 13, 46; SSC 24
See also CA 81-84; CANR 26, 53; DLBY 86; INT CANR-26; MTCW

Adams, Andy 1859-1935 .... TCLC 56
See also YABC 1

Adams, Douglas (Noel) 1952- .... CLC 27, 60; DAM POP
See also AAYA 4; BEST 89:3; CA 106; CANR 34, 64; DLBY 83; JRDA

Adams, Francis 1862-1893 .... NCLC 33

Adams, Henry (Brooks) 1838-1918 TCLC 4, 52; DA; DAB; DAC; DAM MST
See also CA 104; 133; DLB 12, 47, 189

Adams, Richard (George) 1920-CLC 4, 5, 18; DAM NOV
See also AAYA 16; AITN 1, 2; CA 49-52; CANR 3, 35; CLR 20; JRDA; MAICYA; MTCW; SATA 7, 69

Adamson, Joy(-Friederike Victoria) 1910-1980 CLC 17

See also CA 69-72; 93-96; CANR 22; MTCW; SATA 11; SATA-Obit 22

Adcock, Fleur 1934- ....CLC 41
See also CA 25-28R; CAAS 23; CANR 11, 34; DLB 40

Addams, Charles (Samuel) 1912-1988CLC 30
See also CA 61-64; 126; CANR 12

Addams, Jane 1860-1945 .... TCLC 76

Addison, Joseph 1672-1719 .... LC 18
See also CDBLB 1660-1789; DLB 101

Adler, Alfred (F.) 1870-1937 .... TCLC 61
See also CA 119; 159

Adler, C(arole) S(chwerdtfeger) 1932-.. C L C 35
See also AAYA 4; CA 89-92; CANR 19, 40; JRDA; MAICYA; SAAS 15; SATA 26, 63

Adler, Renata 1938- .... CLC 8, 31
See also CA 49-52; CANR 5, 22, 52; MTCW

Ady, Endre 1877-1919 .... TCLC 11
See also CA 107

A.E. 1867-1935 .... TCLC 3, 10
See also Russell, George William

Aeschylus 525B.C.-456B.C. ..CMLC 11; DA; DAB; DAC; DAM DRAM, MST; DC 8; WLCS
See also DLB 176

Aesop 620(?)B.C.-564(?)B.C. .... CMLC 24
See also CLR 14; MAICYA; SATA 64

Africa, Ben
See Bosman, Herman Charles

Afton, Effie
See Harper, Frances Ellen Watkins

Agapida, Fray Antonio
See Irving, Washington

Agee, James (Rufus) 1909-1955 TCLC 1, 19; DAM NOV
See also AITN 1; CA 108; 148; CDALB 1941-1968; DLB 2, 26, 152

Aghill, Gordon
See Silverberg, Robert

Agnon, S(hmuel) Y(osef Halevi) 1888-1970 CLC 4, 8, 14; SSC 30
See also CA 17-18; 25-28R; CANR 60; CAP 2; MTCW

Agrippa von Nettesheim, Henry Cornelius 1486-1535 .... LC 27

Aherne, Owen
See Cassill, R(onald) V(erlin)

Ai 1947- .... CLC 4, 14, 69
See also CA 85-88; CAAS 13; DLB 120

Aickman, Robert (Fordyce) 1914-1981 . C L C 57
See also CA 5-8R; CANR 3

Aiken, Conrad (Potter) 1889-1973CLC 1, 3, 5, 10, 52; DAM NOV, POET; SSC 9
See also CA 5-8R; 45-48; CANR 4, 60; CDALB 1929-1941; DLB 9, 45, 102; MTCW; SATA 3, 30

Aiken, Joan (Delano) 1924- .... CLC 35
See also AAYA 1, 25; CA 9-12R; CANR 4, 23, 34, 64; CLR 1, 19; DLB 161; JRDA; MAICYA; MTCW; SAAS 1; SATA 2, 30, 73

Ainsworth, William Harrison 1805-1882

NCLC 13
See also DLB 21; SATA 24

Aitmatov, Chingiz (Torekulovich) 1928-C L C 71
See also CA 103; CANR 38; MTCW; SATA 56

Akers, Floyd
See Baum, L(yman) Frank

Akhmadulina, Bella Akhatovna 1937-CLC 53; DAM POET
See also CA 65-68

Akhmatova, Anna 1888-1966CLC 11, 25, 64; DAM POET; PC 2
See also CA 19-20; 25-28R; CANR 35; CAP 1; MTCW

Aksakov, Sergei Timofeyvich 1791-1859 NCLC 2

Aksenov, Vassily
See Aksyonov, Vassily (Pavlovich)

Akst, Daniel 1956- .... CLC 109
See also CA 161

Aksyonov, Vassily (Pavlovich) 1932-CLC 22, 37, 101
See also CA 53-56; CANR 12, 48

Akutagawa, Ryunosuke 1892-1927 TCLC 16
See also CA 117; 154

Alain 1868-1951 .... TCLC 41
See also CA 163

Alain-Fournier .... TCLC 6
See also Fournier, Henri Alban
See also DLB 65

Alarcon, Pedro Antonio de 1833-1891NCLC 1

Alas (y Urena), Leopoldo (Enrique Garcia) 1852-1901 .... TCLC 29
See also CA 113; 131; HW

Albee, Edward (Franklin III) 1928-CLC 1, 2, 3, 5, 9, 11, 13, 25, 53, 86; DA; DAB; DAC; DAM DRAM, MST; WLC
See also AITN 1; CA 5-8R; CABS 3; CANR 8, 54; CDALB 1941-1968; DLB 7; INT CANR-8; MTCW

Alberti, Rafael 1902- .... CLC 7
See also CA 85-88; DLB 108

Albert the Great 1200(?)-1280 ...... CMLC 16
See also DLB 115

Alcala-Galiano, Juan Valera y
See Valera y Alcala-Galiano, Juan

Alcott, Amos Bronson 1799-1888 ....NCLC 1
See also DLB 1

Alcott, Louisa May 1832-1888 . NCLC 6, 58; DA; DAB; DAC; DAM MST, NOV; SSC 27; WLC
See also AAYA 20; CDALB 1865-1917; CLR 1, 38; DLB 1, 42, 79; DLBD 14; JRDA; MAICYA; YABC 1

Aldanov, M. A.
See Aldanov, Mark (Alexandrovich)

Aldanov, Mark (Alexandrovich) 1886(?)-1957 TCLC 23
See also CA 118

Aldington, Richard 1892-1962 .... CLC 49
See also CA 85-88; CANR 45; DLB 20, 36, 100, 149

Aldiss, Brian W(ilson) 1925- . CLC 5, 14, 40;

DAM NOV
See also CA 5-8R; CAAS 2; CANR 5, 28, 64;
DLB 14; MTCW; SATA 34

Alegria, Claribel 1924-CLC 75; DAM MULT
See also CA 131; CAAS 15; CANR 66; DLB
145; HW

Alegria, Fernando 1918- .... CLC 57
See also CA 9-12R; CANR 5, 32; HW

Aleichem, Sholom .... TCLC 1, 35
See also Rabinovitch, Sholem

Aleixandre, Vicente 1898-1984 ... CLC 9, 36;
DAM POET; PC 15
See also CA 85-88; 114; CANR 26; DLB 108;
HW; MTCW

Alepoudelis, Odysseus
See Elytis, Odysseus

Aleshkovsky, Joseph 1929-
See Aleshkovsky, Yuz
See also CA 121; 128

Aleshkovsky, Yuz .... CLC 44
See also Aleshkovsky, Joseph

Alexander, Lloyd (Chudley) 1924- .. CLC 35
See also AAYA 1; CA 1-4R; CANR 1, 24, 38,
55; CLR 1, 5, 48; DLB 52; JRDA; MAICYA;
MTCW; SAAS 19; SATA 3, 49, 81

Alexander, Samuel 1859-1938 .... TCLC 77

Alexie, Sherman (Joseph, Jr.) 1966- CLC 96;
DAM MULT
See also CA 138; CANR 65; DLB 175; NNAL

Alfau, Felipe 1902- .... CLC 66
See also CA 137

Alger, Horatio, Jr. 1832-1899 .... NCLC 8
See also DLB 42; SATA 16

Algren, Nelson 1909-1981 .... CLC 4, 10, 33
See also CA 13-16R; 103; CANR 20, 61;
CDALB 1941-1968; DLB 9; DLBY 81, 82;
MTCW

Ali, Ahmed 1910- .... CLC 69
See also CA 25-28R; CANR 15, 34

Alighieri, Dante
See Dante

Allan, John B.
See Westlake, Donald E(dwin)

Allan, Sidney
See Hartmann, Sadakichi

Allan, Sydney
See Hartmann, Sadakichi

Allen, Edward 1948- .... CLC 59

Allen, Paula Gunn 1939- .... CLC 84; DAM
MULT
See also CA 112; 143; CANR 63; DLB 175;
NNAL

Allen, Roland
See Ayckbourn, Alan

Allen, Sarah A.
See Hopkins, Pauline Elizabeth

Allen, Sidney H.
See Hartmann, Sadakichi

Allen, Woody 1935- CLC 16, 52; DAM POP
See also AAYA 10; CA 33-36R; CANR 27, 38,
63; DLB 44; MTCW

Allende, Isabel 1942- . CLC 39, 57, 97; DAM
MULT, NOV; HLC; WLCS
See also AAYA 18; CA 125; 130; CANR 51;
DLB 145; HW; INT 130; MTCW

Alleyn, Ellen
See Rossetti, Christina (Georgina)

Allingham, Margery (Louise) 1904-1966CLC
19
See also CA 5-8R; 25-28R; CANR 4, 58; DLB
77; MTCW

Allingham, William 1824-1889 ...... NCLC 25
See also DLB 35

Allison, Dorothy E. 1949- .... CLC 78
See also CA 140; CANR 66

Allston, Washington 1779-1843 .... NCLC 2
See also DLB 1

Almedingen, E. M. .... CLC 12
See also Almedingen, Martha Edith von
See also SATA 3

Almedingen, Martha Edith von 1898-1971
See Almedingen, E. M.
See also CA 1-4R; CANR 1

Almqvist, Carl Jonas Love 1793-1866 N C L C
42

Alonso, Damaso 1898-1990 .... CLC 14
See also CA 110; 131; 130; DLB 108; HW

Alov
See Gogol, Nikolai (Vasilyevich)

Alta 1942- .... CLC 19
See also CA 57-60

Alter, Robert B(ernard) 1935- .... CLC 34
See also CA 49-52; CANR 1, 47

Alther, Lisa 1944- .... CLC 7, 41
See also CA 65-68; CANR 12, 30, 51; MTCW

Althusser, L.
See Althusser, Louis

Althusser, Louis 1918-1990 .... CLC 106
See also CA 131; 132

Altman, Robert 1925- .... CLC 16
See also CA 73-76; CANR 43

Alvarez, A(lfred) 1929- .... CLC 5, 13
See also CA 1-4R; CANR 3, 33, 63; DLB 14,
40

Alvarez, Alejandro Rodriguez 1903-1965
See Casona, Alejandro
See also CA 131; 93-96; HW

Alvarez, Julia 1950- .... CLC 93
See also AAYA 25; CA 147

Alvaro, Corrado 1896-1956 .... TCLC 60
See also CA 163

Amado, Jorge 1912- CLC 13, 40, 106; DAM
MULT, NOV; HLC
See also CA 77-80; CANR 35; DLB 113;
MTCW

Ambler, Eric 1909- .... CLC 4, 6, 9
See also CA 9-12R; CANR 7, 38; DLB 77;
MTCW

Amichai, Yehuda 1924- .... CLC 9, 22, 57
See also CA 85-88; CANR 46, 60; MTCW

Amichai, Yehudah
See Amichai, Yehuda

Amiel, Henri Frederic 1821-1881 .... NCLC 4

Amis, Kingsley (William) 1922-1995CLC 1, 2,
3, 5, 8, 13, 40, 44; DA; DAB; DAC; DAM
MST, NOV
See also AITN 2; CA 9-12R; 150; CANR 8, 28,
54; CDBLB 1945-1960; DLB 15, 27, 100,
139; DLBY 96; INT CANR-8; MTCW

Amis, Martin (Louis) 1949- CLC 4, 9, 38, 62,
101
See also BEST 90:3; CA 65-68; CANR 8, 27,
54; DLB 14, 194; INT CANR-27

Ammons, A(rchie) R(andolph) 1926-CLC 2, 3,
5, 8, 9, 25, 57, 108; DAM POET; PC 16
See also AITN 1; CA 9-12R; CANR 6, 36, 51;
DLB 5, 165; MTCW

Amo, Tauraatua i
See Adams, Henry (Brooks)

Anand, Mulk Raj 1905- .. CLC 23, 93; DAM
NOV
See also CA 65-68; CANR 32, 64; MTCW

Anatol
See Schnitzler, Arthur

Anaximander c. 610B.C.-c. 546B.C.CMLC 22

Anaya, Rudolfo A(lfonso) 1937- ..... CLC 23;

DAM MULT, NOV; HLC
See also AAYA 20; CA 45-48; CAAS 4; CANR
1, 32, 51; DLB 82; HW 1; MTCW

Andersen, Hans Christian 1805-1875NCLC 7;
DA; DAB; DAC; DAM MST, POP; SSC
6; WLC
See also CLR 6; MAICYA; YABC 1

Anderson, C. Farley
See Mencken, H(enry) L(ouis); Nathan, George
Jean

Anderson, Jessica (Margaret) Queale 1916-
CLC 37
See also CA 9-12R; CANR 4, 62

Anderson, Jon (Victor) 1940-.. CLC 9; DAM
POET
See also CA 25-28R; CANR 20

Anderson, Lindsay (Gordon) 1923-1994C L C
20
See also CA 125; 128; 146

Anderson, Maxwell 1888-1959TCLC 2; DAM
DRAM
See also CA 105; 152; DLB 7

Anderson, Poul (William) 1926- ...... CLC 15
See also AAYA 5; CA 1-4R; CAAS 2; CANR
2, 15, 34, 64; DLB 8; INT CANR-15;
MTCW; SATA 90; SATA-Brief 39

Anderson, Robert (Woodruff) 1917-CLC 23;
DAM DRAM
See also AITN 1; CA 21-24R; CANR 32; DLB
7

Anderson, Sherwood 1876-1941 TCLC 1, 10,
24; DA; DAB; DAC; DAM MST, NOV;
SSC 1; WLC
See also CA 104; 121; CANR 61; CDALB
1917-1929; DLB 4, 9, 86; DLBD 1; MTCW

Andier, Pierre
See Desnos, Robert

Andouard
See Giraudoux, (Hippolyte) Jean

Andrade, Carlos Drummond de .... CLC 18
See also Drummond de Andrade, Carlos

Andrade, Mario de 1893-1945 .... TCLC 43

Andreae, Johann V(alentin) 1586-1654LC 32
See also DLB 164

Andreas-Salome, Lou 1861-1937 ... TCLC 56
See also DLB 66

Andress, Lesley
See Sanders, Lawrence

Andrewes, Lancelot 1555-1626 .... LC 5
See also DLB 151, 172

Andrews, Cicily Fairfield
See West, Rebecca

Andrews, Elton V.
See Pohl, Frederik

Andreyev, Leonid (Nikolaevich) 1871-1919
TCLC 3
See also CA 104

Andric, Ivo 1892-1975 .... CLC 8
See also CA 81-84; 57-60; CANR 43, 60; DLB
147; MTCW

Androvar
See Prado (Calvo), Pedro

Angelique, Pierre
See Bataille, Georges

Angell, Roger 1920- .... CLC 26
See also CA 57-60; CANR 13, 44; DLB 171,
185

Angelou, Maya 1928-CLC 12, 35, 64, 77; BLC;
DA; DAB; DAC; DAM MST, MULT,
POET, POP; WLCS
See also AAYA 7, 20; BW 2; CA 65-68; CANR
19, 42, 65; DLB 38; MTCW; SATA 49

Anna Comnena 1083-1153 .... CMLC 25

Annensky, Innokenty (Fyodorovich) 1856-1909
TCLC 14
See also CA 110; 155
Annunzio, Gabriele d'
See D'Annunzio, Gabriele
Anodos
See Coleridge, Mary E(lizabeth)
Anon, Charles Robert
See Pessoa, Fernando (Antonio Nogueira)
Anouilh, Jean (Marie Lucien Pierre) 1910-1987
CLC 1, 3, 8, 13, 40, 50; DAM DRAM; DC 8
See also CA 17-20R; 123; CANR 32; MTCW
Anthony, Florence
See Ai
Anthony, John
See Ciardi, John (Anthony)
Anthony, Peter
See Shaffer, Anthony (Joshua); Shaffer, Peter (Levin)
Anthony, Piers 1934- ..... CLC 35; DAM POP
See also AAYA 11; CA 21-24R; CANR 28, 56; DLB 8; MTCW; SAAS 22; SATA 84
Antoine, Marc
See Proust, (Valentin-Louis-George-Eugene-)Marcel
Antoninus, Brother
See Everson, William (Oliver)
Antonioni, Michelangelo 1912- .... CLC 20
See also CA 73-76; CANR 45
Antschel, Paul 1920-1970
See Celan, Paul
See also CA 85-88; CANR 33, 61; MTCW
Anwar, Chairil 1922-1949 .... TCLC 22
See also CA 121
Apollinaire, Guillaume 1880-1918TCLC 3, 8, 51; DAM POET; PC 7
See also Kostrowitzki, Wilhelm Apollinaris de
See also CA 152
Appelfeld, Aharon 1932- .... CLC 23, 47
See also CA 112; 133
Apple, Max (Isaac) 1941- .... CLC 9, 33
See also CA 81-84; CANR 19, 54; DLB 130
Appleman, Philip (Dean) 1926- .... CLC 51
See also CA 13-16R; CAAS 18; CANR 6, 29, 56
Appleton, Lawrence
See Lovecraft, H(oward) P(hillips)
Apteryx
See Eliot, T(homas) S(tearns)
Apuleius, (Lucius Madaurensis) 125(?)-175(?)
CMLC 1
Aquin, Hubert 1929-1977 .... CLC 15
See also CA 105; DLB 53
Aragon, Louis 1897-1982 ..CLC 3, 22; DAM NOV, POET
See also CA 69-72; 108; CANR 28; DLB 72; MTCW
Arany, Janos 1817-1882 .... NCLC 34
Arbuthnot, John 1667-1735 .... LC 1
See also DLB 101
Archer, Herbert Winslow
See Mencken, H(enry) L(ouis)
Archer, Jeffrey (Howard) 1940- ..... CLC 28; DAM POP
See also AAYA 16; BEST 89:3; CA 77-80; CANR 22, 52; INT CANR-22
Archer, Jules 1915- .... CLC 12
See also CA 9-12R; CANR 6; SAAS 5; SATA 4, 85
Archer, Lee
See Ellison, Harlan (Jay)
Arden, John 1930-CLC 6, 13, 15; DAM DRAM

See also CA 13-16R; CAAS 4; CANR 31, 65, 67; DLB 13; MTCW
Arenas, Reinaldo 1943-1990 .CLC 41; DAM MULT; HLC
See also CA 124; 128; 133; DLB 145; HW
Arendt, Hannah 1906-1975 .... CLC 66, 98
See also CA 17-20R; 61-64; CANR 26, 60; MTCW
Aretino, Pietro 1492-1556 .... LC 12
Arghezi, Tudor ....CLC 80
See also Theodorescu, Ion N.
Arguedas, Jose Maria 1911-1969CLC 10, 18
See also CA 89-92; DLB 113; HW
Argueta, Manlio 1936- .... CLC 31
See also CA 131; DLB 145; HW
Ariosto, Ludovico 1474-1533 .... LC 6
Aristides
See Epstein, Joseph
Aristophanes 450B.C.-385B.C.CMLC 4; DA; DAB; DAC; DAM DRAM, MST; DC 2; WLCS
See also DLB 176
Arlt, Roberto (Godofredo Christophersen) 1900-1942TCLC 29; DAM MULT; HLC
See also CA 123; 131; CANR 67; HW
Armah, Ayi Kwei 1939-CLC 5, 33; BLC; DAM MULT, POET
See also BW 1; CA 61-64; CANR 21, 64; DLB 117; MTCW
Armatrading, Joan 1950- .... CLC 17
See also CA 114
Arnette, Robert
See Silverberg, Robert
Arnim, Achim von (Ludwig Joachim von Arnim) 1781-1831 ...... NCLC 5; SSC 29
See also DLB 90
Arnim, Bettina von 1785-1859 .... NCLC 38
See also DLB 90
Arnold, Matthew 1822-1888NCLC 6, 29; DA; DAB; DAC; DAM MST, POET; PC 5; WLC
See also CDBLB 1832-1890; DLB 32, 57
Arnold, Thomas 1795-1842 .... NCLC 18
See also DLB 55
Arnow, Harriette (Louisa) Simpson 1908-1986
CLC 2, 7, 18
See also CA 9-12R; 118; CANR 14; DLB 6; MTCW; SATA 42; SATA-Obit 47
Arp, Hans
See Arp, Jean
Arp, Jean 1887-1966 .... CLC 5
See also CA 81-84; 25-28R; CANR 42
Arrabal
See Arrabal, Fernando
Arrabal, Fernando 1932- .... CLC 2, 9, 18, 58
See also CA 9-12R; CANR 15
Arrick, Fran ....CLC 30
See also Gaberman, Judie Angell
Artaud, Antonin (Marie Joseph) 1896-1948
TCLC 3, 36; DAM DRAM
See also CA 104; 149
Arthur, Ruth M(abel) 1905-1979 ......CLC 12
See also CA 9-12R; 85-88; CANR 4; SATA 7, 26
Artsybashev, Mikhail (Petrovich) 1878-1927
TCLC 31
Arundel, Honor (Morfydd) 1919-1973CLC 17
See also CA 21-22; 41-44R; CAP 2; CLR 35; SATA 4; SATA-Obit 24
Arzner, Dorothy 1897-1979 ....CLC 98
Asch, Sholem 1880-1957 .... TCLC 3
See also CA 105
Ash, Shalom

See Asch, Sholem
Ashbery, John (Lawrence) 1927-CLC 2, 3, 4, 6, 9, 13, 15, 25, 41, 77; DAM POET
See also CA 5-8R; CANR 9, 37, 66; DLB 5, 165; DLBY 81; INT CANR-9; MTCW
Ashdown, Clifford
See Freeman, R(ichard) Austin
Ashe, Gordon
See Creasey, John
Ashton-Warner, Sylvia (Constance) 1908-1984
CLC 19
See also CA 69-72; 112; CANR 29; MTCW
Asimov, Isaac 1920-1992 CLC 1, 3, 9, 19, 26, 76, 92; DAM POP
See also AAYA 13; BEST 90:2; CA 1-4R; 137; CANR 2, 19, 36, 60; CLR 12; DLB 8; DLBY 92; INT CANR-19; JRDA; MAICYA; MTCW; SATA 1, 26, 74
Assis, Joaquim Maria Machado de
See Machado de Assis, Joaquim Maria
Astley, Thea (Beatrice May) 1925- ...CLC 41
See also CA 65-68; CANR 11, 43
Aston, James
See White, T(erence) H(anbury)
Asturias, Miguel Angel 1899-1974 CLC 3, 8, 13; DAM MULT, NOV; HLC
See also CA 25-28; 49-52; CANR 32; CAP 2; DLB 113; HW; MTCW
Atares, Carlos Saura
See Saura (Atares), Carlos
Atheling, William
See Pound, Ezra (Weston Loomis)
Atheling, William, Jr.
See Blish, James (Benjamin)
Atherton, Gertrude (Franklin Horn) 1857-1948
TCLC 2
See also CA 104; 155; DLB 9, 78, 186
Atherton, Lucius
See Masters, Edgar Lee
Atkins, Jack
See Harris, Mark
Atkinson, Kate ....CLC 99
Attaway, William (Alexander) 1911-1986
CLC 92; BLC; DAM MULT
See also BW 2; CA 143; DLB 76
Atticus
See Fleming, Ian (Lancaster)
Atwood, Margaret (Eleanor) 1939-CLC 2, 3, 4, 8, 13, 15, 25, 44, 84; DA; DAB; DAC; DAM MST, NOV, POET; PC 8; SSC 2; WLC
See also AAYA 12; BEST 89:2; CA 49-52; CANR 3, 24, 33, 59; DLB 53; INT CANR-24; MTCW; SATA 50
Aubigny, Pierre d'
See Mencken, H(enry) L(ouis)
Aubin, Penelope 1685-1731(?) .... LC 9
See also DLB 39
Auchincloss, Louis (Stanton) 1917-CLC 4, 6, 9, 18, 45; DAM NOV; SSC 22
See also CA 1-4R; CANR 6, 29, 55; DLB 2; DLBY 80; INT CANR-29; MTCW
Auden, W(ystan) H(ugh) 1907-1973CLC 1, 2, 3, 4, 6, 9, 11, 14, 43; DA; DAB; DAC; DAM DRAM, MST, POET; PC 1; WLC
See also AAYA 18; CA 9-12R; 45-48; CANR 5, 61; CDBLB 1914-1945; DLB 10, 20; MTCW
Audiberti, Jacques 1900-1965CLC 38; DAM DRAM
See also CA 25-28R
Audubon, John James 1785-1851 ..NCLC 47
Auel, Jean M(arie) 1936-CLC 31, 107; DAM

POP
See also AAYA 7; BEST 90:4; CA 103; CANR 21, 64; INT CANR-21; SATA 91

Auerbach, Erich 1892-1957 .... **TCLC 43**
See also CA 118; 155

Augier, Emile 1820-1889 .... **NCLC 31**
See also DLB 192

August, John
See De Voto, Bernard (Augustine)

Augustine, St. 354-430 .... **CMLC 6; DAB**

Aurelius
See Bourne, Randolph S(illiman)

Aurobindo, Sri
See Aurobindo Ghose

Aurobindo Ghose 1872-1950 .... **TCLC 63**
See also CA 163

Austen, Jane 1775-1817 **NCLC 1, 13, 19, 33, 51; DA; DAB; DAC; DAM MST, NOV; WLC**
See also AAYA 19; CDBLB 1789-1832; DLB 116

Auster, Paul 1947- .... **CLC 47**
See also CA 69-72; CANR 23, 52

Austin, Frank
See Faust, Frederick (Schiller)

Austin, Mary (Hunter) 1868-1934 . **TCLC 25**
See also CA 109; DLB 9, 78

Autran Dourado, Waldomiro
See Dourado, (Waldomiro Freitas) Autran

Averroes 1126-1198 .... **CMLC 7**
See also DLB 115

Avicenna 980-1037 .... **CMLC 16**
See also DLB 115

Avison, Margaret 1918- **CLC 2, 4, 97; DAC; DAM POET**
See also CA 17-20R; DLB 53; MTCW

Axton, David
See Koontz, Dean R(ay)

Ayckbourn, Alan 1939- **CLC 5, 8, 18, 33, 74; DAB; DAM DRAM**
See also CA 21-24R; CANR 31, 59; DLB 13; MTCW

Aydy, Catherine
See Tennant, Emma (Christina)

Ayme, Marcel (Andre) 1902-1967 ..... **CLC 11**
See also CA 89-92; CANR 67; CLR 25; DLB 72; SATA 91

Ayrton, Michael 1921-1975 .... **CLC 7**
See also CA 5-8R; 61-64; CANR 9, 21

Azorin .... **CLC 11**
See also Martinez Ruiz, Jose

Azuela, Mariano 1873-1952 . **TCLC 3; DAM MULT; HLC**
See also CA 104; 131; HW; MTCW

Baastad, Babbis Friis
See Friis-Baastad, Babbis Ellinor

Bab
See Gilbert, W(illiam) S(chwenck)

Babbis, Eleanor
See Friis-Baastad, Babbis Ellinor

Babel, Isaac
See Babel, Isaak (Emmanuilovich)

Babel, Isaak (Emmanuilovich) 1894-1941(?)
TCLC 2, 13; SSC 16
See also CA 104; 155

Babits, Mihaly 1883-1941 .... **TCLC 14**
See also CA 114

Babur 1483-1530 .... **LC 18**

Bacchelli, Riccardo 1891-1985 .... **CLC 19**
See also CA 29-32R; 117

Bach, Richard (David) 1936- **CLC 14; DAM NOV, POP**
See also AITN 1; BEST 89:2; CA 9-12R; CANR

18; MTCW; SATA 13

Bachman, Richard
See King, Stephen (Edwin)

Bachmann, Ingeborg 1926-1973 .... **CLC 69**
See also CA 93-96; 45-48; DLB 85

Bacon, Francis 1561-1626 .... **LC 18, 32**
See also CDBLB Before 1660; DLB 151

Bacon, Roger 1214(?)-1292 .... **CMLC 14**
See also DLB 115

Bacovia, George .... **TCLC 24**
See also Vasiliu, Gheorghe

Badanes, Jerome 1937- .... **CLC 59**

Bagehot, Walter 1826-1877 .... **NCLC 10**
See also DLB 55

Bagnold, Enid 1889-1981 ...... **CLC 25; DAM DRAM**
See also CA 5-8R; 103; CANR 5, 40; DLB 13, 160, 191; MAICYA; SATA 1, 25

Bagritsky, Eduard 1895-1934 .... **TCLC 60**

Bagrjana, Elisaveta
See Belcheva, Elisaveta

Bagryana, Elisaveta .... **CLC 10**
See also Belcheva, Elisaveta
See also DLB 147

Bailey, Paul 1937- .... **CLC 45**
See also CA 21-24R; CANR 16, 62; DLB 14

Baillie, Joanna 1762-1851 .... **NCLC 2**
See also DLB 93

Bainbridge, Beryl (Margaret) 1933-**CLC 4, 5, 8, 10, 14, 18, 22, 62; DAM NOV**
See also CA 21-24R; CANR 24, 55; DLB 14; MTCW

Baker, Elliott 1922- .... **CLC 8**
See also CA 45-48; CANR 2, 63

Baker, Jean H. .... **TCLC 3, 10**
See also Russell, George William

Baker, Nicholson 1957- . **CLC 61; DAM POP**
See also CA 135; CANR 63

Baker, Ray Stannard 1870-1946 .... **TCLC 47**
See also CA 118

Baker, Russell (Wayne) 1925- .... **CLC 31**
See also BEST 89:4; CA 57-60; CANR 11, 41, 59; MTCW

Bakhtin, M.
See Bakhtin, Mikhail Mikhailovich

Bakhtin, M. M.
See Bakhtin, Mikhail Mikhailovich

Bakhtin, Mikhail
See Bakhtin, Mikhail Mikhailovich

Bakhtin, Mikhail Mikhailovich 1895-1975
CLC 83
See also CA 128; 113

Bakshi, Ralph 1938(?)- .... **CLC 26**
See also CA 112; 138

Bakunin, Mikhail (Alexandrovich) 1814-1876
NCLC 25, 58

Baldwin, James (Arthur) 1924-1987**CLC 1, 2, 3, 4, 5, 8, 13, 15, 17, 42, 50, 67, 90; BLC; DA; DAB; DAC; DAM MST, MULT, NOV, POP; DC 1; SSC 10; WLC**
See also AAYA 4; BW 1; CA 1-4R; 124; CABS 1; CANR 3, 24; CDALB 1941-1968; DLB 2, 7, 33; DLBY 87; MTCW; SATA 9; SATA-Obit 54

Ballard, J(ames) G(raham) 1930-**CLC 3, 6, 14, 36; DAM NOV, POP; SSC 1**
See also AAYA 3; CA 5-8R; CANR 15, 39, 65; DLB 14; MTCW; SATA 93

Balmont, Konstantin (Dmitriyevich) 1867-1943
TCLC 11
See also CA 109; 155

Balzac, Honore de 1799-1850**NCLC 5, 35, 53; DA; DAB; DAC; DAM MST, NOV; SSC**

5; WLC
See also DLB 119

Bambara, Toni Cade 1939-1995 **CLC 19, 88; BLC; DA; DAC; DAM MST, MULT; WLCS**
See also AAYA 5; BW 2; CA 29-32R; 150; CANR 24, 49; DLB 38; MTCW

Bamdad, A.
See Shamlu, Ahmad

Banat, D. R.
See Bradbury, Ray (Douglas)

Bancroft, Laura
See Baum, L(yman) Frank

Banim, John 1798-1842 .... **NCLC 13**
See also DLB 116, 158, 159

Banim, Michael 1796-1874 .... **NCLC 13**
See also DLB 158, 159

Banjo, The
See Paterson, A(ndrew) B(arton)

Banks, Iain
See Banks, Iain M(enzies)

Banks, Iain M(enzies) 1954- .... **CLC 34**
See also CA 123; 128; CANR 61; DLB 194; INT 128

Banks, Lynne Reid .... **CLC 23**
See also Reid Banks, Lynne
See also AAYA 6

Banks, Russell 1940- .... **CLC 37, 72**
See also CA 65-68; CAAS 15; CANR 19, 52; DLB 130

Banville, John 1945- .... **CLC 46**
See also CA 117; 128; DLB 14; INT 128

Banville, Theodore (Faullain) de 1832-1891
NCLC 9

Baraka, Amiri 1934-**CLC 1, 2, 3, 5, 10, 14, 33; BLC; DA; DAC; DAM MST, MULT, POET, POP; DC 6; PC 4; WLCS**
See also Jones, LeRoi
See also BW 2; CA 21-24R; CABS 3; CANR 27, 38, 61; CDALB 1941-1968; DLB 5, 7, 16, 38; DLBD 8; MTCW

Barbauld, Anna Laetitia 1743-1825**NCLC 50**
See also DLB 107, 109, 142, 158

Barbellion, W. N. P. .... **TCLC 24**
See also Cummings, Bruce F(rederick)

Barbera, Jack (Vincent) 1945- .... **CLC 44**
See also CA 110; CANR 45

Barbey d'Aurevilly, Jules Amedee 1808-1889
NCLC 1; SSC 17
See also DLB 119

Barbusse, Henri 1873-1935 .... **TCLC 5**
See also CA 105; 154; DLB 65

Barclay, Bill
See Moorcock, Michael (John)

Barclay, William Ewert
See Moorcock, Michael (John)

Barea, Arturo 1897-1957 .... **TCLC 14**
See also CA 111

Barfoot, Joan 1946- .... **CLC 18**
See also CA 105

Baring, Maurice 1874-1945 .... **TCLC 8**
See also CA 105; DLB 34

Barker, Clive 1952- .... **CLC 52; DAM POP**
See also AAYA 10; BEST 90:3; CA 121; 129; INT 129; MTCW

Barker, George Granville 1913-1991 **CLC 8, 48; DAM POET**
See also CA 9-12R; 135; CANR 7, 38; DLB 20; MTCW

Barker, Harley Granville
See Granville-Barker, Harley
See also DLB 10

Barker, Howard 1946- .... **CLC 37**

See also CA 102; DLB 13

Barker, Pat(ricia) 1943- .... **CLC 32, 94**
See also CA 117; 122; CANR 50; INT 122

Barlow, Joel 1754-1812 .... **NCLC 23**
See also DLB 37

Barnard, Mary (Ethel) 1909- .... **CLC 48**
See also CA 21-22; CAP 2

Barnes, Djuna 1892-1982 CLC 3, 4, 8, 11, 29; SSC 3
See also CA 9-12R; 107; CANR 16, 55; DLB 4, 9, 45; MTCW

Barnes, Julian (Patrick) 1946- CLC 42; DAB
See also CA 102; CANR 19, 54; DLB 194; DLBY 93

Barnes, Peter 1931- .... **CLC 5, 56**
See also CA 65-68; CAAS 12; CANR 33, 34, 64; DLB 13; MTCW

Baroja (y Nessi), Pio 1872-1956 TCLC 8; HLC
See also CA 104

Baron, David
See Pinter, Harold

Baron Corvo
See Rolfe, Frederick (William Serafino Austin Lewis Mary)

Barondess, Sue K(aufman) 1926-1977 CLC 8
See also Kaufman, Sue
See also CA 1-4R; 69-72; CANR 1

Baron de Teive
See Pessoa, Fernando (Antonio Nogueira)

Barres, (Auguste-) Maurice 1862-1923 T C L C 47
See also CA 164; DLB 123

Barreto, Afonso Henrique de Lima
See Lima Barreto, Afonso Henrique de

Barrett, (Roger) Syd 1946- .... **CLC 35**

Barrett, William (Christopher) 1913-1992 CLC 27
See also CA 13-16R; 139; CANR 11, 67; INT CANR-11

Barrie, J(ames) M(atthew) 1860-1937 T C L C 2; DAB; DAM DRAM
See also CA 104; 136; CDBLB 1890-1914; CLR 16; DLB 10, 141, 156; MAICYA; YABC 1

Barrington, Michael
See Moorcock, Michael (John)

Barrol, Grady
See Bograd, Larry

Barry, Mike
See Malzberg, Barry N(athaniel)

Barry, Philip 1896-1949 .... **TCLC 11**
See also CA 109; DLB 7

Bart, Andre Schwarz
See Schwarz-Bart, Andre

Barth, John (Simmons) 1930- CLC 1, 2, 3, 5, 7, 9, 10, 14, 27, 51, 89; DAM NOV; SSC 10
See also AITN 1, 2; CA 1-4R; CABS 1; CANR 5, 23, 49, 64; DLB 2; MTCW

Barthelme, Donald 1931-1989 CLC 1, 2, 3, 5, 6, 8, 13, 23, 46, 59; DAM NOV; SSC 2
See also CA 21-24R; 129; CANR 20, 58; DLB 2; DLBY 80, 89; MTCW; SATA 7; SATA-Obit 62

Barthelme, Frederick 1943- .... **CLC 36**
See also CA 114; 122; DLBY 85; INT 122

Barthes, Roland (Gerard) 1915-1980 CLC 24, 83
See also CA 130; 97-100; CANR 66; MTCW

Barzun, Jacques (Martin) 1907- ...... **CLC 51**
See also CA 61-64; CANR 22

Bashevis, Isaac
See Singer, Isaac Bashevis

Bashkirtseff, Marie 1859-1884 .... **NCLC 27**

Basho
See Matsuo Basho

Bass, Kingsley B., Jr.
See Bullins, Ed

Bass, Rick 1958- .... **CLC 79**
See also CA 126; CANR 53

Bassani, Giorgio 1916- .... **CLC 9**
See also CA 65-68; CANR 33; DLB 128, 177; MTCW

Bastos, Augusto (Antonio) Roa
See Roa Bastos, Augusto (Antonio)

Bataille, Georges 1897-1962 .... **CLC 29**
See also CA 101; 89-92

Bates, H(erbert) E(rnest) 1905-1974 CLC 46; DAB; DAM POP; SSC 10
See also CA 93-96; 45-48; CANR 34; DLB 162, 191; MTCW

Bauchart
See Camus, Albert

Baudelaire, Charles 1821-1867 NCLC 6, 29, 55; DA; DAB; DAC; DAM MST, POET; PC 1; SSC 18; WLC

Baudrillard, Jean 1929- .... **CLC 60**

Baum, L(yman) Frank 1856-1919 ... **TCLC 7**
See also CA 108; 133; CLR 15; DLB 22; JRDA; MAICYA; MTCW; SATA 18

Baum, Louis F.
See Baum, L(yman) Frank

Baumbach, Jonathan 1933- .... **CLC 6, 23**
See also CA 13-16R; CAAS 5; CANR 12, 66; DLBY 80; INT CANR-12; MTCW

Bausch, Richard (Carl) 1945- .... **CLC 51**
See also CA 101; CAAS 14; CANR 43, 61; DLB 130

Baxter, Charles (Morley) 1947- CLC 45, 78; DAM POP
See also CA 57-60; CANR 40, 64; DLB 130

Baxter, George Owen
See Faust, Frederick (Schiller)

Baxter, James K(eir) 1926-1972 .... **CLC 14**
See also CA 77-80

Baxter, John
See Hunt, E(verette) Howard, (Jr.)

Bayer, Sylvia
See Glassco, John

Baynton, Barbara 1857-1929 .... **TCLC 57**

Beagle, Peter S(oyer) 1939- .... **CLC 7, 104**
See also CA 9-12R; CANR 4, 51; DLBY 80; INT CANR-4; SATA 60

Bean, Normal
See Burroughs, Edgar Rice

Beard, Charles A(ustin) 1874-1948 TCLC 15
See also CA 115; DLB 17; SATA 18

Beardsley, Aubrey 1872-1898 .... **NCLC 6**

Beattie, Ann 1947- CLC 8, 13, 18, 40, 63; DAM NOV, POP; SSC 11
See also BEST 90:2; CA 81-84; CANR 53; DLBY 82; MTCW

Beattie, James 1735-1803 .... **NCLC 25**
See also DLB 109

Beauchamp, Kathleen Mansfield 1888-1923
See Mansfield, Katherine
See also CA 104; 134; DA; DAC; DAM MST

Beaumarchais, Pierre-Augustin Caron de 1732-1799 .... **DC 4**
See also DAM DRAM

Beaumont, Francis 1584(?)-1616 LC 33; DC 6
See also CDBLB Before 1660; DLB 58, 121

Beauvoir, Simone (Lucie Ernestine Marie Bertrand) de 1908-1986 CLC 1, 2, 4, 8, 14, 31, 44, 50, 71; DA; DAB; DAC; DAM MST, NOV; WLC
See also CA 9-12R; 118; CANR 28, 61; DLB

Becker, Carl (Lotus) 1873-1945 ..... **TCLC 63**
See also CA 157; DLB 17

Becker, Jurek 1937-1997 .... **CLC 7, 19**
See also CA 85-88; 157; CANR 60; DLB 75

Becker, Walter 1950- .... **CLC 26**

Beckett, Samuel (Barclay) 1906-1989 CLC 1, 2, 3, 4, 6, 9, 10, 11, 14, 18, 29, 57, 59, 83; DA; DAB; DAC; DAM DRAM, MST, NOV; SSC 16; WLC
See also CA 5-8R; 130; CANR 33, 61; CDBLB 1945-1960; DLB 13, 15; DLBY 90; MTCW

Beckford, William 1760-1844 .... **NCLC 16**
See also DLB 39

Beckman, Gunnel 1910- .... **CLC 26**
See also CA 33-36R; CANR 15; CLR 25; MAICYA; SAAS 9; SATA 6

Becque, Henri 1837-1899 .... **NCLC 3**
See also DLB 192

Beddoes, Thomas Lovell 1803-1849 NCLC 3
See also DLB 96

Bede c. 673-735 .... **CMLC 20**
See also DLB 146

Bedford, Donald F.
See Fearing, Kenneth (Flexner)

Beecher, Catharine Esther 1800-1878 N C L C 30
See also DLB 1

Beecher, John 1904-1980 .... **CLC 6**
See also AITN 1; CA 5-8R; 105; CANR 8

Beer, Johann 1655-1700 .... **LC 5**
See also DLB 168

Beer, Patricia 1924- .... **CLC 58**
See also CA 61-64; CANR 13, 46; DLB 40

Beerbohm, Max
See Beerbohm, (Henry) Max(imilian)

Beerbohm, (Henry) Max(imilian) 1872-1956 TCLC 1, 24
See also CA 104; 154; DLB 34, 100

Beer-Hofmann, Richard 1866-1945 TCLC 60
See also CA 160; DLB 81

Begiebing, Robert J(ohn) 1946- .... **CLC 70**
See also CA 122; CANR 40

Behan, Brendan 1923-1964 CLC 1, 8, 11, 15, 79; DAM DRAM
See also CA 73-76; CANR 33; CDBLB 1945-1960; DLB 13; MTCW

Behn, Aphra 1640(?)-1689 LC 1, 30; DA; DAB; DAC; DAM DRAM, MST, NOV, POET; DC 4; PC 13; WLC
See also DLB 39, 80, 131

Behrman, S(amuel) N(athaniel) 1893-1973 CLC 40
See also CA 13-16; 45-48; CAP 1; DLB 7, 44

Belasco, David 1853-1931 .... **TCLC 3**
See also CA 104; DLB 7

Belcheva, Elisaveta 1893- .... **CLC 10**
See also Bagryana, Elisaveta

Beldone, Phil "Cheech"
See Ellison, Harlan (Jay)

Beleno
See Azuela, Mariano

Belinski, Vissarion Grigoryevich 1811-1848 NCLC 5

Belitt, Ben 1911- .... **CLC 22**
See also CA 13-16R; CAAS 4; CANR 7; DLB 5

Bell, Gertrude 1868-1926 .... **TCLC 67**
See also DLB 174

Bell, James Madison 1826-1902 ... **TCLC 43**; BLC; DAM MULT
See also BW 1; CA 122; 124; DLB 50

Bell, Madison Smartt 1957- ...... **CLC 41, 102**

See also CA 111; CANR 28, 54

Bell, Marvin (Hartley) 1937-**CLC 8, 31; DAM POET**
See also CA 21-24R; CAAS 14; CANR 59; DLB 5; MTCW

Bell, W. L. D.
See Mencken, H(enry) L(ouis)

Bellamy, Atwood C.
See Mencken, H(enry) L(ouis)

Bellamy, Edward 1850-1898 .... **NCLC 4**
See also DLB 12

Bellin, Edward J.
See Kuttner, Henry

Belloc, (Joseph) Hilaire (Pierre Sebastien Rene Swanton) 1870-1953 **TCLC 7, 18; DAM POET**
See also CA 106; 152; DLB 19, 100, 141, 174; YABC 1

Belloc, Joseph Peter Rene Hilaire
See Belloc, (Joseph) Hilaire (Pierre Sebastien Rene Swanton)

Belloc, Joseph Pierre Hilaire
See Belloc, (Joseph) Hilaire (Pierre Sebastien Rene Swanton)

Belloc, M. A.
See Lowndes, Marie Adelaide (Belloc)

Bellow, Saul 1915-**CLC 1, 2, 3, 6, 8, 10, 13, 15, 25, 33, 34, 63, 79; DA; DAB; DAC; DAM MST, NOV, POP; SSC 14; WLC**
See also AITN 2; BEST 89:3; CA 5-8R; CABS 1; CANR 29, 53; CDALB 1941-1968; DLB 2, 28; DLBD 3; DLBY 82; MTCW

Belser, Reimond Karel Maria de 1929-
See Ruyslinck, Ward
See also CA 152

Bely, Andrey .... **TCLC 7; PC 11**
See also Bugayev, Boris Nikolayevich

Belyi, Andrei
See Bugayev, Boris Nikolayevich

Benary, Margot
See Benary-Isbert, Margot

Benary-Isbert, Margot 1889-1979 ... **CLC 12**
See also CA 5-8R; 89-92; CANR 4; CLR 12; MAICYA; SATA 2; SATA-Obit 21

Benavente (y Martinez), Jacinto 1866-1954 **TCLC 3; DAM DRAM, MULT**
See also CA 106; 131; HW; MTCW

Benchley, Peter (Bradford) 1940-. **CLC 4, 8; DAM NOV, POP**
See also AAYA 14; AITN 2; CA 17-20R; CANR 12, 35, 66; MTCW; SATA 3, 89

Benchley, Robert (Charles) 1889-1945**T C L C 1, 55**
See also CA 105; 153; DLB 11

Benda, Julien 1867-1956 .... **TCLC 60**
See also CA 120; 154

Benedict, Ruth (Fulton) 1887-1948 **TCLC 60**
See also CA 158

Benedikt, Michael 1935- .... **CLC 4, 14**
See also CA 13-16R; CANR 7; DLB 5

Benet, Juan 1927- .... **CLC 28**
See also CA 143

Benet, Stephen Vincent 1898-1943 . **TCLC 7; DAM POET; SSC 10**
See also CA 104; 152; DLB 4, 48, 102; DLBY 97; YABC 1

Benet, William Rose 1886-1950 ... **TCLC 28; DAM POET**
See also CA 118; 152; DLB 45

Benford, Gregory (Albert) 1941- ..... **CLC 52**
See also CA 69-72; CAAS 27; CANR 12, 24, 49; DLBY 82

Bengtsson, Frans (Gunnar) 1894-1954**T C L C**
48

Benjamin, David
See Slavitt, David R(ytman)

Benjamin, Lois
See Gould, Lois

Benjamin, Walter 1892-1940 .... **TCLC 39**
See also CA 164

Benn, Gottfried 1886-1956 .... **TCLC 3**
See also CA 106; 153; DLB 56

Bennett, Alan 1934-**CLC 45, 77; DAB; DAM MST**
See also CA 103; CANR 35, 55; MTCW

Bennett, (Enoch) Arnold 1867-1931**TCLC 5, 20**
See also CA 106; 155; CDBLB 1890-1914; DLB 10, 34, 98, 135

Bennett, Elizabeth
See Mitchell, Margaret (Munnerlyn)

Bennett, George Harold 1930-
See Bennett, Hal
See also BW 1; CA 97-100

Bennett, Hal ....**CLC 5**
See also Bennett, George Harold
See also DLB 33

Bennett, Jay 1912- ....**CLC 35**
See also AAYA 10; CA 69-72; CANR 11, 42; JRDA; SAAS 4; SATA 41, 87; SATA-Brief 27

Bennett, Louise (Simone) 1919-**CLC 28; BLC; DAM MULT**
See also BW 2; CA 151; DLB 117

Benson, E(dward) F(rederic) 1867-1940 **TCLC 27**
See also CA 114; 157; DLB 135, 153

Benson, Jackson J. 1930- .... **CLC 34**
See also CA 25-28R; DLB 111

Benson, Sally 1900-1972 .... **CLC 17**
See also CA 19-20; 37-40R; CAP 1; SATA 1, 35; SATA-Obit 27

Benson, Stella 1892-1933 .... **TCLC 17**
See also CA 117; 155; DLB 36, 162

Bentham, Jeremy 1748-1832 .... **NCLC 38**
See also DLB 107, 158

Bentley, E(dmund) C(lerihew) 1875-1956 **TCLC 12**
See also CA 108; DLB 70

Bentley, Eric (Russell) 1916- .... **CLC 24**
See also CA 5-8R; CANR 6, 67; INT CANR-6

Beranger, Pierre Jean de 1780-1857**NCLC 34**

Berdyaev, Nicolas
See Berdyaev, Nikolai (Aleksandrovich)

Berdyaev, Nikolai (Aleksandrovich) 1874-1948 **TCLC 67**
See also CA 120; 157

Berdyayev, Nikolai (Aleksandrovich)
See Berdyaev, Nikolai (Aleksandrovich)

Berendt, John (Lawrence) 1939- ...... **CLC 86**
See also CA 146

Berger, Colonel
See Malraux, (Georges-)Andre

Berger, John (Peter) 1926- .... **CLC 2, 19**
See also CA 81-84; CANR 51; DLB 14

Berger, Melvin H. 1927- .... **CLC 12**
See also CA 5-8R; CANR 4; CLR 32; SAAS 2; SATA 5, 88

Berger, Thomas (Louis) 1924-**CLC 3, 5, 8, 11, 18, 38; DAM NOV**
See also CA 1-4R; CANR 5, 28, 51; DLB 2; DLBY 80; INT CANR-28; MTCW

Bergman, (Ernst) Ingmar 1918- **CLC 16, 72**
See also CA 81-84; CANR 33

Bergson, Henri 1859-1941 .... **TCLC 32**
See also CA 164

Bergstein, Eleanor 1938- .... **CLC 4**
See also CA 53-56; CANR 5

Berkoff, Steven 1937- .... **CLC 56**
See also CA 104

Bermant, Chaim (Icyk) 1929- .... **CLC 40**
See also CA 57-60; CANR 6, 31, 57

Bern, Victoria
See Fisher, M(ary) F(rances) K(ennedy)

Bernanos, (Paul Louis) Georges 1888-1948 **TCLC 3**
See also CA 104; 130; DLB 72

Bernard, April 1956- .... **CLC 59**
See also CA 131

Berne, Victoria
See Fisher, M(ary) F(rances) K(ennedy)

Bernhard, Thomas 1931-1989 **CLC 3, 32, 61**
See also CA 85-88; 127; CANR 32, 57; DLB 85, 124; MTCW

Bernhardt, Sarah (Henriette Rosine) 1844-1923 **TCLC 75**
See also CA 157

Berriault, Gina 1926-. **CLC 54, 109; SSC 30**
See also CA 116; 129; CANR 66; DLB 130

Berrigan, Daniel 1921-........................**CLC 4**
See also CA 33-36R; CAAS 1; CANR 11, 43; DLB 5

Berrigan, Edmund Joseph Michael, Jr. 1934-1983
See Berrigan, Ted
See also CA 61-64; 110; CANR 14

Berrigan, Ted .... **CLC 37**
See also Berrigan, Edmund Joseph Michael, Jr.
See also DLB 5, 169

Berry, Charles Edward Anderson 1931-
See Berry, Chuck
See also CA 115

Berry, Chuck ....**CLC 17**
See also Berry, Charles Edward Anderson

Berry, Jonas
See Ashbery, John (Lawrence)

Berry, Wendell (Erdman) 1934- **CLC 4, 6, 8, 27, 46; DAM POET**
See also AITN 1; CA 73-76; CANR 50; DLB 5, 6

Berryman, John 1914-1972**CLC 1, 2, 3, 4, 6, 8, 10, 13, 25, 62; DAM POET**
See also CA 13-16; 33-36R; CABS 2; CANR 35; CAP 1; CDALB 1941-1968; DLB 48; MTCW

Bertolucci, Bernardo 1940- .... **CLC 16**
See also CA 106

Berton, Pierre (Francis De Marigny) 1920- **CLC 104**
See also CA 1-4R; CANR 2, 56; DLB 68

Bertrand, Aloysius 1807-1841 .... **NCLC 31**

Bertran de Born c. 1140-1215 .... **CMLC 5**

Besant, Annie (Wood) 1847-1933 ..... **TCLC 9**
See also CA 105

Bessie, Alvah 1904-1985 .... **CLC 23**
See also CA 5-8R; 116; CANR 2; DLB 26

Bethlen, T. D.
See Silverberg, Robert

Beti, Mongo ...... **CLC 27; BLC; DAM MULT**
See also Biyidi, Alexandre

Betjeman, John 1906-1984 **CLC 2, 6, 10, 34, 43; DAB; DAM MST, POET**
See also CA 9-12R; 112; CANR 33, 56; CDBLB 1945-1960; DLB 20; DLBY 84; MTCW

Bettelheim, Bruno 1903-1990 .... **CLC 79**
See also CA 81-84; 131; CANR 23, 61; MTCW

Betti, Ugo 1892-1953 .... **TCLC 5**
See also CA 104; 155

Betts, Doris (Waugh) 1932- ...... **CLC 3, 6, 28**

See also CA 13-16R; CANR 9, 66; DLBY 82;
INT CANR-9

Bevan, Alistair
See Roberts, Keith (John Kingston)

Bialik, Chaim Nachman 1873-1934 **TCLC 25**

Bickerstaff, Isaac
See Swift, Jonathan

Bidart, Frank 1939- .... **CLC 33**
See also CA 140

Bienek, Horst 1930- .... **CLC 7, 11**
See also CA 73-76; DLB 75

Bierce, Ambrose (Gwinett) 1842-1914(?)
**TCLC 1, 7, 44; DA; DAC; DAM MST; SSC
9; WLC**
See also CA 104; 139; CDALB 1865-1917;
DLB 11, 12, 23, 71, 74, 186

Biggers, Earl Derr 1884-1933 .... **TCLC 65**
See also CA 108; 153

Billings, Josh
See Shaw, Henry Wheeler

Billington, (Lady) Rachel (Mary) 1942-**C L C
43**
See also AITN 2; CA 33-36R; CANR 44

Binyon, T(imothy) J(ohn) 1936- ...... **CLC 34**
See also CA 111; CANR 28

Bioy Casares, Adolfo 1914-1984**CLC 4, 8, 13,
88; DAM MULT; HLC; SSC 17**
See also CA 29-32R; CANR 19, 43, 66; DLB
113; HW; MTCW

Bird, Cordwainer
See Ellison, Harlan (Jay)

Bird, Robert Montgomery 1806-1854**NCLC 1**

Birney, (Alfred) Earle 1904-1995**CLC 1, 4, 6,
11; DAC; DAM MST, POET**
See also CA 1-4R; CANR 5, 20; DLB 88;
MTCW

Bishop, Elizabeth 1911-1979 **CLC 1, 4, 9, 13,
15, 32; DA; DAC; DAM MST, POET; PC
3**
See also CA 5-8R; 89-92; CABS 2; CANR 26,
61; CDALB 1968-1988; DLB 5, 169;
MTCW; SATA-Obit 24

Bishop, John 1935- .... **CLC 10**
See also CA 105

Bissett, Bill 1939-.................... **CLC 18; PC 14**
See also CA 69-72; CAAS 19; CANR 15; DLB
53; MTCW

Bitov, Andrei (Georgievich) 1937-... **CLC 57**
See also CA 142

Biyidi, Alexandre 1932-
See Beti, Mongo
See also BW 1; CA 114; 124; MTCW

Bjarme, Brynjolf
See Ibsen, Henrik (Johan)

Bjornson, Bjornstjerne (Martinius) 1832-1910
TCLC 7, 37
See also CA 104

Black, Robert
See Holdstock, Robert P.

Blackburn, Paul 1926-1971 .... **CLC 9, 43**
See also CA 81-84; 33-36R; CANR 34; DLB
16; DLBY 81

Black Elk 1863-1950**TCLC 33; DAM MULT**
See also CA 144; NNAL

Black Hobart
See Sanders, (James) Ed(ward)

Blacklin, Malcolm
See Chambers, Aidan

Blackmore, R(ichard) D(oddridge) 1825-1900
TCLC 27
See also CA 120; DLB 18

Blackmur, R(ichard) P(almer) 1904-1965
CLC 2, 24

See also CA 11-12; 25-28R; CAP 1; DLB 63

Black Tarantula
See Acker, Kathy

Blackwood, Algernon (Henry) 1869-1951
TCLC 5
See also CA 105; 150; DLB 153, 156, 178

Blackwood, Caroline 1931-1996**CLC 6, 9, 100**
See also CA 85-88; 151; CANR 32, 61, 65; DLB
14; MTCW

Blade, Alexander
See Hamilton, Edmond; Silverberg, Robert

Blaga, Lucian 1895-1961 .... **CLC 75**

Blair, Eric (Arthur) 1903-1950
See Orwell, George
See also CA 104; 132; DA; DAB; DAC; DAM
MST, NOV; MTCW; SATA 29

Blais, Marie-Claire 1939-**CLC 2, 4, 6, 13, 22;
DAC; DAM MST**
See also CA 21-24R; CAAS 4; CANR 38; DLB
53; MTCW

Blaise, Clark 1940- .... **CLC 29**
See also AITN 2; CA 53-56; CAAS 3; CANR
5, 66; DLB 53

Blake, Fairley
See De Voto, Bernard (Augustine)

Blake, Nicholas
See Day Lewis, C(ecil)
See also DLB 77

Blake, William 1757-1827 . **NCLC 13, 37, 57;
DA; DAB; DAC; DAM MST, POET; PC
12; WLC**
See also CDBLB 1789-1832; DLB 93, 163;
MAICYA; SATA 30

Blasco Ibanez, Vicente 1867-1928 **TCLC 12;
DAM NOV**
See also CA 110; 131; HW; MTCW

Blatty, William Peter 1928-**CLC 2; DAM POP**
See also CA 5-8R; CANR 9

Bleeck, Oliver
See Thomas, Ross (Elmore)

Blessing, Lee 1949- .... **CLC 54**

Blish, James (Benjamin) 1921-1975 . **CLC 14**
See also CA 1-4R; 57-60; CANR 3; DLB 8;
MTCW; SATA 66

Bliss, Reginald
See Wells, H(erbert) G(eorge)

Blixen, Karen (Christentze Dinesen) 1885-1962
See Dinesen, Isak
See also CA 25-28; CANR 22, 50; CAP 2;
MTCW; SATA 44

Bloch, Robert (Albert) 1917-1994 .... **CLC 33**
See also CA 5-8R; 146; CAAS 20; CANR 5;
DLB 44; INT CANR-5; SATA 12; SATA-Obit
82

Blok, Alexander (Alexandrovich) 1880-1921
TCLC 5; PC 21
See also CA 104

Blom, Jan
See Breytenbach, Breyten

Bloom, Harold 1930- .... **CLC 24, 103**
See also CA 13-16R; CANR 39; DLB 67

Bloomfield, Aurelius
See Bourne, Randolph S(illiman)

Blount, Roy (Alton), Jr. 1941- .... **CLC 38**
See also CA 53-56; CANR 10, 28, 61; INT
CANR-28; MTCW

Bloy, Leon 1846-1917 .... **TCLC 22**
See also CA 121; DLB 123

Blume, Judy (Sussman) 1938-... **CLC 12, 30;
DAM NOV, POP**
See also AAYA 3; CA 29-32R; CANR 13, 37,
66; CLR 2, 15; DLB 52; JRDA; MAICYA;
MTCW; SATA 2, 31, 79

Blunden, Edmund (Charles) 1896-1974 **C L C
2, 56**
See also CA 17-18; 45-48; CANR 54; CAP 2;
DLB 20, 100, 155; MTCW

Bly, Robert (Elwood) 1926-**CLC 1, 2, 5, 10, 15,
38; DAM POET**
See also CA 5-8R; CANR 41; DLB 5; MTCW

Boas, Franz 1858-1942 .... **TCLC 56**
See also CA 115

Bobette
See Simenon, Georges (Jacques Christian)

Boccaccio, Giovanni 1313-1375 .. **CMLC 13;
SSC 10**

Bochco, Steven 1943- .... **CLC 35**
See also AAYA 11; CA 124; 138

Bodenheim, Maxwell 1892-1954 .... **TCLC 44**
See also CA 110; DLB 9, 45

Bodker, Cecil 1927- .... **CLC 21**
See also CA 73-76; CANR 13, 44; CLR 23;
MAICYA; SATA 14

Boell, Heinrich (Theodor) 1917-1985 **CLC 2,
3, 6, 9, 11, 15, 27, 32, 72; DA; DAB; DAC;
DAM MST, NOV; SSC 23; WLC**
See also CA 21-24R; 116; CANR 24; DLB 69;
DLBY 85; MTCW

Boerne, Alfred
See Doeblin, Alfred

Boethius 480(?)-524(?) .... **CMLC 15**
See also DLB 115

Bogan, Louise 1897-1970 . **CLC 4, 39, 46, 93;
DAM POET; PC 12**
See also CA 73-76; 25-28R; CANR 33; DLB
45, 169; MTCW

Bogarde, Dirk .... **CLC 19**
See also Van Den Bogarde, Derek Jules Gaspard
Ulric Niven
See also DLB 14

Bogosian, Eric 1953- .... **CLC 45**
See also CA 138

Bograd, Larry 1953- .... **CLC 35**
See also CA 93-96; CANR 57; SAAS 21; SATA
33, 89

Boiardo, Matteo Maria 1441-1494 .... **LC 6**

Boileau-Despreaux, Nicolas 1636-1711 **LC 3**

Bojer, Johan 1872-1959 .... **TCLC 64**

Boland, Eavan (Aisling) 1944- .. **CLC 40, 67;
DAM POET**
See also CA 143; CANR 61; DLB 40

Bolt, Lee
See Faust, Frederick (Schiller)

Bolt, Robert (Oxton) 1924-1995 ..... **CLC 14;
DAM DRAM**
See also CA 17-20R; 147; CANR 35, 67; DLB
13; MTCW

Bombet, Louis-Alexandre-Cesar
See Stendhal

Bomkauf
See Kaufman, Bob (Garnell)

Bonaventura .... **NCLC 35**
See also DLB 90

Bond, Edward 1934- **CLC 4, 6, 13, 23; DAM
DRAM**
See also CA 25-28R; CANR 38, 67; DLB 13;
MTCW

Bonham, Frank 1914-1989 .... **CLC 12**
See also AAYA 1; CA 9-12R; CANR 4, 36;
JRDA; MAICYA; SAAS 3; SATA 1, 49;
SATA-Obit 62

Bonnefoy, Yves 1923- .. **CLC 9, 15, 58; DAM
MST, POET**
See also CA 85-88; CANR 33; MTCW

Bontemps, Arna(ud Wendell) 1902-1973**C L C
1, 18; BLC; DAM MULT, NOV, POET**

See also BW 1; CA 1-4R; 41-44R; CANR 4, 35; CLR 6; DLB 48, 51; JRDA; MAICYA; MTCW; SATA 2, 44; SATA-Obit 24

Booth, Martin 1944- .... **CLC 13**
See also CA 93-96; CAAS 2

Booth, Philip 1925- .... **CLC 23**
See also CA 5-8R; CANR 5; DLBY 82

Booth, Wayne C(layson) 1921- .... **CLC 24**
See also CA 1-4R; CAAS 5; CANR 3, 43; DLB 67

Borchert, Wolfgang 1921-1947 .... **TCLC 5**
See also CA 104; DLB 69, 124

Borel, Petrus 1809-1859 .... **NCLC 41**

Borges, Jorge Luis 1899-1986 **CLC 1, 2, 3, 4, 6, 8, 9, 10, 13, 19, 44, 48, 83; DA; DAB; DAC; DAM MST, MULT; HLC; SSC 4; WLC**
See also AAYA 19; CA 21-24R; CANR 19, 33; DLB 113; DLBY 86; HW; MTCW

Borowski, Tadeusz 1922-1951 .... **TCLC 9**
See also CA 106; 154

Borrow, George (Henry) 1803-1881 **NCLC 9**
See also DLB 21, 55, 166

Bosman, Herman Charles 1905-1951 . **T C L C 49**
See also Malan, Herman
See also CA 160

Bosschere, Jean de 1878(?)-1953 ... **TCLC 19**
See also CA 115

Boswell, James 1740-1795 . **LC 4; DA; DAB; DAC; DAM MST; WLC**
See also CDBLB 1660-1789; DLB 104, 142

Bottoms, David 1949- .... **CLC 53**
See also CA 105; CANR 22; DLB 120; DLBY 83

Boucicault, Dion 1820-1890 .... **NCLC 41**

Boucolon, Maryse 1937(?)-
See Conde, Maryse
See also CA 110; CANR 30, 53

Bourget, Paul (Charles Joseph) 1852-1935 **TCLC 12**
See also CA 107; DLB 123

Bourjaily, Vance (Nye) 1922- .... **CLC 8, 62**
See also CA 1-4R; CAAS 1; CANR 2; DLB 2, 143

Bourne, Randolph S(illiman) 1886-1918 **TCLC 16**
See also CA 117; 155; DLB 63

Bova, Ben(jamin William) 1932- ..... **CLC 45**
See also AAYA 16; CA 5-8R; CAAS 18; CANR 11, 56; CLR 3; DLBY 81; INT CANR-11; MAICYA; MTCW; SATA 6, 68

Bowen, Elizabeth (Dorothea Cole) 1899-1973 **CLC 1, 3, 6, 11, 15, 22; DAM NOV; SSC 3, 28**
See also CA 17-18; 41-44R; CANR 35; CAP 2; CDBLB 1945-1960; DLB 15, 162; MTCW

Bowering, George 1935- .... **CLC 15, 47**
See also CA 21-24R; CAAS 16; CANR 10; DLB 53

Bowering, Marilyn R(uthe) 1949- ... **CLC 32**
See also CA 101; CANR 49

Bowers, Edgar 1924- ....**CLC 9**
See also CA 5-8R; CANR 24; DLB 5

Bowie, David .... **CLC 17**
See also Jones, David Robert

Bowles, Jane (Sydney) 1917-1973 **CLC 3, 68**
See also CA 19-20; 41-44R; CAP 2

Bowles, Paul (Frederick) 1910-1986 **CLC 1, 2, 19, 53; SSC 3**
See also CA 1-4R; CAAS 1; CANR 1, 19, 50; DLB 5, 6; MTCW

Box, Edgar
See Vidal, Gore

Boyd, Nancy
See Millay, Edna St. Vincent

Boyd, William 1952- .... **CLC 28, 53, 70**
See also CA 114; 120; CANR 51

Boyle, Kay 1902-1992 **CLC 1, 5, 19, 58; SSC 5**
See also CA 13-16R; 140; CAAS 1; CANR 29, 61; DLB 4, 9, 48, 86; DLBY 93; MTCW

Boyle, Mark
See Kienzle, William X(avier)

Boyle, Patrick 1905-1982 .... **CLC 19**
See also CA 127

Boyle, T. C. 1948-
See Boyle, T(homas) Coraghessan

Boyle, T(homas) Coraghessan 1948- **CLC 36, 55, 90; DAM POP; SSC 16**
See also BEST 90:4; CA 120; CANR 44; DLBY 86

Boz
See Dickens, Charles (John Huffam)

Brackenridge, Hugh Henry 1748-1816 **N C L C 7**
See also DLB 11, 37

Bradbury, Edward P.
See Moorcock, Michael (John)

Bradbury, Malcolm (Stanley) 1932- **CLC 32, 61; DAM NOV**
See also CA 1-4R; CANR 1, 33; DLB 14; MTCW

Bradbury, Ray (Douglas) 1920- **CLC 1, 3, 10, 15, 42, 98; DA; DAB; DAC; DAM MST, NOV, POP; SSC 29; WLC**
See also AAYA 15; AITN 1, 2; CA 1-4R; CANR 2, 30; CDALB 1968-1988; DLB 2, 8; MTCW; SATA 11, 64

Bradford, Gamaliel 1863-1932 ...... **TCLC 36**
See also CA 160; DLB 17

Bradley, David (Henry, Jr.) 1950- .. **CLC 23; BLC; DAM MULT**
See also BW 1; CA 104; CANR 26; DLB 33

Bradley, John Ed(mund, Jr.) 1958- .. **CLC 55**
See also CA 139

Bradley, Marion Zimmer 1930- **CLC 30; DAM POP**
See also AAYA 9; CA 57-60; CAAS 10; CANR 7, 31, 51; DLB 8; MTCW; SATA 90

Bradstreet, Anne 1612(?)-1672 **LC 4, 30; DA; DAC; DAM MST, POET; PC 10**
See also CDALB 1640-1865; DLB 24

Brady, Joan 1939- .... **CLC 86**
See also CA 141

Bragg, Melvyn 1939- .... **CLC 10**
See also BEST 89:3; CA 57-60; CANR 10, 48; DLB 14

Braine, John (Gerard) 1922-1986 **CLC 1, 3, 41**
See also CA 1-4R; 120; CANR 1, 33; CDBLB 1945-1960; DLB 15; DLBY 86; MTCW

Bramah, Ernest 1868-1942 .... **TCLC 72**
See also CA 156; DLB 70

Brammer, William 1930(?)-1978 .... **CLC 31**
See also CA 77-80

Brancati, Vitaliano 1907-1954 .... **TCLC 12**
See also CA 109

Brancato, Robin F(idler) 1936- .... **CLC 35**
See also AAYA 9; CA 69-72; CANR 11, 45; CLR 32; JRDA; SAAS 9; SATA 97

Brand, Max
See Faust, Frederick (Schiller)

Brand, Millen 1906-1980 .... **CLC 7**
See also CA 21-24R; 97-100

Branden, Barbara .... **CLC 44**
See also CA 148

Brandes, Georg (Morris Cohen) 1842-1927 **TCLC 10**

See also CA 105

Brandys, Kazimierz 1916- .... **CLC 62**

Branley, Franklyn M(ansfield) 1915- **CLC 21**
See also CA 33-36R; CANR 14, 39; CLR 13; MAICYA; SAAS 16; SATA 4, 68

Brathwaite, Edward Kamau 1930- **CLC 11; DAM POET**
See also BW 2; CA 25-28R; CANR 11, 26, 47; DLB 125

Brautigan, Richard (Gary) 1935-1984 **CLC 1, 3, 5, 9, 12, 34, 42; DAM NOV**
See also CA 53-56; 113; CANR 34; DLB 2, 5; DLBY 80, 84; MTCW; SATA 56

Brave Bird, Mary 1953-
See Crow Dog, Mary (Ellen)
See also NNAL

Braverman, Kate 1950- .... **CLC 67**
See also CA 89-92

Brecht, (Eugen) Bertolt (Friedrich) 1898-1956 **TCLC 1, 6, 13, 35; DA; DAB; DAC; DAM DRAM, MST; DC 3; WLC**
See also CA 104; 133; CANR 62; DLB 56, 124; MTCW

Brecht, Eugen Berthold Friedrich
See Brecht, (Eugen) Bertolt (Friedrich)

Bremer, Fredrika 1801-1865 .... **NCLC 11**

Brennan, Christopher John 1870-1932 **T C L C 17**
See also CA 117

Brennan, Maeve 1917- ....**CLC 5**
See also CA 81-84

Brent, Linda
See Jacobs, Harriet

Brentano, Clemens (Maria) 1778-1842 **N C L C 1**
See also DLB 90

Brent of Bin Bin
See Franklin, (Stella Maria Sarah) Miles

Brenton, Howard 1942- .... **CLC 31**
See also CA 69-72; CANR 33, 67; DLB 13; MTCW

Breslin, James 1930-1996
See Breslin, Jimmy
See also CA 73-76; CANR 31; DAM NOV; MTCW

Breslin, Jimmy .... **CLC 4, 43**
See also Breslin, James
See also AITN 1; DLB 185

Bresson, Robert 1901- .... **CLC 16**
See also CA 110; CANR 49

Breton, Andre 1896-1966 **CLC 2, 9, 15, 54; PC 15**
See also CA 19-20; 25-28R; CANR 40, 60; CAP 2; DLB 65; MTCW

Breytenbach, Breyten 1939(?)- . **CLC 23, 37; DAM POET**
See also CA 113; 129; CANR 61

Bridgers, Sue Ellen 1942- .... **CLC 26**
See also AAYA 8; CA 65-68; CANR 11, 36; CLR 18; DLB 52; JRDA; MAICYA; SAAS 1; SATA 22, 90

Bridges, Robert (Seymour) 1844-1930 **T C L C 1; DAM POET**
See also CA 104; 152; CDBLB 1890-1914; DLB 19, 98

Bridie, James .... **TCLC 3**
See also Mavor, Osborne Henry
See also DLB 10

Brin, David 1950- .... **CLC 34**
See also AAYA 21; CA 102; CANR 24; INT CANR-24; SATA 65

Brink, Andre (Philippus) 1935- **CLC 18, 36, 106**

See also CA 104; CANR 39, 62; INT 103;
MTCW
Brinsmead, H(esba) F(ay) 1922- ...... **CLC 21**
See also CA 21-24R; CANR 10; CLR 47;
MAICYA; SAAS 5; SATA 18, 78
Brittain, Vera (Mary) 1893(?)-1970 **CLC 23**
See also CA 13-16; 25-28R; CANR 58; CAP 1;
DLB 191; MTCW
Broch, Hermann 1886-1951 .... **TCLC 20**
See also CA 117; DLB 85, 124
Brock, Rose
See Hansen, Joseph
Brodkey, Harold (Roy) 1930-1996 ... **CLC 56**
See also CA 111; 151; DLB 130
Brodsky, Iosif Alexandrovich 1940-1996
See Brodsky, Joseph
See also AITN 1; CA 41-44R; 151; CANR 37;
DAM POET; MTCW
Brodsky, Joseph 1940-1996 **CLC 4, 6, 13, 36,
100; PC 9**
See also Brodsky, Iosif Alexandrovich
Brodsky, Michael (Mark) 1948- .... **CLC 19**
See also CA 102; CANR 18, 41, 58
Bromell, Henry 1947- ....**CLC 5**
See also CA 53-56; CANR 9
Bromfield, Louis (Brucker) 1896-1956**T C L C
11**
See also CA 107; 155; DLB 4, 9, 86
Broner, E(sther) M(asserman) 1930- **CLC 19**
See also CA 17-20R; CANR 8, 25; DLB 28
Bronk, William 1918- .... **CLC 10**
See also CA 89-92; CANR 23; DLB 165
Bronstein, Lev Davidovich
See Trotsky, Leon
Bronte, Anne 1820-1849 .... **NCLC 4**
See also DLB 21
Bronte, Charlotte 1816-1855 **NCLC 3, 8, 33,
58; DA; DAB; DAC; DAM MST, NOV;
WLC**
See also AAYA 17; CDBLB 1832-1890; DLB
21, 159
Bronte, Emily (Jane) 1818-1848**NCLC 16, 35;
DA; DAB; DAC; DAM MST, NOV, POET;
PC 8; WLC**
See also AAYA 17; CDBLB 1832-1890; DLB
21, 32
Brooke, Frances 1724-1789 .... **LC 6**
See also DLB 39, 99
Brooke, Henry 1703(?)-1783 .... **LC 1**
See also DLB 39
Brooke, Rupert (Chawner) 1887-1915 **T C L C
2, 7; DA; DAB; DAC; DAM MST, POET;
WLC**
See also CA 104; 132; CANR 61; CDBLB
1914-1945; DLB 19; MTCW
Brooke-Haven, P.
See Wodehouse, P(elham) G(renville)
Brooke-Rose, Christine 1926(?)- ...... **CLC 40**
See also CA 13-16R; CANR 58; DLB 14
Brookner, Anita 1928- **CLC 32, 34, 51; DAB;
DAM POP**
See also CA 114; 120; CANR 37, 56; DLB 194;
DLBY 87; MTCW
Brooks, Cleanth 1906-1994 .... **CLC 24, 86**
See also CA 17-20R; 145; CANR 33, 35; DLB
63; DLBY 94; INT CANR-35; MTCW
Brooks, George
See Baum, L(yman) Frank
Brooks, Gwendolyn 1917- **CLC 1, 2, 4, 5, 15,
49; BLC; DA; DAC; DAM MST, MULT,
POET; PC 7; WLC**
See also AAYA 20; AITN 1; BW 2; CA 1-4R;
CANR 1, 27, 52; CDALB 1941-1968; CLR

27; DLB 5, 76, 165; MTCW; SATA 6
Brooks, Mel ....**CLC 12**
See also Kaminsky, Melvin
See also AAYA 13; DLB 26
Brooks, Peter 1938- ....**CLC 34**
See also CA 45-48; CANR 1
Brooks, Van Wyck 1886-1963 .... **CLC 29**
See also CA 1-4R; CANR 6; DLB 45, 63, 103
Brophy, Brigid (Antonia) 1929-1995 . **CLC 6,
11, 29, 105**
See also CA 5-8R; 149; CAAS 4; CANR 25,
53; DLB 14; MTCW
Brosman, Catharine Savage 1934- ..... **CLC 9**
See also CA 61-64; CANR 21, 46
Brother Antoninus
See Everson, William (Oliver)
The Brothers Quay
See Quay, Stephen; Quay, Timothy
Broughton, T(homas) Alan 1936- ..... **CLC 19**
See also CA 45-48; CANR 2, 23, 48
Broumas, Olga 1949- .... **CLC 10, 73**
See also CA 85-88; CANR 20
Brown, Alan 1951- ....**CLC 99**
Brown, Charles Brockden 1771-1810 **N C L C
22**
See also CDALB 1640-1865; DLB 37, 59, 73
Brown, Christy 1932-1981 ....**CLC 63**
See also CA 105; 104; DLB 14
Brown, Claude 1937- .. **CLC 30; BLC; DAM
MULT**
See also AAYA 7; BW 1; CA 73-76
Brown, Dee (Alexander) 1908- .. **CLC 18, 47;
DAM POP**
See also CA 13-16R; CAAS 6; CANR 11, 45,
60; DLBY 80; MTCW; SATA 5
Brown, George
See Wertmueller, Lina
Brown, George Douglas 1869-1902 **TCLC 28**
See also CA 162
Brown, George Mackay 1921-1996**CLC 5, 48,
100**
See also CA 21-24R; 151; CAAS 6; CANR 12,
37, 62, 67; DLB 14, 27, 139; MTCW; SATA
35
Brown, (William) Larry 1951- .... **CLC 73**
See also CA 130; 134; INT 133
Brown, Moses
See Barrett, William (Christopher)
Brown, Rita Mae 1944- **CLC 18, 43, 79; DAM
NOV, POP**
See also CA 45-48; CANR 2, 11, 35, 62; INT
CANR-11; MTCW
Brown, Roderick (Langmere) Haig-
See Haig-Brown, Roderick (Langmere)
Brown, Rosellen 1939- ....**CLC 32**
See also CA 77-80; CAAS 10; CANR 14, 44
Brown, Sterling Allen 1901-1989 **CLC 1, 23,
59; BLC; DAM MULT, POET**
See also BW 1; CA 85-88; 127; CANR 26; DLB
48, 51, 63; MTCW
Brown, Will
See Ainsworth, William Harrison
Brown, William Wells 1813-1884 .. **NCLC 2;
BLC; DAM MULT; DC 1**
See also DLB 3, 50
Browne, (Clyde) Jackson 1948(?)- .... **CLC 21**
See also CA 120
Browning, Elizabeth Barrett 1806-1861
**NCLC 1, 16, 61, 66; DA; DAB; DAC; DAM
MST, POET; PC 6; WLC**
See also CDBLB 1832-1890; DLB 32
Browning, Robert 1812-1889 **NCLC 19; DA;
DAB; DAC; DAM MST, POET; PC 2;**

WLCS
See also CDBLB 1832-1890; DLB 32, 163;
YABC 1
Browning, Tod 1882-1962 ....**CLC 16**
See also CA 141; 117
Brownson, Orestes (Augustus) 1803-1876
NCLC 50
Bruccoli, Matthew J(oseph) 1931- ....**CLC 34**
See also CA 9-12R; CANR 7; DLB 103
Bruce, Lenny ....**CLC 21**
See also Schneider, Leonard Alfred
Bruin, John
See Brutus, Dennis
Brulard, Henri
See Stendhal
Brulls, Christian
See Simenon, Georges (Jacques Christian)
Brunner, John (Kilian Houston) 1934-1995
CLC 8, 10; DAM POP
See also CA 1-4R; 149; CAAS 8; CANR 2, 37;
MTCW
Bruno, Giordano 1548-1600 .... **LC 27**
Brutus, Dennis 1924-... **CLC 43; BLC; DAM
MULT, POET**
See also BW 2; CA 49-52; CAAS 14; CANR 2,
27, 42; DLB 117
Bryan, C(ourtlandt) D(ixon) B(arnes) 1936-
CLC 29
See also CA 73-76; CANR 13, 68; DLB 185;
INT CANR-13
Bryan, Michael
See Moore, Brian
Bryant, William Cullen 1794-1878 . **NCLC 6,
46; DA; DAB; DAC; DAM MST, POET;
PC 20**
See also CDALB 1640-1865; DLB 3, 43, 59,
189
Bryusov, Valery Yakovlevich 1873-1924
TCLC 10
See also CA 107; 155
Buchan, John 1875-1940 .... **TCLC 41; DAB;
DAM POP**
See also CA 108; 145; DLB 34, 70, 156; YABC
2
Buchanan, George 1506-1582 .... **LC 4**
Buchheim, Lothar-Guenther 1918- ....**CLC 6**
See also CA 85-88
Buchner, (Karl) Georg 1813-1837 .**NCLC 26**
Buchwald, Art(hur) 1925- ....**CLC 33**
See also AITN 1; CA 5-8R; CANR 21, 67;
MTCW; SATA 10
Buck, Pearl S(ydenstricker) 1892-1973**CLC 7,
11, 18; DA; DAB; DAC; DAM MST, NOV**
See also AITN 1; CA 1-4R; 41-44R; CANR 1,
34; DLB 9, 102; MTCW; SATA 1, 25
Buckler, Ernest 1908-1984 .... **CLC 13; DAC;
DAM MST**
See also CA 11-12; 114; CAP 1; DLB 68; SATA
47
Buckley, Vincent (Thomas) 1925-1988**CLC 57**
See also CA 101
Buckley, William F(rank), Jr. 1925-**CLC 7, 18,
37; DAM POP**
See also AITN 1; CA 1-4R; CANR 1, 24, 53;
DLB 137; DLBY 80; INT CANR-24; MTCW
Buechner, (Carl) Frederick 1926-**CLC 2, 4, 6,
9; DAM NOV**
See also CA 13-16R; CANR 11, 39, 64; DLBY
80; INT CANR-11; MTCW
Buell, John (Edward) 1927- ....**CLC 10**
See also CA 1-4R; DLB 53
Buero Vallejo, Antonio 1916- ..... **CLC 15, 46**
See also CA 106; CANR 24, 49; HW; MTCW

Bufalino, Gesualdo 1920(?)- .... **CLC 74**
See also DLB 196

Bugayev, Boris Nikolayevich 1880-1934
TCLC 7; PC 11
See also Bely, Andrey
See also CA 104; 165

Bukowski, Charles 1920-1994**CLC 2, 5, 9, 41,
82, 108; DAM NOV, POET; PC 18**
See also CA 17-20R; 144; CANR 40, 62; DLB
5, 130, 169; MTCW

Bulgakov, Mikhail (Afanas'evich) 1891-1940
TCLC 2, 16; DAM DRAM, NOV; SSC 18
See also CA 105; 152

Bulgya, Alexander Alexandrovich 1901-1956
TCLC 53
See also Fadeyev, Alexander
See also CA 117

Bullins, Ed 1935- ... **CLC 1, 5, 7; BLC; DAM
DRAM, MULT; DC 6**
See also BW 2; CA 49-52; CAAS 16; CANR
24, 46; DLB 7, 38; MTCW

Bulwer-Lytton, Edward (George Earle Lytton)
1803-1873 .... **NCLC 1, 45**
See also DLB 21

Bunin, Ivan Alexeyevich 1870-1953 **TCLC 6;
SSC 5**
See also CA 104

Bunting, Basil 1900-1985 ..... **CLC 10, 39, 47;
DAM POET**
See also CA 53-56; 115; CANR 7; DLB 20

Bunuel, Luis 1900-1983 .. **CLC 16, 80; DAM
MULT; HLC**
See also CA 101; 110; CANR 32; HW

Bunyan, John 1628-1688 ... **LC 4; DA; DAB;
DAC; DAM MST; WLC**
See also CDBLB 1660-1789; DLB 39

Burckhardt, Jacob (Christoph) 1818-1897
NCLC 49

Burford, Eleanor
See Hibbert, Eleanor Alice Burford

Burgess, Anthony**CLC 1, 2, 4, 5, 8, 10, 13, 15,
22, 40, 62, 81, 94; DAB**
See also Wilson, John (Anthony) Burgess
See also AAYA 25; AITN 1; CDBLB 1960 to
Present; DLB 14, 194

Burke, Edmund 1729(?)-1797 **LC 7, 36; DA;
DAB; DAC; DAM MST; WLC**
See also DLB 104

Burke, Kenneth (Duva) 1897-1993**CLC 2, 24**
See also CA 5-8R; 143; CANR 39; DLB 45,
63; MTCW

Burke, Leda
See Garnett, David

Burke, Ralph
See Silverberg, Robert

Burke, Thomas 1886-1945 .... **TCLC 63**
See also CA 113; 155

Burney, Fanny 1752-1840 .... **NCLC 12, 54**
See also DLB 39

Burns, Robert 1759-1796 ....**PC 6**
See also CDBLB 1789-1832; DA; DAB; DAC;
DAM MST, POET; DLB 109; WLC

Burns, Tex
See L'Amour, Louis (Dearborn)

Burnshaw, Stanley 1906- .... **CLC 3, 13, 44**
See also CA 9-12R; DLB 48; DLBY 97

Burr, Anne 1937- ....**CLC 6**
See also CA 25-28R

Burroughs, Edgar Rice 1875-1950 . **TCLC 2,
32; DAM NOV**
See also AAYA 11; CA 104; 132; DLB 8;
MTCW; SATA 41

Burroughs, William S(eward) 1914-1997**CLC**

1, 2, 5, 15, 22, 42, 75, 109; DA; DAB; DAC;
DAM MST, NOV, POP; WLC**
See also AITN 2; CA 9-12R; 160; CANR 20,
52; DLB 2, 8, 16, 152; DLBY 81, 97; MTCW

Burton, Richard F. 1821-1890 .... **NCLC 42**
See also DLB 55, 184

Busch, Frederick 1941- ..... **CLC 7, 10, 18, 47**
See also CA 33-36R; CAAS 1; CANR 45; DLB
6

Bush, Ronald 1946- ....**CLC 34**
See also CA 136

Bustos, F(rancisco)
See Borges, Jorge Luis

Bustos Domecq, H(onorio)
See Bioy Casares, Adolfo; Borges, Jorge Luis

Butler, Octavia E(stelle) 1947-**CLC 38; DAM
MULT, POP**
See also AAYA 18; BW 2; CA 73-76; CANR
12, 24, 38; DLB 33; MTCW; SATA 84

Butler, Robert Olen (Jr.) 1945-**CLC 81; DAM
POP**
See also CA 112; CANR 66; DLB 173; INT 112

Butler, Samuel 1612-1680 .... **LC 16**
See also DLB 101, 126

Butler, Samuel 1835-1902 . **TCLC 1, 33; DA;
DAB; DAC; DAM MST, NOV; WLC**
See also CA 143; CDBLB 1890-1914; DLB 18,
57, 174

Butler, Walter C.
See Faust, Frederick (Schiller)

Butor, Michel (Marie Francois) 1926-**CLC 1,
3, 8, 11, 15**
See also CA 9-12R; CANR 33, 66; DLB 83;
MTCW

Butts, Mary 1892(?)-1937 .... **TCLC 77**
See also CA 148

Buzo, Alexander (John) 1944- .... **CLC 61**
See also CA 97-100; CANR 17, 39

Buzzati, Dino 1906-1972 .... **CLC 36**
See also CA 160; 33-36R; DLB 177

Byars, Betsy (Cromer) 1928- .... **CLC 35**
See also AAYA 19; CA 33-36R; CANR 18, 36,
57; CLR 1, 16; DLB 52; INT CANR-18;
JRDA; MAICYA; MTCW; SAAS 1; SATA
4, 46, 80

Byatt, A(ntonia) S(usan Drabble) 1936-**C L C
19, 65; DAM NOV, POP**
See also CA 13-16R; CANR 13, 33, 50; DLB
14, 194; MTCW

Byrne, David 1952-...........................**CLC 26**
See also CA 127

Byrne, John Keyes 1926-
See Leonard, Hugh
See also CA 102; INT 102

Byron, George Gordon (Noel) 1788-1824
**NCLC 2, 12; DA; DAB; DAC; DAM MST,
POET; PC 16; WLC**
See also CDBLB 1789-1832; DLB 96, 110

Byron, Robert 1905-1941 .... **TCLC 67**
See also CA 160; DLB 195

C. 3. 3.
See Wilde, Oscar (Fingal O'Flahertie Wills)

Caballero, Fernan 1796-1877 ....**NCLC 10**

Cabell, Branch
See Cabell, James Branch

Cabell, James Branch 1879-1958 .... **TCLC 6**
See also CA 105; 152; DLB 9, 78

Cable, George Washington 1844-1925 **T C L C
4; SSC 4**
See also CA 104; 155; DLB 12, 74; DLBD 13

Cabral de Melo Neto, Joao 1920- ... **CLC 76;
DAM MULT**
See also CA 151

Cabrera Infante, G(uillermo) 1929- ..**CLC 5,
25, 45; DAM MULT; HLC**
See also CA 85-88; CANR 29, 65; DLB 113;
HW; MTCW

Cade, Toni
See Bambara, Toni Cade

Cadmus and Harmonia
See Buchan, John

Caedmon fl. 658-680 .... **CMLC 7**
See also DLB 146

Caeiro, Alberto
See Pessoa, Fernando (Antonio Nogueira)

Cage, John (Milton, Jr.) 1912- .... **CLC 41**
See also CA 13-16R; CANR 9; DLB 193; INT
CANR-9

Cahan, Abraham 1860-1951 .... **TCLC 71**
See also CA 108; 154; DLB 9, 25, 28

Cain, G.
See Cabrera Infante, G(uillermo)

Cain, Guillermo
See Cabrera Infante, G(uillermo)

Cain, James M(allahan) 1892-1977**CLC 3, 11,
28**
See also AITN 1; CA 17-20R; 73-76; CANR 8,
34, 61; MTCW

Caine, Mark
See Raphael, Frederic (Michael)

Calasso, Roberto 1941- .... **CLC 81**
See also CA 143

Calderon de la Barca, Pedro 1600-1681 . **L C
23; DC 3**

Caldwell, Erskine (Preston) 1903-1987**CLC 1,
8, 14, 50, 60; DAM NOV; SSC 19**
See also AITN 1; CA 1-4R; 121; CAAS 1;
CANR 2, 33; DLB 9, 86; MTCW

Caldwell, (Janet Miriam) Taylor (Holland)
1900-1985**CLC 2, 28, 39; DAM NOV, POP**
See also CA 5-8R; 116; CANR 5

Calhoun, John Caldwell 1782-1850**NCLC 15**
See also DLB 3

Calisher, Hortense 1911-**CLC 2, 4, 8, 38; DAM
NOV; SSC 15**
See also CA 1-4R; CANR 1, 22, 67; DLB 2;
INT CANR-22; MTCW

Callaghan, Morley Edward 1903-1990**CLC 3,
14, 41, 65; DAC; DAM MST**
See also CA 9-12R; 132; CANR 33; DLB 68;
MTCW

Callimachus c. 305B.C.-c. 240B.C.**CMLC 18**
See also DLB 176

Calvin, John 1509-1564 .... **LC 37**

Calvino, Italo 1923-1985**CLC 5, 8, 11, 22, 33,
39, 73; DAM NOV; SSC 3**
See also CA 85-88; 116; CANR 23, 61; DLB
196; MTCW

Cameron, Carey 1952- .... **CLC 59**
See also CA 135

Cameron, Peter 1959- .... **CLC 44**
See also CA 125; CANR 50

Campana, Dino 1885-1932 .... **TCLC 20**
See also CA 117; DLB 114

Campanella, Tommaso 1568-1639 ...... **LC 32**

Campbell, John W(ood, Jr.) 1910-1971 **C L C
32**
See also CA 21-22; 29-32R; CANR 34; CAP 2;
DLB 8; MTCW

Campbell, Joseph 1904-1987 .... **CLC 69**
See also AAYA 3; BEST 89:2; CA 1-4R; 124;
CANR 3, 28, 61; MTCW

Campbell, Maria 1940- ....**CLC 85; DAC**
See also CA 102; CANR 54; NNAL

Campbell, (John) Ramsey 1946-**CLC 42; SSC
19**

See also CA 57-60; CANR 7; INT CANR-7

Campbell, (Ignatius) Roy (Dunnachie) 1901-1957 .... **TCLC 5**
See also CA 104; 155; DLB 20

Campbell, Thomas 1777-1844 .... **NCLC 19**
See also DLB 93; 144

Campbell, Wilfred .... **TCLC 9**
See also Campbell, William

Campbell, William 1858(?)-1918
See Campbell, Wilfred
See also CA 106; DLB 92

Campion, Jane .... **CLC 95**
See also CA 138

Campos, Alvaro de
See Pessoa, Fernando (Antonio Nogueira)

Camus, Albert 1913-1960 CLC 1, 2, 4, 9, 11, 14, 32, 63, 69; DA; DAB; DAC; DAM DRAM, MST, NOV; DC 2; SSC 9; WLC
See also CA 89-92; DLB 72; MTCW

Canby, Vincent 1924- .... **CLC 13**
See also CA 81-84

Cancale
See Desnos, Robert

Canetti, Elias 1905-1994 CLC 3, 14, 25, 75, 86
See also CA 21-24R; 146; CANR 23, 61; DLB 85, 124; MTCW

Canin, Ethan 1960- .... **CLC 55**
See also CA 131; 135

Cannon, Curt
See Hunter, Evan

Cao, Lan 1961- .... **CLC 109**

Cape, Judith
See Page, P(atricia) K(athleen)

Capek, Karel 1890-1938 ... **TCLC 6, 37; DA; DAB; DAC; DAM DRAM, MST, NOV; DC 1; WLC**
See also CA 104; 140

Capote, Truman 1924-1984 CLC 1, 3, 8, 13, 19, 34, 38, 58; DA; DAB; DAC; DAM MST, NOV, POP; SSC 2; WLC
See also CA 5-8R; 113; CANR 18, 62; CDALB 1941-1968; DLB 2, 185; DLBY 80, 84; MTCW; SATA 91

Capra, Frank 1897-1991 .... **CLC 16**
See also CA 61-64; 135

Caputo, Philip 1941- .... **CLC 32**
See also CA 73-76; CANR 40

Caragiale, Ion Luca 1852-1912 ...... **TCLC 76**
See also CA 157

Card, Orson Scott 1951- CLC 44, 47, 50; DAM POP
See also AAYA 11; CA 102; CANR 27, 47; INT CANR-27; MTCW; SATA 83

Cardenal, Ernesto 1925- .... **CLC 31; DAM MULT, POET; HLC**
See also CA 49-52; CANR 2, 32, 66; HW; MTCW

Cardozo, Benjamin N(athan) 1870-1938
TCLC 65
See also CA 117; 164

Carducci, Giosue (Alessandro Giuseppe) 1835-1907 .... **TCLC 32**
See also CA 163

Carew, Thomas 1595(?)-1640 .... **LC 13**
See also DLB 126

Carey, Ernestine Gilbreth 1908- ...... **CLC 17**
See also CA 5-8R; SATA 2

Carey, Peter 1943- .... **CLC 40, 55, 96**
See also CA 123; 127; CANR 53; INT 127; MTCW; SATA 94

Carleton, William 1794-1869 .... **NCLC 3**
See also DLB 159

Carlisle, Henry (Coffin) 1926- .... **CLC 33**

See also CA 13-16R; CANR 15

Carlsen, Chris
See Holdstock, Robert P.

Carlson, Ron(ald F.) 1947- .... **CLC 54**
See also CA 105; CANR 27

Carlyle, Thomas 1795-1881 . **NCLC 22; DA; DAB; DAC; DAM MST**
See also CDBLB 1789-1832; DLB 55; 144

Carman, (William) Bliss 1861-1929 **TCLC 7; DAC**
See also CA 104; 152; DLB 92

Carnegie, Dale 1888-1955 .... **TCLC 53**

Carossa, Hans 1878-1956 .... **TCLC 48**
See also DLB 66

Carpenter, Don(ald Richard) 1931-1995 **C L C 41**
See also CA 45-48; 149; CANR 1

Carpentier (y Valmont), Alejo 1904-1980 CLC 8, 11, 38; DAM MULT; HLC
See also CA 65-68; 97-100; CANR 11; DLB 113; HW

Carr, Caleb 1955(?)- .... **CLC 86**
See also CA 147

Carr, Emily 1871-1945 .... **TCLC 32**
See also CA 159; DLB 68

Carr, John Dickson 1906-1977 .... **CLC 3**
See also Fairbairn, Roger
See also CA 49-52; 69-72; CANR 3, 33, 60; MTCW

Carr, Philippa
See Hibbert, Eleanor Alice Burford

Carr, Virginia Spencer 1929- .... **CLC 34**
See also CA 61-64; DLB 111

Carrere, Emmanuel 1957- .... **CLC 89**

Carrier, Roch 1937- CLC 13, 78; DAC; DAM MST
See also CA 130; CANR 61; DLB 53

Carroll, James P. 1943(?)- .... **CLC 38**
See also CA 81-84

Carroll, Jim 1951- .... **CLC 35**
See also AAYA 17; CA 45-48; CANR 42

Carroll, Lewis ...... **NCLC 2, 53; PC 18; WLC**
See also Dodgson, Charles Lutwidge
See also CDBLB 1832-1890; CLR 2, 18; DLB 18, 163, 178; JRDA

Carroll, Paul Vincent 1900-1968 ...... **CLC 10**
See also CA 9-12R; 25-28R; DLB 10

Carruth, Hayden 1921- **CLC 4, 7, 10, 18, 84; PC 10**
See also CA 9-12R; CANR 4, 38, 59; DLB 5, 165; INT CANR-4; MTCW; SATA 47

Carson, Rachel Louise 1907-1964 .. **CLC 71; DAM POP**
See also CA 77-80; CANR 35; MTCW; SATA 23

Carter, Angela (Olive) 1940-1992 **CLC 5, 41, 76; SSC 13**
See also CA 53-56; 136; CANR 12, 36, 61; DLB 14; MTCW; SATA 66; SATA-Obit 70

Carter, Nick
See Smith, Martin Cruz

Carver, Raymond 1938-1988 CLC 22, 36, 53, 55; DAM NOV; SSC 8
See also CA 33-36R; 126; CANR 17, 34, 61; DLB 130; DLBY 84, 88; MTCW

Cary, Elizabeth, Lady Falkland 1585-1639
LC 30

Cary, (Arthur) Joyce (Lunel) 1888-1957
TCLC 1, 29
See also CA 104; 164; CDBLB 1914-1945; DLB 15, 100

Casanova de Seingalt, Giovanni Jacopo 1725-1798 .... **LC 13**

Casares, Adolfo Bioy
See Bioy Casares, Adolfo

Casely-Hayford, J(oseph) E(phraim) 1866-1930
TCLC 24; BLC; DAM MULT
See also BW 2; CA 123; 152

Casey, John (Dudley) 1939- .... **CLC 59**
See also BEST 90:2; CA 69-72; CANR 23

Casey, Michael 1947- .... **CLC 2**
See also CA 65-68; DLB 5

Casey, Patrick
See Thurman, Wallace (Henry)

Casey, Warren (Peter) 1935-1988 ..... **CLC 12**
See also CA 101; 127; INT 101

Casona, Alejandro .... **CLC 49**
See also Alvarez, Alejandro Rodriguez

Cassavetes, John 1929-1989 .... **CLC 20**
See also CA 85-88; 127

Cassian, Nina 1924- .... **PC 17**

Cassill, R(onald) V(erlin) 1919- ... **CLC 4, 23**
See also CA 9-12R; CAAS 1; CANR 7, 45; DLB 6

Cassirer, Ernst 1874-1945 .... **TCLC 61**
See also CA 157

Cassity, (Allen) Turner 1929- .... **CLC 6, 42**
See also CA 17-20R; CAAS 8; CANR 11; DLB 105

Castaneda, Carlos 1931(?)- .... **CLC 12**
See also CA 25-28R; CANR 32, 66; HW; MTCW

Castedo, Elena 1937- .... **CLC 65**
See also CA 132

Castedo-Ellerman, Elena
See Castedo, Elena

Castellanos, Rosario 1925-1974 CLC 66; DAM MULT; HLC
See also CA 131; 53-56; CANR 58; DLB 113; HW

Castelvetro, Lodovico 1505-1571 .... **LC 12**

Castiglione, Baldassare 1478-1529 ..... **LC 12**

Castle, Robert
See Hamilton, Edmond

Castro, Guillen de 1569-1631 .... **LC 19**

Castro, Rosalia de 1837-1885 NCLC 3; DAM MULT

Cather, Willa
See Cather, Willa Sibert

Cather, Willa Sibert 1873-1947 **TCLC 1, 11, 31; DA; DAB; DAC; DAM MST, NOV; SSC 2; WLC**
See also AAYA 24; CA 104; 128; CDALB 1865-1917; DLB 9, 54, 78; DLBD 1; MTCW; SATA 30

Cato, Marcus Porcius 234B.C.-149B.C.
CMLC 21

Catton, (Charles) Bruce 1899-1978 .. **CLC 35**
See also AITN 1; CA 5-8R; 81-84; CANR 7; DLB 17; SATA 2; SATA-Obit 24

Catullus c. 84B.C.-c. 54B.C. .... **CMLC 18**

Cauldwell, Frank
See King, Francis (Henry)

Caunitz, William J. 1933-1996 .... **CLC 34**
See also BEST 89:3; CA 125; 130; 152; INT 130

Causley, Charles (Stanley) 1917- .... **CLC 7**
See also CA 9-12R; CANR 5, 35; CLR 30; DLB 27; MTCW; SATA 3, 66

Caute, (John) David 1936- ..... **CLC 29; DAM NOV**
See also CA 1-4R; CAAS 4; CANR 1, 33, 64; DLB 14

Cavafy, C(onstantine) P(eter) 1863-1933
TCLC 2, 7; DAM POET
See also Kavafis, Konstantinos Petrou

See also CA 148
Cavallo, Evelyn
See Spark, Muriel (Sarah)
Cavanna, Betty .... **CLC 12**
See also Harrison, Elizabeth Cavanna
See also JRDA; MAICYA; SAAS 4; SATA 1,
30
Cavendish, Margaret Lucas 1623-1673**LC 30**
See also DLB 131
Caxton, William 1421(?)-1491(?) .... **LC 17**
See also DLB 170
Cayrol, Jean 1911-..............................**CLC 11**
See also CA 89-92; DLB 83
Cela, Camilo Jose 1916-**CLC 4, 13, 59; DAM MULT; HLC**
See also BEST 90:2; CA 21-24R; CAAS 10;
CANR 21, 32; DLBY 89; HW; MTCW
Celan, Paul .... **CLC 10, 19, 53, 82; PC 10**
See also Antschel, Paul
See also DLB 69
Celine, Louis-Ferdinand CLC 1, 3, 4, 7, 9, 15, 47
See also Destouches, Louis-Ferdinand
See also DLB 72
Cellini, Benvenuto 1500-1571 .... **LC 7**
Cendrars, Blaise 1887-1961 ..... **CLC 18, 106**
See also Sauser-Hall, Frederic
Cernuda (y Bidon), Luis 1902-1963 **CLC 54; DAM POET**
See also CA 131; 89-92; DLB 134; HW
Cervantes (Saavedra), Miguel de 1547-1616
LC 6, 23; DA; DAB; DAC; DAM MST, NOV; SSC 12; WLC
Cesaire, Aime (Fernand) 1913-. **CLC 19, 32; BLC; DAM MULT, POET**
See also BW 2; CA 65-68; CANR 24, 43;
MTCW
Chabon, Michael 1963- .... **CLC 55**
See also CA 139; CANR 57
Chabrol, Claude 1930-..................... **CLC 16**
See also CA 110
Challans, Mary 1905-1983
See Renault, Mary
See also CA 81-84; 111; SATA 23; SATA-Obit
36
Challis, George
See Faust, Frederick (Schiller)
Chambers, Aidan 1934-..................... **CLC 35**
See also CA 25-28R; CANR 12, 31, 58; JRDA;
MAICYA; SAAS 12; SATA 1, 69
Chambers, James 1948-
See Cliff, Jimmy
See also CA 124
Chambers, Jessie
See Lawrence, D(avid) H(erbert Richards)
Chambers, Robert W. 1865-1933 ... **TCLC 41**
See also CA 165
Chandler, Raymond (Thornton) 1888-1959
TCLC 1, 7; SSC 23
See also AAYA 25; CA 104; 129; CANR 60;
CDALB 1929-1941; DLBD 6; MTCW
Chang, Eileen 1921- ....**SSC 28**
Chang, Jung 1952- .... **CLC 71**
See also CA 142
Channing, William Ellery 1780-1842 . **N C L C 17**
See also DLB 1, 59
Chaplin, Charles Spencer 1889-1977**CLC 16**
See also Chaplin, Charlie
See also CA 81-84; 73-76
Chaplin, Charlie
See Chaplin, Charles Spencer
See also DLB 44

Chapman, George 1559(?)-1634**LC 22; DAM DRAM**
See also DLB 62, 121
Chapman, Graham 1941-1989 .... **CLC 21**
See also Monty Python
See also CA 116; 129; CANR 35
Chapman, John Jay 1862-1933 .... **TCLC 7**
See also CA 104
Chapman, Lee
See Bradley, Marion Zimmer
Chapman, Walker
See Silverberg, Robert
Chappell, Fred (Davis) 1936- ..... **CLC 40, 78**
See also CA 5-8R; CAAS 4; CANR 8, 33, 67;
DLB 6, 105
Char, Rene(-Emile) 1907-1988**CLC 9, 11, 14, 55; DAM POET**
See also CA 13-16R; 124; CANR 32; MTCW
Charby, Jay
See Ellison, Harlan (Jay)
Chardin, Pierre Teilhard de
See Teilhard de Chardin, (Marie Joseph) Pierre
Charles I 1600-1649 .... **LC 13**
Charriere, Isabelle de 1740-1805 ... **NCLC 66**
Charyn, Jerome 1937-............... **CLC 5, 8, 18**
See also CA 5-8R; CAAS 1; CANR 7, 61;
DLBY 83; MTCW
Chase, Mary (Coyle) 1907-1981 .... **DC 1**
See also CA 77-80; 105; SATA 17; SATA-Obit
29
Chase, Mary Ellen 1887-1973 ....**CLC 2**
See also CA 13-16; 41-44R; CAP 1; SATA 10
Chase, Nicholas
See Hyde, Anthony
Chateaubriand, Francois Rene de 1768-1848
NCLC 3
See also DLB 119
Chatterje, Sarat Chandra 1876-1936(?)
See Chatterji, Saratchandra
See also CA 109
Chatterji, Bankim Chandra 1838-1894**NCLC 19**
Chatterji, Saratchandra .... **TCLC 13**
See also Chatterje, Sarat Chandra
Chatterton, Thomas 1752-1770 . **LC 3; DAM POET**
See also DLB 109
Chatwin, (Charles) Bruce 1940-1989**CLC 28, 57, 59; DAM POP**
See also AAYA 4; BEST 90:1; CA 85-88; 127;
DLB 194
Chaucer, Daniel
See Ford, Ford Madox
Chaucer, Geoffrey 1340(?)-1400 **LC 17; DA; DAB; DAC; DAM MST, POET; PC 19; WLCS**
See also CDBLB Before 1660; DLB 146
Chaviaras, Strates 1935-
See Haviaras, Stratis
See also CA 105
Chayefsky, Paddy ....**CLC 23**
See also Chayefsky, Sidney
See also DLB 7, 44; DLBY 81
Chayefsky, Sidney 1923-1981
See Chayefsky, Paddy
See also CA 9-12R; 104; CANR 18; DAM
DRAM
Chedid, Andree 1920- ....**CLC 47**
See also CA 145
Cheever, John 1912-1982 **CLC 3, 7, 8, 11, 15, 25, 64; DA; DAB; DAC; DAM MST, NOV, POP; SSC 1; WLC**
See also CA 5-8R; 106; CABS 1; CANR 5, 27;

CDALB 1941-1968; DLB 2, 102; DLBY 80,
82; INT CANR-5; MTCW
Cheever, Susan 1943- .... **CLC 18, 48**
See also CA 103; CANR 27, 51; DLBY 82; INT
CANR-27
Chekhonte, Antosha
See Chekhov, Anton (Pavlovich)
Chekhov, Anton (Pavlovich) 1860-1904**TCLC 3, 10, 31, 55; DA; DAB; DAC; DAM DRAM, MST; SSC 2, 28; WLC**
See also CA 104; 124; SATA 90
Chernyshevsky, Nikolay Gavrilovich 1828-1889
NCLC 1
Cherry, Carolyn Janice 1942-
See Cherryh, C. J.
See also CA 65-68; CANR 10
Cherryh, C. J. .... **CLC 35**
See also Cherry, Carolyn Janice
See also AAYA 24; DLBY 80; SATA 93
Chesnutt, Charles W(addell) 1858-1932
TCLC 5, 39; BLC; DAM MULT; SSC 7
See also BW 1; CA 106; 125; DLB 12, 50, 78;
MTCW
Chester, Alfred 1929(?)-1971 .... **CLC 49**
See also CA 33-36R; DLB 130
Chesterton, G(ilbert) K(eith) 1874-1936
TCLC 1, 6, 64; DAM NOV, POET; SSC 1
See also CA 104; 132; CDBLB 1914-1945;
DLB 10, 19, 34, 70, 98, 149, 178; MTCW;
SATA 27
Chiang Pin-chin 1904-1986
See Ding Ling
See also CA 118
Ch'ien Chung-shu 1910- .... **CLC 22**
See also CA 130; MTCW
Child, L. Maria
See Child, Lydia Maria
Child, Lydia Maria 1802-1880 .... **NCLC 6**
See also DLB 1, 74; SATA 67
Child, Mrs.
See Child, Lydia Maria
Child, Philip 1898-1978 .... **CLC 19, 68**
See also CA 13-14; CAP 1; SATA 47
Childers, (Robert) Erskine 1870-1922 **T C L C 65**
See also CA 113; 153; DLB 70
Childress, Alice 1920-1994**CLC 12, 15, 86, 96; BLC; DAM DRAM, MULT, NOV; DC 4**
See also AAYA 8; BW 2; CA 45-48; 146; CANR
3, 27, 50; CLR 14; DLB 7, 38; JRDA;
MAICYA; MTCW; SATA 7, 48, 81
Chin, Frank (Chew, Jr.) 1940- .... **DC 7**
See also CA 33-36R; DAM MULT
Chislett, (Margaret) Anne 1943-...... **CLC 34**
See also CA 151
Chitty, Thomas Willes 1926- .... **CLC 11**
See also Hinde, Thomas
See also CA 5-8R
Chivers, Thomas Holley 1809-1858**NCLC 49**
See also DLB 3
Chomette, Rene Lucien 1898-1981
See Clair, Rene
See also CA 103
Chopin, Kate TCLC 5, 14; DA; DAB; SSC 8; WLCS
See also Chopin, Katherine
See also CDALB 1865-1917; DLB 12, 78
Chopin, Katherine 1851-1904
See Chopin, Kate
See also CA 104; 122; DAC; DAM MST, NOV
Chretien de Troyes c. 12th cent. - .. **CMLC 10**
Christie
See Ichikawa, Kon

Christie, Agatha (Mary Clarissa) 1890-1976 **CLC 1, 6, 8, 12, 39, 48; DAB; DAC; DAM NOV**
See also AAYA 9; AITN 1, 2; CA 17-20R; 61-64; CANR 10, 37; CDBLB 1914-1945; DLB 13, 77; MTCW; SATA 36

Christie, (Ann) Philippa
See Pearce, Philippa
See also CA 5-8R; CANR 4

Christine de Pizan 1365(?)-1431(?) ...... **LC 9**

Chubb, Elmer
See Masters, Edgar Lee

Chulkov, Mikhail Dmitrievich 1743-1792 **LC 2**
See also DLB 150

Churchill, Caryl 1938- ..... **CLC 31, 55; DC 5**
See also CA 102; CANR 22, 46; DLB 13; MTCW

Churchill, Charles 1731-1764 .... **LC 3**
See also DLB 109

Chute, Carolyn 1947- .... **CLC 39**
See also CA 123

Ciardi, John (Anthony) 1916-1986. **CLC 10, 40, 44; DAM POET**
See also CA 5-8R; 118; CAAS 2; CANR 5, 33; CLR 19; DLB 5; DLBY 86; INT CANR-5; MAICYA; MTCW; SAAS 26; SATA 1, 65; SATA-Obit 46

Cicero, Marcus Tullius 106B.C.-43B.C. **CMLC 3**

Cimino, Michael 1943- .... **CLC 16**
See also CA 105

Cioran, E(mil) M. 1911-1995 .... **CLC 64**
See also CA 25-28R; 149

Cisneros, Sandra 1954- **CLC 69; DAM MULT; HLC**
See also AAYA 9; CA 131; CANR 64; DLB 122, 152; HW

Cixous, Helene 1937- .... **CLC 92**
See also CA 126; CANR 55; DLB 83; MTCW

Clair, Rene .... **CLC 20**
See also Chomette, Rene Lucien

Clampitt, Amy 1920-1994 ..... **CLC 32; PC 19**
See also CA 110; 146; CANR 29; DLB 105

Clancy, Thomas L., Jr. 1947-
See Clancy, Tom
See also CA 125; 131; CANR 62; INT 131; MTCW

Clancy, Tom .... **CLC 45; DAM NOV, POP**
See also Clancy, Thomas L., Jr.
See also AAYA 9; BEST 89:1, 90:1

Clare, John 1793-1864 **NCLC 9; DAB; DAM POET**
See also DLB 55, 96

Clarin
See Alas (y Urena), Leopoldo (Enrique Garcia)

Clark, Al C.
See Goines, Donald

Clark, (Robert) Brian 1932- .... **CLC 29**
See also CA 41-44R; CANR 67

Clark, Curt
See Westlake, Donald E(dwin)

Clark, Eleanor 1913-1996 .... **CLC 5, 19**
See also CA 9-12R; 151; CANR 41; DLB 6

Clark, J. P.
See Clark, John Pepper
See also DLB 117

Clark, John Pepper 1935- ...... **CLC 38; BLC; DAM DRAM, MULT; DC 5**
See also Clark, J. P.
See also BW 1; CA 65-68; CANR 16

Clark, M. R.
See Clark, Mavis Thorpe

Clark, Mavis Thorpe 1909- .... **CLC 12**

See also CA 57-60; CANR 8, 37; CLR 30; MAICYA; SAAS 5; SATA 8, 74

Clark, Walter Van Tilburg 1909-1971 **CLC 28**
See also CA 9-12R; 33-36R; CANR 63; DLB 9; SATA 8

Clarke, Arthur C(harles) 1917- **CLC 1, 4, 13, 18, 35; DAM POP; SSC 3**
See also AAYA 4; CA 1-4R; CANR 2, 28, 55; JRDA; MAICYA; MTCW; SATA 13, 70

Clarke, Austin 1896-1974 .... **CLC 6, 9; DAM POET**
See also CA 29-32; 49-52; CAP 2; DLB 10, 20

Clarke, Austin C(hesterfield) 1934- **CLC 8, 53; BLC; DAC; DAM MULT**
See also BW 1; CA 25-28R; CAAS 16; CANR 14, 32, 68; DLB 53, 125

Clarke, Gillian 1937- .... **CLC 61**
See also CA 106; DLB 40

Clarke, Marcus (Andrew Hislop) 1846-1881 **NCLC 19**

Clarke, Shirley 1925- .... **CLC 16**

Clash, The
See Headon, (Nicky) Topper; Jones, Mick; Simonon, Paul; Strummer, Joe

Claudel, Paul (Louis Charles Marie) 1868-1955 **TCLC 2, 10**
See also CA 104; 165; DLB 192

Clavell, James (duMaresq) 1925-1994 **CLC 6, 25, 87; DAM NOV, POP**
See also CA 25-28R; 146; CANR 26, 48; MTCW

Cleaver, (Leroy) Eldridge 1935- ..... **CLC 30; BLC; DAM MULT**
See also BW 1; CA 21-24R; CANR 16

Cleese, John (Marwood) 1939- .... **CLC 21**
See also Monty Python
See also CA 112; 116; CANR 35; MTCW

Cleishbotham, Jebediah
See Scott, Walter

Cleland, John 1710-1789 .... **LC 2**
See also DLB 39

Clemens, Samuel Langhorne 1835-1910
See Twain, Mark
See also CA 104; 135; CDALB 1865-1917; DA; DAB; DAC; DAM MST, NOV; DLB 11, 12, 23, 64, 74, 186, 189; JRDA; MAICYA; YABC 2

Cleophil
See Congreve, William

Clerihew, E.
See Bentley, E(dmund) C(lerihew)

Clerk, N. W.
See Lewis, C(live) S(taples)

Cliff, Jimmy .... **CLC 21**
See also Chambers, James

Clifton, (Thelma) Lucille 1936- **CLC 19, 66; BLC; DAM MULT, POET; PC 17**
See also BW 2; CA 49-52; CANR 2, 24, 42; CLR 5; DLB 5, 41; MAICYA; MTCW; SATA 20, 69

Clinton, Dirk
See Silverberg, Robert

Clough, Arthur Hugh 1819-1861 ... **NCLC 27**
See also DLB 32

Clutha, Janet Paterson Frame 1924-
See Frame, Janet
See also CA 1-4R; CANR 2, 36; MTCW

Clyne, Terence
See Blatty, William Peter

Cobalt, Martin
See Mayne, William (James Carter)

Cobb, Irvin S. 1876-1944 .... **TCLC 77**
See also DLB 11, 25, 86

Cobbett, William 1763-1835 .... **NCLC 49**
See also DLB 43, 107, 158

Coburn, D(onald) L(ee) 1938- .... **CLC 10**
See also CA 89-92

Cocteau, Jean (Maurice Eugene Clement) 1889-1963 **CLC 1, 8, 15, 16, 43; DA; DAB; DAC; DAM DRAM, MST, NOV; WLC**
See also CA 25-28; CANR 40; CAP 2; DLB 65; MTCW

Codrescu, Andrei 1946- **CLC 46; DAM POET**
See also CA 33-36R; CAAS 19; CANR 13, 34, 53

Coe, Max
See Bourne, Randolph S(illiman)

Coe, Tucker
See Westlake, Donald E(dwin)

Coen, Ethan 1958- .... **CLC 108**
See also CA 126

Coen, Joel 1955- .... **CLC 108**
See also CA 126

The Coen Brothers
See Coen, Ethan; Coen, Joel

Coetzee, J(ohn) M(ichael) 1940- **CLC 23, 33, 66; DAM NOV**
See also CA 77-80; CANR 41, 54; MTCW

Coffey, Brian
See Koontz, Dean R(ay)

Cohan, George M(ichael) 1878-1942 **TCLC 60**
See also CA 157

Cohen, Arthur A(llen) 1928-1986 **CLC 7, 31**
See also CA 1-4R; 120; CANR 1, 17, 42; DLB 28

Cohen, Leonard (Norman) 1934- **CLC 3, 38; DAC; DAM MST**
See also CA 21-24R; CANR 14; DLB 53; MTCW

Cohen, Matt 1942- .... **CLC 19; DAC**
See also CA 61-64; CAAS 18; CANR 40; DLB 53

Cohen-Solal, Annie 19(?)- .... **CLC 50**

Colegate, Isabel 1931- .... **CLC 36**
See also CA 17-20R; CANR 8, 22; DLB 14; INT CANR-22; MTCW

Coleman, Emmett
See Reed, Ishmael

Coleridge, M. E.
See Coleridge, Mary E(lizabeth)

Coleridge, Mary E(lizabeth) 1861-1907 **TCLC 73**
See also CA 116; DLB 19, 98

Coleridge, Samuel Taylor 1772-1834 **NCLC 9, 54; DA; DAB; DAC; DAM MST, POET; PC 11; WLC**
See also CDBLB 1789-1832; DLB 93, 107

Coleridge, Sara 1802-1852 .... **NCLC 31**

Coles, Don 1928- .... **CLC 46**
See also CA 115; CANR 38

Coles, Robert (Martin) 1929- .... **CLC 108**
See also CA 45-48; CANR 3, 32, 66; INT CANR-32; SATA 23

Colette, (Sidonie-Gabrielle) 1873-1954 **TCLC 1, 5, 16; DAM NOV; SSC 10**
See also CA 104; 131; DLB 65; MTCW

Collett, (Jacobine) Camilla (Wergeland) 1813-1895 .... **NCLC 22**

Collier, Christopher 1930- .... **CLC 30**
See also AAYA 13; CA 33-36R; CANR 13, 33; JRDA; MAICYA; SATA 16, 70

Collier, James L(incoln) 1928- **CLC 30; DAM POP**
See also AAYA 13; CA 9-12R; CANR 4, 33, 60; CLR 3; JRDA; MAICYA; SAAS 21; SATA 8, 70

Collier, Jeremy 1650-1726 .... LC 6

Collier, John 1901-1980 .... SSC 19
See also CA 65-68; 97-100; CANR 10; DLB 77

Collingwood, R(obin) G(eorge) 1889(?)-1943 TCLC 67
See also CA 117; 155

Collins, Hunt
See Hunter, Evan

Collins, Linda 1931- .... CLC 44
See also CA 125

Collins, (William) Wilkie 1824-1889NCLC 1, 18
See also CDBLB 1832-1890; DLB 18, 70, 159

Collins, William 1721-1759 . LC 4, 40; DAM POET
See also DLB 109

Collodi, Carlo 1826-1890 .... NCLC 54
See also Lorenzini, Carlo
See also CLR 5

Colman, George 1732-1794
See Glassco, John

Colt, Winchester Remington
See Hubbard, L(afayette) Ron(ald)

Colter, Cyrus 1910- .... CLC 58
See also BW 1; CA 65-68; CANR 10, 66; DLB 33

Colton, James
See Hansen, Joseph

Colum, Padraic 1881-1972 .... CLC 28
See also CA 73-76; 33-36R; CANR 35; CLR 36; MAICYA; MTCW; SATA 15

Colvin, James
See Moorcock, Michael (John)

Colwin, Laurie (E.) 1944-1992CLC 5, 13, 23, 84
See also CA 89-92; 139; CANR 20, 46; DLBY 80; MTCW

Comfort, Alex(ander) 1920-CLC 7; DAM POP
See also CA 1-4R; CANR 1, 45

Comfort, Montgomery
See Campbell, (John) Ramsey

Compton-Burnett, I(vy) 1884(?)-1969CLC 1, 3, 10, 15, 34; DAM NOV
See also CA 1-4R; 25-28R; CANR 4; DLB 36; MTCW

Comstock, Anthony 1844-1915 ...... TCLC 13
See also CA 110

Comte, Auguste 1798-1857 .... NCLC 54

Conan Doyle, Arthur
See Doyle, Arthur Conan

Conde, Maryse 1937- ...... CLC 52, 92; DAM MULT
See also Boucolon, Maryse
See also BW 2

Condillac, Etienne Bonnot de 1714-1780 L C 26

Condon, Richard (Thomas) 1915-1996CLC 4, 6, 8, 10, 45, 100; DAM NOV
See also BEST 90:3; CA 1-4R; 151; CAAS 1; CANR 2, 23; INT CANR-23; MTCW

Confucius 551B.C.-479B.C. . CMLC 19; DA; DAB; DAC; DAM MST; WLCS

Congreve, William 1670-1729 LC 5, 21; DA; DAB; DAC; DAM DRAM, MST, POET; DC 2; WLC
See also CDBLB 1660-1789; DLB 39, 84

Connell, Evan S(helby), Jr. 1924-CLC 4,6,45; DAM NOV
See also AAYA 7; CA 1-4R; CAAS 2; CANR 2, 39; DLB 2; DLBY 81; MTCW

Connelly, Marc(us Cook) 1890-1980 ..CLC 7
See also CA 85-88; 102; CANR 30; DLB 7;

DLBY 80; SATA-Obit 25

Connor, Ralph .... TCLC 31
See also Gordon, Charles William
See also DLB 92

Conrad, Joseph 1857-1924TCLC 1, 6, 13, 25, 43, 57; DA; DAB; DAC; DAM MST, NOV; SSC 9; WLC
See also CA 104; 131; CANR 60; CDBLB 1890-1914; DLB 10, 34, 98, 156; MTCW; SATA 27

Conrad, Robert Arnold
See Hart, Moss

Conroy, Donald Pat(rick) 1945- CLC 30, 74; DAM NOV, POP
See also AAYA 8; AITN 1; CA 85-88; CANR 24, 53; DLB 6; MTCW

Constant (de Rebecque), (Henri) Benjamin 1767-1830 .... NCLC 6
See also DLB 119

Conybeare, Charles Augustus
See Eliot, T(homas) S(tearns)

Cook, Michael 1933- .... CLC 58
See also CA 93-96; CANR 68; DLB 53

Cook, Robin 1940- .... CLC 14; DAM POP
See also BEST 90:2; CA 108; 111; CANR 41; INT 111

Cook, Roy
See Silverberg, Robert

Cooke, Elizabeth 1948- .... CLC 55
See also CA 129

Cooke, John Esten 1830-1886 .... NCLC 5
See also DLB 3

Cooke, John Estes
See Baum, L(yman) Frank

Cooke, M. E.
See Creasey, John

Cooke, Margaret
See Creasey, John

Cook-Lynn, Elizabeth 1930-..CLC 93; DAM MULT
See also CA 133; DLB 175; NNAL

Cooney, Ray .... CLC 62

Cooper, Douglas 1960- .... CLC 86

Cooper, Henry St. John
See Creasey, John

Cooper, J(oan) California .... CLC 56; DAM MULT
See also AAYA 12; BW 1; CA 125; CANR 55

Cooper, James Fenimore 1789-1851NCLC 1, 27, 54
See also AAYA 22; CDALB 1640-1865; DLB 3; SATA 19

Coover, Robert (Lowell) 1932- CLC 3, 7, 15, 32, 46, 87; DAM NOV; SSC 15
See also CA 45-48; CANR 3, 37, 58; DLB 2; DLBY 81; MTCW

Copeland, Stewart (Armstrong) 1952-CLC 26

Coppard, A(lfred) E(dgar) 1878-1957 T C L C 5; SSC 21
See also CA 114; DLB 162; YABC 1

Coppee, Francois 1842-1908 .... TCLC 25

Coppola, Francis Ford 1939- .... CLC 16
See also CA 77-80; CANR 40; DLB 44

Corbiere, Tristan 1845-1875 .... NCLC 43

Corcoran, Barbara 1911- .... CLC 17
See also AAYA 14; CA 21-24R; CAAS 2; CANR 11, 28, 48; DLB 52; JRDA; SAAS 20; SATA 3, 77

Cordelier, Maurice
See Giraudoux, (Hippolyte) Jean

Corelli, Marie 1855-1924 .... TCLC 51
See also Mackay, Mary
See also DLB 34, 156

Corman, Cid 1924- ....CLC 9
See also Corman, Sidney
See also CAAS 2; DLB 5, 193

Corman, Sidney 1924-
See Corman, Cid
See also CA 85-88; CANR 44; DAM POET

Cormier, Robert (Edmund) 1925-CLC 12, 30; DA; DAB; DAC; DAM MST, NOV
See also AAYA 3, 19; CA 1-4R; CANR 5, 23; CDALB 1968-1988; CLR 12; DLB 52; INT CANR-23; JRDA; MAICYA; MTCW; SATA 10, 45, 83

Corn, Alfred (DeWitt III) 1943- ...... CLC 33
See also CA 104; CAAS 25; CANR 44; DLB 120; DLBY 80

Corneille, Pierre 1606-1684 .... LC 28; DAB; DAM MST

Cornwell, David (John Moore) 1931-CLC 9, 15; DAM POP
See also le Carre, John
See also CA 5-8R; CANR 13, 33, 59; MTCW

Corso, (Nunzio) Gregory 1930- .... CLC 1, 11
See also CA 5-8R; CANR 41; DLB 5, 16; MTCW

Cortazar, Julio 1914-1984CLC 2, 3, 5, 10, 13, 15, 33, 34, 92; DAM MULT, NOV; HLC; SSC 7
See also CA 21-24R; CANR 12, 32; DLB 113; HW; MTCW

CORTES, HERNAN 1484-1547 .... LC 31

Corwin, Cecil
See Kornbluth, C(yril) M.

Cosic, Dobrica 1921- .... CLC 14
See also CA 122; 138; DLB 181

Costain, Thomas B(ertram) 1885-1965 . C L C 30
See also CA 5-8R; 25-28R; DLB 9

Costantini, Humberto 1924(?)-1987 CLC 49
See also CA 131; 122; HW

Costello, Elvis 1955- .... CLC 21

Cotes, Cecil V.
See Duncan, Sara Jeannette

Cotter, Joseph Seamon Sr. 1861-1949 T C L C 28; BLC; DAM MULT
See also BW 1; CA 124; DLB 50

Couch, Arthur Thomas Quiller
See Quiller-Couch, SirArthur Thomas

Coulton, James
See Hansen, Joseph

Couperus, Louis (Marie Anne) 1863-1923 TCLC 15
See also CA 115

Coupland, Douglas 1961-CLC 85; DAC; DAM POP
See also CA 142; CANR 57

Court, Wesli
See Turco, Lewis (Putnam)

Courtenay, Bryce 1933- .... CLC 59
See also CA 138

Courtney, Robert
See Ellison, Harlan (Jay)

Cousteau, Jacques-Yves 1910-1997 . CLC 30
See also CA 65-68; 159; CANR 15, 67; MTCW; SATA 38, 98

Cowan, Peter (Walkinshaw) 1914- ....SSC 28
See also CA 21-24R; CANR 9, 25, 50

Coward, Noel (Peirce) 1899-1973CLC 1,9,29, 51; DAM DRAM
See also AITN 1; CA 17-18; 41-44R; CANR 35; CAP 2; CDBLB 1914-1945; DLB 10; MTCW

Cowley, Malcolm 1898-1989 .... CLC 39
See also CA 5-8R; 128; CANR 3, 55; DLB 4,

48; DLBY 81, 89; MTCW

Cowper, William 1731-1800 . **NCLC 8; DAM POET**
See also DLB 104, 109

Cox, William Trevor 1928- .... **CLC 9, 14, 71; DAM NOV**
See also Trevor, William
See also CA 9-12R; CANR 4, 37, 55; DLB 14; INT CANR-37; MTCW

Coyne, P. J.
See Masters, Hilary

Cozzens, James Gould 1903-1978 **CLC 1, 4, 11, 92**
See also CA 9-12R; 81-84; CANR 19; CDALB 1941-1968; DLB 9; DLBD 2; DLBY 84, 97; MTCW

Crabbe, George 1754-1832 .... **NCLC 26**
See also DLB 93

Craddock, Charles Egbert
See Murfree, Mary Noailles

Craig, A. A.
See Anderson, Poul (William)

Craik, Dinah Maria (Mulock) 1826-1887 **NCLC 38**
See also DLB 35, 163; MAICYA; SATA 34

Cram, Ralph Adams 1863-1942 ..... **TCLC 45**
See also CA 160

Crane, (Harold) Hart 1899-1932 **TCLC 2, 5; DA; DAB; DAC; DAM MST, POET; PC 3; WLC**
See also CA 104; 127; CDALB 1917-1929; DLB 4, 48; MTCW

Crane, R(onald) S(almon) 1886-1967 **CLC 27**
See also CA 85-88; DLB 63

Crane, Stephen (Townley) 1871-1900 **TCLC 11, 17, 32; DA; DAB; DAC; DAM MST, NOV, POET; SSC 7; WLC**
See also AAYA 21; CA 109; 140; CDALB 1865-1917; DLB 12, 54, 78; YABC 2

Crase, Douglas 1944- .... **CLC 58**
See also CA 106

Crashaw, Richard 1612(?)-1649 .... **LC 24**
See also DLB 126

Craven, Margaret 1901-1980 . **CLC 17; DAC**
See also CA 103

Crawford, F(rancis) Marion 1854-1909 **TCLC 10**
See also CA 107; DLB 71

Crawford, Isabella Valancy 1850-1887 **NCLC 12**
See also DLB 92

Crayon, Geoffrey
See Irving, Washington

Creasey, John 1908-1973 .... **CLC 11**
See also CA 5-8R; 41-44R; CANR 8, 59; DLB 77; MTCW

Crebillon, Claude Prosper Jolyot de (fils) 1707-1777 .... **LC 28**

Credo
See Creasey, John

Credo, Alvaro J. de
See Prado (Calvo), Pedro

Creeley, Robert (White) 1926- **CLC 1, 2, 4, 8, 11, 15, 36, 78; DAM POET**
See also CA 1-4R; CAAS 10; CANR 23, 43; DLB 5, 16, 169; MTCW

Crews, Harry (Eugene) 1935- **CLC 6, 23, 49**
See also AITN 1; CA 25-28R; CANR 20, 57; DLB 6, 143, 185; MTCW

Crichton, (John) Michael 1942- **CLC 2, 6, 54, 90; DAM NOV, POP**
See also AAYA 10; AITN 2; CA 25-28R; CANR 13, 40, 54; DLBY 81; INT CANR-13; JRDA;

MTCW; SATA 9, 88

Crispin, Edmund .... **CLC 22**
See also Montgomery, (Robert) Bruce
See also DLB 87

Cristofer, Michael 1945(?)- .... **CLC 28; DAM DRAM**
See also CA 110; 152; DLB 7

Croce, Benedetto 1866-1952 .... **TCLC 37**
See also CA 120; 155

Crockett, David 1786-1836 .... **NCLC 8**
See also DLB 3, 11

Crockett, Davy
See Crockett, David

Crofts, Freeman Wills 1879-1957 .. **TCLC 55**
See also CA 115; DLB 77

Croker, John Wilson 1780-1857 ..... **NCLC 10**
See also DLB 110

Crommelynck, Fernand 1885-1970 .. **CLC 75**
See also CA 89-92

Cronin, A(rchibald) J(oseph) 1896-1981 **CLC 32**
See also CA 1-4R; 102; CANR 5; DLB 191; SATA 47; SATA-Obit 25

Cross, Amanda
See Heilbrun, Carolyn G(old)

Crothers, Rachel 1878(?)-1958 ...... **TCLC 19**
See also CA 113; DLB 7

Croves, Hal
See Traven, B.

Crow Dog, Mary (Ellen) (?)- .... **CLC 93**
See also Brave Bird, Mary
See also CA 154

Crowfield, Christopher
See Stowe, Harriet (Elizabeth) Beecher

Crowley, Aleister .... **TCLC 7**
See also Crowley, Edward Alexander

Crowley, Edward Alexander 1875-1947
See Crowley, Aleister
See also CA 104

Crowley, John 1942- .... **CLC 57**
See also CA 61-64; CANR 43; DLBY 82; SATA 65

Crud
See Crumb, R(obert)

Crumarums
See Crumb, R(obert)

Crumb, R(obert) 1943- .... **CLC 17**
See also CA 106

Crumbum
See Crumb, R(obert)

Crumski
See Crumb, R(obert)

Crum the Bum
See Crumb, R(obert)

Crunk
See Crumb, R(obert)

Crustt
See Crumb, R(obert)

Cryer, Gretchen (Kiger) 1935- .... **CLC 21**
See also CA 114; 123

Csath, Geza 1887-1919 .... **TCLC 13**
See also CA 111

Cudlip, David 1933- .... **CLC 34**

Cullen, Countee 1903-1946 **TCLC 4, 37; BLC; DA; DAC; DAM MST, MULT, POET; PC 20; WLCS**
See also BW 1; CA 108; 124; CDALB 1917-1929; DLB 4, 48, 51; MTCW; SATA 18

Cum, R.
See Crumb, R(obert)

Cummings, Bruce F(rederick) 1889-1919
See Barbellion, W. N. P.
See also CA 123

Cummings, E(dward) E(stlin) 1894-1962 **CLC 1, 3, 8, 12, 15, 68; DA; DAB; DAC; DAM MST, POET; PC 5; WLC 2**
See also CA 73-76; CANR 31; CDALB 1929-1941; DLB 4, 48; MTCW

Cunha, Euclides (Rodrigues Pimenta) da 1866-1909 .... **TCLC 24**
See also CA 123

Cunningham, E. V.
See Fast, Howard (Melvin)

Cunningham, J(ames) V(incent) 1911-1985 **CLC 3, 31**
See also CA 1-4R; 115; CANR 1; DLB 5

Cunningham, Julia (Woolfolk) 1916- **CLC 12**
See also CA 9-12R; CANR 4, 19, 36; JRDA; MAICYA; SAAS 2; SATA 1, 26

Cunningham, Michael 1952- .... **CLC 34**
See also CA 136

Cunninghame Graham, R(obert) B(ontine) 1852-1936 .... **TCLC 19**
See also Graham, R(obert) B(ontine) Cunninghame
See also CA 119; DLB 98

Currie, Ellen 19(?)- .... **CLC 44**

Curtin, Philip
See Lowndes, Marie Adelaide (Belloc)

Curtis, Price
See Ellison, Harlan (Jay)

Cutrate, Joe
See Spiegelman, Art

Cynewulf c. 770-c. 840 .... **CMLC 23**

Czaczkes, Shmuel Yosef
See Agnon, S(hmuel) Y(osef Halevi)

Dabrowska, Maria (Szumska) 1889-1965 **CLC 15**
See also CA 106

Dabydeen, David 1955- .... **CLC 34**
See also BW 1; CA 125; CANR 56

Dacey, Philip 1939- .... **CLC 51**
See also CA 37-40R; CAAS 17; CANR 14, 32, 64; DLB 105

Dagerman, Stig (Halvard) 1923-1954 **TCLC 17**
See also CA 117; 155

Dahl, Roald 1916-1990 **CLC 1, 6, 18, 79; DAB; DAC; DAM MST, NOV, POP**
See also AAYA 15; CA 1-4R; 133; CANR 6, 32, 37, 62; CLR 1, 7, 41; DLB 139; JRDA; MAICYA; MTCW; SATA 1, 26, 73; SATA-Obit 65

Dahlberg, Edward 1900-1977 .. **CLC 1, 7, 14**
See also CA 9-12R; 69-72; CANR 31, 62; DLB 48; MTCW

Daitch, Susan 1954- .... **CLC 103**
See also CA 161

Dale, Colin .... **TCLC 18**
See also Lawrence, T(homas) E(dward)

Dale, George E.
See Asimov, Isaac

Daly, Elizabeth 1878-1967 .... **CLC 52**
See also CA 23-24; 25-28R; CANR 60; CAP 2

Daly, Maureen 1921- .... **CLC 17**
See also AAYA 5; CANR 37; JRDA; MAICYA; SAAS 1; SATA 2

Damas, Leon-Gontran 1912-1978 ..... **CLC 84**
See also BW 1; CA 125; 73-76

Dana, Richard Henry Sr. 1787-1879 **NCLC 53**

Daniel, Samuel 1562(?)-1619 .... **LC 24**
See also DLB 62

Daniels, Brett
See Adler, Renata

Dannay, Frederic 1905-1982 . **CLC 11; DAM POP**

See also Queen, Ellery
See also CA 1-4R; 107; CANR 1, 39; DLB 137;
MTCW
D'Annunzio, Gabriele 1863-1938**TCLC 6, 40**
See also CA 104; 155
Danois, N. le
See Gourmont, Remy (-Marie-Charles) de
Dante 1265-1321 .... **CMLC 3, 18; DA; DAB;**
DAC; DAM MST, POET; PC 21; WLCS
d'Antibes, Germain
See Simenon, Georges (Jacques Christian)
Danticat, Edwidge 1969- .... **CLC 94**
See also CA 152
Danvers, Dennis 1947- .... **CLC 70**
Danziger, Paula 1944- .... **CLC 21**
See also AAYA 4; CA 112; 115; CANR 37; CLR
20; JRDA; MAICYA; SATA 36, 63; SATA-
Brief 30
Da Ponte, Lorenzo 1749-1838 .... **NCLC 50**
Dario, Ruben 1867-1916 .... **TCLC 4; DAM**
MULT; HLC; PC 15
See also CA 131; HW; MTCW
Darley, George 1795-1846 .... **NCLC 2**
See also DLB 96
Darwin, Charles 1809-1882 .... **NCLC 57**
See also DLB 57, 166
Daryush, Elizabeth 1887-1977 ..... **CLC 6, 19**
See also CA 49-52; CANR 3; DLB 20
Dashwood, Edmee Elizabeth Monica de la Pas-
ture 1890-1943
See Delafield, E. M.
See also CA 119; 154
Daudet, (Louis Marie) Alphonse 1840-1897
NCLC 1
See also DLB 123
Daumal, Rene 1908-1944 .... **TCLC 14**
See also CA 114
Davenport, Guy (Mattison, Jr.) 1927-**CLC 6,**
14, 38; SSC 16
See also CA 33-36R; CANR 23; DLB 130
Davidson, Avram 1923-
See Queen, Ellery
See also CA 101; CANR 26; DLB 8
Davidson, Donald (Grady) 1893-1968**CLC 2,**
13, 19
See also CA 5-8R; 25-28R; CANR 4; DLB 45
Davidson, Hugh
See Hamilton, Edmond
Davidson, John 1857-1909 .... **TCLC 24**
See also CA 118; DLB 19
Davidson, Sara 1943- ....**CLC 9**
See also CA 81-84; CANR 44, 68; DLB 185
Davie, Donald (Alfred) 1922-1995 **CLC 5, 8,**
10, 31
See also CA 1-4R; 149; CAAS 3; CANR 1, 44;
DLB 27; MTCW
Davies, Ray(mond Douglas) 1944-... **CLC 21**
See also CA 116; 146
Davies, Rhys 1901-1978 .... **CLC 23**
See also CA 9-12R; 81-84; CANR 4; DLB 139,
191
Davies, (William) Robertson 1913-1995 **C L C**
2, 7, 13, 25, 42, 75, 91; DA; DAB; DAC;
DAM MST, NOV, POP; WLC
See also BEST 89:2; CA 33-36R; 150; CANR
17, 42; DLB 68; INT CANR-17; MTCW
Davies, W(illiam) H(enry) 1871-1940**TCLC 5**
See also CA 104; DLB 19, 174
Davies, Walter C.
See Kornbluth, C(yril) M.
Davis, Angela (Yvonne) 1944- **CLC 77; DAM**
MULT
See also BW 2; CA 57-60; CANR 10

Davis, B. Lynch
See Bioy Casares, Adolfo; Borges, Jorge Luis
Davis, Gordon
See Hunt, E(verette) Howard, (Jr.)
Davis, Harold Lenoir 1896-1960 ...... **CLC 49**
See also CA 89-92; DLB 9
Davis, Rebecca (Blaine) Harding 1831-1910
TCLC 6
See also CA 104; DLB 74
Davis, Richard Harding 1864-1916**TCLC 24**
See also CA 114; DLB 12, 23, 78, 79, 189;
DLBD 13
Davison, Frank Dalby 1893-1970 ..... **CLC 15**
See also CA 116
Davison, Lawrence H.
See Lawrence, D(avid) H(erbert Richards)
Davison, Peter (Hubert) 1928- .... **CLC 28**
See also CA 9-12R; CAAS 4; CANR 3, 43; DLB
5
Davys, Mary 1674-1732 .... **LC 1**
See also DLB 39
Dawson, Fielding 1930- .... **CLC 6**
See also CA 85-88; DLB 130
Dawson, Peter
See Faust, Frederick (Schiller)
Day, Clarence (Shepard, Jr.) 1874-1935
TCLC 25
See also CA 108; DLB 11
Day, Thomas 1748-1789 .... **LC 1**
See also DLB 39; YABC 1
Day Lewis, C(ecil) 1904-1972 .. **CLC 1, 6, 10;**
DAM POET; PC 11
See also Blake, Nicholas
See also CA 13-16; 33-36R; CANR 34; CAP 1;
DLB 15, 20; MTCW
Dazai, Osamu 1909-1948 .... **TCLC 11**
See also Tsushima, Shuji
See also CA 164; DLB 182
de Andrade, Carlos Drummond
See Drummond de Andrade, Carlos
Deane, Norman
See Creasey, John
de Beauvoir, Simone (Lucie Ernestine Marie
Bertrand)
See Beauvoir, Simone (Lucie Ernestine Marie
Bertrand) de
de Beer, P.
See Bosman, Herman Charles
de Brissac, Malcolm
See Dickinson, Peter (Malcolm)
de Chardin, Pierre Teilhard
See Teilhard de Chardin, (Marie Joseph) Pierre
Dee, John 1527-1608 .... **LC 20**
Deer, Sandra 1940- .... **CLC 45**
De Ferrari, Gabriella 1941- .... **CLC 65**
See also CA 146
Defoe, Daniel 1660(?)-1731 **LC 1; DA; DAB;**
DAC; DAM MST, NOV; WLC
See also CDBLB 1660-1789; DLB 39, 95, 101;
JRDA; MAICYA; SATA 22
de Gourmont, Remy(-Marie-Charles)
See Gourmont, Remy (-Marie-Charles) de
de Hartog, Jan 1914-.......................... **CLC 19**
See also CA 1-4R; CANR 1
de Hostos, E. M.
See Hostos (y Bonilla), Eugenio Maria de
de Hostos, Eugenio M.
See Hostos (y Bonilla), Eugenio Maria de
Deighton, Len .... **CLC 4, 7, 22, 46**
See also Deighton, Leonard Cyril
See also AAYA 6; BEST 89:2; CDBLB 1960 to
Present; DLB 87
Deighton, Leonard Cyril 1929-

See Deighton, Len
See also CA 9-12R; CANR 19, 33, 68; DAM
NOV, POP; MTCW
Dekker, Thomas 1572(?)-1632 ..**LC 22; DAM**
DRAM
See also CDBLB Before 1660; DLB 62, 172
Delafield, E. M. 1890-1943 .... **TCLC 61**
See also Dashwood, Edmee Elizabeth Monica
de la Pasture
See also DLB 34
de la Mare, Walter (John) 1873-1956**TCLC 4,**
53; DAB; DAC; DAM MST, POET; SSC
14; WLC
See also CA 163; CDBLB 1914-1945; CLR 23;
DLB 162; SATA 16
Delaney, Franey
See O'Hara, John (Henry)
Delaney, Shelagh 1939-**CLC 29; DAM DRAM**
See also CA 17-20R; CANR 30, 67; CDBLB
1960 to Present; DLB 13; MTCW
Delany, Mary (Granville Pendarves) 1700-1788
LC 12
Delany, Samuel R(ay, Jr.) 1942-**CLC 8, 14, 38;**
BLC; DAM MULT
See also AAYA 24; BW 2; CA 81-84; CANR
27, 43; DLB 8, 33; MTCW
De La Ramee, (Marie) Louise 1839-1908
See Ouida
See also SATA 20
de la Roche, Mazo 1879-1961 .... **CLC 14**
See also CA 85-88; CANR 30; DLB 68; SATA
64
De La Salle, Innocent
See Hartmann, Sadakichi
Delbanco, Nicholas (Franklin) 1942- **CLC 6,**
13
See also CA 17-20R; CAAS 2; CANR 29, 55;
DLB 6
del Castillo, Michel 1933- .... **CLC 38**
See also CA 109
Deledda, Grazia (Cosima) 1875(?)-1936
TCLC 23
See also CA 123
Delibes, Miguel .... **CLC 8, 18**
See also Delibes Setien, Miguel
Delibes Setien, Miguel 1920-
See Delibes, Miguel
See also CA 45-48; CANR 1, 32; HW; MTCW
DeLillo, Don 1936-**CLC 8, 10, 13, 27, 39, 54,**
76; DAM NOV, POP
See also BEST 89:1; CA 81-84; CANR 21; DLB
6, 173; MTCW
de Lisser, H. G.
See De Lisser, H(erbert) G(eorge)
See also DLB 117
De Lisser, H(erbert) G(eorge) 1878-1944
TCLC 12
See also de Lisser, H. G.
See also BW 2; CA 109; 152
Deloney, Thomas 1560-1600 .... **LC 41**
Deloria, Vine (Victor), Jr. 1933- ..... **CLC 21;**
DAM MULT
See also CA 53-56; CANR 5, 20, 48; DLB 175;
MTCW; NNAL; SATA 21
Del Vecchio, John M(ichael) 1947- .. **CLC 29**
See also CA 110; DLBD 9
de Man, Paul (Adolph Michel) 1919-1983
CLC 55
See also CA 128; 111; CANR 61; DLB 67;
MTCW
De Marinis, Rick 1934- .... **CLC 54**
See also CA 57-60; CAAS 24; CANR 9, 25, 50
Dembry, R. Emmet

See Murfree, Mary Noailles

Demby, William 1922- . **CLC 53; BLC; DAM MULT**
See also BW 1; CA 81-84; DLB 33

de Menton, Francisco
See Chin, Frank (Chew, Jr.)

Demijohn, Thom
See Disch, Thomas M(ichael)

de Montherlant, Henry (Milon)
See Montherlant, Henry (Milon) de

Demosthenes 384B.C.-322B.C. ...... **CMLC 13**
See also DLB 176

de Natale, Francine
See Malzberg, Barry N(athaniel)

Denby, Edwin (Orr) 1903-1983 .... **CLC 48**
See also CA 138; 110

Denis, Julio
See Cortazar, Julio

Denmark, Harrison
See Zelazny, Roger (Joseph)

Dennis, John 1658-1734 ....**LC 11**
See also DLB 101

Dennis, Nigel (Forbes) 1912-1989 ....**CLC 8**
See also CA 25-28R; 129; DLB 13, 15; MTCW

Dent, Lester 1904(?)-1959 ....**TCLC 72**
See also CA 112; 161

De Palma, Brian (Russell) 1940- ...... **CLC 20**
See also CA 109

De Quincey, Thomas 1785-1859 ....**NCLC 4**
See also CDBLB 1789-1832; DLB 110; 144

Deren, Eleanora 1908(?)-1961
See Deren, Maya
See also CA 111

Deren, Maya 1917-1961 .... **CLC 16, 102**
See also Deren, Eleanora

Derleth, August (William) 1909-1971**CLC 31**
See also CA 1-4R; 29-32R; CANR 4; DLB 9; SATA 5

Der Nister 1884-1950 ....**TCLC 56**

de Routisie, Albert
See Aragon, Louis

Derrida, Jacques 1930- .... **CLC 24, 87**
See also CA 124; 127

Derry Down Derry
See Lear, Edward

Dersonnes, Jacques
See Simenon, Georges (Jacques Christian)

Desai, Anita 1937-**CLC 19, 37, 97; DAB; DAM NOV**
See also CA 81-84; CANR 33, 53; MTCW; SATA 63

de Saint-Luc, Jean
See Glassco, John

de Saint Roman, Arnaud
See Aragon, Louis

Descartes, Rene 1596-1650 .... **LC 20, 35**

De Sica, Vittorio 1901(?)-1974 .... **CLC 20**
See also CA 117

Desnos, Robert 1900-1945 ....**TCLC 22**
See also CA 121; 151

Destouches, Louis-Ferdinand 1894-1961**CLC 9, 15**
See also Celine, Louis-Ferdinand
See also CA 85-88; CANR 28; MTCW

de Tolignac, Gaston
See Griffith, D(avid Lewelyn) W(ark)

Deutsch, Babette 1895-1982 .... **CLC 18**
See also CA 1-4R; 108; CANR 4; DLB 45; SATA 1; SATA-Obit 33

Devenant, William 1606-1649 .... **LC 13**

Devkota, Laxmiprasad 1909-1959 . **TCLC 23**
See also CA 123

De Voto, Bernard (Augustine) 1897-1955

TCLC 29
See also CA 113; 160; DLB 9

De Vries, Peter 1910-1993 **CLC 1, 2, 3, 7, 10, 28, 46; DAM NOV**
See also CA 17-20R; 142; CANR 41; DLB 6; DLBY 82; MTCW

Dexter, John
See Bradley, Marion Zimmer

Dexter, Martin
See Faust, Frederick (Schiller)

Dexter, Pete 1943- ... **CLC 34, 55; DAM POP**
See also BEST 89:2; CA 127; 131; INT 131; MTCW

Diamano, Silmang
See Senghor, Leopold Sedar

Diamond, Neil 1941- ....**CLC 30**
See also CA 108

Diaz del Castillo, Bernal 1496-1584 ... **LC 31**

di Bassetto, Corno
See Shaw, George Bernard

Dick, Philip K(indred) 1928-1982**CLC 10, 30, 72; DAM NOV, POP**
See also AAYA 24; CA 49-52; 106; CANR 2, 16; DLB 8; MTCW

Dickens, Charles (John Huffam) 1812-1870
NCLC 3, 8, 18, 26, 37, 50; DA; DAB; DAC; DAM MST, NOV; SSC 17; WLC
See also CA 23; CDBLB 1832-1890; DLB 21, 55, 70, 159, 166; JRDA; MAICYA; SATA 15

Dickey, James (Lafayette) 1923-1997 **CLC 1, 2, 4, 7, 10, 15, 47, 109; DAM NOV, POET, POP**
See also AITN 1, 2; CA 9-12R; 156; CABS 2; CANR 10, 48, 61; CDALB 1968-1988; DLB 5, 193; DLBD 7; DLBY 82, 93. 96, 97; INT CANR-10; MTCW

Dickey, William 1928-1994 .... **CLC 3, 28**
See also CA 9-12R; 145; CANR 24; DLB 5

Dickinson, Charles 1951- ....**CLC 49**
See also CA 128

Dickinson, Emily (Elizabeth) 1830-1886
NCLC 21; DA; DAB; DAC; DAM MST, POET; PC 1; WLC
See also AAYA 22; CDALB 1865-1917; DLB 1; SATA 29

Dickinson, Peter (Malcolm) 1927-**CLC 12, 35**
See also AAYA 9; CA 41-44R; CANR 31, 58; CLR 29; DLB 87, 161; JRDA; MAICYA; SATA 5, 62, 95

Dickson, Carr
See Carr, John Dickson

Dickson, Carter
See Carr, John Dickson

Diderot, Denis 1713-1784 .... **LC 26**

Didion, Joan 1934-**CLC 1, 3, 8, 14, 32; DAM NOV**
See also AITN 1; CA 5-8R; CANR 14, 52; CDALB 1968-1988; DLB 2, 173, 185; DLBY 81, 86; MTCW

Dietrich, Robert
See Hunt, E(verette) Howard, (Jr.)

Dillard, Annie 1945- . **CLC 9, 60; DAM NOV**
See also AAYA 6; CA 49-52; CANR 3, 43, 62; DLBY 80; MTCW; SATA 10

Dillard, R(ichard) H(enry) W(ilde) 1937-
CLC 5
See also CA 21-24R; CAAS 7; CANR 10; DLB 5

Dillon, Eilis 1920-1994 ....**CLC 17**
See also CA 9-12R; 147; CAAS 3; CANR 4, 38; CLR 26; MAICYA; SATA 2, 74; SATA-Obit 83

Dimont, Penelope
See Mortimer, Penelope (Ruth)

Dinesen, Isak .... **CLC 10, 29, 95; SSC 7**
See also Blixen, Karen (Christentze Dinesen)

Ding Ling ....**CLC 68**
See also Chiang Pin-chin

Disch, Thomas M(ichael) 1940- ... **CLC 7, 36**
See also AAYA 17; CA 21-24R; CAAS 4; CANR 17, 36, 54; CLR 18; DLB 8; MAICYA; MTCW; SAAS 15; SATA 92

Disch, Tom
See Disch, Thomas M(ichael)

d'Isly, Georges
See Simenon, Georges (Jacques Christian)

Disraeli, Benjamin 1804-1881 ....**NCLC 2, 39**
See also DLB 21, 55

Ditcum, Steve
See Crumb, R(obert)

Dixon, Paige
See Corcoran, Barbara

Dixon, Stephen 1936- .... **CLC 52; SSC 16**
See also CA 89-92; CANR 17, 40, 54; DLB 130

Doak, Annie
See Dillard, Annie

Dobell, Sydney Thompson 1824-1874 **NCLC 43**
See also DLB 32

Doblin, Alfred .... **TCLC 13**
See also Doeblin, Alfred

Dobrolyubov, Nikolai Alexandrovich 1836-1861
NCLC 5

Dobson, Austin 1840-1921 .... **TCLC 79**
See also DLB 35; 144

Dobyns, Stephen 1941- ....**CLC 37**
See also CA 45-48; CANR 2, 18

Doctorow, E(dgar) L(aurence) 1931- **CLC 6, 11, 15, 18, 37, 44, 65; DAM NOV, POP**
See also AAYA 22; AITN 2; BEST 89:3; CA 45-48; CANR 2, 33, 51; CDALB 1968-1988; DLB 2, 28, 173; DLBY 80; MTCW

Dodgson, Charles Lutwidge 1832-1898
See Carroll, Lewis
See also CLR 2; DA; DAB; DAC; DAM MST, NOV, POET; MAICYA; YABC 2

Dodson, Owen (Vincent) 1914-1983 **CLC 79; BLC; DAM MULT**
See also BW 1; CA 65-68; 110; CANR 24; DLB 76

Doeblin, Alfred 1878-1957 .... **TCLC 13**
See also Doblin, Alfred
See also CA 110; 141; DLB 66

Doerr, Harriet 1910- .... **CLC 34**
See also CA 117; 122; CANR 47; INT 122

Domecq, H(onorio) Bustos
See Bioy Casares, Adolfo; Borges, Jorge Luis

Domini, Rey
See Lorde, Audre (Geraldine)

Dominique
See Proust, (Valentin-Louis-George-Eugene-) Marcel

Don, A
See Stephen, SirLeslie

Donaldson, Stephen R. 1947- **CLC 46; DAM POP**
See also CA 89-92; CANR 13, 55; INT CANR-13

Donleavy, J(ames) P(atrick) 1926-**CLC 1, 4, 6, 10, 45**
See also AITN 2; CA 9-12R; CANR 24, 49, 62; DLB 6, 173; INT CANR-24; MTCW

Donne, John 1572-1631**LC 10, 24; DA; DAB; DAC; DAM MST, POET; PC 1**
See also CDBLB Before 1660; DLB 121, 151

Donnell, David 1939(?)- .... **CLC 34**
Donoghue, P. S.
See Hunt, E(verette) Howard, (Jr.)
Donoso (Yanez), Jose 1924-1996**CLC 4, 8, 11, 32, 99; DAM MULT; HLC**
See also CA 81-84; 155; CANR 32; DLB 113; HW; MTCW
Donovan, John 1928-1992 .... **CLC 35**
See also AAYA 20; CA 97-100; 137; CLR 3; MAICYA; SATA 72; SATA-Brief 29
Don Roberto
See Cunninghame Graham, R(obert) B(ontine)
Doolittle, Hilda 1886-1961**CLC 3, 8, 14, 31, 34, 73; DA; DAC; DAM MST, POET; PC 5; WLC**
See also H. D.
See also CA 97-100; CANR 35; DLB 4, 45; MTCW
Dorfman, Ariel 1942- ...... **CLC 48, 77; DAM MULT; HLC**
See also CA 124; 130; CANR 67; HW; INT 130
Dorn, Edward (Merton) 1929- ... **CLC 10, 18**
See also CA 93-96; CANR 42; DLB 5; INT 93-96
Dorris, Michael (Anthony) 1945-1997 ..**C L C 109; DAM MULT, NOV**
See also AAYA 20; BEST 90:1; CA 102; 157; CANR 19, 46; DLB 175; NNAL; SATA 75; SATA-Obit 94
Dorris, Michael A.
See Dorris, Michael (Anthony)
Dorsan, Luc
See Simenon, Georges (Jacques Christian)
Dorsange, Jean
See Simenon, Georges (Jacques Christian)
Dos Passos, John (Roderigo) 1896-1970 **C L C 1, 4, 8, 11, 15, 25, 34, 82; DA; DAB; DAC; DAM MST, NOV; WLC**
See also CA 1-4R; 29-32R; CANR 3; CDALB 1929-1941; DLB 4, 9; DLBD 1, 15; DLBY 96; MTCW
Dossage, Jean
See Simenon, Georges (Jacques Christian)
Dostoevsky, Fedor Mikhailovich 1821-1881 **NCLC 2, 7, 21, 33, 43; DA; DAB; DAC; DAM MST, NOV; SSC 2; WLC**
Doughty, Charles M(ontagu) 1843-1926 **TCLC 27**
See also CA 115; DLB 19, 57, 174
Douglas, Ellen .... **CLC 73**
See also Haxton, Josephine Ayres; Williamson, Ellen Douglas
Douglas, Gavin 1475(?)-1522 .... **LC 20**
Douglas, George
See Brown, George Douglas
Douglas, Keith (Castellain) 1920-1944**T C L C 40**
See also CA 160; DLB 27
Douglas, Leonard
See Bradbury, Ray (Douglas)
Douglas, Michael
See Crichton, (John) Michael
Douglas, Norman 1868-1952 .... **TCLC 68**
See also DLB 195
Douglas, William
See Brown, George Douglas
Douglass, Frederick 1817(?)-1895**NCLC 7, 55; BLC; DA; DAC; DAM MST, MULT; WLC**
See also CDALB 1640-1865; DLB 1, 43, 50, 79; SATA 29
Dourado, (Waldomiro Freitas) Autran 1926- **CLC 23, 60**
See also CA 25-28R; CANR 34

Dourado, Waldomiro Autran
See Dourado, (Waldomiro Freitas) Autran
Dove, Rita (Frances) 1952-**CLC 50, 81; DAM MULT, POET; PC 6**
See also BW 2; CA 109; CAAS 19; CANR 27, 42, 68; DLB 120
Dowell, Coleman 1925-1985 .... **CLC 60**
See also CA 25-28R; 117; CANR 10; DLB 130
Dowson, Ernest (Christopher) 1867-1900 **TCLC 4**
See also CA 105; 150; DLB 19, 135
Doyle, A. Conan
See Doyle, Arthur Conan
Doyle, Arthur Conan 1859-1930**TCLC 7; DA; DAB; DAC; DAM MST, NOV; SSC 12; WLC**
See also AAYA 14; CA 104; 122; CDBLB 1890-1914; DLB 18, 70, 156, 178; MTCW; SATA 24
Doyle, Conan
See Doyle, Arthur Conan
Doyle, John
See Graves, Robert (von Ranke)
Doyle, Roddy 1958(?)- ....**CLC 81**
See also AAYA 14; CA 143; DLB 194
Doyle, Sir A. Conan
See Doyle, Arthur Conan
Doyle, Sir Arthur Conan
See Doyle, Arthur Conan
Dr. A
See Asimov, Isaac; Silverstein, Alvin
Drabble, Margaret 1939-**CLC 2, 3, 5, 8, 10, 22, 53; DAB; DAC; DAM MST, NOV, POP**
See also CA 13-16R; CANR 18, 35, 63; CDBLB 1960 to Present; DLB 14, 155; MTCW; SATA 48
Drapier, M. B.
See Swift, Jonathan
Drayham, James
See Mencken, H(enry) L(ouis)
Drayton, Michael 1563-1631 .... **LC 8**
Dreadstone, Carl
See Campbell, (John) Ramsey
Dreiser, Theodore (Herman Albert) 1871-1945 **TCLC 10, 18, 35; DA; DAC; DAM MST, NOV; SSC 30; WLC**
See also CA 106; 132; CDALB 1865-1917; DLB 9, 12, 102, 137; DLBD 1; MTCW
Drexler, Rosalyn 1926- .... **CLC 2, 6**
See also CA 81-84; CANR 68
Dreyer, Carl Theodor 1889-1968 ...... **CLC 16**
See also CA 116
Drieu la Rochelle, Pierre(-Eugene) 1893-1945 **TCLC 21**
See also CA 117; DLB 72
Drinkwater, John 1882-1937 .... **TCLC 57**
See also CA 109; 149; DLB 10, 19, 149
Drop Shot
See Cable, George Washington
Droste-Hulshoff, Annette Freiin von 1797-1848 **NCLC 3**
See also DLB 133
Drummond, Walter
See Silverberg, Robert
Drummond, William Henry 1854-1907**T C L C 25**
See also CA 160; DLB 92
Drummond de Andrade, Carlos 1902-1987 **CLC 18**
See also Andrade, Carlos Drummond de
See also CA 132; 123
Drury, Allen (Stuart) 1918- .... **CLC 37**
See also CA 57-60; CANR 18, 52; INT CANR-

18
Dryden, John 1631-1700**LC 3, 21; DA; DAB; DAC; DAM DRAM, MST, POET; DC 3; WLC**
See also CDBLB 1660-1789; DLB 80, 101, 131
Duberman, Martin (Bauml) 1930- ...... **CLC 8**
See also CA 1-4R; CANR 2, 63
Dubie, Norman (Evans) 1945- .... **CLC 36**
See also CA 69-72; CANR 12; DLB 120
Du Bois, W(illiam) E(dward) B(urghardt) 1868-1963**CLC 1, 2, 13, 64, 96; BLC; DA; DAC; DAM MST, MULT, NOV; WLC**
See also BW 1; CA 85-88; CANR 34; CDALB 1865-1917; DLB 47, 50, 91; MTCW; SATA 42
Dubus, Andre 1936- **CLC 13, 36, 97; SSC 15**
See also CA 21-24R; CANR 17; DLB 130; INT CANR-17
Duca Minimo
See D'Annunzio, Gabriele
Ducharme, Rejean 1941- .... **CLC 74**
See also CA 165; DLB 60
Duclos, Charles Pinot 1704-1772 .... **LC 1**
Dudek, Louis 1918- .... **CLC 11, 19**
See also CA 45-48; CAAS 14; CANR 1; DLB 88
Duerrenmatt, Friedrich 1921-1990 **CLC 1, 4, 8, 11, 15, 43, 102; DAM DRAM**
See also CA 17-20R; CANR 33; DLB 69, 124; MTCW
Duffy, Bruce (?)- .... **CLC 50**
Duffy, Maureen 1933- .... **CLC 37**
See also CA 25-28R; CANR 33, 68; DLB 14; MTCW
Dugan, Alan 1923- .... **CLC 2, 6**
See also CA 81-84; DLB 5
du Gard, Roger Martin
See Martin du Gard, Roger
Duhamel, Georges 1884-1966 .... **CLC 8**
See also CA 81-84; 25-28R; CANR 35; DLB 65; MTCW
Dujardin, Edouard (Emile Louis) 1861-1949 **TCLC 13**
See also CA 109; DLB 123
Dulles, John Foster 1888-1959 .... **TCLC 72**
See also CA 115; 149
Dumas, Alexandre (Davy de la Pailleterie) 1802-1870 ... **NCLC 11; DA; DAB; DAC; DAM MST, NOV; WLC**
See also DLB 119, 192; SATA 18
Dumas, Alexandre 1824-1895 **NCLC 9; DC 1**
See also AAYA 22; DLB 192
Dumas, Claudine
See Malzberg, Barry N(athaniel)
Dumas, Henry L. 1934-1968 .... **CLC 6, 62**
See also BW 1; CA 85-88; DLB 41
du Maurier, Daphne 1907-1989**CLC 6, 11, 59; DAB; DAC; DAM MST, POP; SSC 18**
See also CA 5-8R; 128; CANR 6, 55; DLB 191; MTCW; SATA 27; SATA-Obit 60
Dunbar, Paul Laurence 1872-1906 . **TCLC 2, 12; BLC; DA; DAC; DAM MST, MULT, POET; PC 5; SSC 8; WLC**
See also BW 1; CA 104; 124; CDALB 1865-1917; DLB 50, 54, 78; SATA 34
Dunbar, William 1460(?)-1530(?) .... **LC 20**
See also DLB 132, 146
Duncan, Dora Angela
See Duncan, Isadora
Duncan, Isadora 1877(?)-1927 .... **TCLC 68**
See also CA 118; 149
Duncan, Lois 1934- .... **CLC 26**
See also AAYA 4; CA 1-4R; CANR 2, 23, 36;

CLR 29; JRDA; MAICYA; SAAS 2; SATA
1, 36, 75

Duncan, Robert (Edward) 1919-1988 **CLC 1,
2, 4, 7, 15, 41, 55; DAM POET; PC 2**
See also CA 9-12R; 124; CANR 28, 62; DLB
5, 16, 193; MTCW

Duncan, Sara Jeannette 1861-1922 **TCLC 60**
See also CA 157; DLB 92

Dunlap, William 1766-1839 .... **NCLC 2**
See also DLB 30, 37, 59

Dunn, Douglas (Eaglesham) 1942- **CLC 6, 40**
See also CA 45-48; CANR 2, 33; DLB 40;
MTCW

Dunn, Katherine (Karen) 1945- .... **CLC 71**
See also CA 33-36R

Dunn, Stephen 1939- .... **CLC 36**
See also CA 33-36R; CANR 12, 48, 53; DLB
105

Dunne, Finley Peter 1867-1936 ...... **TCLC 28**
See also CA 108; DLB 11, 23

Dunne, John Gregory 1932- .... **CLC 28**
See also CA 25-28R; CANR 14, 50; DLBY 80

Dunsany, Edward John Moreton Drax Plunkett
1878-1957
See Dunsany, Lord
See also CA 104; 148; DLB 10

Dunsany, Lord .... **TCLC 2, 59**
See also Dunsany, Edward John Moreton Drax
Plunkett
See also DLB 77, 153, 156

du Perry, Jean
See Simenon, Georges (Jacques Christian)

Durang, Christopher (Ferdinand) 1949- **C L C
27, 38**
See also CA 105; CANR 50

Duras, Marguerite 1914-1996 **CLC 3, 6, 11, 20,
34, 40, 68, 100**
See also CA 25-28R; 151; CANR 50; DLB 83;
MTCW

Durban, (Rosa) Pam 1947- .... **CLC 39**
See also CA 123

Durcan, Paul 1944- **CLC 43, 70; DAM POET**
See also CA 134

Durkheim, Emile 1858-1917 .... **TCLC 55**

Durrell, Lawrence (George) 1912-1990 **C L C
1, 4, 6, 8, 13, 27, 41; DAM NOV**
See also CA 9-12R; 132; CANR 40; CDBLB
1945-1960; DLB 15, 27; DLBY 90; MTCW

Durrenmatt, Friedrich
See Duerrenmatt, Friedrich

Dutt, Toru 1856-1877 .... **NCLC 29**

Dwight, Timothy 1752-1817 .... **NCLC 13**
See also DLB 37

Dworkin, Andrea 1946- .... **CLC 43**
See also CA 77-80; CAAS 21; CANR 16, 39;
INT CANR-16; MTCW

Dwyer, Deanna
See Koontz, Dean R(ay)

Dwyer, K. R.
See Koontz, Dean R(ay)

Dye, Richard
See De Voto, Bernard (Augustine)

Dylan, Bob 1941- .... **CLC 3, 4, 6, 12, 77**
See also CA 41-44R; DLB 16

Eagleton, Terence (Francis) 1943-
See Eagleton, Terry
See also CA 57-60; CANR 7, 23, 68; MTCW

Eagleton, Terry .... **CLC 63**
See also Eagleton, Terence (Francis)

Early, Jack
See Scoppettone, Sandra

East, Michael
See West, Morris L(anglo)

Eastaway, Edward
See Thomas, (Philip) Edward

Eastlake, William (Derry) 1917-1997 . **CLC 8**
See also CA 5-8R; 158; CAAS 1; CANR 5, 63;
DLB 6; INT CANR-5

Eastman, Charles A(lexander) 1858-1939
TCLC 55; DAM MULT
See also DLB 175; NNAL; YABC 1

Eberhart, Richard (Ghormley) 1904- **CLC 3,
11, 19, 56; DAM POET**
See also CA 1-4R; CANR 2; CDALB 1941-
1968; DLB 48; MTCW

Eberstadt, Fernanda 1960- .... **CLC 39**
See also CA 136

Echegaray (y Eizaguirre), Jose (Maria Waldo)
1832-1916 .... **TCLC 4**
See also CA 104; CANR 32; HW; MTCW

Echeverria, (Jose) Esteban (Antonino) 1805-
1851 .... **NCLC 18**

Echo
See Proust, (Valentin-Louis-George-Eugene-)
Marcel

Eckert, Allan W. 1931- .... **CLC 17**
See also AAYA 18; CA 13-16R; CANR 14, 45;
INT CANR-14; SAAS 21; SATA 29, 91;
SATA-Brief 27

Eckhart, Meister 1260(?)-1328(?) ... **CMLC 9**
See also DLB 115

Eckmar, F. R.
See de Hartog, Jan

Eco, Umberto 1932- **CLC 28, 60; DAM NOV,
POP**
See also BEST 90:1; CA 77-80; CANR 12, 33,
55; DLB 196; MTCW

Eddison, E(ric) R(ucker) 1882-1945 **TCLC 15**
See also CA 109; 156

Eddy, Mary (Morse) Baker 1821-1910 **T C L C
71**
See also CA 113

Edel, (Joseph) Leon 1907-1997 .. **CLC 29, 34**
See also CA 1-4R; 161; CANR 1, 22; DLB 103;
INT CANR-22

Eden, Emily 1797-1869 .... **NCLC 10**

Edgar, David 1948- ... **CLC 42; DAM DRAM**
See also CA 57-60; CANR 12, 61; DLB 13;
MTCW

Edgerton, Clyde (Carlyle) 1944- ...... **CLC 39**
See also AAYA 17; CA 118; 134; CANR 64;
INT 134

Edgeworth, Maria 1768-1849 .... **NCLC 1, 51**
See also DLB 116, 159, 163; SATA 21

Edmonds, Paul
See Kuttner, Henry

Edmonds, Walter D(umaux) 1903- ... **CLC 35**
See also CA 5-8R; CANR 2; DLB 9; MAICYA;
SAAS 4; SATA 1, 27

Edmondson, Wallace
See Ellison, Harlan (Jay)

Edson, Russell .... **CLC 13**
See also CA 33-36R

Edwards, Bronwen Elizabeth
See Rose, Wendy

Edwards, G(erald) B(asil) 1899-1976 **CLC 25**
See also CA 110

Edwards, Gus 1939- .... **CLC 43**
See also CA 108; INT 108

Edwards, Jonathan 1703-1758 ..... **LC 7; DA;
DAC; DAM MST**
See also DLB 24

Efron, Marina Ivanovna Tsvetaeva
See Tsvetaeva (Efron), Marina (Ivanovna)

Ehle, John (Marsden, Jr.) 1925- .... **CLC 27**
See also CA 9-12R

Ehrenbourg, Ilya (Grigoryevich)
See Ehrenburg, Ilya (Grigoryevich)

Ehrenburg, Ilya (Grigoryevich) 1891-1967
CLC 18, 34, 62
See also CA 102; 25-28R

Ehrenburg, Ilyo (Grigoryevich)
See Ehrenburg, Ilya (Grigoryevich)

Eich, Guenter 1907-1972 .... **CLC 15**
See also CA 111; 93-96; DLB 69, 124

Eichendorff, Joseph Freiherr von 1788-1857
NCLC 8
See also DLB 90

Eigner, Larry .... **CLC 9**
See also Eigner, Laurence (Joel)
See also CAAS 23; DLB 5

Eigner, Laurence (Joel) 1927-1996
See Eigner, Larry
See also CA 9-12R; 151; CANR 6; DLB 193

Einstein, Albert 1879-1955 .... **TCLC 65**
See also CA 121; 133; MTCW

Eiseley, Loren Corey 1907-1977 .... **CLC 7**
See also AAYA 5; CA 1-4R; 73-76; CANR 6

Eisenstadt, Jill 1963- .... **CLC 50**
See also CA 140

Eisenstein, Sergei (Mikhailovich) 1898-1948
TCLC 57
See also CA 114; 149

Eisner, Simon
See Kornbluth, C(yril) M.

Ekeloef, (Bengt) Gunnar 1907-1968 **CLC 27;
DAM POET**
See also CA 123; 25-28R

Ekelof, (Bengt) Gunnar
See Ekeloef, (Bengt) Gunnar

Ekelund, Vilhelm 1880-1949 .... **TCLC 75**

Ekwensi, C. O. D.
See Ekwensi, Cyprian (Odiatu Duaka)

Ekwensi, Cyprian (Odiatu Duaka) 1921- **CLC
4; BLC; DAM MULT**
See also BW 2; CA 29-32R; CANR 18, 42; DLB
117; MTCW; SATA 66

Elaine .... **TCLC 18**
See also Leverson, Ada

El Crummo
See Crumb, R(obert)

Elder, Lonne III 1931-1996 .... **DC 8**
See also BLC; BW 1; CA 81-84; 152; CANR
25; DAM MULT; DLB 7, 38, 44

Elia
See Lamb, Charles

Eliade, Mircea 1907-1986 .... **CLC 19**
See also CA 65-68; 119; CANR 30, 62; MTCW

Eliot, A. D.
See Jewett, (Theodora) Sarah Orne

Eliot, Alice
See Jewett, (Theodora) Sarah Orne

Eliot, Dan
See Silverberg, Robert

Eliot, George 1819-1880 **NCLC 4, 13, 23, 41,
49; DA; DAB; DAC; DAM MST, NOV; PC
20; WLC**
See also CDBLB 1832-1890; DLB 21, 35, 55

Eliot, John 1604-1690 .... **LC 5**
See also DLB 24

Eliot, T(homas) S(tearns) 1888-1965 **CLC 1, 2,
3, 6, 9, 10, 13, 15, 24, 34, 41, 55, 57; DA;
DAB; DAC; DAM DRAM, MST, POET;
PC 5; WLC 2**
See also CA 5-8R; 25-28R; CANR 41; CDALB
1929-1941; DLB 7, 10, 45, 63; DLBY 88;
MTCW

Elizabeth 1866-1941 .... **TCLC 41**

Elkin, Stanley L(awrence) 1930-1995 **CLC 4,**

6, 9, 14, 27, 51, 91; DAM NOV, POP; SSC 12
See also CA 9-12R; 148; CANR 8, 46; DLB 2, 28; DLBY 80; INT CANR-8; MTCW

Elledge, Scott .... **CLC 34**

Elliot, Don
See Silverberg, Robert

Elliott, Don
See Silverberg, Robert

Elliott, George P(aul) 1918-1980 .... **CLC 2**
See also CA 1-4R; 97-100; CANR 2

Elliott, Janice 1931- .... **CLC 47**
See also CA 13-16R; CANR 8, 29; DLB 14

Elliott, Sumner Locke 1917-1991 .... **CLC 38**
See also CA 5-8R; 134; CANR 2, 21

Elliott, William
See Bradbury, Ray (Douglas)

Ellis, A. E. .... **CLC 7**

Ellis, Alice Thomas .... **CLC 40**
See also Haycraft, Anna
See also DLB 194

Ellis, Bret Easton 1964- .. **CLC 39, 71; DAM POP**
See also AAYA 2; CA 118; 123; CANR 51; INT 123

Ellis, (Henry) Havelock 1859-1939 TCLC 14
See also CA 109; DLB 190

Ellis, Landon
See Ellison, Harlan (Jay)

Ellis, Trey 1962- .... **CLC 55**
See also CA 146

Ellison, Harlan (Jay) 1934- ... **CLC 1, 13, 42; DAM POP; SSC 14**
See also CA 5-8R; CANR 5, 46; DLB 8; INT CANR-5; MTCW

Ellison, Ralph (Waldo) 1914-1994 CLC 1, 3, 11, 54, 86; BLC; DA; DAB; DAC; DAM MST, MULT, NOV; SSC 26; WLC
See also AAYA 19; BW 1; CA 9-12R; 145; CANR 24, 53; CDALB 1941-1968; DLB 2, 76; DLBY 94; MTCW

Ellmann, Lucy (Elizabeth) 1956- ..... **CLC 61**
See also CA 128

Ellmann, Richard (David) 1918-1987CLC 50
See also BEST 89:2; CA 1-4R; 122; CANR 2, 28, 61; DLB 103; DLBY 87; MTCW

Elman, Richard (Martin) 1934-1997 CLC 19
See also CA 17-20R; 163; CAAS 3; CANR 47

Elron
See Hubbard, L(afayette) Ron(ald)

Eluard, Paul .... **TCLC 7, 41**
See also Grindel, Eugene

Elyot, Sir Thomas 1490(?)-1546 .... **LC 11**

Elytis, Odysseus 1911-1996 CLC 15, 49, 100; DAM POET; PC 21
See also CA 102; 151; MTCW

Emecheta, (Florence Onye) Buchi 1944-C L C 14, 48; BLC; DAM MULT
See also BW 2; CA 81-84; CANR 27; DLB 117; MTCW; SATA 66

Emerson, Mary Moody 1774-1863 NCLC 66

Emerson, Ralph Waldo 1803-1882 .NCLC 1, 38; DA; DAB; DAC; DAM MST, POET; PC 18; WLC
See also CDALB 1640-1865; DLB 1, 59, 73

Eminescu, Mihail 1850-1889 .... **NCLC 33**

Empson, William 1906-1984CLC 3, 8, 19, 33, 34
See also CA 17-20R; 112; CANR 31, 61; DLB 20; MTCW

Enchi Fumiko (Ueda) 1905-1986 ..... **CLC 31**
See also CA 129; 121

Ende, Michael (Andreas Helmuth) 1929-1995

CLC 31
See also CA 118; 124; 149; CANR 36; CLR 14; DLB 75; MAICYA; SATA 61; SATA-Brief 42; SATA-Obit 86

Endo, Shusaku 1923-1996 CLC 7, 14, 19, 54, 99; DAM NOV
See also CA 29-32R; 153; CANR 21, 54; DLB 182; MTCW

Engel, Marian 1933-1985 .... **CLC 36**
See also CA 25-28R; CANR 12; DLB 53; INT CANR-12

Engelhardt, Frederick
See Hubbard, L(afayette) Ron(ald)

Enright, D(ennis) J(oseph) 1920-CLC 4, 8, 31
See also CA 1-4R; CANR 1, 42; DLB 27; SATA 25

Enzensberger, Hans Magnus 1929- ..CLC 43
See also CA 116; 119

Ephron, Nora 1941- .... **CLC 17, 31**
See also AITN 2; CA 65-68; CANR 12, 39

Epicurus 341B.C.-270B.C. .... **CMLC 21**
See also DLB 176

Epsilon
See Betjeman, John

Epstein, Daniel Mark 1948- .... **CLC 7**
See also CA 49-52; CANR 2, 53

Epstein, Jacob 1956- .... **CLC 19**
See also CA 114

Epstein, Joseph 1937- .... **CLC 39**
See also CA 112; 119; CANR 50, 65

Epstein, Leslie 1938- .... **CLC 27**
See also CA 73-76; CAAS 12; CANR 23

Equiano, Olaudah 1745(?)-1797LC 16; BLC; DAM MULT
See also DLB 37, 50

ER .... **TCLC 33**
See also CA 160; DLB 85

Erasmus, Desiderius 1469(?)-1536 ..... **LC 16**

Erdman, Paul E(mil) 1932- .... **CLC 25**
See also AITN 1; CA 61-64; CANR 13, 43

Erdrich, Louise 1954- ..... CLC 39, 54; DAM MULT, NOV, POP
See also AAYA 10; BEST 89:1; CA 114; CANR 41, 62; DLB 152, 175; MTCW; NNAL; SATA 94

Erenburg, Ilya (Grigoryevich)
See Ehrenburg, Ilya (Grigoryevich)

Erickson, Stephen Michael 1950-
See Erickson, Steve
See also CA 129

Erickson, Steve 1950- .... **CLC 64**
See also Erickson, Stephen Michael
See also CANR 60, 68

Ericson, Walter
See Fast, Howard (Melvin)

Eriksson, Buntel
See Bergman, (Ernst) Ingmar

Ernaux, Annie 1940- .... **CLC 88**
See also CA 147

Eschenbach, Wolfram von
See Wolfram von Eschenbach

Eseki, Bruno
See Mphahlele, Ezekiel

Esenin, Sergei (Alexandrovich) 1895-1925 TCLC 4
See also CA 104

Eshleman, Clayton 1935- .... **CLC 7**
See also CA 33-36R; CAAS 6; DLB 5

Espriella, Don Manuel Alvarez
See Southey, Robert

Espriu, Salvador 1913-1985 .... **CLC 9**
See also CA 154; 115; DLB 134

Espronceda, Jose de 1808-1842 ..... **NCLC 39**

Esse, James
See Stephens, James

Esterbrook, Tom
See Hubbard, L(afayette) Ron(ald)

Estleman, Loren D. 1952-CLC 48; DAM NOV, POP
See also CA 85-88; CANR 27; INT CANR-27; MTCW

Euclid 306B.C.-283B.C. .... **CMLC 25**

Eugenides, Jeffrey 1960(?)- .... **CLC 81**
See also CA 144

Euripides c. 485B.C.-406B.C.CMLC 23; DA; DAB; DAC; DAM DRAM, MST; DC 4; WLCS
See also DLB 176

Evan, Evin
See Faust, Frederick (Schiller)

Evans, Evan
See Faust, Frederick (Schiller)

Evans, Marian
See Eliot, George

Evans, Mary Ann
See Eliot, George

Evarts, Esther
See Benson, Sally

Everett, Percival L. 1956- .... **CLC 57**
See also BW 2; CA 129

Everson, R(onald) G(ilmour) 1903-. CLC 27
See also CA 17-20R; DLB 88

Everson, William (Oliver) 1912-1994 CLC 1, 5, 14
See also CA 9-12R; 145; CANR 20; DLB 5, 16; MTCW

Evtushenko, Evgenii Aleksandrovich
See Yevtushenko, Yevgeny (Alexandrovich)

Ewart, Gavin (Buchanan) 1916-1995CLC 13, 46
See also CA 89-92; 150; CANR 17, 46; DLB 40; MTCW

Ewers, Hanns Heinz 1871-1943 ..... **TCLC 12**
See also CA 109; 149

Ewing, Frederick R.
See Sturgeon, Theodore (Hamilton)

Exley, Frederick (Earl) 1929-1992 CLC 6, 11
See also AITN 2; CA 81-84; 138; DLB 143; DLBY 81

Eynhardt, Guillermo
See Quiroga, Horacio (Sylvestre)

Ezekiel, Nissim 1924- .... **CLC 61**
See also CA 61-64

Ezekiel, Tish O'Dowd 1943- .... **CLC 34**
See also CA 129

Fadeyev, A.
See Bulgya, Alexander Alexandrovich

Fadeyev, Alexander .... **TCLC 53**
See also Bulgya, Alexander Alexandrovich

Fagen, Donald 1948- .... **CLC 26**

Fainzilberg, Ilya Arnoldovich 1897-1937
See Ilf, Ilya
See also CA 120; 165

Fair, Ronald L. 1932- .... **CLC 18**
See also BW 1; CA 69-72; CANR 25; DLB 33

Fairbairn, Roger
See Carr, John Dickson

Fairbairns, Zoe (Ann) 1948- .... **CLC 32**
See also CA 103; CANR 21

Falco, Gian
See Papini, Giovanni

Falconer, James
See Kirkup, James

Falconer, Kenneth
See Kornbluth, C(yril) M.

Falkland, Samuel

See Heijermans, Herman

Fallaci, Oriana 1930- ....**CLC 11**
See also CA 77-80; CANR 15, 58; MTCW

Faludy, George 1913-........................**CLC 42**
See also CA 21-24R

Faludy, Gyoergy
See Faludy, George

Fanon, Frantz 1925-1961**CLC 74; BLC; DAM
MULT**
See also BW 1; CA 116; 89-92

Fanshawe, Ann 1625-1680 ....**LC 11**

Fante, John (Thomas) 1911-1983 .... **CLC 60**
See also CA 69-72; 109; CANR 23; DLB 130;
DLBY 83

Farah, Nuruddin 1945- **CLC 53; BLC; DAM
MULT**
See also BW 2; CA 106; DLB 125

Fargue, Leon-Paul 1876(?)-1947 ... **TCLC 11**
See also CA 109

Farigoule, Louis
See Romains, Jules

Farina, Richard 1936(?)-1966 ....**CLC 9**
See also CA 81-84; 25-28R

Farley, Walter (Lorimer) 1915-1989 **CLC 17**
See also CA 17-20R; CANR 8, 29; DLB 22;
JRDA; MAICYA; SATA 2, 43

Farmer, Philip Jose 1918- .... **CLC 1, 19**
See also CA 1-4R; CANR 4, 35; DLB 8;
MTCW; SATA 93

Farquhar, George 1677-1707 ... **LC 21; DAM
DRAM**
See also DLB 84

Farrell, J(ames) G(ordon) 1935-1979 **CLC 6**
See also CA 73-76; 89-92; CANR 36; DLB 14;
MTCW

Farrell, James T(homas) 1904-1979**CLC 1, 4,
8, 11, 66; SSC 28**
See also CA 5-8R; 89-92; CANR 9, 61; DLB 4,
9, 86; DLBD 2; MTCW

Farren, Richard J.
See Betjeman, John

Farren, Richard M.
See Betjeman, John

Fassbinder, Rainer Werner 1946-1982**CLC 20**
See also CA 93-96; 106; CANR 31

Fast, Howard (Melvin) 1914- **CLC 23; DAM
NOV**
See also AAYA 16; CA 1-4R; CAAS 18; CANR
1, 33, 54; DLB 9; INT CANR-33; SATA 7

Faulcon, Robert
See Holdstock, Robert P.

Faulkner, William (Cuthbert) 1897-1962**CLC
1, 3, 6, 8, 9, 11, 14, 18, 28, 52, 68; DA; DAB;
DAC; DAM MST, NOV; SSC 1; WLC**
See also AAYA 7; CA 81-84; CANR 33;
CDALB 1929-1941; DLB 9, 11, 44, 102;
DLBD 2; DLBY 86, 97; MTCW

Fauset, Jessie Redmon 1884(?)-1961**CLC 19,
54; BLC; DAM MULT**
See also BW 1; CA 109; DLB 51

Faust, Frederick (Schiller) 1892-1944(?)
TCLC 49; DAM POP
See also CA 108; 152

Faust, Irvin 1924- ....**CLC 8**
See also CA 33-36R; CANR 28, 67; DLB 2,
28; DLBY 80

Fawkes, Guy
See Benchley, Robert (Charles)

Fearing, Kenneth (Flexner) 1902-1961 .**C L C
51**
See also CA 93-96; CANR 59; DLB 9

Fecamps, Elise
See Creasey, John

Federman, Raymond 1928- .... **CLC 6, 47**
See also CA 17-20R; CAAS 8; CANR 10, 43;
DLBY 80

Federspiel, J(uerg) F. 1931-...............**CLC 42**
See also CA 146

Feiffer, Jules (Ralph) 1929- ..... **CLC 2, 8, 64;
DAM DRAM**
See also AAYA 3; CA 17-20R; CANR 30, 59;
DLB 7, 44; INT CANR-30; MTCW; SATA
8, 61

Feige, Hermann Albert Otto Maximilian
See Traven, B.

Feinberg, David B. 1956-1994 ....**CLC 59**
See also CA 135; 147

Feinstein, Elaine 1930-.......................**CLC 36**
See also CA 69-72; CAAS 1; CANR 31, 68;
DLB 14, 40; MTCW

Feldman, Irving (Mordecai) 1928- .....**CLC 7**
See also CA 1-4R; CANR 1; DLB 169

Felix-Tchicaya, Gerald
See Tchicaya, Gerald Felix

Fellini, Federico 1920-1993 .... **CLC 16, 85**
See also CA 65-68; 143; CANR 33

Felsen, Henry Gregor 1916- ....**CLC 17**
See also CA 1-4R; CANR 1; SAAS 2; SATA 1

Fenno, Jack
See Calisher, Hortense

Fenton, James Martin 1949- ....**CLC 32**
See also CA 102; DLB 40

Ferber, Edna 1887-1968 .... **CLC 18, 93**
See also AITN 1; CA 5-8R; 25-28R; CANR 68;
DLB 9, 28, 86; MTCW; SATA 7

Ferguson, Helen
See Kavan, Anna

Ferguson, Samuel 1810-1886 ....**NCLC 33**
See also DLB 32

Fergusson, Robert 1750-1774 .... **LC 29**
See also DLB 109

Ferling, Lawrence
See Ferlinghetti, Lawrence (Monsanto)

Ferlinghetti, Lawrence (Monsanto) 1919(?)-
CLC 2, 6, 10, 27; DAM POET; PC 1
See also CA 5-8R; CANR 3, 41; CDALB 1941-
1968; DLB 5, 16; MTCW

Fernandez, Vicente Garcia Huidobro
See Huidobro Fernandez, Vicente Garcia

Ferrer, Gabriel (Francisco Victor) Miro
See Miro (Ferrer), Gabriel (Francisco Victor)

Ferrier, Susan (Edmonstone) 1782-1854
NCLC 8
See also DLB 116

Ferrigno, Robert 1948(?)-..................**CLC 65**
See also CA 140

Ferron, Jacques 1921-1985 ....**CLC 94; DAC**
See also CA 117; 129; DLB 60

Feuchtwanger, Lion 1884-1958 ....**TCLC 3**
See also CA 104; DLB 66

Feuillet, Octave 1821-1890 ....**NCLC 45**
See also DLB 192

Feydeau, Georges (Leon Jules Marie) 1862-
1921 ....**TCLC 22; DAM DRAM**
See also CA 113; 152; DLB 192

Fichte, Johann Gottlieb 1762-1814 **NCLC 62**
See also DLB 90

Ficino, Marsilio 1433-1499 .... **LC 12**

Fiedeler, Hans
See Doeblin, Alfred

Fiedler, Leslie A(aron) 1917- . **CLC 4, 13, 24**
See also CA 9-12R; CANR 7, 63; DLB 28, 67;
MTCW

Field, Andrew 1938-..........................**CLC 44**
See also CA 97-100; CANR 25

Field, Eugene 1850-1895 ....**NCLC 3**
See also DLB 23, 42, 140; DLBD 13; MAICYA;
SATA 16

Field, Gans T.
See Wellman, Manly Wade

Field, Michael ....**TCLC 43**

Field, Peter
See Hobson, Laura Z(ametkin)

Fielding, Henry 1707-1754 **LC 1; DA; DAB;
DAC; DAM DRAM, MST, NOV; WLC**
See also CDBLB 1660-1789; DLB 39, 84, 101

Fielding, Sarah 1710-1768 .... **LC 1**
See also DLB 39

Fierstein, Harvey (Forbes) 1954- .... **CLC 33;
DAM DRAM, POP**
See also CA 123; 129

Figes, Eva 1932-.................................**CLC 31**
See also CA 53-56; CANR 4, 44; DLB 14

Finch, Anne 1661-1720 .... **LC 3; PC 21**
See also DLB 95

Finch, Robert (Duer Claydon) 1900- **CLC 18**
See also CA 57-60; CANR 9, 24, 49; DLB 88

Findley, Timothy 1930- . **CLC 27, 102; DAC;
DAM MST**
See also CA 25-28R; CANR 12, 42; DLB 53

Fink, William
See Mencken, H(enry) L(ouis)

Firbank, Louis 1942-
See Reed, Lou
See also CA 117

Firbank, (Arthur Annesley) Ronald 1886-1926
TCLC 1
See also CA 104; DLB 36

Fisher, M(ary) F(rances) K(ennedy) 1908-1992
CLC 76, 87
See also CA 77-80; 138; CANR 44

Fisher, Roy 1930-................................**CLC 25**
See also CA 81-84; CAAS 10; CANR 16; DLB
40

Fisher, Rudolph 1897-1934 . **TCLC 11; BLC;
DAM MULT; SSC 25**
See also BW 1; CA 107; 124; DLB 51, 102

Fisher, Vardis (Alvero) 1895-1968 ......**CLC 7**
See also CA 5-8R; 25-28R; CANR 68; DLB 9

Fiske, Tarleton
See Bloch, Robert (Albert)

Fitch, Clarke
See Sinclair, Upton (Beall)

Fitch, John IV
See Cormier, Robert (Edmund)

Fitzgerald, Captain Hugh
See Baum, L(yman) Frank

FitzGerald, Edward 1809-1883 ....**NCLC 9**
See also DLB 32

Fitzgerald, F(rancis) Scott (Key) 1896-1940
**TCLC 1, 6, 14, 28, 55; DA; DAB; DAC;
DAM MST, NOV; SSC 6; WLC**
See also AAYA 24; AITN 1; CA 110; 123;
CDALB 1917-1929; DLB 4, 9, 86; DLBD 1,
15, 16; DLBY 81, 96; MTCW

Fitzgerald, Penelope 1916- ... **CLC 19, 51, 61**
See also CA 85-88; CAAS 10; CANR 56; DLB
14, 194

Fitzgerald, Robert (Stuart) 1910-1985**CLC 39**
See also CA 1-4R; 114; CANR 1; DLBY 80

FitzGerald, Robert D(avid) 1902-1987**CLC 19**
See also CA 17-20R

Fitzgerald, Zelda (Sayre) 1900-1948**TCLC 52**
See also CA 117; 126; DLBY 84

Flanagan, Thomas (James Bonner) 1923-
CLC 25, 52
See also CA 108; CANR 55; DLBY 80; INT
108; MTCW

Flaubert, Gustave 1821-1880**NCLC 2, 10, 19,**

62, 66; DA; DAB; DAC; DAM MST, NOV;
SSC 11; WLC
See also DLB 119

Flecker, Herman Elroy
See Flecker, (Herman) James Elroy

Flecker, (Herman) James Elroy 1884-1915
TCLC 43
See also CA 109; 150; DLB 10, 19

Fleming, Ian (Lancaster) 1908-1964 **CLC 3,
30; DAM POP**
See also CA 5-8R; CANR 59; CDBLB 1945-
1960; DLB 87; MTCW; SATA 9

Fleming, Thomas (James) 1927- ...... **CLC 37**
See also CA 5-8R; CANR 10; INT CANR-10;
SATA 8

Fletcher, John 1579-1625 .... **LC 33; DC 6**
See also CDBLB Before 1660; DLB 58

Fletcher, John Gould 1886-1950 .... **TCLC 35**
See also CA 107; DLB 4, 45

Fleur, Paul
See Pohl, Frederik

Flooglebuckle, Al
See Spiegelman, Art

Flying Officer X
See Bates, H(erbert) E(rnest)

Fo, Dario 1926- . **CLC 32, 109; DAM DRAM**
See also CA 116; 128; CANR 68; DLBY 97;
MTCW

Fogarty, Jonathan Titulescu Esq.
See Farrell, James T(homas)

Folke, Will
See Bloch, Robert (Albert)

Follett, Ken(neth Martin) 1949- ..... **CLC 18;
DAM NOV, POP**
See also AAYA 6; BEST 89:4; CA 81-84; CANR
13, 33, 54; DLB 87; DLBY 81; INT CANR-
33; MTCW

Fontane, Theodor 1819-1898 .... **NCLC 26**
See also DLB 129

Foote, Horton 1916-**CLC 51, 91; DAM DRAM**
See also CA 73-76; CANR 34, 51; DLB 26; INT
CANR-34

Foote, Shelby 1916-**CLC 75; DAM NOV, POP**
See also CA 5-8R; CANR 3, 45; DLB 2, 17

Forbes, Esther 1891-1967 .... **CLC 12**
See also AAYA 17; CA 13-14; 25-28R; CAP 1;
CLR 27; DLB 22; JRDA; MAICYA; SATA 2

Forche, Carolyn (Louise) 1950- **CLC 25, 83,
86; DAM POET; PC 10**
See also CA 109; 117; CANR 50; DLB 5, 193;
INT 117

Ford, Elbur
See Hibbert, Eleanor Alice Burford

Ford, Ford Madox 1873-1939**TCLC 1, 15, 39,
57; DAM NOV**
See also CA 104; 132; CDBLB 1914-1945;
DLB 162; MTCW

Ford, Henry 1863-1947 .... **TCLC 73**
See also CA 115; 148

Ford, John 1586-(?) .... **DC 8**
See also CDBLB Before 1660; DAM DRAM;
DLB 58

Ford, John 1895-1973 .... **CLC 16**
See also CA 45-48

Ford, Richard .... **CLC 99**

Ford, Richard 1944- .... **CLC 46**
See also CA 69-72; CANR 11, 47

Ford, Webster
See Masters, Edgar Lee

Foreman, Richard 1937-.................. **CLC 50**
See also CA 65-68; CANR 32, 63

Forester, C(ecil) S(cott) 1899-1966 .. **CLC 35**
See also CA 73-76; 25-28R; DLB 191; SATA

13

Forez
See Mauriac, Francois (Charles)

Forman, James Douglas 1932- .... **CLC 21**
See also AAYA 17; CA 9-12R; CANR 4, 19,
42; JRDA; MAICYA; SATA 8, 70

Fornes, Maria Irene 1930-.......... **CLC 39, 61**
See also CA 25-28R; CANR 28; DLB 7; HW;
INT CANR-28; MTCW

Forrest, Leon (Richard) 1937-1997 .... **CLC 4**
See also BW 2; CA 89-92; 162; CAAS 7; CANR
25, 52; DLB 33

Forster, E(dward) M(organ) 1879-1970 C L C
**1, 2, 3, 4, 9, 10, 13, 15, 22, 45, 77; DA; DAB;
DAC; DAM MST, NOV; SSC 27; WLC**
See also AAYA 2; CA 13-14; 25-28R; CANR
45; CAP 1; CDBLB 1914-1945; DLB 34, 98,
162, 178, 195; DLBD 10; MTCW; SATA 57

Forster, John 1812-1876 .... **NCLC 11**
See also DLB 144, 184

Forsyth, Frederick 1938-**CLC 2, 5, 36; DAM
NOV, POP**
See also BEST 89:4; CA 85-88; CANR 38, 62;
DLB 87; MTCW

Forten, Charlotte L. .... **TCLC 16; BLC**
See also Grimke, Charlotte L(ottie) Forten
See also DLB 50

Foscolo, Ugo 1778-1827 .... **NCLC 8**

Fosse, Bob ....**CLC 20**
See also Fosse, Robert Louis

Fosse, Robert Louis 1927-1987
See Fosse, Bob
See also CA 110; 123

Foster, Stephen Collins 1826-1864 **NCLC 26**

Foucault, Michel 1926-1984 . **CLC 31, 34, 69**
See also CA 105; 113; CANR 34; MTCW

Fouque, Friedrich (Heinrich Karl) de la Motte
1777-1843 .... **NCLC 2**
See also DLB 90

Fourier, Charles 1772-1837 .... **NCLC 51**

Fournier, Henri Alban 1886-1914
See Alain-Fournier
See also CA 104

Fournier, Pierre 1916- .... **CLC 11**
See also Gascar, Pierre
See also CA 89-92; CANR 16, 40

Fowles, John 1926-**CLC 1, 2, 3, 4, 6, 9, 10, 15,
33, 87; DAB; DAC; DAM MST**
See also CA 5-8R; CANR 25; CDBLB 1960 to
Present; DLB 14, 139; MTCW; SATA 22

Fox, Paula 1923- .... **CLC 2, 8**
See also AAYA 3; CA 73-76; CANR 20, 36,
62; CLR 1, 44; DLB 52; JRDA; MAICYA;
MTCW; SATA 17, 60

Fox, William Price (Jr.) 1926- .... **CLC 22**
See also CA 17-20R; CAAS 19; CANR 11; DLB
2; DLBY 81

Foxe, John 1516(?)-1587 .... **LC 14**

Frame, Janet 1924-**CLC 2, 3, 6, 22, 66, 96; SSC
29**
See also Clutha, Janet Paterson Frame

France, Anatole .... **TCLC 9**
See also Thibault, Jacques Anatole Francois
See also DLB 123

Francis, Claude 19(?)-........................ **CLC 50**

Francis, Dick 1920-**CLC 2, 22, 42, 102; DAM
POP**
See also AAYA 5, 21; BEST 89:3; CA 5-8R;
CANR 9, 42, 68; CDBLB 1960 to Present;
DLB 87; INT CANR-9; MTCW

Francis, Robert (Churchill) 1901-1987 . C L C
15
See also CA 1-4R; 123; CANR 1

Frank, Anne(lies Marie) 1929-1945**TCLC 17;
DA; DAB; DAC; DAM MST; WLC**
See also AAYA 12; CA 113; 133; CANR 68;
MTCW; SATA 87; SATA-Brief 42

Frank, Elizabeth 1945- .... **CLC 39**
See also CA 121; 126; INT 126

Frankl, Viktor E(mil) 1905-1997 ..... **CLC 93**
See also CA 65-68; 161

Franklin, Benjamin
See Hasek, Jaroslav (Matej Frantisek)

Franklin, Benjamin 1706-1790 .. **LC 25; DA;
DAB; DAC; DAM MST; WLCS**
See also CDALB 1640-1865; DLB 24, 43, 73

Franklin, (Stella Maria Sarah) Miles 1879-1954
TCLC 7
See also CA 104; 164

Fraser, (Lady) Antonia (Pakenham) 1932-
CLC 32, 107
See also CA 85-88; CANR 44, 65; MTCW;
SATA-Brief 32

Fraser, George MacDonald 1925- ......**CLC 7**
See also CA 45-48; CANR 2, 48

Fraser, Sylvia 1935- .... **CLC 64**
See also CA 45-48; CANR 1, 16, 60

Frayn, Michael 1933-**CLC 3, 7, 31, 47; DAM
DRAM, NOV**
See also CA 5-8R; CANR 30; DLB 13, 14, 194;
MTCW

Fraze, Candida (Merrill) 1945- .... **CLC 50**
See also CA 126

Frazer, J(ames) G(eorge) 1854-1941**TCLC 32**
See also CA 118

Frazer, Robert Caine
See Creasey, John

Frazer, Sir James George
See Frazer, J(ames) G(eorge)

Frazier, Charles 1950- .... **CLC 109**
See also CA 161

Frazier, Ian 1951- .... **CLC 46**
See also CA 130; CANR 54

Frederic, Harold 1856-1898 .... **NCLC 10**
See also DLB 12, 23; DLBD 13

Frederick, John
See Faust, Frederick (Schiller)

Frederick the Great 1712-1786 .... **LC 14**

Fredro, Aleksander 1793-1876 .... **NCLC 8**

Freeling, Nicolas 1927- .... **CLC 38**
See also CA 49-52; CAAS 12; CANR 1, 17,
50; DLB 87

Freeman, Douglas Southall 1886-1953**T C L C
11**
See also CA 109; DLB 17

Freeman, Judith 1946- .... **CLC 55**
See also CA 148

Freeman, Mary Eleanor Wilkins 1852-1930
TCLC 9; SSC 1
See also CA 106; DLB 12, 78

Freeman, R(ichard) Austin 1862-1943 **T C L C
21**
See also CA 113; DLB 70

French, Albert 1943- .... **CLC 86**

French, Marilyn 1929-**CLC 10, 18, 60; DAM
DRAM, NOV, POP**
See also CA 69-72; CANR 3, 31; INT CANR-
31; MTCW

French, Paul
See Asimov, Isaac

Freneau, Philip Morin 1752-1832 ....**NCLC 1**
See also DLB 37, 43

Freud, Sigmund 1856-1939 .... **TCLC 52**
See also CA 115; 133; MTCW

Friedan, Betty (Naomi) 1921- .... **CLC 74**
See also CA 65-68; CANR 18, 45; MTCW

Friedlander, Saul 1932- .... **CLC 90**
See also CA 117; 130
Friedman, B(ernard) H(arper) 1926- . **CLC 7**
See also CA 1-4R; CANR 3, 48
Friedman, Bruce Jay 1930- ...... **CLC 3, 5, 56**
See also CA 9-12R; CANR 25, 52; DLB 2, 28;
INT CANR-25
Friel, Brian 1929- .... **CLC 5, 42, 59; DC 8**
See also CA 21-24R; CANR 33; DLB 13;
MTCW
Friis-Baastad, Babbis Ellinor 1921-1970**CLC 12**
See also CA 17-20R; 134; SATA 7
Frisch, Max (Rudolf) 1911-1991**CLC 3, 9, 14, 18, 32, 44; DAM DRAM, NOV**
See also CA 85-88; 134; CANR 32; DLB 69, 124; MTCW
Fromentin, Eugene (Samuel Auguste) 1820-1876 ....**NCLC 10**
See also DLB 123
Frost, Frederick
See Faust, Frederick (Schiller)
Frost, Robert (Lee) 1874-1963**CLC 1, 3, 4, 9, 10, 13, 15, 26, 34, 44; DA; DAB; DAC; DAM MST, POET; PC 1; WLC**
See also AAYA 21; CA 89-92; CANR 33;
CDALB 1917-1929; DLB 54; DLBD 7;
MTCW; SATA 14
Froude, James Anthony 1818-1894**NCLC 43**
See also DLB 18, 57, 144
Froy, Herald
See Waterhouse, Keith (Spencer)
Fry, Christopher 1907- **CLC 2, 10, 14; DAM DRAM**
See also CA 17-20R; CAAS 23; CANR 9, 30;
DLB 13; MTCW; SATA 66
Frye, (Herman) Northrop 1912-1991**CLC 24, 70**
See also CA 5-8R; 133; CANR 8, 37; DLB 67, 68; MTCW
Fuchs, Daniel 1909-1993 .... **CLC 8, 22**
See also CA 81-84; 142; CAAS 5; CANR 40;
DLB 9, 26, 28; DLBY 93
Fuchs, Daniel 1934- .... **CLC 34**
See also CA 37-40R; CANR 14, 48
Fuentes, Carlos 1928-**CLC 3, 8, 10, 13, 22, 41, 60; DA; DAB; DAC; DAM MST, MULT, NOV; HLC; SSC 24; WLC**
See also AAYA 4; AITN 2; CA 69-72; CANR
10, 32, 68; DLB 113; HW; MTCW
Fuentes, Gregorio Lopez y
See Lopez y Fuentes, Gregorio
Fugard, (Harold) Athol 1932-**CLC 5, 9, 14, 25, 40, 80; DAM DRAM; DC 3**
See also AAYA 17; CA 85-88; CANR 32, 54;
MTCW
Fugard, Sheila 1932- .... **CLC 48**
See also CA 125
Fuller, Charles (H., Jr.) 1939-**CLC 25; BLC; DAM DRAM, MULT; DC 1**
See also BW 2; CA 108; 112; DLB 38; INT 112;
MTCW
Fuller, John (Leopold) 1937- .... **CLC 62**
See also CA 21-24R; CANR 9, 44; DLB 40
Fuller, Margaret .... **NCLC 5, 50**
See also Ossoli, Sarah Margaret (Fuller
marchesa d')
Fuller, Roy (Broadbent) 1912-1991**CLC 4, 28**
See also CA 5-8R; 135; CAAS 10; CANR 53;
DLB 15, 20; SATA 87
Fulton, Alice 1952- .... **CLC 52**
See also CA 116; CANR 57; DLB 193
Furphy, Joseph 1843-1912 .... **TCLC 25**

See also CA 163
Fussell, Paul 1924-..........................**CLC 74**
See also BEST 90:1; CA 17-20R; CANR 8, 21, 35; INT CANR-21; MTCW
Futabatei, Shimei 1864-1909 .... **TCLC 44**
See also CA 162; DLB 180
Futrelle, Jacques 1875-1912 .... **TCLC 19**
See also CA 113; 155
Gaboriau, Emile 1835-1873 .... **NCLC 14**
Gadda, Carlo Emilio 1893-1973 .... **CLC 11**
See also CA 89-92; DLB 177
Gaddis, William 1922- **CLC 1, 3, 6, 8, 10, 19, 43, 86**
See also CA 17-20R; CANR 21, 48; DLB 2;
MTCW
Gage, Walter
See Inge, William (Motter)
Gaines, Ernest J(ames) 1933- **CLC 3, 11, 18, 86; BLC; DAM MULT**
See also AAYA 18; AITN 1; BW 2; CA 9-12R;
CANR 6, 24, 42; CDALB 1968-1988; DLB
2, 33, 152; DLBY 80; MTCW; SATA 86
Gaitskill, Mary 1954- .... **CLC 69**
See also CA 128; CANR 61
Galdos, Benito Perez
See Perez Galdos, Benito
Gale, Zona 1874-1938**TCLC 7; DAM DRAM**
See also CA 105; 153; DLB 9, 78
Galeano, Eduardo (Hughes) 1940- ... **CLC 72**
See also CA 29-32R; CANR 13, 32; HW
Galiano, Juan Valera y Alcala
See Valera y Alcala-Galiano, Juan
Gallagher, Tess 1943- .... **CLC 18, 63; DAM POET; PC 9**
See also CA 106; DLB 120
Gallant, Mavis 1922- ... **CLC 7, 18, 38; DAC; DAM MST; SSC 5**
See also CA 69-72; CANR 29; DLB 53; MTCW
Gallant, Roy A(rthur) 1924- .... **CLC 17**
See also CA 5-8R; CANR 4, 29, 54; CLR 30;
MAICYA; SATA 4, 68
Gallico, Paul (William) 1897-1976 ..... **CLC 2**
See also AITN 1; CA 5-8R; 69-72; CANR 23;
DLB 9, 171; MAICYA; SATA 13
Gallo, Max Louis 1932- .... **CLC 95**
See also CA 85-88
Gallois, Lucien
See Desnos, Robert
Gallup, Ralph
See Whitemore, Hugh (John)
Galsworthy, John 1867-1933**TCLC 1, 45; DA; DAB; DAC; DAM DRAM, MST, NOV; SSC 22; WLC 2**
See also CA 104; 141; CDBLB 1890-1914;
DLB 10, 34, 98, 162; DLBD 16
Galt, John 1779-1839 .... **NCLC 1**
See also DLB 99, 116, 159
Galvin, James 1951- .... **CLC 38**
See also CA 108; CANR 26
Gamboa, Federico 1864-1939 .... **TCLC 36**
Gandhi, M. K.
See Gandhi, Mohandas Karamchand
Gandhi, Mahatma
See Gandhi, Mohandas Karamchand
Gandhi, Mohandas Karamchand 1869-1948
TCLC 59; DAM MULT
See also CA 121; 132; MTCW
Gann, Ernest Kellogg 1910-1991 ...... **CLC 23**
See also AITN 1; CA 1-4R; 136; CANR 1
Garcia, Cristina 1958- .... **CLC 76**
See also CA 141
Garcia Lorca, Federico 1898-1936**TCLC 1, 7, 49; DA; DAB; DAC; DAM DRAM, MST,**

MULT, POET; DC 2; HLC; PC 3; WLC
See also CA 104; 131; DLB 108; HW; MTCW
Garcia Marquez, Gabriel (Jose) 1928-**CLC 2, 3, 8, 10, 15, 27, 47, 55, 68; DA; DAB; DAC; DAM MST, MULT, NOV, POP; HLC; SSC 8; WLC**
See also AAYA 3; BEST 89:1, 90:4; CA 33-36R; CANR 10, 28, 50; DLB 113; HW;
MTCW
Gard, Janice
See Latham, Jean Lee
Gard, Roger Martin du
See Martin du Gard, Roger
Gardam, Jane 1928-..........................**CLC 43**
See also CA 49-52; CANR 2, 18, 33, 54; CLR
12; DLB 14, 161; MAICYA; MTCW; SAAS
9; SATA 39, 76; SATA-Brief 28
Gardner, Herb(ert) 1934- .... **CLC 44**
See also CA 149
Gardner, John (Champlin), Jr. 1933-1982
CLC 2, 3, 5, 7, 8, 10, 18, 28, 34; DAM NOV, POP; SSC 7
See also AITN 1; CA 65-68; 107; CANR 33;
DLB 2; DLBY 82; MTCW; SATA 40; SATA-Obit 31
Gardner, John (Edmund) 1926-**CLC 30; DAM POP**
See also CA 103; CANR 15; MTCW
Gardner, Miriam
See Bradley, Marion Zimmer
Gardner, Noel
See Kuttner, Henry
Gardons, S. S.
See Snodgrass, W(illiam) D(e Witt)
Garfield, Leon 1921-1996 .... **CLC 12**
See also AAYA 8; CA 17-20R; 152; CANR 38,
41; CLR 21; DLB 161; JRDA; MAICYA;
SATA 1, 32, 76; SATA-Obit 90
Garland, (Hannibal) Hamlin 1860-1940
TCLC 3; SSC 18
See also CA 104; DLB 12, 71, 78, 186
Garneau, (Hector de) Saint-Denys 1912-1943
TCLC 13
See also CA 111; DLB 88
Garner, Alan 1934-**CLC 17; DAB; DAM POP**
See also AAYA 18; CA 73-76; CANR 15, 64;
CLR 20; DLB 161; MAICYA; MTCW; SATA
18, 69
Garner, Hugh 1913-1979 .... **CLC 13**
See also CA 69-72; CANR 31; DLB 68
Garnett, David 1892-1981 .... **CLC 3**
See also CA 5-8R; 103; CANR 17; DLB 34
Garos, Stephanie
See Katz, Steve
Garrett, George (Palmer) 1929-**CLC 3, 11, 51; SSC 30**
See also CA 1-4R; CAAS 5; CANR 1, 42, 67;
DLB 2, 5, 130, 152; DLBY 83
Garrick, David 1717-1779 ....**LC 15; DAM DRAM**
See also DLB 84
Garrigue, Jean 1914-1972 .... **CLC 2, 8**
See also CA 5-8R; 37-40R; CANR 20
Garrison, Frederick
See Sinclair, Upton (Beall)
Garth, Will
See Hamilton, Edmond; Kuttner, Henry
Garvey, Marcus (Moziah, Jr.) 1887-1940
TCLC 41; BLC; DAM MULT
See also BW 1; CA 120; 124
Gary, Romain ....**CLC 25**
See also Kacew, Romain
See also DLB 83

Gascar, Pierre ....CLC 11
  See also Fournier, Pierre
Gascoyne, David (Emery) 1916- ...... CLC 45
  See also CA 65-68; CANR 10, 28, 54; DLB 20;
  MTCW
Gaskell, Elizabeth Cleghorn 1810-1865NCLC
  5; DAB; DAM MST; SSC 25
  See also CDBLB 1832-1890; DLB 21, 144, 159
Gass, William H(oward) 1924-CLC 1, 2, 8, 11,
  15, 39; SSC 12
  See also CA 17-20R; CANR 30; DLB 2; MTCW
Gasset, Jose Ortega y
  See Ortega y Gasset, Jose
Gates, Henry Louis, Jr. 1950- CLC 65; DAM
  MULT
  See also BW 2; CA 109; CANR 25, 53; DLB
  67
Gautier, Theophile 1811-1872 .. NCLC 1, 59;
  DAM POET; PC 18; SSC 20
  See also DLB 119
Gawsworth, John
  See Bates, H(erbert) E(rnest)
Gay, Oliver
  See Gogarty, Oliver St. John
Gaye, Marvin (Penze) 1939-1984 .... CLC 26
  See also CA 112
Gebler, Carlo (Ernest) 1954- .... CLC 39
  See also CA 119; 133
Gee, Maggie (Mary) 1948- .... CLC 57
  See also CA 130
Gee, Maurice (Gough) 1931- .... CLC 29
  See also CA 97-100; CANR 67; SATA 46
Gelbart, Larry (Simon) 1923- .... CLC 21, 61
  See also CA 73-76; CANR 45
Gelber, Jack 1932- .... CLC 1, 6, 14, 79
  See also CA 1-4R; CANR 2; DLB 7
Gellhorn, Martha (Ellis) 1908-1998 CLC 14,
  60
  See also CA 77-80; 164; CANR 44; DLBY 82
Genet, Jean 1910-1986CLC 1, 2, 5, 10, 14, 44,
  46; DAM DRAM
  See also CA 13-16R; CANR 18; DLB 72;
  DLBY 86; MTCW
Gent, Peter 1942-............................... CLC 29
  See also AITN 1; CA 89-92; DLBY 82
Gentlewoman in New England, A
  See Bradstreet, Anne
Gentlewoman in Those Parts, A
  See Bradstreet, Anne
George, Jean Craighead 1919- .... CLC 35
  See also AAYA 8; CA 5-8R; CANR 25; CLR 1;
  DLB 52; JRDA; MAICYA; SATA 2, 68
George, Stefan (Anton) 1868-1933TCLC 2, 14
  See also CA 104
Georges, Georges Martin
  See Simenon, Georges (Jacques Christian)
Gerhardi, William Alexander
  See Gerhardie, William Alexander
Gerhardie, William Alexander 1895-1977
  CLC 5
  See also CA 25-28R; 73-76; CANR 18; DLB
  36
Gerstler, Amy 1956- .... CLC 70
  See also CA 146
Gertler, T. .... CLC 34
  See also CA 116; 121; INT 121
Ghalib ....NCLC 39
  See also Ghalib, Hsadullah Khan
Ghalib, Hsadullah Khan 1797-1869
  See Ghalib
  See also DAM POET
Ghelderode, Michel de 1898-1962CLC 6, 11;
  DAM DRAM

See also CA 85-88; CANR 40
Ghiselin, Brewster 1903- ....CLC 23
  See also CA 13-16R; CAAS 10; CANR 13
Ghose, Zulfikar 1935-...........................CLC 42
  See also CA 65-68; CANR 67
Ghosh, Amitav 1956-...........................CLC 44
  See also CA 147
Giacosa, Giuseppe 1847-1906 .... TCLC 7
  See also CA 104
Gibb, Lee
  See Waterhouse, Keith (Spencer)
Gibbon, Lewis Grassic .... TCLC 4
  See also Mitchell, James Leslie
Gibbons, Kaye 1960-CLC 50, 88; DAM POP
  See also CA 151
Gibran, Kahlil 1883-1931 . TCLC 1, 9; DAM
  POET, POP; PC 9
  See also CA 104; 150
Gibran, Khalil
  See Gibran, Kahlil
Gibson, William 1914- .. CLC 23; DA; DAB;
  DAC; DAM DRAM, MST
  See also CA 9-12R; CANR 9, 42; DLB 7; SATA
  66
Gibson, William (Ford) 1948- ... CLC 39, 63;
  DAM POP
  See also AAYA 12; CA 126; 133; CANR 52
Gide, Andre (Paul Guillaume) 1869-1951
  TCLC 5, 12, 36; DA; DAB; DAC; DAM
  MST, NOV; SSC 13; WLC
  See also CA 104; 124; DLB 65; MTCW
Gifford, Barry (Colby) 1946- ....CLC 34
  See also CA 65-68; CANR 9, 30, 40
Gilbert, Frank
  See De Voto, Bernard (Augustine)
Gilbert, W(illiam) S(chwenck) 1836-1911
  TCLC 3; DAM DRAM, POET
  See also CA 104; SATA 36
Gilbreth, Frank B., Jr. 1911- ....CLC 17
  See also CA 9-12R; SATA 2
Gilchrist, Ellen 1935-CLC 34, 48; DAM POP;
  SSC 14
  See also CA 113; 116; CANR 41, 61; DLB 130;
  MTCW
Giles, Molly 1942- ....CLC 39
  See also CA 126
Gill, Patrick
  See Creasey, John
Gilliam, Terry (Vance) 1940- ....CLC 21
  See also Monty Python
  See also AAYA 19; CA 108; 113; CANR 35;
  INT 113
Gillian, Jerry
  See Gilliam, Terry (Vance)
Gilliatt, Penelope (Ann Douglass) 1932-1993
  CLC 2, 10, 13, 53
  See also AITN 2; CA 13-16R; 141; CANR 49;
  DLB 14
Gilman, Charlotte (Anna) Perkins (Stetson)
  1860-1935 ....TCLC 9, 37; SSC 13
  See also CA 106; 150
Gilmour, David 1949-........................CLC 35
  See also CA 138, 147
Gilpin, William 1724-1804 ....NCLC 30
Gilray, J. D.
  See Mencken, H(enry) L(ouis)
Gilroy, Frank D(aniel) 1925-...............CLC 2
  See also CA 81-84; CANR 32, 64; DLB 7
Gilstrap, John 1957(?)- ....CLC 99
  See also CA 160
Ginsberg, Allen 1926-1997CLC 1, 2, 3, 4, 6, 13,
  36, 69, 109; DA; DAB; DAC; DAM MST,
  POET; PC 4; WLC 3

See also AITN 1; CA 1-4R; 157; CANR 2, 41,
  63; CDALB 1941-1968; DLB 5, 16, 169;
  MTCW
Ginzburg, Natalia 1916-1991CLC 5, 11, 54, 70
  See also CA 85-88; 135; CANR 33; DLB 177;
  MTCW
Giono, Jean 1895-1970 ....CLC 4, 11
  See also CA 45-48; 29-32R; CANR 2, 35; DLB
  72; MTCW
Giovanni, Nikki 1943-CLC 2, 4, 19, 64; BLC;
  DA; DAB; DAC; DAM MST, MULT,
  POET; PC 19; WLCS
  See also AAYA 22; AITN 1; BW 2; CA 29-32R;
  CAAS 6; CANR 18, 41, 60; CLR 6; DLB 5,
  41; INT CANR-18; MAICYA; MTCW; SATA
  24
Giovene, Andrea 1904- ....CLC 7
  See also CA 85-88
Gippius, Zinaida (Nikolayevna) 1869-1945
  See Hippius, Zinaida
  See also CA 106
Giraudoux, (Hippolyte) Jean 1882-1944
  TCLC 2, 7; DAM DRAM
  See also CA 104; DLB 65
Gironella, Jose Maria 1917-.............CLC 11
  See also CA 101
Gissing, George (Robert) 1857-1903TCLC 3,
  24, 47
  See also CA 105; DLB 18, 135, 184
Giurlani, Aldo
  See Palazzeschi, Aldo
Gladkov, Fyodor (Vasilyevich) 1883-1958
  TCLC 27
Glanville, Brian (Lester) 1931- ....CLC 6
  See also CA 5-8R; CAAS 9; CANR 3; DLB 15,
  139; SATA 42
Glasgow, Ellen (Anderson Gholson) 1873(?)-
  1945 ....TCLC 2, 7
  See also CA 104; 164; DLB 9, 12
Glaspell, Susan 1882(?)-1948 .... TCLC 55
  See also CA 110; 154; DLB 7, 9, 78; YABC 2
Glassco, John 1909-1981 ....CLC 9
  See also CA 13-16R; 102; CANR 15; DLB 68
Glasscock, Amnesia
  See Steinbeck, John (Ernst)
Glasser, Ronald J. 1940(?)- ....CLC 37
Glassman, Joyce
  See Johnson, Joyce
Glendinning, Victoria 1937-.............CLC 50
  See also CA 120; 127; CANR 59; DLB 155
Glissant, Edouard 1928- . CLC 10, 68; DAM
  MULT
  See also CA 153
Gloag, Julian 1930- ....CLC 40
  See also AITN 1; CA 65-68; CANR 10
Glowacki, Aleksander
  See Prus, Boleslaw
Gluck, Louise (Elisabeth) 1943-CLC 7, 22, 44,
  81; DAM POET; PC 16
  See also CA 33-36R; CANR 40; DLB 5
Glyn, Elinor 1864-1943 ....TCLC 72
  See also DLB 153
Gobineau, Joseph Arthur (Comte) de 1816-
  1882 ....NCLC 17
  See also DLB 123
Godard, Jean-Luc 1930- ....CLC 20
  See also CA 93-96
Godden, (Margaret) Rumer 1907-... CLC 53
  See also AAYA 6; CA 5-8R; CANR 4, 27, 36,
  55; CLR 20; DLB 161; MAICYA; SAAS 12;
  SATA 3, 36
Godoy Alcayaga, Lucila 1889-1957
  See Mistral, Gabriela

See also BW 2; CA 104; 131; DAM MULT; HW; MTCW

Godwin, Gail (Kathleen) 1937- **CLC 5, 8, 22, 31, 69; DAM POP**
See also CA 29-32R; CANR 15, 43; DLB 6; INT CANR-15; MTCW

Godwin, William 1756-1836 .... **NCLC 14**
See also CDBLB 1789-1832; DLB 39, 104, 142, 158, 163

Goebbels, Josef
See Goebbels, (Paul) Joseph

Goebbels, (Paul) Joseph 1897-1945 **TCLC 68**
See also CA 115; 148

Goebbels, Joseph Paul
See Goebbels, (Paul) Joseph

Goethe, Johann Wolfgang von 1749-1832 **NCLC 4, 22, 34; DA; DAB; DAC; DAM DRAM, MST, POET; PC 5; WLC 3**
See also DLB 94

Gogarty, Oliver St. John 1878-1957 **TCLC 15**
See also CA 109; 150; DLB 15, 19

Gogol, Nikolai (Vasilyevich) 1809-1852 **NCLC 5, 15, 31; DA; DAB; DAC; DAM DRAM, MST; DC 1; SSC 4, 29; WLC**

Goines, Donald 1937(?)-1974 **CLC 80; BLC; DAM MULT, POP**
See also AITN 1; BW 1; CA 124; 114; DLB 33

Gold, Herbert 1924- .... **CLC 4, 7, 14, 42**
See also CA 9-12R; CANR 17, 45; DLB 2; DLBY 81

Goldbarth, Albert 1948- .... **CLC 5, 38**
See also CA 53-56; CANR 6, 40; DLB 120

Goldberg, Anatol 1910-1982 .... **CLC 34**
See also CA 131; 117

Goldemberg, Isaac 1945- .... **CLC 52**
See also CA 69-72; CAAS 12; CANR 11, 32; HW

Golding, William (Gerald) 1911-1993 **CLC 1, 2, 3, 8, 10, 17, 27, 58, 81; DA; DAB; DAC; DAM MST, NOV; WLC**
See also AAYA 5; CA 5-8R; 141; CANR 13, 33, 54; CDBLB 1945-1960; DLB 15, 100; MTCW

Goldman, Emma 1869-1940 .... **TCLC 13**
See also CA 110; 150

Goldman, Francisco 1954- .... **CLC 76**
See also CA 162

Goldman, William (W.) 1931- ...... **CLC 1, 48**
See also CA 9-12R; CANR 29; DLB 44

Goldmann, Lucien 1913-1970 .... **CLC 24**
See also CA 25-28; CAP 2

Goldoni, Carlo 1707-1793 **LC 4; DAM DRAM**

Goldsberry, Steven 1949- .... **CLC 34**
See also CA 131

Goldsmith, Oliver 1728-1774 **LC 2; DA; DAB; DAC; DAM DRAM, MST, NOV, POET; DC 8; WLC**
See also CDBLB 1660-1789; DLB 39, 89, 104, 109, 142; SATA 26

Goldsmith, Peter
See Priestley, J(ohn) B(oynton)

Gombrowicz, Witold 1904-1969 **CLC 4, 7, 11, 49; DAM DRAM**
See also CA 19-20; 25-28R; CAP 2

Gomez de la Serna, Ramon 1888-1963 **CLC 9**
See also CA 153; 116; HW

Goncharov, Ivan Alexandrovich 1812-1891 **NCLC 1, 63**

Goncourt, Edmond (Louis Antoine Huot) de 1822-1896 .... **NCLC 7**
See also DLB 123

Goncourt, Jules (Alfred Huot) de 1830-1870 **NCLC 7**

See also DLB 123

Gontier, Fernande 19(?)- .... **CLC 50**

Gonzalez Martinez, Enrique 1871-1952 **TCLC 72**
See also HW

Goodman, Paul 1911-1972 ...... **CLC 1, 2, 4, 7**
See also CA 19-20; 37-40R; CANR 34; CAP 2; DLB 130; MTCW

Gordimer, Nadine 1923- **CLC 3, 5, 7, 10, 18, 33, 51, 70; DA; DAB; DAC; DAM MST, NOV; SSC 17; WLCS**
See also CA 5-8R; CANR 3, 28, 56; INT CANR-28; MTCW

Gordon, Adam Lindsay 1833-1870 **NCLC 21**

Gordon, Caroline 1895-1981 **CLC 6, 13, 29, 83; SSC 15**
See also CA 11-12; 103; CANR 36; CAP 1; DLB 4, 9, 102; DLBY 81; MTCW

Gordon, Charles William 1860-1937
See Connor, Ralph
See also CA 109

Gordon, Mary (Catherine) 1949- **CLC 13, 22**
See also CA 102; CANR 44; DLB 6; DLBY 81; INT 102; MTCW

Gordon, N. J.
See Bosman, Herman Charles

Gordon, Sol 1923- .... **CLC 26**
See also CA 53-56; CANR 4; SATA 11

Gordone, Charles 1925-1995 **CLC 1, 4; DAM DRAM; DC 8**
See also BW 1; CA 93-96; 150; CANR 55; DLB 7; INT 93-96; MTCW

Gore, Catherine 1800-1861 .... **NCLC 65**
See also DLB 116

Gorenko, Anna Andreevna
See Akhmatova, Anna

Gorky, Maxim 1868-1936 **TCLC 8; DAB; SSC 28; WLC**
See also Peshkov, Alexei Maximovich

Goryan, Sirak
See Saroyan, William

Gosse, Edmund (William) 1849-1928 **TCLC 28**
See also CA 117; DLB 57, 144, 184

Gotlieb, Phyllis Fay (Bloom) 1926- .. **CLC 18**
See also CA 13-16R; CANR 7; DLB 88

Gottesman, S. D.
See Kornbluth, C(yril) M.; Pohl, Frederik

Gottfried von Strassburg fl. c. 1210- . **CMLC 10**
See also DLB 138

Gould, Lois .... **CLC 4, 10**
See also CA 77-80; CANR 29; MTCW

Gourmont, Remy (-Marie-Charles) de 1858-1915 .... **TCLC 17**
See also CA 109; 150

Govier, Katherine 1948- .... **CLC 51**
See also CA 101; CANR 18, 40

Goyen, (Charles) William 1915-1983 **CLC 5, 8, 14, 40**
See also AITN 2; CA 5-8R; 110; CANR 6; DLB 2; DLBY 83; INT CANR-6

Goytisolo, Juan 1931- . **CLC 5, 10, 23; DAM MULT; HLC**
See also CA 85-88; CANR 32, 61; HW; MTCW

Gozzano, Guido 1883-1916 .... **PC 10**
See also CA 154; DLB 114

Gozzi, (Conte) Carlo 1720-1806 .... **NCLC 23**

Grabbe, Christian Dietrich 1801-1836 **NCLC 2**
See also DLB 133

Grace, Patricia 1937- .... **CLC 56**

Gracian y Morales, Baltasar 1601-1658 **LC 15**

Gracq, Julien .... **CLC 11, 48**

See also Poirier, Louis
See also DLB 83

Grade, Chaim 1910-1982 .... **CLC 10**
See also CA 93-96; 107

Graduate of Oxford, A
See Ruskin, John

Grafton, Garth
See Duncan, Sara Jeannette

Graham, John
See Phillips, David Graham

Graham, Jorie 1951- .... **CLC 48**
See also CA 111; CANR 63; DLB 120

Graham, R(obert) B(ontine) Cunninghame
See Cunninghame Graham, R(obert) B(ontine)
See also DLB 98, 135, 174

Graham, Robert
See Haldeman, Joe (William)

Graham, Tom
See Lewis, (Harry) Sinclair

Graham, W(illiam) S(ydney) 1918-1986 **CLC 29**
See also CA 73-76; 118; DLB 20

Graham, Winston (Mawdsley) 1910- **CLC 23**
See also CA 49-52; CANR 2, 22, 45, 66; DLB 77

Grahame, Kenneth 1859-1932 **TCLC 64; DAB**
See also CA 108; 136; CLR 5; DLB 34, 141, 178; MAICYA; YABC 1

Grant, Skeeter
See Spiegelman, Art

Granville-Barker, Harley 1877-1946 **TCLC 2; DAM DRAM**
See also Barker, Harley Granville
See also CA 104

Grass, Guenter (Wilhelm) 1927- **CLC 1, 2, 4, 6, 11, 15, 22, 32, 49, 88; DA; DAB; DAC; DAM MST, NOV; WLC**
See also CA 13-16R; CANR 20; DLB 75, 124; MTCW

Gratton, Thomas
See Hulme, T(homas) E(rnest)

Grau, Shirley Ann 1929- .. **CLC 4, 9; SSC 15**
See also CA 89-92; CANR 22; DLB 2; INT CANR-22; MTCW

Gravel, Fern
See Hall, James Norman

Graver, Elizabeth 1964- .... **CLC 70**
See also CA 135

Graves, Richard Perceval 1945- .... **CLC 44**
See also CA 65-68; CANR 9, 26, 51

Graves, Robert (von Ranke) 1895-1985 **CLC 1, 2, 6, 11, 39, 44, 45; DAB; DAC; DAM MST, POET; PC 6**
See also CA 5-8R; 117; CANR 5, 36; CDBLB 1914-1945; DLB 20, 100, 191; DLBY 85; MTCW; SATA 45

Graves, Valerie
See Bradley, Marion Zimmer

Gray, Alasdair (James) 1934- .... **CLC 41**
See also CA 126; CANR 47; DLB 194; INT 126; MTCW

Gray, Amlin 1946- .... **CLC 29**
See also CA 138

Gray, Francine du Plessix 1930- ..... **CLC 22; DAM NOV**
See also BEST 90:3; CA 61-64; CAAS 2; CANR 11, 33; INT CANR-11; MTCW

Gray, John (Henry) 1866-1934 ...... **TCLC 19**
See also CA 119; 162

Gray, Simon (James Holliday) 1936- **CLC 9, 14, 36**
See also AITN 1; CA 21-24R; CAAS 3; CANR 32; DLB 13; MTCW

Gray, Spalding 1941-CLC 49; DAM POP; DC 7
  See also CA 128
Gray, Thomas 1716-1771LC 4, 40; DA; DAB; DAC; DAM MST; PC 2; WLC
  See also CDBLB 1660-1789; DLB 109
Grayson, David
  See Baker, Ray Stannard
Grayson, Richard (A.) 1951- .... CLC 38
  See also CA 85-88; CANR 14, 31, 57
Greeley, Andrew M(oran) 1928- ..... CLC 28; DAM POP
  See also CA 5-8R; CAAS 7; CANR 7, 43; MTCW
Green, Anna Katharine 1846-1935 TCLC 63
  See also CA 112; 159
Green, Brian
  See Card, Orson Scott
Green, Hannah
  See Greenberg, Joanne (Goldenberg)
Green, Hannah 1927(?)-1996 .... CLC 3
  See also CA 73-76; CANR 59
Green, Henry 1905-1973 .... CLC 2, 13, 97
  See also Yorke, Henry Vincent
  See also DLB 15
Green, Julian (Hartridge) 1900-
  See Green, Julien
  See also CA 21-24R; CANR 33; DLB 4, 72; MTCW
Green, Julien .... CLC 3, 11, 77
  See also Green, Julian (Hartridge)
Green, Paul (Eliot) 1894-1981CLC 25; DAM DRAM
  See also AITN 1; CA 5-8R; 103; CANR 3; DLB 7, 9; DLBY 81
Greenberg, Ivan 1908-1973
  See Rahv, Philip
  See also CA 85-88
Greenberg, Joanne (Goldenberg) 1932- C L C 7, 30
  See also AAYA 12; CA 5-8R; CANR 14, 32; SATA 25
Greenberg, Richard 1959(?)- ....,... CLC 57
  See also CA 138
Greene, Bette 1934- .... CLC 30
  See also AAYA 7; CA 53-56; CANR 4; CLR 2; JRDA; MAICYA; SAAS 16; SATA 8
Greene, Gael .... CLC 8
  See also CA 13-16R; CANR 10
Greene, Graham (Henry) 1904-1991CLC 1, 3, 6, 9, 14, 18, 27, 37, 70, 72; DA; DAB; DAC; DAM MST, NOV; SSC 29; WLC
  See also AITN 2; CA 13-16R; 133; CANR 35, 61; CDBLB 1945-1960; DLB 13, 15, 77, 100, 162; DLBY 91; MTCW; SATA 20
Greene, Robert 1558-1592 .... LC 41
  See also DLB 62, 167
Greer, Richard
  See Silverberg, Robert
Gregor, Arthur 1923- .... CLC 9
  See also CA 25-28R; CAAS 10; CANR 11; SATA 36
Gregor, Lee
  See Pohl, Frederik
Gregory, Isabella Augusta (Persse) 1852-1932 TCLC 1
  See also CA 104; DLB 10
Gregory, J. Dennis
  See Williams, John A(lfred)
Grendon, Stephen
  See Derleth, August (William)
Grenville, Kate 1950- .... CLC 61
  See also CA 118; CANR 53

Grenville, Pelham
  See Wodehouse, P(elham) G(renville)
Greve, Felix Paul (Berthold Friedrich) 1879-1948
  See Grove, Frederick Philip
  See also CA 104; 141; DAC; DAM MST
Grey, Zane 1872-1939 .. TCLC 6; DAM POP
  See also CA 104; 132; DLB 9; MTCW
Grieg, (Johan) Nordahl (Brun) 1902-1943 TCLC 10
  See also CA 107
Grieve, C(hristopher) M(urray) 1892-1978 CLC 11, 19; DAM POET
  See also MacDiarmid, Hugh; Pteleon
  See also CA 5-8R; 85-88; CANR 33; MTCW
Griffin, Gerald 1803-1840 .... NCLC 7
  See also DLB 159
Griffin, John Howard 1920-1980 ..... CLC 68
  See also AITN 1; CA 1-4R; 101; CANR 2
Griffin, Peter 1942- .... CLC 39
  See also CA 136
Griffith, D(avid Lewelyn) W(ark) 1875(?)-1948 TCLC 68
  See also CA 119; 150
Griffith, Lawrence
  See Griffith, D(avid Lewelyn) W(ark)
Griffiths, Trevor 1935- .... CLC 13, 52
  See also CA 97-100; CANR 45; DLB 13
Griggs, Sutton Elbert 1872-1930(?)TCLC 77
  See also CA 123; DLB 50
Grigson, Geoffrey (Edward Harvey) 1905-1985 CLC 7, 39
  See also CA 25-28R; 118; CANR 20, 33; DLB 27; MTCW
Grillparzer, Franz 1791-1872 .... NCLC 1
  See also DLB 133
Grimble, Reverend Charles James
  See Eliot, T(homas) S(tearns)
Grimke, Charlotte L(ottie) Forten 1837(?)-1914
  See Forten, Charlotte L.
  See also BW 1; CA 117; 124; DAM MULT, POET
Grimm, Jacob Ludwig Karl 1785-1863NCLC 3
  See also DLB 90; MAICYA; SATA 22
Grimm, Wilhelm Karl 1786-1859 .... NCLC 3
  See also DLB 90; MAICYA; SATA 22
Grimmelshausen, Johann Jakob Christoffel von 1621-1676 .... LC 6
  See also DLB 168
Grindel, Eugene 1895-1952
  See Eluard, Paul
  See also CA 104
Grisham, John 1955- ..... CLC 84; DAM POP
  See also AAYA 14; CA 138; CANR 47
Grossman, David 1954- .... CLC 67
  See also CA 138
Grossman, Vasily (Semenovich) 1905-1964 CLC 41
  See also CA 124; 130; MTCW
Grove, Frederick Philip .... TCLC 4
  See also Greve, Felix Paul (Berthold Friedrich)
  See also DLB 92
Grubb
  See Crumb, R(obert)
Grumbach, Doris (Isaac) 1918-CLC 13, 22, 64
  See also CA 5-8R; CAAS 2; CANR 9, 42; INT CANR-9
Grundtvig, Nicolai Frederik Severin 1783-1872 NCLC 1
Grunge
  See Crumb, R(obert)
Grunwald, Lisa 1959- .... CLC 44

See also CA 120
Guare, John 1938- . CLC 8, 14, 29, 67; DAM DRAM
  See also CA 73-76; CANR 21; DLB 7; MTCW
Gudjonsson, Halldor Kiljan 1902-1998
  See Laxness, Halldor
  See also CA 103; 164
Guenter, Erich
  See Eich, Guenter
Guest, Barbara 1920- .... CLC 34
  See also CA 25-28R; CANR 11, 44; DLB 5, 193
Guest, Judith (Ann) 1936- .CLC 8, 30; DAM NOV, POP
  See also AAYA 7; CA 77-80; CANR 15; INT CANR-15; MTCW
Guevara, Che .... CLC 87; HLC
  See also Guevara (Serna), Ernesto
Guevara (Serna), Ernesto 1928-1967
  See Guevara, Che
  See also CA 127; 111; CANR 56; DAM MULT; HW
Guild, Nicholas M. 1944- .... CLC 33
  See also CA 93-96
Guillemin, Jacques
  See Sartre, Jean-Paul
Guillen, Jorge 1893-1984 .... CLC 11; DAM MULT, POET
  See also CA 89-92; 112; DLB 108; HW
Guillen, Nicolas (Cristobal) 1902-1989 .C L C 48, 79; BLC; DAM MST, MULT, POET; HLC
  See also BW 2; CA 116; 125; 129; HW
Guillevic, (Eugene) 1907- .... CLC 33
  See also CA 93-96
Guillois
  See Desnos, Robert
Guillois, Valentin
  See Desnos, Robert
Guiney, Louise Imogen 1861-1920 TCLC 41
  See also CA 160; DLB 54
Guiraldes, Ricardo (Guillermo) 1886-1927 TCLC 39
  See also CA 131; HW; MTCW
Gumilev, Nikolai (Stepanovich) 1886-1921 TCLC 60
  See also CA 165
Gunesekera, Romesh 1954- .... CLC 91
  See also CA 159
Gunn, Bill ....CLC 5
  See also Gunn, William Harrison
  See also DLB 38
Gunn, Thom(son William) 1929-CLC 3, 6, 18, 32, 81; DAM POET
  See also CA 17-20R; CANR 9, 33; CDBLB 1960 to Present; DLB 27; INT CANR-33; MTCW
Gunn, William Harrison 1934(?)-1989
  See Gunn, Bill
  See also AITN 1; BW 1; CA 13-16R; 128; CANR 12, 25
Gunnars, Kristjana 1948- .... CLC 69
  See also CA 113; DLB 60
Gurdjieff, G(eorgei) I(vanovich) 1877(?)-1949 TCLC 71
  See also CA 157
Gurganus, Allan 1947- ... CLC 70; DAM POP
  See also BEST 90:1; CA 135
Gurney, A(lbert) R(amsdell), Jr. 1930- . C L C 32, 50, 54; DAM DRAM
  See also CA 77-80; CANR 32, 64
Gurney, Ivor (Bertie) 1890-1937 ... TCLC 33
Gurney, Peter

See Gurney, A(lbert) R(amsdell), Jr.

Guro, Elena 1877-1913 .... **TCLC 56**

Gustafson, James M(oody) 1925- .. **CLC 100**
See also CA 25-28R; CANR 37

Gustafson, Ralph (Barker) 1909- .... **CLC 36**
See also CA 21-24R; CANR 8, 45; DLB 88

Gut, Gom
See Simenon, Georges (Jacques Christian)

Guterson, David 1956- .... **CLC 91**
See also CA 132

Guthrie, A(lfred) B(ertram), Jr. 1901-1991
CLC 23
See also CA 57-60; 134; CANR 24; DLB 6;
SATA 62; SATA-Obit 67

Guthrie, Isobel
See Grieve, C(hristopher) M(urray)

Guthrie, Woodrow Wilson 1912-1967
See Guthrie, Woody
See also CA 113; 93-96

Guthrie, Woody .... **CLC 35**
See also Guthrie, Woodrow Wilson

Guy, Rosa (Cuthbert) 1928- .... **CLC 26**
See also AAYA 4; BW 2; CA 17-20R; CANR
14, 34; CLR 13; DLB 33; JRDA; MAICYA;
SATA 14, 62

Gwendolyn
See Bennett, (Enoch) Arnold

H. D. .... **CLC 3, 8, 14, 31, 34, 73; PC 5**
See also Doolittle, Hilda

H. de V.
See Buchan, John

Haavikko, Paavo Juhani 1931- .. **CLC 18, 34**
See also CA 106

Habbema, Koos
See Heijermans, Herman

Habermas, Juergen 1929- .... **CLC 104**
See also CA 109

Habermas, Jurgen
See Habermas, Juergen

Hacker, Marilyn 1942- . **CLC 5, 9, 23, 72, 91;**
DAM POET
See also CA 77-80; CANR 68; DLB 120

Haggard, H(enry) Rider 1856-1925 **TCLC 11**
See also CA 108; 148; DLB 70, 156, 174, 178;
SATA 16

Hagiosy, L.
See Larbaud, Valery (Nicolas)

Hagiwara Sakutaro 1886-1942 **TCLC 60; PC**
18

Haig, Fenil
See Ford, Ford Madox

Haig-Brown, Roderick (Langmere) 1908-1976
CLC 21
See also CA 5-8R; 69-72; CANR 4, 38; CLR
31; DLB 88; MAICYA; SATA 12

Hailey, Arthur 1920- **CLC 5; DAM NOV, POP**
See also AITN 2; BEST 90:3; CA 1-4R; CANR
2, 36; DLB 88; DLBY 82; MTCW

Hailey, Elizabeth Forsythe 1938- .... **CLC 40**
See also CA 93-96; CAAS 1; CANR 15, 48;
INT CANR-15

Haines, John (Meade) 1924- .... **CLC 58**
See also CA 17-20R; CANR 13, 34; DLB 5

Hakluyt, Richard 1552-1616 .... **LC 31**

Haldeman, Joe (William) 1943- .... **CLC 61**
See also CA 53-56; CAAS 25; CANR 6; DLB
8; INT CANR-6

Haley, Alex(ander Murray Palmer) 1921-1992
CLC 8, 12, 76; BLC; DA; DAB; DAC;
DAM MST, MULT, POP
See also BW 2; CA 77-80; 136; CANR 61; DLB
38; MTCW

Haliburton, Thomas Chandler 1796-1865

NCLC 15
See also DLB 11, 99

Hall, Donald (Andrew, Jr.) 1928- **CLC 1, 13,**
37, 59; DAM POET
See also CA 5-8R; CAAS 7; CANR 2, 44, 64;
DLB 5; SATA 23, 97

Hall, Frederic Sauser
See Sauser-Hall, Frederic

Hall, James
See Kuttner, Henry

Hall, James Norman 1887-1951 ..... **TCLC 23**
See also CA 123; SATA 21

Hall, (Marguerite) Radclyffe 1886-1943
TCLC 12
See also CA 110; 150

Hall, Rodney 1935- .... **CLC 51**
See also CA 109

Halleck, Fitz-Greene 1790-1867 .... **NCLC 47**
See also DLB 3

Halliday, Michael
See Creasey, John

Halpern, Daniel 1945- .... **CLC 14**
See also CA 33-36R

Hamburger, Michael (Peter Leopold) 1924-
CLC 5, 14
See also CA 5-8R; CAAS 4; CANR 2, 47; DLB
27

Hamill, Pete 1935- .... **CLC 10**
See also CA 25-28R; CANR 18

Hamilton, Alexander 1755(?)-1804 **NCLC 49**
See also DLB 37

Hamilton, Clive
See Lewis, C(live) S(taples)

Hamilton, Edmond 1904-1977 .... **CLC 1**
See also CA 1-4R; CANR 3; DLB 8

Hamilton, Eugene (Jacob) Lee
See Lee-Hamilton, Eugene (Jacob)

Hamilton, Franklin
See Silverberg, Robert

Hamilton, Gail
See Corcoran, Barbara

Hamilton, Mollie
See Kaye, M(ary) M(argaret)

Hamilton, (Anthony Walter) Patrick 1904-1962
CLC 51
See also CA 113; DLB 10

Hamilton, Virginia 1936- .... **CLC 26; DAM**
MULT
See also AAYA 2, 21; BW 2; CA 25-28R;
CANR 20, 37; CLR 1, 11, 40; DLB 33, 52;
INT CANR-20; JRDA; MAICYA; MTCW;
SATA 4, 56, 79

Hammett, (Samuel) Dashiell 1894-1961 **C L C**
3, 5, 10, 19, 47; SSC 17
See also AITN 1; CA 81-84; CANR 42; CDALB
1929-1941; DLBD 6; DLBY 96; MTCW

Hammon, Jupiter 1711(?)-1800(?) . **NCLC 5;**
BLC; DAM MULT, POET; PC 16
See also DLB 31, 50

Hammond, Keith
See Kuttner, Henry

Hamner, Earl (Henry), Jr. 1923- ...... **CLC 12**
See also AITN 2; CA 73-76; DLB 6

Hampton, Christopher (James) 1946- **CLC 4**
See also CA 25-28R; DLB 13; MTCW

Hamsun, Knut .... **TCLC 2, 14, 49**
See also Pedersen, Knut

Handke, Peter 1942- **CLC 5, 8, 10, 15, 38; DAM**
DRAM, NOV
See also CA 77-80; CANR 33; DLB 85, 124;
MTCW

Hanley, James 1901-1985 ..... **CLC 3, 5, 8, 13**
See also CA 73-76; 117; CANR 36; DLB 191;

MTCW

Hannah, Barry 1942- .... **CLC 23, 38, 90**
See also CA 108; 110; CANR 43, 68; DLB 6;
INT 110; MTCW

Hannon, Ezra
See Hunter, Evan

Hansberry, Lorraine (Vivian) 1930-1965 **CLC**
17, 62; BLC; DA; DAB; DAC; DAM
DRAM, MST, MULT; DC 2
See also AAYA 25; BW 1; CA 109; 25-28R;
CABS 3; CANR 58; CDALB 1941-1968;
DLB 7, 38; MTCW

Hansen, Joseph 1923- .... **CLC 38**
See also CA 29-32R; CAAS 17; CANR 16, 44,
66; INT CANR-16

Hansen, Martin A. 1909-1955 .... **TCLC 32**

Hanson, Kenneth O(stlin) 1922- .... **CLC 13**
See also CA 53-56; CANR 7

Hardwick, Elizabeth 1916- .... **CLC 13; DAM**
NOV
See also CA 5-8R; CANR 3, 32; DLB 6; MTCW

Hardy, Thomas 1840-1928 **TCLC 4, 10, 18, 32,**
48, 53, 72; DA; DAB; DAC; DAM MST,
NOV, POET; PC 8; SSC 2; WLC
See also CA 104; 123; CDBLB 1890-1914;
DLB 18, 19, 135; MTCW

Hare, David 1947- .... **CLC 29, 58**
See also CA 97-100; CANR 39; DLB 13;
MTCW

Harewood, John
See Van Druten, John (William)

Harford, Henry
See Hudson, W(illiam) H(enry)

Hargrave, Leonie
See Disch, Thomas M(ichael)

Harjo, Joy 1951- .... **CLC 83; DAM MULT**
See also CA 114; CANR 35, 67; DLB 120, 175;
NNAL

Harlan, Louis R(udolph) 1922- .... **CLC 34**
See also CA 21-24R; CANR 25, 55

Harling, Robert 1951(?)- .... **CLC 53**
See also CA 147

Harmon, William (Ruth) 1938- .... **CLC 38**
See also CA 33-36R; CANR 14, 32, 35; SATA
65

Harper, F. E. W.
See Harper, Frances Ellen Watkins

Harper, Frances E. W.
See Harper, Frances Ellen Watkins

Harper, Frances E. Watkins
See Harper, Frances Ellen Watkins

Harper, Frances Ellen
See Harper, Frances Ellen Watkins

Harper, Frances Ellen Watkins 1825-1911
TCLC 14; BLC; DAM MULT, POET; PC
21
See also BW 1; CA 111; 125; DLB 50

Harper, Michael S(teven) 1938- ... **CLC 7, 22**
See also BW 1; CA 33-36R; CANR 24; DLB
41

Harper, Mrs. F. E. W.
See Harper, Frances Ellen Watkins

Harris, Christie (Lucy) Irwin 1907- . **CLC 12**
See also CA 5-8R; CANR 6; CLR 47; DLB 88;
JRDA; MAICYA; SAAS 10; SATA 6, 74

Harris, Frank 1856-1931 .... **TCLC 24**
See also CA 109; 150; DLB 156

Harris, George Washington 1814-1869 **N C L C**
23
See also DLB 3, 11

Harris, Joel Chandler 1848-1908 ... **TCLC 2;**
SSC 19
See also CA 104; 137; CLR 49; DLB 11, 23,

42, 78, 91; MAICYA; YABC 1

Harris, John (Wyndham Parkes Lucas) Beynon 1903-1969
See Wyndham, John
See also CA 102; 89-92

Harris, MacDonald ....CLC 9
See also Heiney, Donald (William)

Harris, Mark 1922- ....CLC 19
See also CA 5-8R; CAAS 3; CANR 2, 55; DLB 2; DLBY 80

Harris, (Theodore) Wilson 1921-.....CLC 25
See also BW 2; CA 65-68; CAAS 16; CANR 11, 27; DLB 117; MTCW

Harrison, Elizabeth Cavanna 1909-
See Cavanna, Betty
See also CA 9-12R; CANR 6, 27

Harrison, Harry (Max) 1925- ....CLC 42
See also CA 1-4R; CANR 5, 21; DLB 8; SATA 4

Harrison, James (Thomas) 1937-CLC 6, 14, 33, 66; SSC 19
See also CA 13-16R; CANR 8, 51; DLBY 82; INT CANR-8

Harrison, Jim
See Harrison, James (Thomas)

Harrison, Kathryn 1961-.................CLC 70
See also CA 144; CANR 68

Harrison, Tony 1937- ....CLC 43
See also CA 65-68; CANR 44; DLB 40; MTCW

Harriss, Will(ard Irvin) 1922- ....CLC 34
See also CA 111

Harson, Sley
See Ellison, Harlan (Jay)

Hart, Ellis
See Ellison, Harlan (Jay)

Hart, Josephine 1942(?)-CLC 70; DAM POP
See also CA 138

Hart, Moss 1904-1961CLC 66; DAM DRAM
See also CA 109; 89-92; DLB 7

Harte, (Francis) Bret(t) 1836(?)-1902TCLC 1, 25; DA; DAC; DAM MST; SSC 8; WLC
See also CA 104; 140; CDALB 1865-1917; DLB 12, 64, 74, 79, 186; SATA 26

Hartley, L(eslie) P(oles) 1895-1972CLC 2, 22
See also CA 45-48; 37-40R; CANR 33; DLB 15, 139; MTCW

Hartman, Geoffrey H. 1929- ....CLC 27
See also CA 117; 125; DLB 67

Hartmann, Sadakichi 1867-1944 ...TCLC 73
See also CA 157; DLB 54

Hartmann von Aue c. 1160-c. 1205CMLC 15
See also DLB 138

Hartmann von Aue 1170-1210 ......CMLC 15

Haruf, Kent 1943- ....CLC 34
See also CA 149

Harwood, Ronald 1934-.........CLC 32; DAM DRAM, MST
See also CA 1-4R; CANR 4, 55; DLB 13

Hasegawa Tatsunosuke
See Futabatei, Shimei

Hasek, Jaroslav (Matej Frantisek) 1883-1923 TCLC 4
See also CA 104; 129; MTCW

Hass, Robert 1941- ... CLC 18, 39, 99; PC 16
See also CA 111; CANR 30, 50; DLB 105; SATA 94

Hastings, Hudson
See Kuttner, Henry

Hastings, Selina ....CLC 44

Hathorne, John 1641-1717 ....LC 38

Hatteras, Amelia
See Mencken, H(enry) L(ouis)

Hatteras, Owen .... TCLC 18

See also Mencken, H(enry) L(ouis); Nathan, George Jean

Hauptmann, Gerhart (Johann Robert) 1862-1946 ....TCLC 4; DAM DRAM
See also CA 104; 153; DLB 66, 118

Havel, Vaclav 1936-... CLC 25, 58, 65; DAM DRAM; DC 6
See also CA 104; CANR 36, 63; MTCW

Haviaras, Stratis ....CLC 33
See also Chaviaras, Strates

Hawes, Stephen 1475(?)-1523(?) ....LC 17

Hawkes, John (Clendennin Burne, Jr.) 1925-CLC 1, 2, 3, 4, 7, 9, 14, 15, 27, 49
See also CA 1-4R; CANR 2, 47, 64; DLB 2, 7; DLBY 80; MTCW

Hawking, S. W.
See Hawking, Stephen W(illiam)

Hawking, Stephen W(illiam) 1942- CLC 63, 105
See also AAYA 13; BEST 89:1; CA 126; 129; CANR 48

Hawthorne, Julian 1846-1934 ....TCLC 25
See also CA 165

Hawthorne, Nathaniel 1804-1864 NCLC 39; DA; DAB; DAC; DAM MST, NOV; SSC 3, 29; WLC
See also AAYA 18; CDALB 1640-1865; DLB 1, 74; YABC 2

Haxton, Josephine Ayres 1921-
See Douglas, Ellen
See also CA 115; CANR 41

Hayaseca y Eizaguirre, Jorge
See Echegaray (y Eizaguirre), Jose (Maria Waldo)

Hayashi Fumiko 1904-1951 ....TCLC 27
See also CA 161; DLB 180

Haycraft, Anna
See Ellis, Alice Thomas
See also CA 122

Hayden, Robert E(arl) 1913-1980 CLC 5, 9, 14, 37; BLC; DA; DAC; DAM MST, MULT, POET; PC 6
See also BW 1; CA 69-72; 97-100; CABS 2; CANR 24; CDALB 1941-1968; DLB 5, 76; MTCW; SATA 19; SATA-Obit 26

Hayford, J(oseph) E(phraim) Casely
See Casely-Hayford, J(oseph) E(phraim)

Hayman, Ronald 1932-......................CLC 44
See also CA 25-28R; CANR 18, 50; DLB 155

Haywood, Eliza (Fowler) 1693(?)-1756 LC 1

Hazlitt, William 1778-1830 ....NCLC 29
See also DLB 110, 158

Hazzard, Shirley 1931- ....CLC 18
See also CA 9-12R; CANR 4; DLBY 82; MTCW

Head, Bessie 1937-1986 .. CLC 25, 67; BLC; DAM MULT
See also BW 2; CA 29-32R; 119; CANR 25; DLB 117; MTCW

Headon, (Nicky) Topper 1956(?)- .....CLC 30

Heaney, Seamus (Justin) 1939- CLC 5, 7, 14, 25, 37, 74, 91; DAB; DAM POET; PC 18; WLCS
See also CA 85-88; CANR 25, 48; CDBLB 1960 to Present; DLB 40; DLBY 95; MTCW

Hearn, (Patricio) Lafcadio (Tessima Carlos) 1850-1904 ....TCLC 9
See also CA 105; DLB 12, 78

Hearne, Vicki 1946-...........................CLC 56
See also CA 139

Hearon, Shelby 1931-.........................CLC 63
See also AITN 2; CA 25-28R; CANR 18, 48

Heat-Moon, William Least ....CLC 29

See also Trogdon, William (Lewis)
See also AAYA 9

Hebbel, Friedrich 1813-1863NCLC 43; DAM DRAM
See also DLB 129

Hebert, Anne 1916-CLC 4, 13, 29; DAC; DAM MST, POET
See also CA 85-88; DLB 68; MTCW

Hecht, Anthony (Evan) 1923- CLC 8, 13, 19; DAM POET
See also CA 9-12R; CANR 6; DLB 5, 169

Hecht, Ben 1894-1964 ....CLC 8
See also CA 85-88; DLB 7, 9, 25, 26, 28, 86

Hedayat, Sadeq 1903-1951 ....TCLC 21
See also CA 120

Hegel, Georg Wilhelm Friedrich 1770-1831 NCLC 46
See also DLB 90

Heidegger, Martin 1889-1976 ....CLC 24
See also CA 81-84; 65-68; CANR 34; MTCW

Heidenstam, (Carl Gustaf) Verner von 1859-1940 ....TCLC 5
See also CA 104

Heifner, Jack 1946- ....CLC 11
See also CA 105; CANR 47

Heijermans, Herman 1864-1924 ....TCLC 24
See also CA 123

Heilbrun, Carolyn G(old) 1926- ......CLC 25
See also CA 45-48; CANR 1, 28, 58

Heine, Heinrich 1797-1856 ....NCLC 4, 54
See also DLB 90

Heinemann, Larry (Curtiss) 1944-.. CLC 50
See also CA 110; CAAS 21; CANR 31; DLBD 9; INT CANR-31

Heiney, Donald (William) 1921-1993
See Harris, MacDonald
See also CA 1-4R; 142; CANR 3, 58

Heinlein, Robert A(nson) 1907-1988CLC 1, 3, 8, 14, 26, 55; DAM POP
See also AAYA 17; CA 1-4R; 125; CANR 1, 20, 53; DLB 8; JRDA; MAICYA; MTCW; SATA 9, 69; SATA-Obit 56

Helforth, John
See Doolittle, Hilda

Hellenhofferu, Vojtech Kapristian z
See Hasek, Jaroslav (Matej Frantisek)

Heller, Joseph 1923-CLC 1, 3, 5, 8, 11, 36, 63; DA; DAB; DAC; DAM MST, NOV, POP; WLC
See also AAYA 24; AITN 1; CA 5-8R; CABS 1; CANR 8, 42, 66; DLB 2, 28; DLBY 80; INT CANR-8; MTCW

Hellman, Lillian (Florence) 1906-1984CLC 2, 4, 8, 14, 18, 34, 44, 52; DAM DRAM; DC 1
See also AITN 1, 2; CA 13-16R; 112; CANR 33; DLB 7; DLBY 84; MTCW

Helprin, Mark 1947-CLC 7, 10, 22, 32; DAM NOV, POP
See also CA 81-84; CANR 47, 64; DLBY 85; MTCW

Helvetius, Claude-Adrien 1715-1771 . LC 26

Helyar, Jane Penelope Josephine 1933-
See Poole, Josephine
See also CA 21-24R; CANR 10, 26; SATA 82

Hemans, Felicia 1793-1835 ....NCLC 29
See also DLB 96

Hemingway, Ernest (Miller) 1899-1961 C L C 1, 3, 6, 8, 10, 13, 19, 30, 34, 39, 41, 44, 50, 61, 80; DA; DAB; DAC; DAM MST, NOV; SSC 25; WLC
See also AAYA 19; CA 77-80; CANR 34; CDALB 1917-1929; DLB 4, 9, 102; DLBD 1, 15, 16; DLBY 81, 87, 96; MTCW

Hempel, Amy 1951- .... **CLC 39**
See also CA 118; 137
Henderson, F. C.
See Mencken, H(enry) L(ouis)
Henderson, Sylvia
See Ashton-Warner, Sylvia (Constance)
Henderson, Zenna (Chlarson) 1917-1983**S S C 29**
See also CA 1-4R; 133; CANR 1; DLB 8; SATA 5
Henley, Beth .... **CLC 23; DC 6**
See also Henley, Elizabeth Becker
See also CABS 3; DLBY 86
Henley, Elizabeth Becker 1952-
See Henley, Beth
See also CA 107; CANR 32; DAM DRAM, MST; MTCW
Henley, William Ernest 1849-1903 .. **TCLC 8**
See also CA 105; DLB 19
Hennissart, Martha
See Lathen, Emma
See also CA 85-88; CANR 64
Henry, O. .... **TCLC 1, 19; SSC 5; WLC**
See also Porter, William Sydney
Henry, Patrick 1736-1799 .... **LC 25**
Henryson, Robert 1430(?)-1506(?) ..... **LC 20**
See also DLB 146
Henry VIII 1491-1547 .... **LC 10**
Henschke, Alfred
See Klabund
Hentoff, Nat(han Irving) 1925- .... **CLC 26**
See also AAYA 4; CA 1-4R; CAAS 6; CANR 5, 25; CLR 1; INT CANR-25; JRDA; MAICYA; SATA 42, 69; SATA-Brief 27
Heppenstall, (John) Rayner 1911-1981 . **C L C 10**
See also CA 1-4R; 103; CANR 29
Heraclitus c. 540B.C.-c. 450B.C. .... **CMLC 22**
See also DLB 176
Herbert, Frank (Patrick) 1920-1986 **CLC 12, 23, 35, 44, 85; DAM POP**
See also AAYA 21; CA 53-56; 118; CANR 5, 43; DLB 8; INT CANR-5; MTCW; SATA 9, 37; SATA-Obit 47
Herbert, George 1593-1633 ..... **LC 24; DAB; DAM POET; PC 4**
See also CDBLB Before 1660; DLB 126
Herbert, Zbigniew 1924- ...**CLC 9, 43; DAM POET**
See also CA 89-92; CANR 36; MTCW
Herbst, Josephine (Frey) 1897-1969 **CLC 34**
See also CA 5-8R; 25-28R; DLB 9
Hergesheimer, Joseph 1880-1954 ... **TCLC 11**
See also CA 109; DLB 102, 9
Herlihy, James Leo 1927-1993 .... **CLC 6**
See also CA 1-4R; 143; CANR 2
Hermogenes fl. c. 175- .... **CMLC 6**
Hernandez, Jose 1834-1886 .... **NCLC 17**
Herodotus c. 484B.C.-429B.C. .... **CMLC 17**
See also DLB 176
Herrick, Robert 1591-1674**LC 13; DA; DAB; DAC; DAM MST, POP; PC 9**
See also DLB 126
Herring, Guilles
See Somerville, Edith
Herriot, James 1916-1995**CLC 12; DAM POP**
See also Wight, James Alfred
See also AAYA 1; CA 148; CANR 40; SATA 86
Herrmann, Dorothy 1941- .... **CLC 44**
See also CA 107
Herrmann, Taffy
See Herrmann, Dorothy

Hersey, John (Richard) 1914-1993**CLC 1, 2, 7, 9, 40, 81, 97; DAM POP**
See also CA 17-20R; 140; CANR 33; DLB 6, 185; MTCW; SATA 25; SATA-Obit 76
Herzen, Aleksandr Ivanovich 1812-1870 **NCLC 10, 61**
Herzl, Theodor 1860-1904 .... **TCLC 36**
Herzog, Werner 1942- .... **CLC 16**
See also CA 89-92
Hesiod c. 8th cent. B.C.- .... **CMLC 5**
See also DLB 176
Hesse, Hermann 1877-1962**CLC 1, 2, 3, 6, 11, 17, 25, 69; DA; DAB; DAC; DAM MST, NOV; SSC 9; WLC**
See also CA 17-18; CAP 2; DLB 66; MTCW; SATA 50
Hewes, Cady
See De Voto, Bernard (Augustine)
Heyen, William 1940- .... **CLC 13, 18**
See also CA 33-36R; CAAS 9; DLB 5
Heyerdahl, Thor 1914- .... **CLC 26**
See also CA 5-8R; CANR 5, 22, 66; MTCW; SATA 2, 52
Heym, Georg (Theodor Franz Arthur) 1887-1912 .... **TCLC 9**
See also CA 106
Heym, Stefan 1913- .... **CLC 41**
See also CA 9-12R; CANR 4; DLB 69
Heyse, Paul (Johann Ludwig von) 1830-1914 **TCLC 8**
See also CA 104; DLB 129
Heyward, (Edwin) DuBose 1885-1940 **T C L C 59**
See also CA 108; 157; DLB 7, 9, 45; SATA 21
Hibbert, Eleanor Alice Burford 1906-1993 **CLC 7; DAM POP**
See also BEST 90:4; CA 17-20R; 140; CANR 9, 28, 59; SATA 2; SATA-Obit 74
Hichens, Robert (Smythe) 1864-1950 . **T C L C 64**
See also CA 162; DLB 153
Higgins, George V(incent) 1939-**CLC 4, 7, 10, 18**
See also CA 77-80; CAAS 5; CANR 17, 51; DLB 2; DLBY 81; INT CANR-17; MTCW
Higginson, Thomas Wentworth 1823-1911 **TCLC 36**
See also CA 162; DLB 1, 64
Highet, Helen
See MacInnes, Helen (Clark)
Highsmith, (Mary) Patricia 1921-1995**CLC 2, 4, 14, 42, 102; DAM NOV, POP**
See also CA 1-4R; 147; CANR 1, 20, 48, 62; MTCW
Highwater, Jamake (Mamake) 1942(?)- **C L C 12**
See also AAYA 7; CA 65-68; CAAS 7; CANR 10, 34; CLR 17; DLB 52; DLBY 85; JRDA; MAICYA; SATA 32, 69; SATA-Brief 30
Highway, Tomson 1951-**CLC 92; DAC; DAM MULT**
See also CA 151; NNAL
Higuchi, Ichiyo 1872-1896 .... **NCLC 49**
Hijuelos, Oscar 1951- **CLC 65; DAM MULT, POP; HLC**
See also AAYA 25; BEST 90:1; CA 123; CANR 50; DLB 145; HW
Hikmet, Nazim 1902(?)-1963 .... **CLC 40**
See also CA 141; 93-96
Hildegard von Bingen 1098-1179 . **CMLC 20**
See also DLB 148
Hildesheimer, Wolfgang 1916-1991 ..**CLC 49**
See also CA 101; 135; DLB 69, 124

Hill, Geoffrey (William) 1932- **CLC 5, 8, 18, 45; DAM POET**
See also CA 81-84; CANR 21; CDBLB 1960 to Present; DLB 40; MTCW
Hill, George Roy 1921- .... **CLC 26**
See also CA 110; 122
Hill, John
See Koontz, Dean R(ay)
Hill, Susan (Elizabeth) 1942- . **CLC 4; DAB; DAM MST, NOV**
See also CA 33-36R; CANR 29; DLB 14, 139; MTCW
Hillerman, Tony 1925- ..**CLC 62; DAM POP**
See also AAYA 6; BEST 89:1; CA 29-32R; CANR 21, 42, 65; SATA 6
Hillesum, Etty 1914-1943 .... **TCLC 49**
See also CA 137
Hilliard, Noel (Harvey) 1929- .... **CLC 15**
See also CA 9-12R; CANR 7
Hillis, Rick 1956- .... **CLC 66**
See also CA 134
Hilton, James 1900-1954 .... **TCLC 21**
See also CA 108; DLB 34, 77; SATA 34
Himes, Chester (Bomar) 1909-1984**CLC 2, 4, 7, 18, 58, 108; BLC; DAM MULT**
See also BW 2; CA 25-28R; 114; CANR 22; DLB 2, 76, 143; MTCW
Hinde, Thomas ....**CLC 6, 11**
See also Chitty, Thomas Willes
Hindin, Nathan
See Bloch, Robert (Albert)
Hine, (William) Daryl 1936- .... **CLC 15**
See also CA 1-4R; CAAS 15; CANR 1, 20; DLB 60
Hinkson, Katharine Tynan
See Tynan, Katharine
Hinton, S(usan) E(loise) 1950- **CLC 30; DA; DAB; DAC; DAM MST, NOV**
See also AAYA 2; CA 81-84; CANR 32, 62; CLR 3, 23; JRDA; MAICYA; MTCW; SATA 19, 58
Hippius, Zinaida .... **TCLC 9**
See also Gippius, Zinaida (Nikolayevna)
Hiraoka, Kimitake 1925-1970
See Mishima, Yukio
See also CA 97-100; 29-32R; DAM DRAM; MTCW
Hirsch, E(ric) D(onald), Jr. 1928- ..... **CLC 79**
See also CA 25-28R; CANR 27, 51; DLB 67; INT CANR-27; MTCW
Hirsch, Edward 1950- .... **CLC 31, 50**
See also CA 104; CANR 20, 42; DLB 120
Hitchcock, Alfred (Joseph) 1899-1980**CLC 16**
See also AAYA 22; CA 159; 97-100; SATA 27; SATA-Obit 24
Hitler, Adolf 1889-1945 .... **TCLC 53**
See also CA 117; 147
Hoagland, Edward 1932- .... **CLC 28**
See also CA 1-4R; CANR 2, 31, 57; DLB 6; SATA 51
Hoban, Russell (Conwell) 1925- . **CLC 7, 25; DAM NOV**
See also CA 5-8R; CANR 23, 37, 66; CLR 3; DLB 52; MAICYA; MTCW; SATA 1, 40, 78
Hobbes, Thomas 1588-1679 .... **LC 36**
See also DLB 151
Hobbs, Perry
See Blackmur, R(ichard) P(almer)
Hobson, Laura Z(ametkin) 1900-1986**CLC 7, 25**
See also CA 17-20R; 118; CANR 55; DLB 28; SATA 52
Hochhuth, Rolf 1931- ...**CLC 4, 11, 18; DAM**

DRAM
See also CA 5-8R; CANR 33; DLB 124; MTCW
Hochman, Sandra 1936- .... **CLC 3, 8**
See also CA 5-8R; DLB 5
Hochwaelder, Fritz 1911-1986**CLC 36; DAM
DRAM**
See also CA 29-32R; 120; CANR 42; MTCW
Hochwalder, Fritz
See Hochwaelder, Fritz
Hocking, Mary (Eunice) 1921-......... **CLC 13**
See also CA 101; CANR 18, 40
Hodgins, Jack 1938- .... **CLC 23**
See also CA 93-96; DLB 60
Hodgson, William Hope 1877(?)-1918 **T C L C
13**
See also CA 111; 164; DLB 70, 153, 156, 178
Hoeg, Peter 1957- .... **CLC 95**
See also CA 151
Hoffman, Alice 1952- ... **CLC 51; DAM NOV**
See also CA 77-80; CANR 34, 66; MTCW
Hoffman, Daniel (Gerard) 1923-**CLC 6, 13, 23**
See also CA 1-4R; CANR 4; DLB 5
Hoffman, Stanley 1944- .... **CLC 5**
See also CA 77-80
Hoffman, William M(oses) 1939-..... **CLC 40**
See also CA 57-60; CANR 11
Hoffmann, E(rnst) T(heodor) A(madeus) 1776-
1822 .... **NCLC 2; SSC 13**
See also DLB 90; SATA 27
Hofmann, Gert 1931- .... **CLC 54**
See also CA 128
Hofmannsthal, Hugo von 1874-1929**TCLC 11;
DAM DRAM; DC 4**
See also CA 106; 153; DLB 81, 118
Hogan, Linda 1947- ... **CLC 73; DAM MULT**
See also CA 120; CANR 45; DLB 175; NNAL
Hogarth, Charles
See Creasey, John
Hogarth, Emmett
See Polonsky, Abraham (Lincoln)
Hogg, James 1770-1835 .... **NCLC 4**
See also DLB 93, 116, 159
Holbach, Paul Henri Thiry Baron 1723-1789
LC 14
Holberg, Ludvig 1684-1754 .... **LC 6**
Holden, Ursula 1921- .... **CLC 18**
See also CA 101; CAAS 8; CANR 22
Holderlin, (Johann Christian) Friedrich 1770-
1843 .... **NCLC 16; PC 4**
Holdstock, Robert
See Holdstock, Robert P.
Holdstock, Robert P. 1948- .... **CLC 39**
See also CA 131
Holland, Isabelle 1920- .... **CLC 21**
See also AAYA 11; CA 21-24R; CANR 10, 25,
47; JRDA; MAICYA; SATA 8, 70
Holland, Marcus
See Caldwell, (Janet Miriam) Taylor (Holland)
Hollander, John 1929- .... **CLC 2, 5, 8, 14**
See also CA 1-4R; CANR 1, 52; DLB 5; SATA
13
Hollander, Paul
See Silverberg, Robert
Holleran, Andrew 1943(?)- .... **CLC 38**
See also CA 144
Hollinghurst, Alan 1954- .... **CLC 55, 91**
See also CA 114
Hollis, Jim
See Summers, Hollis (Spurgeon, Jr.)
Holly, Buddy 1936-1959 .... **TCLC 65**
Holmes, Gordon
See Shiel, M(atthew) P(hipps)
Holmes, John

See Souster, (Holmes) Raymond
Holmes, John Clellon 1926-1988 ......**CLC 56**
See also CA 9-12R; 125; CANR 4; DLB 16
Holmes, Oliver Wendell, Jr. 1841-1935**T C L C
77**
See also CA 114
Holmes, Oliver Wendell 1809-1894 **NCLC 14**
See also CDALB 1640-1865; DLB 1, 189;
SATA 34
Holmes, Raymond
See Souster, (Holmes) Raymond
Holt, Victoria
See Hibbert, Eleanor Alice Burford
Holub, Miroslav 1923- ....**CLC 4**
See also CA 21-24R; CANR 10
Homer c. 8th cent. B.C.- ... **CMLC 1, 16; DA;
DAB; DAC; DAM MST, POET; WLCS**
See also DLB 176
Honig, Edwin 1919-............................**CLC 33**
See also CA 5-8R; CAAS 8; CANR 4, 45; DLB
5
Hood, Hugh (John Blagdon) 1928-**CLC 15, 28**
See also CA 49-52; CAAS 17; CANR 1, 33;
DLB 53
Hood, Thomas 1799-1845 ....**NCLC 16**
See also DLB 96
Hooker, (Peter) Jeremy 1941- ....**CLC 43**
See also CA 77-80; CANR 22; DLB 40
hooks, bell ....**CLC 94**
See also Watkins, Gloria
Hope, A(lec) D(erwent) 1907- ...... **CLC 3, 51**
See also CA 21-24R; CANR 33; MTCW
Hope, Brian
See Creasey, John
Hope, Christopher (David Tully) 1944- **C L C
52**
See also CA 106; CANR 47; SATA 62
Hopkins, Gerard Manley 1844-1889 .. **N C L C
17; DA; DAB; DAC; DAM MST, POET;
PC 15; WLC**
See also CDBLB 1890-1914; DLB 35, 57
Hopkins, John (Richard) 1931-...........**CLC 4**
See also CA 85-88
Hopkins, Pauline Elizabeth 1859-1930**T C L C
28; BLC; DAM MULT**
See also BW 2; CA 141; DLB 50
Hopkinson, Francis 1737-1791 ....**LC 25**
See also DLB 31
Hopley-Woolrich, Cornell George 1903-1968
See Woolrich, Cornell
See also CA 13-14; CANR 58; CAP 1
Horatio
See Proust, (Valentin-Louis-George-Eugene-)
Marcel
Horgan, Paul (George Vincent O'Shaughnessy)
1903-1995 ....**CLC 9, 53; DAM NOV**
See also CA 13-16R; 147; CANR 9, 35; DLB
102; DLBY 85; INT CANR-9; MTCW;
SATA 13; SATA-Obit 84
Horn, Peter
See Kuttner, Henry
Hornem, Horace Esq.
See Byron, George Gordon (Noel)
Horney, Karen (Clementine Theodore
Danielsen) 1885-1952 ....**TCLC 71**
See also CA 114; 165
Hornung, E(rnest) W(illiam) 1866-1921
TCLC 59
See also CA 108; 160; DLB 70
Horovitz, Israel (Arthur) 1939-**CLC 56; DAM
DRAM**
See also CA 33-36R; CANR 46, 59; DLB 7
Horvath, Odon von

See Horvath, Oedoen von
See also DLB 85, 124
Horvath, Oedoen von 1901-1938 ... **TCLC 45**
See also Horvath, Odon von
See also CA 118
Horwitz, Julius 1920-1986 .... **CLC 14**
See also CA 9-12R; 119; CANR 12
Hospital, Janette Turner 1942- .... **CLC 42**
See also CA 108; CANR 48
Hostos, E. M. de
See Hostos (y Bonilla), Eugenio Maria de
Hostos, Eugenio M. de
See Hostos (y Bonilla), Eugenio Maria de
Hostos, Eugenio Maria
See Hostos (y Bonilla), Eugenio Maria de
Hostos (y Bonilla), Eugenio Maria de 1839-
1903 .... **TCLC 24**
See also CA 123; 131; HW
Houdini
See Lovecraft, H(oward) P(hillips)
Hougan, Carolyn 1943- .... **CLC 34**
See also CA 139
Household, Geoffrey (Edward West) 1900-1988
CLC 11
See also CA 77-80; 126; CANR 58; DLB 87;
SATA 14; SATA-Obit 59
Housman, A(lfred) E(dward) 1859-1936
**TCLC 1, 10; DA; DAB; DAC; DAM MST,
POET; PC 2; WLCS**
See also CA 104; 125; DLB 19; MTCW
Housman, Laurence 1865-1959 .... **TCLC 7**
See also CA 106; 155; DLB 10; SATA 25
Howard, Elizabeth Jane 1923-..... **CLC 7, 29**
See also CA 5-8R; CANR 8, 62
Howard, Maureen 1930-......... **CLC 5, 14, 46**
See also CA 53-56; CANR 31; DLBY 83; INT
CANR-31; MTCW
Howard, Richard 1929- .... **CLC 7, 10, 47**
See also AITN 1; CA 85-88; CANR 25; DLB 5;
INT CANR-25
Howard, Robert E(rvin) 1906-1936 **TCLC 8**
See also CA 105; 157
Howard, Warren F.
See Pohl, Frederik
Howe, Fanny 1940- .... **CLC 47**
See also CA 117; CAAS 27; SATA-Brief 52
Howe, Irving 1920-1993 .... **CLC 85**
See also CA 9-12R; 141; CANR 21, 50; DLB
67; MTCW
Howe, Julia Ward 1819-1910 .... **TCLC 21**
See also CA 117; DLB 1, 189
Howe, Susan 1937- .... **CLC 72**
See also CA 160; DLB 120
Howe, Tina 1937- .... **CLC 48**
See also CA 109
Howell, James 1594(?)-1666 .... **LC 13**
See also DLB 151
Howells, W. D.
See Howells, William Dean
Howells, William D.
See Howells, William Dean
Howells, William Dean 1837-1920**TCLC 7, 17,
41**
See also CA 104; 134; CDALB 1865-1917;
DLB 12, 64, 74, 79, 189
Howes, Barbara 1914-1996 .... **CLC 15**
See also CA 9-12R; 151; CAAS 3; CANR 53;
SATA 5
Hrabal, Bohumil 1914-1997 .... **CLC 13, 67**
See also CA 106; 156; CAAS 12; CANR 57
Hsun, Lu
See Lu Hsun
Hubbard, L(afayette) Ron(ald) 1911-1986

CLC 43; DAM POP
See also CA 77-80; 118; CANR 52
Huch, Ricarda (Octavia) 1864-1947TCLC 13
See also CA 111; DLB 66
Huddle, David 1942- .... CLC 49
See also CA 57-60; CAAS 20; DLB 130
Hudson, Jeffrey
See Crichton, (John) Michael
Hudson, W(illiam) H(enry) 1841-1922 T C L C
29
See also CA 115; DLB 98, 153, 174; SATA 35
Hueffer, Ford Madox
See Ford, Ford Madox
Hughart, Barry 1934- .... CLC 39
See also CA 137
Hughes, Colin
See Creasey, John
Hughes, David (John) 1930- .... CLC 48
See also CA 116; 129; DLB 14
Hughes, Edward James
See Hughes, Ted
See also DAM MST, POET
Hughes, (James) Langston 1902-1967CLC 1,
5, 10, 15, 35, 44, 108; BLC; DA; DAB;
DAC; DAM DRAM, MST, MULT, POET;
DC 3; PC 1; SSC 6; WLC
See also AAYA 12; BW 1; CA 1-4R; 25-28R;
CANR 1, 34; CDALB 1929-1941; CLR 17;
DLB 4, 7, 48, 51, 86; JRDA; MAICYA;
MTCW; SATA 4, 33
Hughes, Richard (Arthur Warren) 1900-1976
CLC 1, 11; DAM NOV
See also CA 5-8R; 65-68; CANR 4; DLB 15,
161; MTCW; SATA 8; SATA-Obit 25
Hughes, Ted 1930- CLC 2, 4, 9, 14, 37; DAB;
DAC; PC 7
See also Hughes, Edward James
See also CA 1-4R; CANR 1, 33, 66; CLR 3;
DLB 40, 161; MAICYA; MTCW; SATA 49;
SATA-Brief 27
Hugo, Richard F(ranklin) 1923-1982 CLC 6,
18, 32; DAM POET
See also CA 49-52; 108; CANR 3; DLB 5
Hugo, Victor (Marie) 1802-1885NCLC 3, 10,
21; DA; DAB; DAC; DAM DRAM, MST,
NOV, POET; PC 17; WLC
See also DLB 119, 192; SATA 47
Huidobro, Vicente
See Huidobro Fernandez, Vicente Garcia
Huidobro Fernandez, Vicente Garcia 1893-
1948 .... TCLC 31
See also CA 131; HW
Hulme, Keri 1947- .... CLC 39
See also CA 125; INT 125
Hulme, T(homas) E(rnest) 1883-1917 T C L C
21
See also CA 117; DLB 19
Hume, David 1711-1776 .... LC 7
See also DLB 104
Humphrey, William 1924-1997 .... CLC 45
See also CA 77-80; 160; CANR 68; DLB 6
Humphreys, Emyr Owen 1919- .... CLC 47
See also CA 5-8R; CANR 3, 24; DLB 15
Humphreys, Josephine 1945- ..... CLC 34, 57
See also CA 121; 127; INT 127
Huneker, James Gibbons 1857-1921TCLC 65
See also DLB 71
Hungerford, Pixie
See Brinsmead, H(esba) F(ay)
Hunt, E(verette) Howard, (Jr.) 1918- . CLC 3
See also AITN 1; CA 45-48; CANR 2, 47
Hunt, Kyle
See Creasey, John

Hunt, (James Henry) Leigh 1784-1859N C L C
1; DAM POET
Hunt, Marsha 1946- .... CLC 70
See also BW 2; CA 143
Hunt, Violet 1866-1942 .... TCLC 53
See also DLB 162
Hunter, E. Waldo
See Sturgeon, Theodore (Hamilton)
Hunter, Evan 1926- . CLC 11, 31; DAM POP
See also CA 5-8R; CANR 5, 38, 62; DLBY 82;
INT CANR-5; MTCW; SATA 25
Hunter, Kristin (Eggleston) 1931- ....CLC 35
See also AITN 1; BW 1; CA 13-16R; CANR
13; CLR 3; DLB 33; INT CANR-13;
MAICYA; SAAS 10; SATA 12
Hunter, Mollie 1922- .... CLC 21
See also McIlwraith, Maureen Mollie Hunter
See also AAYA 13; CANR 37; CLR 25; DLB
161; JRDA; MAICYA; SAAS 7; SATA 54
Hunter, Robert (?)-1734 .... LC 7
Hurston, Zora Neale 1903-1960CLC 7, 30, 61;
BLC; DA; DAC; DAM MST, MULT, NOV;
SSC 4; WLCS
See also AAYA 15; BW 1; CA 85-88; CANR
61; DLB 51, 86; MTCW
Huston, John (Marcellus) 1906-1987 CLC 20
See also CA 73-76; 123; CANR 34; DLB 26
Hustvedt, Siri 1955- .... CLC 76
See also CA 137
Hutten, Ulrich von 1488-1523 .... LC 16
See also DLB 179
Huxley, Aldous (Leonard) 1894-1963 CLC 1,
3, 4, 5, 8, 11, 18, 35, 79; DA; DAB; DAC;
DAM MST, NOV; WLC
See also AAYA 11; CA 85-88; CANR 44;
CDBLB 1914-1945; DLB 36, 100, 162, 195;
MTCW; SATA 63
Huxley, T. H. 1825-1895 .... NCLC 67
See also DLB 57
Huysmans, Joris-Karl 1848-1907TCLC 7, 69
See also CA 104; 165; DLB 123
Hwang, David Henry 1957-... CLC 55; DAM
DRAM; DC 4
See also CA 127; 132; INT 132
Hyde, Anthony 1946- .... CLC 42
See also CA 136
Hyde, Margaret O(ldroyd) 1917- ..... CLC 21
See also CA 1-4R; CANR 1, 36; CLR 23; JRDA;
MAICYA; SAAS 8; SATA 1, 42, 76
Hynes, James 1956(?)-......................... CLC 65
See also CA 164
Ian, Janis 1951- .... CLC 21
See also CA 105
Ibanez, Vicente Blasco
See Blasco Ibanez, Vicente
Ibarguengoitia, Jorge 1928-1983 ...... CLC 37
See also CA 124; 113; HW
Ibsen, Henrik (Johan) 1828-1906 TCLC 2, 8,
16, 37, 52; DA; DAB; DAC; DAM DRAM,
MST; DC 2; WLC
See also CA 104; 141
Ibuse Masuji 1898-1993 .... CLC 22
See also CA 127; 141; DLB 180
Ichikawa, Kon 1915- .... CLC 20
See also CA 121
Idle, Eric 1943- .... CLC 21
See also Monty Python
See also CA 116; CANR 35
Ignatow, David 1914-1997 .. CLC 4, 7, 14, 40
See also CA 9-12R; 162; CAAS 3; CANR 31,
57; DLB 5
Ihimaera, Witi 1944- .... CLC 46
See also CA 77-80

Ilf, Ilya .... TCLC 21
See also Fainzilberg, Ilya Arnoldovich
Illyes, Gyula 1902-1983 .... PC 16
See also CA 114; 109
Immermann, Karl (Lebrecht) 1796-1840
NCLC 4, 49
See also DLB 133
Inchbald, Elizabeth 1753-1821 ...... NCLC 62
See also DLB 39, 89
Inclan, Ramon (Maria) del Valle
See Valle-Inclan, Ramon (Maria) del
Infante, G(uillermo) Cabrera
See Cabrera Infante, G(uillermo)
Ingalls, Rachel (Holmes) 1940- .... CLC 42
See also CA 123; 127
Ingamells, Rex 1913-1955 .... TCLC 35
Inge, William (Motter) 1913-1973 CLC 1, 8,
19; DAM DRAM
See also CA 9-12R; CDALB 1941-1968; DLB
7; MTCW
Ingelow, Jean 1820-1897 .... NCLC 39
See also DLB 35, 163; SATA 33
Ingram, Willis J.
See Harris, Mark
Innaurato, Albert (F.) 1948(?)- .. CLC 21, 60
See also CA 115; 122; INT 122
Innes, Michael
See Stewart, J(ohn) I(nnes) M(ackintosh)
Innis, Harold Adams 1894-1952 .... TCLC 77
See also DLB 88
Ionesco, Eugene 1909-1994CLC 1, 4, 6, 9, 11,
15, 41, 86; DA; DAB; DAC; DAM DRAM,
MST; WLC
See also CA 9-12R; 144; CANR 55; MTCW;
SATA 7; SATA-Obit 79
Iqbal, Muhammad 1873-1938 .... TCLC 28
Ireland, Patrick
See O'Doherty, Brian
Iron, Ralph
See Schreiner, Olive (Emilie Albertina)
Irving, John (Winslow) 1942-CLC 13, 23, 38;
DAM NOV, POP
See also AAYA 8; BEST 89:3; CA 25-28R;
CANR 28; DLB 6; DLBY 82; MTCW
Irving, Washington 1783-1859 . NCLC 2, 19;
DA; DAB; DAM MST; SSC 2; WLC
See also CDALB 1640-1865; DLB 3, 11, 30,
59, 73, 74, 186; YABC 2
Irwin, P. K.
See Page, P(atricia) K(athleen)
Isaacs, Susan 1943-........ CLC 32; DAM POP
See also BEST 89:1; CA 89-92; CANR 20, 41,
65; INT CANR-20; MTCW
Isherwood, Christopher (William Bradshaw)
1904-1986.... CLC 1, 9, 11, 14, 44; DAM
DRAM, NOV
See also CA 13-16R; 117; CANR 35; DLB 15,
195; DLBY 86; MTCW
Ishiguro, Kazuo 1954- CLC 27, 56, 59; DAM
NOV
See also BEST 90:2; CA 120; CANR 49; DLB
194; MTCW
Ishikawa, Hakuhin
See Ishikawa, Takuboku
Ishikawa, Takuboku 1886(?)-1912 TCLC 15;
DAM POET; PC 10
See also CA 113; 153
Iskander, Fazil 1929- .... CLC 47
See also CA 102
Isler, Alan (David) 1934-................... CLC 91
See also CA 156
Ivan IV 1530-1584 .... LC 17
Ivanov, Vyacheslav Ivanovich 1866-1949

TCLC 33
See also CA 122

Ivask, Ivar Vidrik 1927-1992 .... **CLC 14**
See also CA 37-40R; 139; CANR 24

Ives, Morgan
See Bradley, Marion Zimmer

J. R. S.
See Gogarty, Oliver St. John

Jabran, Kahlil
See Gibran, Kahlil

Jabran, Khalil
See Gibran, Kahlil

Jackson, Daniel
See Wingrove, David (John)

Jackson, Jesse 1908-1983 .... **CLC 12**
See also BW 1; CA 25-28R; 109; CANR 27; CLR 28; MAICYA; SATA 2, 29; SATA-Obit 48

Jackson, Laura (Riding) 1901-1991
See Riding, Laura
See also CA 65-68; 135; CANR 28; DLB 48

Jackson, Sam
See Trumbo, Dalton

Jackson, Sara
See Wingrove, David (John)

Jackson, Shirley 1919-1965 . **CLC 11, 60, 87; DA; DAC; DAM MST; SSC 9; WLC**
See also AAYA 9; CA 1-4R; 25-28R; CANR 4, 52; CDALB 1941-1968; DLB 6; SATA 2

Jacob, (Cyprien-)Max 1876-1944 .... **TCLC 6**
See also CA 104

Jacobs, Harriet 1813(?)-1897 .... **NCLC 67**

Jacobs, Jim 1942- .... **CLC 12**
See also CA 97-100; INT 97-100

Jacobs, W(illiam) W(ymark) 1863-1943 **TCLC 22**
See also CA 121; DLB 135

Jacobsen, Jens Peter 1847-1885 ..... **NCLC 34**

Jacobsen, Josephine 1908- .... **CLC 48, 102**
See also CA 33-36R; CAAS 18; CANR 23, 48

Jacobson, Dan 1929- .... **CLC 4, 14**
See also CA 1-4R; CANR 2, 25, 66; DLB 14; MTCW

Jacqueline
See Carpentier (y Valmont), Alejo

Jagger, Mick 1944- .... **CLC 17**

Jahiz, Al- c. 776-869 .... **CMLC 25**

Jahiz, al- c. 780-c. 869 .... **CMLC 25**

Jakes, John (William) 1932- .. **CLC 29; DAM NOV, POP**
See also BEST 89:4; CA 57-60; CANR 10, 43, 66; DLBY 83; INT CANR-10; MTCW; SATA 62

James, Andrew
See Kirkup, James

James, C(yril) L(ionel) R(obert) 1901-1989 **CLC 33**
See also BW 2; CA 117; 125; 128; CANR 62; DLB 125; MTCW

James, Daniel (Lewis) 1911-1988
See Santiago, Danny
See also CA 125

James, Dynely
See Mayne, William (James Carter)

James, Henry Sr. 1811-1882 .... **NCLC 53**

James, Henry 1843-1916 **TCLC 2, 11, 24, 40, 47, 64; DA; DAB; DAC; DAM MST, NOV; SSC 8; WLC**
See also CA 104; 132; CDALB 1865-1917; DLB 12, 71, 74, 189; DLBD 13; MTCW

James, M. R.
See James, Montague (Rhodes)
See also DLB 156

James, Montague (Rhodes) 1862-1936 **T C L C 6; SSC 16**
See also CA 104

James, P. D. .... **CLC 18, 46**
See also White, Phyllis Dorothy James
See also BEST 90:2; CDBLB 1960 to Present; DLB 87

James, Philip
See Moorcock, Michael (John)

James, William 1842-1910 .... **TCLC 15, 32**
See also CA 109

James I 1394-1437 .... **LC 20**

Jameson, Anna 1794-1860 .... **NCLC 43**
See also DLB 99, 166

Jami, Nur al-Din 'Abd al-Rahman 1414-1492 **LC 9**

Jammes, Francis 1868-1938 .... **TCLC 75**

Jandl, Ernst 1925- .... **CLC 34**

Janowitz, Tama 1957- ... **CLC 43; DAM POP**
See also CA 106; CANR 52

Japrisot, Sebastien 1931- .... **CLC 90**

Jarrell, Randall 1914-1965 **CLC 1, 2, 6, 9, 13, 49; DAM POET**
See also CA 5-8R; 25-28R; CABS 2; CANR 6, 34; CDALB 1941-1968; CLR 6; DLB 48, 52; MAICYA; MTCW; SATA 7

Jarry, Alfred 1873-1907 . **TCLC 2, 14; DAM DRAM; SSC 20**
See also CA 104; 153; DLB 192

Jarvis, E. K.
See Bloch, Robert (Albert); Ellison, Harlan (Jay); Silverberg, Robert

Jeake, Samuel, Jr.
See Aiken, Conrad (Potter)

Jean Paul 1763-1825 .... **NCLC 7**

Jefferies, (John) Richard 1848-1887 **NCLC 47**
See also DLB 98, 141; SATA 16

Jeffers, (John) Robinson 1887-1962 **CLC 2, 3, 11, 15, 54; DA; DAC; DAM MST, POET; PC 17; WLC**
See also CA 85-88; CANR 35; CDALB 1917-1929; DLB 45; MTCW

Jefferson, Janet
See Mencken, H(enry) L(ouis)

Jefferson, Thomas 1743-1826 .... **NCLC 11**
See also CDALB 1640-1865; DLB 31

Jeffrey, Francis 1773-1850 .... **NCLC 33**
See also DLB 107

Jelakowitch, Ivan
See Heijermans, Herman

Jellicoe, (Patricia) Ann 1927- .... **CLC 27**
See also CA 85-88; DLB 13

Jen, Gish .... **CLC 70**
See also Jen, Lillian

Jen, Lillian 1956(?)-
See Jen, Gish
See also CA 135

Jenkins, (John) Robin 1912- .... **CLC 52**
See also CA 1-4R; CANR 1; DLB 14

Jennings, Elizabeth (Joan) 1926- . **CLC 5, 14**
See also CA 61-64; CAAS 5; CANR 8, 39, 66; DLB 27; MTCW; SATA 66

Jennings, Waylon 1937- .... **CLC 21**

Jensen, Johannes V. 1873-1950 ...... **TCLC 41**

Jensen, Laura (Linnea) 1948- .... **CLC 37**
See also CA 103

Jerome, Jerome K(lapka) 1859-1927 **TCLC 23**
See also CA 119; DLB 10, 34, 135

Jerrold, Douglas William 1803-1857 **NCLC 2**
See also DLB 158, 159

Jewett, (Theodora) Sarah Orne 1849-1909 **TCLC 1, 22; SSC 6**
See also CA 108; 127; DLB 12, 74; SATA 15

Jewsbury, Geraldine (Endsor) 1812-1880 **NCLC 22**
See also DLB 21

Jhabvala, Ruth Prawer 1927- **CLC 4, 8, 29, 94; DAB; DAM NOV**
See also CA 1-4R; CANR 2, 29, 51; DLB 139, 194; INT CANR-29; MTCW

Jibran, Kahlil
See Gibran, Kahlil

Jibran, Khalil
See Gibran, Kahlil

Jiles, Paulette 1943- .... **CLC 13, 58**
See also CA 101

Jimenez (Mantecon), Juan Ramon 1881-1958 **TCLC 4; DAM MULT, POET; HLC; PC 7**
See also CA 104; 131; DLB 134; HW; MTCW

Jimenez, Ramon
See Jimenez (Mantecon), Juan Ramon

Jimenez Mantecon, Juan
See Jimenez (Mantecon), Juan Ramon

Jin, Ha 1956- .... **CLC 109**
See also CA 152

Joel, Billy .... **CLC 26**
See also Joel, William Martin

Joel, William Martin 1949-
See Joel, Billy
See also CA 108

John of the Cross, St. 1542-1591 .... **LC 18**

Johnson, B(ryan) S(tanley William) 1933-1973 **CLC 6, 9**
See also CA 9-12R; 53-56; CANR 9; DLB 14, 40

Johnson, Benj. F. of Boo
See Riley, James Whitcomb

Johnson, Benjamin F. of Boo
See Riley, James Whitcomb

Johnson, Charles (Richard) 1948- **CLC 7, 51, 65; BLC; DAM MULT**
See also BW 2; CA 116; CAAS 18; CANR 42, 66; DLB 33

Johnson, Denis 1949- .... **CLC 52**
See also CA 117; 121; DLB 120

Johnson, Diane 1934- .... **CLC 5, 13, 48**
See also CA 41-44R; CANR 17, 40, 62; DLBY 80; INT CANR-17; MTCW

Johnson, Eyvind (Olof Verner) 1900-1976 **CLC 14**
See also CA 73-76; 69-72; CANR 34

Johnson, J. R.
See James, C(yril) L(ionel) R(obert)

Johnson, James Weldon 1871-1938 **TCLC 3, 19; BLC; DAM MULT, POET**
See also BW 1; CA 104; 125; CDALB 1917-1929; CLR 32; DLB 51; MTCW; SATA 31

Johnson, Joyce 1935- .... **CLC 58**
See also CA 125; 129

Johnson, Lionel (Pigot) 1867-1902 **TCLC 19**
See also CA 117; DLB 19

Johnson, Mel
See Malzberg, Barry N(athaniel)

Johnson, Pamela Hansford 1912-1981 **CLC 1, 7, 27**
See also CA 1-4R; 104; CANR 2, 28; DLB 15; MTCW

Johnson, Robert 1911(?)-1938 .... **TCLC 69**

Johnson, Samuel 1709-1784 **LC 15; DA; DAB; DAC; DAM MST; WLC**
See also CDBLB 1660-1789; DLB 39, 95, 104, 142

Johnson, Uwe 1934-1984 .. **CLC 5, 10, 15, 40**
See also CA 1-4R; 112; CANR 1, 39; DLB 75; MTCW

Johnston, George (Benson) 1913- .... **CLC 51**
    See also CA 1-4R; CANR 5, 20; DLB 88
Johnston, Jennifer 1930- .... **CLC 7**
    See also CA 85-88; DLB 14
Jolley, (Monica) Elizabeth 1923-**CLC 46; SSC
    19**
    See also CA 127; CAAS 13; CANR 59
Jones, Arthur Llewellyn 1863-1947
    See Machen, Arthur
    See also CA 104
Jones, D(ouglas) G(ordon) 1929- ..... **CLC 10**
    See also CA 29-32R; CANR 13; DLB 53
Jones, David (Michael) 1895-1974**CLC 2, 4, 7,
    13, 42**
    See also CA 9-12R; 53-56; CANR 28; CDBLB
    1945-1960; DLB 20, 100; MTCW
Jones, David Robert 1947-
    See Bowie, David
    See also CA 103
Jones, Diana Wynne 1934- .... **CLC 26**
    See also AAYA 12; CA 49-52; CANR 4, 26,
    56; CLR 23; DLB 161; JRDA; MAICYA;
    SAAS 7; SATA 9, 70
Jones, Edward P. 1950- .... **CLC 76**
    See also BW 2; CA 142
Jones, Gayl 1949- ...... **CLC 6, 9; BLC; DAM
    MULT**
    See also BW 2; CA 77-80; CANR 27, 66; DLB
    33; MTCW
Jones, James 1921-1977 ...... **CLC 1, 3, 10, 39**
    See also AITN 1, 2; CA 1-4R; 69-72; CANR 6;
    DLB 2, 143; MTCW
Jones, John J.
    See Lovecraft, H(oward) P(hillips)
Jones, LeRoi .... **CLC 1, 2, 3, 5, 10, 14**
    See also Baraka, Amiri
Jones, Louis B. .... **CLC 65**
    See also CA 141
Jones, Madison (Percy, Jr.) 1925- .... **CLC 4**
    See also CA 13-16R; CAAS 11; CANR 7, 54;
    DLB 152
Jones, Mervyn 1922- .... **CLC 10, 52**
    See also CA 45-48; CAAS 5; CANR 1; MTCW
Jones, Mick 1956(?)- .... **CLC 30**
Jones, Nettie (Pearl) 1941- .... **CLC 34**
    See also BW 2; CA 137; CAAS 20
Jones, Preston 1936-1979 .... **CLC 10**
    See also CA 73-76; 89-92; DLB 7
Jones, Robert F(rancis) 1934- .... **CLC 7**
    See also CA 49-52; CANR 2, 61
Jones, Rod 1953- .... **CLC 50**
    See also CA 128
Jones, Terence Graham Parry 1942- **CLC 21**
    See also Jones, Terry; Monty Python
    See also CA 112; 116; CANR 35; INT 116
Jones, Terry
    See Jones, Terence Graham Parry
    See also SATA 67; SATA-Brief 51
Jones, Thom 1945(?)- .... **CLC 81**
    See also CA 157
Jong, Erica 1942- **CLC 4, 6, 8, 18, 83; DAM
    NOV, POP**
    See also AITN 1; BEST 90:2; CA 73-76; CANR
    26, 52; DLB 2, 5, 28, 152; INT CANR-26;
    MTCW
Jonson, Ben(jamin) 1572(?)-1637 .. **LC 6, 33;
    DA; DAB; DAC; DAM DRAM, MST,
    POET; DC 4; PC 17; WLC**
    See also CDBLB Before 1660; DLB 62, 121
Jordan, June 1936- .... **CLC 5, 11, 23; DAM
    MULT, POET**
    See also AAYA 2; BW 2; CA 33-36R; CANR
    25; CLR 10; DLB 38; MAICYA; MTCW;

SATA 4
Jordan, Pat(rick M.) 1941- .... **CLC 37**
    See also CA 33-36R
Jorgensen, Ivar
    See Ellison, Harlan (Jay)
Jorgenson, Ivar
    See Silverberg, Robert
Josephus, Flavius c. 37-100 .... **CMLC 13**
Josipovici, Gabriel 1940- .... **CLC 6, 43**
    See also CA 37-40R; CAAS 8; CANR 47; DLB
    14
Joubert, Joseph 1754-1824 .... **NCLC 9**
Jouve, Pierre Jean 1887-1976 .... **CLC 47**
    See also CA 65-68
Jovine, Francesco 1902-1950 .... **TCLC 79**
Joyce, James (Augustine Aloysius) 1882-1941
    **TCLC 3, 8, 16, 35, 52; DA; DAB; DAC;
    DAM MST, NOV, POET; SSC 3, 26; WLC**
    See also CA 104; 126; CDBLB 1914-1945;
    DLB 10, 19, 36, 162; MTCW
Jozsef, Attila 1905-1937 .... **TCLC 22**
    See also CA 116
Juana Ines de la Cruz 1651(?)-1695 ..... **LC 5**
Judd, Cyril
    See Kornbluth, C(yril) M.; Pohl, Frederik
Julian of Norwich 1342(?)-1416(?) .... **LC 6**
    See also DLB 146
Junger, Sebastian 1962- .... **CLC 109**
    See also CA 165
Juniper, Alex
    See Hospital, Janette Turner
Junius
    See Luxemburg, Rosa
Just, Ward (Swift) 1935- .... **CLC 4, 27**
    See also CA 25-28R; CANR 32; INT CANR-
    32
Justice, Donald (Rodney) 1925- .. **CLC 6, 19,
    102; DAM POET**
    See also CA 5-8R; CANR 26, 54; DLBY 83;
    INT CANR-26
Juvenal c. 55-c. 127 .... **CMLC 8**
Juvenis
    See Bourne, Randolph S(illiman)
Kacew, Romain 1914-1980
    See Gary, Romain
    See also CA 108; 102
Kadare, Ismail 1936- ....**CLC 52**
    See also CA 161
Kadohata, Cynthia ....**CLC 59**
    See also CA 140
Kafka, Franz 1883-1924**TCLC 2, 6, 13, 29, 47,
    53; DA; DAB; DAC; DAM MST, NOV;
    SSC 5, 29; WLC**
    See also CA 105; 126; DLB 81; MTCW
Kahanovitsch, Pinkhes
    See Der Nister
Kahn, Roger 1927- ....**CLC 30**
    See also CA 25-28R; CANR 44; DLB 171;
    SATA 37
Kain, Saul
    See Sassoon, Siegfried (Lorraine)
Kaiser, Georg 1878-1945 .... **TCLC 9**
    See also CA 106; DLB 124
Kaletski, Alexander 1946- .... **CLC 39**
    See also CA 118; 143
Kalidasa fl. c. 400- .... **CMLC 9**
Kallman, Chester (Simon) 1921-1975 **CLC 2**
    See also CA 45-48; 53-56; CANR 3
Kaminsky, Melvin 1926-
    See Brooks, Mel
    See also CA 65-68; CANR 16
Kaminsky, Stuart M(elvin) 1934- ..... **CLC 59**
    See also CA 73-76; CANR 29, 53

Kane, Francis
    See Robbins, Harold
Kane, Paul
    See Simon, Paul (Frederick)
Kane, Wilson
    See Bloch, Robert (Albert)
Kanin, Garson 1912- .... **CLC 22**
    See also AITN 1; CA 5-8R; CANR 7; DLB 7
Kaniuk, Yoram 1930- .... **CLC 19**
    See also CA 134
Kant, Immanuel 1724-1804 ..... **NCLC 27, 67**
    See also DLB 94
Kantor, MacKinlay 1904-1977 .... **CLC 7**
    See also CA 61-64; 73-76; CANR 60, 63; DLB
    9, 102
Kaplan, David Michael 1946- .... **CLC 50**
Kaplan, James 1951- .... **CLC 59**
    See also CA 135
Karageorge, Michael
    See Anderson, Poul (William)
Karamzin, Nikolai Mikhailovich 1766-1826
    NCLC 3
    See also DLB 150
Karapanou, Margarita 1946- .... **CLC 13**
    See also CA 101
Karinthy, Frigyes 1887-1938 .... **TCLC 47**
Karl, Frederick R(obert) 1927- ....**CLC 34**
    See also CA 5-8R; CANR 3, 44
Kastel, Warren
    See Silverberg, Robert
Kataev, Evgeny Petrovich 1903-1942
    See Petrov, Evgeny
    See also CA 120
Kataphusin
    See Ruskin, John
Katz, Steve 1935- ....**CLC 47**
    See also CA 25-28R; CAAS 14, 64; CANR 12;
    DLBY 83
Kauffman, Janet 1945- .... **CLC 42**
    See also CA 117; CANR 43; DLBY 86
Kaufman, Bob (Garnell) 1925-1986 .**CLC 49**
    See also BW 1; CA 41-44R; 118; CANR 22;
    DLB 16, 41
Kaufman, George S. 1889-1961**CLC 38; DAM
    DRAM**
    See also CA 108; 93-96; DLB 7; INT 108
Kaufman, Sue .... **CLC 3, 8**
    See also Barondess, Sue K(aufman)
Kavafis, Konstantinos Petrou 1863-1933
    See Cavafy, C(onstantine) P(eter)
    See also CA 104
Kavan, Anna 1901-1968 .... **CLC 5, 13, 82**
    See also CA 5-8R; CANR 6, 57; MTCW
Kavanagh, Dan
    See Barnes, Julian (Patrick)
Kavanagh, Patrick (Joseph) 1904-1967 **C L C
    22**
    See also CA 123; 25-28R; DLB 15, 20; MTCW
Kawabata, Yasunari 1899-1972 **CLC 2, 5, 9,
    18, 107; DAM MULT; SSC 17**
    See also CA 93-96; 33-36R; DLB 180
Kaye, M(ary) M(argaret) 1909- ....**CLC 28**
    See also CA 89-92; CANR 24, 60; MTCW;
    SATA 62
Kaye, Mollie
    See Kaye, M(ary) M(argaret)
Kaye-Smith, Sheila 1887-1956 .... **TCLC 20**
    See also CA 118; DLB 36
Kaymor, Patrice Maguilene
    See Senghor, Leopold Sedar
Kazan, Elia 1909- .... **CLC 6, 16, 63**
    See also CA 21-24R; CANR 32
Kazantzakis, Nikos 1883(?)-1957 **TCLC 2, 5,**

33
See also CA 105; 132; MTCW

Kazin, Alfred 1915- .... **CLC 34, 38**
See also CA 1-4R; CAAS 7; CANR 1, 45; DLB 67

Keane, Mary Nesta (Skrine) 1904-1996
See Keane, Molly
See also CA 108; 114; 151

Keane, Molly .... **CLC 31**
See also Keane, Mary Nesta (Skrine)
See also INT 114

Keates, Jonathan 1946(?)- .... **CLC 34**
See also CA 163

Keaton, Buster 1895-1966 .... **CLC 20**

Keats, John 1795-1821 . **NCLC 8; DA; DAB; DAC; DAM MST, POET; PC 1; WLC**
See also CDBLB 1789-1832; DLB 96, 110

Keene, Donald 1922- .... **CLC 34**
See also CA 1-4R; CANR 5

Keillor, Garrison .... **CLC 40**
See also Keillor, Gary (Edward)
See also AAYA 2; BEST 89:3; DLBY 87; SATA 58

Keillor, Gary (Edward) 1942-
See Keillor, Garrison
See also CA 111; 117; CANR 36, 59; DAM POP; MTCW

Keith, Michael
See Hubbard, L(afayette) Ron(ald)

Keller, Gottfried 1819-1890NCLC 2; SSC 26
See also DLB 129

Keller, Nora Okja .... **CLC 109**

Kellerman, Jonathan 1949-...**CLC 44; DAM POP**
See also BEST 90:1; CA 106; CANR 29, 51; INT CANR-29

Kelley, William Melvin 1937-........... **CLC 22**
See also BW 1; CA 77-80; CANR 27; DLB 33

Kellogg, Marjorie 1922- .... **CLC 2**
See also CA 81-84

Kellow, Kathleen
See Hibbert, Eleanor Alice Burford

Kelly, M(ilton) T(erry) 1947- .... **CLC 55**
See also CA 97-100; CAAS 22; CANR 19, 43

Kelman, James 1946- .... **CLC 58, 86**
See also CA 148; DLB 194

Kemal, Yashar 1923- .... **CLC 14, 29**
See also CA 89-92; CANR 44

Kemble, Fanny 1809-1893 .... **NCLC 18**
See also DLB 32

Kemelman, Harry 1908-1996 .... **CLC 2**
See also AITN 1; CA 9-12R; 155; CANR 6; DLB 28

Kempe, Margery 1373(?)-1440(?) .... **LC 6**
See also DLB 146

Kempis, Thomas a 1380-1471 .... **LC 11**

Kendall, Henry 1839-1882 .... **NCLC 12**

Keneally, Thomas (Michael) 1935- **CLC 5, 8, 10, 14, 19, 27, 43; DAM NOV**
See also CA 85-88; CANR 10, 50; MTCW

Kennedy, Adrienne (Lita) 1931- ..... **CLC 66; BLC; DAM MULT; DC 5**
See also BW 2; CA 103; CAAS 20; CABS 3; CANR 26, 53; DLB 38

Kennedy, John Pendleton 1795-1870NCLC 2
See also DLB 3

Kennedy, Joseph Charles 1929-
See Kennedy, X. J.
See also CA 1-4R; CANR 4, 30, 40; SATA 14, 86

Kennedy, William 1928- ..CLC 6, 28, 34, 53; **DAM NOV**
See also AAYA 1; CA 85-88; CANR 14, 31;

DLB 143; DLBY 85; INT CANR-31; MTCW; SATA 57

Kennedy, X. J. .... **CLC 8, 42**
See also Kennedy, Joseph Charles
See also CAAS 9; CLR 27; DLB 5; SAAS 22

Kenny, Maurice (Francis) 1929- ..... **CLC 87; DAM MULT**
See also CA 144; CAAS 22; DLB 175; NNAL

Kent, Kelvin
See Kuttner, Henry

Kenton, Maxwell
See Southern, Terry

Kenyon, Robert O.
See Kuttner, Henry

Kerouac, Jack .... CLC 1, 2, 3, 5, 14, 29, 61
See also Kerouac, Jean-Louis Lebris de
See also AAYA 25; CDALB 1941-1968; DLB 2, 16; DLBD 3; DLBY 95

Kerouac, Jean-Louis Lebris de 1922-1969
See Kerouac, Jack
See also AITN 1; CA 5-8R; 25-28R; CANR 26, 54; DA; DAB; DAC; DAM MST, NOV, POET, POP; MTCW; WLC

Kerr, Jean 1923- .... CLC 22
See also CA 5-8R; CANR 7; INT CANR-7

Kerr, M. E. .... **CLC 12, 35**
See also Meaker, Marijane (Agnes)
See also AAYA 2, 23; CLR 29; SAAS 1

Kerr, Robert ....CLC 55

Kerrigan, (Thomas) Anthony 1918-CLC 4, 6
See also CA 49-52; CAAS 11; CANR 4

Kerry, Lois
See Duncan, Lois

Kesey, Ken (Elton) 1935- CLC 1, 3, 6, 11, 46, 64; **DA; DAB; DAC; DAM MST, NOV, POP; WLC**
See also AAYA 25; CA 1-4R; CANR 22, 38, 66; CDALB 1968-1988; DLB 2, 16; MTCW; SATA 66

Kesselring, Joseph (Otto) 1902-1967CLC 45; **DAM DRAM, MST**
See also CA 150

Kessler, Jascha (Frederick) 1929-.......CLC 4
See also CA 17-20R; CANR 8, 48

Kettelkamp, Larry (Dale) 1933- ....CLC 12
See also CA 29-32R; CANR 16; SAAS 3; SATA 2

Key, Ellen 1849-1926 .... TCLC 65

Keyber, Conny
See Fielding, Henry

Keyes, Daniel 1927-CLC 80; **DA; DAC; DAM MST, NOV**
See also AAYA 23; CA 17-20R; CANR 10, 26, 54; SATA 37

Keynes, John Maynard 1883-1946 TCLC 64
See also CA 114; 162, 163; DLBD 10

Khanshendel, Chiron
See Rose, Wendy

Khayyam, Omar 1048-1131 CMLC 11; **DAM POET; PC 8**

Kherdian, David 1931-.................... CLC 6, 9
See also CA 21-24R; CAAS 2; CANR 39; CLR 24; JRDA; MAICYA; SATA 16, 74

Khlebnikov, Velimir .... TCLC 20
See also Khlebnikov, Viktor Vladimirovich

Khlebnikov, Viktor Vladimirovich 1885-1922
See Khlebnikov, Velimir
See also CA 117

Khodasevich, Vladislav (Felitsianovich) 1886-1939 .... TCLC 15
See also CA 115

Kielland, Alexander Lange 1849-1906TCLC 5

See also CA 104

Kiely, Benedict 1919- .... CLC 23, 43
See also CA 1-4R; CANR 2; DLB 15

Kienzle, William X(avier) 1928- ..... **CLC 25; DAM POP**
See also CA 93-96; CAAS 1; CANR 9, 31, 59; INT CANR-31; MTCW

Kierkegaard, Soren 1813-1855 ...... NCLC 34

Killens, John Oliver 1916-1987 .... CLC 10
See also BW 2; CA 77-80; 123; CAAS 2; CANR 26; DLB 33

Killigrew, Anne 1660-1685 .... LC 4
See also DLB 131

Kim
See Simenon, Georges (Jacques Christian)

Kincaid, Jamaica 1949- .. **CLC 43, 68; BLC; DAM MULT, NOV**
See also AAYA 13; BW 2; CA 125; CANR 47, 59; DLB 157

King, Francis (Henry) 1923-CLC 8, 53; **DAM NOV**
See also CA 1-4R; CANR 1, 33; DLB 15, 139; MTCW

King, Kennedy
See Brown, George Douglas

King, Martin Luther, Jr. 1929-1968 CLC 83; **BLC; DA; DAB; DAC; DAM MST, MULT; WLCS**
See also BW 2; CA 25-28; CANR 27, 44; CAP 2; MTCW; SATA 14

King, Stephen (Edwin) 1947-CLC 12, 26, 37, 61; **DAM NOV, POP; SSC 17**
See also AAYA 1, 17; BEST 90:1; CA 61-64; CANR 1, 30, 52; DLB 143; DLBY 80; JRDA; MTCW; SATA 9, 55

King, Steve
See King, Stephen (Edwin)

King, Thomas 1943- .... **CLC 89; DAC; DAM MULT**
See also CA 144; DLB 175; NNAL; SATA 96

Kingman, Lee .... CLC 17
See also Natti, (Mary) Lee
See also SAAS 3; SATA 1, 67

Kingsley, Charles 1819-1875 .... NCLC 35
See also DLB 21, 32, 163, 190; YABC 2

Kingsley, Sidney 1906-1995 .... CLC 44
See also CA 85-88; 147; DLB 7

Kingsolver, Barbara 1955-CLC 55, 81; **DAM POP**
See also AAYA 15; CA 129; 134; CANR 60; INT 134

Kingston, Maxine (Ting Ting) Hong 1940- **CLC 12, 19, 58; DAM MULT, NOV; WLCS**
See also AAYA 8; CA 69-72; CANR 13, 38; DLB 173; DLBY 80; INT CANR-13; MTCW; SATA 53

Kinnell, Galway 1927- CLC 1, 2, 3, 5, 13, 29
See also CA 9-12R; CANR 10, 34, 66; DLB 5; DLBY 87; INT CANR-34; MTCW

Kinsella, Thomas 1928- .... CLC 4, 19
See also CA 17-20R; CANR 15; DLB 27; MTCW

Kinsella, W(illiam) P(atrick) 1935- CLC 27, 43; **DAC; DAM NOV, POP**
See also AAYA 7; CA 97-100; CAAS 7; CANR 21, 35, 66; INT CANR-21; MTCW

Kipling, (Joseph) Rudyard 1865-1936 T C L C 8, 17; **DA; DAB; DAC; DAM MST, POET; PC 3; SSC 5; WLC**
See also CA 105; 120; CANR 33; CDBLB 1890-1914; CLR 39; DLB 19, 34, 141, 156; MAICYA; MTCW; YABC 2

Kirkup, James 1918- .... **CLC 1**
    See also CA 1-4R; CAAS 4; CANR 2; DLB 27;
    SATA 12
Kirkwood, James 1930(?)-1989 .... **CLC 9**
    See also AITN 2; CA 1-4R; 128; CANR 6, 40
Kirshner, Sidney
    See Kingsley, Sidney
Kis, Danilo 1935-1989 .... **CLC 57**
    See also CA 109; 118; 129; CANR 61; DLB
    181; MTCW
Kivi, Aleksis 1834-1872 .... **NCLC 30**
Kizer, Carolyn (Ashley) 1925-**CLC 15, 39, 80;**
    DAM POET
    See also CA 65-68; CAAS 5; CANR 24; DLB
    5, 169
Klabund 1890-1928 .... **TCLC 44**
    See also CA 162; DLB 66
Klappert, Peter 1942- .... **CLC 57**
    See also CA 33-36R; DLB 5
Klein, A(braham) M(oses) 1909-1972**CLC 19;**
    DAB; DAC; DAM MST
    See also CA 101; 37-40R; DLB 68
Klein, Norma 1938-1989 .... **CLC 30**
    See also AAYA 2; CA 41-44R; 128; CANR 15,
    37; CLR 2, 19; INT CANR-15; JRDA;
    MAICYA; SAAS 1; SATA 7, 57
Klein, T(heodore) E(ibon) D(onald) 1947-
    CLC 34
    See also CA 119; CANR 44
Kleist, Heinrich von 1777-1811 **NCLC 2, 37;**
    DAM DRAM; SSC 22
    See also DLB 90
Klima, Ivan 1931- .... **CLC 56; DAM NOV**
    See also CA 25-28R; CANR 17, 50
Klimentov, Andrei Platonovich 1899-1951
    See Platonov, Andrei
    See also CA 108
Klinger, Friedrich Maximilian von 1752-1831
    NCLC 1
    See also DLB 94
Klingsor the Magician
    See Hartmann, Sadakichi
Klopstock, Friedrich Gottlieb 1724-1803
    NCLC 11
    See also DLB 97
Knapp, Caroline 1959-........................ **CLC 99**
    See also CA 154
Knebel, Fletcher 1911-1993 .... **CLC 14**
    See also AITN 1; CA 1-4R; 140; CAAS 3;
    CANR 1, 36; SATA 36; SATA-Obit 75
Knickerbocker, Diedrich
    See Irving, Washington
Knight, Etheridge 1931-1991 **CLC 40; BLC;**
    DAM POET; PC 14
    See also BW 1; CA 21-24R; 133; CANR 23;
    DLB 41
Knight, Sarah Kemble 1666-1727 .... **LC 7**
    See also DLB 24
Knister, Raymond 1899-1932 .... **TCLC 56**
    See also DLB 68
Knowles, John 1926- ..**CLC 1, 4, 10, 26; DA;**
    DAC; DAM MST, NOV
    See also AAYA 10; CA 17-20R; CANR 40;
    CDALB 1968-1988; DLB 6; MTCW; SATA
    8, 89
Knox, Calvin M.
    See Silverberg, Robert
Knox, John c. 1505-1572 .... **LC 37**
    See also DLB 132
Knye, Cassandra
    See Disch, Thomas M(ichael)
Koch, C(hristopher) J(ohn) 1932- ... **CLC 42**
    See also CA 127

Koch, Christopher
    See Koch, C(hristopher) J(ohn)
Koch, Kenneth 1925- .... **CLC 5, 8, 44; DAM**
    POET
    See also CA 1-4R; CANR 6, 36, 57; DLB 5;
    INT CANR-36; SATA 65
Kochanowski, Jan 1530-1584 .... **LC 10**
Kock, Charles Paul de 1794-1871 ..**NCLC 16**
Koda Shigeyuki 1867-1947
    See Rohan, Koda
    See also CA 121
Koestler, Arthur 1905-1983**CLC 1, 3, 6, 8, 15,**
    33
    See also CA 1-4R; 109; CANR 1, 33; CDBLB
    1945-1960; DLBY 83; MTCW
Kogawa, Joy Nozomi 1935- .. **CLC 78; DAC;**
    DAM MST, MULT
    See also CA 101; CANR 19, 62
Kohout, Pavel 1928- .... **CLC 13**
    See also CA 45-48; CANR 3
Koizumi, Yakumo
    See Hearn, (Patricio) Lafcadio (Tessima Carlos)
Kolmar, Gertrud 1894-1943 .... **TCLC 40**
Komunyakaa, Yusef 1947- .... **CLC 86, 94**
    See also CA 147; DLB 120
Konrad, George
    See Konrad, Gyoergy
Konrad, Gyoergy 1933- .... **CLC 4, 10, 73**
    See also CA 85-88
Konwicki, Tadeusz 1926- .... **CLC 8, 28, 54**
    See also CA 101; CAAS 9; CANR 39, 59;
    MTCW
Koontz, Dean R(ay) 1945- ..... **CLC 78; DAM**
    NOV, POP
    See also AAYA 9; BEST 89:3, 90:2; CA 108;
    CANR 19, 36, 52; MTCW; SATA 92
Kopit, Arthur (Lee) 1937-**CLC 1, 18, 33; DAM**
    DRAM
    See also AITN 1; CA 81-84; CABS 3; DLB 7;
    MTCW
Kops, Bernard 1926- .... **CLC 4**
    See also CA 5-8R; DLB 13
Kornbluth, C(yril) M. 1923-1958 .... **TCLC 8**
    See also CA 105; 160; DLB 8
Korolenko, V. G.
    See Korolenko, Vladimir Galaktionovich
Korolenko, Vladimir
    See Korolenko, Vladimir Galaktionovich
Korolenko, Vladimir G.
    See Korolenko, Vladimir Galaktionovich
Korolenko, Vladimir Galaktionovich 1853-
    1921 .... **TCLC 22**
    See also CA 121
Korzybski, Alfred (Habdank Skarbek) 1879-
    1950 .... **TCLC 61**
    See also CA 123; 160
Kosinski, Jerzy (Nikodem) 1933-1991**CLC 1,**
    2, 3, 6, 10, 15, 53, 70; DAM NOV
    See also CA 17-20R; 134; CANR 9, 46; DLB
    2; DLBY 82; MTCW
Kostelanetz, Richard (Cory) 1940-...**CLC 28**
    See also CA 13-16R; CAAS 8; CANR 38
Kostrowitzki, Wilhelm Apollinaris de 1880-
    1918
    See Apollinaire, Guillaume
    See also CA 104
Kotlowitz, Robert 1924- .... **CLC 4**
    See also CA 33-36R; CANR 36
Kotzebue, August (Friedrich Ferdinand) von
    1761-1819 .... **NCLC 25**
    See also DLB 94
Kotzwinkle, William 1938- ...... **CLC 5, 14, 35**
    See also CA 45-48; CANR 3, 44; CLR 6; DLB

    173; MAICYA; SATA 24, 70
Kowna, Stancy
    See Szymborska, Wislawa
Kozol, Jonathan 1936- .... **CLC 17**
    See also CA 61-64; CANR 16, 45
Kozoll, Michael 1940(?)-.................... **CLC 35**
Kramer, Kathryn 19(?)- .... **CLC 34**
Kramer, Larry 1935-**CLC 42; DAM POP; DC**
    8
    See also CA 124; 126; CANR 60
Krasicki, Ignacy 1735-1801 .... **NCLC 8**
Krasinski, Zygmunt 1812-1859 .... **NCLC 4**
Kraus, Karl 1874-1936 .... **TCLC 5**
    See also CA 104; DLB 118
Kreve (Mickevicius), Vincas 1882-1954**TCLC**
    27
Kristeva, Julia 1941- .... **CLC 77**
    See also CA 154
Kristofferson, Kris 1936-.................... **CLC 26**
    See also CA 104
Krizanc, John 1956- .... **CLC 57**
Krleza, Miroslav 1893-1981 .... **CLC 8**
    See also CA 97-100; 105; CANR 50; DLB 147
Kroetsch, Robert 1927-**CLC 5, 23, 57; DAC;**
    DAM POET
    See also CA 17-20R; CANR 8, 38; DLB 53;
    MTCW
Kroetz, Franz
    See Kroetz, Franz Xaver
Kroetz, Franz Xaver 1946- .... **CLC 41**
    See also CA 130
Kroker, Arthur (W.) 1945-................... **CLC 77**
    See also CA 161
Kropotkin, Peter (Aleksieevich) 1842-1921
    TCLC 36
    See also CA 119
Krotkov, Yuri 1917-............................ **CLC 19**
    See also CA 102
Krumb
    See Crumb, R(obert)
Krumgold, Joseph (Quincy) 1908-1980 **C L C**
    12
    See also CA 9-12R; 101; CANR 7; MAICYA;
    SATA 1, 48; SATA-Obit 23
Krumwitz
    See Crumb, R(obert)
Krutch, Joseph Wood 1893-1970 ...... **CLC 24**
    See also CA 1-4R; 25-28R; CANR 4; DLB 63
Krutzch, Gus
    See Eliot, T(homas) S(tearns)
Krylov, Ivan Andreevich 1768(?)-1844**N C L C**
    1
    See also DLB 150
Kubin, Alfred (Leopold Isidor) 1877-1959
    TCLC 23
    See also CA 112; 149; DLB 81
Kubrick, Stanley 1928-........................ **CLC 16**
    See also CA 81-84; CANR 33; DLB 26
Kumin, Maxine (Winokur) 1925- **CLC 5, 13,**
    28; DAM POET; PC 15
    See also AITN 2; CA 1-4R; CAAS 8; CANR 1,
    21; DLB 5; MTCW; SATA 12
Kundera, Milan 1929-..**CLC 4, 9, 19, 32, 68;**
    DAM NOV; SSC 24
    See also AAYA 2; CA 85-88; CANR 19, 52;
    MTCW
Kunene, Mazisi (Raymond) 1930- ....**CLC 85**
    See also BW 1; CA 125; DLB 117
Kunitz, Stanley (Jasspon) 1905-**CLC 6,11,14;**
    PC 19
    See also CA 41-44R; CANR 26, 57; DLB 48;
    INT CANR-26; MTCW
Kunze, Reiner 1933-........................... **CLC 10**

See also CA 93-96; DLB 75

Kuprin, Aleksandr Ivanovich 1870-1938
TCLC 5
See also CA 104

Kureishi, Hanif 1954(?)- .... **CLC 64**
See also CA 139; DLB 194

Kurosawa, Akira 1910-**CLC 16; DAM MULT**
See also AAYA 11; CA 101; CANR 46

Kushner, Tony 1957(?)-**CLC 81; DAM DRAM**
See also CA 144

Kuttner, Henry 1915-1958 .... **TCLC 10**
See also Vance, Jack
See also CA 107; 157; DLB 8

Kuzma, Greg 1944- .... **CLC 7**
See also CA 33-36R

Kuzmin, Mikhail 1872(?)-1936 ...... **TCLC 40**

Kyd, Thomas 1558-1594**LC 22; DAM DRAM;
DC 3**
See also DLB 62

Kyprianos, Iossif
See Samarakis, Antonis

La Bruyere, Jean de 1645-1696 .... **LC 17**

Lacan, Jacques (Marie Emile) 1901-1981
CLC 75
See also CA 121; 104

Laclos, Pierre Ambroise Francois Choderlos de
1741-1803 .... **NCLC 4**

La Colere, Francois
See Aragon, Louis

Lacolere, Francois
See Aragon, Louis

La Deshabilleuse
See Simenon, Georges (Jacques Christian)

Lady Gregory
See Gregory, Isabella Augusta (Persse)

Lady of Quality, A
See Bagnold, Enid

**La Fayette, Marie (Madelaine Pioche de la
Vergne Comtes** 1634-1693 .... **LC 2**

Lafayette, Rene
See Hubbard, L(afayette) Ron(ald)

Laforgue, Jules 1860-1887**NCLC 5, 53; PC 14;
SSC 20**

Lagerkvist, Paer (Fabian) 1891-1974 **CLC 7,
10, 13, 54; DAM DRAM, NOV**
See also Lagerkvist, Par
See also CA 85-88; 49-52; MTCW

Lagerkvist, Par .... **SSC 12**
See also Lagerkvist, Paer (Fabian)

Lagerloef, Selma (Ottiliana Lovisa) 1858-1940
TCLC 4, 36
See also Lagerlof, Selma (Ottiliana Lovisa)
See also CA 108; SATA 15

Lagerlof, Selma (Ottiliana Lovisa)
See Lagerloef, Selma (Ottiliana Lovisa)
See also CLR 7; SATA 15

La Guma, (Justin) Alex(ander) 1925-1985
CLC 19; DAM NOV
See also BW 1; CA 49-52; 118; CANR 25; DLB
117; MTCW

Laidlaw, A. K.
See Grieve, C(hristopher) M(urray)

Lainez, Manuel Mujica
See Mujica Lainez, Manuel
See also HW

Laing, R(onald) D(avid) 1927-1989 . **CLC 95**
See also CA 107; 129; CANR 34; MTCW

Lamartine, Alphonse (Marie Louis Prat) de
1790-1869**NCLC 11; DAM POET; PC 16**

Lamb, Charles 1775-1834..... **NCLC 10; DA;
DAB; DAC; DAM MST; WLC**
See also CDBLB 1789-1832; DLB 93, 107, 163;
SATA 17

Lamb, Lady Caroline 1785-1828 ... **NCLC 38**
See also DLB 116

Lamming, George (William) 1927- **CLC 2, 4,
66; BLC; DAM MULT**
See also BW 2; CA 85-88; CANR 26; DLB 125;
MTCW

L'Amour, Louis (Dearborn) 1908-1988 . **C L C
25, 55; DAM NOV, POP**
See also AAYA 16; AITN 2; BEST 89:2; CA 1-
4R; 125; CANR 3, 25, 40; DLBY 80; MTCW

Lampedusa, Giuseppe (Tomasi) di 1896-1957
TCLC 13
See also Tomasi di Lampedusa, Giuseppe
See also CA 164; DLB 177

Lampman, Archibald 1861-1899 ... **NCLC 25**
See also DLB 92

Lancaster, Bruce 1896-1963 .... **CLC 36**
See also CA 9-10; CAP 1; SATA 9

Lanchester, John .... **CLC 99**

Landau, Mark Alexandrovich
See Aldanov, Mark (Alexandrovich)

Landau-Aldanov, Mark Alexandrovich
See Aldanov, Mark (Alexandrovich)

Landis, Jerry
See Simon, Paul (Frederick)

Landis, John 1950- .... **CLC 26**
See also CA 112; 122

Landolfi, Tommaso 1908-1979 .... **CLC 11, 49**
See also CA 127; 117; DLB 177

Landon, Letitia Elizabeth 1802-1838 . **N C L C
15**
See also DLB 96

Landor, Walter Savage 1775-1864 **NCLC 14**
See also DLB 93, 107

Landwirth, Heinz 1927-
See Lind, Jakov
See also CA 9-12R; CANR 7

Lane, Patrick 1939- .... **CLC 25; DAM POET**
See also CA 97-100; CANR 54; DLB 53; INT
97-100

Lang, Andrew 1844-1912 .... **TCLC 16**
See also CA 114; 137; DLB 98, 141, 184;
MAICYA; SATA 16

Lang, Fritz 1890-1976 .... **CLC 20, 103**
See also CA 77-80; 69-72; CANR 30

Lange, John
See Crichton, (John) Michael

Langer, Elinor 1939- .... **CLC 34**
See also CA 121

Langland, William 1330(?)-1400(?) ... **LC 19;
DA; DAB; DAC; DAM MST, POET**
See also DLB 146

Langstaff, Launcelot
See Irving, Washington

Lanier, Sidney 1842-1881 ..... **NCLC 6; DAM
POET**
See also DLB 64; DLBD 13; MAICYA; SATA
18

Lanyer, Aemilia 1569-1645 .... **LC 10, 30**
See also DLB 121

Lao Tzu .... **CMLC 7**

Lapine, James (Elliot) 1949- .... **CLC 39**
See also CA 123; 130; CANR 54; INT 130

Larbaud, Valery (Nicolas) 1881-1957**TCLC 9**
See also CA 106; 152

Lardner, Ring
See Lardner, Ring(gold) W(ilmer)

Lardner, Ring W., Jr.
See Lardner, Ring(gold) W(ilmer)

Lardner, Ring(gold) W(ilmer) 1885-1933
TCLC 2, 14
See also CA 104; 131; CDALB 1917-1929;
DLB 11, 25, 86; DLBD 16; MTCW

Laredo, Betty
See Codrescu, Andrei

Larkin, Maia
See Wojciechowska, Maia (Teresa)

Larkin, Philip (Arthur) 1922-1985**CLC 3, 5, 8,
9, 13, 18, 33, 39, 64; DAB; DAM MST,
POET; PC 21**
See also CA 5-8R; 117; CANR 24, 62; CDBLB
1960 to Present; DLB 27; MTCW

Larra (y Sanchez de Castro), Mariano Jose de
1809-1837 .... **NCLC 17**

Larsen, Eric 1941- .... **CLC 55**
See also CA 132

Larsen, Nella 1891-1964**CLC 37; BLC; DAM
MULT**
See also BW 1; CA 125; DLB 51

Larson, Charles R(aymond) 1938- .. **CLC 31**
See also CA 53-56; CANR 4

Larson, Jonathan 1961-1996 .... **CLC 99**
See also CA 156

Las Casas, Bartolome de 1474-1566 ... **LC 31**

Lasch, Christopher 1932-1994 .... **CLC 102**
See also CA 73-76; 144; CANR 25; MTCW

Lasker-Schueler, Else 1869-1945 ... **TCLC 57**
See also DLB 66, 124

Laski, Harold 1893-1950 .... **TCLC 79**

Latham, Jean Lee 1902- .... **CLC 12**
See also AITN 1; CA 5-8R; CANR 7; MAICYA;
SATA 2, 68

Latham, Mavis
See Clark, Mavis Thorpe

Lathen, Emma .... **CLC 2**
See also Hennissart, Martha; Latsis, Mary J(ane)

Lathrop, Francis
See Leiber, Fritz (Reuter, Jr.)

Latsis, Mary J(ane) 1927(?)-1997
See Lathen, Emma
See also CA 85-88; 162

Lattimore, Richmond (Alexander) 1906-1984
CLC 3
See also CA 1-4R; 112; CANR 1

Laughlin, James 1914-1997 .... **CLC 49**
See also CA 21-24R; 162; CAAS 22; CANR 9,
47; DLB 48; DLBY 96, 97

Laurence, (Jean) Margaret (Wemyss) 1926-
1987 .. **CLC 3, 6, 13, 50, 62; DAC; DAM
MST; SSC 7**
See also CA 5-8R; 121; CANR 33; DLB 53;
MTCW; SATA-Obit 50

Laurent, Antoine 1952- .... **CLC 50**

Lauscher, Hermann
See Hesse, Hermann

Lautreamont, Comte de 1846-1870**NCLC 12;
SSC 14**

Laverty, Donald
See Blish, James (Benjamin)

Lavin, Mary 1912-1996**CLC 4, 18, 99; SSC 4**
See also CA 9-12R; 151; CANR 33; DLB 15;
MTCW

Lavond, Paul Dennis
See Kornbluth, C(yril) M.; Pohl, Frederik

Lawler, Raymond Evenor 1922- ...... **CLC 58**
See also CA 103

Lawrence, D(avid) H(erbert Richards) 1885-
1930**TCLC 2, 9, 16, 33, 48, 61; DA; DAB;
DAC; DAM MST, NOV, POET; SSC 4, 19;
WLC**
See also CA 104; 121; CDBLB 1914-1945;
DLB 10, 19, 36, 98, 162, 195; MTCW

Lawrence, T(homas) E(dward) 1888-1935
TCLC 18
See also Dale, Colin
See also CA 115; DLB 195

Lawrence of Arabia
  See Lawrence, T(homas) E(dward)
Lawson, Henry (Archibald Hertzberg) 1867-
    1922 .... **TCLC 27; SSC 18**
  See also CA 120
Lawton, Dennis
  See Faust, Frederick (Schiller)
Laxness, Halldor .... **CLC 25**
  See also Gudjonsson, Halldor Kiljan
Layamon fl. c. 1200- .... **CMLC 10**
  See also DLB 146
Laye, Camara 1928-1980 .. **CLC 4, 38; BLC;**
    DAM MULT
  See also BW 1; CA 85-88; 97-100; CANR 25;
    MTCW
Layton, Irving (Peter) 1912-**CLC 2, 15; DAC;**
    DAM MST, POET
  See also CA 1-4R; CANR 2, 33, 43, 66; DLB
    88; MTCW
Lazarus, Emma 1849-1887 .... **NCLC 8**
Lazarus, Felix
  See Cable, George Washington
Lazarus, Henry
  See Slavitt, David R(ytman)
Lea, Joan
  See Neufeld, John (Arthur)
Leacock, Stephen (Butler) 1869-1944**TCLC 2;**
    DAC; DAM MST
  See also CA 104; 141; DLB 92
Lear, Edward 1812-1888 .... **NCLC 3**
  See also CLR 1; DLB 32, 163, 166; MAICYA;
    SATA 18
Lear, Norman (Milton) 1922- .... **CLC 12**
  See also CA 73-76
Leavis, F(rank) R(aymond) 1895-1978**CLC 24**
  See also CA 21-24R; 77-80; CANR 44; MTCW
Leavitt, David 1961- ...... **CLC 34; DAM POP**
  See also CA 116; 122; CANR 50, 62; DLB 130;
    INT 122
Leblanc, Maurice (Marie Emile) 1864-1941
    TCLC 49
  See also CA 110
Lebowitz, Fran(ces Ann) 1951(?)-**CLC 11, 36**
  See also CA 81-84; CANR 14, 60; INT CANR-
    14; MTCW
Lebrecht, Peter
  See Tieck, (Johann) Ludwig
le Carre, John .... **CLC 3, 5, 9, 15, 28**
  See also Cornwell, David (John Moore)
  See also BEST 89:4; CDBLB 1960 to Present;
    DLB 87
Le Clezio, J(ean) M(arie) G(ustave) 1940-
    CLC 31
  See also CA 116; 128; DLB 83
Leconte de Lisle, Charles-Marie-Rene 1818-
    1894 .... **NCLC 29**
Le Coq, Monsieur
  See Simenon, Georges (Jacques Christian)
Leduc, Violette 1907-1972 .... **CLC 22**
  See also CA 13-14; 33-36R; CAP 1
Ledwidge, Francis 1887(?)-1917 .... **TCLC 23**
  See also CA 123; DLB 20
Lee, Andrea 1953-**CLC 36; BLC; DAM MULT**
  See also BW 1; CA 125
Lee, Andrew
  See Auchincloss, Louis (Stanton)
Lee, Chang-rae 1965- .... **CLC 91**
  See also CA 148
Lee, Don L. ....**CLC 2**
  See also Madhubuti, Haki R.
Lee, George W(ashington) 1894-1976**CLC 52;**
    BLC; DAM MULT
  See also BW 1; CA 125; DLB 51

Lee, (Nelle) Harper 1926- .. **CLC 12, 60; DA;**
    DAB; DAC; DAM MST, NOV; WLC
  See also AAYA 13; CA 13-16R; CANR 51;
    CDALB 1941-1968; DLB 6; MTCW; SATA
    11
Lee, Helen Elaine 1959(?)- .... **CLC 86**
  See also CA 148
Lee, Julian
  See Latham, Jean Lee
Lee, Larry
  See Lee, Lawrence
Lee, Laurie 1914-1997 **CLC 90; DAB; DAM**
    POP
  See also CA 77-80; 158; CANR 33; DLB 27;
    MTCW
Lee, Lawrence 1941-1990 .... **CLC 34**
  See also CA 131; CANR 43
Lee, Manfred B(ennington) 1905-1971**CLC 11**
  See also Queen, Ellery
  See also CA 1-4R; 29-32R; CANR 2; DLB 137
Lee, Shelton Jackson 1957(?)-**CLC 105; DAM**
    MULT
  See also Lee, Spike
  See also BW 2; CA 125; CANR 42
Lee, Spike
  See Lee, Shelton Jackson
  See also AAYA 4
Lee, Stan 1922- .... **CLC 17**
  See also AAYA 5; CA 108; 111; INT 111
Lee, Tanith 1947- .... **CLC 46**
  See also AAYA 15; CA 37-40R; CANR 53;
    SATA 8, 88
Lee, Vernon .... **TCLC 5**
  See also Paget, Violet
  See also DLB 57, 153, 156, 174, 178
Lee, William
  See Burroughs, William S(eward)
Lee, Willy
  See Burroughs, William S(eward)
Lee-Hamilton, Eugene (Jacob) 1845-1907
    TCLC 22
  See also CA 117
Leet, Judith 1935- .... **CLC 11**
Le Fanu, Joseph Sheridan 1814-1873**NCLC 9,**
    58; DAM POP; SSC 14
  See also DLB 21, 70, 159, 178
Leffland, Ella 1931- .... **CLC 19**
  See also CA 29-32R; CANR 35; DLBY 84; INT
    CANR-35; SATA 65
Leger, Alexis
  See Leger, (Marie-Rene Auguste) Alexis Saint-
    Leger
Leger, (Marie-Rene Auguste) Alexis Saint-
    Leger 1887-1975 **CLC 11; DAM POET**
  See also Perse, St.-John
  See also CA 13-16R; 61-64; CANR 43; MTCW
Leger, Saintleger
  See Leger, (Marie-Rene Auguste) Alexis Saint-
    Leger
Le Guin, Ursula K(roeber) 1929- **CLC 8, 13,**
    22, 45, 71; DAB; DAC; DAM MST, POP;
    SSC 12
  See also AAYA 9; AITN 1; CA 21-24R; CANR
    9, 32, 52; CDALB 1968-1988; CLR 3, 28;
    DLB 8, 52; INT CANR-32; JRDA; MAICYA;
    MTCW; SATA 4, 52
Lehmann, Rosamond (Nina) 1901-1990**CLC 5**
  See also CA 77-80; 131; CANR 8; DLB 15
Leiber, Fritz (Reuter, Jr.) 1910-1992 **CLC 25**
  See also CA 45-48; 139; CANR 2, 40; DLB 8;
    MTCW; SATA 45; SATA-Obit 73
Leibniz, Gottfried Wilhelm von 1646-1716**LC**
    35

See also DLB 168
Leimbach, Martha 1963-
  See Leimbach, Marti
  See also CA 130
Leimbach, Marti ....**CLC 65**
  See also Leimbach, Martha
Leino, Eino .... **TCLC 24**
  See also Loennbohm, Armas Eino Leopold
Leiris, Michel (Julien) 1901-1990 ..... **CLC 61**
  See also CA 119; 128; 132
Leithauser, Brad 1953- .... **CLC 27**
  See also CA 107; CANR 27; DLB 120
Lelchuk, Alan 1938- ....**CLC 5**
  See also CA 45-48; CAAS 20; CANR 1
Lem, Stanislaw 1921- .... **CLC 8, 15, 40**
  See also CA 105; CAAS 1; CANR 32; MTCW
Lemann, Nancy 1956- .... **CLC 39**
  See also CA 118; 136
Lemonnier, (Antoine Louis) Camille 1844-1913
    TCLC 22
  See also CA 121
Lenau, Nikolaus 1802-1850 .... **NCLC 16**
L'Engle, Madeleine (Camp Franklin) 1918-
    CLC 12; DAM POP
  See also AAYA 1; AITN 2; CA 1-4R; CANR 3,
    21, 39, 66; CLR 1, 14; DLB 52; JRDA;
    MAICYA; MTCW; SAAS 15; SATA 1, 27,
    75
Lengyel, Jozsef 1896-1975 ....**CLC 7**
  See also CA 85-88; 57-60
Lenin 1870-1924
  See Lenin, V. I.
  See also CA 121
Lenin, V. I. .... **TCLC 67**
  See also Lenin
Lennon, John (Ono) 1940-1980 . **CLC 12, 35**
  See also CA 102
Lennox, Charlotte Ramsay 1729(?)-1804
    NCLC 23
  See also DLB 39
Lentricchia, Frank (Jr.) 1940- .... **CLC 34**
  See also CA 25-28R; CANR 19
Lenz, Siegfried 1926- .... **CLC 27**
  See also CA 89-92; DLB 75
Leonard, Elmore (John, Jr.) 1925-**CLC 28, 34,**
    71; DAM POP
  See also AAYA 22; AITN 1; BEST 89:1, 90:4;
    CA 81-84; CANR 12, 28, 53; DLB 173; INT
    CANR-28; MTCW
Leonard, Hugh ....**CLC 19**
  See also Byrne, John Keyes
  See also DLB 13
Leonov, Leonid (Maximovich) 1899-1994
    CLC 92; DAM NOV
  See also CA 129; MTCW
Leopardi, (Conte) Giacomo 1798-1837**NCLC**
    22
Le Reveler
  See Artaud, Antonin (Marie Joseph)
Lerman, Eleanor 1952- ....**CLC 9**
  See also CA 85-88
Lerman, Rhoda 1936- .... **CLC 56**
  See also CA 49-52
Lermontov, Mikhail Yuryevich 1814-1841
    NCLC 47; PC 18
Leroux, Gaston 1868-1927 .... **TCLC 25**
  See also CA 108; 136; SATA 65
Lesage, Alain-Rene 1668-1747 .... **LC 28**
Leskov, Nikolai (Semyonovich) 1831-1895
    NCLC 25
Lessing, Doris (May) 1919-**CLC 1, 2, 3, 6, 10,**
    15, 22, 40, 94; DA; DAB; DAC; DAM MST,
    NOV; SSC 6; WLCS

See also CA 9-12R; CAAS 14; CANR 33, 54;
CDBLB 1960 to Present; DLB 15, 139;
DLBY 85; MTCW
Lessing, Gotthold Ephraim 1729-1781 **LC 8**
See also DLB 97
Lester, Richard 1932- .... **CLC 20**
Lever, Charles (James) 1806-1872 .**NCLC 23**
See also DLB 21
Leverson, Ada 1865(?)-1936(?) ...... **TCLC 18**
See also Elaine
See also CA 117; DLB 153
Levertov, Denise 1923-1997 .**CLC 1, 2, 3, 5, 8,**
15, 28, 66; DAM POET; PC 11
See also CA 1-4R; 163; CAAS 19; CANR 3,
29, 50; DLB 5, 165; INT CANR-29; MTCW
Levi, Jonathan .... **CLC 76**
Levi, Peter (Chad Tigar) 1931- .... **CLC 41**
See also CA 5-8R; CANR 34; DLB 40
Levi, Primo 1919-1987 . **CLC 37, 50; SSC 12**
See also CA 13-16R; 122; CANR 12, 33, 61;
DLB 177; MTCW
Levin, Ira 1929- .... **CLC 3, 6; DAM POP**
See also CA 21-24R; CANR 17, 44; MTCW;
SATA 66
Levin, Meyer 1905-1981 .**CLC 7; DAM POP**
See also AITN 1; CA 9-12R; 104; CANR 15;
DLB 9, 28; DLBY 81; SATA 21; SATA-Obit
27
Levine, Norman 1924- .... **CLC 54**
See also CA 73-76; CAAS 23; CANR 14; DLB
88
Levine, Philip 1928- .. **CLC 2, 4, 5, 9, 14, 33;**
DAM POET
See also CA 9-12R; CANR 9, 37, 52; DLB 5
Levinson, Deirdre 1931- .... **CLC 49**
See also CA 73-76
Levi-Strauss, Claude 1908- .... **CLC 38**
See also CA 1-4R; CANR 6, 32, 57; MTCW
Levitin, Sonia (Wolff) 1934- .... **CLC 17**
See also AAYA 13; CA 29-32R; CANR 14, 32;
JRDA; MAICYA; SAAS 2; SATA 4, 68
Levon, O. U.
See Kesey, Ken (Elton)
Levy, Amy 1861-1889 .... **NCLC 59**
See also DLB 156
Lewes, George Henry 1817-1878 ...**NCLC 25**
See also DLB 55, 144
Lewis, Alun 1915-1944 .... **TCLC 3**
See also CA 104; DLB 20, 162
Lewis, C. Day
See Day Lewis, C(ecil)
Lewis, C(live) S(taples) 1898-1963**CLC 1, 3, 6,**
14, 27; DA; DAB; DAC; DAM MST, NOV,
POP; WLC
See also AAYA 3; CA 81-84; CANR 33;
CDBLB 1945-1960; CLR 3, 27; DLB 15,
100, 160; JRDA; MAICYA; MTCW; SATA
13
Lewis, Janet 1899- .... **CLC 41**
See also Winters, Janet Lewis
See also CA 9-12R; CANR 29, 63; CAP 1;
DLBY 87
Lewis, Matthew Gregory 1775-1818**NCLC 11,**
62
See also DLB 39, 158, 178
Lewis, (Harry) Sinclair 1885-1951 . **TCLC 4,**
13, 23, 39; DA; DAB; DAC; DAM MST,
NOV; WLC
See also CA 104; 133; CDALB 1917-1929;
DLB 9, 102; DLBD 1; MTCW
Lewis, (Percy) Wyndham 1882(?)-1957**T C L C**
2, 9
See also CA 104; 157; DLB 15

Lewisohn, Ludwig 1883-1955 .... **TCLC 19**
See also CA 107; DLB 4, 9, 28, 102
Lewton, Val 1904-1951 .... **TCLC 76**
Leyner, Mark 1956- .... **CLC 92**
See also CA 110; CANR 28, 53
Lezama Lima, Jose 1910-1976**CLC 4, 10, 101;**
DAM MULT
See also CA 77-80; DLB 113; HW
L'Heureux, John (Clarke) 1934- .... **CLC 52**
See also CA 13-16R; CANR 23, 45
Liddell, C. H.
See Kuttner, Henry
Lie, Jonas (Lauritz Idemil) 1833-1908(?)
TCLC 5
See also CA 115
Lieber, Joel 1937-1971 .... **CLC 6**
See also CA 73-76; 29-32R
Lieber, Stanley Martin
See Lee, Stan
Lieberman, Laurence (James) 1935- .**CLC 4,**
36
See also CA 17-20R; CANR 8, 36
Lieksman, Anders
See Haavikko, Paavo Juhani
Li Fei-kan 1904-
See Pa Chin
See also CA 105
Lifton, Robert Jay 1926- .... **CLC 67**
See also CA 17-20R; CANR 27; INT CANR-
27; SATA 66
Lightfoot, Gordon 1938- .... **CLC 26**
See also CA 109
Lightman, Alan P(aige) 1948- .... **CLC 81**
See also CA 141; CANR 63
Ligotti, Thomas (Robert) 1953-**CLC 44; SSC**
16
See also CA 123; CANR 49
Li Ho 791-817 .... **PC 13**
Liliencron, (Friedrich Adolf Axel) Detlev von
1844-1909 .... **TCLC 18**
See also CA 117
Lilly, William 1602-1681 .... **LC 27**
Lima, Jose Lezama
See Lezama Lima, Jose
Lima Barreto, Afonso Henrique de 1881-1922
TCLC 23
See also CA 117
Limonov, Edward 1944- .... **CLC 67**
See also CA 137
Lin, Frank
See Atherton, Gertrude (Franklin Horn)
Lincoln, Abraham 1809-1865 .... **NCLC 18**
Lind, Jakov .... **CLC 1, 2, 4, 27, 82**
See also Landwirth, Heinz
See also CAAS 4
Lindbergh, Anne (Spencer) Morrow 1906-
CLC 82; DAM NOV
See also CA 17-20R; CANR 16; MTCW; SATA
33
Lindsay, David 1878-1945 .... **TCLC 15**
See also CA 113
Lindsay, (Nicholas) Vachel 1879-1931 **T C L C**
17; DA; DAC; DAM MST, POET; WLC
See also CA 114; 135; CDALB 1865-1917;
DLB 54; SATA 40
Linke-Poot
See Doeblin, Alfred
Linney, Romulus 1930- .... **CLC 51**
See also CA 1-4R; CANR 40, 44
Linton, Eliza Lynn 1822-1898 .... **NCLC 41**
See also DLB 18
Li Po 701-763 .... **CMLC 2**
Lipsius, Justus 1547-1606 .... **LC 16**

Lipsyte, Robert (Michael) 1938-**CLC 21; DA;**
DAC; DAM MST, NOV
See also AAYA 7; CA 17-20R; CANR 8, 57;
CLR 23; JRDA; MAICYA; SATA 5, 68
Lish, Gordon (Jay) 1934- ...**CLC 45; SSC 18**
See also CA 113; 117; DLB 130; INT 117
Lispector, Clarice 1925-1977 .... **CLC 43**
See also CA 139; 116; DLB 113
Littell, Robert 1935(?)- .... **CLC 42**
See also CA 109; 112; CANR 64
Little, Malcolm 1925-1965
See Malcolm X
See also BW 1; CA 125; 111; DA; DAB; DAC;
DAM MST, MULT; MTCW
Littlewit, Humphrey Gent.
See Lovecraft, H(oward) P(hillips)
Litwos
See Sienkiewicz, Henryk (Adam Alexander
Pius)
Liu E 1857-1909 .... **TCLC 15**
See also CA 115
Lively, Penelope (Margaret) 1933- . **CLC 32,**
50; DAM NOV
See also CA 41-44R; CANR 29, 67; CLR 7;
DLB 14, 161; JRDA; MAICYA; MTCW;
SATA 7, 60
Livesay, Dorothy (Kathleen) 1909-**CLC 4, 15,**
79; DAC; DAM MST, POET
See also AITN 2; CA 25-28R; CAAS 8; CANR
36, 67; DLB 68; MTCW
Livy c. 59B.C.-c. 17 .... **CMLC 11**
Lizardi, Jose Joaquin Fernandez de 1776-1827
NCLC 30
Llewellyn, Richard
See Llewellyn Lloyd, Richard Dafydd Vivian
See also DLB 15
Llewellyn Lloyd, Richard Dafydd Vivian 1906-
1983 .... **CLC 7, 80**
See also Llewellyn, Richard
See also CA 53-56; 111; CANR 7; SATA 11;
SATA-Obit 37
Llosa, (Jorge) Mario (Pedro) Vargas
See Vargas Llosa, (Jorge) Mario (Pedro)
Lloyd, Manda
See Mander, (Mary) Jane
Lloyd Webber, Andrew 1948-
See Webber, Andrew Lloyd
See also AAYA 1; CA 116; 149; DAM DRAM;
SATA 56
Llull, Ramon c. 1235-c. 1316 .... **CMLC 12**
Locke, Alain (Le Roy) 1886-1954 .. **TCLC 43**
See also BW 1; CA 106; 124; DLB 51
Locke, John 1632-1704 .... **LC 7, 35**
See also DLB 101
Locke-Elliott, Sumner
See Elliott, Sumner Locke
Lockhart, John Gibson 1794-1854 ..**NCLC 6**
See also DLB 110, 116, 144
Lodge, David (John) 1935- ....**CLC 36; DAM**
POP
See also BEST 90:1; CA 17-20R; CANR 19,
53; DLB 14, 194; INT CANR-19; MTCW
Lodge, Thomas 1558-1625 .... **LC 41**
See also DLB 172
Lodge, Thomas 1558-1625 .... **LC 41**
Loennbohm, Armas Eino Leopold 1878-1926
See Leino, Eino
See also CA 123
Loewinsohn, Ron(ald William) 1937-**CLC 52**
See also CA 25-28R
Logan, Jake
See Smith, Martin Cruz
Logan, John (Burton) 1923-1987 .... **CLC 5**

See also CA 77-80; 124; CANR 45; DLB 5

Lo Kuan-chung 1330(?)-1400(?) .... **LC 12**

Lombard, Nap
See Johnson, Pamela Hansford

London, Jack.. **TCLC 9, 15, 39; SSC 4; WLC**
See also London, John Griffith
See also AAYA 13; AITN 2; CDALB 1865-
1917; DLB 8, 12, 78; SATA 18

London, John Griffith 1876-1916
See London, Jack
See also CA 110; 119; DA; DAB; DAC; DAM
MST, NOV; JRDA; MAICYA; MTCW

Long, Emmett
See Leonard, Elmore (John, Jr.)

Longbaugh, Harry
See Goldman, William (W.)

Longfellow, Henry Wadsworth 1807-1882
**NCLC 2, 45; DA; DAB; DAC; DAM MST,
POET; WLCS**
See also CDALB 1640-1865; DLB 1, 59; SATA
19

Longley, Michael 1939-...................... **CLC 29**
See also CA 102; DLB 40

Longus fl. c. 2nd cent. - .... **CMLC 7**

Longway, A. Hugh
See Lang, Andrew

Lonnrot, Elias 1802-1884 .... **NCLC 53**

Lopate, Phillip 1943-......................... **CLC 29**
See also CA 97-100; DLBY 80; INT 97-100

Lopez Portillo (y Pacheco), Jose 1920- . **C L C
46**
See also CA 129; HW

Lopez y Fuentes, Gregorio 1897(?)-1966**C L C
32**
See also CA 131; HW

Lorca, Federico Garcia
See Garcia Lorca, Federico

Lord, Bette Bao 1938-....................... **CLC 23**
See also BEST 90:3; CA 107; CANR 41; INT
107; SATA 58

Lord Auch
See Bataille, Georges

Lord Byron
See Byron, George Gordon (Noel)

Lorde, Audre (Geraldine) 1934-1992**CLC 18,
71; BLC; DAM MULT, POET; PC 12**
See also BW 1; CA 25-28R; 142; CANR 16,
26, 46; DLB 41; MTCW

Lord Houghton
See Milnes, Richard Monckton

Lord Jeffrey
See Jeffrey, Francis

Lorenzini, Carlo 1826-1890
See Collodi, Carlo
See also MAICYA; SATA 29

Lorenzo, Heberto Padilla
See Padilla (Lorenzo), Heberto

Loris
See Hofmannsthal, Hugo von

Loti, Pierre .... **TCLC 11**
See also Viaud, (Louis Marie) Julien
See also DLB 123

Louie, David Wong 1954- .... **CLC 70**
See also CA 139

Louis, Father M.
See Merton, Thomas

Lovecraft, H(oward) P(hillips) 1890-1937
TCLC 4, 22; DAM POP; SSC 3
See also AAYA 14; CA 104; 133; MTCW

Lovelace, Earl 1935- .... **CLC 51**
See also BW 2; CA 77-80; CANR 41; DLB 125;
MTCW

Lovelace, Richard 1618-1657 .... **LC 24**

See also DLB 131

Lowell, Amy 1874-1925 .... **TCLC 1, 8; DAM
POET; PC 13**
See also CA 104; 151; DLB 54, 140

Lowell, James Russell 1819-1891 ....**NCLC 2**
See also CDALB 1640-1865; DLB 1, 11, 64,
79, 189

Lowell, Robert (Traill Spence, Jr.) 1917-1977
**CLC 1, 2, 3, 4, 5, 8, 9, 11, 15, 37; DA; DAB;
DAC; DAM MST, NOV; PC 3; WLC**
See also CA 9-12R; 73-76; CABS 2; CANR 26,
60; DLB 5, 169; MTCW

Lowndes, Marie Adelaide (Belloc) 1868-1947
TCLC 12
See also CA 107; DLB 70

Lowry, (Clarence) Malcolm 1909-1957**T C L C
6, 40**
See also CA 105; 131; CANR 62; CDBLB
1945-1960; DLB 15; MTCW

Lowry, Mina Gertrude 1882-1966
See Loy, Mina
See also CA 113

Loxsmith, John
See Brunner, John (Kilian Houston)

Loy, Mina .... **CLC 28; DAM POET; PC 16**
See also Lowry, Mina Gertrude
See also DLB 4, 54

Loyson-Bridet
See Schwob, (Mayer Andre) Marcel

Lucas, Craig 1951- .... **CLC 64**
See also CA 137

Lucas, E(dward) V(errall) 1868-1938 **T C L C
73**
See also DLB 98, 149, 153; SATA 20

Lucas, George 1944- .... **CLC 16**
See also AAYA 1, 23; CA 77-80; CANR 30;
SATA 56

Lucas, Hans
See Godard, Jean-Luc

Lucas, Victoria
See Plath, Sylvia

Ludlam, Charles 1943-1987 .... **CLC 46, 50**
See also CA 85-88; 122

Ludlum, Robert 1927-**CLC 22, 43; DAM NOV,
POP**
See also AAYA 10; BEST 89:1, 90:3; CA 33-
36R; CANR 25, 41, 68; DLBY 82; MTCW

Ludwig, Ken .... **CLC 60**

Ludwig, Otto 1813-1865 .... **NCLC 4**
See also DLB 129

Lugones, Leopoldo 1874-1938 .... **TCLC 15**
See also CA 116; 131; HW

Lu Hsun 1881-1936 .... **TCLC 3; SSC 20**
See also Shu-Jen, Chou

Lukacs, George .... **CLC 24**
See also Lukacs, Gyorgy (Szegeny von)

Lukacs, Gyorgy (Szegeny von) 1885-1971
See Lukacs, George
See also CA 101; 29-32R; CANR 62

Luke, Peter (Ambrose Cyprian) 1919-1995
CLC 38
See also CA 81-84; 147; DLB 13

Lunar, Dennis
See Mungo, Raymond

Lurie, Alison 1926-.............. **CLC 4, 5, 18, 39**
See also CA 1-4R; CANR 2, 17, 50; DLB 2;
MTCW; SATA 46

Lustig, Arnost 1926-.......................... **CLC 56**
See also AAYA 3; CA 69-72; CANR 47; SATA
56

Luther, Martin 1483-1546 .... **LC 9, 37**
See also DLB 179

Luxemburg, Rosa 1870(?)-1919 ..... **TCLC 63**

See also CA 118

Luzi, Mario 1914-................................**CLC 13**
See also CA 61-64; CANR 9; DLB 128

Lyly, John 1554(?)-1606**LC 41; DAM DRAM;
DC 7**
See also DLB 62, 167

L'Ymagier
See Gourmont, Remy (-Marie-Charles) de

Lynch, B. Suarez
See Bioy Casares, Adolfo; Borges, Jorge Luis

Lynch, David (K.) 1946- .... **CLC 66**
See also CA 124; 129

Lynch, James
See Andreyev, Leonid (Nikolaevich)

Lynch Davis, B.
See Bioy Casares, Adolfo; Borges, Jorge Luis

Lyndsay, Sir David 1490-1555 .... **LC 20**

Lynn, Kenneth S(chuyler) 1923-.......**CLC 50**
See also CA 1-4R; CANR 3, 27, 65

Lynx
See West, Rebecca

Lyons, Marcus
See Blish, James (Benjamin)

Lyre, Pinchbeck
See Sassoon, Siegfried (Lorraine)

Lytle, Andrew (Nelson) 1902-1995 ...**CLC 22**
See also CA 9-12R; 150; DLB 6; DLBY 95

Lyttelton, George 1709-1773 .... **LC 10**

Maas, Peter 1929-..............................**CLC 29**
See also CA 93-96; INT 93-96

Macaulay, Rose 1881-1958 .... **TCLC 7, 44**
See also CA 104; DLB 36

Macaulay, Thomas Babington 1800-1859
NCLC 42
See also CDBLB 1832-1890; DLB 32, 55

MacBeth, George (Mann) 1932-1992**CLC 2, 5,
9**
See also CA 25-28R; 136; CANR 61, 66; DLB
40; MTCW; SATA 4; SATA-Obit 70

MacCaig, Norman (Alexander) 1910-**CLC 36;
DAB; DAM POET**
See also CA 9-12R; CANR 3, 34; DLB 27

MacCarthy, (Sir Charles Otto) Desmond 1877-
1952 .... **TCLC 36**

MacDiarmid, Hugh**CLC 2, 4, 11, 19, 63; PC 9**
See also Grieve, C(hristopher) M(urray)
See also CDBLB 1945-1960; DLB 20

MacDonald, Anson
See Heinlein, Robert A(nson)

Macdonald, Cynthia 1928- .... **CLC 13, 19**
See also CA 49-52; CANR 4, 44; DLB 105

MacDonald, George 1824-1905 .... **TCLC 9**
See also CA 106; 137; DLB 18, 163, 178;
MAICYA; SATA 33

Macdonald, John
See Millar, Kenneth

MacDonald, John D(ann) 1916-1986 **CLC 3,
27, 44; DAM NOV, POP**
See also CA 1-4R; 121; CANR 1, 19, 60; DLB
8; DLBY 86; MTCW

Macdonald, John Ross
See Millar, Kenneth

Macdonald, Ross .... **CLC 1, 2, 3, 14, 34, 41**
See also Millar, Kenneth
See also DLBD 6

MacDougal, John
See Blish, James (Benjamin)

MacEwen, Gwendolyn (Margaret) 1941-1987
CLC 13, 55
See also CA 9-12R; 124; CANR 7, 22; DLB
53; SATA 50; SATA-Obit 55

Macha, Karel Hynek 1810-1846 ....**NCLC 46**

Machado (y Ruiz), Antonio 1875-1939**T C L C**

3
See also CA 104; DLB 108

Machado de Assis, Joaquim Maria 1839-1908 **TCLC 10; BLC; SSC 24**
See also CA 107; 153

Machen, Arthur .... **TCLC 4; SSC 20**
See also Jones, Arthur Llewellyn
See also DLB 36, 156, 178

Machiavelli, Niccolo 1469-1527 **LC 8, 36; DA; DAB; DAC; DAM MST; WLCS**

MacInnes, Colin 1914-1976 .... **CLC 4, 23**
See also CA 69-72; 65-68; CANR 21; DLB 14; MTCW

MacInnes, Helen (Clark) 1907-1985 **CLC 27, 39; DAM POP**
See also CA 1-4R; 117; CANR 1, 28, 58; DLB 87; MTCW; SATA 22; SATA-Obit 44

Mackay, Mary 1855-1924
See Corelli, Marie
See also CA 118

Mackenzie, Compton (Edward Montague) 1883-1972 .... **CLC 18**
See also CA 21-22; 37-40R; CAP 2; DLB 34, 100

Mackenzie, Henry 1745-1831 .... **NCLC 41**
See also DLB 39

Mackintosh, Elizabeth 1896(?)-1952
See Tey, Josephine
See also CA 110

MacLaren, James
See Grieve, C(hristopher) M(urray)

Mac Laverty, Bernard 1942- .... **CLC 31**
See also CA 116; 118; CANR 43; INT 118

MacLean, Alistair (Stuart) 1922(?)-1987 **CLC 3, 13, 50, 63; DAM POP**
See also CA 57-60; 121; CANR 28, 61; MTCW; SATA 23; SATA-Obit 50

Maclean, Norman (Fitzroy) 1902-1990 . **CLC 78; DAM POP; SSC 13**
See also CA 102; 132; CANR 49

MacLeish, Archibald 1892-1982 **CLC 3, 8, 14, 68; DAM POET**
See also CA 9-12R; 106; CANR 33, 63; DLB 4, 7, 45; DLBY 82; MTCW

MacLennan, (John) Hugh 1907-1990 **CLC 2, 14, 92; DAC; DAM MST**
See also CA 5-8R; 142; CANR 33; DLB 68; MTCW

MacLeod, Alistair 1936- **CLC 56; DAC; DAM MST**
See also CA 123; DLB 60

Macleod, Fiona
See Sharp, William

MacNeice, (Frederick) Louis 1907-1963 **CLC 1, 4, 10, 53; DAB; DAM POET**
See also CA 85-88; CANR 61; DLB 10, 20; MTCW

MacNeill, Dand
See Fraser, George MacDonald

Macpherson, James 1736-1796 .... **LC 29**
See also DLB 109

Macpherson, (Jean) Jay 1931- .... **CLC 14**
See also CA 5-8R; DLB 53

MacShane, Frank 1927- .... **CLC 39**
See also CA 9-12R; CANR 3, 33; DLB 111

Macumber, Mari
See Sandoz, Mari(e Susette)

Madach, Imre 1823-1864 .... **NCLC 19**

Madden, (Jerry) David 1933- .... **CLC 5, 15**
See also CA 1-4R; CAAS 3; CANR 4, 45; DLB 6; MTCW

Maddern, Al(an)
See Ellison, Harlan (Jay)

Madhubuti, Haki R. 1942- **CLC 6, 73; BLC; DAM MULT, POET; PC 5**
See also Lee, Don L.
See also BW 2; CA 73-76; CANR 24, 51; DLB 5, 41; DLBD 8

Maepenn, Hugh
See Kuttner, Henry

Maepenn, K. H.
See Kuttner, Henry

Maeterlinck, Maurice 1862-1949 .... **TCLC 3; DAM DRAM**
See also CA 104; 136; DLB 192; SATA 66

Maginn, William 1794-1842 .... **NCLC 8**
See also DLB 110, 159

Mahapatra, Jayanta 1928- .... **CLC 33; DAM MULT**
See also CA 73-76; CAAS 9; CANR 15, 33, 66

Mahfouz, Naguib (Abdel Aziz Al-Sabilgi) 1911(?)-
See Mahfuz, Najib
See also BEST 89:2; CA 128; CANR 55; DAM NOV; MTCW

Mahfuz, Najib .... **CLC 52, 55**
See also Mahfouz, Naguib (Abdel Aziz Al-Sabilgi)
See also DLBY 88

Mahon, Derek 1941- .... **CLC 27**
See also CA 113; 128; DLB 40

Mailer, Norman 1923- **CLC 1, 2, 3, 4, 5, 8, 11, 14, 28, 39, 74; DA; DAB; DAC; DAM MST, NOV, POP**
See also AITN 2; CA 9-12R; CABS 1; CANR 28; CDALB 1968-1988; DLB 2, 16, 28, 185; DLBD 3; DLBY 80, 83; MTCW

Maillet, Antonine 1929- .... **CLC 54; DAC**
See also CA 115; 120; CANR 46; DLB 60; INT 120

Mais, Roger 1905-1955 .... **TCLC 8**
See also BW 1; CA 105; 124; DLB 125; MTCW

Maistre, Joseph de 1753-1821 .... **NCLC 37**

Maitland, Frederic 1850-1906 .... **TCLC 65**

Maitland, Sara (Louise) 1950- .... **CLC 49**
See also CA 69-72; CANR 13, 59

Major, Clarence 1936- **CLC 3, 19, 48; BLC; DAM MULT**
See also BW 2; CA 21-24R; CAAS 6; CANR 13, 25, 53; DLB 33

Major, Kevin (Gerald) 1949- .. **CLC 26; DAC**
See also AAYA 16; CA 97-100; CANR 21, 38; CLR 11; DLB 60; INT CANR-21; JRDA; MAICYA; SATA 32, 82

Maki, James
See Ozu, Yasujiro

Malabaila, Damiano
See Levi, Primo

Malamud, Bernard 1914-1986 **CLC 1, 2, 3, 5, 8, 9, 11, 18, 27, 44, 78, 85; DA; DAB; DAC; DAM MST, NOV, POP; SSC 15; WLC**
See also AAYA 16; CA 5-8R; 118; CABS 1; CANR 28, 62; CDALB 1941-1968; DLB 2, 28, 152; DLBY 80, 86; MTCW

Malan, Herman
See Bosman, Herman Charles; Bosman, Herman Charles

Malaparte, Curzio 1898-1957 .... **TCLC 52**

Malcolm, Dan
See Silverberg, Robert

Malcolm X .... **CLC 82; BLC; WLCS**
See also Little, Malcolm

Malherbe, Francois de 1555-1628 .... **LC 5**

Mallarme, Stephane 1842-1898 **NCLC 4, 41; DAM POET; PC 4**

Mallet-Joris, Francoise 1930- .... **CLC 11**

See also CA 65-68; CANR 17; DLB 83

Malley, Ern
See McAuley, James Phillip

Mallowan, Agatha Christie
See Christie, Agatha (Mary Clarissa)

Maloff, Saul 1922- .... **CLC 5**
See also CA 33-36R

Malone, Louis
See MacNeice, (Frederick) Louis

Malone, Michael (Christopher) 1942- **CLC 43**
See also CA 77-80; CANR 14, 32, 57

Malory, (Sir) Thomas 1410(?)-1471(?) **LC 11; DA; DAB; DAC; DAM MST; WLCS**
See also CDBLB Before 1660; DLB 146; SATA 59; SATA-Brief 33

Malouf, (George Joseph) David 1934- **CLC 28, 86**
See also CA 124; CANR 50

Malraux, (Georges-)Andre 1901-1976 **CLC 1, 4, 9, 13, 15, 57; DAM NOV**
See also CA 21-22; 69-72; CANR 34, 58; CAP 2; DLB 72; MTCW

Malzberg, Barry N(athaniel) 1939- .... **CLC 7**
See also CA 61-64; CAAS 4; CANR 16; DLB 8

Mamet, David (Alan) 1947- **CLC 9, 15, 34, 46, 91; DAM DRAM; DC 4**
See also AAYA 3; CA 81-84; CABS 3; CANR 15, 41, 67; DLB 7; MTCW

Mamoulian, Rouben (Zachary) 1897-1987 **CLC 16**
See also CA 25-28R; 124

Mandelstam, Osip (Emilievich) 1891(?)-1938(?) **TCLC 2, 6; PC 14**
See also CA 104; 150

Mander, (Mary) Jane 1877-1949 ... **TCLC 31**
See also CA 162

Mandeville, John fl. 1350- .... **CMLC 19**
See also DLB 146

Mandiargues, Andre Pieyre de .... **CLC 41**
See also Pieyre de Mandiargues, Andre
See also DLB 83

Mandrake, Ethel Belle
See Thurman, Wallace (Henry)

Mangan, James Clarence 1803-1849 **NCLC 27**

Maniere, J.-E.
See Giraudoux, (Hippolyte) Jean

Manley, (Mary) Delariviere 1672(?)-1724 **LC 1**
See also DLB 39, 80

Mann, Abel
See Creasey, John

Mann, Emily 1952- .... **DC 7**
See also CA 130; CANR 55

Mann, (Luiz) Heinrich 1871-1950 ... **TCLC 9**
See also CA 106; 164; DLB 66

Mann, (Paul) Thomas 1875-1955 **TCLC 2, 8, 14, 21, 35, 44, 60; DA; DAB; DAC; DAM MST, NOV; SSC 5; WLC**
See also CA 104; 128; DLB 66; MTCW

Mannheim, Karl 1893-1947 .... **TCLC 65**

Manning, David
See Faust, Frederick (Schiller)

Manning, Frederic 1887(?)-1935 ... **TCLC 25**
See also CA 124

Manning, Olivia 1915-1980 .... **CLC 5, 19**
See also CA 5-8R; 101; CANR 29; MTCW

Mano, D. Keith 1942- .... **CLC 2, 10**
See also CA 25-28R; CAAS 6; CANR 26, 57; DLB 6

Mansfield, Katherine **TCLC 2, 8, 39; DAB; SSC 9, 23; WLC**
See also Beauchamp, Kathleen Mansfield

See also DLB 162

Manso, Peter 1940- .... **CLC 39**
    See also CA 29-32R; CANR 44

Mantecon, Juan Jimenez
    See Jimenez (Mantecon), Juan Ramon

Manton, Peter
    See Creasey, John

Man Without a Spleen, A
    See Chekhov, Anton (Pavlovich)

Manzoni, Alessandro 1785-1873 .... **NCLC 29**

Mapu, Abraham (ben Jekutiel) 1808-1867
    NCLC 18

Mara, Sally
    See Queneau, Raymond

Marat, Jean Paul 1743-1793 .... **LC 10**

Marcel, Gabriel Honore 1889-1973 . **CLC 15**
    See also CA 102; 45-48; MTCW

Marchbanks, Samuel
    See Davies, (William) Robertson

Marchi, Giacomo
    See Bassani, Giorgio

Margulies, Donald .... **CLC 76**

Marie de France c. 12th cent. - .... **CMLC 8**

Marie de l'Incarnation 1599-1672 ...... **LC 10**

Marier, Captain Victor
    See Griffith, D(avid Lewelyn) W(ark)

Mariner, Scott
    See Pohl, Frederik

Marinetti, Filippo Tommaso 1876-1944**TCLC
    10**
    See also CA 107; DLB 114

Marivaux, Pierre Carlet de Chamblain de 1688-
    1763 .... **LC 4; DC 7**

Markandaya, Kamala .... **CLC 8, 38**
    See also Taylor, Kamala (Purnaiya)

Markfield, Wallace 1926- .... **CLC 8**
    See also CA 69-72; CAAS 3; DLB 2, 28

Markham, Edwin 1852-1940 .... **TCLC 47**
    See also CA 160; DLB 54, 186

Markham, Robert
    See Amis, Kingsley (William)

Marks, J
    See Highwater, Jamake (Mamake)

Marks-Highwater, J
    See Highwater, Jamake (Mamake)

Markson, David M(errill) 1927- ...... **CLC 67**
    See also CA 49-52; CANR 1

Marley, Bob .... **CLC 17**
    See also Marley, Robert Nesta

Marley, Robert Nesta 1945-1981
    See Marley, Bob
    See also CA 107; 103

Marlowe, Christopher 1564-1593**LC 22; DA;
    DAB; DAC; DAM DRAM, MST; DC 1;
    WLC**
    See also CDBLB Before 1660; DLB 62

Marlowe, Stephen 1928-
    See Queen, Ellery
    See also CA 13-16R; CANR 6, 55

Marmontel, Jean-Francois 1723-1799 . **LC 2**

Marquand, John P(hillips) 1893-1960**CLC 2,
    10**
    See also CA 85-88; DLB 9, 102

Marques, Rene 1919-1979 ..... **CLC 96; DAM
    MULT; HLC**
    See also CA 97-100; 85-88; DLB 113; HW

Marquez, Gabriel (Jose) Garcia
    See Garcia Marquez, Gabriel (Jose)

Marquis, Don(ald Robert Perry) 1878-1937
    TCLC 7
    See also CA 104; DLB 11, 25

Marric, J. J.
    See Creasey, John

Marryat, Frederick 1792-1848 .... **NCLC 3**
    See also DLB 21, 163

Marsden, James
    See Creasey, John

Marsh, (Edith) Ngaio 1899-1982 **CLC 7, 53;
    DAM POP**
    See also CA 9-12R; CANR 6, 58; DLB 77;
    MTCW

Marshall, Garry 1934- .... **CLC 17**
    See also AAYA 3; CA 111; SATA 60

Marshall, Paule 1929-**CLC 27, 72; BLC; DAM
    MULT; SSC 3**
    See also BW 2; CA 77-80; CANR 25; DLB 157;
    MTCW

Marsten, Richard
    See Hunter, Evan

Marston, John 1576-1634**LC 33; DAM DRAM**
    See also DLB 58, 172

Martha, Henry
    See Harris, Mark

Marti, Jose 1853-1895**NCLC 63; DAM MULT;
    HLC**

Martial c. 40-c. 104 .... **PC 10**

Martin, Ken
    See Hubbard, L(afayette) Ron(ald)

Martin, Richard
    See Creasey, John

Martin, Steve 1945- .... **CLC 30**
    See also CA 97-100; CANR 30; MTCW

Martin, Valerie 1948- .... **CLC 89**
    See also BEST 90:2; CA 85-88; CANR 49

Martin, Violet Florence 1862-1915 **TCLC 51**

Martin, Webber
    See Silverberg, Robert

Martindale, Patrick Victor
    See White, Patrick (Victor Martindale)

Martin du Gard, Roger 1881-1958 **TCLC 24**
    See also CA 118; DLB 65

Martineau, Harriet 1802-1876 .... **NCLC 26**
    See also DLB 21, 55, 159, 163, 166, 190; YABC
    2

Martines, Julia
    See O'Faolain, Julia

Martinez, Enrique Gonzalez
    See Gonzalez Martinez, Enrique

Martinez, Jacinto Benavente y
    See Benavente (y Martinez), Jacinto

Martinez Ruiz, Jose 1873-1967
    See Azorin; Ruiz, Jose Martinez
    See also CA 93-96; HW

Martinez Sierra, Gregorio 1881-1947**TCLC 6**
    See also CA 115

Martinez Sierra, Maria (de la O'LeJarraga)
    1874-1974 .... **TCLC 6**
    See also CA 115

Martinsen, Martin
    See Follett, Ken(neth Martin)

Martinson, Harry (Edmund) 1904-1978**C L C
    14**
    See also CA 77-80; CANR 34

Marut, Ret
    See Traven, B.

Marut, Robert
    See Traven, B.

Marvell, Andrew 1621-1678**LC 4; DA; DAB;
    DAC; DAM MST, POET; PC 10; WLC**
    See also CDBLB 1660-1789; DLB 131

Marx, Karl (Heinrich) 1818-1883 . **NCLC 17**
    See also DLB 129

Masaoka Shiki .... **TCLC 18**
    See also Masaoka Tsunenori

Masaoka Tsunenori 1867-1902
    See Masaoka Shiki

See also CA 117

Masefield, John (Edward) 1878-1967**CLC 11,
    47; DAM POET**
    See also CA 19-20; 25-28R; CANR 33; CAP 2;
    CDBLB 1890-1914; DLB 10, 19, 153, 160;
    MTCW; SATA 19

Maso, Carole 19(?)- .... **CLC 44**

Mason, Bobbie Ann 1940-**CLC 28, 43, 82; SSC
    4**
    See also AAYA 5; CA 53-56; CANR 11, 31,
    58; DLB 173; DLBY 87; INT CANR-31;
    MTCW

Mason, Ernst
    See Pohl, Frederik

Mason, Lee W.
    See Malzberg, Barry N(athaniel)

Mason, Nick 1945- .... **CLC 35**

Mason, Tally
    See Derleth, August (William)

Mass, William
    See Gibson, William

Masters, Edgar Lee 1868-1950 **TCLC 2, 25;
    DA; DAC; DAM MST, POET; PC 1;
    WLCS**
    See also CA 104; 133; CDALB 1865-1917;
    DLB 54; MTCW

Masters, Hilary 1928- .... **CLC 48**
    See also CA 25-28R; CANR 13, 47

Mastrosimone, William 19(?)- .... **CLC 36**

Mathe, Albert
    See Camus, Albert

Mather, Cotton 1663-1728 .... **LC 38**
    See also CDALB 1640-1865; DLB 24, 30, 140

Mather, Increase 1639-1723 .... **LC 38**
    See also DLB 24

Matheson, Richard Burton 1926- ..... **CLC 37**
    See also CA 97-100; DLB 8, 44; INT 97-100

Mathews, Harry 1930- .... **CLC 6, 52**
    See also CA 21-24R; CAAS 6; CANR 18, 40

Mathews, John Joseph 1894-1979 .. **CLC 84;
    DAM MULT**
    See also CA 19-20; 142; CANR 45; CAP 2;
    DLB 175; NNAL

Mathias, Roland (Glyn) 1915- .... **CLC 45**
    See also CA 97-100; CANR 19, 41; DLB 27

Matsuo Basho 1644-1694 .... **PC 3**
    See also DAM POET

Mattheson, Rodney
    See Creasey, John

Matthews, Greg 1949- .... **CLC 45**
    See also CA 135

Matthews, William (Procter, III) 1942-1997
    CLC 40
    See also CA 29-32R; 162; CAAS 18; CANR
    12, 57; DLB 5

Matthias, John (Edward) 1941- .... **CLC 9**
    See also CA 33-36R; CANR 56

Matthiessen, Peter 1927-**CLC 5, 7, 11, 32, 64;
    DAM NOV**
    See also AAYA 6; BEST 90:4; CA 9-12R;
    CANR 21, 50; DLB 6, 173; MTCW; SATA
    27

Maturin, Charles Robert 1780(?)-1824**NCLC
    6**
    See also DLB 178

Matute (Ausejo), Ana Maria 1925- .. **CLC 11**
    See also CA 89-92; MTCW

Maugham, W. S.
    See Maugham, W(illiam) Somerset

Maugham, W(illiam) Somerset 1874-1965
    **CLC 1, 11, 15, 67, 93; DA; DAB; DAC;
    DAM DRAM, MST, NOV; SSC 8; WLC**
    See also CA 5-8R; 25-28R; CANR 40; CDBLB

1914-1945; DLB 10, 36, 77, 100, 162, 195;
MTCW; SATA 54

Maugham, William Somerset
See Maugham, W(illiam) Somerset

Maupassant, (Henri Rene Albert) Guy de 1850-
1893NCLC **1, 42; DA; DAB; DAC; DAM
MST; SSC 1; WLC**
See also DLB 123

Maupin, Armistead 1944-CLC **95; DAM POP**
See also CA 125; 130; CANR 58; INT 130

Maurhut, Richard
See Traven, B.

Mauriac, Claude 1914-1996 .... **CLC 9**
See also CA 89-92; 152; DLB 83

Mauriac, Francois (Charles) 1885-1970 C L C
4, 9, 56; SSC 24
See also CA 25-28; CAP 2; DLB 65; MTCW

Mavor, Osborne Henry 1888-1951
See Bridie, James
See also CA 104

Maxwell, William (Keepers, Jr.) 1908-CLC **19**
See also CA 93-96; CANR 54; DLBY 80; INT
93-96

May, Elaine 1932- .... **CLC 16**
See also CA 124; 142; DLB 44

Mayakovski, Vladimir (Vladimirovich) 1893-
1930 .... **TCLC 4, 18**
See also CA 104; 158

Mayhew, Henry 1812-1887 .... **NCLC 31**
See also DLB 18, 55, 190

Mayle, Peter 1939(?)- .... **CLC 89**
See also CA 139; CANR 64

Maynard, Joyce 1953- .... **CLC 23**
See also CA 111; 129; CANR 64

Mayne, William (James Carter) 1928-CLC **12**
See also AAYA 20; CA 9-12R; CANR 37; CLR
25; JRDA; MAICYA; SAAS 11; SATA 6, 68

Mayo, Jim
See L'Amour, Louis (Dearborn)

Maysles, Albert 1926- .... **CLC 16**
See also CA 29-32R

Maysles, David 1932- .... **CLC 16**

Mazer, Norma Fox 1931- .... **CLC 26**
See also AAYA 5; CA 69-72; CANR 12, 32,
66; CLR 23; JRDA; MAICYA; SAAS 1;
SATA 24, 67

Mazzini, Guiseppe 1805-1872 .... **NCLC 34**

McAuley, James Phillip 1917-1976 . **CLC 45**
See also CA 97-100

McBain, Ed
See Hunter, Evan

McBrien, William Augustine 1930- . **CLC 44**
See also CA 107

McCaffrey, Anne (Inez) 1926-CLC **17; DAM
NOV, POP**
See also AAYA 6; AITN 2; BEST 89:2; CA 25-
28R; CANR 15, 35, 55; CLR 49; DLB 8;
JRDA; MAICYA; MTCW; SAAS 11; SATA
8, 70

McCall, Nathan 1955(?)- .... **CLC 86**
See also CA 146

McCann, Arthur
See Campbell, John W(ood, Jr.)

McCann, Edson
See Pohl, Frederik

McCarthy, Charles, Jr. 1933-
See McCarthy, Cormac
See also CANR 42; DAM POP

McCarthy, Cormac 1933- CLC **4, 57, 59, 101**
See also McCarthy, Charles, Jr.
See also DLB 6, 143

McCarthy, Mary (Therese) 1912-1989CLC **1,
3, 5, 14, 24, 39, 59; SSC 24**

See also CA 5-8R; 129; CANR 16, 50, 64; DLB
2; DLBY 81; INT CANR-16; MTCW

McCartney, (James) Paul 1942-. **CLC 12, 35**
See also CA 146

McCauley, Stephen (D.) 1955- .... **CLC 50**
See also CA 141

McClure, Michael (Thomas) 1932-CLC **6, 10**
See also CA 21-24R; CANR 17, 46; DLB 16

McCorkle, Jill (Collins) 1958-........... **CLC 51**
See also CA 121; DLBY 87

McCourt, Frank 1930- .... **CLC 109**
See also CA 157

McCourt, James 1941- .... **CLC 5**
See also CA 57-60

McCoy, Horace (Stanley) 1897-1955TCLC **28**
See also CA 108; 155; DLB 9

McCrae, John 1872-1918 .... **TCLC 12**
See also CA 109; DLB 92

McCreigh, James
See Pohl, Frederik

McCullers, (Lula) Carson (Smith) 1917-1967
CLC **1, 4, 10, 12, 48, 100; DA; DAB; DAC;
DAM MST, NOV; SSC 9, 24; WLC**
See also AAYA 21; CA 5-8R; 25-28R; CABS
1, 3; CANR 18; CDALB 1941-1968; DLB
2, 7, 173; MTCW; SATA 27

McCulloch, John Tyler
See Burroughs, Edgar Rice

McCullough, Colleen 1938(?)- CLC **27, 107;
DAM NOV, POP**
See also CA 81-84; CANR 17, 46, 67; MTCW

McDermott, Alice 1953-.................... **CLC 90**
See also CA 109; CANR 40

McElroy, Joseph 1930- .... **CLC 5, 47**
See also CA 17-20R

McEwan, Ian (Russell) 1948- .... CLC **13, 66;
DAM NOV**
See also BEST 90:4; CA 61-64; CANR 14, 41;
DLB 14, 194; MTCW

McFadden, David 1940-.................... **CLC 48**
See also CA 104; DLB 60; INT 104

McFarland, Dennis 1950-.................. **CLC 65**
See also CA 165

McGahern, John 1934-CLC **5, 9, 48; SSC 17**
See also CA 17-20R; CANR 29, 68; DLB 14;
MTCW

McGinley, Patrick (Anthony) 1937- .**CLC 41**
See also CA 120; 127; CANR 56; INT 127

McGinley, Phyllis 1905-1978 .... **CLC 14**
See also CA 9-12R; 77-80; CANR 19; DLB 11,
48; SATA 2, 44; SATA-Obit 24

McGinniss, Joe 1942- .... **CLC 32**
See also AITN 2; BEST 89:2; CA 25-28R;
CANR 26; DLB 185; INT CANR-26

McGivern, Maureen Daly
See Daly, Maureen

McGrath, Patrick 1950-..................... **CLC 55**
See also CA 136; CANR 65

McGrath, Thomas (Matthew) 1916-1990CLC
28, 59; DAM POET
See also CA 9-12R; 132; CANR 6, 33; MTCW;
SATA 41; SATA-Obit 66

McGuane, Thomas (Francis III) 1939-CLC **3,
7, 18, 45**
See also AITN 2; CA 49-52; CANR 5, 24, 49;
DLB 2; DLBY 80; INT CANR-24; MTCW

McGuckian, Medbh 1950- ..... CLC **48; DAM
POET**
See also CA 143; DLB 40

McHale, Tom 1942(?)-1982 .... **CLC 3, 5**
See also AITN 1; CA 77-80; 106

McIlvanney, William 1936- .... **CLC 42**
See also CA 25-28R; CANR 61; DLB 14

McIlwraith, Maureen Mollie Hunter
See Hunter, Mollie
See also SATA 2

McInerney, Jay 1955- ... **CLC 34; DAM POP**
See also AAYA 18; CA 116; 123; CANR 45,
68; INT 123

McIntyre, Vonda N(eel) 1948- .... **CLC 18**
See also CA 81-84; CANR 17, 34; MTCW

McKay, ClaudeTCLC **7, 41; BLC; DAB; PC 2**
See also McKay, Festus Claudius
See also DLB 4, 45, 51, 117

McKay, Festus Claudius 1889-1948
See McKay, Claude
See also BW 1; CA 104; 124; DA; DAC; DAM
MST, MULT, NOV, POET; MTCW; WLC

McKuen, Rod 1933- .... **CLC 1, 3**
See also AITN 1; CA 41-44R; CANR 40

McLoughlin, R. B.
See Mencken, H(enry) L(ouis)

McLuhan, (Herbert) Marshall 1911-1980
CLC **37, 83**
See also CA 9-12R; 102; CANR 12, 34, 61;
DLB 88; INT CANR-12; MTCW

McMillan, Terry (L.) 1951-CLC **50, 61; DAM
MULT, NOV, POP**
See also AAYA 21; BW 2; CA 140; CANR 60

McMurtry, Larry (Jeff) 1936-CLC **2, 3, 7, 11,
27, 44; DAM NOV, POP**
See also AAYA 15; AITN 2; BEST 89:2; CA 5-
8R; CANR 19, 43, 64; CDALB 1968-1988;
DLB 2, 143; DLBY 80, 87; MTCW

McNally, T. M. 1961-........................ **CLC 82**

McNally, Terrence 1939- ... CLC **4, 7, 41, 91;
DAM DRAM**
See also CA 45-48; CANR 2, 56; DLB 7

McNamer, Deirdre 1950- .... **CLC 70**

McNeile, Herman Cyril 1888-1937
See Sapper
See also DLB 77

McNickle, (William) D'Arcy 1904-1977 C L C
89; DAM MULT
See also CA 9-12R; 85-88; CANR 5, 45; DLB
175; NNAL; SATA-Obit 22

McPhee, John (Angus) 1931- .... **CLC 36**
See also BEST 90:1; CA 65-68; CANR 20, 46,
64; DLB 185; MTCW

McPherson, James Alan 1943-... CLC **19, 77**
See also BW 1; CA 25-28R; CAAS 17; CANR
24; DLB 38; MTCW

McPherson, William (Alexander) 1933- C L C
34
See also CA 69-72; CANR 28; INT CANR-28

Mead, Margaret 1901-1978 .... **CLC 37**
See also AITN 1; CA 1-4R; 81-84; CANR 4;
MTCW; SATA-Obit 20

Meaker, Marijane (Agnes) 1927-
See Kerr, M. E.
See also CA 107; CANR 37, 63; INT 107;
JRDA; MAICYA; MTCW; SATA 20, 61

Medoff, Mark (Howard) 1940- ... CLC **6, 23;
DAM DRAM**
See also AITN 1; CA 53-56; CANR 5; DLB 7;
INT CANR-5

Medvedev, P. N.
See Bakhtin, Mikhail Mikhailovich

Meged, Aharon
See Megged, Aharon

Meged, Aron
See Megged, Aharon

Megged, Aharon 1920-........................**CLC 9**
See also CA 49-52; CAAS 13; CANR 1

Mehta, Ved (Parkash) 1934-............. **CLC 37**
See also CA 1-4R; CANR 2, 23; MTCW

Melanter
  See Blackmore, R(ichard) D(oddridge)
Melikow, Loris
  See Hofmannsthal, Hugo von
Melmoth, Sebastian
  See Wilde, Oscar (Fingal O'Flahertie Wills)
Meltzer, Milton 1915- .... **CLC 26**
  See also AAYA 8; CA 13-16R; CANR 38; CLR
  13; DLB 61; JRDA; MAICYA; SAAS 1;
  SATA 1, 50, 80
Melville, Herman 1819-1891**NCLC 3, 12, 29,
  45, 49; DA; DAB; DAC; DAM MST, NOV;
  SSC 1, 17; WLC**
  See also AAYA 25; CDALB 1640-1865; DLB
  3, 74; SATA 59
Menander c. 342B.C.-c. 292B.C. .... **CMLC 9;
  DAM DRAM; DC 3**
  See also DLB 176
Mencken, H(enry) L(ouis) 1880-1956 **T C L C
  13**
  See also CA 105; 125; CDALB 1917-1929;
  DLB 11, 29, 63, 137; MTCW
Mendelsohn, Jane 1965(?)- .... **CLC 99**
  See also CA 154
Mercer, David 1928-1980**CLC 5; DAM DRAM**
  See also CA 9-12R; 102; CANR 23; DLB 13;
  MTCW
Merchant, Paul
  See Ellison, Harlan (Jay)
Meredith, George 1828-1909 .. **TCLC 17, 43;
  DAM POET**
  See also CA 117; 153; CDBLB 1832-1890;
  DLB 18, 35, 57, 159
Meredith, William (Morris) 1919-**CLC 4, 13,
  22, 55; DAM POET**
  See also CA 9-12R; CAAS 14; CANR 6, 40;
  DLB 5
Merezhkovsky, Dmitry Sergeyevich 1865-1941
  TCLC 29
Merimee, Prosper 1803-1870**NCLC 6, 65; SSC
  7**
  See also DLB 119, 192
Merkin, Daphne 1954- .... **CLC 44**
  See also CA 123
Merlin, Arthur
  See Blish, James (Benjamin)
Merrill, James (Ingram) 1926-1995**CLC 2, 3,
  6, 8, 13, 18, 34, 91; DAM POET**
  See also CA 13-16R; 147; CANR 10, 49, 63;
  DLB 5, 165; DLBY 85; INT CANR-10;
  MTCW
Merriman, Alex
  See Silverberg, Robert
Merritt, E. B.
  See Waddington, Miriam
Merton, Thomas 1915-1968**CLC 1, 3, 11, 34,
  83; PC 10**
  See also CA 5-8R; 25-28R; CANR 22, 53; DLB
  48; DLBY 81; MTCW
Merwin, W(illiam) S(tanley) 1927- **CLC 1, 2,
  3, 5, 8, 13, 18, 45, 88; DAM POET**
  See also CA 13-16R; CANR 15, 51; DLB 5,
  169; INT CANR-15; MTCW
Metcalf, John 1938- .... **CLC 37**
  See also CA 113; DLB 60
Metcalf, Suzanne
  See Baum, L(yman) Frank
Mew, Charlotte (Mary) 1870-1928 .. **TCLC 8**
  See also CA 105; DLB 19, 135
Mewshaw, Michael 1943- .... **CLC 9**
  See also CA 53-56; CANR 7, 47; DLBY 80
Meyer, June
  See Jordan, June

Meyer, Lynn
  See Slavitt, David R(ytman)
Meyer-Meyrink, Gustav 1868-1932
  See Meyrink, Gustav
  See also CA 117
Meyers, Jeffrey 1939- .... **CLC 39**
  See also CA 73-76; CANR 54; DLB 111
Meynell, Alice (Christina Gertrude Thompson)
  1847-1922 .... **TCLC 6**
  See also CA 104; DLB 19, 98
Meyrink, Gustav .... **TCLC 21**
  See also Meyer-Meyrink, Gustav
  See also DLB 81
Michaels, Leonard 1933- **CLC 6, 25; SSC 16**
  See also CA 61-64; CANR 21, 62; DLB 130;
  MTCW
Michaux, Henri 1899-1984 .... **CLC 8, 19**
  See also CA 85-88; 114
Micheaux, Oscar 1884-1951 .... **TCLC 76**
  See also DLB 50
Michelangelo 1475-1564 .... **LC 12**
Michelet, Jules 1798-1874 .... **NCLC 31**
Michener, James A(lbert) 1907(?)-1997 **C L C
  1, 5, 11, 29, 60, 109; DAM NOV, POP**
  See also AITN 1; BEST 90:1; CA 5-8R; 161;
  CANR 21, 45, 68; DLB 6; MTCW
Mickiewicz, Adam 1798-1855 .... **NCLC 3**
Middleton, Christopher 1926- .... **CLC 13**
  See also CA 13-16R; CANR 29, 54; DLB 40
Middleton, Richard (Barham) 1882-1911
  TCLC 56
  See also DLB 156
Middleton, Stanley 1919- .... **CLC 7, 38**
  See also CA 25-28R; CAAS 23; CANR 21, 46;
  DLB 14
Middleton, Thomas 1580-1627 **LC 33; DAM
  DRAM, MST; DC 5**
  See also DLB 58
Migueis, Jose Rodrigues 1901- .... **CLC 10**
Mikszath, Kalman 1847-1910 .... **TCLC 31**
Miles, Jack .... **CLC 100**
Miles, Josephine (Louise) 1911-1985**CLC 1, 2,
  14, 34, 39; DAM POET**
  See also CA 1-4R; 116; CANR 2, 55; DLB 48
Militant
  See Sandburg, Carl (August)
Mill, John Stuart 1806-1873 .... **NCLC 11, 58**
  See also CDBLB 1832-1890; DLB 55, 190
Millar, Kenneth 1915-1983 .... **CLC 14; DAM
  POP**
  See also Macdonald, Ross
  See also CA 9-12R; 110; CANR 16, 63; DLB
  2; DLBD 6; DLBY 83; MTCW
Millay, E. Vincent
  See Millay, Edna St. Vincent
Millay, Edna St. Vincent 1892-1950**TCLC 4,
  49; DA; DAB; DAC; DAM MST, POET;
  PC 6; WLCS**
  See also CA 104; 130; CDALB 1917-1929;
  DLB 45; MTCW
Miller, Arthur 1915-**CLC 1, 2, 6, 10, 15, 26, 47,
  78; DA; DAB; DAC; DAM DRAM, MST;
  DC 1; WLC**
  See also AAYA 15; AITN 1; CA 1-4R; CABS
  3; CANR 2, 30, 54; CDALB 1941-1968;
  DLB 7; MTCW
Miller, Henry (Valentine) 1891-1980**CLC 1, 2,
  4, 9, 14, 43, 84; DA; DAB; DAC; DAM
  MST, NOV; WLC**
  See also CA 9-12R; 97-100; CANR 33, 64;
  CDALB 1929-1941; DLB 4, 9; DLBY 80;
  MTCW
Miller, Jason 1939(?)- .... **CLC 2**

  See also AITN 1; CA 73-76; DLB 7
Miller, Sue 1943- .... **CLC 44; DAM POP**
  See also BEST 90:3; CA 139; CANR 59; DLB
  143
Miller, Walter M(ichael, Jr.) 1923-**CLC 4, 30**
  See also CA 85-88; DLB 8
Millett, Kate 1934- .... **CLC 67**
  See also AITN 1; CA 73-76; CANR 32, 53;
  MTCW
Millhauser, Steven (Lewis) 1943-**CLC 21, 54,
  109**
  See also CA 110; 111; CANR 63; DLB 2; INT
  111
Millin, Sarah Gertrude 1889-1968 ...**CLC 49**
  See also CA 102; 93-96
Milne, A(lan) A(lexander) 1882-1956**TCLC 6;
  DAB; DAC; DAM MST**
  See also CA 104; 133; CLR 1, 26; DLB 10, 77,
  100, 160; MAICYA; MTCW; YABC 1
Milner, Ron(ald) 1938- **CLC 56; BLC; DAM
  MULT**
  See also AITN 1; BW 1; CA 73-76; CANR 24;
  DLB 38; MTCW
Milnes, Richard Monckton 1809-1885 **N C L C
  61**
  See also DLB 32, 184
Milosz, Czeslaw 1911- **CLC 5, 11, 22, 31, 56,
  82; DAM MST, POET; PC 8; WLCS**
  See also CA 81-84; CANR 23, 51; MTCW
Milton, John 1608-1674 ..... **LC 9; DA; DAB;
  DAC; DAM MST, POET; PC 19; WLC**
  See also CDBLB 1660-1789; DLB 131, 151
Min, Anchee 1957-............................. **CLC 86**
  See also CA 146
Minehaha, Cornelius
  See Wedekind, (Benjamin) Frank(lin)
Miner, Valerie 1947-........................... **CLC 40**
  See also CA 97-100; CANR 59
Minimo, Duca
  See D'Annunzio, Gabriele
Minot, Susan 1956-............................. **CLC 44**
  See also CA 134
Minus, Ed 1938-................................ **CLC 39**
Miranda, Javier
  See Bioy Casares, Adolfo
Mirbeau, Octave 1848-1917 .... **TCLC 55**
  See also DLB 123, 192
Miro (Ferrer), Gabriel (Francisco Victor) 1879-
  1930 .... **TCLC 5**
  See also CA 104
Mishima, Yukio 1925-1970**CLC 2, 4, 6, 9, 27;
  DC 1; SSC 4**
  See also Hiraoka, Kimitake
  See also DLB 182
Mistral, Frederic 1830-1914 .... **TCLC 51**
  See also CA 122
Mistral, Gabriela .... **TCLC 2; HLC**
  See also Godoy Alcayaga, Lucila
Mistry, Rohinton 1952- .... **CLC 71; DAC**
  See also CA 141
Mitchell, Clyde
  See Ellison, Harlan (Jay); Silverberg, Robert
Mitchell, James Leslie 1901-1935
  See Gibbon, Lewis Grassic
  See also CA 104; DLB 15
Mitchell, Joni 1943- .... **CLC 12**
  See also CA 112
Mitchell, Joseph (Quincy) 1908-1996**CLC 98**
  See also CA 77-80; 152; DLB 185; DLBY 96
Mitchell, Margaret (Munnerlyn) 1900-1949
  TCLC 11; DAM NOV, POP
  See also AAYA 23; CA 109; 125; CANR 55;
  DLB 9; MTCW

Mitchell, Peggy
  See Mitchell, Margaret (Munnerlyn)
Mitchell, S(ilas) Weir 1829-1914 ... **TCLC 36**
  See also CA 165
Mitchell, W(illiam) O(rmond) 1914-1998**CLC 25; DAC; DAM MST**
  See also CA 77-80; 165; CANR 15, 43; DLB 88
Mitford, Mary Russell 1787-1855 ...**NCLC 4**
  See also DLB 110, 116
Mitford, Nancy 1904-1973 .... **CLC 44**
  See also CA 9-12R; DLB 191
Miyamoto, Yuriko 1899-1951 .... **TCLC 37**
  See also DLB 180
Miyazawa, Kenji 1896-1933 .... **TCLC 76**
  See also CA 157
Mizoguchi, Kenji 1898-1956 .... **TCLC 72**
Mo, Timothy (Peter) 1950(?)-........... **CLC 46**
  See also CA 117; DLB 194; MTCW
Modarressi, Taghi (M.) 1931- .... **CLC 44**
  See also CA 121; 134; INT 134
Modiano, Patrick (Jean) 1945- .... **CLC 18**
  See also CA 85-88; CANR 17, 40; DLB 83
Moerck, Paal
  See Roelvaag, O(le) E(dvart)
Mofolo, Thomas (Mokopu) 1875(?)-1948 **TCLC 22; BLC; DAM MULT**
  See also CA 121; 153
Mohr, Nicholasa 1938-**CLC 12; DAM MULT; HLC**
  See also AAYA 8; CA 49-52; CANR 1, 32, 64; CLR 22; DLB 145; HW; JRDA; SAAS 8; SATA 8, 97
Mojtabai, A(nn) G(race) 1938- **CLC 5, 9, 15, 29**
  See also CA 85-88
Moliere 1622-1673 . **LC 28; DA; DAB; DAC; DAM DRAM, MST; WLC**
Molin, Charles
  See Mayne, William (James Carter)
Molnar, Ferenc 1878-1952 .. **TCLC 20; DAM DRAM**
  See also CA 109; 153
Momaday, N(avarre) Scott 1934- **CLC 2, 19, 85, 95; DA; DAB; DAC; DAM MST, MULT, NOV, POP; WLCS**
  See also AAYA 11; CA 25-28R; CANR 14, 34, 68; DLB 143, 175; INT CANR-14; MTCW; NNAL; SATA 48; SATA-Brief 30
Monette, Paul 1945-1995 .... **CLC 82**
  See also CA 139; 147
Monroe, Harriet 1860-1936............ **TCLC 12**
  See also CA 109; DLB 54, 91
Monroe, Lyle
  See Heinlein, Robert A(nson)
Montagu, Elizabeth 1917- ....**NCLC 7**
  See also CA 9-12R
Montagu, Mary (Pierrepont) Wortley 1689-1762 ....**LC 9; PC 16**
  See also DLB 95, 101
Montagu, W. H.
  See Coleridge, Samuel Taylor
Montague, John (Patrick) 1929- **CLC 13, 46**
  See also CA 9-12R; CANR 9; DLB 40; MTCW
Montaigne, Michel (Eyquem) de 1533-1592 **LC 8; DA; DAB; DAC; DAM MST; WLC**
Montale, Eugenio 1896-1981**CLC 7, 9, 18; PC 13**
  See also CA 17-20R; 104; CANR 30; DLB 114; MTCW
Montesquieu, Charles-Louis de Secondat 1689-1755 .... **LC 7**
Montgomery, (Robert) Bruce 1921-1978

See Crispin, Edmund
  See also CA 104
Montgomery, L(ucy) M(aud) 1874-1942
  TCLC 51; DAC; DAM MST
  See also AAYA 12; CA 108; 137; CLR 8; DLB 92; DLBD 14; JRDA; MAICYA; YABC 1
Montgomery, Marion H., Jr. 1925- ....**CLC 7**
  See also AITN 1; CA 1-4R; CANR 3, 48; DLB 6
Montgomery, Max
  See Davenport, Guy (Mattison, Jr.)
Montherlant, Henry (Milon) de 1896-1972
  CLC 8, 19; DAM DRAM
  See also CA 85-88; 37-40R; DLB 72; MTCW
Monty Python
  See Chapman, Graham; Cleese, John (Marwood); Gilliam, Terry (Vance); Idle, Eric; Jones, Terence Graham Parry; Palin, Michael (Edward)
  See also AAYA 7
Moodie, Susanna (Strickland) 1803-1885
  NCLC 14
  See also DLB 99
Mooney, Edward 1951-
  See Mooney, Ted
  See also CA 130
Mooney, Ted ....**CLC 25**
  See also Mooney, Edward
Moorcock, Michael (John) 1939-**CLC 5, 27, 58**
  See also CA 45-48; CAAS 5; CANR 2, 17, 38, 64; DLB 14; MTCW; SATA 93
Moore, Brian 1921- **CLC 1, 3, 5, 7, 8, 19, 32, 90; DAB; DAC; DAM MST**
  See also CA 1-4R; CANR 1, 25, 42, 63; MTCW
Moore, Edward
  See Muir, Edwin
Moore, George Augustus 1852-1933**TCLC 7; SSC 19**
  See also CA 104; DLB 10, 18, 57, 135
Moore, Lorrie .... **CLC 39, 45, 68**
  See also Moore, Marie Lorena
Moore, Marianne (Craig) 1887-1972**CLC 1, 2, 4, 8, 10, 13, 19, 47; DA; DAB; DAC; DAM MST, POET; PC 4; WLCS**
  See also CA 1-4R; 33-36R; CANR 3, 61; CDALB 1929-1941; DLB 45; DLBD 7; MTCW; SATA 20
Moore, Marie Lorena 1957-
  See Moore, Lorrie
  See also CA 116; CANR 39
Moore, Thomas 1779-1852 .... **NCLC 6**
  See also DLB 96, 144
Morand, Paul 1888-1976 .... **CLC 41; SSC 22**
  See also CA 69-72; DLB 65
Morante, Elsa 1918-1985 .... **CLC 8, 47**
  See also CA 85-88; 117; CANR 35; DLB 177; MTCW
Moravia, Alberto 1907-1990**CLC 2, 7, 11, 27, 46; SSC 26**
  See also Pincherle, Alberto
  See also DLB 177
More, Hannah 1745-1833 .... **NCLC 27**
  See also DLB 107, 109, 116, 158
More, Henry 1614-1687 .... **LC 9**
  See also DLB 126
More, Sir Thomas 1478-1535 .... **LC 10, 32**
Moreas, Jean .... **TCLC 18**
  See also Papadiamantopoulos, Johannes
Morgan, Berry 1919- .... **CLC 6**
  See also CA 49-52; DLB 6
Morgan, Claire
  See Highsmith, (Mary) Patricia
Morgan, Edwin (George) 1920- ....**CLC 31**

See also CA 5-8R; CANR 3, 43; DLB 27
Morgan, (George) Frederick 1922- . **CLC 23**
  See also CA 17-20R; CANR 21
Morgan, Harriet
  See Mencken, H(enry) L(ouis)
Morgan, Jane
  See Cooper, James Fenimore
Morgan, Janet 1945- .... **CLC 39**
  See also CA 65-68
Morgan, Lady 1776(?)-1859 .... **NCLC 29**
  See also DLB 116, 158
Morgan, Robin 1941- ....**CLC 2**
  See also CA 69-72; CANR 29, 68; MTCW; SATA 80
Morgan, Scott
  See Kuttner, Henry
Morgan, Seth 1949(?)-1990 .... **CLC 65**
  See also CA 132
Morgenstern, Christian 1871-1914 . **TCLC 8**
  See also CA 105
Morgenstern, S.
  See Goldman, William (W.)
Moricz, Zsigmond 1879-1942 .... **TCLC 33**
  See also CA 165
Morike, Eduard (Friedrich) 1804-1875**NCLC 10**
  See also DLB 133
Moritz, Karl Philipp 1756-1793 .... **LC 2**
  See also DLB 94
Morland, Peter Henry
  See Faust, Frederick (Schiller)
Morren, Theophil
  See Hofmannsthal, Hugo von
Morris, Bill 1952- .... **CLC 76**
Morris, Julian
  See West, Morris L(anglo)
Morris, Steveland Judkins 1950(?)-
  See Wonder, Stevie
  See also CA 111
Morris, William 1834-1896 .... **NCLC 4**
  See also CDBLB 1832-1890; DLB 18, 35, 57, 156, 178, 184
Morris, Wright 1910- ...... **CLC 1, 3, 7, 18, 37**
  See also CA 9-12R; CANR 21; DLB 2; DLBY 81; MTCW
Morrison, Arthur 1863-1945 .... **TCLC 72**
  See also CA 120; 157; DLB 70, 135
Morrison, Chloe Anthony Wofford
  See Morrison, Toni
Morrison, James Douglas 1943-1971
  See Morrison, Jim
  See also CA 73-76; CANR 40
Morrison, Jim .... **CLC 17**
  See also Morrison, James Douglas
Morrison, Toni 1931-**CLC 4, 10, 22, 55, 81, 87; BLC; DA; DAB; DAC; DAM MST, MULT, NOV, POP**
  See also AAYA 1, 22; BW 2; CA 29-32R; CANR 27, 42, 67; CDALB 1968-1988; DLB 6, 33, 143; DLBY 81; MTCW; SATA 57
Morrison, Van 1945- .... **CLC 21**
  See also CA 116
Morrissy, Mary 1958- .... **CLC 99**
Mortimer, John (Clifford) 1923-**CLC 28, 43; DAM DRAM, POP**
  See also CA 13-16R; CANR 21; CDBLB 1960 to Present; DLB 13; INT CANR-21; MTCW
Mortimer, Penelope (Ruth) 1918- ....**CLC 5**
  See also CA 57-60; CANR 45
Morton, Anthony
  See Creasey, John
Mosca, Gaetano 1858-1941 .... **TCLC 75**
Mosher, Howard Frank 1943- .... **CLC 62**

See also CA 139; CANR 65

Mosley, Nicholas 1923- .... **CLC 43, 70**
See also CA 69-72; CANR 41, 60; DLB 14

Mosley, Walter 1952- **CLC 97; DAM MULT, POP**
See also AAYA 17; BW 2; CA 142; CANR 57

Moss, Howard 1922-1987 **CLC 7, 14, 45, 50; DAM POET**
See also CA 1-4R; 123; CANR 1, 44; DLB 5

Mossgiel, Rab
See Burns, Robert

Motion, Andrew (Peter) 1952- .... **CLC 47**
See also CA 146; DLB 40

Motley, Willard (Francis) 1909-1965 **CLC 18**
See also BW 1; CA 117; 106; DLB 76, 143

Motoori, Norinaga 1730-1801 .... **NCLC 45**

Mott, Michael (Charles Alston) 1930- **CLC 15, 34**
See also CA 5-8R; CAAS 7; CANR 7, 29

Mountain Wolf Woman 1884-1960 .. **CLC 92**
See also CA 144; NNAL

Moure, Erin 1955- .... **CLC 88**
See also CA 113; DLB 60

Mowat, Farley (McGill) 1921- **CLC 26; DAC; DAM MST**
See also AAYA 1; CA 1-4R; CANR 4, 24, 42, 68; CLR 20; DLB 68; INT CANAR-24; JRDA; MAICYA; MTCW; SATA 3, 55

Moyers, Bill 1934- .... **CLC 74**
See also AITN 2; CA 61-64; CANR 31, 52

Mphahlele, Es'kia
See Mphahlele, Ezekiel
See also DLB 125

Mphahlele, Ezekiel 1919-1983 **CLC 25; BLC; DAM MULT**
See also Mphahlele, Es'kia
See also BW 2; CA 81-84; CANR 26

Mqhayi, S(amuel) E(dward) K(rune Loliwe) 1875-1945 **TCLC 25; BLC; DAM MULT**
See also CA 153

Mrozek, Slawomir 1930- .... **CLC 3, 13**
See also CA 13-16R; CAAS 10; CANR 29; MTCW

Mrs. Belloc-Lowndes
See Lowndes, Marie Adelaide (Belloc)

Mtwa, Percy (?)- .... **CLC 47**

Mueller, Lisel 1924- .... **CLC 13, 51**
See also CA 93-96; DLB 105

Muir, Edwin 1887-1959 .... **TCLC 2**
See also CA 104; DLB 20, 100, 191

Muir, John 1838-1914 .... **TCLC 28**
See also CA 165; DLB 186

Mujica Lainez, Manuel 1910-1984 .. **CLC 31**
See also Lainez, Manuel Mujica
See also CA 81-84; 112; CANR 32; HW

Mukherjee, Bharati 1940- **CLC 53; DAM NOV**
See also BEST 89:2; CA 107; CANR 45; DLB 60; MTCW

Muldoon, Paul 1951- **CLC 32, 72; DAM POET**
See also CA 113; 129; CANR 52; DLB 40; INT 129

Mulisch, Harry 1927- .... **CLC 42**
See also CA 9-12R; CANR 6, 26, 56

Mull, Martin 1943- .... **CLC 17**
See also CA 105

Mulock, Dinah Maria
See Craik, Dinah Maria (Mulock)

Munford, Robert 1737(?)-1783 .... **LC 5**
See also DLB 31

Mungo, Raymond 1946- .... **CLC 72**
See also CA 49-52; CANR 2

Munro, Alice 1931- .... **CLC 6, 10, 19, 50, 95; DAC; DAM MST, NOV; SSC 3; WLCS**

See also AITN 2; CA 33-36R; CANR 33, 53; DLB 53; MTCW; SATA 29

Munro, H(ector) H(ugh) 1870-1916
See Saki
See also CA 104; 130; CDBLB 1890-1914; DA; DAB; DAC; DAM MST, NOV; DLB 34, 162; MTCW; WLC

Murasaki, Lady .... **CMLC 1**

Murdoch, (Jean) Iris 1919- **CLC 1, 2, 3, 4, 6, 8, 11, 15, 22, 31, 51; DAB; DAC; DAM MST, NOV**
See also CA 13-16R; CANR 8, 43, 68; CDBLB 1960 to Present; DLB 14, 194; INT CANR-8; MTCW

Murfree, Mary Noailles 1850-1922 ... **SSC 22**
See also CA 122; DLB 12, 74

Murnau, Friedrich Wilhelm
See Plumpe, Friedrich Wilhelm

Murphy, Richard 1927- .... **CLC 41**
See also CA 29-32R; DLB 40

Murphy, Sylvia 1937- .... **CLC 34**
See also CA 121

Murphy, Thomas (Bernard) 1935- ... **CLC 51**
See also CA 101

Murray, Albert L. 1916- .... **CLC 73**
See also BW 2; CA 49-52; CANR 26, 52; DLB 38

Murray, Judith Sargent 1751-1820 **NCLC 63**
See also DLB 37

Murray, Les(lie) A(llan) 1938- **CLC 40; DAM POET**
See also CA 21-24R; CANR 11, 27, 56

Murry, J. Middleton
See Murry, John Middleton

Murry, John Middleton 1889-1957 **TCLC 16**
See also CA 118; DLB 149

Musgrave, Susan 1951- .... **CLC 13, 54**
See also CA 69-72; CANR 45

Musil, Robert (Edler von) 1880-1942 . **T C L C 12, 68; SSC 18**
See also CA 109; CANR 55; DLB 81, 124

Muske, Carol 1945- .... **CLC 90**
See also Muske-Dukes, Carol (Anne)

Muske-Dukes, Carol (Anne) 1945-
See Muske, Carol
See also CA 65-68; CANR 32

Musset, (Louis Charles) Alfred de 1810-1857 **NCLC 7**
See also DLB 192

My Brother's Brother
See Chekhov, Anton (Pavlovich)

Myers, L(eopold) H(amilton) 1881-1944 **TCLC 59**
See also CA 157; DLB 15

Myers, Walter Dean 1937- ..... **CLC 35; BLC; DAM MULT, NOV**
See also AAYA 4, 23; BW 2; CA 33-36R; CANR 20, 42, 67; CLR 4, 16, 35; DLB 33; INT CANR-20; JRDA; MAICYA; SAAS 2; SATA 41, 71; SATA-Brief 27

Myers, Walter M.
See Myers, Walter Dean

Myles, Symon
See Follett, Ken(neth Martin)

Nabokov, Vladimir (Vladimirovich) 1899-1977 **CLC 1, 2, 3, 6, 8, 11, 15, 23, 44, 46, 64; DA; DAB; DAC; DAM MST, NOV; SSC 11; WLC**
See also CA 5-8R; 69-72; CANR 20; CDALB 1941-1968; DLB 2; DLBD 3; DLBY 80, 91; MTCW

Nagai Kafu 1879-1959 .... **TCLC 51**
See also Nagai Sokichi

See also DLB 180

Nagai Sokichi 1879-1959
See Nagai Kafu
See also CA 117

Nagy, Laszlo 1925-1978 .... **CLC 7**
See also CA 129; 112

Naipaul, Shiva(dhar Srinivasa) 1945-1985 **CLC 32, 39; DAM NOV**
See also CA 110; 112; 116; CANR 33; DLB 157; DLBY 85; MTCW

Naipaul, V(idiadhar) S(urajprasad) 1932- **CLC 4, 7, 9, 13, 18, 37, 105; DAB; DAC; DAM MST, NOV**
See also CA 1-4R; CANR 1, 33, 51; CDBLB 1960 to Present; DLB 125; DLBY 85; MTCW

Nakos, Lilika 1899(?)- .... **CLC 29**

Narayan, R(asipuram) K(rishnaswami) 1906- **CLC 7, 28, 47; DAM NOV; SSC 25**
See also CA 81-84; CANR 33, 61; MTCW; SATA 62

Nash, (Fredric) Ogden 1902-1971 . **CLC 23; DAM POET; PC 21**
See also CA 13-14; 29-32R; CANR 34, 61; CAP 1; DLB 11; MAICYA; MTCW; SATA 2, 46

Nashe, Thomas 1567-1601(?) .... **LC 41**
See also DLB 167

Nashe, Thomas 1567-1601 .... **LC 41**

Nathan, Daniel
See Dannay, Frederic

Nathan, George Jean 1882-1958 .... **TCLC 18**
See also Hatteras, Owen
See also CA 114; DLB 137

Natsume, Kinnosuke 1867-1916
See Natsume, Soseki
See also CA 104

Natsume, Soseki 1867-1916 .... **TCLC 2, 10**
See also Natsume, Kinnosuke
See also DLB 180

Natti, (Mary) Lee 1919-
See Kingman, Lee
See also CA 5-8R; CANR 2

Naylor, Gloria 1950- **CLC 28, 52; BLC; DA; DAC; DAM MST, MULT, NOV, POP; WLCS**
See also AAYA 6; BW 2; CA 107; CANR 27, 51; DLB 173; MTCW

Neihardt, John Gneisenau 1881-1973 **CLC 32**
See also CA 13-14; CANR 65; CAP 1; DLB 9, 54

Nekrasov, Nikolai Alekseevich 1821-1878 **NCLC 11**

Nelligan, Emile 1879-1941 .... **TCLC 14**
See also CA 114; DLB 92

Nelson, Willie 1933- .... **CLC 17**
See also CA 107

Nemerov, Howard (Stanley) 1920-1991 **CLC 2, 6, 9, 36; DAM POET**
See also CA 1-4R; 134; CABS 2; CANR 1, 27, 53; DLB 5, 6; DLBY 83; INT CANR-27; MTCW

Neruda, Pablo 1904-1973 **CLC 1, 2, 5, 7, 9, 28, 62; DA; DAB; DAC; DAM MST, MULT, POET; HLC; PC 4; WLC**
See also CA 19-20; 45-48; CAP 2; HW; MTCW

Nerval, Gerard de 1808-1855 **NCLC 1, 67; PC 13; SSC 18**

Nervo, (Jose) Amado (Ruiz de) 1870-1919 **TCLC 11**
See also CA 109; 131; HW

Nessi, Pio Baroja y
See Baroja (y Nessi), Pio

Nestroy, Johann 1801-1862 .... **NCLC 42**

See also DLB 133
Netterville, Luke
   See O'Grady, Standish (James)
Neufeld, John (Arthur) 1938- .... **CLC 17**
   See also AAYA 11; CA 25-28R; CANR 11, 37,
   56; MAICYA; SAAS 3; SATA 6, 81
Neville, Emily Cheney 1919- .... **CLC 12**
   See also CA 5-8R; CANR 3, 37; JRDA;
   MAICYA; SAAS 2; SATA 1
Newbound, Bernard Slade 1930-
   See Slade, Bernard
   See also CA 81-84; CANR 49; DAM DRAM
Newby, P(ercy) H(oward) 1918-1997 **CLC 2,
   13; DAM NOV**
   See also CA 5-8R; 161; CANR 32, 67; DLB
   15; MTCW
Newlove, Donald 1928- .... **CLC 6**
   See also CA 29-32R; CANR 25
Newlove, John (Herbert) 1938-........ **CLC 14**
   See also CA 21-24R; CANR 9, 25
Newman, Charles 1938- .... **CLC 2, 8**
   See also CA 21-24R
Newman, Edwin (Harold) 1919- ...... **CLC 14**
   See also AITN 1; CA 69-72; CANR 5
Newman, John Henry 1801-1890...**NCLC 38**
   See also DLB 18, 32, 55
Newton, Suzanne 1936-...................... **CLC 35**
   See also CA 41-44R; CANR 14; JRDA; SATA
   5, 77
Nexo, Martin Andersen 1869-1954 **TCLC 43**
Nezval, Vitezslav 1900-1958 .... **TCLC 44**
   See also CA 123
Ng, Fae Myenne 1957(?)- .... **CLC 81**
   See also CA 146
Ngema, Mbongeni 1955-................... **CLC 57**
   See also BW 2; CA 143
Ngugi, James T(hiong'o) .... **CLC 3, 7, 13**
   See also Ngugi wa Thiong'o
Ngugi wa Thiong'o 1938-**CLC 36; BLC; DAM
   MULT, NOV**
   See also Ngugi, James T(hiong'o)
   See also BW 2; CA 81-84; CANR 27, 58; DLB
   125; MTCW
Nichol, B(arrie) P(hillip) 1944-1988 **CLC 18**
   See also CA 53-56; DLB 53; SATA 66
Nichols, John (Treadwell) 1940- ...... **CLC 38**
   See also CA 9-12R; CAAS 2; CANR 6; DLBY
   82
Nichols, Leigh
   See Koontz, Dean R(ay)
Nichols, Peter (Richard) 1927-**CLC 5, 36, 65**
   See also CA 104; CANR 33; DLB 13; MTCW
Nicolas, F. R. E.
   See Freeling, Nicolas
Niedecker, Lorine 1903-1970 .... **CLC 10, 42;
   DAM POET**
   See also CA 25-28; CAP 2; DLB 48
Nietzsche, Friedrich (Wilhelm) 1844-1900
   TCLC 10, 18, 55
   See also CA 107; 121; DLB 129
Nievo, Ippolito 1831-1861 .... **NCLC 22**
Nightingale, Anne Redmon 1943-
   See Redmon, Anne
   See also CA 103
Nik. T. O.
   See Annensky, Innokenty (Fyodorovich)
Nin, Anais 1903-1977**CLC 1, 4, 8, 11, 14, 60;
   DAM NOV, POP; SSC 10**
   See also AITN 2; CA 13-16R; 69-72; CANR
   22, 53; DLB 2, 4, 152; MTCW
Nishiwaki, Junzaburo 1894-1982 .... **PC 15**
   See also CA 107
Nissenson, Hugh 1933- .... **CLC 4, 9**

See also CA 17-20R; CANR 27; DLB 28
Niven, Larry .... **CLC 8**
   See also Niven, Laurence Van Cott
   See also DLB 8
Niven, Laurence Van Cott 1938-
   See Niven, Larry
   See also CA 21-24R; CAAS 12; CANR 14, 44,
   66; DAM POP; MTCW; SATA 95
Nixon, Agnes Eckhardt 1927- .... **CLC 21**
   See also CA 110
Nizan, Paul 1905-1940 .... **TCLC 40**
   See also CA 161; DLB 72
Nkosi, Lewis 1936- ...... **CLC 45; BLC; DAM
   MULT**
   See also BW 1; CA 65-68; CANR 27; DLB 157
Nodier, (Jean) Charles (Emmanuel) 1780-1844
   NCLC 19
   See also DLB 119
Nolan, Christopher 1965- .... **CLC 58**
   See also CA 111
Noon, Jeff 1957-................................. **CLC 91**
   See also CA 148
Norden, Charles
   See Durrell, Lawrence (George)
Nordhoff, Charles (Bernard) 1887-1947
   TCLC 23
   See also CA 108; DLB 9; SATA 23
Norfolk, Lawrence 1963- .... **CLC 76**
   See also CA 144
Norman, Marsha 1947-**CLC 28; DAM DRAM;
   DC 8**
   See also CA 105; CABS 3; CANR 41; DLBY
   84
Norris, Frank 1870-1902 .... **SSC 28**
   See also Norris, (Benjamin) Frank(lin, Jr.)
   See also CDALB 1865-1917; DLB 12, 71, 186
Norris, (Benjamin) Frank(lin, Jr.) 1870-1902
   TCLC 24
   See also Norris, Frank
   See also CA 110; 160
Norris, Leslie 1921- .... **CLC 14**
   See also CA 11-12; CANR 14; CAP 1; DLB 27
North, Andrew
   See Norton, Andre
North, Anthony
   See Koontz, Dean R(ay)
North, Captain George
   See Stevenson, Robert Louis (Balfour)
North, Milou
   See Erdrich, Louise
Northrup, B. A.
   See Hubbard, L(afayette) Ron(ald)
North Staffs
   See Hulme, T(homas) E(rnest)
Norton, Alice Mary
   See Norton, Andre
   See also MAICYA; SATA 1, 43
Norton, Andre 1912- .... **CLC 12**
   See also Norton, Alice Mary
   See also AAYA 14; CA 1-4R; CANR 68; DLB
   8, 52; JRDA; MTCW; SATA 91
Norton, Caroline 1808-1877 .... **NCLC 47**
   See also DLB 21, 159
Norway, Nevil Shute 1899-1960
   See Shute, Nevil
   See also CA 102; 93-96
Norwid, Cyprian Kamil 1821-1883**NCLC 17**
Nosille, Nabrah
   See Ellison, Harlan (Jay)
Nossack, Hans Erich 1901-1978.......... **CLC 6**
   See also CA 93-96; 85-88; DLB 69
Nostradamus 1503-1566 .... **LC 27**
Nosu, Chuji

See Ozu, Yasujiro
Notenburg, Eleanora (Genrikhovna) von
   See Guro, Elena
Nova, Craig 1945-.......................... **CLC 7, 31**
   See also CA 45-48; CANR 2, 53
Novak, Joseph
   See Kosinski, Jerzy (Nikodem)
Novalis 1772-1801 .... **NCLC 13**
   See also DLB 90
Novis, Emile
   See Weil, Simone (Adolphine)
Nowlan, Alden (Albert) 1933-1983 . **CLC 15;
   DAC; DAM MST**
   See also CA 9-12R; CANR 5; DLB 53
Noyes, Alfred 1880-1958 .... **TCLC 7**
   See also CA 104; DLB 20
Nunn, Kem .... **CLC 34**
   See also CA 159
Nye, Robert 1939-...**CLC 13, 42; DAM NOV**
   See also CA 33-36R; CANR 29, 67; DLB 14;
   MTCW; SATA 6
Nyro, Laura 1947- .... **CLC 17**
Oates, Joyce Carol 1938-**CLC 1, 2, 3, 6, 9, 11,
   15, 19, 33, 52, 108; DA; DAB; DAC; DAM
   MST, NOV, POP; SSC 6; WLC**
   See also AAYA 15; AITN 1; BEST 89:2; CA 5-
   8R; CANR 25, 45; CDALB 1968-1988; DLB
   2, 5, 130; DLBY 81; INT CANR-25; MTCW
O'Brien, Darcy 1939- .... **CLC 11**
   See also CA 21-24R; CANR 8, 59
O'Brien, E. G.
   See Clarke, Arthur C(harles)
O'Brien, Edna 1936- **CLC 3, 5, 8, 13, 36, 65;
   DAM NOV; SSC 10**
   See also CA 1-4R; CANR 6, 41, 65; CDBLB
   1960 to Present; DLB 14; MTCW
O'Brien, Fitz-James 1828-1862 ..... **NCLC 21**
   See also DLB 74
O'Brien, Flann .... **CLC 1, 4, 5, 7, 10, 47**
   See also O Nuallain, Brian
O'Brien, Richard 1942- .... **CLC 17**
   See also CA 124
O'Brien, (William) Tim(othy) 1946- .**CLC 7,
   19, 40, 103; DAM POP**
   See also AAYA 16; CA 85-88; CANR 40, 58;
   DLB 152; DLBD 9; DLBY 80
Obstfelder, Sigbjoern 1866-1900 ... **TCLC 23**
   See also CA 123
O'Casey, Sean 1880-1964**CLC 1, 5, 9, 11, 15,
   88; DAB; DAC; DAM DRAM, MST;
   WLCS**
   See also CA 89-92; CANR 62; CDBLB 1914-
   1945; DLB 10; MTCW
O'Cathasaigh, Sean
   See O'Casey, Sean
Ochs, Phil 1940-1976 .... **CLC 17**
   See also CA 65-68
O'Connor, Edwin (Greene) 1918-1968**CLC 14**
   See also CA 93-96; 25-28R
O'Connor, (Mary) Flannery 1925-1964 **C L C
   1, 2, 3, 6, 10, 13, 15, 21, 66, 104; DA; DAB;
   DAC; DAM MST, NOV; SSC 1, 23; WLC**
   See also AAYA 7; CA 1-4R; CANR 3, 41;
   CDALB 1941-1968; DLB 2, 152; DLBD 12;
   DLBY 80; MTCW
O'Connor, Frank .... **CLC 23; SSC 5**
   See also O'Donovan, Michael John
   See also DLB 162
O'Dell, Scott 1898-1989 .... **CLC 30**
   See also AAYA 3; CA 61-64; 129; CANR 12,
   30; CLR 1, 16; DLB 52; JRDA; MAICYA;
   SATA 12, 60
Odets, Clifford 1906-1963**CLC 2, 28, 98; DAM**

DRAM; DC 6
  See also CA 85-88; CANR 62; DLB 7, 26;
    MTCW
O'Doherty, Brian 1934- .... **CLC 76**
  See also CA 105
O'Donnell, K. M.
  See Malzberg, Barry N(athaniel)
O'Donnell, Lawrence
  See Kuttner, Henry
O'Donovan, Michael John 1903-1966**CLC 14**
  See also O'Connor, Frank
  See also CA 93-96
Oe, Kenzaburo 1935- **CLC 10, 36, 86; DAM**
    NOV; SSC 20
  See also CA 97-100; CANR 36, 50; DLB 182;
    DLBY 94; MTCW
O'Faolain, Julia 1932- .... **CLC 6, 19, 47, 108**
  See also CA 81-84; CAAS 2; CANR 12, 61;
    DLB 14; MTCW
O'Faolain, Sean 1900-1991 **CLC 1, 7, 14, 32,**
    70; SSC 13
  See also CA 61-64; 134; CANR 12, 66; DLB
    15, 162; MTCW
O'Flaherty, Liam 1896-1984**CLC 5, 34; SSC 6**
  See also CA 101; 113; CANR 35; DLB 36, 162;
    DLBY 84; MTCW
Ogilvy, Gavin
  See Barrie, J(ames) M(atthew)
O'Grady, Standish (James) 1846-1928**T C L C**
    5
  See also CA 104; 157
O'Grady, Timothy 1951- .... **CLC 59**
  See also CA 138
O'Hara, Frank 1926-1966 . **CLC 2, 5, 13, 78;**
    DAM POET
  See also CA 9-12R; 25-28R; CANR 33; DLB
    5, 16, 193; MTCW
O'Hara, John (Henry) 1905-1970**CLC 1, 2, 3,**
    6, 11, 42; DAM NOV; SSC 15
  See also CA 5-8R; 25-28R; CANR 31, 60;
    CDALB 1929-1941; DLB 9, 86; DLBD 2;
    MTCW
O Hehir, Diana 1922- .... **CLC 41**
  See also CA 93-96
Okigbo, Christopher (Ifenayichukwu) 1932-
    1967 ... **CLC 25, 84; BLC; DAM MULT,**
    POET; PC 7
  See also BW 1; CA 77-80; DLB 125; MTCW
Okri, Ben 1959-................................. **CLC 87**
  See also BW 2; CA 130; 138; CANR 65; DLB
    157; INT 138
Olds, Sharon 1942- .... **CLC 32, 39, 85; DAM**
    POET
  See also CA 101; CANR 18, 41, 66; DLB 120
Oldstyle, Jonathan
  See Irving, Washington
Olesha, Yuri (Karlovich) 1899-1960 ...**CLC 8**
  See also CA 85-88
Oliphant, Laurence 1829(?)-1888 .. **NCLC 47**
  See also DLB 18, 166
Oliphant, Margaret (Oliphant Wilson) 1828-
    1897 .... **NCLC 11, 61; SSC 25**
  See also DLB 18, 159, 190
Oliver, Mary 1935- .... **CLC 19, 34, 98**
  See also CA 21-24R; CANR 9, 43; DLB 5, 193
Olivier, Laurence (Kerr) 1907-1989 **CLC 20**
  See also CA 111; 150; 129
Olsen, Tillie 1913-**CLC 4, 13; DA; DAB; DAC;**
    DAM MST; SSC 11
  See also CA 1-4R; CANR 1, 43; DLB 28; DLBY
    80; MTCW
Olson, Charles (John) 1910-1970**CLC 1, 2, 5,**
    6, 9, 11, 29; DAM POET; PC 19

  See also CA 13-16; 25-28R; CABS 2; CANR
    35, 61; CAP 1; DLB 5, 16, 193; MTCW
Olson, Toby 1937-............................. **CLC 28**
  See also CA 65-68; CANR 9, 31
Olyesha, Yuri
  See Olesha, Yuri (Karlovich)
Ondaatje, (Philip) Michael 1943-**CLC 14, 29,**
    51, 76; DAB; DAC; DAM MST
  See also CA 77-80; CANR 42; DLB 60
Oneal, Elizabeth 1934-
  See Oneal, Zibby
  See also CA 106; CANR 28; MAICYA; SATA
    30, 82
Oneal, Zibby .... **CLC 30**
  See also Oneal, Elizabeth
  See also AAYA 5; CLR 13; JRDA
O'Neill, Eugene (Gladstone) 1888-1953**TCLC**
    1, 6, 27, 49; DA; DAB; DAC; DAM DRAM,
    MST; WLC
  See also AITN 1; CA 110; 132; CDALB 1929-
    1941; DLB 7; MTCW
Onetti, Juan Carlos 1909-1994 ... **CLC 7, 10;**
    DAM MULT, NOV; SSC 23
  See also CA 85-88; 145; CANR 32, 63; DLB
    113; HW; MTCW
O Nuallain, Brian 1911-1966
  See O'Brien, Flann
  See also CA 21-22; 25-28R; CAP 2
Ophuls, Max 1902-1957 .... **TCLC 79**
  See also CA 113
Opie, Amelia 1769-1853 .... **NCLC 65**
  See also DLB 116, 159
Oppen, George 1908-1984 ...... **CLC 7, 13, 34**
  See also CA 13-16R; 113; CANR 8; DLB 5,
    165
Oppenheim, E(dward) Phillips 1866-1946
    TCLC 45
  See also CA 111; DLB 70
Opuls, Max
  See Ophuls, Max
Origen c. 185-c. 254 .... **CMLC 19**
Orlovitz, Gil 1918-1973 .... **CLC 22**
  See also CA 77-80; 45-48; DLB 2, 5
Orris
  See Ingelow, Jean
Ortega y Gasset, Jose 1883-1955 ....**TCLC 9;**
    DAM MULT; HLC
  See also CA 106; 130; HW; MTCW
Ortese, Anna Maria 1914- ....**CLC 89**
  See also DLB 177
Ortiz, Simon J(oseph) 1941-..**CLC 45; DAM**
    MULT, POET; PC 17
  See also CA 134; DLB 120, 175; NNAL
Orton, Joe .... **CLC 4, 13, 43; DC 3**
  See also Orton, John Kingsley
  See also CDBLB 1960 to Present; DLB 13
Orton, John Kingsley 1933-1967
  See Orton, Joe
  See also CA 85-88; CANR 35, 66; DAM
    DRAM; MTCW
Orwell, George **TCLC 2, 6, 15, 31, 51; DAB;**
    WLC
  See also Blair, Eric (Arthur)
  See also CDBLB 1945-1960; DLB 15, 98, 195
Osborne, David
  See Silverberg, Robert
Osborne, George
  See Silverberg, Robert
Osborne, John (James) 1929-1994**CLC 1, 2, 5,**
    11, 45; DA; DAB; DAC; DAM DRAM,
    MST; WLC
  See also CA 13-16R; 147; CANR 21, 56;
    CDBLB 1945-1960; DLB 13; MTCW

Osborne, Lawrence 1958-................. **CLC 50**
Oshima, Nagisa 1932- .... **CLC 20**
  See also CA 116; 121
Oskison, John Milton 1874-1947 . **TCLC 35;**
    DAM MULT
  See also CA 144; DLB 175; NNAL
Ossoli, Sarah Margaret (Fuller marchesa d')
    1810-1850
  See Fuller, Margaret
  See also SATA 25
Ostrovsky, Alexander 1823-1886**NCLC 30, 57**
Otero, Blas de 1916-1979 .... **CLC 11**
  See also CA 89-92; DLB 134
Otto, Whitney 1955-.......................... **CLC 70**
  See also CA 140
Ouida .... **TCLC 43**
  See also De La Ramee, (Marie) Louise
  See also DLB 18, 156
Ousmane, Sembene 1923- .... **CLC 66; BLC**
  See also BW 1; CA 117; 125; MTCW
Ovid 43B.C.-18(?)**CMLC 7; DAM POET; PC**
    2
Owen, Hugh
  See Faust, Frederick (Schiller)
Owen, Wilfred (Edward Salter) 1893-1918
    TCLC 5, 27; DA; DAB; DAC; DAM MST,
    POET; PC 19; WLC
  See also CA 104; 141; CDBLB 1914-1945;
    DLB 20
Owens, Rochelle 1936- ....**CLC 8**
  See also CA 17-20R; CAAS 2; CANR 39
Oz, Amos 1939-**CLC 5, 8, 11, 27, 33, 54; DAM**
    NOV
  See also CA 53-56; CANR 27, 47, 65; MTCW
Ozick, Cynthia 1928-**CLC 3, 7, 28, 62; DAM**
    NOV, POP; SSC 15
  See also BEST 90:1; CA 17-20R; CANR 23,
    58; DLB 28, 152; DLBY 82; INT CANR-
    23; MTCW
Ozu, Yasujiro 1903-1963 .... **CLC 16**
  See also CA 112
Pacheco, C.
  See Pessoa, Fernando (Antonio Nogueira)
Pa Chin ....**CLC 18**
  See also Li Fei-kan
Pack, Robert 1929- .... **CLC 13**
  See also CA 1-4R; CANR 3, 44; DLB 5
Padgett, Lewis
  See Kuttner, Henry
Padilla (Lorenzo), Heberto 1932- ..... **CLC 38**
  See also AITN 1; CA 123; 131; HW
Page, Jimmy 1944- .... **CLC 12**
Page, Louise 1955-............................. **CLC 40**
  See also CA 140
Page, P(atricia) K(athleen) 1916- **CLC 7, 18;**
    DAC; DAM MST; PC 12
  See also CA 53-56; CANR 4, 22, 65; DLB 68;
    MTCW
Page, Thomas Nelson 1853-1922 .... **SSC 23**
  See also CA 118; DLB 12, 78; DLBD 13
Pagels, Elaine Hiesey 1943- .... **CLC 104**
  See also CA 45-48; CANR 2, 24, 51
Paget, Violet 1856-1935
  See Lee, Vernon
  See also CA 104
Paget-Lowe, Henry
  See Lovecraft, H(oward) P(hillips)
Paglia, Camille (Anna) 1947- ....**CLC 68**
  See also CA 140
Paige, Richard
  See Koontz, Dean R(ay)
Paine, Thomas 1737-1809 .... **NCLC 62**
  See also CDALB 1640-1865; DLB 31, 43, 73,

158

Pakenham, Antonia
See Fraser, (Lady) Antonia (Pakenham)
Palamas, Kostes 1859-1943 .... **TCLC 5**
See also CA 105
Palazzeschi, Aldo 1885-1974 .... **CLC 11**
See also CA 89-92; 53-56; DLB 114
Paley, Grace 1922-**CLC 4, 6, 37; DAM POP; SSC 8**
See also CA 25-28R; CANR 13, 46; DLB 28; INT CANR-13; MTCW
Palin, Michael (Edward) 1943- .... **CLC 21**
See also Monty Python
See also CA 107; CANR 35; SATA 67
Palliser, Charles 1947- .... **CLC 65**
See also CA 136
Palma, Ricardo 1833-1919 .... **TCLC 29**
Pancake, Breece Dexter 1952-1979
See Pancake, Breece D'J
See also CA 123; 109
Pancake, Breece D'J .... **CLC 29**
See also Pancake, Breece Dexter
See also DLB 130
Panko, Rudy
See Gogol, Nikolai (Vasilyevich)
Papadiamantis, Alexandros 1851-1911**T C L C 29**
Papadiamantopoulos, Johannes 1856-1910
See Moreas, Jean
See also CA 117
Papini, Giovanni 1881-1956 .... **TCLC 22**
See also CA 121
Paracelsus 1493-1541 .... **LC 14**
See also DLB 179
Parasol, Peter
See Stevens, Wallace
Pardo Bazán, Emilia 1851-1921 ....**SSC 30**
Pareto, Vilfredo 1848-1923 .... **TCLC 69**
Parfenie, Maria
See Codrescu, Andrei
Parini, Jay (Lee) 1948- .... **CLC 54**
See also CA 97-100; CAAS 16; CANR 32
Park, Jordan
See Kornbluth, C(yril) M.; Pohl, Frederik
Park, Robert E(zra) 1864-1944 ...... **TCLC 73**
See also CA 122; 165
Parker, Bert
See Ellison, Harlan (Jay)
Parker, Dorothy (Rothschild) 1893-1967**C L C 15, 68; DAM POET; SSC 2**
See also CA 19-20; 25-28R; CAP 2; DLB 11, 45, 86; MTCW
Parker, Robert B(rown) 1932-**CLC 27; DAM NOV, POP**
See also BEST 89:4; CA 49-52; CANR 1, 26, 52; INT CANR-26; MTCW
Parkin, Frank 1940- .... **CLC 43**
See also CA 147
Parkman, Francis, Jr. 1823-1893 ...**NCLC 12**
See also DLB 1, 30, 186
Parks, Gordon (Alexander Buchanan) 1912-**CLC 1, 16; BLC; DAM MULT**
See also AITN 2; BW 2; CA 41-44R; CANR 26, 66; DLB 33; SATA 8
Parmenides c. 515B.C.-c. 450B.C. **CMLC 22**
See also DLB 176
Parnell, Thomas 1679-1718 .... **LC 3**
See also DLB 94
Parra, Nicanor 1914- ...... **CLC 2, 102; DAM MULT; HLC**
See also CA 85-88; CANR 32; HW; MTCW
Parrish, Mary Frances
See Fisher, M(ary) F(rances) K(ennedy)

Parson
See Coleridge, Samuel Taylor
Parson Lot
See Kingsley, Charles
Partridge, Anthony
See Oppenheim, E(dward) Phillips
Pascal, Blaise 1623-1662 .... **LC 35**
Pascoli, Giovanni 1855-1912 .... **TCLC 45**
Pasolini, Pier Paolo 1922-1975 . **CLC 20, 37, 106; PC 17**
See also CA 93-96; 61-64; CANR 63; DLB 128, 177; MTCW
Pasquini
See Silone, Ignazio
Pastan, Linda (Olenik) 1932- **CLC 27; DAM POET**
See also CA 61-64; CANR 18, 40, 61; DLB 5
Pasternak, Boris (Leonidovich) 1890-1960 **CLC 7, 10, 18, 63; DA; DAB; DAC; DAM MST, NOV, POET; PC 6; WLC**
See also CA 127; 116; MTCW
Patchen, Kenneth 1911-1972 ... **CLC 1, 2, 18; DAM POET**
See also CA 1-4R; 33-36R; CANR 3, 35; DLB 16, 48; MTCW
Pater, Walter (Horatio) 1839-1894 .. **NCLC 7**
See also CDBLB 1832-1890; DLB 57, 156
Paterson, A(ndrew) B(arton) 1864-1941 **TCLC 32**
See also CA 155; SATA 97
Paterson, Katherine (Womeldorf) 1932-**C L C 12, 30**
See also AAYA 1; CA 21-24R; CANR 28, 59; CLR 7; DLB 52; JRDA; MAICYA; MTCW; SATA 13, 53, 92
Patmore, Coventry Kersey Dighton 1823-1896 **NCLC 9**
See also DLB 35, 98
Paton, Alan (Stewart) 1903-1988 **CLC 4, 10, 25, 55, 106; DA; DAB; DAC; DAM MST, NOV; WLC**
See also CA 13-16; 125; CANR 22; CAP 1; MTCW; SATA 11; SATA-Obit 56
Paton Walsh, Gillian 1937-
See Walsh, Jill Paton
See also CANR 38; JRDA; MAICYA; SAAS 3; SATA 4, 72
Patton, George S. 1885-1945 .... **TCLC 79**
Paulding, James Kirke 1778-1860 ... **NCLC 2**
See also DLB 3, 59, 74
Paulin, Thomas Neilson 1949-
See Paulin, Tom
See also CA 123; 128
Paulin, Tom .... **CLC 37**
See also Paulin, Thomas Neilson
See also DLB 40
Paustovsky, Konstantin (Georgievich) 1892-1968 .... **CLC 40**
See also CA 93-96; 25-28R
Pavese, Cesare 1908-1950 ... **TCLC 3; PC 13; SSC 19**
See also CA 104; DLB 128, 177
Pavic, Milorad 1929- .... **CLC 60**
See also CA 136; DLB 181
Payne, Alan
See Jakes, John (William)
Paz, Gil
See Lugones, Leopoldo
Paz, Octavio 1914-1998**CLC 3, 4, 6, 10, 19, 51, 65; DA; DAB; DAC; DAM MST, MULT, POET; HLC; PC 1; WLC**
See also CA 73-76; 165; CANR 32, 65; DLBY 90; HW; MTCW

p'Bitek, Okot 1931-1982**CLC 96; BLC; DAM MULT**
See also BW 2; CA 124; 107; DLB 125; MTCW
Peacock, Molly 1947- .... **CLC 60**
See also CA 103; CAAS 21; CANR 52; DLB 120
Peacock, Thomas Love 1785-1866 .**NCLC 22**
See also DLB 96, 116
Peake, Mervyn 1911-1968 .... **CLC 7, 54**
See also CA 5-8R; 25-28R; CANR 3; DLB 15, 160; MTCW; SATA 23
Pearce, Philippa .... **CLC 21**
See also Christie, (Ann) Philippa
See also CLR 9; DLB 161; MAICYA; SATA 1, 67
Pearl, Eric
See Elman, Richard (Martin)
Pearson, T(homas) R(eid) 1956- ...... **CLC 39**
See also CA 120; 130; INT 130
Peck, Dale 1967- .... **CLC 81**
See also CA 146
Peck, John 1941- ....**CLC 3**
See also CA 49-52; CANR 3
Peck, Richard (Wayne) 1934-........... **CLC 21**
See also AAYA 1, 24; CA 85-88; CANR 19, 38; CLR 15; INT CANR-19; JRDA; MAICYA; SAAS 2; SATA 18, 55, 97
Peck, Robert Newton 1928- ..... **CLC 17; DA; DAC; DAM MST**
See also AAYA 3; CA 81-84; CANR 31, 63; CLR 45; JRDA; MAICYA; SAAS 1; SATA 21, 62
Peckinpah, (David) Sam(uel) 1925-1984**C L C 20**
See also CA 109; 114
Pedersen, Knut 1859-1952
See Hamsun, Knut
See also CA 104; 119; CANR 63; MTCW
Peeslake, Gaffer
See Durrell, Lawrence (George)
Peguy, Charles Pierre 1873-1914 ... **TCLC 10**
See also CA 107
Pena, Ramon del Valle y
See Valle-Inclan, Ramon (Maria) del
Pendennis, Arthur Esquir
See Thackeray, William Makepeace
Penn, William 1644-1718 .... **LC 25**
See also DLB 24
PEPECE
See Prado (Calvo), Pedro
Pepys, Samuel 1633-1703 **LC 11; DA; DAB; DAC; DAM MST; WLC**
See also CDBLB 1660-1789; DLB 101
Percy, Walker 1916-1990**CLC 2, 3, 6, 8, 14, 18, 47, 65; DAM NOV, POP**
See also CA 1-4R; 131; CANR 1, 23, 64; DLB 2; DLBY 80, 90; MTCW
Perec, Georges 1936-1982 .... **CLC 56**
See also CA 141; DLB 83
Pereda (y Sanchez de Porrua), Jose Maria de 1833-1906 .... **TCLC 16**
See also CA 117
Pereda y Porrua, Jose Maria de
See Pereda (y Sanchez de Porrua), Jose Maria de
Peregoy, George Weems
See Mencken, H(enry) L(ouis)
Perelman, S(idney) J(oseph) 1904-1979 **C L C 3, 5, 9, 15, 23, 44, 49; DAM DRAM**
See also AITN 1, 2; CA 73-76; 89-92; CANR 18; DLB 11, 44; MTCW
Peret, Benjamin 1899-1959 .... **TCLC 20**
See also CA 117

Peretz, Isaac Loeb 1851(?)-1915 .. **TCLC 16;
SSC 26**
See also CA 109
Peretz, Yitzkhok Leibush
See Peretz, Isaac Loeb
Perez Galdos, Benito 1843-1920 .... **TCLC 27**
See also CA 125; 153; HW
Perrault, Charles 1628-1703 .... **LC 2**
See also MAICYA; SATA 25
Perry, Brighton
See Sherwood, Robert E(mmet)
Perse, St.-John .... **CLC 4, 11, 46**
See also Leger, (Marie-Rene Auguste) Alexis
Saint-Leger
Perutz, Leo 1882-1957 .... **TCLC 60**
See also DLB 81
Peseenz, Tulio F.
See Lopez y Fuentes, Gregorio
Pesetsky, Bette 1932- .... **CLC 28**
See also CA 133; DLB 130
Peshkov, Alexei Maximovich 1868-1936
See Gorky, Maxim
See also CA 105; 141; DA; DAC; DAM DRAM,
MST, NOV
Pessoa, Fernando (Antonio Nogueira) 1898-
1935 .... **TCLC 27; HLC; PC 20**
See also CA 125
Peterkin, Julia Mood 1880-1961 ...... **CLC 31**
See also CA 102; DLB 9
Peters, Joan K(aren) 1945- .... **CLC 39**
See also CA 158
Peters, Robert L(ouis) 1924- .... **CLC 7**
See also CA 13-16R; CAAS 8; DLB 105
Petofi, Sandor 1823-1849 .... **NCLC 21**
Petrakis, Harry Mark 1923- .... **CLC 3**
See also CA 9-12R; CANR 4, 30
Petrarch 1304-1374 **CMLC 20; DAM POET;
PC 8**
Petrov, Evgeny .... **TCLC 21**
See also Kataev, Evgeny Petrovich
Petry, Ann (Lane) 1908-1997 ... **CLC 1, 7, 18**
See also BW 1; CA 5-8R; 157; CAAS 6; CANR
4, 46; CLR 12; DLB 76; JRDA; MAICYA;
MTCW; SATA 5; SATA-Obit 94
Petursson, Halligrimur 1614-1674 .... **LC 8**
Phaedrus 18(?)B.C.-55(?) .... **CMLC 25**
Philips, Katherine 1632-1664 .... **LC 30**
See also DLB 131
Philipson, Morris H. 1926- .... **CLC 53**
See also CA 1-4R; CANR 4
Phillips, Caryl 1958- . **CLC 96; DAM MULT**
See also BW 2; CA 141; CANR 63; DLB 157
Phillips, David Graham 1867-1911 **TCLC 44**
See also CA 108; DLB 9, 12
Phillips, Jack
See Sandburg, Carl (August)
Phillips, Jayne Anne 1952- **CLC 15, 33; SSC 16**
See also CA 101; CANR 24, 50; DLBY 80; INT
CANR-24; MTCW
Phillips, Richard
See Dick, Philip K(indred)
Phillips, Robert (Schaeffer) 1938- ... **CLC 28**
See also CA 17-20R; CAAS 13; CANR 8; DLB
105
Phillips, Ward
See Lovecraft, H(oward) P(hillips)
Piccolo, Lucio 1901-1969 .... **CLC 13**
See also CA 97-100; DLB 114
Pickthall, Marjorie L(owry) C(hristie) 1883-
1922 .... **TCLC 21**
See also CA 107; DLB 92
Pico della Mirandola, Giovanni 1463-1494**LC
15**

Piercy, Marge 1936- **CLC 3, 6, 14, 18, 27, 62**
See also CA 21-24R; CAAS 1; CANR 13, 43,
66; DLB 120; MTCW
Piers, Robert
See Anthony, Piers
Pieyre de Mandiargues, Andre 1909-1991
See Mandiargues, Andre Pieyre de
See also CA 103; 136; CANR 22
Pilnyak, Boris .... **TCLC 23**
See also Vogau, Boris Andreyevich
Pincherle, Alberto 1907-1990 ... **CLC 11, 18;
DAM NOV**
See also Moravia, Alberto
See also CA 25-28R; 132; CANR 33, 63;
MTCW
Pinckney, Darryl 1953- .... **CLC 76**
See also BW 2; CA 143
Pindar 518B.C.-446B.C. ..... **CMLC 12; PC 19**
See also DLB 176
Pineda, Cecile 1942- .... **CLC 39**
See also CA 118
Pinero, Arthur Wing 1855-1934 .. **TCLC 32;
DAM DRAM**
See also CA 110; 153; DLB 10
Pinero, Miguel (Antonio Gomez) 1946-1988
CLC 4, 55
See also CA 61-64; 125; CANR 29; HW
Pinget, Robert 1919-1997 .... **CLC 7, 13, 37**
See also CA 85-88; 160; DLB 83
Pink Floyd
See Barrett, (Roger) Syd; Gilmour, David; Ma-
son, Nick; Waters, Roger; Wright, Rick
Pinkney, Edward 1802-1828 .... **NCLC 31**
Pinkwater, Daniel Manus 1941- .... **CLC 35**
See also Pinkwater, Manus
See also AAYA 1; CA 29-32R; CANR 12, 38;
CLR 4; JRDA; MAICYA; SAAS 3; SATA 46,
76
Pinkwater, Manus
See Pinkwater, Daniel Manus
See also SATA 8
Pinsky, Robert 1940-**CLC 9, 19, 38, 94; DAM
POET**
See also CA 29-32R; CAAS 4; CANR 58;
DLBY 82
Pinta, Harold
See Pinter, Harold
Pinter, Harold 1930-**CLC 1, 3, 6, 9, 11, 15, 27,
58, 73; DA; DAB; DAC; DAM DRAM,
MST; WLC**
See also CA 5-8R; CANR 33, 65; CDBLB 1960
to Present; DLB 13; MTCW
Piozzi, Hester Lynch (Thrale) 1741-1821
NCLC 57
See also DLB 104, 142
Pirandello, Luigi 1867-1936**TCLC 4, 29; DA;
DAB; DAC; DAM DRAM, MST; DC 5;
SSC 22; WLC**
See also CA 104; 153
Pirsig, Robert M(aynard) 1928-**CLC 4, 6, 73;
DAM POP**
See also CA 53-56; CANR 42; MTCW; SATA
39
Pisarev, Dmitry Ivanovich 1840-1868 **N C L C
25**
Pix, Mary (Griffith) 1666-1709 .... **LC 8**
See also DLB 80
Pixerecourt, (Rene Charles) Guilbert de 1773-
1844 .... **NCLC 39**
See also DLB 192
Plaatje, Sol(omon) T(shekisho) 1876-1932
TCLC 73
See also BW 2; CA 141

Plaidy, Jean
See Hibbert, Eleanor Alice Burford
Planche, James Robinson 1796-1880**NCLC 42**
Plant, Robert 1948- .... **CLC 12**
Plante, David (Robert) 1940- **CLC 7, 23, 38;
DAM NOV**
See also CA 37-40R; CANR 12, 36, 58; DLBY
83; INT CANR-12; MTCW
Plath, Sylvia 1932-1963 **CLC 1, 2, 3, 5, 9, 11,
14, 17, 50, 51, 62; DA; DAB; DAC; DAM
MST, POET; PC 1; WLC**
See also AAYA 13; CA 19-20; CANR 34; CAP
2; CDALB 1941-1968; DLB 5, 6, 152;
MTCW; SATA 96
Plato 428(?)B.C.-348(?)B.C. .... **CMLC 8; DA;
DAB; DAC; DAM MST; WLCS**
See also DLB 176
Platonov, Andrei .... **TCLC 14**
See also Klimentov, Andrei Platonovich
Platt, Kin 1911- .... **CLC 26**
See also AAYA 11; CA 17-20R; CANR 11;
JRDA; SAAS 17; SATA 21, 86
Plautus c. 251B.C.-184B.C. .. **CMLC 24; DC 6**
Plick et Plock
See Simenon, Georges (Jacques Christian)
Plimpton, George (Ames) 1927- .... **CLC 36**
See also AITN 1; CA 21-24R; CANR 32; DLB
185; MTCW; SATA 10
Pliny the Elder c. 23-79 .... **CMLC 23**
Plomer, William Charles Franklin 1903-1973
CLC 4, 8
See also CA 21-22; CANR 34; CAP 2; DLB
20, 162, 191; MTCW; SATA 24
Plowman, Piers
See Kavanagh, Patrick (Joseph)
Plum, J.
See Wodehouse, P(elham) G(renville)
Plumly, Stanley (Ross) 1939- .... **CLC 33**
See also CA 108; 110; DLB 5, 193; INT 110
Plumpe, Friedrich Wilhelm 1888-1931**T C L C
53**
See also CA 112
Po Chu-i 772-846 .... **CMLC 24**
Poe, Edgar Allan 1809-1849**NCLC 1, 16, 55;
DA; DAB; DAC; DAM MST, POET; PC
1; SSC 1, 22; WLC**
See also AAYA 14; CDALB 1640-1865; DLB
3, 59, 73, 74; SATA 23
Poet of Titchfield Street, The
See Pound, Ezra (Weston Loomis)
Pohl, Frederik 1919- .... **CLC 18; SSC 25**
See also AAYA 24; CA 61-64; CAAS 1; CANR
11, 37; DLB 8; INT CANR-11; MTCW;
SATA 24
Poirier, Louis 1910-
See Gracq, Julien
See also CA 122; 126
Poitier, Sidney 1927- .... **CLC 26**
See also BW 1; CA 117
Polanski, Roman 1933- .... **CLC 16**
See also CA 77-80
Poliakoff, Stephen 1952- .... **CLC 38**
See also CA 106; DLB 13
Police, The
See Copeland, Stewart (Armstrong); Summers,
Andrew James; Sumner, Gordon Matthew
Polidori, John William 1795-1821 . **NCLC 51**
See also DLB 116
Pollitt, Katha 1949- .... **CLC 28**
See also CA 120; 122; CANR 66; MTCW
Pollock, (Mary) Sharon 1936-**CLC 50; DAC;
DAM DRAM, MST**
See also CA 141; DLB 60

Polo, Marco 1254-1324 .... **CMLC 15**
Polonsky, Abraham (Lincoln) 1910- **CLC 92**
See also CA 104; DLB 26; INT 104
Polybius c. 200B.C.-c. 118B.C. ...... **CMLC 17**
See also DLB 176
Pomerance, Bernard 1940-.... **CLC 13; DAM DRAM**
See also CA 101; CANR 49
Ponge, Francis (Jean Gaston Alfred) 1899-1988 **CLC 6, 18; DAM POET**
See also CA 85-88; 126; CANR 40
Pontoppidan, Henrik 1857-1943 .... **TCLC 29**
Poole, Josephine .... **CLC 17**
See also Helyar, Jane Penelope Josephine
See also SAAS 2; SATA 5
Popa, Vasko 1922-1991 .... **CLC 19**
See also CA 112; 148; DLB 181
Pope, Alexander 1688-1744 **LC 3; DA; DAB; DAC; DAM MST, POET; WLC**
See also CDBLB 1660-1789; DLB 95, 101
Porter, Connie (Rose) 1959(?)- .... **CLC 70**
See also BW 2; CA 142; SATA 81
Porter, Gene(va Grace) Stratton 1863(?)-1924 **TCLC 21**
See also CA 112
Porter, Katherine Anne 1890-1980**CLC 1,3,7, 10, 13, 15, 27, 101; DA; DAB; DAC; DAM MST, NOV; SSC 4**
See also AITN 2; CA 1-4R; 101; CANR 1, 65; DLB 4, 9, 102; DLBD 12; DLBY 80; MTCW; SATA 39; SATA-Obit 23
Porter, Peter (Neville Frederick) 1929-**CLC 5, 13, 33**
See also CA 85-88; DLB 40
Porter, William Sydney 1862-1910
See Henry, O.
See also CA 104; 131; CDALB 1865-1917; DA; DAB; DAC; DAM MST; DLB 12, 78, 79; MTCW; YABC 2
Portillo (y Pacheco), Jose Lopez
See Lopez Portillo (y Pacheco), Jose
Post, Melville Davisson 1869-1930 **TCLC 39**
See also CA 110
Potok, Chaim 1929- . **CLC 2, 7, 14, 26; DAM NOV**
See also AAYA 15; AITN 1, 2; CA 17-20R; CANR 19, 35, 64; DLB 28, 152; INT CANR-19; MTCW; SATA 33
Potter, (Helen) Beatrix 1866-1943
See Webb, (Martha) Beatrice (Potter)
See also MAICYA
Potter, Dennis (Christopher George) 1935-1994 **CLC 58, 86**
See also CA 107; 145; CANR 33, 61; MTCW
Pound, Ezra (Weston Loomis) 1885-1972 **CLC 1, 2, 3, 4, 5, 7, 10, 13, 18, 34, 48, 50; DA; DAB; DAC; DAM MST, POET; PC 4; WLC**
See also CA 5-8R; 37-40R; CANR 40; CDALB 1917-1929; DLB 4, 45, 63; DLBD 15; MTCW
Povod, Reinaldo 1959-1994 .... **CLC 44**
See also CA 136; 146
Powell, Adam Clayton, Jr. 1908-1972**CLC 89; BLC; DAM MULT**
See also BW 1; CA 102; 33-36R
Powell, Anthony (Dymoke) 1905-**CLC 1, 3, 7, 9, 10, 31**
See also CA 1-4R; CANR 1, 32, 62; CDBLB 1945-1960; DLB 15; MTCW
Powell, Dawn 1897-1965 .... **CLC 66**
See also CA 5-8R; DLBY 97
Powell, Padgett 1952-....................... **CLC 34**

See also CA 126; CANR 63
Power, Susan 1961- .... **CLC 91**
Powers, J(ames) F(arl) 1917-**CLC 1, 4, 8, 57; SSC 4**
See also CA 1-4R; CANR 2, 61; DLB 130; MTCW
Powers, John J(ames) 1945-
See Powers, John R.
See also CA 69-72
Powers, John R. .... **CLC 66**
See also Powers, John J(ames)
Powers, Richard (S.) 1957- .... **CLC 93**
See also CA 148
Pownall, David 1938- .... **CLC 10**
See also CA 89-92; CAAS 18; CANR 49; DLB 14
Powys, John Cowper 1872-1963**CLC 7, 9, 15, 46**
See also CA 85-88; DLB 15; MTCW
Powys, T(heodore) F(rancis) 1875-1953 **TCLC 9**
See also CA 106; DLB 36, 162
Prado (Calvo), Pedro 1886-1952 .... **TCLC 75**
See also CA 131; HW
Prager, Emily 1952- .... **CLC 56**
Pratt, E(dwin) J(ohn) 1883(?)-1964 **CLC 19; DAC; DAM POET**
See also CA 141; 93-96; DLB 92
Premchand .... **TCLC 21**
See also Srivastava, Dhanpat Rai
Preussler, Otfried 1923- .... **CLC 17**
See also CA 77-80; SATA 24
Prevert, Jacques (Henri Marie) 1900-1977 **CLC 15**
See also CA 77-80; 69-72; CANR 29, 61; MTCW; SATA-Obit 30
Prevost, Abbe (Antoine Francois) 1697-1763 **LC 1**
Price, (Edward) Reynolds 1933-**CLC 3, 6, 13, 43, 50, 63; DAM NOV; SSC 22**
See also CA 1-4R; CANR 1, 37, 57; DLB 2; INT CANR-37
Price, Richard 1949- .... **CLC 6, 12**
See also CA 49-52; CANR 3; DLBY 81
Prichard, Katharine Susannah 1883-1969 **CLC 46**
See also CA 11-12; CANR 33; CAP 1; MTCW; SATA 66
Priestley, J(ohn) B(oynton) 1894-1984**CLC 2, 5, 9, 34; DAM DRAM, NOV**
See also CA 9-12R; 113; CANR 33; CDBLB 1914-1945; DLB 10, 34, 77, 100, 139; DLBY 84; MTCW
Prince 1958(?)-................................. **CLC 35**
Prince, F(rank) T(empleton) 1912-... **CLC 22**
See also CA 101; CANR 43; DLB 20
Prince Kropotkin
See Kropotkin, Peter (Aleksieevich)
Prior, Matthew 1664-1721 .... **LC 4**
See also DLB 95
Prishvin, Mikhail 1873-1954 .... **TCLC 75**
Pritchard, William H(arrison) 1932- **CLC 34**
See also CA 65-68; CANR 23; DLB 111
Pritchett, V(ictor) S(awdon) 1900-1997 **C L C 5, 13, 15, 41; DAM NOV; SSC 14**
See also CA 61-64; 157; CANR 31, 63; DLB 15, 139; MTCW
Private 19022
See Manning, Frederic
Probst, Mark 1925- .... **CLC 59**
See also CA 130
Prokosch, Frederic 1908-1989 ..... **CLC 4, 48**
See also CA 73-76; 128; DLB 48

Prophet, The
See Dreiser, Theodore (Herman Albert)
Prose, Francine 1947- .... **CLC 45**
See also CA 109; 112; CANR 46
Proudhon
See Cunha, Euclides (Rodrigues Pimenta) da
Proulx, Annie
See Proulx, E(dna) Annie
Proulx, E(dna) Annie 1935-... **CLC 81; DAM POP**
See also CA 145; CANR 65
Proust, (Valentin-Louis-George-Eugene-) Marcel 1871-1922 **TCLC 7, 13, 33; DA; DAB; DAC; DAM MST, NOV; WLC**
See also CA 104; 120; DLB 65; MTCW
Prowler, Harley
See Masters, Edgar Lee
Prus, Boleslaw 1845-1912 .... **TCLC 48**
Pryor, Richard (Franklin Lenox Thomas) 1940- **CLC 26**
See also CA 122
Przybyszewski, Stanislaw 1868-1927**TCLC 36**
See also CA 160; DLB 66
Pteleon
See Grieve, C(hristopher) M(urray)
See also DAM POET
Puckett, Lute
See Masters, Edgar Lee
Puig, Manuel 1932-1990**CLC 3, 5, 10, 28, 65; DAM MULT; HLC**
See also CA 45-48; CANR 2, 32, 63; DLB 113; HW; MTCW
Pulitzer, Joseph 1847-1911 .... **TCLC 76**
See also CA 114; DLB 23
Purdy, Al(fred Wellington) 1918-**CLC 3, 6, 14, 50; DAC; DAM MST, POET**
See also CA 81-84; CAAS 17; CANR 42, 66; DLB 88
Purdy, James (Amos) 1923- **CLC 2, 4, 10, 28, 52**
See also CA 33-36R; CAAS 1; CANR 19, 51; DLB 2; INT CANR-19; MTCW
Pure, Simon
See Swinnerton, Frank Arthur
Pushkin, Alexander (Sergeyevich) 1799-1837 **NCLC 3, 27; DA; DAB; DAC; DAM DRAM, MST, POET; PC 10; SSC 27; WLC**
See also SATA 61
P'u Sung-ling 1640-1715 .... **LC 3**
Putnam, Arthur Lee
See Alger, Horatio, Jr.
Puzo, Mario 1920-**CLC 1, 2, 6, 36, 107; DAM NOV, POP**
See also CA 65-68; CANR 4, 42, 65; DLB 6; MTCW
Pygge, Edward
See Barnes, Julian (Patrick)
Pyle, Ernest Taylor 1900-1945
See Pyle, Ernie
See also CA 115; 160
Pyle, Ernie 1900-1945 .... **TCLC 75**
See also Pyle, Ernest Taylor
See also DLB 29
Pym, Barbara (Mary Crampton) 1913-1980 **CLC 13, 19, 37**
See also CA 13-14; 97-100; CANR 13, 34; CAP 1; DLB 14; DLBY 87; MTCW
Pynchon, Thomas (Ruggles, Jr.) 1937-**CLC 2, 3, 6, 9, 11, 18, 33, 62, 72; DA; DAB; DAC; DAM MST, NOV, POP; SSC 14; WLC**
See also BEST 90:2; CA 17-20R; CANR 22, 46; DLB 2, 173; MTCW

Pythagoras c. 570B.C.-c. 500B.C. . **CMLC 22**
  See also DLB 176
Qian Zhongshu
  See Ch'ien Chung-shu
Qroll
  See Dagerman, Stig (Halvard)
Quarrington, Paul (Lewis) 1953- ..... **CLC 65**
  See also CA 129; CANR 62
Quasimodo, Salvatore 1901-1968 .... **CLC 10**
  See also CA 13-16; 25-28R; CAP 1; DLB 114;
  MTCW
Quay, Stephen 1947- .... **CLC 95**
Quay, Timothy 1947-......................... **CLC 95**
Queen, Ellery .... **CLC 3, 11**
  See also Dannay, Frederic; Davidson, Avram;
  Lee, Manfred B(ennington); Marlowe,
  Stephen; Sturgeon, Theodore (Hamilton);
  Vance, John Holbrook
Queen, Ellery, Jr.
  See Dannay, Frederic; Lee, Manfred
  B(ennington)
Queneau, Raymond 1903-1976 **CLC 2, 5, 10,
  42**
  See also CA 77-80; 69-72; CANR 32; DLB 72;
  MTCW
Quevedo, Francisco de 1580-1645 ...... **LC 23**
Quiller-Couch, SirArthur Thomas 1863-1944
  TCLC 53
  See also CA 118; DLB 135, 153, 190
Quin, Ann (Marie) 1936-1973 .... **CLC 6**
  See also CA 9-12R; 45-48; DLB 14
Quinn, Martin
  See Smith, Martin Cruz
Quinn, Peter 1947- .... **CLC 91**
Quinn, Simon
  See Smith, Martin Cruz
Quiroga, Horacio (Sylvestre) 1878-1937
  TCLC 20; DAM MULT; HLC
  See also CA 117; 131; HW; MTCW
Quoirez, Francoise 1935-..................... **CLC 9**
  See also Sagan, Francoise
  See also CA 49-52; CANR 6, 39; MTCW
Raabe, Wilhelm 1831-1910 .... **TCLC 45**
  See also DLB 129
Rabe, David (William) 1940-... **CLC 4, 8, 33;
  DAM DRAM**
  See also CA 85-88; CABS 3; CANR 59; DLB 7
Rabelais, Francois 1483-1553**LC 5; DA; DAB;
  DAC; DAM MST; WLC**
Rabinovitch, Sholem 1859-1916
  See Aleichem, Sholom
  See also CA 104
Rachilde 1860-1953 .... **TCLC 67**
  See also DLB 123, 192
Racine, Jean 1639-1699 . **LC 28; DAB; DAM
  MST**
Radcliffe, Ann (Ward) 1764-1823**NCLC 6, 55**
  See also DLB 39, 178
Radiguet, Raymond 1903-1923 ...... **TCLC 29**
  See also CA 162; DLB 65
Radnoti, Miklos 1909-1944............. **TCLC 16**
  See also CA 118
Rado, James 1939-............................. **CLC 17**
  See also CA 105
Radvanyi, Netty 1900-1983
  See Seghers, Anna
  See also CA 85-88; 110
Rae, Ben
  See Griffiths, Trevor
Raeburn, John (Hay) 1941-.............. **CLC 34**
  See also CA 57-60
Ragni, Gerome 1942-1991 .... **CLC 17**
  See also CA 105; 134

Rahv, Philip 1908-1973 .... **CLC 24**
  See also Greenberg, Ivan
  See also DLB 137
Raimund, Ferdinand Jakob 1790-1836**NCLC
  69**
  See also DLB 90
Raine, Craig 1944- .... **CLC 32, 103**
  See also CA 108; CANR 29, 51; DLB 40
Raine, Kathleen (Jessie) 1908- ..... **CLC 7, 45**
  See also CA 85-88; CANR 46; DLB 20; MTCW
Rainis, Janis 1865-1929 .... **TCLC 29**
Rakosi, Carl 1903-.............................**CLC 47**
  See also Rawley, Callman
  See also CAAS 5; DLB 193
Raleigh, Richard
  See Lovecraft, H(oward) P(hillips)
Raleigh, Sir Walter 1554(?)-1618 . **LC 31, 39**
  See also CDBLB Before 1660; DLB 172
Rallentando, H. P.
  See Sayers, Dorothy L(eigh)
Ramal, Walter
  See de la Mare, Walter (John)
Ramon, Juan
  See Jimenez (Mantecon), Juan Ramon
Ramos, Graciliano 1892-1953 .... **TCLC 32**
Rampersad, Arnold 1941- .... **CLC 44**
  See also BW 2; CA 127; 133; DLB 111; INT
  133
Rampling, Anne
  See Rice, Anne
Ramsay, Allan 1684(?)-1758 .... **LC 29**
  See also DLB 95
Ramuz, Charles-Ferdinand 1878-1947**T C L C
  33**
  See also CA 165
Rand, Ayn 1905-1982**CLC 3, 30, 44, 79; DA;
  DAC; DAM MST, NOV, POP; WLC**
  See also AAYA 10; CA 13-16R; 105; CANR
  27; MTCW
Randall, Dudley (Felker) 1914-**CLC 1; BLC;
  DAM MULT**
  See also BW 1; CA 25-28R; CANR 23; DLB
  41
Randall, Robert
  See Silverberg, Robert
Ranger, Ken
  See Creasey, John
Ransom, John Crowe 1888-1974**CLC 2, 4, 5,
  11, 24; DAM POET**
  See also CA 5-8R; 49-52; CANR 6, 34; DLB
  45, 63; MTCW
Rao, Raja 1909- ...... **CLC 25, 56; DAM NOV**
  See also CA 73-76; CANR 51; MTCW
Raphael, Frederic (Michael) 1931-**CLC 2, 14**
  See also CA 1-4R; CANR 1; DLB 14
Ratcliffe, James P.
  See Mencken, H(enry) L(ouis)
Rathbone, Julian 1935-..................... **CLC 41**
  See also CA 101; CANR 34
Rattigan, Terence (Mervyn) 1911-1977**CLC 7;
  DAM DRAM**
  See also CA 85-88; 73-76; CDBLB 1945-1960;
  DLB 13; MTCW
Ratushinskaya, Irina 1954- .... **CLC 54**
  See also CA 129; CANR 68
Raven, Simon (Arthur Noel) 1927-... **CLC 14**
  See also CA 81-84
Ravenna, Michael
  See Welty, Eudora
Rawley, Callman 1903-
  See Rakosi, Carl
  See also CA 21-24R; CANR 12, 32
Rawlings, Marjorie Kinnan 1896-1953**TCLC
  4**
  See also AAYA 20; CA 104; 137; DLB 9, 22,
  102; JRDA; MAICYA; YABC 1
Ray, Satyajit 1921-1992 .. **CLC 16, 76; DAM
  MULT**
  See also CA 114; 137
Read, Herbert Edward 1893-1968 ..... **CLC 4**
  See also CA 85-88; 25-28R; DLB 20, 149
Read, Piers Paul 1941- .... **CLC 4, 10, 25**
  See also CA 21-24R; CANR 38; DLB 14; SATA
  21
Reade, Charles 1814-1884 .... **NCLC 2**
  See also DLB 21
Reade, Hamish
  See Gray, Simon (James Holliday)
Reading, Peter 1946- .... **CLC 47**
  See also CA 103; CANR 46; DLB 40
Reaney, James 1926- ... **CLC 13; DAC; DAM
  MST**
  See also CA 41-44R; CAAS 15; CANR 42; DLB
  68; SATA 43
Rebreanu, Liviu 1885-1944 .... **TCLC 28**
  See also CA 165
Rechy, John (Francisco) 1934- **CLC 1, 7, 14,
  18, 107; DAM MULT; HLC**
  See also CA 5-8R; CAAS 4; CANR 6, 32, 64;
  DLB 122; DLBY 82; HW; INT CANR-6
Redcam, Tom 1870-1933 .... **TCLC 25**
Reddin, Keith .... **CLC 67**
Redgrove, Peter (William) 1932- . **CLC 6, 41**
  See also CA 1-4R; CANR 3, 39; DLB 40
Redmon, Anne ....**CLC 22**
  See also Nightingale, Anne Redmon
  See also DLBY 86
Reed, Eliot
  See Ambler, Eric
Reed, Ishmael 1938-**CLC 2, 3, 5, 6, 13, 32, 60;
  BLC; DAM MULT**
  See also BW 2; CA 21-24R; CANR 25, 48; DLB
  2, 5, 33, 169; DLBD 8; MTCW
Reed, John (Silas) 1887-1920 .... **TCLC 9**
  See also CA 106
Reed, Lou ....**CLC 21**
  See also Firbank, Louis
Reeve, Clara 1729-1807 .... **NCLC 19**
  See also DLB 39
Reich, Wilhelm 1897-1957 .... **TCLC 57**
Reid, Christopher (John) 1949- ....**CLC 33**
  See also CA 140; DLB 40
Reid, Desmond
  See Moorcock, Michael (John)
Reid Banks, Lynne 1929-
  See Banks, Lynne Reid
  See also CA 1-4R; CANR 6, 22, 38; CLR 24;
  JRDA; MAICYA; SATA 22, 75
Reilly, William K.
  See Creasey, John
Reiner, Max
  See Caldwell, (Janet Miriam) Taylor (Holland)
Reis, Ricardo
  See Pessoa, Fernando (Antonio Nogueira)
Remarque, Erich Maria 1898-1970 **CLC 21;
  DA; DAB; DAC; DAM MST, NOV**
  See also CA 77-80; 29-32R; DLB 56; MTCW
Remizov, A.
  See Remizov, Aleksei (Mikhailovich)
Remizov, A. M.
  See Remizov, Aleksei (Mikhailovich)
Remizov, Aleksei (Mikhailovich) 1877-1957
  TCLC 27
  See also CA 125; 133
Renan, Joseph Ernest 1823-1892 ... **NCLC 26**
Renard, Jules 1864-1910 .... **TCLC 17**

See also CA 117
Renault, Mary .... **CLC 3, 11, 17**
 See also Challans, Mary
 See also DLBY 83
Rendell, Ruth (Barbara) 1930- . **CLC 28, 48;**
  DAM POP
 See also Vine, Barbara
 See also CA 109; CANR 32, 52; DLB 87; INT
  CANR-32; MTCW
Renoir, Jean 1894-1979 .... **CLC 20**
 See also CA 129; 85-88
Resnais, Alain 1922- .... **CLC 16**
Reverdy, Pierre 1889-1960 .... **CLC 53**
 See also CA 97-100; 89-92
Rexroth, Kenneth 1905-1982 **CLC 1, 2, 6, 11,**
  22, 49; DAM POET; PC 20
 See also CA 5-8R; 107; CANR 14, 34, 63;
  CDALB 1941-1968; DLB 16, 48, 165;
  DLBY 82; INT CANR-14; MTCW
Reyes, Alfonso 1889-1959 .... **TCLC 33**
 See also CA 131; HW
Reyes y Basoalto, Ricardo Eliecer Neftali
 See Neruda, Pablo
Reymont, Wladyslaw (Stanislaw) 1868(?)-1925
  TCLC 5
 See also CA 104
Reynolds, Jonathan 1942- .... **CLC 6, 38**
 See also CA 65-68; CANR 28
Reynolds, Joshua 1723-1792 .... **LC 15**
 See also DLB 104
Reynolds, Michael Shane 1937- .... **CLC 44**
 See also CA 65-68; CANR 9
Reznikoff, Charles 1894-1976 ....**CLC 9**
 See also CA 33-36; 61-64; CAP 2; DLB 28, 45
Rezzori (d'Arezzo), Gregor von 1914-**CLC 25**
 See also CA 122; 136
Rhine, Richard
 See Silverstein, Alvin
Rhodes, Eugene Manlove 1869-1934**TCLC 53**
R'hoone
 See Balzac, Honore de
Rhys, Jean 1890(?)-1979 **CLC 2, 4, 6, 14, 19,**
  51; DAM NOV; SSC 21
 See also CA 25-28R; 85-88; CANR 35, 62;
  CDBLB 1945-1960; DLB 36, 117, 162;
  MTCW
Ribeiro, Darcy 1922-1997 .... **CLC 34**
 See also CA 33-36R; 156
Ribeiro, Joao Ubaldo (Osorio Pimentel) 1941-
  CLC 10, 67
 See also CA 81-84
Ribman, Ronald (Burt) 1932- .... **CLC 7**
 See also CA 21-24R; CANR 46
Ricci, Nino 1959- .... **CLC 70**
 See also CA 137
Rice, Anne 1941- .... **CLC 41; DAM POP**
 See also AAYA 9; BEST 89:2; CA 65-68; CANR
  12, 36, 53
Rice, Elmer (Leopold) 1892-1967 **CLC 7, 49;**
  DAM DRAM
 See also CA 21-22; 25-28R; CAP 2; DLB 4, 7;
  MTCW
Rice, Tim(othy Miles Bindon) 1944- **CLC 21**
 See also CA 103; CANR 46
Rich, Adrienne (Cecile) 1929-**CLC 3, 6, 7, 11,**
  18, 36, 73, 76; DAM POET; PC 5
 See also CA 9-12R; CANR 20, 53; DLB 5, 67;
  MTCW
Rich, Barbara
 See Graves, Robert (von Ranke)
Rich, Robert
 See Trumbo, Dalton
Richard, Keith .... **CLC 17**

See also Richards, Keith
Richards, David Adams 1950- **CLC 59; DAC**
 See also CA 93-96; CANR 60; DLB 53
Richards, I(vor) A(rmstrong) 1893-1979**CLC**
  14, 24
 See also CA 41-44R; 89-92; CANR 34; DLB
  27
Richards, Keith 1943-
 See Richard, Keith
 See also CA 107
Richardson, Anne
 See Roiphe, Anne (Richardson)
Richardson, Dorothy Miller 1873-1957**TCLC**
  3
 See also CA 104; DLB 36
Richardson, Ethel Florence (Lindesay) 1870-
  1946
 See Richardson, Henry Handel
 See also CA 105
Richardson, Henry Handel .... **TCLC 4**
 See also Richardson, Ethel Florence (Lindesay)
Richardson, John 1796-1852**NCLC 55; DAC**
 See also DLB 99
Richardson, Samuel 1689-1761 .... **LC 1; DA;**
  DAB; DAC; DAM MST, NOV; WLC
 See also CDBLB 1660-1789; DLB 39
Richler, Mordecai 1931-**CLC 3, 5, 9, 13, 18, 46,**
  70; DAC; DAM MST, NOV
 See also AITN 1; CA 65-68; CANR 31, 62; CLR
  17; DLB 53; MAICYA; MTCW; SATA 44,
  98; SATA-Brief 27
Richter, Conrad (Michael) 1890-1968**CLC 30**
 See also AAYA 21; CA 5-8R; 25-28R; CANR
  23; DLB 9; MTCW; SATA 3
Ricostranza, Tom
 See Ellis, Trey
Riddell, Charlotte 1832-1906 .... **TCLC 40**
 See also CA 165; DLB 156
Riding, Laura .... **CLC 3, 7**
 See also Jackson, Laura (Riding)
Riefenstahl, Berta Helene Amalia 1902-
 See Riefenstahl, Leni
 See also CA 108
Riefenstahl, Leni .... **CLC 16**
 See also Riefenstahl, Berta Helene Amalia
Riffe, Ernest
 See Bergman, (Ernst) Ingmar
Riggs, (Rolla) Lynn 1899-1954 ..... **TCLC 56;**
  DAM MULT
 See also CA 144; DLB 175; NNAL
Riley, James Whitcomb 1849-1916**TCLC 51;**
  DAM POET
 See also CA 118; 137; MAICYA; SATA 17
Riley, Tex
 See Creasey, John
Rilke, Rainer Maria 1875-1926**TCLC 1, 6, 19;**
  DAM POET; PC 2
 See also CA 104; 132; CANR 62; DLB 81;
  MTCW
Rimbaud, (Jean Nicolas) Arthur 1854-1891
  NCLC 4, 35; DA; DAB; DAC; DAM MST,
  POET; PC 3; WLC
Rinehart, Mary Roberts 1876-1958**TCLC 52**
 See also CA 108
Ringmaster, The
 See Mencken, H(enry) L(ouis)
Ringwood, Gwen(dolyn Margaret) Pharis
  1910-1984 .... **CLC 48**
 See also CA 148; 112; DLB 88
Rio, Michel 19(?)- .... **CLC 43**
Ritsos, Giannes
 See Ritsos, Yannis
Ritsos, Yannis 1909-1990 .... **CLC 6, 13, 31**

See also CA 77-80; 133; CANR 39, 61; MTCW
Ritter, Erika 1948(?)- .... **CLC 52**
Rivera, Jose Eustasio 1889-1928 ... **TCLC 35**
 See also CA 162; HW
Rivers, Conrad Kent 1933-1968 ....**CLC 1**
 See also BW 1; CA 85-88; DLB 41
Rivers, Elfrida
 See Bradley, Marion Zimmer
Riverside, John
 See Heinlein, Robert A(nson)
Rizal, Jose 1861-1896 ....**NCLC 27**
Roa Bastos, Augusto (Antonio) 1917-**CLC 45;**
  DAM MULT; HLC
 See also CA 131; DLB 113; HW
Robbe-Grillet, Alain 1922- **CLC 1, 2, 4, 6, 8,**
  10, 14, 43
 See also CA 9-12R; CANR 33, 65; DLB 83;
  MTCW
Robbins, Harold 1916-1997 ..... **CLC 5; DAM**
  NOV
 See also CA 73-76; 162; CANR 26, 54; MTCW
Robbins, Thomas Eugene 1936-
 See Robbins, Tom
 See also CA 81-84; CANR 29, 59; DAM NOV,
  POP; MTCW
Robbins, Tom .... **CLC 9, 32, 64**
 See also Robbins, Thomas Eugene
 See also BEST 90:3; DLBY 80
Robbins, Trina 1938- .... **CLC 21**
 See also CA 128
Roberts, Charles G(eorge) D(ouglas) 1860-1943
  TCLC 8
 See also CA 105; CLR 33; DLB 92; SATA 88;
  SATA-Brief 29
Roberts, Elizabeth Madox 1886-1941 **TCLC**
  68
 See also CA 111; DLB 9, 54, 102; SATA 33;
  SATA-Brief 27
Roberts, Kate 1891-1985 .... **CLC 15**
 See also CA 107; 116
Roberts, Keith (John Kingston) 1935-**CLC 14**
 See also CA 25-28R; CANR 46
Roberts, Kenneth (Lewis) 1885-1957**TCLC 23**
 See also CA 109; DLB 9
Roberts, Michele (B.) 1949- .... **CLC 48**
 See also CA 115; CANR 58
Robertson, Ellis
 See Ellison, Harlan (Jay); Silverberg, Robert
Robertson, Thomas William 1829-1871**NCLC**
  35; DAM DRAM
Robeson, Kenneth
 See Dent, Lester
Robinson, Edwin Arlington 1869-1935**TCLC**
  5; DA; DAC; DAM MST, POET; PC 1
 See also CA 104; 133; CDALB 1865-1917;
  DLB 54; MTCW
Robinson, Henry Crabb 1775-1867**NCLC 15**
 See also DLB 107
Robinson, Jill 1936- .... **CLC 10**
 See also CA 102; INT 102
Robinson, Kim Stanley 1952-........... **CLC 34**
 See also CA 126
Robinson, Lloyd
 See Silverberg, Robert
Robinson, Marilynne 1944- .... **CLC 25**
 See also CA 116
Robinson, Smokey .... **CLC 21**
 See also Robinson, William, Jr.
Robinson, William, Jr. 1940-
 See Robinson, Smokey
 See also CA 116
Robison, Mary 1949- .... **CLC 42, 98**
 See also CA 113; 116; DLB 130; INT 116

Rod, Edouard 1857-1910 .... **TCLC 52**
Roddenberry, Eugene Wesley 1921-1991
　See Roddenberry, Gene
　See also CA 110; 135; CANR 37; SATA 45;
　　SATA-Obit 69
Roddenberry, Gene .... **CLC 17**
　See also Roddenberry, Eugene Wesley
　See also AAYA 5; SATA-Obit 69
Rodgers, Mary 1931- .... **CLC 12**
　See also CA 49-52; CANR 8, 55; CLR 20; INT
　　CANR-8; JRDA; MAICYA; SATA 8
Rodgers, W(illiam) R(obert) 1909-1969**CLC 7**
　See also CA 85-88; DLB 20
Rodman, Eric
　See Silverberg, Robert
Rodman, Howard 1920(?)-1985 .... **CLC 65**
　See also CA 118
Rodman, Maia
　See Wojciechowska, Maia (Teresa)
Rodriguez, Claudio 1934- .... **CLC 10**
　See also DLB 134
Roelvaag, O(le) E(dvart) 1876-1931**TCLC 17**
　See also CA 117; DLB 9
Roethke, Theodore (Huebner) 1908-1963**CLC
　1, 3, 8, 11, 19, 46, 101; DAM POET; PC 15**
　See also CA 81-84; CABS 2; CDALB 1941-
　　1968; DLB 5; MTCW
Rogers, Samuel 1763-1855 .... **NCLC 69**
　See also DLB 93
Rogers, Thomas Hunton 1927- .... **CLC 57**
　See also CA 89-92; INT 89-92
Rogers, Will(iam Penn Adair) 1879-1935
　　TCLC 8, 71; DAM MULT
　See also CA 105; 144; DLB 11; NNAL
Rogin, Gilbert 1929- .... **CLC 18**
　See also CA 65-68; CANR 15
Rohan, Koda .... **TCLC 22**
　See also Koda Shigeyuki
Rohlfs, Anna Katharine Green
　See Green, Anna Katharine
Rohmer, Eric .... **CLC 16**
　See also Scherer, Jean-Marie Maurice
Rohmer, Sax .... **TCLC 28**
　See also Ward, Arthur Henry Sarsfield
　See also DLB 70
Roiphe, Anne (Richardson) 1935- . **CLC 3, 9**
　See also CA 89-92; CANR 45; DLBY 80; INT
　　89-92
Rojas, Fernando de 1465-1541 .... **LC 23**
Rolfe, Frederick (William Serafino Austin
　　Lewis Mary) 1860-1913 .... **TCLC 12**
　See also CA 107; DLB 34, 156
Rolland, Romain 1866-1944 .... **TCLC 23**
　See also CA 118; DLB 65
Rolle, Richard c. 1300-c. 1349 ...... **CMLC 21**
　See also DLB 146
Rolvaag, O(le) E(dvart)
　See Roelvaag, O(le) E(dvart)
Romain Arnaud, Saint
　See Aragon, Louis
Romains, Jules 1885-1972 .... **CLC 7**
　See also CA 85-88; CANR 34; DLB 65; MTCW
Romero, Jose Ruben 1890-1952 ..... **TCLC 14**
　See also CA 114; 131; HW
Ronsard, Pierre de 1524-1585 .... **LC 6; PC 11**
Rooke, Leon 1934- .. **CLC 25, 34; DAM POP**
　See also CA 25-28R; CANR 23, 53
Roosevelt, Theodore 1858-1919 ..... **TCLC 69**
　See also CA 115; DLB 47, 186
Roper, William 1498-1578 .... **LC 10**
Roquelaure, A. N.
　See Rice, Anne
Rosa, Joao Guimaraes 1908-1967 ... **CLC 23**

See also CA 89-92; DLB 113
Rose, Wendy 1948-**CLC 85; DAM MULT; PC
　13**
　See also CA 53-56; CANR 5, 51; DLB 175;
　　NNAL; SATA 12
Rosen, R. D.
　See Rosen, Richard (Dean)
Rosen, Richard (Dean) 1949- .... **CLC 39**
　See also CA 77-80; CANR 62; INT CANR-30
Rosenberg, Isaac 1890-1918 .... **TCLC 12**
　See also CA 107; DLB 20
Rosenblatt, Joe .... **CLC 15**
　See also Rosenblatt, Joseph
Rosenblatt, Joseph 1933-
　See Rosenblatt, Joe
　See also CA 89-92; INT 89-92
Rosenfeld, Samuel
　See Tzara, Tristan
Rosenstock, Sami
　See Tzara, Tristan
Rosenstock, Samuel
　See Tzara, Tristan
Rosenthal, M(acha) L(ouis) 1917-1996 . **C L C
　28**
　See also CA 1-4R; 152; CAAS 6; CANR 4, 51;
　　DLB 5; SATA 59
Ross, Barnaby
　See Dannay, Frederic
Ross, Bernard L.
　See Follett, Ken(neth Martin)
Ross, J. H.
　See Lawrence, T(homas) E(dward)
Ross, Martin
　See Martin, Violet Florence
　See also DLB 135
Ross, (James) Sinclair 1908- **CLC 13; DAC;
　DAM MST; SSC 24**
　See also CA 73-76; DLB 88
Rossetti, Christina (Georgina) 1830-1894
　　**NCLC 2, 50, 66; DA; DAB; DAC; DAM
　MST, POET; PC 7; WLC**
　See also DLB 35, 163; MAICYA; SATA 20
Rossetti, Dante Gabriel 1828-1882 **NCLC 4;
　DA; DAB; DAC; DAM MST, POET; WLC**
　See also CDBLB 1832-1890; DLB 35
Rossner, Judith (Perelman) 1935-**CLC 6, 9, 29**
　See also AITN 2; BEST 90:3; CA 17-20R;
　　CANR 18, 51; DLB 6; INT CANR-18;
　　MTCW
Rostand, Edmond (Eugene Alexis) 1868-1918
　　**TCLC 6, 37; DA; DAB; DAC; DAM
　DRAM, MST**
　See also CA 104; 126; DLB 192; MTCW
Roth, Henry 1906-1995 ..... **CLC 2, 6, 11, 104**
　See also CA 11-12; 149; CANR 38, 63; CAP 1;
　　DLB 28; MTCW
Roth, Philip (Milton) 1933-**CLC 1, 2, 3, 4, 6, 9,
　15, 22, 31, 47, 66, 86; DA; DAB; DAC;
　DAM MST, NOV, POP; SSC 26; WLC**
　See also BEST 90:3; CA 1-4R; CANR 1, 22,
　　36, 55; CDALB 1968-1988; DLB 2, 28, 173;
　　DLBY 82; MTCW
Rothenberg, Jerome 1931- .... **CLC 6, 57**
　See also CA 45-48; CANR 1; DLB 5, 193
Roumain, Jacques (Jean Baptiste) 1907-1944
　　TCLC 19; BLC; DAM MULT
　See also BW 1; CA 117; 125
Rourke, Constance (Mayfield) 1885-1941
　　TCLC 12
　See also CA 107; YABC 1
Rousseau, Jean-Baptiste 1671-1741 ..... **LC 9**
Rousseau, Jean-Jacques 1712-1778**LC 14, 36;
　DA; DAB; DAC; DAM MST; WLC**

Roussel, Raymond 1877-1933 .... **TCLC 20**
　See also CA 117
Rovit, Earl (Herbert) 1927- .... **CLC 7**
　See also CA 5-8R; CANR 12
Rowe, Nicholas 1674-1718 .... **LC 8**
　See also DLB 84
Rowley, Ames Dorrance
　See Lovecraft, H(oward) P(hillips)
Rowson, Susanna Haswell 1762(?)-1824
　　NCLC 5, 69
　See also DLB 37
Roy, Arundhati 1960(?)- .... **CLC 109**
　See also CA 163; DLBY 97
Roy, Gabrielle 1909-1983 **CLC 10, 14; DAB;
　DAC; DAM MST**
　See also CA 53-56; 110; CANR 5, 61; DLB 68;
　　MTCW
Royko, Mike 1932-1997 .... **CLC 109**
　See also CA 89-92; 157; CANR 26
Rozewicz, Tadeusz 1921- ... **CLC 9, 23; DAM
　POET**
　See also CA 108; CANR 36, 66; MTCW
Ruark, Gibbons 1941- .... **CLC 3**
　See also CA 33-36R; CAAS 23; CANR 14, 31,
　　57; DLB 120
Rubens, Bernice (Ruth) 1923- .... **CLC 19, 31**
　See also CA 25-28R; CANR 33, 65; DLB 14;
　　MTCW
Rubin, Harold
　See Robbins, Harold
Rudkin, (James) David 1936- .... **CLC 14**
　See also CA 89-92; DLB 13
Rudnik, Raphael 1933- .... **CLC 7**
　See also CA 29-32R
Ruffian, M.
　See Hasek, Jaroslav (Matej Frantisek)
Ruiz, Jose Martinez .... **CLC 11**
　See also Martinez Ruiz, Jose
Rukeyser, Muriel 1913-1980**CLC 6, 10, 15, 27;
　DAM POET; PC 12**
　See also CA 5-8R; 93-96; CANR 26, 60; DLB
　　48; MTCW; SATA-Obit 22
Rule, Jane (Vance) 1931- .... **CLC 27**
　See also CA 25-28R; CAAS 18; CANR 12; DLB
　　60
Rulfo, Juan 1918-1986 .... **CLC 8, 80; DAM
　MULT; HLC; SSC 25**
　See also CA 85-88; 118; CANR 26; DLB 113;
　　HW; MTCW
Rumi, Jalal al-Din 1297-1373 .... **CMLC 20**
Runeberg, Johan 1804-1877 .... **NCLC 41**
Runyon, (Alfred) Damon 1884(?)-1946**T C L C
　10**
　See also CA 107; 165; DLB 11, 86, 171
Rush, Norman 1933- .... **CLC 44**
　See also CA 121; 126; INT 126
Rushdie, (Ahmed) Salman 1947-**CLC 23, 31,
　55, 100; DAB; DAC; DAM MST, NOV,
　POP; WLCS**
　See also BEST 89:3; CA 108; 111; CANR 33,
　　56; DLB 194; INT 111; MTCW
Rushforth, Peter (Scott) 1945- .... **CLC 19**
　See also CA 101
Ruskin, John 1819-1900 .... **TCLC 63**
　See also CA 114; 129; CDBLB 1832-1890;
　　DLB 55, 163, 190; SATA 24
Russ, Joanna 1937- .... **CLC 15**
　See also CA 25-28R; CANR 11, 31, 65; DLB
　　8; MTCW
Russell, George William 1867-1935
　See Baker, Jean H.
　See also CA 104; 153; CDBLB 1890-1914;
　　DAM POET

Russell, (Henry) Ken(neth Alfred) 1927-**CLC 16**
See also CA 105
Russell, William Martin 1947- .... **CLC 60**
See also CA 164
Rutherford, Mark .... **TCLC 25**
See also White, William Hale
See also DLB 18
Ruyslinck, Ward 1929- .... **CLC 14**
See also Belser, Reimond Karel Maria de
Ryan, Cornelius (John) 1920-1974 ..... **CLC 7**
See also CA 69-72; 53-56; CANR 38
Ryan, Michael 1946- .... **CLC 65**
See also CA 49-52; DLBY 82
Ryan, Tim
See Dent, Lester
Rybakov, Anatoli (Naumovich) 1911-**CLC 23, 53**
See also CA 126; 135; SATA 79
Ryder, Jonathan
See Ludlum, Robert
Ryga, George 1932-1987**CLC 14; DAC; DAM MST**
See also CA 101; 124; CANR 43; DLB 60
S. H.
See Hartmann, Sadakichi
S. S.
See Sassoon, Siegfried (Lorraine)
Saba, Umberto 1883-1957 .... **TCLC 33**
See also CA 144; DLB 114
Sabatini, Rafael 1875-1950 .... **TCLC 47**
See also CA 162
Sabato, Ernesto (R.) 1911-**CLC 10, 23; DAM MULT; HLC**
See also CA 97-100; CANR 32, 65; DLB 145; HW; MTCW
Sacastru, Martin
See Bioy Casares, Adolfo
Sacher-Masoch, Leopold von 1836(?)-1895 **NCLC 31**
Sachs, Marilyn (Stickle) 1927- .... **CLC 35**
See also AAYA 2; CA 17-20R; CANR 13, 47; CLR 2; JRDA; MAICYA; SAAS 2; SATA 3, 68
Sachs, Nelly 1891-1970 .... **CLC 14, 98**
See also CA 17-18; 25-28R; CAP 2
Sackler, Howard (Oliver) 1929-1982 **CLC 14**
See also CA 61-64; 108; CANR 30; DLB 7
Sacks, Oliver (Wolf) 1933- .... **CLC 67**
See also CA 53-56; CANR 28, 50; INT CANR-28; MTCW
Sadakichi
See Hartmann, Sadakichi
Sade, Donatien Alphonse Francois Comte 1740-1814 .... **NCLC 47**
Sadoff, Ira 1945- .... **CLC 9**
See also CA 53-56; CANR 5, 21; DLB 120
Saetone
See Camus, Albert
Safire, William 1929- .... **CLC 10**
See also CA 17-20R; CANR 31, 54
Sagan, Carl (Edward) 1934-1996 .... **CLC 30**
See also AAYA 2; CA 25-28R; 155; CANR 11, 36; MTCW; SATA 58; SATA-Obit 94
Sagan, Francoise .... **CLC 3, 6, 9, 17, 36**
See also Quoirez, Francoise
See also DLB 83
Sahgal, Nayantara (Pandit) 1927- ... **CLC 41**
See also CA 9-12R; CANR 11
Saint, H(arry) F. 1941- .... **CLC 50**
See also CA 127
St. Aubin de Teran, Lisa 1953-
See Teran, Lisa St. Aubin de

See also CA 118; 126; INT 126
Saint Birgitta of Sweden c. 1303-1373**CMLC 24**
Sainte-Beuve, Charles Augustin 1804-1869 **NCLC 5**
Saint-Exupery, Antoine (Jean Baptiste Marie Roger) de 1900-1944**TCLC 2, 56; DAM NOV; WLC**
See also CA 108; 132; CLR 10; DLB 72; MAICYA; MTCW; SATA 20
St. John, David
See Hunt, E(verette) Howard, (Jr.)
Saint-John Perse
See Leger, (Marie-Rene Auguste) Alexis Saint-Leger
Saintsbury, George (Edward Bateman) 1845-1933 .... **TCLC 31**
See also CA 160; DLB 57, 149
Sait Faik .... **TCLC 23**
See also Abasiyanik, Sait Faik
Saki .... **TCLC 3; SSC 12**
See also Munro, H(ector) H(ugh)
Sala, George Augustus .... **NCLC 46**
Salama, Hannu 1936- .... **CLC 18**
Salamanca, J(ack) R(ichard) 1922-**CLC 4, 15**
See also CA 25-28R
Sale, J. Kirkpatrick
See Sale, Kirkpatrick
Sale, Kirkpatrick 1937- .... **CLC 68**
See also CA 13-16R; CANR 10
Salinas, Luis Omar 1937- ...... **CLC 90; DAM MULT; HLC**
See also CA 131; DLB 82; HW
Salinas (y Serrano), Pedro 1891(?)-1951 **TCLC 17**
See also CA 117; DLB 134
Salinger, J(erome) D(avid) 1919-**CLC 1, 3, 8, 12, 55, 56; DA; DAB; DAC; DAM MST, NOV, POP; SSC 2, 28; WLC**
See also AAYA 2; CA 5-8R; CANR 39; CDALB 1941-1968; CLR 18; DLB 2, 102, 173; MAICYA; MTCW; SATA 67
Salisbury, John
See Caute, (John) David
Salter, James 1925- .... **CLC 7, 52, 59**
See also CA 73-76; DLB 130
Saltus, Edgar (Everton) 1855-1921 . **TCLC 8**
See also CA 105
Saltykov, Mikhail Evgrafovich 1826-1889 **NCLC 16**
Samarakis, Antonis 1919- .... **CLC 5**
See also CA 25-28R; CAAS 16; CANR 36
Sanchez, Florencio 1875-1910 .... **TCLC 37**
See also CA 153; HW
Sanchez, Luis Rafael 1936- .... **CLC 23**
See also CA 128; DLB 145; HW
Sanchez, Sonia 1934-..... **CLC 5; BLC; DAM MULT; PC 9**
See also BW 2; CA 33-36R; CANR 24, 49; CLR 18; DLB 41; DLBD 8; MAICYA; MTCW; SATA 22
Sand, George 1804-1876**NCLC 2, 42, 57; DA; DAB; DAC; DAM MST, NOV; WLC**
See also DLB 119, 192
Sandburg, Carl (August) 1878-1967**CLC 1, 4, 10, 15, 35; DA; DAB; DAC; DAM MST, POET; PC 2; WLC**
See also AAYA 24; CA 5-8R; 25-28R; CANR 35; CDALB 1865-1917; DLB 17, 54; MAICYA; MTCW; SATA 8
Sandburg, Charles
See Sandburg, Carl (August)
Sandburg, Charles A.

See Sandburg, Carl (August)
Sanders, (James) Ed(ward) 1939-.... **CLC 53**
See also CA 13-16R; CAAS 21; CANR 13, 44; DLB 16
Sanders, Lawrence 1920-1998**CLC 41; DAM POP**
See also BEST 89:4; CA 81-84; 165; CANR 33, 62; MTCW
Sanders, Noah
See Blount, Roy (Alton), Jr.
Sanders, Winston P.
See Anderson, Poul (William)
Sandoz, Mari(e Susette) 1896-1966 . **CLC 28**
See also CA 1-4R; 25-28R; CANR 17, 64; DLB 9; MTCW; SATA 5
Saner, Reg(inald Anthony) 1931- .... **CLC 9**
See also CA 65-68
Sannazaro, Jacopo 1456(?)-1530 .... **LC 8**
Sansom, William 1912-1976 **CLC 2, 6; DAM NOV; SSC 21**
See also CA 5-8R; 65-68; CANR 42; DLB 139; MTCW
Santayana, George 1863-1952 .... **TCLC 40**
See also CA 115; DLB 54, 71; DLBD 13
Santiago, Danny .... **CLC 33**
See also James, Daniel (Lewis)
See also DLB 122
Santmyer, Helen Hoover 1895-1986 **CLC 33**
See also CA 1-4R; 118; CANR 15, 33; DLBY 84; MTCW
Santoka, Taneda 1882-1940 .... **TCLC 72**
Santos, Bienvenido N(uqui) 1911-1996 . **CLC 22; DAM MULT**
See also CA 101; 151; CANR 19, 46
Sapper .... **TCLC 44**
See also McNeile, Herman Cyril
Sapphire 1950- .... **CLC 99**
Sappho fl. 6th cent. B.C.- ...... **CMLC 3; DAM POET; PC 5**
See also DLB 176
Sarduy, Severo 1937-1993 .... **CLC 6, 97**
See also CA 89-92; 142; CANR 58; DLB 113; HW
Sargeson, Frank 1903-1982 .... **CLC 31**
See also CA 25-28R; 106; CANR 38
Sarmiento, Felix Ruben Garcia
See Dario, Ruben
Saroyan, William 1908-1981**CLC 1, 8, 10, 29, 34, 56; DA; DAB; DAC; DAM DRAM, MST, NOV; SSC 21; WLC**
See also CA 5-8R; 103; CANR 30; DLB 7, 9, 86; DLBY 81; MTCW; SATA 23; SATA-Obit 24
Sarraute, Nathalie 1900-**CLC 1, 2, 4, 8, 10, 31, 80**
See also CA 9-12R; CANR 23, 66; DLB 83; MTCW
Sarton, (Eleanor) May 1912-1995 **CLC 4, 14, 49, 91; DAM POET**
See also CA 1-4R; 149; CANR 1, 34, 55; DLB 48; DLBY 81; INT CANR-34; MTCW; SATA 36; SATA-Obit 86
Sartre, Jean-Paul 1905-1980**CLC 1, 4, 7, 9, 13, 18, 24, 44, 50, 52; DA; DAB; DAC; DAM DRAM, MST, NOV; DC 3; WLC**
See also CA 9-12R; 97-100; CANR 21; DLB 72; MTCW
Sassoon, Siegfried (Lorraine) 1886-1967**CLC 36; DAB; DAM MST, NOV, POET; PC 12**
See also CA 104; 25-28R; CANR 36; DLB 20, 191; MTCW
Satterfield, Charles
See Pohl, Frederik

Saul, John (W. III) 1942-**CLC 46; DAM NOV, POP**
See also AAYA 10; BEST 90:4; CA 81-84; CANR 16, 40; SATA 98

Saunders, Caleb
See Heinlein, Robert A(nson)

Saura (Atares), Carlos 1932- .... **CLC 20**
See also CA 114; 131; HW

Sauser-Hall, Frederic 1887-1961 ..... **CLC 18**
See also Cendrars, Blaise
See also CA 102; 93-96; CANR 36, 62; MTCW

Saussure, Ferdinand de 1857-1913 **TCLC 49**

Savage, Catharine
See Brosman, Catharine Savage

Savage, Thomas 1915- .... **CLC 40**
See also CA 126; 132; CAAS 15; INT 132

Savan, Glenn 19(?)- .... **CLC 50**

Sayers, Dorothy L(eigh) 1893-1957 **TCLC 2, 15; DAM POP**
See also CA 104; 119; CANR 60; CDBLB 1914-1945; DLB 10, 36, 77, 100; MTCW

Sayers, Valerie 1952-......................... **CLC 50**
See also CA 134; CANR 61

Sayles, John (Thomas) 1950- . **CLC 7, 10, 14**
See also CA 57-60; CANR 41; DLB 44

Scammell, Michael 1935- .... **CLC 34**
See also CA 156

Scannell, Vernon 1922- .... **CLC 49**
See also CA 5-8R; CANR 8, 24, 57; DLB 27; SATA 59

Scarlett, Susan
See Streatfeild, (Mary) Noel

Schaeffer, Susan Fromberg 1941- **CLC 6, 11, 22**
See also CA 49-52; CANR 18, 65; DLB 28; MTCW; SATA 22

Schary, Jill
See Robinson, Jill

Schell, Jonathan 1943- .... **CLC 35**
See also CA 73-76; CANR 12

Schelling, Friedrich Wilhelm Joseph von 1775-1854 .... **NCLC 30**
See also DLB 90

Schendel, Arthur van 1874-1946 ... **TCLC 56**

Scherer, Jean-Marie Maurice 1920-
See Rohmer, Eric
See also CA 110

Schevill, James (Erwin) 1920-............. **CLC 7**
See also CA 5-8R; CAAS 12

Schiller, Friedrich 1759-1805 . **NCLC 39, 69; DAM DRAM**
See also DLB 94

Schisgal, Murray (Joseph) 1926- .... **CLC 6**
See also CA 21-24R; CANR 48

Schlee, Ann 1934- .... **CLC 35**
See also CA 101; CANR 29; SATA 44; SATA-Brief 36

Schlegel, August Wilhelm von 1767-1845 **NCLC 15**
See also DLB 94

Schlegel, Friedrich 1772-1829 .... **NCLC 45**
See also DLB 90

Schlegel, Johann Elias (von) 1719(?)-1749**LC 5**

Schlesinger, Arthur M(eier), Jr. 1917-**CLC 84**
See also AITN 1; CA 1-4R; CANR 1, 28, 58; DLB 17; INT CANR-28; MTCW; SATA 61

Schmidt, Arno (Otto) 1914-1979 ...... **CLC 56**
See also CA 128; 109; DLB 69

Schmitz, Aron Hector 1861-1928
See Svevo, Italo
See also CA 104; 122; MTCW

Schnackenberg, Gjertrud 1953- ...... **CLC 40**

See also CA 116; DLB 120

Schneider, Leonard Alfred 1925-1966
See Bruce, Lenny
See also CA 89-92

Schnitzler, Arthur 1862-1931**TCLC 4; SSC 15**
See also CA 104; DLB 81, 118

Schoenberg, Arnold 1874-1951 ...... **TCLC 75**
See also CA 109

Schonberg, Arnold
See Schoenberg, Arnold

Schopenhauer, Arthur 1788-1860 ..**NCLC 51**
See also DLB 90

Schor, Sandra (M.) 1932(?)-1990 ...... **CLC 65**
See also CA 132

Schorer, Mark 1908-1977 ....**CLC 9**
See also CA 5-8R; 73-76; CANR 7; DLB 103

Schrader, Paul (Joseph) 1946- ....**CLC 26**
See also CA 37-40R; CANR 41; DLB 44

Schreiner, Olive (Emilie Albertina) 1855-1920 **TCLC 9**
See also CA 105; 154; DLB 18, 156, 190

Schulberg, Budd (Wilson) 1914-.. **CLC 7, 48**
See also CA 25-28R; CANR 19; DLB 6, 26, 28; DLBY 81

Schulz, Bruno 1892-1942**TCLC 5, 51; SSC 13**
See also CA 115; 123

Schulz, Charles M(onroe) 1922- ....**CLC 12**
See also CA 9-12R; CANR 6; INT CANR-6; SATA 10

Schumacher, E(rnst) F(riedrich) 1911-1977 **CLC 80**
See also CA 81-84; 73-76; CANR 34

Schuyler, James Marcus 1923-1991**CLC 5, 23; DAM POET**
See also CA 101; 134; DLB 5, 169; INT 101

Schwartz, Delmore (David) 1913-1966**CLC 2, 4, 10, 45, 87; PC 8**
See also CA 17-18; 25-28R; CANR 35; CAP 2; DLB 28, 48; MTCW

Schwartz, Ernst
See Ozu, Yasujiro

Schwartz, John Burnham 1965- ....**CLC 59**
See also CA 132

Schwartz, Lynne Sharon 1939- ....**CLC 31**
See also CA 103; CANR 44

Schwartz, Muriel A.
See Eliot, T(homas) S(tearns)

Schwarz-Bart, Andre 1928- ....**CLC 2, 4**
See also CA 89-92

Schwarz-Bart, Simone 1938-...............**CLC 7**
See also BW 2; CA 97-100

Schwob, (Mayer Andre) Marcel 1867-1905 **TCLC 20**
See also CA 117; DLB 123

Sciascia, Leonardo 1921-1989 . **CLC 8, 9, 41**
See also CA 85-88; 130; CANR 35; DLB 177; MTCW

Scoppettone, Sandra 1936- ....**CLC 26**
See also AAYA 11; CA 5-8R; CANR 41; SATA 9, 92

Scorsese, Martin 1942- .... **CLC 20, 89**
See also CA 110; 114; CANR 46

Scotland, Jay
See Jakes, John (William)

Scott, Duncan Campbell 1862-1947 **TCLC 6; DAC**
See also CA 104; 153; DLB 92

Scott, Evelyn 1893-1963 ....**CLC 43**
See also CA 104; 112; CANR 64; DLB 9, 48

Scott, F(rancis) R(eginald) 1899-1985**CLC 22**
See also CA 101; 114; DLB 88; INT 101

Scott, Frank
See Scott, F(rancis) R(eginald)

Scott, Joanna 1960- ....**CLC 50**
See also CA 126; CANR 53

Scott, Paul (Mark) 1920-1978 ...... **CLC 9, 60**
See also CA 81-84; 77-80; CANR 33; DLB 14; MTCW

Scott, Walter 1771-1832 .. **NCLC 15, 69; DA; DAB; DAC; DAM MST, NOV, POET; PC 13; WLC**
See also AAYA 22; CDBLB 1789-1832; DLB 93, 107, 116, 144, 159; YABC 2

Scribe, (Augustin) Eugene 1791-1861 **NCLC 16; DAM DRAM; DC 5**
See also DLB 192

Scrum, R.
See Crumb, R(obert)

Scudery, Madeleine de 1607-1701 .... **LC 2**

Scum
See Crumb, R(obert)

Scumbag, Little Bobby
See Crumb, R(obert)

Seabrook, John
See Hubbard, L(afayette) Ron(ald)

Sealy, I. Allan 1951- ....**CLC 55**

Search, Alexander
See Pessoa, Fernando (Antonio Nogueira)

Sebastian, Lee
See Silverberg, Robert

Sebastian Owl
See Thompson, Hunter S(tockton)

Sebestyen, Ouida 1924-.....................**CLC 30**
See also AAYA 8; CA 107; CANR 40; CLR 17; JRDA; MAICYA; SAAS 10; SATA 39

Secundus, H. Scriblerus
See Fielding, Henry

Sedges, John
See Buck, Pearl S(ydenstricker)

Sedgwick, Catharine Maria 1789-1867**NCLC 19**
See also DLB 1, 74

Seelye, John 1931- ....**CLC 7**

Seferiades, Giorgos Stylianou 1900-1971
See Seferis, George
See also CA 5-8R; 33-36R; CANR 5, 36; MTCW

Seferis, George ....**CLC 5, 11**
See also Seferiades, Giorgos Stylianou

Segal, Erich (Wolf) 1937- ..**CLC 3, 10; DAM POP**
See also BEST 89:1; CA 25-28R; CANR 20, 36, 65; DLBY 86; INT CANR-20; MTCW

Seger, Bob 1945- ....**CLC 35**

Seghers, Anna ....**CLC 7**
See also Radvanyi, Netty
See also DLB 69

Seidel, Frederick (Lewis) 1936- ....**CLC 18**
See also CA 13-16R; CANR 8; DLBY 84

Seifert, Jaroslav 1901-1986 .. **CLC 34, 44, 93**
See also CA 127; MTCW

Sei Shonagon c. 966-1017(?) ....**CMLC 6**

Selby, Hubert, Jr. 1928-**CLC 1, 2, 4, 8; SSC 20**
See also CA 13-16R; CANR 33; DLB 2

Selzer, Richard 1928- ....**CLC 74**
See also CA 65-68; CANR 14

Sembene, Ousmane
See Ousmane, Sembene

Senancour, Etienne Pivert de 1770-1846 **NCLC 16**
See also DLB 119

Sender, Ramon (Jose) 1902-1982**CLC 8; DAM MULT; HLC**
See also CA 5-8R; 105; CANR 8; HW; MTCW

Seneca, Lucius Annaeus 4B.C.-65 **CMLC 6; DAM DRAM; DC 5**

Senghor, Leopold Sedar 1906-**CLC 54; BLC; DAM MULT, POET**
    See also BW 2; CA 116; 125; CANR 47; MTCW
Serling, (Edward) Rod(man) 1924-1975 **C L C 30**
    See also AAYA 14; AITN 1; CA 162; 57-60; DLB 26
Serna, Ramon Gomez de la
    See Gomez de la Serna, Ramon
Serpieres
    See Guillevic, (Eugene)
Service, Robert
    See Service, Robert W(illiam)
    See also DAB; DLB 92
Service, Robert W(illiam) 1874(?)-1958 **TCLC 15; DA; DAC; DAM MST, POET; WLC**
    See also Service, Robert
    See also CA 115; 140; SATA 20
Seth, Vikram 1952-**CLC 43, 90; DAM MULT**
    See also CA 121; 127; CANR 50; DLB 120; INT 127
Seton, Cynthia Propper 1926-1982 . **CLC 27**
    See also CA 5-8R; 108; CANR 7
Seton, Ernest (Evan) Thompson 1860-1946 **TCLC 31**
    See also CA 109; DLB 92; DLBD 13; JRDA; SATA 18
Seton-Thompson, Ernest
    See Seton, Ernest (Evan) Thompson
Settle, Mary Lee 1918- .... **CLC 19, 61**
    See also CA 89-92; CAAS 1; CANR 44; DLB 6; INT 89-92
Seuphor, Michel
    See Arp, Jean
Sevigne, Marie (de Rabutin-Chantal) Marquise de 1626-1696 .... **LC 11**
Sewall, Samuel 1652-1730 .... **LC 38**
    See also DLB 24
Sexton, Anne (Harvey) 1928-1974**CLC 2, 4, 6, 8, 10, 15, 53; DA; DAB; DAC; DAM MST, POET; PC 2; WLC**
    See also CA 1-4R; 53-56; CABS 2; CANR 3, 36; CDALB 1941-1968; DLB 5, 169; MTCW; SATA 10
Shaara, Michael (Joseph, Jr.) 1929-1988**C L C 15; DAM POP**
    See also AITN 1; CA 102; 125; CANR 52; DLBY 83
Shackleton, C. C.
    See Aldiss, Brian W(ilson)
Shacochis, Bob .... **CLC 39**
    See also Shacochis, Robert G.
Shacochis, Robert G. 1951-
    See Shacochis, Bob
    See also CA 119; 124; INT 124
Shaffer, Anthony (Joshua) 1926- .... **CLC 19; DAM DRAM**
    See also CA 110; 116; DLB 13
Shaffer, Peter (Levin) 1926-**CLC 5, 14, 18, 37, 60; DAB; DAM DRAM, MST; DC 7**
    See also CA 25-28R; CANR 25, 47; CDBLB 1960 to Present; DLB 13; MTCW
Shakey, Bernard
    See Young, Neil
Shalamov, Varlam (Tikhonovich) 1907(?)-1982 **CLC 18**
    See also CA 129; 105
Shamlu, Ahmad 1925-....................... **CLC 10**
Shammas, Anton 1951- .... **CLC 55**
Shange, Ntozake 1948-**CLC 8, 25, 38, 74; BLC; DAM DRAM, MULT; DC 3**
    See also AAYA 9; BW 2; CA 85-88; CABS 3; CANR 27, 48; DLB 38; MTCW

Shanley, John Patrick 1950- .... **CLC 75**
    See also CA 128; 133
Shapcott, Thomas W(illiam) 1935- ... **CLC 38**
    See also CA 69-72; CANR 49
Shapiro, Jane .... **CLC 76**
Shapiro, Karl (Jay) 1913-... **CLC 4, 8, 15, 53**
    See also CA 1-4R; CAAS 6; CANR 1, 36, 66; DLB 48; MTCW
Sharp, William 1855-1905 .... **TCLC 39**
    See also CA 160; DLB 156
Sharpe, Thomas Ridley 1928-
    See Sharpe, Tom
    See also CA 114; 122; INT 122
Sharpe, Tom .... **CLC 36**
    See also Sharpe, Thomas Ridley
    See also DLB 14
Shaw, Bernard .... **TCLC 45**
    See also Shaw, George Bernard
    See also BW 1
Shaw, G. Bernard
    See Shaw, George Bernard
Shaw, George Bernard 1856-1950**TCLC 3, 9, 21; DA; DAB; DAC; DAM DRAM, MST; WLC**
    See also Shaw, Bernard
    See also CA 104; 128; CDBLB 1914-1945; DLB 10, 57, 190; MTCW
Shaw, Henry Wheeler 1818-1885 ..**NCLC 15**
    See also DLB 11
Shaw, Irwin 1913-1984 **CLC 7, 23, 34; DAM DRAM, POP**
    See also AITN 1; CA 13-16R; 112; CANR 21; CDALB 1941-1968; DLB 6, 102; DLBY 84; MTCW
Shaw, Robert 1927-1978 .... **CLC 5**
    See also AITN 1; CA 1-4R; 81-84; CANR 4; DLB 13, 14
Shaw, T. E.
    See Lawrence, T(homas) E(dward)
Shawn, Wallace 1943- .... **CLC 41**
    See also CA 112
Shea, Lisa 1953-................................. **CLC 86**
    See also CA 147
Sheed, Wilfrid (John Joseph) 1930-**CLC 2, 4, 10, 53**
    See also CA 65-68; CANR 30, 66; DLB 6; MTCW
Sheldon, Alice Hastings Bradley 1915(?)-1987
    See Tiptree, James, Jr.
    See also CA 108; 122; CANR 34; INT 108; MTCW
Sheldon, John
    See Bloch, Robert (Albert)
Shelley, Mary Wollstonecraft (Godwin) 1797-1851**NCLC 14, 59; DA; DAB; DAC; DAM MST, NOV; WLC**
    See also AAYA 20; CDBLB 1789-1832; DLB 110, 116, 159, 178; SATA 29
Shelley, Percy Bysshe 1792-1822 . **NCLC 18; DA; DAB; DAC; DAM MST, POET; PC 14; WLC**
    See also CDBLB 1789-1832; DLB 96, 110, 158
Shepard, Jim 1956- .... **CLC 36**
    See also CA 137; CANR 59; SATA 90
Shepard, Lucius 1947- .... **CLC 34**
    See also CA 128; 141
Shepard, Sam 1943-**CLC 4, 6, 17, 34, 41, 44; DAM DRAM; DC 5**
    See also AAYA 1; CA 69-72; CABS 3; CANR 22; DLB 7; MTCW
Shepherd, Michael
    See Ludlum, Robert
Sherburne, Zoa (Morin) 1912- .... **CLC 30**

    See also AAYA 13; CA 1-4R; CANR 3, 37; MAICYA; SAAS 18; SATA 3
Sheridan, Frances 1724-1766 .... **LC 7**
    See also DLB 39, 84
Sheridan, Richard Brinsley 1751-1816**NCLC 5; DA; DAB; DAC; DAM DRAM, MST; DC 1; WLC**
    See also CDBLB 1660-1789; DLB 89
Sherman, Jonathan Marc .... **CLC 55**
Sherman, Martin 1941(?)- .... **CLC 19**
    See also CA 116; 123
Sherwin, Judith Johnson 1936- ... **CLC 7, 15**
    See also CA 25-28R; CANR 34
Sherwood, Frances 1940- .... **CLC 81**
    See also CA 146
Sherwood, Robert E(mmet) 1896-1955**T C L C 3; DAM DRAM**
    See also CA 104; 153; DLB 7, 26
Shestov, Lev 1866-1938 .... **TCLC 56**
Shevchenko, Taras 1814-1861 .... **NCLC 54**
Shiel, M(atthew) P(hipps) 1865-1947**TCLC 8**
    See also Holmes, Gordon
    See also CA 106; 160; DLB 153
Shields, Carol 1935-................ **CLC 91; DAC**
    See also CA 81-84; CANR 51
Shields, David 1956- .... **CLC 97**
    See also CA 124; CANR 48
Shiga, Naoya 1883-1971 ..... **CLC 33; SSC 23**
    See also CA 101; 33-36R; DLB 180
Shilts, Randy 1951-1994 .... **CLC 85**
    See also AAYA 19; CA 115; 127; 144; CANR 45; INT 127
Shimazaki, Haruki 1872-1943
    See Shimazaki Toson
    See also CA 105; 134
Shimazaki Toson 1872-1943 .... **TCLC 5**
    See also Shimazaki, Haruki
    See also DLB 180
Sholokhov, Mikhail (Aleksandrovich) 1905-1984 .... **CLC 7, 15**
    See also CA 101; 112; MTCW; SATA-Obit 36
Shone, Patric
    See Hanley, James
Shreve, Susan Richards 1939- .... **CLC 23**
    See also CA 49-52; CAAS 5; CANR 5, 38; MAICYA; SATA 46, 95; SATA-Brief 41
Shue, Larry 1946-1985**CLC 52; DAM DRAM**
    See also CA 145; 117
Shu-Jen, Chou 1881-1936
    See Lu Hsun
    See also CA 104
Shulman, Alix Kates 1932- .... **CLC 2, 10**
    See also CA 29-32R; CANR 43; SATA 7
Shuster, Joe 1914- .... **CLC 21**
Shute, Nevil .... **CLC 30**
    See also Norway, Nevil Shute
Shuttle, Penelope (Diane) 1947-.......... **CLC 7**
    See also CA 93-96; CANR 39; DLB 14, 40
Sidney, Mary 1561-1621 .... **LC 19, 39**
Sidney, Sir Philip 1554-1586 **LC 19, 39; DA; DAB; DAC; DAM MST, POET**
    See also CDBLB Before 1660; DLB 167
Siegel, Jerome 1914-1996 .... **CLC 21**
    See also CA 116; 151
Siegel, Jerry
    See Siegel, Jerome
Sienkiewicz, Henryk (Adam Alexander Pius) 1846-1916 .... **TCLC 3**
    See also CA 104; 134
Sierra, Gregorio Martinez
    See Martinez Sierra, Gregorio
Sierra, Maria (de la O'LeJarraga) Martinez
    See Martinez Sierra, Maria (de la O'LeJarraga)

Sigal, Clancy 1926- ....**CLC 7**
See also CA 1-4R

Sigourney, Lydia Howard (Huntley) 1791-1865 **NCLC 21**
See also DLB 1, 42, 73

Siguenza y Gongora, Carlos de 1645-1700**L C 8**

Sigurjonsson, Johann 1880-1919 ... **TCLC 27**

Sikelianos, Angelos 1884-1951 .... **TCLC 39**

Silkin, Jon 1930- .... **CLC 2, 6, 43**
See also CA 5-8R; CAAS 5; DLB 27

Silko, Leslie (Marmon) 1948-**CLC 23, 74; DA; DAC; DAM MST, MULT, POP; WLCS**
See also AAYA 14; CA 115; 122; CANR 45, 65; DLB 143, 175; NNAL

Sillanpaa, Frans Eemil 1888-1964 ... **CLC 19**
See also CA 129; 93-96; MTCW

Sillitoe, Alan 1928- .... **CLC 1, 3, 6, 10, 19, 57**
See also AITN 1; CA 9-12R; CAAS 2; CANR 8, 26, 55; CDBLB 1960 to Present; DLB 14, 139; MTCW; SATA 61

Silone, Ignazio 1900-1978 .... **CLC 4**
See also CA 25-28; 81-84; CANR 34; CAP 2; MTCW

Silver, Joan Micklin 1935- .... **CLC 20**
See also CA 114; 121; INT 121

Silver, Nicholas
See Faust, Frederick (Schiller)

Silverberg, Robert 1935- **CLC 7; DAM POP**
See also AAYA 24; CA 1-4R; CAAS 3; CANR 1, 20, 36; DLB 8; INT CANR-20; MAICYA; MTCW; SATA 13, 91

Silverstein, Alvin 1933- .... **CLC 17**
See also CA 49-52; CANR 2; CLR 25; JRDA; MAICYA; SATA 8, 69

Silverstein, Virginia B(arbara Opshelor) 1937- **CLC 17**
See also CA 49-52; CANR 2; CLR 25; JRDA; MAICYA; SATA 8, 69

Sim, Georges
See Simenon, Georges (Jacques Christian)

Simak, Clifford D(onald) 1904-1988**CLC 1, 55**
See also CA 1-4R; 125; CANR 1, 35; DLB 8; MTCW; SATA-Obit 56

Simenon, Georges (Jacques Christian) 1903-1989 .. **CLC 1, 2, 3, 8, 18, 47; DAM POP**
See also CA 85-88; 129; CANR 35; DLB 72; DLBY 89; MTCW

Simic, Charles 1938- ....**CLC 6, 9, 22, 49, 68; DAM POET**
See also CA 29-32R; CAAS 4; CANR 12, 33, 52, 61; DLB 105

Simmel, Georg 1858-1918 .... **TCLC 64**
See also CA 157

Simmons, Charles (Paul) 1924- .... **CLC 57**
See also CA 89-92; INT 89-92

Simmons, Dan 1948- ...... **CLC 44; DAM POP**
See also AAYA 16; CA 138; CANR 53

Simmons, James (Stewart Alexander) 1933- **CLC 43**
See also CA 105; CAAS 21; DLB 40

Simms, William Gilmore 1806-1870 **NCLC 3**
See also DLB 3, 30, 59, 73

Simon, Carly 1945- .... **CLC 26**
See also CA 105

Simon, Claude 1913-1984 ..**CLC 4, 9, 15, 39; DAM NOV**
See also CA 89-92; CANR 33; DLB 83; MTCW

Simon, (Marvin) Neil 1927-**CLC 6, 11, 31, 39, 70; DAM DRAM**
See also AITN 1; CA 21-24R; CANR 26, 54; DLB 7; MTCW

Simon, Paul (Frederick) 1941(?)- ..... **CLC 17**

See also CA 116; 153

Simonon, Paul 1956(?)- .... **CLC 30**

Simpson, Harriette
See Arnow, Harriette (Louisa) Simpson

Simpson, Louis (Aston Marantz) 1923-**CLC 4, 7, 9, 32; DAM POET**
See also CA 1-4R; CAAS 4; CANR 1, 61; DLB 5; MTCW

Simpson, Mona (Elizabeth) 1957- ....**CLC 44**
See also CA 122; 135; CANR 68

Simpson, N(orman) F(rederick) 1919-**CLC 29**
See also CA 13-16R; DLB 13

Sinclair, Andrew (Annandale) 1935- .**CLC 2, 14**
See also CA 9-12k; CAAS 5; CANR 14, 38; DLB 14; MTCW

Sinclair, Emil
See Hesse, Hermann

Sinclair, Iain 1943- ....**CLC 76**
See also CA 132

Sinclair, Iain MacGregor
See Sinclair, Iain

Sinclair, Irene
See Griffith, D(avid Lewelyn) W(ark)

Sinclair, Mary Amelia St. Clair 1865(?)-1946
See Sinclair, May
See also CA 104

Sinclair, May .... **TCLC 3, 11**
See also Sinclair, Mary Amelia St. Clair
See also DLB 36, 135

Sinclair, Roy
See Griffith, D(avid Lewelyn) W(ark)

Sinclair, Upton (Beall) 1878-1968 **CLC 1, 11, 15, 63; DA; DAB; DAC; DAM MST, NOV; WLC**
See also CA 5-8R; 25-28R; CANR 7; CDALB 1929-1941; DLB 9; INT CANR-7; MTCW; SATA 9

Singer, Isaac
See Singer, Isaac Bashevis

Singer, Isaac Bashevis 1904-1991**CLC 1, 3, 6, 9, 11, 15, 23, 38, 69; DA; DAB; DAC; DAM MST, NOV; SSC 3; WLC**
See also CA 1-4R; 134; CANR 1, 39; CDALB 1941-1968; CLR 1; DLB 6, 28, 52; DLBY 91; JRDA; MAICYA; MTCW; SATA 3, 27; SATA-Obit 68

Singer, Israel Joshua 1893-1944 .... **TCLC 33**

Singh, Khushwant 1915- .... **CLC 11**
See also CA 9-12R; CAAS 9; CANR 6

Singleton, Ann
See Benedict, Ruth (Fulton)

Sinjohn, John
See Galsworthy, John

Sinyavsky, Andrei (Donatevich) 1925-1997 **CLC 8**
See also CA 85-88; 159

Sirin, V.
See Nabokov, Vladimir (Vladimirovich)

Sissman, L(ouis) E(dward) 1928-1976**CLC 9, 18**
See also CA 21-24R; 65-68; CANR 13; DLB 5

Sisson, C(harles) H(ubert) 1914- .... **CLC 8**
See also CA 1-4R; CAAS 3; CANR 3, 48; DLB 27

Sitwell, Dame Edith 1887-1964 **CLC 2, 9, 67; DAM POET; PC 3**
See also CA 9-12R; CANR 35; CDBLB 1945-1960; DLB 20; MTCW

Siwaarmill, H. P.
See Sharp, William

Sjoewall, Maj 1935- .... **CLC 7**
See also CA 65-68

Sjowall, Maj
See Sjoewall, Maj

Skelton, Robin 1925-1997 .... **CLC 13**
See also AITN 2; CA 5-8R; 160; CAAS 5; CANR 28; DLB 27, 53

Skolimowski, Jerzy 1938- .... **CLC 20**
See also CA 128

Skram, Amalie (Bertha) 1847-1905 **TCLC 25**
See also CA 165

Skvorecky, Josef (Vaclav) 1924- **CLC 15, 39, 69; DAC; DAM NOV**
See also CA 61-64; CAAS 1; CANR 10, 34, 63; MTCW

Slade, Bernard .... **CLC 11, 46**
See also Newbound, Bernard Slade
See also CAAS 9; DLB 53

Slaughter, Carolyn 1946- .... **CLC 56**
See also CA 85-88

Slaughter, Frank G(ill) 1908- .... **CLC 29**
See also AITN 2; CA 5-8R; CANR 5; INT CANR-5

Slavitt, David R(ytman) 1935- ..... **CLC 5, 14**
See also CA 21-24R; CAAS 3; CANR 41; DLB 5, 6

Slesinger, Tess 1905-1945 .... **TCLC 10**
See also CA 107; DLB 102

Slessor, Kenneth 1901-1971 .... **CLC 14**
See also CA 102; 89-92

Slowacki, Juliusz 1809-1849 .... **NCLC 15**

Smart, Christopher 1722-1771 ..**LC 3; DAM POET; PC 13**
See also DLB 109

Smart, Elizabeth 1913-1986 .... **CLC 54**
See also CA 81-84; 118; DLB 88

Smiley, Jane (Graves) 1949-**CLC 53, 76; DAM POP**
See also CA 104; CANR 30, 50; INT CANR-30

Smith, A(rthur) J(ames) M(arshall) 1902-1980 **CLC 15; DAC**
See also CA 1-4R; 102; CANR 4; DLB 88

Smith, Adam 1723-1790 .... **LC 36**
See also DLB 104

Smith, Alexander 1829-1867 .... **NCLC 59**
See also DLB 32, 55

Smith, Anna Deavere 1950- .... **CLC 86**
See also CA 133

Smith, Betty (Wehner) 1896-1972 ..... **CLC 19**
See also CA 5-8R; 33-36R; DLBY 82; SATA 6

Smith, Charlotte (Turner) 1749-1806 **N C L C 23**
See also DLB 39, 109

Smith, Clark Ashton 1893-1961 .... **CLC 43**
See also CA 143

Smith, Dave .... **CLC 22, 42**
See also Smith, David (Jeddie)
See also CAAS 7; DLB 5

Smith, David (Jeddie) 1942-
See Smith, Dave
See also CA 49-52; CANR 1, 59; DAM POET

Smith, Florence Margaret 1902-1971
See Smith, Stevie
See also CA 17-18; 29-32R; CANR 35; CAP 2; DAM POET; MTCW

Smith, Iain Crichton 1928- .... **CLC 64**
See also CA 21-24R; DLB 40, 139

Smith, John 1580(?)-1631 .... **LC 9**

Smith, Johnston
See Crane, Stephen (Townley)

Smith, Joseph, Jr. 1805-1844 .... **NCLC 53**

Smith, Lee 1944- .... **CLC 25, 73**
See also CA 114; 119; CANR 46; DLB 143; DLBY 83; INT 119

Smith, Martin
See Smith, Martin Cruz
Smith, Martin Cruz 1942- ..... **CLC 25; DAM MULT, POP**
See also BEST 89:4; CA 85-88; CANR 6, 23, 43, 65; INT CANR-23; NNAL
Smith, Mary-Ann Tirone 1944- .... **CLC 39**
See also CA 118; 136
Smith, Patti 1946- .... **CLC 12**
See also CA 93-96; CANR 63
Smith, Pauline (Urmson) 1882-1959 **TCLC 25**
Smith, Rosamond
See Oates, Joyce Carol
Smith, Sheila Kaye
See Kaye-Smith, Sheila
Smith, Stevie .... **CLC 3, 8, 25, 44; PC 12**
See also Smith, Florence Margaret
See also DLB 20
Smith, Wilbur (Addison) 1933-........ **CLC 33**
See also CA 13-16R; CANR 7, 46, 66; MTCW
Smith, William Jay 1918- .... **CLC 6**
See also CA 5-8R; CANR 44; DLB 5; MAICYA; SAAS 22; SATA 2, 68
Smith, Woodrow Wilson
See Kuttner, Henry
Smolenskin, Peretz 1842-1885 .... **NCLC 30**
Smollett, Tobias (George) 1721-1771 ... **LC 2**
See also CDBLB 1660-1789; DLB 39, 104
Snodgrass, W(illiam) D(e Witt) 1926-**CLC 2, 6, 10, 18, 68; DAM POET**
See also CA 1-4R; CANR 6, 36, 65; DLB 5; MTCW
Snow, C(harles) P(ercy) 1905-1980 **CLC 1, 4, 6, 9, 13, 19; DAM NOV**
See also CA 5-8R; 101; CANR 28; CDBLB 1945-1960; DLB 15, 77; MTCW
Snow, Frances Compton
See Adams, Henry (Brooks)
Snyder, Gary (Sherman) 1930-**CLC 1, 2, 5, 9, 32; DAM POET; PC 21**
See also CA 17-20R; CANR 30, 60; DLB 5, 16, 165
Snyder, Zilpha Keatley 1927-........... **CLC 17**
See also AAYA 15; CA 9-12R; CANR 38; CLR 31; JRDA; MAICYA; SAAS 2; SATA 1, 28, 75
Soares, Bernardo
See Pessoa, Fernando (Antonio Nogueira)
Sobh, A.
See Shamlu, Ahmad
Sobol, Joshua .... **CLC 60**
Soderberg, Hjalmar 1869-1941 ..... **TCLC 39**
Sodergran, Edith (Irene)
See Soedergran, Edith (Irene)
Soedergran, Edith (Irene) 1892-1923 . **T C L C 31**
Softly, Edgar
See Lovecraft, H(oward) P(hillips)
Softly, Edward
See Lovecraft, H(oward) P(hillips)
Sokolov, Raymond 1941- .... **CLC 7**
See also CA 85-88
Solo, Jay
See Ellison, Harlan (Jay)
Sologub, Fyodor .... **TCLC 9**
See also Teternikov, Fyodor Kuzmich
Solomons, Ikey Esquir
See Thackeray, William Makepeace
Solomos, Dionysios 1798-1857 .... **NCLC 15**
Solwoska, Mara
See French, Marilyn
Solzhenitsyn, Aleksandr I(sayevich) 1918-
CLC 1, 2, 4, 7, 9, 10, 18, 26, 34, 78; DA;

DAB; DAC; DAM MST, NOV; WLC
See also AITN 1; CA 69-72; CANR 40, 65; MTCW
Somers, Jane
See Lessing, Doris (May)
Somerville, Edith 1858-1949 .... **TCLC 51**
See also DLB 135
Somerville & Ross
See Martin, Violet Florence; Somerville, Edith
Sommer, Scott 1951-........................... **CLC 25**
See also CA 106
Sondheim, Stephen (Joshua) 1930-. **CLC 30, 39; DAM DRAM**
See also AAYA 11; CA 103; CANR 47, 68
Song, Cathy 1955- .... **PC 21**
See also CA 154; DLB 169
Sontag, Susan 1933-**CLC 1, 2, 10, 13, 31, 105; DAM POP**
See also CA 17-20R; CANR 25/ 51; DLB 2, 67; MTCW
Sophocles 496(?)B.C.-406(?)B.C. .. **CMLC 2; DA; DAB; DAC; DAM DRAM, MST; DC 1; WLCS**
See also DLB 176
Sordello 1189-1269 .... **CMLC 15**
Sorel, Julia
See Drexler, Rosalyn
Sorrentino, Gilbert 1929-**CLC 3, 7, 14, 22, 40**
See also CA 77-80; CANR 14, 33; DLB 5, 173; DLBY 80; INT CANR-14
Soto, Gary 1952-. **CLC 32, 80; DAM MULT; HLC**
See also AAYA 10; CA 119; 125; CANR 50; CLR 38; DLB 82; HW; INT 125; JRDA; SATA 80
Soupault, Philippe 1897-1990 .... **CLC 68**
See also CA 116; 147; 131
Souster, (Holmes) Raymond 1921-**CLC 5, 14; DAC; DAM POET**
See also CA 13-16R; CAAS 14; CANR 13, 29, 53; DLB 88; SATA 63
Southern, Terry 1924(?)-1995 .... **CLC 7**
See also CA 1-4R; 150; CANR 1, 55; DLB 2
Southey, Robert 1774-1843 .... **NCLC 8**
See also DLB 93, 107, 142; SATA 54
Southworth, Emma Dorothy Eliza Nevitte
1819-1899 .... **NCLC 26**
Souza, Ernest
See Scott, Evelyn
Soyinka, Wole 1934-**CLC 3, 5, 14, 36, 44; BLC; DA; DAB; DAC; DAM DRAM, MST, MULT; DC 2; WLC**
See also BW 2; CA 13-16R; CANR 27, 39; DLB 125; MTCW
Spackman, W(illiam) M(ode) 1905-1990 **C L C 46**
See also CA 81-84; 132
Spacks, Barry (Bernard) 1931-......... **CLC 14**
See also CA 154; CANR 33; DLB 105
Spanidou, Irini 1946- .... **CLC 44**
Spark, Muriel (Sarah) 1918-**CLC 2, 3, 5, 8, 13, 18, 40, 94; DAB; DAC; DAM MST, NOV; SSC 10**
See also CA 5-8R; CANR 12, 36; CDBLB 1945-1960; DLB 15, 139; INT CANR-12; MTCW
Spaulding, Douglas
See Bradbury, Ray (Douglas)
Spaulding, Leonard
See Bradbury, Ray (Douglas)
Spence, J. A. D.
See Eliot, T(homas) S(tearns)
Spencer, Elizabeth 1921- .... **CLC 22**
See also CA 13-16R; CANR 32, 65; DLB 6;

MTCW; SATA 14
Spencer, Leonard G.
See Silverberg, Robert
Spencer, Scott 1945- .... **CLC 30**
See also CA 113; CANR 51; DLBY 86
Spender, Stephen (Harold) 1909-1995**CLC 1, 2, 5, 10, 41, 91; DAM POET**
See also CA 9-12R; 149; CANR 31, 54; CDBLB 1945-1960; DLB 20; MTCW
Spengler, Oswald (Arnold Gottfried) 1880-1936
TCLC 25
See also CA 118
Spenser, Edmund 1552(?)-1599**LC 5, 39; DA; DAB; DAC; DAM MST, POET; PC 8; WLC**
See also CDBLB Before 1660; DLB 167
Spicer, Jack 1925-1965 **CLC 8, 18, 72; DAM POET**
See also CA 85-88; DLB 5, 16, 193
Spiegelman, Art 1948- .... **CLC 76**
See also AAYA 10; CA 125; CANR 41, 55
Spielberg, Peter 1929-......................... **CLC 6**
See also CA 5-8R; CANR 4, 48; DLBY 81
Spielberg, Steven 1947-..................... **CLC 20**
See also AAYA 8, 24; CA 77-80; CANR 32; SATA 32
Spillane, Frank Morrison 1918-
See Spillane, Mickey
See also CA 25-28R; CANR 28, 63; MTCW; SATA 66
Spillane, Mickey .... **CLC 3, 13**
See also Spillane, Frank Morrison
Spinoza, Benedictus de 1632-1677 .... **LC 9**
Spinrad, Norman (Richard) 1940- .. **CLC 46**
See also CA 37-40R; CAAS 19; CANR 20; DLB 8; INT CANR-20
Spitteler, Carl (Friedrich Georg) 1845-1924
TCLC 12
See also CA 109; DLB 129
Spivack, Kathleen (Romola Drucker) 1938-
CLC 6
See also CA 49-52
Spoto, Donald 1941- .... **CLC 39**
See also CA 65-68; CANR 11, 57
Springsteen, Bruce (F.) 1949- .... **CLC 17**
See also CA 111
Spurling, Hilary 1940- .... **CLC 34**
See also CA 104; CANR 25, 52
Spyker, John Howland
See Elman, Richard (Martin)
Squires, (James) Radcliffe 1917-1993**CLC 51**
See also CA 1-4R; 140; CANR 6, 21
Srivastava, Dhanpat Rai 1880(?)-1936
See Premchand
See also CA 118
Stacy, Donald
See Pohl, Frederik
Stael, Germaine de 1766-1817
See Stael-Holstein, Anne Louise Germaine Necker Baronn
See also DLB 119
Stael-Holstein, Anne Louise Germaine Necker Baronn 1766-1817 .... **NCLC 3**
See also Stael, Germaine de
See also DLB 192
Stafford, Jean 1915-1979**CLC 4, 7, 19, 68; SSC 26**
See also CA 1-4R; 85-88; CANR 3, 65; DLB 2, 173; MTCW; SATA-Obit 22
Stafford, William (Edgar) 1914-1993 **CLC 4, 7, 29; DAM POET**
See also CA 5-8R; 142; CAAS 3; CANR 5, 22; DLB 5; INT CANR-22

Stagnelius, Eric Johan 1793-1823 .**NCLC 61**
Staines, Trevor
    See Brunner, John (Kilian Houston)
Stairs, Gordon
    See Austin, Mary (Hunter)
Stannard, Martin 1947- .... **CLC 44**
    See also CA 142; DLB 155
Stanton, Elizabeth Cady 1815-1902**TCLC 73**
    See also DLB 79
Stanton, Maura 1946- ....**CLC 9**
    See also CA 89-92; CANR 15; DLB 120
Stanton, Schuyler
    See Baum, L(yman) Frank
Stapledon, (William) Olaf 1886-1950 . **T C L C
    22**
    See also CA 111; 162; DLB 15
Starbuck, George (Edwin) 1931-1996**CLC 53;
    DAM POET**
    See also CA 21-24R; 153; CANR 23
Stark, Richard
    See Westlake, Donald E(dwin)
Staunton, Schuyler
    See Baum, L(yman) Frank
Stead, Christina (Ellen) 1902-1983 **CLC 2, 5,
    8, 32, 80**
    See also CA 13-16R; 109; CANR 33, 40;
    MTCW
Stead, William Thomas 1849-1912 **TCLC 48**
Steele, Richard 1672-1729 .... **LC 18**
    See also CDBLB 1660-1789; DLB 84, 101
Steele, Timothy (Reid) 1948- .... **CLC 45**
    See also CA 93-96; CANR 16, 50; DLB 120
Steffens, (Joseph) Lincoln 1866-1936. **T C L C
    20**
    See also CA 117
Stegner, Wallace (Earle) 1909-1993**CLC 9, 49,
    81; DAM NOV; SSC 27**
    See also AITN 1; BEST 90:3; CA 1-4R; 141;
    CAAS 9; CANR 1, 21, 46; DLB 9; DLBY
    93; MTCW
Stein, Gertrude 1874-1946**TCLC 1, 6, 28, 48;
    DA; DAB; DAC; DAM MST, NOV, POET;
    PC 18; WLC**
    See also CA 104; 132; CDALB 1917-1929;
    DLB 4, 54, 86; DLBD 15; MTCW
Steinbeck, John (Ernst) 1902-1968 **CLC 1, 5,
    9, 13, 21, 34, 45, 75; DA; DAB; DAC; DAM
    DRAM, MST, NOV; SSC 11; WLC**
    See also AAYA 12; CA 1-4R; 25-28R; CANR
    1, 35; CDALB 1929-1941; DLB 7, 9; DLBD
    2; MTCW; SATA 9
Steinem, Gloria 1934- .... **CLC 63**
    See also CA 53-56; CANR 28, 51; MTCW
Steiner, George 1929- ... **CLC 24; DAM NOV**
    See also CA 73-76; CANR 31, 67; DLB 67;
    MTCW; SATA 62
Steiner, K. Leslie
    See Delany, Samuel R(ay, Jr.)
Steiner, Rudolf 1861-1925 .... **TCLC 13**
    See also CA 107
Stendhal 1783-1842**NCLC 23, 46; DA; DAB;
    DAC; DAM MST, NOV; SSC 27; WLC**
    See also DLB 119
Stephen, Adeline Virginia
    See Woolf, (Adeline) Virginia
Stephen, SirLeslie 1832-1904 .... **TCLC 23**
    See also CA 123; DLB 57, 144, 190
Stephen, Sir Leslie
    See Stephen, SirLeslie
Stephen, Virginia
    See Woolf, (Adeline) Virginia
Stephens, James 1882(?)-1950 .... **TCLC 4**
    See also CA 104; DLB 19, 153, 162

Stephens, Reed
    See Donaldson, Stephen R.
Steptoe, Lydia
    See Barnes, Djuna
Sterchi, Beat 1949- ....**CLC 65**
Sterling, Brett
    See Bradbury, Ray (Douglas); Hamilton,
    Edmond
Sterling, Bruce 1954- ....**CLC 72**
    See also CA 119; CANR 44
Sterling, George 1869-1926 .... **TCLC 20**
    See also CA 117; 165; DLB 54
Stern, Gerald 1925- .... **CLC 40, 100**
    See also CA 81-84; CANR 28; DLB 105
Stern, Richard (Gustave) 1928- ... **CLC 4, 39**
    See also CA 1-4R; CANR 1, 25, 52; DLBY 87;
    INT CANR-25
Sternberg, Josef von 1894-1969 ....**CLC 20**
    See also CA 81-84
Sterne, Laurence 1713-1768**LC 2; DA; DAB;
    DAC; DAM MST, NOV; WLC**
    See also CDBLB 1660-1789; DLB 39
Sternheim, (William Adolf) Carl 1878-1942
    TCLC 8
    See also CA 105; DLB 56, 118
Stevens, Mark 1951- ....**CLC 34**
    See also CA 122
Stevens, Wallace 1879-1955 **TCLC 3, 12, 45;
    DA; DAB; DAC; DAM MST, POET; PC
    6; WLC**
    See also CA 104; 124; CDALB 1929-1941;
    DLB 54; MTCW
Stevenson, Anne (Katharine) 1933-**CLC 7, 33**
    See also CA 17-20R; CAAS 9; CANR 9, 33;
    DLB 40; MTCW
Stevenson, Robert Louis (Balfour) 1850-1894
    **NCLC 5, 14, 63; DA; DAB; DAC; DAM
    MST, NOV; SSC 11; WLC**
    See also AAYA 24; CDBLB 1890-1914; CLR
    10, 11; DLB 18, 57, 141, 156, 174; DLBD
    13; JRDA; MAICYA; YABC 2
Stewart, J(ohn) I(nnes) M(ackintosh) 1906-
    1994 .... **CLC 7, 14, 32**
    See also CA 85-88; 147; CAAS 3; CANR 47;
    MTCW
Stewart, Mary (Florence Elinor) 1916-**CLC 7,
    35; DAB**
    See also CA 1-4R; CANR 1, 59; SATA 12
Stewart, Mary Rainbow
    See Stewart, Mary (Florence Elinor)
Stifle, June
    See Campbell, Maria
Stifter, Adalbert 1805-1868**NCLC 41; SSC 28**
    See also DLB 133
Still, James 1906- ....**CLC 49**
    See also CA 65-68; CAAS 17; CANR 10, 26;
    DLB 9; SATA 29
Sting
    See Sumner, Gordon Matthew
Stirling, Arthur
    See Sinclair, Upton (Beall)
Stitt, Milan 1941- ....**CLC 29**
    See also CA 69-72
Stockton, Francis Richard 1834-1902
    See Stockton, Frank R.
    See also CA 108; 137; MAICYA; SATA 44
Stockton, Frank R. ....**TCLC 47**
    See also Stockton, Francis Richard
    See also DLB 42, 74; DLBD 13; SATA-Brief
    32
Stoddard, Charles
    See Kuttner, Henry
Stoker, Abraham 1847-1912

See Stoker, Bram
    See also CA 105; DA; DAC; DAM MST, NOV;
    SATA 29
Stoker, Bram 1847-1912**TCLC 8; DAB; WLC**
    See also Stoker, Abraham
    See also AAYA 23; CA 150; CDBLB 1890-
    1914; DLB 36, 70, 178
Stolz, Mary (Slattery) 1920- ....**CLC 12**
    See also AAYA 8; AITN 1; CA 5-8R; CANR
    13, 41; JRDA; MAICYA; SAAS 3; SATA 10,
    71
Stone, Irving 1903-1989 ..**CLC 7; DAM POP**
    See also AITN 1; CA 1-4R; 129; CAAS 3;
    CANR 1, 23; INT CANR-23; MTCW; SATA
    3; SATA-Obit 64
Stone, Oliver (William) 1946- ....**CLC 73**
    See also AAYA 15; CA 110; CANR 55
Stone, Robert (Anthony) 1937-**CLC 5, 23, 42**
    See also CA 85-88; CANR 23, 66; DLB 152;
    INT CANR-23; MTCW
Stone, Zachary
    See Follett, Ken(neth Martin)
Stoppard, Tom 1937-**CLC 1, 3, 4, 5, 8, 15, 29,
    34, 63, 91; DA; DAB; DAC; DAM DRAM,
    MST; DC 6; WLC**
    See also CA 81-84; CANR 39, 67; CDBLB
    1960 to Present; DLB 13; DLBY 85; MTCW
Storey, David (Malcolm) 1933-**CLC 2, 4, 5, 8;
    DAM DRAM**
    See also CA 81-84; CANR 36; DLB 13, 14;
    MTCW
Storm, Hyemeyohsts 1935- ...... **CLC 3; DAM
    MULT**
    See also CA 81-84; CANR 45; NNAL
Storm, (Hans) Theodor (Woldsen) 1817-1888
    NCLC 1; SSC 27
Storni, Alfonsina 1892-1938 . **TCLC 5; DAM
    MULT; HLC**
    See also CA 104; 131; HW
Stoughton, William 1631-1701 .... **LC 38**
    See also DLB 24
Stout, Rex (Todhunter) 1886-1975 .....**CLC 3**
    See also AITN 2; CA 61-64
Stow, (Julian) Randolph 1935- .. **CLC 23, 48**
    See also CA 13-16R; CANR 33; MTCW
Stowe, Harriet (Elizabeth) Beecher 1811-1896
    **NCLC 3, 50; DA; DAB; DAC; DAM MST,
    NOV; WLC**
    See also CDALB 1865-1917; DLB 1, 12, 42,
    74, 189; JRDA; MAICYA; YABC 1
Strachey, (Giles) Lytton 1880-1932 **TCLC 12**
    See also CA 110; DLB 149; DLBD 10
Strand, Mark 1934-**CLC 6, 18, 41, 71; DAM
    POET**
    See also CA 21-24R; CANR 40, 65; DLB 5;
    SATA 41
Straub, Peter (Francis) 1943-..**CLC 28, 107;
    DAM POP**
    See also BEST 89:1; CA 85-88; CANR 28, 65;
    DLBY 84; MTCW
Strauss, Botho 1944- ....**CLC 22**
    See also CA 157; DLB 124
Streatfeild, (Mary) Noel 1895(?)-1986**CLC 21**
    See also CA 81-84; 120; CANR 31; CLR 17;
    DLB 160; MAICYA; SATA 20; SATA-Obit
    48
Stribling, T(homas) S(igismund) 1881-1965
    CLC 23
    See also CA 107; DLB 9
Strindberg, (Johan) August 1849-1912**T C L C
    1, 8, 21, 47; DA; DAB; DAC; DAM DRAM,
    MST; WLC**
    See also CA 104; 135

Stringer, Arthur 1874-1950 .... **TCLC 37**
   See also CA 161; DLB 92
Stringer, David
   See Roberts, Keith (John Kingston)
Stroheim, Erich von 1885-1957 ..... **TCLC 71**
Strugatskii, Arkadii (Natanovich) 1925-1991
   CLC 27
   See also CA 106; 135
Strugatskii, Boris (Natanovich) 1933-**CLC 27**
   See also CA 106
Strummer, Joe 1953(?)- .... **CLC 30**
Stuart, Don A.
   See Campbell, John W(ood, Jr.)
Stuart, Ian
   See MacLean, Alistair (Stuart)
Stuart, Jesse (Hilton) 1906-1984**CLC 1, 8, 11,
   14, 34**
   See also CA 5-8R; 112; CANR 31; DLB 9, 48,
   102; DLBY 84; SATA 2; SATA-Obit 36
Sturgeon, Theodore (Hamilton) 1918-1985
   CLC 22, 39
   See also Queen, Ellery
   See also CA 81-84; 116; CANR 32; DLB 8;
   DLBY 85; MTCW
Sturges, Preston 1898-1959 .... **TCLC 48**
   See also CA 114; 149; DLB 26
Styron, William 1925-**CLC 1, 3, 5, 11, 15, 60;
   DAM NOV, POP; SSC 25**
   See also BEST 90:4; CA 5-8R; CANR 6, 33;
   CDALB 1968-1988; DLB 2, 143; DLBY 80;
   INT CANR-6; MTCW
Suarez Lynch, B.
   See Bioy Casares, Adolfo; Borges, Jorge Luis
Su Chien 1884-1918
   See Su Man-shu
   See also CA 123
Suckow, Ruth 1892-1960 .... **SSC 18**
   See also CA 113; DLB 9, 102
Sudermann, Hermann 1857-1928 .. **TCLC 15**
   See also CA 107; DLB 118
Sue, Eugene 1804-1857 .... **NCLC 1**
   See also DLB 119
Sueskind, Patrick 1949- .... **CLC 44**
   See also Suskind, Patrick
Sukenick, Ronald 1932- .... **CLC 3, 4, 6, 48**
   See also CA 25-28R; CAAS 8; CANR 32; DLB
   173; DLBY 81
Suknaski, Andrew 1942- .... **CLC 19**
   See also CA 101; DLB 53
Sullivan, Vernon
   See Vian, Boris
Sully Prudhomme 1839-1907 .... **TCLC 31**
Su Man-shu .... **TCLC 24**
   See also Su Chien
Summerforest, Ivy B.
   See Kirkup, James
Summers, Andrew James 1942- .... **CLC 26**
Summers, Andy
   See Summers, Andrew James
Summers, Hollis (Spurgeon, Jr.) 1916-**CLC 10**
   See also CA 5-8R; CANR 3; DLB 6
**Summers, (Alphonsus Joseph-Mary Augustus)
   Montague** 1880-1948 .... **TCLC 16**
   See also CA 118; 163
Sumner, Gordon Matthew 1951- ..... **CLC 26**
Surtees, Robert Smith 1803-1864 ..**NCLC 14**
   See also DLB 21
Susann, Jacqueline 1921-1974 .... **CLC 3**
   See also AITN 1; CA 65-68; 53-56; MTCW
Su Shih 1036-1101 .... **CMLC 15**
Suskind, Patrick
   See Sueskind, Patrick
   See also CA 145

Sutcliff, Rosemary 1920-1992**CLC 26; DAB;
   DAC; DAM MST, POP**
   See also AAYA 10; CA 5-8R; 139; CANR 37;
   CLR 1, 37; JRDA; MAICYA; SATA 6, 44,
   78; SATA-Obit 73
Sutro, Alfred 1863-1933 .... **TCLC 6**
   See also CA 105; DLB 10
Sutton, Henry
   See Slavitt, David R(ytman)
Svevo, Italo 1861-1928 . **TCLC 2, 35; SSC 25**
   See also Schmitz, Aron Hector
Swados, Elizabeth (A.) 1951- ....**CLC 12**
   See also CA 97-100; CANR 49; INT 97-100
Swados, Harvey 1920-1972 ....**CLC 5**
   See also CA 5-8R; 37-40R; CANR 6; DLB 2
Swan, Gladys 1934- ....**CLC 69**
   See also CA 101; CANR 17, 39
Swarthout, Glendon (Fred) 1918-1992**CLC 35**
   See also CA 1-4R; 139; CANR 1, 47; SATA 26
Sweet, Sarah C.
   See Jewett, (Theodora) Sarah Orne
Swenson, May 1919-1989**CLC 4, 14, 61, 106;
   DA; DAB; DAC; DAM MST, POET; PC
   14**
   See also CA 5-8R; 130; CANR 36, 61; DLB 5;
   MTCW; SATA 15
Swift, Augustus
   See Lovecraft, H(oward) P(hillips)
Swift, Graham (Colin) 1949- ...... **CLC 41, 88**
   See also CA 117; 122; CANR 46; DLB 194
Swift, Jonathan 1667-1745 **LC 1; DA; DAB;
   DAC; DAM MST, NOV, POET; PC 9;
   WLC**
   See also CDBLB 1660-1789; DLB 39, 95, 101;
   SATA 19
Swinburne, Algernon Charles 1837-1909
   **TCLC 8, 36; DA; DAB; DAC; DAM MST,
   POET; WLC**
   See also CA 105; 140; CDBLB 1832-1890;
   DLB 35, 57
Swinfen, Ann ....**CLC 34**
Swinnerton, Frank Arthur 1884-1982**CLC 31**
   See also CA 108; DLB 34
Swithen, John
   See King, Stephen (Edwin)
Sylvia
   See Ashton-Warner, Sylvia (Constance)
Symmes, Robert Edward
   See Duncan, Robert (Edward)
Symonds, John Addington 1840-1893 **N C L C
   34**
   See also DLB 57, 144
Symons, Arthur 1865-1945 .... **TCLC 11**
   See also CA 107; DLB 19, 57, 149
Symons, Julian (Gustave) 1912-1994 **CLC 2,
   14, 32**
   See also CA 49-52; 147; CAAS 3; CANR 3,
   33, 59; DLB 87, 155; DLBY 92; MTCW
Synge, (Edmund) J(ohn) M(illington) 1871-
   1909 .. **TCLC 6, 37; DAM DRAM; DC 2**
   See also CA 104; 141; CDBLB 1890-1914;
   DLB 10, 19
Syruc, J.
   See Milosz, Czeslaw
Szirtes, George 1948- ....**CLC 46**
   See also CA 109; CANR 27, 61
Szymborska, Wislawa 1923-..............**CLC 99**
   See also CA 154; DLBY 96
T. O., Nik
   See Annensky, Innokenty (Fyodorovich)
Tabori, George 1914- ....**CLC 19**
   See also CA 49-52; CANR 4
Tagore, Rabindranath 1861-1941**TCLC 3, 53;**

   DAM DRAM, POET; PC 8
   See also CA 104; 120; MTCW
Taine, Hippolyte Adolphe 1828-1893 . **N C L C
   15**
Talese, Gay 1932- .... **CLC 37**
   See also AITN 1; CA 1-4R; CANR 9, 58; DLB
   185; INT CANR-9; MTCW
Tallent, Elizabeth (Ann) 1954- .... **CLC 45**
   See also CA 117; DLB 130
Tally, Ted 1952-.................................. **CLC 42**
   See also CA 120; 124; INT 124
Tamayo y Baus, Manuel 1829-1898 . **NCLC 1**
Tammsaare, A(nton) H(ansen) 1878-1940
   TCLC 27
   See also CA 164
Tam'si, Tchicaya U
   See Tchicaya, Gerald Felix
Tan, Amy (Ruth) 1952-**CLC 59; DAM MULT,
   NOV, POP**
   See also AAYA 9; BEST 89:3; CA 136; CANR
   54; DLB 173; SATA 75
Tandem, Felix
   See Spitteler, Carl (Friedrich Georg)
Tanizaki, Jun'ichiro 1886-1965**CLC 8, 14, 28;
   SSC 21**
   See also CA 93-96; 25-28R; DLB 180
Tanner, William
   See Amis, Kingsley (William)
Tao Lao
   See Storni, Alfonsina
Tarassoff, Lev
   See Troyat, Henri
Tarbell, Ida M(inerva) 1857-1944 . **TCLC 40**
   See also CA 122; DLB 47
Tarkington, (Newton) Booth 1869-1946**TCLC
   9**
   See also CA 110; 143; DLB 9, 102; SATA 17
Tarkovsky, Andrei (Arsenyevich) 1932-1986
   CLC 75
   See also CA 127
Tartt, Donna 1964(?)- .... **CLC 76**
   See also CA 142
Tasso, Torquato 1544-1595 .... **LC 5**
Tate, (John Orley) Allen 1899-1979**CLC 2, 4,
   6, 9, 11, 14, 24**
   See also CA 5-8R; 85-88; CANR 32; DLB 4,
   45, 63; MTCW
Tate, Ellalice
   See Hibbert, Eleanor Alice Burford
Tate, James (Vincent) 1943- ..... **CLC 2, 6, 25**
   See also CA 21-24R; CANR 29, 57; DLB 5,
   169
Tavel, Ronald 1940- ....**CLC 6**
   See also CA 21-24R; CANR 33
Taylor, C(ecil) P(hilip) 1929-1981 .... **CLC 27**
   See also CA 25-28R; 105; CANR 47
Taylor, Edward 1642(?)-1729 ..... **LC 11; DA;
   DAB; DAC; DAM MST, POET**
   See also DLB 24
Taylor, Eleanor Ross 1920- ....**CLC 5**
   See also CA 81-84
Taylor, Elizabeth 1912-1975 ..... **CLC 2, 4, 29**
   See also CA 13-16R; CANR 9; DLB 139;
   MTCW; SATA 13
Taylor, Frederick Winslow 1856-1915 **T C L C
   76**
Taylor, Henry (Splawn) 1942- .... **CLC 44**
   See also CA 33-36R; CAAS 7; CANR 31; DLB
   5
Taylor, Kamala (Purnaiya) 1924-
   See Markandaya, Kamala
   See also CA 77-80
Taylor, Mildred D. .... **CLC 21**

See also AAYA 10; BW 1; CA 85-88; CANR
25; CLR 9; DLB 52; JRDA; MAICYA; SAAS
5; SATA 15, 70
Taylor, Peter (Hillsman) 1917-1994CLC **1, 4,
18, 37, 44, 50, 71; SSC 10**
See also CA 13-16R; 147; CANR 9, 50; DLBY
81, 94; INT CANR-9; MTCW
Taylor, Robert Lewis 1912- .... CLC **14**
See also CA 1-4R; CANR 3, 64; SATA 10
Tchekhov, Anton
See Chekhov, Anton (Pavlovich)
Tchicaya, Gerald Felix 1931-1988 . CLC **101**
See also CA 129; 125
Tchicaya U Tam'si
See Tchicaya, Gerald Felix
Teasdale, Sara 1884-1933 .... TCLC **4**
See also CA 104; 163; DLB 45; SATA 32
Tegner, Esaias 1782-1846 .... NCLC **2**
Teilhard de Chardin, (Marie Joseph) Pierre
1881-1955 .... TCLC **9**
See also CA 105
Temple, Ann
See Mortimer, Penelope (Ruth)
Tennant, Emma (Christina) 1937-CLC **13, 52**
See also CA 65-68; CAAS 9; CANR 10, 38,
59; DLB 14
Tenneshaw, S. M.
See Silverberg, Robert
Tennyson, Alfred 1809-1892 ... NCLC **30, 65;
DA; DAB; DAC; DAM MST, POET; PC
6; WLC**
See also CDBLB 1832-1890; DLB 32
Teran, Lisa St. Aubin de .... CLC **36**
See also St. Aubin de Teran, Lisa
Terence 195(?)B.C.-159B.C. CMLC **14; DC 7**
Teresa de Jesus, St. 1515-1582 .... LC **18**
Terkel, Louis 1912-
See Terkel, Studs
See also CA 57-60; CANR 18, 45, 67; MTCW
Terkel, Studs .... CLC **38**
See also Terkel, Louis
See also AITN 1
Terry, C. V.
See Slaughter, Frank G(ill)
Terry, Megan 1932- .... CLC **19**
See also CA 77-80; CABS 3; CANR 43; DLB 7
Tertz, Abram
See Sinyavsky, Andrei (Donatevich)
Tesich, Steve 1943(?)-1996 .... CLC **40, 69**
See also CA 105; 152; DLBY 83
Teternikov, Fyodor Kuzmich 1863-1927
See Sologub, Fyodor
See also CA 104
Tevis, Walter 1928-1984 .... CLC **42**
See also CA 113
Tey, Josephine .... TCLC **14**
See also Mackintosh, Elizabeth
See also DLB 77
Thackeray, William Makepeace 1811-1863
NCLC **5, 14, 22, 43; DA; DAB; DAC; DAM
MST, NOV; WLC**
See also CDBLB 1832-1890; DLB 21, 55, 159,
163; SATA 23
Thakura, Ravindranatha
See Tagore, Rabindranath
Tharoor, Shashi 1956- .... CLC **70**
See also CA 141
Thelwell, Michael Miles 1939- .... CLC **22**
See also BW 2; CA 101
Theobald, Lewis, Jr.
See Lovecraft, H(oward) P(hillips)
Theodorescu, Ion N. 1880-1967
See Arghezi, Tudor

See also CA 116
Theriault, Yves 1915-1983 .... CLC **79; DAC;
DAM MST**
See also CA 102; DLB 88
Theroux, Alexander (Louis) 1939- CLC **2, 25**
See also CA 85-88; CANR 20, 63
Theroux, Paul (Edward) 1941- CLC **5, 8, 11,
15, 28, 46; DAM POP**
See also BEST 89:4; CA 33-36R; CANR 20,
45; DLB 2; MTCW; SATA 44
Thesen, Sharon 1946- ....CLC **56**
See also CA 163
Thevenin, Denis
See Duhamel, Georges
Thibault, Jacques Anatole Francois 1844-1924
See France, Anatole
See also CA 106; 127; DAM NOV; MTCW
Thiele, Colin (Milton) 1920- ....CLC **17**
See also CA 29-32R; CANR 12, 28, 53; CLR
27; MAICYA; SAAS 2; SATA 14, 72
Thomas, Audrey (Callahan) 1935-CLC **7, 13,
37, 107; SSC 20**
See also AITN 2; CA 21-24R; CAAS 19; CANR
36, 58; DLB 60; MTCW
Thomas, D(onald) M(ichael) 1935-. CLC **13,
22, 31**
See also CA 61-64; CAAS 11; CANR 17, 45;
CDBLB 1960 to Present; DLB 40; INT
CANR-17; MTCW
Thomas, Dylan (Marlais) 1914-1953TCLC **1,
8, 45; DA; DAB; DAC; DAM DRAM,
MST, POET; PC 2; SSC 3; WLC**
See also CA 104; 120; CANR 65; CDBLB
1945-1960; DLB 13, 20, 139; MTCW; SATA
60
Thomas, (Philip) Edward 1878-1917 . TCLC
10; DAM POET
See also CA 106; 153; DLB 19
Thomas, Joyce Carol 1938- .... CLC **35**
See also AAYA 12; BW 2; CA 113; 116; CANR
48; CLR 19; DLB 33; INT 116; JRDA;
MAICYA; MTCW; SAAS 7; SATA 40, 78
Thomas, Lewis 1913-1993 .... CLC **35**
See also CA 85-88; 143; CANR 38, 60; MTCW
Thomas, Paul
See Mann, (Paul) Thomas
Thomas, Piri 1928- ....CLC **17**
See also CA 73-76; HW
Thomas, R(onald) S(tuart) 1913- CLC **6, 13,
48; DAB; DAM POET**
See also CA 89-92; CAAS 4; CANR 30;
CDBLB 1960 to Present; DLB 27; MTCW
Thomas, Ross (Elmore) 1926-1995 ...CLC **39**
See also CA 33-36R; 150; CANR 22, 63
Thompson, Francis Clegg
See Mencken, H(enry) L(ouis)
Thompson, Francis Joseph 1859-1907TCLC **4**
See also CA 104; CDBLB 1890-1914; DLB 19
Thompson, Hunter S(tockton) 1939- .CLC **9,
17, 40, 104; DAM POP**
See also BEST 89:1; CA 17-20R; CANR 23,
46; DLB 185; MTCW
Thompson, James Myers
See Thompson, Jim (Myers)
Thompson, Jim (Myers) 1906-1977(?)CLC **69**
See also CA 140
Thompson, Judith ....CLC **39**
Thomson, James 1700-1748 ... LC **16, 29, 40;
DAM POET**
See also DLB 95
Thomson, James 1834-1882 NCLC **18; DAM
POET**
See also DLB 35

Thoreau, Henry David 1817-1862NCLC **7, 21,
61; DA; DAB; DAC; DAM MST; WLC**
See also CDALB 1640-1865; DLB 1
Thornton, Hall
See Silverberg, Robert
Thucydides c. 455B.C.-399B.C. ..... CMLC **17**
See also DLB 176
Thurber, James (Grover) 1894-1961 .CLC **5,
11, 25; DA; DAB; DAC; DAM DRAM,
MST, NOV; SSC 1**
See also CA 73-76; CANR 17, 39; CDALB
1929-1941; DLB 4, 11, 22, 102; MAICYA;
MTCW; SATA 13
Thurman, Wallace (Henry) 1902-1934T C L C
6; BLC; DAM MULT
See also BW 1; CA 104; 124; DLB 51
Ticheburn, Cheviot
See Ainsworth, William Harrison
Tieck, (Johann) Ludwig 1773-1853 NCLC **5,
46**
See also DLB 90
Tiger, Derry
See Ellison, Harlan (Jay)
Tilghman, Christopher 1948(?)- ....CLC **65**
See also CA 159
Tillinghast, Richard (Williford) 1940-CLC **29**
See also CA 29-32R; CAAS 23; CANR 26, 51
Timrod, Henry 1828-1867 ....NCLC **25**
See also DLB 3
Tindall, Gillian (Elizabeth) 1938-.......CLC **7**
See also CA 21-24R; CANR 11, 65
Tiptree, James, Jr. .... CLC **48, 50**
See also Sheldon, Alice Hastings Bradley
See also DLB 8
Titmarsh, Michael Angelo
See Thackeray, William Makepeace
**Tocqueville, Alexis (Charles Henri Maurice
Clerel Comte)** 1805-1859 ...NCLC **7, 63**
Tolkien, J(ohn) R(onald) R(euel) 1892-1973
CLC **1, 2, 3, 8, 12, 38; DA; DAB; DAC;
DAM MST, NOV, POP; WLC**
See also AAYA 10; AITN 1; CA 17-18; 45-48;
CANR 36; CAP 2; CDBLB 1914-1945; DLB
15, 160; JRDA; MAICYA; MTCW; SATA 2,
32; SATA-Obit 24
Toller, Ernst 1893-1939 .... TCLC **10**
See also CA 107; DLB 124
Tolson, M. B.
See Tolson, Melvin B(eaunorus)
Tolson, Melvin B(eaunorus) 1898(?)-1966
CLC **36, 105; BLC; DAM MULT, POET**
See also BW 1; CA 124; 89-92; DLB 48, 76
Tolstoi, Aleksei Nikolaevich
See Tolstoy, Alexey Nikolaevich
Tolstoy, Alexey Nikolaevich 1882-1945T C L C
18
See also CA 107; 158
Tolstoy, Count Leo
See Tolstoy, Leo (Nikolaevich)
Tolstoy, Leo (Nikolaevich) 1828-1910TCLC **4,
11, 17, 28, 44, 79; DA; DAB; DAC; DAM
MST, NOV; SSC 9, 30; WLC**
See also CA 104; 123; SATA 26
Tomasi di Lampedusa, Giuseppe 1896-1957
See Lampedusa, Giuseppe (Tomasi) di
See also CA 111
Tomlin, Lily ....CLC **17**
See also Tomlin, Mary Jean
Tomlin, Mary Jean 1939(?)-
See Tomlin, Lily
See also CA 117
Tomlinson, (Alfred) Charles 1927-CLC **2, 4, 6,
13, 45; DAM POET; PC 17**

See also CA 5-8R; CANR 33; DLB 40

Tomlinson, H(enry) M(ajor) 1873-1958**TCLC 71**
See also CA 118; 161; DLB 36, 100, 195

Tonson, Jacob
See Bennett, (Enoch) Arnold

Toole, John Kennedy 1937-1969 **CLC 19, 64**
See also CA 104; DLBY 81

Toomer, Jean 1894-1967 .... **CLC 1, 4, 13, 22; BLC; DAM MULT; PC 7; SSC 1; WLCS**
See also BW 1; CA 85-88; CDALB 1917-1929; DLB 45, 51; MTCW

Torley, Luke
See Blish, James (Benjamin)

Tornimparte, Alessandra
See Ginzburg, Natalia

Torre, Raoul della
See Mencken, H(enry) L(ouis)

Torrey, E(dwin) Fuller 1937- .... **CLC 34**
See also CA 119

Torsvan, Ben Traven
See Traven, B.

Torsvan, Benno Traven
See Traven, B.

Torsvan, Berick Traven
See Traven, B.

Torsvan, Berwick Traven
See Traven, B.

Torsvan, Bruno Traven
See Traven, B.

Torsvan, Traven
See Traven, B.

Tournier, Michel (Edouard) 1924-**CLC 6, 23, 36, 95**
See also CA 49-52; CANR 3, 36; DLB 83; MTCW; SATA 23

Tournimparte, Alessandra
See Ginzburg, Natalia

Towers, Ivar
See Kornbluth, C(yril) M.

Towne, Robert (Burton) 1936(?)- ..... **CLC 87**
See also CA 108; DLB 44

Townsend, Sue .... **CLC 61**
See also Townsend, Susan Elaine
See also SATA 55, 93; SATA-Brief 48

Townsend, Susan Elaine 1946-
See Townsend, Sue
See also CA 119; 127; CANR 65; DAB; DAC; DAM MST

Townshend, Peter (Dennis Blandford) 1945-
CLC 17, 42
See also CA 107

Tozzi, Federigo 1883-1920 .... **TCLC 31**
See also CA 160

Traill, Catharine Parr 1802-1899 ..**NCLC 31**
See also DLB 99

Trakl, Georg 1887-1914 .... **TCLC 5; PC 20**
See also CA 104; 165

Transtroemer, Tomas (Goesta) 1931-**CLC 52, 65; DAM POET**
See also CA 117; 129; CAAS 17

Transtromer, Tomas Gosta
See Transtroemer, Tomas (Goesta)

Traven, B. (?)-1969 .... **CLC 8, 11**
See also CA 19-20; 25-28R; CAP 2; DLB 9, 56; MTCW

Treitel, Jonathan 1959- .... **CLC 70**

Tremain, Rose 1943- .... **CLC 42**
See also CA 97-100; CANR 44; DLB 14

Tremblay, Michel 1942- **CLC 29, 102; DAC; DAM MST**
See also CA 116; 128; DLB 60; MTCW

Trevanian .... **CLC 29**

See also Whitaker, Rod(ney)

Trevor, Glen
See Hilton, James

Trevor, William 1928- ..**CLC 7, 9, 14, 25, 71; SSC 21**
See also Cox, William Trevor
See also DLB 14, 139

Trifonov, Yuri (Valentinovich) 1925-1981
CLC 45
See also CA 126; 103; MTCW

Trilling, Lionel 1905-1975 ...... **CLC 9, 11, 24**
See also CA 9-12R; 61-64; CANR 10; DLB 28, 63; INT CANR-10; MTCW

Trimball, W. H.
See Mencken, H(enry) L(ouis)

Tristan
See Gomez de la Serna, Ramon

Tristram
See Housman, A(lfred) E(dward)

Trogdon, William (Lewis) 1939-
See Heat-Moon, William Least
See also CA 115; 119; CANR 47; INT 119

Trollope, Anthony 1815-1882**NCLC 6,33; DA; DAB; DAC; DAM MST, NOV; SSC 28; WLC**
See also CDBLB 1832-1890; DLB 21, 57, 159; SATA 22

Trollope, Frances 1779-1863 .... **NCLC 30**
See also DLB 21, 166

Trotsky, Leon 1879-1940 .... **TCLC 22**
See also CA 118

Trotter (Cockburn), Catharine 1679-1749**L C 8**
See also DLB 84

Trout, Kilgore
See Farmer, Philip Jose

Trow, George W. S. 1943- .... **CLC 52**
See also CA 126

Troyat, Henri 1911- .... **CLC 23**
See also CA 45-48; CANR 2, 33, 67; MTCW

Trudeau, G(arretson) B(eekman) 1948-
See Trudeau, Garry B.
See also CA 81-84; CANR 31; SATA 35

Trudeau, Garry B. .... **CLC 12**
See also Trudeau, G(arretson) B(eekman)
See also AAYA 10; AITN 2

Truffaut, Francois 1932-1984 .. **CLC 20, 101**
See also CA 81-84; 113; CANR 34

Trumbo, Dalton 1905-1976 .... **CLC 19**
See also CA 21-24R; 69-72; CANR 10; DLB 26

Trumbull, John 1750-1831 .... **NCLC 30**
See also DLB 31

Trundlett, Helen B.
See Eliot, T(homas) S(tearns)

Tryon, Thomas 1926-1991 . **CLC 3, 11; DAM POP**
See also AITN 1; CA 29-32R; 135; CANR 32; MTCW

Tryon, Tom
See Tryon, Thomas

Ts'ao Hsueh-ch'in 1715(?)-1763 .... **LC 1**

Tsushima, Shuji 1909-1948
See Dazai, Osamu
See also CA 107

Tsvetaeva (Efron), Marina (Ivanovna) 1892-1941 .... **TCLC 7, 35; PC 14**
See also CA 104; 128; MTCW

Tuck, Lily 1938- .... **CLC 70**
See also CA 139

Tu Fu 712-770 .... **PC 9**
See also DAM MULT

Tunis, John R(oberts) 1889-1975 ...... **CLC 12**

See also CA 61-64; CANR 62; DLB 22, 171; JRDA; MAICYA; SATA 37; SATA-Brief 30

Tuohy, Frank .... **CLC 37**
See also Tuohy, John Francis
See also DLB 14, 139

Tuohy, John Francis 1925-
See Tuohy, Frank
See also CA 5-8R; CANR 3, 47

Turco, Lewis (Putnam) 1934- ...... **CLC 11, 63**
See also CA 13-16R; CAAS 22; CANR 24, 51; DLBY 84

Turgenev, Ivan 1818-1883 .... **NCLC 21; DA; DAB; DAC; DAM MST, NOV; DC 7; SSC 7; WLC**

Turgot, Anne-Robert-Jacques 1727-1781 **L C 26**

Turner, Frederick 1943- .... **CLC 48**
See also CA 73-76; CAAS 10; CANR 12, 30, 56; DLB 40

Tutu, Desmond M(pilo) 1931-**CLC 80; BLC; DAM MULT**
See also BW 1; CA 125; CANR 67

Tutuola, Amos 1920-1997**CLC 5, 14, 29; BLC; DAM MULT**
See also BW 2; CA 9-12R; 159; CANR 27, 66; DLB 125; MTCW

Twain, Mark   **TCLC 6, 12, 19, 36, 48, 59; SSC 26; WLC**
See also Clemens, Samuel Langhorne
See also AAYA 20; DLB 11, 12, 23, 64, 74

Tyler, Anne 1941- . **CLC 7, 11, 18, 28, 44, 59, 103; DAM NOV, POP**
See also AAYA 18; BEST 89:1; CA 9-12R; CANR 11, 33, 53; DLB 6, 143; DLBY 82; MTCW; SATA 7, 90

Tyler, Royall 1757-1826 .... **NCLC 3**
See also DLB 37

Tynan, Katharine 1861-1931 .... **TCLC 3**
See also CA 104; DLB 153

Tyutchev, Fyodor 1803-1873 .... **NCLC 34**

Tzara, Tristan 1896-1963 ...... **CLC 47; DAM POET**
See also CA 153; 89-92

Uhry, Alfred 1936-... **CLC 55; DAM DRAM, POP**
See also CA 127; 133; INT 133

Ulf, Haerved
See Strindberg, (Johan) August

Ulf, Harved
See Strindberg, (Johan) August

Ulibarri, Sabine R(eyes) 1919-**CLC 83; DAM MULT**
See also CA 131; DLB 82; HW

Unamuno (y Jugo), Miguel de 1864-1936
TCLC 2, 9; DAM MULT, NOV; HLC; SSC 11
See also CA 104; 131; DLB 108; HW; MTCW

Undercliffe, Errol
See Campbell, (John) Ramsey

Underwood, Miles
See Glassco, John

Undset, Sigrid 1882-1949**TCLC 3; DA; DAB; DAC; DAM MST, NOV; WLC**
See also CA 104; 129; MTCW

Ungaretti, Giuseppe 1888-1970**CLC 7, 11, 15**
See also CA 19-20; 25-28R; CAP 2; DLB 114

Unger, Douglas 1952- .... **CLC 34**
See also CA 130

Unsworth, Barry (Forster) 1930- .... **CLC 76**
See also CA 25-28R; CANR 30, 54; DLB 194

Updike, John (Hoyer) 1932-**CLC 1, 2, 3, 5, 7, 9, 13, 15, 23, 34, 43, 70; DA; DAB; DAC; DAM MST, NOV, POET, POP; SSC 13, 27;**

WLC
　See also CA 1-4R; CABS 1; CANR 4, 33, 51;
　　CDALB 1968-1988; DLB 2, 5, 143; DLBD
　　3; DLBY 80, 82, 97; MTCW
Upshaw, Margaret Mitchell
　See Mitchell, Margaret (Munnerlyn)
Upton, Mark
　See Sanders, Lawrence
Urdang, Constance (Henriette) 1922-CLC 47
　See also CA 21-24R; CANR 9, 24
Uriel, Henry
　See Faust, Frederick (Schiller)
Uris, Leon (Marcus) 1924- CLC 7, 32; DAM
　NOV, POP
　See also AITN 1, 2; BEST 89:2; CA 1-4R;
　　CANR 1, 40, 65; MTCW; SATA 49
Urmuz
　See Codrescu, Andrei
Urquhart, Jane 1949- ....CLC 90; DAC
　See also CA 113; CANR 32, 68
Ustinov, Peter (Alexander) 1921-........CLC 1
　See also AITN 1; CA 13-16R; CANR 25, 51;
　　DLB 13
U Tam'si, Gerald Felix Tchicaya
　See Tchicaya, Gerald Felix
U Tam'si, Tchicaya
　See Tchicaya, Gerald Felix
Vachss, Andrew (Henry) 1942- ...... CLC 106
　See also CA 118; CANR 44
Vachss, Andrew H.
　See Vachss, Andrew (Henry)
Vaculik, Ludvik 1926- ....CLC 7
　See also CA 53-56
Vaihinger, Hans 1852-1933 .... TCLC 71
　See also CA 116
Valdez, Luis (Miguel) 1940- ..CLC 84; DAM
　MULT; HLC
　See also CA 101; CANR 32; DLB 122; HW
Valenzuela, Luisa 1938- CLC 31, 104; DAM
　MULT; SSC 14
　See also CA 101; CANR 32, 65; DLB 113; HW
Valera y Alcala-Galiano, Juan 1824-1905
　TCLC 10
　See also CA 106
Valery, (Ambroise) Paul (Toussaint Jules) 1871-
　1945 .... TCLC 4, 15; DAM POET; PC 9
　See also CA 104; 122; MTCW
Valle-Inclan, Ramon (Maria) del 1866-1936
　TCLC 5; DAM MULT; HLC
　See also CA 106; 153; DLB 134
Vallejo, Antonio Buero
　See Buero Vallejo, Antonio
Vallejo, Cesar (Abraham) 1892-1938TCLC 3,
　56; DAM MULT; HLC
　See also CA 105; 153; HW
Vallette, Marguerite Eymery
　See Rachilde
Valle Y Pena, Ramon del
　See Valle-Inclan, Ramon (Maria) del
Van Ash, Cay 1918- ....CLC 34
Vanbrugh, Sir John 1664-1726 LC 21; DAM
　DRAM
　See also DLB 80
Van Campen, Karl
　See Campbell, John W(ood, Jr.)
Vance, Gerald
　See Silverberg, Robert
Vance, Jack ....CLC 35
　See also Kuttner, Henry; Vance, John Holbrook
　See also DLB 8
Vance, John Holbrook 1916-
　See Queen, Ellery; Vance, Jack
　See also CA 29-32R; CANR 17, 65; MTCW

Van Den Bogarde, Derek Jules Gaspard Ulric
　Niven 1921-
　See Bogarde, Dirk
　See also CA 77-80
Vandenburgh, Jane ....CLC 59
Vanderhaeghe, Guy 1951- ....CLC 41
　See also CA 113
van der Post, Laurens (Jan) 1906-1996CLC 5
　See also CA 5-8R; 155; CANR 35
van de Wetering, Janwillem 1931- ... CLC 47
　See also CA 49-52; CANR 4, 62
Van Dine, S. S. .... TCLC 23
　See also Wright, Willard Huntington
Van Doren, Carl (Clinton) 1885-1950 T C L C
　18
　See also CA 111
Van Doren, Mark 1894-1972 .... CLC 6, 10
　See also CA 1-4R; 37-40R; CANR 3; DLB 45;
　　MTCW
Van Druten, John (William) 1901-1957TCLC
　2
　See also CA 104; 161; DLB 10
Van Duyn, Mona (Jane) 1921- CLC 3, 7, 63;
　DAM POET
　See also CA 9-12R; CANR 7, 38, 60; DLB 5
Van Dyne, Edith
　See Baum, L(yman) Frank
van Itallie, Jean-Claude 1936- ....CLC 3
　See also CA 45-48; CAAS 2; CANR 1, 48; DLB
　　7
van Ostaijen, Paul 1896-1928 .... TCLC 33
　See also CA 163
Van Peebles, Melvin 1932-.CLC 2, 20; DAM
　MULT
　See also BW 2; CA 85-88; CANR 27, 67
Vansittart, Peter 1920- ....CLC 42
　See also CA 1-4R; CANR 3, 49
Van Vechten, Carl 1880-1964 ....CLC 33
　See also CA 89-92; DLB 4, 9, 51
Van Vogt, A(lfred) E(lton) 1912-.........CLC 1
　See also CA 21-24R; CANR 28; DLB 8; SATA
　　14
Varda, Agnes 1928- ....CLC 16
　See also CA 116; 122
Vargas Llosa, (Jorge) Mario (Pedro) 1936-
　CLC 3, 6, 9, 10, 15, 31, 42, 85; DA; DAB;
　DAC; DAM MST, MULT, NOV; HLC
　See also CA 73-76; CANR 18, 32, 42, 67; DLB
　　145; HW; MTCW
Vasiliu, Gheorghe 1881-1957
　See Bacovia, George
　See also CA 123
Vassa, Gustavus
　See Equiano, Olaudah
Vassilikos, Vassilis 1933- .... CLC 4, 8
　See also CA 81-84
Vaughan, Henry 1621-1695 .... LC 27
　See also DLB 131
Vaughn, Stephanie ....CLC 62
Vazov, Ivan (Minchov) 1850-1921 . TCLC 25
　See also CA 121; DLB 147
Veblen, Thorstein (Bunde) 1857-1929 T C L C
　31
　See also CA 115; 165
Vega, Lope de 1562-1635 .... LC 23
Venison, Alfred
　See Pound, Ezra (Weston Loomis)
Verdi, Marie de
　See Mencken, H(enry) L(ouis)
Verdu, Matilde
　See Cela, Camilo Jose
Verga, Giovanni (Carmelo) 1840-1922T C L C
　3; SSC 21

　See also CA 104; 123
Vergil 70B.C.-19B.C. ....CMLC 9; DA; DAB;
　DAC; DAM MST, POET; PC 12; WLCS
Verhaeren, Emile (Adolphe Gustave) 1855-1916
　TCLC 12
　See also CA 109
Verlaine, Paul (Marie) 1844-1896NCLC 2, 51;
　DAM POET; PC 2
Verne, Jules (Gabriel) 1828-1905TCLC 6, 52
　See also AAYA 16; CA 110; 131; DLB 123;
　　JRDA; MAICYA; SATA 21
Very, Jones 1813-1880 ....NCLC 9
　See also DLB 1
Vesaas, Tarjei 1897-1970 ....CLC 48
　See also CA 29-32R
Vialis, Gaston
　See Simenon, Georges (Jacques Christian)
Vian, Boris 1920-1959 ....TCLC 9
　See also CA 106; 164; DLB 72
Viaud, (Louis Marie) Julien 1850-1923
　See Loti, Pierre
　See also CA 107
Vicar, Henry
　See Felsen, Henry Gregor
Vicker, Angus
　See Felsen, Henry Gregor
Vidal, Gore 1925-CLC 2, 4, 6, 8, 10, 22, 33, 72;
　DAM NOV, POP
　See also AITN 1; BEST 90:2; CA 5-8R; CANR
　　13, 45, 65; DLB 6, 152; INT CANR-13;
　　MTCW
Viereck, Peter (Robert Edwin) 1916-.CLC 4
　See also CA 1-4R; CANR 1, 47; DLB 5
Vigny, Alfred (Victor) de 1797-1863NCLC 7;
　DAM POET
　See also DLB 119, 192
Vilakazi, Benedict Wallet 1906-1947TCLC 37
Villiers de l'Isle Adam, Jean Marie Mathias
　Philippe Auguste Comte 1838-1889
　NCLC 3; SSC 14
　See also DLB 123
Villon, Francois 1431-1463(?) ....PC 13
Vinci, Leonardo da 1452-1519 .... LC 12
Vine, Barbara ....CLC 50
　See also Rendell, Ruth (Barbara)
　See also BEST 90:4
Vinge, Joan D(ennison) 1948-CLC 30; SSC 24
　See also CA 93-96; SATA 36
Violis, G.
　See Simenon, Georges (Jacques Christian)
Visconti, Luchino 1906-1976 ....CLC 16
　See also CA 81-84; 65-68; CANR 39
Vittorini, Elio 1908-1966 .... CLC 6, 9, 14
　See also CA 133; 25-28R
Vizenor, Gerald Robert 1934-CLC 103; DAM
　MULT
　See also CA 13-16R; CAAS 22; CANR 5, 21,
　　44, 67; DLB 175; NNAL
Vizinczey, Stephen 1933- ....CLC 40
　See also CA 128; INT 128
Vliet, R(ussell) G(ordon) 1929-1984 . CLC 22
　See also CA 37-40R; 112; CANR 18
Vogau, Boris Andreyevich 1894-1937(?)
　See Pilnyak, Boris
　See also CA 123
Vogel, Paula A(nne) 1951- ....CLC 76
　See also CA 108
Voight, Ellen Bryant 1943-...............CLC 54
　See also CA 69-72; CANR 11, 29, 55; DLB 120
Voigt, Cynthia 1942- ....CLC 30
　See also AAYA 3; CA 106; CANR 18, 37, 40;
　　CLR 13,48; INT CANR-18; JRDA;
　　MAICYA; SATA 48, 79; SATA-Brief 33

Voinovich, Vladimir (Nikolaevich) 1932-**C L C 10, 49**
See also CA 81-84; CAAS 12; CANR 33, 67; MTCW

Vollmann, William T. 1959-... **CLC 89; DAM NOV, POP**
See also CA 134; CANR 67

Voloshinov, V. N.
See Bakhtin, Mikhail Mikhailovich

Voltaire 1694-1778 **LC 14; DA; DAB; DAC; DAM DRAM, MST; SSC 12; WLC**

von Daeniken, Erich 1935- .... **CLC 30**
See also AITN 1; CA 37-40R; CANR 17, 44

von Daniken, Erich
See von Daeniken, Erich

von Heidenstam, (Carl Gustaf) Verner
See Heidenstam, (Carl Gustaf) Verner von

von Heyse, Paul (Johann Ludwig)
See Heyse, Paul (Johann Ludwig von)

von Hofmannsthal, Hugo
See Hofmannsthal, Hugo von

von Horvath, Odon
See Horvath, Oedoen von

von Horvath, Oedoen
See Horvath, Oedoen von

von Liliencron, (Friedrich Adolf Axel) Detlev
See Liliencron, (Friedrich Adolf Axel) Detlev von

Vonnegut, Kurt, Jr. 1922-**CLC 1, 2, 3, 4, 5, 8, 12, 22, 40, 60; DA; DAB; DAC; DAM MST, NOV, POP; SSC 8; WLC**
See also AAYA 6; AITN 1; BEST 90:4; CA 1-4R; CANR 1, 25, 49; CDALB 1968-1988; DLB 2, 8, 152; DLBD 3; DLBY 80; MTCW

Von Rachen, Kurt
See Hubbard, L(afayette) Ron(ald)

von Rezzori (d'Arezzo), Gregor
See Rezzori (d'Arezzo), Gregor von

von Sternberg, Josef
See Sternberg, Josef von

Vorster, Gordon 1924- .... **CLC 34**
See also CA 133

Vosce, Trudie
See Ozick, Cynthia

Voznesensky, Andrei (Andreievich) 1933-**CLC 1, 15, 57; DAM POET**
See also CA 89-92; CANR 37; MTCW

Waddington, Miriam 1917- .... **CLC 28**
See also CA 21-24R; CANR 12, 30; DLB 68

Wagman, Fredrica 1937- .... **CLC 7**
See also CA 97-100; INT 97-100

Wagner, Linda W.
See Wagner-Martin, Linda (C.)

Wagner, Linda Welshimer
See Wagner-Martin, Linda (C.)

Wagner, Richard 1813-1883 .... **NCLC 9**
See also DLB 129

Wagner-Martin, Linda (C.) 1936- ... **CLC 50**
See also CA 159

Wagoner, David (Russell) 1926- **CLC 3, 5, 15**
See also CA 1-4R; CAAS 3; CANR 2; DLB 5; SATA 14

Wah, Fred(erick James) 1939- .... **CLC 44**
See also CA 107; 141; DLB 60

Wahloo, Per 1926-1975 .... **CLC 7**
See also CA 61-64

Wahloo, Peter
See Wahloo, Per

Wain, John (Barrington) 1925-1994 **CLC 2, 11, 15, 46**
See also CA 5-8R; 145; CAAS 4; CANR 23, 54; CDBLB 1960 to Present; DLB 15, 27, 139, 155; MTCW

Wajda, Andrzej 1926- .... **CLC 16**
See also CA 102

Wakefield, Dan 1932- .... **CLC 7**
See also CA 21-24R; CAAS 7

Wakoski, Diane 1937-. **CLC 2, 4, 7, 9, 11, 40; DAM POET; PC 15**
See also CA 13-16R; CAAS 1; CANR 9, 60; DLB 5; INT CANR-9

Wakoski-Sherbell, Diane
See Wakoski, Diane

Walcott, Derek (Alton) 1930-**CLC 2, 4, 9, 14, 25, 42, 67, 76; BLC; DAB; DAC; DAM MST, MULT, POET; DC 7**
See also BW 2; CA 89-92; CANR 26, 47; DLB 117; DLBY 81; MTCW

Waldman, Anne 1945- .... **CLC 7**
See also CA 37-40R; CAAS 17; CANR 34; DLB 16

Waldo, E. Hunter
See Sturgeon, Theodore (Hamilton)

Waldo, Edward Hamilton
See Sturgeon, Theodore (Hamilton)

Walker, Alice (Malsenior) 1944- **CLC 5, 6, 9, 19, 27, 46, 58, 103; BLC; DA; DAB; DAC; DAM MST, MULT, NOV, POET, POP; SSC 5; WLCS**
See also AAYA 3; BEST 89:4; BW 2; CA 37-40R; CANR 9, 27, 49, 66; CDALB 1968-1988; DLB 6, 33, 143; INT CANR-27; MTCW; SATA 31

Walker, David Harry 1911-1992 .... **CLC 14**
See also CA 1-4R; 137; CANR 1; SATA 8; SATA-Obit 71

Walker, Edward Joseph 1934-
See Walker, Ted
See also CA 21-24R; CANR 12, 28, 53

Walker, George F. 1947- . **CLC 44, 61; DAB; DAC; DAM MST**
See also CA 103; CANR 21, 43, 59; DLB 60

Walker, Joseph A. 1935- .... **CLC 19; DAM DRAM, MST**
See also BW 1; CA 89-92; CANR 26; DLB 38

Walker, Margaret (Abigail) 1915- **CLC 1, 6; BLC; DAM MULT; PC 20**
See also BW 2; CA 73-76; CANR 26, 54; DLB 76, 152; MTCW

Walker, Ted .... **CLC 13**
See also Walker, Edward Joseph
See also DLB 40

Wallace, David Foster 1962- .... **CLC 50**
See also CA 132; CANR 59

Wallace, Dexter
See Masters, Edgar Lee

Wallace, (Richard Horatio) Edgar 1875-1932 **TCLC 57**
See also CA 115; DLB 70

Wallace, Irving 1916-1990 . **CLC 7, 13; DAM NOV, POP**
See also AITN 1; CA 1-4R; 132; CAAS 1; CANR 1, 27; INT CANR-27; MTCW

Wallant, Edward Lewis 1926-1962**CLC 5, 10**
See also CA 1-4R; CANR 22; DLB 2, 28, 143; MTCW

Walley, Byron
See Card, Orson Scott

Walpole, Horace 1717-1797 .... **LC 2**
See also DLB 39, 104

Walpole, Hugh (Seymour) 1884-1941**TCLC 5**
See also CA 104; 165; DLB 34

Walser, Martin 1927- .... **CLC 27**
See also CA 57-60; CANR 8, 46; DLB 75, 124

Walser, Robert 1878-1956 **TCLC 18; SSC 20**
See also CA 118; 165; DLB 66

Walsh, Jill Paton .... **CLC 35**
See also Paton Walsh, Gillian
See also AAYA 11; CLR 2; DLB 161; SAAS 3

Walter, Villiam Christian
See Andersen, Hans Christian

Wambaugh, Joseph (Aloysius, Jr.) 1937-**C L C 3, 18; DAM NOV, POP**
See also AITN 1; BEST 89:3; CA 33-36R; CANR 42, 65; DLB 6; DLBY 83; MTCW

Wang Wei 699(?)-761(?) .... **PC 18**

Ward, Arthur Henry Sarsfield 1883-1959
See Rohmer, Sax
See also CA 108

Ward, Douglas Turner 1930- .... **CLC 19**
See also BW 1; CA 81-84; CANR 27; DLB 7, 38

Ward, Mary Augusta
See Ward, Mrs. Humphry

Ward, Mrs. Humphry 1851-1920 .. **TCLC 55**
See also DLB 18

Ward, Peter
See Faust, Frederick (Schiller)

Warhol, Andy 1928(?)-1987 .... **CLC 20**
See also AAYA 12; BEST 89:4; CA 89-92; 121; CANR 34

Warner, Francis (Robert le Plastrier) 1937-**CLC 14**
See also CA 53-56; CANR 11

Warner, Marina 1946- .... **CLC 59**
See also CA 65-68; CANR 21, 55; DLB 194

Warner, Rex (Ernest) 1905-1986 ..... **CLC 45**
See also CA 89-92; 119; DLB 15

Warner, Susan (Bogert) 1819-1885 **NCLC 31**
See also DLB 3, 42

Warner, Sylvia (Constance) Ashton
See Ashton-Warner, Sylvia (Constance)

Warner, Sylvia Townsend 1893-1978 **CLC 7, 19; SSC 23**
See also CA 61-64; 77-80; CANR 16, 60; DLB 34, 139; MTCW

Warren, Mercy Otis 1728-1814 ...... **NCLC 13**
See also DLB 31

Warren, Robert Penn 1905-1989**CLC 1, 4, 6, 8, 10, 13, 18, 39, 53, 59; DA; DAB; DAC; DAM MST, NOV, POET; SSC 4; WLC**
See also AITN 1; CA 13-16R; 129; CANR 10, 47; CDALB 1968-1988; DLB 2, 48, 152; DLBY 80, 89; INT CANR-10; MTCW; SATA 46; SATA-Obit 63

Warshofsky, Isaac
See Singer, Isaac Bashevis

Warton, Thomas 1728-1790 ..... **LC 15; DAM POET**
See also DLB 104, 109

Waruk, Kona
See Harris, (Theodore) Wilson

Warung, Price 1855-1911 .... **TCLC 45**

Warwick, Jarvis
See Garner, Hugh

Washington, Alex
See Harris, Mark

Washington, Booker T(aliaferro) 1856-1915 **TCLC 10; BLC; DAM MULT**
See also BW 1; CA 114; 125; SATA 28

Washington, George 1732-1799 .... **LC 25**
See also DLB 31

Wassermann, (Karl) Jakob 1873-1934 **T C L C 6**
See also CA 104; DLB 66

Wasserstein, Wendy 1950-... **CLC 32, 59, 90; DAM DRAM; DC 4**
See also CA 121; 129; CABS 3; CANR 53; INT 129; SATA 94

Waterhouse, Keith (Spencer) 1929-. **CLC 47**
    See also CA 5-8R; CANR 38, 67; DLB 13, 15;
    MTCW
Waters, Frank (Joseph) 1902-1995 .. **CLC 88**
    See also CA 5-8R; 149; CAAS 13; CANR 3,
    18, 63; DLBY 86
Waters, Roger 1944- .... **CLC 35**
Watkins, Frances Ellen
    See Harper, Frances Ellen Watkins
Watkins, Gerrold
    See Malzberg, Barry N(athaniel)
Watkins, Gloria 1955(?)-
    See hooks, bell
    See also BW 2; CA 143
Watkins, Paul 1964- .... **CLC 55**
    See also CA 132; CANR 62
Watkins, Vernon Phillips 1906-1967 **CLC 43**
    See also CA 9-10; 25-28R; CAP 1; DLB 20
Watson, Irving S.
    See Mencken, H(enry) L(ouis)
Watson, John H.
    See Farmer, Philip Jose
Watson, Richard F.
    See Silverberg, Robert
Waugh, Auberon (Alexander) 1939- ..**CLC 7**
    See also CA 45-48; CANR 6, 22; DLB 14, 194
Waugh, Evelyn (Arthur St. John) 1903-1966
    CLC 1, 3, 8, 13, 19, 27, 44, 107; DA; DAB;
    DAC; DAM MST, NOV, POP; WLC
    See also CA 85-88; 25-28R; CANR 22; CDBLB
    1914-1945; DLB 15, 162, 195; MTCW
Waugh, Harriet 1944- .... **CLC 6**
    See also CA 85-88; CANR 22
Ways, C. R.
    See Blount, Roy (Alton), Jr.
Waystaff, Simon
    See Swift, Jonathan
Webb, (Martha) Beatrice (Potter) 1858-1943
    TCLC 22
    See also Potter, (Helen) Beatrix
    See also CA 117
Webb, Charles (Richard) 1939- .... **CLC 7**
    See also CA 25-28R
Webb, James H(enry), Jr. 1946- ...... **CLC 22**
    See also CA 81-84
Webb, Mary (Gladys Meredith) 1881-1927
    TCLC 24
    See also CA 123; DLB 34
Webb, Mrs. Sidney
    See Webb, (Martha) Beatrice (Potter)
Webb, Phyllis 1927- .... **CLC 18**
    See also CA 104; CANR 23; DLB 53
Webb, Sidney (James) 1859-1947 .. **TCLC 22**
    See also CA 117; 163; DLB 190
Webber, Andrew Lloyd .... **CLC 21**
    See also Lloyd Webber, Andrew
Weber, Lenora Mattingly 1895-1971 **CLC 12**
    See also CA 19-20; 29-32R; CAP 1; SATA 2;
    SATA-Obit 26
Weber, Max 1864-1920 .... **TCLC 69**
    See also CA 109
Webster, John 1579(?)-1634(?) ... **LC 33; DA;**
    DAB; DAC; DAM DRAM, MST; DC 2;
    WLC
    See also CDBLB Before 1660; DLB 58
Webster, Noah 1758-1843 .... **NCLC 30**
Wedekind, (Benjamin) Frank(lin) 1864-1918
    TCLC 7; DAM DRAM
    See also CA 104; 153; DLB 118
Weidman, Jerome 1913- .... **CLC 7**
    See also AITN 2; CA 1-4R; CANR 1; DLB 28
Weil, Simone (Adolphine) 1909-1943 **TCLC 23**
    See also CA 117; 159

Weinstein, Nathan
    See West, Nathanael
Weinstein, Nathan von Wallenstein
    See West, Nathanael
Weir, Peter (Lindsay) 1944- .... **CLC 20**
    See also CA 113; 123
Weiss, Peter (Ulrich) 1916-1982 **CLC 3, 15, 51;**
    DAM DRAM
    See also CA 45-48; 106; CANR 3; DLB 69, 124
Weiss, Theodore (Russell) 1916- **CLC 3, 8, 14**
    See also CA 9-12R; CAAS 2; CANR 46; DLB
    5
Welch, (Maurice) Denton 1915-1948 **TCLC 22**
    See also CA 121; 148
Welch, James 1940- ..... **CLC 6, 14, 52; DAM**
    MULT, POP
    See also CA 85-88; CANR 42, 66; DLB 175;
    NNAL
Weldon, Fay 1931- .. **CLC 6, 9, 11, 19, 36, 59;**
    DAM POP
    See also CA 21-24R; CANR 16, 46, 63; CDBLB
    1960 to Present; DLB 14, 194; INT CANR-
    16; MTCW
Wellek, Rene 1903-1995 .... **CLC 28**
    See also CA 5-8R; 150; CAAS 7; CANR 8; DLB
    63; INT CANR-8
Weller, Michael 1942- .... **CLC 10, 53**
    See also CA 85-88
Weller, Paul 1958- .... **CLC 26**
Wellershoff, Dieter 1925- .... **CLC 46**
    See also CA 89-92; CANR 16, 37
Welles, (George) Orson 1915-1985 **CLC 20, 80**
    See also CA 93-96; 117
Wellman, Mac 1945- .... **CLC 65**
Wellman, Manly Wade 1903-1986 .... **CLC 49**
    See also CA 1-4R; 118; CANR 6, 16, 44; SATA
    6; SATA-Obit 47
Wells, Carolyn 1869(?)-1942 .... **TCLC 35**
    See also CA 113; DLB 11
Wells, H(erbert) G(eorge) 1866-1946 **TCLC 6,**
    12, 19; DA; DAB; DAC; DAM MST, NOV;
    SSC 6; WLC
    See also AAYA 18; CA 110; 121; CDBLB 1914-
    1945; DLB 34, 70, 156, 178; MTCW; SATA
    20
Wells, Rosemary 1943- .... **CLC 12**
    See also AAYA 13; CA 85-88; CANR 48; CLR
    16; MAICYA; SAAS 1; SATA 18, 69
Welty, Eudora 1909- **CLC 1, 2, 5, 14, 22, 33,**
    105; DA; DAB; DAC; DAM MST, NOV;
    SSC 1, 27; WLC
    See also CA 9-12R; CABS 1; CANR 32, 65;
    CDALB 1941-1968; DLB 2, 102, 143;
    DLBD 12; DLBY 87; MTCW
Wen I-to 1899-1946 .... **TCLC 28**
Wentworth, Robert
    See Hamilton, Edmond
Werfel, Franz (Viktor) 1890-1945 ... **TCLC 8**
    See also CA 104; 161; DLB 81, 124
Wergeland, Henrik Arnold 1808-1845 **N C L C**
    5
Wersba, Barbara 1932- .... **CLC 30**
    See also AAYA 2; CA 29-32R; CANR 16, 38;
    CLR 3; DLB 52; JRDA; MAICYA; SAAS 2;
    SATA 1, 58
Wertmueller, Lina 1928- .... **CLC 16**
    See also CA 97-100; CANR 39
Wescott, Glenway 1901-1987 .... **CLC 13**
    See also CA 13-16R; 121; CANR 23; DLB 4,
    9, 102
Wesker, Arnold 1932- .... **CLC 3, 5, 42; DAB;**
    DAM DRAM
    See also CA 1-4R; CAAS 7; CANR 1, 33;

    CDBLB 1960 to Present; DLB 13; MTCW
Wesley, Richard (Errol) 1945- .... **CLC 7**
    See also BW 1; CA 57-60; CANR 27; DLB 38
Wessel, Johan Herman 1742-1785 .... **LC 7**
West, Anthony (Panther) 1914-1987 **CLC 50**
    See also CA 45-48; 124; CANR 3, 19; DLB 15
West, C. P.
    See Wodehouse, P(elham) G(renville)
West, (Mary) Jessamyn 1902-1984 **CLC 7, 17**
    See also CA 9-12R; 112; CANR 27; DLB 6;
    DLBY 84; MTCW; SATA-Obit 37
West, Morris L(anglo) 1916- .... **CLC 6, 33**
    See also CA 5-8R; CANR 24, 49, 64; MTCW
West, Nathanael 1903-1940 **TCLC 1, 14, 44;**
    SSC 16
    See also CA 104; 125; CDALB 1929-1941;
    DLB 4, 9, 28; MTCW
West, Owen
    See Koontz, Dean R(ay)
West, Paul 1930- .... **CLC 7, 14, 96**
    See also CA 13-16R; CAAS 7; CANR 22, 53;
    DLB 14; INT CANR-22
West, Rebecca 1892-1983 ... **CLC 7, 9, 31, 50**
    See also CA 5-8R; 109; CANR 19; DLB 36;
    DLBY 83; MTCW
Westall, Robert (Atkinson) 1929-1993 **CLC 17**
    See also AAYA 12; CA 69-72; 141; CANR 18,
    68; CLR 13; JRDA; MAICYA; SAAS 2;
    SATA 23, 69; SATA-Obit 75
Westlake, Donald E(dwin) 1933- **CLC 7, 33;**
    DAM POP
    See also CA 17-20R; CAAS 13; CANR 16, 44,
    65; INT CANR-16
Westmacott, Mary
    See Christie, Agatha (Mary Clarissa)
Weston, Allen
    See Norton, Andre
Wetcheek, J. L.
    See Feuchtwanger, Lion
Wetering, Janwillem van de
    See van de Wetering, Janwillem
Wetherell, Elizabeth
    See Warner, Susan (Bogert)
Whale, James 1889-1957 .... **TCLC 63**
Whalen, Philip 1923- .... **CLC 6, 29**
    See also CA 9-12R; CANR 5, 39; DLB 16
Wharton, Edith (Newbold Jones) 1862-1937
    TCLC 3, 9, 27, 53; DA; DAB; DAC; DAM
    MST, NOV; SSC 6; WLC
    See also AAYA 25; CA 104; 132; CDALB 1865-
    1917; DLB 4, 9, 12, 78, 189; DLBD 13;
    MTCW
Wharton, James
    See Mencken, H(enry) L(ouis)
Wharton, William (a pseudonym) **CLC 18, 37**
    See also CA 93-96; DLBY 80; INT 93-96
Wheatley (Peters), Phillis 1754(?)-1784 **LC 3;**
    BLC; DA; DAC; DAM MST, MULT,
    POET; PC 3; WLC
    See also CDALB 1640-1865; DLB 31, 50
Wheelock, John Hall 1886-1978 .... **CLC 14**
    See also CA 13-16R; 77-80; CANR 14; DLB
    45
White, E(lwyn) B(rooks) 1899-1985 **CLC 10,**
    34, 39; DAM POP
    See also AITN 2; CA 13-16R; 116; CANR 16,
    37; CLR 1, 21; DLB 11, 22; MAICYA;
    MTCW; SATA 2, 29; SATA-Obit 44
White, Edmund (Valentine III) 1940- **CLC 27;**
    DAM POP
    See also AAYA 7; CA 45-48; CANR 3, 19, 36,
    62; MTCW
White, Patrick (Victor Martindale) 1912-1990

CLC 3, 4, 5, 7, 9, 18, 65, 69
See also CA 81-84; 132; CANR 43; MTCW
White, Phyllis Dorothy James 1920-
See James, P. D.
See also CA 21-24R; CANR 17, 43, 65; DAM
POP; MTCW
White, T(erence) H(anbury) 1906-1964 **C L C
30**
See also AAYA 22; CA 73-76; CANR 37; DLB
160; JRDA; MAICYA; SATA 12
White, Terence de Vere 1912-1994 .. **CLC 49**
See also CA 49-52; 145; CANR 3
White, Walter F(rancis) 1893-1955 **TCLC 15**
See also White, Walter
See also BW 1; CA 115; 124; DLB 51
White, William Hale 1831-1913
See Rutherford, Mark
See also CA 121
Whitehead, E(dward) A(nthony) 1933-**CLC 5**
See also CA 65-68; CANR 58
Whitemore, Hugh (John) 1936- .... **CLC 37**
See also CA 132; INT 132
Whitman, Sarah Helen (Power) 1803-1878
NCLC 19
See also DLB 1
Whitman, Walt(er) 1819-1892 .. **NCLC 4, 31;
DA; DAB; DAC; DAM MST, POET; PC
3; WLC**
See also CDALB 1640-1865; DLB 3, 64; SATA
20
Whitney, Phyllis A(yame) 1903- ..... **CLC 42;
DAM POP**
See also AITN 2; BEST 90:3; CA 1-4R; CANR
3, 25, 38, 60; JRDA; MAICYA; SATA 1, 30
Whittemore, (Edward) Reed (Jr.) 1919-**CLC 4**
See also CA 9-12R; CAAS 8; CANR 4; DLB 5
Whittier, John Greenleaf 1807-1892**NCLC 8,
59**
See also DLB 1
Whittlebot, Hernia
See Coward, Noel (Peirce)
Wicker, Thomas Grey 1926-
See Wicker, Tom
See also CA 65-68; CANR 21, 46
Wicker, Tom ....**CLC 7**
See also Wicker, Thomas Grey
Wideman, John Edgar 1941- **CLC 5, 34, 36,
67; BLC; DAM MULT**
See also BW 2; CA 85-88; CANR 14, 42, 67;
DLB 33, 143
Wiebe, Rudy (Henry) 1934-... **CLC 6, 11, 14;
DAC; DAM MST**
See also CA 37-40R; CANR 42, 67; DLB 60
Wieland, Christoph Martin 1733-1813**N C L C
17**
See also DLB 97
Wiene, Robert 1881-1938 .... **TCLC 56**
Wieners, John 1934-...........................**CLC 7**
See also CA 13-16R; DLB 16
Wiesel, Elie(zer) 1928- **CLC 3, 5, 11, 37; DA;
DAB; DAC; DAM MST, NOV; WLCS 2**
See also AAYA 7; AITN 1; CA 5-8R; CAAS 4;
CANR 8, 40, 65; DLB 83; DLBY 87; INT
CANR-8; MTCW; SATA 56
Wiggins, Marianne 1947- .... **CLC 57**
See also BEST 89:3; CA 130; CANR 60
Wight, James Alfred 1916-
See Herriot, James
See also CA 77-80; SATA 55; SATA-Brief 44
Wilbur, Richard (Purdy) 1921-**CLC 3, 6, 9, 14,
53; DA; DAB; DAC; DAM MST, POET**
See also CA 1-4R; CABS 2; CANR 2, 29; DLB
5, 169; INT CANR-29; MTCW; SATA 9

Wild, Peter 1940-................................**CLC 14**
See also CA 37-40R; DLB 5
Wilde, Oscar (Fingal O'Flahertie Wills)
1854(?)-1900**TCLC 1, 8, 23, 41; DA; DAB;
DAC; DAM DRAM, MST, NOV; SSC 11;
WLC**
See also CA 104; 119; CDBLB 1890-1914;
DLB 10, 19, 34, 57, 141, 156, 190; SATA 24
Wilder, Billy ....**CLC 20**
See also Wilder, Samuel
See also DLB 26
Wilder, Samuel 1906-
See Wilder, Billy
See also CA 89-92
Wilder, Thornton (Niven) 1897-1975**CLC 1, 5,
6, 10, 15, 35, 82; DA; DAB; DAC; DAM
DRAM, MST, NOV; DC 1; WLC**
See also AITN 2; CA 13-16R; 61-64; CANR
40; DLB 4, 7, 9; DLBY 97; MTCW
Wilding, Michael 1942-.......................**CLC 73**
See also CA 104; CANR 24, 49
Wiley, Richard 1944- ....**CLC 44**
See also CA 121; 129
Wilhelm, Kate ....**CLC 7**
See also Wilhelm, Katie Gertrude
See also AAYA 20; CAAS 5; DLB 8; INT
CANR-17
Wilhelm, Katie Gertrude 1928-
See Wilhelm, Kate
See also CA 37-40R; CANR 17, 36, 60; MTCW
Wilkins, Mary
See Freeman, Mary Eleanor Wilkins
Willard, Nancy 1936- .... **CLC 7, 37**
See also CA 89-92; CANR 10, 39, 68; CLR 5;
DLB 5, 52; MAICYA; MTCW; SATA 37, 71;
SATA-Brief 30
Williams, C(harles) K(enneth) 1936-**CLC 33,
56; DAM POET**
See also CA 37-40R; CAAS 26; CANR 57; DLB
5
Williams, Charles
See Collier, James L(incoln)
Williams, Charles (Walter Stansby) 1886-1945
TCLC 1, 11
See also CA 104; 163; DLB 100, 153
Williams, (George) Emlyn 1905-1987**CLC 15;
DAM DRAM**
See also CA 104; 123; CANR 36; DLB 10, 77;
MTCW
Williams, Hugo 1942-..........................**CLC 42**
See also CA 17-20R; CANR 45; DLB 40
Williams, J. Walker
See Wodehouse, P(elham) G(renville)
Williams, John A(lfred) 1925-..... **CLC 5, 13;
BLC; DAM MULT**
See also BW 2; CA 53-56; CAAS 3; CANR 6,
26, 51; DLB 2, 33; INT CANR-6
Williams, Jonathan (Chamberlain) 1929-
CLC 13
See also CA 9-12R; CAAS 12; CANR 8; DLB
5
Williams, Joy 1944- ....**CLC 31**
See also CA 41-44R; CANR 22, 48
Williams, Norman 1952- ....**CLC 39**
See also CA 118
Williams, Sherley Anne 1944-**CLC 89; BLC;
DAM MULT, POET**
See also BW 2; CA 73-76; CANR 25; DLB 41;
INT CANR-25; SATA 78
Williams, Shirley
See Williams, Sherley Anne
Williams, Tennessee 1911-1983**CLC 1, 2, 5, 7,
8, 11, 15, 19, 30, 39, 45, 71; DA; DAB;**

DAC; DAM DRAM, MST; DC 4; WLC
See also AITN 1, 2; CA 5-8R; 108; CABS 3;
CANR 31; CDALB 1941-1968; DLB 7;
DLBD 4; DLBY 83; MTCW
Williams, Thomas (Alonzo) 1926-1990**CLC 14**
See also CA 1-4R; 132; CANR 2
Williams, William C.
See Williams, William Carlos
Williams, William Carlos 1883-1963**CLC 1, 2,
5, 9, 13, 22, 42, 67; DA; DAB; DAC; DAM
MST, POET; PC 7**
See also CA 89-92; CANR 34; CDALB 1917-
1929; DLB 4, 16, 54, 86; MTCW
Williamson, David (Keith) 1942- ..... **CLC 56**
See also CA 103; CANR 41
Williamson, Ellen Douglas 1905-1984
See Douglas, Ellen
See also CA 17-20R; 114; CANR 39
Williamson, Jack .... **CLC 29**
See also Williamson, John Stewart
See also CAAS 8; DLB 8
Williamson, John Stewart 1908-
See Williamson, Jack
See also CA 17-20R; CANR 23
Willie, Frederick
See Lovecraft, H(oward) P(hillips)
Willingham, Calder (Baynard, Jr.) 1922-1995
CLC 5, 51
See also CA 5-8R; 147; CANR 3; DLB 2, 44;
MTCW
Willis, Charles
See Clarke, Arthur C(harles)
Willy
See Colette, (Sidonie-Gabrielle)
Willy, Colette
See Colette, (Sidonie-Gabrielle)
Wilson, A(ndrew) N(orman) 1950-.. **CLC 33**
See also CA 112; 122; DLB 14, 155, 194
Wilson, Angus (Frank Johnstone) 1913-1991
CLC 2, 3, 5, 25, 34; SSC 21
See also CA 5-8R; 134; CANR 21; DLB 15,
139, 155; MTCW
Wilson, August 1945- **CLC 39, 50, 63; BLC;
DA; DAB; DAC; DAM DRAM, MST,
MULT; DC 2; WLCS**
See also AAYA 16; BW 2; CA 115; 122; CANR
42, 54; MTCW
Wilson, Brian 1942- .... **CLC 12**
Wilson, Colin 1931- .... **CLC 3, 14**
See also CA 1-4R; CAAS 5; CANR 1, 22, 33;
DLB 14, 194; MTCW
Wilson, Dirk
See Pohl, Frederik
Wilson, Edmund 1895-1972**CLC 1, 2, 3, 8, 24**
See also CA 1-4R; 37-40R; CANR 1, 46; DLB
63; MTCW
Wilson, Ethel Davis (Bryant) 1888(?)-1980
CLC 13; DAC; DAM POET
See also CA 102; DLB 68; MTCW
Wilson, John 1785-1854 ....**NCLC 5**
Wilson, John (Anthony) Burgess 1917-1993
See Burgess, Anthony
See also CA 1-4R; 143; CANR 2, 46; DAC;
DAM NOV; MTCW
Wilson, Lanford 1937- **CLC 7, 14, 36; DAM
DRAM**
See also CA 17-20R; CABS 3; CANR 45; DLB
7
Wilson, Robert M. 1944- .... **CLC 7, 9**
See also CA 49-52; CANR 2, 41; MTCW
Wilson, Robert McLiam 1964-......... **CLC 59**
See also CA 132
Wilson, Sloan 1920-...........................**CLC 32**

See also CA 1-4R; CANR 1, 44
Wilson, Snoo 1948- .... **CLC 33**
    See also CA 69-72
Wilson, William S(mith) 1932- .... **CLC 49**
    See also CA 81-84
Wilson, Woodrow 1856-1924 .... **TCLC 73**
    See also DLB 47
Winchilsea, Anne (Kingsmill) Finch Counte
    1661-1720
    See Finch, Anne
Windham, Basil
    See Wodehouse, P(elham) G(renville)
Wingrove, David (John) 1954- .... **CLC 68**
    See also CA 133
Wintergreen, Jane
    See Duncan, Sara Jeannette
Winters, Janet Lewis .... **CLC 41**
    See also Lewis, Janet
    See also DLBY 87
Winters, (Arthur) Yvor 1900-1968 **CLC 4, 8,**
    32
    See also CA 11-12; 25-28R; CAP 1; DLB 48;
    MTCW
Winterson, Jeanette 1959-**CLC 64; DAM POP**
    See also CA 136; CANR 58
Winthrop, John 1588-1649 .... **LC 31**
    See also DLB 24, 30
Wiseman, Frederick 1930- .... **CLC 20**
    See also CA 159
Wister, Owen 1860-1938 .... **TCLC 21**
    See also CA 108; 162; DLB 9, 78, 186; SATA
    62
Witkacy
    See Witkiewicz, Stanislaw Ignacy
Witkiewicz, Stanislaw Ignacy 1885-1939
    TCLC 8
    See also CA 105; 162
Wittgenstein, Ludwig (Josef Johann) 1889-1951
    TCLC 59
    See also CA 113; 164
Wittig, Monique 1935(?)- .... **CLC 22**
    See also CA 116; 135; DLB 83
Wittlin, Jozef 1896-1976 .... **CLC 25**
    See also CA 49-52; 65-68; CANR 3
Wodehouse, P(elham) G(renville) 1881-1975
    CLC 1, 2, 5, 10, 22; DAB; DAC; DAM
    NOV; SSC 2
    See also AITN 2; CA 45-48; 57-60; CANR 3,
    33; CDBLB 1914-1945; DLB 34, 162;
    MTCW; SATA 22
Woiwode, L.
    See Woiwode, Larry (Alfred)
Woiwode, Larry (Alfred) 1941- ... **CLC 6, 10**
    See also CA 73-76; CANR 16; DLB 6; INT
    CANR-16
Wojciechowska, Maia (Teresa) 1927-**CLC 26**
    See also AAYA 8; CA 9-12R; CANR 4, 41; CLR
    1; JRDA; MAICYA; SAAS 1; SATA 1, 28,
    83
Wolf, Christa 1929- .... **CLC 14, 29, 58**
    See also CA 85-88; CANR 45; DLB 75; MTCW
Wolfe, Gene (Rodman) 1931- **CLC 25; DAM**
    POP
    See also CA 57-60; CAAS 9; CANR 6, 32, 60;
    DLB 8
Wolfe, George C. 1954- .... **CLC 49**
    See also CA 149
Wolfe, Thomas (Clayton) 1900-1938**TCLC 4,**
    13, 29, 61; DA; DAB; DAC; DAM MST,
    NOV; WLC
    See also CA 104; 132; CDALB 1929-1941;
    DLB 9, 102; DLBD 2, 16; DLBY 85, 97;
    MTCW

Wolfe, Thomas Kennerly, Jr. 1931-
    See Wolfe, Tom
    See also CA 13-16R; CANR 9, 33; DAM POP;
    DLB 185; INT CANR-9; MTCW
Wolfe, Tom .... **CLC 1, 2, 9, 15, 35, 51**
    See also Wolfe, Thomas Kennerly, Jr.
    See also AAYA 8; AITN 2; BEST 89:1; DLB
    152
Wolff, Geoffrey (Ansell) 1937- .... **CLC 41**
    See also CA 29-32R; CANR 29, 43
Wolff, Sonia
    See Levitin, Sonia (Wolff)
Wolff, Tobias (Jonathan Ansell) 1945-..**C L C**
    39, 64
    See also AAYA 16; BEST 90:2; CA 114; 117;
    CAAS 22; CANR 54; DLB 130; INT 117
Wolfram von Eschenbach c. 1170-c. 1220
    CMLC 5
    See also DLB 138
Wolitzer, Hilma 1930- .... **CLC 17**
    See also CA 65-68; CANR 18, 40; INT CANR-
    18; SATA 31
Wollstonecraft, Mary 1759-1797 .... **LC 5**
    See also CDBLB 1789-1832; DLB 39, 104, 158
Wonder, Stevie .... **CLC 12**
    See also Morris, Steveland Judkins
Wong, Jade Snow 1922- .... **CLC 17**
    See also CA 109
Woodberry, George Edward 1855-1930
    TCLC 73
    See also CA 165; DLB 71, 103
Woodcott, Keith
    See Brunner, John (Kilian Houston)
Woodruff, Robert W.
    See Mencken, H(enry) L(ouis)
Woolf, (Adeline) Virginia 1882-1941**TCLC 1,**
    5, 20, 43, 56; DA; DAB; DAC; DAM MST,
    NOV; SSC 7; WLC
    See also CA 104; 130; CANR 64; CDBLB
    1914-1945; DLB 36, 100, 162; DLBD 10;
    MTCW
Woolf, Virginia Adeline
    See Woolf, (Adeline) Virginia
Woollcott, Alexander (Humphreys) 1887-1943
    TCLC 5
    See also CA 105; 161; DLB 29
Woolrich, Cornell 1903-1968 .... **CLC 77**
    See also Hopley-Woolrich, Cornell George
Wordsworth, Dorothy 1771-1855 ..**NCLC 25**
    See also DLB 107
Wordsworth, William 1770-1850..**NCLC 12,**
    38; DA; DAB; DAC; DAM MST, POET;
    PC 4; WLC
    See also CDBLB 1789-1832; DLB 93, 107
Wouk, Herman 1915-**CLC 1, 9, 38; DAM NOV,**
    POP
    See also CA 5-8R; CANR 6, 33, 67; DLBY 82;
    INT CANR-6; MTCW
Wright, Charles (Penzel, Jr.) 1935-**CLC 6, 13,**
    28
    See also CA 29-32R; CAAS 7; CANR 23, 36,
    62; DLB 165; DLBY 82; MTCW
Wright, Charles Stevenson 1932- ... **CLC 49;**
    BLC 3; DAM MULT, POET
    See also BW 1; CA 9-12R; CANR 26; DLB 33
Wright, Jack R.
    See Harris, Mark
Wright, James (Arlington) 1927-1980**CLC 3,**
    5, 10, 28; DAM POET
    See also AITN 2; CA 49-52; 97-100; CANR 4,
    34, 64; DLB 5, 169; MTCW
Wright, Judith (Arandell) 1915- **CLC 11, 53;**
    PC 14

See also CA 13-16R; CANR 31; MTCW; SATA
    14
Wright, L(aurali) R. 1939- .... **CLC 44**
    See also CA 138
Wright, Richard (Nathaniel) 1908-1960 **C L C**
    1, 3, 4, 9, 14, 21, 48, 74; BLC; DA; DAB;
    DAC; DAM MST, MULT, NOV; SSC 2;
    WLC
    See also AAYA 5; BW 1; CA 108; CANR 64;
    CDALB 1929-1941; DLB 76, 102; DLBD
    2; MTCW
Wright, Richard B(ruce) 1937- .... **CLC 6**
    See also CA 85-88; DLB 53
Wright, Rick 1945- .... **CLC 35**
Wright, Rowland
    See Wells, Carolyn
Wright, Stephen 1946- .... **CLC 33**
Wright, Willard Huntington 1888-1939
    See Van Dine, S. S.
    See also CA 115; DLBD 16
Wright, William 1930- .... **CLC 44**
    See also CA 53-56; CANR 7, 23
Wroth, LadyMary 1587-1653(?) .... **LC 30**
    See also DLB 121
Wu Ch'eng-en 1500(?)-1582(?) .... **LC 7**
Wu Ching-tzu 1701-1754 .... **LC 2**
Wurlitzer, Rudolph 1938(?)- .... **CLC 2, 4, !5**
    See also CA 85-88; DLB 173
Wycherley, William 1641-1715**LC 8, 21; DAM**
    DRAM
    See also CDBLB 1660-1789; DLB 80
Wylie, Elinor (Morton Hoyt) 1885-1928
    TCLC 8
    See also CA 105; 162; DLB 9, 45
Wylie, Philip (Gordon) 1902-1971 ....**CLC 43**
    See also CA 21-22; 33-36R; CAP 2; DLB 9
Wyndham, John .... **CLC 19**
    See also Harris, John (Wyndham Parkes Lucas)
    Beynon
Wyss, Johann David Von 1743-1818**NCLC 10**
    See also JRDA; MAICYA; SATA 29; SATA-
    Brief 27
Xenophon c. 430B.C.-c. 354B.C. ... **CMLC 17**
    See also DLB 176
Yakumo Koizumi
    See Hearn, (Patricio) Lafcadio (Tessima Carlos)
Yanez, Jose Donoso
    See Donoso (Yanez), Jose
Yanovsky, Basile S.
    See Yanovsky, V(assily) S(emenovich)
Yanovsky, V(assily) S(emenovich) 1906-1989
    CLC 2, 18
    See also CA 97-100; 129
Yates, Richard 1926-1992 .... **CLC 7, 8, 23**
    See also CA 5-8R; 139; CANR 10, 43; DLB 2;
    DLBY 81, 92; INT CANR-10
Yeats, W. B.
    See Yeats, William Butler
Yeats, William Butler 1865-1939**TCLC 1, 11,**
    18, 31; DA; DAB; DAC; DAM DRAM,
    MST, POET; PC 20; WLC
    See also CA 104; 127; CANR 45; CDBLB
    1890-1914; DLB 10, 19, 98, 156; MTCW
Yehoshua, A(braham) B. 1936- .. **CLC 13, 31**
    See also CA 33-36R; CANR 43
Yep, Laurence Michael 1948- ....**CLC 35**
    See also AAYA 5; CA 49-52; CANR 1, 46; CLR
    3, 17; DLB 52; JRDA; MAICYA; SATA 7,
    69
Yerby, Frank G(arvin) 1916-1991 **CLC 1, 7,**
    22; BLC; DAM MULT
    See also BW 1; CA 9-12R; 136; CANR 16, 52;
    DLB 76; INT CANR-16; MTCW

Yesenin, Sergei Alexandrovich
See Esenin, Sergei (Alexandrovich)
Yevtushenko, Yevgeny (Alexandrovich) 1933-
CLC 1, 3, 13, 26, 51; DAM POET
See also CA 81-84; CANR 33, 54; MTCW
Yezierska, Anzia 1885(?)-1970 .... **CLC 46**
See also CA 126; 89-92; DLB 28; MTCW
Yglesias, Helen 1915- .... **CLC 7, 22**
See also CA 37-40R; CAAS 20; CANR 15, 65;
INT CANR-15; MTCW
Yokomitsu Riichi 1898-1947 .... **TCLC 47**
Yonge, Charlotte (Mary) 1823-1901 **TCLC 48**
See also CA 109; 163; DLB 18, 163; SATA 17
York, Jeremy
See Creasey, John
York, Simon
See Heinlein, Robert A(nson)
Yorke, Henry Vincent 1905-1974 ..... **CLC 13**
See also Green, Henry
See also CA 85-88; 49-52
Yosano Akiko 1878-1942 .... **TCLC 59; PC 11**
See also CA 161
Yoshimoto, Banana .... **CLC 84**
See also Yoshimoto, Mahoko
Yoshimoto, Mahoko 1964-
See Yoshimoto, Banana
See also CA 144
Young, Al(bert James) 1939- . **CLC 19; BLC;**
DAM MULT
See also BW 2; CA 29-32R; CANR 26, 65; DLB
33
Young, Andrew (John) 1885-1971 ...... **CLC 5**
See also CA 5-8R; CANR 7, 29
Young, Collier
See Bloch, Robert (Albert)
Young, Edward 1683-1765 .... **LC 3, 40**
See also DLB 95
Young, Marguerite (Vivian) 1909-1995 **C L C**
82
See also CA 13-16; 150; CAP 1
Young, Neil 1945- .... **CLC 17**

See also CA 110
Young Bear, Ray A. 1950- ..... **CLC 94; DAM**
MULT
See also CA 146; DLB 175; NNAL
Yourcenar, Marguerite 1903-1987 **CLC 19, 38,**
50, 87; DAM NOV
See also CA 69-72; CANR 23, 60; DLB 72;
DLBY 88; MTCW
Yurick, Sol 1925- .... **CLC 6**
See also CA 13-16R; CANR 25
Zabolotskii, Nikolai Alekseevich 1903-1958
TCLC 52
See also CA 116; 164
Zamiatin, Yevgenii
See Zamyatin, Evgeny Ivanovich
Zamora, Bernice (B. Ortiz) 1938-... **CLC 89;**
DAM MULT; HLC
See also CA 151; DLB 82; HW
Zamyatin, Evgeny Ivanovich 1884-1937
TCLC 8, 37
See also CA 105
Zangwill, Israel 1864-1926 .... **TCLC 16**
See also CA 109; DLB 10, 135
Zappa, Francis Vincent, Jr. 1940-1993
See Zappa, Frank
See also CA 108; 143; CANR 57
Zappa, Frank .... **CLC 17**
See also Zappa, Francis Vincent, Jr.
Zaturenska, Marya 1902-1982 ...... **CLC 6, 11**
See also CA 13-16R; 105; CANR 22
Zeami 1363-1443 .... **DC 7**
Zelazny, Roger (Joseph) 1937-1995 . **CLC 21**
See also AAYA 7; CA 21-24R; 148; CANR 26,
60; DLB 8; MTCW; SATA 57; SATA-Brief
39
Zhdanov, Andrei A(lexandrovich) 1896-1948
TCLC 18
See also CA 117
Zhukovsky, Vasily 1783-1852 .... **NCLC 35**
Ziegenhagen, Eric .... **CLC 55**

Zimmer, Jill Schary
See Robinson, Jill
Zimmerman, Robert
See Dylan, Bob
Zindel, Paul 1936- **CLC 6, 26; DA; DAB; DAC;**
DAM DRAM, MST, NOV; DC 5
See also AAYA 2; CA 73-76; CANR 31, 65;
CLR 3, 45; DLB 7, 52; JRDA; MAICYA;
MTCW; SATA 16, 58
Zinov'Ev, A. A.
See Zinoviev, Alexander (Aleksandrovich)
Zinoviev, Alexander (Aleksandrovich) 1922-
CLC 19
See also CA 116; 133; CAAS 10
Zoilus
See Lovecraft, H(oward) P(hillips)
Zola, Emile (Edouard Charles Antoine) 1840-
1902 **TCLC 1, 6, 21, 41; DA; DAB; DAC;**
DAM MST, NOV; WLC
See also CA 104; 138; DLB 123
Zoline, Pamela 1941- .... **CLC 62**
See also CA 161
Zorrilla y Moral, Jose 1817-1893 .... **NCLC 6**
Zoshchenko, Mikhail (Mikhailovich) 1895-1958
TCLC 15; SSC 15
See also CA 115; 160
Zuckmayer, Carl 1896-1977 .... **CLC 18**
See also CA 69-72; DLB 56, 124
Zuk, Georges
See Skelton, Robin
Zukofsky, Louis 1904-1978 **CLC 1, 2, 4, 7, 11,**
18; DAM POET; PC 11
See also CA 9-12R; 77-80; CANR 39; DLB 5,
165; MTCW
Zweig, Paul 1935-1984 .... **CLC 34, 42**
See also CA 85-88; 113
Zweig, Stefan 1881-1942 .... **TCLC 17**
See also CA 112; DLB 81, 118
Zwingli, Huldreich 1484-1531 .... **LC 37**
See also DLB 179

Literary Criticism Series
Cumulative Topic Index

This index lists all topic entries in Gale's *Classical and Medieval Literature Criticism, Contemporary Literary Criticism, Literature Criticism from 1400 to 1800, Nineteenth-Century Literature Criticism,* and *Twentieth-Century Literary Criticism.*

Age of Johnson LC 15: 1-87
  Johnson's London, 3-15
  aesthetics of neoclassicism, 15-36
  "age of prose and reason," 36-45
  clubmen and bluestockings, 45-56
  printing technology, 56-62
  periodicals: "a map of busy life," 62-74
  transition, 74-86

Age of Spenser LC 39: 1-70
  Overviews, 2-21
  Literary Style, 22-34
  Poets and the Crown, 34-70

AIDS in Literature CLC 81: 365-416

Alcohol and Literature TCLC 70: 1-58
  overview, 2-8
  fiction, 8-48
  poetry and drama, 48-58

American Abolitionism NCLC 44: 1-73
  overviews, 2-26
  abolitionist ideals, 26-46
  the literature of abolitionism, 46-72

American Black Humor Fiction TCLC 54: 1-85
  characteristics of black humor, 2-13
  origins and development, 13-38
  black humor distinguished from related literary trends, 38-60
  black humor and society, 60-75
  black humor reconsidered, 75-83

American Civil War in Literature NCLC 32: 1-109
  overviews, 2-20
  regional perspectives, 20-54
  fiction popular during the war, 54-79
  the historical novel, 79-108

American Frontier in Literature NCLC 28: 1-103
  definitions, 2-12
  development, 12-17

nonfiction writing about the frontier, 17-30
  frontier fiction, 30-45
  frontier protagonists, 45-66
  portrayals of Native Americans, 66-86
  feminist readings, 86-98
  twentieth-century reaction against frontier literature, 98-100

American Humor Writing NCLC 52: 1-59
  overviews, 2-12
  the Old Southwest, 12-42
  broader impacts, 42-5
  women humorists, 45-58

***American Mercury,* The** TCLC 74: 1-80

American Popular Song, Golden Age of TCLC 42: 1-49
  background and major figures, 2-34
  the lyrics of popular songs, 34-47

American Proletarian Literature TCLC 54: 86-175
  overviews, 87-95
  American proletarian literature and the American Communist Party, 95-111
  ideology and literary merit, 111-7
  novels, 117-36
  Gastonia, 136-48
  drama, 148-54
  journalism, 154-9
  proletarian literature in the United States, 159-74

American Romanticism NCLC 44: 74-138
  overviews, 74-84
  sociopolitical influences, 84-104
  Romanticism and the American frontier, 104-15
  thematic concerns, 115-37

American Western Literature TCLC 46: 1-100
  definition and development of American Western literature, 2-7
  characteristics of the Western novel, 8-

23
  Westerns as history and fiction, 23-34
  critical reception of American Western literature, 34-41
  the Western hero, 41-73
  women in Western fiction, 73-91
  later Western fiction, 91-9

Art and Literature TCLC 54: 176-248
  overviews, 176-93
  definitions, 193-219
  influence of visual arts on literature, 219-31
  spatial form in literature, 231-47

Arthurian Literature CMLC 10: 1-127
  historical context and literary beginnings, 2-27
  development of the legend through Malory, 27-64
  development of the legend from Malory to the Victorian Age, 65-81
  themes and motifs, 81-95
  principal characters, 95-125

Arthurian Revival NCLC 36: 1-77
  overviews, 2-12
  Tennyson and his influence, 12-43
  other leading figures, 43-73
  the Arthurian legend in the visual arts, 73-6

Australian Literature TCLC 50: 1-94
  origins and development, 2-21
  characteristics of Australian literature, 21-33
  historical and critical perspectives, 33-41
  poetry, 41-58
  fiction, 58-76
  drama, 76-82
  Aboriginal literature, 82-91

Beat Generation, Literature of the TCLC 42: 50-102
  overviews, 51-9
  the Beat generation as a social phenom-

enon, 59-62
development, 62-5
Beat literature, 66-96
influence, 97-100

The Bell Curve Controversy CLC 91: 281-330

***Bildungsroman* in Nineteenth-Century Literature** NCLC 20: 92-168
surveys, 93-113
in Germany, 113-40
in England, 140-56
female *Bildungsroman,* 156-67

Bloomsbury Group TCLC 34: 1-73
history and major figures, 2-13
definitions, 13-7
influences, 17-27
thought, 27-40
prose, 40-52
and literary criticism, 52-4
political ideals, 54-61
response to, 61-71

Bly, Robert, *Iron John: A Book about Men and Men's Work* CLC 70: 414-62

The Book of J CLC 65: 289-311

Buddhism and Literature TCLC 70: 59-164
eastern literature, 60-113
western literature, 113-63

Businessman in American Literature TCLC 26: 1-48
portrayal of the businessman, 1-32
themes and techniques in business fiction, 32-47

Catholicism in Nineteenth-Century American Literature NCLC 64: 1-58
overviews, 3-14
polemical literature, 14-46
Catholicism in literature, 47-57

Celtic Mythology CMLC 26: 1-111
overviews, 2-22
Celtic myth as literature and history, 22-48
Celtic religion: Druids and divinities, 48-80
Fionn MacCuhaill and the Fenian cycle, 80-111

Celtic Twilight
See **Irish Literary Renaissance**

Chartist Movement and Literature, The

NCLC 60: 1-84
overview: nineteenth-century working-class fiction, 2-19
Chartist fiction and poetry, 19-73
the Chartist press, 73-84

Children's Literature, Nineteenth-Century NCLC 52: 60-135
overviews, 61-72
moral tales, 72-89
fairy tales and fantasy, 90-119
making men/making women, 119-34

Civic Critics, Russian NCLC 20: 402-46
principal figures and background, 402-9
and Russian Nihilism, 410-6
aesthetic and critical views, 416-45

The Cockney School NCLC 68: 1-64
overview, 2-7
Blackwood's Magazine and the contemporary critical response, 7-24
the political and social import of the Cockneys and their critics, 24-63

Colonial America: The Intellectual Background LC 25: 1-98
overviews, 2-17
philosophy and politics, 17-31
early religious influences in Colonial America, 31-60
consequences of the Revolution, 60-78
religious influences in post-revolution-ary America, 78-87
colonial literary genres, 87-97

Colonialism in Victorian English Literature NCLC 56: 1-77
overviews, 2-34
colonialism and gender, 34-51
monsters and the occult, 51-76

Columbus, Christopher, Books on the Quincentennial of His Arrival in the New World CLC 70: 329-60

Comic Books TCLC 66: 1-139
historical and critical perspectives, 2-48
superheroes, 48-67
underground comix, 67-88
comic books and society, 88-122
adult comics and graphic novels, 122-36

Connecticut Wits NCLC 48: 1-95
general overviews, 2-40
major works, 40-76
intellectual context, 76-95

Crime in Literature TCLC 54: 249-307
evolution of the criminal figure in

literature, 250-61
crime and society, 261-77
literary perspectives on crime and punishment, 277-88
writings by criminals, 288-306

Czechoslovakian Literature of the Twentieth Century TCLC 42: 103-96
through World War II, 104-35
de-Stalinization, the Prague Spring, and contemporary literature, 135-72
Slovak literature, 172-85
Czech science fiction, 185-93

Dadaism TCLC 46: 101-71
background and major figures, 102-16
definitions, 116-26
manifestos and commentary by Dadaists, 126-40
theater and film, 140-58
nature and characteristics of Dadaist writing, 158-70

Darwinism and Literature NCLC 32: 110-206
background, 110-31
direct responses to Darwin, 131-71
collateral effects of Darwinism, 171-205

Death in Nineteenth-Century British Literature NCLC 68: 65-142
overviews, 66-92
responses to death, 92-102
feminist perspectives, 103-17
striving for immortality, 117-41

Death in Literature TCLC 78:1-183
fiction, 2-115
poetry, 115-46
drama, 146-81

de Man, Paul, Wartime Journalism of CLC 55: 382-424

Detective Fiction, Nineteenth-Century NCLC 36: 78-148
origins of the genre, 79-100
history of nineteenth-century detective fiction, 101-33
significance of nineteenth-century detective fiction, 133-46

Detective Fiction, Twentieth-Century TCLC 38: 1-96
genesis and history of the detective story, 3-22
defining detective fiction, 22-32
evolution and varieties, 32-77
the appeal of detective fiction, 77-90

Disease and Literature TCLC 66: 140-283
  overviews, 141-65
  disease in nineteenth-century literature, 165-81
  tuberculosis and literature, 181-94
  women and disease in literature, 194-221
  plague literature, 221-53
  AIDS in literature, 253-82

The Double in Nineteenth-Century Literature NCLC 40: 1-95
  genesis and development of the theme, 2-15
  the double and Romanticism, 16-27
  sociological views, 27-52
  psychological interpretations, 52-87
  philosophical considerations, 87-95

Dramatic Realism NCLC 44: 139-202
  overviews, 140-50
  origins and definitions, 150-66
  impact and influence, 166-93
  realist drama and tragedy, 193-201

Drugs and Literature TCLC 78: 184-282
  overviews, 185-201
  pre-twentieth-century literature, 201-42
  twentieth-century literature, 242-82

Eastern Mythology CMLC 26: 112-92
  heroes and kings, 113-51
  cross-cultural perspective, 151-69
  relations to history and society, 169-92

Electronic "Books": Hypertext and Hyperfiction CLC 86: 367-404
  books vs. CD-ROMS, 367-76
  hypertext and hyperfiction, 376-95
  implications for publishing, libraries, and the public, 395-403

Eliot, T. S., Centenary of Birth CLC 55: 345-75

Elizabethan Drama LC 22: 140-240
  origins and influences, 142-67
  characteristics and conventions, 167-83
  theatrical production, 184-200
  histories, 200-12
  comedy, 213-20
  tragedy, 220-30

Elizabethan Prose Fiction LC 41: 1-70
  overviews, 1-15
  origins and influences, 15-43
  style and structure, 43-69

The Encyclopedists LC 26: 172-253
  overviews, 173-210

  intellectual background, 210-32
  views on esthetics, 232-41
  views on women, 241-52

English Caroline Literature LC 13: 221-307
  background, 222-41
  evolution and varieties, 241-62
  the Cavalier mode, 262-75
  court and society, 275-91
  politics and religion, 291-306

English Decadent Literature of the 1890s NCLC 28: 104-200
  fin de siècle: the Decadent period, 105-19
  definitions, 120-37
  major figures: "the tragic generation," 137-50
  French literature and English literary Decadence, 150-7
  themes, 157-61
  poetry, 161-82
  periodicals, 182-96

English Essay, Rise of the LC 18: 238-308
  definitions and origins, 236-54
  influence on the essay, 254-69
  historical background, 269-78
  the essay in the seventeenth century, 279-93
  the essay in the eighteenth century, 293-307

English Mystery Cycle Dramas LC 34: 1-88
  overviews, 1-27
  the nature of dramatic performances, 27-42
  the medieval worldview and the mystery cycles, 43-67
  the doctrine of repentance and the mystery cycles, 67-76
  the fall from grace in the mystery cycles, 76-88

English Romantic Hellenism NCLC 68: 143-250
  overviews, 144-69
  historical development of English Romantic Hellenism, 169-91
  inflience of Greek mythology on the Romantics, 191-229
  influence of Greek literature, art, and culture on the Romantics, 229-50

English Romantic Poetry NCLC 28: 201-327
  overviews and reputation, 202-37
  major subjects and themes, 237-67

  forms of Romantic poetry, 267-78
  politics, society, and Romantic poetry, 278-99
  philosophy, religion, and Romantic poetry, 299-324

Espionage Literature TCLC 50: 95-159
  overviews, 96-113
  espionage fiction/formula fiction, 113-26
  spies in fact and fiction, 126-38
  the female spy, 138-44
  social and psychological perspectives, 144-58

European Romanticism NCLC 36: 149-284
  definitions, 149-77
  origins of the movement, 177-82
  Romantic theory, 182-200
  themes and techniques, 200-23
  Romanticism in Germany, 223-39
  Romanticism in France, 240-61
  Romanticism in Italy, 261-4
  Romanticism in Spain, 264-8
  impact and legacy, 268-82

Existentialism and Literature TCLC 42: 197-268
  overviews and definitions, 198-209
  history and influences, 209-19
  Existentialism critiqued and defended, 220-35
  philosophical and religious perspectives, 235-41
  Existentialist fiction and drama, 241-67

Familiar Essay NCLC 48: 96-211
  definitions and origins, 97-130
  overview of the genre, 130-43
  elements of form and style, 143-59
  elements of content, 159-73
  the Cockneys: Hazlitt, Lamb, and Hunt, 173-91
  status of the genre, 191-210

Fear in Literature TCLC 74: 81-258
  overviews, 81
  pre-twentieth-century literature, 123
  twentieth-century literature, 182

Feminism in the 1990s: Commentary on Works by Naomi Wolf, Susan Faludi, and Camille Paglia CLC 76: 377-415

Feminist Criticism in 1990 CLC 65: 312-60

Fifteenth-Century English Literature LC 17: 248-334

background, 249-72
poetry, 272-315
drama, 315-23
prose, 323-33

Film and Literature TCLC 38: 97-226
overviews, 97-119
film and theater, 119-34
film and the novel, 134-45
the art of the screenplay, 145-66
genre literature/genre film, 167-79
the writer and the film industry, 179-90
authors on film adaptations of their
works, 190-200
fiction into film: comparative essays,
200-23

French Drama in the Age of Louis XIV LC
28: 94-185
overview, 95-127
tragedy, 127-46
comedy, 146-66
tragicomedy, 166-84

French Enlightenment LC 14: 81-145
the question of definition, 82-9
Le siècle des lumières, 89-94
women and the salons, 94-105
censorship, 105-15
the philosophy of reason, 115-31
influence and legacy, 131-44

French Realism NCLC 52: 136-216
origins and definitions, 137-70
issues and influence, 170-98
realism and representation, 198-215

French Revolution and English Literature
NCLC 40: 96-195
history and theory, 96-123
romantic poetry, 123-50
the novel, 150-81
drama, 181-92
children's literature, 192-5

Futurism, Italian TCLC 42: 269-354
principles and formative influences,
271-9
manifestos, 279-88
literature, 288-303
theater, 303-19
art, 320-30
music, 330-6
architecture, 336-9
and politics, 339-46
reputation and significance, 346-51

Gaelic Revival
See **Irish Literary Renaissance**

**Gates, Henry Louis, Jr., and African-
American Literary Criticism** CLC 65:
361-405

Gay and Lesbian Literature CLC 76: 416-
39

German Exile Literature TCLC 30: 1-58
the writer and the Nazi state, 1-10
definition of, 10-4
life in exile, 14-32
surveys, 32-50
Austrian literature in exile, 50-2
German publishing in the United States,
52-7

German Expressionism TCLC 34: 74-160
history and major figures, 76-85
aesthetic theories, 85-109
drama, 109-26
poetry, 126-38
film, 138-42
painting, 142-7
music, 147-53
and politics, 153-8

***Glasnost* and Contemporary Soviet
Literature** CLC 59: 355-97

Gothic Novel NCLC 28: 328-402
development and major works, 328-34
definitions, 334-50
themes and techniques, 350-78
in America, 378-85
in Scotland, 385-91
influence and legacy, 391-400

Graphic Narratives CLC 86: 405-32
history and overviews, 406-21
the "Classics Illustrated" series, 421-2
reviews of recent works, 422-32

Greek Historiography CMLC 17: 1-49

Greek Mythology CMLC-26 193-320
overviews, 194-209
origins and development of Greek
mythology, 209-29
cosmogonies and divinities in Greek
mythology, 229-54
heroes and heroines in Greek mythology, 254-80
women in Greek mythology, 280-320

Harlem Renaissance TCLC 26: 49-125
principal issues and figures, 50-67
the literature and its audience, 67-74
theme and technique in poetry, fiction,
and drama, 74-115
and American society, 115-21

achievement and influence, 121-2

Havel, Václav, Playwright and President
CLC 65: 406-63

Historical Fiction, Nineteenth-Century
NCLC 48: 212-307
definitions and characteristics, 213-36
Victorian historical fiction, 236-65
American historical fiction, 265-88
realism in historical fiction, 288-306

**Holocaust and the Atomic Bomb: Fifty
Years Later** CLC 91: 331-82
the Holocaust remembered, 333-52
Anne Frank revisited, 352-62
the atomic bomb and American memory,
362-81

Holocaust Denial Literature TCLC 58: 1-
110
overviews, 1-30
Robert Faurisson and Noam Chomsky,
30-52
Holocaust denial literature in America,
52-71
library access to Holocaust denial
literature, 72-5
the authenticity of Anne Frank's diary,
76-90
David Irving and the "normalization" of
Hitler, 90-109

Holocaust, Literature of the TCLC 42:
355-450
historical overview, 357-61
critical overview, 361-70
diaries and memoirs, 370-95
novels and short stories, 395-425
poetry, 425-41
drama, 441-8

**Homosexuality in Nineteenth-Century
Literature** NCLC 56: 78-182
defining homosexuality, 80-111
Greek love, 111-44
trial and danger, 144-81

**Hungarian Literature of the Twentieth
Century** TCLC 26: 126-88
surveys of, 126-47
Nyugat and early twentieth-century
literature, 147-56
mid-century literature, 156-68
and politics, 168-78
since the 1956 revolt, 178-87

Hysteria in Nineteenth-Century Literature
NCLC 64: 59-184
the history of hysteria, 60-75

the gender of hysteria, 75-103
hysteria and women's narratives, 103-57
hysteria in nineteenth-century poetry, 157-83

Imagism TCLC 74: 259-454
history and development, 260
major figures, 288
sources and influences, 352
Imagism and other movements, 397
influence and legacy, 431

Indian Literature in English TCLC 54: 308-406
overview, 309-13
origins and major figures, 313-25
the Indo-English novel, 325-55
Indo-English poetry, 355-67
Indo-English drama, 367-72
critical perspectives on Indo-English literature, 372-80
modern Indo-English literature, 380-9
Indo-English authors on their work, 389-404

Industrial Revolution in Literature, The NCLC 56: 183-273
historical and cultural perspectives, 184-201
contemporary reactions to the machine, 201-21
themes and symbols in literature, 221-73

The Irish Famine as Represented in Nineteenth-Century Literature NCLC 64: 185-261
overviews, 187-98
historical background, 198-212
famine novels, 212-34
famine poetry, 234-44
famine letters and eye-witness accounts, 245-61

Irish Literary Renaissance TCLC 46: 172-287
overview, 173-83
development and major figures, 184-202
influence of Irish folklore and mythology, 202-22
Irish poetry, 222-34
Irish drama and the Abbey Theatre, 234-56
Irish fiction, 256-86

Irish Nationalism and Literature NCLC 44: 203-73
the Celtic element in literature, 203-19
anti-Irish sentiment and the Celtic response, 219-34
literary ideals in Ireland, 234-45

literary expressions, 245-73

Italian Futurism
See **Futurism, Italian**

Italian Humanism LC 12: 205-77
origins and early development, 206-18
revival of classical letters, 218-23
humanism and other philosophies, 224-39
humanisms and humanists, 239-46
the plastic arts, 246-57
achievement and significance, 258-76

Italian Romanticism NCLC 60: 85-145
origins and overviews, 86-101
Italian Romantic theory, 101-25
the language of Romanticism, 125-45

Jacobean Drama LC 33: 1-37
the Jacobean worldview: an era of transition, 2-14
the moral vision of Jacobean drama, 14-22
Jacobean tragedy, 22-3
the Jacobean masque, 23-36

Jewish-American Fiction TCLC 62: 1-181
overviews, 2-24
major figures, 24-48
Jewish writers and American life, 48-78
Jewish characters in American fiction, 78-108
themes in Jewish-American fiction, 108-43
Jewish-American women writers, 143-59
the Holocaust and Jewish-American fiction, 159-81

Knickerbocker Group, The NCLC 56: 274-341
overviews, 276-314
Knickerbocker periodicals, 314-26
writers and artists, 326-40

Lake Poets, The NCLC 52: 217-304
characteristics of the Lake Poets and their works, 218-27
literary influences and collaborations, 227-66
defining and developing Romantic ideals, 266-84
embracing Conservatism, 284-303

Larkin, Philip, Controversy CLC 81: 417-64

Latin American Literature, Twentieth-

Century TCLC 58: 111-98
historical and critical perspectives, 112-36
the novel, 136-45
the short story, 145-9
drama, 149-60
poetry, 160-7
the writer and society, 167-86
Native Americans in Latin American literature, 186-97

Madness in Twentieth-Century Literature TCLC 50: 160-225
overviews, 161-71
madness and the creative process, 171-86
suicide, 186-91
madness in American literature, 191-207
madness in German literature, 207-13
madness and feminist artists, 213-24

Memoirs of Trauma CLC 109: 419-466
overview, 420
criticism, 429

Metaphysical Poets LC 24: 356-439
early definitions, 358-67
surveys and overviews, 367-92
cultural and social influences, 392-406
stylistic and thematic variations, 407-38

Modern Essay, The TCLC 58: 199-273
overview, 200-7
the essay in the early twentieth century, 207-19
characteristics of the modern essay, 219-32
modern essayists, 232-45
the essay as a literary genre, 245-73

Modern Japanese Literature TCLC 66: 284-389
poetry, 285-305
drama, 305-29
fiction, 329-61
western influences, 361-87

Modernism TCLC 70: 165-275
definitions, 166-184
Modernism and earlier influences, 184-200
stylistic and thematic traits, 200-229
poetry and drama, 229-242
redefining Modernism, 242-275

Muckraking Movement in American Journalism TCLC 34: 161-242
development, principles, and major figures, 162-70
publications, 170-9

social and political ideas, 179-86
targets, 186-208
fiction, 208-19
decline, 219-29
impact and accomplishments, 229-40

Multiculturalism in Literature and Education CLC 70: 361-413

Music and Modern Literature TCLC 62: 182-329
overviews, 182-211
musical form/literary form, 211-32
music in literature, 232-50
the influence of music on literature, 250-73
literature and popular music, 273-303
jazz and poetry, 303-28

Native American Literature CLC 76: 440-76

Natural School, Russian NCLC 24: 205-40
history and characteristics, 205-25
contemporary criticism, 225-40

Naturalism NCLC 36: 285-382
definitions and theories, 286-305
critical debates on Naturalism, 305-16
Naturalism in theater, 316-32
European Naturalism, 332-61
American Naturalism, 361-72
the legacy of Naturalism, 372-81

Negritude TCLC 50: 226-361
origins and evolution, 227-56
definitions, 256-91
Negritude in literature, 291-343
Negritude reconsidered, 343-58

New Criticism TCLC 34: 243-318
development and ideas, 244-70
debate and defense, 270-99
influence and legacy, 299-315

The New World in Renaissance Literature LC 31: 1-51
overview, 1-18
utopia vs. terror, 18-31
explorers and Native Americans, 31-51

New York Intellectuals and *Partisan Review* TCLC 30: 117-98
development and major figures, 118-28
influence of Judaism, 128-39
Partisan Review, 139-57
literary philosophy and practice, 157-75
political philosophy, 175-87
achievement and significance, 187-97

The New Yorker TCLC 58: 274-357
overviews, 274-95
major figures, 295-304
New Yorker style, 304-33
fiction, journalism, and humor at *The New Yorker,* 333-48
the new *New Yorker,* 348-56

Newgate Novel NCLC 24: 166-204
development of Newgate literature, 166-73
Newgate Calendar, 173-7
Newgate fiction, 177-95
Newgate drama, 195-204

Nigerian Literature of the Twentieth Century TCLC 30: 199-265
surveys of, 199-227
English language and African life, 227-45
politics and the Nigerian writer, 245-54
Nigerian writers and society, 255-62

Nineteenth-Century Native American Autobiography NCLC 64: 262-389
overview, 263-8
problems of authorship, 268-81
the evolution of Native American autobiography, 281-304
political issues, 304-15
gender and autobiography, 316-62
autobiographical works during the turn of the century, 362-88

Norse Mythology CMLC-26: 321-85
history and mythological tradition, 322-44
Eddic poetry, 344-74
Norse mythology and other traditions, 374-85

Northern Humanism LC 16: 281-356
background, 282-305
precursor of the Reformation, 305-14
the Brethren of the Common Life, the Devotio Moderna, and education, 314-40
the impact of printing, 340-56

Novel of Manners, The NCLC 56: 342-96
social and political order, 343-53
domestic order, 353-73
depictions of gender, 373-83
the American novel of manners, 383-95

Nuclear Literature: Writings and Criticism in the Nuclear Age TCLC 46: 288-390
overviews, 290-301
fiction, 301-35

poetry, 335-8
nuclear war in Russo-Japanese literature, 338-55
nuclear war and women writers, 355-67
the nuclear referent and literary criticism, 367-88

Occultism in Modern Literature TCLC 50: 362-406
influence of occultism on literature, 363-72
occultism, literature, and society, 372-87
fiction, 387-96
drama, 396-405

Opium and the Nineteenth-Century Literary Imagination NCLC 20: 250-301
original sources, 250-62
historical background, 262-71
and literary society, 271-9
and literary creativity, 279-300

Periodicals, Nineteenth-Century British NCLC 24: 100-65
overviews, 100-30
in the Romantic Age, 130-41
in the Victorian era, 142-54
and the reviewer, 154-64

Plath, Sylvia, and the Nature of Biography CLC 86: 433-62
the nature of biography, 433-52
reviews of *The Silent Woman,* 452-61

Political Theory from the 15th to the 18th Century LC 36: 1-55
Overview, 1-26
Natural Law, 26-42
Empiricism, 42-55

Polish Romanticism NCLC 52: 305-71
overviews, 306-26
major figures, 326-40
Polish Romantic drama, 340-62
influences, 362-71

Popular Literature TCLC 70: 279-382
overviews, 280-324
"formula" fiction, 324-336
readers of popular literature, 336-351
evolution of popular literature, 351-382

Pre-Raphaelite Movement NCLC 20: 302-401
overview, 302-4
genesis, 304-12
Germ and *Oxford and Cambridge Magazine,* 312-20
Robert Buchanan and the "Fleshly School of Poetry," 320-31

satires and parodies, 331-4
surveys, 334-51
aesthetics, 351-75
sister arts of poetry and painting, 375-94
influence, 394-9

Preromanticism LC 40: 1-56
overviews, 2-14
defining the period, 14-23
new directions in poetry and prose, 23-
45
the focus on the self, 45-56

Presocratic Philosophy CMLC 22: 1-56
overviews, 3-24
the Ionians and the Pythagoreans, 25-35
Heraclitus, the Eleatics, and the
Atomists, 36-47
the Sophists, 47-55

Protestant Reformation, Literature of the
LC 37: 1-83
overviews, 1-49
humanism and scholasticism, 49-69
the reformation and literature, 69-82

Psychoanalysis and Literature TCLC 38:
227-338
overviews, 227-46
Freud on literature, 246-51
psychoanalytic views of the literary
process, 251-61
psychoanalytic theories of response to
literature, 261-88
psychoanalysis and literary criticism,
288-312
psychoanalysis as literature/literature as
psychoanalysis, 313-34

Rap Music CLC 76: 477-50

Renaissance Natural Philosophy LC 27:
201-87
cosmology, 201-28
astrology, 228-54
magic, 254-86

Restoration Drama LC 21: 184-275
general overviews, 185-230
Jeremy Collier stage controversy, 230-9
other critical interpretations, 240-75

Revising the Literary Canon CLC 81:
465-509

Robin Hood, Legend of LC 19: 205-58
origins and development of the Robin
Hood legend, 206-20
representations of Robin Hood, 220-44
Robin Hood as hero, 244-56

Rushdie, Salman, *Satanic Verses* Contro-
versy CLC 55 214-63; 59: 404-56

Russian Nihilism NCLC 28: 403-47
definitions and overviews, 404-17
women and Nihilism, 417-27
literature as reform: the Civic Critics,
427-33
Nihilism and the Russian novel:
Turgenev and Dostoevsky, 433-47

Russian Thaw TCLC 26: 189-247
literary history of the period, 190-206
theoretical debate of socialist realism,
206-11
Novy Mir, 211-7
Literary Moscow, 217-24
Pasternak, *Zhivago,* and the Nobel
Prize, 224-7
poetry of liberation, 228-31
Brodsky trial and the end of the Thaw,
231-6
achievement and influence, 236-46

Salem Witch Trials LC-38: 1-145
overviews, 2-30
historical background, 30-65
judicial background, 65-78
the search for causes, 78-115
the role of women in the trials, 115-44

Salinger, J. D., Controversy Surrounding
In Search of J. D. Salinger CLC 55: 325-
44

Science Fiction, Nineteenth-Century
NCLC 24: 241-306
background, 242-50
definitions of the genre, 251-6
representative works and writers, 256-75
themes and conventions, 276-305

Scottish Chaucerians LC 20: 363-412

Scottish Poetry, Eighteenth-Century LC
29: 95-167
overviews, 96-114
the Scottish Augustans, 114-28
the Scots Vernacular Revival, 132-63
Scottish poetry after Burns, 163-6

Sentimental Novel, The NCLC 60: 146-
245
overviews, 147-58
the politics of domestic fiction, 158-79
a literature of resistance and repression,
179-212
the reception of sentimental fiction, 213-
44

Sherlock Holmes Centenary TCLC 26:
248-310
Doyle's life and the composition of the
Holmes stories, 248-59
life and character of Holmes, 259-78
method, 278-9
Holmes and the Victorian world, 279-92
Sherlockian scholarship, 292-301
Doyle and the development of the
detective story, 301-7
Holmes's continuing popularity, 307-9

Slave Narratives, American NCLC 20: 1-
91
background, 2-9
overviews, 9-24
contemporary responses, 24-7
language, theme, and technique, 27-70
historical authenticity, 70-5
antecedents, 75-83
role in development of Black American
literature, 83-8

Spanish Civil War Literature TCLC 26:
311-85
topics in, 312-33
British and American literature, 333-59
French literature, 359-62
Spanish literature, 362-73
German literature, 373-5
political idealism and war literature,
375-83

Spanish Golden Age Literature LC 23:
262-332
overviews, 263-81
verse drama, 281-304
prose fiction, 304-19
lyric poetry, 319-31

Spasmodic School of Poetry NCLC 24:
307-52
history and major figures, 307-21
the Spasmodics on poetry, 321-7
Firmilian and critical disfavor, 327-39
theme and technique, 339-47
influence, 347-51

Steinbeck, John, Fiftieth Anniversary of
The Grapes of Wrath CLC 59: 311-54

Sturm und Drang NCLC 40: 196-276
definitions, 197-238
poetry and poetics, 238-58
drama, 258-75

Supernatural Fiction in the Nineteenth
Century NCLC 32: 207-87
major figures and influences, 208-35
the Victorian ghost story, 236-54

Topic Index

the influence of science and occultism,
254-66
supernatural fiction and society, 266-86

Supernatural Fiction, Modern TCLC 30:
59-116
evolution and varieties, 60-74
"decline" of the ghost story, 74-86
as a literary genre, 86-92
technique, 92-101
nature and appeal, 101-15

Surrealism TCLC 30: 334-406
history and formative influences, 335-43
manifestos, 343-54
philosophic, aesthetic, and political
principles, 354-75
poetry, 375-81
novel, 381-6
drama, 386-92
film, 392-8
painting and sculpture, 398-403
achievement, 403-5

Symbolism, Russian TCLC 30: 266-333
doctrines and major figures, 267-92
theories, 293-8
and French Symbolism, 298-310
themes in poetry, 310-4
theater, 314-20
and the fine arts, 320-32

Symbolist Movement, French NCLC 20:
169-249
background and characteristics, 170-86
principles, 186-91
attacked and defended, 191-7
influences and predecessors, 197-211
and Decadence, 211-6
theater, 216-26
prose, 226-33
decline and influence, 233-47

Television and Literature TCLC 78: 283-
426
television and literacy, 283-98
reading vs. watching, 298-341
adaptations, 341-62
literary genres and television, 362-90
television genres and literature, 390-410
children's literature/children's television, 410-25

Theater of the Absurd TCLC 38: 339-415
"The Theater of the Absurd," 340-7
major plays and playwrights, 347-58
and the concept of the absurd, 358-86
theatrical techniques, 386-94

predecessors of, 394-402
influence of, 402-13

Tin Pan Alley
See **American Popular Song, Golden Age
of**

Transcendentalism, American NCLC 24:
1-99
overviews, 3-23
contemporary documents, 23-41
theological aspects of, 42-52
and social issues, 52-74
literature of, 74-96

Travel Writing in the Nineteenth Century
NCLC 44: 274-392
the European grand tour, 275-303
the Orient, 303-47
North America, 347-91

Travel Writing in the Twentieth Century
TCLC 30: 407-56
conventions and traditions, 407-27
and fiction writing, 427-43
comparative essays on travel writers,
443-54

True-Crime Literature CLC 99: 333-433
history and analysis, 334-407
reviews of true-crime publications, 407-
23
writing instruction, 424-29
author profiles, 429-33

Ulysses **and the Process of Textual
Reconstruction** TCLC 26: 386-416
evaluations of the new *Ulysses,* 386-94
editorial principles and procedures, 394-
401
theoretical issues, 401-16

Utopian Literature, Nineteenth-Century
NCLC 24: 353-473
definitions, 354-74
overviews, 374-88
theory, 388-408
communities, 409-26
fiction, 426-53
women and fiction, 454-71

Utopian Literature, Renaissance LC-32:
1-63
overviews, 2-25
classical background, 25-33
utopia and the social contract, 33-9
origins in mythology, 39-48
utopia and the Renaissance country

house, 48-52
influence of millenarianism, 52-62

Vampire in Literature TCLC 46: 391-454
origins and evolution, 392-412
social and psychological perspectives,
413-44
vampire fiction and science fiction, 445-
53

Victorian Autobiography NCLC 40: 277-
363
development and major characteristics,
278-88
themes and techniques, 289-313
the autobiographical tendency in
Victorian prose and poetry, 313-47
Victorian women's autobiographies,
347-62

Victorian Fantasy Literature NCLC 60:
246-384
overviews, 247-91
major figures, 292-366
women in Victorian fantasy literature,
366-83

Victorian Hellenism NCLC 68: 251-376
overviews, 252-78
the meanings of Hellenism, 278-335
the literary influence, 335-75

Victorian Novel NCLC 32: 288-454
development and major characteristics,
290-310
themes and techniques, 310-58
social criticism in the Victorian novel,
359-97
urban and rural life in the Victorian
novel, 397-406
women in the Victorian novel, 406-25
Mudie's Circulating Library, 425-34
the late-Victorian novel, 434-51

Vietnam War in Literature and Film CLC
91: 383-437
overview, 384-8
prose, 388-412
film and drama, 412-24
poetry, 424-35

Vorticism TCLC 62: 330-426
Wyndham Lewis and Vorticism, 330-8
characteristics and principles of
Vorticism, 338-65
Lewis and Pound, 365-82

Vorticist writing, 382-416
Vorticist painting, 416-26

Women's Diaries, Nineteenth-Century
NCLC 48: 308-54
    overview, 308-13
    diary as history, 314-25
    sociology of diaries, 325-34
    diaries as psychological scholarship,
        334-43
    diary as autobiography, 343-8
    diary as literature, 348-53

Women Writers, Seventeenth-Century LC
30: 2-58
    overview, 2-15
    women and education, 15-9
    women and autobiography, 19-31
    women's diaries, 31-9
    early feminists, 39-58

World War I Literature TCLC 34: 392-486
    overview, 393-403
    English, 403-27
    German, 427-50

American, 450-66
French, 466-74
and modern history, 474-82

Yellow Journalism NCLC 36: 383-456
    overviews, 384-96
    major figures, 396-413

Young Playwrights Festival
    1988—CLC 55: 376-81
    1989—CLC 59: 398-403
    1990—CLC 65: 444-8

Topic Index

Contemporary Literary Criticism
Cumulative Nationality Index

ALBANIAN

Kadare, Ismail **52**

ALGERIAN

Althusser, Louis **106**
Camus, Albert **1, 2, 4, 9, 11, 14, 32, 63, 69**
Cixous, Helene **92**
Cohen-Solal, Annie **50**

AMERICAN

Abbey, Edward **36, 59**
Abbott, Lee K(ittredge) **48**
Abish, Walter **22**
Abrams, M(eyer) H(oward) **24**
Acker, Kathy **45**
Adams, Alice (Boyd) **6, 13, 46**
Addams, Charles (Samuel) **30**
Adler, C(arole) S(chwerdtfeger) **35**
Adler, Renata **8, 31**
Ai **4, 14, 69**
Aiken, Conrad (Potter) **1, 3, 5, 10, 52**
Albee, Edward (Franklin III) **1, 2, 3, 5, 9, 11, 13, 25, 53, 86**
Alexander, Lloyd (Chudley) **35**
Alexie, Sherman (Joseph Jr.) **96**
Algren, Nelson **4, 10, 33**
Allen, Edward **59**
Allen, Paula Gunn **84**
Allen, Woody **16, 52**
Allison, Dorothy E. **78**
Alta **19**
Alter, Robert B(ernard) **34**
Alther, Lisa **7, 41**
Altman, Robert **16**
Alvarez, Julia **93**
Ammons, A(rchie) R(andolph) **2, 3, 5, 8, 9, 25, 57, 108**
Anaya, Rudolfo A(lfonso) **23**
Anderson, Jon (Victor) **9**
Anderson, Poul (William) **15**
Anderson, Robert (Woodruff) **23**
Angell, Roger **26**
Angelou, Maya **12, 35, 64, 77**
Anthony, Piers **35**
Apple, Max (Isaac) **9, 33**
Appleman, Philip (Dean) **51**
Archer, Jules **12**
Arendt, Hannah **66, 98**
Arnow, Harriette (Louisa) Simpson **2, 7, 18**
Arrick, Fran **30**
Arzner, Dorothy **98**
Ashbery, John (Lawrence) **2, 3, 4, 6, 9, 13, 15, 25, 41, 77**
Asimov, Isaac **1, 3, 9, 19, 26, 76, 92**
Attaway, William (Alexander) **92**
Auchincloss, Louis (Stanton) **4, 6, 9, 18, 45**
Auden, W(ystan) H(ugh) **1, 2, 3, 4, 6, 9, 11, 14, 43**
Auel, Jean M(arie) **31, 107**
Auster, Paul **47**
Bach, Richard (David) **14**
Badanes, Jerome **59**
Baker, Elliott **8**
Baker, Nicholson **61**

Baker, Russell (Wayne) **31**
Bakshi, Ralph **26**
Baldwin, James (Arthur) **1, 2, 3, 4, 5, 8, 13, 15, 17, 42, 50, 67, 90**
Bambara, Toni Cade **19, 88**
Banks, Russell **37, 72**
Baraka, Amiri **1, 2, 3, 5, 10, 14, 33**
Barbera, Jack (Vincent) **44**
Barnard, Mary (Ethel) **48**
Barnes, Djuna **3, 4, 8, 11, 29**
Barondess, Sue K(aufman) **8**
Barrett, William (Christopher) **27**
Barth, John (Simmons) **1, 2, 3, 5, 7, 9, 10, 14, 27, 51, 89**
Barthelme, Donald **1, 2, 3, 5, 6, 8, 13, 23, 46, 59**
Barthelme, Frederick **36**
Barzun, Jacques (Martin) **51**
Bass, Rick **79**
Baumbach, Jonathan **6, 23**
Bausch, Richard (Carl) **51**
Baxter, Charles (Morley) **45, 78**
Beagle, Peter S(oyer) **7, 104**
Beattie, Ann **8, 13, 18, 40, 63**
Becker, Walter **26**
Beecher, John **6**
Begiebing, Robert J(ohn) **70**
Behrman, S(amuel) N(athaniel) **40**
Belitt, Ben **22**
Bell, Madison Smartt **41, 102**
Bell, Marvin (Hartley) **8, 31**
Bellow, Saul **1, 2, 3, 6, 8, 10, 13, 15, 25, 33, 34, 63, 79**
Benary-Isbert, Margot **12**
Benchley, Peter (Bradford) **4, 8**
Benedikt, Michael **4, 14**
Benford, Gregory (Albert) **52**
Bennett, Hal **5**
Bennett, Jay **35**
Benson, Jackson J. **34**
Benson, Sally **17**
Bentley, Eric (Russell) **24**
Berendt, John (Lawrence) **86**
Berger, Melvin H. **12**
Berger, Thomas (Louis) **3, 5, 8, 11, 18, 38**
Bergstein, Eleanor **4**
Bernard, April **59**
Berriault, Gina **54, 109**
Berrigan, Daniel **4**
Berrigan, Ted **37**
Berry, Chuck **17**
Berry, Wendell (Erdman) **4, 6, 8, 27, 46**
Berryman, John **1, 2, 3, 4, 6, 8, 10, 13, 25, 62**
Bessie, Alvah **23**
Bettelheim, Bruno **79**
Betts, Doris (Waugh) **3, 6, 28**
Bidart, Frank **33**
Bishop, Elizabeth **1, 4, 9, 13, 15, 32**
Bishop, John **10**
Blackburn, Paul **9, 43**
Blackmur, R(ichard) P(almer) **2, 24**
Blaise, Clark **29**
Blatty, William Peter **2**
Blessing, Lee **54**

Blish, James (Benjamin) **14**
Bloch, Robert (Albert) **33**
Bloom, Harold **24, 103**
Blount, Roy (Alton) Jr. **38**
Blume, Judy (Sussman) **12, 30**
Bly, Robert (Elwood) **1, 2, 5, 10, 15, 38**
Bochco, Steven **35**
Bogan, Louise **4, 39, 46, 93**
Bogosian, Eric **45**
Bograd, Larry **35**
Bonham, Frank **12**
Bontemps, Arna(ud Wendell) **1, 18**
Booth, Philip **23**
Booth, Wayne C(layson) **24**
Bottoms, David **53**
Bourjaily, Vance (Nye) **8, 62**
Bova, Ben(jamin William) **45**
Bowers, Edgar **9**
Bowles, Jane (Sydney) **3, 68**
Bowles, Paul (Frederick) **1, 2, 19, 53**
Boyle, Kay **1, 5, 19, 58**
Boyle, T(homas) Coraghessan **36, 55, 90**
Bradbury, Ray (Douglas) **1, 3, 10, 15, 42, 98**
Bradley, David (Henry Jr.) **23**
Bradley, John Ed(mund Jr.) **55**
Bradley, Marion Zimmer **30**
Brady, Joan **86**
Brammer, William **31**
Brancato, Robin F(idler) **35**
Brand, Millen **7**
Branden, Barbara **44**
Branley, Franklyn M(ansfield) **21**
Brautigan, Richard (Gary) **1, 3, 5, 9, 12, 34, 42**
Braverman, Kate **67**
Brennan, Maeve **5**
Breslin, Jimmy **4, 43**
Bridgers, Sue Ellen **26**
Brin, David **34**
Brodkey, Harold (Roy) **56**
Brodsky, Joseph **4, 6, 13, 36, 100**
Brodsky, Michael (Mark) **19**
Bromell, Henry **5**
Broner, E(sther) M(asserman) **19**
Bronk, William **10**
Brooks, Cleanth **24, 86**
Brooks, Gwendolyn **1, 2, 4, 5, 15, 49**
Brooks, Mel **12**
Brooks, Peter **34**
Brooks, Van Wyck **29**
Brosman, Catharine Savage **9**
Broughton, T(homas) Alan **19**
Broumas, Olga **10, 73**
Brown, Alan **99**
Brown, Claude **30**
Brown, Dee (Alexander) **18, 47**
Brown, Rita Mae **18, 43, 79**
Brown, Rosellen **32**
Brown, Sterling Allen **1, 23, 59**
Brown, (William) Larry **73**
Browne, (Clyde) Jackson **21**
Browning, Tod **16**
Bruccoli, Matthew J(oseph) **34**
Bruce, Lenny **21**

Bryan, C(ourtlandt) D(ixon) B(arnes) 29
Buchwald, Art(hur) 33
Buck, Pearl S(ydenstricker) 7, 11, 18
Buckley, William F(rank) Jr. 7, 18, 37
Buechner, (Carl) Frederick 2, 4, 6, 9
Bukowski, Charles 2, 5, 9, 41, 82, 108
Bullins, Ed 1, 5, 7
Burke, Kenneth (Duva) 2, 24
Burnshaw, Stanley 3, 13, 44
Burr, Anne 6
Burroughs, William S(eward) 1, 2, 5, 15, 22, 42, 75, 109
Busch, Frederick 7, 10, 18, 47
Bush, Ronald 34
Butler, Octavia E(stelle) 38
Butler, Robert Olen (Jr.) 81
Byars, Betsy (Cromer) 35
Byrne, David 26
Cage, John (Milton Jr.) 41
Cain, James M(allahan) 3, 11, 28
Caldwell, Erskine (Preston) 1, 8, 14, 50, 60
Caldwell, (Janet Miriam) Taylor (Holland) 2, 28, 39
Calisher, Hortense 2, 4, 8, 38
Cameron, Carey 59
Cameron, Peter 44
Campbell, John W(ood Jr.) 32
Campbell, Joseph 69
Campion, Jane 95
Canby, Vincent 13
Canin, Ethan 55
Capote, Truman 1, 3, 8, 13, 19, 34, 38, 58
Capra, Frank 16
Caputo, Philip 32
Card, Orson Scott 44, 47, 50
Carey, Ernestine Gilbreth 17
Carlisle, Henry (Coffin) 33
Carlson, Ron(ald F.) 54
Carpenter, Don(ald Richard) 41
Carr, Caleb 86
Carr, John Dickson 3
Carr, Virginia Spencer 34
Carroll, James P. 38
Carroll, Jim 35
Carruth, Hayden 4, 7, 10, 18, 84
Carson, Rachel Louise 71
Carver, Raymond 22, 36, 53, 55
Casey, John (Dudley) 59
Casey, Michael 2
Casey, Warren (Peter) 12
Cassavetes, John 20
Cassill, R(onald) V(erlin) 4, 23
Cassity, (Allen) Turner 6, 42
Castaneda, Carlos 12
Castedo, Elena 65
Catton, (Charles) Bruce 35
Caunitz, William J. 34
Cavanna, Betty 12
Chabon, Michael 55
Chappell, Fred (Davis) 40, 78
Charyn, Jerome 5, 8, 18
Chase, Mary Ellen 2
Chayefsky, Paddy 23
Cheever, John 3, 7, 8, 11, 15, 25, 64
Cheever, Susan 18, 48
Cherryh, C. J. 35
Chester, Alfred 49
Childress, Alice 12, 15, 86, 96
Chute, Carolyn 39
Ciardi, John (Anthony) 10, 40, 44
Cimino, Michael 16
Cisneros, Sandra 69
Clampitt, Amy 32

Clancy, Tom 45
Clark, Eleanor 5, 19
Clark, Walter Van Tilburg 28
Clarke, Shirley 16
Clavell, James (duMaresq) 6, 25, 87
Cleaver, (Leroy) Eldridge 30
Clifton, (Thelma) Lucille 19, 66
Coburn, D(onald) L(ee) 10
Codrescu, Andrei 46
Coen, Ethan 108
Coen, Joel 108
Cohen, Arthur A(llen) 7, 31
Coles, Robert (Martin) 108
Collier, Christopher 30
Collier, James L(incoln) 30
Collins, Linda 44
Colter, Cyrus 58
Colum, Padraic 28
Colwin, Laurie (E.) 5, 13, 23, 84
Condon, Richard (Thomas) 4, 6, 8, 10, 45, 100
Connell, Evan S(helby) Jr. 4, 6, 45
Connelly, Marc(us Cook) 7
Conroy, Donald Pat(rick) 30, 74
Cook, Robin 14
Cooke, Elizabeth 55
Cook-Lynn, Elizabeth 93
Cooper, J(oan) California 56
Coover, Robert (Lowell) 3, 7, 15, 32, 46, 87
Coppola, Francis Ford 16
Corcoran, Barbara 17
Corman, Cid 9
Cormier, Robert (Edmund) 12, 30
Corn, Alfred (DeWitt III) 33
Corso, (Nunzio) Gregory 1, 11
Costain, Thomas B(ertram) 30
Cowley, Malcolm 39
Cozzens, James Gould 1, 4, 11, 92
Crane, R(onald) S(almon) 27
Crase, Douglas 58
Creeley, Robert (White) 1, 2, 4, 8, 11, 15, 36, 78
Crews, Harry (Eugene) 6, 23, 49
Crichton, (John) Michael 2, 6, 54, 90
Cristofer, Michael 28
Crow Dog, Mary (Ellen) 93
Crowley, John 57
Crumb, R(obert) 17
Cryer, Gretchen (Kiger) 21
Cudlip, David 34
Cummings, E(dward) E(stlin) 1, 3, 8, 12, 15, 68
Cunningham, J(ames) V(incent) 3, 31
Cunningham, Julia (Woolfolk) 12
Cunningham, Michael 34
Currie, Ellen 44
Dacey, Philip 51
Dahlberg, Edward 1, 7, 14
Daitch, Susan 103
Daly, Elizabeth 52
Daly, Maureen 17
Dannay, Frederic 11
Danticat, Edwidge 94
Danvers, Dennis 70
Danziger, Paula 21
Davenport, Guy (Mattison Jr.) 6, 14, 38
Davidson, Donald (Grady) 2, 13, 19
Davidson, Sara 9
Davis, Angela (Yvonne) 77
Davis, Harold Lenoir 49
Davison, Peter (Hubert) 28
Dawson, Fielding 6
Deer, Sandra 45

Delany, Samuel R(ay Jr.) 8, 14, 38
Delbanco, Nicholas (Franklin) 6, 13
DeLillo, Don 8, 10, 13, 27, 39, 54, 76
Deloria, Vine (Victor) Jr. 21
Del Vecchio, John M(ichael) 29
de Man, Paul (Adolph Michel) 55
De Marinis, Rick 54
Demby, William 53
Denby, Edwin (Orr) 48
De Palma, Brian (Russell) 20
Deren, Maya 16, 102
Derleth, August (William) 31
Deutsch, Babette 18
De Vries, Peter 1, 2, 3, 7, 10, 28, 46
Dexter, Pete 34, 55
Diamond, Neil 30
Dick, Philip K(indred) 10, 30, 72
Dickey, James (Lafayette) 1, 2, 4, 7, 10, 15, 47, 109
Dickey, William 3, 28
Dickinson, Charles 49
Didion, Joan 1, 3, 8, 14, 32
Dillard, Annie 9, 60
Dillard, R(ichard) H(enry) W(ilde) 5
Disch, Thomas M(ichael) 7, 36
Dixon, Stephen 52
Dobyns, Stephen 37
Doctorow, E(dgar) L(aurence) 6, 11, 15, 18, 37, 44, 65
Dodson, Owen (Vincent) 79
Doerr, Harriet 34
Donaldson, Stephen R. 46
Donleavy, J(ames) P(atrick) 1, 4, 6, 10, 45
Donovan, John 35
Doolittle, Hilda 3, 8, 14, 31, 34, 73
Dorn, Edward (Merton) 10, 18
Dorris, Michael (Anthony) 109
Dos Passos, John (Roderigo) 1, 4, 8, 11, 15, 25, 34, 82
Douglas, Ellen 73
Dove, Rita (Frances) 50, 81
Dowell, Coleman 60
Drexler, Rosalyn 2, 6
Drury, Allen (Stuart) 37
Duberman, Martin (Bauml) 8
Dubie, Norman (Evans) 36
Du Bois, W(illiam) E(dward) B(urghardt) 1, 2, 13, 64, 96
Dubus, Andre 13, 36, 97
Duffy, Bruce 50
Dugan, Alan 2, 6
Dumas, Henry L. 6, 62
Duncan, Lois 26
Duncan, Robert (Edward) 1, 2, 4, 7, 15, 41, 55
Dunn, Katherine (Karen) 71
Dunn, Stephen 36
Dunne, John Gregory 28
Durang, Christopher (Ferdinand) 27, 38
Durban, (Rosa) Pam 39
Dworkin, Andrea 43
Dylan, Bob 3, 4, 6, 12, 77
Eastlake, William (Derry) 8
Eberhart, Richard (Ghormley) 3, 11, 19, 56
Eberstadt, Fernanda 39
Eckert, Allan W. 17
Edel, (Joseph) Leon 29, 34
Edgerton, Clyde (Carlyle) 39
Edmonds, Walter D(umaux) 35
Edson, Russell 13
Edwards, Gus 43
Ehle, John (Marsden Jr.) 27
Eigner, Larry 9
Eiseley, Loren Corey 7

Eisenstadt, Jill **50**
Eliade, Mircea **19**
Eliot, T(homas) S(tearns) **1, 2, 3, 6, 9, 10, 13, 15, 24, 34, 41, 55, 57**
Elkin, Stanley L(awrence) **4, 6, 9, 14, 27, 51, 91**
Elledge, Scott **34**
Elliott, George P(aul) **2**
Ellis, Bret Easton **39, 71**
Ellison, Harlan (Jay) **1, 13, 42**
Ellison, Ralph (Waldo) **1, 3, 11, 54, 86**
Ellmann, Lucy (Elizabeth) **61**
Ellmann, Richard (David) **50**
Elman, Richard (Martin) **19**
Ephron, Nora **17, 31**
Epstein, Daniel Mark **7**
Epstein, Jacob **19**
Epstein, Joseph **39**
Epstein, Leslie **27**
Erdman, Paul E(mil) **25**
Erdrich, Louise **39, 54**
Erickson, Steve **64**
Eshleman, Clayton **7**
Estleman, Loren D. **48**
Eugenides, Jeffrey **81**
Everett, Percival L. **57**
Everson, William (Oliver) **1, 5, 14**
Exley, Frederick (Earl) **6, 11**
Ezekiel, Tish O'Dowd **34**
Fagen, Donald **26**
Fair, Ronald L. **18**
Fante, John (Thomas) **60**
Farina, Richard **9**
Farley, Walter (Lorimer) **17**
Farmer, Philip Jose **1, 19**
Farrell, James T(homas) **1, 4, 8, 11, 66**
Fast, Howard (Melvin) **23**
Faulkner, William (Cuthbert) **1, 3, 6, 8, 9, 11, 14, 18, 28, 52, 68**
Fauset, Jessie Redmon **19, 54**
Faust, Irvin **8**
Fearing, Kenneth (Flexner) **51**
Federman, Raymond **6, 47**
Feiffer, Jules (Ralph) **2, 8, 64**
Feinberg, David B. **59**
Feldman, Irving (Mordecai) **7**
Felsen, Henry Gregor **17**
Ferber, Edna **18, 93**
Ferlinghetti, Lawrence (Monsanto) **2, 6, 10, 27**
Ferrigno, Robert **65**
Fiedler, Leslie A(aron) **4, 13, 24**
Field, Andrew **44**
Fierstein, Harvey (Forbes) **33**
Fisher, M(ary) F(rances) K(ennedy) **76, 87**
Fisher, Vardis (Alvero) **7**
Fitzgerald, Robert (Stuart) **39**
Flanagan, Thomas (James Bonner) **25, 52**
Fleming, Thomas (James) **37**
Foote, Horton **51, 91**
Foote, Shelby **75**
Forbes, Esther **12**
Forche, Carolyn (Louise) **25, 83, 86**
Ford, John **16**
Ford, Richard **46**
Ford, Richard **99**
Foreman, Richard **50**
Forman, James Douglas **21**
Fornes, Maria Irene **39, 61**
Forrest, Leon (Richard) **4**
Fosse, Bob **20**
Fox, Paula **2, 8**
Fox, William Price (Jr.) **22**

Francis, Robert (Churchill) **15**
Frank, Elizabeth **39**
Fraze, Candida (Merrill) **50**
Frazier, Ian **46**
Freeman, Judith **55**
French, Albert **86**
French, Marilyn **10, 18, 60**
Friedan, Betty (Naomi) **74**
Friedman, B(ernard) H(arper) **7**
Friedman, Bruce Jay **3, 5, 56**
Frost, Robert (Lee) **1, 3, 4, 9, 10, 13, 15, 26, 34, 44**
Fuchs, Daniel **34**
Fuchs, Daniel **8, 22**
Fuller, Charles (H. Jr.) **25**
Fulton, Alice **52**
Fussell, Paul **74**
Gaddis, William **1, 3, 6, 8, 10, 19, 43, 86**
Gaines, Ernest J(ames) **3, 11, 18, 86**
Gaitskill, Mary **69**
Gallagher, Tess **18, 63**
Gallant, Roy A(rthur) **17**
Gallico, Paul (William) **2**
Galvin, James **38**
Gann, Ernest Kellogg **23**
Garcia, Cristina **76**
Gardner, Herb(ert) **44**
Gardner, John (Champlin) Jr. **2, 3, 5, 7, 8, 10, 18, 28, 34**
Garrett, George (Palmer) **3, 11, 51**
Garrigue, Jean **2, 8**
Gass, William H(oward) **1, 2, 8, 11, 15, 39**
Gates, Henry Louis Jr. **65**
Gaye, Marvin (Penze) **26**
Gelbart, Larry (Simon) **21, 61**
Gelber, Jack **1, 6, 14, 79**
Gellhorn, Martha (Ellis) **14, 60**
Gent, Peter **29**
George, Jean Craighead **35**
Gertler, T. **34**
Ghiselin, Brewster **23**
Gibbons, Kaye **50, 88**
Gibson, William **23**
Gibson, William (Ford) **39, 63**
Gifford, Barry (Colby) **34**
Gilbreth, Frank B. Jr. **17**
Gilchrist, Ellen **34, 48**
Giles, Molly **39**
Gilliam, Terry (Vance) **21**
Gilroy, Frank D(aniel) **2**
Gilstrap, John **99**
Ginsberg, Allen **1, 2, 3, 4, 6, 13, 36, 69, 109**
Giovanni, Nikki **2, 4, 19, 64**
Glasser, Ronald J. **37**
Gluck, Louise (Elisabeth) **7, 22, 44, 81**
Godwin, Gail (Kathleen) **5, 8, 22, 31, 69**
Goines, Donald **80**
Gold, Herbert **4, 7, 14, 42**
Goldbarth, Albert **5, 38**
Goldman, Francisco **76**
Goldman, William (W.) **1, 48**
Goldsberry, Steven **34**
Goodman, Paul **1, 2, 4, 7**
Gordon, Caroline **6, 13, 29, 83**
Gordon, Mary (Catherine) **13, 22**
Gordon, Sol **26**
Gordone, Charles **1, 4**
Gould, Lois **4, 10**
Goyen, (Charles) William **5, 8, 14, 40**
Graham, Jorie **48**
Grau, Shirley Ann **4, 9**
Graver, Elizabeth **70**
Gray, Amlin **29**

Gray, Francine du Plessix **22**
Gray, Spalding **49**
Grayson, Richard (A.) **38**
Greeley, Andrew M(oran) **28**
Green, Hannah **3**
Green, Julien **3, 11, 77**
Green, Paul (Eliot) **25**
Greenberg, Joanne (Goldenberg) **7, 30**
Greenberg, Richard **57**
Greene, Bette **30**
Greene, Gael **8**
Gregor, Arthur **9**
Griffin, John Howard **68**
Griffin, Peter **39**
Grisham, John **84**
Grumbach, Doris (Isaac) **13, 22, 64**
Grunwald, Lisa **44**
Guare, John **8, 14, 29, 67**
Guest, Barbara **34**
Guest, Judith (Ann) **8, 30**
Guild, Nicholas M. **33**
Gunn, Bill **5**
Gurganus, Allan **70**
Gurney, A(lbert) R(amsdell) Jr. **32, 50, 54**
Gustafson, James M(oody) **100**
Guterson, David **91**
Guthrie, A(lfred) B(ertram) Jr. **23**
Guthrie, Woody **35**
Guy, Rosa (Cuthbert) **26**
Hacker, Marilyn **5, 9, 23, 72, 91**
Hailey, Elizabeth Forsythe **40**
Haines, John (Meade) **58**
Haldeman, Joe (William) **61**
Haley, Alex(ander Murray Palmer) **8, 12, 76**
Hall, Donald (Andrew Jr.) **1, 13, 37, 59**
Halpern, Daniel **14**
Hamill, Pete **10**
Hamilton, Edmond **1**
Hamilton, Virginia **26**
Hammett, (Samuel) Dashiell **3, 5, 10, 19, 47**
Hamner, Earl (Henry) Jr. **12**
Hannah, Barry **23, 38, 90**
Hansberry, Lorraine (Vivian) **17, 62**
Hansen, Joseph **38**
Hanson, Kenneth O(stlin) **13**
Hardwick, Elizabeth **13**
Harjo, Joy **83**
Harlan, Louis R(udolph) **34**
Harling, Robert **53**
Harmon, William (Ruth) **38**
Harper, Michael S(teven) **7, 22**
Harris, MacDonald **9**
Harris, Mark **19**
Harrison, Harry (Max) **42**
Harrison, James (Thomas) **6, 14, 33, 66**
Harrison, Kathryn **70**
Harriss, Will(ard Irvin) **34**
Hart, Moss **66**
Hartman, Geoffrey H. **27**
Haruf, Kent **34**
Hass, Robert **18, 39, 99**
Haviaras, Stratis **33**
Hawkes, John (Clendennin Burne Jr.) **1, 2, 3, 4, 7, 9, 14, 15, 27, 49**
Hayden, Robert E(arl) **5, 9, 14, 37**
Hayman, Ronald **44**
H. D. **3, 8, 14, 31, 34, 73**
Hearne, Vicki **56**
Hearon, Shelby **63**
Heat-Moon, William Least **29**
Hecht, Anthony (Evan) **8, 13, 19**
Hecht, Ben **8**
Heifner, Jack **11**

Nationality Index

Heilbrun, Carolyn G(old) 25
Heinemann, Larry (Curtiss) 50
Heinlein, Robert A(nson) 1, 3, 8, 14, 26, 55
Heller, Joseph 1, 3, 5, 8, 11, 36, 63
Hellman, Lillian (Florence) 2, 4, 8, 14, 18, 34, 44, 52
Helprin, Mark 7, 10, 22, 32
Hemingway, Ernest (Miller) 1, 3, 6, 8, 10, 13, 19, 30, 34, 39, 41, 44, 50, 61, 80
Hempel, Amy 39
Henley, Beth 23
Hentoff, Nat(han Irving) 26
Herbert, Frank (Patrick) 12, 23, 35, 44, 85
Herbst, Josephine (Frey) 34
Herlihy, James Leo 6
Herrmann, Dorothy 44
Hersey, John (Richard) 1, 2, 7, 9, 40, 81, 97
Heyen, William 13, 18
Higgins, George V(incent) 4, 7, 10, 18
Highsmith, (Mary) Patricia 2, 4, 14, 42, 102
Highwater, Jamake (Mamake) 12
Hijuelos, Oscar 65
Hill, George Roy 26
Hillerman, Tony 62
Himes, Chester (Bomar) 2, 4, 7, 18, 58, 108
Hinton, S(usan) E(loise) 30
Hirsch, Edward 31, 50
Hirsch, E(ric) D(onald) Jr. 79
Hoagland, Edward 28
Hoban, Russell (Conwell) 7, 25
Hobson, Laura Z(ametkin) 7, 25
Hochman, Sandra 3, 8
Hoffman, Alice 51
Hoffman, Daniel (Gerard) 6, 13, 23
Hoffman, Stanley 5
Hoffman, William M(oses) 40
Hogan, Linda 73
Holland, Isabelle 21
Hollander, John 2, 5, 8, 14
Holleran, Andrew 38
Holmes, John Clellon 56
Honig, Edwin 33
hooks, bell 94
Horgan, Paul (George Vincent O'Shaughnessy) 9, 53
Horovitz, Israel (Arthur) 56
Horwitz, Julius 14
Hougan, Carolyn 34
Howard, Maureen 5, 14, 46
Howard, Richard 7, 10, 47
Howe, Fanny 47
Howe, Irving 85
Howe, Susan 72
Howe, Tina 48
Howes, Barbara 15
Hubbard, L(afayette) Ron(ald) 43
Huddle, David 49
Hughart, Barry 39
Hughes, (James) Langston 1, 5, 10, 15, 35, 44, 108
Hugo, Richard F(ranklin) 6, 18, 32
Humphrey, William 45
Humphreys, Josephine 34, 57
Hunt, E(verette) Howard (Jr.) 3
Hunt, Marsha 70
Hunter, Evan 11, 31
Hunter, Kristin (Eggleston) 35
Hurston, Zora Neale 7, 30, 61
Huston, John (Marcellus) 20
Hustvedt, Siri 76
Hwang, David Henry 55
Hyde, Margaret O(ldroyd) 21
Hynes, James 65

Ian, Janis 21
Ignatow, David 4, 7, 14, 40
Ingalls, Rachel (Holmes) 42
Inge, William (Motter) 1, 8, 19
Innaurato, Albert (F.) 21, 60
Irving, John (Winslow) 13, 23, 38
Isaacs, Susan 32
Isler, Alan (David) 91
Ivask, Ivar Vidrik 14
Jackson, Jesse 12
Jackson, Shirley 11, 60, 87
Jacobs, Jim 12
Jacobsen, Josephine 48, 102
Jakes, John (William) 29
Janowitz, Tama 43
Jarrell, Randall 1, 2, 6, 9, 13, 49
Jeffers, (John) Robinson 2, 3, 11, 15, 54
Jen, Gish 70
Jennings, Waylon 21
Jensen, Laura (Linnea) 37
Joel, Billy 26
Johnson, Charles (Richard) 7, 51, 65
Johnson, Denis 52
Johnson, Diane 5, 13, 48
Johnson, Joyce 58
Jones, Edward P. 76
Jones, Gayl 6, 9
Jones, James 1, 3, 10, 39
Jones, LeRoi 1, 2, 3, 5, 10, 14
Jones, Louis B. 65
Jones, Madison (Percy Jr.) 4
Jones, Nettie (Pearl) 34
Jones, Preston 10
Jones, Robert F(rancis) 7
Jones, Thom 81
Jong, Erica 4, 6, 8, 18, 83
Jordan, June 5, 11, 23
Jordan, Pat(rick M.) 37
Just, Ward (Swift) 4, 27
Justice, Donald (Rodney) 6, 19, 102
Kadohata, Cynthia 59
Kahn, Roger 30
Kaletski, Alexander 39
Kallman, Chester (Simon) 2
Kaminsky, Stuart M(elvin) 59
Kanin, Garson 22
Kantor, MacKinlay 7
Kaplan, David Michael 50
Kaplan, James 59
Karl, Frederick R(obert) 34
Katz, Steve 47
Kauffman, Janet 42
Kaufman, Bob (Garnell) 49
Kaufman, George S. 38
Kaufman, Sue 3, 8
Kazan, Elia 6, 16, 63
Kazin, Alfred 34, 38
Keaton, Buster 20
Keene, Donald 34
Keillor, Garrison 40
Kellerman, Jonathan 44
Kelley, William Melvin 22
Kellogg, Marjorie 2
Kemelman, Harry 2
Kennedy, Adrienne (Lita) 66
Kennedy, William 6, 28, 34, 53
Kennedy, X. J. 8, 42
Kenny, Maurice (Francis) 87
Kerouac, Jack 1, 2, 3, 5, 14, 29, 61
Kerr, Jean 22
Kerr, M. E. 12, 35
Kerr, Robert 55
Kerrigan, (Thomas) Anthony 4, 6

Kesey, Ken (Elton) 1, 3, 6, 11, 46, 64
Kesselring, Joseph (Otto) 45
Kessler, Jascha (Frederick) 4
Kettelkamp, Larry (Dale) 12
Keyes, Daniel 80
Kherdian, David 6, 9
Kienzle, William X(avier) 25
Killens, John Oliver 10
Kincaid, Jamaica 43, 68
King, Martin Luther Jr. 83
King, Stephen (Edwin) 12, 26, 37, 61
King, Thomas 89
Kingman, Lee 17
Kingsley, Sidney 44
Kingsolver, Barbara 55, 81
Kingston, Maxine (Ting Ting) Hong 12, 19, 58
Kinnell, Galway 1, 2, 3, 5, 13, 29
Kirkwood, James 9
Kizer, Carolyn (Ashley) 15, 39, 80
Klappert, Peter 57
Klein, Norma 30
Klein, T(heodore) E(ibon) D(onald) 34
Knapp, Caroline 99
Knebel, Fletcher 14
Knight, Etheridge 40
Knowles, John 1, 4, 10, 26
Koch, Kenneth 5, 8, 44
Komunyakaa, Yusef 86, 94
Koontz, Dean R(ay) 78
Kopit, Arthur (Lee) 1, 18, 33
Kosinski, Jerzy (Nikodem) 1, 2, 3, 6, 10, 15, 53, 70
Kostelanetz, Richard (Cory) 28
Kotlowitz, Robert 4
Kotzwinkle, William 5, 14, 35
Kozol, Jonathan 17
Kozoll, Michael 35
Kramer, Kathryn 34
Kramer, Larry 42
Kristofferson, Kris 26
Krumgold, Joseph (Quincy) 12
Krutch, Joseph Wood 24
Kubrick, Stanley 16
Kumin, Maxine (Winokur) 5, 13, 28
Kunitz, Stanley (Jasspon) 6, 11, 14
Kushner, Tony 81
Kuzma, Greg 7
L'Amour, Louis (Dearborn) 25, 55
Lancaster, Bruce 36
Landis, John 26
Langer, Elinor 34
Lapine, James (Elliot) 39
Larsen, Eric 55
Larsen, Nella 37
Larson, Charles R(aymond) 31
Lasch, Christopher 102
Latham, Jean Lee 12
Lattimore, Richmond (Alexander) 3
Laughlin, James 49
Lear, Norman (Milton) 12
Leavitt, David 34
Lebowitz, Fran(ces Ann) 11, 36
Lee, Andrea 36
Lee, Chang-rae 91
Lee, Don L. 2
Lee, George W(ashington) 52
Lee, Helen Elaine 86
Lee, Lawrence 34
Lee, Manfred B(ennington) 11
Lee, (Nelle) Harper 12, 60
Lee, Shelton Jackson 105
Lee, Stan 17

Leet, Judith **11**
Leffland, Ella **19**
Le Guin, Ursula K(roeber) **8, 13, 22, 45, 71**
Leiber, Fritz (Reuter Jr.) **25**
Leimbach, Marti **65**
Leithauser, Brad **27**
Lelchuk, Alan **5**
Lemann, Nancy **39**
L'Engle, Madeleine (Camp Franklin) **12**
Lentricchia, Frank (Jr.) **34**
Leonard, Elmore (John Jr.) **28, 34, 71**
Lerman, Eleanor **9**
Lerman, Rhoda **56**
Lester, Richard **20**
Levertov, Denise **1, 2, 3, 5, 8, 15, 28, 66**
Levi, Jonathan **76**
Levin, Ira **3, 6**
Levin, Meyer **7**
Levine, Philip **2, 4, 5, 9, 14, 33**
Levinson, Deirdre **49**
Levitin, Sonia (Wolff) **17**
Lewis, Janet **41**
Leyner, Mark **92**
L'Heureux, John (Clarke) **52**
Lieber, Joel **6**
Lieberman, Laurence (James) **4, 36**
Lifton, Robert Jay **67**
Lightman, Alan P(aige) **81**
Ligotti, Thomas (Robert) **44**
Lindbergh, Anne (Spencer) Morrow **82**
Linney, Romulus **51**
Lipsyte, Robert (Michael) **21**
Lish, Gordon (Jay) **45**
Littell, Robert **42**
Loewinsohn, Ron(ald William) **52**
Logan, John (Burton) **5**
Lopate, Phillip **29**
Lord, Bette Bao **23**
Lorde, Audre (Geraldine) **18, 71**
Louie, David Wong **70**
Lowell, Robert (Traill Spence Jr.) **1, 2, 3, 4, 5, 8, 9, 11, 15, 37**
Loy, Mina **28**
Lucas, Craig **64**
Lucas, George **16**
Ludlam, Charles **46, 50**
Ludlum, Robert **22, 43**
Ludwig, Ken **60**
Lurie, Alison **4, 5, 18, 39**
Lynch, David (K.) **66**
Lynn, Kenneth S(chuyler) **50**
Lytle, Andrew (Nelson) **22**
Maas, Peter **29**
Macdonald, Cynthia **13, 19**
MacDonald, John D(ann) **3, 27, 44**
Macdonald, Ross **1, 2, 3, 14, 34, 41**
MacInnes, Helen (Clark) **27, 39**
Maclean, Norman (Fitzroy) **78**
MacLeish, Archibald **3, 8, 14, 68**
MacShane, Frank **39**
Madden, (Jerry) David **5, 15**
Madhubuti, Haki R. **6, 73**
Mailer, Norman **1, 2, 3, 4, 5, 8, 11, 14, 28, 39, 74**
Major, Clarence **3, 19, 48**
Malamud, Bernard **1, 2, 3, 5, 8, 9, 11, 18, 27, 44, 78, 85**
Malcolm X **82**
Maloff, Saul **5**
Malone, Michael (Christopher) **43**
Malzberg, Barry N(athaniel) **7**
Mamet, David (Alan) **9, 15, 34, 46, 91**
Mamoulian, Rouben (Zachary) **16**

Mano, D. Keith **2, 10**
Manso, Peter **39**
Margulies, Donald **76**
Markfield, Wallace **8**
Markson, David M(errill) **67**
Marquand, John P(hillips) **2, 10**
Marques, Rene **96**
Marshall, Garry **17**
Marshall, Paule **27, 72**
Martin, Steve **30**
Martin, Valerie **89**
Maso, Carole **44**
Mason, Bobbie Ann **28, 43, 82**
Masters, Hilary **48**
Mastrosimone, William **36**
Matheson, Richard Burton **37**
Mathews, Harry **6, 52**
Mathews, John Joseph **84**
Matthews, William (Procter, III) **40**
Matthias, John (Edward) **9**
Matthiessen, Peter **5, 7, 11, 32, 64**
Maupin, Armistead **95**
Maxwell, William (Keepers Jr.) **19**
May, Elaine **16**
Maynard, Joyce **23**
Maysles, Albert **16**
Maysles, David **16**
Mazer, Norma Fox **26**
McBrien, William Augustine **44**
McCaffrey, Anne (Inez) **17**
McCall, Nathan **86**
McCarthy, Cormac **4, 57, 59, 101**
McCarthy, Mary (Therese) **1, 3, 5, 14, 24, 39, 59**
McCauley, Stephen (D.) **50**
McClure, Michael (Thomas) **6, 10**
McCorkle, Jill (Collins) **51**
McCourt, James **23**
McCullers, (Lula) Carson (Smith) **1, 4, 10, 12, 48, 100**
McDermott, Alice **90**
McElroy, Joseph **5, 47**
McFarland, Dennis **65**
McGinley, Phyllis **14**
McGinniss, Joe **32**
McGrath, Thomas (Matthew) **28, 59**
McGuane, Thomas (Francis III) **3, 7, 18, 45**
McHale, Tom **3, 5**
McInerney, Jay **34**
McIntyre, Vonda N(eel) **18**
McKuen, Rod **1, 3**
McMillan, Terry (L.) **50, 61**
McMurtry, Larry (Jeff) **2, 3, 7, 11, 27, 44**
McNally, Terrence **4, 7, 41, 91**
McNally, T. M. **82**
McNamer, Deirdre **70**
McNickle, (William) D'Arcy **89**
McPhee, John (Angus) **36**
McPherson, James Alan **19, 77**
McPherson, William (Alexander) **34**
Mead, Margaret **37**
Medoff, Mark (Howard) **6, 23**
Mehta, Ved (Parkash) **37**
Meltzer, Milton **26**
Mendelsohn, Jane **99**
Meredith, William (Morris) **4, 13, 22, 55**
Merkin, Daphne **44**
Merrill, James (Ingram) **2, 3, 6, 8, 13, 18, 34, 91**
Merton, Thomas **1, 3, 11, 34, 83**
Merwin, W(illiam) S(tanley) **1, 2, 3, 5, 8, 13, 18, 45, 88**
Mewshaw, Michael **9**

Meyers, Jeffrey **39**
Michaels, Leonard **6, 25**
Michener, James A(lbert) **1, 5, 11, 29, 60, 109**
Miles, Jack **100**
Miles, Josephine (Louise) **1, 2, 14, 34, 39**
Millar, Kenneth **14**
Miller, Arthur **1, 2, 6, 10, 15, 26, 47, 78**
Miller, Henry (Valentine) **1, 2, 4, 9, 14, 43, 84**
Miller, Jason **2**
Miller, Sue **44**
Miller, Walter M(ichael Jr.) **4, 30**
Millett, Kate **67**
Millhauser, Steven (Lewis) **21, 54, 109**
Milner, Ron(ald) **56**
Miner, Valerie **40**
Minot, Susan **44**
Minus, Ed **39**
Mitchell, Joseph (Quincy) **98**
Modarressi, Taghi (M.) **44**
Mohr, Nicholasa **12**
Mojtabai, A(nn) G(race) **5, 9, 15, 29**
Momaday, N(avarre) Scott **2, 19, 85, 95**
Monette, Paul **82**
Montague, John (Patrick) **13, 46**
Montgomery, Marion H. Jr. **7**
Mooney, Ted **25**
Moore, Lorrie **39, 45, 68**
Moore, Marianne (Craig) **1, 2, 4, 8, 10, 13, 19, 47**
Morgan, Berry **6**
Morgan, (George) Frederick **23**
Morgan, Robin **2**
Morgan, Seth **65**
Morris, Bill **76**
Morris, Wright **1, 3, 7, 18, 37**
Morrison, Jim **17**
Morrison, Toni **4, 10, 22, 55, 81, 87**
Mosher, Howard Frank **62**
Mosley, Walter **97**
Moss, Howard **7, 14, 45, 50**
Motley, Willard (Francis) **18**
Mountain Wolf Woman **92**
Moyers, Bill **74**
Mueller, Lisel **13, 51**
Mukherjee, Bharati **53**
Mull, Martin **17**
Mungo, Raymond **72**
Murphy, Sylvia **34**
Murray, Albert L. **73**
Muske, Carol **90**
Myers, Walter Dean **35**
Nabokov, Vladimir (Vladimirovich) **1, 2, 3, 6, 8, 11, 15, 23, 44, 46, 64**
Nash, (Frediric) Ogden **23**
Naylor, Gloria **28, 52**
Neihardt, John Gneisenau **32**
Nelson, Willie **17**
Nemerov, Howard (Stanley) **2, 6, 9, 36**
Neufeld, John (Arthur) **17**
Neville, Emily Cheney **12**
Newlove, Donald **6**
Newman, Charles **2, 8**
Newman, Edwin (Harold) **14**
Newton, Suzanne **35**
Nichols, John (Treadwell) **38**
Niedecker, Lorine **10, 42**
Nin, Anais **1, 4, 8, 11, 14, 60**
Nissenson, Hugh **4, 9**
Niven, Larry **8**
Nixon, Agnes Eckhardt **21**
Norman, Marsha **28**
Norton, Andre **12**
Nova, Craig **7, 31**

Nunn, Kem 34
Nyro, Laura 17
Oates, Joyce Carol 1, 2, 3, 6, 9, 11, 15, 19, 33, 52, 108
O'Brien, Darcy 11
O'Brien, (William) Tim(othy) 7, 19, 40, 103
Ochs, Phil 17
O'Connor, Edwin (Greene) 14
O'Connor, (Mary) Flannery 1, 2, 3, 6, 10, 13, 15, 21, 66, 104
O'Dell, Scott 30
Odets, Clifford 2, 28, 98
O'Donovan, Michael John 14
O'Grady, Timothy 59
O'Hara, Frank 2, 5, 13, 78
O'Hara, John (Henry) 1, 2, 3, 6, 11, 42
O Hehir, Diana 41
Olds, Sharon 32, 39, 85
Oliver, Mary 19, 34, 98
Olsen, Tillie 4, 13
Olson, Charles (John) 1, 2, 5, 6, 9, 11, 29
Olson, Toby 28
Oneal, Zibby 30
Oppen, George 7, 13, 34
Orlovitz, Gil 22
Ortiz, Simon J(oseph) 45
Otto, Whitney 70
Owens, Rochelle 8
Ozick, Cynthia 3, 7, 28, 62
Pack, Robert 13
Pagels, Elaine Hiesey 104
Paglia, Camille (Anna) 68
Paley, Grace 4, 6, 37
Palliser, Charles 65
Pancake, Breece D'J 29
Parini, Jay (Lee) 54
Parker, Dorothy (Rothschild) 15, 68
Parker, Robert B(rown) 27
Parks, Gordon (Alexander Buchanan) 1, 16
Pastan, Linda (Olenik) 27
Patchen, Kenneth 1, 2, 18
Paterson, Katherine (Womeldorf) 12, 30
Peacock, Molly 60
Pearson, T(homas) R(eid) 39
Peck, John 3
Peck, Richard (Wayne) 21
Peck, Robert Newton 17
Peckinpah, (David) Sam(uel) 20
Percy, Walker 2, 3, 6, 8, 14, 18, 47, 65
Perelman, S(idney) J(oseph) 3, 5, 9, 15, 23, 44, 49
Pesetsky, Bette 28
Peterkin, Julia Mood 31
Peters, Joan K(aren) 39
Peters, Robert L(ouis) 7
Petrakis, Harry Mark 3
Petry, Ann (Lane) 1, 7, 18
Philipson, Morris H. 53
Phillips, Jayne Anne 15, 33
Phillips, Robert (Schaeffer) 28
Piercy, Marge 3, 6, 14, 18, 27, 62
Pinckney, Darryl 76
Pineda, Cecile 39
Pinkwater, Daniel Manus 35
Pinsky, Robert 9, 19, 38, 94
Pirsig, Robert M(aynard) 4, 6, 73
Plante, David (Robert) 7, 23, 38
Plath, Sylvia 1, 2, 3, 5, 9, 11, 14, 17, 50, 51, 62
Platt, Kin 26
Plimpton, George (Ames) 36
Plumly, Stanley (Ross) 33
Pohl, Frederik 18

Poitier, Sidney 26
Pollitt, Katha 28
Polonsky, Abraham (Lincoln) 92
Pomerance, Bernard 13
Porter, Connie (Rose) 70
Porter, Katherine Anne 1, 3, 7, 10, 13, 15, 27, 101
Potok, Chaim 2, 7, 14, 26
Pound, Ezra (Weston Loomis) 1, 2, 3, 4, 5, 7, 10, 13, 18, 34, 48, 50
Povod, Reinaldo 44
Powell, Adam Clayton Jr. 89
Powell, Dawn 66
Powell, Padgett 34
Power, Susan 91
Powers, J(ames) F(arl) 1, 4, 8, 57
Powers, John R. 66
Powers, Richard (S.) 93
Prager, Emily 56
Price, (Edward) Reynolds 3, 6, 13, 43, 50, 63
Price, Richard 6, 12
Prince 35
Pritchard, William H(arrison) 34
Probst, Mark 59
Prokosch, Frederic 4, 48
Prose, Francine 45
Pryor, Richard (Franklin Lenox Thomas) 26
Purdy, James (Amos) 2, 4, 10, 28, 52
Puzo, Mario 1, 2, 6, 36, 107
Pynchon, Thomas (Ruggles Jr.) 2, 3, 6, 9, 11, 18, 33, 62, 72
Quay, Stephen 95
Quay, Timothy 95
Queen, Ellery 3, 11
Quinn, Peter 91
Rabe, David (William) 4, 8, 33
Rado, James 17
Raeburn, John (Hay) 34
Ragni, Gerome 17
Rahv, Philip 24
Rakosi, Carl 47
Rampersad, Arnold 44
Rand, Ayn 3, 30, 44, 79
Randall, Dudley (Felker) 1
Ransom, John Crowe 2, 4, 5, 11, 24
Raphael, Frederic (Michael) 2, 14
Rechy, John (Francisco) 1, 7, 14, 18, 107
Reddin, Keith 67
Redmon, Anne 22
Reed, Ishmael 2, 3, 5, 6, 13, 32, 60
Reed, Lou 21
Remarque, Erich Maria 21
Rexroth, Kenneth 1, 2, 6, 11, 22, 49
Reynolds, Jonathan 6, 38
Reynolds, Michael Shane 44
Reznikoff, Charles 9
Ribman, Ronald (Burt) 7
Rice, Anne 41
Rice, Elmer (Leopold) 7, 49
Rich, Adrienne (Cecile) 3, 6, 7, 11, 18, 36, 73, 76
Richter, Conrad (Michael) 30
Riding, Laura 3, 7
Ringwood, Gwen(dolyn Margaret) Pharis 48
Rivers, Conrad Kent 1
Robbins, Harold 5
Robbins, Tom 9, 32, 64
Robbins, Trina 21
Robinson, Jill 10
Robinson, Kim Stanley 34
Robinson, Marilynne 25
Robinson, Smokey 21
Robison, Mary 42, 98

Roddenberry, Gene 17
Rodgers, Mary 12
Rodman, Howard 65
Roethke, Theodore (Huebner) 1, 3, 8, 11, 19, 46, 101
Rogers, Thomas Hunton 57
Rogin, Gilbert 18
Roiphe, Anne (Richardson) 3, 9
Rooke, Leon 25, 34
Rose, Wendy 85
Rosen, Richard (Dean) 39
Rosenthal, M(acha) L(ouis) 28
Rossner, Judith (Perelman) 6, 9, 29
Roth, Henry 2, 6, 11, 104
Roth, Philip (Milton) 1, 2, 3, 4, 6, 9, 15, 22, 31, 47, 66, 86
Rothenberg, Jerome 6, 57
Rovit, Earl (Herbert) 7
Royko, Mike 109
Ruark, Gibbons 3
Rudnik, Raphael 7
Rukeyser, Muriel 6, 10, 15, 27
Rule, Jane (Vance) 27
Rush, Norman 44
Russ, Joanna 15
Ryan, Cornelius (John) 7
Ryan, Michael 65
Sachs, Marilyn (Stickle) 35
Sackler, Howard (Oliver) 14
Sadoff, Ira 9
Safire, William 10
Sagan, Carl (Edward) 30
Saint, H(arry) F. 50
Salamanca, J(ack) R(ichard) 4, 15
Sale, Kirkpatrick 68
Salinas, Luis Omar 90
Salinger, J(erome) D(avid) 1, 3, 8, 12, 55, 56
Salter, James 7, 52, 59
Sanchez, Sonia 5
Sandburg, Carl (August) 1, 4, 10, 15, 35
Sanders, (James) Ed(ward) 53
Sanders, Lawrence 41
Sandoz, Mari(e Susette) 28
Saner, Reg(inald Anthony) 9
Santiago, Danny 33
Santmyer, Helen Hoover 33
Santos, Bienvenido N(uqui) 22
Sapphire 99
Saroyan, William 1, 8, 10, 29, 34, 56
Sarton, (Eleanor) May 4, 14, 49, 91
Saul, John (W. III) 46
Savage, Thomas 40
Savan, Glenn 50
Sayers, Valerie 50
Sayles, John (Thomas) 7, 10, 14
Schaeffer, Susan Fromberg 6, 11, 22
Schell, Jonathan 35
Schevill, James (Erwin) 7
Schisgal, Murray (Joseph) 6
Schlesinger, Arthur M(eier) Jr. 84
Schnackenberg, Gjertrud 40
Schor, Sandra (M.) 65
Schorer, Mark 9
Schrader, Paul (Joseph) 26
Schulberg, Budd (Wilson) 7, 48
Schulz, Charles M(onroe) 12
Schuyler, James Marcus 5, 23
Schwartz, Delmore (David) 2, 4, 10, 45, 87
Schwartz, John Burnham 59
Schwartz, Lynne Sharon 31
Scoppettone, Sandra 26
Scorsese, Martin 20, 89
Scott, Evelyn 43

Scott, Joanna **50**
Sebestyen, Ouida **30**
Seelye, John **7**
Segal, Erich (Wolf) **3, 10**
Seger, Bob **35**
Seidel, Frederick (Lewis) **18**
Selby, Hubert Jr. **1, 2, 4, 8**
Selzer, Richard **74**
Serling, (Edward) Rod(man) **30**
Seton, Cynthia Propper **27**
Settle, Mary Lee **19, 61**
Sexton, Anne (Harvey) **2, 4, 6, 8, 10, 15, 53**
Shaara, Michael (Joseph Jr.) **15**
Shacochis, Bob **39**
Shange, Ntozake **8, 25, 38, 74**
Shanley, John Patrick **75**
Shapiro, Jane **76**
Shapiro, Karl (Jay) **4, 8, 15, 53**
Shaw, Irwin **7, 23, 34**
Shawn, Wallace **41**
Shea, Lisa **86**
Sheed, Wilfrid (John Joseph) **2, 4, 10, 53**
Shepard, Jim **36**
Shepard, Lucius **34**
Shepard, Sam **4, 6, 17, 34, 41, 44**
Sherburne, Zoa (Morin) **30**
Sherman, Jonathan Marc **55**
Sherman, Martin **19**
Sherwin, Judith Johnson **7, 15**
Shields, Carol **91**
Shields, David **97**
Shilts, Randy **85**
Shreve, Susan Richards **23**
Shue, Larry **52**
Shulman, Alix Kates **2, 10**
Shuster, Joe **21**
Siegel, Jerome **21**
Sigal, Clancy **7**
Silko, Leslie (Marmon) **23, 74**
Silver, Joan Micklin **20**
Silverberg, Robert **7**
Silverstein, Alvin **17**
Silverstein, Virginia B(arbara Opshelor) **17**
Simak, Clifford D(onald) **1, 55**
Simic, Charles **6, 9, 22, 49, 68**
Simmons, Charles (Paul) **57**
Simmons, Dan **44**
Simon, Carly **26**
Simon, (Marvin) Neil **6, 11, 31, 39, 70**
Simon, Paul (Frederick) **17**
Simpson, Louis (Aston Marantz) **4, 7, 9, 32**
Simpson, Mona (Elizabeth) **44**
Sinclair, Upton (Beall) **1, 11, 15, 63**
Singer, Isaac Bashevis **1, 3, 6, 9, 11, 15, 23, 38, 69**
Sissman, L(ouis) E(dward) **9, 18**
Slaughter, Frank G(ill) **29**
Slavitt, David R(ytman) **5, 14**
Smiley, Jane (Graves) **53, 76**
Smith, Anna Deavere **86**
Smith, Betty (Wehner) **19**
Smith, Clark Ashton **43**
Smith, Dave **22, 42**
Smith, Lee **25, 73**
Smith, Martin Cruz **25**
Smith, Mary-Ann Tirone **39**
Smith, Patti **12**
Smith, William Jay **6**
Snodgrass, W(illiam) D(e Witt) **2, 6, 10, 18, 68**
Snyder, Gary (Sherman) **1, 2, 5, 9, 32**
Snyder, Zilpha Keatley **17**
Sokolov, Raymond **7**

Sommer, Scott **25**
Sondheim, Stephen (Joshua) **30, 39**
Sontag, Susan **1, 2, 10, 13, 31, 105**
Sorrentino, Gilbert **3, 7, 14, 22, 40**
Soto, Gary **32, 80**
Southern, Terry **7**
Spackman, W(illiam) M(ode) **46**
Spacks, Barry (Bernard) **14**
Spanidou, Irini **44**
Spencer, Elizabeth **22**
Spencer, Scott **30**
Spicer, Jack **8, 18, 72**
Spiegelman, Art **76**
Spielberg, Peter **6**
Spielberg, Steven **20**
Spillane, Mickey **3, 13**
Spinrad, Norman (Richard) **46**
Spivack, Kathleen (Romola Drucker) **6**
Spoto, Donald **39**
Springsteen, Bruce (F.) **17**
Squires, (James) Radcliffe **51**
Stafford, Jean **4, 7, 19, 68**
Stafford, William (Edgar) **4, 7, 29**
Stanton, Maura **9**
Starbuck, George (Edwin) **53**
Steele, Timothy (Reid) **45**
Stegner, Wallace (Earle) **9, 49, 81**
Steinbeck, John (Ernst) **1, 5, 9, 13, 21, 34, 45, 75**
Steinem, Gloria **63**
Steiner, George **24**
Sterling, Bruce **72**
Stern, Gerald **40, 100**
Stern, Richard (Gustave) **4, 39**
Sternberg, Josef von **20**
Stevens, Mark **34**
Stevenson, Anne (Katharine) **7, 33**
Still, James **49**
Stitt, Milan **29**
Stolz, Mary (Slattery) **12**
Stone, Irving **7**
Stone, Oliver (William) **73**
Stone, Robert (Anthony) **5, 23, 42**
Storm, Hyemeyohsts **3**
Stout, Rex (Todhunter) **3**
Strand, Mark **6, 18, 41, 71**
Straub, Peter (Francis) **28, 107**
Stribling, T(homas) S(igismund) **23**
Stuart, Jesse (Hilton) **1, 8, 11, 14, 34**
Sturgeon, Theodore (Hamilton) **22, 39**
Styron, William **1, 3, 5, 11, 15, 60**
Sukenick, Ronald **3, 4, 6, 48**
Summers, Hollis (Spurgeon Jr.) **10**
Susann, Jacqueline **3**
Swados, Elizabeth (A.) **12**
Swados, Harvey **5**
Swan, Gladys **69**
Swarthout, Glendon (Fred) **35**
Swenson, May **4, 14, 61, 106**
Talese, Gay **37**
Tallent, Elizabeth (Ann) **45**
Tally, Ted **42**
Tan, Amy (Ruth) **59**
Tartt, Donna **76**
Tate, James (Vincent) **2, 6, 25**
Tate, (John Orley) Allen **2, 4, 6, 9, 11, 14, 24**
Tavel, Ronald **6**
Taylor, Eleanor Ross **5**
Taylor, Henry (Splawn) **44**
Taylor, Mildred D. **21**
Taylor, Peter (Hillsman) **1, 4, 18, 37, 44, 50, 71**
Taylor, Robert Lewis **14**

Terkel, Studs **38**
Terry, Megan **19**
Tesich, Steve **40, 69**
Tevis, Walter **42**
Theroux, Alexander (Louis) **2, 25**
Theroux, Paul (Edward) **5, 8, 11, 15, 28, 46**
Thomas, Audrey (Callahan) **7, 13, 37, 107**
Thomas, Joyce Carol **35**
Thomas, Lewis **35**
Thomas, Piri **17**
Thomas, Ross (Elmore) **39**
Thompson, Hunter S(tockton) **9, 17, 40, 104**
Thompson, Jim (Myers) **69**
Thurber, James (Grover) **5, 11, 25**
Tilghman, Christopher **65**
Tillinghast, Richard (Williford) **29**
Tiptree, James Jr. **48, 50**
Tolson, Melvin B(eaunorus) **36, 105**
Tomlin, Lily **17**
Toole, John Kennedy **19, 64**
Toomer, Jean **1, 4, 13, 22**
Torrey, E(dwin) Fuller **34**
Towne, Robert (Burton) **87**
Traven, B. **8, 11**
Trevanian **29**
Trilling, Lionel **9, 11, 24**
Trow, George W. S. **52**
Trudeau, Garry B. **12**
Trumbo, Dalton **19**
Tryon, Thomas **3, 11**
Tuck, Lily **70**
Tunis, John R(oberts) **12**
Turco, Lewis (Putnam) **11, 63**
Turner, Frederick **48**
Tyler, Anne **7, 11, 18, 28, 44, 59, 103**
Uhry, Alfred **55**
Ulibarri, Sabine R(eyes) **83**
Unger, Douglas **34**
Updike, John (Hoyer) **1, 2, 3, 5, 7, 9, 13, 15, 23, 34, 43, 70**
Urdang, Constance (Henriette) **47**
Uris, Leon (Marcus) **7, 32**
Vachss, Andrew (Henry) **106**
Valdez, Luis (Miguel) **84**
Van Ash, Cay **34**
Vance, Jack **35**
Vandenburgh, Jane **59**
Van Doren, Mark **6, 10**
Van Duyn, Mona (Jane) **3, 7, 63**
Van Peebles, Melvin **2, 20**
Van Vechten, Carl **33**
Vaughn, Stephanie **62**
Vidal, Gore **2, 4, 6, 8, 10, 22, 33, 72**
Viereck, Peter (Robert Edwin) **4**
Vinge, Joan D(ennison) **30**
Vizenor, Gerald Robert **103**
Vliet, R(ussell) G(ordon) **22**
Vogel, Paula A(nne) **76**
Voight, Ellen Bryant **54**
Voigt, Cynthia **30**
Vollmann, William T. **89**
Vonnegut, Kurt Jr. **1, 2, 3, 4, 5, 8, 12, 22, 40, 60**
Wagman, Fredrica **7**
Wagner-Martin, Linda (C.) **50**
Wagoner, David (Russell) **3, 5, 15**
Wakefield, Dan **7**
Wakoski, Diane **2, 4, 7, 9, 11, 40**
Waldman, Anne **7**
Walker, Alice (Malsenior) **5, 6, 9, 19, 27, 46, 58, 103**
Walker, Joseph A. **19**
Walker, Margaret (Abigail) **1, 6**

Nationality Index

Wallace, David Foster **50**
Wallace, Irving **7, 13**
Wallant, Edward Lewis **5, 10**
Wambaugh, Joseph (Aloysius Jr.) **3, 18**
Ward, Douglas Turner **19**
Warhol, Andy **20**
Warren, Robert Penn **1, 4, 6, 8, 10, 13, 18, 39, 53, 59**
Wasserstein, Wendy **32, 59, 90**
Waters, Frank (Joseph) **88**
Watkins, Paul **55**
Webb, Charles (Richard) **7**
Webb, James H(enry) Jr. **22**
Weber, Lenora Mattingly **12**
Weidman, Jerome **7**
Weiss, Theodore (Russell) **3, 8, 14**
Welch, James **6, 14, 52**
Wellek, Rene **28**
Weller, Michael **10, 53**
Welles, (George) Orson **20, 80**
Wellman, Mac **65**
Wellman, Manly Wade **49**
Wells, Rosemary **12**
Welty, Eudora **1, 2, 5, 14, 22, 33, 105**
Wersba, Barbara **30**
Wescott, Glenway **13**
Wesley, Richard (Errol) **7**
West, (Mary) Jessamyn **7, 17**
West, Paul **7, 14, 96**
Westlake, Donald E(dwin) **7, 33**
Whalen, Philip **6, 29**
Wharton, William (a pseudonym) **18, 37**
Wheelock, John Hall **14**
White, Edmund (Valentine III) **27**
White, E(lwyn) B(rooks) **10, 34, 39**
Whitney, Phyllis A(yame) **42**
Whittemore, (Edward) Reed (Jr.) **4**
Wicker, Tom **7**
Wideman, John Edgar **5, 34, 36, 67**
Wieners, John **7**
Wiesel, Elie(zer) **3, 5, 11, 37**
Wiggins, Marianne **57**
Wilbur, Richard (Purdy) **3, 6, 9, 14, 53**
Wild, Peter **14**
Wilder, Billy **20**
Wilder, Thornton (Niven) **1, 5, 6, 10, 15, 35, 82**
Wiley, Richard **44**
Wilhelm, Kate **7**
Willard, Nancy **7, 37**
Williams, C(harles) K(enneth) **33, 56**
Williams, John A(lfred) **5, 13**
Williams, Jonathan (Chamberlain) **13**
Williams, Joy **31**
Williams, Norman **39**
Williams, Sherley Anne **89**
Williams, Tennessee **1, 2, 5, 7, 8, 11, 15, 19, 30, 39, 45, 71**
Williams, Thomas (Alonzo) **14**
Williams, William Carlos **1, 2, 5, 9, 13, 22, 42, 67**
Williamson, Jack **29**
Willingham, Calder (Baynard Jr.) **5, 51**
Wilson, August **39, 50, 63**
Wilson, Brian **12**
Wilson, Edmund **1, 2, 3, 8, 24**
Wilson, Lanford **7, 14, 36**
Wilson, Robert M. **7, 9**
Wilson, Sloan **32**
Wilson, William S(mith) **49**
Winters, (Arthur) Yvor **4, 8, 32**
Winters, Janet Lewis **41**
Wiseman, Frederick **20**

Wodehouse, P(elham) G(renville) **1, 2, 5, 10, 22**
Woiwode, Larry (Alfred) **6, 10**
Wojciechowska, Maia (Teresa) **26**
Wolfe, Gene (Rodman) **25**
Wolfe, George C. **49**
Wolfe, Tom **1, 2, 9, 15, 35, 51**
Wolff, Geoffrey (Ansell) **41**
Wolff, Tobias (Jonathan Ansell) **39, 64**
Wolitzer, Hilma **17**
Wonder, Stevie **12**
Wong, Jade Snow **17**
Woolrich, Cornell **77**
Wouk, Herman **1, 9, 38**
Wright, Charles (Penzel Jr.) **6, 13, 28**
Wright, Charles Stevenson **49**
Wright, James (Arlington) **3, 5, 10, 28**
Wright, Richard (Nathaniel) **1, 3, 4, 9, 14, 21, 48, 74**
Wright, Stephen **33**
Wright, William **44**
Wurlitzer, Rudolph **2, 4, 15**
Wylie, Philip (Gordon) **43**
Yates, Richard **7, 8, 23**
Yep, Laurence Michael **35**
Yerby, Frank G(arvin) **1, 7, 22**
Yglesias, Helen **7, 22**
Young, Al(bert James) **19**
Young, Marguerite (Vivian) **82**
Young Bear, Ray A. **94**
Yurick, Sol **6**
Zamora, Bernice (B. Ortiz) **89**
Zappa, Frank **17**
Zaturenska, Marya **6, 11**
Zelazny, Roger (Joseph) **21**
Ziegenhagen, Eric **55**
Zindel, Paul **6, 26**
Zoline, Pamela **62**
Zukofsky, Louis **1, 2, 4, 7, 11, 18**
Zweig, Paul **34, 42**

ANTIGUAN
Edwards, Gus **43**
Kincaid, Jamaica **43, 68**

ARGENTINIAN
Bioy Casares, Adolfo **4, 8, 13, 88**
Borges, Jorge Luis **1, 2, 3, 4, 6, 8, 9, 10, 13, 19, 44, 48, 83**
Cortazar, Julio **2, 3, 5, 10, 13, 15, 33, 34, 92**
Costantini, Humberto **49**
Dorfman, Ariel **48, 77**
Guevara, Che **87**
Mujica Lainez, Manuel **31**
Puig, Manuel **3, 5, 10, 28, 65**
Sabato, Ernesto (R.) **10, 23**
Valenzuela, Luisa **31, 104**

ARMENIAN
Mamoulian, Rouben (Zachary) **16**

AUSTRALIAN
Anderson, Jessica (Margaret) Queale **37**
Astley, Thea (Beatrice May) **41**
Brinsmead, H(esba) F(ay) **21**
Buckley, Vincent (Thomas) **57**
Buzo, Alexander (John) **61**
Carey, Peter **40, 55, 96**
Clark, Mavis Thorpe **12**
Clavell, James (duMaresq) **6, 25, 87**
Courtenay, Bryce **59**
Davison, Frank Dalby **15**
Elliott, Sumner Locke **38**

FitzGerald, Robert D(avid) **19**
Grenville, Kate **61**
Hall, Rodney **51**
Hazzard, Shirley **18**
Hope, A(lec) D(erwent) **3, 51**
Hospital, Janette Turner **42**
Jolley, (Monica) Elizabeth **46**
Jones, Rod **50**
Keneally, Thomas (Michael) **5, 8, 10, 14, 19, 27, 43**
Koch, C(hristopher) J(ohn) **42**
Lawler, Raymond Evenor **58**
Malouf, (George Joseph) David **28, 86**
Matthews, Greg **45**
McAuley, James Phillip **45**
McCullough, Colleen **27, 107**
Murray, Les(lie) A(llan) **40**
Porter, Peter (Neville Frederick) **5, 13, 33**
Prichard, Katharine Susannah **46**
Shapcott, Thomas W(illiam) **38**
Slessor, Kenneth **14**
Stead, Christina (Ellen) **2, 5, 8, 32, 80**
Stow, (Julian) Randolph **23, 48**
Thiele, Colin (Milton) **17**
Weir, Peter (Lindsay) **20**
West, Morris L(anglo) **6, 33**
White, Patrick (Victor Martindale) **3, 4, 5, 7, 9, 18, 65, 69**
Wilding, Michael **73**
Williamson, David (Keith) **56**
Wright, Judith (Arandell) **11, 53**

AUSTRIAN
Adamson, Joy(-Friederike Victoria) **17**
Bachmann, Ingeborg **69**
Bernhard, Thomas **3, 32, 61**
Bettelheim, Bruno **79**
Frankl, Viktor E(mil) **93**
Gregor, Arthur **9**
Handke, Peter **5, 8, 10, 15, 38**
Hochwaelder, Fritz **36**
Jandl, Ernst **34**
Lang, Fritz **20, 103**
Lind, Jakov **1, 2, 4, 27, 82**
Sternberg, Josef von **20**
Wellek, Rene **28**
Wilder, Billy **20**

BARBADIAN
Brathwaite, Edward Kamau **11**
Clarke, Austin C(hesterfield) **8, 53**
Kennedy, Adrienne (Lita) **66**
Lamming, George (William) **2, 4, 66**

BELGIAN
Crommelynck, Fernand **75**
Ghelderode, Michel de **6, 11**
Levi-Strauss, Claude **38**
Mallet-Joris, Francoise **11**
Michaux, Henri **8, 19**
Sarton, (Eleanor) May **4, 14, 49, 91**
Simenon, Georges (Jacques Christian) **1, 2, 3, 8, 18, 47**
van Itallie, Jean-Claude **3**
Yourcenar, Marguerite **19, 38, 50, 87**

BOTSWANAN
Head, Bessie **25, 67**

BRAZILIAN
Amado, Jorge **13, 40, 106**
Andrade, Carlos Drummond de **18**
Cabral de Melo Neto, Joao **76**

Dourado, (Waldomiro Freitas) Autran **23, 60**
Drummond de Andrade, Carlos **18**
Lispector, Clarice **43**
Ribeiro, Darcy **34**
Ribeiro, Joao Ubaldo (Osorio Pimentel) **10, 67**
Rosa, Joao Guimaraes **23**

BULGARIAN
Bagryana, Elisaveta **10**
Belcheva, Elisaveta **10**
Canetti, Elias **3, 14, 25, 75, 86**
Kristeva, Julia **77**

CAMEROONIAN
Beti, Mongo **27**

CANADIAN
Acorn, Milton **15**
Aquin, Hubert **15**
Atwood, Margaret (Eleanor) **2, 3, 4, 8, 13, 15, 25, 44, 84**
Avison, Margaret **2, 4, 97**
Barfoot, Joan **18**
Bellow, Saul **1, 2, 3, 6, 8, 10, 13, 15, 25, 33, 34, 63, 79**
Berton, Pierre (Francis De Marigny) **104**
Birney, (Alfred) Earle **1, 4, 6, 11**
Bissett, Bill **18**
Blais, Marie-Claire **2, 4, 6, 13, 22**
Blaise, Clark **29**
Bowering, George **15, 47**
Bowering, Marilyn R(uthe) **32**
Buckler, Ernest **13**
Buell, John (Edward) **10**
Callaghan, Morley Edward **3, 14, 41, 65**
Campbell, Maria **85**
Carrier, Roch **13, 78**
Child, Philip **19, 68**
Chislett, (Margaret) Anne **34**
Clarke, Austin C(hesterfield) **8, 53**
Cohen, Leonard (Norman) **3, 38**
Cohen, Matt **19**
Coles, Don **46**
Cook, Michael **58**
Cooper, Douglas **86**
Coupland, Douglas **85**
Craven, Margaret **17**
Davies, (William) Robertson **2, 7, 13, 25, 42, 75, 91**
de la Roche, Mazo **14**
Donnell, David **34**
Ducharme, Rejean **74**
Dudek, Louis **11, 19**
Engel, Marian **36**
Everson, R(onald) G(ilmour) **27**
Faludy, George **42**
Ferron, Jacques **94**
Finch, Robert (Duer Claydon) **18**
Findley, Timothy **27, 102**
Fraser, Sylvia **64**
Frye, (Herman) Northrop **24, 70**
Gallant, Mavis **7, 18, 38**
Garner, Hugh **13**
Gilmour, David **35**
Glassco, John **9**
Gotlieb, Phyllis Fay (Bloom) **18**
Govier, Katherine **51**
Gunnars, Kristjana **69**
Gustafson, Ralph (Barker) **36**
Haig-Brown, Roderick (Langmere) **21**
Hailey, Arthur **5**
Harris, Christie (Lucy) Irwin **12**

Hebert, Anne **4, 13, 29**
Highway, Tomson **92**
Hillis, Rick **66**
Hine, (William) Daryl **15**
Hodgins, Jack **23**
Hood, Hugh (John Blagdon) **15, 28**
Hospital, Janette Turner **42**
Hyde, Anthony **42**
Jacobsen, Josephine **48, 102**
Jiles, Paulette **13, 58**
Johnston, George (Benson) **51**
Jones, D(ouglas) G(ordon) **10**
Kelly, M(ilton) T(erry) **55**
King, Thomas **89**
Kinsella, W(illiam) P(atrick) **27, 43**
Klein, A(braham) M(oses) **19**
Kogawa, Joy Nozomi **78**
Krizanc, John **57**
Kroetsch, Robert **5, 23, 57**
Kroker, Arthur (W.) **77**
Lane, Patrick **25**
Laurence, (Jean) Margaret (Wemyss) **3, 6, 13, 50, 62**
Layton, Irving (Peter) **2, 15**
Levine, Norman **54**
Lightfoot, Gordon **26**
Livesay, Dorothy (Kathleen) **4, 15, 79**
MacEwen, Gwendolyn (Margaret) **13, 55**
MacLennan, (John) Hugh **2, 14, 92**
MacLeod, Alistair **56**
Macpherson, (Jean) Jay **14**
Maillet, Antonine **54**
Major, Kevin (Gerald) **26**
McFadden, David **48**
McLuhan, (Herbert) Marshall **37, 83**
Metcalf, John **37**
Mitchell, Joni **12**
Mitchell, W(illiam) O(rmond) **25**
Moore, Brian **1, 3, 5, 7, 8, 19, 32, 90**
Morgan, Janet **39**
Moure, Erin **88**
Mowat, Farley (McGill) **26**
Munro, Alice **6, 10, 19, 50, 95**
Musgrave, Susan **13, 54**
Newlove, John (Herbert) **14**
Nichol, B(arrie) P(hillip) **18**
Nowlan, Alden (Albert) **15**
Ondaatje, (Philip) Michael **14, 29, 51, 76**
Page, P(atricia) K(athleen) **7, 18**
Pollock, (Mary) Sharon **50**
Pratt, E(dwin) J(ohn) **19**
Purdy, Al(fred Wellington) **3, 6, 14, 50**
Quarrington, Paul (Lewis) **65**
Reaney, James **13**
Ricci, Nino **70**
Richards, David Adams **59**
Richler, Mordecai **3, 5, 9, 13, 18, 46, 70**
Ringwood, Gwen(dolyn Margaret) Pharis **48**
Ritter, Erika **52**
Rooke, Leon **25, 34**
Rosenblatt, Joe **15**
Ross, (James) Sinclair **13**
Roy, Gabrielle **10, 14**
Rule, Jane (Vance) **27**
Ryga, George **14**
Scott, F(rancis) R(eginald) **22**
Shields, Carol **91**
Skelton, Robin **13**
Skvorecky, Josef (Vaclav) **15, 39, 69**
Slade, Bernard **11, 46**
Smart, Elizabeth **54**
Smith, A(rthur) J(ames) M(arshall) **15**
Souster, (Holmes) Raymond **5, 14**

Suknaski, Andrew **19**
Theriault, Yves **79**
Thesen, Sharon **56**
Thomas, Audrey (Callahan) **7, 13, 37, 107**
Thompson, Judith **39**
Tremblay, Michel **29, 102**
Urquhart, Jane **90**
Vanderhaeghe, Guy **41**
Van Vogt, A(lfred) E(lton) **1**
Vizinczey, Stephen **40**
Waddington, Miriam **28**
Wah, Fred(erick James) **44**
Walker, David Harry **14**
Walker, George F. **44, 61**
Webb, Phyllis **18**
Wiebe, Rudy (Henry) **6, 11, 14**
Wilson, Ethel Davis (Bryant) **13**
Wright, L(aurali) R. **44**
Wright, Richard B(ruce) **6**
Young, Neil **17**

CHILEAN
Alegria, Fernando **57**
Allende, Isabel **39, 57, 97**
Donoso (Yanez), Jose **4, 8, 11, 32, 99**
Dorfman, Ariel **48, 77**
Neruda, Pablo **1, 2, 5, 7, 9, 28, 62**
Parra, Nicanor **2, 102**

CHINESE
Chang, Jung **71**
Ch'ien Chung-shu **22**
Ding Ling **68**
Lord, Bette Bao **23**
Mo, Timothy (Peter) **46**
Pa Chin **18**
Peake, Mervyn **7, 54**
Wong, Jade Snow **17**

COLOMBIAN
Garcia Marquez, Gabriel (Jose) **2, 3, 8, 10, 15, 27, 47, 55, 68**

CONGOLESE
Tchicaya, Gerald Felix **101**

CUBAN
Arenas, Reinaldo **41**
Cabrera Infante, G(uillermo) **5, 25, 45**
Calvino, Italo **5, 8, 11, 22, 33, 39, 73**
Carpentier (y Valmont), Alejo **8, 11, 38**
Fornes, Maria Irene **39, 61**
Garcia, Cristina **76**
Guevara, Che **87**
Guillen, Nicolas (Cristobal) **48, 79**
Lezama Lima, Jose **4, 10, 101**
Padilla (Lorenzo), Heberto **38**
Sarduy, Severo **6, 97**

CZECH
Friedlander, Saul **90**
Havel, Vaclav **25, 58, 65**
Holub, Miroslav **4**
Hrabal, Bohumil **13, 67**
Klima, Ivan **56**
Kohout, Pavel **13**
Kundera, Milan **4, 9, 19, 32, 68**
Lustig, Arnost **56**
Seifert, Jaroslav **34, 44, 93**
Skvorecky, Josef (Vaclav) **15, 39, 69**
Vaculik, Ludvik **7**

DANISH

Abell, Kjeld 15
Bodker, Cecil 21
Dinesen, Isak 10, 29, 95
Dreyer, Carl Theodor 16
Hoeg, Peter 95

DUTCH
de Hartog, Jan 19
Mulisch, Harry 42
Ruyslinck, Ward 14
van de Wetering, Janwillem 47

EGYPTIAN
Chedid, Andree 47
Mahfuz, Najib 52, 55

ENGLISH
Ackroyd, Peter 34, 52
Adams, Douglas (Noel) 27, 60
Adams, Richard (George) 4, 5, 18
Adcock, Fleur 41
Aickman, Robert (Fordyce) 57
Aiken, Joan (Delano) 35
Aldington, Richard 49
Aldiss, Brian W(ilson) 5, 14, 40
Allingham, Margery (Louise) 19
Almedingen, E. M. 12
Alvarez, A(lfred) 5, 13
Ambler, Eric 4, 6, 9
Amis, Kingsley (William) 1, 2, 3, 5, 8, 13, 40, 44
Amis, Martin (Louis) 4, 9, 38, 62, 101
Anderson, Lindsay (Gordon) 20
Anthony, Piers 35
Archer, Jeffrey (Howard) 28
Arden, John 6, 13, 15
Armatrading, Joan 17
Arthur, Ruth M(abel) 12
Arundel, Honor (Morfydd) 17
Atkinson, Kate 99
Auden, W(ystan) H(ugh) 1, 2, 3, 4, 6, 9, 11, 14, 43
Ayckbourn, Alan 5, 8, 18, 33, 74
Ayrton, Michael 7
Bagnold, Enid 25
Bailey, Paul 45
Bainbridge, Beryl (Margaret) 4, 5, 8, 10, 14, 18, 22, 62
Ballard, J(ames) G(raham) 3, 6, 14, 36
Banks, Lynne Reid 23
Barker, Clive 52
Barker, George Granville 8, 48
Barker, Howard 37
Barker, Pat(ricia) 32, 94
Barnes, Julian (Patrick) 42
Barnes, Peter 5, 56
Barrett, (Roger) Syd 35
Bates, H(erbert) E(rnest) 46
Beer, Patricia 58
Bennett, Alan 45, 77
Berger, John (Peter) 2, 19
Berkoff, Steven 56
Bermant, Chaim (Icyk) 40
Betjeman, John 2, 6, 10, 34, 43
Billington, (Lady) Rachel (Mary) 43
Binyon, T(imothy) J(ohn) 34
Blunden, Edmund (Charles) 2, 56
Bogarde, Dirk 19
Bolt, Robert (Oxton) 14
Bond, Edward 4, 6, 13, 23
Booth, Martin 13
Bowen, Elizabeth (Dorothea Cole) 1, 3, 6, 11, 15, 22

Bowie, David 17
Boyd, William 28, 53, 70
Bradbury, Malcolm (Stanley) 32, 61
Bragg, Melvyn 10
Braine, John (Gerard) 1, 3, 41
Brenton, Howard 31
Brittain, Vera (Mary) 23
Brooke-Rose, Christine 40
Brookner, Anita 32, 34, 51
Brophy, Brigid (Antonia) 6, 11, 29, 105
Brunner, John (Kilian Houston) 8, 10
Bunting, Basil 10, 39, 47
Burgess, Anthony 1, 2, 4, 5, 8, 10, 13, 15, 22, 40, 62, 81, 94
Byatt, A(ntonia) S(usan Drabble) 19, 65
Caldwell, (Janet Miriam) Taylor (Holland) 2, 28, 39
Campbell, (John) Ramsey 42
Carter, Angela (Olive) 5, 41, 76
Causley, Charles (Stanley) 7
Caute, (John) David 29
Chambers, Aidan 35
Chaplin, Charles Spencer 16
Chapman, Graham 21
Chatwin, (Charles) Bruce 28, 57, 59
Chitty, Thomas Willes 11
Christie, Agatha (Mary Clarissa) 1, 6, 8, 12, 39, 48
Churchill, Caryl 31, 55
Clark, (Robert) Brian 29
Clarke, Arthur C(harles) 1, 4, 13, 18, 35
Cleese, John (Marwood) 21
Colegate, Isabel 36
Comfort, Alex(ander) 7
Compton-Burnett, I(vy) 1, 3, 10, 15, 34
Cooney, Ray 62
Copeland, Stewart (Armstrong) 26
Cornwell, David (John Moore) 9, 15
Costello, Elvis 21
Coward, Noel (Peirce) 1, 9, 29, 51
Creasey, John 11
Crispin, Edmund 22
Dabydeen, David 34
Dahl, Roald 1, 6, 18, 79
Daryush, Elizabeth 6, 19
Davie, Donald (Alfred) 5, 8, 10, 31
Davies, Rhys 23
Day Lewis, C(ecil) 1, 6, 10
Deighton, Len 4, 7, 22, 46
Delaney, Shelagh 29
Dennis, Nigel (Forbes) 8
Dickinson, Peter (Malcolm) 12, 35
Drabble, Margaret 2, 3, 5, 8, 10, 22, 53
Duffy, Maureen 37
du Maurier, Daphne 6, 11, 59
Durrell, Lawrence (George) 1, 4, 6, 8, 13, 27, 41
Eagleton, Terry 63
Edgar, David 42
Edwards, G(erald) B(asil) 25
Eliot, T(homas) S(tearns) 1, 2, 3, 6, 9, 10, 13, 15, 24, 34, 41, 55, 57
Elliott, Janice 47
Ellis, A. E. 7
Ellis, Alice Thomas 40
Empson, William 3, 8, 19, 33, 34
Enright, D(ennis) J(oseph) 4, 8, 31
Ewart, Gavin (Buchanan) 13, 46
Fairbairns, Zoe (Ann) 32
Farrell, J(ames) G(ordon) 6
Feinstein, Elaine 36
Fenton, James Martin 32
Figes, Eva 31

Fisher, Roy 25
Fitzgerald, Penelope 19, 51, 61
Fleming, Ian (Lancaster) 3, 30
Follett, Ken(neth Martin) 18
Forester, C(ecil) S(cott) 35
Forster, E(dward) M(organ) 1, 2, 3, 4, 9, 10, 13, 15, 22, 45, 77
Forsyth, Frederick 2, 5, 36
Fowles, John 1, 2, 3, 4, 6, 9, 10, 15, 33, 87
Francis, Dick 2, 22, 42, 102
Fraser, George MacDonald 7
Fraser, (Lady) Antonia (Pakenham) 32, 107
Frayn, Michael 3, 7, 31, 47
Freeling, Nicolas 38
Fry, Christopher 2, 10, 14
Fugard, Sheila 48
Fuller, John (Leopold) 62
Fuller, Roy (Broadbent) 4, 28
Gardam, Jane 43
Gardner, John (Edmund) 30
Garfield, Leon 12
Garner, Alan 17
Garnett, David 3
Gascoyne, David (Emery) 45
Gee, Maggie (Mary) 57
Gerhardie, William Alexander 5
Gilliatt, Penelope (Ann Douglass) 2, 10, 13, 53
Glanville, Brian (Lester) 6
Glendinning, Victoria 50
Gloag, Julian 40
Godden, (Margaret) Rumer 53
Golding, William (Gerald) 1, 2, 3, 8, 10, 17, 27, 58, 81
Graham, Winston (Mawdsley) 23
Graves, Richard Perceval 44
Graves, Robert (von Ranke) 1, 2, 6, 11, 39, 44, 45
Gray, Simon (James Holliday) 9, 14, 36
Green, Henry 2, 13, 97
Greene, Graham (Henry) 1, 3, 6, 9, 14, 18, 27, 37, 70, 72
Griffiths, Trevor 13, 52
Grigson, Geoffrey (Edward Harvey) 7, 39
Gunn, Thom(son William) 3, 6, 18, 32, 81
Haig-Brown, Roderick (Langmere) 21
Hailey, Arthur 5
Hall, Rodney 51
Hamburger, Michael (Peter Leopold) 5, 14
Hamilton, (Anthony Walter) Patrick 51
Hampton, Christopher (James) 4
Hare, David 29, 58
Harrison, Tony 43
Hartley, L(eslie) P(oles) 2, 22
Harwood, Ronald 32
Hastings, Selina 44
Hawking, Stephen W(illiam) 63, 105
Headon, (Nicky) Topper 30
Heppenstall, (John) Rayner 10
Herriot, James 12
Hibbert, Eleanor Alice Burford 7
Hill, Geoffrey (William) 5, 8, 18, 45
Hill, Susan (Elizabeth) 4
Hinde, Thomas 6, 11
Hitchcock, Alfred (Joseph) 16
Hocking, Mary (Eunice) 13
Holden, Ursula 18
Holdstock, Robert P. 39
Hollinghurst, Alan 55, 91
Hooker, (Peter) Jeremy 43
Hopkins, John (Richard) 4
Household, Geoffrey (Edward West) 11
Howard, Elizabeth Jane 7, 29

Hughes, David (John) 48
Hughes, Richard (Arthur Warren) 1, 11
Hughes, Ted 2, 4, 9, 14, 37
Huxley, Aldous (Leonard) 1, 3, 4, 5, 8, 11, 18, 35, 79
Idle, Eric 21
Ingalls, Rachel (Holmes) 42
Isherwood, Christopher (William Bradshaw) 1, 9, 11, 14, 44
Ishiguro, Kazuo 27, 56, 59
Jacobson, Dan 4, 14
Jagger, Mick 17
James, C(yril) L(ionel) R(obert) 33
James, P. D. 18, 46
Jellicoe, (Patricia) Ann 27
Jennings, Elizabeth (Joan) 5, 14
Jhabvala, Ruth Prawer 4, 8, 29, 94
Johnson, B(ryan) S(tanley William) 6, 9
Johnson, Pamela Hansford 1, 7, 27
Jolley, (Monica) Elizabeth 46
Jones, David (Michael) 2, 4, 7, 13, 42
Jones, Diana Wynne 26
Jones, Mervyn 10, 52
Jones, Mick 30
Josipovici, Gabriel 6, 43
Kavan, Anna 5, 13, 82
Kaye, M(ary) M(argaret) 28
Keates, Jonathan 34
King, Francis (Henry) 8, 53
Kirkup, James 1
Koestler, Arthur 1, 3, 6, 8, 15, 33
Kops, Bernard 4
Kureishi, Hanif 64
Lanchester, John 99
Larkin, Philip (Arthur) 3, 5, 8, 9, 13, 18, 33, 39, 64
Leavis, F(rank) R(aymond) 24
le Carré, John 3, 5, 9, 15, 28
Lee, Laurie 90
Lee, Tanith 46
Lehmann, Rosamond (Nina) 5
Lennon, John (Ono) 12, 35
Lessing, Doris (May) 1, 2, 3, 6, 10, 15, 22, 40, 94
Levertov, Denise 1, 2, 3, 5, 8, 15, 28, 66
Levi, Peter (Chad Tigar) 41
Lewis, C(live) S(taples) 1, 3, 6, 14, 27
Lively, Penelope (Margaret) 32, 50
Lodge, David (John) 36
Loy, Mina 28
Luke, Peter (Ambrose Cyprian) 38
MacInnes, Colin 4, 23
Mackenzie, Compton (Edward Montague) 18
Macpherson, (Jean) Jay 14
Maitland, Sara (Louise) 49
Manning, Olivia 5, 19
Markandaya, Kamala 8, 38
Masefield, John (Edward) 11, 47
Mason, Nick 35
Maugham, W(illiam) Somerset 1, 11, 15, 67, 93
Mayle, Peter 89
Mayne, William (James Carter) 12
McEwan, Ian (Russell) 13, 66
McGrath, Patrick 55
Mercer, David 5
Metcalf, John 37
Middleton, Christopher 13
Middleton, Stanley 7, 38
Mitford, Nancy 44
Mo, Timothy (Peter) 46
Moorcock, Michael (John) 5, 27, 58
Mortimer, John (Clifford) 28, 43

Mortimer, Penelope (Ruth) 5
Mosley, Nicholas 43, 70
Mott, Michael (Charles Alston) 15, 34
Murdoch, (Jean) Iris 1, 2, 3, 4, 6, 8, 11, 15, 22, 31, 51
Naipaul, V(idiadhar) S(urajprasad) 4, 7, 9, 13, 18, 37, 105
Newby, P(ercy) H(oward) 2, 13
Nichols, Peter (Richard) 5, 36, 65
Noon, Jeff 91
Norfolk, Lawrence 76
Nye, Robert 13, 42
O'Brien, Richard 17
O'Faolain, Julia 6, 19, 47, 108
Olivier, Laurence (Kerr) 20
Orton, Joe 4, 13, 43
Osborne, John (James) 1, 2, 5, 11, 45
Osborne, Lawrence 50
Page, Jimmy 12
Page, Louise 40
Page, P(atricia) K(athleen) 7, 18
Palin, Michael (Edward) 21
Parkin, Frank 43
Paulin, Tom 37
Peake, Mervyn 7, 54
Pearce, Philippa 21
Phillips, Caryl 96
Pinter, Harold 1, 3, 6, 9, 11, 15, 27, 58, 73
Plant, Robert 12
Poliakoff, Stephen 38
Poole, Josephine 17
Potter, Dennis (Christopher George) 58, 86
Powell, Anthony (Dymoke) 1, 3, 7, 9, 10, 31
Pownall, David 10
Powys, John Cowper 7, 9, 15, 46
Priestley, J(ohn) B(oynton) 2, 5, 9, 34
Prince, F(rank) T(empleton) 22
Pritchett, V(ictor) S(awdon) 5, 13, 15, 41
Pym, Barbara (Mary Crampton) 13, 19, 37
Quin, Ann (Marie) 6
Raine, Craig 32, 103
Raine, Kathleen (Jessie) 7, 45
Rathbone, Julian 41
Rattigan, Terence (Mervyn) 7
Raven, Simon (Arthur Noel) 14
Read, Herbert Edward 4
Read, Piers Paul 4, 10, 25
Reading, Peter 47
Redgrove, Peter (William) 6, 41
Reid, Christopher (John) 33
Renault, Mary 3, 11, 17
Rendell, Ruth (Barbara) 28, 48
Rhys, Jean 2, 4, 6, 14, 19, 51
Rice, Tim(othy Miles Bindon) 21
Richard, Keith 17
Richards, I(vor) A(rmstrong) 14, 24
Roberts, Keith (John Kingston) 14
Roberts, Michele (B.) 48
Rudkin, (James) David 14
Rushdie, (Ahmed) Salman 23, 31, 55, 100
Rushforth, Peter (Scott) 19
Russell, (Henry) Ken(neth Alfred) 16
Russell, William Martin 60
Sacks, Oliver (Wolf) 67
Sansom, William 2, 6
Sassoon, Siegfried (Lorraine) 36
Scammell, Michael 34
Scannell, Vernon 49
Schlee, Ann 35
Schumacher, E(rnst) F(riedrich) 80
Scott, Paul (Mark) 9, 60
Shaffer, Anthony (Joshua) 19
Shaffer, Peter (Levin) 5, 14, 18, 37, 60

Sharpe, Tom 36
Shaw, Robert 5
Sheed, Wilfrid (John Joseph) 2, 4, 10, 53
Shute, Nevil 30
Shuttle, Penelope (Diane) 7
Silkin, Jon 2, 6, 43
Sillitoe, Alan 1, 3, 6, 10, 19, 57
Simonon, Paul 30
Simpson, N(orman) F(rederick) 29
Sinclair, Andrew (Annandale) 2, 14
Sinclair, Iain 76
Sisson, C(harles) H(ubert) 8
Sitwell, Dame Edith 2, 9, 67
Slaughter, Carolyn 56
Smith, Stevie 3, 8, 25, 44
Snow, C(harles) P(ercy) 1, 4, 6, 9, 13, 19
Spender, Stephen (Harold) 1, 2, 5, 10, 41, 91
Spurling, Hilary 34
Stannard, Martin 44
Stewart, J(ohn) I(nnes) M(ackintosh) 7, 14, 32
Stewart, Mary (Florence Elinor) 7, 35
Stoppard, Tom 1, 3, 4, 5, 8, 15, 29, 34, 63, 91
Storey, David (Malcolm) 2, 4, 5, 8
Streatfeild, (Mary) Noel 21
Strummer, Joe 30
Summers, Andrew James 26
Sumner, Gordon Matthew 26
Sutcliff, Rosemary 26
Swift, Graham (Colin) 41, 88
Swinfen, Ann 34
Swinnerton, Frank Arthur 31
Symons, Julian (Gustave) 2, 14, 32
Szirtes, George 46
Taylor, Elizabeth 2, 4, 29
Tennant, Emma (Christina) 13, 52
Teran, Lisa St. Aubin de 36
Thomas, D(onald) M(ichael) 13, 22, 31
Tindall, Gillian (Elizabeth) 7
Tolkien, J(ohn) R(onald) R(euel) 1, 2, 3, 8, 12, 38
Tomlinson, (Alfred) Charles 2, 4, 6, 13, 45
Townshend, Peter (Dennis Blandford) 17, 42
Treitel, Jonathan 70
Tremain, Rose 42
Tuohy, Frank 37
Turner, Frederick 48
Unsworth, Barry (Forster) 76
Ustinov, Peter (Alexander) 1
Vansittart, Peter 42
Vine, Barbara 50
Wain, John (Barrington) 2, 11, 15, 46
Walker, Ted 13
Walsh, Jill Paton 35
Warner, Francis (Robert le Plastrier) 14
Warner, Marina 59
Warner, Rex (Ernest) 45
Warner, Sylvia Townsend 7, 19
Waterhouse, Keith (Spencer) 47
Waters, Roger 35
Waugh, Auberon (Alexander) 7
Waugh, Evelyn (Arthur St. John) 1, 3, 8, 13, 19, 27, 44, 107
Waugh, Harriet 6
Webber, Andrew Lloyd 21
Weldon, Fay 6, 9, 11, 19, 36, 59
Weller, Paul 26
Wesker, Arnold 3, 5, 42
West, Anthony (Panther) 50
West, Paul 7, 14, 96
West, Rebecca 7, 9, 31, 50
Westall, Robert (Atkinson) 17
White, Patrick (Victor Martindale) 3, 4, 5, 7, 9, 18, 65, 69

White, T(erence) H(anbury) 30
Whitehead, E(dward) A(nthony) 5
Whitemore, Hugh (John) 37
Wilding, Michael 73
Williams, Hugo 42
Wilson, A(ndrew) N(orman) 33
Wilson, Angus (Frank Johnstone) 2, 3, 5, 25, 34
Wilson, Colin 3, 14
Wilson, Snoo 33
Wingrove, David (John) 68
Winterson, Jeanette 64
Wodehouse, P(elham) G(renville) 1, 2, 5, 10, 22
Wright, Rick 35
Wyndham, John 19
Yorke, Henry Vincent 13
Young, Andrew (John) 5

ESTONIAN
Ivask, Ivar Vidrik 14

FIJI ISLANDER
Prichard, Katharine Susannah 46

FILIPINO
Santos, Bienvenido N(uqui) 22

FINNISH
Haavikko, Paavo Juhani 18, 34
Salama, Hannu 18
Sillanpaa, Frans Eemil 19

FRENCH
Adamov, Arthur 4, 25
Anouilh, Jean (Marie Lucien Pierre) 1, 3, 8, 13, 40, 50
Aragon, Louis 3, 22
Audiberti, Jacques 38
Ayme, Marcel (Andre) 11
Barthes, Roland (Gerard) 24, 83
Bataille, Georges 29
Baudrillard, Jean 60
Beauvoir, Simone (Lucie Ernestine Marie Bertrand) de 1, 2, 4, 8, 14, 31, 44, 50, 71
Beckett, Samuel (Barclay) 1, 2, 3, 4, 6, 9, 10, 11, 14, 18, 29, 57, 59, 83
Bonnefoy, Yves 9, 15, 58
Bresson, Robert 16
Breton, Andre 2, 9, 15, 54
Butor, Michel (Marie Francois) 1, 3, 8, 11, 15
Camus, Albert 1, 2, 4, 9, 11, 14, 32, 63, 69
Carrere, Emmanuel 89
Cayrol, Jean 11
Celine, Louis-Ferdinand 1, 3, 4, 7, 9, 15, 47
Cendrars, Blaise 18, 106
Chabrol, Claude 16
Char, Rene(-Emile) 9, 11, 14, 55
Chedid, Andree 47
Cixous, Helene 92
Clair, Rene 20
Cocteau, Jean (Maurice Eugene Clement) 1, 8, 15, 16, 43
Cousteau, Jacques-Yves 30
del Castillo, Michel 38
Derrida, Jacques 24, 87
Destouches, Louis-Ferdinand 9, 15
Duhamel, Georges 8
Duras, Marguerite 3, 6, 11, 20, 34, 40, 68, 100
Ernaux, Annie 88
Federman, Raymond 6, 47
Foucault, Michel 31, 34, 69
Fournier, Pierre 11

Francis, Claude 50
Gallo, Max Louis 95
Gary, Romain 25
Gascar, Pierre 11
Genet, Jean 1, 2, 5, 10, 14, 44, 46
Giono, Jean 4, 11
Godard, Jean-Luc 20
Goldmann, Lucien 24
Gontier, Fernande 50
Gracq, Julien 11, 48
Gray, Francine du Plessix 22
Green, Julien 3, 11, 77
Guillevic, (Eugene) 33
Ionesco, Eugene 1, 4, 6, 9, 11, 15, 41, 86
Japrisot, Sebastien 90
Jouve, Pierre Jean 47
Kristeva, Julia 77
Lacan, Jacques (Marie Emile) 75
Laurent, Antoine 50
Le Clezio, J(ean) M(arie) G(ustave) 31
Leduc, Violette 22
Leger, (Marie-Rene Auguste) Alexis Saint-Leger 11
Leiris, Michel (Julien) 61
Levi-Strauss, Claude 38
Mallet-Joris, Francoise 11
Malraux, (Georges-)Andre 1, 4, 9, 13, 15, 57
Mandiargues, Andre Pieyre de 41
Marcel, Gabriel Honore 15
Mauriac, Claude 9
Mauriac, Francois (Charles) 4, 9, 56
Merton, Thomas 1, 3, 11, 34, 83
Modiano, Patrick (Jean) 18
Montherlant, Henry (Milon) de 8, 19
Morand, Paul 41
Nin, Anais 1, 4, 8, 11, 14, 60
Perec, Georges 56
Perse, St.-John 4, 11, 46
Pinget, Robert 7, 13, 37
Ponge, Francis (Jean Gaston Alfred) 6, 18
Prevert, Jacques (Henri Marie) 15
Queneau, Raymond 2, 5, 10, 42
Quoirez, Francoise 9
Renoir, Jean 20
Resnais, Alain 16
Reverdy, Pierre 53
Rio, Michel 43
Robbe-Grillet, Alain 1, 2, 4, 6, 8, 10, 14, 43
Rohmer, Eric 16
Romains, Jules 7
Sachs, Nelly 14, 98
Sagan, Francoise 3, 6, 9, 17, 36
Sarduy, Severo 6, 97
Sarraute, Nathalie 1, 2, 4, 8, 10, 31, 80
Sartre, Jean-Paul 1, 4, 7, 9, 13, 18, 24, 44, 50, 52
Sauser-Hall, Frederic 18
Schwarz-Bart, Andre 2, 4
Schwarz-Bart, Simone 7
Simenon, Georges (Jacques Christian) 1, 2, 3, 8, 18, 47
Simon, Claude 4, 9, 15, 39
Soupault, Philippe 68
Steiner, George 24
Tournier, Michel (Edouard) 6, 23, 36, 95
Troyat, Henri 23
Truffaut, Francois 20, 101
Tuck, Lily 70
Tzara, Tristan 47
Varda, Agnes 16
Wittig, Monique 22
Yourcenar, Marguerite 19, 38, 50, 87

FRENCH GUINEAN
Damas, Leon-Gontran 84

GERMAN
Amichai, Yehuda 9, 22, 57
Arendt, Hannah 66, 98
Arp, Jean 5
Becker, Jurek 7, 19
Benary-Isbert, Margot 12
Bienek, Horst 7, 11
Boell, Heinrich (Theodor) 2, 3, 6, 9, 11, 15, 27, 32, 72
Buchheim, Lothar-Guenther 6
Bukowski, Charles 2, 5, 9, 41, 82, 108
Eich, Guenter 15
Ende, Michael (Andreas Helmuth) 31
Enzensberger, Hans Magnus 43
Fassbinder, Rainer Werner 20
Figes, Eva 31
Grass, Guenter (Wilhelm) 1, 2, 4, 6, 11, 15, 22, 32, 49, 88
Habermas, Juergen 104
Hamburger, Michael (Peter Leopold) 5, 14
Heidegger, Martin 24
Herzog, Werner 16
Hesse, Hermann 1, 2, 3, 6, 11, 17, 25, 69
Heym, Stefan 41
Hildesheimer, Wolfgang 49
Hochhuth, Rolf 4, 11, 18
Hofmann, Gert 54
Johnson, Uwe 5, 10, 15, 40
Kroetz, Franz Xaver 41
Kunze, Reiner 10
Lenz, Siegfried 27
Levitin, Sonia (Wolff) 17
Mueller, Lisel 13, 51
Nossack, Hans Erich 6
Preussler, Otfried 17
Remarque, Erich Maria 21
Riefenstahl, Leni 16
Sachs, Nelly 14, 98
Schmidt, Arno (Otto) 56
Schumacher, E(rnst) F(riedrich) 80
Seghers, Anna 7
Strauss, Botho 22
Sueskind, Patrick 44
Walser, Martin 27
Weiss, Peter (Ulrich) 3, 15, 51
Wellershoff, Dieter 46
Wolf, Christa 14, 29, 58
Zuckmayer, Carl 18

GHANIAN
Armah, Ayi Kwei 5, 33

GREEK
Broumas, Olga 10, 73
Elytis, Odysseus 15, 49, 100
Haviaras, Stratis 33
Karapanou, Margarita 13
Nakos, Lilika 29
Ritsos, Yannis 6, 13, 31
Samarakis, Antonis 5
Seferis, George 5, 11
Spanidou, Irini 44
Vassilikos, Vassilis 4, 8

GUADELOUPEAN
Conde, Maryse 52, 92
Schwarz-Bart, Simone 7

GUATEMALAN
Asturias, Miguel Angel 3, 8, 13

GUINEAN
Laye, Camara **4, 38**

GUYANESE
Dabydeen, David **34**
Harris, (Theodore) Wilson **25**

HUNGARIAN
Faludy, George **42**
Koestler, Arthur **1, 3, 6, 8, 15, 33**
Konrad, Gyoergy **4, 10, 73**
Lengyel, Jozsef **7**
Lukacs, George **24**
Nagy, Laszlo **7**
Szirtes, George **46**
Tabori, George **19**
Vizinczey, Stephen **40**

ICELANDIC
Gunnars, Kristjana **69**
Laxness, Halldor **25**

INDIAN
Ali, Ahmed **69**
Anand, Mulk Raj **23, 93**
Desai, Anita **19, 37, 97**
Ezekiel, Nissim **61**
Ghosh, Amitav **44**
Mahapatra, Jayanta **33**
Markandaya, Kamala **8, 38**
Mehta, Ved (Parkash) **37**
Mistry, Rohinton **71**
Mukherjee, Bharati **53**
Narayan, R(asipuram) K(rishnaswami) **7, 28, 47**
Rao, Raja **25, 56**
Ray, Satyajit **16, 76**
Rushdie, (Ahmed) Salman **23, 31, 55, 100**
Sahgal, Nayantara (Pandit) **41**
Sealy, I. Allan **55**
Seth, Vikram **43, 90**
Singh, Khushwant **11**
Tharoor, Shashi **70**
White, T(erence) H(anbury) **30**

IRANIAN
Modarressi, Taghi (M.) **44**
Shamlu, Ahmad **10**

IRISH
Banville, John **46**
Beckett, Samuel (Barclay) **1, 2, 3, 4, 6, 9, 10, 11, 14, 18, 29, 57, 59, 83**
Behan, Brendan **1, 8, 11, 15, 79**
Blackwood, Caroline **6, 9, 100**
Boland, Eavan (Aisling) **40, 67**
Bowen, Elizabeth (Dorothea Cole) **1, 3, 6, 11, 15, 22**
Boyle, Patrick **19**
Brennan, Maeve **5**
Brown, Christy **63**
Carroll, Paul Vincent **10**
Clarke, Austin **6, 9**
Colum, Padraic **28**
Cox, William Trevor **9, 14, 71**
Day Lewis, C(ecil) **1, 6, 10**
Dillon, Eilis **17**
Donleavy, J(ames) P(atrick) **1, 4, 6, 10, 45**
Doyle, Roddy **81**
Durcan, Paul **43, 70**
Friel, Brian **5, 42, 59**
Gebler, Carlo (Ernest) **39**

Hanley, James **3, 5, 8, 13**
Hart, Josephine **70**
Heaney, Seamus (Justin) **5, 7, 14, 25, 37, 74, 91**
Johnston, Jennifer **7**
Kavanagh, Patrick (Joseph) **22**
Keane, Molly **31**
Kiely, Benedict **23, 43**
Kinsella, Thomas **4, 19**
Lavin, Mary **4, 18, 99**
Leonard, Hugh **19**
Longley, Michael **29**
Mac Laverty, Bernard **31**
MacNeice, (Frederick) Louis **1, 4, 10, 53**
Mahon, Derek **27**
McGahern, John **5, 9, 48**
McGinley, Patrick (Anthony) **41**
McGuckian, Medbh **48**
Montague, John (Patrick) **13, 46**
Moore, Brian **1, 3, 5, 7, 8, 19, 32, 90**
Morrison, Van **21**
Morrissy, Mary **99**
Muldoon, Paul **32, 72**
Murphy, Richard **41**
Murphy, Thomas (Bernard) **51**
Nolan, Christopher **58**
O'Brien, Edna **3, 5, 8, 13, 36, 65**
O'Brien, Flann **1, 4, 5, 7, 10, 47**
O'Casey, Sean **1, 5, 9, 11, 15, 88**
O'Connor, Frank **23**
O'Doherty, Brian **76**
O'Faolain, Julia **6, 19, 47, 108**
O'Faolain, Sean **1, 7, 14, 32, 70**
O'Flaherty, Liam **5, 34**
Paulin, Tom **37**
Rodgers, W(illiam) R(obert) **7**
Simmons, James (Stewart Alexander) **43**
Trevor, William **7, 9, 14, 25, 71**
White, Terence de Vere **49**
Wilson, Robert McLiam **59**

ISRAELI
Agnon, S(hmuel) Y(osef Halevi) **4, 8, 14**
Amichai, Yehuda **9, 22, 57**
Appelfeld, Aharon **23, 47**
Bakshi, Ralph **26**
Friedlander, Saul **90**
Grossman, David **67**
Kaniuk, Yoram **19**
Levin, Meyer **7**
Megged, Aharon **9**
Oz, Amos **5, 8, 11, 27, 33, 54**
Shammas, Anton **55**
Sobol, Joshua **60**
Yehoshua, A(braham) B. **13, 31**

ITALIAN
Antonioni, Michelangelo **20**
Bacchelli, Riccardo **19**
Bassani, Giorgio **9**
Bertolucci, Bernardo **16**
Bufalino, Gesualdo **74**
Buzzati, Dino **36**
Calasso, Roberto **81**
Calvino, Italo **5, 8, 11, 22, 33, 39, 73**
De Sica, Vittorio **20**
Eco, Umberto **28, 60**
Fallaci, Oriana **11**
Fellini, Federico **16, 85**
Fo, Dario **32, 109**
Gadda, Carlo Emilio **11**
Ginzburg, Natalia **5, 11, 54, 70**
Giovene, Andrea **7**

Landolfi, Tommaso **11, 49**
Levi, Primo **37, 50**
Luzi, Mario **13**
Montale, Eugenio **7, 9, 18**
Morante, Elsa **8, 47**
Moravia, Alberto **2, 7, 11, 27, 46**
Ortese, Anna Maria **89**
Palazzeschi, Aldo **11**
Pasolini, Pier Paolo **20, 37, 106**
Piccolo, Lucio **13**
Pincherle, Alberto **11, 18**
Quasimodo, Salvatore **10**
Ricci, Nino **70**
Sciascia, Leonardo **8, 9, 41**
Silone, Ignazio **4**
Ungaretti, Giuseppe **7, 11, 15**
Visconti, Luchino **16**
Vittorini, Elio **6, 9, 14**
Wertmueller, Lina **16**

JAMAICAN
Bennett, Louise (Simone) **28**
Cliff, Jimmy **21**
Marley, Bob **17**
Thelwell, Michael Miles **22**

JAPANESE
Abe, Kobo **8, 22, 53, 81**
Enchi Fumiko (Ueda) **31**
Endo, Shusaku **7, 14, 19, 54, 99**
Ibuse Masuji **22**
Ichikawa, Kon **20**
Ishiguro, Kazuo **27, 56, 59**
Kawabata, Yasunari **2, 5, 9, 18, 107**
Kurosawa, Akira **16**
Mishima, Yukio **2, 4, 6, 9, 27**
Oe, Kenzaburo **10, 36, 86**
Oshima, Nagisa **20**
Ozu, Yasujiro **16**
Shiga, Naoya **33**
Tanizaki, Jun'ichiro **8, 14, 28**
Yoshimoto, Banana **84**

KENYAN
Ngugi, James T(hiong'o) **3, 7, 13**
Ngugi wa Thiong'o **36**

MARTINICAN
Cesaire, Aime (Fernand) **19, 32**
Fanon, Frantz **74**
Glissant, Edouard **10, 68**

MEXICAN
Castellanos, Rosario **66**
Fuentes, Carlos **3, 8, 10, 13, 22, 41, 60**
Ibarguengoitia, Jorge **37**
Lopez Portillo (y Pacheco), Jose **46**
Lopez y Fuentes, Gregorio **32**
Paz, Octavio **3, 4, 6, 10, 19, 51, 65**
Rulfo, Juan **8, 80**

MOROCCAN
Arrabal, Fernando **2, 9, 18, 58**

NEW ZEALANDER
Adcock, Fleur **41**
Ashton-Warner, Sylvia (Constance) **19**
Baxter, James K(eir) **14**
Campion, Jane **95**
Frame, Janet **2, 3, 6, 22, 66, 96**
Gee, Maurice (Gough) **29**
Grace, Patricia **56**
Hilliard, Noel (Harvey) **15**

Nationality Index

Hulme, Keri **39**
Ihimaera, Witi **46**
Marsh, (Edith) Ngaio **7, 53**
Sargeson, Frank **31**

NICARAGUAN
Alegria, Claribel **75**
Cardenal, Ernesto **31**

NIGERIAN
Achebe, (Albert) Chinua(lumogu) **1, 3, 5, 7,**
   11, 26, 51, 75
Clark, John Pepper **38**
Ekwensi, Cyprian (Odiatu Duaka) **4**
Emecheta, (Florence Onye) Buchi **14, 48**
Okigbo, Christopher (Ifenayichukwu) **25, 84**
Okri, Ben **87**
Soyinka, Wole **3, 5, 14, 36, 44**
Tutuola, Amos **5, 14, 29**

NORTHERN IRISH
Simmons, James (Stewart Alexander) **43**
Wilson, Robert McLiam **59**

NORWEGIAN
Friis-Baastad, Babbis Ellinor **12**
Heyerdahl, Thor **26**
Vesaas, Tarjei **48**

PAKISTANI
Ali, Ahmed **69**
Ghose, Zulfikar **42**

PARAGUAYAN
Roa Bastos, Augusto (Antonio) **45**

PERUVIAN
Allende, Isabel **39, 57, 97**
Arguedas, Jose Maria **10, 18**
Goldemberg, Isaac **52**
Vargas Llosa, (Jorge) Mario (Pedro) **3, 6, 9,**
   10, 15, 31, 42, 85

POLISH
Agnon, S(hmuel) Y(osef Halevi) **4, 8, 14**
Becker, Jurek **7, 19**
Bermant, Chaim (Icyk) **40**
Bienek, Horst **7, 11**
Brandys, Kazimierz **62**
Dabrowska, Maria (Szumska) **15**
Gombrowicz, Witold **4, 7, 11, 49**
Herbert, Zbigniew **9, 43**
Konwicki, Tadeusz **8, 28, 54**
Kosinski, Jerzy (Nikodem) **1, 2, 3, 6, 10, 15,**
   53, 70
Lem, Stanislaw **8, 15, 40**
Milosz, Czeslaw **5, 11, 22, 31, 56, 82**
Mrozek, Slawomir **3, 13**
Polanski, Roman **16**
Rozewicz, Tadeusz **9, 23**
Singer, Isaac Bashevis **1, 3, 6, 9, 11, 15, 23,**
   38, 69
Skolimowski, Jerzy **20**
Szymborska, Wislawa **99**
Wajda, Andrzej **16**
Wittlin, Jozef **25**
Wojciechowska, Maia (Teresa) **26**

PORTUGUESE
Migueis, Jose Rodrigues **10**

PUERTO RICAN
Marques, Rene **96**

Pinero, Miguel (Antonio Gomez) **4, 55**
Sanchez, Luis Rafael **23**

ROMANIAN
Appelfeld, Aharon **23, 47**
Arghezi, Tudor **80**
Blaga, Lucian **75**
Celan, Paul **10, 19, 53, 82**
Cioran, E(mil) M. **64**
Codrescu, Andrei **46**
Ionesco, Eugene **1, 4, 6, 9, 11, 15, 41, 86**
Rezzori (d'Arezzo), Gregor von **25**
Tzara, Tristan **47**
Wiesel, Elie(zer) **3, 5, 11, 37**

RUSSIAN
Aitmatov, Chingiz (Torekulovich) **71**
Akhmadulina, Bella Akhatovna **53**
Akhmatova, Anna **11, 25, 64**
Aksyonov, Vassily (Pavlovich) **22, 37, 101**
Aleshkovsky, Yuz **44**
Almedingen, E. M. **12**
Asimov, Isaac **1, 3, 9, 19, 26, 76, 92**
Bakhtin, Mikhail Mikhailovich **83**
Bitov, Andrei (Georgievich) **57**
Brodsky, Joseph **4, 6, 13, 36, 100**
Deren, Maya **16, 102**
Ehrenburg, Ilya (Grigoryevich) **18, 34, 62**
Eliade, Mircea **19**
Gary, Romain **25**
Goldberg, Anatol **34**
Grade, Chaim **10**
Grossman, Vasily (Semenovich) **41**
Iskander, Fazil **47**
Kaletski, Alexander **39**
Krotkov, Yuri **19**
Leonov, Leonid (Maximovich) **92**
Limonov, Edward **67**
Nabokov, Vladimir (Vladimirovich) **1, 2, 3, 6,**
   8, 11, 15, 23, 44, 46, 64
Olesha, Yuri (Karlovich) **8**
Pasternak, Boris (Leonidovich) **7, 10, 18, 63**
Paustovsky, Konstantin (Georgievich) **40**
Rahv, Philip **24**
Rand, Ayn **3, 30, 44, 79**
Ratushinskaya, Irina **54**
Rybakov, Anatoli (Naumovich) **23, 53**
Sarraute, Nathalie **1, 2, 4, 8, 10, 31, 80**
Shalamov, Varlam (Tikhonovich) **18**
Sholokhov, Mikhail (Aleksandrovich) **7, 15**
Sinyavsky, Andrei (Donatevich) **8**
Solzhenitsyn, Aleksandr I(sayevich) **1, 2, 4, 7,**
   9, 10, 18, 26, 34, 78
Strugatskii, Arkadii (Natanovich) **27**
Strugatskii, Boris (Natanovich) **27**
Tarkovsky, Andrei (Arsenyevich) **75**
Trifonov, Yuri (Valentinovich) **45**
Troyat, Henri **23**
Voinovich, Vladimir (Nikolaevich) **10, 49**
Voznesensky, Andrei (Andreievich) **1, 15, 57**
Yanovsky, V(assily) S(emenovich) **2, 18**
Yevtushenko, Yevgeny (Alexandrovich) **1, 3,**
   13, 26, 51
Yezierska, Anzia **46**
Zaturenska, Marya **6, 11**
Zinoviev, Alexander (Aleksandrovich) **19**

SALVADORAN
Alegria, Claribel **75**
Argueta, Manlio **31**

SCOTTISH
Banks, Iain M(enzies) **34**

Brown, George Mackay **5, 48, 100**
Cronin, A(rchibald) J(oseph) **32**
Dunn, Douglas (Eaglesham) **6, 40**
Graham, W(illiam) S(ydney) **29**
Gray, Alasdair (James) **41**
Grieve, C(hristopher) M(urray) **11, 19**
Hunter, Mollie **21**
Jenkins, (John) Robin **52**
Kelman, James **58, 86**
Laing, R(onald) D(avid) **95**
MacBeth, George (Mann) **2, 5, 9**
MacCaig, Norman (Alexander) **36**
MacDiarmid, Hugh **2, 4, 11, 19, 63**
MacInnes, Helen (Clark) **27, 39**
MacLean, Alistair (Stuart) **3, 13, 50, 63**
McIlvanney, William **42**
Morgan, Edwin (George) **31**
Smith, Iain Crichton **64**
Spark, Muriel (Sarah) **2, 3, 5, 8, 13, 18, 40, 94**
Taylor, C(ecil) P(hilip) **27**
Walker, David Harry **14**
Young, Andrew (John) **5**

SENEGALESE
Ousmane, Sembene **66**
Senghor, Leopold Sedar **54**

SOMALIAN
Farah, Nuruddin **53**

SOUTH AFRICAN
Abrahams, Peter (Henry) **4**
Breytenbach, Breyten **23, 37**
Brink, Andre (Philippus) **18, 36, 106**
Brutus, Dennis **43**
Coetzee, J(ohn) M(ichael) **23, 33, 66**
Courtenay, Bryce **59**
Fugard, (Harold) Athol **5, 9, 14, 25, 40, 80**
Fugard, Sheila **48**
Gordimer, Nadine **3, 5, 7, 10, 18, 33, 51, 70**
Harwood, Ronald **32**
Head, Bessie **25, 67**
Hope, Christopher (David Tully) **52**
Kunene, Mazisi (Raymond) **85**
La Guma, (Justin) Alex(ander) **19**
Millin, Sarah Gertrude **49**
Mphahlele, Ezekiel **25**
Mtwa, Percy **47**
Ngema, Mbongeni **57**
Nkosi, Lewis **45**
Paton, Alan (Stewart) **4, 10, 25, 55, 106**
Plomer, William Charles Franklin **4, 8**
Prince, F(rank) T(empleton) **22**
Smith, Wilbur (Addison) **33**
Tolkien, J(ohn) R(onald) R(euel) **1, 2, 3, 8, 12,**
   38
Tutu, Desmond M(pilo) **80**
van der Post, Laurens (Jan) **5**
Vorster, Gordon **34**

SPANISH
Alberti, Rafael **7**
Aleixandre, Vicente **9, 36**
Alfau, Felipe **66**
Alonso, Damaso **14**
Arrabal, Fernando **2, 9, 18, 58**
Azorin **11**
Benet, Juan **28**
Buero Vallejo, Antonio **15, 46**
Bunuel, Luis **16, 80**
Casona, Alejandro **49**
Castedo, Elena **65**
Cela, Camilo Jose **4, 13, 59**

Cernuda (y Bidon), Luis **54**
del Castillo, Michel **38**
Delibes, Miguel **8, 18**
Espriu, Salvador **9**
Gironella, Jose Maria **11**
Gomez de la Serna, Ramon **9**
Goytisolo, Juan **5, 10, 23**
Guillen, Jorge **11**
Matute (Ausejo), Ana Maria **11**
Otero, Blas de **11**
Rodriguez, Claudio **10**
Ruiz, Jose Martinez **11**
Saura (Atares), Carlos **20**
Sender, Ramon (Jose) **8**

SRI LANKAN
Gunesekera, Romesh **91**

ST. LUCIAN
Walcott, Derek (Alton) **2, 4, 9, 14, 25, 42, 67, 76**

SWEDISH
Beckman, Gunnel **26**
Bergman, (Ernst) Ingmar **16, 72**
Ekeloef, (Bengt) Gunnar **27**
Johnson, Eyvind (Olof Verner) **14**
Lagerkvist, Paer (Fabian) **7, 10, 13, 54**
Martinson, Harry (Edmund) **14**
Sjoewall, Maj **7**
Spiegelman, Art **76**
Transtroemer, Tomas (Goesta) **52, 65**
Wahloo, Per **7**

Weiss, Peter (Ulrich) **3, 15, 51**

SWISS
Canetti, Elias **3, 14, 25, 75, 86**
Cendrars, Blaise **18, 106**
Duerrenmatt, Friedrich **1, 4, 8, 11, 15, 43, 102**
Frisch, Max (Rudolf) **3, 9, 14, 18, 32, 44**
Hesse, Hermann **1, 2, 3, 6, 11, 17, 25, 69**
Pinget, Robert **7, 13, 37**
Sauser-Hall, Frederic **18**
Sterchi, Beat **65**
von Daeniken, Erich **30**

TRINIDADIAN
Guy, Rosa (Cuthbert) **26**
James, C(yril) L(ionel) R(obert) **33**
Lovelace, Earl **51**
Naipaul, Shiva(dhar Srinivasa) **32, 39**
Naipaul, V(idiadhar) S(urajprasad) **4, 7, 9, 13, 18, 37, 105**

TURKISH
Hikmet, Nazim **40**
Kemal, Yashar **14, 29**
Seferis, George **5, 11**

UGANDAN
p'Bitek, Okot **96**

URUGUAYAN
Galeano, Eduardo (Hughes) **72**
Onetti, Juan Carlos **7, 10**

WELSH
Abse, Dannie **7, 29**
Arundel, Honor (Morfydd) **17**
Clarke, Gillian **61**
Dahl, Roald **1, 6, 18, 79**
Davies, Rhys **23**
Francis, Dick **2, 22, 42, 102**
Hughes, Richard (Arthur Warren) **1, 11**
Humphreys, Emyr Owen **47**
Jones, David (Michael) **2, 4, 7, 13, 42**
Jones, Terence Graham Parry **21**
Levinson, Deirdre **49**
Llewellyn Lloyd, Richard Dafydd Vivian **7, 80**
Mathias, Roland (Glyn) **45**
Norris, Leslie **14**
Roberts, Kate **15**
Rubens, Bernice (Ruth) **19, 31**
Thomas, R(onald) S(tuart) **6, 13, 48**
Watkins, Vernon Phillips **43**
Williams, (George) Emlyn **15**

YUGOSLAVIAN
Andric, Ivo **8**
Cosic, Dobrica **14**
Kis, Danilo **57**
Krleza, Miroslav **8**
Pavic, Milorad **60**
Popa, Vasko **19**
Simic, Charles **6, 9, 22, 49, 68**
Tesich, Steve **40, 69**

Nationality Index

CLC-109 **Title Index**

About Face (Fo)
   See *Clascon trombette e penacchi*
Accidental Death of an Anarchist (Fo)
   See *Morte accidentale di un anarchico*
"Actue Crisis Identity" (Royko) **109**:405
"After the Big Parade" (Ginsberg) **109**:318
Alaska (Michener) **109**:376-77, 381, 386
"Alice, Falling" (Millhauser) **109**:157-58, 160-61
"Alinsky No in Their League" (Royko) **109**:408
Almost By Chance A Woman: Elizabeth (Fo)
   See *Elisabetta: Quasi per Caso una Donna*
Alnilam (Dickey) **109**:236, 240, 241, 257
"America" (Ginsberg) **109**:337, 355
"American Change" (Ginsberg) **109**:364
Angela's Ashes (McCourt) **109**:146-55
"Anna Lisa's Nose" (Berriault) **109**:96
"Anything" (Dorris) **109**:307
Apo-33 Bulletin A Metabolic Regulator (Burroughs) **109**:184
"Approaching Prayer" (Dickey) **109**:237, 273
Archangels Don't Play Pinball (Fo) **109**:118-19, 121
"Autumn Leaves" (Ginsberg) **109**:329
Babel to Byzantium (Dickey) **109**:245
"Barnum Museum" (Millhauser) **109**:158, 161
The Barnum Museum (Millhauser) **109**:157-60, 165, 167, 169-70, 174
"The Beginning Is Also the End" (Burroughs) **109**:196
"Behind the Blue Curtain" (Millhauser) **109**:157, 160
Between Silences (Jin) **109**:52-3
"Between Two Prisoners" (Dickey) **109**:238
The Black Rider (Burroughs) **109**:182
"Black Shroud" (Ginsberg) **109**:364
"The Blue Angel" (Ginsberg) **109**:358
Boss: Richard J. Daley of Chicago (Royko) **109**:399, 401-02, 404
"The Bricklayers' Lunch Hour" (Ginsberg) **109**:353
The Bridge at Andau (Michener) **109**:375, 378-79, 382
The Bridges of Toko-Ri (Michener) **109**:376, 378-79, 382
The Broken Cord: A Family's Ongoing Struggle with Fetal Alcohol Syndrome (Dorris) **109**:296-99, 304-05, 307-08, 310-11, 313
Buckdancer's Choice (Dickey) **109**:243-44
"Bugs in the Bug" (Royko) **109**:406
"The Bystander" (Berriault) **109**:96
Can't Pay? Won't Pay! (Fo) **109**:143
Caravans (Michener) **109**:376, 378-79, 382
Caribbean (Michener) **109**:377, 382, 386
The Cat Inside (Burroughs) **109**:182
Centennial (Michener) **109**:375, 377-79, 381, 383
The Central Motion (Dickey) **109**:245
A Century of Sonnets (Michener) **109**:380
"Chances R" (Ginsberg) **109**:364
"Charnel Ground" (Ginsberg) **109**:329
Chesapeake (Michener) **109**:375, 377, 379, 381, 388
Clascon trombette e penacchi (Fo) **109**:109-11, 119-20, 136-37, 139, 143, 146

Cloud Chamber (Dorris) **109**:296-300, 311-13
Cold Mountain (Frazier) **109**:48-51
Collected Poems, 1947-1980 (Ginsberg) **109**:331, 338, 352, 356, 358, 364
La Colpa é sempre del diavolo (Fo) **109**:115
Comfort Woman (Keller) **109**:63-6
Conference of Victims (Berriault) **109**:90
Coppia aperta (Fo) **109**:109
Cosmopolatain Greetings (Ginsberg) **109**:316, 318, 329
The Covenant (Michener) **109**:375, 379, 381, 386
The Crown of Columbus (Dorris) **109**:296-98, 307-09
"The Dark Smoke" (Dorris) **109**:309-10
"The Day Slats Fell for a Girl" (Royko) **109**:407
Deliverance (Dickey) **109**:243, 245, 257-63, 276-77, 279-80, 282-83, 285-86
The Descent (Berriault) **109**:90
Devil with Boobs (Fo) **109**:143
"The Diary of K. W." (Berriault) **109**:96-7
Don't Grow Old (Ginsberg) **109**:338
"Dragon Head" (Jin) **109**:52, 54
"Dream Record: June 1955" (Ginsberg) **109**:358
The Drifters (Michener) **109**:375, 378-79
"Drinking From a Helmet" (Dickey) **109**:237
Drowning with Others (Dickey) **109**:244-45
The Eagle and the Raven (Michener) **109**:326
"The Eagle's Mile" (Dickey) **109**:246-47, 251, 273
The Eagle's Mile (Dickey) **109**:236, 245-46, 264
"Earnest Money" (Dorris) **109**:307, 310
"Ecologue" (Ginsberg) **109**:364
Edwin Mullhouse: The Life and Death of an American Writer, 1943-1954, by Jeffrey Cartwright (Millhauser) **109**:161-62, 165-70, 173-74
"Ego Confessions" (Ginsberg) **109**:333
"The Eighth Voyage of Sinbad" (Millhauser) **109**:157-59, 161
"Eisenheim the Illusionist" (Millhauser) **109**:157-58, 161, 171
Elisabetta: Quasi per Caso una Donna (Fo) **109**:101, 116, 119, 140
Empty Mirror (Ginsberg) **109**:340, 353, 371
"The Energized Man" (Dickey) **109**:249
"Ether" (Ginsberg) **109**:325
"The Eye-Beaters" (Dickey) **109**:267-68, 273, 292
The Eye-Beaters, Blood, Victory, Madness, Buckhead, and Mercy (Dickey) **109**:245, 264, 267-69, 272
Fabulazzo Osceno (Fo) **109**:101, 109
"Facing Shadows" (Jin) **109**:53
The Fall of America: Poems of These States 1965-1971 (Ginsberg) **109**:357, 362
"Falling" (Dickey) **109**:246-48, 250-52, 254-56, 266, 283, 293
"Felis Catus" (Berriault) **109**:96
"The Firebombing" (Dickey) **109**:238, 244, 266, 272, 281-82
The Fires of Spring (Michener) **109**:377
The Floating World (Michener) **109**:376, 379, 382

"Footnote to Howl" (Ginsberg) **109**:347, 350, 359, 370
"For the Death of Lombardi" (Dickey) **109**:245
From the Realm of Morpheus (Millhauser) **109**:157, 170, 174
The Future of Social Studies (Michener) **109**:376
"A Game of Clue" (Millhauser) **109**:158, 160
The Gates of Wrath: Rhymed Poems, 1948-1952 (Ginsberg) **109**:352-53
Ghost of a Chance (Burroughs) **109**:182
La giullarata (Fo) **109**:114-15
"God and the Article Writer" (Berriault) **109**:92-3, 95
The God of Small Things (Roy) **109**:68-78
The Grammelot of Zanni (Fo) **109**:102
"The Grass Still Grows, the River Still Flows" (Dorris) **109**:310
Guests (Dorris) **109**:309
Harlequin (Fo) **109**:129-34
"Has Pinochle Lost Its Whack?" (Royko) **109**:406
Hawaii (Michener) **109**:375-81, 383, 385-86, 388
Helmets (Dickey) **109**:244
"The Houses of the City" (Berriault) **109**:96
"Howl" (Ginsberg) **109**:316-17, 323-28, 332-33, 335-37, 347-52, 355, 358, 369-72
Howl, and Other Poems (Ginsberg) **109**:334, 337-42, 344, 350, 352-54, 356, 362, 363
Hydrogen Box (Ginsberg) **109**:356
I May Be Wrong, But I Doubt It (Royko) **109**:404
Il Fanfani rapito (Fo) **109**:104
In the Penny Arcade (Millhauser) **109**:157-58, 169-70, 174
Indian Journals, March 1962-May 1963 (Ginsberg) **109**:351
"The Infinite Passion of Expectation" (Berriault) **109**:94
The Infinite Passion of Expectation (Berriault) **109**:90, 92, 98
Into the Stone (Dickey) **109**:236, 244, 265
"The Invention of Robert Herendeen" (Millhauser) **109**:158-59, 161
Isabella, tre caravelle e un cacciaballe (Fo) **109**:113, 115
"The Island Ven" (Berriault) **109**:97
"Jeopardy" (Dorris) **109**:308
"Journal Night Thoughts" (Ginsberg) **109**:345
Journals: Early Fifties, Early Sixties (Ginsberg) **109**:348, 351
Journals Mid-Fifties (1954-1958) (Ginsberg) **109**:350-51
Journey (Michener) **109**:376, 381
"Just Say Yes Calypso" (Ginsberg) **109**:318
"Kaddish" (Ginsberg) **109**:324-26, 330, 332-33, 336, 338, 351, 358-62, 364, 371-72
Kaddish, and Other Poems (Ginsberg) **109**:328, 338-43, 348, 352, 359, 362-63
Kent State: What Happened and Why (Michener) **109**:375, 378-79, 382
"Klassik Komix #1" (Millhauser) **109**:160
"Kral Majales" (Ginsberg) **109**:346-47, 355-56
"Laugh and Learn" (Royko) **109**:408
"Laugh? I Thought I'd Die" (Royko) **109**:408
Legacy (Michener) **109**:382, 386
The Letters of William S. Burroughs (Burroughs)

109:227

"The Light at Birth" (Berriault)   **109**:98

The Lights of Earth (Berriault)   **109**:90, 94

"The Lion for Real" (Ginsberg)   **109**:356

Literary Reflections (Michener)   **109**:383

Little Kingdoms (Millhauser)   **109**:165, 167, 170, 174

"Lives of the Saints" (Berriault)   **109**:95

"Love in the Air" (Jin)   **109**:54

"Love Poem on a Theme by Whitman" (Ginsberg)   **109**:354, 358

"LSD" (Ginsberg)   **109**:325

"Madness" (Dickey)   **109**:272

Una madre (Fo)   **109**:109

"Maintaining a Home" (Dorris)   **109**:311

"Malest Cornifici Tuo Catullo" (Ginsberg)   **109**:358

"Manhattan May Day Midnight" (Ginsberg)   **109**:364

Manuale minimo dell'Attore (Fo)   **109**:113, 119, 131, 135

"Many Loves" (Ginsberg)   **109**:357

"Marijuana Notation" (Ginsberg)   **109**:325

"Marriage No Field of Daisies" (Royko)   **109**:407

Martin Dressler: The Tale of an American Dreamer (Millhauser)   **109**:165-69, 171-74

"May Day Sermon" (Dickey)   **109**:266-68, 273

"May Days" (Ginsberg)   **109**:329

"Mercy" (Dickey)   **109**:267-69, 272

"Mescaline" (Ginsberg)   **109**:325

Mexico (Michener)   **109**:383, 386

"Mike's View" (Royko)   **109**:395

"Millions in His Firing Squad" (Royko)   **109**:408

Mind Breaths: Poems, 1972-1977 (Ginsberg)   **109**:331

Minutes to Go (Burroughs)   **109**:183, 194-95

Miracle in Saville (Michener)   **109**:383

"Miss Jee" (Jin)   **109**:52

Mistero Buffo (Fo)   **109**:101, 104-06, 108-09, 113-18, 124-25, 127, 131, 142, 146

"The Mistress" (Berriault)   **109**:96

The Mistress and Other Stories (Berriault)   **109**:90

Monkey Bridge (Cao)   **109**:44-5

Morning Girl (Dorris)   **109**:306-07, 309

Morte accidentale di un anarchico (Fo)   **109**:104, 106, 117-18, 120-21, 136, 142, 144-45

"Mr. Morgan" (Michener)   **109**:378

"Mrs. Grobnik a Checker-Upper" (Royko)   **109**:407

"Mugging" (Ginsberg)   **109**:365

"My Best Soldier" (Jin)   **109**:54

My Education: A Book of Dreams (Burroughs)   **109**:182, 230-31

Naked Lunch (Burroughs)   **109**:180-91, 194-95, 197, 207, 210-16, 220-22, 224, 226, 227-31

Native Americans: 500 Years After, A Guide to Research in Native American Studies (Dorris)   **109**:296

"Nights in the Gardens of Spain" (Berriault)   **109**:97

"Nitrous Oxide" (Ginsberg)   **109**:325

"Notes on the Decline of Outrage" (Dickey)   **109**:239

Nova Express (Burroughs)   **109**:183, 186, 195-96, 207, 209, 212, 229

The Novel (Michener)   **109**:383

"Ocean of Words" (Jin)   **109**:54

Ocean of Words (Jin)   **109**:53-4

"The Olympian" (Dickey)   **109**:246

Open Couple (Fo)   **109**:119

Orgasmo Adulto Escapes from the Zoo (Fo)

109:119

"The Other" (Dickey)   **109**:235

"Oui" (Dorris)   **109**:309

"The Overcoat" (Berriault)   **109**:96

Paper Trail (Dorris)   **109**:298, 310

"Paradise Park" (Millhauser)   **109**:170

"Paterson" (Ginsberg)   **109**:354

The Perfect Storm (Junger)   **109**:56-62

"A Perfectly, Clear View of Basketball" (Royko)   **109**:408

"The Performance" (Dickey)   **109**:238, 287

"Personals" (Ginsberg)   **109**:364

"Pine" (Dickey)   **109**:266-67, 270-72

The Place of Dead Roads (Burroughs)   **109**:197-99, 201

"Please, Master" (Ginsberg)   **109**:333, 357, 364, 366

Poems, 1957-1967 (Dickey)   **109**:264

Poland (Michener)   **109**:375, 377, 379, 382, 386, 388

The Pope and the Witch (Fo)   **109**:142, 144

Port of Saints (Burroughs)   **109**:195

Portrait of a Romantic (Millhauser)   **109**:170, 174

"Power of Love" (Dorris)   **109**:311

Presidential Lottery (Michener)   **109**:383, 386

Puella (Dickey)   **109**:245, 264-65

"Pull My Daisy" (Ginsberg)   **109**:365

"Qiana" (Dorris)   **109**:307

Queer (Burroughs)   **109**:221, 229

"Rain" (Millhauser)   **109**:160

"Reactive Agent Tape Cut by Lee the Agent in Interzone" (Burroughs)   **109**:195

Recessional (Michener)   **109**:383, 386, 388-89

"Reincarnation I" (Dickey)   **109**:273

"Reincarnation II" (Dickey)   **109**:247, 273

"A Report" (Jin)   **109**:54

Report of the Country Chairman (Michener)   **109**:375, 378-79, 383, 386

"The Resurection of Lazarus" (Fo)   **109**:125

Return to Paradise (Michener)   **109**:378, 382

Rooms in the House of Stone (Dorris)   **109**:310

Route Two and Back (Dorris)   **109**:298

"Rumble in Bavaria" (Royko)   **109**:406

Ruski (Burroughs)   **109**:182

"San-Fran-York on the Lake" (Royko)   **109**:405

"Save a Kitty from Extinction" (Royko)   **109**:407

Sayonara (Michener)   **109**:376, 378-79, 382

Scion (Dickey)   **109**:245

"The Search for J. Kruper" (Berriault)   **109**:94

Selected Poems 1947-1995 (Ginsberg)   **109**:362-63, 365

Self-Interviews (Dickey)   **109**:249-50

"The Sepia Postcard" (Millhauser)   **109**:157-58

"Shark in the Window" (Dickey)   **109**:244

"The Shark's Parlor" (Dickey)   **109**:266

"The Sheep Child" (Dickey)   **109**:273

"Shining Agate" (Dorris)   **109**:309

Slats Grobnik and Some Other Friends (Royko)   **109**:404

"Sleeping Out at Easter" (Dickey)   **109**:265

The Soft Machine (Burroughs)   **109**:183, 185-86, 191, 194-96, 199, 207, 212, 229

The Son (Berriault)   **109**:90, 92

"Soul and Money" (Berriault)   **109**:95

The Source (Michener)   **109**:375, 377, 379, 380, 382, 386

Space (Michener)   **109**:378-79, 381, 386

Spare Ass Annie (Burroughs)   **109**:185

Sports in America (Michener)   **109**:382

St. Burl's Obituary (Akst)   **109**:39-42

"Stolen Pleasures" (Berriault)   **109**:97

"The Stone Boy" (Berriault)   **109**:95

Storia della Tigre (Fo)   **109**:101, 108, 115

"The Strength of Fields" (Dickey)   **109**:243

The Strength of Fields (Dickey)   **109**:245

"The Sublime Child" (Berriault)   **109**:96

"Sunflower Sutra" (Ginsberg)   **109**:333, 365

"A Supermarket in California" (Ginsberg)   **109**:355

The Suspect in Poetry (Dickey)   **109**:244

"Sweet Boy, Give me Yr Ass" (Ginsberg)   **109**:358

T. V. Baby Poems (Ginsberg)   **109**:338

Tales of the South Pacific (Michener)   **109**:375-80, 382, 384, 385, 387, 388

"Television Is a Baby Crawling Toward That Death Chamber" (Ginsberg)   **109**:344

Texas (Michener)   **109**:376-77, 379-81, 383, 386

The Third Mind (Burroughs)   **109**:182

"This Form of Life Needs Sex" (Ginsberg)   **109**:358

This Noble Land (Michener)   **109**:383

The Ticket That Exploded (Burroughs)   **109**:183, 186, 195, 207, 212, 229

Time (Burroughs)   **109**:184

"To the Butterflies" (Dickey)   **109**:246

To the White Sea (Dickey)   **109**:236, 257-60, 262-63, 273, 275, 287

"Too Late" (Jin)   **109**:54

Trumpets and Rasperrries (Fo)
   See *Clascon trombette e penacchi*

Tutti unitil tutti insiemel ma scusa quello non e 'il padrone? (Fo)   **109**:104, 112

Two Poems in the Air (Dickey)   **109**:244

Under the Red Flag (Jin)   **109**:54

"Until They Sail" (Michener)   **109**:378

Up Against It (Royko)   **109**:404

"The Vegetable King" (Dickey)   **109**:272

"Victory" (Dickey)   **109**:267, 273-75

The Voice of Asia (Michener)   **109**:376, 379, 382

"Wales Visitation" (Ginsberg)   **109**:347

We Won't Pay! We Won't Pay! (Fo)   **109**:100-01, 119-20, 122, 144, 146

The Western Lands (Burroughs)   **109**:197-99, 201, 230

White Shroud (Ginsberg)   **109**:324, 338, 356, 358

"Who Actually Creates Gaps?" (Royko)   **109**:405

"Who Be Kind To" (Ginsberg)   **109**:347

"Who Is It Can Tell Me Who I Am?" (Berriault)   **109**:94-7

"Why I'm Jewish" (Ginsberg)   **109**:328

"Wichita Vortex Sutra" (Ginsberg)   **109**:347, 372

Wichita Vortex Sutra (Ginsberg)   **109**:338

The Wild Boys: A Book of the Dead (Burroughs)   **109**:184, 195

The Window (Dorris)   **109**:298

"Woman In the Rose Colored Dress" (Berriault)   **109**:96

Women in Their Beds: New and Selected Stories (Berriault)   **109**:95, 98

Working Men (Dorris)   **109**:298, 307-10

The World Is My Home: A Memoir (Michener)   **109**:375, 381, 385, 387-89

"Written in My Dream by W.C. Williams" (Ginsberg)   **109**:324

"Yage" (Ginsberg)   **109**:325

The Yage Letters (Burroughs)   **109**:184, 187

A Yellow Raft in Blue Water (Dorris)   **109**:296-97, 299-301, 303, 306, 308-13

"Yiddishe Kopf" (Ginsberg)   **109**:328

The Zodiac (Dickey)   **109**:245, 264

ISBN 0-7876-2032-7

90000

9 780787 620325